More Than Just a Textbook

Internet Resources

Step 1 Connect to IL Math Online glencoe.com

Step 2 Connect to online resources by using QuickPass codes. You can connect directly to the chapter you want.

MC3323c1 — Enter this code with the appropriate chapter number.

For Students

Connect to the student edition ***eBook*** that contains all of the following online assets. You don't need to take your textbook home every night.

- Personal Tutor
- Extra Examples
- Self-Check Quizzes
- Multilingual eGlossary
- Concepts in Motion
- Chapter Test Practice
- Test Practice
- Study to Go
- Hotmath Math Homework Help Homework Help

For Teachers

Connect to professional development content at glencoe.com and the ***eBook Advance Tracker*** at AdvanceTracker.com.

For Parents

Connect to glencoe.com for access to the ***eBook*** and all the resources for students and teachers that are listed above.

Glencoe McGraw-Hill

Illinois Math Connects

Concepts, Skills, and Problem Solving

Course 3

Authors

Day • Frey • Howard • Hutchens • Luchin • McClain • Molix-Bailey
Ott • Pelfrey • Price • Vielhaber • Willard

McGraw Hill Glencoe

About the Cover

If you like to read the sports page, you know that math is an integral part of sports because statistics is used to summarize and compare data sets. But there's more math than that! The soccer field is composed of rectangles and circles. Even the soccer ball is covered with pentagons and hexagons. Maybe most importantly, the speed of the goalie as she makes a save can be described by an algebraic function. You'll learn more about geometry in Chapter 6 and functions in Chapters 9 and 10.

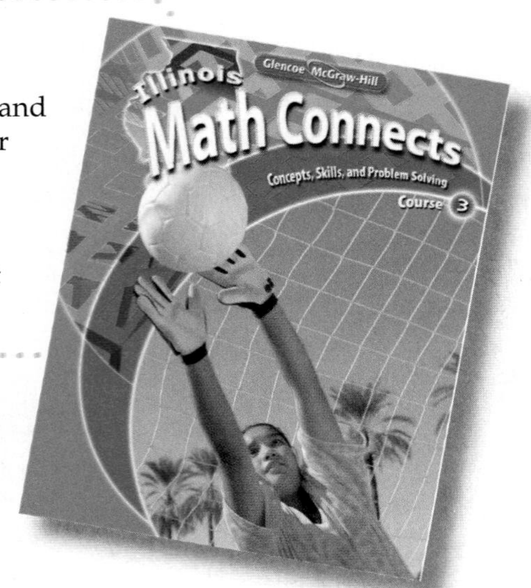

The McGraw-Hill Companies

Send all inquiries to:
Glencoe/McGraw-Hill
8787 Orion Place
Columbus, OH 43240-4027

ISBN: 978-0-07-888332-3
MHID: 0-07-888332-6

Printed in the United States of America.

1 2 3 4 5 6 7 8 9 10 027/055 17 16 15 14 13 12 11 10 09 08

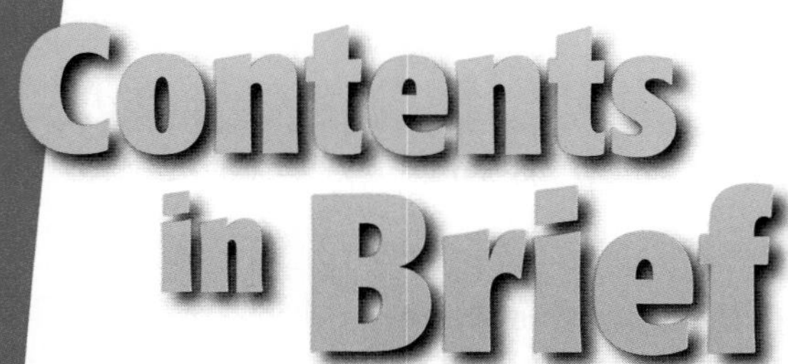

Contents in Brief

The Curriculum Focal Points identify key mathematical ideas for this grade. They are not discrete topics or a checklist to be mastered; rather, they provide a framework for the majority of instruction at a particular grade level and the foundation for future mathematics study. The complete document may be viewed at www.nctm.org/focalpoints.

KEY

G8-FP1 Grade 8 Focal Point 1

G8-FP2 Grade 8 Focal Point 2

G8-FP3 Grade 8 Focal Point 3

G8-FP4C Grade 8 Focal Point 4 Connection

G8-FP5C Grade 8 Focal Point 5 Connection

G8-FP6C Grade 8 Focal Point 6 Connection

G8-FP7C Grade 8 Focal Point 7 Connection

G8-FP1 Algebra: **Analyzing and representing linear functions and solving linear equations and systems of linear equations**

Students use linear functions, linear equations, and systems of linear equations to represent, analyze, and solve a variety of problems. They recognize a proportion ($y/x = k$, or $y = kx$) as a special case of a linear equation of the form $y = mx + b$, understanding that the constant of proportionality (k) is the slope and the resulting graph is a line through the origin. Students understand that the slope (m) of a line is a constant rate of change, so if the input, or x-coordinate, changes by a specific amount, a, the output, or y-coordinate, changes by the amount ma. Students translate among verbal, tabular, graphical, and algebraic representations of functions (recognizing that tabular and graphical representations are usually only partial representations), and they describe how such aspects of a function as slope and y-intercept appear in different representations. Students solve systems of two linear equations in two variables and relate the systems to pairs of lines that intersect, are parallel, or are the same line, in the plane. Students use linear equations, systems of linear equations, linear functions, and their understanding of the slope of a line to analyze situations and solve problems.

G8-FP2 Geometry and Measurement: **Analyzing two- and three-dimensional space and figures by using distance and angle**

Students use fundamental facts about distance and angles to describe and analyze figures and situations in two- and three-dimensional space and to solve problems, including those with multiple steps. They prove that particular configurations of lines give rise to similar triangles because of the congruent angles created when a transversal cuts parallel lines. Students apply this reasoning about similar triangles to solve a variety of problems, including those that ask them to find heights and distances. They use facts about the angles that are created when a transversal cuts parallel lines to explain why the sum of the measures of the angles in a triangle is 180 degrees, and they apply this fact about triangles to find unknown measures of angles. Students explain why the Pythagorean theorem is valid by using a variety of methods—for example, by decomposing a square in two different ways. They apply the Pythagorean theorem to find distances between points in the Cartesian coordinate plane to measure lengths and analyze polygons and polyhedra.

G8-FP3 Data Analysis and Number and Operations and Algebra: **Analyzing and summarizing data sets**

Students use descriptive statistics, including mean, median, and range, to summarize and compare data sets, and they organize and display data to pose and answer questions. They compare the information provided by the mean and the median and investigate the different effects that changes in data values have on these measures of center. They understand that a measure of center alone does not thoroughly describe a data set because very different data sets can share the same measure of center. Students select the mean or the median as the appropriate measure of center for a given purpose.

Connections to the Focal Points

G8-FP4C **Algebra:** Students encounter some nonlinear functions (such as the inverse proportions that they studied in grade 7 as well as basic quadratic and exponential functions) whose rates of change contrast with the constant rate of change of linear functions. They view arithmetic sequences, including those arising from patterns or problems, as linear functions whose inputs are counting numbers. They apply ideas about linear functions to solve problems involving rates such as motion at a constant speed.

G8-FP5C **Geometry:** Given a line in a coordinate plane, students understand that all "slope triangles"—triangles created by a vertical "rise" line segment (showing the change in y), a horizontal "run" line segment (showing the change in x), and a segment of the line itself—are similar. They also understand the relationship of these similar triangles to the constant slope of a line.

G8-FP6C **Data Analysis:** Building on their work in previous grades to organize and display data to pose and answer questions, students now see numerical data as an aggregate, which they can often summarize with one or several numbers. In addition to the median, students determine the 25th and 75th percentiles (1st and 3rd quartiles) to obtain information about the spread of data. They may use box-and-whisker plots to convey this information. Students make scatterplots to display bivariate data, and they informally estimate lines of best fit to make and test conjectures.

G8-FP7C **Number and Operations:** Students use exponents and scientific notation to describe very large and very small numbers. They use square roots when they apply the Pythagorean theorem.

Authors

Roger Day, Ph.D.
Mathematics Department Chair
Pontiac Township High School
Pontiac, Illinois

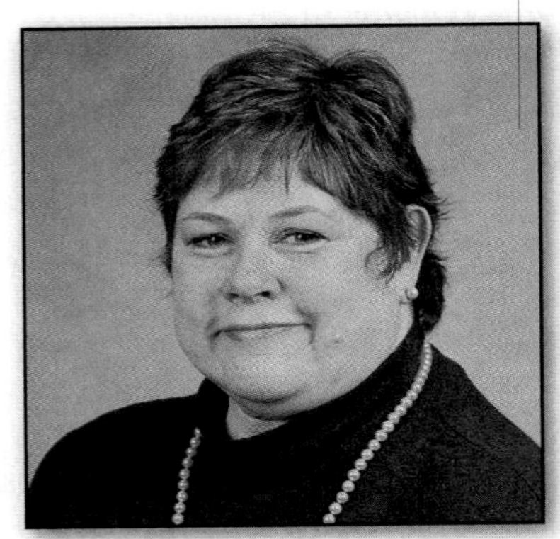

Patricia Frey, Ed.D.
Math Coordinator at Westminster Community Charter School
Buffalo, New York

Arthur C. Howard
Mathematics Teacher
Houston Christian High School
Houston, Texas

Deborah A. Hutchens, Ed.D.
Principal
Chesapeake, Virginia

Beatrice Luchin
Mathematics Consultant
League City, Texas

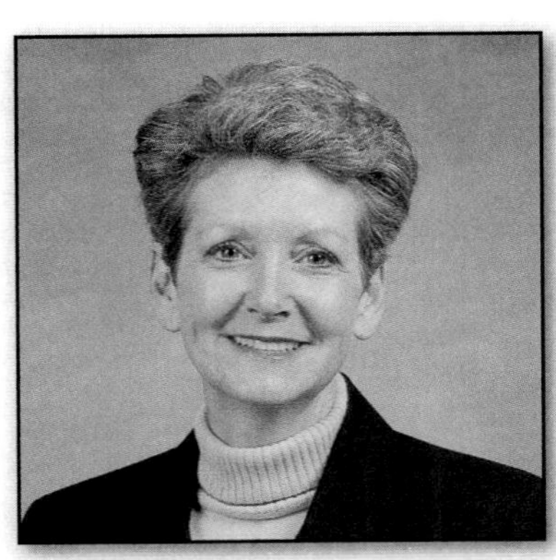

Kay McClain, Ed.D.
Assistant Professor
Vanderbilt University
Nashville, Tennessee

IL Math Online Meet the Authors at glencoe.com

Authors

Rhonda J. Molix-Bailey
Mathematics Consultant
Mathematics by Design
DeSoto, Texas

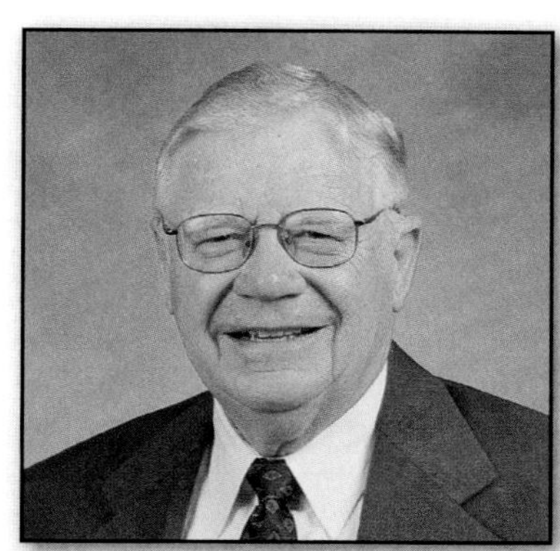

Jack M. Ott, Ph.D.
Distinguished Professor of Secondary Education Emeritus
University of South Carolina
Columbia, South Carolina

Ronald Pelfrey, Ed.D.
Mathematics Specialist
Appalachian Rural Systemic Initiative and Mathematics Consultant
Lexington, Kentucky

Jack Price, Ed.D.
Professor Emeritus
California State Polytechnic University
Pomona, California

Kathleen Vielhaber
Mathematics Consultant
St. Louis, Missouri

Teri Willard, Ed.D.
Assistant Professor
Department of Mathematics
Central Washington University
Ellensburg, Washington

Contributing Author

FOLDABLES **Dinah Zike**
Educational Consultant
Dinah-Might Activities, Inc.
San Antonio, Texas

Master the Illinois Learning Standards in 3 Easy Steps

1 Practice the Standards Daily

- Each lesson addresses Illinois Learning Standards covered in that lesson.

IL Learning Standards

6.B.3c Identify and apply properties of real numbers including pi, squares, and square roots. **8.D.3c** Apply properties of powers, perfect squares and square roots.

- Questions aligned to the standards in a format like those on the Illinois Standards Achievement Test provide you with ongoing opportunities to sharpen your test-taking skills.

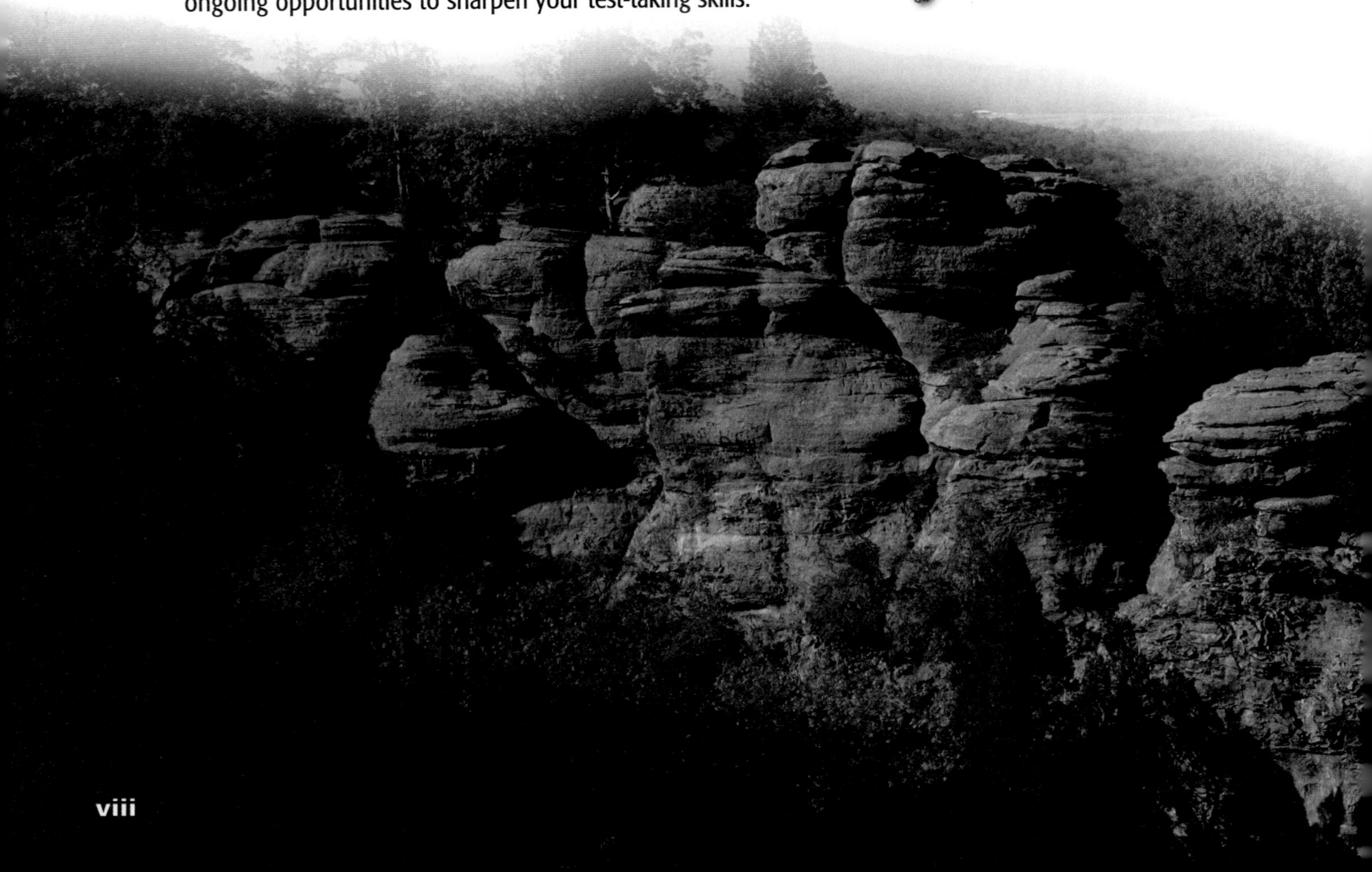

2 Practice the Standards throughout the Chapter

- Every chapter contains a completely worked-out Illinois Standards Achievement Test Example to help you solve problems that are similar to those you might find on that test.

ISAT EXAMPLE

- Every chapter contains two full pages of ISAT Practice with Test-Taking Tips.

ISAT Practice

3 Practice the Standards Before the Test

- If you've followed steps 1 and 2, you should be more than ready for the test. But just in case you want to make sure, use pages IL1–IL25 to practice questions that are organized by standard. Lesson references are included, should you need a little refresher.

Illinois Reviewers

Each Illinois Reviewer reviewed gave feedback and suggestions for improving the effectiveness of the PreK–8 *Math Connects* program.

Patricia A. Bruzek
Mathematics Teacher
Glenn Westlake Middle School
Lombard, Illinois

Monica Engel
Educator Second Grade
Pioneer Elementary School
Bolingbrook, Illinois

Katherine A. Frontier
Elementary Teacher
Laidlaw
Western Springs, Illinois

Peter Gatz
Student Services Coordinator
Brooks Elementary
Aurora, Illinois

Becky Gorniack
Middle School Mathematics Teacher
Fremont Middle School
Mundelein, Illinois

Lauren May, NBCT
4th Grade Teacher
May Watts Elementary School
Naperville, Illinois

Jen Neufeld
3rd Grade Teacher
Kendall
Naperville, Illinois

Phyllis L. Pacilli
Elementary Education Teacher
Fullerton Elementary
Addison, Illinois

Casey Condran Plackett
7th Grade Mathematics Teacher
Kennedy Junior High School
Lisle, Illinois

Dr. John A. Rhodes
Director of Mathematics
Indian Prairie SD #204
Aurora, Illinois

Jennifer L. Rodriguez
Mathematics Teacher
Glen Crest Middle School
Glen Ellyn, Illinois

Petra Siprian
Teacher
Army Trail Elementary School
Addison, Illinois

Christine F. Weiss
3rd Grade Teacher
Robert C. Hill Elementary School
Romeoville, Illinois

Consultants

Glencoe/McGraw-Hill wishes to thank the following professionals for their feedback. They were instrumental in providing valuable input toward the development of this program in these specific areas.

Mathematical Content

Viken Hovsepian
Professor of Mathematics
Rio Hondo College
Whittier, California

Grant A. Fraser, Ph.D.
Professor of Mathematics
California State University, Los Angeles
Los Angeles, California

Arthur K. Wayman, Ph.D.
Professor of Mathematics Emeritus
California State University, Long Beach
Long Beach, California

English Language Learners

Josefina V. Tinajero, Ph.D.
Dean, College of Education
The University of Texas at El Paso
El Paso, Texas

Gifted and Talented

Ed Zaccaro
Author and Consultant
Bellevue, Iowa

Graphing Calculator

Ruth M. Casey
National Mathematics Consultant
National Instructor, Teachers Teaching with Technology
Frankfort, Kentucky

Learning Disabilities

Kate Garnett, Ph.D.
Chairperson, Coordinator Learning Disabilities
School of Education
Department of Special Education
Hunter College, CUNY
New York, New York

Mathematical Fluency

Jason Mutford
Mathematics Instructor
Coxsackie-Athens Central School District
Coxsackie, New York

Pre-AP

Dixie Ross
Mathematics Teacher
Pflugerville High School
Pflugerville, Texas

Reading and Vocabulary

Douglas Fisher, Ph.D.
Professor of Language and Literacy Education
San Diego State University
San Diego, California

Lynn T. Havens
Director of Project CRISS
Kalispell, Montana

Reviewers

Each reviewer reviewed at least two chapters of the Student Edition, giving feedback and suggestions for improving the effectiveness of the mathematics instruction.

Sheila J. Allen
Mathematics Teacher
A.I. Root Middle School
Medina, Ohio

Paula Barnes
Mathematics Teacher
Minisink Valley CSD
Slate Hill, New York

Deborah Barnett
Mathematics Consultant
Lake Shore Public Schools
St. Clair Shores, Michigan

Laurel W. Blackburn
Teacher/Mathematics Department Chair
Hillcrest Middle School
Simpsonville, South Carolina

Drista Bowser
Mathematics Teacher
New Windsor Middle School
New Windsor, Maryland

Matthew Bowser
Teacher
Oil City Middle School
Oil City, Pennsylvania

Susan M. Brewer
Mathematics Teacher
Brunswick Middle School
Brunswick, Maryland

Patricia A. Bruzek
Mathematics Teacher
Glenn Westlake Middle School
Lombard, Illinois

Luanne Budd
Supervisor of Mathematics
Randolph Township
Randolph, New Jersey

Ella Violet Burch
Mathematics Teacher
Penns Grove High School
Carneys Point, New Jersey

Hailey Caldwell
7th Grade Mathematics Teacher
Greenville Middle Academy of Traditional Studies
Greenville, South Carolina

Linda K. Chandler
7th Grade Mathematics Teacher
Willard Middle School
Willard, Ohio

Debra M. Cline
7th Grade Mathematics Teacher
Thomas Jefferson Middle School
Winston-Salem, North Carolina

Randall G. Crites
Principal
Bunker R-3
Bunker, Missouri

Rose Dickinson
Science and Mathematics Teacher
Seneca Middle School
Clinton Township, Michigan

Joyce Wolfe Dodd
6th Grade Mathematics Teacher
Bryson Middle School
Simpsonville, South Carolina

John G. Doyle
Middle School Chairperson/Mathematics Teacher
Wyoming Valley West School District
Kingston, Pennsylvania

Katie England
Secondary Mathematics Resource Teacher
Carroll County Public Schools
Westminster, Maryland

Carol A. Fincannon
6th Grade Mathematics Teacher
Southwood Middle School
Anderson, South Carolina

Sally J. Fulmer
7th Grade Mathematics Teacher/Department Chair
C.E. Williams Middle School
Charleston, South Carolina

Marian K. Geist
Mathematics Teacher/Leadership Team
Baker Prairie Middle School
Canby, Oregon

Becky Gorniack
Middle School Mathematics Teacher
Fremont Middle School
Mundelein, Illinois

Donna Tutterow Hamilton
Curriculum Facilitator
Corriher Lipe Middle School
Landis, North Carolina

Danny Liebertz
8th Grade Mathematics Instructor
Fowler Middle School
Tigard, Oregon

Marie Merkel
Learning Support
North Pocono School District
Scranton, Pennsylvania

Tonda North
Algebra 1/8th Grade Mathematics Teacher
Indian Valley Middle School
Enon, Ohio

Natasha L.M. Nuttbrock
7th Grade Mathematics Teacher
Ferguson Middle School
Beavercreek, Ohio

Paul Penn
Curriculum Team Leader, Mathematics
Lima City Schools
Lima, Ohio

Casey Condran Plackett
7th Grade Mathematics Teacher
Kennedy Junior High School
Lisle, Illinois

E. Elaine Rafferty
Mathematics Consultant
Summerville, South Carolina

Edward M. Repko
Mathematics Teacher
Kilbourne Middle School
Worthington, Ohio

Alfreda Reynolds
Teacher
Charlotte-Mecklenburg School System
Charlotte, North Carolina

Alice Roberts
Mathematics Teacher
Oakdale Middle School
Ijamsville, Maryland

Jennifer L. Rodriguez
Mathematics Teacher
Glen Crest Middle School
Glen Ellyn, Illinois

Natalie Rohaley
6th Grade Mathematics
Riverside Middle School
Greer, South Carolina

Annika Lee Schilling
Mathematics and Science Teacher
Duniway Middle School
McMinnville, Oregon

Sherry Scott
Mathematics Teacher
E.A. Tighe School
Margate, New Jersey

Eli Shaheen
Mathematics Teacher/Department Chair
Plum Senior High School
Pittsburgh, Pennsylvania

Kelly Eady Shaw
7th Grade Mathematics Teacher
Rawlinson Road Middle School
Rock Hill, South Carolina

Evan J. Silver
Mathematics Teacher
Walkersville Middle School
Frederick, Maryland

Charlotte A. Thore
6th/7th Grade Mathematics Teacher
Northwest School of the Arts
Charlotte, North Carolina

Gene A. Tournoux
Mathematics Department Head
Shaker Heights High School
Shaker Heights, Ohio

Pamela J. Trainer
Mathematics Teacher
Roland-Grise Middle School
Wilmington, North Carolina

David A. Trez
Mathematics Teacher
Bloomfield Middle School
Bloomfield, New Jersey

Pauline D. Von Hoffer
Mathematics Teacher
Wentzville School District
Wentzville, Missouri

Kentucky Consultants

Jenn Crase
8th Grade Mathematics Teacher/Department Chair
South Oldham Middle School
Crestwood, Kentucky

Max DeBoer Lux
8th Grade Mathematics
Summit View Middle School
Independence, Kentucky

Jennifer Wells Phipps
Middle School Mathematics Teacher
Corbin Middle School
Corbin, Kentucky

Bea Torrence
Teacher/Mathematics Content Leader
Camp Ernst Middle School
Burlington, Kentucky

J. Ron Vanover
Advanced Placement Calculus
Boone County High School
Florence, Kentucky

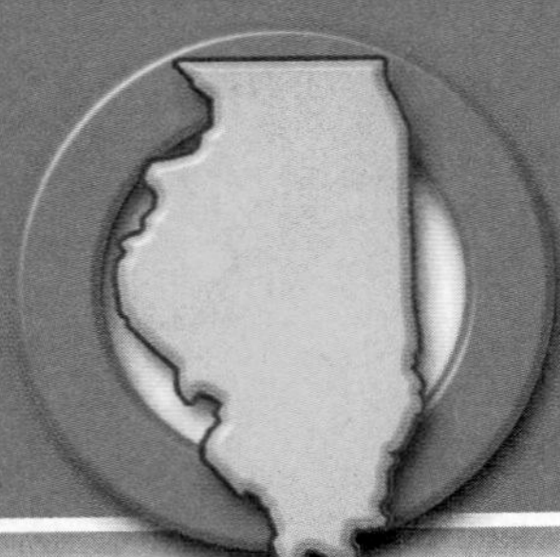

Illinois Learning Standards, Middle/Junior High School, Correlated to *Illinois Math Connects*, Course 3

Lessons in which the standard is the primary focus are indicated in **bold.**

Goals and Standards		Lessons	Page References
STATE GOAL 6: Demonstrate and apply a knowledge and sense of numbers, including numeration and operations (addition, subtraction, multiplication, division), patterns, ratios and proportions.			
6.A. Demonstrate knowledge and use of numbers and their representations in a broad range of theoretical and practical settings.			
6.A.3	Represent fractions, decimals, percentages, exponents and scientific notation in equivalent forms.	**2-1, 2-2, 2-9, 2-10, 5-1, 5-2,** 5-3, 5-4	**84–89, 91–95, 126–133, 252–261,** 263–271
6.B. Investigate, represent and solve problems using number facts, operations (addition, subtraction, multiplication, division) and their properties, algorithms and relationships.			
6.B.3a	Solve practical computation problems involving whole numbers, integers and rational numbers.	*Used throughout the text.* For example, 1-4, 1-5, 2-3, 2-4	*Used throughout the text.* For example, 41–50, 96–107
6.B.3b	Apply primes, factors, divisors, multiples, common factors and common multiples in solving problems.	Start Smart 2, Also covered in *Illinois Math Connects* Courses 1-2	6–7, Also covered in *Illinois Math Connects* Courses 1-2
6.B.3c	Identify and apply properties of real numbers including pi, squares, and square roots.	**3-1, 3-4, Explore 3-5, 3-5, 3-6, Extend 3-6, 3-7**	**144–147, 155–159, 161–178**
6.C. Compute and estimate using mental mathematics, paper-and-pencil methods, calculators and computers.			
6.C.3a	Select computational procedures and solve problems with whole numbers, fractions, decimals, percents and proportions.	*Used throughout the text.* For example, 2-3, 2-6, 4-5, 5-1	*Used throughout the text.* For example, 96–101, 114–118, 210–214, 252–255
6.C.3b	Show evidence that computational results using whole numbers, fractions, decimals, percents and proportions are correct and/or that estimates are reasonable.	*Used throughout the text.* For example, 4-5, 5-4, 5-5, 5-6	*Used throughout the text.* For example, 210–214, 268–273, 275–278
6.D. Solve problems using comparison of quantities, ratios, proportions and percents.			
6.D.3	Apply ratios and proportions to solve practical problems.	**4-1,** 4-2, 4-3, 4-4, **4-5, 4-7, Extend 4-7, 4-8, Extend 4-8, 4-9, 4-10, 5-1, 5-3,** 5-8, **Explore 7-9, 7-9, 9-4, 9-5, Extend 9-5,** 12-2, 12-3	**190–193,** 194–209, **210–214, 218–241, 252–255, 263–267,** 284–289, **397–404, 481–493,** 637–647
STATE GOAL 7: Estimate, make and use measurements of objects, quantities and relationships and determine acceptable levels of accuracy.			
7.A. Measure and compare quantities using appropriate units, instruments and methods.			
7.A.3a	Measure length, capacity, weight/mass and angles using sophisticated instruments (e.g., compass, protractor, trundle wheel).	Extend 7-1, **Extend 9-5,** CSB2, **CSB3, CSB4,** Also covered in *Illinois Math Connects* Courses 1-2	358–359, **493,** 732–734, **735, 736,** Also covered in *Illinois Math Connects* Courses 1-2

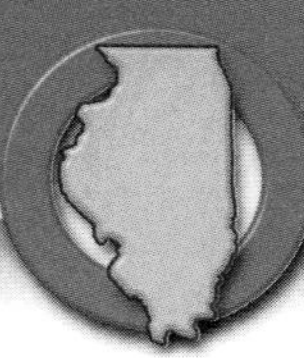

Goals and Standards		Lessons	Page References
7.A.3b	Apply the concepts and attributes of length, capacity, weight/mass, perimeter, area, volume, time, temperature and angle measures in practical situations.	**Explore 3-5, 3-5, 3-6, 3-7, 6-1, 6-3, 7-1, Explore 7-3, 7-3, 7-5, 7-6, Explore 7-7, 7-7, Extend 7-7, 7-8, CSB3, CSB4, CSB7, CSB8, CSB9, CSB10**	**161–167, 173–178, 306–311, 316–319, 352–359, 362–367, 373–378, 380–396, 735, 736, 739–745**
7.B. Estimate measurements and determine acceptable levels of accuracy.			
7.B.3	Select and apply instruments including rulers and protractors and units of measure to the degree of accuracy required.	Extend 7-1, **Extend 9-5,** CSB2, **CSB3, CSB4,** Also covered in *Illinois Math Connects* Courses 1-2	358–359, **493,** 732–734, **735, 736,** Also covered in *Illinois Math Connects* Courses 1-2
7.C. Select and use appropriate technology, instruments and formulas to solve problems, interpret results and communicate findings.			
7.C.3a	Construct a simple scale drawing for a given situation.	**4-10**	**236–241**
7.C.3b	Use concrete and graphic models and appropriate formulas to find perimeters, areas, surface areas and volumes of two- and three-dimensional regions.	**7-1, Explore 7-3, 7-3, 7-5, 7-6, Explore 7-7, 7-7, 7-8, CSB7, CSB8**	**352–359, 362–367, 373–378, 380–391, 393–396, 739–741**
STATE GOAL 8: Use algebraic and analytical methods to identify and describe patterns and relationships in data, solve problems and predict results.			
8.A. Describe numerical relationships using variables and patterns.			
8.A.3a	Apply the basic properties of commutative, associative, distributive, transitive, inverse, identity, zero, equality and order of operations to solve problems.	**1-2, 1-4, 1-9, 1-10, 8-1,** Also covered in *Illinois Math Connects* Courses 1-2	**29–34, 43–45, 65–73, 416–421,** Also covered in *Illinois Math Connects* Courses 1-2
8.A.3b	Solve problems using linear expressions, equations and inequalities.	**1-2, 1-7, 1-9, 1-10, 2-7, 4-5, 5-7, 5-8, 5-9, Extend 5-9, 10-2, 10-4, Extend 10-4, 10-5, 10-6, 10-7, 10-8, 8-1, 8-2, 8-3, Explore 8-4, 8-4, 8-6, 8-7, 8-8, 9-3, 9-4, 9-5, Extend 9-5, 9-6, Extend 9-6, 9-7, 10-1, LA 1, LA 2, LA 3, LA 6**	**29–34, 57–61, 65–73, 119–123, 210–214, 279–294, 416–437, 441–453, 475–493, 495–507, 528–537, 540–548, 550–562, LA2–LA11, LA19–LA21**
8.B. Interpret and describe numerical relationships using tables, graphs and symbols.			
8.B.3	Use graphing technology and algebraic methods to analyze and predict linear relationships and make generalizations from linear patterns.	**9-1,** 9-2, Extend 9-2, 9-3, 9-4, 9-5, Extend 9-5, 9-6, **Extend 9-6,** 9-7, **9-8, 9-9, Extend 9-9,** 10-1, LA 6	**464–468,** 469–493, 495–499, **500–501,** 502–507, **508–517,** 528–533, 519–521
8.C. Solve problems using systems of numbers and their properties.			
8.C.3	Apply the properties of numbers and operations including inverses in algebraic settings derived from economics, business and the sciences.	**1-2, 1-9, 1-10, 2-7, 5-3, 8-2, Explore 8-4, 8-4, 8-6, 8-7, 8-8**	**29–34, 65–69, 70–73, 119–123, 263–267, 422–426, 432–437, 441–444, 445–448, 449–453**

LA = Looking Ahead; CSB = Concepts and Skills Bank; RSP = Reading to Solve Problems

Goals and Standards		Lessons	Page References
8.D. Use algebraic concepts and procedures to represent and solve problems.			
8.D.3a	Solve problems using numeric, graphic or symbolic representations of variables, expressions, equations and inequalities.	**1-2, 1-7, 1-9, 1-10, 2-7, 4-5, 8-1, 8-2, 8-3, Explore 8-4, 8-4, 8-6, 8-7, 8-8, 9-3, 9-4, 9-5, Extend 9-5, 9-6, Extend 9-6, 9-7, 10-1, 10-2, 10-4, LA 1, LA 2, LA 3, LA 6**	**29–34, 57–61, 65–73, 119–123, 210–214, 416–437, 441–453, 475–493, 495–507, 528–537, 540–543, LA2–LA11, LA19–LA21**
8.D.3b	Propose and solve problems using proportions, formulas and linear functions.	**4-2, 4-5, 4-9, 5-3, 9-2, Extend 9-2, 9-3, 9-5, 9-6, Extend 9-6, 10-1, LA 6**	**194–197, 210–214, 232–235, 263–267, 469–480, 487–492, 495–501, 528–533, LA19–LA21**
8.D.3c	Apply properties of powers, perfect squares and square roots.	**2-9, 3-1, 3-2,** Explore 3-5, 3-5, 3-6, Extend 3-6, 3-7, 10-5, 10-7, 10-8	**126–129, 144–151,** 161–178, 545–548, 555–558, 559–562
STATE GOAL 9: Use geometric methods to analyze, categorize and draw conclusions about points, lines, planes and space.			
9.A. Demonstrate and apply geometric concepts involving points, lines, planes and space.			
9.A.3a	Draw or construct two- and three-dimensional geometric figures including prisms, pyramids, cylinders and cones.	**Extend 6-1, Extend 6-4, Extend 7-1,** 7-6, 7-7, **Extend 7-7**	**312–313, 324–325, 358–359,** 380–384, 386–391, **392**
9.A.3b	Draw transformation images of figures, with and without the use of technology.	**4-8, Extend 4-8, 6-6, 6-7**	**225–231, 332–341**
9.A.3c	Use concepts of symmetry, congruency, similarity, scale, perspective, and angles to describe and analyze two- and three-dimensional shapes found in practical applications (e.g., geodesic domes, A-frame houses, basketball courts, inclined planes, art forms, blueprints).	**4-7, Extend 4-7, 4-8, Extend 4-8, 4-9, 4-10, 6-1, Extend 6-1, 6-3, 6-4, Extend 6-4, 6-5,** Explore 7-9, 7-9, CSB2, CSB3, CSB5, CSB6	**218–241, 306–313, 316–325, 327–331,** 397–404, 732–734, 735, 737, 738
9.B. Identify, describe, classify and compare relationships using points, lines, planes and solids.			
9.B.3	Identify, describe, classify and compare two- and three-dimensional geometric figures and models according to their properties.	**6-1, Extend 6-1, 6-3, 6-4, Extend 6-4, 6-5, 7-4, 7-9, CSB1, CSB5, CSB6, CSB8**	**306–311, 312–313, 316–319, 320–323, 324–325, 327–331, 368–372, 399–404, 730–731, 737, 738, 741**
9.C. Construct convincing arguments and proofs to solve problems.			
9.C.3a	Construct, develop and communicate logical arguments (informal proofs) about geometric figures and patterns.	6-1, Extend 6-1, 6-2, 6-3, 6-4, Extend 6-4, 6-5, Extend 7-1, Explore 7-9	306–325, 358–359, 397–398
9.C.3b	Develop and solve problems using geometric relationships and models, with and without the use of technology.	6-1, Extend 6-1, 6-3, 6-4, Extend 6-4, 6-5, 6-6, 6-7, Explore 7-9, 7-9, 10-3	306–313, 316–325, 327–341, 397–404, 538–539

Goals and Standards		Lessons	Page References
9.D. Use trigonometric ratios and circular functions to solve problems.			
9.D.3	Compute distances, lengths and measures of angles using proportions, the Pythagorean theorem and its converse.	**Explore 3-5, 3-5, 3-6, 3-7**	**161, 162–166, 167–171, 173–178**
STATE GOAL 10: Collect, organize and analyze data using statistical methods; predict results; and interpret uncertainty using concepts of probability.			
10.A. Organize, describe and make predictions from existing data.			
10.A.3a	Construct, read and interpret tables, graphs (including circle graphs) and charts to organize and represent data.	**11-1, 11-2, Extend 11-2, 11-3, Extend 11-3, 11-6, Extend 11-6, 11-7, 11-8, CSB13, CSB15**	**574–590, 605–621, 749–750, 752–753**
10.A.3b	Compare the mean, median, mode and range, with and without the use of technology.	**11-4, Extend 11-4,** 11-5	**591–596, 597,** 599
10.A.3c	Test the reasonableness of an argument based on data and communicate their findings.	11-3, 11-6, 11-7, 11-8, CSB14, CSB15	582–588, 605–610, 612–621, 751–753
10.B. Formulate questions, design data collection methods, gather and analyze data and communicate findings.			
10.B.3	Formulate questions (e.g., relationships between car age and mileage, average incomes and years of schooling), devise and conduct experiments or simulations, gather data, draw conclusions and communicate results to an audience using traditional methods and contemporary technologies.	**12-5**	**653–658**
10.C. Determine, describe and apply the probabilities of events.			
10.C.3a	Determine the probability and odds of events using fundamental counting principles.	**12-2, 12-3, CSB11**	**637–647, 746**
10.C.3b	Analyze problem situations (e.g., board games, grading scales) and make predictions about results.	**12-2, 12-3, Extend 12-3,** 12-4, **CSB12**	**637–649,** 650–651, **747–748**

LA = Looking Ahead; CSB = Concepts and Skills Bank; RSP = Reading to Solve Problems

Contents

Start Smart

ILS

Unit 1

Number and Operations: Rational and Real Numbers

Chapter 1 Algebra: Integers

ILS

Focal Points and Connections
See page iv for key.

G8-FP1 Algebra

ISAT PRACTICE

H.O.T. Problems
Higher Order Thinking

Table of Contents

Algebra: Rational Numbers

G8-FP1 Algebra
G8-FP7C Number and Operations

Real Numbers and the Pythagorean Theorem

ILS

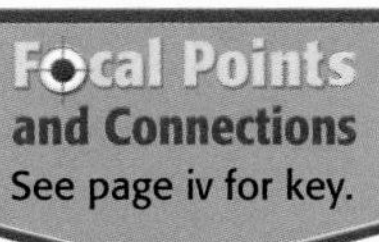

G8-FP2 Geometry and Measurement
G8-FP7C Number and Operations

H.O.T. Problems
Higher Order Thinking

Unit 2

Patterns, Relationships, and Algebraic Thinking

Chapter 4 Proportions and Similarity

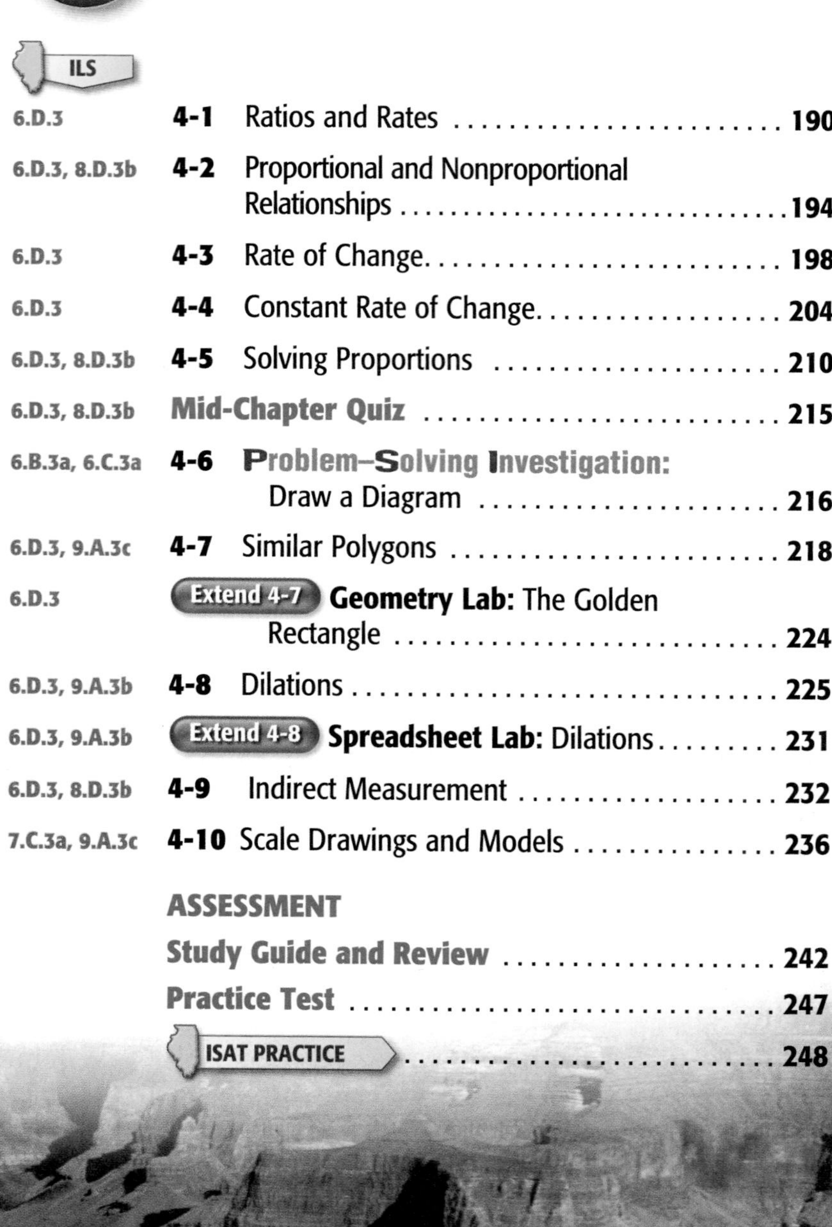

ILS

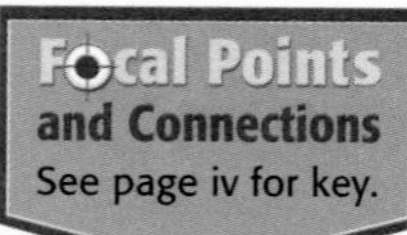

Focal Points and Connections
See page iv for key.

G8-FP1 Algebra

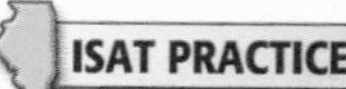

ISAT PRACTICE

- Extended Response 249
- Multiple Choice 193, 197, 203, 209, 214, 222, 223, 230, 235, 241
- Short Response/Grid In 214, 249
- Worked Out Example 221

H.O.T. Problems
Higher Order Thinking

- Challenge 193, 197, 203, 209, 214, 223, 230, 235, 241
- Find the Error 240
- Number Sense 203
- Open Ended 197, 203, 209, 214, 230, 235, 240
- Which One Doesn't Belong? 193

Percent

G8-FP1 Algebra

ISAT PRACTICE

H.O.T. Problems
Higher Order Thinking

Table of Contents

Unit 3

Geometry and Measurement

Geometry and Spatial Reasoning

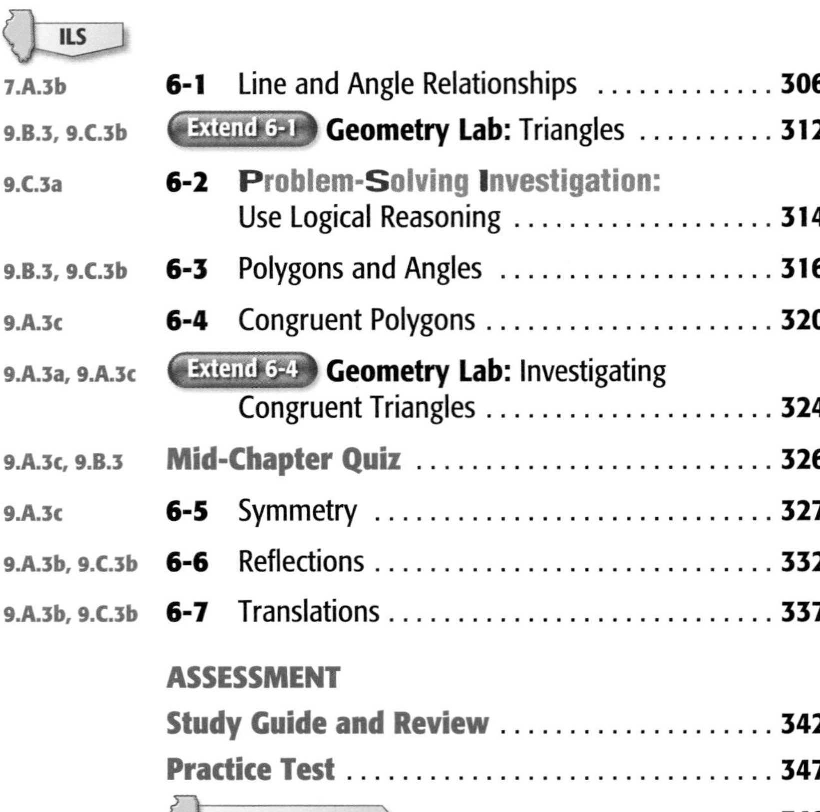

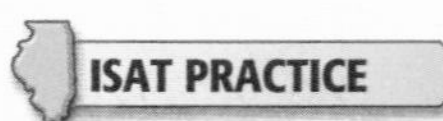

Focal Points and Connections
See page iv for key.

G8-FP2 Geometry and Measurement

ISAT PRACTICE

- Extended Response 349
- Multiple Choice 311, 319, 323, 331, 336, 339, 341
- Short Response/Grid In 323, 349
- Worked Out Example 338

H.O.T. Problems
Higher Order Thinking

- Challenge 311, 318, 323, 331, 336, 341
- Open Ended 310, 336
- Reasoning 310, 341

Measurement: Area and Volume

ILS

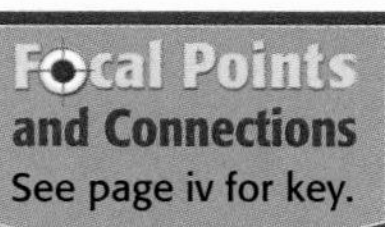

G8-FP2 Geometry and Measurement

ISAT PRACTICE

- Extended Response 411
- Multiple Choice 357, 367, 372, 378, 384, 391, 396, 402, 404
- Short Response/Grid In 378, 411
- Worked Out Example 401

H.O.T. Problems
Higher Order Thinking

- Challenge 357, 367, 372, 377, 384, 391, 396, 403
- Find the Error 377
- Number Sense 356, 391
- Open Ended 356, 372, 377, 384, 396, 403
- Reasoning 391
- Select the Tool 378
- Select the Technique 403

Unit 4

Algebraic Thinking: Linear and Nonlinear Functions

Algebra: More Equations and Inequalities

ILS

ASSESSMENT

G8-FP1 Algebra

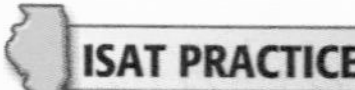

H.O.T. Problems
Higher Order Thinking

Algebra: Linear Functions

ILS

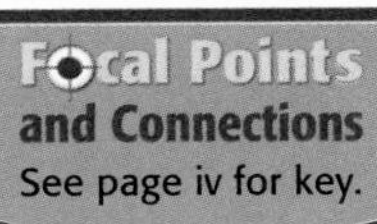

G8-FP1 Algebra
G8-FP5C Geometry

ISAT PRACTICE

H.O.T. Problems
Higher Order Thinking

Table of Contents

Algebra: Nonlinear Functions and Polynomials

ILS

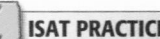

Focal Points and Connections
See page iv for key.

G8-FP4C Algebra

ISAT PRACTICE

- Extended Response 569
- Multiple Choice 533, 537, 543, 548, 554, 558, 562
- Short Response/Grid In 548, 569
- Worked Out Example 551

H.O.T. Problems
Higher Order Thinking

- Challenge 532, 537, 543, 548, 554, 558, 562
- Number Sense 554
- Open Ended 532, 537, 543, 548, 554, 558, 562
- Which One Doesn't Belong? 532

Unit 5

Statistics, Data Analysis, and Probability

Statistics

ILS

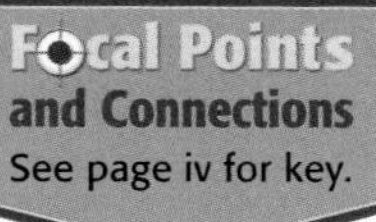

G8-FP3 Data Analysis and Number and Operations and Algebra
G8-FP6C Data Analysis

ISAT PRACTICE

H.O.T. Problems
Higher Order Thinking

Chapter 12 Probability

ILS

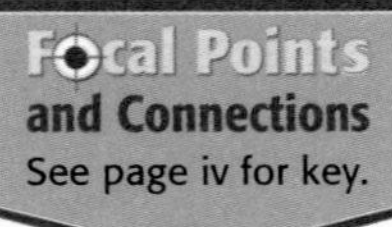

G8-FP3 Data Analysis and Number and Operations and Algebra

ISAT PRACTICE

- Extended Response 665
- Multiple Choice 633, 636, 642, 647, 658
- Short Response/Grid In 647, 665
- Worked Out Example 638

H.O.T. Problems
Higher Order Thinking

- Challenge 635, 642, 646, 657
- Find the Error 641
- Number Sense 635
- Open Ended 635, 641, 646

GET READY FOR THE

Illinois Standards Achievement Test

In March, you will take your Grade 8 Illinois Standards Achievement Test (ISAT) for Mathematics. You will apply the concepts and skills that you have learned throughout the year in order to answer multiple-choice, short-response, and extended-response questions.

Multiple-Choice Items

For multiple-choice questions, you will select the correct response from four answer choices. Your teacher will provide you with an answer sheet to fill in your answer choices.

Short- and Extended-Response Items

For short- and extended-response questions, you will write answers to open-ended questions. You are required to show your work to receive full credit. In some cases, you will be required to explain, in words, how you arrived at your response.

How Can I Get Ready?

The Illinois Standards Achievement Test you will take in March covers the Illinois Learning Standards for Mathematics. The following pages give you practice questions similar to those found on the test. You can use these practice pages in the weeks before the test to determine if you are ready. If you are struggling with any of the items, lesson references are provided so that you can go back and review from the pages in your textbook.

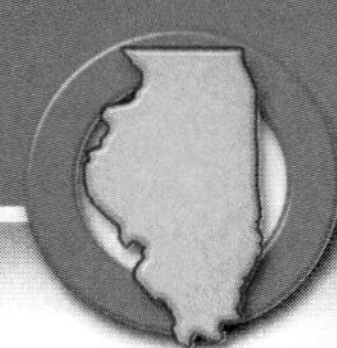

Number Sense

1

Pablo's checking account balance is $168. What is his balance after he uses the ATM to withdraw $45 on Monday and $20 on Tuesday? (Lesson 1-4) **(6.8.09)**

A $103
B $123
C $143
D $238

2

The projected population of Illinois in 2030 is about 15,140,000. Which of the following represents this projected population in scientific notation? (Lesson 2-10) **(6.8.04)**

A 0.1514×10^6
B 1.514×10^6
C 1.514×10^7
D 15.14×10^7

3

José earns $16.50 for 3 hours of babysitting. At this rate, how much will he earn for babysitting 5 hours? (Lesson 4-5) **(6.8.15)**

A $5.50
B $27.50
C $34.50
D $82.50

4

Between which two whole numbers is $\sqrt{58}$? (Lesson 3-2) **(6.8.14)**

A 4 and 5
B 5 and 6
C 6 and 7
D 7 and 8

5

If 5 pounds of cherries are needed to bake 3 cherry pies, how many pounds of cherries does a bakery need to bake 125 cherry pies? (Lesson 4-5) **(6.8.16)**

A 75 pounds
B $180\frac{1}{3}$ pounds
C $208\frac{1}{3}$ pounds
D 375 pounds

6

Caitlyn is filling a small pool in her backyard. The pool is filling at a rate of 6 gallons per minute. How much water will be in the pool after 15 minutes? (Lesson 1-6) **(6.B.16)**

A 21 gallons
B 36 gallons
C 66 gallons
D 90 gallons

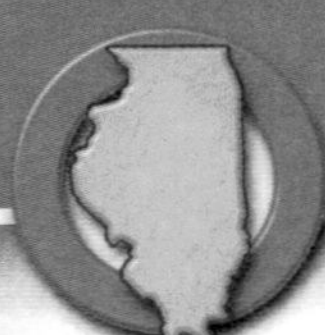

7

A pair of tennis shoes have a regular price of \$64. They are on sale for \$48. What is the percent of decrease in the price of the shoes? (Lesson 5-8) **(6.8.18)**

A 13%
B 20%
C 25%
D 75%

8

What is the value of x in the following proportion? (Lesson 4-5) **(6.8.18)**

$$\frac{10}{6} = \frac{5.5}{x}$$

A 3.3
B 3.75
C 9.16
D 10.9

9

Of newly manufactured cell phones, 12 were defective and 75 passed inspection. What ratio compares the number of defective cell phones to the total number of cell phones manufactured? (Lesson 4-1) **(6.8.15)**

A 1 : 9
B 4 : 25
C 2 : 15
D 3 : 25

10

Raul figures that the diagonal of his vegetable garden is $\sqrt{7}$ feet long. He wants to determine how long this distance is in feet. Between which two whole numbers is $\sqrt{7}$ located? (Lesson 3-1) **(6.8.07)**

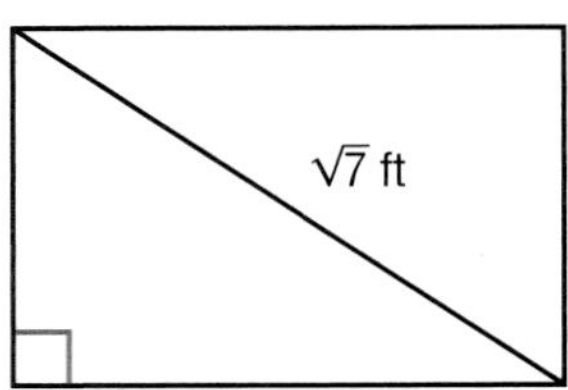

2, 3	3, 4	4, 5	5, 6
A	**B**	**C**	**D**

11

Find $\frac{7}{8} - \frac{5}{12}$. (Lesson 2-6) **(6.8.09)**

$\frac{1}{12}$	$\frac{5}{12}$	$\frac{11}{24}$	$\frac{1}{2}$
A	**B**	**C**	**D**

12

Write the expression $6 \cdot x \cdot x \cdot x \cdot x \cdot y \cdot y$ using exponents. (Lesson 2-9) **(6.8.05)**

A $6x^4y^2$
B $6x^5y^2$
C $6x^2y^4$
D $6x^4y$

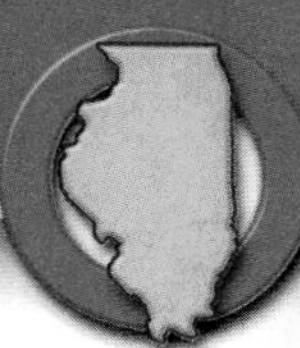

13

When finding the sum of $-\frac{6}{7}$ and $\frac{2}{3}$, what is the least common denominator? (Lesson 2-6) **(6.8.08, 6.8.13)**

A 7
B 10
C 14
D 21

14

The thickness of a strand of human hair is $\frac{3}{50{,}000}$ meter. What is the decimal form of this number? (Lesson 5-2) **(6.8.03)**

A 0.000006
B 0.00006
C 0.0006
D 0.006

15

Chen bought a dress for the homecoming dance and spent \$70.53, including \$5.53 in tax. Which equation could be used to find the cost of the dress before tax? (Lesson 1-9) **(6.8.18)**

A $x - 5.53 = 70.53$
B $x + 5.53 = 70.53$
C $x + 70.53 = 5.53$
D $x - 70.53 = 5.53$

16

Which point on the number line below is the coordinate of 0.4375? (Lesson 2-2) **(6.8.07)**

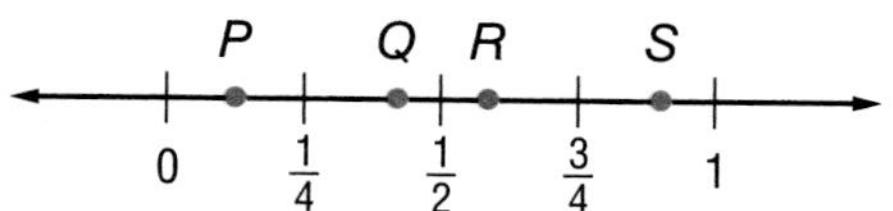

A Point P
B Point Q
C Point R
D Point S

17

The total cost of Mason's birthday dinner was \$64.55. If his parents want to leave a 20% tip, which of the following would be a reasonable amount for the tip? (Lesson 5-4) **(6.8.18)**

A \$6.50
B \$10.00
C \$11.00
D \$13.00

18

A bag of dog food contains $7\frac{1}{2}$ pounds of food. Each day, Joaquin's dog eats $\frac{1}{4}$ pound of food. For how many days will this bag of dog food last? (Lesson 2-4) **(6.8.16)**

15	18	30	60
A	**B**	**C**	**D**

19

On her 14th birthday, Josie measured $60\frac{1}{4}$ inches tall. On her 13th birthday, she measured $57\frac{1}{2}$ inches tall. How much did Josie grow between her 13th and 14th birthdays? (Lesson 2-5) **(6.8.09)**

A $2\frac{1}{2}$ inches
B $2\frac{3}{4}$ inches
C $3\frac{1}{4}$ inches
D $3\frac{1}{2}$ inches

20

A recipe calls for $2\frac{1}{4}$ cups of flour, $\frac{1}{3}$ cup of sugar, and $\frac{1}{4}$ cup of brown sugar. What is the total amount of dry ingredients in this cookie recipe? (Lesson 2-6) **(6.8.09)**

A $2\frac{3}{4}$ cups
B $2\frac{5}{6}$ cups
C $3\frac{1}{6}$ cups
D $3\frac{1}{4}$ cups

21

Which of the following numbers has the greatest value? (Lessons 3-1, 3-2) **(6.8.06)**

A 3.5^2
B 12
C $\sqrt{140}$
D $-\sqrt{169}$

22

Jordana wrote the following statement on the board. Which property is demonstrated by this statement? (Lesson 1-2) **(6.8.11)**

$$(2 \times 3) \times 6 = 2 \times (3 \times 6)$$

A Commutative Property
B Associative Property
C Distributive Property
D Identify Property

23

The label on a jar of salsa says that it contains $8\frac{1}{2}$ servings. If each serving size is $\frac{1}{4}$ cup, how many cups of salsa are in the jar of salsa? (Lesson 2-3) **(6.8.16)**

A $1\frac{5}{8}$ cups
B 2 cups
C $2\frac{1}{8}$ cups
D $2\frac{1}{4}$ cups

24

Of 52 students in the choir, 24 are boys. Which ratio compares the number of girls to boys in the choir? (Lesson 4-1) **(6.8.15)**

7 : 6	7 : 5	6 : 5	5 : 7
A	**B**	**C**	**D**

25

Which of the following is an example of the Identity Property? (Lesson 1-2) **(6.8.11)**

A $5 \cdot x = x \cdot 5$

B $\frac{3}{5} \cdot \frac{5}{3} = 1$

C $7x \cdot 1 = 7x$

D $-6a \cdot 0 = 0$

26

If 85% of the eighth-grade students are going to the spring dance, what fraction of the students are not going to the spring dance? (Lesson 5-1) **(6.8.17)**

A $\frac{3}{20}$

B $\frac{1}{5}$

C $\frac{1}{4}$

D $\frac{17}{20}$

27

A lacrosse team played twenty-five games, eighteen of which they won. What percent of the games did they win? (Lesson 5-1) **(6.8.17)**

A 14%

B 66%

C 72%

D 86%

28

Refer to the figures below. The area of trapezoid M is 138 square feet. The area of trapezoid N is 46 square feet. If trapezoid M is similar to trapezoid N, what is the value of x? (Lesson 4-5) **(6.8.16)**

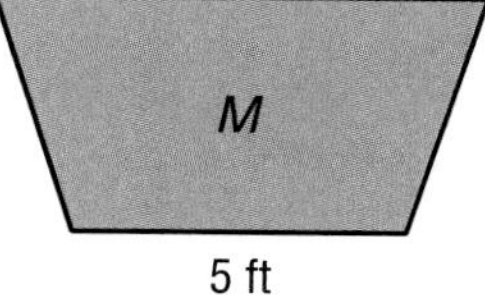

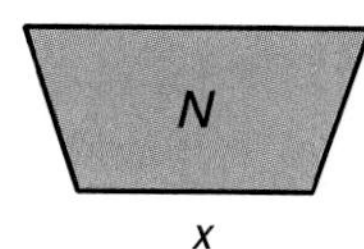

A 2 feet 6 inches

B 1 foot 11 inches

C 1 foot 8 inches

D 1 foot 4 inches

29

A whole number is squared. The result is between 1,200 and 1,400. Between which two numbers is the whole number? (Lesson 3-2) **(6.8.07)**

A 32 and 35

B 35 and 38

C 36 and 39

D 40 and 43

30

Which of the following rational numbers is the greatest? (Lesson 5-2) **(6.8.06)**

$3\frac{5}{7}$	3.14	348%	$\frac{19}{5}$
A	**B**	**C**	**D**

31

Which of the following expressions could not be used to describe the model shown below? (Lesson 3-1) **(6.8.02)**

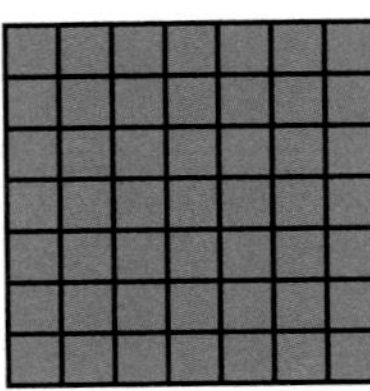

A $7 \cdot 7$
B $7 + 7 + 7 + 7 + 7$
C 49
D 7^2

32

Which of the following proportions could be used to find what number is 38% of 120? (Lesson 5-3) **(6.8.16)**

A $\frac{n}{120} = \frac{38}{100}$
B $\frac{n}{100} = \frac{38}{120}$
C $\frac{n}{38} = \frac{120}{100}$
D $\frac{120}{n} = \frac{38}{100}$

33

Estimate $5\frac{1}{5} \cdot 6\frac{2}{3}$. Then find the actual product. Explain whether or not your estimate is reasonable. (Lesson 2-3) **(6.8.09)**

34

Coal lies under 37,000 square miles of Illinois. This is about 65% of the state's surface. Write 65% as a fraction in simplest form. (Lesson 5-3) **(6.8.03)**

35

Addison decided to backpack with friends over the weekend. The first day, they traveled $\frac{1}{2}$ of the total distance that they wanted to travel for the entire weekend. The second day, they traveled an additional $\frac{1}{3}$ of this total distance. How much of the total distance do they need to travel on the third day in order to complete the trip? (Lesson 2-6) **(8.8.06)**

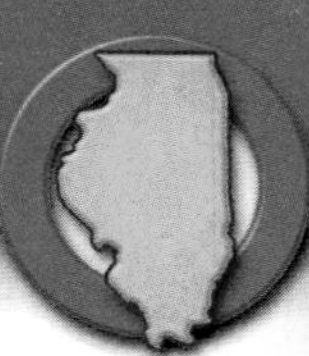

Measurement

1

What is the circumference of the above ground pool shown to the nearest tenth of a foot? (Lesson 7-1) **(7.8.02)**

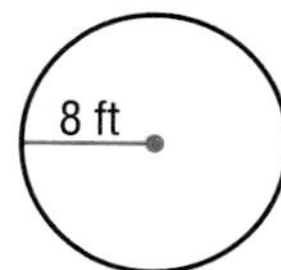

A 25.1 feet
B 50.3 feet
C 100.5 feet
D 201.1 feet

2

Mason is making a scale drawing of the Sears Tower. The height of the building in his drawing is 20 centimeters. If the actual height of the Sears Tower is 442 meters, what is the scale factor of his drawing? (Lesson 4-10) **(7.8.06)**

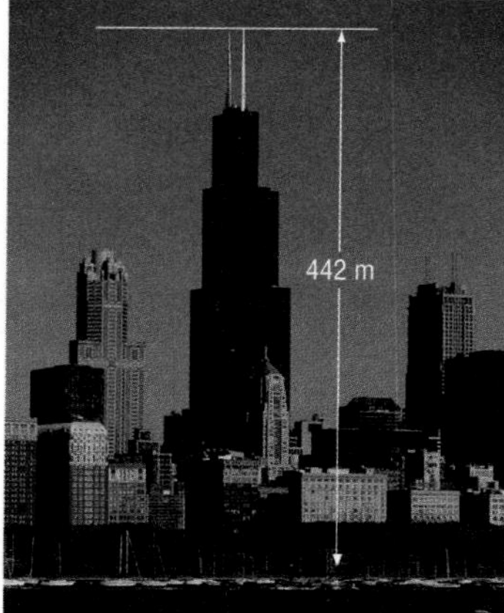

A 1 : 221
B 1 : 442
C 1 : 2,210
D 1 : 4,420

3

Which of the following represents the shaded portion of the figure below? (Lesson 5-1) **(7.8.02)**

A 30%
B $44.\overline{4}\%$
C $55.\overline{5}\%$
D 80%

4

The area of each square in the figure below is 16 square units. What is the perimeter of the figure? (Lesson 3-1) **(7.8.02)**

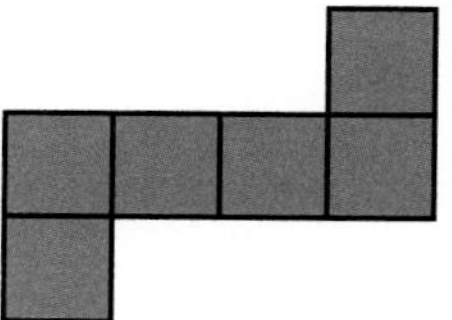

A 24 units
B 56 units
C 76 units
D 224 units

5

The Brookfield Zoo Carousel in Brookfield has a diameter of 54 feet. What is the circumference of this carousel to the nearest tenth of a foot? (Lesson 7-1) **(7.8.02)**

A 84.8 feet
B 169.6 feet
C 2,290.2 feet
D 9,160.9 feet

6

What is the measure of the angle shown below? (page 735) **(7.8.01)**

40°	100°	130°	140°
A	**B**	**C**	**D**

7

What is the area of a triangle with a height of 6 feet and a base of 11.4 feet? (page 739) **(7.8.02)**

A 8.7 ft^2
B 17.4 ft^2
C 34.2 ft^2
D 68.4 ft^2

8

What is the surface area of the prism shown below? (Lesson 7-7) **(7.8.04)**

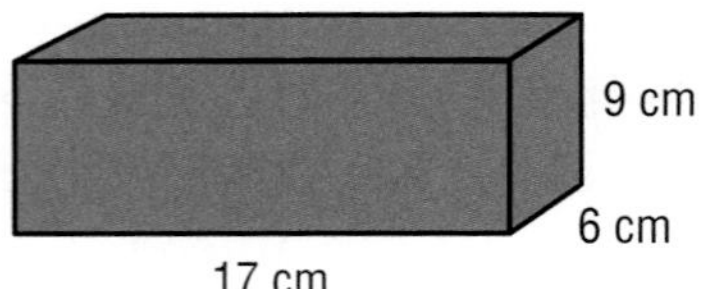

A 309 cm^2
B 618 cm^2
C 918 cm^2
D 1,836 cm^2

9

The label for a tuna can has a surface area of 80 square centimeters. If the radius of the can is 4.25 centimeters, what is the height of the tuna can label to the nearest centimeter? (Lesson 7-7) **(7.8.04)**

A 2 centimeters
B 3 centimeters
C 6 centimeters
D 9 centimeters

10

A map has a scale of 2 inches = 100 miles. How many inches on the map would represent 550 miles? (Lesson 4-10) **(7.8.06)**

A 5.5 inches
B 11 inches
C 18 inches
D 33 inches

11

The Benitezes' house is on a rectangular lot that is 30 meters wide by 72 meters long. What is the perimeter of the lot? (page 739) **(7.8.02)**

A 102 meters
B 132 meters
C 204 meters
D 2,160 meters

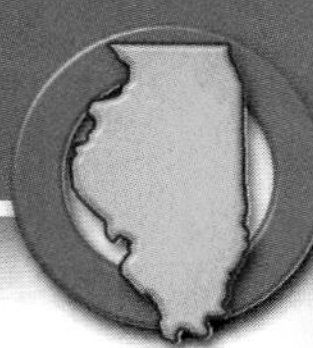

12

Which of the following tools could you use to find the value of x in the figure below? (page 735) **(7.8.01)**

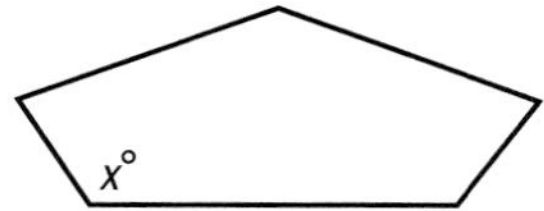

A centimeter rule
B protractor
C compass
D tape measure

13

A soup can has a diameter of 3.5 inches and a height of 6 inches. What is the volume of the soup can to the nearest tenth? (Lesson 7-5) **(7.8.04)**

A 57.7 in^3
B 99.0 in^3
C 113.1 in^3
D 230.9 in^3

14

What is the perimeter of the square shown below? (Lesson 3-1) **(7.8.02)**

Area = 49 ft^2

A 14 feet
B 28 feet
C 49 feet
D 98 feet

15

Will's dad is building a deck in their backyard. What is the area of the deck shown below? (Lesson 7-3) **(7.8.02)**

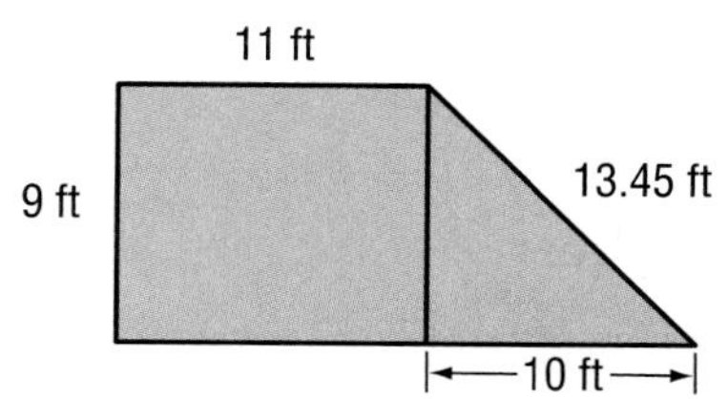

A 60.525 ft^2
B 99 ft^2
C 159.525 ft^2
D 233.5 ft^2

16

For a class project, Darnell's group needs to measure the length of a car to the nearest foot. Which of the following tools should they use? (page 735) **(7.8.01)**

A centimeter ruler
B protractor
C compass
D tape measure

17

A certain bird flies at the rate of 12 feet per second. Convert 12 feet per second to yards per minute. (page 742) **(7.8.05)**

A 0.6 yard per minute
B 36 yards per minute
C 240 yards per minute
D 2,160 yards per minute

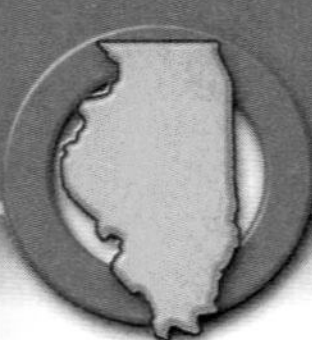

18

A circle has a radius of 1.85 feet. Which of the following is the best estimate for the circumference of the circle? (Lesson 7-1) **(7.8.03)**

A 6 feet
B 12 feet
C 18 feet
D 24 feet

19

Mr. Benton needs 4 pounds of red potatoes to make potato salad. What tool should he use to make sure he buys enough potatoes? (page 735) **(7.8.01)**

A centimeter ruler
B scale
C trundle wheel
D protractor

20

Shea is using wrapping paper to wrap a box that is 10 inches by 7 inches by 3 inches. What is the minimum amount of wrapping paper that Shea needs? (Lesson 7-7) **(7.8.04)**

21

The volume of the square prism at the right is 540 cubic yards. What is the height of the prism? Explain how you solved the problem. (Lesson 7-6) **(7.8.04)**

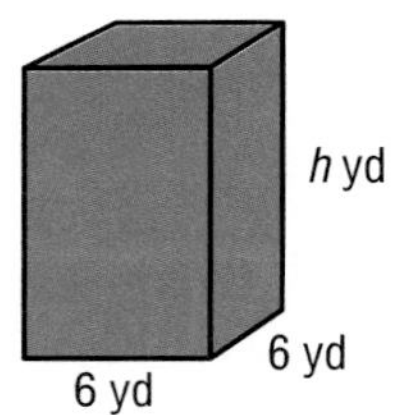

22

An archery target has a diameter of 80 inches. Each ring of color is 4 inches wide. (Lesson 7-1) **(7.8.02)**

- Explain how you could find the area of the white ring.
- Use your method from above to find the area of the blue ring. Use 3.14 for π. Show your work. Round to the nearest hundredth.

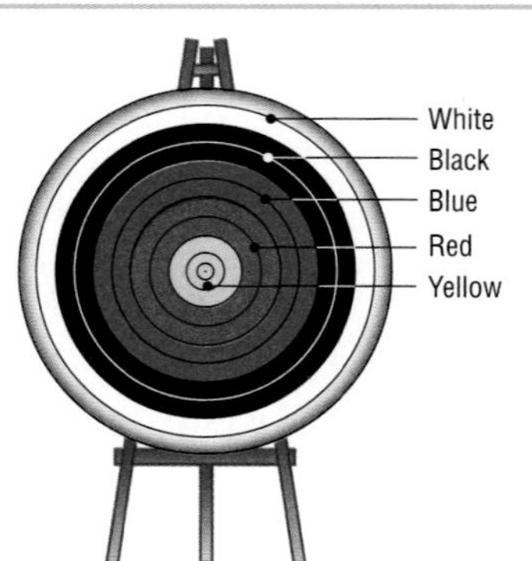

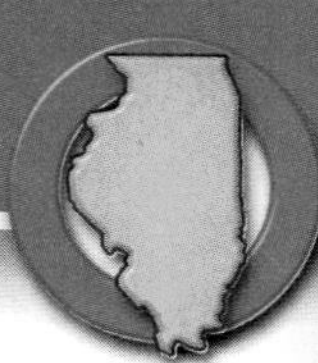

Algebra

1

What are the solutions of the equation $d^2 = 64$? (Lesson 3-1) **(6.8.09)**

A 8 and −8
B 16 and −16
C 32 and −32
D 64 and −64

2

Which of the following is equivalent to $3(x - 9)$? (Lesson 1-2) **(8.8.03)**

A $3x - 9$
B $3x - 27$
C $3x + 27$
D $3x - 3$

3

Elisa's mom is ordering tulip bulbs from a flower catalog. The price of each bulb is \$0.75. She has \$14 to spend and the shipping is \$3 for any size order. Which equation represents the maximum number of bulbs b that Elisa's mom can order? (Lesson 8-3) **(8.8.11)**

Tulip Bulbs	
price per bulb	\$0.75
shipping	\$3

A $0.75b + 3 = 14$
B $b + 3 = 14$
C $b + 3 = \frac{14}{0.75}$
D $0.75b = 14 + 3$

4

When the equation $y = 3x + 5$ is graphed on a coordinate plane, what is the y-coordinate when the x-coordinate is −2? (Lesson 9-3) **(8.8.07)**

A −11
B −6
C −1
D 11

5

What is the value of d in the equation $\frac{d}{3} + 20 = 14$? (Lesson 8-2) **(8.8.12)**

A	B	C	D
102	42	22	−18

6

Ana is filling up a small swimming pool in her backyard. Which of the following graphs could represent the amount of water w in the pool after t time? (Lesson 9-4) **(8.8.08)**

A
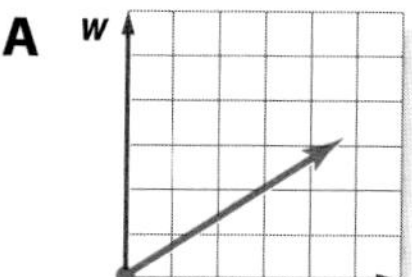

C
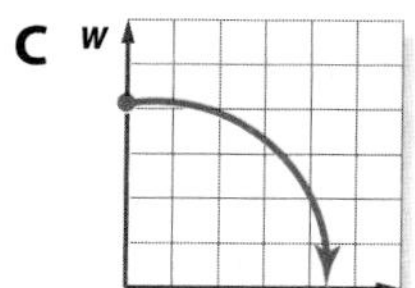

B **D**
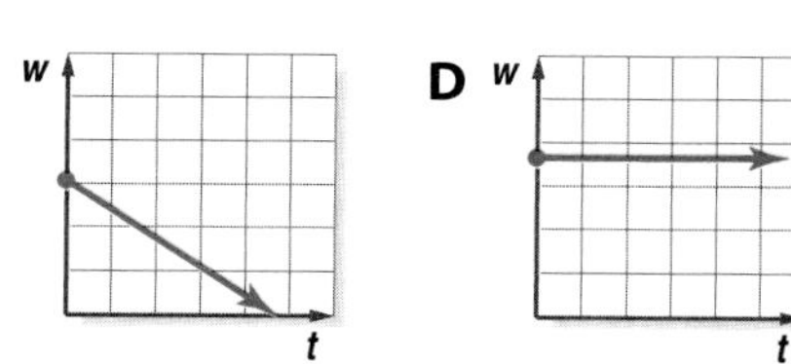

7

Jacob spent \$275 on lawn equipment. He charges \$10 per hour to mow lawns. The equation $y = 10x - 275$ represents the amount of money he will earn for mowing x hours over the summer. After how many hours of mowing lawns will Jacob have earned \$375? (Lesson 9-3) **(8.8.13)**

45 h	60 h	65 h	100 h
A	**B**	**C**	**D**

8

Which expression can be used to find the perimeter of the rectangle shown below? (Lesson 8-1) **(8.8.02)**

$2x + 5$

$6x + 3$

A $8x + 8$
B $8x + 16$
C $12x + 15$
D $16x + 16$

9

If $w - 16 \leq -7$, then which of the following values could not be a value of w? (Lesson 8-7) **(8.8.10)**

A -8
B 0
C 9
D 11

10

A line has slope of $\frac{2}{3}$ and a y-intercept of 4. Which of the following represents the equation of the line? (Lesson 9-6) **(8.8.08)**

A $3x - 2y = 12$
B $-2x + 3y = 12$
C $2x + 3y = -4$
D $-3x + 2y = -4$

11

Which of the following equations does not have a solution of -4? (Lessons 1-9, 1-10) **(8.8.12)**

A $-6x = 24$
B $x + (-7) = 11$
C $-9 = x - 5$
D $\frac{x}{-2} = 2$

12

Which of the following expressions represents the nth term of the sequence below? (Lesson 9-1) **(8.8.01)**

3, 5, 7, 9, 11, 13, …

A $2n$
B $2n + 1$
C $2n + 3$
D $2n + 5$

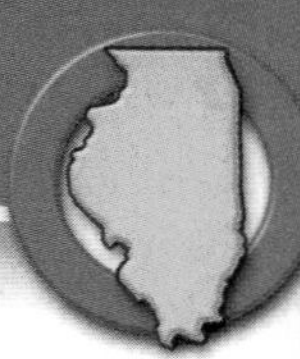

13

Translate the following statement into an algebraic equation. (Lesson 8-3) **(8.8.11)**

three more than four times a number is five more than six

A $3 + 4 + x = 5 + 6$
B $3 - 4x = 5 - 6$
C $3 + 4x = 5 + 6$
D $4x - 3 = 5 + 6$

14

The table below shows the admission prices to a local amusement park. Which equation represents this situation? (Lesson 9-3) **(8.8.11)**

Number of Visitors (V)	1	2	3	4
Total Price ($\$t$)	12	24	36	48

A $t = v + 12$
B $t = \frac{v}{12}$
C $t = 12v$
D $t = 4 + v + 12$

15

To rent a jet ski, there is a flat rate of \$15 plus \$10 per hour. Which equation represents the total cost t for renting a jet ski for h hours? (Lesson 9-3) **(8.8.11)**

A $t = 10h + 15$
B $t = 25h$
C $t = 15h - 10$
D $t = 15h + 10$

16

The average lifespan of American women in recent years can be represented by the equation $y = 0.2t + 73$, where t represents the number of years since 1960. Which of the following statements is true? (Lesson 9-6) **(8.8.09)**

A The y-intercept of the line is 0.2.
B The slope of the line is 73.
C The y-intercept of the line is 1960.
D The slope of the line is 0.2.

17

In baseball, the field is a square with 90 feet between each base. Let s represent this distance. The distance from home plate to second base can be found by the expression $\sqrt{(s^2 + s^2)}$. Find this distance. (Lesson 3-2) **(8.8.05)**

A 19.0 feet
B 90.1 feet
C 127.3 feet
D 134.2 feet

18

Name the first step in solving the equation below. (Lesson 8-2) **(8.8.12)**

$$4x + 7 = -9$$

A Divide each side by 4.
B Subtract 7 from each side.
C Divide each side by −9.
D Add 7 to each side.

19

Which of the following statements is not true about the line graphed below? (Lesson 9-6) **(8.8.07)**

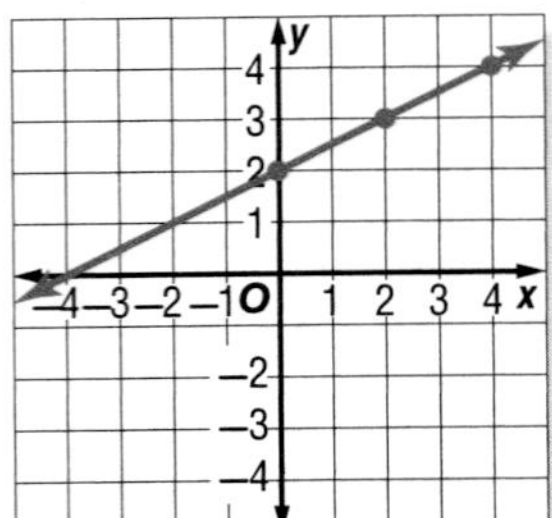

A The slope of the line is $\frac{1}{2}$.

B The y-intercept of the line is 2.

C The x-intercept of the line is -4.

D The equation of the line is $y = \frac{1}{2}x - 2$.

20

What is the value of x in the equation $-47 = x - 16$? (Lesson 1-9) **(8.8.12)**

-63	-31	31	63
A	**B**	**C**	**D**

21

At a restaurant, children 5 and under eat for free. Which inequality represents the age of children that eat free? (Lesson 8-6) **(8.8.10)**

A $a < 5$
B $a \leq 5$
C $a > 5$
D $a \geq 5$

22

Which equation can be represented by the graph below? (Lesson 10-2) **(8.8.08)**

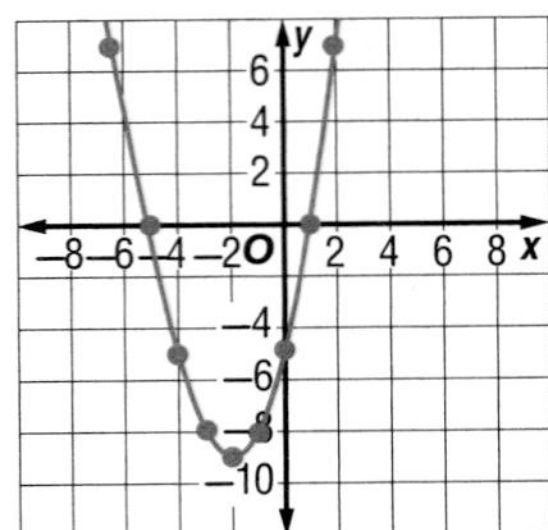

A $y = x^2 + 4x - 5$
B $y = x^2 + 4x - 15$
C $y = x^2 + 5x - 5$
D $y = 2x^2 + 4x - 5$

23

What is the exponent of d when the expression $7c^3d^5$ is raised to the third power? (Lesson 10-7) **(8.8.03)**

6	8	9	15
A	**B**	**C**	**D**

24

What is the product of $6a^3$ and $5a^4b$? (Lesson 10-5) **(8.8.03)**

A $11a^{12}b$
B $11a^7b$
C $30a^{12}b$
D $30a^7b$

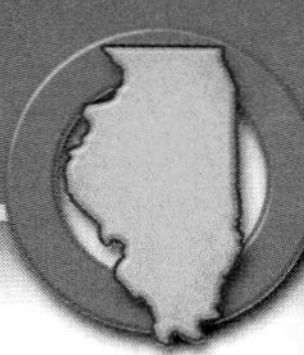

25

The equation for the speed of a ball that is thrown straight up in the air is given by $v = 128 - 32t$, where v is the velocity and t is the number of seconds after the ball is thrown. What is the slope of the equation? **(Lesson 9-6) (8.8.11)**

A 128
B 32
C −32
D −128

26

A company has 32 sales associates. It plans to increase the number of sales associates by four each month until it has doubled its current number of sales associates. Which equation can be used to determine m, the number of months it will take for the number of sales associates to double? **(Lesson 8-3) (8.8.11)**

A $4m + 32 = 64$
B $4m + 32m = 64$
C $2m + 32 = 64$
D $2(4m + 32) = 64$

27

In a group of 64 people, 3 out of 8 people are left-handed. **(Lesson 4-2) (8.8.13)**

- Describe how you would determine how many more people are right-handed in this group than are left-handed.
- Use your method from described above to solve the problem. Show your work.

28

What is the rate of change for the linear function represented in the table? **(Lesson 4-3) (8.8.06)**

Time (min)	Distance (mi)
20	124
25	155
30	186
35	217

29

Ms. Banderra wants to find the gas mileage of her car. She put 13.5 gallons of gas in her car and had driven 378 miles. Write and solve an equation that Ms. Banderra can use to find her car's gas mileage. **(Lesson 1-10) (8.8.13)**

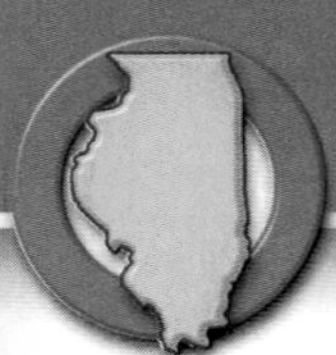

Geometry

1

Which of the following statements is not true about the figure shown below? (Lesson 7-4) **(9.8.01)**

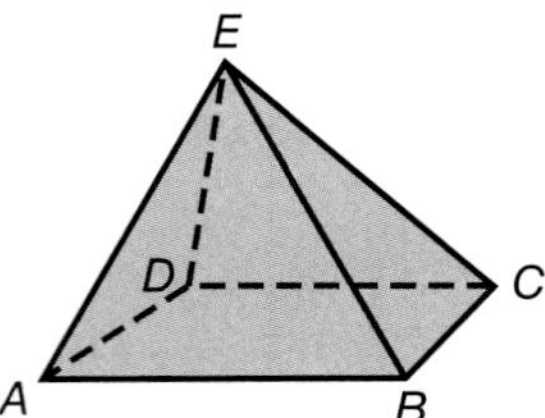

A One of the faces of the figure is $\triangle AEB$.
B Point D is a vertex of the figure.
C Figure $ABCE$ is the base of the pyramid.
D One of the edges of the figure is line DC.

2

Two angles are supplementary if the sum of their measures is 180°. The two angles shown are supplementary. Which of the following is an equation that can be used to find the measure of angle X? (Lesson 6-1) **(9.8.09)**

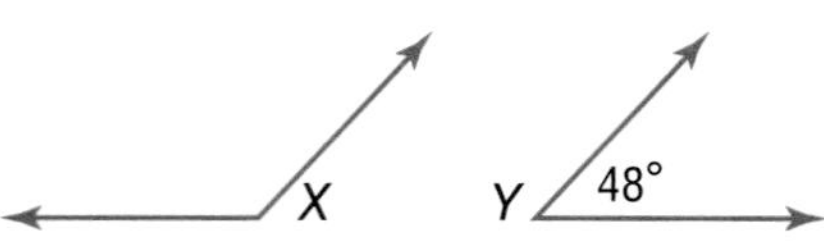

A $x + 48 = 180$
B $x + 48 = 90$
C $48 - x = 180$
D $48 - x = 90$

3

Does the figure shown below have rotational symmetry? If yes, what is its angle of rotation? (Lesson 6-5) **(9.8.06)**

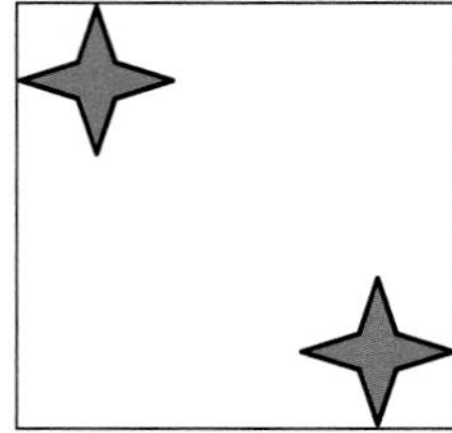

A Yes; the angle of rotation is 90°.
B Yes; the angle of rotation is 180°.
C Yes; the angle of rotation is 270°.
D No

4

Given triangle ABC, what are the coordinates of C' when a dilation of $\frac{1}{2}$ is applied? (Lesson 4-8) **(9.8.06)**

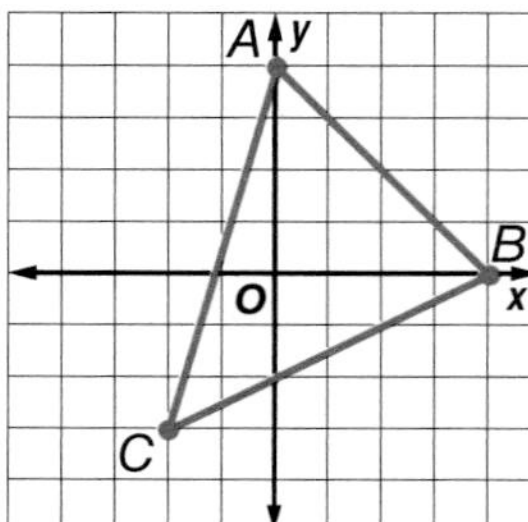

A (–2, –3)
B (–2, –1.5)
C (–1, –1.5)
D (–1, –2)

5

A circle has a diameter of 15 meters. Which statement is correct concerning the relationship between the circle's circumference and the irrational number π? **(Lesson 7-1) (9.8.04)**

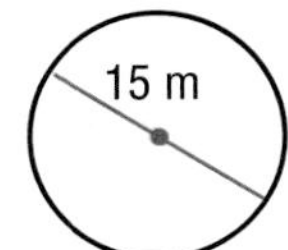

A The circle's circumference is five times larger than π.
B The ratio of π to the circle's circumference is equal to 15 meters.
C The circle's circumference is equal to the ratio of the circle's diameter to π.
D The ratio of the circle's circumference to π is equal to 15 meters.

6

Edmund designed the company logo below. What is the overall shape of the logo? **(Lesson 6-3) (9.8.01)**

A hexagon
B pentagon
C heptagon
D quadrilateral

7

Triangle ABC is similar to $\triangle LMN$. What is the value of $\overline{MN}$ if $\overline{AC}$ is 6 centimeters, $\overline{LN}$ is 8 centimeters, and $\overline{BC}$ is 15 centimeters? **(Lesson 4-7) (9.8.11)**

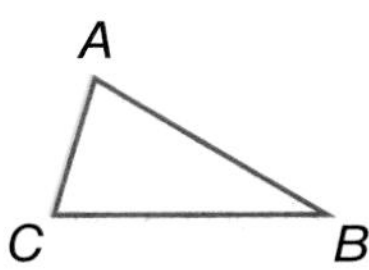

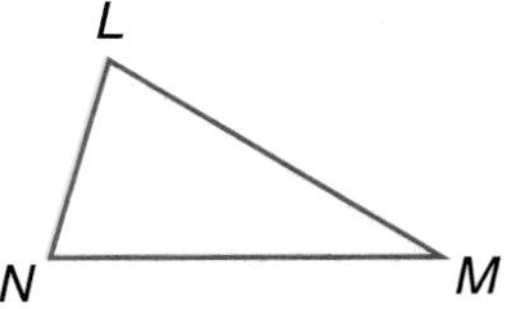

A 20 centimeters
B 18 centimeters
C 11.25 centimeters
D 3.2 centimeters

8

What is the value of x in the A-frame house shown below? **(page 737) (9.8.02)**

A 22
B 34
C 44
D 112

9

In the figure shown below, $a \parallel b$ and n is a transversal. If $m\angle 6 = 105°$, what is the measure of $\angle 5$? (Lesson 6-1) **(9.8.08)**

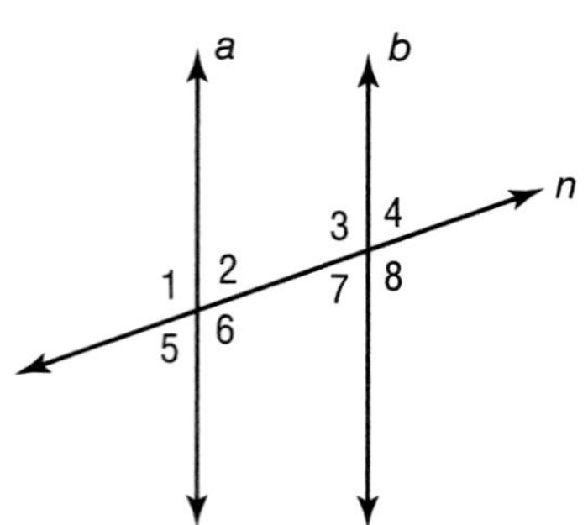

A 15°
B 75°
C 105°
D 150°

10

Mykia correctly found the surface area of a cylinder. Her teacher asked her to come to the board to show her class how she found the surface area. What two-dimensional figures can she draw on the board to help her explain how she found the surface area? (Explore 7-7) **(9.8.10)**

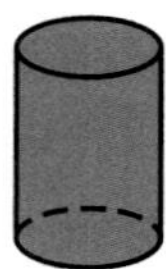

A a rectangle and two squares
B a rectangle and two circles
C two rectangles and a circle
D a rectangle and a circle

11

Julia is building a skateboard ramp. If the ramp is 12.5 feet tall and 15 feet long, how long is the base of the ramp? (Lesson 3-5) **(9.8.03)**

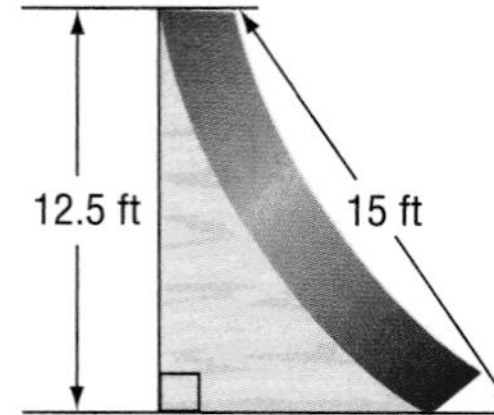

A 8.3 feet
B 16.6 feet
C 33.2 feet
D 68.75 feet

12

Triangle LMN has vertices $L(-2, -2)$, $M(4, -1)$, and $N(1, 5)$. What are the coordinates of M' after a translation 3 units left and 2 units up? (Lesson 6-7) **(9.8.05, 9.8.06)**

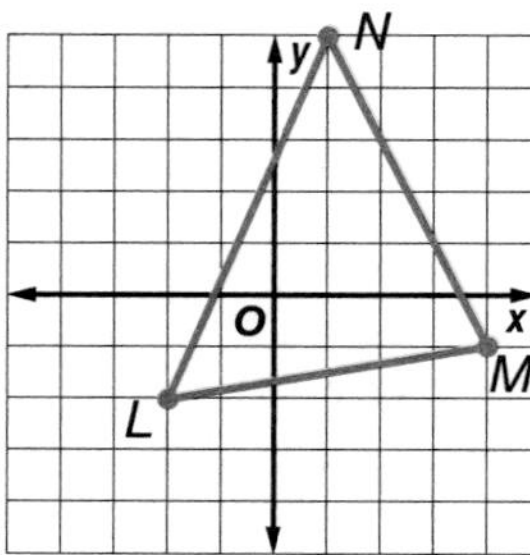

A (7, 1)
B (1, 1)
C (−2, 7)
D (2, 2)

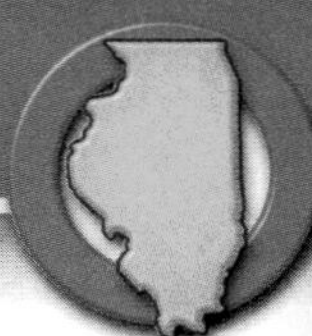

13

What is the sum of the interior angle measures of a hexagon? (Lesson 6-3) **(9.8.01)**

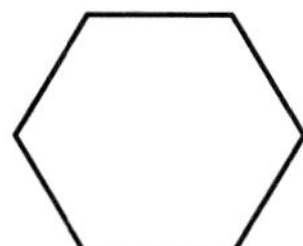

A 720°
B 840°
C 1,080°
D 1,440°

14

Which of the following statements best represents the expression $|x| = 7$? (Lesson 1-3) **(9.8.12)**

A The absolute value of 7 is −7.
B The distance between x and 0 on the number line is 7 units.
C The opposite of 7 is −7.
D The multiplicative inverse of 7 is $\frac{1}{7}$.

15

Which of the following three-dimensional figures has two circular bases? (Lesson 7-4) **(9.8.01)**

A triangular pyramid
B cone
C rectangular prism
D cylinder

16

Khung is drawing a picture of a shoebox. What type of three-dimensional figure is Khung drawing? (Lesson 7-4) **(9.8.01)**

A rectangular prism
B triangular prism
C cylinder
D rectangular pyramid

17

The side lengths of a right triangle are 12 inches, 35 inches, and x inches. What is the value of x, the hypotenuse of the triangle? (Lesson 3-5) **(9.8.03)**

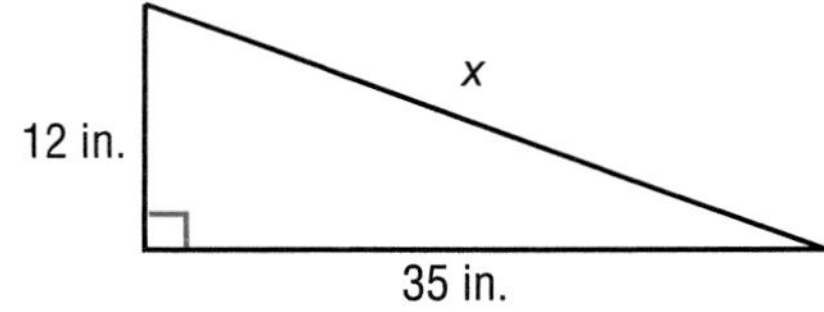

A 13.4 inches
B 32.9 inches
C 37 inches
D 39 inches

18

Meagan drew a square pyramid. How many edges does this figure have? (Lesson 7-4) **(9.8.01)**

A 5
B 6
C 7
D 8

19

In the figure shown below, which term describes the relationship of $\angle 2$ and $\angle 3$? (Lesson 6-1) **(9.8.08)**

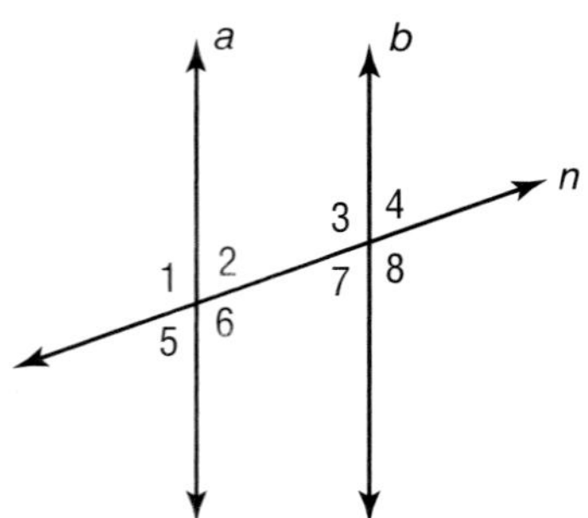

A alternate interior angles
B alternate exterior angles
C corresponding angles
D vertical angles

20

The two rectangles below represent the screen size of two different handheld games. The rectangles are similar. What is the area of the larger screen? (Lesson 4-7) **(9.8.11)**

4 in.

$A = 8$ in^2

8 in.

$A = x$ in^2

A 48 in^2
B 32 in^2
C 16 in^2
D 8 in^2

21

Felipe is building a model of an airplane with an actual length of 35 meters. What other information is needed to find x, the width of the propeller in Felipe's model? (Lesson 4-10) **(9.8.11)**

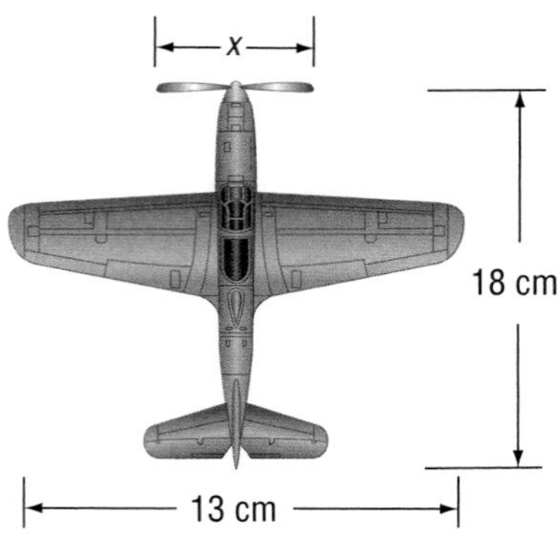

A the actual width of the airplane
B the actual width of the propeller
C the scale factor used
D the average speed of the airplane

22

Which of the following side lengths of a triangle form a right triangle? (Lesson 3-5) **(9.8.03)**

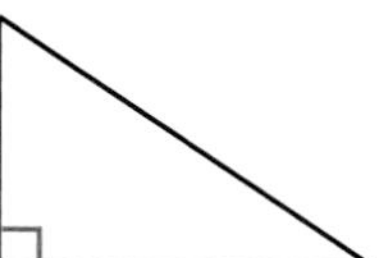

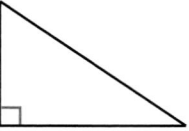

A 5 centimeters, 12 centimeters, 15 centimeters
B 7 inches, 20 inches, 25 inches
C 10 feet, 24 feet, 30 feet
D 15 yards, 20 yards, 25 yards

23

The vertices of $\triangle PQR$ are $P(-4, 2)$, $Q(-1, 5)$, and $R(3, 1)$. Graph the triangle and its image after a reflection over the x-axis. **(Lesson 6-6) (9.8.06)**

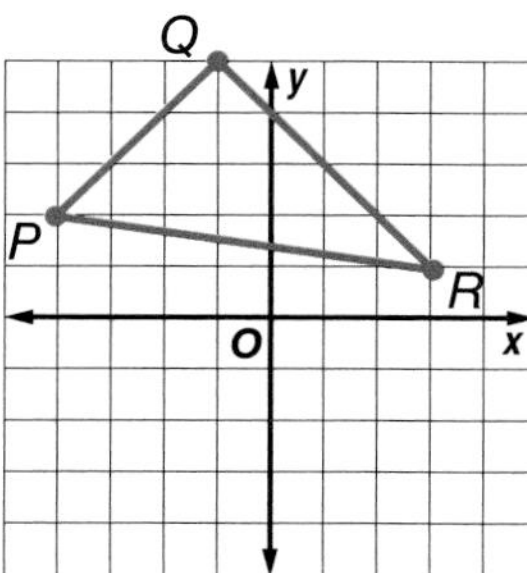

24

A teacher puts a mirror on the floor facing up and has a student stand at a distance of two feet from the edge of the mirror. The teacher stands so that she can just see the top of the student's head in the mirror and measures that distance. She then can determine the student's height. The diagram shows this situation. Write a proportion that can be used to find the teacher's height h if the measured distance and the student's height are both known. **(Lesson 4-9) (9.8.11)**

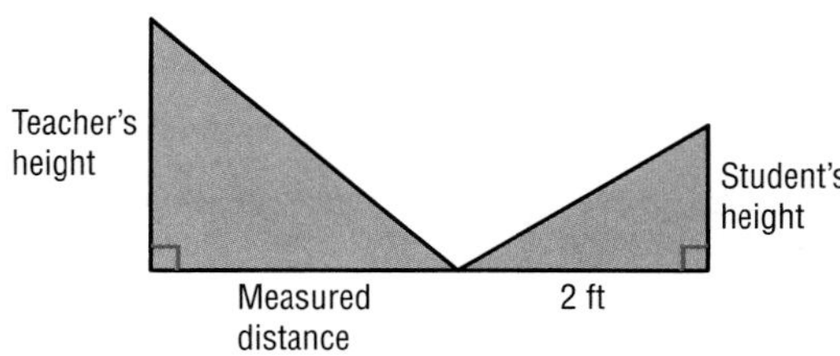

25

Under a dilation, the picture at the right has been reduced in size. What was the scale factor? Justify your response. **(Lesson 4-8) (9.8.06, 9.8.11)**

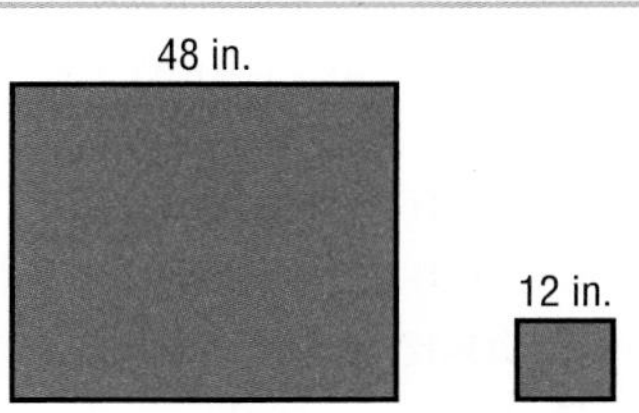

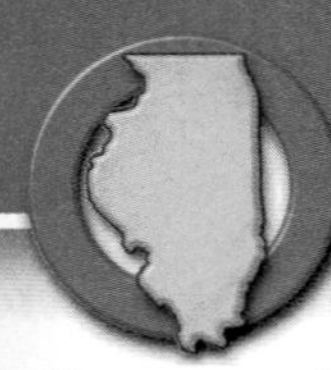

Data Analysis, Statistics, and Probability

1

The stem-and-leaf plot shows the ages of all the people in Felisa's family, including her parents, siblings, grandparents, aunts, uncles, and cousins. What is the median age of the members of Felisa's family? (Lesson 11-7) **(10.8.05)**

Age of Felisa's Family Members

Stem	Leaf
0	1 1 3 7 8 9
1	0 0 0 2 6
2	
3	2 4 7 9
4	1 2
5	
6	2 7 8

$3 | 2 = 32$

A 10 **B** 12 **C** 14 **D** 16

2

Mr. Brown's math class had the following test scores. Which is an appropriate display to show the measures of variation for the test scores? (Lesson 11-8) **(10.8.02)**

Math Test Scores									
80	75	90	95	65	65	80	85	70	100

A stem-and-leaf plot
B box-and-whisker plot
C histogram
D scatter plot

3

Which of the following data sets has the greatest range? (Lesson 11-4) **(10.8.05)**

A {11, 28, 13, 37, 45, 6, 52}
B {213, 220, 211, 217, 225, 218}
C {95, 96, 90, 85, 76, 81}
D {578, 544, 539, 570, 548, 553}

4

The production records of a tennis racket manufacturing company show that 4 out of every 80 tennis rackets have a defect. What is the probability that a randomly selected tennis racket manufactured at the company will not have a defect? (Lesson 12-3) **(10.8.06)**

A 5% **B** 20% **C** 85% **D** 95%

5

Mrs. Sato is buying a new car. The type of car she wants to buy comes in 2-door or 4-door, 3 different interior colors, and 5 different exterior colors. How many possible outcomes does Mrs. Sato have to choose from? (Lesson 12-1) **(10.8.07)**

A 10 **B** 20 **C** 30 **D** 60

6

A spinner has 4 equal sections colored yellow, blue, green, and red. What is the probability of landing on blue? (Lesson 12-2) **(10.8.06)**

$\frac{1}{4}$	$\frac{1}{3}$	$\frac{1}{2}$	$\frac{3}{4}$
A	**B**	**C**	**D**

7

The circle graph below shows the favorite sport of students. If 200 eighth-grade students were surveyed, how many more students favor baseball than volleyball? (Lesson 11-3) **(10.8.01)**

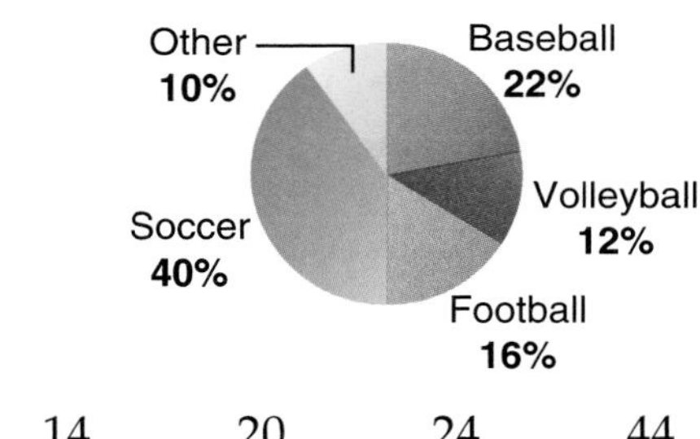

14	20	24	44
A	**B**	**C**	**D**

8

Which of the following data displays would be best to show the number of participants in a race according to age intervals? (Lesson 11-8) **(10.8.02)**

A stem-and-leaf plot
B box-and-whisker plot
C line graph
D histogram

9

A bag contains 3 purple marbles and 7 pink marbles. Once a marble is selected, it is not replaced. What is the probability of selecting a purple marble and then a pink marble? (Lesson 12-2) **(10.8.06)**

A $\frac{7}{30}$
B $\frac{3}{10}$
C $\frac{10}{19}$
D $\frac{7}{9}$

10

The number of points the Lions scored in each basketball game this season is represented in the box-and-whisker plot below. Which of the following statements is not a reasonable conclusion? (Lesson 11-6) **(10.8.01)**

Points Scored

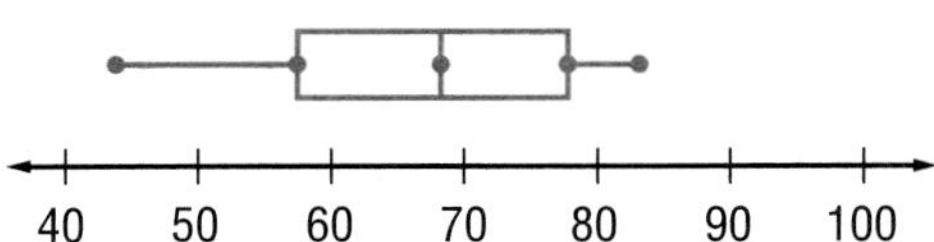

A The median number of points scored this season was 69.
B The greatest number of points scored was 99.
C The minimum number of points scored was 57.
D Most of the games the team scored between 57 and 77 points.

11

The number of pounds of recycled paper for each class at a junior high school is shown in the table below. Which measure would the school use to show they recycled a lot of paper? (Lesson 11-4) **(10.8.05)**

15	22	12	30	16
27	16	31	24	19

A mean
B median
C mode
D range

12

Dasha said that the number that best represented the following set of data is 28. Which measure is this? (Lesson 11-4) **(10.8.05)**

16, 25, 30, 16, 40, 26, 28, 29, 33

A mean
B median
C mode
D range

13

A fruit bowl has 6 apples and 4 oranges. If one piece of fruit is selected at random and then a second piece of fruit is selected at random without replacing the first piece of fruit, what is the probability that both pieces of fruit will be apples? (Lesson 12-2) **(10.8.06)**

A $\frac{1}{2}$
B $\frac{1}{3}$
C $\frac{1}{4}$
D $\frac{1}{5}$

14

Using the circle graph below, which of the following statements is a reasonable conclusion? (Lesson 11-3) **(10.8.01)**

Cost of Owning a Dog

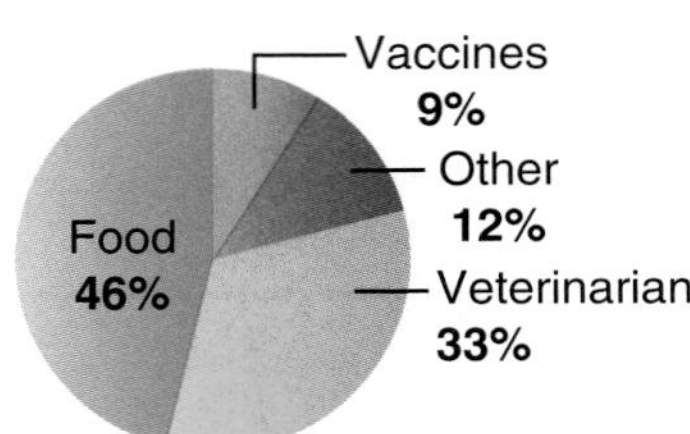

A Veterinary costs are the greatest.
B The cost of dog food is more than half the total cost of owning a dog.
C The cost of dog food is about five times the cost of vaccines.
D The cost of vaccines is about one fourth the total cost of owning a dog.

15

Last week, Aiyanna biked 12, 9, 6, 4, 6, and 11 miles. Which measure is the greatest? (Lesson 11-4) **(10.8.05)**

A mean
B median
C mode
D range

16

How many outcomes are there when a number cube is rolled four times? (Lesson 12-1) **(10.8.07)**

A 216
B 256
C 864
D 1,296

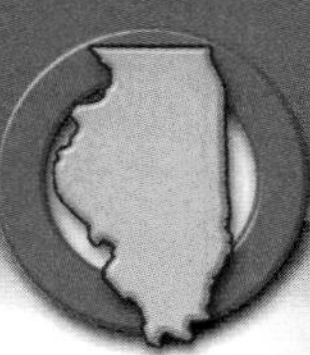

17

The spinner shown below is used for a board game. Which of the following is a reasonable prediction? (Lesson 12-2) **(10.8.06)**

A Rolling an even number is more likely than rolling an odd number.
B Rolling a prime number is less likely than rolling a composite number.
C Rolling a number less than 5 is more likely than rolling a number greater than 5.
D Rolling a multiple of 3 is more likely than rolling a factor of 6.

18

Tyrell has the following scores on six math quizzes: 78, 85, 90, 71, 90, and 83. If his teacher drops the lowest quiz score, which of the following statements is true concerning the measures of central tendency? (Lesson 11-4) **(10.8.05)**

A The mean will decrease.
B The mean will increase.
C The median will decrease.
D The mode will increase.

19

Owen wants to take a survey of his classmates to determine the number of hours each person spends watching TV during a typical week. What type of graph might be the best way for Owen to display his results? Explain your reasoning. (Lesson 11-8) **(10.8.02)**

20

The scatter plot shows the number of gallons of ice cream sold at various temperatures. Determine whether the data in the scatter plot shows a positive, negative, or no relationship. Explain your answer. (Lesson 9-9) **(10.8.01)**

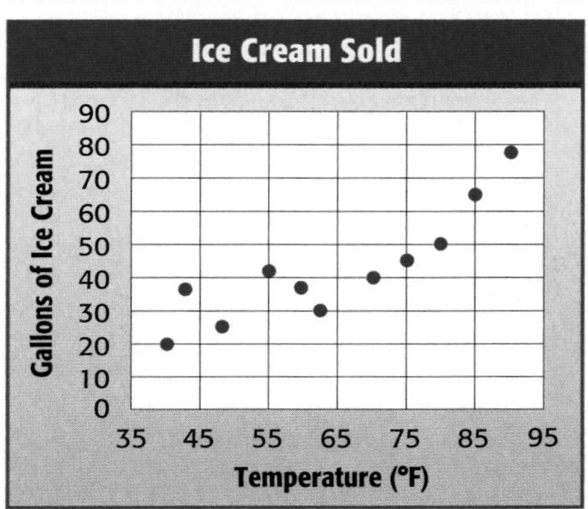

To the Student

As you gear up to study mathematics, you are probably wondering, "What will I learn this year?" You will focus on these three areas:

- **Algebra:** Analyze and represent linear functions, and solve linear equations.
- **Geometry and Measurement:** Analyze two- and three-dimensional figures.
- **Data Analysis:** Analyze and summarize data sets.

Along the way, you'll learn more about problem solving, how to use the tools and language of mathematics, and how to THINK mathematically.

How to Use Your Math Book

Have you ever been in class and not understood all of what was being presented? Or, you understood everything in class, but got stuck on how to solve some of the homework problems? Don't worry. You can find answers in your math book!

- Read the MAIN IDEA at the beginning of the lesson.
- Find the New Vocabulary words, **highlighted in yellow**, and read their definitions.
- Review the EXAMPLE problems, solved step-by-step, to remind you of the day's material.
- Refer to the HOMEWORK HELP boxes that show you which examples may help with your homework problems.
- Go to IL Math Online where you can find extra examples to coach you through difficult problems.
- Review the notes you've taken on your FOLDABLES™.
- Find the answers to odd-numbered problems in the back of the book. Use them to see if you are solving the problems correctly.

Scavenger Hunt

Let's Get Started

Use the Scavenger Hunt below to learn where things are located in each chapter.

1. What is the title of Chapter 1?
2. How can you tell what you'll learn in Lesson 1-1?
3. In the margin of Lesson 1-2, there is a Vocabulary Link. What can you learn from that feature?
4. What is the key concept presented in Lesson 1-2?
5. Sometimes you may ask, "When am I ever going to use this?" Name a situation that uses the concepts from Lesson 1-3.
6. How many examples are presented in Lesson 1-3?
7. What is the title of the feature in Lesson 1-3 that tells you how to read inequality symbols?
8. What is the Web address where you could find extra examples?
9. Suppose you're doing your homework on page 38 and you get stuck on Exercise 19. Where could you find help?
10. What problem-solving strategy is presented in the Problem-Solving Investigation in Lesson 1-8?
11. List the new vocabulary words that are presented in Lesson 1-9.
12. What is the Web address that would allow you to take a self-check quiz to be sure you understand the lesson?
13. There is a Real-World Career mentioned in Lesson 1-10. What is it?
14. On what pages will you find the Study Guide and Review for Chapter 1?
15. Suppose you can't figure out how to do Exercise 25 in the Study Guide and Review on page 76. Where could you find help?

MATH SYMBOLS

Let's Review!

Lincoln's Boyhood Home

Lesson 1

A Plan for Problem Solving

Let's Hit the Trail!

Pere Marquette State Park, 5 miles west of Grafton, is Illinois' largest state park with an area of 8,050 acres. The park offers year-round activities including boating, biking, hiking, horseback riding, and camping. The table gives the distance of the park's scenic hiking trails.

Trail	Distance (mi)
Dogwood	0.5
Fern Hollow	2.5
Goat Cliff	1.5
Hickory	0.5
Hickory North	1
Hickory South	1.5
Oak	0.25
Rattlesnake	0.25
Ravine	0.5
Ridge	0.25

Source: Great River Road

What is the combined length in miles of the park's scenic hiking trails?

You can use the four-step problem-solving plan to solve many kinds of problems. The four steps are Understand, Plan, Solve, and Check.

Understand

- **Read the problem carefully.**
- **What facts do you know?**
- **What do you need to find?**

You know the length in miles of each hiking trail. You need to find the combined length in miles of the hiking trails.

Plan

- **How do the facts relate to each other?**
- **Plan a strategy to solve the problem.**

To find the combined length of the park's hiking trails, add the length of each of the park's hiking trails.

Solve

- **Use your plan to solve the problem.**
  $0.5 + 2.5 + 1.5 + 0.5 + 1 + 1.5 + 0.25 + 0.25 + 0.5 + 0.25 = 8.75$

So, the combined length in miles of the park's hiking trails is 8.75 miles.

Check

- **Look back at the problem.**
- **Does your answer make sense?**
- **If not, solve the problem another way.**

Add the miles that are whole numbers. $2 + 1 + 1 + 1 = 5$

There are 6 half-mile portions. This is equal to 3 miles.

There are 3 quarter-mile portions. This is equal to 0.75 mile.

Since $5 + 3 + 0.75 = 8.75$, the answer makes sense.

CHECK Your Understanding

1. How much longer in miles is the Fern Hollow Trail than the Ridge Trail?

2. WRITING IN MATH Pere Marquette State Park offers a 50-minute horseback riding tour along a 2.5-mile trail. Explain how you could use the four-step problem-solving plan to determine the average number of minutes each mile on the tour lasts. Then solve the problem.

6.B.3b Apply primes, factors, divisors, multiples, common factors and common multiples in solving problems.

Illinois Start Smart

Lesson 2

Number Sense

Go For 3!

Normal is home to Illinois State University and the Redbirds women's basketball team. The table below gives the number of points the Redbirds women's basketball team scored during each game of the 2007-2008 season.

Points Scored per Game
Redbirds Women's Basketball
(2007–2008 Season)

81	79	70	82	75	69	94	71	78	77	77
82	79	71	82	78	75	82	74	66	69	87
77	95	71	88	62	79	91	77	68	70	61

Source: Illinois State University

Prime or Composite Numbers

When a whole number greater than 1 has exactly two factors, 1 and itself, it is called a *prime number*. When a whole number greater than 1 has more than two factors, it is called a *composite number*.

Use the scores from the table on page 6 and determine if they are *prime* or *composite* numbers.

1. 78 **2.** 94 **3.** 61

4. 81 **5.** 79 **6.** 77

Prime Factorization

When a number is expressed as a product of factors that are all prime, the expression is called the *prime factorization* of the number. Every number has a unique set of prime factors.

A *factor tree* is useful in finding the prime factorization of a number. A factor of 60 is shown at the right. So, the prime factorization of 60 is $2^2 \times 3 \times 5$.

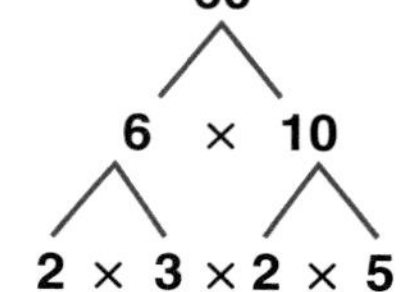

Use the data from page 6 to write the prime factorization of each score.

7. 81 **8.** 70 **9.** 77

10. **WRITING IN MATH** Use the table showing selected team statistics of the Redbirds women's basketball team for the 2007-2008 season. Explain how to determine if each number is prime or composite. Then determine which numbers are prime, if any, and which numbers are composite, if any.

Team Statistics (2007–2008 Season)

Statistic	Number
Rebounds	1,308
Assists	580
Turnovers	447
Steals	230
Blocks	121

Source: Illinois State University

8.A.2b Construct and solve number sentences using a variable to represent an unknown quantity.

Lesson 3

Algebra and Analytical Methods

Hook, Line, and Sinker!

The state fish of Illinois is the bluegill. The average adult bluegill is about 10 inches long and weighs one pound. It can live up to eleven years in quiet, weedy ponds, lakes, and bays. The table shows the average lengths of several other fish common to Illinois.

Fish	Average Length (in.)
Bowfin	18
Brown Trout	20
Channel Catfish	13
Freshwater Drum	14
Lake Trout	22
Smallmouth Bass	15

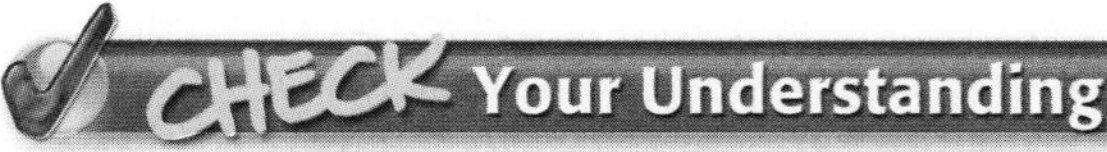

CHECK Your Understanding — Variables and Equations

Use the table on page 8 to answer the following questions.

1. The average length of a bowfin is 12 inches more than that of a rock bass. Write an equation that can be used to find the average length of a rock bass.

2. Solve the equation you created in Exercise 1. What is the average length of a rock bass?

3. The average length of a smallmouth bass is three times as long as that of a white perch. Write an equation that can be used to find the average length of a white perch.

4. Solve the equation you created in Exercise 3. What is the average length of a white perch?

5. The average length of a channel catfish is half the average length of an Atlantic salmon. Write an equation that can be used to find the average length of an Atlantic salmon.

6. Solve the equation you created in Exercise 5. What is the average length of an Atlantic salmon?

7. **WRITING IN MATH** Write a real-world problem to represent the equation $14 = a + 8$. Then solve the equation.

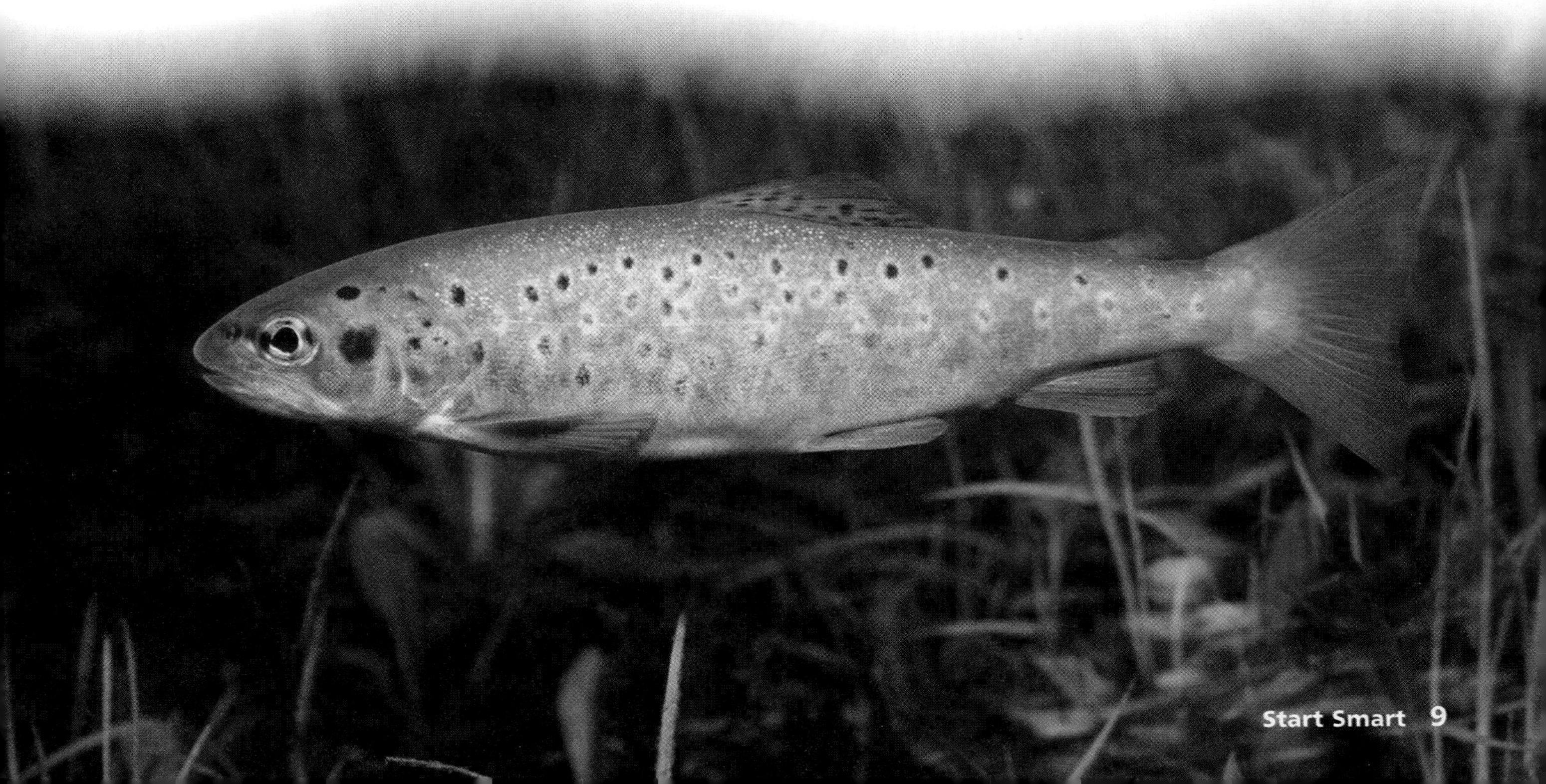

9.A.2b Identify and describe how geometric figures are used in practical settings (e.g., construction, art, advertising).

Illinois Start Smart

Geometry

Designed by Frank Lloyd Wright, the Hollis Root House, in Glencoe, exhibits prominent horizontal lines. Built in 1915, it is still a popular tourist attraction.

CHECK Your Understanding — Parallel and Perpendicular Lines

Pairs of lines can be parallel or intersecting. When lines are parallel, they are always the same distance apart; they will never intersect. When pairs of lines intersect at 90-degree angles, they are considered perpendicular lines. When classifying pairs of lines in two-dimensional photos, it is important to keep in mind the actual object is three-dimensional.

Use the photo of the Hollis Root House to classify each pair of lines as *parallel, perpendicular,* or *neither.*

1. the blue and yellow lines

2. the yellow and red lines

3. the purple and blue lines

4. the green and yellow lines

CHECK Your Understanding

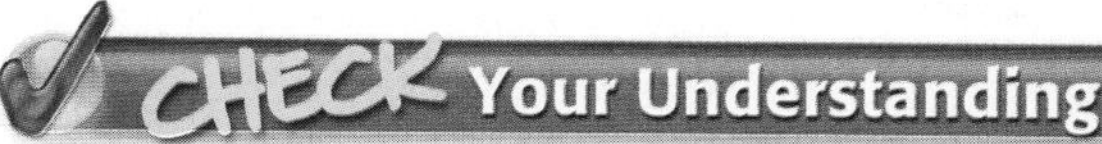

Classify Triangles

Triangles can be classified by their interior angle measurements. An *acute triangle* has three acute angles. A *right triangle* has one right angle and two acute angles. An *obtuse triangle* has one obtuse angle and two acute angles.

Use the photo below of the W. Irving Clark Residence, in LaGrange, to classify each triangle as *acute, right,* or *obtuse.*

5. the red triangle

6. the blue triangle

7. the green triangle

8. the yellow triangle

9. **WRITING IN MATH** Use the Internet or another source to find a photo of another building in Illinois that uses parallel lines, perpendicular lines, or triangles. Write a few sentences describing the geometry in the photo.

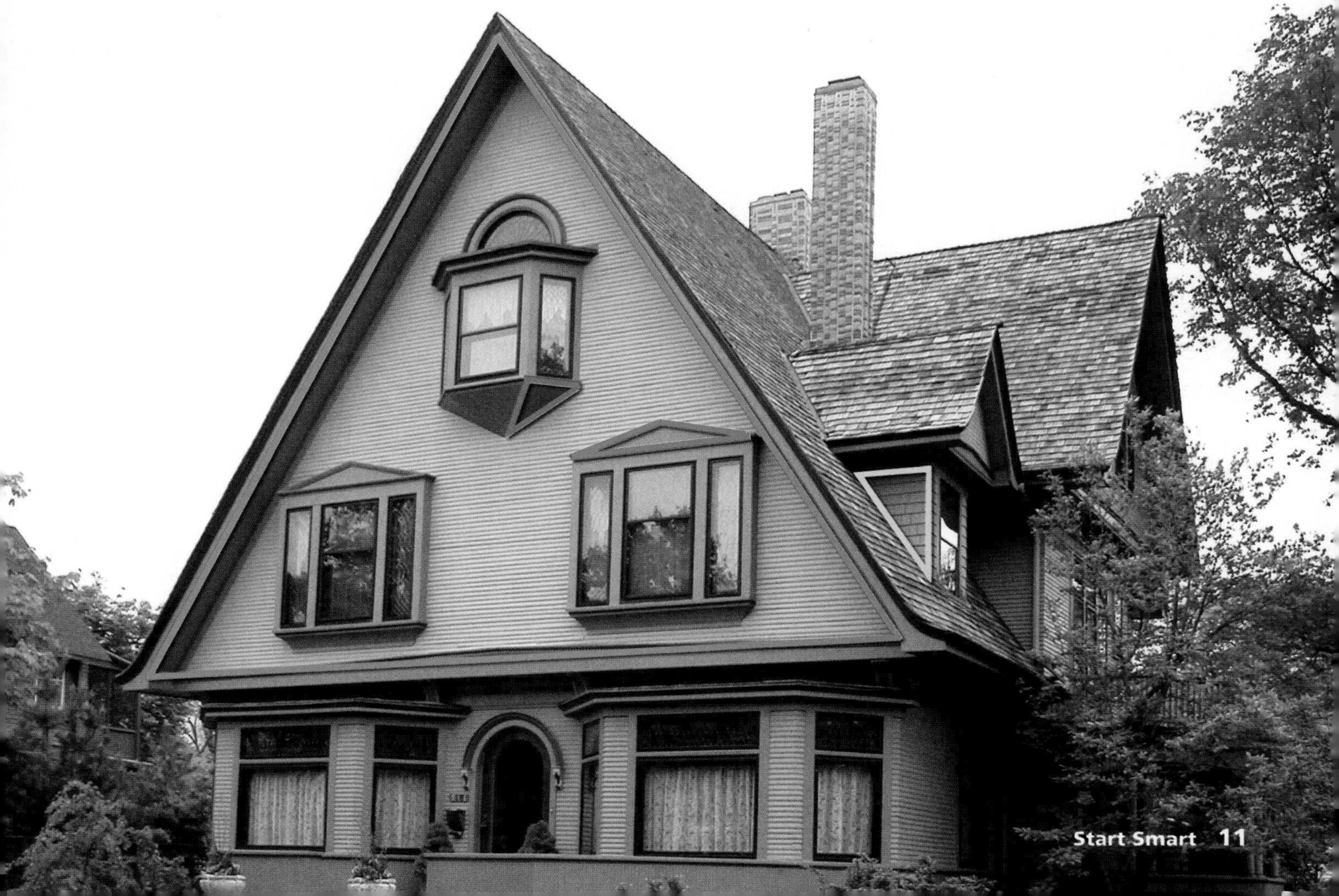

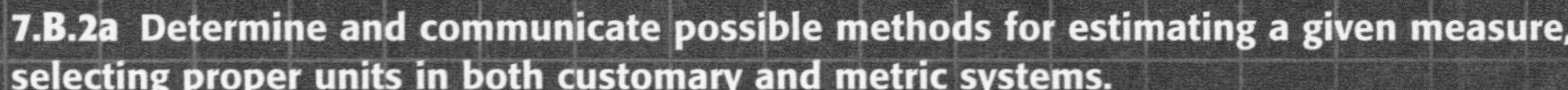

Illinois Start Smart

Lesson 5

Estimation and Measurement

And the Winner Is . . .

Over 80% of the world's canned pumpkin is processed in Morton. In 1978, Morton was nicknamed "The Pumpkin Capital of the World." The Morton Pumpkin Festival is held every fall and offers carnival rides, foot races, food tents, craft shows, parades, and a pumpkin weigh-off. The table gives the weight in pounds of the pumpkins that won selected categories during a recent Pumpkin Festival.

Category	Weight (lb)
King Pumpkin 1st	125
King Pumpkin 2nd	83.5
King Pumpkin 3rd	75
Queen Pumpkin	64
Closest to 41 lb (for the 41st Festival)	40.5

Source: Morton Chamber of Commerce

Converting Between Customary Units

You know that one pound is equal to 16 ounces and that 2,000 pounds is equal to one ton.

Use the table on page 12 to answer each question.

1. What is the weight in ounces of the pumpkin that won the category of Queen Pumpkin?

2. What fraction of one ton is the weight of the pumpkin that won the category of King Pumpkin 1st? Write in simplest form.

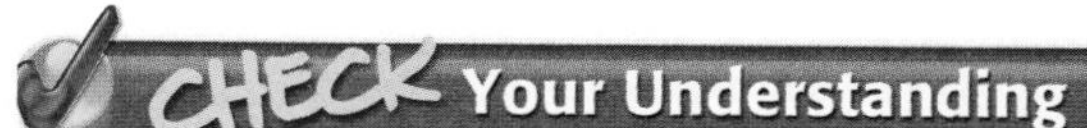

Estimation

Use the table on page 12 to answer each question.

3. About how many times heavier did the pumpkin that won the category of King Pumpkin 1st weigh than the pumpkin that won the category of Queen Pumpkin?

4. About how many times as heavy was the pumpkin that won the category of Closest to 41 lb as the pumpkin that won the category of King Pumpkin 1st?

5. The pumpkin that won the category of Tiniest Pumpkin weighed 50 grams. If one ounce is approximately equal to 28.35 grams, about how many ounces did the pumpkin that won this category weigh?

6. About what fraction of one pound is the weight of the pumpkin that won the category of Tiniest Pumpkin?

7. **WRITING IN MATH** Use the table on page 12 to write and solve a real-world problem involving measurement or estimation.

The LaSalle Bank Chicago Marathon is a yearly event in which 45,000 runners run a 26.2-mile course winding through Chicago. The Chicago Marathon celebrated its 30th anniversary in 2007, and nine runners have participated in the marathon for each of those 30 years. The table below gives the times for the top 5 men and top 5 women finishes of a recent year.

Top 5 Men's Times (h:min:sec)	Top 5 Women's Times (h:min:sec)
2:21:42	2:40:14
2:26:34	2:49:59
2:26:55	2:50:50
2:29:06	2:51:58
2:29:42	2:56:24

These data can be arranged in a histogram. A histogram is similar to a bar graph and shows the number of pieces of data in equal intervals. A frequency table is often used to create a histogram.

Frequency Tables

1. Complete the frequency table using the data about race times.

Race Times for Top 5 Men and Top 5 Women		
Time	Tally	Frequency
2:20:00–2:29:59		
2:30:00–2:39:59		
2:40:00–2:49:59		
2:50:00–2:59:59		

2. Which interval has the greatest number of scores?

3. How many runners finished the marathon in less than 2 hours and 40 minutes?

Histograms

4. Complete the histogram using the frequency table you completed for Exercise 1.

5. According to the histogram created, during what times were there no runners crossing the finish line?

6. **WRITING IN MATH** Explain how a race organizer can use the frequency table or histogram above to predict how many runners will finish the marathon in under three hours next year.

Illinois Data File

The following pages contain data that you will use throughout the book.

Chicagoland Speedway, Joliet

Acres of Land: 930
Acres of Parking: 500
Number of Seats: 75,000
Height of Grandstands: 15 stories
Length of Grandstands: 2,480 feet long
Garages: 4; 120 bays; 11,050 square feet
Pit Road: 43 stalls

Source: Chicagoland Speedway

Peoria Weather

Forecast for Peoria, Illinois March 1–5 of a Recent Year			
Day	**High Temperatures**	**Probability of Precipitation**	**Cloud Cover**
March 1	38°	20%	Mostly Sunny
March 2	47°	30%	Cloudy
March 3	39°	40%	Cloudy
March 4	30°	60%	Mostly Cloudy
March 5	36°	10%	Partly Cloudy

Source: The Weather Channel

Champaign, Illinois

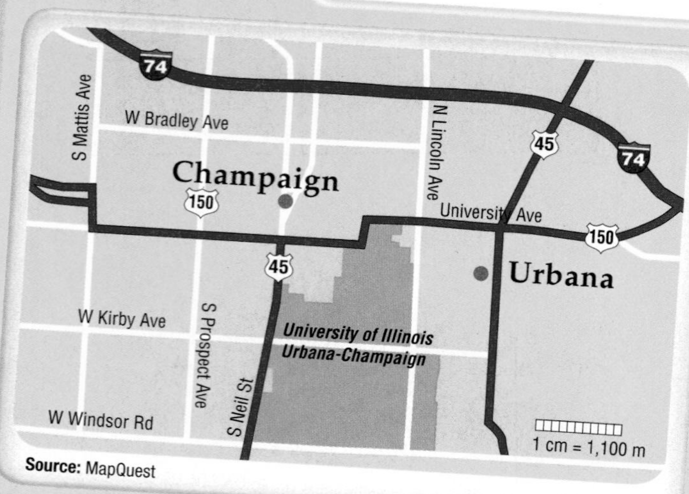

Source: MapQuest

Marina City, Chicago, Illinois

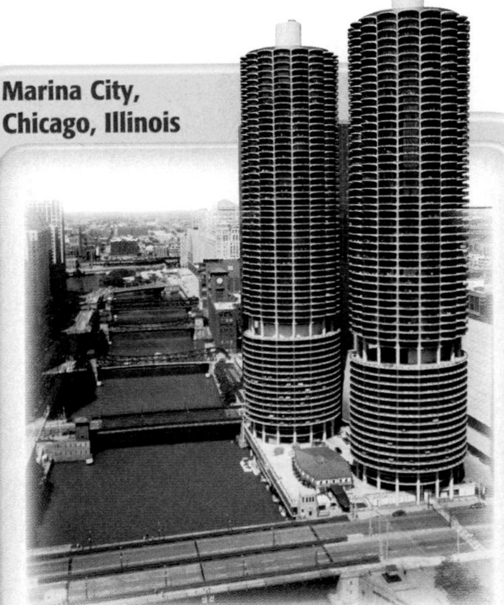

Built in 1959, the Marina City twin buildings are comprised of apartments and parking space. The bottom 20 stories are comprised of a continuous parking ramp that has space for 450 vehicles. The top 40 stories are comprised of 450 apartments. Each tower is 587 feet tall and contains almost no interior right angles.

Source: Great Buildings

Chicago-Style Deep Dish Pizza Crust

Chicago-Style Deep Dish Pizza Crust

Ingredients:

- 2 packages dry yeast ("Quick Rise")
- 2 cups tepid water (90° F)
- $\frac{1}{2}$ cup salad oil
- 4 tablespoons olive oil
- $\frac{1}{2}$ cup cornmeal
- $5\frac{1}{2}$ cups flour

Source: All Recipes

Stadium Capacities

Stadium Capacities

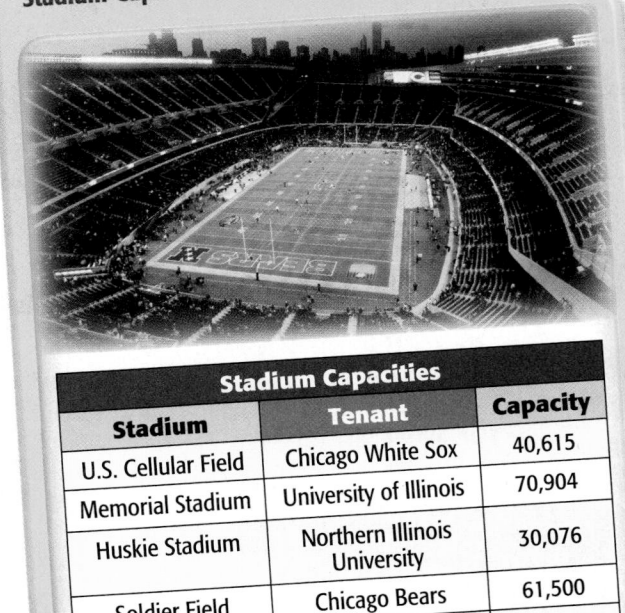

Stadium	Tenant	Capacity
U.S. Cellular Field	Chicago White Sox	40,615
Memorial Stadium	University of Illinois	70,904
Huskie Stadium	Northern Illinois University	30,076
Soldier Field	Chicago Bears	61,500
Wrigley Field	Chicago Cubs	41,118

Calumet City, Illinois

Source: MapQuest

Monarch Butterfly

The Monarch Butterfly was chosen as the state insect of Illinois in 1975. It undergoes 4 physical changes during its lifetime: tiny egg, caterpillar, caterpillar with protective covering, and butterfly. This process takes about a month. Monarchs from Illinois travel to California for winter. Only about 1% survive the journey back to Illinois.

Source: Illinois Department of Natural Resources

Illinois Minerals

Mineral	Average Crystal Length
Aragonite	1.5 cm
Calcite	8 cm
Dolomite	5 mm
Galena	1 cm
Millerite	2 cm
Pyrite	5 mm
Quartz	1 cm
Smithsonite	1 mm

Source: Mineralogical Record

Galena

Eighty-five percent of Galena's buildings are in a National Register Historic District.

Population: 3,460

Number of Annual Visitors: more than 1,000,000

Source: City of Galena

Lewis and Clark National Historic Trail

Starting in Illinois in 1804, the Lewis and Clark Expedition traveled to the Pacific Ocean over a two-year period. Today, the Lewis and Clark National Historic Trail gives visitors the opportunity to experience and learn about the expedition. The following map shows the 3,700-mile trail that travels through 11 states.

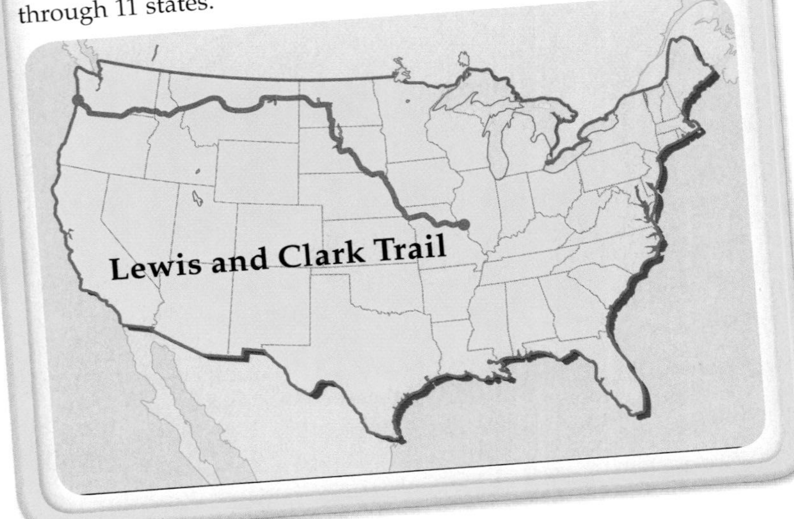

Illinois State Fair, Springfield

Approximate Attendance of Illinois State Fair by Year	
Year	**Attendance**
2003	650,000
2004	671,333
2005	672,615
2006	705,000

Source: Illinois State Fair

DÉJÀVU Roller Coaster

Amusement Park: Six Flags Great America

Opening Date: 2001

Height: 196 feet

Length: 1,203 feet

Top Speed: 65 miles per hour

Angle of Descent: 90°

G-Force: 4.5

Source: Roller Coaster Database

Exploration Station®

Exploration Station®, located in Bourbonnais, is a hands-on discovery center for children of all ages. The table below shows the admission prices.

Admission Prices		
Type	Age Range	Price ($)
Adults	18–54 years	5.00
Children	12 months–17 years	4.00
Seniors	55 years and older	4.00
Children	under 12 months	Free

Source: Exploration Station

Windy City Thunderbolts, Crestwood

Windy City Thunderbolts Baseball Team		
Season	Wins	Losses
2004	37	57
2005	39	57
2006	41	54
2007	68	28

Wrigley Field, Chicago

Distances from Home Plate	Leftfield	Left-Centerfield	Centerfield	Right-Centerfield	Rightfield
Distance (ft)	355	368	400	368	353

Source: Major League Baseball

Lowest Temperatures

Lowest Temperature Record by Month, Springfield, IL					
J	F	M	A	M	J
−21	−22	−12	19	28	40
J	A	S	O	N	D
48	43	32	17	−3	−21

Source: National Oceanic and Atmospheric Association

Unit 1

Number and Operations: Rational and Real Numbers

Focus

Use appropriate operations and strategies to solve problems.

CHAPTER 1
Algebra: Integers

BIG Idea Use algebraic terminology, expressions, equations, inequalities, and graphs to express quantitative relationships.

CHAPTER 2
Algebra: Rational Numbers

BIG Idea Use equations with rational numbers to solve problems.

BIG Idea Use scientific notation to express equivalent forms of rational numbers.

CHAPTER 3
Real Numbers and the Pythagorean Theorem

BIG Idea Apply the Pythagorean Theorem to find distances in the coordinate plane and to solve problems.

Problem Solving in Music

Real-World Unit Project

Music To My Ears Grab some sheet music. You're about to compose music! In this project, you'll learn about the connection between math and music. Along the way, you'll research Pythagoras' findings of music and learn how to make music harmonious. You'll need your problem-solving skills and an ear for music. This is one project that's sure to be on the music charts!

IL Math Online Log on to glencoe.com to begin.

Algebra: Integers

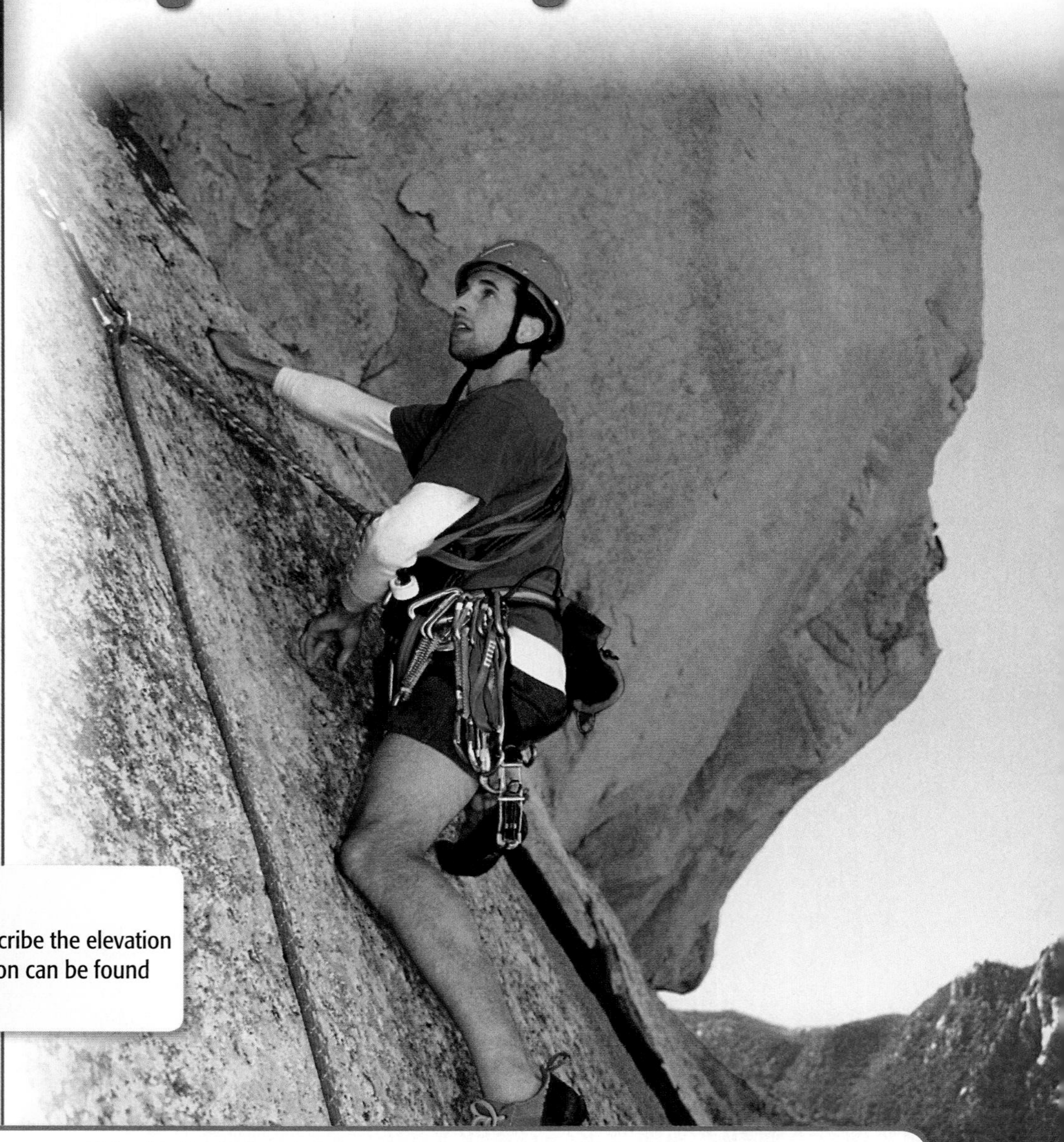

Illinois Learning Standards

6.B.3a Solve practical computation problems involving whole numbers, integers and rational numbers.
8.A.3a Apply the basic properties of commutative, associative, distributive, transitive, inverse, identity, zero, equality and order of operations to solve problems.

Key Vocabulary

algebraic expression (p. 29)
equation (p. 57)
integer (p. 35)
variable (p. 29)

Real-World Link

Terrain Integers can be used to describe the elevation of a rock climber. Changes in elevation can be found by adding or subtracting integers.

Algebra: Integers Make this Foldable to help you organize your notes. Begin with a piece of 11″ × 17″ paper.

1. **Fold** the paper in sixths lengthwise.
2. **Open and fold** a 4″ tab along the short side. Then fold the rest in half. 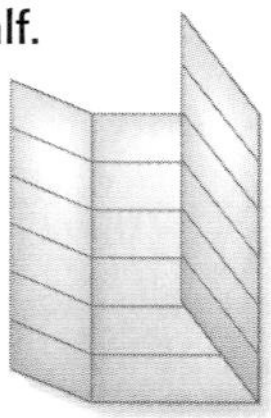
3. **Draw** lines along the folds and label as shown.

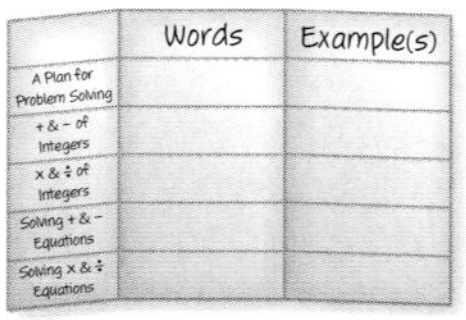

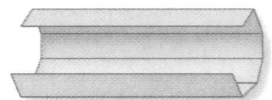

GET READY for Chapter 1

Diagnose Readiness You have two options for checking Prerequisite Skills.

Option 2

IL Math Online Take the Online Readiness Quiz at glencoe.com.

Option 1

Take the Quick Check below. Refer to the Quick Review for help.

QUICK Practice

Add. (Prior Grade)

1. $64 + 13$
2. $10.32 + 4.7$
3. $2.5 + 77$
4. $38 + 156$
5. **SHOPPING** Mrs. Wilson spent \$80.20, \$72.10, \$68.50, and \$60.70 on school clothes for her children. Find the total amount she spent. (Prior Grade)

Subtract. (Prior Grade)

6. $200 - 48$
7. $59 - 26$
8. $3.3 - 0.7$
9. $73.5 - 0.87$

Multiply. (Prior Grade)

10. $3 \times 5 \times 2$
11. 2.8×5
12. 12.7×6
13. $4 \times 9 \times 3$
14. **TRAVEL** The Perez family drove for 5.75 hours at 55 miles per hour. How far did they drive? (Prior Grade)

Divide. (Prior Grade)

15. $244 \div 0.2$
16. $72 \div 9$
17. $96 \div 3$
18. $100 \div 0.5$
19. $2 \div 5$
20. $0.36 \div 0.3$
21. **BAGELS** A bag of 8 assorted bagels sells for \$6.32. What is the price per bagel? (Prior Grade)

QUICK Review

Example 1 **Find 14.63 + 2.9.**

$$\begin{array}{r} 14.63 \\ +\ \ 2.90 \\ \hline 17.53 \end{array}$$

Line up the decimal points.
Annex a zero.

Example 2 **Find 82 − 14.61.**

$$\begin{array}{r} 82.00 \\ -\ 14.61 \\ \hline 67.39 \end{array}$$

Annex two zeroes.

Example 3 **Find 8.7 × 6.**

$$\begin{array}{rl} 8.7 & \leftarrow \text{1 decimal place} \\ \times\ \ 6 & \leftarrow \text{+0 decimal places} \\ \hline 52.2 & \leftarrow \text{1 decimal place} \end{array}$$

Example 4 **Find 4.77 ÷ 0.9.**

$0.9\overline{)4.77} \rightarrow 09.\overline{)47.7}$ Multiply both numbers by the same power of 10.

$$\begin{array}{r} 5.3 \\ 9\overline{)47.7} \\ -45 \\ \hline 27 \\ -27 \\ \hline 0 \end{array}$$

Place the decimal point and divide as with whole numbers.

1-1 A Plan for Problem Solving

MAIN IDEA

Solve problems using the four-step plan.

IL Learning Standards

6.B.3a Solve practical computation problems involving whole numbers, integers and rational numbers.

New Vocabulary

conjecture

IL Math Online

glencoe.com
- Extra Examples
- Personal Tutor
- Self-Check Quiz

MINI Lab

Bees build their homes by constructing hexagons out of wax. The first three patterns in a row can be shown using toothpicks.

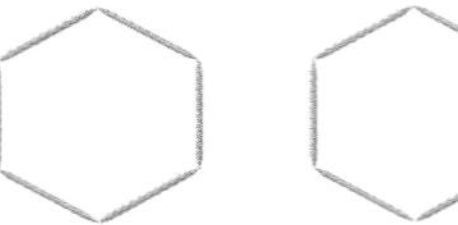
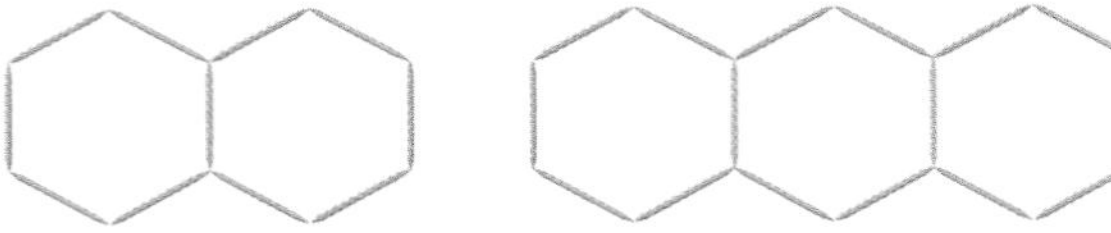

1. How many toothpicks does it take to make each of these three patterns?
2. Predict how many toothpicks it will take to make a row of 4 hexagons.
3. How many toothpicks will it take to make a row of 6 hexagons? Explain your reasoning.

Some problems, like the one above, can be solved by using one or more problem-solving strategies.

No matter which strategy you use, you can always use the four-step plan to solve a problem.

Understand
- Determine what information is given in the problem and what you need to find.
- Do you have all the information you need?
- Is there too much information?

Plan
- Visualize the problem and select a strategy for solving it. There may be several strategies that you can use.
- Estimate what you think the answer should be.
- Make an educated guess or a **conjecture**.

Solve
- Solve the problem by carrying out your plan.
- If your plan doesn't work, try another.

Check
- Examine your answer carefully.
- See if your answer fits the facts given in the problem.
- Compare your answer to your estimate.
- You may also want to check your answer by solving the problem again in a different way.
- If the answer is not reasonable, make a new plan and start again.

Real-World EXAMPLE

1 **BEEHIVES** The picture at the right shows a cross-section of a beehive with two cells outlined. If each side of a cell is one unit, the perimeter of one cell is 6 units. What would be the perimeter if there were 10 cells in a row?

Number of Cells	1	2	3	4	5	6
Perimeter	6	10	14	18	22	26

Study Tip

Understand In the Mini Lab, each row of hexagons used an inside toothpick. Example 1 is just the perimeter.

Understand From the Mini Lab, you know how many toothpicks are needed to make a row of 6 hexagons.

Plan You might recognize a pattern in the number of toothpicks used to outline any number of cells. One method for solving this problem is to look for a pattern.

Solve First, look for the pattern. Then, extend the pattern.

Number of Cells	1	2	3	4	5	6	7	8	9	10
Perimeter	6	10	14	18	22	26	30	34	38	42

+4 +4 +4 +4 +4 +4 +4 +4 +4

It would take 42 toothpicks to build the tenth row of the hive, or the perimeter of a figure with 10 cells in a row is 42.

Study Tip

Reasonableness Always check to be sure your answer is reasonable. If the answer seems unreasonable, solve the problem again.

Check The perimeter is a little more than four times the number of cells. To build the tenth row, it would take a little more than 4×10 toothpicks. So, 42 toothpicks is reasonable.

CHECK Your Progress

a. **INTERNET** The table shows the number of visitors, rounded to the nearest thousand, to a new Web site on each of the first five days after the Web site places an ad in a newspaper. If this pattern continues, about how many visitors should the Web site receive on day 8?

Day	Visitors
1	15,000
2	30,000
3	60,000
4	120,000
5	240,000

Some problems can be solved by a combination of operations.

Use the Four-Step Plan

Reading Math

Word Problems It is important to read a problem more than once before attempting to solve it. You may discover important details that you overlooked when you read the problem the first time.

2 **ANIMALS** **Refer to the graphic. If a cheetah and a giant tortoise travel at their top speed for 1 minute, how much farther does the cheetah travel?**

Animal Speed

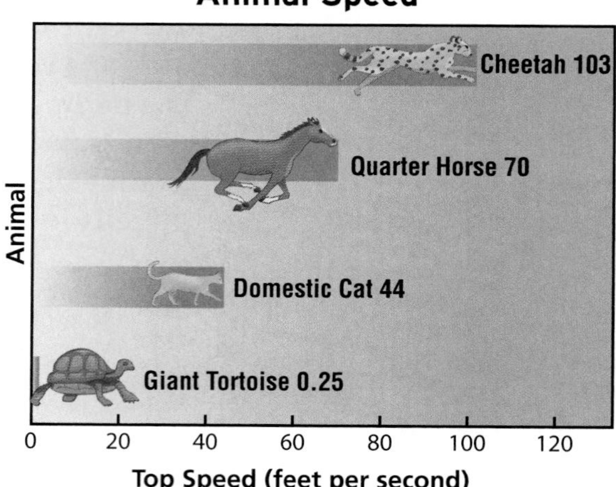

Top Speed (feet per second)

Understand *What do you know?*
You know the top speeds for a cheetah and a giant tortoise in feet per second.

What are you trying to find?
You need to find the difference in the distances traveled by a cheetah and a giant tortoise in 1 minute.

Plan Begin by determining the distance each animal traveled in 1 minute. Since 1 minute is 60 seconds, multiply each top speed by 60. Then, subtract to find the difference of the distances traveled by the two animals.

Estimate $100 \times 60 = 6{,}000$ and $0.25 \times 60 = 15$
$6{,}000 - 15 = 5{,}985$

Solve

$103 \times 60 = 6{,}180$ Distance cheetah travels in 1 minute
$0.25 \times 60 = 15$ Distance giant tortoise travels in 1 minute
$6{,}180 - 15 = 6{,}165$ Difference in distances traveled

A cheetah will travel 6,165 feet farther than a giant tortoise in 1 minute.

Check Is your answer reasonable? The answer is close to the estimate, so the answer is reasonable.

CHECK Your Progress

b. **FOOD** Almost 90 million jars of a popular brand of peanut butter are sold annually. Use the four-step plan to determine the approximate number of jars sold every second.

CHECK Your Understanding

Example 1 (p. 25)

1. **PAPER** A card is made using triangles as shown below. If one side of the triangle is 1 unit, use the four-step plan to determine the perimeter of the 10th figure in this pattern.

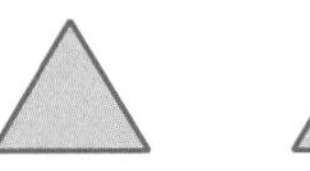
Figure 1

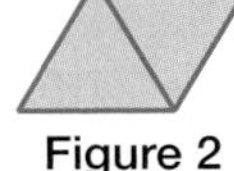
Figure 2

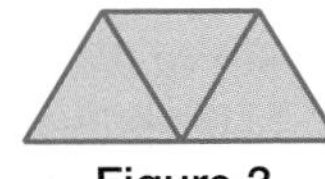
Figure 3

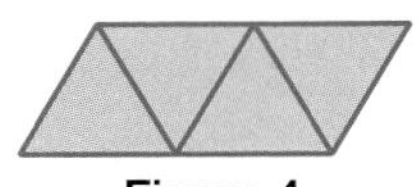
Figure 4

Example 2 (p. 26)

HOCKEY For Exercises 2 and 3, use the following information.

Jaromir Jagr of the New York Rangers led the league in scoring for 5 years. The number of points he scored those years is shown in the table at the right.

Year	Points Scored
1995	70
1998	102
1999	127
2000	96
2001	121

Source: ESPN

2. About how many more goals did he score in the last two years than in the first two years?
3. Estimate the total number of points Jagr scored in those 5 years.

Practice and Problem Solving

HOMEWORK HELP

For Exercises	See Examples
4–5	1
6–7	2

Use the four-step plan to solve each problem.

4. **PATTERNS** How many blue squares are needed for the fifth figure in this pattern?

Figure 1 Figure 2

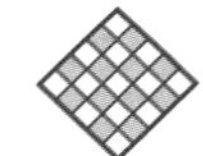
Figure 3

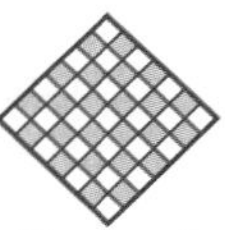
Figure 4

5. **PATTERNS** How many toothpicks are needed to make the 10th figure in this pattern?

Figure 1 Figure 2

Figure 3 Figure 4

6. **CLASS TRIP** Mr. Bassett's science classes are going to the Natural History Museum. A tour guide is needed for each group of eight students. His classes have 28 students, 35 students, 22 students, 33 students, and 22 students. How many tour guides are needed?

7. **POPULATION** In a recent year, the population of Delaware was 783,600. Delaware covers 1,953 square miles of land. North Carolina's land area is 48,710 square miles, and its population that year was 8,049,313. Which state had a greater number of people per square mile? by how much? Round your answer to the nearest whole number.

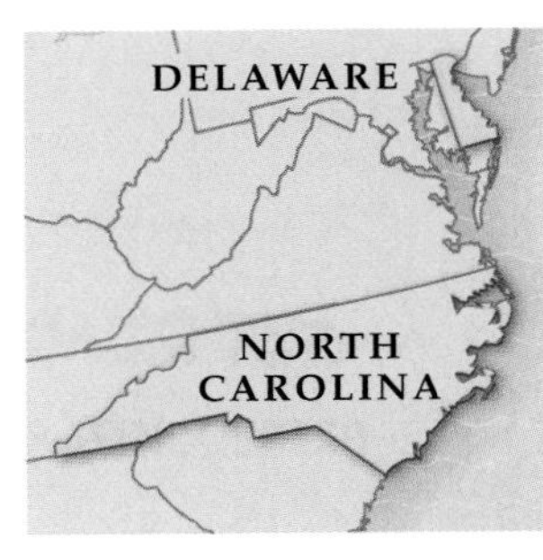

Use the four-step plan to solve each problem.

8. **COOKING** The local market is selling cucumbers for $0.79 each and tomatoes for $0.56 each. How many cucumbers and tomatoes could be bought with exactly $5.96?

9. **JOBS** Mr. Desmond stocks the vending machines at Taylor Elementary every 9 school days and King Middle School every 6 school days. In September, he stocked both schools on the 27th. How many school days earlier had he stocked the vending machines at both schools on the same day?

GEOMETRY For Exercises 10 and 11, draw the next two figures in each pattern.

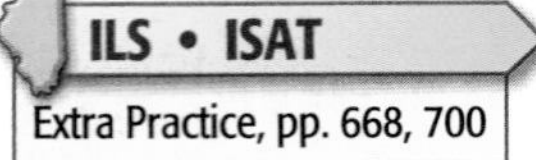

10.

11.

H.O.T. Problems

12. **OPEN ENDED** Refer to the Mini Lab at the beginning of the lesson. Describe another method you could use to find the number of toothpicks it takes to make a row that is 14 cells long.

13. **CHALLENGE** Draw the next figure in the pattern at the right. How many white tiles are needed when 21 green tiles are used? Explain.

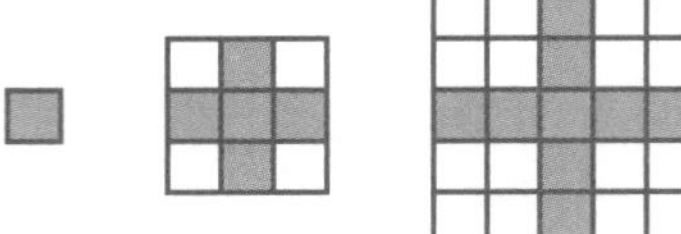

14. **SELECT A TECHNIQUE** Handy Crafts will paint a custom design on the back of a cell phone for $3.25. Which of the following techniques should one use to determine the fewest number of phones that will need to be painted in order to earn $58.29 for the painting supplies? Justify your selection(s). Then use the technique(s) to solve the problem.

mental math | estimation | paper/pencil

15. **WRITING IN MATH** Summarize the four-step problem-solving plan.

ISAT PRACTICE 6.B.3a

16. **SHORT RESPONSE** The Diversity Club wants to purchase 3 posters for each of the 75 classrooms at the school. Each poster costs $3.75. Estimate the cost of the posters.

17. The next figure in the pattern will have what fraction of its area shaded?

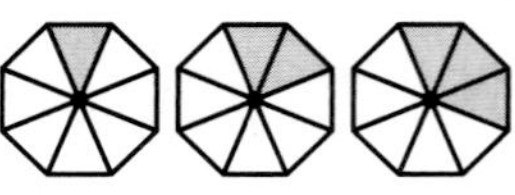

F $\frac{3}{8}$ H $\frac{5}{8}$

G $\frac{1}{2}$ J $\frac{3}{4}$

GET READY for the Next Lesson

PREREQUISITE SKILL Add, subtract, multiply, or divide.

18. $15 + 45$ 19. $1{,}287 - 978$ 20. 4×3.6 21. $280 \div 0.4$

Variables, Expressions, and Properties

MAIN IDEA

Evaluate expressions and identify properties.

IL Learning Standards

8.A.3a Apply the basic properties of commutative, associative, distributive, transitive, inverse, **identity,** zero, equality and order of operations **to solve problems.**
8.D.3a Solve problems using numeric, graphic or symbolic representations of variables, expressions, equations and inequalities. *Also addresses 8.A.3b, 8.C.3.*

New Vocabulary

variable
algebra
algebraic expression
evaluate
numerical expression
order of operations
powers
property
counterexample

IL Math Online

glencoe.com
- Concepts in Motion
- Extra Examples
- Personal Tutor
- Self-Check Quiz
- Reading in the Content Area

MINI Lab

The figures at the right are formed using toothpicks. If each toothpick is a unit, the perimeter of the first figure is 6 units.

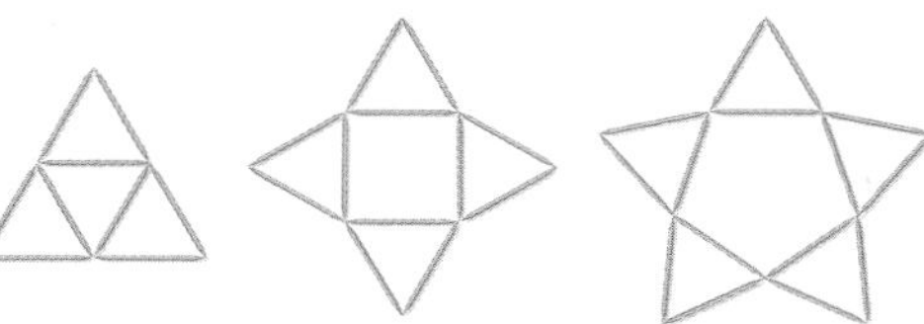

1. Copy and complete the table. What is the relationship between the number of triangles used to make the figure and the perimeter of the figure?
2. What would be the perimeter of Figure 10?

Figure Number	Number of Triangles	Perimeter
1	3	6
2	4	8
3	5	
4	6	
5	7	
6	8	

A **variable** is a symbol, usually a letter, used to represent a number. You can use the variable n to represent the number of triangles in the Mini Lab above.

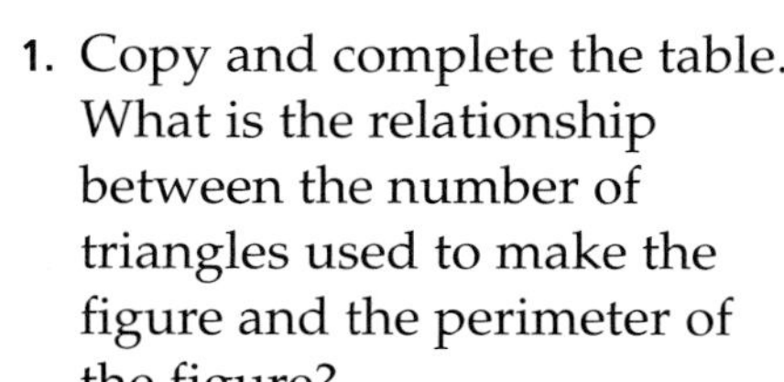

The branch of mathematics that involves expressions with variables is called **algebra**. The expression $2 \times n$ is called an **algebraic expression** because it contains a variable, a number, and at least one operation.

To **evaluate** or find the value of an algebraic expression, first replace the variable or variables with the known values to produce a **numerical expression**, one with only numbers and operations. Then find the value of the expression using the **order of operations**.

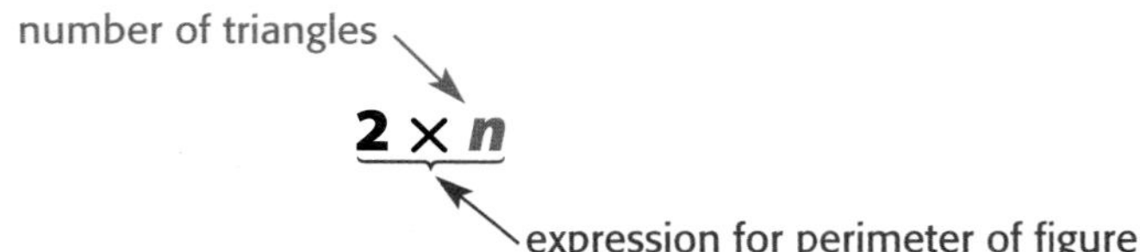

Order of Operations — Key Concept

1. Perform all operations within grouping symbols first; start with the innermost grouping symbols.
2. Evaluate all powers before other operations.
3. Multiply and divide in order from left to right.
4. Add and subtract in order from left to right.

Algebra uses special ways of showing multiplication. Since the multiplication symbol $\times$ can be confused with the variable x, 2 times n is usually written as $2 \cdot n$, $2(n)$, or $2n$.

Expressions such as 7^2 and x^3 are called **powers** and represent repeated multiplication.

7 squared or $7 \cdot 7$ → 7^2 x^3 ← x cubed or $x \cdot x \cdot x$

Study Tip

Parentheses Parentheses around a single number do not necessarily mean that multiplication should be performed first. Remember to multiply or divide in order from left to right.

$20 \div 4(2) = 5(2)$ or 10

EXAMPLES Evaluate Algebraic Expressions

1 Evaluate $6(x - y)^2$ if $x = 7$ and $y = 4$.

$6(x - y)^2 = 6(7 - 4)^2$ Replace x with 7 and y with 4.

$= 6(3)^2$ Perform operations in the parentheses first.

$= 6 \cdot 9$ or 54 Evaluate the power. Then multiply.

2 Evaluate $g^2 - 2g - 4$ if $g = 5$.

$g^2 - 2g - 4 = (5)^2 - 2(5) - 4$ Replace g with 5.

$= 25 - 2(5) - 4$ Evaluate powers before other operations.

$= 25 - 10 - 4$ Multiply 2 and 5.

$= 15 - 4$ or 11 Subtract from left to right.

CHECK Your Progress

Evaluate each expression if $c = 3$ and $d = 7$.

a. $6c + 4 - 3d$ b. $4(d - c)^2 + 1$ c. $d^2 + 5d - 6$

The fraction bar is another grouping symbol. Evaluate the expressions in the numerator and denominator separately before dividing.

EXAMPLE Evaluate Algebraic Fractions

3 Evaluate $\frac{4 + 6m}{2n - 8}$ if $m = 9$ and $n = 5$.

$\frac{4 + 6m}{2n - 8} = \frac{4 + 6(9)}{2(5) - 8}$ Replace m with 9 and n with 5.

$= \frac{58}{2(5) - 8}$ Evaluate the numerator.

$= \frac{58}{2}$ or 29 Evaluate the denominator. Then divide.

CHECK Your Progress

Evaluate each expression if $p = 5$ and $q = 12$.

d. $\frac{3p - 6}{8 - p}$ e. $\frac{4q}{q + 2(p + 1)}$ f. $\frac{q^2}{4p - 2}$

A **property** is a feature of an object or a rule that is always true. The following properties are true for all numbers.

Property	Algebra	Arithmetic
Commutative	$a + b = b + a$ $a \cdot b = b \cdot a$	$6 + 1 = 1 + 6$ $7 \cdot 3 = 3 \cdot 7$
Associative	$a + (b + c) = (a + b) + c$ $a \cdot (b \cdot c) = (a \cdot b) \cdot c$	$2 + (3 + 8) = (2 + 3) + 8$ $3 \cdot (4 \cdot 5) = (3 \cdot 4) \cdot 5$
Distributive	$a(b + c) = ab + ac$ $a(b - c) = ab - ac$	$4(6 + 2) = 4 \cdot 6 + 4 \cdot 2$ $3(7 - 5) = 3 \cdot 7 - 3 \cdot 5$
Identity	$a + 0 = a$ $a \cdot 1 = a$	$9 + 0 = 9$ $5 \cdot 1 = 5$

EXAMPLE Identify Properties

4 **Name the property shown by the statement $2 \cdot (5 \cdot n) = (2 \cdot 5) \cdot n$.**

The order of the numbers and variables did not change but their grouping did. This is the Associative Property of Multiplication.

CHECK Your Progress

Name the property shown by each statement.

g. $42 + x + y = 42 + y + x$

h. $3x + 0 = 3x$

You may wonder whether any of the properties applies to subtraction or division. If you can find a **counterexample**, an example that shows that a conjecture is false, the property does not apply.

Vocabulary Link
Conjecture
Everyday Use a guess
Math Use an informed guess based on known information

EXAMPLE Find a Counterexample

5 **State whether the following conjecture is *true* or *false*. If *false*, provide a counterexample.**

Division of whole numbers is commutative.

Write two division expressions using the Commutative Property.

$15 \div 3 \stackrel{?}{=} 3 \div 15$ State the conjecture.

$5 \neq \frac{1}{5}$ Divide.

We found a counterexample. That is, $15 \div 3 \neq 3 \div 15$. So, division is *not* commutative. The conjecture is false.

CHECK Your Progress

i. State whether the following conjecture is *true* or *false*. If *false*, provide a counterexample.

The difference of two different whole numbers is always less than either of the two numbers.

CHECK Your Understanding

Examples 1–3 (p. 30)

Evaluate each expression if $a = 2$, $b = 7$, and $c = 4$.

1. $(a + b)^2$
2. $4(a + b - c)^2$
3. $c^2 - 2c + 5$
4. $b^2 - 2a + 10$
5. $\frac{bc}{2}$
6. $\frac{c^2}{b - 5}$

Example 3 (p. 30)

7. **TEMPERATURE** The expression $\frac{c}{4} + 37$ gives the approximate temperature of the air in degrees Fahrenheit, given the number of chirps c per minute made by a cricket. If Brandon estimates that a cricket has chirped 140 times in the past minute, what is the approximate temperature of the air in degrees Fahrenheit?

Example 4 (p. 31)

Name the property shown by each statement.

8. $3(m + n) = 3m + 3n$
9. $6(5 \cdot y) = (6 \cdot 5)y$

Example 5 (p. 31)

10. State whether the following conjecture is *true* or *false*. If *false*, provide a counterexample.

Subtraction of whole numbers is associative.

Practice and Problem Solving

HOMEWORK HELP	
For Exercises	See Examples
11–22	1–3
23, 24	3
25–32	4
33–36	5

Evaluate each expression if $w = 2$, $x = 6$, $y = 4$, and $z = 5$.

11. $2x + y$
12. $3z - 2w$
13. $9 + 7x - y$
14. $12 + z - x$
15. wx^2
16. $(wx)^2$
17. $\frac{x^2 - 3}{2z + 1}$
18. $\frac{wz^2}{y + 6}$

Evaluate each expression if $a = 4$, $b = 3$, and $c = 6$.

19. $3(c - b)^2 - a$
20. $2(ab - 9)^2 \div c$
21. $3b^2 + 2b - 7$
22. $2c^2 - 4c + 5$

23. **MEASUREMENT** When a temperature in degrees Fahrenheit F is known, the expression $\frac{5F - 160}{9}$ can be used to find the temperature in degrees Celsius C. If a thermometer shows that the temperature is 50°F, what is the temperature in degrees Celsius?

24. **TRAVEL** The cost of renting a car in dollars from EZ Rent-A-Car for a day is given by the expression $\frac{270 + m}{10}$, where m is the number of miles driven. How much would it cost to rent a car for one day and drive 50 miles?

Name the property shown by each statement.

25. $1(12 \cdot 4) = 12 \cdot 4$
26. $14(16 \cdot 32) = (14 \cdot 16)32$
27. $a + (b + 12) = (b + 12) + a$
28. $(5 + x) + 0 = 5 + x$
29. $15(3 + 6) = 15(3) + 15(6)$
30. $16 + (c + 17) = (16 + c) + 17$
31. $9(ab) = (9a)b$
32. $y \cdot 7 = 7y$

State whether each conjecture is *true* or *false*. If *false*, provide a counterexample.

33. The sum of two even numbers is always even.
34. The sum of two odd numbers is always odd.
35. Division of whole numbers is associative.
36. Subtraction of whole numbers is commutative.

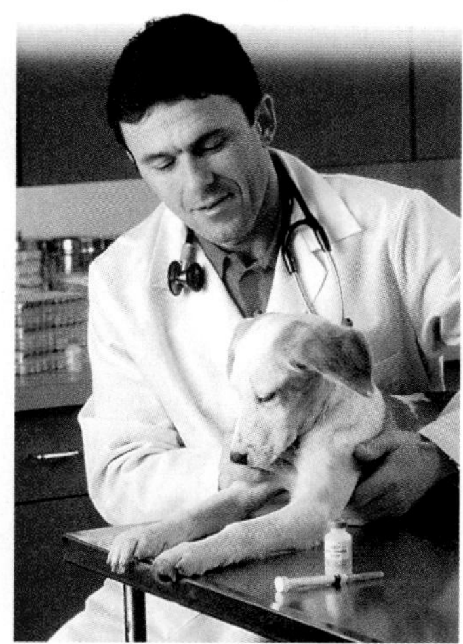

Real-World Link The average dog visits its veterinarian almost twice as many times as the average cat or horse.

Source: The American Veterinary Medical Association

37. **DOGS** You can estimate the number of households in a community that own a dog by evaluating the expression $\frac{c}{n} \cdot p$, where n is the number of people per household, c is the population, and p is the fraction of households owning a dog. Suppose there are approximately 2.62 people per household and 0.365 of the households own a dog. How many households own a dog in a community with a population of 50,000?

38. **PHYSICAL SCIENCE** The distance in feet an object falls t seconds after it is released is given by the expression $\frac{gt^2}{2}$, where g is the force of gravity. How many feet will a stone fall 3 seconds after it is released from the top of a cliff? Assume a force of gravity of 16 feet per second squared.

For Exercises 39 and 40, the first four figures in a pattern are given. Write an expression for the total number of dots in any figure. Then evaluate the expression for the tenth figure in the pattern.

39.

40.

RECREATION For Exercises 41–43, use the following information.
A group is planning to go to an amusement park. There are two parks in the area, Fun World and Coaster City. The cost in dollars for n admission tickets to Fun World is $37n$. If the group has 15 or more people, the cost at Coaster City is $30n + 75$. If the group has fewer than 15 people, the cost at Coaster City is $40n$. As few as 10 people or as many as 25 people might go.

41. Find the cost for each possible group size if they go to Fun World.
42. Find the cost for each possible group size if they go to Coaster City.
43. Write a recommendation that details which park they should go to based on the number of people they expect to attend. Justify your answer.

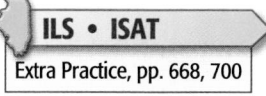

ILS • ISAT
Extra Practice, pp. 668, 700

H.O.T. Problems

44. **OPEN ENDED** Write an equation that illustrates the Commutative Property of Multiplication.

CHALLENGE Decide whether each equation is *true* or *false*. If *false*, copy the equation and insert parentheses to make it true.

45. $8 \cdot 4 - 3 \cdot 2 = 26$ 46. $8 + 2^3 \div 4 = 4$ 47. $6 + 7 \cdot 2 + 5 = 55$

48. FIND THE ERROR Regina and Camila are evaluating $10 \div 2 \times 5$. Who is correct? Explain.

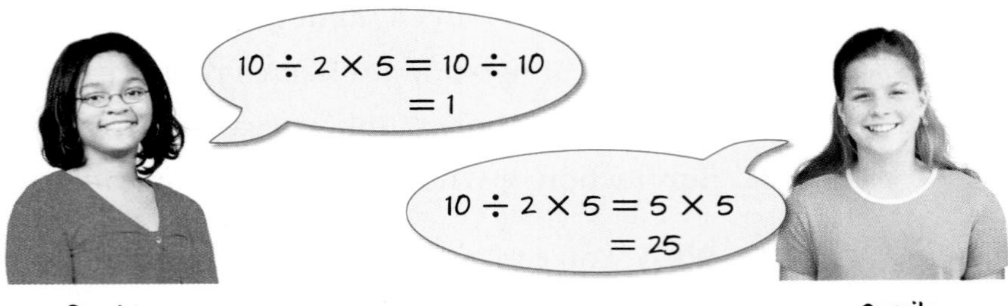

49. WRITING IN MATH Compare the everyday meaning of the term variable with its mathematical definition.

ISAT PRACTICE 8.A.3a, 8.D.3a

50. The expression $6s^2$ can be used to find the surface area of a cube, where s is the length of an edge of the cube. What is the surface area of the cube shown below?

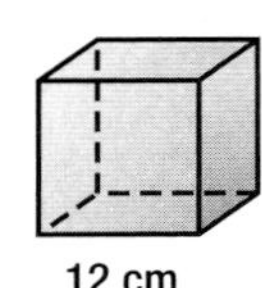

A 144 cm^2

B 432 cm^2

C 864 cm^2

D $5{,}184 \text{ cm}^2$

51. Which equation is an example of the Commutative Property?

F $4 \cdot 1 = 4$

G $16 + 0 = 16$

H $w + (3 + 2) = w + (2 + 3)$

J $d(9 \cdot f) = (d \cdot 9)f$

52. If $r = 4$ and $t = 3$, then $rt - 2r =$

A 4

B 6

C 19

D 40

Spiral Review

Use the four-step plan to solve each problem.

53. SHOPPING Beng went to a jeans store with a $25 gift card. He purchased a pair of shorts for $23.67. How much money is left on the gift card? (Lesson 1-1)

54. BABYSITTING Kayla earned $30 babysitting last weekend. She wants to buy 3 CDs that cost $7.89, $12.25, and $11.95. Does she have enough money to purchase the CDs? Explain your reasoning. (Lesson 1-1)

GET READY for the Next Lesson

PREREQUISITE SKILL Replace each ● with <, >, or = to make a true sentence.

55. 4 ● 9 **56.** 7 ● 7 **57.** 8 ● 5 **58.** 3 ● 2

1-3 Integers and Absolute Value

MAIN IDEA

Compare and order integers and find absolute value.

IL Learning Standards

6.B.3a Solve practical computation problems involving whole numbers, **integers** and rational numbers.

New Vocabulary

negative number
positive number
integer
coordinate
inequality
absolute value

IL Math Online

glencoe.com

- Extra Examples
- Personal Tutor
- Self-Check Quiz

GET READY for the Lesson

TEMPERATURE A record high temperature of +114°F was recorded for Kentucky in 1930. In 1963, the record low temperature of −34°F was recorded.

KENTUCKY

1. What does a temperature of −34°F represent?
2. Which temperature is closer to zero?

With zero as the starting point, you can express 34 degrees below zero as negative 34 or −34. A **negative number** is a number less than zero. A **positive number** like 114 is a number greater than zero.

Numbers like −34 and 114 are called integers. An **integer** is any number from the set {..., −4, −3, −2, −1, 0, 1, 2, 3, 4, ...}, where ... means *continues without end*.

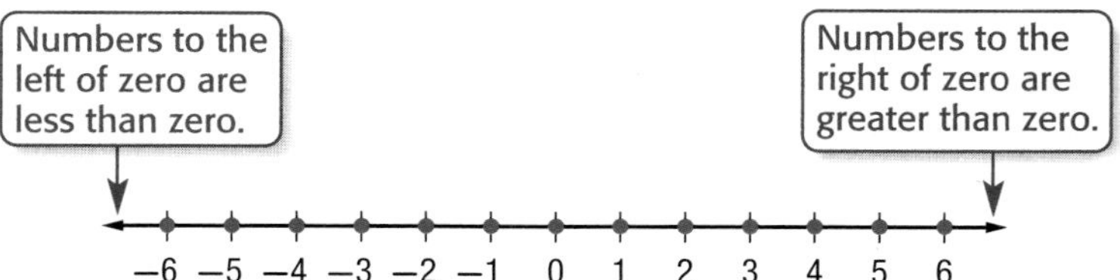

Numbers to the left of zero are less than zero.
Numbers to the right of zero are greater than zero.
−6 −5 −4 −3 −2 −1 0 1 2 3 4 5 6

To graph an integer, locate the point corresponding to the integer on a number line. The number that corresponds to a point is called its **coordinate**. The number line below shows the graphs of points with coordinates −5 and 4.

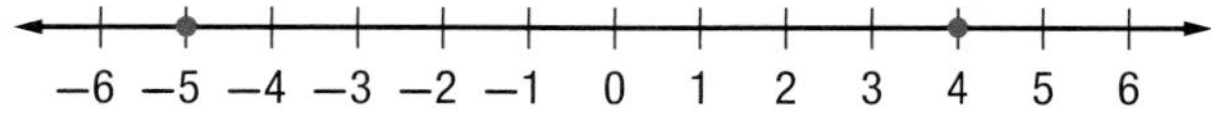

−6 −5 −4 −3 −2 −1 0 1 2 3 4 5 6

Notice that −5 is to the left of 4 on the number line. This means that −5 is less than 4. A mathematical sentence indicating that two quantities are not equal is called an **inequality**. Inequalities contain symbols like < and >.

−5 is less than 4. ⟶ $-5 < 4$ $\quad$ $4 > -5$ ⟵ 4 is greater than −5.

Reading Math

Inequality Symbols
$<$ is less than
$>$ is greater than

EXAMPLE Compare Integers

1 Replace the ● with $<$ or $>$ to make -2 ● -4 a true sentence.

Graph each integer on a number line.

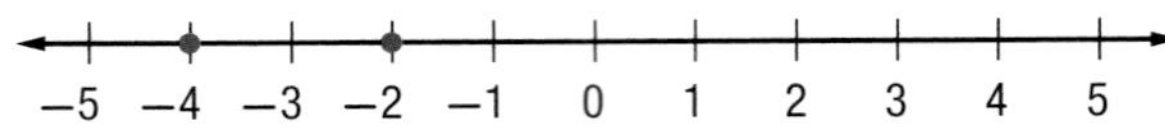

Since -2 is to the right of -4, $-2 > -4$.

CHECK Your Progress

Replace each ● with $<$ or $>$ to make a true sentence.

a. -3 ● 2

b. -5 ● -6

c. -1 ● 1

The distance between a number and 0 on a number line is called its **absolute value**. On the number line below, notice that -4 and 4 are each 4 units from 0, even though they are on opposite sides of 0. They have the same absolute value, 4.

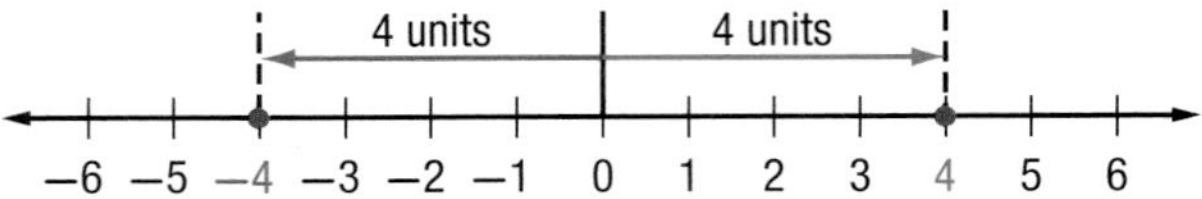

The symbol for absolute value is two vertical bars on either side of the number.

The absolute value of -4 is 4. → $|-4| = 4$ $|4| = 4$ ← The absolute value of 4 is 4.

Study Tip

Absolute Value
Since distance cannot be negative, the absolute value of a number is always positive or zero.

EXAMPLES Expressions with Absolute Value

2 Evaluate $|-7|$.

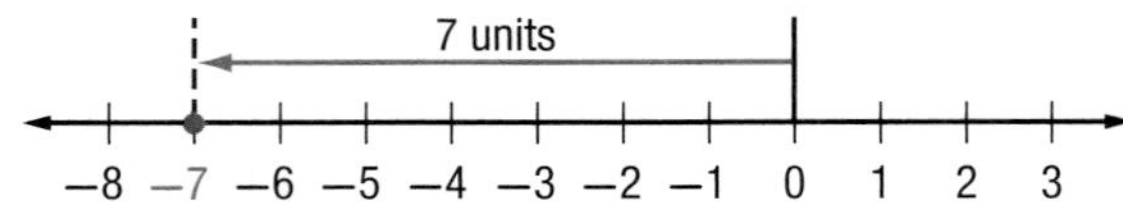

The graph of -7 is 7 units to the left of 0 on the number line.

$|-7| = 7$

3 Evaluate $|5| + |-6|$.

$|5| + |-6| = 5 + |-6|$	The absolute value of 5 is 5.
$= 5 + 6$	The absolute value of -6 is 6.
$= 11$	Simplify.

4 Evaluate $|5 - 3| + |8 - 10|$.

$|5 - 3| + |8 - 10| = |2| + |-2|$	Simplify the absolute value expressions.
$= 2 + |-2|$	The absolute value of 2 is 2.
$= 2 + 2$	The absolute value of -2 is 2.
$= 4$	Simplify.

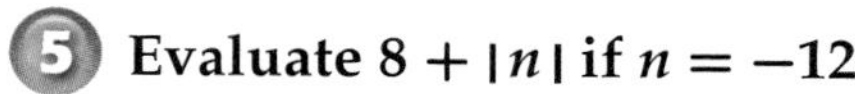

5 **Evaluate $8 + |n|$ if $n = -12$.**

$8 + |n| = 8 + |-12|$ Replace n with -12.

$= 8 + 12$ or 20 $|-12| = 12$

CHECK Your Progress **Evaluate each expression.**

d. $|14|$

e. $|-8| - |-2|$

f. $|7 - 4| + |12 - 15|$

g. $|a| - 2$, if $a = -5$

You can also use an absolute value expression to find the distance between a number and zero on a number line.

Real-World EXAMPLE

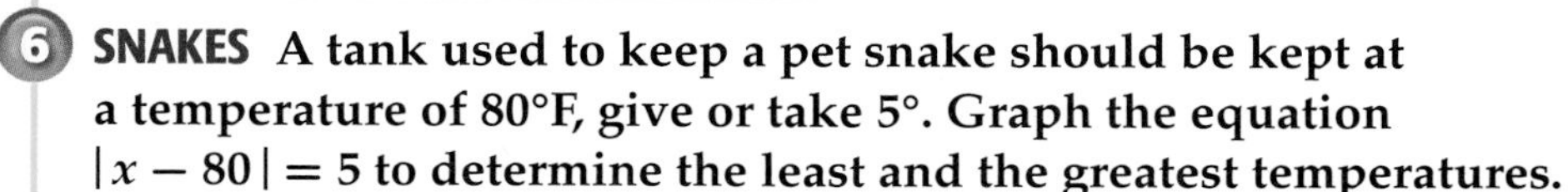

6 **SNAKES** **A tank used to keep a pet snake should be kept at a temperature of 80°F, give or take 5°. Graph the equation $|x - 80| = 5$ to determine the least and the greatest temperatures.**

$|x - 80| = 5$ means that the distance between x and 80 is 5 units. Start at 80 and move 5 units in either direction to find the value of x.

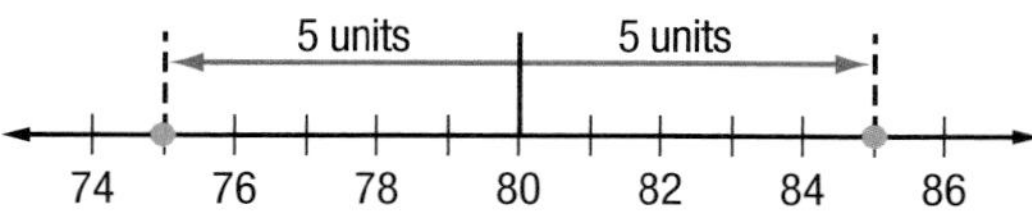

The distance from 80 to 75 is 5 units.

The distance from 80 to 85 is 5 units.

The solution set is {75, 85}.

CHECK Your Progress

h. The average lifespan of an elephant in the wild is 65 years, give or take 6 years. Graph the equation $|y - 65| = 6$ on a number line to determine the least and greatest average age of an elephant.

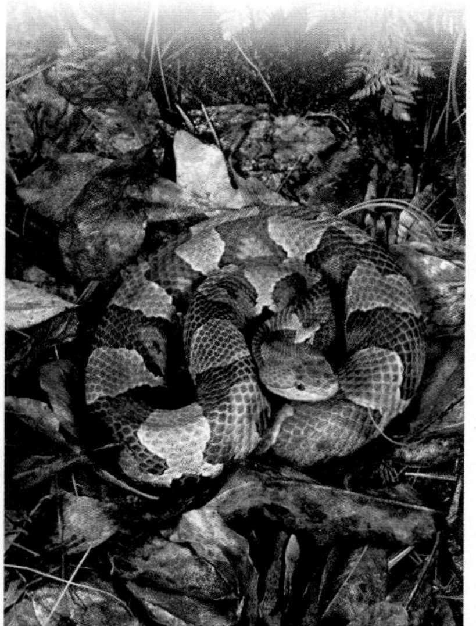

Real-World Link

Snakes are cold-blooded, which means that they cannot regulate their body temperature. Their body temperature will reflect the temperature of their surroundings, and these animals cannot survive temperature extremes.

Source: TrailQuest

CHECK Your Understanding

Example 1 (p. 36)

Replace each ● with < or > to make a true sentence.

1. $1 ● -5$
2. $-1 ● -2$
3. $-4 ● 3$
4. $-7 ● -3$

Examples 2-4 (p. 36)

Evaluate each expression.

5. $|5|$
6. $|-9|$
7. $|6 - 3| - |2 - 4|$
8. $|-8| - |-2|$

Example 5 (p. 37)

Evaluate each expression if $x = -10$ and $y = 6$.

9. $3 + |x|$
10. $|y| + 12$
11. $|x| - y$

Example 6 (p. 37)

12. **PROFIT** In order to ensure a profit, the average cost of a CD must be \$16, give or take \$3. Graph the equation $|c - 16| = 3$ to determine the least and greatest cost of a CD.

Practice and Problem Solving

HOMEWORK HELP	
For Exercises	See Examples
13–24	1
25–30	2–4
31–34	5
35–38	6

Replace each ● with <, >, or = to make a true sentence.

13. $0 \bullet -1$
14. $5 \bullet -6$
15. $-9 \bullet -7$
16. $-6 \bullet -1$
17. $-7 \bullet -2$
18. $0 \bullet 12$
19. $-9 \bullet -10$
20. $4 \bullet -11$
21. $-3 \bullet 0$
22. $-15 \bullet 14$
23. $-8 \bullet -8$
24. $-13 \bullet -13$

Evaluate each expression.

25. $|-14|$
26. $|25|$
27. $|0| + |-18|$
28. $|2| - |-13|$
29. $|6 - 8| + |9 - 5|$
30. $|14 - 7| - |5 - 8|$

Evaluate each expression if $a = 5$, $b = -8$, $c = -3$, and $d = 9$.

31. $|b| + 7$
32. $a - |c|$
33. $d + |b|$
34. $6|b| + d$

Graph the equation to determine the solutions.

35. $|x - 15| = 10$
36. $|a - 7| = 4$

37. **SOCCER** A professional soccer player is in his prime at age 26, plus or minus 7 years. This range can be modeled by the equation $|x - 26| = 7$. Graph the equation on a number line to determine the least and the greatest ages.

38. **MONEY** The Perez family spends an average of $435 per month on groceries, give or take $22. This range can be modeled by the equation $|y - 435| = 22$. Graph the equation on a number line to determine the least and the greatest money spent.

CHEMISTRY For Exercises 39–42, use the table at the right.

Gas	Freezing Point (°F) at Sea Level
hydrogen	−435°
krypton	−251°
oxygen	−369°
helium	−458°
argon	−309°

39. Which of these gases freezes at the coldest temperature?

40. Which of these gases freezes at the warmest temperature?

41. The freezing point for xenon at sea level is about 200 degrees warmer than the freezing point for oxygen. What is the approximate freezing point of xenon? Justify your answer using a number line.

42. How many degrees lower is the freezing point for oxygen at sea level than the freezing point for argon? Justify your answer using a number line.

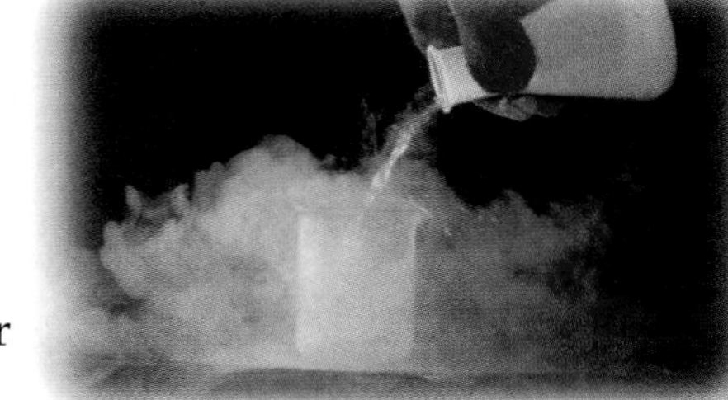

ILS • ISAT

Extra Practice, pp. 668, 700

H.O.T. Problems

CHALLENGE Determine whether each statement is *always, sometimes,* or *never* true. Explain your reasoning.

43. The absolute value of a positive integer is a negative integer.

44. If a and b are integers and $a > b$, then $|a| > |b|$.

45. If a and b are integers, $a - |b| \leq a + b$.

46. **Which One Doesn't Belong?** Identify the phrase that cannot be described by the same integer as the other three. Explain your reasoning.

a loss of 8 pounds	8 miles above sea level	giving away $8	8° below normal

47. **WRITING IN MATH** Explain why the absolute value of a number is never negative.

ISAT PRACTICE 6.B.3a

48. The table shows the number of laps selected race cars finished behind the winner of a race.

Car Number	Laps Behind Winner
3	−1
8	−12
15	−3
24	0
48	−8

Which list shows the finishing order of the cars from first to fifth?

A 8, 48, 15, 3, 24 **C** 24, 3, 15, 48, 8
B 3, 8, 15, 24, 48 **D** 48, 24, 15, 8, 3

49. If $x = -2$ and $y = 2$, then which of the following statements is false?

F $|x| > 1$
G $|x| = |y|$
H $|y| < 1$
J $|x| = y$

50. Which expression has the *greatest* value?

A $|-25|$
B $|-16|$
C $|18|$
D $|22|$

Spiral Review

ALGEBRA Evaluate each expression if $m = 3$, $n = 2$, $p = 10$, and $r = 15$. (Lesson 1-2)

51. $r - 4n$
52. $2m^2 - p + 3$
53. $\dfrac{3p + m}{r - 2n}$

54. **SCIENCE** A chemist pours table salt into a beaker. If the beaker plus the salt has a mass of 84.7 grams and the beaker itself has a mass of 63.3 grams, what is the mass of the salt? (Lesson 1-1)

GET READY for the Next Lesson

PREREQUISITE SKILL Add or subtract.

55. $9 + 14$
56. $100 - 57$
57. $47 - 19$
58. $18 + 34 + 13$

Explore 1-4

Algebra Lab
Adding Integers

In this lab, you will investigate the relationship between positive and negative addends and their sums. In previous courses, you have used algebra tiles to model addition. Two examples are shown below.

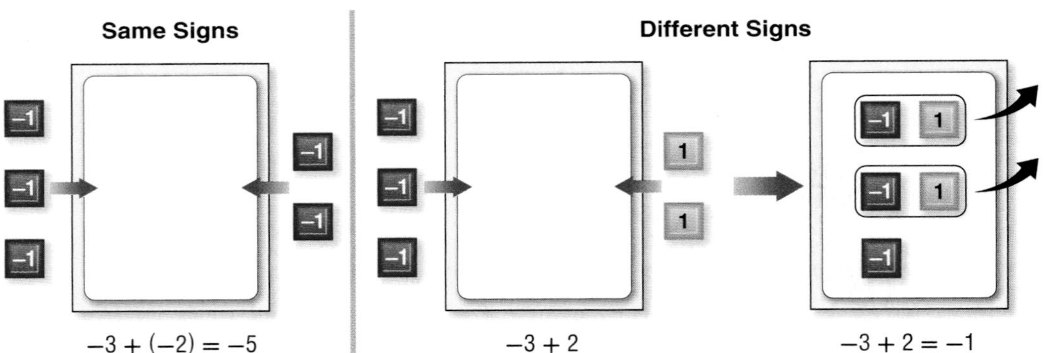

ACTIVITY

Copy and complete the addition table from 4 through −4. The first few rows have been done for you. Use algebra tiles if necessary.

Addition Table									
+	4	3	2	1	0	−1	−2	−3	−4
4	8	7	6	5	4	3	2	1	0
3	7	6	5	4	3	2	1	0	−1
2	6	5	4	3	2	1	0	−1	−2
1									

Analyze the Results

1. **MAKE A CONJECTURE** Locate all of the positive sums in the table. Describe the addends that result in a positive sum.
2. **MAKE A CONJECTURE** Locate all of the negative sums in the table. Describe the addends that result in a negative sum.
3. **MAKE A CONJECTURE** Locate all of the sums that are zero. Describe the addends that result in a sum of zero.
4. Does it appear that the Identity Property, the Commutative Property, and the Associative Property are true for addition of integers? If so, write two examples for each that illustrate the property. If not, give a counterexample.

1-4 Adding Integers

MAIN IDEA

Add integers.

IL Learning Standards

6.B.3a Solve practical computation problems involving whole numbers, **integers** and rational numbers.
8.A.3a Apply the basic properties of commutative, associative, distributive, transitive, **inverse,** identity, zero, equality and order of operations **to solve problems.**

New Vocabulary

opposites
additive inverse

IL Math Online

glencoe.com

- Concepts in Motion
- Extra Examples
- Personal Tutor
- Self-Check Quiz

GET READY for the Lesson

MUSIC Jack was downloading songs onto his MP3 player. It costs $1 for each song. He borrowed money from his brother to cover the cost of the songs.

1. Write an integer that describes the amount of money Jack owes his brother for the three days he downloads songs.
2. Write an addition sentence that describes this situation.

The equation $-2 + (-4) + (-3) = -9$ is an example of adding integers with the same sign. Notice that the sign of the sum is the same as the sign of each addend.

EXAMPLE Add Integers with the Same Sign

1 Find $-4 + (-2)$.

Use a number line.

- Start at zero.
- Move 4 units left.
- From there, move 2 units left.

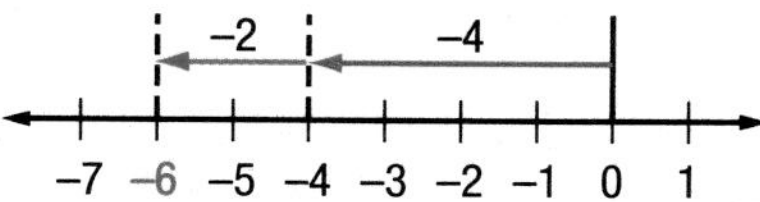

So, $-4 + (-2) = -6$.

CHECK Your Progress

Add. Use a number line if necessary.

a. $-3 + (-2)$ b. $1 + 5$ c. $-5 + (-4)$

Add Integers with the Same Sign

Key Concept

Words To add integers with the same sign, add their absolute values. The sum has the same sign as the integers.

Examples $-7 + (-3) = -10$ $5 + 4 = 9$

A number line can also help you add integers with different signs.

Study Tip

Adding Integers on a Number Line
Always start at zero. Move right to model a positive integer and left to model a negative integer.

EXAMPLES Add Integers with Different Signs

2 Find 5 + (−2).

Use a number line.

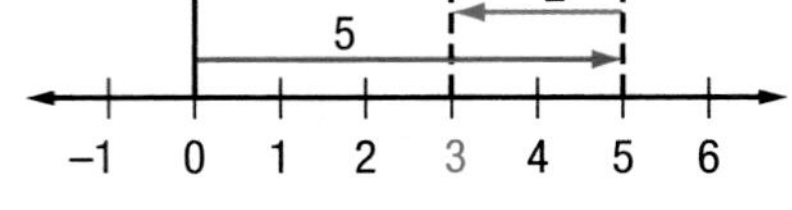

- Start at zero.
- Move 5 units right.
- From there, move 2 units left.

5 + (−2) = 3

3 Find −4 + 3.

Use a number line.

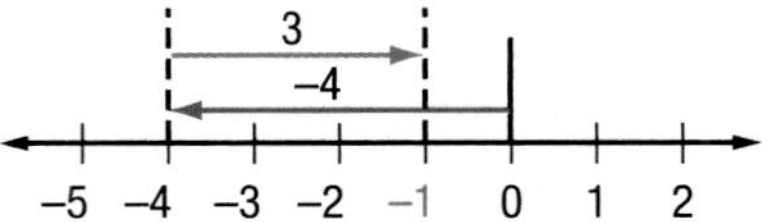

- Start at zero.
- Move 4 units left.
- From there, move 3 units right.

−4 + 3 = −1

 **CHECK Your Progress**

Add. Use a number line if necessary.

d. 7 + (−5) **e.** −6 + 4 **f.** −1 + 8

These examples suggest a rule for adding integers with different signs.

Add Integers with Different Signs — Key Concept

Words	To add integers with different signs, subtract their absolute values. The sum has the same sign as the integer with the greater absolute value.
Examples	8 + (−3) = 5 −8 + 3 = −5

EXAMPLE Add Integers with Different Signs

 **Find −14 + 9.**

−14 + 9 = −5 To find −14 + 9, subtract |9| from |−14|. The sum is negative because |−14| > |9|.

 **CHECK Your Progress**

Add.

g. −20 + 4 **h.** 17 + (−6) **i.** −8 + 27

Two numbers with the same absolute value but different signs are called **opposites**. For example, -2 and 2 are opposites. An integer and its opposite are also called **additive inverses**.

Additive Inverse Property

Key Concept

Words The sum of any number and its additive inverse is zero.

Examples

Numbers	Algebra
$7 + (-7) = 0$	$x + (-x) = 0$

The Commutative, Associative, and Identity Properties, along with the Additive Inverse Property, can help you add three or more integers.

EXAMPLE Add Three or More Integers

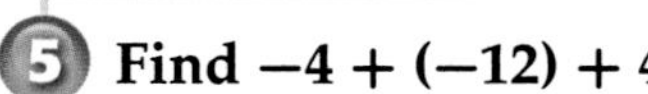

5 Find $-4 + (-12) + 4$.

$-4 + (-12) + 4 = -4 + 4 + (-12)$ Commutative Property

$= 0 + (-12)$ Additive Inverse Property

$= -12$ Identity Property of Addition

CHECK Your Progress

Add.

j. $33 + 16 + (-33)$

k. $3 + (-2) + (-10) + 6$

Real-World Link

One out of every five Americans does not have a checking account.

Source: Harper's Magazine

Real-World EXAMPLE

6 ATM Erik's savings account balance is \$235. What is his balance after he uses the ATM to withdraw \$58 and \$67?

Withdrawing money *decreases* your account balance. The integers for this situation are -58 and -67. Add these integers to the starting balance to find the new balance.

$235 + (-58) + (-67) = 235 + [-58 + (-67)]$ Associative Property

$= 235 + (-125)$ $-58 + (-67) = -125$

$= 110$ Simplify.

Erik's balance is now \$110.

CHECK Your Progress

l. **BANKING** A checking account has a starting balance of \$130. What is the balance after writing checks for \$58 and \$62, then making a deposit of \$150?

CHECK Your Understanding

Add.

Examples 1–4 (pp. 41–42)

1. $-4 + (-5)$
2. $-18 + (-8)$
3. $-3 + (-12)$
4. $10 + (-6)$
5. $7 + (-18)$
6. $-9 + 16$

Example 5 (p. 43)

7. $11 + 9 + (-3)$
8. $8 + (-6) + 5$
9. $3 + (-15) + 1$

Example 6 (p. 43)

10. **MOUNTAINEERING** A rock climber climbed 125 feet up a cliff, climbed 56 feet up another cliff, then rappelled down 200 feet. How far was she from her starting point?

Practice and Problem Solving

HOMEWORK HELP	
For Exercises	See Examples
11–16	1
17–22	2–4
23–28	5
29, 30	6

Add.

11. $14 + 8$
12. $12 + 17$
13. $-14 + (-6)$
14. $-21 + (-13)$
15. $-5 + (-31)$
16. $-7 + (-24)$
17. $20 + (-5)$
18. $45 + (-4)$
19. $-15 + 8$
20. $-19 + 2$
21. $-10 + 34$
22. $-17 + 28$
23. $5 + 18 + (-22)$
24. $8 + 13 + (-14)$
25. $-17 + (-4) + 10$
26. $-26 + (-8) + 2$
27. $-12 + 9 + (-15)$
28. $-34 + 19 + (-16)$

TIDES For Exercises 29 and 30, use the table at the right that shows the change in water levels in feet due to tides.

Day	Beginning Water Level	Change to Low Tide	Change to High Tide
Mon	20	−22	+24
Tues	22	−25	+23
Wed	21	−23	+20

29. What is the water level change for each day's low tide?
30. On what day(s) was the final water level the lowest?

Write an addition expression to describe each situation. Then find each sum and explain its meaning.

31. **AIRPLANES** A pilot descended 350 feet to avoid a thunderstorm, then ascended 400 feet.

32. **MONEY** Gregg earned \$27 mowing lawns, then spent \$15 on a movie.

33. **STOCK** A stock cost \$46 on Wednesday. The price changed −\$3 on Thursday and +\$5 on Friday. What was the stock worth at the end of the day on Friday?

Add.

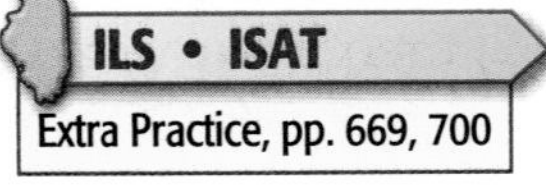

Extra Practice, pp. 669, 700

34. $-47 + (-41) + (-33)$
35. $-51 + (-38) + (-44)$
36. $-31 + (-26) + (-60)$
37. $-13 + 6 + (-8) + 13$
38. $9 + (-4) + 12 + (-9)$
39. $-14 + 2 + (-15) + 7$

H.O.T. Problems

40. **OPEN ENDED** Give an example of a positive and a negative integer with a negative sum. Then find their sum.

41. **CHALLENGE** Determine whether the following statement is *always*, *sometimes*, or *never* true. Give examples to justify your answer.

If x and y are integers, then $|x + y| = |x| + |y|$.

42. **WRITING IN MATH** Find the sum of −8, 25, and −2 mentally by applying the properties of numbers. Justify the process.

ISAT PRACTICE 6.B.3a, 8.A.3a

43. A golfer played 5 rounds of a tournament. What was the golfer's final score after Monday's round?

Day	Score
Thursday	+2
Friday	−1
Saturday	+3
Sunday	−4
Monday	−3

A +1 **C** −1

B −3 **D** +3

44. Marcus started the month with a balance of $75 in his checking account. He made a deposit of $12.50 and wrote three checks in the amounts of $25, $58.75, and $32. What is the balance of his checking account?

F $3.75

G $0

H −$18.75

J −$28.25

Spiral Review

Replace each ● with <, >, or = to make a true sentence. (Lesson 1-3)

45. −6 ● −11 46. 5 ● −5 47. 5 ● |8| 48. |−7| ● −7

49. **STATISTICS** The graph shows the number of television viewers for each network for one week in March 2007. Estimate the total number of viewers for the top two networks. (Lesson 1-1)

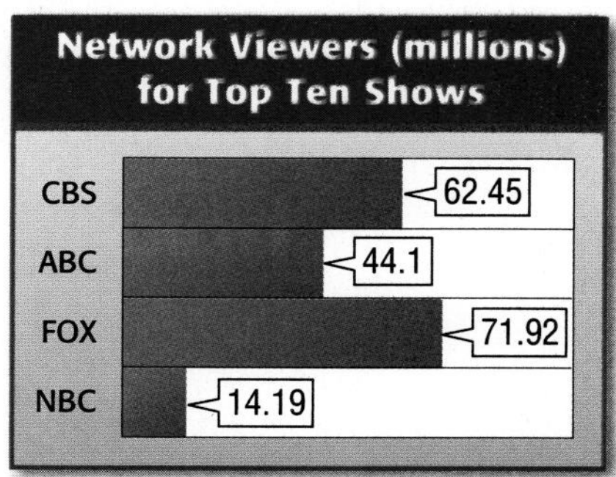

Source: Nielsen Media

50. **MEASUREMENT** The area A of a triangle can be found using the formula $A = \frac{1}{2}bh$, where b is the base of the triangle and h is the height. Find the area of the triangle if the base is 7 centimeters and the height is 4 centimeters. (Lesson 1-2)

GET READY for the Next Lesson

PREREQUISITE SKILL Evaluate each expression if $x = 3$, $y = 9$, and $z = 5$. (Lesson 1-2)

51. $x + 14$ 52. $z - 2$ 53. $y - z$ 54. $x + y - z$

1-5 Subtracting Integers

MAIN IDEA
Subtract integers.
IL Learning Standards
6.B.3a Solve practical computation problems involving whole numbers, integers and rational numbers.
IL Math Online
glencoe.com
• Concepts In Motion
• Extra Examples
• Personal Tutor
• Self-Check Quiz

MINI Lab

You can use algebra tiles to model the subtraction of two integers. Follow these steps to model 2 − 5. Remember that *subtract* means *take away* or *remove*.

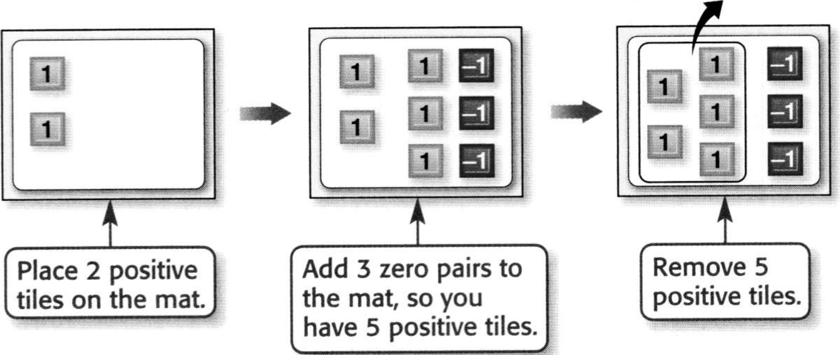

Since 3 negative tiles remain, $2 - 5 = -3$.

1. How does this result compare with the result of $2 + (-5)$?
2. Use algebra tiles to find $-3 - 4$.
3. How does this result compare to $-3 + (-4)$?
4. Use algebra tiles to find each difference and sum. Compare the results in each group.

   a. $3 - 6; 3 + (-6)$ b. $-4 - 2; -4 + (-2)$

When you subtract 5, as shown in the Mini Lab, the result is the same as adding −5.

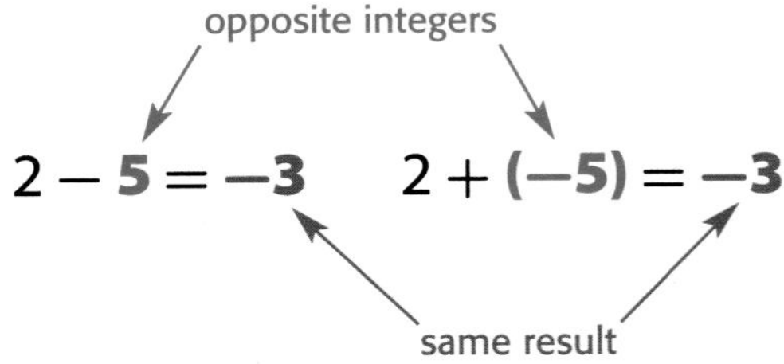

This and other examples suggest a method for subtracting integers.

Subtract Integers — Key Concept

Words To subtract an integer, add its opposite or additive inverse.

Examples

Numbers	Algebra
$4 - 7 = 4 + (-7)$ or -3	$a - b = a + (-b)$

EXAMPLES Subtract a Positive Integer

1 **Find 9 − 12.**

$9 - 12 = 9 + (-12)$ To subtract 12, add −12.

$= -3$ Add.

2 **Find −6 − 8.**

$-6 - 8 = -6 + (-8)$ To subtract 8, add −8.

$= -14$ Add.

CHECK Your Progress **Subtract.**

a. $3 - 8$ b. $-5 - 4$ c. $10 - 7$

EXAMPLES Subtract a Negative Integer

3 **Find 7 − (−15).**

$7 - (-15) = 7 + 15$ or 22 To subtract −15, add 15.

4 **CHEMISTRY** **The melting point of mercury is about −39°C and the melting point of aluminum is about 660°C. Find the difference between these temperatures.**

$660 - (-39) = 660 + 39$ or 699 To subtract −39, add 39.

The difference between the temperatures is about 699°C.

CHECK Your Progress **Subtract.**

d. $6 - (-7)$ e. $-5 - (-19)$ f. $-14 - (-2)$

EXAMPLES Evaluate Algebraic Expressions

Evaluate each expression if $a = 9$, $b = -8$, and $c = -2$.

5 $14 - b$

$14 - b = 14 - (-8)$ Replace *b* with −8.

$= 14 + 8$ or 22 To subtract −8, add 8.

6 $c - a^2$

$c - a^2 = -2 - 9^2$ Replace *c* with −2 and *a* with 9.

$= -2 - 81$ Simplify 9^2.

$= -2 + (-81)$ or −83 To subtract 81, add −81.

Study Tip

Common Error
In Example 5, a common error is to replace *b* with 8 instead of its correct value of −8. Prevent this error by inserting a set of parentheses before replacing *b* with its value.

$14 - b = 14 - (\quad)$
$= 14 - (-8)$

CHECK Your Progress

Evaluate each expression if $x = -5$ and $y = 7$.

g. $x - (-8)$ h. $-3 - y$ i. $y^2 - x + 3$

CHECK Your Understanding

Examples 1–4 (p. 47)

Subtract.

1. $8 - 13$
2. $5 - 24$
3. $-4 - 10$
4. $-6 - 3$
5. $7 - (-3)$
6. $2 - (-8)$
7. $-2 - (-6)$
8. $-18 - (-7)$

Example 3 (p. 47)

9. **WEATHER** The temperature in Spearfish, South Dakota, rose from −4°F to 45°F in two minutes. By how many degrees did the temperature change?

Examples 5, 6 (p. 47)

Evaluate each expression if $n = 10$, $m = -4$, and $p = -12$.

10. $n - 17$
11. $m - p$
12. $p + n - m$

Practice and Problem Solving

HOMEWORK HELP	
For Exercises	See Examples
13–16	1
17–20	2
21–24	3
25–28	4
29–30	1–4
31–38	5, 6

Subtract.

13. $14 - 8$
14. $17 - 12$
15. $5 - 9$
16. $1 - 8$
17. $-16 - 4$
18. $-15 - 12$
19. $-3 - 14$
20. $-6 - 13$
21. $9 - (-5)$
22. $10 - (-2)$
23. $5 - (-11)$
24. $17 - (-14)$
25. $-5 - (-4)$
26. $-18 - (-7)$
27. $-3 - (-6)$
28. $-9 - (-20)$

CONTINENTS For Exercises 29 and 30, use the table at the right.

29. Which continent has the greatest difference in elevation? by how much?
30. Find the difference between the lowest points of Antarctica and Asia.

Continent	Lowest Elevation (feet)	Highest Elevation (feet)
North America	−282	20,320
South America	−131	22,834
Europe	−92	18,510
Asia	−1,339	29,028
Africa	−512	19,340
Australia	−52	7,310
Antarctica	−8,327	16,066

Source: *New York Times Almanac*

Evaluate each expression if $a = -3$, $b = 14$, and $c = -8$.

31. $b - 20$
32. $c - 15$
33. $a - c$
34. $a - b$
35. $b - a$
36. $c - b$
37. $(b - a)^2 + c$
38. $a - c - b^2$

GOLF For Exercises 39 and 40, use the table that shows the results of an LPGA tournament.

39. Which player had the greatest difference in scores? by how much?
40. What was the difference between Se Ri Pak's score for round 1 and Cristie Kerr's score for round 1?

Player	Round				Total
	1	2	3	4	
Se Ri Pak	−1	−3	−1	−3	−8
Karrie Webb	−2	−2	0	−4	−8
Mi Hyun Kim	−4	−1	−1	−1	−7
Ai Miyazato	−4	0	−3	0	−7
Cristie Kerr	−6	+2	+2	−4	−6

Source: LPGA

ILS • ISAT
Extra Practice, pp. 669, 700

Simplify.

41. $31 - (-3) - (-18)$
42. $-20 - [6 + (-28)]$
43. $(-3 + 8) - (-21 - 10)$

H.O.T. Problems

44. **OPEN ENDED** Write an expression involving the subtraction of a negative integer. Then write an equivalent addition expression.

45. **FIND THE ERROR** Anna and David are finding $-5 - (-8)$. Who is correct? Explain your reasoning.

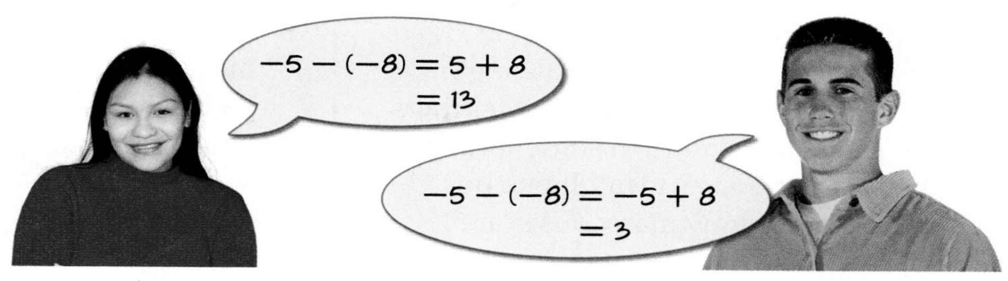

CHALLENGE For Exercises 46 and 47, determine whether the statement is *true* or *false*. If *false*, give a counterexample.

46. If x and y are positive integers, then $x - y$ is a positive integer.

47. Subtraction of integers is commutative.

48. **WRITING IN MATH** Write a problem about a real-world situation involving subtraction of integers for which the answer is -4.

ISAT PRACTICE **6.B.3a**

49. The temperature on Mars can range from 70°F to −225°F. Find the difference in temperatures.

A 300°F
B 295°F
C 155°F
D −155°F

50. Find the difference in elevation for the mountain shown.

F 2,136 feet
G 2,130 feet
H 2,018 feet
J 2,028 feet

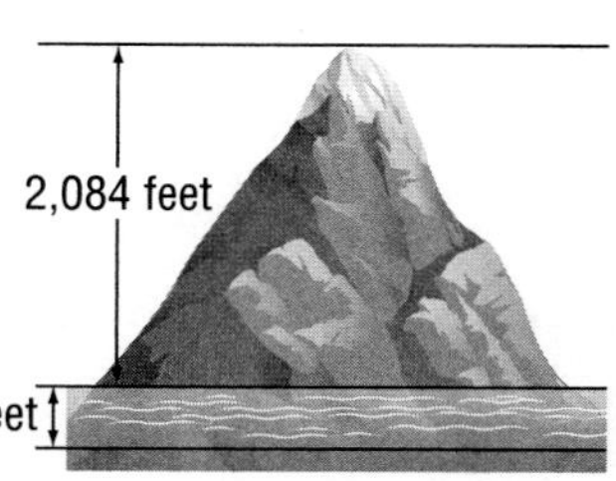

Spiral Review

51. **FINANCES** Mrs. Palmer deposited $829.32 into her checking account. The balance before the deposit was $532.26. She then wrote checks for $450.00, $79.97, and $126.57. Find her new checking account balance. (Lesson 1-4)

Evaluate each expression. (Lesson 1-3)

52. $|-14| + |3|$

53. $|20| - |-5|$

54. $|13 - (-7)|$

55. $|-12 + (-25)|$

GET READY for the Next Lesson

PREREQUISITE SKILL Find the mean for each set of data.

56. 1, 2, 3, 6, 8

57. 12, 13, 14, 16, 17, 18

58. 40, 45, 55, 60, 75, 85

CHAPTER 1

Mid-Chapter Quiz

Lessons 1-1 through 1-5

IL Learning Standards

6.B.3a, 8.A.3a

1. **FIELD TRIP** Two 8th-grade teams, the Tigers and the Waves, are going to Washington, D.C. There are 123 students and 4 teachers on the Tigers team and 115 students and 4 teachers on the Waves team. If one bus holds 64 people, how many buses are needed for the trip? (Lesson 1-1)

2. **MULTIPLE CHOICE** A landscaper plants bushes in a row across the back and down two sides of a yard. A bush is planted at each of the four corners and at every 4 meters. Which expression would give the number of bushes that are planted? (Lesson 1-1)

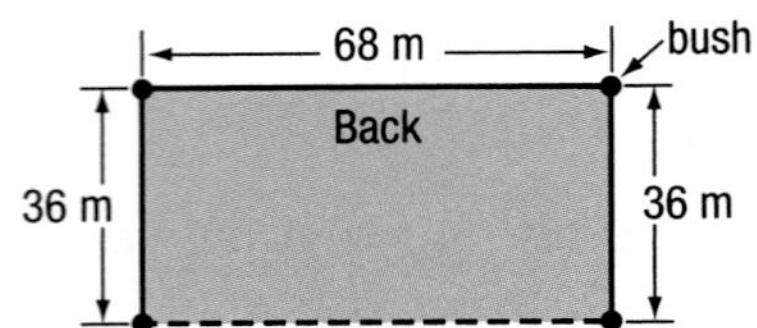

A $2 \times (36 \div 4) + (68 \div 4)$

B $2 + 2 \times (36 \div 4) + (64 \div 4)$

C $4 + 2 \times (36 \div 4) + (68 \div 4)$

D $2 \times (36 \div 4) + 2 \times (68 \div 4)$

Evaluate each expression if $x = 3$, $y = 6$, and $z = 2$. (Lesson 1-2)

3. $x^2 + y^2 + z^2$

4. $\frac{xy}{z} - 4z$

5. **MEASUREMENT** The expression $2\ell + 2w$ gives the perimeter of a rectangle with length ℓ and width w. What amount of fencing would Mr. Nakagawa need in order to fence his tomato garden that is 12 feet long and 9 feet wide? (Lesson 1-2)

Replace each ● with <, >, or = to make a true sentence. (Lesson 1-3)

6. -3 ● 2

7. $|-4|$ ● $|4|$

8. **MULTIPLE CHOICE** The table gives several of the highest and lowest elevations, in meters, on Earth's land surface.

Name	Location	Elevation
Mt. Everest	Nepal	8,850
Lake Assal	Djibouti	–156
Mt. McKinley	Alaska	6,194
Death Valley	California	–86
Dead Sea	Israel	–400

Choose the group of elevations that is listed in order from least to greatest. (Lesson 1-3)

F −86, −156, −400, 6,194, 8,850

G 8,850, 6,194, −400, −156, −86

H −400, −156, −86, 6,194, 8,850

J −156, −86, −400, 6,194, 8,850

Add or subtract. (Lessons 1-4, 1-5)

9. $-7 + 2 + (-1)$

10. $-3 - (-4)$

11. $2 - 6$

12. $-5 + (-8)$

13. $-5 + 9$

14. $-11 + 15 + 11 + (-6)$

15. $12 + (-4) - 7$

16. $-7 + 14 + (-1) + 13$

17. $-4 + -7$

18. $(-1) + (-5) + 18 - 3$

19. **MULTIPLE CHOICE** If $|y| = 5$, what is the value of y? (Lesson 1-3)

A −25 or 25

B 0 or 5

C −5 or 5

D −5 or 0

20. **ELEVATORS** In one hour, an elevator traveled up 5 floors, down 2 floors, up 8 floors, down 6 floors, up 11 floors, and down 14 floors. If the elevator started on the seventh floor, on which floor is it now? (Lessons 1-4, 1-5)

Multiplying and Dividing Integers

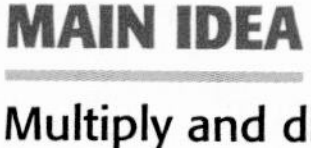

MAIN IDEA

Multiply and divide integers.

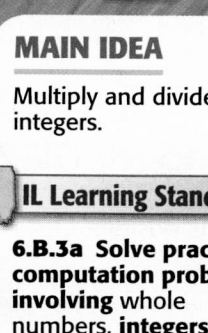

IL Learning Standards

6.B.3a Solve practical computation problems involving whole numbers, **integers** and rational numbers.

IL Math Online

glencoe.com
- Extra Examples
- Personal Tutor
- Self-Check Quiz

GET READY for the Lesson

PLANES An airplane descends 500 feet each minute to reach the runway. The table shows the change in the plane's elevation.

Time (minutes)	Change in Elevation (feet)
1	−500
2	−1,000
⋮	⋮

1. Write an addition sentence that could be used to find the change in the plane's elevation after 3 seconds. Then find the sum.
2. Write a multiplication sentence that could be used to find this same change in elevation. Explain your reasoning.
3. Write a multiplication sentence that could be used to find the change in the plane's elevation after 12 seconds. Then find the product.

Multiplication is repeated addition. So, 3(−500) means that −500 is used as an addend 3 times.

$$3(-500) = -500 + (-500) + (-500)$$
$$= -1{,}500$$

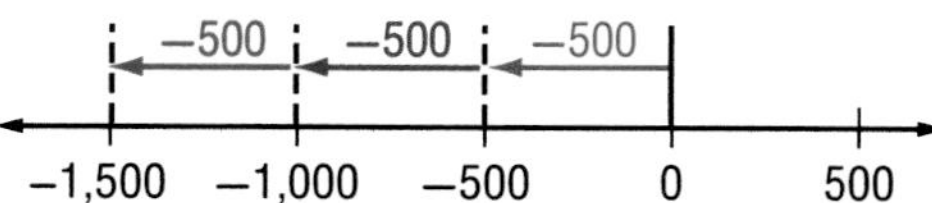

By the Commutative Property of Multiplication, 3(−500) = −500(3). This example suggests the following rule.

Multiply Integers with Different Signs — Key Concept

Words The product of two integers with different signs is negative.

Examples 2(−5) = −10 −5(2) = −10

EXAMPLES

1 Find 6(−8).

6(−8) = −48 The factors have different signs. The product is negative.

2 Find −9(2).

−9(2) = −18 The factors have different signs. The product is negative.

CHECK Your Progress **Multiply.**

a. 5(−3) b. −8(6) c. −2(4)

The product of two positive integers is positive. What is the sign of the product of two negative integers? Look at the pattern below.

Review Vocabulary

factors numbers that are multiplied together

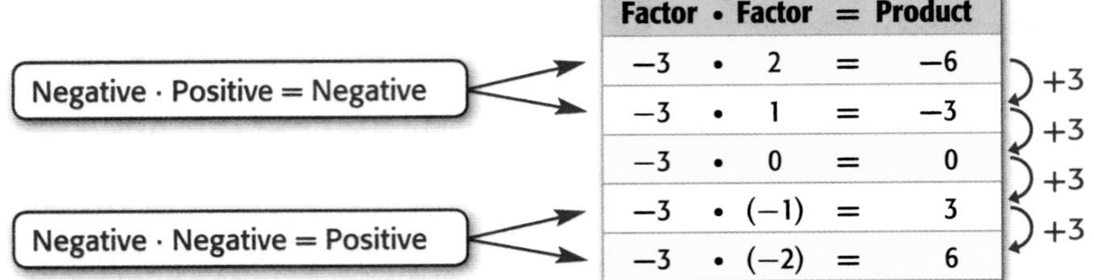

Factor	•	Factor	=	Product
−3	•	2	=	−6
−3	•	1	=	−3
−3	•	0	=	0
−3	•	(−1)	=	3
−3	•	(−2)	=	6

Multiply Integers with the Same Sign

Key Concept

Words The product of two integers with the same sign is positive.

Examples $2(5) = 10$ $\quad -2(-5) = 10$

EXAMPLE Multiply Integers with the Same Sign

3 Find $-4(-3)$.

$-4(-3) = 12$ The factors have the same sign. The product is positive.

CHECK Your Progress Multiply.

d. $-3(-7)$ e. $6(4)$ f. $(-5)^2$

To multiply more than two integers, use the Commutative and Associative Properties of Multiplication.

EXAMPLE Multiply More than Two Integers

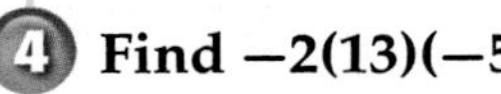

4 Find $-2(13)(-5)$.

METHOD 1 Use the Associative Property.

$-2(13)(-5) = [-2(13)](-5)$ Associative Property

$= -26(-5)$ $-2(13) = -26$

$= 130$ $-26(-5) = 130$

METHOD 2 Use the Commutative Property.

$-2(13)(-5) = -2(-5)(13)$ Commutative Property

$= 10(13)$ $-2(-5) = 10$

$= 130$ $10(13) = 130$

Study Tip

Method of Computation Mental Math Look for products that are multiples of ten to make the multiplication simpler.

CHOOSE Your Method Multiply.

g. $4(-2)(-5)$ h. $-1(-3)(-8)$ i. $(-2)^3$

Examine the following multiplication sentences and their related division sentences.

Reading Math

Division In a division sentence like $12 \div 3 = 4$, the number you are dividing, 12, is called the *dividend*. The number you are dividing by, 3, is called the *divisor*. The result is called the *quotient*.

Multiplication Sentence	Related Division Sentences	
$4(3) = 12$	$12 \div 3 = 4$	$12 \div 4 = 3$
$-4(3) = -12$	$-12 \div 3 = -4$	$-12 \div -4 = 3$
$4(-3) = -12$	$-12 \div (-3) = 4$	$-12 \div 4 = -3$
$-4(-3) = 12$	$12 \div (-3) = -4$	$12 \div (-4) = -3$

These examples suggest that the rules for dividing integers are similar to the rules for multiplying integers.

Divide Integers

Key Concept

Words The quotient of two integers with different signs is negative. The quotient of two integers with the same sign is positive.

Examples $16 \div (-8) = -2$ $\quad -16 \div (-8) = 2$

EXAMPLES Divide Integers

5 **Find $-24 \div 3$.** The dividend and the divisor have different signs.

$-24 \div 3 = -8$ The quotient is negative.

6 **Find $\frac{-30}{-15}$.** The signs are the same.

$\frac{-30}{-15} = 2$ The quotient is positive.

CHECK Your Progress **Divide.**

j. $-28 \div (-7)$ k. $\frac{36}{-2}$ l. $\frac{-40}{8}$

You can use all of the rules you have learned for adding, subtracting, multiplying, and dividing integers to evaluate algebraic expressions.

EXAMPLE Evaluate Algebraic Expressions

7 **Evaluate $-2a - b$ if $a = -3$ and $b = -5$.**

$-2a - b = -2(-3) - (-5)$ Replace a with -3 and b with -5.

$= 6 - (-5)$ The product of -2 and -3 is positive.

$= 6 + 5$ To subtract -5, add 5.

$= 11$ Add.

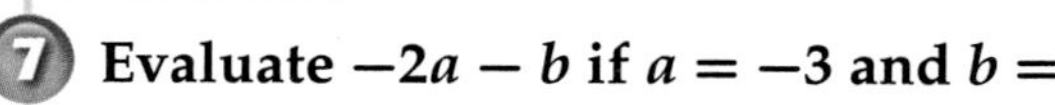

CHECK Your Progress

Evaluate each expression if $a = -4$, $b = 5$, and $c = -6$.

m. $c + 3a$ n. $\frac{-10}{a + b}$ o. $ab + c^2$

Real-World EXAMPLE

8 TEMPERATURE For six consecutive days, the average temperature in Asheville was lower than normal. The number of degrees the average temperature differed from the normal temperature is shown. Find the mean (average) of those variations.

Day	Variation (°F)
1	−6
2	−1
3	−8
4	−7
5	−12
6	−8

To find the mean of a set of numbers, find the sum of the numbers. Then divide the sum by how many numbers there are in the set.

$$\frac{-6 + (-1) + (-8) + (-7) + (-12) + (-8)}{6} = \frac{-42}{6}$$ Find the sum of the set of numbers. Divide by the number in the set.

$$= -7$$ Simplify.

The temperature was an average of 7 degrees lower than normal.

CHECK Your Progress

p. **FOOTBALL** On five plays, the Hawks completed passes for 15, −2, 8, 4, and 5 yards. What was average number of yards per pass?

Multiplying and Dividing Integers — Concept Summary

- The product or quotient of two integers with the same sign is positive.
- The product or quotient of two integers with different signs is negative.

CHECK Your Understanding

Examples 1–4 (pp. 51–52)

Multiply.

1. $4(-5)$
2. $3(-6)$
3. $-3(7)$
4. $-7(-2)$
5. $(-3)^2$
6. $-4(5)(-7)$

Examples 5, 6 (p. 53)

Divide.

7. $-16 \div 4$
8. $21 \div (-3)$
9. $-72 \div (-8)$
10. $\frac{22}{11}$
11. $\frac{-25}{-5}$
12. $\frac{-96}{12}$

Example 7 (p. 53)

Evaluate each expression if $a = -5$, $b = 8$, and $c = -12$.

13. $4a + 9$
14. $\frac{b - c}{a}$
15. $3b - a^2$

Example 8 (p. 54)

16. **FOOTBALL** During a scoring drive, a football team gained or lost yards on each play as shown. What was the average number of yards per play?

Yards Gained or Lost					
+6	−2	+8	0	+23	−4
+5	+12	−4	−3	+18	+1

Practice and Problem Solving

HOMEWORK HELP

For Exercises	See Examples
17–22, 29, 30	1, 2
23–26	3
27, 28	4
31–40	5, 6
41–44	7
45–48	8

Multiply.

17. $7(-8)$ 18. $8(-9)$ 19. $-5 \cdot 8$ 20. $-12 \cdot 7$

21. $-4(9)$ 22. $-6(8)$ 23. $-4(-6)$ 24. $-14(-2)$

25. $(-4)^2$ 26. $(-7)^2$ 27. $-6(-2)(-7)$ 28. $-3(-3)(-4)$

29. **COOKING** The boiling point of water at sea level is 212°F. For every 500 feet above sea level, the boiling point decreases by about 1°F. Find the boiling point of water at an elevation of 2,500 feet above sea level.

30. **HEALTH** The average person loses 50 to 80 hairs per day to make way for new growth. If you lost 65 hairs per day for 15 days without regrowing any, what would be the change in the number of hairs you have?

Divide.

31. $50 \div (-5)$ 32. $-60 \div 3$ 33. $45 \div 9$ 34. $-34 \div (-2)$

35. $\frac{-84}{4}$ 36. $\frac{28}{-7}$ 37. $\frac{-72}{-6}$ 38. $\frac{64}{8}$

39. **FARMING** During a seven-day period, the level of a pond receded 28 centimeters. Find the average daily change in the level of the pond.

40. **SWIMMING** With the drain open, a pool loses water at a rate of 9 gallons per minute. At that rate, how long will it take to drain 486 gallons of water?

ALGEBRA Evaluate each expression if $w = -2$, $x = 3$, $y = -4$, and $z = -5$.

41. $x + 6y$ 42. $9 - wz$ 43. $\frac{w - x}{z}$ 44. $\frac{8y}{x^2 - 5}$

STATISTICS Find the mean of each set of integers.

45. $-4, 6, -10, -3, -8, 1$ 46. $12, -14, -15, 18, -19, -17, -21$

47. $-2, -7, -6, 5, -10$ 48. $-14, -17, -20, -16, -13$

49. **AVIATION** A weather research airplane began descending from an altitude of 36,000 feet above its base, at a rate of 125 feet per minute. How long did it take for the plane to land at its base?

Multiply or divide.

50. $(2)^2 \cdot (-6)^2$ 51. $(-4)^3$ 52. $-2(4)(-3)(-10)$

ALGEBRA Evaluate each expression if $a = 12$, $b = -4$, and $c = -8$.

53. $\frac{6c}{a} - b$ 54. $\frac{-96}{b - a} + c$ 55. $-c^2 - 25$ 56. $(3b + 2)^2 \div (-4)$

57. **MOVIES** Predict the number of theater admissions in 2010 if the average change per year following 2004 remains the same as the average change per year from 2002 to 2004. Justify your answer.

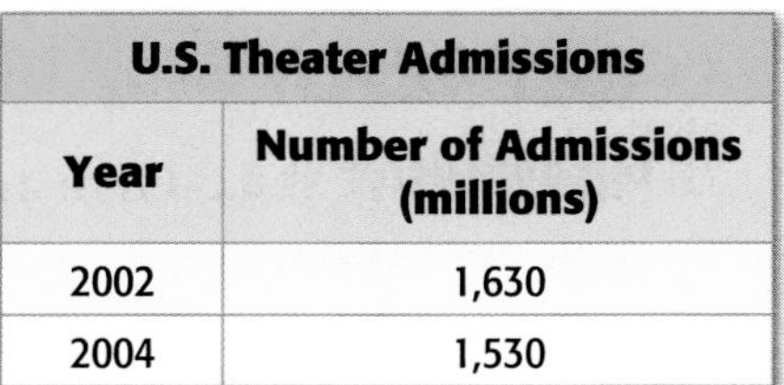

U.S. Theater Admissions

Year	Number of Admissions (millions)
2002	1,630
2004	1,530

Source: National Association of Theater Owners

ILS • ISAT
Extra Practice, pp. 669, 700

H.O.T. Problems

58. **OPEN ENDED** Name two integers that have a quotient of −7.

NUMBER SENSE Find the sign of each of the following if n is a negative number. Explain your reasoning.

59. n^2
60. n^3
61. n^4
62. n^5

CHALLENGE The sum of any two whole numbers is always a whole number. So, the set of whole numbers (0, 1, 2, 3, ...) is said to be *closed* under addition. This is an example of the *Closure Property*. State whether each statement is *true* or *false*. If *false*, give a counterexample.

63. The set of whole numbers is closed under subtraction.
64. The set of integers is closed under multiplication.
65. **WRITING IN MATH** Determine the sign of the product of −2, −3, and −4. Explain your reasoning.

ISAT PRACTICE 6.B.3a

66. A shoreline receded at a rate of 5 inches per day for two consecutive weeks. How much did the shoreline's position change in all?

A −10 in. C −50 in.
B −15 in. D −70 in.

67. The temperature at 6:00 P.M. was 10°F. Between 6:00 P.M. and midnight, the temperature dropped 4° three different times. What was the temperature at midnight?

F −12° H 0°
G −2° J 2°

Spiral Review

Subtract. (Lesson 1-5)

68. 12 − 18
69. −5 − (−14)
70. −3 − 20
71. 7 − (−15)

Add. (Lesson 1-4)

72. −9 + 2 + (−8)
73. −24 + (−11) + 24
74. −21 + 5 + (−14)
75. −7 + (−3) + 6

76. **SHOPPING** Gabriel went to the store to buy DVDs. Each DVD costs $20. If he buys four DVDs, he can get a fifth DVD free. How much will he save per DVD if he buys four? (Lesson 1-1)

GET READY for the Next Lesson

PREREQUISITE SKILL Give an example of a word or phrase that could indicate each operation.

Example: addition ⟶ the sum of

77. subtraction
78. multiplication
79. division

1-7 Writing Equations

MAIN IDEA

Write algebraic equations from verbal sentences and problem situations.

IL Learning Standards

8.A.3b Solve problems using linear expressions, **equations** and inequalities.
8.D.3a Solve problems using numeric, graphic **or symbolic representations of variables,** expressions, **equations** and inequalities.

New Vocabulary

equation
define a variable

IL Math Online

glencoe.com
- Extra Examples
- Personal Tutor
- Self-Check Quiz

GET READY for the Lesson

UNIFORMS Cheerleading uniforms cost $32 each. The Weberstown booster club wants to purchase uniforms for the team.

Number of Uniforms	Total Cost
1	$32
3	$96
5	$160

1. What is the relationship between the number of uniforms and the total cost?
2. Write an expression representing the total cost for n uniforms.
3. What does the equation $32n = 384$ represent in this situation?

An **equation** is a mathematical sentence containing two expressions separated by an equals sign (=). An important skill in algebra is modeling situations using equations.

1 WORDS Describe the situation. Use only the most important words.

2 VARIABLE **Define a variable** by assigning a variable to represent the unknown quantity.

3 EQUATION Translate your verbal model into an algebraic equation.

To translate your verbal model, look for common words or phrases that suggest one of the four operations.

EXAMPLE Write an Algebraic Equation

1 **GAMES Eduardo had a score of –150 points in the first round of a game. His final score after two rounds was 75 points. Write an equation to find his second round score.**

Words	1st round score	plus	2nd round score	was	final score.
Variable	Let s represent the 2nd round score.				
Equation	$-150 + s = 75$				

CHECK Your Progress **Write an equation to model each situation.**

a. The winning time of 27 seconds was 2 seconds shorter than Tina's.

b. A drop of 4°F per hour for the last several hours resulted in a total temperature change of −24°F.

Real-World EXAMPLE

2 **CARS** **For the average consumer, a hybrid SUV would cost $1,473 less per year in gas to drive than a regular SUV. Use the information at the left to write an equation that could be used to find the yearly gas cost for a regular SUV.**

Words	Gas cost for a hybrid SUV	is	$1,473 less than	gas cost for a regular SUV.
Variable	Let g represent gas cost for a regular SUV.			
Equation	$1,386 = g - 1,473$			

Real-World Link Hybrid cars operate on a combination of gasoline and electricity. The electricity is generated by the brakes of a car and stored in a battery. The estimated gas costs for a hybrid SUV is $1,386 per year.
Source: U.S. Department of Energy

CHECK Your Progress

c. **DANCE** The change in attendance from last year's spring dance was −45 students. The attendance this year was 128 students. Write an equation that could be used to find the attendance last year.

You can also write an equation with two variables to express the relationship between two unknown quantities.

ISAT EXAMPLE 8.A.3b, 8.D.3a

3 **The number of pounds of insects a bat can eat is 2.5 times its own body weight. Given b, a bat's body weight in pounds, which equation can be used to find p, the pounds of insects it can eat?**

A $b = 2.5 \cdot p$ **C** $b = 2.5 + p$

B $p = b + 2.5$ **D** $p = 2.5 \cdot b$

Read the Item

The phrase *2.5 times its own body weight* indicates multiplication. So, you can eliminate B and C.

Solve the Item

Pounds of insects eaten is 2.5 times body weight.

$$p = 2.5 \cdot b$$

The solution is D.

Test-Taking Tip

Reading Choices Read all answer choices carefully before deciding on the correct answer. Often two choices will look very similar.

CHECK Your Progress

d. A state's number of electoral votes is 2 more than its number of Representatives. Given r, a state's number of Representatives, which equation can be used to find e, the state's number of electoral votes?

F $e = 2r$ **G** $e = r \div 2$ **H** $e = r + 2$ **J** $e = 2 - r$

CHECK Your Understanding

Example 1 (p. 57) **Define a variable. Then write an equation to model each situation.**

1. Kevin's score of 20 points was four times Corey's score.
2. The total was \$28 after a \$4 tip was added to the bill.

Example 2 (p. 58) **Define a variable. Then write an equation that could be used to solve each problem.**

3. **SUBMARINES** A submarine dove 75 feet below its original depth. If the submarine's new depth is −600 feet, what was its original depth?
4. **TESTING** The total time given to take a state test is equally divided among the 3 subjects tested. If the time given for each subject test is 45 minutes, how many minutes long is the entire test?

Example 3 (p. 58)

5. **MULTIPLE CHOICE** Javier is 4 years younger than his sister Rita. Given j, Javier's age, which equation can be used to find r, Rita's age?

   A $j = r \div 4$ **B** $j = r + 4$ **C** $j = r - 4$ **D** $j = 4r$

Practice and Problem Solving

HOMEWORK HELP	
For Exercises	See Examples
6–11	1
12–15	2
16–19	3

Define a variable. Then write an equation to model each situation.

6. After dropping 12°C, the temperature outside was −5°C.
7. Jamal's score of 82 was 5 points less than the class average.
8. At 30 meters per second, a cheetah's top speed is three times that of the top speed of the fastest recorded human.
9. An archaelogical site is excavated to a level of −75 centimeters over several days for an average dirt removal of 15 centimeters each day.
10. A class of 24 students separated into equal-sized teams results in 6 students per team.
11. When the money was divided among the four grade levels, each grade received \$235.

Define a variable. Then write an equation that could be used to solve each problem.

12. **PETS** Nikki's cat is 5 pounds heavier than her sister's cat. If Nikki's cat weighs 9 pounds, how much does her sister's cat weigh?
13. **MEASUREMENT** A triangle's base is one-fourth its height. If the base is 15 meters long, what is the height of the triangle?
14. **CREDIT** For charging the cost of 4 equally priced shirts, Antonio's father's credit card statement shows an entry of −\$74. What would the statement have shown for a charge of just one shirt?

15. **GOLF** The table shows some of the top 20 leaders in a golf tournament after the first round. If the 6th place participant is 5 strokes behind the leader, what was the leader's score after the first round?

6.	Poole	−3
7.	Shaw	−2
8.	Kendrick	−2
9.	Rodriguez	1

Real-World Link The earliest year a musical group can be inducted into the Rock and Roll Hall of Fame is 25 years after the year its first album debuted.
Source: Rock and Roll Hall of Fame

Write an equation that could be used to express the relationship between the two quantities.

16. **HEALTH** Your heart rate r in beats per minute is the number of times your heart beats h in 15 seconds multiplied by 4. Given h, write an equation to find r.

17. **CARS** Ashley's car travels 24 miles per gallon of gas. Given d, the distance the car travels, write an equation to find g, the gallons of gas used.

18. **FRAMING** A mat for a picture frame should be cut so that its width is $\frac{1}{8}$ inch less than the frame's opening. Given p, the width of the frame's opening, write an equation to find m, the width of the mat.

19. **MEASUREMENT** A seam allowance indicates that the total length of fabric needed is $\frac{1}{2}$ inch more than that measured. Given t, the total length of fabric needed, write an equation to find m, the length measured.

20. **MUSIC** Refer to the information at the left. If an artist was inducted in 2009, write an equation that could be used to find the latest year the artist's first album could have debuted.

Write an equation to model the relationship between the quantities in each table.

21.

Yards, y	Feet, f
1	3
2	6
3	9
4	12
y	f

22.

Centimeters, c	Meters, m
200	2
300	3
400	4
500	5
c	m

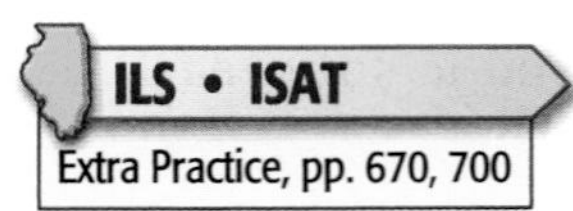

Extra Practice, pp. 670, 700

23. **MAPS** The scale on a map indicates that 1 inch on the map represents an actual distance of 20 miles. Create a table of values showing the number of miles represented by 1, 2, 3, 4, and m inches on the map. Given m, a distance on the map, write an equation to find a, the actual distance.

H.O.T. Problems

CHALLENGE For Exercises 24–26, consider the sequence 2, 4, 6, 8, ...

24. Express the relationship between a number in this sequence and its position using words. For example, 6 is the third number in this sequence.

25. Define two variables and write an equation to express this relationship.

26. Describe how this relationship would change, using words and a new equation, if the sequence were changed to 0, 2, 4, 6, 8, ...

27. **FIND THE ERROR** Zoe and Toshi are translating the verbal sentence *14 is 6 less than a number* into an algebraic equation. Who is correct? Explain.

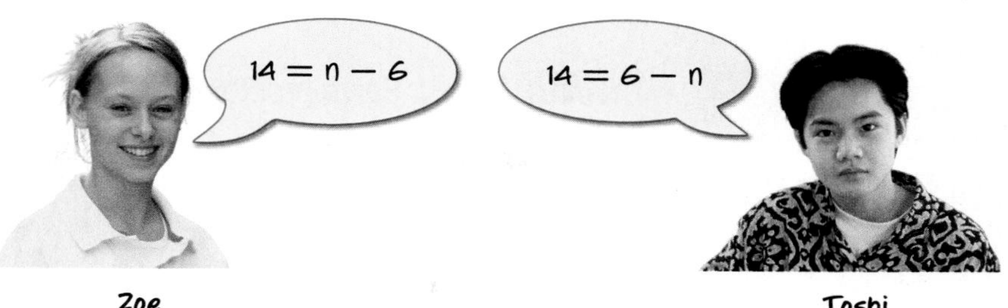

28. **WRITING IN MATH** Analyze the meaning of the equations $\ell = 2w$ and $w = 2\ell$ if ℓ represents the length of a rectangle and w its width. Then draw a rectangle that demonstrates each relationship.

ISAT PRACTICE 8.A.3b, 8.D.3a

29. The length of an actual car is 87 times its corresponding length of a model of the car. Given a, an actual length of the car, which equation can be used to find m, the corresponding model length?

A $a = 87 + m$

B $a = 87 - m$

C $a = 87 \cdot m$

D $a = 87 \div m$

30. The sides of each square are 1 unit long. Which equation can be used to represent the perimeter of the figure that contains x squares?

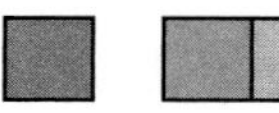

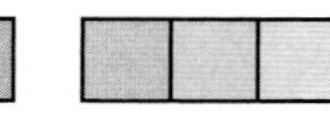

Figure 1 Figure 2 Figure 3

F $P = 4x$

G $P = 4x - 2$

H $P = 2x + 2$

J $P = 2x - 2$

Spiral Review

Multiply or divide. (Lesson 1-6)

31. $-9(10)$

32. $-5(-14)$

33. $34 \div (-17)$

34. $\frac{-105}{-5}$

35. **SPACE** On Mercury, the temperatures range from 805°F during the day to −275°F at night. Find the change in temperature from day to night.

GET READY for the Next Lesson

36. **PREREQUISITE SKILL** When Jason joined the football team, he had 8 plays memorized. By the end of the 1st week, he had 10 memorized. By the end of the 2nd week, he had 14 memorized. By the end of the 3rd week, he had 20 memorized. If he continues to learn at this pace, how many plays will he have memorized after 8 weeks? (Lesson 1-1)

1-8 Problem-Solving Investigation

MAIN IDEA: Solve problems by working backward.

ILS 6.B.3a Solve practical computation problems involving whole numbers, integers and rational numbers.

P.S.I. TEAM +

e-Mail: WORK BACKWARD

ALEX: Stephanie and I decided to trade video games. I gave Stephanie one fourth of my video games in exchange for 6 video games. Then I sold 3 video games and gave 2 video games to my brother. I ended up with 16 video games.

YOUR MISSION: Work backward to find how many video games Alex started with.

Understand	You know how many video games Alex now has. You know how many video games he gave away, sold, or traded. You need to determine how many video games he started with.
Plan	Start with the ending number of video games and work backward.
Solve	Alex has 16 video games — 16 **Go back** Add the games he gave to his brother. $+2$ — 18 **Go back** Add the games he sold. $+3$ — 21 **Go back** Subtract the games he traded with Stephanie. -6 — 15 **Go back** This number is $\frac{3}{4}$ of his games. $\times\frac{4}{3}$ — 20 Alex had 20 video games at the beginning.
Check	Assume Alex had 20 video games. Work forward, adding and subtracting the games he traded, sold, or gave away.

Analyze The Strategy

1. Tell why the *work backward* strategy is the best way to solve this problem.
2. Explain how you can check a solution when you solve by working backward.
3. **WRITING IN MATH** Write a problem that can be solved by working backward. Then write the steps you would take to find the solution to your problem.

Mixed Problem Solving

For Exercises 4–6, solve using the *work backward* strategy.

4. **PARTY** Aurora collected money for a birthday party for a friend. Jacy made the first donation. Guillermo doubled Jacy's donation. Rosa's mother tripled what Aurora collected and she now has $120. Find how much Jacy donated.

5. **SCHEDULE** Nyoko needs to be at school at 7:45 A.M. It takes her 25 minutes to walk to school, 25 minutes to eat breakfast, and 35 minutes to get dressed. At what time should Nyoko wake up in order to get to school 5 minutes early?

6. **SHOPPING** Janelle has $75 to spend on a dress. She buys a dress that is on sale for half price and then applies an in-store coupon for $10 off. After paying an additional sales tax of $1.80, she receives $37.20 in change. What was the original price of the dress?

Use any strategy to solve Exercises 7–12. Some strategies are shown below.

7. **SAVINGS** Examine the graph below.

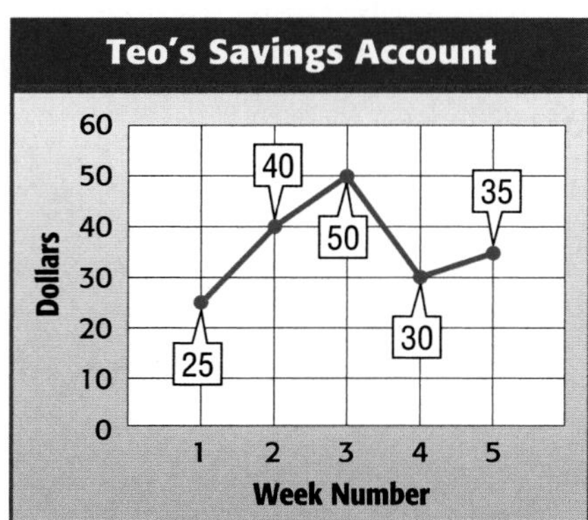

The activity in Teo's savings account is reflected in the graph. If after week 5, he continues to save at the same rate between weeks 2 and 3, in what week will his balance be at least $100?

8. **ANALYZE TABLES** The table gives the average television viewing time in hours:minutes for teens and children.

Group	Nightly 8–11 P.M.	Total per Week
Teens (ages 12–17)	5:38	19:19
Children (ages 2–11)	4:58	21:00

Source: Nielsen Media Research

How many more minutes each week do children spend watching television at times other than 8–11 P.M. than teens do?

9. **FURNITURE** Ms. Ruiz makes an initial down payment of $150 when purchasing a sofa. She pays the remaining cost of the sofa over 12 months, at no additional charge. If her monthly payment is $37.50, what was the original price of the sofa?

10. **ANALYZE TABLES** The table gives information about two different airplanes.

Airplane	Top Speed (mph)	Flight Length (mi)	Operating Cost per Hour
B747-400	534	3,960	$8,443
B727-200	430	644	$4,075

Source: *The World Almanac*

How much greater is the operating cost of a B747-400 than a B727-200 if each plane flies at its top speed for its maximum length of flight?

11. **PEACE PRIZE** Mother Teresa of Calcutta, India, received the Nobel Peace Prize in 1979. She died in 1997 at the age of 87. How old was she when she received the Nobel Prize?

12. **SCHOOL SUPPLIES** A bookstore sells gel pens for $1.15 and notebooks for $3.85. How many of each could you buy for exactly $13.45?

READING to SOLVE PROBLEMS

Simplify the Problem

ILS **Preparation for 8.A.3b** Solve problems using linear expressions, equations and inequalities.

Have you ever tried to solve a long word problem and didn't know where to start? Always start by reading the problem carefully.

Step 1

Look for key words like *more* or *less* to understand how the numbers are related.

It is estimated that 12.4 million pounds of potato chips were consumed during a recent Super Bowl. This was 3.1 million pounds more than the number of pounds of tortilla chips consumed. How many pounds of tortilla chips were consumed?

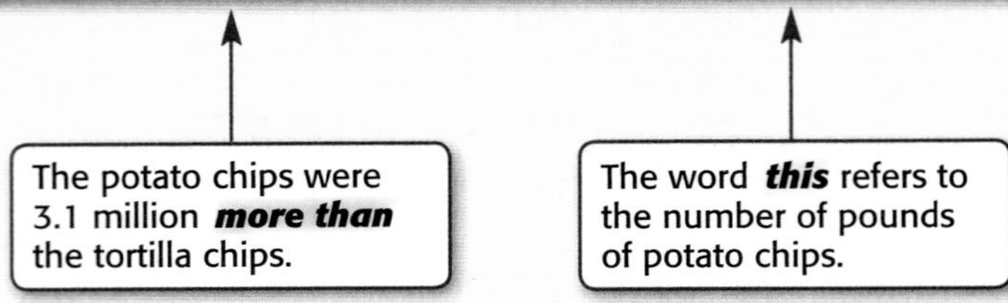

The potato chips were 3.1 million ***more than*** the tortilla chips.
The word ***this*** refers to the number of pounds of potato chips.

Step 2

Now, try to write the important information in only one sentence.

The number of pounds of potato chips was 3.1 million pounds more than the number of pounds of tortilla chips.

Step 3

Replace any phrases with numbers that you know.

12.4 million was 3.1 million more than the number of pounds of tortilla chips.

Before you write an equation, use the three steps described above to simplify the problem.

PRACTICE

Refer to page 59. For each exercise below, simplify the problem by writing the important information in only one sentence. Replace any phrases with numbers that you know. Do not write an equation.

1. Exercise 3 **2.** Exercise 12 **3.** Exercise 13

1-9

Solving Addition and Subtraction Equations

MAIN IDEA

Solve equations using the Subtraction and Addition Properties of Equality.

IL Learning Standards

8.A.3b Solve problems using linear expressions, **equations** and inequalities.
8.D.3a Solve problems using numeric, graphic **or symbolic representations of variables,** expressions, **equations** and inequalities. *Also addresses 8.A.3a, 8.C.3.*

New Vocabulary

solve
solution
inverse operations

IL Math Online

glencoe.com

- Extra Examples
- Personal Tutor
- Self-Check Quiz

MINI Lab

When you **solve** an equation, you are finding the values of the variable that make the equation true. These values are called the **solutions** of the equation. You can use algebra tiles and an equation mat to solve $x + (-3) = -7$.

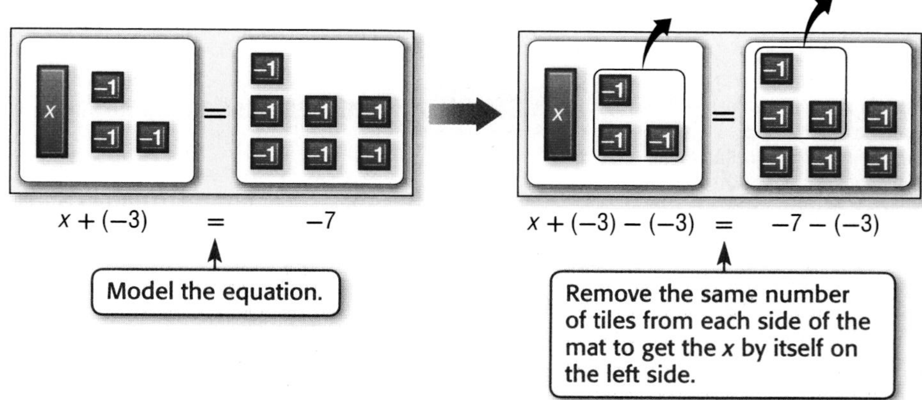
x
–1
–1
–1
=
–1
–1
–1
–1
–1
–1
–1
x + (–3) = –7
Model the equation.
x + (–3) – (–3) = –7 – (–3)
Remove the same number of tiles from each side of the mat to get the x by itself on the left side.

The number of tiles remaining on the right side of the mat represents the value of x. So, -4 is the solution of the equation $x + (-3) = -7$.

Solve each equation using algebra tiles.

1. $x + 1 = 4$
2. $x + 3 = 7$
3. $x + (-4) = -5$
4. Explain how you would find a value of x that makes $x + (-3) = -8$ true without using algebra tiles.

In the Mini Lab, you solved the equation $x + (-3) = -7$ by *removing*, or subtracting, the same number of positive counters from each side of the mat. This suggests the **Subtraction Property of Equality**, which can be used to solve addition equations like $x + (-3) = -7$ or $x + 4 = 6$.

Subtraction Property of Equality

Key Concept

Words If you subtract the same number from each side of an equation, the two sides remain equal.

Examples

Numbers	Algebra
$7 = 7$	$x + 4 = 6$
$7 - 3 = 7 - 3$	$x + 4 - 4 = 6 - 4$
$4 = 4$	$x = 2$

You can use this property to solve any addition equation. Remember to check your solution by substituting it back into the original equation.

Study Tip

Isolating the Variable When trying to decide which value to subtract from each side of an addition equation, remember that your goal is to get the variable by itself on one side of the equation. This is called *isolating the variable.*

EXAMPLE Solve an Addition Equation

1 Solve $x + 5 = 3$. Check your solution.

METHOD 1 Use the vertical method.

$x + 5 = 3$	Write the equation.
$-5 = -5$	Subtract 5 from each side.
$x = -2$	

METHOD 2 Use the horizontal method.

$x + 5 = 3$	Write the equation.
$x + 5 - 5 = 3 - 5$	Subtract 5 from each side.
$x = -2$	

The solution is -2.

Check	$x + 5 = 3$	Write the original equation.
	$-2 + 5 \stackrel{?}{=} 3$	Replace *x* with -2. Is this sentence true?
	$3 = 3$	The sentence is true.

CHOOSE Your Method

Solve each equation. Check your solution.

a. $a + 6 = 2$ b. $y + 3 = -8$ c. $5 = n + 4$

Addition and subtraction are called **inverse operations** because they "undo" each other. For this reason, you can use the **Addition Property of Equality** to solve subtraction equations like $x - 7 = -5$.

Addition Property of Equality

Key Concept

Words If you add the same number to each side of an equation, the two sides remain equal.

Examples

Numbers	Algebra
$7 = 7$	$x - 5 = 6$
$7 + 3 = 7 + 3$	$x - 5 + 5 = 6 + 5$
$10 = 10$	$x = 11$

EXAMPLE Solve an Addition Equation

2 **MEASUREMENT** Two angles are supplementary if the sum of their measures is 180°. The two angles shown are supplementary. Write and solve an equation to find the measure of angle X.

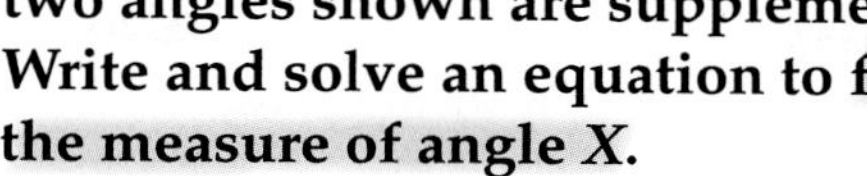

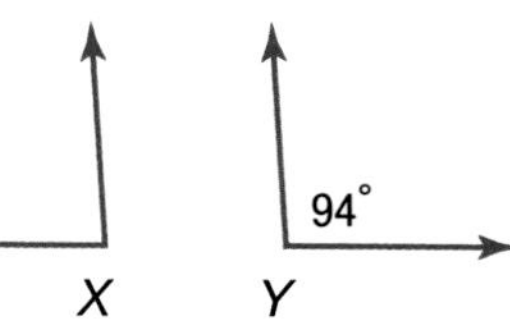

Words	The sum of the measures is 180°.
Variable	Let x represent the measure of angle X.
Equation	$x + 94 = 180$

$x + 94 = 180$	Write the equation.
$x + 94 - 94 = 180 - 94$	Subtract 94 from each side.
$x = 86$	Simplify.

The measure of angle X is 86°.

CHECK Your Progress

d. **READING** A novel is ranked 7th on a best-seller list. This is a change of −8 from its position last week. Write and solve an equation to determine the novel's ranking last week.

EXAMPLE Solve a Subtraction Equation

3 Solve $-6 = y - 7$.

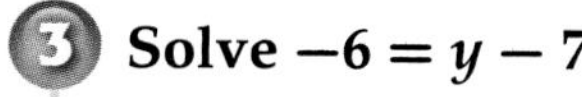

METHOD 1 **Use the vertical method.**

$-6 = y - 7$	Write the equation.
$\underline{+7 = \quad +7}$	Add 7 to each side.
$1 = y$	$-6 + 7 = 1$ and $-7 + 7 = 0$

METHOD 2 **Use the horizontal method.**

$-6 = y - 7$	Write the equation.
$-6 + 7 = y - 7 + 7$	Add 7 to each side.
$1 = y$	$-6 + 7 = 1$ and $-7 + 7 = 0$

The solution is 1. Check the solution.

> **Study Tip**
>
> **Position of the Variable** You could also begin solving Example 3 by rewriting the equation so that the variable is on the left side of the equation.
>
> $-6 = y - 7$
>
> ↓
>
> $y - 7 = -6$

CHOOSE Your Method Solve each equation.

e. $x - 8 = -3$

f. $b - 4 = -10$

g. $7 = p - 12$

CHECK Your Understanding

Example 1 (p. 66)

Solve each equation. Check your solution.

1. $a + 4 = 10$
2. $2 = z + 7$
3. $x + 9 = -3$

Example 2 (p. 67)

4. **RUGS** The length of a rectangular rug is 12 inches shorter than its width. If the length is 30 inches, write and solve an equation to find the width.

Example 3 (p. 67)

Solve each equation. Check your solution.

5. $y - 2 = 5$
6. $n - 5 = -6$
7. $-8 = d - 11$

Practice and Problem Solving

HOMEWORK HELP

For Exercises	See Examples
8–13	1
14–19	3
20–23	2

Solve each equation. Check your solution.

8. $x + 5 = 18$
9. $n + 3 = 20$
10. $9 = p + 11$
11. $1 = a + 7$
12. $y + 12 = -3$
13. $w + 8 = -6$
14. $m - 15 = 3$
15. $b - 9 = -8$
16. $g - 2 = -13$
17. $-16 = t - 6$
18. $-4 = r - 20$
19. $k - 14 = -7$

20. **MEASUREMENT** Two angles are supplementary if the sum of their measures is 180°. The two angles shown are supplementary. Write and solve an equation to find the measure of angle B.

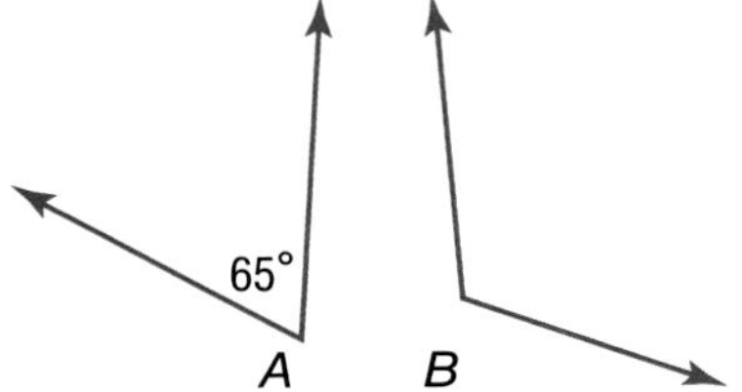

21. **BANKING** After you withdraw \$50 from your savings account, the balance is \$124. Write and solve an equation to find your starting balance.

22. **TEMPERATURE** On one day in Fairfield, Montana, the temperature dropped 84°F from noon to midnight. If the temperature at midnight was −21°F, write and solve an equation to determine the noon temperature that day.

23. **TREES** Before planting a tree, Manuel digs a hole with a depth 18 inches below ground level. Once planted, the top of the tree is 54 inches above ground. Write and solve an equation to find the height of the tree Manuel planted.

ANALYZE TABLES For Exercises 24 and 25, use the table.

24. Lauren Jackson averaged 2.5 point per game less than Seimone Augustus. Write and solve an equation to find Augustus's average points scored per game.

25. Sheryl Swoopes averaged 6.4 fewer points per game than Seimone Augustus. Write and solve an equation to find how many points Swoopes averaged per game.

2006 WNBA Regular Season Points Leaders

Player	AVG
Diana Taurasi	25.3
Seimone Augustus	p
Lisa Leslie	20
Lauren Jackson	19.4

Source: WNBA

26. **STOCK MARKET** The changes in the price of a certain stock each day from Monday to Thursday of one week were $-\$2.25$, $+\$0.50$, $+\$1.50$, and $+\$0.75$. If the overall change in the stock price for the week was $-\$0.50$, write an equation that can be used to find the change in the price on Friday and explain two methods of solving this equation. Then solve the equation and explain its meaning in the context of the situation.

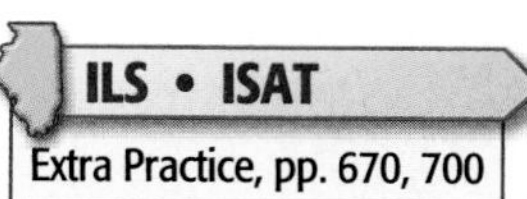

H.O.T. Problems

27. **OPEN ENDED** Write one addition equation and one subtraction equation that each have -3 as a solution.

28. **Which One Doesn't Belong?** Identify the equation that does not belong with the other three. Explain your reasoning.

$y + 4 = 2$	$x + 6 = 4$	$t + 5 = -3$	$1 + m = -1$

29. **CHALLENGE** Solve $|x| + 5 = 7$. Explain your reasoning.

30. **WRITING IN MATH** Write a problem about a real-world situation that can be answered by solving the equation $x + 60 = 20$. Then solve the equation and explain the meaning of its solution in the context of your problem.

ISAT PRACTICE 8.A.3b, 8.D.3a

31. A scuba diver dives 125 feet below the surface of the water, then ascends 42 feet. What is her depth?

A $+167$ feet

B $+83$ feet

C -83 feet

D -167 feet

32. The bill for dinner came to \$15.68 and included a \$3.25 tip. Which equation could be used to find the cost of dinner before the tip?

F $x - 3.25 = 15.68$

G $x + 3.25 = 15.68$

H $x + 15.68 = 3.25$

J $x - 15.68 = 3.25$

Spiral Review

33. **TRAVEL** James needs to drive an average of 575 miles a day for three days in order to make it to his vacation destination on time. If he drives 630 miles the first day and 480 miles the second day, how many miles does he need to drive on the third day to meet his goal? (Lesson 1-8)

ALGEBRA Write an equation to model each situation. (Lesson 1-7)

34. Lindsay, 59 inches tall, is 5 inches shorter than her sister.

35. After cutting the recipe in half, Ricardo needed 3 cups of flour.

GET READY for the Next Lesson

PREREQUISITE SKILL Multiply. (Lesson 1-6)

36. $3(9)$

37. $-2(18)$

38. $-5(-11)$

39. $4(-15)$

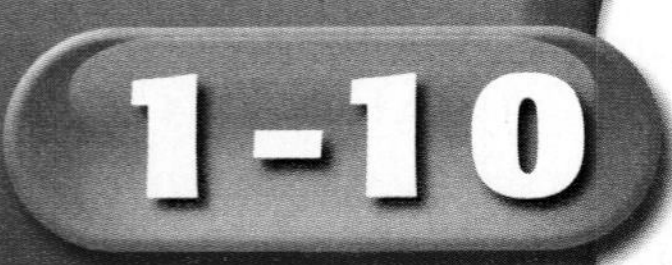

Solving Multiplication and Division Equations

MAIN IDEA

Solve equations by using the Division and Multiplication Properties of Equality.

IL Learning Standards

8.A.3b Solve problems using linear expressions, **equations** and inequalities.
8.D.3a Solve problems using numeric, graphic **or symbolic representations of variables,** expressions, **equations** and inequalities. *Also addresses 8.A.3a, 8.C.3.*

IL Math Online

glencoe.com

- Extra Examples
- Personal Tutor
- Self-Check Quiz

GET READY for the Lesson

TRANSPORTATION High speed trains are very popular in Europe and Asia and can travel at speeds of 150 miles per hour or more. That's almost three times the speed of a car on the highway!

1. If h represents the number of hours the train has traveled, write a multiplication equation you could use to find how long it would take the train to travel 675 miles.

Hour	Distance
1	$150(1) = 150$
2	$150(2) = 300$
3	$150(3) = 450$
⋮	⋮
h	?

The equation $150h = 675$ models the relationship described above. To undo the multiplication of 150, divide each side of the equation by 150.

EXAMPLE Solve a Multiplication Equation

1 Solve $150h = 675$.

$150h = 675$	Write the equation.
$\frac{150h}{150} = \frac{675}{150}$	Divide each side of the equation by 150.
$1h = 4.5$	$150 \div 150 = 1$ and $675 \div 150 = 4.5$
$h = 4.5$	Identity Property; $1h = h$

CHECK Your Progress

Solve each equation. Check your solution.

a. $8x = 72$ b. $-4n = 28$ c. $-12 = -6k$

In Example 1, you used the **Division Property of Equality** to solve a multiplication equation.

Division Property of Equality

Key Concept

Words If you divide each side of an equation by the same nonzero number, the two sides remain equal.

Examples

Numbers	Algebra
$12 = 12$	$5x = -60$
$\frac{12}{4} = \frac{12}{4}$	$\frac{5x}{5} = \frac{-60}{5}$
$3 = 3$	$x = -12$

Reading Math

Division Expressions
Remember, $\frac{a}{-3}$ means *a divided by −3.*

You can use the **Multiplication Property of Equality** to solve equations.

Multiplication Property of Equality — Key Concept

Words If you multiply each side of an equation by the same number, the two sides remain equal.

Examples

Numbers	Algebra
$5 = 5$	$\frac{x}{2} = 8$
$5(-4) = 5(-4)$	$\frac{x}{2}(2) = 8(2)$
$-20 = -20$	$x = 16$

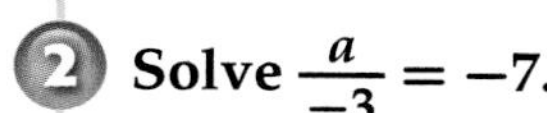

EXAMPLE Solve a Division Equation

2 **Solve $\frac{a}{-3} = -7$.**

$\frac{a}{-3} = -7$	Write the equation.
$\frac{a}{-3}(-3) = -7(-3)$	Multiply each side by −3.
$a = 21$	$-7 \cdot (-3) = 21$

CHECK Your Progress **Solve each equation.**

d. $\frac{y}{-4} = -8$ e. $\frac{m}{5} = -9$ f. $30 = \frac{b}{-2}$

Real-World EXAMPLE

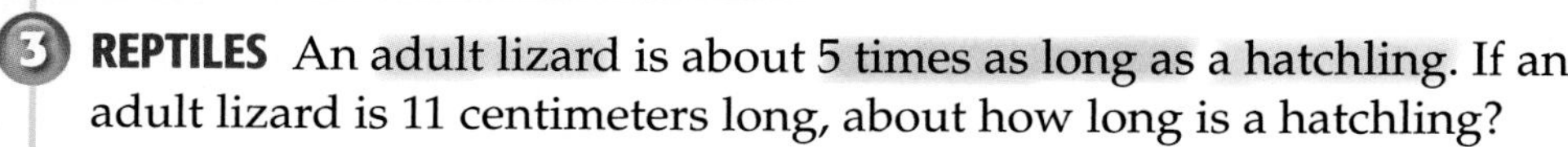

3 **REPTILES** An adult lizard is about 5 times as long as a hatchling. If an adult lizard is 11 centimeters long, about how long is a hatchling?

Words	Adult length is 5 times hatchling length.
Variable	Let g represent the length of a hatchling.
Equation	$11 = 5 \cdot g$

$11 = 5g$	Write the equation.
$\frac{11}{5} = \frac{5g}{5}$	Divide each side by 5.
$2.2 = g$	$11 \div 5 = 2.2$

A lizard hatchling is about 2.2 centimeters long.

Real-World Career . . .
How Does a Zoologist Use Math?
Zoologists use equations to predict the growth of animal populations.

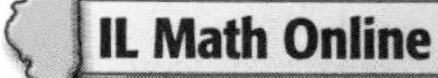

IL Math Online

For more information, go to glencoe.com.

CHECK Your Progress

g. **METEOROLOGY** The recorded amount of precipitation is one-tenth the amount of fallen snow. If Redfield, New York, received 13.6 inches of precipitation in one week, how many inches of snow fell?

CHECK Your Understanding

Examples 1, 2 (pp. 70, 71)

Solve each equation. Check your solution.

1. $5b = 40$
2. $-7k = 14$
3. $-18 = -3n$
4. $\frac{p}{9} = 9$
5. $\frac{a}{12} = -3$
6. $22 = \frac{m}{-2}$

Example 3 (p. 71)

7. **FUNDRAISING** King Middle School is selling cards as a fundraiser and receives $\frac{3}{4}$ of the proceeds. Write and solve a multiplication equation to find how much they need to sell in order to raise $1,350.

Practice and Problem Solving

HOMEWORK HELP	
For Exercises	See Examples
8–13	1
14–19	2
20, 21	3

Solve each equation. Check your solution.

8. $4c = 44$
9. $9b = 72$
10. $34 = -2x$
11. $36 = -18y$
12. $-32 = 8d$
13. $-35 = 5n$
14. $\frac{m}{7} = 10$
15. $\frac{u}{9} = 6$
16. $\frac{h}{-3} = 33$
17. $20 = \frac{q}{-5}$
18. $-8 = \frac{c}{12}$
19. $\frac{r}{24} = -3$

20. **MAMMALS** A koala eats an average of 2.5 pounds of leaves from eucalyptus trees each day. If a small tree has 30 pounds of leaves on it, write and solve a multiplication equation to find how many days the leaves will last.

21. **SCHOOL ACTIVITIES** The drama club sold 1,200 tickets for the school musical. If the total ticket sales were $6,000, write and solve a multiplication equation to find the cost per ticket.

MEASUREMENT For Exercises 22–26, refer to the table. Write and solve an equation to find each quantity.

Customary System Conversions (capacity)
1 tablespoon = 3 teaspoons
1 cup = 16 tablespoons
1 cup = 8 fluid ounces
1 pint = 2 cups
1 quart = 2 pints
1 gallon = 4 quarts

22. the number of cups in 96 teaspoons
23. the number of cups in 64 tablespoons
24. the number of gallons in 24 quarts
25. the number of gallons in 120 pints
26. the number of gallons in 128 fluid ounces

Solve each equation.

27. $7 = \frac{-56}{z}$
28. $\frac{10}{x} = -5$
29. $\frac{-126}{a} = -21$
30. $-17 = \frac{136}{g}$

31. **PHYSICAL SCIENCE** The amount of work, measured in foot-pounds, is equal to the amount of force applied, measured in pounds, times the distance, in feet, the object moved. How far do you have to lift a 45-pound object to produce 180 foot-pounds of work?

ILS • ISAT
Extra Practice, pp. 671, 700

H.O.T. Problems

32. **OPEN ENDED** Describe a real-world situation in which you would use a division equation to solve a problem. Then write your equation.

33. **NUMBER SENSE** Without solving the equation, tell what you know about the value of x in $\frac{x}{25} = 300$.

34. **CHALLENGE** If an object is traveling at a rate of speed r, then the distance d the object travels after a time t is given by the equation $d = rt$. Rewrite this equation so that it expresses the value of r in terms of t and d.

35. **WRITING IN MATH** Explain how to solve $-4a = 84$. Be sure to state which property you use and why you used it.

ISAT PRACTICE 8.A.3b, 8.D.3a

36. Grace paid \$2.24 for 4 granola bars. All 4 granola bars were the same price. How much did each granola bar cost?

    A \$0.52

    B \$0.56

    C \$1.24

    D \$1.56

37. Jason paid half of what Tony paid for new shoes. If Jason paid \$38 for his shoes, which equation can be used to find the amount s that Tony paid for his shoes?

    F $s = \frac{32}{8}$

    G $s = 38 - \frac{1}{2}$

    H $s = 2(38)$

    J $s + \frac{1}{2} = 38$

Spiral Review

38. **SPORTS** At a recent track meet, Lucia tried to break her school's high jump record, but fell short by 4 inches. Write and solve an equation to find the height of Lucia's jump. (Lesson 1-9)

ALGEBRA Write an equation to model each situation. (Lesson 1-7)

39. Eight feet longer than she jumped is 15 feet.

40. The temperature fell 28°F from 6 A.M. to 17°F at 11 A.M.

41. Three friends shared a \$9 parking fee equally.

Find each product or quotient. (Lesson 1-6)

42. $-23(-12)$
43. $-25(7)$
44. $22 \cdot (-20)$
45. $4 \cdot 8 \cdot (-14)$
46. $-180 \div 15$
47. $147 \div (-21)$
48. $-162 \div 9$
49. $-208 \div (-16)$

Write an integer for each situation. (Lesson 1-3)

50. a gain of 4 ounces
51. earning \$45
52. 2 miles below sea level
53. a decrease of 5 miles per gallon

CHAPTER 1 Study Guide and Review

IL Math Online glencoe.com
- STUDY TO GO
- Vocabulary Review

GET READY to Study

Be sure the following Big Ideas are noted in your Foldable.

BIG Ideas

Order of Operations (Lesson 1-2)

1. Do all operations within grouping symbols first.
2. Evaluate all powers before other operations.
3. Multiply and divide in order from left to right.
4. Add and subtract in order from left to right.

Operations With Integers (Lessons 1-4 to 1-6)

- To add integers with the same sign, add their absolute values. The sum has the same sign as the integers.
- To add integers with different signs, subtract their absolute values. The sum has the sign of the integer with the greater absolute value.
- To subtract an integer, add its opposite or additive inverse.
- The product or quotient of two integers with the same sign is positive.
- The product or quotient of two integers with different signs is negative.

Solving Equations (Lessons 1-9, 1-10)

- If you add or subtract the same number to or from each side of an equation, the two sides remain equal.
- If you multiply or divide each side of an equation by the same nonzero number, the two sides remain equal.

Key Vocabulary

absolute value (p. 36)
additive inverse (p. 43)
algebra (p. 29)
algebraic expression (p. 29)
coordinate (p. 35)
counterexample (p. 31)
define a variable (p. 57)
equation (p. 57)
evaluate (p. 29)
inequality (p. 35)
integer (p. 35)
inverse operations (p. 66)
negative number (p. 35)
numerical expression (p. 29)
opposites (p. 43)
order of operations (p. 29)
powers (p. 30)
solution (p. 65)
solve (p. 65)
variable (p. 29)

Vocabulary Check

State whether each sentence is *true* or *false*. If *false*, replace the underlined word or number to make a true sentence.

1. Operations that "undo" each other are called order of operations.
2. The symbol for absolute value is | |.
3. A mathematical sentence that contains an equals sign is an inequality.
4. An integer is a number less than zero.
5. A property is an example that shows that a conjecture is false.
6. The value of the variable that makes the equation true is called the solution.
7. The number that corresponds to a point is called its coordinate.
8. A power is a symbol, usually a letter, used to represent the number.
9. An expression that contains a variable is an algebraic expression.

Lesson-by-Lesson Review

1-1 A Plan for Problem Solving (pp. 24–28)

6.B.3a

Use the four-step plan to solve each problem.

10. **CHARITY WALK** Krystal knows that she can walk about 1.5 meters per second. If she can maintain that pace, about how long should it take her to complete a 10-kilometer charity walk?

11. **PHONES** Abigail was shopping for a new cellular phone. Plan A costs $40 for 500 free minutes plus $0.20 per minute after that. If Abigail uses 650 minutes in a month, how much will her bill be?

12. **SHOPPING** Miguel went to the store to buy jeans. Each pair costs $24. If he buys two pairs, he can get the second pair for half price. How much will he save per pair if he buys two pairs?

Example 1 **Josie needs to fence three sides of her yard, and the house will supply the fourth side. Two of the sides are 25 feet long, and the third side is 35 feet long. If the fencing costs $10 per foot, how much will it cost Josie to fence her yard?**

Understand You know the lengths of the sides and the cost of the fencing. You need to find the total cost.

Plan Add the lengths of the 3 sides, then multiply that by $10.
Estimate $25 + 25 + 40 = 90$ and $90 \times \$10 = \$900$

Solve $25 + 25 + 35 = 85$ and $85 \times \$10 = \$850$
The cost is $850.

Check The answer of $850 is close to the estimate of $900, so the answer is reasonable.

1-2 Variables, Expressions, and Properties (pp. 29–34)

8.A.3a, 8.D.3a

Evaluate each expression if $a = 6$, $b = 2$, and $c = 1$.

13. $a(b + 4)$
14. $3b^2$
15. $3a + 2b + c$
16. $\frac{(a + 2)^2}{bc}$

17. **WEATHER** The time s in seconds between seeing lightning and hearing thunder can be used to estimate a storm's distance in miles. Use the expression $\frac{s}{5}$ to determine how far away a storm is if this time is 15 seconds. (Lesson 1-2)

Example 2 **Evaluate $x^2 + yx - z^2$ if $x = 4$, $y = 2$, and $z = 1$.**

$x^2 + yx - z^2$	Write the expression.
$= 4^2 + (2)(4) - (1)^2$	$x = 4$, $y = 2$, and $z = 1$
$= 16 + (2)(4) - 1$	Evaluate powers first.
$= 16 + 8 - 1$	Multiply.
$= 23$	Add and subtract.

Study Guide and Review

1-3 Integers and Absolute Value (pp. 35–39)

6.B.3a

Replace each ● with <, >, or = to make a true sentence.

18. -8 ● 7

19. -2 ● -6

20. **BASKETBALL** On average, the varsity team wins games by a margin of 13 points, give or take 5 points. This range can be modeled by the equation $|p - 13| = 5$. Graph this equation on a number line to determine the least and the greatest margin of points.

Evaluate each expression.

21. $|-5|$

22. $|-12| - |4|$

Example 3 **Replace the ● in -3 ● -7 with <, >, or = to make a true sentence.**

Graph the integers on a number line.

−8 −7 −6 −5 −4 −3 −2 −1 0 1

Since -3 is to the right of -7, $-3 > -7$.

Example 4 **Evaluate $|-3|$.**

Since the graph of -3 is 3 units from 0 on the number line, the absolute value of -3 is 3.

1-4 Adding Integers (pp. 41–45)

6.B.3a, 8.A.3a

Add.

23. $-54 + 21$

24. $100 + (-75)$

25. $-14 + (-20)$

26. $38 + (-46)$

27. $-14 + 37 + (-20) + 2$

28. **TEMPERATURE** Vostok, Antarctica, may be the coldest place on Earth with an average low temperarture of $-89.6°$ F. If the average high temperature is 63.9° higher than the average low, find the average high temperature.

Example 5 **Find $-16 + (-11)$.**

$-16 + (-11)$ — Add $|-16|$ and $|-11|$. Both numbers are negative, so the sum is negative.
$= -27$

Example 6 **Find $-7 + 20$.**

$-7 + 20$ — Subtract $|-7|$ from $|20|$. The sum is positive because $|20| > |-7|$.
$= 13$

1-5 Subtracting Integers (pp. 46–49)

6.B.3a

Subtract.

29. $-2 - (-5)$

30. $11 - 15$

31. **GEOGRAPHY** At an elevation of -52 feet, Lake Eyre is the lowest point in Australia. How much lower than Lake Eyre is the Valdes Peninsula in South America, which has an elevation of -131 ft?

Example 7 **Find $-27 - (-6)$.**

$-27 - (-6) = -27 + 6$ — To subtract -6, add 6.
$= -21$ — Add.

Mixed Problem Solving
For mixed problem-solving practice, see page 700.

1-6 Multiplying and Dividing Integers (pp. 51–56)

6.B.3a

Multiply or divide.

32. $-4(-25)$
33. $-7(3)$
34. $-15(-4)(-1)$
35. $180 \div (-15)$
36. $-170 \div (-5)$
37. $-88 \div 8$
38. **GAMES** José's score in each of 6 rounds of a game was −2. What was his overall score for these six rounds?

Example 8 **Find 3(−20).**

$3(-20) = -60$ The factors have different signs. The product is negative.

Example 9 **Find −48 ÷ (−12).**

$-48 \div (-12) = 4$ The dividend and the divisor have the same sign. The quotient is positive.

1-7 Writing Equations (pp. 57–61)

8.A.3b, 8.D.3a

39. **SPORTS** An athlete's long jump attempt measured 670 centimeters. This was 5 centimeters less than her best jump. Define a variable. Then write an equation that could be used to find the measure of her best jump.
40. **ALGEBRA** Lauren uses a copier to reduce the length of an image so it is $\frac{1}{4}$ of its original size. Given ℓ, the length of the image, write an equation to find the length n of the new image.

Example 10 **Tennessee became a state 4 years after Kentucky. If Tennessee became a state in 1796, write an equation that could be used to find the year Kentucky became a state.**

Words Tennessee's year is 4 years after Kentucky year.

Variable Let y represent Kentucky's year.

Equation $1796 = y + 4$

1-8 PSI: Work Backward (pp. 62–63)

6.B.3a

Solve. Use the *work backward* strategy.

41. **TRAVEL** Alonzo's flight to Phoenix departs at 7:15 P.M. It takes 30 minutes to drive to the airport from his home, and it is recommended that he arrive at the airport 2 hours prior to departure. What time should Alonzo leave his house?
42. **TICKETS** After Candace purchased tickets to the play for herself and her two brothers, ticket sales totaled $147. If tickets were $5.25 each, how many tickets were sold before her purchase?

Example 11 **Fourteen years ago, Samuel's parents had their oldest child, Isabel. Six years later, Julia was born. If Samuel was born last year, how many years older than Samuel is Julia?**

Since Samuel was born last year, he must be one year old. Since Isabel was born fourteen years ago, she must be fourteen years old. Since Julia was born six years after Isabel, she must be eight years old. This means that Julia is seven years older than Samuel.

Study Guide and Review

1-9 Solving Addition and Subtraction Equations (pp. 65–69)

8.A.3b, 8.D.3a

Solve each equation. Check your solution.

43. $n + 40 = 90$
44. $x - 3 = 10$
45. $c - 30 = -18$
46. $9 = a + 31$
47. $d + 14 = -1$
48. $27 = y - 12$
49. **MOVIES** Thirty-two people arrived at the movie during the previews. If there were 150 people at the movie when it started, how many were there before the previews?
50. **WEATHER** On August 15, the monthly rainfall for a city was 2 inches below average. On August 31, the monthly total was 1 inch above average. Write and solve an addition equation to determine the amount of rainfall between August 15 and August 31.

Example 12 Solve $5 + k = 18$.

$5 + k = 18$	Write the equation.
$5 - 5 + k = 18 - 5$	Subtract 5 from each side.
$k = 13$	$18 - 5 = 13$

Example 13 Solve $n - 13 = -62$.

$n - 13 = -62$	Write the equation.
$n - 13 + 13 = -62 + 13$	Add 13 to each side.
$n = -49$	$-62 + 13 = -49$

1-10 Solving Multiplication and Division Equations (pp. 70–73)

8.A.3b, 8.D.3a

Solve each equation. Check your solution.

51. $15x = -75$
52. $-4x = 52$
53. $\frac{s}{7} = 42$
54. $\frac{y}{-10} = -15$
55. **MONEY** Toni borrowed \$168 from her father to buy clothes. She plans to pay \$28 a month toward this debt. Write and solve an equation to find how many months it will take to repay her father.
56. **CARS** Mr. Mitchell bought 12 quarts of motor oil for \$36. Write and solve an equation to find the cost of each quart of motor oil.

Example 14 Solve $60 = 5t$.

$60 = 5t$	Write the equation.
$\frac{60}{5} = \frac{5t}{5}$	Divide each side by 5.
$12 = t$	Simplify.

Example 15 Solve $\frac{m}{-2} = 8$.

$\frac{m}{-2} = 8$	Write the equation.
$\left(\frac{m}{-2}\right)(-2) = 8(-2)$	Multiply each side by −2.
$m = -16$	Simplify.

Chapter 1 Practice Test

IL Math Online glencoe.com

• Chapter Test

1. **ANALYZE TABLES** The table gives the annual number of hours worked by citizens in four countries in a recent year.

Country	Annual Hours Worked
United States	1,877
Japan	1,840
Canada	1,801
United Kingdom	1,708

On average, how many more hours per week did a person in the United States work that year than a person in the United Kingdom?

Evaluate each expression if $a = 3$, $b = 2$, and $c = -5$.

2. $(2c + b) \div b - 3$
3. $4a^2 - 5a - 12$

4. **CELL PHONES** The monthly charge in dollars for a specific cell phone company is given by the expression $40 + \frac{x - 500}{2}$, where x is the number of minutes of phone usage. Find the charge if a person uses 622 minutes.

Replace each ● with <, >, or = to make a true sentence.

5. -8 ● -11
6. $|13|$ ● -13

7. **MULTIPLE CHOICE** Evaluate the following expression:

$$|12 - 7| - |3 - 6|$$

A -8

B -2

C 2

D 8

8. Find the value of $|y| - |x|$ if $x = -4$ and $y = -9$.

Add, subtract, multiply, or divide.

9. $-27 + 8$
10. $-105 \div 15$
11. $\frac{-70}{-5}$
12. $-4 - (-35)$
13. $7(-10)(-4)$
14. $-9 + (-11)$
15. $8(-9)$
16. $13 - 61$

17. **MULTIPLE CHOICE** What is the absolute value of -7?

F -7

G $-\frac{1}{7}$

H $\frac{1}{7}$

J 7

18. **MEASUREMENT** A circle's radius is half its diameter. Given d, the diameter, write an equation that could be used to find r, the radius.

19. **JEANS** A store set the price it sold a pair of jeans for by tripling the amount it had paid for the jeans. After a month, the jeans were marked down by \$5. Two weeks later, the price was divided in half. Finally, the price was reduced by \$3, down to \$14.99. How much did the store pay for the jeans?

Solve each equation. Check your solution.

20. $x + 15 = -3$
21. $-7 = a - 11$
22. $\frac{n}{-2} = 16$
23. $-96 = 8y$

24. **TRANSPORTATION** An airplane flies over a submarine that is cruising at a depth of -326 feet. The distance between the two is 1,176 feet. Write and solve an equation to find the airplane's altitude.

25. **DANCES** There are 54 people remaining after 37 left a dance. Write and solve an equation to find the number of people who were originally at the dance.

CHAPTER 1

ISAT Practice

Chapter 1

IL Math Online glencoe.com
• Test Practice

PART 1 Multiple Choice

Read each question. Then fill in the correct answer on the answer sheet provided by your teacher or on a sheet of paper.

1. Kristy, Atepa, and Heather sold a total of 47 magazines this weekend. Atepa sold 3 more magazines than Heather, and Kristy sold twice as many magazines as Heather. Which is a reasonable conclusion about the number of magazines sold by the students?

   A Atepa sold the least number of magazines.

   B Kristy and Atepa sold the same number of magazines.

   C Heather sold exactly half of the total number of magazines.

   D Kristy sold the most magazines.

2. Two siblings agreed to split the cost of a television and a DVD player evenly. They spent a total of $335.00 on the television and $95.00 on the DVD player. Find the amount that each sibling paid.

   F $430.00 **H** $215.00

   G $265.00 **J** $210.00

3. Which of the following numerical expressions results in a positive number?

   A $(-4) + (-7)$ **C** $(-4) + (7)$

   B $(4) + (-7)$ **D** $(-4) + (7) + (-4)$

4. An electrician received d dollars for a job. She had to pay $75 for supplies. On her next job, she received $3m$ dollars. Which expression represents the amount of money she has now?

   F $d - 75 - 3m$ **H** $d + 75 - 3m$

   G $d + 75 + 3m$ **J** $d - 75 + 3m$

5. If $|r| = 2$, what is the value of r?

   A -2 or 0 **C** 0 or 2

   B -2 or 2 **D** -4 or 4

TEST-TAKING TIP

Question 5 In some instances, the quickest and easiest way to answer a multiple-choice question is to simply try each choice to see which one works.

6. Santos received some money from his grandmother for his birthday. He spent $12.75 each for 3 CDs. Then he spent $5.20 for lunch. Later he bought a T-shirt for $8.90. If he had $7.65 left over, which of the following expressions can be used to find how much money Santos received for his birthday?

   F $3(12.75) + 5.20 + 8.90 + 7.65$

   G $3(12.75) + 5.20 + 8.90 - 7.65$

   H $3(12.75 + 5.20 + 8.90 + 7.65)$

   J $3(12.75 + 5.20 + 8.90 - 7.65)$

7. Aisha evaluated the expression $|-27 + 3| - |-3 - 5|$ by performing the following steps.

$$\begin{aligned} |-27 + 3| - |-3 - 5| &= |-24| - |-8| \\ &= 24 + 8 \\ &= 32 \end{aligned}$$

   What did Aisha do incorrectly in evaluating the expression?

   A She evaluated $|-24|$ as 24 when she should have evaluated $|-24|$ as -24.

   B She added 24 and 8 when she should have subtracted 8 from 24.

   C She evaluated $|-3 - 5|$ as $|-8|$ when she should have evaluated $|-3 - 5|$ as $|-2|$.

   D She added 24 and 8 when she should have subtracted -8 from -24.

Preparing for ISAT

For test-taking strategies and practice, see pages 712–729.

8. Add six to the quotient of a number and three. The answer is 14. Which of the following equations matches these statements?

   F $14 = \frac{x}{3} + 6$

   G $6 = 14 + \frac{x}{3}$

   H $14 = \frac{x + 6}{3}$

   J $6 = \frac{x + 14}{3}$

9. The table below shows the train travel times from Cleveland (CLE) to Chicago (CHI).

Depart CLE	Arrive CHI
2:30 A.M.	8:45 A.M.
7:45 A.M.	1:45 P.M.
8:20 P.M.	2:25 A.M.
2:00 P.M.	8:20 P.M.

Which of the following statements about the travel times is true?

   A The train leaving at 2:30 A.M. has the least travel time.

   B The train leaving at 7:45 A.M. has the greatest travel time.

   C The train leaving at 8:20 P.M. has the least travel time.

   D The train leaving at 2:00 P.M. has the greatest travel time.

10. If $x = 5$ and $y = \frac{1}{4}$, then $y(13 - x) =$

   F 2 H 4

   G 3 J 6

PART 2 Short Response/Grid In

Record your answers on the answer sheet provided by your teacher or on a sheet of paper.

11. Mandy wants to buy a new couch that costs \$1,299. For the next 8 months, she plans to save an equal amount of money each month to pay for the couch. To the nearest dollar, how much will she need to save each month?

12. A golfer's score on the first day of the tournament was +3. On the last day, her score was a −6. What was the change in her score from the first day to the last day?

13. The formula $P = I - E$ can be used to find the profit P of a business given the income I and expenses E. If a business had an income of \$25,350 and expenses of \$27,210 in March, what is the business' profit in March?

PART 3 Extended Response

Record your answers on the answer sheet provided by your teacher or on a sheet of paper. Show your work.

14. Below, n, p, r, and t each represent a different integer. If $n = -4$ and $t \neq 1$, find each of the following values. Explain your reasoning using the properties of integers.

$$n \times p = n$$
$$t \times r = r$$
$$n + t = r$$

   a. p

   b. r

   c. t

NEED EXTRA HELP?														
If You Missed Question...	1	2	3	4	5	6	7	8	9	10	11	12	13	14
Go to Lesson...	1-1	1-6	1-4	1-7	1-3	1-1	1-3	1-7	1-1	1-2	1-1	1-5	1-5	1-3
IL Learning Standards	6.B.3a	6.B.3a	6.B.3a	8.A.3b	6.B.3a	6.B.3a	6.B.3a	8.A.3a	6.B.3a	8.A.3a	6.B.3a	6.B.3a	6.B.3a	6.B.3a

Algebra: Rational Numbers

Illinois Learning Standards

6.B.3a Solve practical computation problems involving whole numbers, integers and rational numbers.
6.C.3a Select computational procedures and solve problems with whole numbers, fractions, decimals, percents and proportions.

Key Vocabulary

exponent (p. 126)
rational number (p. 84)
reciprocals (p. 102)
scientific notation (p. 130)

Real-World Link

Astronomy Measurements used in astronomy are frequently expressed as powers of 10. For example, the distance from Earth to the Sun can be written as 9.3×10^7 miles.

Algebra: Rational Numbers Make this Foldable to help you organize your notes. Begin with five sheets of $8\frac{1}{2}'' \times 11''$ paper.

1. **Place** 5 sheets of paper $\frac{3}{4}$ inch apart.

2. **Roll** up the bottom edges. All tabs should be the same size.

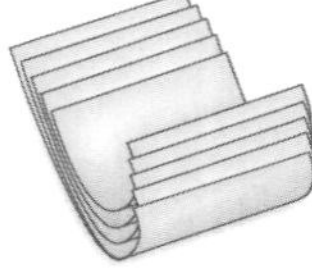

3. **Staple** along the fold.

4. **Label** the tabs with the lesson numbers.

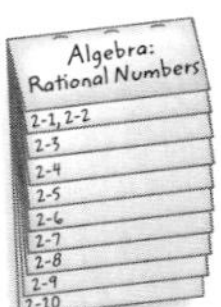

GET READY for Chapter 2

Diagnose Readiness You have two options for checking Prerequisite Skills.

Option 2

IL Math Online Take the Online Readiness Quiz at glencoe.com.

Option 1

Take the Quick Check below. Refer to the Quick Review for help.

QUICK Quiz

Add or subtract. (Lessons 1-4 and 1-5)

1. $-13 + 4$
2. $28 + (-9)$
3. $-8 - 6$
4. $23 - (-15)$
5. **TEMPERATURE** The high temperature for Saturday was 13°F, and the low temperature was −4°F. What was the difference between the high and low temperatures? (Lesson 1-5)

Multiply or divide. (Lesson 1-6)

6. $6(-14)$
7. $36 \div (-4)$
8. $-86 \div (-2)$
9. $-3(-9)$

Solve each equation. (Lessons 1-9 and 1-10)

10. $-12x = 144$
11. $a + 9 = 37$
12. $-18 = y - 42$
13. $25 = \frac{n}{5}$

Find the least common multiple (LCM) of each set of numbers.

(Prior Grade)

14. 12, 16
15. 24, 9
16. 10, 5, 6
17. 3, 7, 9

QUICK Review

Example 1

Find −27 + 13.

$-27 + 13 = -14$ — $|-27| - |13| = |14|$ The sum is negative because $|-27| > |13|$.

Example 2

Find −11 − 8.

$-11 - 8 = -11 + (-8)$ — To subtract 8, add −8.

$-11 + (-8) = -19$ — $|-11| + |-8| = 19$ Both numbers are negative so the sum is negative.

Example 3

Find −12(7).

$-12(7) = -84$ — The factors have different signs. The product is negative.

Example 4

Solve −8x = 64.

$-8x = 64$ — Write the equation.

$\frac{-8x}{-8} = \frac{64}{-8}$ — Divide each side of the equation by −8.

$x = -8$ — Simplify.

Example 5

Find the LCM of 9, 12, and 18.

multiples of 9: 0, 9, 18, 27, 36, 45, ...
multiples of 12: 0, 12, 24, 36, 48, ...
multiples of 18: 0, 18, 36, 54, ...

The LCM of 9, 12, and 18 is 36.

2-1 Rational Numbers

MAIN IDEA

Express rational numbers as decimals and decimals as fractions.

IL Learning Standards

6.A.3 Represent fractions, decimals, percentages, exponents and scientific notation **in equivalent forms.**

New Vocabulary

rational number
terminating decimal
repeating decimal
bar notation

IL Math Online

glencoe.com
- Extra Examples
- Personal Tutor
- Self-Check Quiz
- Reading in the Content Area

GET READY for the Lesson

MARINE LIFE There are over 360 different species of sharks, which are divided into 30 families. The most common shark species found around Florida are listed below.

Shark Species	Color	Average Length (feet)
Sharpnose shark	brown to green-gray	3
Bonnethead shark	gray or gray-brown	3
Blacknose shark	green-gray	5
Blacktip	blue-gray	6
Spinner shark	gray-bronze	6
Sandbar shark	brown or gray	6
Nurse shark	yellow-brown	7
Scalloped hammerhead shark	gray-brown	8
Lemon shark	yellow-gray	9

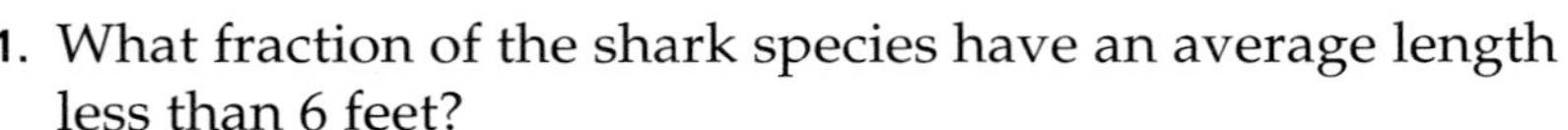

1. What fraction of the shark species have an average length less than 6 feet?
2. What fraction of the shark species are a shade of blue?
3. What fraction of the shark species are not a shade of gray?

Numbers that can be written as fractions are called **rational numbers**. Since -7 can be written as $\frac{-7}{1}$ and $2\frac{2}{3}$ can be written as $\frac{8}{3}$, -7 and $2\frac{2}{3}$ are rational numbers. All integers, fractions, and mixed numbers are rational numbers.

Rational Numbers

Key Concept

Words Rational numbers are numbers that can be written as fractions.

Algebra $\frac{a}{b}$, where a and b are integers and $b \neq 0$.

Model

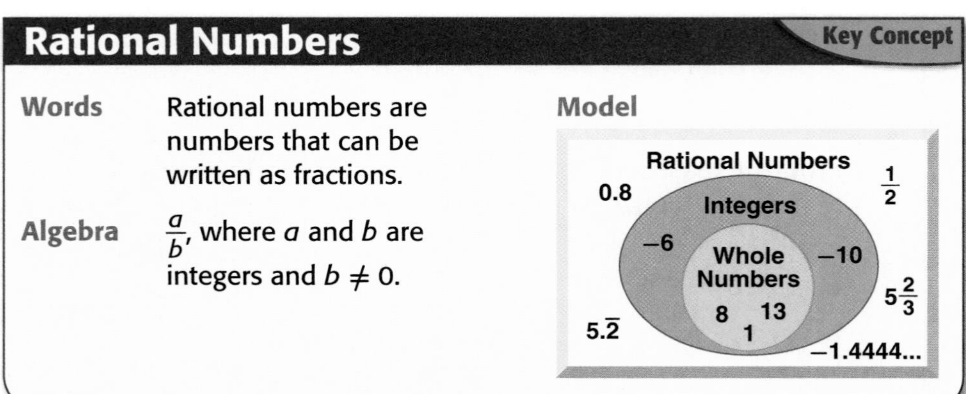

Any fraction, positive or negative, can be expressed as a decimal by dividing the numerator by the denominator.

EXAMPLE Write a Fraction as a Decimal

Write $\frac{5}{8}$ as a decimal.

$\frac{5}{8}$ means $5 \div 8$.

$$\begin{array}{r} 0.625 \\ 8\overline{)5.000} \\ -\underline{48} \\ 20 \\ -\underline{16} \\ 40 \\ -\underline{40} \\ 0 \end{array}$$

Divide 5 by 8.

Vocabulary Link
Terminating
Everyday Use bringing to an end
Math Use a decimal that ends

CHECK Your Progress

Write each fraction or mixed number as a decimal.

a. $\frac{3}{4}$ b. $\frac{-3}{5}$ c. $4\frac{13}{25}$

Every rational number can be written as either a terminating or repeating decimal. A decimal like 0.625 is called a **terminating decimal** because the division ends, or terminates, with a remainder of 0.

If the division does not end, a pattern of digits repeats. **Repeating decimals** have a pattern in their digits that repeats without end. Instead of the three dots at the end of the decimal, **bar notation** is often used to indicate that a digit or group of digits repeats.

Study Tip

Common Error
The bar is placed above the repeating part. To write 8.636363... in bar notation, write $8.\overline{63}$, not $8.\overline{6}$ or $8.\overline{636}$. To write 0.3444... in bar notation, write $0.3\overline{4}$, not $0.\overline{34}$.

$0.333... = 0.\overline{3}$ $-0.282828... = -0.\overline{28}$ $60.7151515... = 60.7\overline{15}$

EXAMPLE Write a Repeating Decimal

2 Write $-1\frac{2}{3}$ as a decimal.

$-1\frac{2}{3}$ can be rewritten as $\frac{-5}{3}$.

Divide 5 by 3 and add a negative sign.

The mixed number $-1\frac{2}{3}$ can be written as $-1.\overline{6}$.

$$\begin{array}{r} 1.6... \\ 3\overline{)5.0} \\ -\underline{3} \\ 20 \\ -\underline{18} \\ 2 \end{array}$$

CHECK Your Progress

Write each fraction as a decimal.

d. $\frac{7}{12}$ e. $-\frac{2}{9}$ f. $3\frac{1}{11}$ g. $-2\frac{14}{15}$

Repeating decimals often occur in real-world situations. However, they are usually rounded to a certain place-value position.

Real-World EXAMPLE

Real-World Career . . .
How Does a Sports Statistician Use Math?
A baseball statistician uses decimal equivalents to determine batting averages and winning averages. A batting average is the number of hits divided by the number of times at bat.

IL Math Online
For more information, go to glencoe.com.

3 **BASEBALL In a recent season, New York Yankees shortstop Derek Jeter had 6 hits in 22 at-bats. To the nearest thousandth, find his batting average.**

To find his batting average, divide the number of hits, 6, by the number of at-bats, 22.

6 [÷] 22 [ENTER] 0.27272727

Look at the digit to the right of the thousandths place. Round up since $7 > 5$.

Derek Jeter's batting average was 0.273.

CHECK Your Progress

h. **AUTO RACING** In a recent season, NASCAR driver Jimmie Johnson won 6 of the 36 total races held. To the nearest thousandth, find the fraction of races he won.

Terminating and repeating decimals are also rational numbers because you can write them as fractions.

EXAMPLES Write Decimals as Fractions

4 **Write 0.45 as a fraction.**

$0.45 = \frac{45}{100}$ — 0.45 is 45 hundredths.

$= \frac{9}{20}$ — Simplify.

5 **ALGEBRA Write $0.\overline{5}$ as a fraction in simplest form.**

Assign a variable to the value $0.\overline{5}$. Let $N = 0.555...$. Then perform operations on N to determine its fractional value.

Study Tip
Repeating Decimals
If 2 digits repeat, multiply each side by 100.

$N = 0.555...$	
$10(N) = 10(0.555...)$	Multiply each side by 10 because 1 digit repeats.
$10N = 5.555...$	Multiplying by 10 moves the decimal point 1 place to the right.
$-\ N = 0.555...$	Subtract $N = 0.555...$ to eliminate the repeating part.
$9N = 5$	Simplify.
$N = \frac{5}{9}$	Divide each side by 9.

The decimal $0.\overline{5}$ can be written as $\frac{5}{9}$.

CHECK Your Progress

Write each decimal as a fraction or mixed number in simplest form.

i. -0.14 j. 8.75 k. $0.\overline{27}$ l. $-1.\overline{4}$

CHECK Your Understanding

Examples 1, 2 (p. 85)

Write each fraction or mixed number as a decimal.

1. $\frac{4}{5}$
2. $\frac{9}{16}$
3. $-1\frac{29}{40}$
4. $\frac{5}{9}$
5. $4\frac{5}{6}$
6. $-7\frac{5}{33}$

Example 3 (p. 86)

7. **BASEBALL** In a recent season, Cleveland pitcher C. C. Sabathia won 12 of the 28 games he started. To the nearest thousandth, find his winning average.

Examples 4, 5 (p. 86)

Write each decimal as a fraction or mixed number in simplest form.

8. 0.6
9. 0.32
10. −1.55
11. $-0.\overline{5}$
12. $-3.\overline{8}$
13. $2.\overline{15}$

Practice and Problem Solving

HOMEWORK HELP

For Exercises	See Examples
14–21	1
22–25	2
26–29	3
30–33	4
34–37	5

Write each fraction or mixed number as a decimal.

14. $\frac{3}{4}$
15. $\frac{2}{5}$
16. $\frac{7}{80}$
17. $\frac{33}{40}$
18. $-\frac{7}{16}$
19. $-\frac{5}{32}$
20. $2\frac{1}{8}$
21. $5\frac{5}{16}$
22. $\frac{4}{33}$
23. $-\frac{6}{11}$
24. $-6\frac{13}{15}$
25. $-7\frac{8}{45}$

FAMILIES **For Exercises 26–29, refer to the table at the right about the students at Carter Junior High.**

Number of Siblings	Fraction of Students
None	$\frac{1}{15}$
One	$\frac{1}{3}$
Two	$\frac{5}{12}$
Three	$\frac{1}{6}$
Four or more	$\frac{1}{60}$

26. Express the fraction of students with no siblings as a decimal.
27. Find the decimal equivalent for the number of students with three siblings.
28. Write the fraction of students with one sibling as a decimal. Round to the nearest thousandth.
29. Write the fraction of students with two siblings as a decimal. Round to the nearest thousandth.

Write each decimal as a fraction or mixed number in simplest form.

30. –0.4
31. 0.5
32. 5.55
33. –7.32
34. $0.\overline{2}$
35. $-0.\overline{45}$
36. $-3.\overline{09}$
37. $2.\overline{7}$

38. **ELECTRONICS** A computer manufacturer produces circuit chips that are 0.00032 inch thick. Write this measure as a fraction in simplest form.

39. **FIND THE DATA** Refer to the Data File on pages 16–19. Choose some data and write a real-world problem in which you would express a fraction as a decimal.

WEATHER For Exercises 40–42, write the rainfall amount for each day as a fraction or mixed number.

Day	Rainfall (inches)
Friday	0.08
Saturday	2.4
Sunday	0.035

40. Friday
41. Saturday
42. Sunday

MEASUREMENT For Exercises 43–46, write the length of each insect as a fraction and as a decimal.

43. 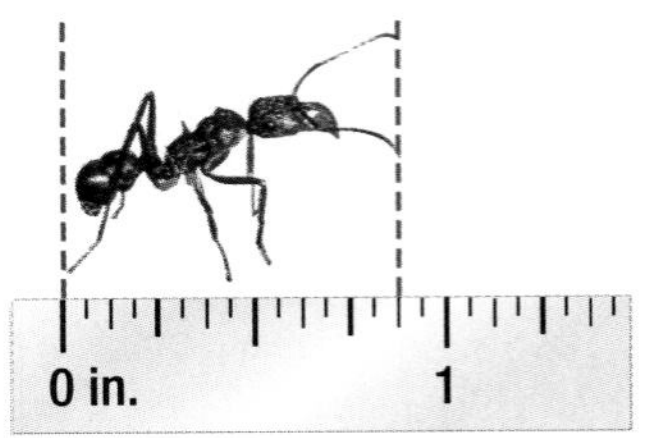

44. 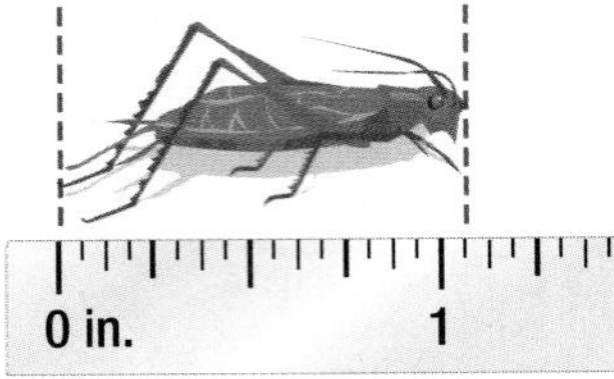

45. 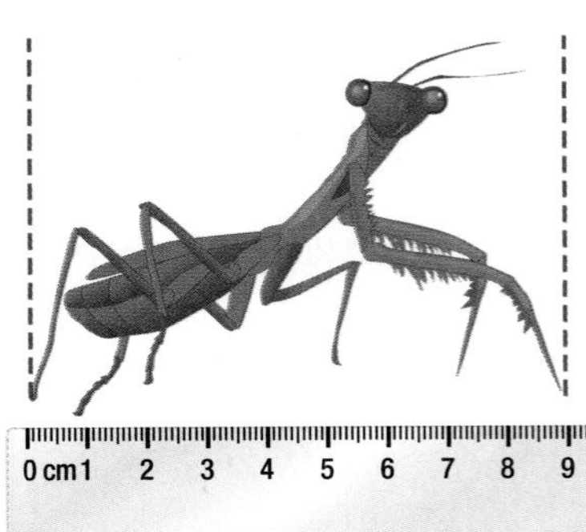

46. 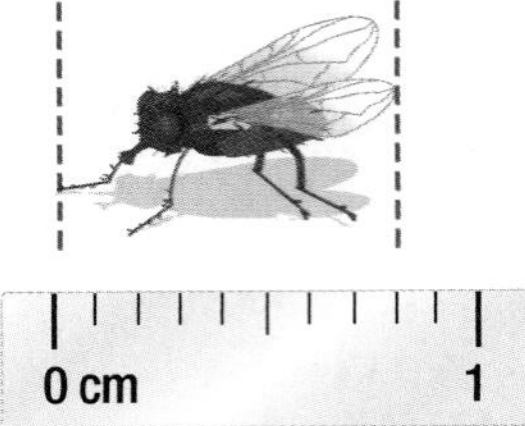

47. **WEATHER** Carla recorded the rainfall totals for several months and compared them to the average monthly totals for her town. Her results are shown in the table. Write each decimal as a fraction or mixed number in simplest form. (*Hint*: −1 means 1 inch less than the average monthly total.)

Month	Above/Below Average (in.)
May	1.06
June	0.24
July	−2.72
August	−3.40

48. **FROZEN YOGURT** The table shows five popular flavors according to the results of a survey. What is the decimal value of those who liked vanilla, chocolate, or strawberry? Round to the nearest hundredth.

Flavor	Fraction
Vanilla	$\frac{3}{10}$
Chocolate	$\frac{1}{11}$
Strawberry	$\frac{1}{18}$
Cookies and Cream	$\frac{2}{55}$
Rocky Road	$\frac{1}{66}$

ILS • ISAT
Extra Practice, pp. 671, 701

H.O.T. Problems

49. **OPEN ENDED** Give an example of a repeating decimal where two digits repeat. Explain why your number is a rational number.

50. **Which One Doesn't Belong?** Identify the fraction that does not belong with the other three. Explain your reasoning.

$\frac{1}{8}$ $\frac{1}{4}$ $\frac{1}{6}$ $\frac{4}{5}$

51. **CHALLENGE** Explain why any rational number is either a terminating or repeating decimal.

52. **WRITING IN MATH** Compare 0.1 and $0.\overline{1}$, 0.13 and $0.\overline{13}$, and 0.157 and $0.\overline{157}$ when written as fractions. Make a conjecture about expressing repeating decimals like these as fractions.

ISAT PRACTICE 6.A.3

53. Which of the following is equivalent to $\frac{13}{5}$?

A 2.4

B 2.45

C 2.55

D 2.6

54. **SHORT RESPONSE** Felisa made 0.9 of her free throws in her last basketball game. Write this decimal as a fraction in simplest form.

55. Janet wants to buy a pair of jeans that cost $29.99. The sign on the display says that the jeans are $\frac{1}{3}$ off. Which expression can be used to estimate the discount?

F $0.033 \times \$30$

G $0.33 \times \$30$

H $1.3 \times \$30$

J $33.3 \times \$30$

Spiral Review

56. The product of two integers is 72. If one integer is –18, what is the other integer? (Lesson 1-10)

ALGEBRA Solve each equation. Check your solution. (Lesson 1-9)

57. $t + 17 = -5$

58. $a - 5 = 14$

59. $5 = 9 + x$

60. $m - 5 = -14$

61. **TIME** The time zones of the world are sometimes expressed in relation to *Greenwich Mean Time GMT*. If Eastern Standard Time is expressed as GMT −5:00 and Pacific Standard Time is expressed as GMT −8:00, what is the difference between Eastern and Pacific Standard Time? (Lesson 1-5)

62. Graph the set of integers {−2, 5, −3, 0, −5, 1} on a number line. Order the integers from least to greatest. (Lesson 1-3)

GET READY for the Next Lesson

PREREQUISITE SKILL Find the least common multiple for each pair of numbers. (Page 735)

63. 15, 5

64. 6, 9

65. 8, 6

66. 3, 5

READING to SOLVE PROBLEMS

New Vocabulary

New vocabulary terms are clues about important concepts and the key to understanding word problems. Your textbook helps you find those clues by highlighting them in yellow, as **terminating decimal** is highlighted on page 85.

Learning new vocabulary is more than just memorizing the definiton. Whenever you see a highlighted word, stop and ask yourself these questions.

- **How does this fit with what I already know?**
- **How is this alike or different from something I learned earlier?**

Organize your answers in a word map like the one below.

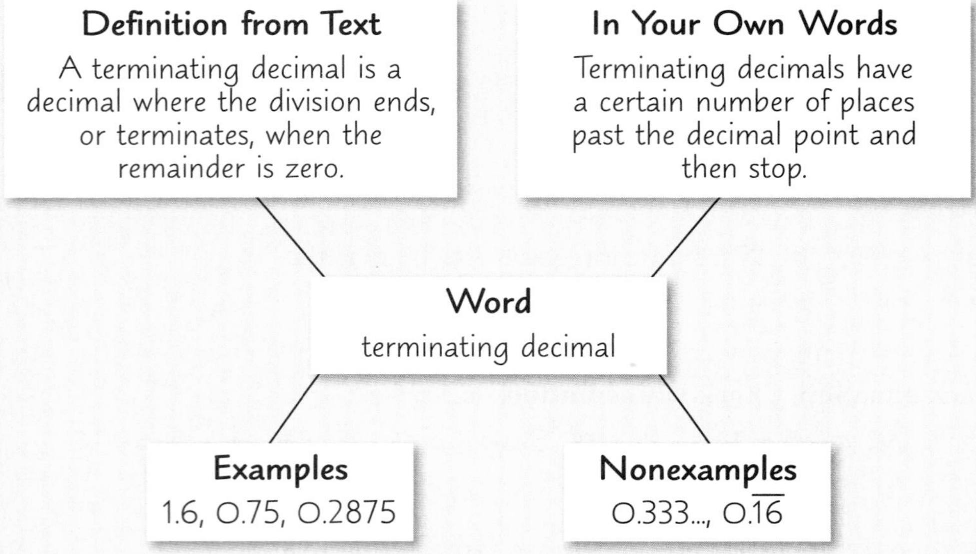

Definition from Text
A terminating decimal is a decimal where the division ends, or terminates, when the remainder is zero.
In Your Own Words
Terminating decimals have a certain number of places past the decimal point and then stop.
Word
terminating decimal
Examples
1.6, 0.75, 0.2875
Nonexamples
0.333..., $0.\overline{16}$

PRACTICE

Make a word map for each term. The term is defined on the given page.

1. rational number (p. 84)
2. integer (p. 35)
3. composite figure (p. 363)
4. quadratic function (p. 534)

Comparing and Ordering Rational Numbers

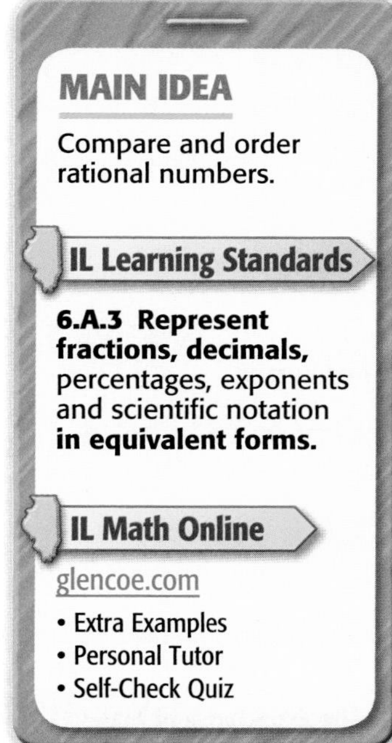

MAIN IDEA
Compare and order rational numbers.
IL Learning Standards
6.A.3 Represent fractions, decimals, percentages, exponents and scientific notation in equivalent forms.
IL Math Online
glencoe.com
• Extra Examples
• Personal Tutor
• Self-Check Quiz

GET READY for the Lesson

POPCORN Kip surveyed his class to find what kind of popcorn students like best. The results of the survey are shown in the table.

Favorite Kinds of Popcorn

Popcorn	Fraction of Students
Buttered	$\frac{5}{12}$
Cheddar	$\frac{3}{16}$
Caramel	$\frac{1}{8}$
Plain	$\frac{1}{6}$

1. Do more or less than half of the students prefer buttered popcorn? Explain how you know.
2. Which category is preferred by more students, caramel or plain? Explain.
3. Which category of popcorn is preferred by about one fourth of the class? Explain.
4. Using estimation, order the fractions from least to greatest.

Sometimes you can use estimation to compare rational numbers. Another method is to rename each fraction using the least common denominator and then compare the numerators.

EXAMPLE Compare Positive Rational Numbers

1 **Replace ● with <, >, or = to make $\frac{5}{8}$ ● $\frac{3}{4}$ a true sentence.**

Rename the fractions using the least common denominator.

For $\frac{5}{8}$ and $\frac{3}{4}$, the least common denominator is 8.

$\frac{5}{8} = \frac{5 \cdot 1}{8 \cdot 1}$ or $\frac{5}{8}$

$\frac{3}{4} = \frac{3 \cdot 2}{4 \cdot 2}$ or $\frac{6}{8}$

Since $\frac{5}{8} < \frac{6}{8}$, $\frac{5}{8} < \frac{3}{4}$.

Replace each ● with <, >, or = to make a true sentence.

a. $\frac{3}{4}$ ● $\frac{7}{12}$ b. $\frac{5}{6}$ ● $\frac{7}{8}$ c. $1\frac{4}{9}$ ● $1\frac{2}{5}$

You can also compare and order rational numbers by expressing them as decimals.

EXAMPLE Compare Using Decimals

2 Replace ● with <, >, or = to make $\frac{8}{9}$ ● 0.8 a true sentence.

$\frac{8}{9}$ ● 0.8

0.888... ● 0.80 — Express $\frac{8}{9}$ as a decimal. In the hundredths place, 8 > 0.

So, $\frac{8}{9} > 0.8$.

CHECK Your Progress

Replace each ● with <, >, or = to make a true sentence.

d. $\frac{1}{3}$ ● 0.3 e. 0.22 ● $\frac{11}{50}$ f. $2\frac{5}{12}$ ● 2.42

Real-World Link American males born after 1990 have an average life expectancy of about 74 years. **Source:** Centers for Disease Control

Real-World EXAMPLE Order Rational Numbers

3 HEALTH The average life expectancies of males for several countries are shown in the table. Order the countries from least to greatest male life expectancy.

Life Expectancy of Males	
Country	Approximate Age (years)
Australia	76.9
France	$74\frac{4}{5}$
Spain	$75\frac{1}{3}$
United Kingdom	75
United States	$74\frac{1}{4}$

Source: MapQuest

Express each number as a decimal.

Australia: 76.9 = 76.90

France: $74\frac{4}{5} = 74.80$

Spain: $75\frac{1}{3} = 75.\overline{3}$

United Kingdom: 75 = 75.00

United States: $74\frac{1}{4} = 74.25$

From least to greatest life expectancy, the countries are United States, France, United Kingdom, Spain, and Australia.

CHECK Your Progress

g. **ELECTRONICS** The overall width in inches of several widescreen televisions are 38.3, $38\frac{3}{5}$, $38\frac{2}{3}$, $38.\overline{4}$, and $38\frac{9}{16}$. Order the widths from least to greatest.

h. **TOOLS** Sophia has five wrenches measuring $\frac{3}{8}$ inch, $\frac{1}{4}$ inch, $\frac{5}{16}$ inch, $\frac{1}{2}$ inch, and $\frac{3}{4}$ inch. What is the order of the measures from *least* to *greatest*?

Just as positive and negative integers can be represented on a number line, so can positive and negative rational numbers.

$-\frac{4}{10}\ -\frac{3}{10}\ -\frac{2}{10}\ -\frac{1}{10}\ \ 0\ \ \frac{1}{10}\ \ \frac{2}{10}\ \ \frac{3}{10}\ \ \frac{4}{10}$

−0.4 −0.3 −0.2 −0.1 0 0.1 0.2 0.3 0.4

You can use a number line to help you compare and order negative rational numbers.

EXAMPLES Compare Negative Rational Numbers

Replace each ● with <, >, or = to make a true sentence.

4 **−2.4 ● −2.45**

Graph the decimals on a number line.

−2.50 −2.48 −2.46 −2.44 −2.42 −2.40

Since −2.4 is to the right of −2.45, −2.4 > −2.45.

Study Tip

Number Line On a number line, a number to the left is always less than a number to the right.

5 $-\frac{7}{8}$ ● $-\frac{6}{8}$

Since the denominators are the same, compare the numerators.

$-7 < -6$, so $-\frac{7}{8} < -\frac{6}{8}$.

CHECK Your Progress

Replace each ● with <, >, or = to make a true sentence.

i. $-\frac{9}{16}$ ● $-\frac{12}{16}$ j. −3.15 ● −3.17 k. $-\frac{7}{10}$ ● $-\frac{4}{5}$

CHECK Your Understanding

Examples 1–4 (pp. 91–93)

Replace each ● with <, >, or = to make a true sentence.

1. $\frac{1}{2}$ ● $\frac{5}{12}$
2. $\frac{9}{25}$ ● $\frac{3}{10}$
3. $\frac{3}{11}$ ● 0.25
4. $3\frac{5}{8}$ ● 3.625
5. $-\frac{10}{18}$ ● $-\frac{16}{18}$
6. $-\frac{4}{5}$ ● $-\frac{7}{10}$
7. $-0.\overline{6}$ ● $-0.\overline{67}$
8. $-2.\overline{4}$ ● −2.42

Example 5 (p. 93)

9. **OCEANOGRAPHY** The tide heights for several cities are shown in the table. Order the cities from least tide height to greatest.

City	Tide Height (ft)	City	Tide Height (ft)
Baltimore, MD	$1.\overline{6}$	Key West, FL	$1.8\overline{3}$
Galveston, TX	$1\frac{5}{12}$	Mobile, AL	1.5
Gulfport, MS	$1\frac{1}{6}$	Washington, DC	$1\frac{17}{20}$

Practice and Problem Solving

HOMEWORK HELP

For Exercises	See Examples
10, 11	1
12–15	2
16, 17	3
18–23	4
24–29	5

Replace each $\bullet$ with $<$, $>$, or $=$ to make a true sentence.

10. $\frac{2}{3} \bullet \frac{7}{9}$
11. $\frac{3}{5} \bullet \frac{5}{8}$
12. $0.5 \bullet \frac{7}{12}$
13. $0.75 \bullet \frac{11}{15}$
14. $6\frac{15}{32} \bullet 6.5$
15. $2\frac{21}{30} \bullet 2.7$

16. **HOBBIES** Renata makes jewelry using beads measuring $\frac{7}{16}$, $\frac{3}{8}$, $\frac{5}{32}$, $\frac{9}{16}$, and $\frac{1}{4}$. If these are all measurements in inches, how should she arrange them in a necklace if she wants them from greatest to least?

17. **PHOTOGRAPHY** Cameras often have multiple shutter speeds. Some common shutter speeds in seconds are $\frac{1}{125}$, $0.0\overline{6}$, $\frac{1}{60}$, 0.125, 0.004, and $\frac{1}{4}$. List these speeds in order from the fastest to the slowest.

Replace each $\bullet$ with $<$, $>$, or $=$ to make a true sentence.

18. $-4.8 \bullet -4.6$
19. $-5.25 \bullet -5.24$
20. $-22.9 \bullet -22.09$
21. $-2.07 \bullet -2.6$
22. $-4.3 \bullet -4.37$
23. $-2.8 \bullet -2.86$
24. $-\frac{3}{11} \bullet -\frac{1}{11}$
25. $-\frac{4}{10} \bullet -\frac{7}{10}$
26. $-\frac{1}{6} \bullet -\frac{1}{12}$
27. $-\frac{3}{5} \bullet -\frac{7}{15}$
28. $-1\frac{3}{8} \bullet -1\frac{2}{3}$
29. $-5\frac{4}{7} \bullet -5\frac{3}{5}$

Graph the following numbers on a number line.

30. $-3\frac{2}{5}$, -3.68, -3.97, $-4\frac{3}{4}$
31. -2.9, -2.95, $-2\frac{1}{4}$, $-2\frac{1}{2}$
32. -5.25, $-5\frac{1}{3}$, $-4\frac{7}{8}$, -4.6
33. 3.7, 2.9, $-4\frac{1}{8}$, $1\frac{1}{5}$

34. **STATISTICS** If you order a set of numbers from least to greatest, the middle number is the *median*. Find the median of -18.5°C, -18°C, and 20.2°C.

35. **ANALYZE TABLES** The table shows the regular season records of five college baseball teams during a recent season. Which team had the best record? (*Hint:* Divide the number of games won by the number of games played.)

Team	Games Won	Games Played
Stetson University	38	60
University of Alabama	41	60
Clemson University	47	61
University of North Carolina	45	58
Jacksonville State University	35	57

36. **ATTENDANCE** The school play was attended by $\frac{5}{6}$ of the 6th grade, $\frac{3}{4}$ of the 7th grade, and $\frac{4}{5}$ of the 8th grade. Which grade has the greatest part of its class attend the play?

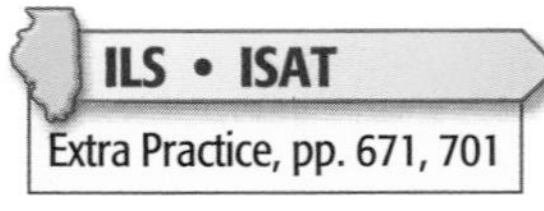

H.O.T. Problems

37. **NUMBER SENSE** Are the fractions $\frac{5}{11}$, $\frac{5}{12}$, $\frac{5}{13}$, and $\frac{5}{14}$ arranged in order from least to greatest or from greatest to least? Explain.

38. **OPEN ENDED** Name two fractions that are less than $\frac{1}{2}$ and two fractions that are greater than $\frac{1}{2}$.

39. **CHALLENGE** Are there any rational numbers between $0.\overline{2}$ and $\frac{2}{9}$? Explain.

40. **WRITING IN MATH** Explain why 0.28 is less than $0.\overline{28}$.

ISAT PRACTICE 6.A.3

41. Which fraction is between $-\frac{3}{4}$ and $-\frac{2}{3}$?

A $-\frac{1}{2}$

B $-\frac{3}{5}$

C $-\frac{5}{7}$

D $-\frac{7}{8}$

42. Which point on the number line below is the coordinate of 0.425?

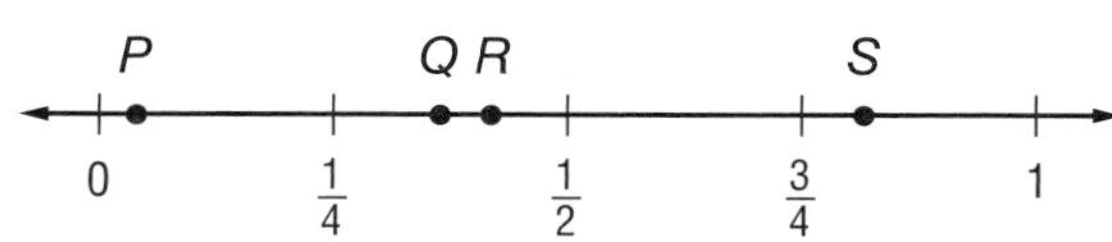

F Point P

G Point Q

H Point R

J Point S

Spiral Review

43. **HOCKEY** The sheet of ice that covers a hockey rink is created in two layers. First, an $\frac{1}{8}$-inch layer of ice is made for the lines to be painted on. Then, a $\frac{6}{8}$-inch layer of ice is added on top of the painted layer, for a total thickness of $\frac{7}{8}$ inch. Write the total thickness of the ice as a decimal. (Lesson 2-1)

ALGEBRA Solve each equation. Check your solution. (Lesson 1-10)

44. $\frac{y}{7} = 22$

45. $4p = -60$

46. $20 = \frac{t}{15}$

47. $81 = -3d$

48. $\frac{a}{6} = -108$

49. $-4n = -96$

50. **WEATHER** After the temperature had fallen 10°F, the temperature was −8°F. Write and solve a subtraction equation to find the starting temperature. (Lesson 1-9)

GET READY for the Next Lesson

PREREQUISITE SKILL Multiply. (Lesson 1-6)

51. $-4(-7)$

52. $8(-12)$

53. $(-3)17$

54. $23(-5)$

2-3 Multiplying Positive and Negative Fractions

MAIN IDEA

Multiply positive and negative fractions.

IL Learning Standards

6.B.3a Solve practical computation problems involving whole numbers, integers and **rational numbers.**
6.C.3a Select computational procedures and solve problems with whole numbers, **fractions**, decimals, percents and proportions.

New Vocabulary

dimensional analysis

IL Math Online

glencoe.com

- Concepts in Motion
- Extra Examples
- Personal Tutor
- Self-Check Quiz

MINI Lab

You can use an area model to find $\frac{1}{3}$ of $\frac{2}{5}$. The model also represents the product of $\frac{1}{3}$ and $\frac{2}{5}$.

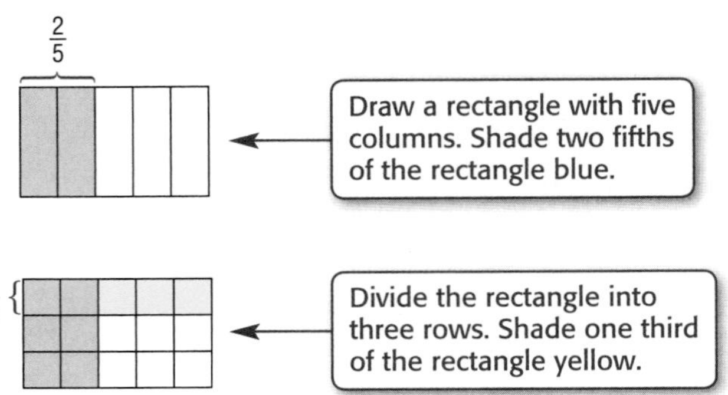

2/5
Draw a rectangle with five columns. Shade two fifths of the rectangle blue.
1/3
Divide the rectangle into three rows. Shade one third of the rectangle yellow.

The green shaded area represents $\frac{1}{3}$ of $\frac{2}{5}$.

1. What is the product of $\frac{1}{3}$ and $\frac{2}{5}$?
2. Use an area model to find each product.

   a. $\frac{3}{4} \cdot \frac{1}{2}$
   b. $\frac{2}{5} \cdot \frac{2}{3}$
   c. $\frac{1}{4} \cdot \frac{3}{5}$
   d. $\frac{2}{3} \cdot \frac{4}{5}$

3. What is the relationship between the numerators of the factors and the numerator of the product?
4. What is the relationship between the denominators of the factors and the denominator of the product?

The Mini Lab suggests the rule for multiplying fractions.

Multiply Fractions — Key Concept

Words To multiply fractions, multiply the numerators and multiply the denominators.

Examples

Numbers $\frac{2}{3} \cdot \frac{4}{5} = \frac{8}{15}$

Algebra $\frac{a}{b} \cdot \frac{c}{d} = \frac{ac}{bd}$, where b and $d \neq 0$.

You can use the rules for multiplying integers to determine the sign of the product of any two signed numbers.

EXAMPLE Multiply Positive Fractions

Review Vocabulary

greatest common factor (GCF) the greatest of the common factors of two or more numbers; *Example:* the GFC of 8 and 12 is 4.

1 **Find $\frac{4}{9} \cdot \frac{3}{5}$. Write in simplest form.**

$\frac{4}{9} \cdot \frac{3}{5} = \frac{4}{\cancel{9}_3} \cdot \frac{\cancel{3}^1}{5}$ Divide 9 and 3 by their GCF, 3.

$= \frac{4 \cdot 1}{3 \cdot 5}$ ←Multiply the numerators. ←Multiply the denominators.

$= \frac{4}{15}$ Simplify.

CHECK Your Progress

a. $\frac{1}{4} \cdot \frac{2}{3}$ b. $\frac{5}{12} \cdot \frac{3}{20}$ c. $\frac{7}{10} \cdot \frac{7}{16}$

EXAMPLE Multiply Negative Fractions

Study Tip

Negative Fractions $-\frac{5}{6}$, $\frac{-5}{6}$, and $\frac{5}{-6}$ are all equivalent fractions.

2 **Find $-\frac{5}{6} \cdot \frac{3}{8}$. Write in simplest form.**

$-\frac{5}{6} \cdot \frac{3}{8} = \frac{-5}{\cancel{6}_2} \cdot \frac{\cancel{3}^1}{8}$ Divide 6 and 3 by their GCF, 3.

$= \frac{-5 \cdot 1}{2 \cdot 8}$ ←Multiply the numerators. ←Multiply the denominators.

$= -\frac{5}{16}$ The fractions have different signs, so the product is negative.

CHECK Your Progress

d. $\frac{8}{9} \cdot -\frac{3}{4}$ e. $-\frac{3}{5} \cdot \frac{7}{9}$ f. $\left(-\frac{1}{2}\right)\left(-\frac{6}{7}\right)$

To multiply mixed numbers, first rename them as improper fractions.

EXAMPLE Multiply Mixed Numbers

3 **Find $4\frac{1}{2} \cdot 2\frac{2}{3}$. Write in simplest form.** **Estimate** $4 \times 3 = 12$

$4\frac{1}{2} \cdot 2\frac{2}{3} = \frac{9}{2} \cdot \frac{8}{3}$ $4\frac{1}{2} = \frac{9}{2}$, $2\frac{2}{3} = \frac{8}{3}$

$= \frac{\cancel{9}^3}{\cancel{2}_1} \cdot \frac{\cancel{8}^4}{\cancel{3}_1}$ Divide out common factors.

$= \frac{3 \cdot 4}{1 \cdot 1}$ ←Multiply the numerators. ←Multiply the denominators.

$= \frac{12}{1}$ or 12 Simplify. Compare to the estimate.

CHECK Your Progress

g. $1\frac{1}{2} \cdot 1\frac{2}{3}$ h. $\frac{5}{7} \cdot 1\frac{3}{5}$ i. $\left(-2\frac{1}{6}\right)\left(-1\frac{1}{5}\right)$

Real-World EXAMPLE

4 **ROLLER COASTERS** **A roller coaster at an amusement park is 160 feet tall. If a new roller coaster is built that is $2\frac{3}{5}$ times the height of the existing coaster, what is the height of the new roller coaster?**

The new coaster is $2\frac{3}{5}$ times as tall as the current coaster.

$2\frac{3}{5} \cdot 160 = \frac{13}{5} \cdot \frac{160}{1}$ — $2\frac{3}{5} = \frac{13}{5}$, $160 = \frac{160}{1}$

$= \frac{2{,}080}{5}$ or 416 — The new roller coaster will be 416 feet high.

CHECK Your Progress

j. **CARPENTRY** A piece of lumber is $4\frac{1}{4}$ feet long. If you need a piece of lumber that is $\frac{2}{3}$ this size, how long a piece do you need?

Real-World Link
Marine One is the helicopter used to transport the President and Vice-President. The latest model is the VH-71, which has a cruising speed of 172 miles per hour. It has 200 square feet of cabin space, almost double the previous model.
Source: Lockheed Martin

Dimensional analysis is the process of including units of measurement when you compute. You can use dimensional analysis to check whether your answers are reasonable.

EXAMPLE Use Dimensional Analysis

5 **AIRCRAFT** **Refer to the information at the left. Suppose a VH-71 helicopter is traveling at its cruising speed. How far will it travel in $1\frac{3}{4}$ hours?**

Words	Distance equals the rate multiplied by the time.
Variable	Let d represent the distance.
Equation	$d = 172$ miles per hour $\cdot 1\frac{3}{4}$ hours

$d = \frac{172 \text{ miles}}{1 \text{ hour}} \cdot 1\frac{3}{4} \text{ hours}$ — Write the equation.

$d = \frac{172 \text{ miles}}{1 \text{ hour}} \cdot \frac{7}{4} \cdot \frac{\text{hours}}{1}$ — $1\frac{3}{4} = \frac{7}{4}$

$d = \frac{\overset{43}{\cancel{172}} \text{ miles}}{1 \cancel{\text{hour}}} \cdot \frac{7}{\underset{1}{\cancel{4}}} \cdot \frac{\cancel{\text{hours}}}{1}$ — Divide by common factors and units.

$d = 301$ miles

At its cruising speed, a VH-71 will travel 301 miles in $1\frac{3}{4}$ hours.

Check for Reasonableness The problem asks for the distance. When you divide the common units, the answer is expressed in miles.

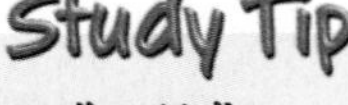

Study Tip

Canceling Units
Only units that are in both the numerator and in the denominator can be canceled out.

CHECK Your Progress

k. **AIRCRAFT** Refer to the information about the VH-71 aircraft. What is the size of its cabin space in square yards? (*Hint:* 1 square yard = 9 square feet)

CHECK Your Understanding

Examples 1–3 (p. 97)

Multiply. Write in simplest form.

1. $\frac{3}{5} \cdot \frac{5}{7}$
2. $\frac{4}{5} \cdot \frac{3}{8}$
3. $\frac{6}{7} \cdot \frac{7}{6}$
4. $-\frac{1}{8} \cdot \frac{4}{9}$
5. $-\frac{2}{9} \cdot \left(\frac{3}{8}\right)$
6. $\left(-\frac{12}{13}\right)\left(-\frac{2}{3}\right)$
7. $1\frac{1}{3} \cdot 5\frac{1}{2}$
8. $2\frac{1}{2} \cdot 1\frac{2}{5}$
9. $-6\frac{3}{4} \cdot 1\frac{7}{9}$

Example 4 (p. 98)

10. **GEOGRAPHY** Rhode Island is the smallest state in the United States. Its area is about $\frac{1}{6}$ the area of New Hampshire. If the area of New Hampshire is about 9,270 square miles, what is the approximate area of Rhode Island?

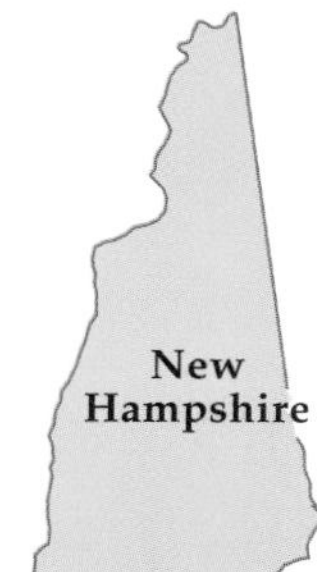

Example 5 (p. 98)

11. **FRUIT** Terrence bought $2\frac{5}{8}$ pounds of grapes that cost \$2 per pound. What was the total cost of the grapes? Use dimensional analysis to check the reasonableness of the answer.

Practice and Problem Solving

HOMEWORK HELP

For Exercises	See Examples
12–15	1
16–19	2
20–23	3
24, 25	4
26–27	5

Multiply. Write in simplest form.

12. $\frac{1}{12} \cdot \frac{4}{7}$
13. $\frac{3}{16} \cdot \frac{1}{9}$
14. $\frac{5}{8} \cdot \frac{4}{5}$
15. $\frac{9}{10} \cdot \frac{2}{3}$
16. $-\frac{9}{10} \cdot \frac{2}{3}$
17. $\left(-\frac{12}{25}\right)\frac{15}{32}$
18. $\left(-\frac{3}{5}\right)\left(-\frac{1}{3}\right)$
19. $\left(-\frac{4}{7}\right)\left(-\frac{1}{20}\right)$
20. $3\frac{1}{3} \cdot \frac{1}{4}$
21. $4\frac{1}{4} \cdot 3\frac{1}{3}$
22. $-3\frac{3}{8} \cdot \left(-\frac{2}{3}\right)$
23. $-\frac{5}{6} \cdot \left(-1\frac{4}{5}\right)$
24. **FOOD** There are $3\frac{1}{2}$ servings of green beans in a certain can. Each serving is $\frac{1}{2}$ cup of beans. How many cups of green beans does the can contain?
25. **MEASUREMENT** Tiffany has a photograph of the volleyball team that measures $3\frac{1}{2}$ inches by 5 inches. She digitally reduces each dimension to $\frac{2}{3}$ its size. What are the lengths of the sides of the new photograph?

Solve each problem. Use dimensional analysis to check the reasonableness of the answer.

26. **BAKING** A recipe calls for $\frac{3}{4}$ cup of sugar per batch of cookies. If Gabe wants to make 6 batches of cookies, how many cups of sugar does he need?
27. **POPULATION** The population density measures how many people live within a certain area. In a certain city, there are about 150,000 people per square mile. How many people live in an area of $2\frac{1}{4}$ square miles?

ALGEBRA **Evaluate each expression if $r = -\frac{1}{4}$, $s = \frac{2}{5}$, $t = \frac{8}{9}$, and $v = -\frac{2}{3}$.**

28. rs
29. rt
30. stv
31. rtv

Find each product. Write in simplest form.

32. $\frac{1}{3} \cdot \left(-\frac{3}{8}\right) \cdot \frac{4}{5}$
33. $\frac{1}{2} \cdot \frac{2}{5} \cdot \frac{3}{4}$
34. $\left(-\frac{2}{5}\right) \cdot \frac{1}{6} \cdot \left(-\frac{5}{2}\right)$
35. $2\frac{2}{7} \cdot 1\frac{5}{9} \cdot 2\frac{2}{5}$
36. $3\frac{1}{3} \cdot 1\frac{1}{2} \cdot 5$
37. $10 \cdot 3.78 \cdot \frac{1}{5}$
38. $\frac{1}{5} \cdot 0.25$
39. $-\frac{2}{9} \cdot 0.\overline{3}$
40. $-\frac{7}{16} \cdot (-2.375)$

GEOGRAPHY **For Exercises 41–43, refer to the table and the information below. Round answers to the nearest whole number.**

There are about 57 million square miles of land on Earth covering seven continents.

Continent	Approximate Fraction of Earth's Landmass
Africa	$\frac{1}{5}$
Antarctica	$\frac{9}{100}$
Asia	$\frac{3}{10}$
Australia	$\frac{11}{200}$
Europe	$\frac{7}{100}$
North America	$\frac{33}{200}$
South America	$\frac{3}{25}$

41. What is the approximate land area of Europe?
42. What is the approximate land area of Asia?
43. Only about $\frac{3}{10}$ of Australia's land area is able to support agriculture. What fraction of Earth's land is this?

ALGEBRA **Evaluate each expression if $a = -1\frac{1}{5}$, $b = 2\frac{7}{9}$, $c = -2\frac{1}{4}$, and $d = 4\frac{1}{2}$. Express in simplest form.**

44. abd^2
45. b^2c^2
46. $\frac{1}{2}a^2d$
47. $-3ac(-bd)$

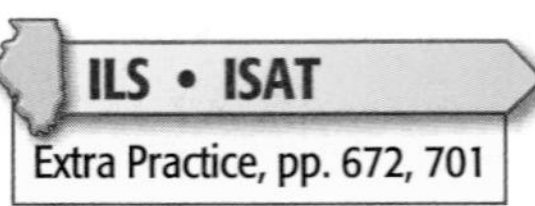

48. **RESEARCH** Use the Internet or other resource to find a recipe for spaghetti sauce. Change the recipe to make $\frac{2}{3}$ of the amount. Then change the recipe to make $1\frac{1}{2}$ the amount.

H.O.T. Problems

49. **FIND THE ERROR** Brad and Jorge are multiplying $2\frac{1}{2}$ and $3\frac{1}{4}$. Who is correct? Explain your reasoning.

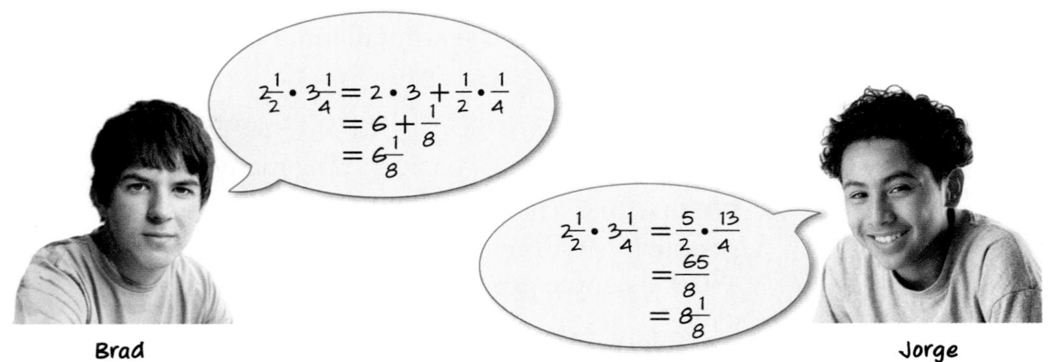

$2\frac{1}{2} \cdot 3\frac{1}{4} = 2 \cdot 3 + \frac{1}{2} \cdot \frac{1}{4}$
$= 6 + \frac{1}{8}$
$= 6\frac{1}{8}$
$2\frac{1}{2} \cdot 3\frac{1}{4} = \frac{5}{2} \cdot \frac{13}{4}$
$= \frac{65}{8}$
$= 8\frac{1}{8}$
Brad
Jorge

50. **OPEN ENDED** Select two fractions with a product greater than $\frac{1}{2}$ and less than 1. Use a number line to justify your answer.

51. **CHALLENGE** Find the missing fraction. $\frac{3}{4} \cdot \blacksquare = \frac{9}{14}$

52. **WRITING IN MATH** Explain why the product of $\frac{1}{2}$ and $\frac{7}{8}$ is less than $\frac{1}{2}$.

ISAT PRACTICE 6.B.3a, 6.C.3a

53. A whole number greater than one is multiplied by a positive fraction less than one. The product is always

A greater than the whole number.

B between the fraction and the whole number.

C less than the fraction.

D all of the above.

54. Find the area of the parallelogram. Use the formula $A = bh$.

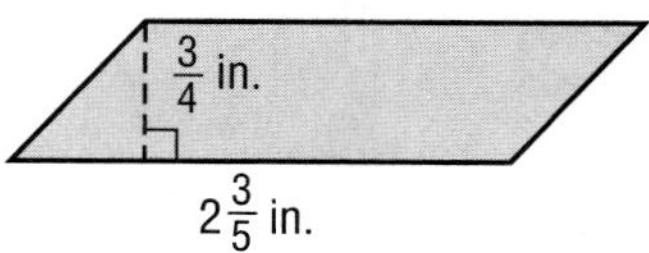

F $\frac{5}{9}$ in^2

G $2\frac{3}{10}$ in^2

H $1\frac{19}{20}$ in^2

J $\frac{4}{5}$ in^2

Spiral Review

Replace each ● with <, >, or = to make a true sentence. (Lesson 2-2)

55. $\frac{1}{2} \bullet \frac{4}{7}$

56. $\frac{2}{7} \bullet 0.\overline{28}$

57. $-\frac{4}{9} \bullet -0.\overline{4}$

BIOLOGY For Exercises 58–60, write the weight of each animal as a fraction or mixed number. (Lesson 2-1)

58. queen bee

59. hummingbird

60. hamster

Animal	Weight (ounces)
Queen Bee	0.004
Hummingbird	0.11
Hamster	3.5

Source: *Animals as Our Companions*

Write an equation to model the relationship between the quantities in each table. (Lesson 1-7)

61.

Servings, *s*	Total Calories, *C*
2	300
5	750
7	1,050
s	*C*

62.

Regular Price, *p*	Sale Price, *s*
$8	$6
$12	$9
$16	$12
p	*s*

GET READY for the Next Lesson

PREREQUISITE SKILL Divide. (Lesson 1-6)

63. $51 \div (-17)$

64. $-81 \div (-3)$

65. $-92 \div 4$

66. $-105 \div (-7)$

2-4 Dividing Positive and Negative Fractions

MAIN IDEA

Divide positive and negative fractions.

IL Learning Standards

6.B.3a Solve practical computation problems involving whole numbers, integers and **rational numbers.**
6.C.3a Select computational procedures and solve problems with whole numbers, **fractions,** decimals, percents and proportions.

New Vocabulary

multiplicative inverses
reciprocals

IL Math Online

glencoe.com

- Concepts in Motion
- Extra Examples
- Personal Tutor
- Self-Check Quiz

GET READY for the Lesson

ANIMALS An antelope is one of the fastest animals on Earth. It can run about 60 miles per hour. A squirrel runs one-fifth of that speed.

1. Find the value of $60 \div 5$.
2. Find the value of $60 \times \frac{1}{5}$.
3. Compare the values of $60 \div 5$ and $60 \times \frac{1}{5}$.
4. What can you conclude about the relationship between dividing by 5 and multiplying by $\frac{1}{5}$?

Two numbers with a product of 1 are **multiplicative inverses**, or **reciprocals**, of each other. For example, 5 and $\frac{1}{5}$ are multiplicative inverses because $5 \cdot \frac{1}{5} = 1$.

Inverse Property of Multiplication — Key Concept

Words The product of a number and its multiplicative inverse is 1.

Symbols

Numbers	**Algebra**
$\frac{3}{4} \cdot \frac{4}{3} = 1$	$\frac{a}{b} \cdot \frac{b}{a} = 1$, where a and $b \neq 0$

EXAMPLE Find a Multiplicative Inverse

1 Write the multiplicative inverse of $-5\frac{2}{3}$.

$-5\frac{2}{3} = -\frac{17}{3}$ Write $-5\frac{2}{3}$ as an improper fraction.

Since $-\frac{17}{3}\left(-\frac{3}{17}\right) = 1$, the multiplicative inverse of $-5\frac{2}{3}$ is $-\frac{3}{17}$.

CHECK Your Progress

Write the multiplicative inverse of each number.

a. $-2\frac{1}{3}$ b. $-\frac{5}{8}$ c. 7

Study Tip

Complex Fractions Recall that a fraction bar represents division. So, $\frac{a}{b} \div \frac{c}{d} = \frac{\frac{a}{b}}{\frac{c}{d}}$.

Multiplicative inverses are used in division. Consider $\frac{a}{b} \div \frac{c}{d}$, which can be written as a fraction.

$\frac{\frac{a}{b}}{\frac{c}{d}} = \frac{\frac{a}{b} \cdot \frac{d}{c}}{\frac{c}{d} \cdot \frac{d}{c}}$ Multiply the numerator and denominator by $\frac{d}{c}$, the multiplicative inverse of $\frac{c}{d}$.

$= \frac{\frac{a}{b} \cdot \frac{d}{c}}{1}$ $\frac{c}{d} \cdot \frac{d}{c} = 1$

$= \frac{a}{b} \cdot \frac{d}{c}$

Divide Fractions — Key Concept

Words To divide by a fraction, multiply by its multiplicative inverse.

Symbols

Numbers $\frac{2}{5} \div \frac{3}{4} = \frac{2}{5} \cdot \frac{4}{3}$

Algebra $\frac{a}{b} \div \frac{c}{d} = \frac{a}{b} \cdot \frac{d}{c}$, where b, c, and $d \neq 0$

EXAMPLES Divide Fractions and Mixed Numbers

Divide. Write in simplest form.

2 $-\frac{4}{5} \div \frac{6}{7}$

$-\frac{4}{5} \div \frac{6}{7} = -\frac{4}{5} \cdot \frac{7}{6}$ Multiply by the multiplicative inverse of $\frac{6}{7}$, which is $\frac{7}{6}$.

$= -\frac{\overset{2}{\cancel{4}}}{5} \cdot \frac{7}{\underset{3}{\cancel{6}}}$ Divide −4 and 6 by their GCF, 2.

$= -\frac{14}{15}$ Multiply.

3 $4\frac{2}{3} \div \left(-3\frac{1}{2}\right)$

$4\frac{2}{3} \div \left(-3\frac{1}{2}\right) = \frac{14}{3} \div \left(-\frac{7}{2}\right)$ $4\frac{2}{3} = \frac{14}{3}$, $-3\frac{1}{2} = -\frac{7}{2}$

$= \frac{14}{3} \cdot \left(-\frac{2}{7}\right)$ The multiplicative inverse of $-\frac{7}{2}$ is $-\frac{2}{7}$.

$= \frac{\overset{2}{\cancel{14}}}{3} \cdot \left(-\frac{2}{\underset{1}{\cancel{7}}}\right)$ Divide 14 and 7 by their GCF, 7.

$= -\frac{4}{3}$ or $-1\frac{1}{3}$ Multiply.

Study Tip

Dividing By a Whole Number When dividing by a whole number, rename it as an improper fraction first. Then multiply by its reciprocal.

CHECK Your Progress

d. $\frac{3}{4} \div \frac{1}{2}$

e. $-\frac{1}{4} \div \frac{7}{8}$

f. $-\frac{2}{3} \div \left(-\frac{3}{5}\right)$

g. $2\frac{3}{4} \div \left(-2\frac{1}{5}\right)$

h. $1\frac{1}{2} \div 2\frac{1}{3}$

i. $-1\frac{1}{2} \div 12$

Real-World Link The width of the blue portion of the Stars and Stripes is $\frac{7}{13}$ of the width of the entire flag. The width of each stripe is $\frac{1}{13}$ of the width of the entire flag.
Source: *United States Code*

Real-World EXAMPLE

4 **CRAFTS** **Lina's class is making flags for the school's International Day celebration. She needs $1\frac{1}{6}$ feet of paper for the blue portion on each flag. If the class has a 21-foot roll of blue paper, how many flags can she make?**

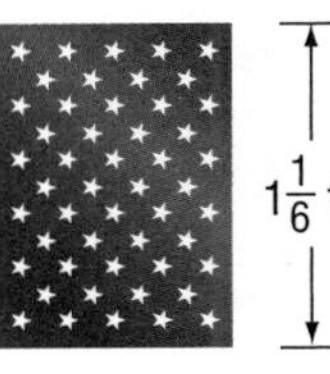

Divide 21 by $1\frac{1}{6}$.

$21 \div 1\frac{1}{6} = \frac{21}{1} \div \frac{7}{6}$ Write 21 as $\frac{21}{1}$. Write $1\frac{1}{6}$ as $\frac{7}{6}$.

$= \frac{\overset{3}{\cancel{21}}}{1} \cdot \frac{6}{\underset{1}{\cancel{7}}}$ Multiply by the multiplicative inverse of $\frac{7}{6}$, which is $\frac{6}{7}$. Divide 7 and 21 by their GCF, 7.

$= \frac{18}{1}$ or 18 Simplify.

Lina's class can make 18 flags using the 21-foot roll of paper.

CHECK Your Progress

j. **LUMBER** How many $1\frac{1}{2}$-inch-thick boards are in a stack that is 36 inches tall?

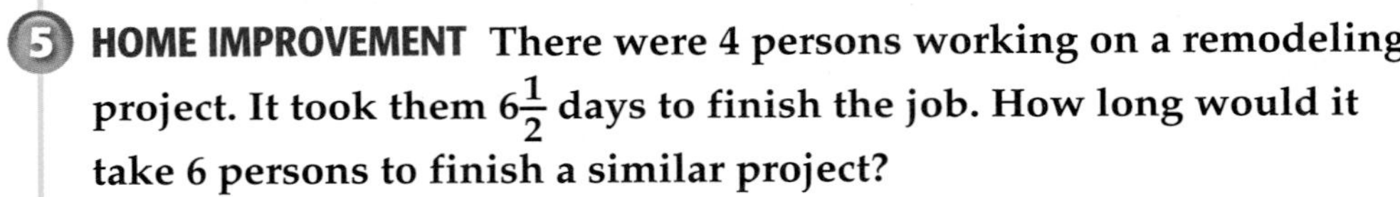

Real-World EXAMPLE

5 **HOME IMPROVEMENT** **There were 4 persons working on a remodeling project. It took them $6\frac{1}{2}$ days to finish the job. How long would it take 6 persons to finish a similar project?**

If 4 persons each worked $6\frac{1}{2}$ days, the project required $4 \times 6\frac{1}{2}$ *person-days* of work. Divide this number by 6 persons to find the number of days it will take to complete the other project.

$4 \times 6\frac{1}{2}$ person-days $\div$ 6 persons

$= \frac{4 \times 6\frac{1}{2} \cancel{\text{person}}\text{-days}}{1} \times \frac{1}{6 \cancel{\text{persons}}}$ Multiply by the multiplicative inverse of 6, which is $\frac{1}{6}$.

$= \frac{26}{6}$ or $4\frac{1}{3}$ days Simplify.

Check for Reasonableness The problem asks for the number of days. When you divide the common units, the answer is expressed in days.

Study Tip
Dimensional Analysis You can also use dimensional analysis to check the reasonableness of the answer.

CHECK Your Progress

k. **TRAVEL** Geoff plans to travel 480 miles. If his car gets an average of 32 miles per gallon of gasoline, approximately how much gasoline will he use? Use dimensional analysis to check the reasonableness of the answer.

CHECK Your Understanding

Example 1 (p. 102)

Write the multiplicative inverse of each number.

1. $\frac{5}{7}$
2. -12
3. $-2\frac{3}{4}$

Example 2 (p. 103)

Divide. Write in simplest form.

4. $\frac{2}{3} \div \frac{3}{4}$
5. $\frac{5}{8} \div \frac{1}{2}$
6. $\frac{3}{8} \div \left(-\frac{9}{10}\right)$
7. $-\frac{7}{16} \div \left(-\frac{7}{8}\right)$

Example 3 (p. 103)

8. $\frac{4}{5} \div 8$
9. $\frac{9}{10} \div 3$
10. $-5\frac{5}{6} \div \left(-4\frac{2}{3}\right)$
11. $-3\frac{7}{12} \div 6\frac{5}{6}$

Examples 4, 5 (p. 104)

12. **BIRDS** The smallest owl found in the United States is the Elf Owl, which weighs $1\frac{1}{2}$ ounces. One of the largest owls is the Eurasian Eagle Owl, which weighs nearly 10 pounds or 156 ounces.

How many times heavier is the Eurasian Eagle Owl than the Elf Owl?

Elf Owl

Eurasian Eagle Owl

Practice and Problem Solving

HOMEWORK HELP

For Exercises	See Examples
13–18	1
19–26	2
27–34	3
35, 36	4
37, 38	5

Write the multiplicative inverse of each number.

13. $-\frac{7}{9}$
14. $-\frac{5}{8}$
15. 15
16. 18
17. $3\frac{2}{5}$
18. $4\frac{1}{8}$

Divide. Write in simplest form.

19. $\frac{2}{5} \div \frac{3}{4}$
20. $\frac{3}{8} \div \frac{2}{3}$
21. $\frac{2}{3} \div \frac{5}{6}$
22. $\frac{2}{5} \div \frac{1}{10}$
23. $-\frac{4}{5} \div \frac{3}{4}$
24. $\frac{3}{10} \div \left(-\frac{2}{3}\right)$
25. $-\frac{5}{9} \div \left(-\frac{2}{3}\right)$
26. $-\frac{7}{12} \div \left(-\frac{5}{6}\right)$
27. $\frac{2}{5} \div 4$
28. $\frac{9}{16} \div 3$
29. $\frac{4}{5} \div 6$
30. $\frac{6}{7} \div 4$
31. $3\frac{3}{4} \div 2\frac{1}{2}$
32. $7\frac{1}{2} \div 2\frac{1}{10}$
33. $-12\frac{1}{4} \div 4\frac{2}{3}$
34. $10\frac{1}{5} \div \left(-\frac{3}{15}\right)$

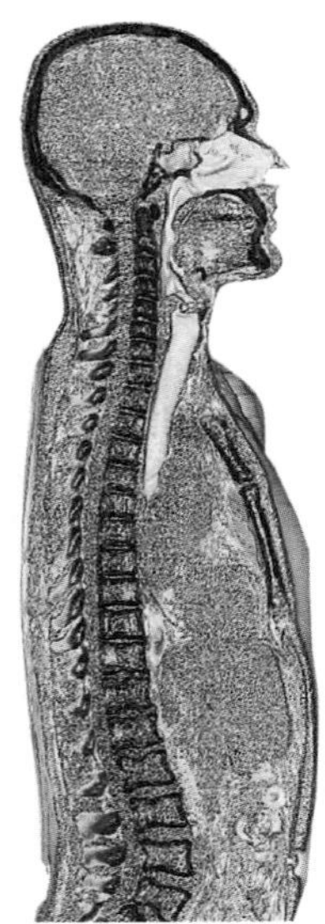

Real-World Link 99% of the mass of the human body is made up of six elements: oxygen, carbon, hydrogen, nitrogen, calcium, and phosphorus.

HUMAN BODY For Exercises 35 and 36, use the information below and at the right.

The table shows the composition of a healthy adult male's body. Examples of body cell mass are muscle, body organs, and blood. Examples of supporting tissue are blood plasma and bones.

Composition of Human Body	
Component	**Fraction of Body Weight**
Body Cell Mass	$\frac{11}{20}$
Supporting Tissue	$\frac{3}{10}$
Body Fat	$\frac{3}{20}$

35. How many times more of a healthy adult male's body weight is made up of body cell mass than body fat?

36. How many times more of a healthy adult male's body weight is made up of body cell mass than supporting tissue?

For Exercises 37 and 38, use dimensional analysis to check the reasonableness of each answer.

37. **PAINTING** It took 3 persons $2\frac{1}{2}$ hours to paint a large room. How long would it take 5 persons to paint a similar room?

38. **VACATION** The Sumner family is planning a vacation. The destination is 350 miles away. If they drive at an average speed of 62 miles per hour, approximately how long will it take to get there?

39. **BIOLOGY** How many of the small hummingbirds need to be placed end-to-end to have the same length as the large hummingbird?

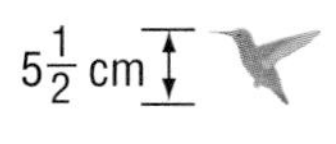

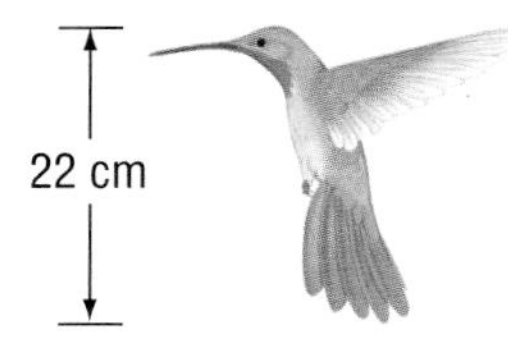

40. **LIBRARIES** Pilar is storing a set of art books on a shelf that has $11\frac{1}{4}$ inches of shelf space. If each book is $\frac{3}{4}$ inch wide, how many books can be stored on the shelf?

41. **GEOMETRY** The circumference C, or distance around a circle, can be approximated using the formula $C = \frac{44}{7}r$, where r is the radius of the circle. What is the radius of the circle at the right? Round to the nearest tenth.

r

$C = 53.2$ m

42. **BAKING** Emily is baking chocolate cupcakes. Each batch of 20 cupcakes requires $\frac{2}{3}$ cup of cocoa. If Emily has $3\frac{1}{4}$ cups of cocoa, how many full batches of cupcakes will she be able to make and how much cocoa will she have left over?

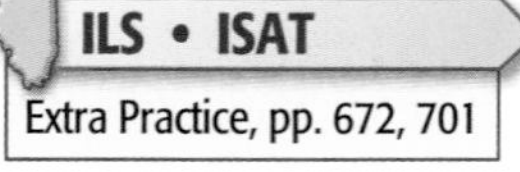

Extra Practice, pp. 672, 701

H.O.T. Problems

43. **OPEN ENDED** Select a fraction between 0 and 1. Identify both its additive and multiplicative inverses. Explain your reasoning.

44. **CHALLENGE** Give a counterexample to the statement *The quotient of two fractions between 0 and 1 is never a whole number.*

45. **NUMBER SENSE** Which is greater: $30 \cdot \frac{3}{4}$ or $30 \div \frac{3}{4}$? Explain.

CHALLENGE Use mental math to find each value.

46. $\frac{43}{594} \cdot \frac{641}{76} \div \frac{641}{594}$

47. $\frac{783}{241} \cdot \frac{241}{783} \div \frac{72}{53}$

48. **WRITING IN MATH** Write a real-world problem that can be solved by dividing fractions or mixed numbers. Solve the problem.

ISAT PRACTICE 6.B.3a, 6.C.3a

49. One batch of a muffin recipe calls for $\frac{2}{3}$ cup of flour and $\frac{3}{4}$ cup of strawberries. Claudio's father used $1\frac{2}{3}$ cups of flour and $1\frac{7}{8}$ cups of strawberries. How many batches of muffins did he make?

A 3

B $2\frac{1}{2}$

C 2

D $1\frac{3}{4}$

50. Mr. Jones is doing a science experiment with his class of 20 students. Each student needs $\frac{3}{4}$ cup of vinegar. If he currently has 15 cups of vinegar, which equation could Mr. Jones use to determine if he has enough vinegar for his entire class?

F $x = 15 \div 20$

G $x = 15 \div \frac{3}{4}$

H $x = 20 - (15)$

J $x = 15(20)$

Spiral Review

Multiply. Write in simplest form. (Lesson 2-3)

51. $\frac{1}{2} \cdot \frac{3}{4}$

52. $\frac{7}{12} \cdot \frac{4}{7}$

53. $1\frac{2}{3} \cdot 4\frac{1}{5}$

54. $\frac{2}{3} \cdot 3\frac{1}{4}$

55. **ACTIVITIES** At Westland Middle School, $\frac{2}{3}$ of the students play sports, and $\frac{5}{8}$ of the students participate in band. Does a greater fraction of students play sports or participate in band? (Lesson 2-2)

56. **ALGEBRA** Write an equation using two variables that could be used to determine the population of Asia if it is about three million less than five times the population of Africa. (Lesson 1-7)

Write an integer to describe each situation. (Lesson 1-3)

57. 10 candy bars short of his goal

58. 7 bonus points

GET READY for the Next Lesson

PREREQUISITE SKILL Add or subtract. (Lessons 1-4 and 1-5)

59. $-7 + 15$

60. $-9 + (-4)$

61. $-3 - 15$

62. $12 - (-17)$

2-5 Adding and Subtracting Like Fractions

MAIN IDEA

Add and subtract fractions with like denominators.

IL Learning Standards

6.B.3a Solve practical computation problems involving whole numbers, integers and **rational numbers.**
6.C.3a Select computational procedures and solve problems with whole numbers, **fractions,** decimals, percents and proportions.

New Vocabulary

like fractions

IL Math Online

glencoe.com

- Extra Examples
- Personal Tutor
- Self-Check Quiz

GET READY for the Lesson

APPLES Oleta and her family went to a local orchard to pick apples. The amount each person picked is shown at the right.

Person	Amount Picked (baskets)
Oleta	$1\frac{1}{4}$
Mr. Davis	2
Mrs. Davis	$1\frac{3}{4}$
Alvin	$\frac{2}{4}$

1. What is the sum of the whole-number parts of the baskets of apples?
2. How many $\frac{1}{4}$ baskets are there?
3. Can you combine all of the apples into a bushel that holds five baskets? Explain.

Fractions that have the same denominators are called **like fractions**.

Add and Subtract Like Fractions — Key Concept

Words To add or subtract like fractions, add or subtract the numerators and write the result over the denominator.

Examples

Numbers	Algebra
$\frac{1}{5} + \frac{3}{5} = \frac{4}{5}$	$\frac{a}{c} + \frac{b}{c} = \frac{a+b}{c}$, where $c \neq 0$
$\frac{7}{8} - \frac{3}{8} = \frac{4}{8}$ or $\frac{1}{2}$	$\frac{a}{c} - \frac{b}{c} = \frac{a-b}{c}$, where $c \neq 0$

You can use the rules for adding integers to determine the sign of the sum of any two signed numbers.

EXAMPLE Add Like Fractions

1 Find $\frac{5}{8} + \left(-\frac{7}{8}\right)$. Write in simplest form.

$\frac{5}{8} + \left(-\frac{7}{8}\right) = \frac{5 + (-7)}{8}$ ←Add the numerators. ←The denominators are the same.

$= \frac{-2}{8}$ or $-\frac{1}{4}$ Simplify.

CHECK Your Progress

a. $\frac{5}{9} + \frac{7}{9}$

b. $-\frac{5}{9} + \frac{1}{9}$

c. $-\frac{1}{6} + \left(-\frac{5}{6}\right)$

EXAMPLE Subtract Like Fractions

2 **Find $-\frac{8}{9} - \frac{7}{9}$. Write in simplest form.**

$$-\frac{8}{9} - \frac{7}{9} = -\frac{8}{9} + \left(-\frac{7}{9}\right)$$

$$= \frac{-8 + (-7)}{9}$$ Subtract the numerators by adding the opposite of 7.

$$= \frac{-15}{9} \text{ or } -1\frac{2}{3}$$ Rename $\frac{-15}{9}$ as $-1\frac{6}{9}$ or $-1\frac{2}{3}$.

Study Tip

Look Back You can review adding integers in Lesson 1-4.

CHECK Your Progress

d. $-\frac{4}{5} - \frac{3}{5}$ e. $\frac{3}{8} - \frac{5}{8}$ f. $\frac{5}{7} - \left(-\frac{4}{7}\right)$

To add or subtract mixed numbers, add or subtract the whole numbers and the fractions separately. Then simplify.

EXAMPLE Add Mixed Numbers

3 **Find $5\frac{7}{9} + 8\frac{4}{9}$. Write in simplest form.**

$$5\frac{7}{9} + 8\frac{4}{9} = (5 + 8) + \left(\frac{7}{9} + \frac{4}{9}\right)$$ Add the whole numbers and fractions separately.

$$= 13 + \frac{7 + 4}{9}$$ Add the numerators.

$$= 13\frac{11}{9} \text{ or } 14\frac{2}{9}$$ $\frac{11}{9} = 1\frac{2}{9}$

CHECK Your Progress

g. $9\frac{5}{8} - 3\frac{3}{8}$ h. $8 - 6\frac{2}{9}$ i. $-8\frac{5}{9} + \left(-6\frac{2}{9}\right)$

Sometimes you need to regroup before you can subtract.

Real-World Link Dressage is an Olympic sport where a horse and rider must go through a series of tests. These tests require very controlled movements for the horse and require years of training.

Real-World EXAMPLE

4 **ANIMALS** Horses are measured by a unit called a *handbreadth* or hand. How much taller is a horse that is $14\frac{1}{4}$ hands tall than one that is $12\frac{3}{4}$ hands tall?

$14\frac{1}{4} \rightarrow 13\frac{5}{4}$ $14\frac{1}{4} = 13 + 1 + \frac{1}{4}$ or $13\frac{5}{4}$

$-12\frac{3}{4} \rightarrow -12\frac{3}{4}$ Subtract the whole numbers and fractions separately.

$1\frac{2}{4}$ or $1\frac{1}{2}$ The first horse is $1\frac{1}{2}$ hands taller.

CHECK Your Progress

j. **BAKING** A recipe for chocolate cookies calls for $2\frac{3}{4}$ cups of flour. If Alexis has $1\frac{1}{4}$ cups of flour, how much more will she need?

CHECK Your Understanding

Examples 1–3 (pp. 108–109)

Add or subtract. Write in simplest form.

1. $\frac{2}{5} + \left(-\frac{4}{5}\right)$
2. $-\frac{3}{4} + \frac{1}{4}$
3. $-\frac{4}{9} + \left(-\frac{7}{9}\right)$
4. $-\frac{7}{10} - \frac{9}{10}$
5. $\frac{3}{8} - \frac{7}{8}$
6. $-\frac{5}{6} - \left(-\frac{2}{6}\right)$
7. $5\frac{4}{9} - 2\frac{2}{9}$
8. $-1\frac{3}{7} + \left(-2\frac{2}{7}\right)$
9. $10 - 3\frac{5}{16}$

Example 4 (p. 109)

10. **HOMEWORK** Venus wrote a report for her middle school history class in $2\frac{1}{4}$ hours. Her sister Tia is in high school, and she wrote a history paper in $4\frac{3}{4}$ hours. How much longer did it take Tia to write her paper?

Practice and Problem Solving

HOMEWORK HELP

For Exercises	See Examples
11–14	1
15–18	2
19–26	3
27, 28	4

Add or subtract. Write in simplest form.

11. $-\frac{1}{9} + \frac{4}{9}$
12. $-\frac{3}{7} + \left(-\frac{2}{7}\right)$
13. $-\frac{5}{12} + \frac{7}{12}$
14. $\frac{8}{9} + \left(-\frac{5}{9}\right)$
15. $-\frac{4}{5} - \frac{3}{5}$
16. $\frac{15}{16} - \frac{9}{16}$
17. $\frac{1}{12} - \frac{7}{12}$
18. $\frac{2}{9} - \frac{8}{9}$
19. $3\frac{5}{8} + 7\frac{5}{8}$
20. $9\frac{5}{9} + 4\frac{7}{9}$
21. $8\frac{1}{10} + \left(-2\frac{9}{10}\right)$
22. $8\frac{5}{12} + \left(-5\frac{11}{12}\right)$
23. $-1\frac{5}{6} - 3\frac{5}{6}$
24. $-3\frac{3}{4} - 7\frac{3}{4}$
25. $7 - 5\frac{2}{5}$
26. $9 - 6\frac{3}{7}$

27. **HOME IMPROVEMENT** Andrew has $42\frac{1}{3}$ feet of molding to use as borders around the windows of his house. If he uses $23\frac{2}{3}$ feet of the molding on the front windows, how much remains for the back windows?

28. **WEATHER** One year, Brady's hometown of Powell received about $42\frac{6}{10}$ inches of snow. The following year only $14\frac{3}{10}$ inches of snow fell. What is the difference in the amount of snow between the two years?

Simplify each expression.

29. $-7\frac{4}{5} + 3\frac{1}{5} - \left(2\frac{3}{5}\right)$
30. $-8\frac{1}{8} - \left(-3\frac{5}{8}\right) + 6\frac{3}{8}$

MEASUREMENT Find the perimeter of each rectangle.

31. $12\frac{1}{4}$ in. $25\frac{3}{4}$ in.

32. 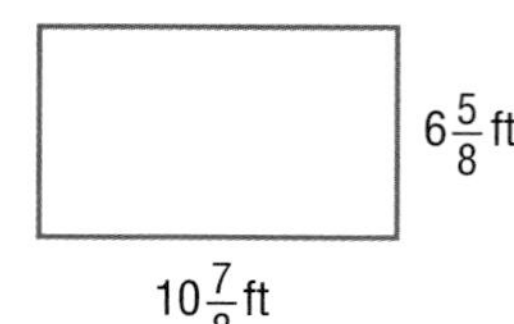

ALGEBRA **Evaluate each expression for the given values.**

33. $a - b$ if $a = 5\frac{1}{3}$ and $b = -2\frac{1}{3}$

34. $x + y$ if $x = -\frac{5}{12}$ and $y = -\frac{1}{12}$

35. $n - m$ if $m = 5\frac{2}{3}$ and $n = -2\frac{2}{3}$

36. $s - t$ if $s = -\frac{1}{2}$ and $t = -2\frac{1}{2}$

37. **TRACK** In the 4 × 100-meter relay, each team member runs one 100-meter leg of the race. Find the total time for the team.

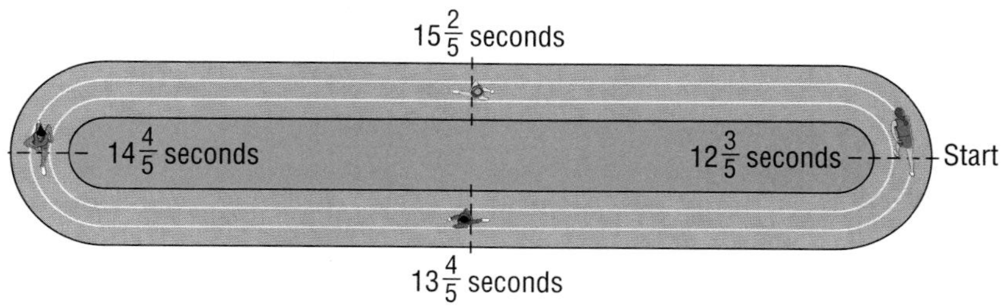

38. **HOMEWORK** Rob recorded the amount of time he spent on homework last week. Express his total time for the week in terms of hours and minutes.

Day	Time
Mon	$2\frac{1}{6}$ h
Tue	$2\frac{1}{2}$ h
Wed	$1\frac{3}{4}$ h
Thu	$2\frac{5}{12}$ h
Fri	$1\frac{1}{4}$ h

39. **PLUMBING** A plumber has a pipe that is $64\frac{5}{8}$ inches long. The plumber cuts $2\frac{7}{8}$ inches off the end of the pipe, then cuts off an additional $1\frac{3}{8}$ inches. How long is the remaining pipe after the last cut is made?

ILS • ISAT
Extra Practice, pp. 672, 701

H.O.T. Problems

40. **OPEN ENDED** Write a subtraction problem with a difference of $\frac{2}{9}$.

41. **FIND THE ERROR** Heather and Raini are adding $\frac{1}{7}$ and $\frac{3}{7}$. Who is correct? Explain your reasoning.

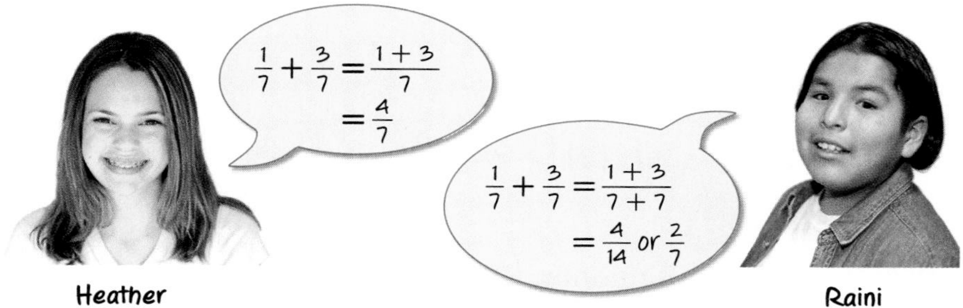

42. **CHALLENGE** Explain how you could use mental math to find the following sum. Then find the sum.

$$3\frac{2}{3} + 4\frac{2}{5} + 2\frac{1}{6} + 2\frac{5}{6} + 1\frac{1}{3} + \frac{3}{5}$$

43. **WRITING IN MATH** Write a real-world situation that can be solved by adding or subtracting mixed numbers. Then solve the problem.

ISAT PRACTICE 6.B.3a, 6.C.3a

44. Esteban is $63\frac{1}{8}$ inches tall. Haley is $59\frac{5}{8}$ inches tall. How much taller is Esteban than Haley? Write in simplest form.

A $4\frac{1}{2}$ in.

B $4\frac{1}{4}$ in.

C $3\frac{3}{4}$ in.

D $3\frac{1}{2}$ in.

45. Use the figure shown below.

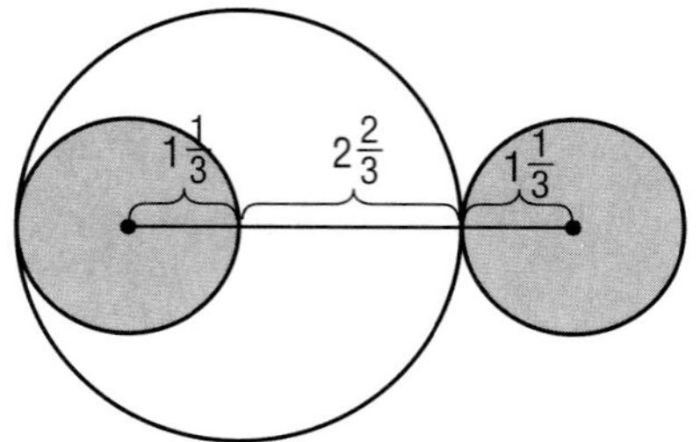

What is the length of the segment connecting the centers of the two smaller circles?

F $6\frac{1}{3}$ units **H** $5\frac{2}{3}$ units

G $5\frac{1}{3}$ units **J** $4\frac{5}{3}$ units

Spiral Review

Divide. Write in simplest form. (Lesson 2-4)

46. $\frac{3}{5} \div \frac{6}{7}$ 47. $\frac{7}{8} \div 2\frac{4}{5}$ 48. $-3\frac{1}{4} \div 2\frac{1}{2}$

49. Find the product of $-\frac{7}{8}$ and $-\frac{6}{7}$. (Lesson 2-3)

50. **NUTRITION** Refer to the table at the right. There is 2.3 times the recommended daily allowance of vitamin C in a 5.5-ounce serving of kiwifruit. Write an equation to represent the amount of vitamin C recommended for each day. (Lesson 1-7)

Fruit	Vitamin C (mg in 5.5 oz)
Orange	52
Strawberries	63
Kiwifruit	103.5

Source: Food and Drug Administration

Evaluate each expression. (Lesson 1-3)

51. $|-20| - |17|$ 52. $|31| - |-10|$ 53. $|5 + 9|$ 54. $|8 - 17|$

55. **HEALTH** In a typical minute, 15 breaths are taken. About how many breaths are taken in one day? (Lesson 1-1)

GET READY for the Next Lesson

PREREQUISITE SKILL Find the least common multiple (LCM) of each set of numbers.

56. 14, 21 57. 18, 9, 6 58. 6, 4, 9 59. 5, 10, 20

Mid-Chapter Quiz

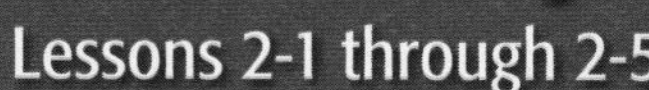

Lessons 2-1 through 2-5

IL Learning Standards
6.B.3a, 6.C.3a

1. **MEASUREMENT** One centimeter is about 0.392 inch. What fraction of an inch is this? (Lesson 2-1)

2. Write $1\frac{7}{16}$ as a decimal. (Lesson 2-1)

3. Write $0.\overline{4}$ as a fraction in simplest form. (Lesson 2-1)

Replace each ● with <, >, or = to make a true sentence. (Lesson 2-2)

4. $\frac{1}{3}$ ● $\frac{1}{4}$

5. $-\frac{2}{5}$ ● $-\frac{3}{10}$

6. $0.\overline{12}$ ● $\frac{4}{33}$

7. $-7.833\ldots$ ● -7.8

8. **MULTIPLE CHOICE** The table gives the durations, in hours, of several human spaceflights.

Mission	Year	Duration (h)
Challenger (41–B)	1984	$191\frac{4}{15}$
Discovery (51–A)	1984	$191\frac{3}{4}$
Endeavour (STS–57)	1992	$190\frac{1}{2}$
Discovery (STS–103)	1999	$191\frac{1}{6}$

Which of the following correctly orders these durations from least to greatest? (Lesson 2-2)

A $190\frac{1}{2}, 191\frac{1}{6}, 191\frac{3}{4}, 191\frac{4}{15}$

B $191\frac{3}{4}, 191\frac{1}{6}, 191\frac{4}{15}, 190\frac{1}{2}$

C $190\frac{1}{2}, 191\frac{1}{6}, 191\frac{4}{15}, 191\frac{3}{4}$

D $191\frac{1}{6}, 191\frac{4}{15}, 190\frac{1}{2}, 191\frac{3}{4}$

Multiply. Write in simplest form. (Lesson 2-3)

9. $\left(-\frac{1}{3}\right) \cdot \frac{7}{8}$

10. $\left(-2\frac{3}{4}\right) \cdot \left(-\frac{1}{5}\right)$

11. **WEATHER** The table shows the approximate number of sunny days each year for certain cities. Oklahoma City has about $\frac{3}{5}$ as many sunny days as Phoenix. About how many sunny days each year are there in Oklahoma City? (Lesson 2-3)

Sunny Days Per Year	
City	**Days**
Austin, TX	120
Denver, CO	115
Phoenix, AZ	215
Sacramento, CA	195
Santa Fe, NM	175

Source: National Oceanic and Atmospheric Administration

Divide. Write in simplest form. (Lesson 2-4)

12. $\frac{1}{2} \div \left(-\frac{3}{4}\right)$

13. $\left(-1\frac{1}{3}\right) \div \left(-\frac{1}{4}\right)$

14. **MULTIPLE CHOICE** A board that is $25\frac{1}{2}$ feet long is cut into pieces that are each $1\frac{1}{2}$ feet long. Which of the steps below would give the number of pieces into which the board is cut? (Lesson 2-4)

F Multiply $1\frac{1}{2}$ by $25\frac{1}{2}$.

G Divide $25\frac{1}{2}$ by $1\frac{1}{2}$.

H Add $25\frac{1}{2}$ to $1\frac{1}{2}$.

J Subtract $1\frac{1}{2}$ from $25\frac{1}{2}$.

Add or subtract. Write in simplest form. (Lesson 2-5)

15. $\frac{1}{5} + \left(-\frac{4}{5}\right)$

16. $-3\frac{4}{7} - 3\frac{6}{7}$

2-6 Adding and Subtracting Unlike Fractions

MAIN IDEA

Add and subtract fractions with like denominators.

IL Learning Standards

6.B.3a Solve practical computation problems involving whole numbers, integers and **rational numbers.**
6.C.3a Select computational procedures and solve problems with whole numbers, **fractions,** decimals, percents and proportions.

New Vocabulary

unlike fractions

IL Math Online

glencoe.com
- Extra Examples
- Personal Tutor
- Self-Check Quiz

GET READY for the Lesson

BAKING A cookie recipe calls for the ingredients at the right along with various amounts of flour, eggs, and baking soda.

1. What are the denominators of the fractions?
2. What is the least common multiple of the denominators?
3. Find the missing value in $\frac{1}{2} = \frac{?}{6}$.

Oatmeal Cookies
$\frac{2}{3}$ cup sugar
$\frac{2}{3}$ cup packed brown sugar
$\frac{1}{2}$ cup butter, softened
$\frac{1}{2}$ cup butter shortening
$\frac{1}{2}$ teaspoon baking powder
$\frac{1}{2}$ teaspoon salt

Fractions with unlike denominators are called **unlike fractions**. To add or subtract unlike fractions, rename the fractions using prime factors to find the least common denominator. Then add or subtract as with like fractions.

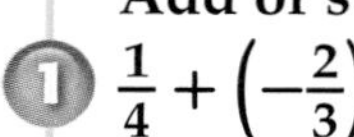

EXAMPLES Add and Subtract Unlike Fractions

Add or subtract. Write in simplest form.

1 $\frac{1}{4} + \left(-\frac{2}{3}\right)$

$\frac{1}{4} + \left(-\frac{2}{3}\right) = \frac{1}{4} \cdot \frac{3}{3} + \left(-\frac{2}{3}\right) \cdot \frac{4}{4}$ The LCD is 3 • 4 or 12.

$= \frac{3}{12} + \left(-\frac{8}{12}\right)$ Rename using the LCD.

$= \frac{3 + (-8)}{12}$ or $-\frac{5}{12}$ Add the numerators. Then simplify.

2 $-\frac{8}{63} - \left(-\frac{7}{99}\right)$

$-\frac{8}{63} + \frac{7}{99} = -\frac{8}{63} \cdot \frac{11}{11} + \frac{7}{99} \cdot \frac{7}{7}$ $63 = 3 \cdot 3 \cdot 7,\ 99 = 3 \cdot 3 \cdot 11$
The LCD is 3 • 3 • 7 • 11 or 693.

$= -\frac{88}{693} + \frac{49}{693}$ Rename using the LCD.

$= \frac{-88 + 49}{693}$ Add the numerators.

$= -\frac{39}{693}$ or $-\frac{13}{231}$ Simplify.

CHECK Your Progress

a. $-\frac{5}{6} + \left(-\frac{1}{2}\right)$ b. $\frac{1}{14} + \frac{3}{49}$ c. $-\frac{5}{16} + \frac{3}{10}$

EXAMPLE Add and Subtract Mixed Numbers

Study Tip

Estimation
Think: $-6\frac{2}{9}$ is about -6 and $4\frac{5}{6}$ is about 5. Since $-6 + 5$ is about -1, the answer is about -1. The answer seems reasonable.

3 **Find $-6\frac{2}{9} + 4\frac{5}{6}$. Write in simplest form.**

$-6\frac{2}{9} + 4\frac{5}{6} = -\frac{56}{9} + \frac{29}{6}$ Write as improper fractions.

$= -\frac{112}{18} + \frac{87}{18}$ $\frac{-56}{9} \cdot \frac{2}{2} = -\frac{112}{18}$ and $\frac{29}{6} \cdot \frac{3}{3} = \frac{87}{18}$

$= \frac{-112 + 87}{18}$ Add the numerators.

$= \frac{-25}{18}$ or $-1\frac{7}{18}$ Simplify.

CHECK Your Progress

Add or subtract. Write in simplest form.

d. $-\frac{5}{12} + \left(-\frac{1}{8}\right)$ e. $-3\frac{1}{2} + 8\frac{1}{3}$ f. $2\frac{3}{4} - 6\frac{1}{3}$ g. $-1\frac{2}{5} + \left(-3\frac{1}{3}\right)$

ISAT EXAMPLE 6.B.3a, 6.C.3a

4 **Four students volunteered to work at an animal shelter after school. They worked $2\frac{1}{3}$ hours, $1\frac{5}{6}$ hours, $2\frac{1}{4}$ hours, and $1\frac{7}{8}$ hours. How much time did the students volunteer in all?**

A $6\frac{5}{12}$ hours
B $8\frac{7}{24}$ hours
C $11\frac{7}{24}$ hours
D $12\frac{1}{3}$ hours

Read the Item

You need to find the sum of four mixed numbers.

Solve the Item

It would take some time to change each of the fractions to ones with a common denominator. However, notice that all four of the numbers have a value of about 2. Since 2×4 equals 8, the answer will be about 8. Notice that only one of the choices is close to 8. The answer is B.

Test-Taking Tip

Use Estimation If a test question would take an excessive amount of time to work, try estimating the answer. Then look for the appropriate answer choice.

CHECK Your Progress

h. Amanda is planning a rectangular vegetable garden using a roll of border fencing that is $45\frac{3}{4}$ feet long. If she makes the width of the garden $10\frac{1}{2}$ feet, what must the length be?

F $12\frac{3}{8}$ ft
G $17\frac{1}{2}$ ft
H $24\frac{3}{4}$ ft
J $35\frac{1}{4}$ ft

CHECK Your Understanding

Examples 1–3 (pp. 114–115)

Add or subtract. Write in simplest form.

1. $\frac{3}{4} + \left(-\frac{1}{6}\right)$
2. $-\frac{5}{8} + \frac{1}{2}$
3. $-\frac{4}{9} + \left(-\frac{2}{3}\right)$
4. $\frac{7}{8} - \frac{3}{4}$
5. $\frac{7}{13} - \frac{2}{9}$
6. $\frac{14}{15} - \left(-\frac{12}{21}\right)$
7. $-3\frac{2}{5} + 1\frac{5}{6}$
8. $3\frac{5}{8} - 1\frac{1}{3}$
9. $-4\frac{7}{12} - \left(-3\frac{7}{72}\right)$

Example 4 (p. 115)

10. **MULTIPLE CHOICE** Tamera played a computer game for $1\frac{1}{4}$ hours, studied for $2\frac{1}{4}$ hours, and did some chores for $\frac{1}{2}$ hour. How much time did Tamera spend on all of these tasks?

A $2\frac{1}{2}$ h **B** $3\frac{1}{4}$ h **C** 4 h **D** $4\frac{1}{2}$ h

Practice and Problem Solving

HOMEWORK HELP	
For Exercises	See Examples
11–14	1
15–18	2
19–26	3
42, 43	4

Add or subtract. Write in simplest form.

11. $\frac{1}{4} + \left(-\frac{7}{12}\right)$
12. $-\frac{3}{8} + \frac{5}{6}$
13. $-\frac{6}{7} + \left(-\frac{1}{2}\right)$
14. $-\frac{5}{9} + \left(-\frac{3}{8}\right)$
15. $\frac{1}{3} - \frac{7}{8}$
16. $\frac{4}{5} - \left(-\frac{2}{15}\right)$
17. $-\frac{2}{9} - \left(-\frac{3}{11}\right)$
18. $-\frac{7}{15} - \left(-\frac{12}{25}\right)$
19. $3\frac{1}{5} + \left(-8\frac{1}{2}\right)$
20. $1\frac{1}{6} + \left(-6\frac{2}{3}\right)$
21. $8\frac{3}{7} - \left(-6\frac{1}{2}\right)$
22. $7\frac{3}{4} - \left(-1\frac{1}{8}\right)$
23. $-4\frac{3}{4} - 5\frac{5}{8}$
24. $-8\frac{1}{3} - 4\frac{5}{6}$
25. $-15\frac{5}{8} + 11\frac{2}{3}$
26. $-22\frac{2}{5} + 15\frac{5}{6}$

27. **HIKING** The map shows a hiking trail at a campground. If the distance along the trail from the campground to Silver Lake is $4\frac{1}{10}$ miles, how far is it from Glacier Ridge to Silver Lake?

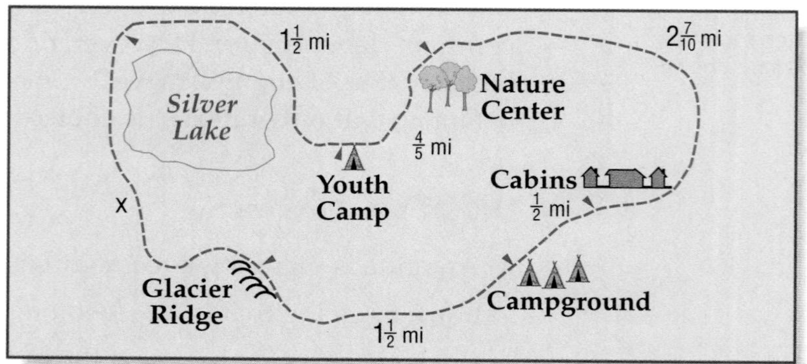

ALGEBRA Evaluate each expression for the given values.

28. $c - d$ if $c = -\frac{3}{4}$ and $d = -12\frac{7}{8}$
29. $r - s$ if $r = -\frac{5}{8}$ and $s = 2\frac{5}{6}$

30. **FOOTBALL** The top four finalists for the 2006 Heisman Trophy were Troy Smith, Darren McFadden, Brady Quinn, and Steve Slaton. Use the information at the right to determine what fraction of the first place votes Steve Slaton received.

Player	School	Fraction of Vote
Troy Smith	Ohio State	$\frac{9}{10}$
Darren McFadden	Arkansas	$\frac{1}{20}$
Brady Quinn	Notre Dame	$\frac{1}{50}$
Steve Slaton	West Virginia	

Source: Heisman Memorial Trophy

31. **PHOTOGRAPHY** Two 4-inch by 6-inch digital photographs are printed on an $8\frac{1}{2}$-inch by 11-inch sheet of photo paper. After the photos are printed, Aaron cuts them from the sheet. What is the area of the remaining photo paper?

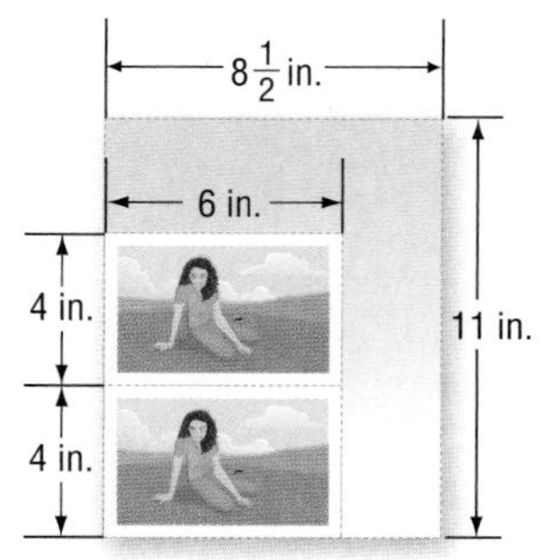

MEASUREMENT **Find the missing measure for each figure.**

32.

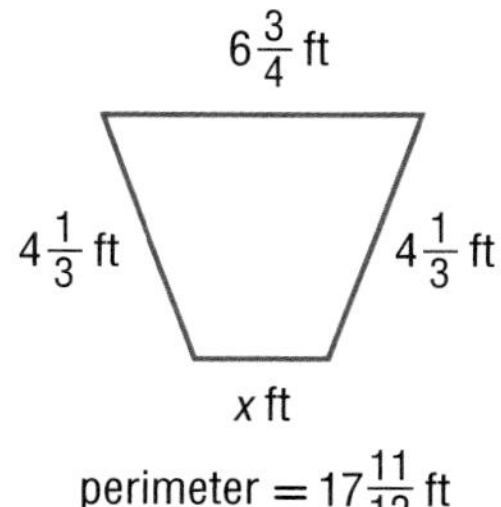

33.

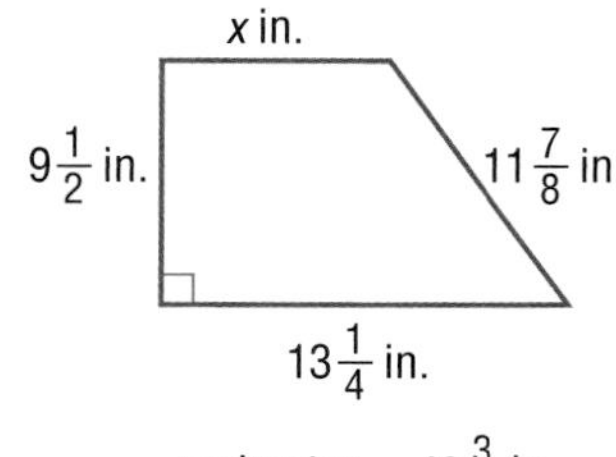

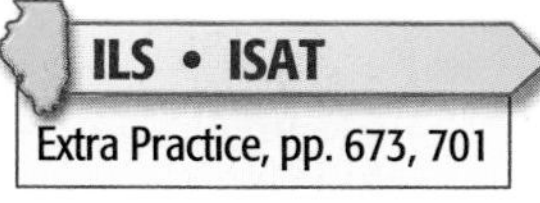

Extra Practice, pp. 673, 701

34. **FIND THE DATA** Refer to the Data File on pages 16–19. Choose some data and write a real-world problem in which you would add or subtract unlike fractions or mixed numbers.

H.O.T. Problems

35. **OPEN ENDED** Write a subtraction problem using unlike fractions with a least common denominator of 12. Find the difference.

36. **NUMBER SENSE** Without doing the computation, determine whether $\frac{4}{7} + \frac{5}{9}$ is greater than, less than, or equal to 1. Explain.

37. **CHALLENGE** Suppose a bucket is placed under two faucets. If one faucet is turned on alone, the bucket will be filled in 5 minutes. If the other faucet is turned on alone, the bucket will be filled in 3 minutes. Write the fraction of the bucket that will be filled in 1 minute if both faucets are turned on.

WRITING IN MATH **For Exercises 38–41, write an expression for each statement. Then find the answer.**

38. $\frac{3}{4}$ of $\frac{2}{3}$

39. $\frac{3}{4}$ more than $\frac{2}{3}$

40. $\frac{3}{4}$ less than $\frac{2}{3}$

41. $\frac{3}{4}$ divided into $\frac{2}{3}$

ISAT PRACTICE 6.B.3a, 6.C.3a

42. A recipe for snack mix contains $2\frac{1}{3}$ cups of mixed nuts, $3\frac{1}{2}$ cups of granola, and $\frac{3}{4}$ cup raisins. What is the total amount of snack mix?

    A $5\frac{2}{3}$ c

    B $5\frac{7}{12}$ c

    C $6\frac{2}{3}$ c

    D $6\frac{7}{12}$ c

43. Which of the following shows the next step using the least common denominator to simplify $\frac{3}{4} - \frac{2}{3}$?

    F $\left(\frac{3}{4} \times \frac{5}{5}\right) - \left(\frac{2}{3} \times \frac{6}{6}\right)$

    G $\left(\frac{3}{4} \times \frac{6}{6}\right) - \left(\frac{2}{3} \times \frac{5}{5}\right)$

    H $\left(\frac{3}{4} \times \frac{3}{3}\right) - \left(\frac{2}{3} \times \frac{4}{4}\right)$

    J $\left(\frac{3}{4} \times \frac{4}{4}\right) - \left(\frac{2}{3} \times \frac{3}{3}\right)$

Spiral Review

Add or subtract. Write in simplest form. (Lesson 2-5)

44. $-\frac{7}{11} + \frac{5}{11}$

45. $-\frac{7}{15} - \frac{4}{15}$

46. $5\frac{4}{5} - 7\frac{1}{5}$

47. **ALGEBRA** Find $a \div b$ if $a = 3\frac{1}{2}$ and $b = -\frac{7}{8}$. (Lesson 2-4)

POPULATION For Exercises 48 and 49, use the graphic at the right. (Lesson 1-7)

48. Write and solve a multiplication equation to determine the number of hours it would take for the population of the United States to increase by 1 million.

49. Write and solve a multiplication equation to determine the number of days it would take for the U.S. population to increase by 1 million.

Population Hourly Change

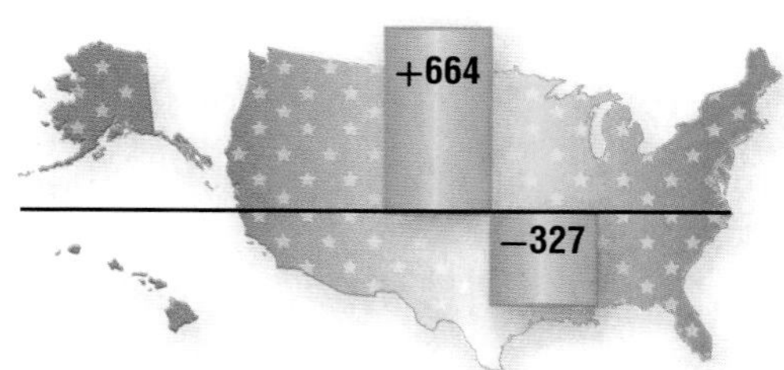

Source: U.S. Census Bureau

50. **INVESTMENTS** Mr. Coffey purchased stock for \$50 per share. The next day the value of the stock dropped \$12. On the second and third days, the value dropped another \$16, then rose \$25. What was the value of the stock at the end of the third day? (Lesson 1-4)

GET READY for the Next Lesson

PREREQUISITE SKILL Solve each equation. Check your solution. (Lessons 1-9 and 1-10)

51. $d - 13 = -44$

52. $-18t = 270$

53. $-34 = y + 22$

54. $-5 = \frac{a}{16}$

2-7 Solving Equations with Rational Numbers

MAIN IDEA

Solve equations involving rational numbers.

IL Learning Standards

8.A.3b Solve problems using linear expressions, **equations** and inequalities.
8.D.3a Solve problems using numeric, graphic or **symbolic representations of variables**, expressions, **equations** and inequalities. *Also addresses 6.B.3a, 6.C.3a, 8.C.3.*

IL Math Online

glencoe.com

- Extra Examples
- Personal Tutor
- Self-Check Quiz

GET READY for the Lesson

RACING In a recent year, NASCAR driver Matt Kenseth won a race in Tennessee with an average speed of 90 miles per hour. This was $\frac{2}{3}$ his average speed the previous week in Michigan. If s represents his average speed in Michigan, you can write the equation $90 = \frac{2}{3}s$.

1. Multiply each side of the equation by 3. Then divide each side by 2. Write the result.
2. Multiply each side of the equation by the multiplicative inverse of $\frac{2}{3}$. Write the result.
3. What was Kenseth's average speed in Michigan?
4. Which method of solving the equation seems most efficient?

You have used properties of equality to solve equations with integers. The same properties can also be used to solve equations with rational numbers.

EXAMPLES Solve by Using Addition or Subtraction

1 Solve $p - 7.36 = 2.84$.

$p - 7.36 = 2.84$	Write the equation.
$p - 7.36 + 7.36 = 2.84 + 7.36$	Add 7.36 to each side.
$p = 10.2$	Simplify.

2 Solve $\frac{1}{2} = t + \frac{3}{4}$.

$\frac{1}{2} = t + \frac{3}{4}$	Write the equation.
$\frac{1}{2} - \frac{3}{4} = t + \frac{3}{4} - \frac{3}{4}$	Subtract $\frac{3}{4}$ from each side.
$\frac{1}{2} - \frac{3}{4} = t$	Simplify.
$\frac{2}{4} - \frac{3}{4} = t$	Rename $\frac{1}{2}$.
$-\frac{1}{4} = t$	Simplify.

CHECK Your Progress

a. $t - 7.81 = 4.32$

b. $y + \frac{2}{5} = -\frac{1}{2}$

c. $1\frac{5}{6} = 2\frac{1}{3} + a$

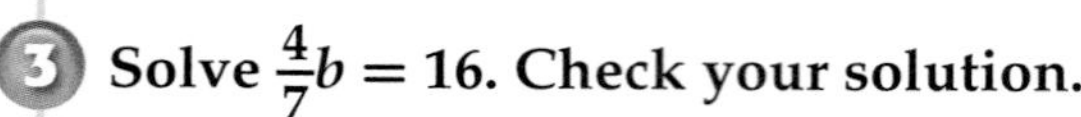

EXAMPLES Solve by Using Multiplication or Division

3 **Solve $\frac{4}{7}b = 16$. Check your solution.**

$\frac{4}{7}b = 16$	Write the equation.
$\frac{7}{4}\left(\frac{4}{7}b\right) = \frac{7}{4}(16)$	Multiply each side by $\frac{7}{4}$, the reciprocal of $\frac{4}{7}$.
$b = 28$	Simplify. Check the solution.

4 **Solve $58.4 = -7.3m$. Check your solution.**

$58.4 = -7.3m$	Write the equation.
$\frac{58.4}{-7.3} = \frac{-7.3m}{-7.3}$	Divide each side by -7.3.
$-8 = m$	Simplify. Check the solution.

CHECK Your Progress

d. $-12 = \frac{4}{5}r$ e. $-\frac{2}{3}n = -\frac{3}{5}$ f. $7.2v = -36$

Real-World Link
In the 2006 World Cup, Italy defeated France 6 to 4 in a shootout.
Source: CBS

Real-World EXAMPLE

5 **SOCCER During practice, a soccer player completed 18 goals, which were $\frac{9}{25}$ of his goal attempts. Write and solve an equation to determine his goal attempts at that practice.**

Words	$\frac{9}{25}$ of goal attempts is 18.
Variable	Let g represent goal attempts.
Equation	$\frac{9}{25}g = 18$

$\frac{9}{25}g = 18$	Write the equation.
$\frac{25}{9}\left(\frac{9}{25}g\right) = \frac{25}{9}(18)$	Multiply each side by $\frac{25}{9}$, the reciprocal of $\frac{9}{25}$.
$g \approx 50$	Simplify.

The soccer player had 50 goal attempts.

CHECK Your Progress

g. **COMMUNICATION** Larissa pays \$0.25 per minute for long distance calls on her cell phone. Her long distance charge last month was \$5. Write and solve an equation that could be used to determine the number of minutes she used to make long distance calls.

CHECK Your Understanding

Solve each equation. Check your solution.

Examples 1, 2 (p. 119)

1. $t + 0.25 = -4.12$
2. $v - 8.34 = -3.77$
3. $a - \frac{3}{4} = -\frac{3}{8}$
4. $c + \frac{5}{8} = -1\frac{9}{16}$

Examples 3, 4 (p. 120)

5. $-45 = \frac{5}{6}d$
6. $-\frac{7}{10}n = 18$
7. $-26.5 = -5.3w$
8. $2.6x = 22.75$

Example 5 (p. 120)

9. **SOLAR SYSTEM** The planet Mercury takes 0.24 Earth-year to make one revolution around the Sun. Write and solve a multiplication equation to determine the number of revolutions Mercury makes in 27.3 Earth-years.

Practice and Problem Solving

HOMEWORK HELP	
For Exercises	See Examples
10–15	1, 2
16–21	3, 4
22, 23	5

Solve each equation. Check your solution.

10. $q + 0.45 = 1.29$
11. $a - 1.72 = 5.81$
12. $-\frac{1}{2} = m - \frac{2}{3}$
13. $-\frac{5}{9} = f + \frac{1}{3}$
14. $g - (-1.5) = 2.35$
15. $-1.3 = n - (-6.12)$
16. $-\frac{4}{7}b = 16$
17. $-\frac{2}{9}p = -8$
18. $-1.92 = -0.32s$
19. $-8.4 = 1.2t$
20. $\frac{t}{3.2} = -4.5$
21. $\frac{h}{-5.75} = -2.2$

22. **CURRENCY** Thirteen European Union countries use the *euro* as their currency. One U.S. dollar is equal to $\frac{3}{4}$ euro. Javier wants to buy a shirt in Spain that costs 24 euros. Write and solve a multiplication equation to find the number of U.S. dollars the shirt would cost.

23. **RECREATION** Refer to the graphic. Write and solve a multiplication equation to determine how many times more visitors t visit the Golden Gate National Recreation Area than the Great Smokey Mountains National Park. Round your answer to the nearest tenth.

Solve each equation. Check your solution.

24. $3.5g = -\frac{7}{8}$
25. $-7.5r = -3\frac{1}{3}$
26. $4\frac{1}{6} = -3.\overline{3}c$
27. $-4.2 = \frac{x}{7}$

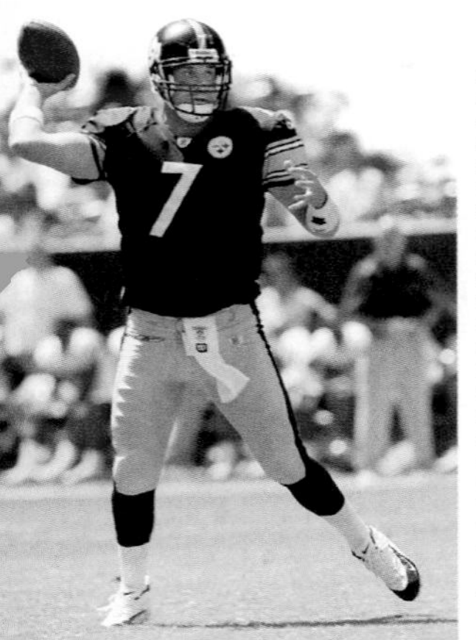

Real-World Link As of 2007, Ben Roethlisberger held the record as the youngest quarterback to win the Super Bowl.

Source: National Football League

28. **FOOTBALL** In his rookie season, Ben Roethlisberger completed 196 passes with a season pass-completion rate of 0.664. Write and solve an equation to determine the number of passes Ben Roethlisberger attempted during his rookie season.

29. **COMPUTERS** Stephan's CD recorder can write 5.3 megabytes of data per second. If he uses a CD with a 700 megabyte capacity, how long will it take to record the entire CD?

MEASUREMENT **Find the area of each rectangle.**

30. 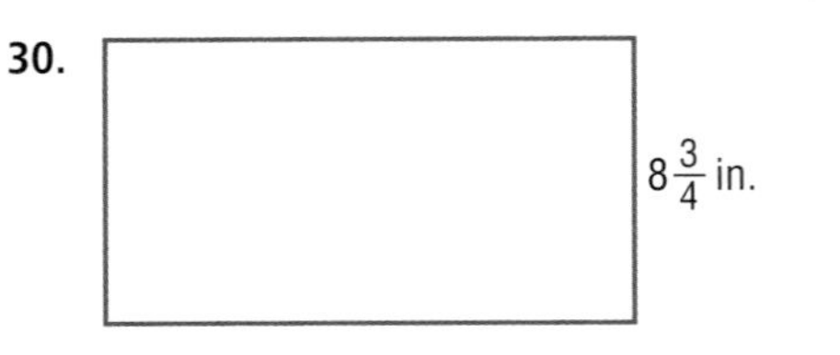

Perimeter $= 38\frac{1}{2}$ in.

31. 4.84 m

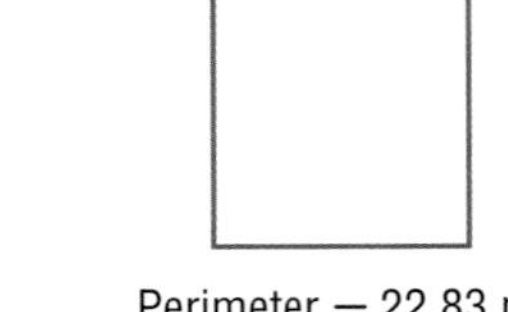

Perimeter = 22.83 m

32. **TRAVEL** Mr. Harris filled the gas tank of his car. Gasoline cost $2.95 per gallon, and Mr. Harris spent a total of $39.53. If his car can travel 32.5 miles per gallon of gasoline, how far can he travel with the gasoline he just purchased?

33. **MEASUREMENT** Andy has a board that he is going to use to make shelves for a craft fair. The board is 108 inches long. If each shelf is $9\frac{5}{8}$ inches long, write and solve an equation to find how many shelves he can make using this board.

ILS • ISAT
Extra Practice, pp. 673, 701

MEASUREMENT **Find the missing measure in each triangle.**

34. h

15 in.

$A = 45\text{ in}^2$

35. 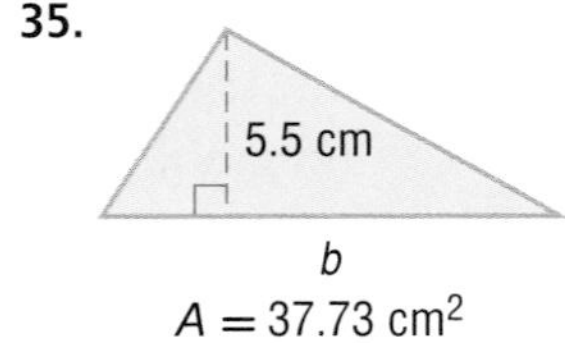

H.O.T. Problems

36. **OPEN ENDED** Write an equation with rational numbers that has a solution of $\frac{1}{4}$.

37. **Which One Doesn't Belong?** Identify the expression that does not have the same value as the other three. Explain your reasoning.

$-6\left(-\frac{1}{6}x\right)$	$\frac{3}{5}\left(\frac{5}{3}x\right)$	$-\frac{1}{4}\left(\frac{1}{4}x\right)$	$\frac{6}{7}\left(\frac{7}{6}x\right)$

38. **CHALLENGE** During a clearance sale, sweaters were marked at $\frac{1}{4}$ the original price. Patrice had a coupon for $\frac{1}{3}$ off the marked price of any sweater. If Patrice paid $24 for a sweater, what was the original price of the sweater?

39. **WRITING IN MATH** Explain how to solve $-\frac{2}{3}x = 14$ using properties of equality. Use the term *multiplicative inverse* in your explanation.

ISAT PRACTICE 8.A.3b, 8.D.3a

40. The area of the triangle is $13\frac{1}{2}$ square inches. What is the height of the triangle? Use the formula $A = \frac{1}{2}bh$.

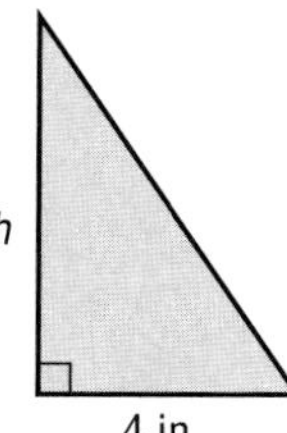

A $4\frac{1}{2}$ inches

B $3\frac{3}{8}$ inches

C $6\frac{3}{4}$ inches

D $5\frac{7}{8}$ inches

41. The difference of a number x and 2.3 is 1.8. Which equation shows this relationship?

F $x + 2.3 = 1.8$

G $x - 2.3 = 1.8$

H $\frac{x}{2.3} = 1.8$

J $x - 1.8 = 2.3$

42. If $a = 6$ and $b = 4$, then $5a - ab =$

A 6

B 24

C 30

D 54

Spiral Review

Add or subtract. Write in simplest form. (Lesson 2-6)

43. $\frac{1}{6} + \frac{1}{7}$

44. $\frac{7}{8} - \frac{1}{6}$

45. $-5\frac{1}{2} - 6\frac{4}{5}$

46. $2\frac{1}{2} + 5\frac{2}{3}$

47. GEOMETRY Find the perimeter of the triangle. (Lesson 2-5)

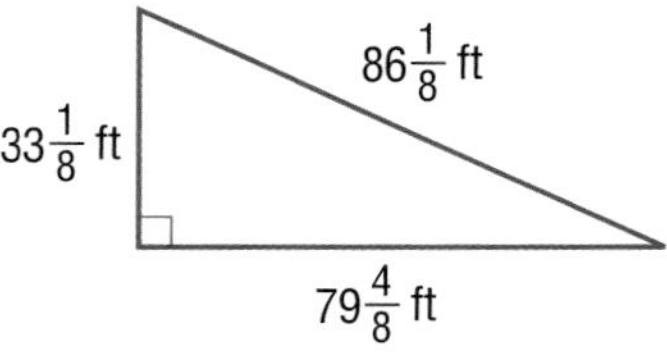

48. VEGETABLES Hudson purchased $3\frac{2}{5}$ pounds of vegetables that cost $3 per pound. What was the total cost of the vegetables? (Lesson 2-3)

49. ALGEBRA The sum of two integers is 24. One of the integers is −6. Write and solve an equation to find the other integer. (Lesson 1-9)

Add. (Lesson 1-4)

50. $-48 + 13 + (-16)$

51. $35 + 17 + (-25)$

52. $-50 + (-62) + 3$

53. $27 + (-30) + (-26)$

GET READY for the Next Lesson

54. PREREQUISITE SKILL Kishi wants to buy a digital music player that costs $250 with tax. So far, she has saved $120. If she saves $15 each week, in how many weeks will she be able to purchase the digital music player? Use the *four-step plan.* (Lesson 1-1)

2-8 Problem-Solving Investigation

MAIN IDEA: Look for a pattern to solve problems.

6.B.3a Solve practical computation problems involving whole numbers, integers and rational numbers. 6.C.3a Select computational procedures and solve problems with whole numbers, fractions, decimals, percents and proportions.

P.S.I. TEAM +

e-Mail: LOOK FOR A PATTERN

DREW: In phys ed class, we are participating in the Presidential Physical Fitness Challenge. My goal is to complete more than the required 56 curl-ups per minute. The first, second, third, and fourth weeks I completed 8, 12, 18, and 26, respectively.

YOUR MISSION: Look for a pattern to find how many weeks will pass until Drew can complete more than 56 curl-ups.

Understand	You know the number of curl-ups Drew completed for the first four weeks. You want to know how many weeks it will take him to complete more than 56 curl-ups.
Plan	Look for a pattern in the number he completes every week. Then continue the pattern to find when he will complete more than 56 curl-ups.
Solve	(see table below) Drew should complete more than 56 curl-ups during the seventh week.
Check	Check your pattern to make sure the answer is correct.

+1 +1 +1 +1 +1 +1

Week	1	2	3	4	5	6	7
Number of Curl-ups	8	12	18	26	36	48	62

+4 +6 +8 +10 +12 +14

Drew should complete more than 56 curl-ups during the seventh week.

Analyze The Strategy

1. Describe how to continue the pattern in the second row. Find the number of curl-ups Drew can do after 8 weeks.
2. **WRITING IN MATH** Write a problem that can be solved by finding a pattern. Describe a pattern.

Mixed Problem Solving

ILS • ISAT

Extra Practice, pp. 673, 701

For Exercises 3–5, look for a pattern. Then use the pattern to solve the problem.

3. **PHYSICAL SCIENCE** A ball was dropped from a height of 27 inches. After the first, second, and third bounces, the heights were 18 inches, 12 inches, and 8 inches, respectively. Describe the pattern in the heights. After which bounce will the height of the ball be less than 3 inches?

4. **GEOMETRY** Draw the next two figures in the pattern.

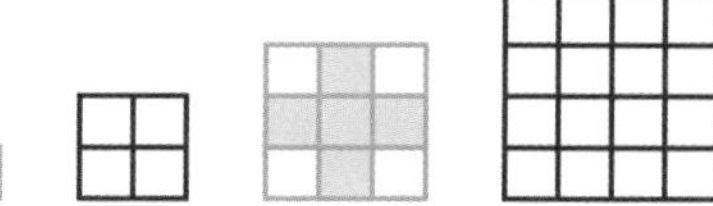

5. **MUSEUMS** A science museum offers discount passes for group admission. If this pattern continues, how many people would be admitted if a group buys 31 passes?

Passes	People Admitted
2	3
5	7
7	10
12	17

Use any strategy to solve Exercises 6–14. Some strategies are shown below.

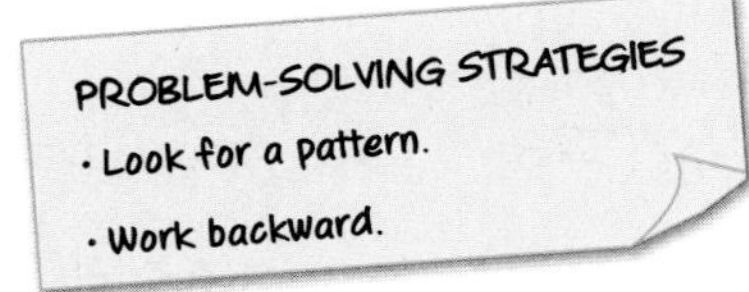

PROBLEM-SOLVING STRATEGIES
• Look for a pattern.
• Work backward.

6. **GEOMETRY** Find the perimeters of the next two figures in the pattern.The length of each side of a triangle is 4 meters.

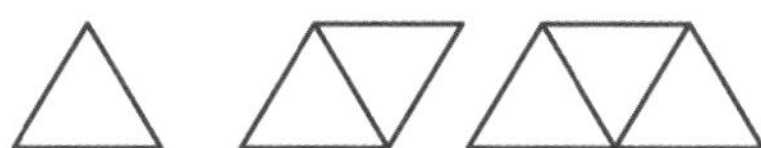

7. **MONEY** To attend the class trip, each student will have to pay $7.50 for transportation, and $5.00 for food. If there are 360 students in the class, how much money will need to be collected for the trip?

8. **TIME** Carlos and his friends are going out for dinner and a movie. The movie starts at 8:10 P.M., and they want to arrive 20 minutes before it starts. Dinner will take 1 hour 15 minutes, and the total travel time is 55 minutes. At what time should they plan to leave Carlos's house?

9. **WORK** Denzel can paint 12 square feet of a wall in 4 minutes. If there are 384 square feet of wall space to paint, after how much time will he have only 96 square feet left to paint?

10. **THEATER** A theater is designed with 12 seats in the first row, 17 seats in the second row, 22 seats in the third row, and so on. How many seats are in the ninth row?

11. **MUSIC THEORY** Musical notes have values that follow a pattern. The first three notes are: whole note, half note, quarter note. Name the next three notes in the pattern.

12. **INSECTS** The longest insect in the world is the stick insect whose length reaches 15 inches. The smallest insect is the fairy fly whose length is only 0.01 inch. How many times longer is the stick insect than the fairy fly?

13. **ANALYZE TABLES** In computer terminology, a bit is the smallest unit of data. A byte is equal to 8 bits. The table below gives the equivalences for several units of data.

Unit of Data	Equivalence
1 byte	8 bits
1 kilobyte (kB)	1,024 bytes
1 megabyte (MB)	1,024 kilobytes
1 gigabyte (GB)	1,024 megabytes

How many bits are in 1 MB?

14. **JOBS** Lola is mowing lawns as part of her summer job. She can mow $\frac{2}{3}$ lawn in $\frac{1}{2}$ hour. How many lawns can she mow in 6 hours?

2-9 Powers and Exponents

MAIN IDEA

Use powers and exponents in expressions.

IL Learning Standards

6.A.3 Represent fractions, decimals, percentages, **exponents** and scientific notation in equivalent forms.
8.D.3c Apply properties of powers, perfect squares and square roots.

New Vocabulary

power
base
exponent

IL Math Online

glencoe.com

- Extra Examples
- Personal Tutor
- Self-Check Quiz

GET READY for the Lesson

SAVINGS Hector decided to start saving money by putting a penny in a piggy bank, then doubling the amount he saves each week.

Week	0	1	2	3	4	5	6
Savings	1¢	2¢	4¢	8¢	16¢	32¢	64¢

1. How many 2s are multiplied to find his savings in Week 4? Week 5?
2. How much money will Hector save in Week 8?
3. When will he have enough to buy a pair of shoes for $80?

A product of repeated factors can be expressed as a **power**, that is, using an exponent and a base.

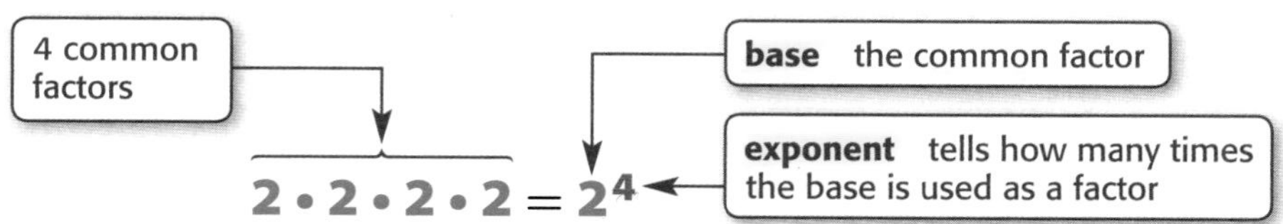

EXAMPLES Write Expressions Using Powers

Write each expression using exponents.

1 $\frac{1}{2} \cdot \frac{1}{2} \cdot \frac{1}{2} \cdot 3 \cdot 3 \cdot 3 \cdot 3$

$\frac{1}{2} \cdot \frac{1}{2} \cdot \frac{1}{2} \cdot 3 \cdot 3 \cdot 3 \cdot 3 = \left(\frac{1}{2} \cdot \frac{1}{2} \cdot \frac{1}{2}\right) \cdot (3 \cdot 3 \cdot 3 \cdot 3)$ Associative Property

$= \left(\frac{1}{2}\right)^3 \cdot 3^4$ Definition of exponents

2 $a \cdot b \cdot b \cdot a \cdot b$

$a \cdot b \cdot b \cdot a \cdot b = a \cdot a \cdot b \cdot b \cdot b$ Commutative Property

$= (a \cdot a) \cdot (b \cdot b \cdot b)$ Associative Property

$= a^2 \cdot b^3$ Definition of exponents

CHECK Your Progress

Write each expression using exponents.

a. $\frac{2}{3} \cdot 7 \cdot \frac{2}{3} \cdot \frac{2}{3} \cdot 7 \cdot \frac{2}{3}$ b. $m \cdot m \cdot n \cdot n \cdot n \cdot m$ c. $3 \cdot a \cdot b \cdot 2 \cdot 3 \cdot a$

Exponents can also be negative. Consider the pattern in the powers of 10.

Negative powers are the result of repeated division.

Exponential Form	Standard Form
10^3	1,000
10^2	100
10^1	10
10^0	1
10^{-1}	$\frac{1}{10}$
10^{-2}	$\frac{1}{100}$

$1{,}000 \div 10 = 100$

$100 \div 10 = 10$

$10 \div 10 = 1$

$1 \div 10 = \frac{1}{10}$ or $\frac{1}{10^1}$

$\frac{1}{10} \div 10 = \frac{1}{100}$ or $\frac{1}{10^2}$

Study Tip

Negative Exponents Remember that 10^{-2} equals $\frac{1}{10^2}$, not -100 or -20.

The pattern suggests the following definition for zero exponents and negative exponents.

Zero and Negative Exponents

Key Concept

Words Any nonzero number to the zero power is 1. Any nonzero number to the negative n power is the multiplicative inverse of its nth power.

Examples

Numbers	Algebra
$5^0 = 1$	$x^0 = 1, x \neq 0$
$7^{-3} = \frac{1}{7} \cdot \frac{1}{7} \cdot \frac{1}{7}$ or $\frac{1}{7^3}$	$x^{-n} = \frac{1}{x^n}, x \neq 0$

EXAMPLES Evaluate Powers

Study Tip

Calculator Keystrokes To use a calculator to evaluate $\left(\frac{2}{3}\right)^4$, follow these keystrokes (2 ÷ 3

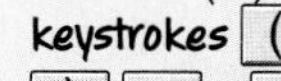 

) ^ 4 ENTER .1975308642.

To turn the decimal into a fraction, enter MATH 1 ENTER $\frac{16}{81}$.

3 **Evaluate $\left(\frac{2}{3}\right)^4$.**

$\left(\frac{2}{3}\right)^4 = \frac{2}{3} \cdot \frac{2}{3} \cdot \frac{2}{3} \cdot \frac{2}{3}$ Write the power as a product.

$= \frac{16}{81}$ Multiply.

4 **Evaluate 4^{-3}.**

$4^{-3} = \frac{1}{4^3}$ Write the power using a positive exponent.

$= \frac{1}{64}$ $4^3 = 4 \cdot 4 \cdot 4$ or 64

5 **ALGEBRA Evaluate $a^2 \cdot b^4$ if $a = 3$ and $b = 5$.**

$a^2 \cdot b^4 = 3^2 \cdot 5^4$ Replace a with 3 and b with 5.

$= (3 \cdot 3) \cdot (5 \cdot 5 \cdot 5 \cdot 5)$ Write the powers as products.

$= 9 \cdot 625$ or 5,625 Multiply.

CHECK Your Progress

Evaluate each expression.

d. $\left(\frac{1}{15}\right)^3$

e. 5^{-4}

f. $c^3 \cdot d^2$ if $c = -4$ and $d = 9$

CHECK Your Understanding

Examples 1, 2 (p. 126)

Write each expression using exponents.

1. $2 \cdot 2 \cdot 2 \cdot 3 \cdot 3 \cdot 3$
2. $r \cdot s \cdot r \cdot r \cdot s \cdot s \cdot r \cdot r$
3. $\frac{1}{2} \cdot p \cdot k \cdot \frac{1}{2} \cdot p \cdot p \cdot k$

Examples 3, 4 (p. 127)

Evaluate each expression.

4. 2^6
5. $\left(\frac{1}{7}\right)^3$
6. 6^{-3}
7. 3^{-5}

Example 5 (p. 127)

8. **EARTH SCIENCE** There are approximately 10^{21} kilograms of water on Earth. This includes oceans, rivers, lakes, ice caps, and water vapor in the atmosphere. Evaluate 10^{21}.

9. **ALGEBRA** Evaluate $x^2 \cdot y^4$ if $x = 2$ and $y = 10$.

Practice and Problem Solving

HOMEWORK HELP	
For Exercises	See Examples
10–15	1
16–23	2–3
24–27	4

Write each expression using exponents.

10. $8 \cdot 8 \cdot a$
11. $5 \cdot q \cdot 3 \cdot q \cdot q \cdot 3$
12. $m \cdot \frac{1}{4} \cdot p \cdot m \cdot \frac{1}{4}$
13. $d \cdot 2 \cdot 2 \cdot d \cdot k \cdot d \cdot k$
14. $2 \cdot 7 \cdot a \cdot 9 \cdot b \cdot a \cdot 7 \cdot b \cdot 9 \cdot b \cdot a$
15. $x \cdot \frac{1}{6} \cdot y \cdot y \cdot \frac{1}{6} \cdot 5 \cdot y \cdot 5 \cdot x \cdot \frac{1}{6} \cdot y \cdot y$

Evaluate each expression.

16. 2^3
17. $\left(\frac{1}{3}\right)^4$
18. $3^3 \cdot 4^2$
19. $3^2 \cdot \left(\frac{1}{5}\right)^2$
20. 5^{-4}
21. 9^{-3}
22. 7^{-2}
23. 4^{-3}

ALGEBRA Evaluate each expression.

24. $g^5 \cdot h$, if $g = 2$ and $h = 7$
25. $x^3 \cdot y^4$, if $x = 1$ and $y = 3$
26. $a^2 \cdot m^6$, if $a = \frac{1}{2}$ and $m = 2$
27. $k^4 \cdot d$, if $k = 3$ and $d = \frac{5}{6}$

PLANETS For Exercises 28–31, refer to the the information at the right. Write your answers in standard form.

28. How far is Earth from the Sun?
29. How far is Saturn from the Sun?
30. How far is Neptune from the Sun?
31. How much farther is Neptune than Saturn from the Sun?

Planetary Distances from the Sun	
Planet	**Distance (miles)**
Mercury	$3.6 \cdot 10^7$
Venus	$6.7 \cdot 10^7$
Earth	$9.3 \cdot 10^7$
Mars	$1.42 \cdot 10^8$
Jupiter	$4.84 \cdot 10^8$
Saturn	$8.87 \cdot 10^8$
Uranus	$1.8 \cdot 10^9$
Neptune	$2.8 \cdot 10^9$

Source: *World Almanac for Kids*

Evaluate each expression.

32. $5 \cdot 2^3 \cdot 7^2$
33. $2^2 \cdot 7 \cdot 10^4$
34. $2^3 \cdot 7^{-2}$
35. $5^{-2} \cdot 2^{-7}$
36. $4 \cdot 2^5 \cdot 5^{-3}$
37. $3^{-2} \cdot 5 \cdot 7^{-3}$
38. $\dfrac{3^3 \cdot 10^2}{3^2 \cdot 10^4}$
39. $\dfrac{4^2 \cdot 3^5 \cdot 2^4}{4^3 \cdot 3^5 \cdot 2^2}$
40. $(0.2)^3 \cdot \left(\frac{1}{2}\right)^4$

ILS • ISAT

Extra Practice, pp. 674, 701

H.O.T. Problems

41. **NUMBER SENSE** Without evaluating the powers, order 6^{-3}, 6^2, and 6^0 from least to greatest. Explain your reasoning.

42. **CHALLENGE** Complete the following pattern.

$$3^4 = 81, 3^3 = 27, 3^2 = 9, 3^1 = 3, 3^0 = \blacksquare, 3^{-1} = \blacksquare, 3^{-2} = \blacksquare, 3^{-3} = \blacksquare$$

43. **OPEN ENDED** Write an expression with a negative exponent with a value between 0 and $\frac{1}{2}$.

44. **CHALLENGE** Select several fractions between 0 and 1. Find the values of each fraction after it is raised to the −1 power. Explain the relationship between the −1 power and the original fraction.

45. **WRITING IN MATH** Explain the difference between the expressions $(-4)^2$ and 4^{-2}.

ISAT PRACTICE 6.A.3, 8.D.3c

46. To find the volume of a cube, multiply its length, its width, and its height.

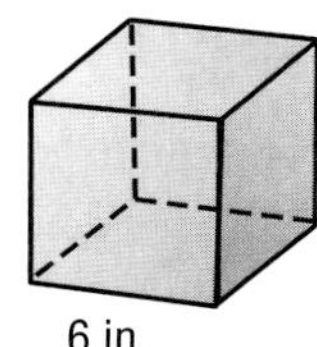

What is the volume of the cube expressed as a power?

A 6^2
B 6^3
C 6^4
D 6^6

47. Which is equivalent to $2^3 \cdot 3^4$?

F $3 \cdot 3 \cdot 4 \cdot 4 \cdot 4$
G $2 \cdot 2 \cdot 2 \cdot 3 \cdot 3 \cdot 3 \cdot 3$
H $2 \cdot 2 \cdot 2 \cdot 3 \cdot 3 \cdot 3$
J $6 \cdot 12$

48. $\left(\frac{3}{4}\right)^3 =$

A $\frac{9}{12}$
B $\frac{9}{16}$
C $\frac{9}{64}$
D $\frac{27}{64}$

Spiral Review

49. **BICYCLING** The table shows the relationship between the time Melody rides her bike and the distance that she rides. If she continues riding at the same rate, how far will she ride in 1 hour? Use the *look for a pattern* strategy. (Lesson 2-8)

Time (min)	Distance (mi)
5	1
15	3
25	5

50. **CLUBS** Shawnda has rectangular pictures that measure $3\frac{1}{2}$ inches high by 5 inches wide. Write and solve a multiplication equation to determine how many pictures can fit on a poster that is 42 inches high. (Lesson 2-7)

GET READY for the Next Lesson

PREREQUISITE SKILL **Write each number.**

51. two million
52. three hundred twenty
53. twenty-six hundred

2-10 Scientific Notation

MAIN IDEA

Express numbers in scientific notation.

IL Learning Standards

6.A.3 Represent fractions, decimals, percentages, exponents and **scientific notation in equivalent forms.**

New Vocabulary

scientific notation

IL Math Online

glencoe.com

- Extra Examples
- Personal Tutor
- Self-Check Quiz

MINI Lab

1. Copy and complete each table below.

Expression	Product
$8.7 \times 10^1 = 8.7 \times 10$	87
$8.7 \times 10^2 = 8.7 \times 100$	
$8.7 \times 10^3 = 8.7 \times$ ■	

Expression	Product
$8.7 \times 10^{-1} = 8.7 \times \frac{1}{10}$	0.87
$8.7 \times 10^{-2} = 8.7 \times \frac{1}{100}$	
$8.7 \times 10^{-3} = 8.7 \times$ ■	

2. If 8.7 is multiplied by a positive power of 10, what relationship exists between the decimal point's new position and the exponent?
3. When 8.7 is multiplied by a negative power of 10, how does the new position of the decimal point relate to the negative exponent?

Scientific notation is a compact way of writing numbers with absolute values that are very large or very small.

factor greater than or equal to 1, but less than 10 → 8.7×10^{-4} ← power of 10 written in exponential form

Scientific Notation to Standard Form — Key Concept

- Multiplying by a positive power of 10 moves the decimal point right.
- Multiplying by a negative power of 10 moves the decimal point left.
- The number of places the decimal point moves is the absolute value of the exponent.

EXAMPLES Express Numbers in Standard Form

1 Write 5.34×10^4 in standard form.

$5.34 \times 10^4 = 53{,}400.$ The decimal point moves 4 places right.

2 Write 3.27×10^{-3} in standard form.

$3.27 \times 10^{-3} = 0.00327$ The decimal point moves 3 places left.

CHECK Your Progress

Write each number in standard form.

a. 7.42×10^5 b. 6.1×10^{-2} c. 3.714×10^2

Standard Form to Scientific Notation

Key Concept

To write a number in scientific notation, follow these steps.

1. Move the decimal point to the right of the first nonzero digit.
2. Count the number of places you moved the decimal point.
3. Find the power of 10. If the absolute value of the original number was between 0 and 1, the exponent is negative. Otherwise, the exponent is positive.

EXAMPLES Write Numbers in Scientific Notation

3 **Write 3,725,000 in scientific notation.**

$3,725,000 = 3.725 \times 1,000,000$ The decimal point moves 6 places.

$= 3.725 \times 10^6$ Since $3,725,000 > 1$, the exponent is positive.

4 **Write 0.000316 in scientific notation.**

$0.000316 = 3.16 \times 0.0001$ The decimal point moves 4 places.

$= 3.16 \times 10^{-4}$ Since $0 < 0.000316 < 1$, the exponent is negative.

CHECK Your Progress

Write each number in scientific notation.

d. 14,140,000 **e.** 0.00876 **f.** 0.114

Real-World EXAMPLE

5 **TOURISM** **Refer to the table at the right. Order the countries according to the amount of money visitors spent in the United States from greatest to least.**

Dollars Spent by International Visitors in the U.S.	
Country	**Dollars Spent**
Canada	1.03×10^7
India	1.83×10^6
Mexico	7.15×10^6
United Kingdom	1.06×10^7

Source: Department of Commerce

Canada and United Kingdom ↓ ; Mexico and India ↓

Step 1 $\begin{Bmatrix} 1.06 \times 10^7 \\ 1.03 \times 10^7 \end{Bmatrix} > \begin{Bmatrix} 7.15 \times 10^6 \\ 1.83 \times 10^6 \end{Bmatrix}$

Step 2 $1.06 > 1.03$ $7.15 > 1.83$

United Kingdom, Canada, Mexico, India

Top U.S. Cities Visited by Overseas Travelers	
U.S. City	**Number of Arrivals**
Boston	7.21×10^5
Las Vegas	1.3×10^6
Los Angeles	2.2×10^6
Metro D.C. area	9.01×10^5
New York	4.0×10^6
Orlando	1.8×10^6
San Francisco	1.6×10^6

Real-World Link

The table lists seven of the top U.S. cities visited by overseas travelers in a recent year.

Source: Infoplease

CHECK Your Progress

g. **TRAVEL** Refer to the information at the left. Order the cities according to the number of arrivals from least to greatest.

CHECK Your Understanding

Examples 1, 2 (p. 130)

Write each number in standard form.

1. 7.32×10^4
2. 9.931×10^5
3. 4.55×10^{-1}
4. 6.02×10^{-4}

Examples 3, 4 (p. 131)

Write each number in scientific notation.

5. 277,000
6. 8,785,000,000
7. 0.00004955
8. 0.524

Example 5 (p. 131)

9. **MUSIC** The table at the right lists the total value of music shipments for four years. List the years from least to greatest dollar amount.

Year	Music Shipments ($)
2003	1.19×10^{10}
2004	1.23×10^{10}
2005	1.22×10^{10}
2006	1.15×10^{10}

Source: Recording Industry Association of America

Practice and Problem Solving

HOMEWORK HELP

For Exercises	See Examples
10–13	1
14–17	2
18–21	3
22–25	4
26–29	5

Write each number in standard form.

10. 2.08×10^2
11. 3.16×10^3
12. 7.113×10^7
13. 4.265×10^6
14. 7.8×10^{-3}
15. 1.1×10^{-4}
16. 8.73×10^{-4}
17. 2.52×10^{-5}

Write each number in scientific notation.

18. 6,700
19. 43,000
20. 52,300,000
21. 147,000,000
22. 0.037
23. 0.0072
24. 0.00000707
25. 0.0000901

26. **CHEMISTRY** The table shows the mass in grams of one atom of each of several elements. List the elements in order from the least mass to greatest mass per atom.

Element	Mass per Atom
Carbon	1.995×10^{-23} g
Gold	3.272×10^{-22} g
Hydrogen	1.674×10^{-24} g
Oxygen	2.658×10^{-23} g
Silver	1.792×10^{-22} g

Source: *Chemistry: Concepts and Applications*

27. **GEOGRAPHY** The areas of the world's oceans are listed in the table. Order the oceans according to their area from least to greatest.

World's Oceans	
Ocean	**Area (mi^2)**
Atlantic	2.96×10^7
Arctic	5.43×10^6
Indian	2.65×10^7
Pacific	6.0×10^7
Southern	7.85×10^6

Source: *NY TImes Almanac*

Arrange these numbers in increasing order.

28. 216,000,000, 2.2×10^3, 3.1×10^7, 310,000
29. -4.56×10^{-3}, 4.56×10^2, -4.56×10^2, 4.56×10^{-2}

ASTRONOMY For Exercises 30 and 31, use the information below.

A light year is used to measure distances in the solar system. A light year is 5,865,696,000,000 miles.

30. Write the number of miles in a light year in scientific notation.

31. The star Sirius is about 8.6 light years away from Earth. Use scientific notation to write the distance in miles.

32. **CHEMISTRY** The diameter of a carbon atom is about 3.0×10^{-10} meter. Write this number using standard form.

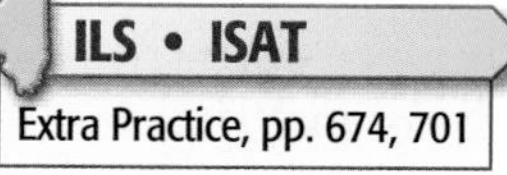

33. **DINOSAURS** The giganotosaurus weighed about 1.6×10^4 pounds. The microceratops weighed about 1.1×10^1. How many times heavier was the giganotosaurus than the microceratops? Write your answer in standard form. Round to the nearest tenth.

H.O.T. Problems

34. **NUMBER SENSE** Determine whether 1.2×10^5 or 1.2×10^6 is closer to one million. Explain.

35. **CHALLENGE** Compute and express each value in scientific notation.

a. $\frac{(130{,}000)(0.0057)}{0.0004}$

b. $\frac{(90{,}000)(0.0016)}{(200{,}000)(30{,}000)(0.00012)}$

36. **WRITING IN MATH** Determine whether a decimal times a power of 10 is *sometimes*, *always*, or *never* expressed in scientific notation. Explain.

ISAT PRACTICE 6.A.3

37. Which shows 0.0000035 in scientific notation?

A 3.5×10^6

B 3.5×10^5

C 3.5×10^{-5}

D 3.5×10^{-6}

38. The average width of a strand of a spider web is 7.0×10^{-6} meter. Which expression represents this number in standard form?

F 7,000,000 m

G 700,000 m

H 0.00007 m

J 0.000007 m

Spiral Review

39. **ALGEBRA** Evaluate $a^5 \cdot b^2$ if $a = 2$ and $b = 3$. (Lesson 2-9)

ALGEBRA Solve each equation. Check your solution. (Lesson 2-7)

40. $t + 3\frac{1}{3} = 2\frac{1}{2}$

41. $-\frac{2}{3}y = 14$

42. $\frac{p}{1.3} = 2.4$

43. $-1\frac{3}{4} = n - 4\frac{1}{6}$

44. **LANGUAGE** There are about one billion people who speak Mandarin. This is 492 million more than those who speak English. How many speak English? (Lesson 1-1)

CHAPTER 2 Study Guide and Review

IL Math Online glencoe.com
- STUDY TO GO
- Vocabulary Review

GET READY to Study

Be sure the following Big Ideas are noted in your Foldable.

BIG Ideas

Rational Numbers (Lesson 2-1)

- A rational number is any number that can be expressed in the form $\frac{a}{b}$, where a and b are integers and $b \neq 0$.

Multiplying and Dividing Fractions
(Lessons 2-3 and 2-4)

- To multiply fractions, multiply the numerators and multiply the denominators.
- To divide by a fraction, multiply by its multiplicative inverse.

Adding and Subtracting Fractions
(Lessons 2-5 and 2-6)

- To add or subtract fractions, rename the fractions using the least common denominator. Then add or subtract and simplify, if necessary.

Powers and Scientific Notation
(Lessons 2-9 and 2-10)

- A number is expressed in scientific notation when it is written as the product of a factor and a power of 10. The factor must be greater than or equal to 1 and less than 10.

Key Vocabulary

bar notation (p. 85)
base (p. 126)
dimensional analysis (p. 98)
exponent (p. 126)
like fraction (p. 108)
multiplicative inverses (p. 102)
power (p. 126)
rational number (p. 84)
reciprocals (p. 102)
repeating decimal (p. 85)
scientific notation (p. 130)
terminating decimal (p. 85)
unlike fraction (p. 114)

Vocabulary Check

State whether each sentence is *true* or *false*. If *false*, replace the underlined word or number to make a true sentence.

1. Like fractions have the same denominator.
2. The number that is expressed using an exponent is a rational number.
3. Dimensional analysis is the process of including units of measurement in computation.
4. The number $0.\overline{3}$ is a repeating decimal.
5. Numbers that can be written as fractions are called reciprocals.
6. The number 4.05×10^8 is written in bar notation.
7. The number 2.75 is a terminating decimal.
8. The base tells how many times a number is used as a factor.
9. Two numbers with a product of 1 are multiplicative inverses of each other.
10. The number 5^4 is a power.

Lesson-by-Lesson Review

Rational Numbers (pp. 84–89)

6.A.3

Write each fraction or mixed number as a decimal.

11. $1\frac{1}{3}$
12. $-\frac{5}{8}$
13. $-2\frac{3}{10}$
14. $\frac{5}{9}$

Write each decimal as a fraction or mixed number in simplest form.

15. 0.3
16. −7.14
17. $4.\overline{3}$
18. $-5.\overline{7}$
19. **HISTORY** Thirteen of the 50 states in the United States were the original colonies. Write this fraction as a decimal.
20. **BIOLOGY** The average rate of human hair growth is about 0.4 inch per month. Write this decimal as a fraction in simplest form.

Example 1 **Write $\frac{3}{5}$ as a decimal.**

$\frac{3}{5}$ means $3 \div 5$.

$$\begin{array}{r} 0.6 \\ 5\overline{)3.0} \\ -3\,0 \\ \hline 0 \end{array}$$

The fraction $\frac{3}{5}$ can be written as 0.6.

Example 2 **Write 0.28 as a fraction in simplest form.**

$0.28 = \frac{28}{100}$ — 0.28 is 28 hundredths.

$= \frac{7}{25}$ — Simplify.

The decimal 0.28 can be written as $\frac{7}{25}$.

2-2

Comparing and Ordering Rational Numbers (pp. 91–95)

6.A.3

Replace each ● with <, >, or = to make a true sentence.

21. $\frac{2}{3}$ ● $\frac{8}{9}$
22. $-0.\overline{24}$ ● $-\frac{8}{33}$
23. $-\frac{1}{2}$ ● $-\frac{55}{110}$
24. $\frac{5}{6}$ ● $\frac{3}{4}$
25. Order $-\frac{1}{2}$, 0.75, $-\frac{3}{4}$, 0 from least to greatest.
26. **BOOKS** The heights of Olivia's books are $4\frac{9}{16}$ inches, $6\frac{5}{8}$ inches, $\frac{15}{2}$ inches, and $\frac{19}{4}$ inches. What would be the order of the books if Olivia places them on a shelf in order from least to greatest height?

Example 3 **Replace ● with <, >, or = to make $\frac{2}{5}$ ● 0.34 a true sentence.**

$\frac{2}{5} = 0.4$

Since $0.4 > 0.34$, $\frac{2}{5} > 0.34$.

Example 4 **Replace ● with <, >, or = to make $-\frac{3}{4}$ ● $-\frac{7}{12}$ a true sentence.**

For $-\frac{3}{4}$ and $-\frac{7}{12}$, the least common denominator is 12.

$-\frac{3}{4} = -\frac{3 \cdot 3}{4 \cdot 3}$ or $-\frac{9}{12}$

Since $-9 < -7$, $-\frac{9}{12} < -\frac{7}{12}$.

So, $-\frac{3}{4} < -\frac{7}{12}$.

2-3 Multiplying Positive and Negative Fractions (pp. 96–101)

6.B.3a, 6.C.3a

Multiply. Write in simplest form.

27. $\frac{3}{5} \cdot 1\frac{2}{3}$

28. $-\frac{2}{3} \cdot \left(-\frac{2}{3}\right)$

29. $\frac{5}{6} \cdot \frac{3}{5}$

30. $\frac{1}{2} \cdot \frac{10}{11}$

31. **COOKING** Crystal is making $1\frac{1}{2}$ times a recipe. The original recipe calls for $3\frac{1}{2}$ cups of milk. How many cups of milk does she need?

Example 5 Find $\frac{2}{3} \cdot \frac{5}{7}$. Write in simplest form.

$\frac{2}{3} \cdot \frac{5}{7} = \frac{2 \cdot 5}{3 \cdot 7}$ ← Multiply the numerators. ← Multiply the denominators.

$= \frac{10}{21}$ Simplify.

2-4 Dividing Positive and Negative Fractions (pp. 102–107)

6.B.3a, 6.C.3a

Divide. Write in simplest form.

32. $\frac{7}{9} \div \frac{1}{3}$

33. $\frac{7}{12} \div \left(-\frac{2}{3}\right)$

34. $-4\frac{2}{5} \div (-2)$

35. $6\frac{1}{6} \div \left(-1\frac{2}{3}\right)$

36. **DESIGN** Marcus wishes to space letters equally across the top of a page. If each letter is 1.7 inches wide, and the paper is $8\frac{1}{2}$ inches wide, what is the maximum number of letters that he can fit across the top of the page?

Example 6 Find $-\frac{5}{6} \div \frac{3}{5}$. Write in simplest form.

$-\frac{5}{6} \div \frac{3}{5} = -\frac{5}{6} \cdot \frac{5}{3}$ Multiply by the multiplicative inverse.

$= -\frac{25}{18}$ Simplify.

$= -1\frac{7}{18}$ Write as a mixed number.

2-5 Adding and Subtracting Like Fractions (pp. 108–112)

6.B.3a, 6.C.3a

Add or subtract. Write in simplest form.

37. $\frac{5}{11} + \frac{6}{11}$

38. $\frac{1}{28} + \left(-\frac{3}{28}\right)$

39. $\frac{1}{8} - \frac{7}{8}$

40. $12\frac{4}{5} - 5\frac{3}{5}$

41. **JOBS** Jeremy worked $5\frac{3}{20}$ hours on Monday. On Tuesday, he worked $2\frac{13}{20}$ hours. How much longer did Jeremy work on Monday than on Tuesday?

Example 7 Find $\frac{1}{5} - \frac{3}{5}$. Write in simplest form.

$\frac{1}{5} - \frac{3}{5} = \frac{1-3}{5}$ ← Subtract the numerators. ← The denominators are the same.

$= \frac{-2}{5}$ Simplify.

$= -\frac{2}{5}$

Mixed Problem Solving
For mixed problem-solving practice, see page 701.

2-6 Adding and Subtracting Unlike Fractions (pp. 114–118)

6.B.3a, 6.C.3a

Add or subtract. Write in simplest form.

42. $-\frac{2}{3} + \frac{3}{5}$
43. $\frac{5}{12} - \left(-\frac{7}{15}\right)$
44. $-4\frac{1}{2} - 6\frac{2}{3}$
45. $5 - 1\frac{2}{5}$
46. $7\frac{3}{4} + 3\frac{4}{5}$
47. $5\frac{3}{5} - 12\frac{1}{2}$
48. **PIZZA** A pizza has 3 toppings with no toppings overlapping. Pepperoni tops $\frac{1}{3}$ of the pizza and mushrooms top $\frac{2}{5}$. The rest is topped with sausage. What fraction is topped with sausage?

Example 8 Find $\frac{3}{4} + \frac{1}{3}$. Write in simplest form.

$\frac{3}{4} + \frac{1}{3} = \frac{9}{12} + \frac{4}{12}$ Rename the fractions.

$= \frac{9+4}{12}$ Add the numerators.

$= \frac{13}{12}$ Simplify.

$= 1\frac{1}{12}$

2-7 Solving Equations with Rational Numbers (pp. 119–123)

8.A.3b, 8.D.3a

Solve each equation.

49. $d - (-0.8) = 4$
50. $\frac{x}{4} = -2.2$
51. $\frac{3}{4}n = \frac{7}{8}$
52. $-7.2 = \frac{r}{1.6}$
53. **AGE** Trevor is $\frac{3}{8}$ of Maria's age. Trevor is 15. Write and solve a multiplication equation to find Maria's age.

Example 9 Solve $t + \frac{1}{3} = \frac{5}{6}$.

$t + \frac{1}{3} = \frac{5}{6}$ Write the equation.

$t + \frac{1}{3} - \frac{1}{3} = \frac{5}{6} - \frac{1}{3}$ Subtract $\frac{1}{3}$ from each side.

$t = \frac{1}{2}$ Simplify.

2-8 PSI: Look for a Pattern (pp. 124–125)

6.B.3a, 6.C.3a

Solve. Use the *look for a pattern* strategy.

54. **ALGEBRA** Find the next two numbers in the sequence 3, 6, 9, 12, … .
55. **RUNNING** Marcy can run one lap in 65 seconds. Each additional lap takes her 2 seconds longer to run than the previous lap. How many minutes will it take her to run three miles? (1 mile = 4 laps)
56. **GEOMETRY** What is the total number of rectangles, of any size, in the figure below?

Example 10 Raul's phone plan charges a flat monthly rate of \$4.95 and \$0.06 per minute. If Raul spent a total of \$7.35 last month, how many minutes did he use?

Look for a pattern.

Minutes	Charges	Total
0	4.95 + 0(0.06)	\$4.95
10	4.95 + 10(0.06)	\$5.55
20	4.95 + 20(0.06)	\$6.15
30	4.95 + 30(0.06)	\$6.75
40	4.95 + 40(0.06)	\$7.35

So, Raul used 40 minutes last month.

2-9 Powers and Exponents (pp. 126–129)

6.A.3, 8.D.3c

Write each expression using exponents.

57. $3 \cdot 3 \cdot 3 \cdot 3 \cdot 3$
58. $2 \cdot 2 \cdot 5 \cdot 5 \cdot 5$
59. $x \cdot x \cdot x \cdot x \cdot y$
60. $4 \cdot 4 \cdot 9 \cdot 9$

Evaluate each expression.

61. 5^4
62. $\left(\frac{1}{3}\right)^2 \cdot \left(\frac{2}{5}\right)^2$
63. 5^{-3}
64. $\left(\frac{3}{4}\right)^2 \cdot \left(\frac{1}{2}\right)^3$
65. **PHONE TREES** To close school for the day, the principal calls six parents, who in turn call six more parents. If each of those parents calls six more parents, how many calls will be made by the parents in this last group?

Example 11

Write $3 \cdot 3 \cdot 3 \cdot 7 \cdot 7$ using exponents.

$3 \cdot 3 \cdot 3 \cdot 7 \cdot 7 = 3^3 \cdot 7^2$

Example 12

Evaluate 7^3.

$7^3 = 7 \cdot 7 \cdot 7$ or 343

Example 13

Evaluate 3^{-6}.

$3^{-6} = \frac{1}{3^6}$ Write the power using a positive exponent

$= \frac{1}{729}$ $3^6 = 3 \cdot 3 \cdot 3 \cdot 3 \cdot 3 \cdot 3$ or 729

2-10 Scientific Notation (pp. 130–133)

6.A.3

Write each number in standard form.

66. 3.2×10^{-3}
67. 6.71×10^4
68. 1.72×10^5
69. 1.5×10^{-2}
70. **ANIMALS** The smallest mammal is the Kitti's hog-nosed bat weighing about 4.375×10^{-3} pound. Write this weight in standard form.

Write each number in scientific notation.

71. 0.000064
72. 0.000351
73. 87,500,000
74. 7,410,000
75. **SPACE** The distance from Earth to the Sun is approximately 93 million miles. Write this distance in standard form and in scientific notation.

Example 14

Write 3.21×10^{-6} in standard form.

$3.21 \times 10^{-6} = 0.00000321$ Move the decimal point 6 places to the left.

Example 15

Write 7.25×10^5 in standard form.

$7.25 \times 10^5 = 725000$ Move the decimal point 5 places to the right.

Example 16

Write 0.004 in scientific notation.

$0.004 = 4 \times 0.001$ The decimal point moves 3 places.

$= 4 \times 10^{-3}$ Since $0 < 0.004 < 1$, the exponent is negative.

Chapter 2 Practice Test

IL Math Online glencoe.com
• Chapter Test

Write each fraction or mixed number as a decimal.

1. $4\frac{5}{6}$

2. $-\frac{7}{20}$

3. **FROGS** The Gold Frog grows to only 0.375 inch. Write this length as a fraction in simplest form.

4. **ENERGY** The United States produces about $\frac{9}{50}$ of the world's energy and consumes about $\frac{6}{25}$ of the world's energy. Does the United States produce more energy than it uses or vice versa? Explain your reasoning.

5. **MULTIPLE CHOICE** A recipe for two dozen cookies calls for $1\frac{3}{4}$ cups of flour. In order to make eight dozen cookies, how many cups of flour should be used?

   A $16\frac{1}{2}$

   B 14

   C $9\frac{1}{4}$

   D 7

Add, subtract, multiply, or divide. Write in simplest form.

6. $-5\frac{1}{4} \cdot \left(-2\frac{1}{3}\right)$

7. $-6 \div \frac{1}{8}$

8. $-\frac{3}{8} + \frac{4}{9}$

9. $\left(-1\frac{7}{8}\right) - \left(-3\frac{1}{4}\right)$

10. **ANALYZE TABLES** The table shows the time of the back and forth swing of a pendulum and its length. How long is a pendulum with a swing of 5 seconds?

Time of Swing	Length of Pendulum
1 second	1 unit
2 seconds	4 units
3 seconds	9 units
4 seconds	16 units

11. **BAKING** Madison needs $2\frac{2}{3}$ cups of flour, but she can only find her $\frac{1}{3}$ measuring cup. How many times will she need to fill the measuring cup with flour to get the amount she needs?

Solve each equation. Check your solution.

12. $x - \frac{5}{6} = \frac{1}{3}$

13. $16 = \frac{2}{3}y$

14. Write the expression $4 \cdot 4 \cdot a \cdot a \cdot b \cdot 3 \cdot 4 \cdot 3 \cdot a$ using exponents.

Evaluate each expression.

15. 6^{-4}

16. $k^3 \cdot g^{-2}$ if $k = 4$ and $g = 8$

17. **EXTREME SPORTS** In 2003, San Antonio, Texas, hosted the first ever summer Global X Games while Whistler, British Columbia, in Canada hosted the winter games. Team USA won the gold medal with a total of $7^2 \cdot 2^2$ points. Evaluate the number of points won by Team USA.

18. Write 8.83×10^{-7} in standard form.

19. Write 25,000 in scientific notation.

20. **MULTIPLE CHOICE** The following table gives the approximate diameter, in miles, for several planets.

Planet	Diameter
Mercury	3.032×10^3
Saturn	7.4975×10^4
Neptune	3.0603×10^4
Earth	7.926×10^3

Which list below correctly orders these planets from least to greatest diameters?

F Mercury, Neptune, Saturn, Earth
G Mercury, Earth, Neptune, Saturn
H Mercury, Neptune, Earth, Saturn
J Neptune, Mercury, Earth, Saturn

ISAT Practice

Cumulative, Chapters 1–2

IL Math Online glencoe.com
• Test Practice

PART 1 Multiple Choice

Read each question. Then fill in the correct answer on the answer sheet provided by your teacher or on a sheet of paper.

1. A carpenter estimates that it will take one person 54 hours to complete a job. He plans to have three people work on the job for two days. How many hours each day will the workers need to work to complete the job?

   A 8 hours C 12 hours
   B 9 hours D 18 hours

2. The weight of a paper clip is 9.0×10^{-4} kilograms. Which of the following represents this weight in standard notation?

   F 0.00000009
   G 0.000009
   H 0.00009
   J 0.0009

3. After reading the salon prices listed below, Alex chose Special No. 1. She wanted to find her total savings. Her first step was to find the sum of \$19 plus 2 times \$4. What should Alex do next to find her total savings?

Hair Salon Prices		
Trim	\$12	**Special #1** Haircut, style, and shampoo \$25
Haircut	\$19	
Shampoo	\$4	
Style	\$4	**Special #2** Haircut, style, shampoo, and highlights \$75
Highlights	\$55	
Perm	\$50	

   A Subtract \$75 from the sum.
   B Divide the sum by 3.
   C Subtract \$25 from the sum.
   D Add \$4 to the sum.

4. Which number equals $(3)^{-3}$?

   F $-\frac{1}{27}$
   G -9
   H $\frac{1}{27}$
   J 9

5. Which fraction is equivalent to $\frac{3}{5} + \frac{3}{10}$?

   A $\frac{6}{15}$ C $\frac{9}{50}$
   B $\frac{9}{10}$ D $\frac{9}{15}$

6. A jar of mixed nuts contains $2\frac{1}{2}$ pounds of peanuts, $1\frac{1}{3}$ pounds of cashews, and $1\frac{5}{6}$ pounds of walnuts. What is the total weight of the contents of the jar?

   F $4\frac{1}{6}$ pounds
   G $4\frac{1}{2}$ pounds
   H $5\frac{2}{3}$ pounds
   J $6\frac{1}{3}$ pounds

TEST-TAKING TIP

Question 6 If the test question would take an excessive amount of time to work, try estimating the answer. Then look for the appropriate answer choice.

7. The distance from Earth to the Sun is 92,900,000 miles. Which expression represents this number in scientific notation?

   A 92.9×10^6 C 9.29×10^6
   B 9.29×10^7 D 929×10^5

Preparing for ISAT

For test-taking strategies and practice, see pages 712–729.

8. The table shows the atomic weights of certain elements.

Element	Atomic Weight (amu)
Argon	39.948
Zinc	65.39
Lead	207.2
Oxygen	15.9994
Titanium	47.867
Mercury	200.59

Which element has an atomic weight that is exactly 160.642 less than the atomic weight of Mercury?

F argon
G titanium
H oxygen
J zinc

9. A pizzeria sells large pizzas for \$11.50, medium pizzas for \$8.75, and small pizzas for \$6.50. Suppose a scout group orders 3 large pizzas, 2 medium pizzas, and 2 small pizzas. Which equation can be used to find the total cost of the pizzas?

A $t = (3 + 2 + 2)(11.50 + 8.75 + 6.50)$

B $t = (3)(11.50) + 2(8.75) + 2(6.50)$

C $t = (3 + 2 + 2)\left(\frac{11.50 + 8.75 + 6.50}{3}\right)$

D $t = (3)(11.50) + 8.75 + 2(6.50)$

10. What does y^3 equal when $y = -4$?

F -64

G -12

H $\frac{1}{64}$

J $\frac{1}{12}$

PART 2 Short Response/Grid In

Record your answers on the answer sheet provided by your teacher or on a sheet of paper.

11. The table shows the number of shoppers in a store on each of the first four days after its grand opening. If this pattern continues, about how many shoppers should the store receive on day 6?

Day	1	2	3	4
Shoppers	550	610	670	730

12. Cindy has 55 minutes before she has to leave to go to school. She spends 15 minutes reading the newspaper. Then she spends 4 minutes brushing her teeth and another 15 minutes watching television. Write a numerical expression that can be used to find the amount of time she has left before she has to leave.

PART 3 Extended Response

Record your answers on the answer sheet provided by your teacher or on a sheet of paper. Show your work.

13. The container for a child's set of blocks is 9 inches by 9 inches by 9 inches. The blocks measure 3 inches by 3 inches by 3 inches.

a. Describe how to determine the number of blocks needed to fill the container.

b. Write and simplify an expression to solve the problem.

c. How many blocks will it take?

NEED EXTRA HELP?													
If You Missed Question...	1	2	3	4	5	6	7	8	9	10	11	12	13
Go to Lesson...	2-3	2-10	1-1	2-9	2-6	2-6	2-10	2-7	1-7	2-9	1-1	1-7	2-9
IL Learning Standards	6.B.3a	6.A.3	6.B.3a	6.A.3	6.B.3a	6.B.3a	6.A.3	8.A.3b	8.A.3a	6.A.3	6.B.3a	8.A.3a	6.A.3

Real Numbers and the Pythagorean Theorem

Illinois Learning Standards

8.D.3c Apply properties of powers, perfect squares and square roots.
9.D.3 Compute distances, lengths and measures of angles using proportions, the Pythagorean theorem and its converse.

Key Vocabulary

ordered pair (p. 173)
Pythagorean Theorem (p. 162)
real number (p. 155)
square root (p. 144)

Real-World Link

Buildings The Transamerica Pyramid in San Francisco, California, is 853 feet high. To determine the approximate distance you can see from the top of the tower, multiply 1.23 by $\sqrt{853}$.

Real Numbers and the Pythagorean Theorem Make this Foldable to help you organize your notes. Begin with two sheets of $8\frac{1}{2}'' \times 11''$ notebook paper.

1. **Fold** one sheet in half from top to bottom. Cut along the fold from edges to margin.

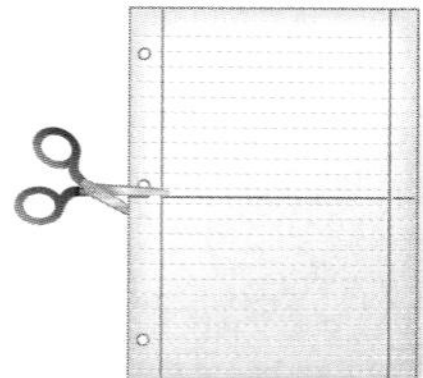

2. **Fold** the other sheet in half. Cut along the fold between the margins.

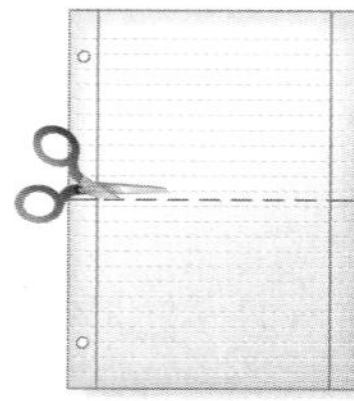

3. **Insert** the first sheet through the second sheet and align the folds.

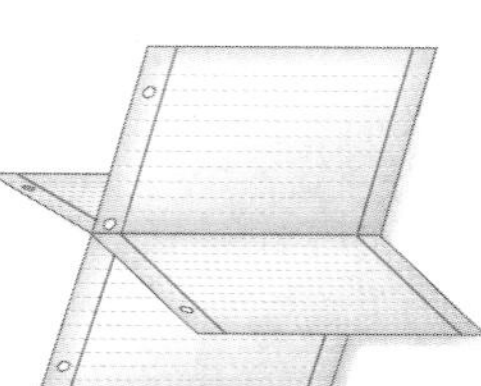

4. **Label** each page with a lesson number and title.

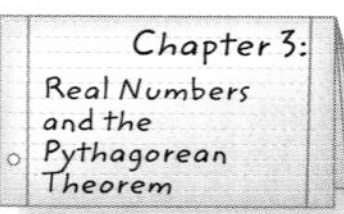

GET READY for Chapter 3

Diagnose Readiness You have two options for checking Prerequisite Skills.

Option 2

IL Math Online Take the Online Readiness Quiz at glencoe.com.

Option 1

Take the Quick Check below. Refer to the Quick Review for help.

QUICK Practice

Graph each point on a coordinate plane. (Prior Grade)

1. $A(-1, 3)$
2. $B(2, -4)$
3. $C(-2, -3)$
4. $D(-4, 0)$

Evaluate each expression. (Lesson 2-9)

5. $2^2 + 4^2$
6. $3^2 + 3^2$
7. $10^2 + 8^2$
8. $7^2 + 5^2$
9. **AGES** Find the sum of the squares of Tina's age and Warren's age if Tina is 13 years old and Warren is 15 years old. (Lesson 2-9)

Solve each equation. Check your solution. (Lesson 1-9)

10. $x + 13 = 45$
11. $56 + d = 71$
12. $101 = 39 + a$
13. $62 = 45 + m$
14. **MARBLES** Barry has 18 more marbles than Heidi. If Barry has 92 marbles, how many marbles does Heidi have? (Lesson 1-9)

QUICK Review

Example 1

Graph the points $P(-3, 4)$, $M(2, -1)$, $R(4, 0)$, and $W(-1, -3)$.

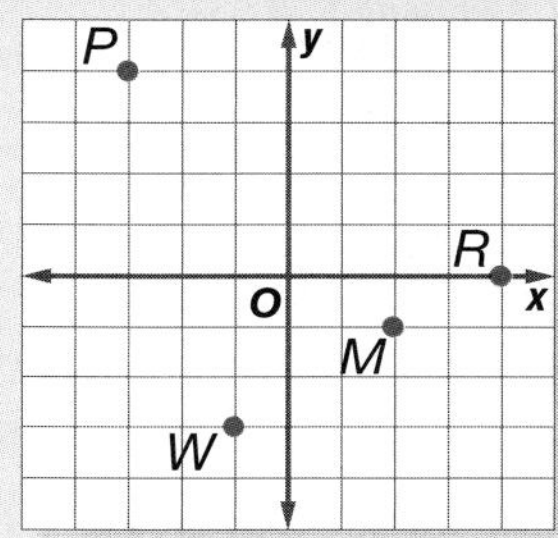

The first number in an ordered pair tells you to move left or right from the origin. The second number tells you to move up or down.

Example 2

Find $6^2 + 4^2$.

$6^2 + 4^2 = 36 + 16$	Evaluate 6^2 and 4^2.
$= 52$	Simplify.

Example 3

Solve $49 + b = 72$.

$49 + b = 72$	Write the equation.
$-49 \quad -49$	Subtract 49 from each side.
$b = 23$	

3-1 Square Roots

MAIN IDEA

Find square roots of perfect squares.

IL Learning Standards

6.B.3c Identify and apply properties of real numbers including pi, **squares, and square roots.**
8.D.3c Apply properties of powers, perfect squares and square roots.

New Vocabulary

perfect square
square root
radical sign

IL Math Online

glencoe.com

- Concepts In Motion
- Extra Examples
- Personal Tutor
- Self-Check Quiz
- Reading in the Content Area

MINI Lab

Continue the pattern of square tiles until you reach 5 tiles on each side.

1. Copy and complete the following table.

Tiles on a Side	1	2	3	4	5
Total Number of Tiles in the Square Arrangement	1	4			

2. Suppose a square arrangement has 36 tiles. How many tiles are on a side?
3. What is the relationship between the number of tiles on a side and the number of tiles in the arrangement?

Numbers such as 1, 4, 9, 16, and 25 are called **perfect squares** because they are squares of integers. Squaring a number and finding a square root are inverse operations. A **square root** of a number is one of its two equal factors. The symbol $\sqrt{\ }$, called a **radical sign**, is used to indicate a positive square root. Every positive number has *both* a negative and a positive square root.

EXAMPLES Find Square Roots

Find each square root.

1 $\sqrt{64}$

$\sqrt{64}$ indicates the *positive* square root. Since $8^2 = 64$, $\sqrt{64} = 8$.

2 $-\sqrt{\frac{25}{36}}$

$-\sqrt{\frac{25}{36}}$ indicates the *negative* square root of $\frac{25}{36}$.

Since $\left(-\frac{5}{6}\right)^2 = \frac{25}{36}$, $-\sqrt{\frac{25}{36}} = -\frac{5}{6}$.

3 $\pm\sqrt{1.21}$

$\pm\sqrt{1.21}$ indicates *both* the positive and negative square roots of 1.21.
Since $1.1^2 = 1.21$ and $(-1.1)^2 = 1.21$, $\pm\sqrt{1.21} = \pm 1.1$, or 1.1 and -1.1.

CHECK Your Progress **Find each square root.**

a. $\sqrt{\frac{9}{16}}$

b. $-\sqrt{49}$

c. $\pm\sqrt{0.81}$

By the definition of a square root, if $n^2 = a$, then $n = \pm\sqrt{a}$. You can use this relationship to solve equations that involve squares.

EXAMPLE Use Square Roots to Solve an Equation

4 ALGEBRA Solve $t^2 = 169$. Check your solution(s).

$t^2 = 169$	Write the equation.
$t = \pm\sqrt{169}$	Definition of square root
$t = 13$ and -13	**Check** $13 \cdot 13 = 169$ and $(-13)(-13) = 169$ ✓

The equation has two solutions, 13 and −13.

CHECK Your Progress

Solve each equation. Check your solution(s).

d. $289 = a^2$ **e.** $m^2 = 0.09$ **f.** $y^2 = \frac{4}{25}$

In most real-world situations, a negative square root does not make sense. Only the positive or *principal* square root is considered.

Real-World EXAMPLE

5 HISTORY The base of the Great Pyramid covers an area of about 562,500 square feet. Determine the length of each side of the base.

Real-World Link The Great Pyramid of Khufu is the largest of the ancient pyramids.
Source: Infoplease

Words	Area is equal to the square of the length of a side.
Variable	Let s represent the length of a side.
Equation	$s^2 = 562{,}500$

$s^2 = 562{,}500$	Write the equation.
$s = \pm\sqrt{562{,}500}$	Definition of square root

To find $\sqrt{562{,}500}$, find two equal factors of 562,500.

$562{,}500 = 2 \cdot 2 \cdot 3 \cdot 3 \cdot 5 \cdot 5 \cdot 5 \cdot 5 \cdot 5 \cdot 5$	Find the prime factors.
$= (2 \cdot 3 \cdot 5 \cdot 5 \cdot 5)(2 \cdot 3 \cdot 5 \cdot 5 \cdot 5)$	Regroup into two equal factors.

So, $s = 2 \cdot 3 \cdot 5 \cdot 5 \cdot 5$ or 750.

Since distance cannot be negative, the length of each side is 750 feet.

CHECK Your Progress

g. CONCERTS A concert crew needs to set up 900 chairs on the floor level. If the chairs are placed in a square arrangement, how many should be in each row?

CHECK Your Understanding

Examples 1–3 (p. 144)

Find each square root.

1. $\sqrt{25}$
2. $\sqrt{0.64}$
3. $-\sqrt{1.69}$
4. $-\sqrt{\frac{16}{81}}$
5. $\pm\sqrt{100}$
6. $\pm\sqrt{\frac{49}{144}}$

Example 4 (p. 145)

ALGEBRA Solve each equation. Check your solution(s).

7. $p^2 = 36$
8. $t^2 = \frac{1}{9}$
9. $6.25 = r^2$

Example 5 (p. 145)

10. **GAMES** A checkerboard is a large square that is made up of 32 small red squares and 32 small black squares. How many small squares are along one side of a checkerboard?

Practice and Problem Solving

HOMEWORK HELP	
For Exercises	See Examples
11–14	1
15–18	2
19–22	3
23–30	4
31, 32	5

Find each square root.

11. $\sqrt{16}$
12. $-\sqrt{81}$
13. $-\sqrt{484}$
14. $\pm\sqrt{36}$
15. $\sqrt{\frac{121}{324}}$
16. $-\sqrt{\frac{64}{225}}$
17. $\pm\sqrt{\frac{9}{49}}$
18. $-\sqrt{\frac{16}{25}}$
19. $-\sqrt{2.56}$
20. $\pm\sqrt{1.44}$
21. $\sqrt{0.25}$
22. $\pm\sqrt{0.0196}$

ALGEBRA Solve each equation. Check your solution(s).

23. $v^2 = 81$
24. $b^2 = 100$
25. $144 = s^2$
26. $225 = y^2$
27. $w^2 = \frac{36}{100}$
28. $\frac{9}{64} = c^2$
29. $0.0169 = d^2$
30. $a^2 = 1.21$

31. **PHOTOGRAPHY** A group of 169 students needs to be seated in a square formation for a yearbook photo. How many students should be in each row?

32. **MARCHING BAND** A marching band wants to form a square in the middle of the field. If there are 225 members in the band, how many should be in each row?

ALGEBRA Solve each equation. Check your solution(s).

33. $\sqrt{x} = 5$
34. $\sqrt{y} = 20$
35. $\sqrt{z} = 10.5$

MEASUREMENT The formula for the perimeter of a square is $P = 4s$, where s is the length of a side. Find the perimeter of each square.

36. Area = 121 square inches

37. Area = 25 square feet

38. Area = 36 square meters

ILS • ISAT

Extra Practice, pp. 674, 702

H.O.T. Problems

39. **OPEN ENDED** Create an equation that can be solved by finding the square root of a perfect square.

40. **CHALLENGE** Find each value.

a. $\left(\sqrt{36}\right)^2$ b. $\left(\sqrt{\frac{25}{81}}\right)^2$ c. $\left(\sqrt{1.99}\right)^2$ d. $\left(\sqrt{x}\right)^2$

41. **NUMBER SENSE** Under what condition is $\sqrt{x} > \sqrt{25}$?

42. **WRITING IN MATH** Read the cartoon. Then find $\sqrt{1{,}296}$. Create a cartoon of your own that uses the square root of a perfect square.

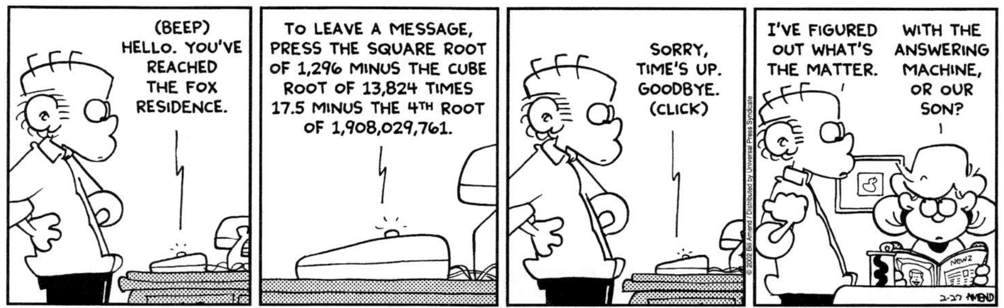

ISAT PRACTICE 6.B.3c, 8.D.3c

43. The area of each square is 16 square units.

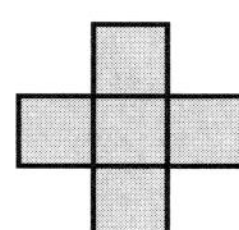

Find the perimeter of the figure.

A 16 units C 40 units

B 32 units D 48 units

44. Mr. Freeman's farm has a square cornfield. Find the area of the cornfield if the sides are measured in whole numbers.

F 164,000 ft^2

G 170,150 ft^2

H 170,586 ft^2

J 174,724 ft^2

Spiral Review

45. **SPACE** The radius of the Sun is 6.96×10^8 meters. Write this distance in standard form. (Lesson 2-10)

Write each expression using exponents. (Lesson 2-9)

46. $6 \cdot 6 \cdot 6$

47. $2 \cdot 3 \cdot 3 \cdot 2 \cdot 2 \cdot 2$

48. $s \cdot t \cdot t \cdot s \cdot s \cdot t \cdot s$

49. What is the absolute value of -18? (Lesson 1-3)

GET READY for the Next Lesson

PREREQUISITE SKILL Between which two perfect squares does each number lie? (Lesson 2-2)

50. 57

51. 68

52. 33

53. 40

3-2 Estimating Square Roots

MAIN IDEA

Estimate square roots.

IL Learning Standards

8.D.3c Apply properties of powers, perfect squares and **square roots.**

IL Math Online

glencoe.com
- Extra Examples
- Personal Tutor
- Self-Check Quiz

MINI Lab

STEP 1 On dot paper, draw and cut out a square like the one at the right. The area of section A is $\frac{1}{2}(2 \cdot 2)$ or 2 square units. So, the shaded square has an area of 8 square units.

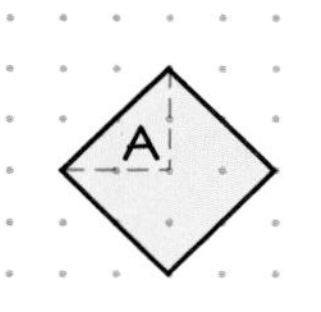

STEP 2 Draw a number line on your dot paper so that 1 unit equals the distance between dots.

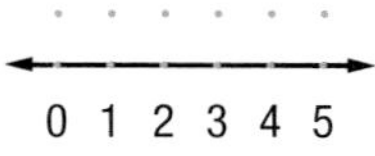

1. Place your square on the number line. Between what two consecutive whole numbers is $\sqrt{8}$, the side length of the square, located?
2. Between what two perfect squares is 8 located?
3. Estimate the length of a side of the square. Verify your estimate by using a calculator to compute the value of $\sqrt{8}$.

In the Mini Lab, you found that $\sqrt{8}$ is not a whole number since 8 is not a perfect square.

The number line below shows that $\sqrt{8}$ is between 2 and 3. Since 8 is closer to 9 than 4, the best positive whole number estimate for $\sqrt{8}$ is 3.

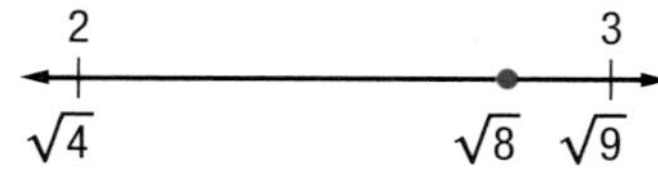

EXAMPLES Estimate Square Roots

Estimate $\sqrt{83}$ to the nearest whole number.

- The largest perfect square less than 83 is 81. $\sqrt{81} = 9$
- The smallest perfect square greater than 83 is 100. $\sqrt{100} = 10$

Plot each square root on a number line. Then estimate $\sqrt{83}$.

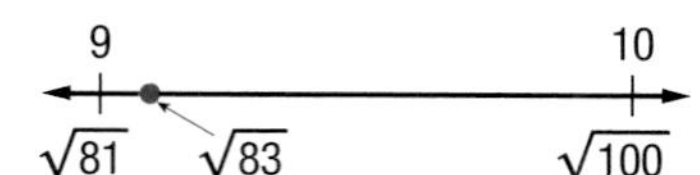

$81 < 83 < 100$	Write an inequality.
$9^2 < 83 < 10^2$	$81 = 9^2$ and $100 = 10^2$
$\sqrt{9^2} < \sqrt{83} < \sqrt{10^2}$	Find the square root of each number.
$9 < \sqrt{83} < 10$	Simplify.

So, $\sqrt{83}$ is between 9 and 10. Since $\sqrt{83}$ is closer to $\sqrt{81}$ than $\sqrt{100}$, the best whole number estimate for $\sqrt{83}$ is 9.

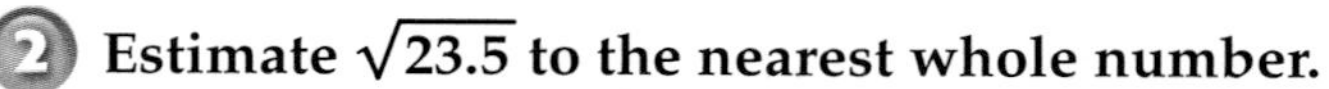

2 **Estimate $\sqrt{23.5}$ to the nearest whole number.**

- The largest perfect square less than 23.5 is 16. $\sqrt{16} = 4$
- The smallest perfect square greater than 23.5 is 25. $\sqrt{25} = 5$

$16 < 23.5 < 25$	Write an inequality.
$4^2 < 23.5 < 5^2$	$16 = 4^2$ and $25 = 5^2$
$\sqrt{4^2} < \sqrt{23.5} < \sqrt{5^2}$	Find the square root of each number.
$4 < \sqrt{23.5} < 5$	Simplify.

So, $\sqrt{23.5}$ is between 4 and 5. Since 23.5 is closer to 25 than 16, the best whole number estimate for $\sqrt{23.5}$ is 5.

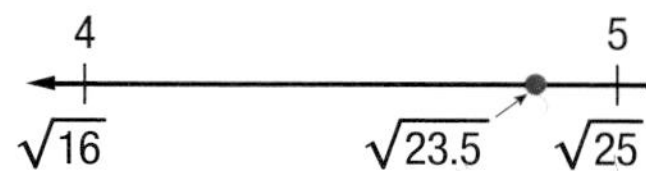

Reading Math

Inequalities
16 < 23.5 < 25 is read *16 is less than 23.5 is less than 25* or *23.5 is between 16 and 25.*

CHECK Your Progress

Estimate to the nearest whole number.

a. $\sqrt{35}$ b. $\sqrt{44.8}$ c. $\sqrt{170}$

Real-World EXAMPLE

3 **NATURE** **The *golden rectangle* is found frequently in the nautilus shell. The length of the longer side divided by the length of the shorter side is equal to $\frac{1 + \sqrt{5}}{2}$. Estimate this value.**

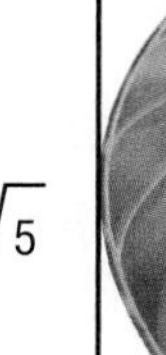
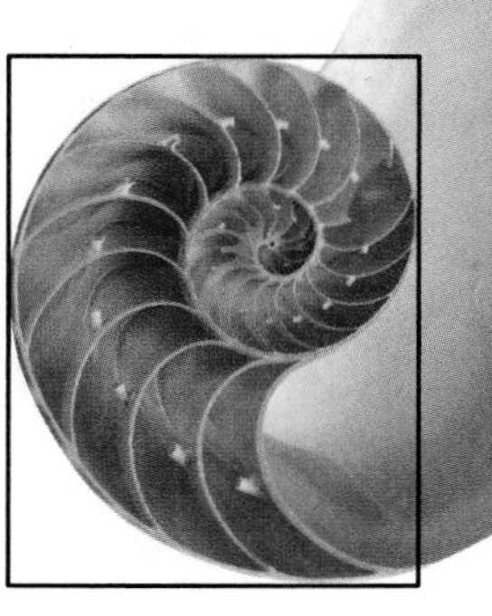

First estimate the value of $\sqrt{5}$.

$4 < 5 < 9$	4 and 9 are the closest perfect squares.
$2^2 < 5 < 3^2$	$4 = 2^2$ and $9 = 3^2$
$\sqrt{2^2} < \sqrt{5} < \sqrt{3^2}$	Find the square root of each number.
$2 < \sqrt{5} < 3$	Simplify.

Since 5 is closer to 4 than 9, the best whole number estimate for $\sqrt{5}$ is 2. Use this value to evaluate the expression.

$$\frac{1 + \sqrt{5}}{2} \approx \frac{1 + 2}{2} \text{ or } 1.5$$

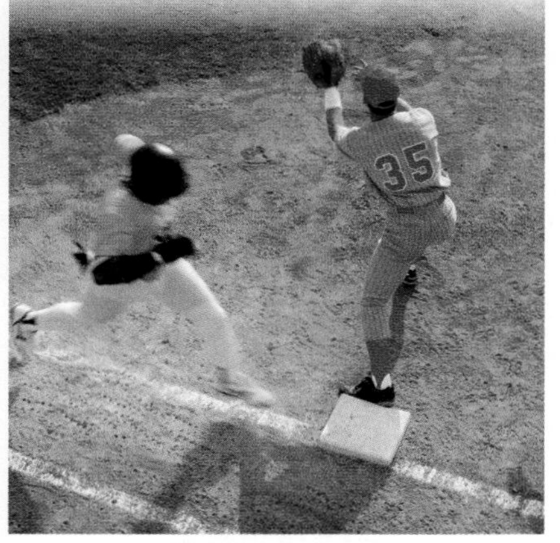

Real-World Link
Major league baseball has very specific requirements for the size of first, second, and third base. They are to be 15 inches square, filled with a soft material, and no more than 5 inches thick nor less than 3 inches thick.
Source: MLB

CHECK Your Progress

d. **BASEBALL** In Little League, the bases are squares with sides of 14 inches. The expression $\sqrt{(s^2 + s^2)}$ represents the distance *across* a square of side length s. Estimate the distance across a base to the nearest inch.

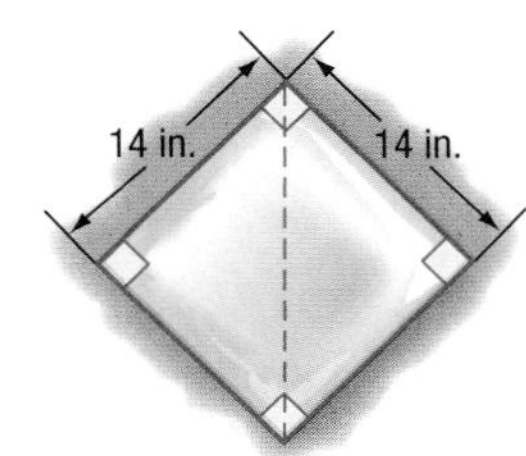

CHECK Your Understanding

Examples 1, 2 (pp. 148–149)

Estimate to the nearest whole number.

1. $\sqrt{28}$
2. $\sqrt{60}$
3. $\sqrt{135}$
4. $\sqrt{13.5}$
5. $\sqrt{38.7}$
6. $\sqrt{79.2}$

Example 3 (p. 149)

7. **SCIENCE** The number of swings back and forth of a pendulum of length L, in inches, each minute is $\frac{375}{\sqrt{L}}$. About how many swings will a 40-inch pendulum make each minute?

Practice and Problem Solving

HOMEWORK HELP	
For Exercises	See Examples
8–15	1, 2
16, 17	3

Estimate to the nearest whole number.

8. $\sqrt{44}$
9. $\sqrt{23}$
10. $\sqrt{125}$
11. $\sqrt{197}$
12. $\sqrt{15.6}$
13. $\sqrt{23.5}$
14. $\sqrt{85.1}$
15. $\sqrt{38.4}$

16. **GEOMETRY** The radius of a circle with area A is approximately $\sqrt{\frac{A}{3}}$. If a pizza has an area of 78 square inches, estimate its radius.

17. **CAVES** The formula $t = \frac{\sqrt{h}}{4}$ represents the time t in seconds that it takes an object to fall from a height of h feet. Suppose a rock falls from a 125-foot-high cave ceiling. Estimate how long will it take to reach the ground.

Estimate to the nearest whole number.

18. $\sqrt{5\frac{1}{5}}$
19. $\sqrt{21\frac{7}{10}}$
20. $\sqrt{17\frac{3}{4}}$

Order from least to greatest.

21. $7, 9, \sqrt{50}, \sqrt{85}$
22. $\sqrt{91}, 7, 5, \sqrt{38}$
23. $\sqrt{62}, 6, \sqrt{34}, 8$

ALGEBRA Estimate the solution of each equation to the nearest integer.

24. $y^2 = 55$
25. $d^2 = 95$
26. $p^2 = 6.8$

27. **FIND THE DATA** Refer to the Data File on pages 16–19. Choose some data and write a real-world problem in which you would estimate a square root.

28. **HOME IMPROVEMENT** Jacob is buying the grass seed shown at the right. Estimate the largest square area Jacob could seed if he purchases 5 bags. State the length of the side of this area.

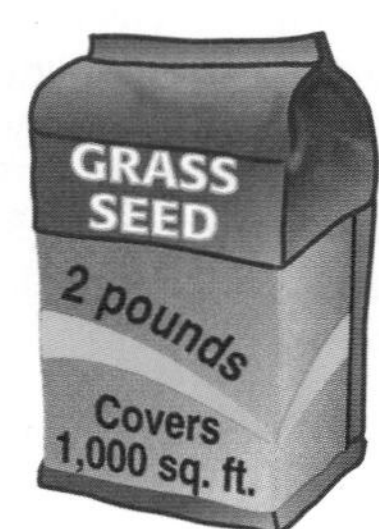

29. **NUMBER SENSE** Without a calculator, determine which is greater, $\sqrt{94}$ or 10. Explain your reasoning.

ILS • ISAT
Extra Practice, pp. 675, 702

H.O.T. Problems

30. **OPEN ENDED** Find two numbers that have square roots between 7 and 8. One number should have a square root closer to 7, and the other number should have a square root closer to 8. Justify your answer.

31. **FIND THE ERROR** Jordan and Dario are estimating $\sqrt{200}$. Who is correct? Explain your reasoning.

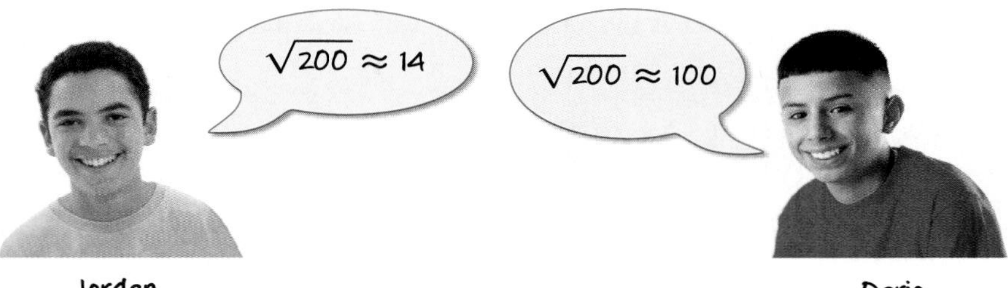

32. **CHALLENGE** If $x^3 = y$, then x is the cube root of y. Explain how to estimate the cube root of 30. Find the cube root of 30 to the nearest whole number.

33. **WRITING IN MATH** Explain how to graph $\sqrt{78}$ on a number line.

ISAT PRACTICE 8.D.3c

34. A whole number is squared. The result is between 950 and 1,000. The number is between

A 26 and 28.

B 28 and 30.

C 30 and 32.

D 32 and 34.

35. Point N on the number line best represents which square root?

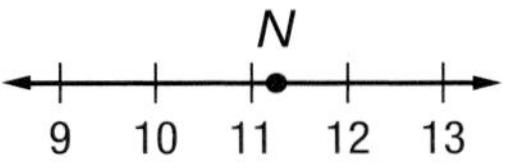

F $\sqrt{140}$ **H** $\sqrt{116}$

G $\sqrt{121}$ **J** $\sqrt{126}$

Spiral Review

36. **ALGEBRA** Find a number that, when squared, equals 8,100. (Lesson 3-1)

37. **LANGUAGE** It is estimated that over 836 million people speak Mandarin Chinese. Write this number in scientific notation. (Lesson 2-10)

Multiply or divide. (Lesson 1-6)

38. $(-5)(-13)$ 39. $(-2)(5)(7)$ 40. $72 \div (-2)$ 41. $-80 \div (-16)$

GET READY for the Next Lesson

42. **PREREQUISITE SKILL** To attend a field trip to an art museum, each student will have to pay $6.50 for transportation and $10.00 for admission and lunch. Find the total amount of money to be collected for a class of 240 students. (Lesson 1-1)

3-3 Problem-Solving Investigation

MAIN IDEA: Use a Venn diagram to solve problems.

ILS **6.B.3a Solve practical computation problems involving whole numbers, integers and rational numbers. 6.C.3a Select computational procedures and solve problems with whole numbers,** fractions, **decimals,** percents and proportions.

P.S.I. TEAM +

e-Mail: USE A VENN DIAGRAM

AMY: There are 15 girls on the cheerleading squad, and four of them are in my math class. Seven of them are in my Spanish class, and two are in both my math and Spanish classes.

YOUR MISSION: Use a Venn diagram to find how many girls on the cheerleading squad are not in Amy's math or Spanish class.

Understand	You know how many cheerleaders are in Amy's math class and Spanish class. You know how many are in both classes.
Plan	Make a Venn diagram to organize the information.
Solve	Draw and label two overlapping circles to represent the two classes. Since 2 cheerleaders are in both classes, place a 2 in the section that is part of both circles. Use subtraction to determine the number for each of the other sections. only math: $4 - 2 = 2$ only in Spanish: $7 - 2 = 5$ neither math nor Spanish classes: $15 - 2 - 2 - 5 = 6$ So, 6 girls on the cheerleading squad are not in Amy's math or Spanish class.
Check	Check each circle to see if the appropriate number of students is represented.

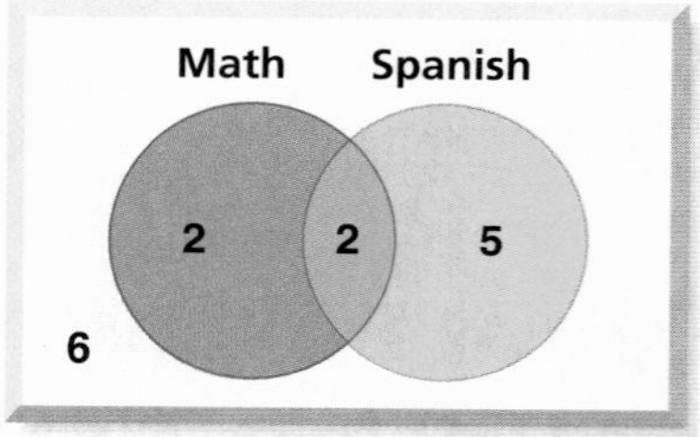

Analyze The Strategy

1. Describe how to determine the number of students who are in either Amy's math or Spanish class but not both using the above Venn diagram.
2. **WRITING IN MATH** Explain what each section of the Venn diagram above represents and the number of students that belong to that category.

Mixed Problem Solving

ILS • ISAT

Extra Practice, pp. 675, 702

Use a Venn diagram to solve Exercises 3–5.

3. **MASCOTS** Nick conducted a survey of 85 students about a new school mascot. The results showed that 40 students liked Tigers, and 31 students liked Bears. Of those students, 12 liked both Tigers and Bears. How many students liked neither Tigers nor Bears?

4. **MARKETING** A survey showed that 70 customers bought white bread, 63 bought wheat bread, and 35 bought rye bread. Of those who bought exactly two types of bread, 12 bought wheat and white, 5 bought white and rye, and 7 bought wheat and rye. Two customers bought all three. How many customers bought only wheat bread?

5. **PETS** Dr. Poston is a veterinarian. One week she treated 20 dogs, 16 cats, and 11 birds. Some owners had more than one pet, as shown in the table below.

Pet	Number of Owners
dog and cat	7
dog and bird	5
cat and bird	3
dog, cat, and bird	2

How many owners had only a dog as a pet?

Use any strategy to solve Exercises 6–11. Some strategies are shown below.

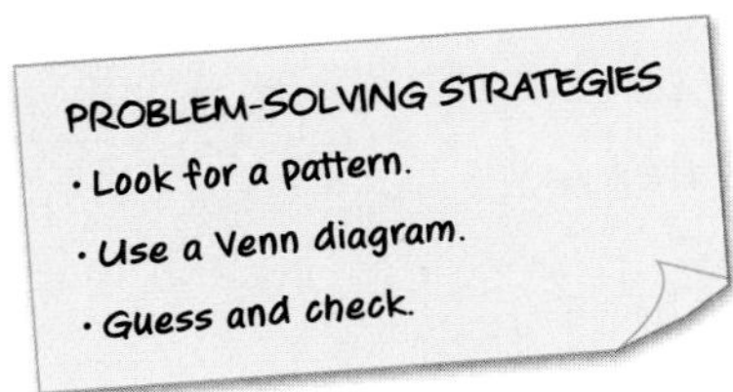

6. **ALGEBRA** What are the next two numbers in the pattern?

864, 432, 216, 108, ■, ■

7. **MONEY** The soccer team sponsored a car wash to pay for their new uniforms. They charged \$3 for a car and \$5 for an SUV. During the first two hours they washed 19 vehicles and earned \$71. How many of each type of vehicle did they wash?

8. **SCIENCE** As part of an experiment, Javier tested the battery life of AA batteries when used to power a CD player. His results are shown in the graph below. If the pattern continues, about how much power will remain after 4 hours?

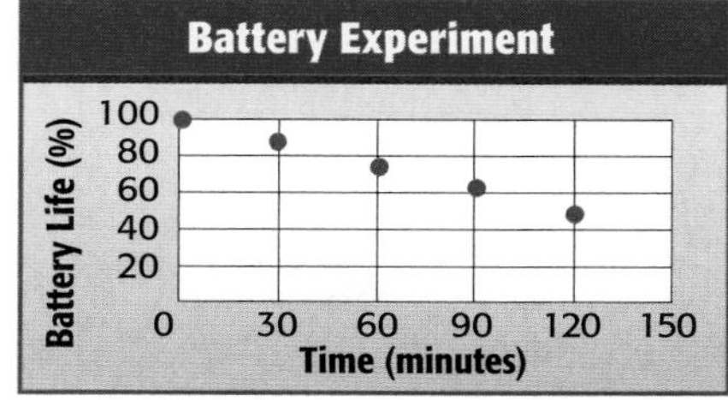

9. **SPORTS** Student Council surveyed a group of 24 students. The results showed that 14 students liked softball, and 18 liked basketball. Of these, 8 liked both. How many students liked just softball and how many liked just basketball?

10. **JOBS** James is looking at three different after-school jobs that are posted on the job board. The first job pays \$6.25 per hour for 20 hours of work each week. The second job pays \$12.75 per day for two hours of work, 5 days a week. The third job pays \$105 for 15 hours of work each week. If he wants to apply for the job with the best hourly rate, which job should he choose? Explain your reasoning.

11. **ROLLER COASTERS** The Silver Streak roller coaster can accommodate 1,296 people in one hour. The coaster has 12 vehicles. If each vehicle carries 4 passengers, how many runs are made in one hour?

READING to SOLVE PROBLEMS

The Language of Mathematics

The language of mathematics is very specific. But many of the words you use in mathematics are also used in everyday language as well as scientific language. Sometimes the everyday or scientific usage can give you clues to the mathematical meaning. Here are some examples.

Usage	Example
Some words are used in English and in mathematics, but have distinct meanings.	leg
Some words are used in science and in mathematics, but the meanings are different.	$x + 4 = -2$ $x = -6$ solution
Some words are used only in mathematics.	hypotenuse

PRACTICE

Explain how the mathematical meaning of each word compares to its everyday meaning.

1. factor
2. leg
3. rational
4. root

Explain how the mathematical meaning of each word compares to its meaning in science.

5. radical
6. variable

Some words are used in English and in mathematics, but the mathematical meaning is more precise. Explain how the mathematical meaning of each word is more precise than the everday meaning.

7. similar
8. real

3-4 The Real Number System

MAIN IDEA

Identify and classify numbers in the real number system.

IL Learning Standards

6.B.3c Identify and apply properties of real numbers including pi, squares, **and square roots.**

New Vocabulary

irrational number
real number

IL Math Online

glencoe.com

- Extra Examples
- Personal Tutor
- Self-Check Quiz

GET READY for the Lesson

SPORTS Major League baseball has rules for the dimensions of the baseball diamond.

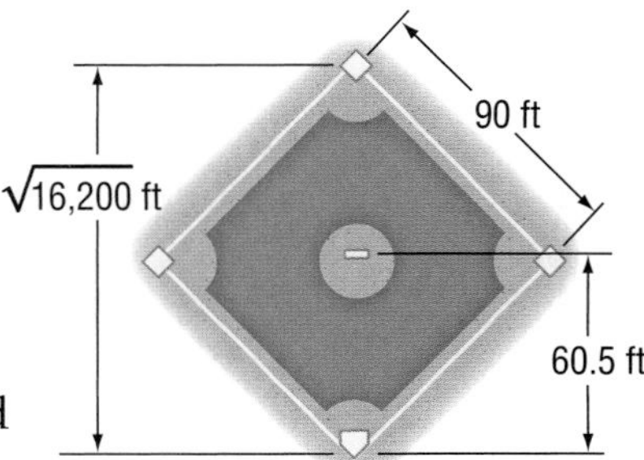

1. The distance from the pitching mound to home plate is 60.5 feet. Is 60.5 a rational number? Explain.
2. The distance from first base to second base is 90 feet. Is 90 a rational number? Explain.
3. The distance from home plate to second base is $\sqrt{16{,}200}$ feet. Can this square root be written as a rational number? Explain.

A calculator gives a decimal value of 127.2792206 for $\sqrt{16{,}200}$. Although this continues on and on, it does not repeat. Since the decimal does not terminate or repeat, $\sqrt{16{,}200}$ cannot be written as a fraction. Therefore, it is *not* a rational number. Numbers that are not rational are called **irrational numbers**. The square root of any number that is not a perfect square number is irrational.

Irrational Numbers — Key Concept

Words An irrational number is a number that cannot be expressed as the quotient $\frac{a}{b}$, where a and b are integers and $b \neq 0$.

Examples $\sqrt{2} \approx 1.414213562...$ $\quad -\sqrt{3} \approx -1.732050807...$

The set of rational numbers and the set of irrational numbers together make up the set of **real numbers.** Study the Venn diagram below.

Real Numbers

Rational Numbers | Irrational Numbers
Integers
Whole Numbers

Review Vocabulary

rational number any number that can be expressed in the form $\frac{a}{b}$, where a and b are integers and $b \neq 0$ (Lesson 2-1)

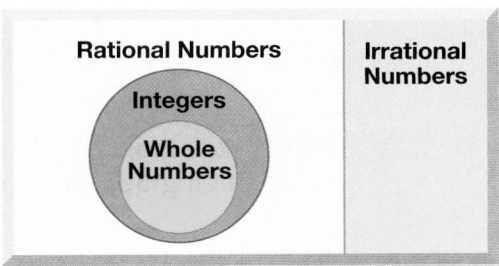

EXAMPLES Classify Numbers

Name all sets of numbers to which each real number belongs.

1. **0.252525...** The decimal ends in a repeating pattern. It is a rational number because it is equivalent to $\frac{25}{99}$.

> **Study Tip**
> **Classifying Numbers** Always simplify numbers before classifying them.

2. $\sqrt{36}$ Since $\sqrt{36} = 6$, it is a whole number, an integer, and a rational number.

3. $-\sqrt{7}$ $-\sqrt{7} \approx -2.645751311\ldots$ Since the decimal does not terminate or repeat, it is an irrational number.

a. $\sqrt{10}$ b. $-2\frac{2}{5}$ c. $\sqrt{100}$

Real numbers follow the properties that are true for whole numbers, integers, and rational numbers.

Real Number Properties (Key Concept)

Property	Arithmetic	Algebra
Commutative	$3.2 + 2.5 = 2.5 + 3.2$ $5.1 \cdot 2.8 = 2.8 \cdot 5.1$	$a + b = b + a$ $a \cdot b = b \cdot a$
Associative	$(2 + 1) + 5 = 2 + (1 + 5)$ $(3 \cdot 4) \cdot 6 = 3 \cdot (4 \cdot 6)$	$(a + b) + c = a + (b + c)$ $(a \cdot b) \cdot c = a \cdot (b \cdot c)$
Distributive	$2(3 + 5) = 2 \cdot 3 + 2 \cdot 5$	$a(b + c) = a \cdot b + a \cdot c$
Identity	$\sqrt{8} + 0 = \sqrt{8}$ $\sqrt{7} \cdot 1 = \sqrt{7}$	$a + 0 = a$ $a \cdot 1 = a$
Additive Inverse	$4 + (-4) = 0$	$a + (-a) = 0$
Multiplicative Inverse	$\frac{2}{3} \cdot \frac{3}{2} = 1$	$\frac{a}{b} \cdot \frac{b}{a} = 1$, where $a, b \neq 0$

EXAMPLE Graph Real Numbers

> **Study Tip**
> **Mental Math** Remember that a negative number is always less than a positive number. Therefore, you can determine that a number like $-\sqrt{3}$ is less than 1.7 without computation.

4. **Estimate $\sqrt{6}$ and $-\sqrt{3}$ to the nearest tenth. Then graph $\sqrt{6}$ and $-\sqrt{3}$ on a number line.**

$\sqrt{6} \approx 2.449489743\ldots$ or about 2.4   Use a calculator.

$-\sqrt{3} \approx -1.7320508075\ldots$ or about -1.7 Use a calculator.

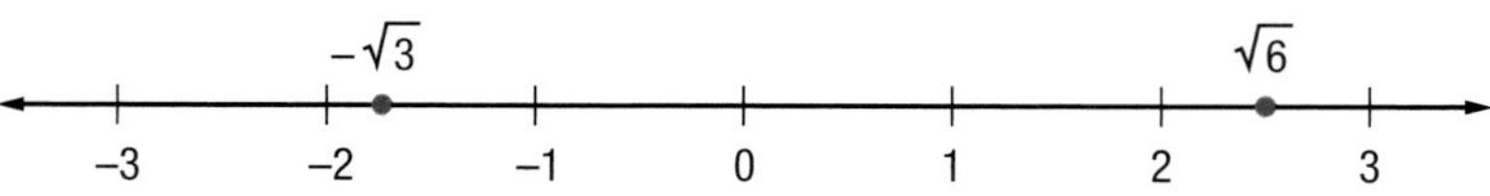

CHECK Your Progress **Estimate each square root to the nearest tenth. Then graph the square root on a number line.**

d. $\sqrt{5}$ e. $-\sqrt{7}$ f. $\sqrt{22}$

EXAMPLES Compare Real Numbers

Replace each ● with <, >, or = to make a true sentence.

5 $\sqrt{7}$ ● $2\frac{2}{3}$

Write each number as a decimal.

$\sqrt{7} \approx 2.645751311\ldots$

$2\frac{2}{3} = 2.666666666\ldots$

Since 2.645751311…is less than 2.66666666…, $\sqrt{7} < 2\frac{2}{3}$.

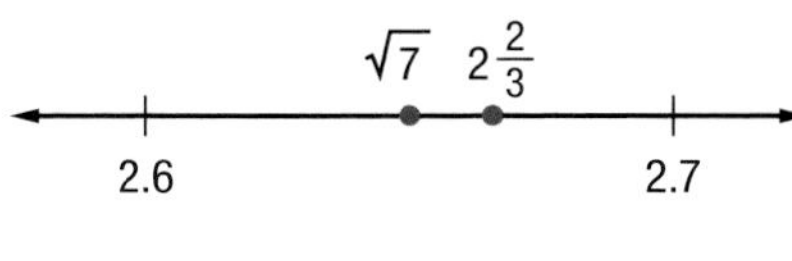

Study Tip

Calculator Use To find $\sqrt{7}$ on a calculator, use the keystrokes [2nd] [x²] 7 [ENTER] 2.645751311

6 $1.\overline{5}$ ● $\sqrt{2.25}$

Write $\sqrt{2.25}$ as a decimal.

$\sqrt{2.25} = 1.5$

$1.\overline{5} = 1.555555555\ldots$

Since 1.555555555… is greater than 1.5, $1.\overline{5} > \sqrt{2.25}$.

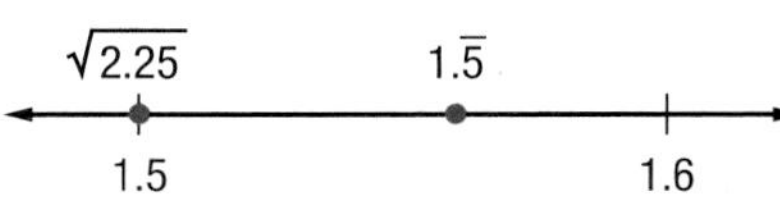

CHECK Your Progress

g. $\sqrt{11}$ ● $3\frac{1}{3}$ h. $\sqrt{17}$ ● 4.03 i. $\sqrt{6.25}$ ● $2\frac{1}{2}$

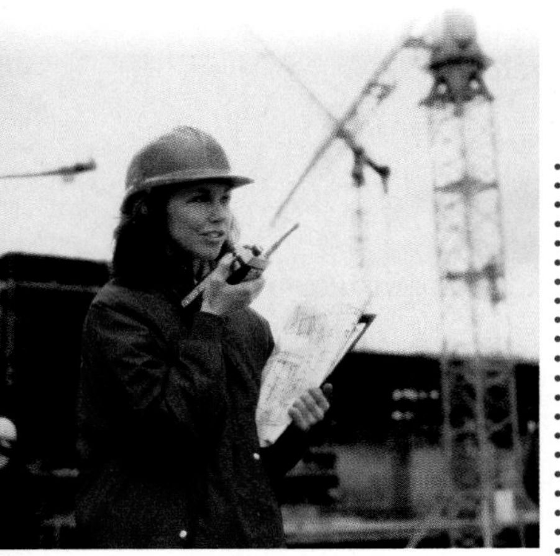

Real-World Career …
How Does a Building Contractor Use Math? Building contractors must manage budgets and order materials. They often use geometry when they plan for roofing or flooring materials.

IL Math Online

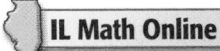

For more information, go to glencoe.com.

Real-World EXAMPLE

7 **SKYSCRAPERS On a clear day, the number of miles a person can see to the horizon is about 1.23 times the square root of his or her distance from the ground, in feet. Suppose Ricardo is at the top of Aon Center and Kia is at the top of the Sears Tower. How much farther can Kia see than Ricardo?**

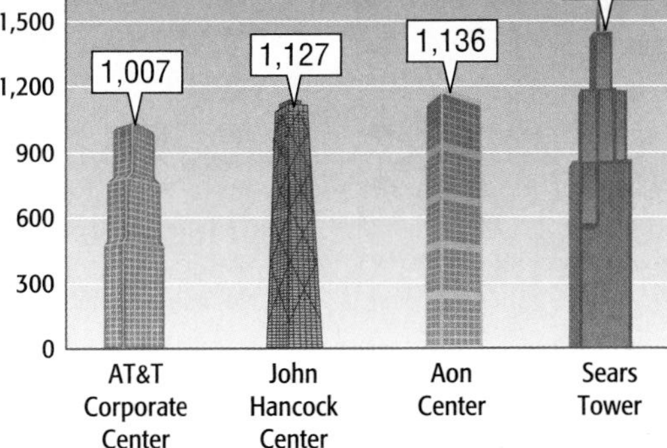

Use a calculator to approximate the distance each person can see.

Ricardo: $1.23\sqrt{1{,}136} \approx 41.46$ Kia: $1.23\sqrt{1{,}451} \approx 46.85$

Kia can see about 46.85 − 41.46 or 5.39 miles farther than Ricardo.

CHECK Your Progress

j. **MEASUREMENT** How much greater is the perimeter of a square with area 250 square meters than a square with area 125 square meters?

CHECK Your Understanding

Examples 1–3 (p. 156)

Name all sets of numbers to which each real number belongs.

1. $0.050505\ldots$ 2. $-\sqrt{64}$ 3. $\sqrt{17}$ 4. $-3\frac{1}{4}$

Example 4 (p. 156)

Estimate each square root to the nearest tenth. Then graph the square root on a number line.

5. $\sqrt{2}$ 6. $-\sqrt{18}$

Examples 5, 6 (p. 157)

Replace each ● with <, >, or = to make a true sentence.

7. $\sqrt{15}$ ● 3.5 8. $\sqrt{2.25}$ ● $1\frac{1}{2}$ 9. $2.\overline{21}$ ● $\sqrt{5.2}$

Example 7 (p. 157)

10. **AREA** The formula $A = \sqrt{s(s-a)(s-b)(s-c)}$ can be used to find the area A of a triangle. The variables a, b, and c are the side measures, and s is one-half the perimeter. Use the formula to find the area of the triangle at the right.

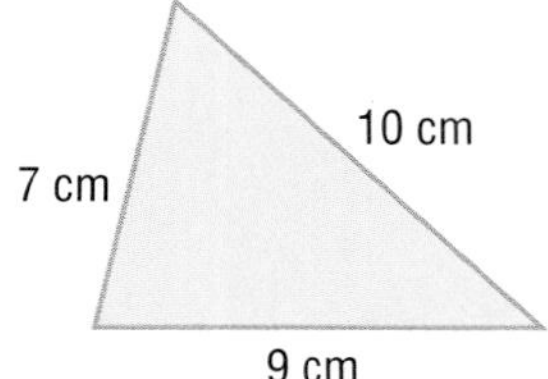

Practice and Problem Solving

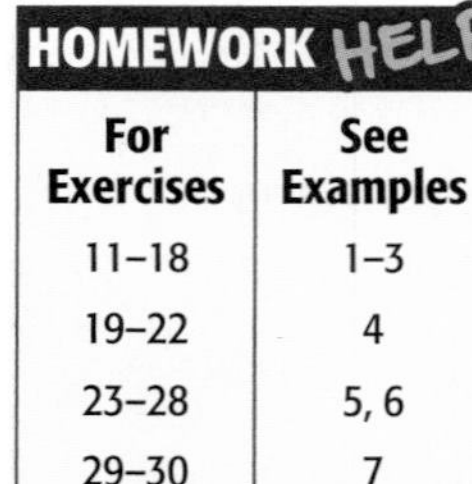

HOMEWORK HELP

For Exercises	See Examples
11–18	1–3
19–22	4
23–28	5, 6
29–30	7

Name all sets of numbers to which each real number belongs.

11. 14 12. $\frac{2}{3}$ 13. $-\sqrt{16}$ 14. $-\sqrt{20}$

15. 4.83 16. $7.\overline{2}$ 17. $-\sqrt{90}$ 18. $\frac{12}{4}$

Estimate each square root to the nearest tenth. Then graph the square root on a number line.

19. $\sqrt{6}$ 20. $\sqrt{8}$ 21. $-\sqrt{22}$ 22. $-\sqrt{27}$

Replace each ● with <, >, or = to make a true sentence.

23. $\sqrt{10}$ ● 3.2 24. $\sqrt{12}$ ● 3.5 25. $6\frac{1}{3}$ ● $\sqrt{40}$

26. $2\frac{2}{5}$ ● $\sqrt{5.76}$ 27. $5\frac{1}{6}$ ● $5.1\overline{6}$ 28. $\sqrt{6.2}$ ● $2.\overline{4}$

29. **ROADS** The equation $s = \sqrt{30fd}$ can be used to find the speed s in miles per hour, of a car given the length d in feet of a skid mark and the friction factor f of the road. Police measured a skid mark of 90 feet on a dry concrete road. If the speed limit is 35 mph, was the car speeding? Explain.

Friction Factor		
Road	**Concrete**	**Tar**
Wet	0.4	0.5
Dry	0.8	1.0

30. **HEALTH** The surface area in square meters of the human body can be found using the expression $\sqrt{\frac{hm}{3{,}600}}$, where h is the height in centimeters and m is the mass in kilograms. Find the surface area of a 15-year-old boy with a height of 183 centimeters and a mass of 74 kilograms.

31. **ALGEBRA** In the sequence 4, 12, ■, 108, 324, the missing number can be found by simplifying $\sqrt{ab}$ where a and b are the numbers on either side of the missing number. Find the missing number.

Order each set of numbers from least to greatest.

ILS • ISAT
Extra Practice, pp. 675, 702

32. $\sqrt{5}, \sqrt{3}, 2.25, 2.\overline{2}$

33. $3.01, 3.\overline{1}, 3.\overline{01}, \sqrt{9}$

34. $-4.1, \sqrt{17}, -4.\overline{1}, 4.01$

35. $-\sqrt{5}, \sqrt{6}, -2.5, 2.5$

H.O.T. Problems

36. **OPEN ENDED** Give a counterexample for the statement *all square roots are irrational numbers*. Explain your reasoning.

CHALLENGE For Exercises 37–39, tell whether the following statement is *always, sometimes,* or *never* true. If a statement is not always true, explain.

37. Integers are rational numbers.

38. Rational numbers are integers.

39. The product of a rational number and an irrational number is irrational.

40. **WRITING IN MATH** Write a real-world problem in which you would need to approximate a square root. Then, solve the problem.

ISAT PRACTICE 6.B.3c

41. Which is an irrational number?

A -6

B $\frac{2}{3}$

C $\sqrt{9}$

D $\sqrt{3}$

42. Which number represents the point graphed on the number line?

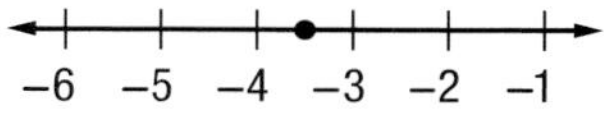

F $-\sqrt{12}$

G $-\sqrt{10}$

H $-\sqrt{15}$

J $-\sqrt{8}$

Spiral Review

43. **SPORTS** Students were surveyed about the sports in which they participate. Thirty-five play baseball, 31 play basketball, and 28 play soccer. Of these, 7 play only baseball and basketball, 9 play only basketball and soccer, 6 play only baseball and soccer, and 5 play all three sports. How many students were surveyed? Use a Venn diagram. (Lesson 3-3)

44. Order 7, $\sqrt{53}$, $\sqrt{32}$, and 6 from least to greatest. (Lesson 3-2)

ALGEBRA Solve each equation. (Lesson 3-1)

45. $t^2 = 25$

46. $y^2 = \frac{1}{49}$

47. $0.64 = a^2$

GET READY for the Next Lesson

PREREQUISITE SKILL Evaluate each expression. (Lesson 2-9)

48. $3^2 + 5^2$

49. $6^2 + 4^2$

50. $9^2 + 11^2$

51. $4^2 + 7^2$

CHAPTER 3

Mid-Chapter Quiz

Lessons 3-1 through 3-4

IL Learning Standards
6.B.3c, 8.D.3c

Find each square root. (Lesson 3-1)

1. $\sqrt{1}$
2. $\pm\sqrt{81}$
3. $\pm\sqrt{36}$
4. $-\sqrt{121}$
5. $-\sqrt{\frac{1}{25}}$
6. $\sqrt{0.09}$

7. **MEASUREMENT** What is the length of a side of the square? (Lesson 3-1)

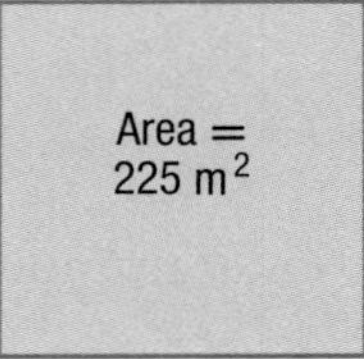

8. **MULTIPLE CHOICE** The area of a square picture frame is 529 square centimeters. How long is each side of the frame? (Lesson 3-1)
   - **A** 26 cm
   - **B** 25 cm
   - **C** 23 cm
   - **D** 21 cm

9. **FOOTBALL** A group of 121 football players needs to be in a square formation for practice. How many players should be in each row? (Lesson 3-1)

Estimate to the nearest whole number. (Lesson 3-2)

10. $\sqrt{90}$
11. $\sqrt{28}$
12. $\sqrt{226}$
13. $\sqrt{17}$
14. $\sqrt{21}$
15. $\sqrt{75}$

16. **ALGEBRA** Estimate the solution(s) of $x^2 = 50$ to the nearest integer. (Lesson 3-2)

17. **MEASUREMENT** The radius of a circle with area A is approximately $\sqrt{\frac{A}{3}}$. If a pie has an area of 42 square inches, estimate its radius. (Lesson 3-2)

18. **MULTIPLE CHOICE** Point P on the number line best represents which square root? (Lesson 3-2)

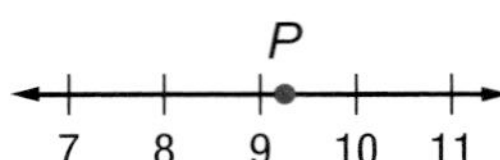

   - **F** $\sqrt{85}$
   - **G** $\sqrt{81}$
   - **H** $\sqrt{98}$
   - **J** $\sqrt{79}$

19. **MARKETING** A survey showed 83 customers bought wheat cereal, 83 bought rice cereal, and 20 bought corn cereal. Of those who bought exactly two boxes of cereal, 6 bought corn and wheat, 10 bought rice and corn, and 12 bought rice and wheat. Four customers bought all three. How many customers bought only rice cereal? (Lesson 3-3)

20. **FOOD** Napoli's pizza conducted a survey of 75 customers. The results showed that 35 customers liked mushroom pizza, 41 liked pepperoni pizza, and 11 liked both mushroom and pepperoni pizza. How many liked neither mushroom nor pepperoni pizza? Use a Venn diagram. (Lesson 3-3)

Name all sets of numbers to which each real number belongs. (Lesson 3-4)

21. $\frac{2}{3}$
22. $\sqrt{25}$
23. $-\sqrt{15}$
24. $\sqrt{3}$
25. 10
26. $-\sqrt{4}$

Replace each ● with <, >, or = to make a true sentence. (Lesson 3-4)

27. $\sqrt{15}$ ● 4.1
28. 6.5 ● $\sqrt{45}$
29. $\sqrt{35}$ ● 5.75
30. $3.\overline{3}$ ● $\sqrt{10}$

Explore 3-5

Geometry Lab
The Pythagorean Theorem

MAIN IDEA

Find the relationship among the sides of a right triangle.

IL Learning Standards

9.D.3 Compute distances, lengths and measures of angles **using** proportions, **the Pythagorean theorem** and its converse. *Also addresses 6.B.3c, 7.A.3b, 8.D.3c.*

You can use centimeter grid paper to find the area of squares and triangles. In this lab, you will investigate the relationship among the sides of a right triangle.

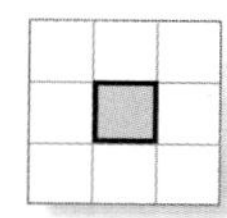

Area = 1 cm²

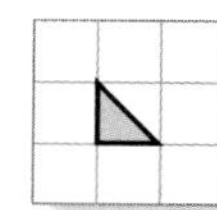

Area = $\frac{1}{2}$ cm²

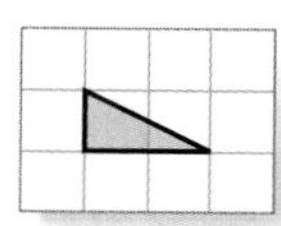

Area = 1 cm²

ACTIVITY

STEP 1 Draw each figure on centimeter grid paper. In each figure, the sides of three squares form a right triangle.

Triangle 1

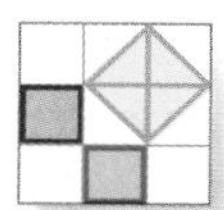

Triangle 2

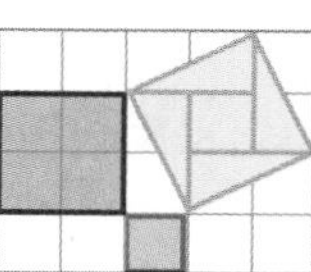

Triangle 3

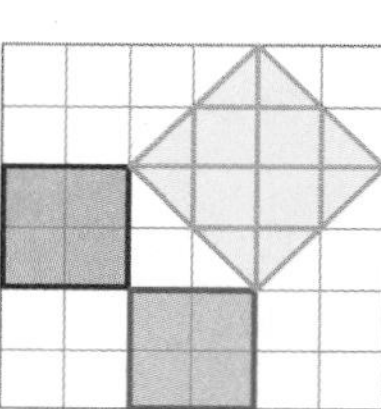

STEP 2 Find the area of each square that is attached to the triangle. Record this information in a table like the one shown.

Triangle	Area of Blue Square (cm²)	Area of Green Square (cm²)	Area of Yellow Square (cm²)
1			
2			
3			

Analyze the Results

1. What relationship exists among the areas of the three squares in each triangle?
2. On centimeter grid paper, draw a right triangle with the two shorter sides 3 centimeters and 4 centimeters long. If squares were attached to each side of this triangle, what would be the area of each square? Use a ruler to measure the length of the third side of the triangle.
3. **MAKE A CONJECTURE** Determine the length of the longest side of a right triangle if the length of the two shorter sides are 6 centimeters and 8 centimeters long.

3-5 The Pythagorean Theorem

MAIN IDEA

Use the Pythagorean Theorem.

IL Learning Standards

9.D.3 Compute distances, lengths and measures of angles **using** proportions, **the Pythagorean theorem and its converse.** *Also addresses 6.B.3c, 7.A.3b, 8.D.3c.*

New Vocabulary

legs
hypotenuse
Pythagorean Theorem
converse

IL Math Online

glencoe.com

- Extra Examples
- Personal Tutor
- Self-Check Quiz

MINI Lab

SPORTS When viewed from the side, the shape of some wooden skateboarding ramps is a right triangle. The dimensions of four possible ramps of this type are given in the table. Copy this table.

Ramp Design	Height, *H* (ft)	Base, *B* (ft)
A	3	4
B	6	8
C	5	12
D	7	24

STEP 1 Draw a side-view model of each ramp on grid paper, letting the width of one grid equal 1 foot.

STEP 2 Cut each ramp out and use your grid paper to find the length of the ramp, which is the longest side of your model. Write these measures in a new column labeled *length, L (ft).*

STEP 3 Finally, add a column labeled $H^2 + B^2$. Calculate each of these values and place them in your table.

1. What is the relationship between the values in the $H^2 + B^2$ column and the values in the L column?
2. How could you use a value in the $H^2 + B^2$ column to find a corresponding value in the L column?

A right triangle is a triangle with one right angle.

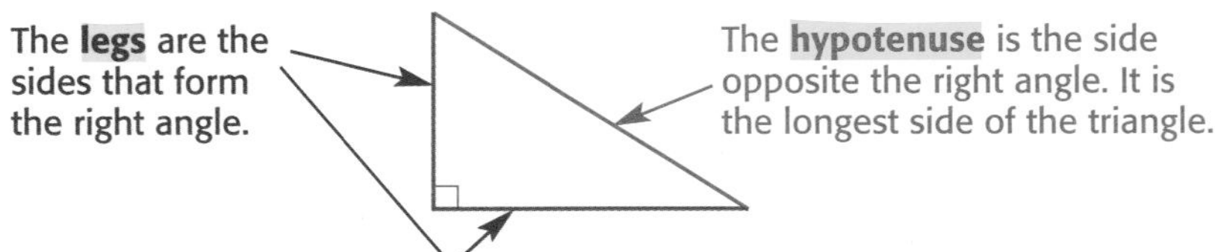

The **legs** are the sides that form the right angle.
The **hypotenuse** is the side opposite the right angle. It is the longest side of the triangle.

The **Pythagorean Theorem** describes the relationship between the lengths of the legs and the hypotenuse for *any* right triangle.

Pythagorean Theorem — Key Concept

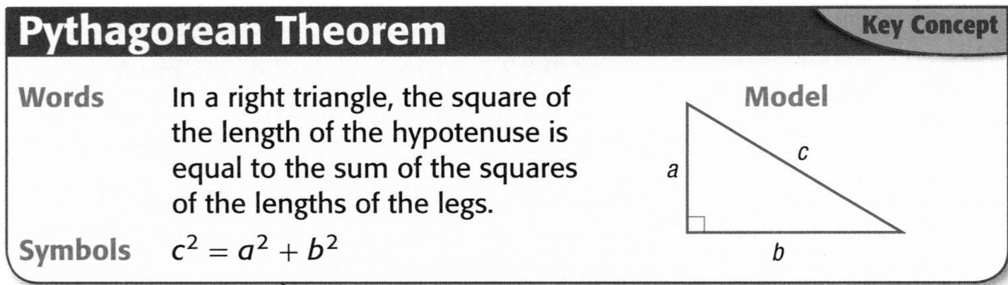

Words In a right triangle, the square of the length of the hypotenuse is equal to the sum of the squares of the lengths of the legs.

Symbols $c^2 = a^2 + b^2$

Model

You can use the Pythagorean Theorem to find the length of a side of a right triangle when you know the other two sides.

EXAMPLES Find a Missing Length

Write an equation you could use to find the length of the missing side of each right triangle. Then find the missing length. Round to the nearest tenth if necessary.

Reading Math

Right Angle The symbol ⌉ indicates an angle with a measure of 90°.

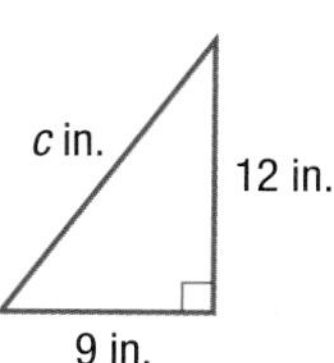

$c^2 = a^2 + b^2$	Pythagorean Theorem
$c^2 = 9^2 + 12^2$	Replace a with 9 and b with 12.
$c^2 = 81 + 144$	Evaluate 9^2 and 12^2.
$c^2 = 225$	Add 81 and 144.
$c = \pm\sqrt{225}$	Definition of square root
$c = 15$ or -15	Simplify.

The equation has two solutions, 15 and −15. However, the length of a side must be positive. So, the hypotenuse is 15 inches long.

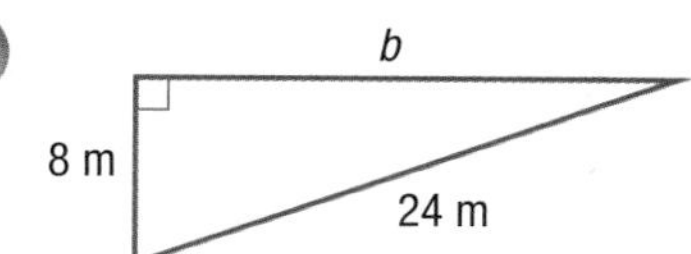

$a^2 + b^2 = c^2$	Pythagorean Theorem
$8^2 + b^2 = 24^2$	Replace a with 8 and c with 24.
$64 + b^2 = 576$	Evaluate 8^2 and 24^2.
$64 - 64 + b^2 = 576 - 64$	Subtract 64 from each side.
$b^2 = 512$	Simplify.
$b = \pm\sqrt{512}$	Definition of square root
$b \approx 22.6$ or -22.6	Use a calculator.

The length of side b is about 22.6 meters.

Study Tip

Check for Reasonableness The hypotenuse is always the longest side in a right triangle. Since 22.6 is less than 24, the answer is reasonable.

CHECK Your Progress

a.

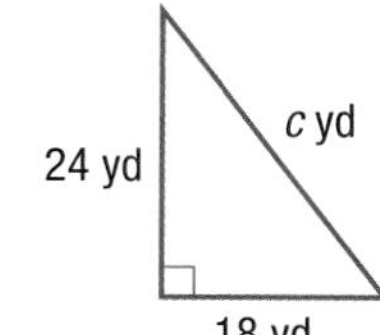

b.

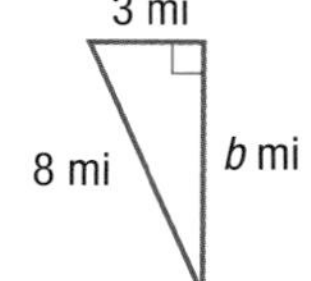

c.

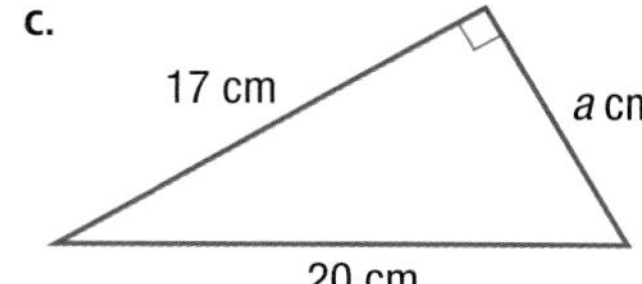

If you reverse the parts of the Pythagorean Theorem, you have formed its **converse**. The converse of the Pythagorean Theorem is also true.

Converse of Pythagorean Theorem

Key Concept

If the sides of a triangle have lengths a, b, and c units such that $c^2 = a^2 + b^2$, then the triangle is a right triangle.

EXAMPLE Identify a Right Triangle

Study Tip

Draw a Picture When solving a problem, it is often helpful to draw a picture to represent the situation.

3 **The measures of three sides of a triangle are 5 inches, 12 inches, and 13 inches. Determine whether the triangle is a right triangle.**

$c^2 = a^2 + b^2$	Pythagorean Theorem
$13^2 \stackrel{?}{=} 5^2 + 12^2$	$c = 13$, $a = 5$, $b = 12$
$169 \stackrel{?}{=} 25 + 144$	Evaluate 13^2, 5^2, and 12^2.
$169 = 169$ ✓	Simplify.

The triangle is a right triangle.

CHECK Your Progress **Determine whether each triangle with sides of given lengths is a right triangle. Justify your answer.**

d. 36 mi, 48 mi, 60 mi **e.** 4 ft, 7 ft, 5 ft

CHECK Your Understanding

Write an equation you could use to find the length of the missing side of each right triangle. Then find the missing length. Round to the nearest tenth if necessary.

Example 1 (p. 163)

1.

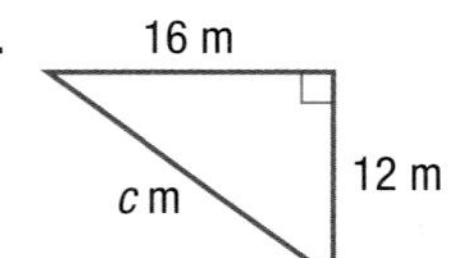

2.

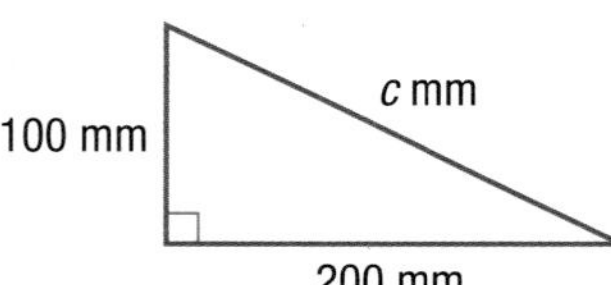

Example 2 (p. 163)

3.

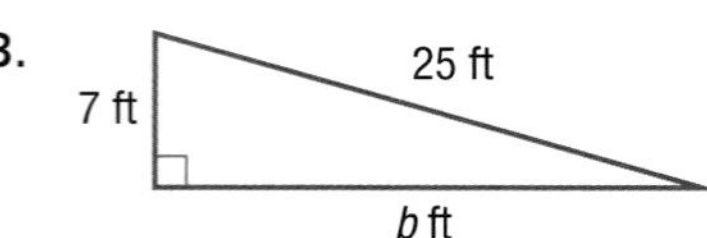

4.

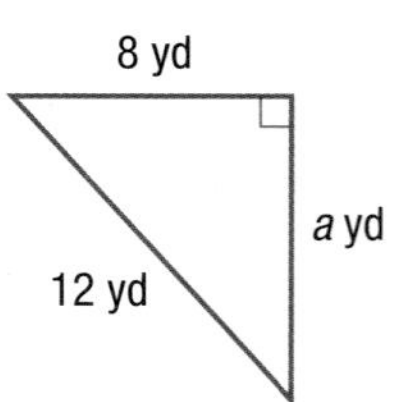

Example 1 (p. 163)

5. The hypotenuse of a right triangle is 12 inches, and one of its legs is 7 inches. Find the length of the other leg. Round to the nearest tenth if necessary.

Example 3 (p. 164)

Determine whether each triangle with sides of given lengths is a right triangle. Justify your answer.

6. 5 in., 10 in., 12 in. **7.** 9 m, 40 m, 41 m

Practice and Problem Solving

HOMEWORK HELP

For Exercises	See Examples
8, 9	1
10–13	2
14–19	3

Write an equation you could use to find the length of the missing side of each right triangle. Then find the missing length. Round to the nearest tenth if necessary.

8. 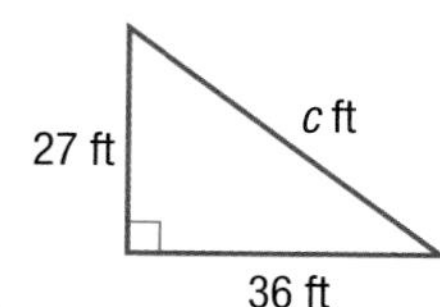

9. 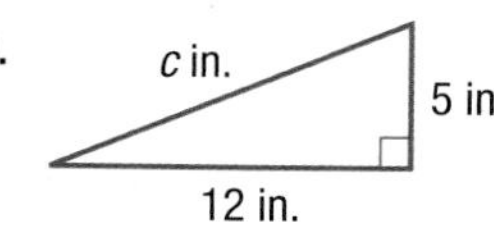

10. 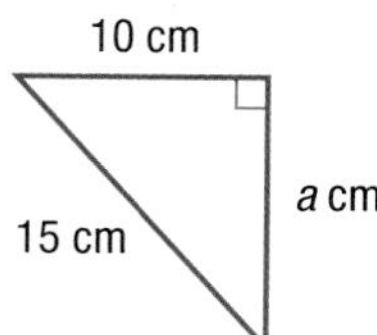

11. 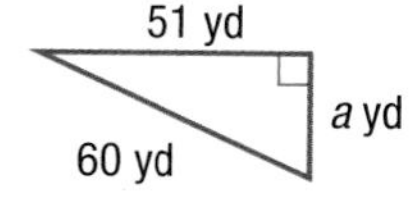

12. 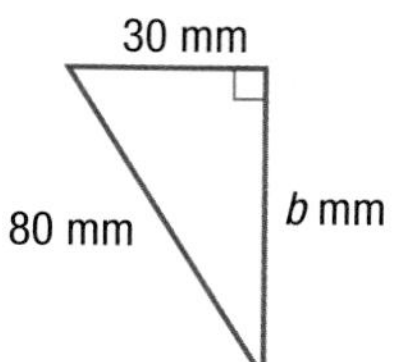

13. 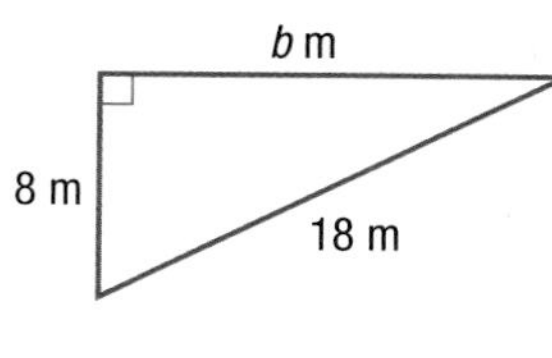

Determine whether each triangle with sides of given lengths is a right triangle. Justify your answer.

14. 28 yd, 195 yd, 197 yd
15. 30 cm, 122 cm, 125 cm
16. 24 m, 143 m, 145 m
17. 135 in., 140 in., 175 in.
18. 56 ft, 65 ft, 16 ft
19. 44 cm, 70 cm, 55 cm

20. **POSTAGE** An envelope is classified as a *large* envelope if the length exceeds 11.5 inches. Is the envelope below a large envelope?

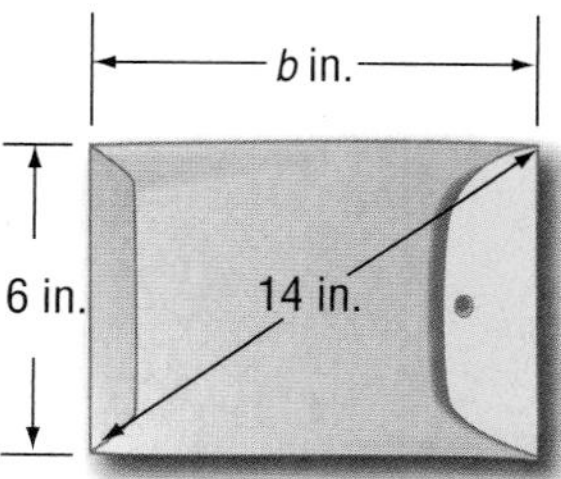

21. **GEOGRAPHY** Calculate the length of the diagonal of the state of Wyoming.

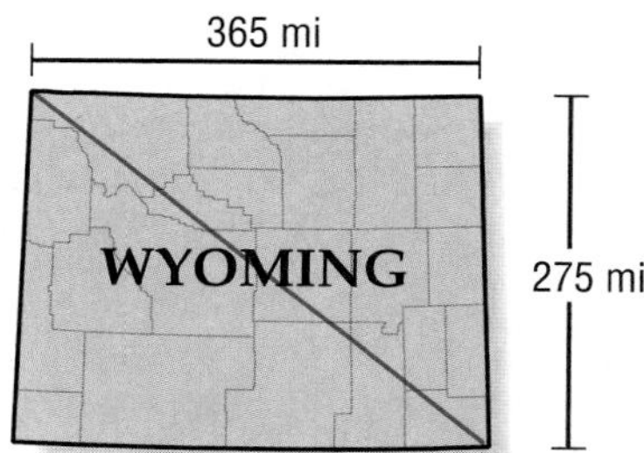

Write an equation you could use to find the length of the missing side of each right triangle. Then find the missing length. Round to the nearest tenth if necessary.

22. b, 99 mm; c, 101 mm
23. a, 48 yd; b, 55 yd
24. a, 17 ft; c, 20 ft
25. a, 23 in.; b, 18 in.
26. b, 4.5 m; c, 9.4 m
27. b, 5.1 m; c, 12.3 m

28. **TRAVEL** The Research Triangle in North Carolina is formed by Raleigh, Durham, and Chapel Hill. Is this triangle a right triangle? Explain.

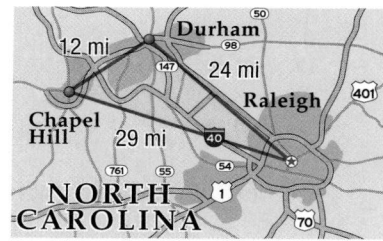

12 mi
Durham
24 mi
Raleigh
Chapel Hill
29 mi
NORTH CAROLINA

ILS • ISAT

Extra Practice, pp. 676, 702

H.O.T. Problems

29. **OPEN ENDED** State three measures that could be the side measures of a right triangle. Justify your answer.

30. **FIND THE ERROR** Jacinta and Akio are finding the length of the third side of the right triangle. Who is correct? Explain your reasoning.

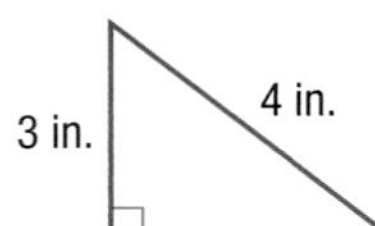

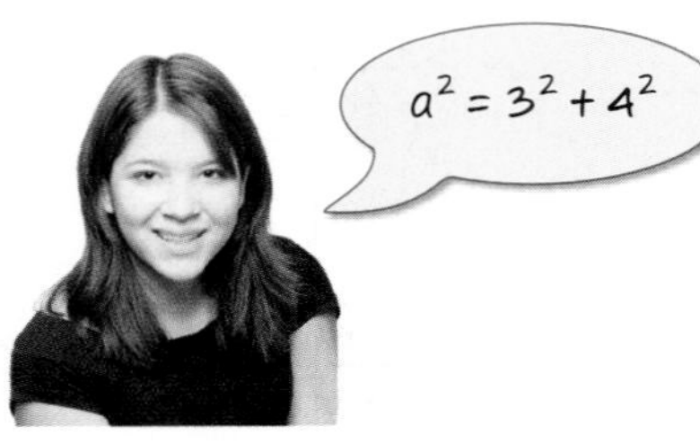

31. **CHALLENGE** The whole numbers 3, 4, and 5 are called Pythagorean triples because they satisfy the Pythagorean Theorem. Find three other sets of Pythagorean triples.

32. **WRITING IN MATH** Explain why you can use any two sides of a right triangle to find the third side.

ISAT PRACTICE 9.D.3

33. What is the perimeter of the triangle *ABC*?

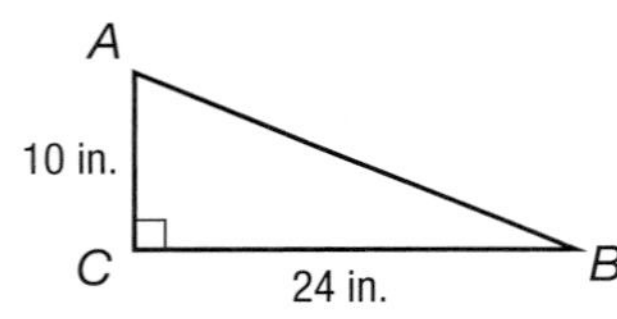

A 26 in.
B 34 in.
C 60 in.
D 68 in.

34. **SHORT RESPONSE** The base of a ten-foot ladder stands six feet from a house.

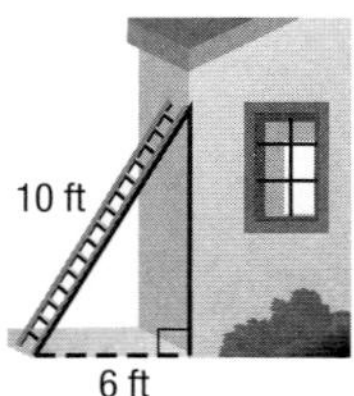

How many feet up the side of the house does the ladder reach?

Spiral Review

Replace each ● with <, >, or = to make each a true sentence. (Lesson 3-4)

35. $\sqrt{12}$ ● 3.5
36. $\sqrt{41}$ ● 6.4
37. $5.\overline{6}$ ● $\frac{17}{3}$
38. $\sqrt{55}$ ● $7.\overline{4}$

39. **ALGEBRA** Estimate the solution of $x^2 = 77$ to the nearest integer. (Lesson 3-2)

GET READY for the Next Lesson

PREREQUISITE SKILL Solve each equation. Check your solution. (Lesson 1-9)

40. $57 = x + 24$
41. $82 = 54 + y$
42. $71 = 35 + z$
43. $64 = a + 27$

3-6 Using The Pythagorean Theorem

MAIN IDEA

Solve problems using the Pythagorean Theorem.

IL Learning Standards

9.D.3 Compute distances, lengths and measures of angles **using** proportions, **the Pythagorean theorem and its converse.** *Also addresses 6.B.3c, 7.A.3b, 8.D.3c.*

IL Math Online

glencoe.com

- Extra Examples
- Personal Tutor
- Self-Check Quiz

GET READY for the Lesson

PARASAILING In parasailing, a towrope is used to attach a parasailor to a boat.

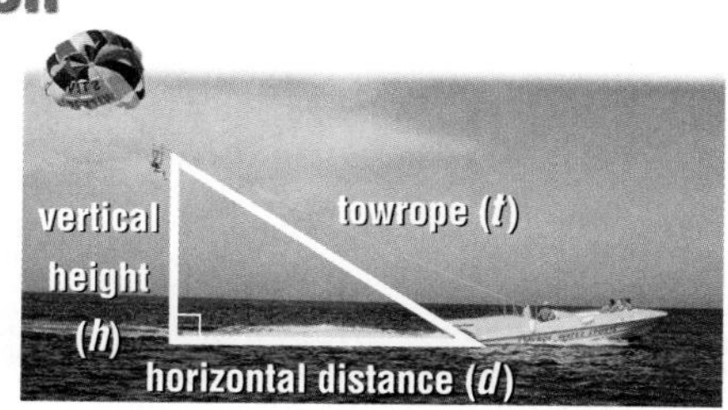

1. What type of triangle is formed by the horizontal distance, the vertical height, and the length of the towrope?
2. Write an equation that can be used to find the length of the towrope.

The Pythagorean Theorem can be used to solve a variety of problems.

Real-World EXAMPLE

1 PARASAILING Find the height of the parasailor above the surface of the water.

Notice that the vertical and horizontal distances, along with the length of the rope, form a right triangle. Use the Pythagorean Theorem.

$c^2 = a^2 + b^2$	Pythagorean Theorem
$200^2 = a^2 + 135^2$	Replace c with 200 and b with 135.
$40{,}000 = a^2 + 18{,}225$	Evaluate 200^2 and 135^2.
$40{,}000 - 18{,}225 = a^2 + 18{,}225 - 18{,}225$	Subtract 18,225 from each side.
$21{,}775 = a^2$	Simplify.
$\pm\sqrt{21{,}775} = a$	Definition of square root
$148 \text{ or } -148 \approx a$	Simplify.

The parasailor is about 148 feet above the surface of the water.

CHECK Your Progress

a. **AVIATION** Write an equation that can be used to find the distance between the planes. Then solve. Round to the nearest tenth.

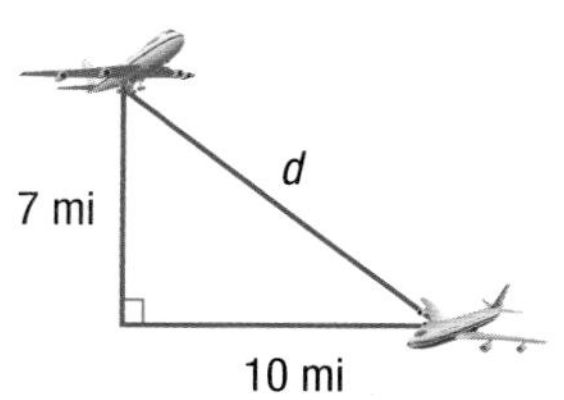

ISAT EXAMPLE 9.D.3

2 A circular lawn sprinkler with a range of 25 feet is placed 20 feet from the edge of a lawn. Find the length of the section of the lawn's edge that is within the range of the sprinkler.

A 15 ft

B 20 ft

C 25 ft

D 30 ft

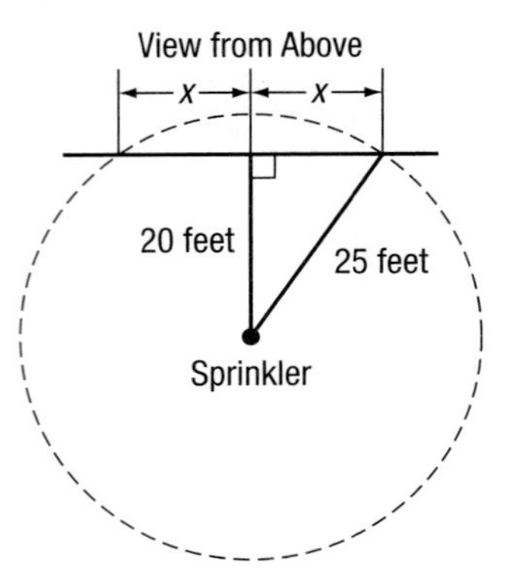

Read the Item

From the diagram, you know that the distance of the sprinkler from the lawn's edge, the sprinkler's range, and a section of the lawn's edge all form a right triangle. The section of the lawn's edge within the range of the sprinkler is twice the section forming the right triangle.

Solve the Item

Use the Pythagorean Theorem.

$a^2 + b^2 = c^2$	Pythagorean Theorem
$20^2 + x^2 = 25^2$	$a = 20$, $b = x$, and $c = 25$.
$400 + x^2 = 625$	Evaluate 20^2 and 25^2.
$400 - 400 + x^2 = 625 - 400$	Subtract 400 from each side.
$x^2 = 225$	Simplify.
$x = \pm\sqrt{225}$	Definition of square root
$x = 15$ or -15	Simplify.

The length of the section of the lawn's edge within the sprinkler's range is $x + x$ or $15 + 15 = 30$ feet. Therefore, choice D is correct.

Test-Taking Tip

Pythagorean Triples Look for measures that are multiples of a 3-4-5 right triangle.
$25 = 5 \cdot 5$
$20 = 4 \cdot 5$
$x = 3 \cdot 5$ or 15

CHECK Your Progress

b. If the *rise* of the stairs of a building is 5 feet and the *run* is 12 feet, how long is it from point A to point B?

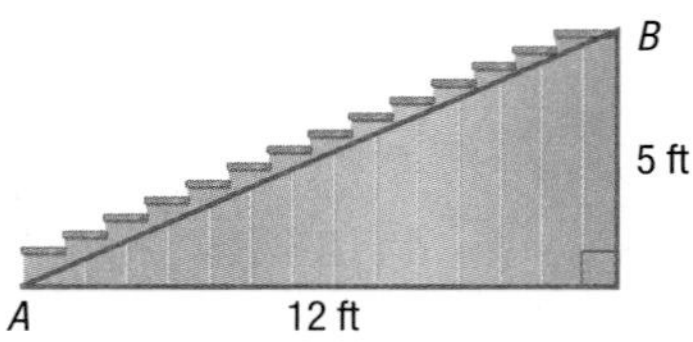

F 13 ft

G 12 ft

H 11 ft

J 10 ft

CHECK Your Understanding

Example 1 (p. 167)

Write an equation that can be used to answer the question. Then solve. Round to the nearest tenth if necessary.

1. What is the height of the tent?

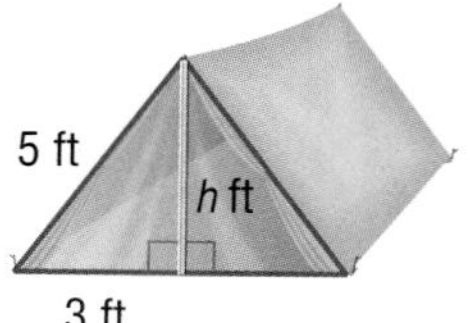

2. How high is the wheel chair ramp?

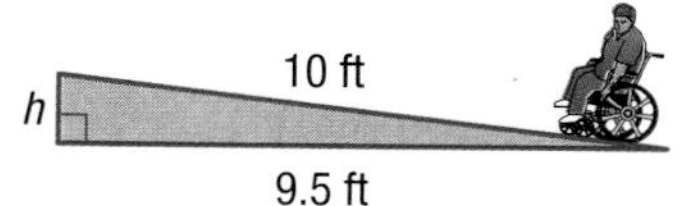

3. **GEOMETRY** An *isosceles* right triangle is a right triangle in which both legs are equal in length. If one leg of an isosceles triangle is 4 inches long, what is the length of the hypotenuse?

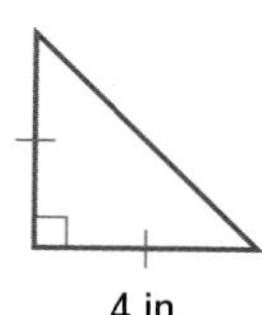

Example 2 (p. 168)

4. **MULTIPLE CHOICE** Abigail designed a stained glass window in the shape of a kite. What is the perimeter of the window?

   A 108 in.
   B 114 in.
   C 162 in.
   D 168 in.

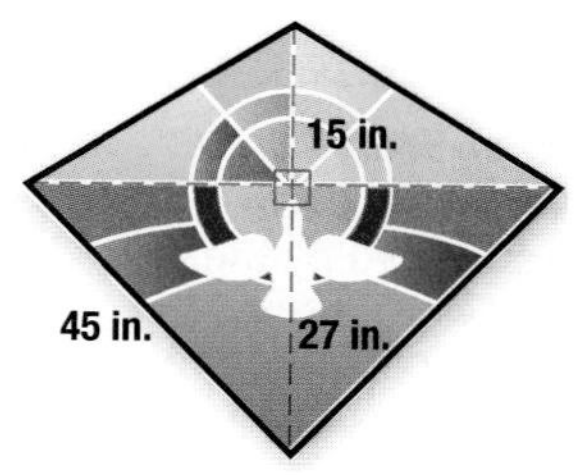

Practice and Problem Solving

HOMEWORK HELP	
For Exercises	See Examples
5–10	1
21, 22	2

Write an equation that can be used to answer the question. Then solve. Round to the nearest tenth if necessary.

5. How far up the tree is the cat?

6. How deep is the water?

7. How far away is the bird?

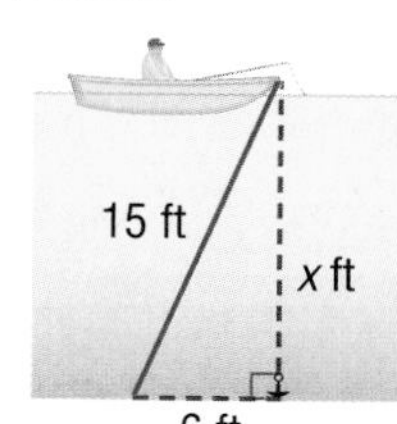

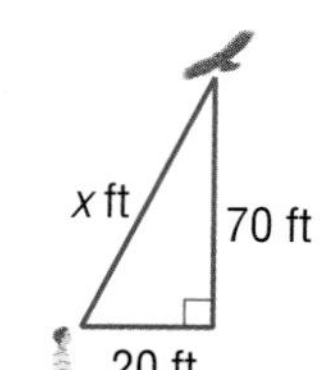

For Exercises 8–10, use the map of the Woodlands Camp at the right. Round your answers to the nearest tenth.

8. How far is it from Sycamore cabin to Oak cabin?

9. A camper in Hickory cabin wants to visit a friend in Elm cabin. How much farther is it if she walks to the Mess Hall first?

10. A group of campers walk from Elm cabin to Maple cabin, then to the Mess Hall. How far do they walk?

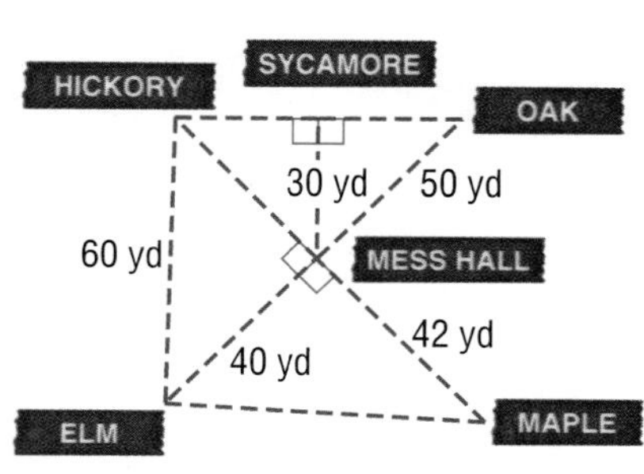

11. **DISTANCE** Antoine wants to go from his house to his grandmother's house. How much distance is saved if he takes Main Street instead of Market and Exchange?

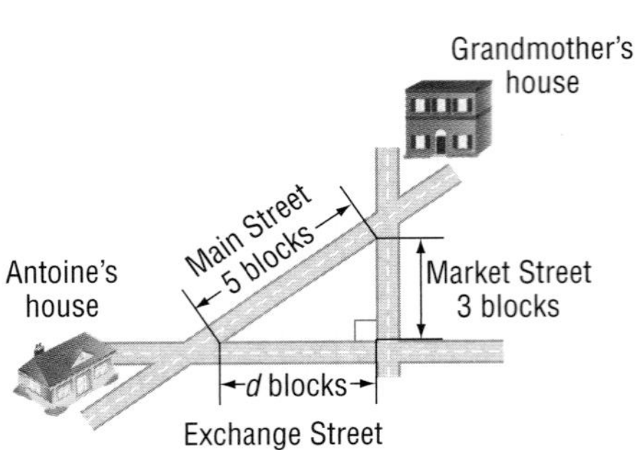

12. **GEOGRAPHY** Suppose Greenville, Rock Hill, and Columbia form a right triangle. What is the distance from Columbia to Greenville?

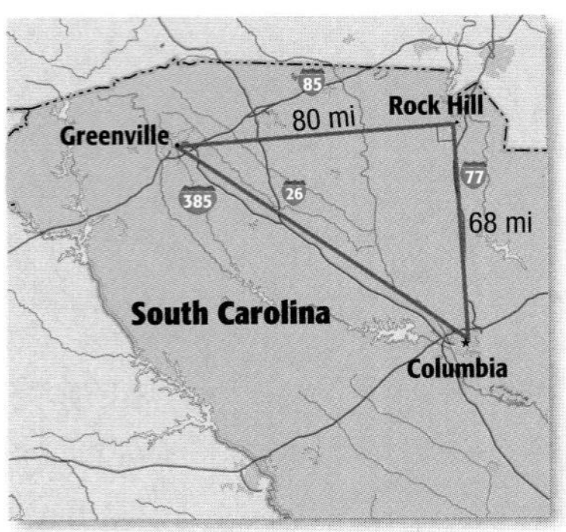

Real-World Link Televisions are advertised by their diagonal measure. The most common sizes are 27–32 inches.

13. **ENTERTAINMENT** Connor loves to watch movies in the widescreen format on his television. He wants to buy a new television with a screen that is at least 25 inches by 13.6 inches. What diagonal size television meets Connor's requirements?

14. **ENGINEERING** Engineers often use trusses in their designs of bridges. What is the length of the beam needed for the base of this design?

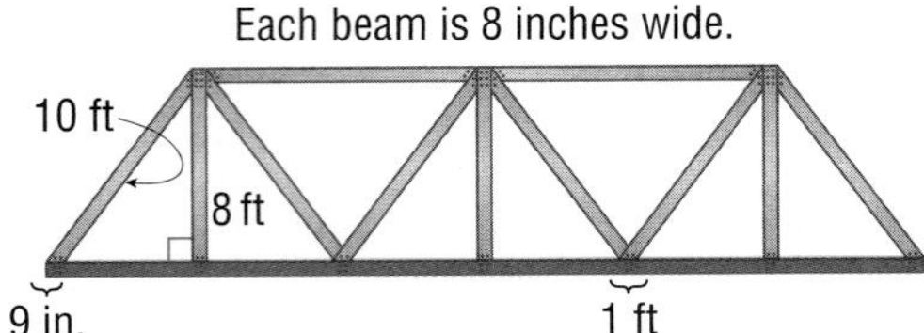

15. **GEOMETRY** Find the length of the hypotenuse *AB*. The length of segment *AD* is congruent to the length of segment *DE*. Round your answer to the nearest tenth.

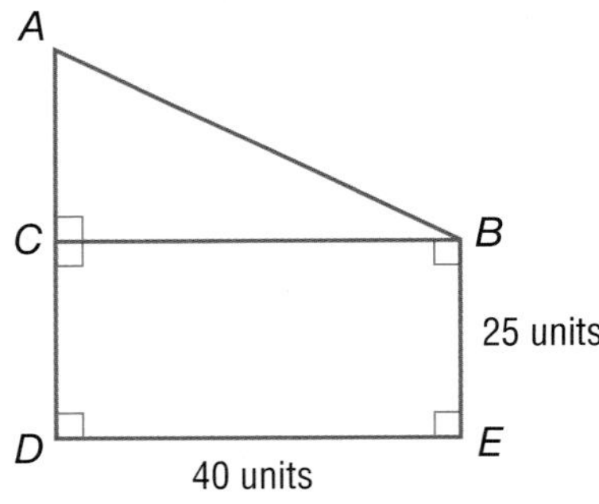

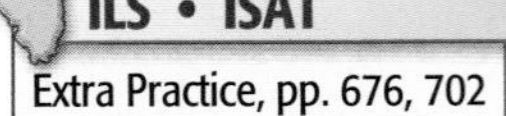

Extra Practice, pp. 676, 702

16. **FIND THE DATA** Refer to the Data File on pages 16–19. Choose some data and write a real-world problem in which you would use the Pythagorean Theorem.

H.O.T. Problems

17. **OPEN ENDED** Write a problem that can be solved by using the Pythagorean Theorem. Then explain how to solve the problem.

18. **Which One Doesn't Belong?** Each set of numbers represents the side measures of a triangle. Identify the set that does not belong with the other three. Explain your reasoning.

3–4–5   12–35–37   3–5–7   6–8–10

19. **CHALLENGE** Suppose a ladder 20 feet long is placed against a vertical wall 20 feet high. How far would the top of the ladder move down the wall by pulling out the bottom of the ladder 5 feet? Explain your reasoning.

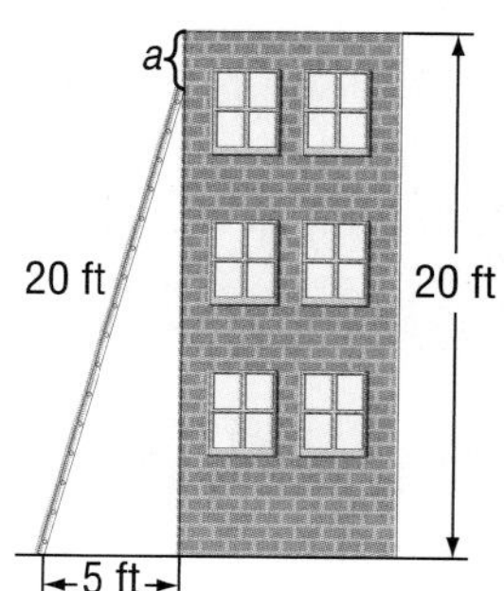

20. **WRITING IN MATH** The length of the hypotenuse of an isosceles right triangle is $\sqrt{288}$ units. Explain how to find the length of a leg.

ISAT PRACTICE 9.D.3

21. Ms. Johnson designed a rectangular garden. She plans to build a walkway through the garden as shown.

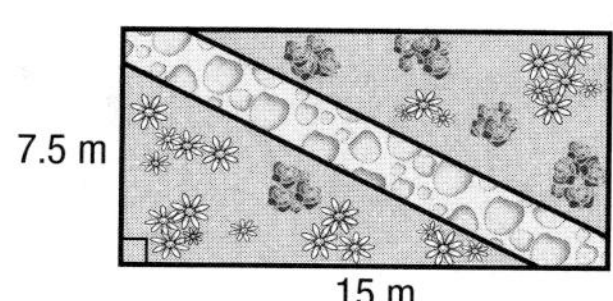

Which measure is closest to the length of the walkway?

A 8 m

B 11 m

C 17 m

D 23 m

22. A hot air balloon is tethered to the ground as shown.

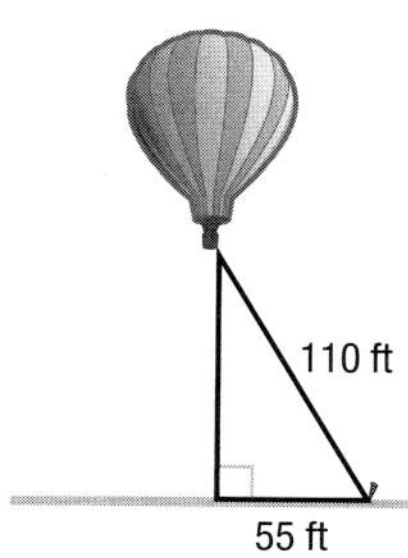

How high above the ground is the balloon?

F 55.0 ft **H** 123.0 ft

G 95.3 ft **J** 163.5 ft

Spiral Review

23. **GEOMETRY** Determine whether a triangle with sides 20 inches, 48 inches, and 52 inches long is a right triangle. Justify your anwer. (Lesson 3-5)

24. Order $\sqrt{45}$, $6.\overline{6}$, 6.75, and 6.7 from least to greatest. (Lesson 3-4)

Add or subtract. Write in simplest form. (Lesson 2-6)

25. $-3\frac{2}{3} + \left(-5\frac{3}{4}\right)$

26. $-1\frac{1}{8} - 7\frac{3}{4}$

27. $\frac{3}{5} - 4\frac{1}{2}$

28. $4\frac{7}{8} + \left(-6\frac{5}{6}\right)$

29. **ARCHAEOLOGY** Stone tools found in Ethiopia are estimated to be 2.5 million years old. That is about 700,000 years older than similar tools found in Tanzania. Write and solve an addition equation to find the age of the tools found in Tanzania. (Lesson 1-9)

GET READY for the Next Lesson

PREREQUISITE SKILL **Graph each point on the same coordinate plane.**

30. $T(5, 2)$

31. $A(-1, 3)$

32. $M(-5, 0)$

33. $D(-2, -4)$

Extend 3-6

Geometry Lab
Graphing Irrational Numbers

MAIN IDEA

Graph irrational numbers.

IL Learning Standards

6.B.3c Identify and apply properties of real numbers including pi, squares, and **square roots.**
8.D.3c Apply properties of powers, perfect squares and **square roots.**

In Lesson 3-2, you found approximate locations for irrational numbers on a number line. You can also accurately graph irrational numbers.

ACTIVITY

Graph $\sqrt{34}$ on a number line as accurately as possible.

STEP 1 Find two numbers with squares that have a sum of 34.

$34 = 25 + 9$ The hypotenuse of a right triangle with legs that measure 5 and 3 units will measure $\sqrt{34}$ units.

$34 = 5^2 + 3^2$

STEP 2 Draw a number line on grid paper. Then draw a right triangle with legs that measure 5 and 3 units.

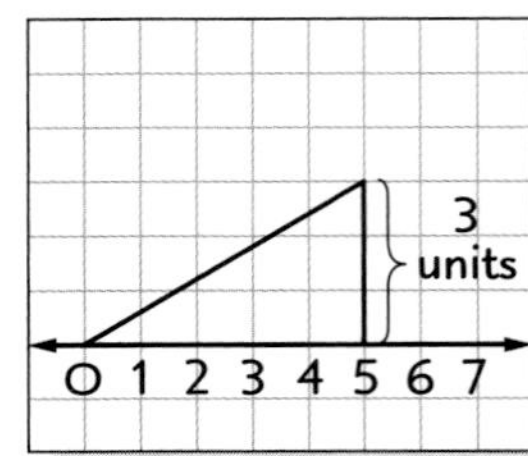

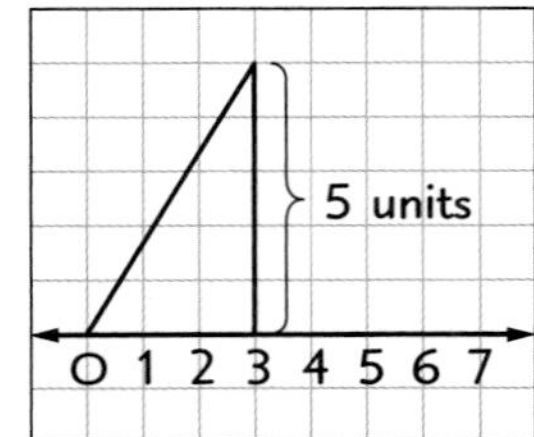

STEP 3 Adjust your compass to the length of the hypotenuse. Place the compass at 0 and draw an arc that intersects the number line. The point of intersection corresponds to the number $\sqrt{34}$.

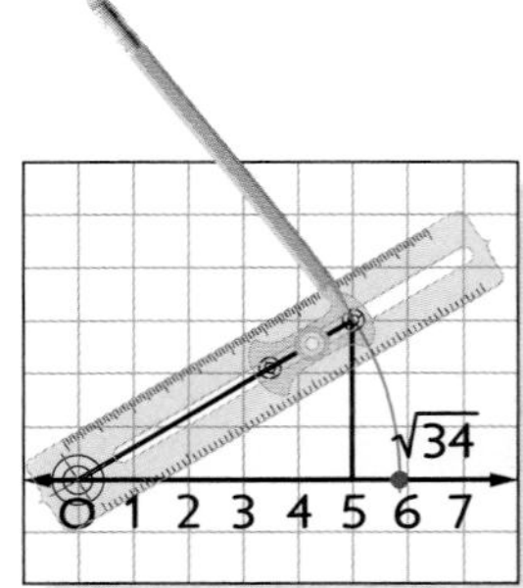

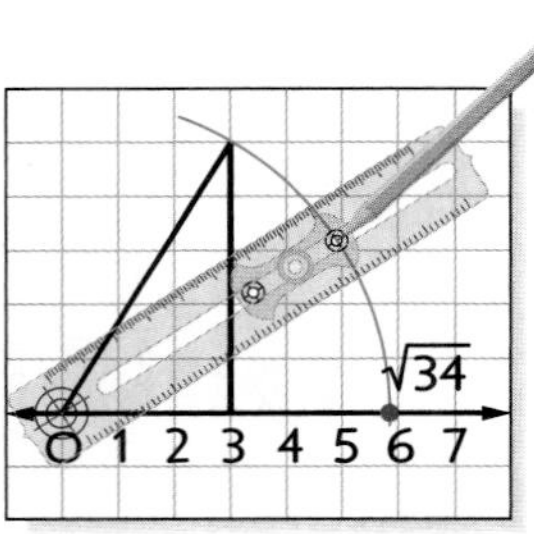

CHECK Your Progress **Graph each irrational number.**

a. $\sqrt{10}$ b. $\sqrt{13}$ c. $\sqrt{17}$ d. $\sqrt{8}$

ANALYZE THE RESULTS

1. Explain how you decide what lengths to make the legs of the right triangle when graphing an irrational number.
2. Explain how the graph of $\sqrt{2}$ can be used to graph $\sqrt{3}$.
3. **MAKE A CONJECTURE** Do you think you could graph the square root of any whole number? Explain your reasoning.

3-7 Geometry: Distance on the Coordinate Plane

MAIN IDEA

Graph rational numbers on the coordinate plane. Find the distance between two points on the coordinate plane.

IL Learning Standards

8.D.3c Apply properties of powers, perfect squares and **square roots.**
9.D.3 Compute distances, lengths and measures of angles **using** proportions, **the Pythagorean theorem** and its converse. *Also addresses 6.B.3c, 7.A.3b.*

New Vocabulary

coordinate plane
origin
y-axis
x-axis
quadrants
ordered pair
x-coordinate
abscissa
y-coordinate
ordinate

IL Math Online

glencoe.com
- Extra Examples
- Personal Tutor
- Self-Check Quiz

GET READY for the Lesson

MOUNTAIN BIKING Evan was biking on a trail. A map of the trail is shown at the right. His brother timed his ride from point *A* to point *B*.

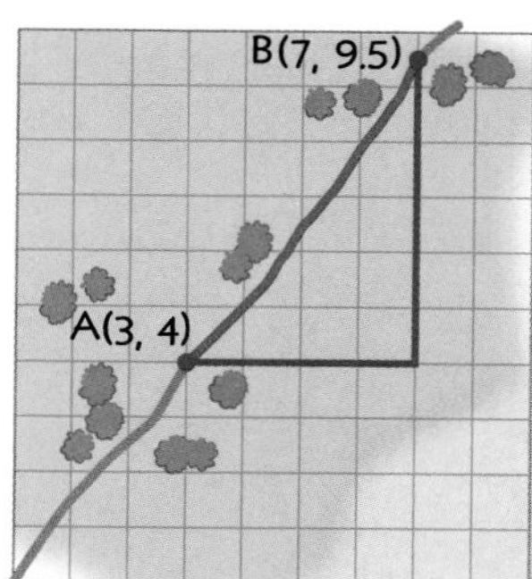
B(7, 9.5)
A(3, 4)

1. What does each colored line on the graph represent?
2. What type of triangle is formed by the lines?
3. What are the lengths of the two blue lines?

Recall that you can locate a point by using a coordinate system similar to the grid used by the mountain biker. It is called a **coordinate plane**.

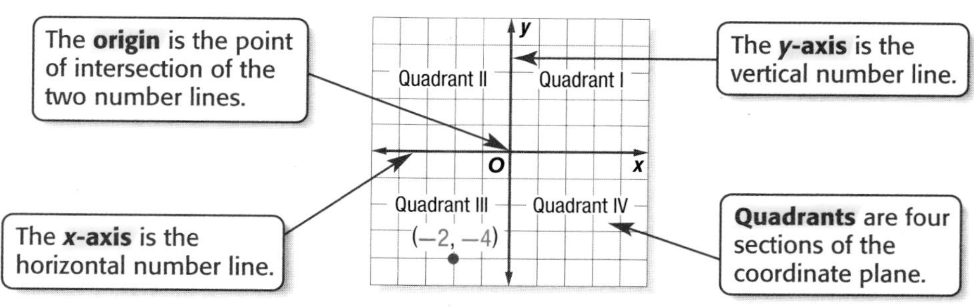
The **origin** is the point of intersection of the two number lines.
The ***y*-axis** is the vertical number line.
The ***x*-axis** is the horizontal number line.
Quadrants are four sections of the coordinate plane.
y
Quadrant II
Quadrant I
O
x
Quadrant III
Quadrant IV
(−2, −4)

Any point on the coordinate plane can be graphed by using an **ordered pair** of numbers. The first number in the ordered pair is the ***x*-coordinate** or **abscissa**. The second number is the ***y*-coordinate** or **ordinate**.

EXAMPLES Name an Ordered Pair

1 **Name the ordered pair for point *P*.**

- Start at the origin.
- Move right to find the *x*-coordinate of point *P*, which is $3\frac{1}{2}$.
- Move up to find the *y*-coordinate, which is 2.

So, the ordered pair for point *P* is $\left(3\frac{1}{2}, 2\right)$.

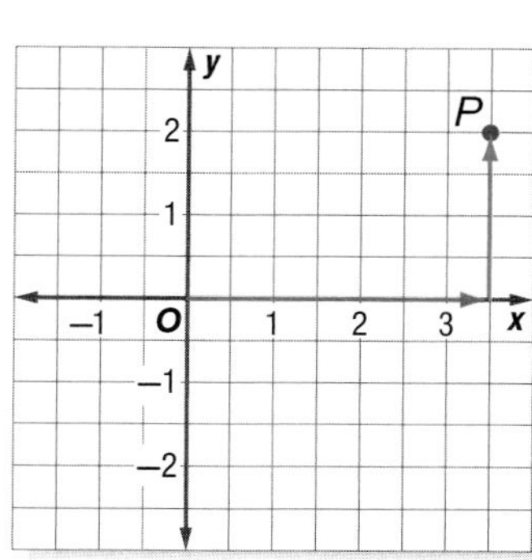
y
P
2
1
−1
O
1
2
3
x
−1
−2

2 **Name the ordered pair for point Q.**

- Start at the origin.
- Move left to find the x-coordinate of point Q, which is $-4\frac{1}{2}$.
- Move down to find the y-coordinate, which is $-1\frac{1}{2}$.

So, the ordered pair for point Q is $\left(-4\frac{1}{2}, -1\frac{1}{2}\right)$.

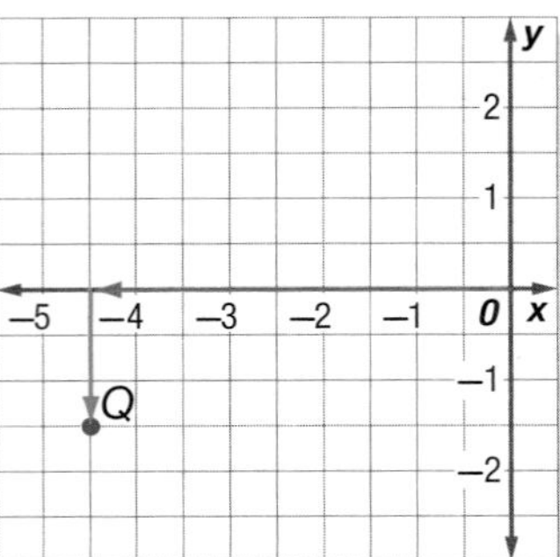

CHECK Your Progress

Name the ordered pair for each point.

a. J

b. K

c. L

d. M

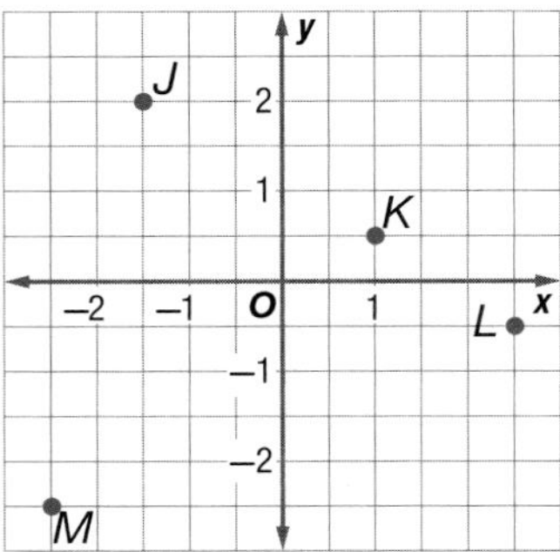

EXAMPLES Graphing Ordered Pairs

Graph and label each point.

3 **$A(0.5, 1.75)$**

- Start at the origin and move 0.5 unit to the right. Then move up 1.75 units.
- Draw a dot and label it $A(0.5, 1.75)$.

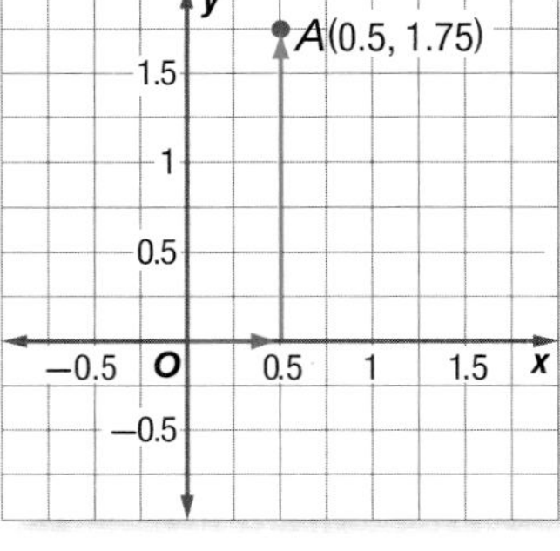

Study Tip

Graphing
Since both coordinates are negative, be sure you move left and then down.

4 $B\left(-2, -3\frac{1}{4}\right)$

- Start at the origin and move 2 units to the left. Then move down $3\frac{1}{4}$ or 3.25 units.
- Draw a dot and label it $B\left(-2, -3\frac{1}{4}\right)$.

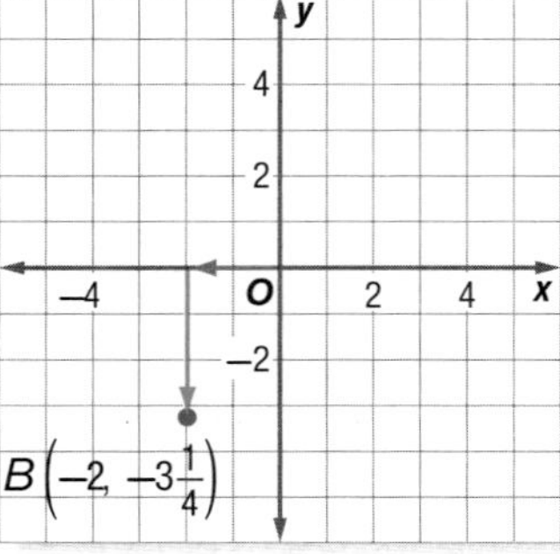

CHECK Your Progress

Graph and label each point.

e. $R\left(2\frac{1}{4}, 3\frac{1}{2}\right)$

f. $S(-1.5, 3)$

g. $T\left(-\frac{1}{2}, -3\frac{3}{4}\right)$

You can use the Pythagorean Theorem to find the distance between two points on the coordinate plane.

Study Tip

Distance
To find the distance between two points on the coordinate plane, graph the points then draw a right triangle with c as the hypotenuse.

EXAMPLE Find Distance on the Coordinate Plane

5 **Graph the ordered pairs (3, 0) and (7, −5). Then find the distance c between the two points.**

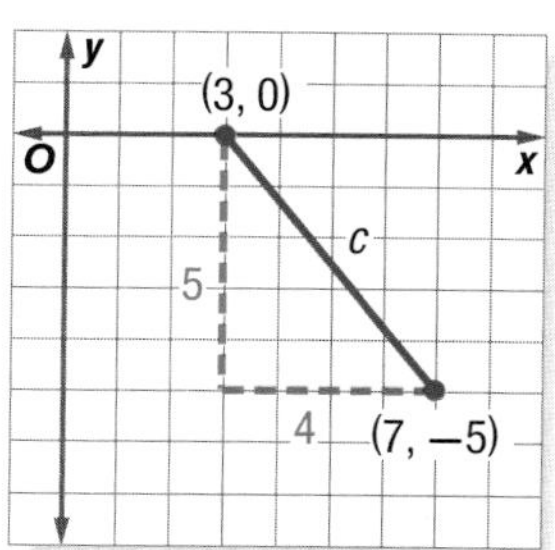

$c^2 = a^2 + b^2$	Pythagorean Theorem
$c^2 = 4^2 + 5^2$	Replace a with 4 and b with 5.
$c^2 = 41$	$4^2 + 5^2 = 16 + 25$ or 41
$\sqrt{c^2} = \pm\sqrt{41}$	Definition of square root
$c \approx \pm 6.4$	Use a calculator.

The points are about 6.4 units apart.

CHECK Your Progress

Graph each pair of ordered pairs. Then find the distance between the points. Round to the nearest tenth.

h. (2, 0), (5, −4) i. (1, 3), (−2, 4) j. (−3,−4), (2, −1)

Real-World EXAMPLE

Real-World Link
The United States Military Academy, also known as West Point, graduates more than 900 officers each year. The same is true for the United States Naval Academy, which is located in Annapolis.
Source: U.S. Military Academy

6 **MAPS On the map, each unit represents 45 miles. West Point, New York, is located at $\left(1\frac{1}{2}, 2\right)$ and Annapolis, Maryland, is located at $\left(-1\frac{1}{2}, -1\frac{1}{2}\right)$. What is the approximate distance between West Point and Annapolis?**

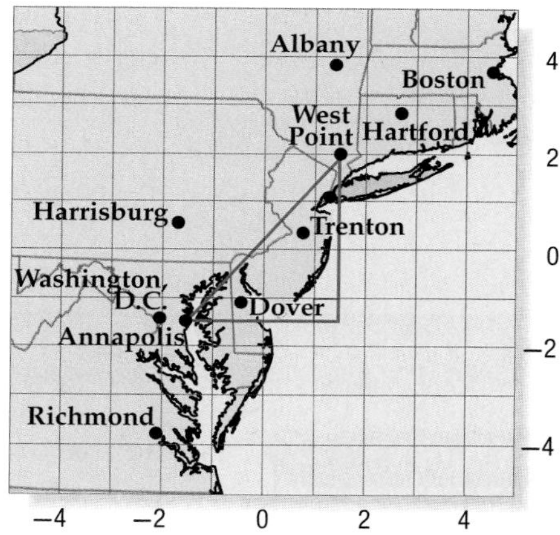

Let c represent the distance between West Point and Annapolis. Then $a = 3$ and $b = 3.5$.

$c^2 = a^2 + b^2$	Pythagorean Theorem
$c^2 = 3^2 + 3.5^2$	Replace a with 3 and b with 3.5.
$c^2 = 21.25$	$3^2 + 3.5^2 = 9 + 12.25$ or 21.25
$\sqrt{c^2} = \pm\sqrt{21.25}$	Definition of square root
$c \approx \pm 4.6$	The map distance is about 4.6 units.

Since each map unit equals 45 miles, the distance between the cities is $4.6 \cdot 45$ or about 207 miles.

CHECK Your Progress

k. **SPORTS** Cromwell field is located at $\left(2\frac{1}{2}, 3\frac{1}{2}\right)$ and Dedeaux Field at $\left(1\frac{1}{2}, 4\frac{1}{2}\right)$ on a map. Graph these points. If each map unit is 0.1 mile, about how far apart are the fields?

CHECK Your Understanding

Examples 1, 2 (pp. 173–174)

Name the ordered pair for each point.

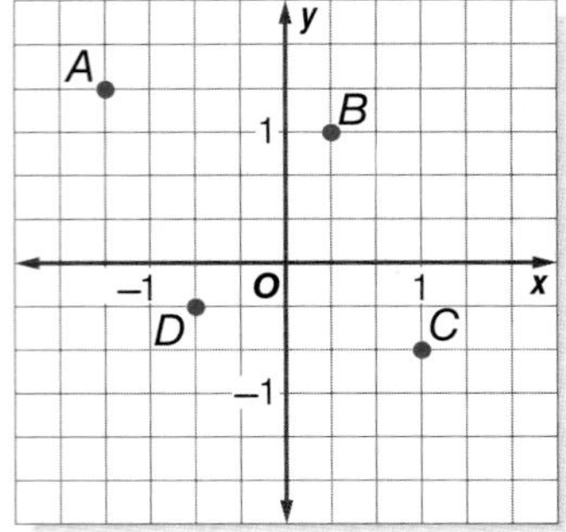

1. A
2. B
3. C
4. D

Examples 3, 4 (p. 174)

Graph and label each point.

5. $J\left(\frac{1}{4}, 3\frac{1}{2}\right)$
6. $K\left(-1, -2\frac{3}{4}\right)$
7. $L(4.5, -2.25)$
8. $M(-2.5, 2.5)$

Example 5 (p. 175)

Graph each pair of ordered pairs. Then find the distance between the points. Round to the nearest tenth if necessary.

9. (1, 5), (3, 1)
10. (−1, 0), (2, 7)
11. (−5.5, −2), (2.5, 3)

12. **GEOMETRY** Square $ABCD$ is graphed on the coordinate plane. What is the length of each side? What is the area? Round to the nearest tenth.

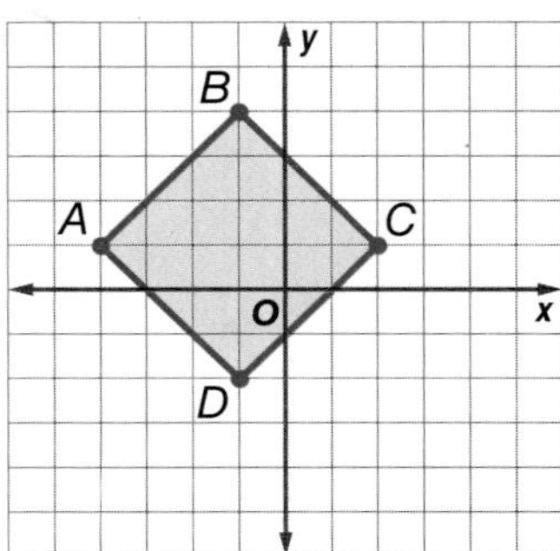

Example 6 (p. 175)

13. **PARKS** On a park map, the ranger station is located at (2.5, 3.5) and the nature center is located at (0.5, 4). Each unit in the map is equal to 0.5 mile. Graph the ordered pairs. What is the approximate distance between the ranger station and the nature center?

Practice and Problem Solving

HOMEWORK HELP	
For Exercises	See Examples
14–21	1
22–27	2, 3
28–33	4, 5
34–35	6

Name the ordered pair for each point.

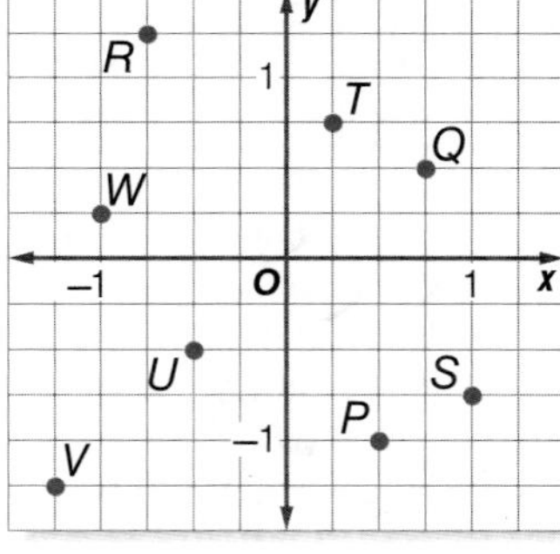

14. P
15. Q
16. R
17. S
18. T
19. U
20. V
21. W

Graph and label each point.

22. $E\left(\frac{3}{4}, 2\frac{1}{4}\right)$
23. $F\left(\frac{2}{5}, 1\frac{1}{2}\right)$
24. $G\left(-3, 4\frac{2}{3}\right)$
25. $H\left(-2\frac{1}{4}, 3\frac{4}{5}\right)$
26. $J(4.3, -3.1)$
27. $K(-3.75, -0.5)$

Graph each pair of ordered pairs. Then find the distance between the points. Round to the nearest tenth if necessary.

28. (4, 5), (2, 2)
29. (6, 2), (1, 0)
30. (−3, 4), (1, 3)
31. (−5, 1), (2, 4)
32. (2.5, −1), (−3.5, −5)
33. (4, −2.3), (−1, −6.3)

34. **NAVIGATION** A ferry sets sail from an island located at (4, 12) on the map at the right. Its destination is Ferry Landing B at (6, 2). How far will the ferry travel if each unit on the grid is 0.5 mile?

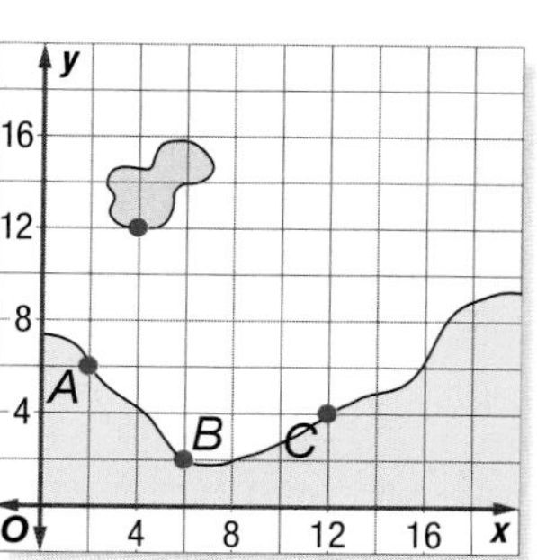

35. **GEOGRAPHY** On a map of Florida, Clearwater is located at (3, 2.5), and Jacksonville is located at (8.5, 14.5). Each unit on the map equals 16.5 miles. Graph the ordered pairs. What is the approximate distance between the cities?

Find the area of each rectangle.

36.

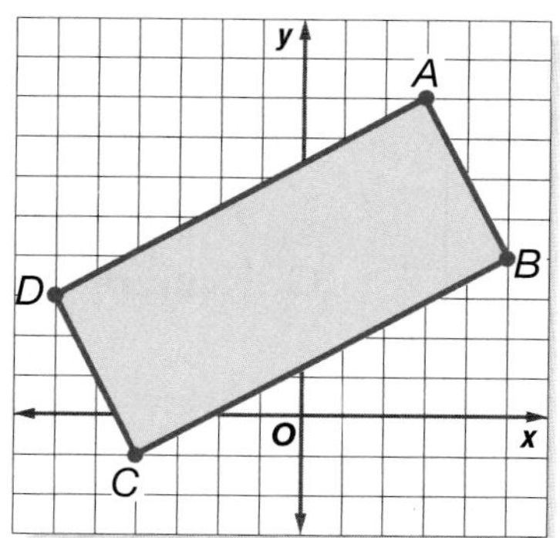

37.

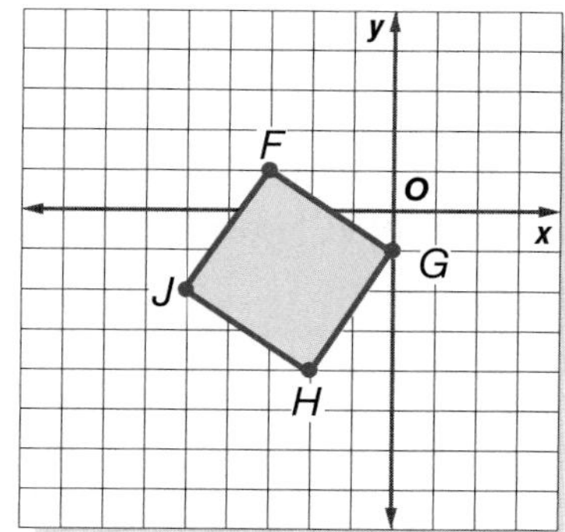

38. **TRAVEL** Chicago, Illinois, has a longitude of 88° W and a latitude of 42° N. Indianapolis, Indiana, is located at 86° W and 40° N. At this longitude/latitude, each degree is about 53 miles. Find the distance between Chicago and Indianapolis.

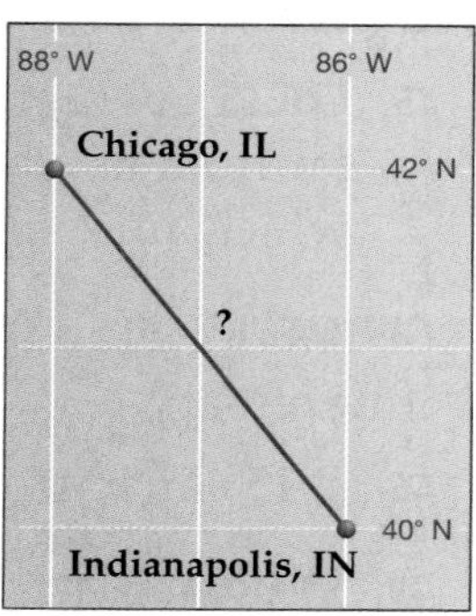

ILS • ISAT
Extra Practice, pp. 676, 702

39. **GEOMETRY** If one point is located at (−5, 4) and another point is located at (−8, −2), find the distance between the points.

H.O.T. Problems

40. **CHALLENGE** Apply what you have learned about distance on the coordinate plane to determine the coordinates of the endpoints of a line segment that is neither horizontal nor vertical and has a length of 5 units.

41. **SELECT A TOOL** Kendra needs to find the distance between the points $A(-2.4, 3.7)$ and $B(4.6, -1.3)$. Which of the following tools will be most useful to Kendra? Justify your selection(s). Then use the tool(s) to solve the problem.

calculator | paper and pencil | real objects

42. **WRITING IN MATH** In your own words, explain how to find the length of a non-vertical and a non-horizontal segment whose endpoints are (x_1, y_1) and (x_2, y_2).

ISAT PRACTICE 8.D.3c, 9.D.3

43. The map shows the location of the towns of Springfield, Centerville, and Point Pleasant.

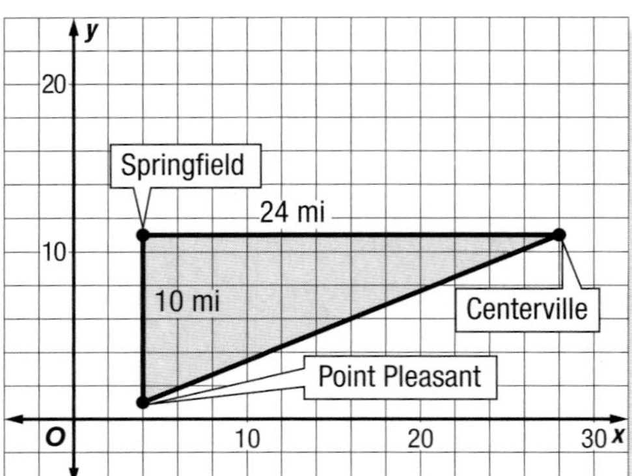

What is the shortest distance between Centerville and Point Pleasant?

A 14 mi **C** 26 mi

B 22 mi **D** 34 mi

44. Rectangle *ABCD* is graphed on the coordinate plane.

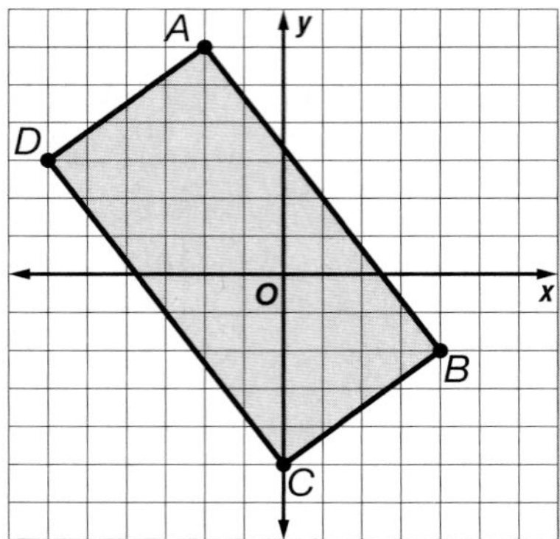

Find the area of rectangle *ABCD*.

F 30 units^2 **H** 60 units^2

G 50 units^2 **J** 100 units^2

Spiral Review

45. CHESS A knight moves two spaces over then one space up. About how far from its starting position is a knight that makes two moves, both of which are 2 spaces right and 1 space up? (Lesson 3-6)

GEOMETRY Find the missing side of each right triangle. Round to the nearest tenth if necessary. (Lesson 3-5)

46. a, 15 cm; b, 18 cm **47.** b, 14 in.; c, 17 in. **48.** a, 36 km; b, 40 km

49. ENERGY Electricity costs $6\frac{1}{2}$¢ per kilowatt-hour. Of that cost, $3\frac{1}{4}$¢ goes toward the cost of the fuel. What fraction of the cost goes toward fuel? (Lesson 2-4)

ALGEBRA Write and solve an equation to find each number. (Lesson 1-10)

50. The product of a number and 8 is 56.

51. The quotient of a number and 7 is -14.

Problem Solving in Music

Real-World Unit Project

Music To My Ears It's time to complete your project. Use the information you have gathered about the mathematical relationship between notes and frequency to write your own music. Be sure to include a report explaining how your music is harmonious.

IL Math Online Unit Project at glencoe.com

CHAPTER 3 Study Guide and Review

IL Math Online glencoe.com
• STUDY TO GO
• Vocabulary Review

FOLDABLES Study Organizer GET READY to Study

Be sure the following Big Ideas are noted in your Foldable.

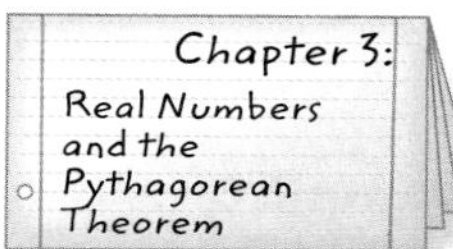

BIG Ideas

Square Roots and Irrational Numbers

(Lessons 3-1, 3-2, and 3-4)

- A square root of a number is one of its two equal factors.
- An irrational number is a number that cannot be expressed as $\frac{a}{b}$, where a and b are integers and $b \neq 0$.

Pythagorean Theorem (Lessons 3-5 to 3-7)

- In a right triangle, the square of the length of the hypotenuse is equal to the sum of the squares of the lengths of the legs.

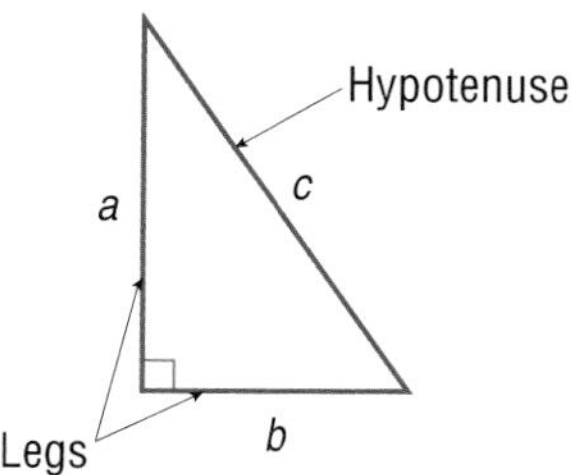

- If the sides of a triangle have lengths a, b, and c units such that $c^2 = a^2 + b^2$, then the triangle is a right triangle.

Key Vocabulary

coordinate plane (p. 173)
hypotenuse (p. 162)
irrational number (p. 155)
legs (p. 162)
perfect square (p. 144)
Pythagorean Theorem (p. 162)
radical sign (p. 144)
real number (p. 155)
square root (p. 144)
Venn diagram (p. 152)

Vocabulary Check

State whether each sentence is *true* or *false*. If *false*, replace the underlined word or number to make a true sentence.

1. The number <u>11</u> is a perfect square.
2. The symbol that is used to indicate a square root is the <u>radical sign</u>.
3. A <u>real number</u> is a number that cannot be expressed as the quotient of two integers.
4. If the measures of the sides of a triangle are 6 inches, 8 inches and 10 inches, then the triangle <u>is</u> a right triangle.
5. The opposite of squaring a number is finding a <u>converse.</u>
6. A Venn diagram uses overlapping <u>rectangles</u> to organize information and solve problems.
7. The hypotenuse is the <u>shortest</u> side of a right triangle.
8. The Pythagorean Theorem states that the sum of the squares of the lengths of the <u>legs</u> of a right triangle equals the square of the length of the hypotenuse.

Lesson-by-Lesson Review

3-1 Square Roots (pp. 144–147)

6.B.3c, 8.D.3c

Find each square root.

9. $\sqrt{81}$
10. $\pm\sqrt{225}$
11. $-\sqrt{64}$
12. $\sqrt{6.25}$

13. **SEWING** A quilter made 256 small squares for a larger quilt. If the quilt is shaped like a square, how many small squares will she use on each side?

Example 1 Find $\sqrt{36}$.

Since $6^2 = 36$, $\sqrt{36} = 6$.

Example 2 Find $-\sqrt{169}$.

Since $(-13)^2 = 169$, $-\sqrt{169} = -13$.

Example 3 Find $\pm\sqrt{1.21}$.

Since $(1.1)^2 = 1.21$ and $(-1.1)^2 = 1.21$, $\pm\sqrt{1.21} = \pm 1.1$.

3-2 Estimating Square Roots (pp. 148–151)

8.D.3c

Estimate to the nearest whole number.

14. $\sqrt{32}$
15. $\sqrt{42}$
16. $\sqrt{230}$
17. $\sqrt{96}$
18. $\sqrt{150}$
19. $\sqrt{8}$
20. $\sqrt{50.1}$
21. $\sqrt{19.25}$

22. **ALGEBRA** Estimate the solution of $b^2 = 60$ to the nearest integer.

Example 4 Estimate $\sqrt{135}$ to the nearest whole number.

$121 < 135 < 144$ Write an inequality.

$11^2 < 135 < 12^2$ $121 = 11^2$ and $144 = 12^2$

$11 < \sqrt{135} < 12$ Take the square root of each number.

Since 135 is closer to 144 than to 121, the best whole number estimate is 12.

3-3 PSI: Use a Venn Diagram (pp. 152–153)

6.B.3a, 6.C.3a

23. **APARTMENTS** An apartment complex offers 15 apartments with a view of the river, 8 with two bedrooms, and 6 that have both selections. How many have only a view of the river?

24. **LANGUAGE** At Madison Middle School, 95% of the students speak English fluently, 65% speak Spanish fluently, and 60% speak both English and Spanish fluently. What percent of the students speak only Spanish fluently?

Example 5 The Venn diagram shows the number of dog and cat owners.

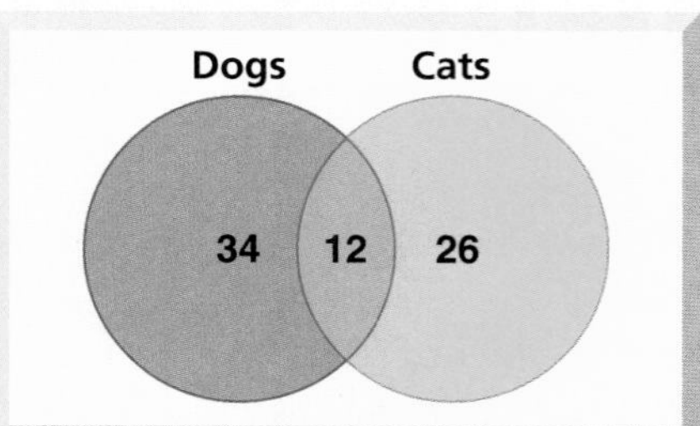

So, 34 people own only dogs, 26 people own only cats, and 12 own both.

Mixed Problem Solving
For mixed problem-solving practice, see page 702.

3-4 The Real Number System (pp. 155–159)

6.B.3c

Name all sets of numbers to which each real number belongs.

25. $-\sqrt{19}$
26. $0.\overline{3}$
27. 7.43
28. -12
29. $\sqrt{32}$
30. 101

31. **MEASUREMENT** The area of a square vegetable garden is 360 square meters. To the nearest hundredth meter, what is the perimeter of the garden?

Example 6 Name all sets of numbers to which $-\sqrt{33}$ belongs.

$-\sqrt{33} \approx -5.744562647$

Since the decimal does not terminate or repeat, it is an irrational number.

3-5 The Pythagorean Theorem (pp. 162–166)

9.D.3

Write an equation you could use to find the length of the missing side of each right triangle. Then find the missing length. Round to the nearest tenth if necessary.

32. 33.

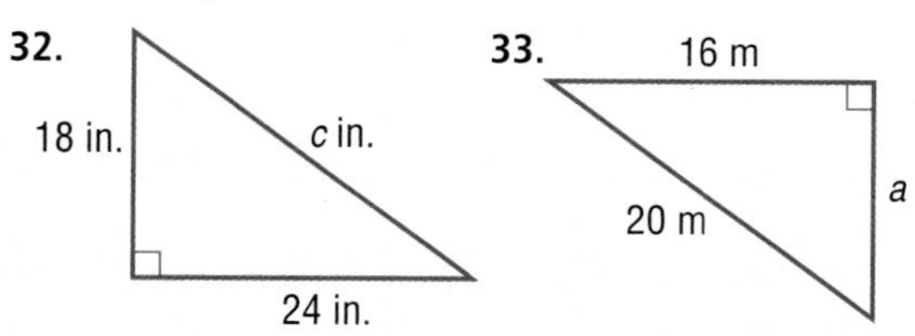

34. 35.

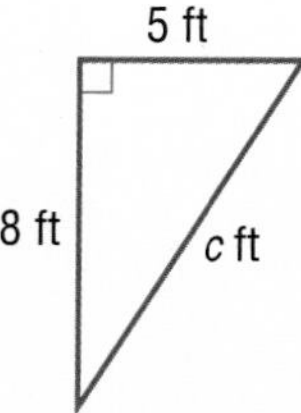

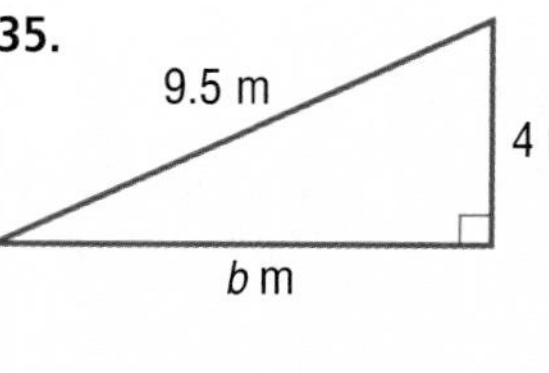

36. a, 5 in.; c, 6 in.
37. a, 6 cm; b, 7 cm

38. **GEOMETRY** Lolita drew a right triangle where the hypotenuse was 17 inches and one of the legs was 8 inches. What was the length of the third side?

Example 7 Write an equation you could use to find the length of the hypotenuse of the right triangle. Then find the missing length.

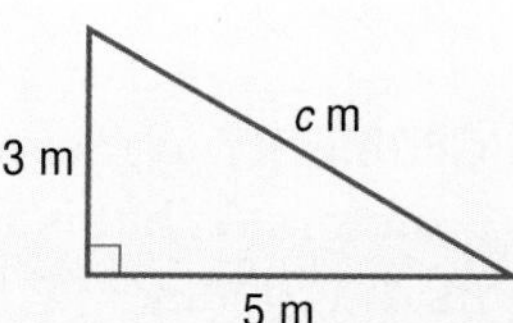

$c^2 = a^2 + b^2$	Pythagorean Theorem
$c^2 = 3^2 + 5^2$	Replace a with 3 and b with 5.
$c^2 = 9 + 25$	Evaluate 3^2 and 5^2.
$c^2 = 34$	Simplify.
$c = \pm\sqrt{34}$	Definition of square root
$c \approx \pm 5.8$	Use a calculator.

The hypotenuse is about 5.8 meters long.

3-6 Using the Pythagorean Theorem (pp. 167–171)

9.D.3

Write an equation that can be used to answer the question. Then solve. Round to the nearest tenth if necessary.

39. How high does the ladder reach?

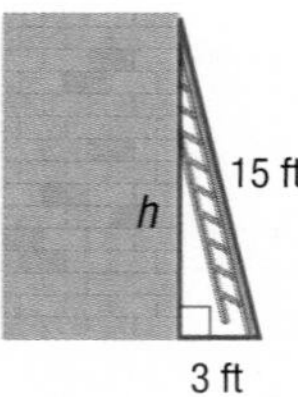

40. How wide is the kite?

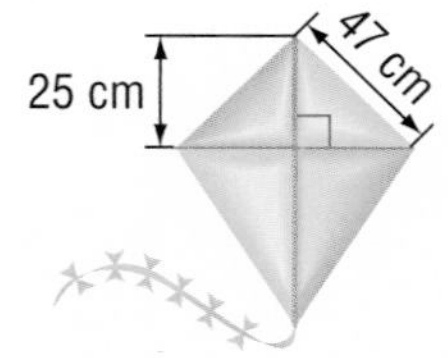

41. How wide is the television?

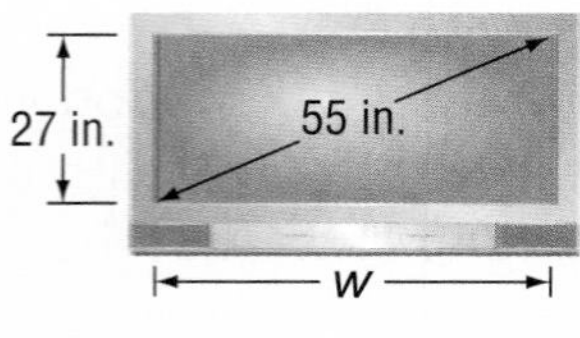

42. How far is the helicopter from the car?

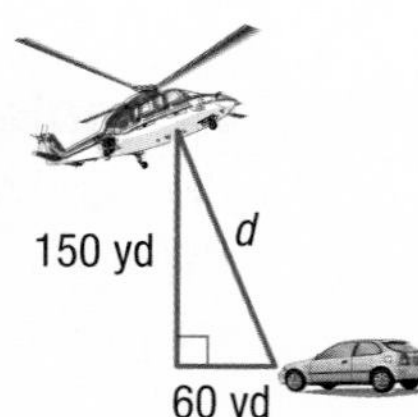

43. **GEOMETRY** A rectangle is 12 meters by 7 meters. What is the length of one of its diagonals?

Example 8 Write an equation that can be used to find the height of the pole where the wire is attached. Then solve.

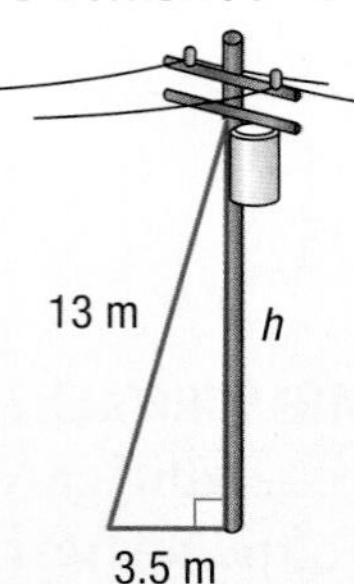

Use the Pythagorean Theorem to write the equation $13^2 = 3.5^2 + h^2$. Then solve the equation.

$$13^2 = 3.5^2 + h^2$$
$$169 = 12.25 + h^2$$
$$169 - 12.25 = 12.25 + h^2 - 12.25$$
$$156.75 = h^2$$
$$\pm\sqrt{156.75} = h$$
$$\pm 12.5 \approx h$$

The height of the pole where the wire is attached is about 12.5 feet.

3-7 Geometry: Distance on the Coordinate Plane (pp. 173–178)

8.D.3c, 9.D.3

Graph each pair of ordered pairs. Then find the distance between the points. Round to the nearest tenth if necessary.

44. (0, −3), (5, 5)
45. (−1, 2), (4, 8)
46. (−2, 1.5), (2, 3.6)
47. (−6, 2), (−4, 5)
48. (3, 4.2), (−2.1, 0)
49. (−1, 3), (2, 4)

50. **GEOMETRY** The coordinates of points R and S are (4, 3) and (1, 6). What is the distance between the points? Round to the nearest tenth if necessary.

Example 9 Graph the ordered pairs (2, 3) and (−1, 1). Then find the distance between the points.

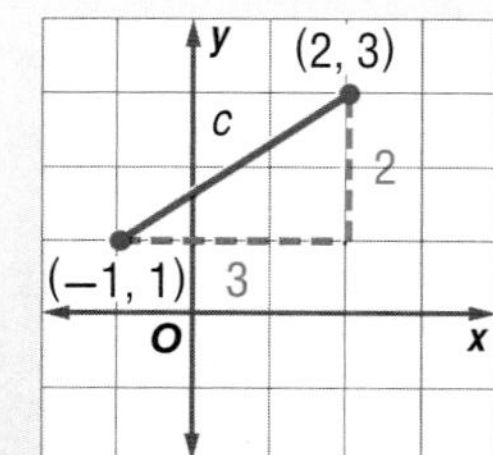

$$c^2 = a^2 + b^2$$
$$c^2 = 3^2 + 2^2$$
$$c^2 = 9 + 4$$
$$c^2 = 13$$
$$c = \sqrt{13}$$
$$c \approx 3.6$$

The distance is about 3.6 units.

Chapter 3 Practice Test

IL Math Online glencoe.com
• Chapter Test

Find each square root.

1. $\sqrt{225}$
2. $-\sqrt{0.25}$
3. $\pm\sqrt{\frac{36}{49}}$

4. **MULTIPLE CHOICE** Which list shows the numbers in order from least to greatest?

   A $2.\overline{2}, 2\frac{1}{5}, 2.25, \sqrt{5}$

   B $2\frac{1}{5}, 2.\overline{2}, \sqrt{5}, 2.25$

   C $\sqrt{5}, 2.25, 2\frac{1}{5}, 2.\overline{2}$

   D $2.25, \sqrt{5}, 2.\overline{2}, 2\frac{1}{5}$

Estimate to the nearest whole number.

5. $\sqrt{67}$
6. $\sqrt{118}$
7. $\sqrt{82}$

Name all sets of numbers to which each real number belongs.

8. $-\sqrt{64}$
9. $6.\overline{13}$
10. $\sqrt{14}$

11. **FOOD** Gino's Pizzeria conducted a survey of 50 customers. The results showed that 15 people liked cheese pizza and 25 liked pepperoni. Of those customers, 4 people liked both cheese and pepperoni pizza. How many people liked neither cheese nor pepperoni pizza? Use a Venn diagram.

Write an equation you could use to find each length of the missing side of each right triangle. Then find the missing length. Round to the nearest tenth if necessary.

12.

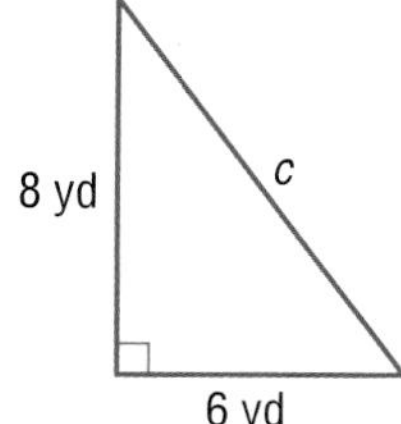

13.

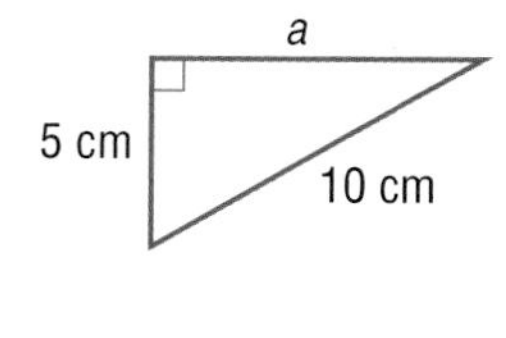

14. a, 55 in.; b, 48 in.
15. b, 12 ft; c, 20 ft

Determine whether each triangle with sides of given lengths is a right triangle. Justify your answer.

16. 12 in., 20 in., 24 in.
17. 34 cm, 30 cm, 16 cm
18. 15 ft, 25 ft, 20 ft
19. 7 yd, 14 yd, 35 yd

20. **MULTIPLE CHOICE** Justin is flying a kite.

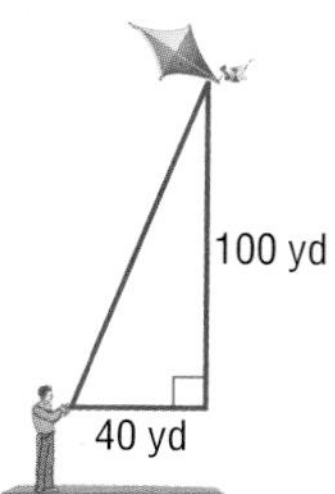

Which is closest to the length of the string?

F 70 yd
G 92 yd
H 108 yd
J 146 yd

21. **MEASUREMENT** Find the perimeter of a right triangle with legs of 10 inches and 8 inches.

22. **SURVEYING** A survey team calculated the distance across a river from point A to point B. How wide is the river at this point? Round to the nearest tenth.

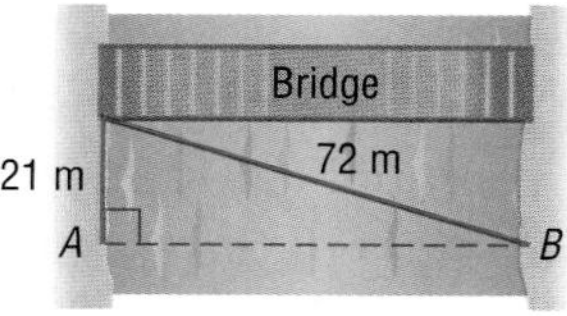

Graph each pair of ordered pairs. Then find the distance between points. Round to the nearest tenth if necessary.

23. $(-2, -2), (5, 6)$
24. $\left(\frac{1}{3}, 1\right), \left(-1\frac{1}{3}, 1\frac{2}{3}\right)$
25. $(-0.5, 0.25), (0.25, -0.75)$

CHAPTER 3 ISAT Practice

Cumulative, Chapters 1–3

IL Math Online glencoe.com
- Test Practice

PART 1 Multiple Choice

Read each question. Then fill in the correct answer on the answer sheet provided by your teacher or on a sheet of paper.

1. Erin jogged along the track around the outer edge of a park. She ran two miles along the one edge and then 3 miles along the other edge. She then cut across the park as shown by the dotted line. How far did she jog to get back to her starting point?

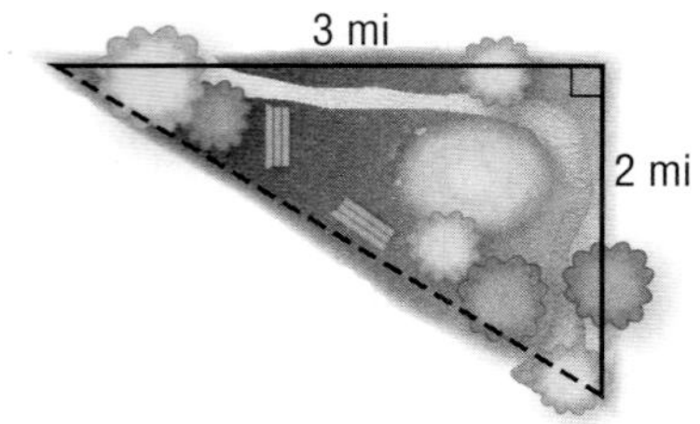

A 3 miles
B 3.6 miles
C 5.2 miles
D 13 miles

2. Michelle had to choose the number closest to 5. Which irrational number should she choose?

F $\sqrt{30}$
G $\sqrt{27}$
H $\sqrt{20}$
J $\sqrt{18}$

3. The Moon is about 3.84×10^5 kilometers from Earth. Which of the following represents this number in standard notation?

A 38,400,000 km
B 3,840,000 km
C 384,000 km
D 38,400 km

4. The square root of 250 is between

F 14 and 15.
G 15 and 16.
H 16 and 17.
J 17 and 18.

5. The proposed location of a new water tower intersects a section of an existing service road. Find x, the inside length of the section of road that is intersected by the water tower.

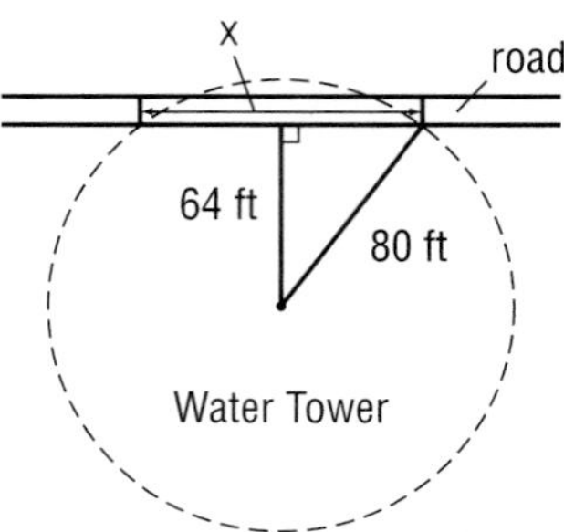

A 36 ft
B 48 ft
C 96 ft
D 112 ft

TEST-TAKING TIP

Question 5 Remember that the hypotenuse of a right triangle is always opposite the right angle.

6. Zack, Luke, and Charlie ordered a large pizza for $11.99, breadsticks for $2.99, and chicken wings for $5.99. If the three friends agree to split the cost of the food evenly, about how much will each friend pay?

F $20.79
G $7.93
H $7.32
J $6.99

7. Out of 100 students surveyed at Central Middle School, 48 are in the band, 52 play a sport, and 50 are in the drama club. Sixteen students are in both the band and the drama club, 22 students are in the drama club and play a sport, and 18 students are in the band and play a sport. Six students are in the band, play a sport, and are in the drama club. How many students are only in the drama club?

A 20 students
B 18 students
C 12 students
D 6 students

Preparing for ISAT
For test-taking strategies and practice, see pages 712–729.

8. Molly multiplied her age by 3 and subtracted 2 from the product. She then divided the difference by 4, and added 7 to the quotient. The result was 14. Which could be the first step in finding Molly's age?

   F Add 14 and 7.

   G Subtract 7 from 14.

   H Multiply 14 by 4.

   J Divide 14 by 3.

9. The diameter of a red blood cell is about 0.00074 centimeter. Which expression represents this number in scientific notation?

   A 7.4×10^4 **C** 7.4×10^{-3}

   B 7.4×10^3 **D** 7.4×10^{-4}

10. Which point on the number line best represents $\sqrt{8}$?

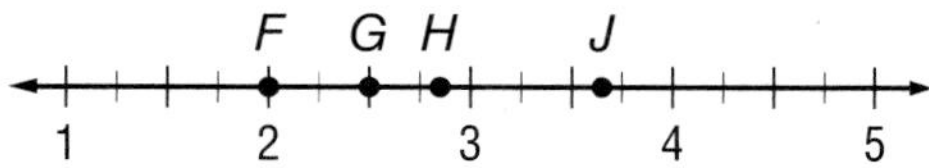

   F point *F*

   G point *G*

   H point *H*

   J point *J*

11. Ms. Leigh wants to organize the desks in the study hall into a square. If she has 64 desks, how many should be in each row?

   A 7

   B 8

   C 9

   D 10

PART 2 Short Response/Grid In

Record your answers on the answer sheet provided by your teacher or on a sheet of paper.

12. On Monday, the high temperature in Las Vegas, Nevada, was 101°F, and the high temperature in Columbus, Ohio, was 76°F. How many degrees warmer was it in Las Vegas than Columbus?

13. Write a fraction that is between $\frac{4}{5}$ and $\frac{5}{6}$?

14. The table below shows the height of three siblings. How much taller is Roberto than Juana?

Sibling	Height (inches)
Juana	$61\frac{1}{4}$
Maria	$57\frac{3}{4}$
Roberto	$69\frac{1}{8}$

15. Student admission to the movies is \$6.25. What is the total cost, in dollars, of tickets for you and four other students?

PART 3 Extended Response

Record your answers on the answer sheet provided by your teacher or on a sheet of paper. Show your work.

16. Find the length of the diagonal $\overline{AB}$ in the rectangular prism below. (*Hint:* First find the length of $\overline{BC}$.)

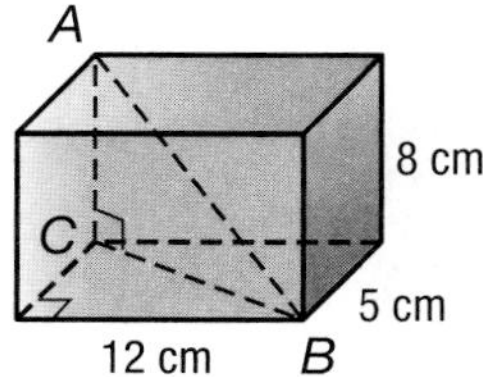

NEED EXTRA HELP?																
If You Missed Question...	1	2	3	4	5	6	7	8	9	10	11	12	13	14	15	16
Go to Lesson...	3-6	3-2	2-10	3-2	3-6	1-1	3-3	1-7	2-10	3-2	3-1	1-5	2-2	2-5	1-6	3-7
IL Learning Standards	9.D.3	8.D.3c	6.A.3	8.D.3c	9.D.3	6.B.3a	6.B.3a	8.A.3a	6.A.3	8.D.3c	6.B.3c	6.B.3a	6.A.3	6.B.3a	6.B.3a	8.D.3c

Unit 2

Patterns, Relationships, and Algebraic Thinking

Focus

Solve problems using proportional relationships.

CHAPTER 4
Proportions and Similarity

BIG Idea Identify proportional and nonproportional linear relationships.

BIG Idea Understand that a proportion is a linear equation.

CHAPTER 5
Percent

BIG Idea Use proportional reasoning to solve a wide variety of percent problems, including discounts, interest, taxes, tips, and percent of change.

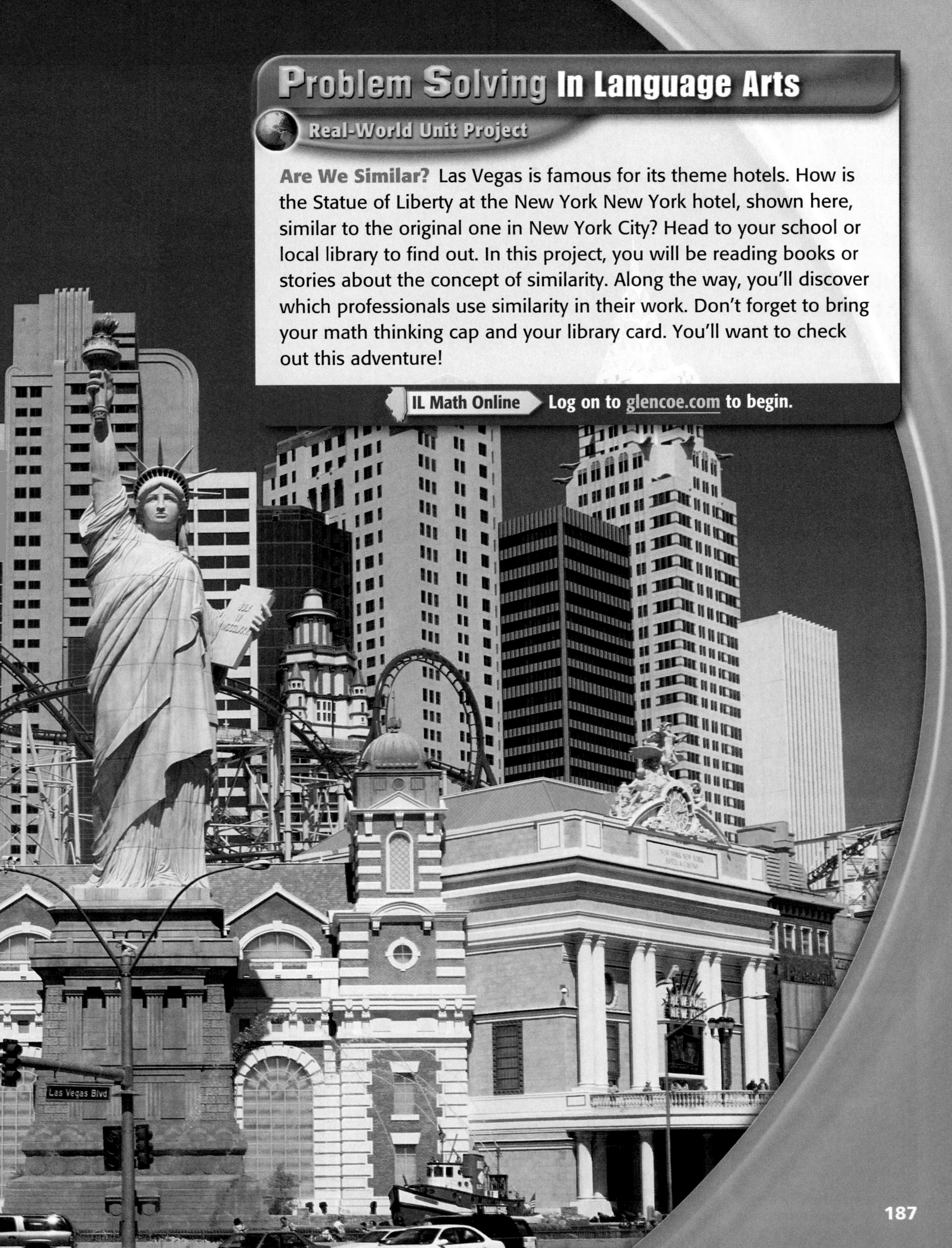

Problem Solving In Language Arts

Real-World Unit Project

Are We Similar? Las Vegas is famous for its theme hotels. How is the Statue of Liberty at the New York New York hotel, shown here, similar to the original one in New York City? Head to your school or local library to find out. In this project, you will be reading books or stories about the concept of similarity. Along the way, you'll discover which professionals use similarity in their work. Don't forget to bring your math thinking cap and your library card. You'll want to check out this adventure!

IL Math Online Log on to glencoe.com to begin.

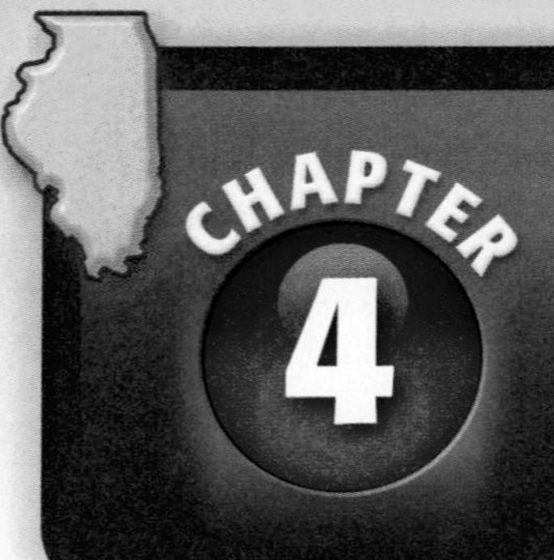

CHAPTER 4

Proportions and Similarity

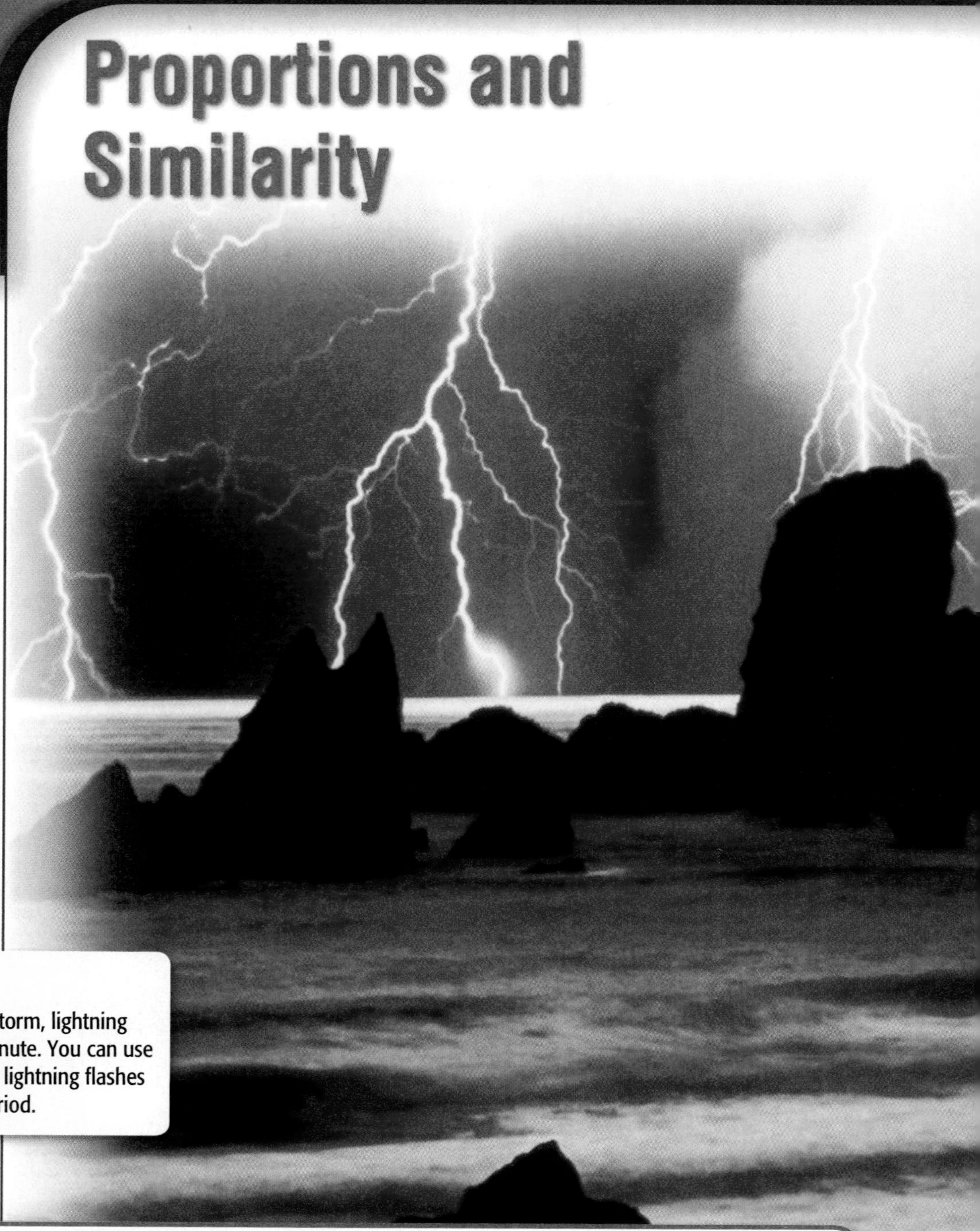

Illinois Learning Standards

6.D.3 Apply ratios and proportions to solve practical problems.
8.D.3b Propose and solve problems using proportions, formulas and linear functions.

Key Vocabulary

constant of proportionality (p. 212)
proportion (p. 210)
ratio (p. 190)
scale factor (p. 219)

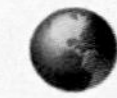

Real-World Link

Lightning During a severe thunderstorm, lightning flashed an average of 8 times per minute. You can use this rate to determine the number of lightning flashes that occurred during a 15-minute period.

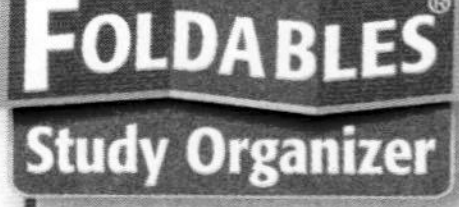

FOLDABLES® Study Organizer

Proportions and Similarity Make this Foldable to help you organize your notes. Begin with a plain sheet of 11″ by 17″ paper.

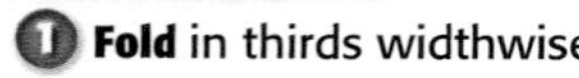

1. **Fold** in thirds widthwise.

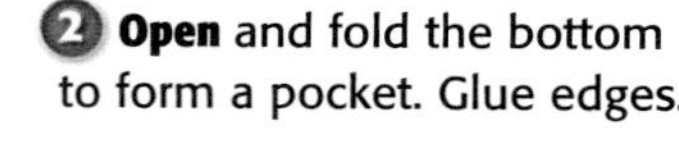

2. **Open** and fold the bottom to form a pocket. Glue edges.

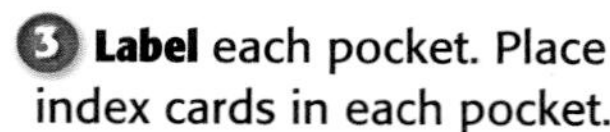

3. **Label** each pocket. Place index cards in each pocket.

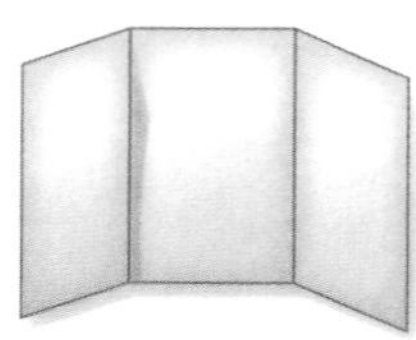

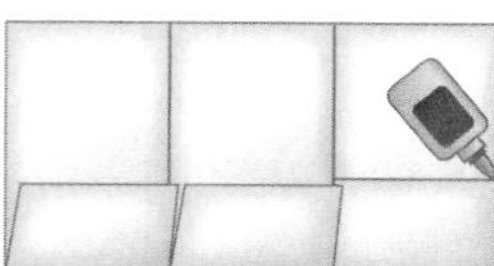

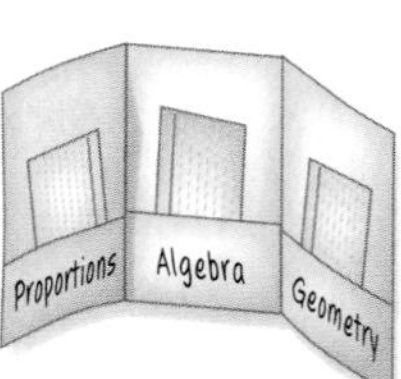

GET READY for Chapter 4

Diagnose Readiness You have two options for checking Prerequisite Skills.

Option 2

IL Math Online Take the Online Readiness Quiz at glencoe.com.

Option 1

Take the Quick Check below. Refer to the Quick Review for help.

QUICK Quiz

Simplify each fraction. (Prior Grade)

1. $\frac{10}{24}$
2. $\frac{88}{104}$
3. $\frac{36}{81}$
4. $\frac{49}{91}$
5. **MONEY** Devon spent \$18 of the \$45 that he saved. Write a fraction in simplest form that represents the portion of his savings he spent. (Prior Grade)

Evaluate each expression. (Prior Grade)

6. $\frac{6-2}{5+5}$
7. $\frac{7-4}{8-4}$
8. $\frac{3-1}{1+9}$
9. $\frac{5+7}{8-6}$

Solve each equation. (Lesson 1-10)

10. $5 \cdot 6 = x \cdot 2$
11. $c \cdot 1.5 = 3 \cdot 7$
12. $12 \cdot z = 9 \cdot 4$
13. $7 \cdot 2 = 8 \cdot g$
14. $3 \cdot 11 = 4 \cdot y$
15. $b \cdot 6 = 7 \cdot 9$
16. **NUMBER SENSE** The product of a number and four is equal to the product of eight and twelve. Find the number. (Lesson 1-10)

QUICK Review

Example 1

Simplify $\frac{54}{81}$.

$\frac{54}{81} = \frac{2}{3}$ (÷ 27 numerator and denominator) — Divide the numerator and denominator by their GCF, 27.

Example 2

Evaluate $\frac{11+4}{9-4}$.

$\frac{11+4}{9-4} = \frac{15}{5}$ — Simplify the numerator and denominator.

$= 3$ — Simplify.

Example 3

Solve $4 \cdot 6 = 8 \cdot p$.

$4 \cdot 6 = 8 \cdot p$ — Write the equation.

$\frac{24}{8} = \frac{8p}{8}$ — Multiply 4 by 6 and 8 by p.

$3 = p$ — Divide each side by 8.

4-1 Ratios and Rates

GET READY for the Lesson

ART To make orange paint for an art project, Mark uses 2 drops of yellow paint for every 4 drops of red paint.

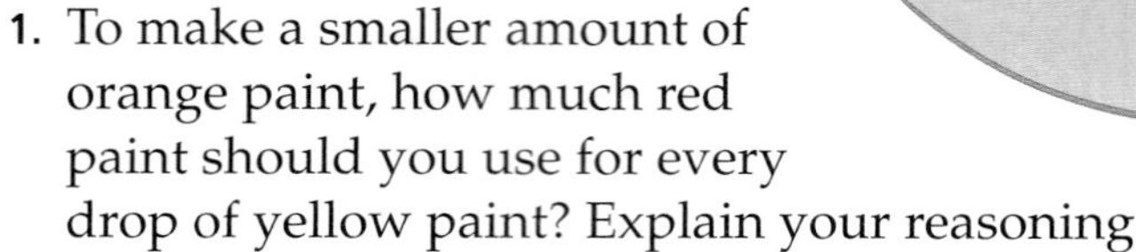

1. To make a smaller amount of orange paint, how much red paint should you use for every drop of yellow paint? Explain your reasoning.

A **ratio** is a comparison of two numbers or quantities by division. If an orange paint contains 2 drops of yellow paint and 4 drops of red paint, the ratio comparing yellow paint to red paint can be written as follows.

2 to **4**   **2** : **4** $\frac{2}{4}$

EXAMPLES Write Ratios in Simplest Form

Express each ratio in simplest form.

1 3 nonfiction books out of 12 books

$\frac{3 \text{ books}}{12 \text{ books}} = \frac{1}{4}$ Divide the numerator and denominator by the greatest common factor, 3. Divide out common units.

The ratio of nonfiction books to books is $\frac{1}{4}$ or 1 out of 4.

2 20 minutes of exercise to 1 hour of studying

When writing ratios that compare quantities with the same kinds of units, convert so that they have the same unit.

$\frac{20 \text{ minutes}}{1 \text{ hour}} = \frac{20 \text{ minutes}}{60 \text{ minutes}}$ Convert 1 hour to 60 minutes.

$= \frac{1 \text{ minute}}{3 \text{ minutes}}$ Divide the numerator and the denominator by 20. Divide out common units.

The ratio of exercise to study in simplest form is $\frac{1}{3}$ or 1:3.

CHECK Your Progress

a. 16 pepperoni pizzas out of 24 pizzas

b. 8 ounces of butter to 1 pound of flour

MAIN IDEA

Express ratios as fractions in simplest form and determine unit rates.

IL Learning Standards

6.D.3 Apply ratios and proportions **to solve practical problems.**

New Vocabulary

ratio
rate
unit rate

IL Math Online

glencoe.com

- Extra Examples
- Personal Tutor
- Self-Check Quiz

A **rate** is a ratio that compares two quantities with different types of units such as $5 for 2 pounds or 130 miles in 2 hours. When a rate is simplified so it has a denominator of 1, it is called a **unit rate**.

EXAMPLE Find a Unit Rate

3 JOBS Lloyd worked one Saturday for 6 hours and earned $40.00. What was Lloyd's average rate of pay in dollars per hour?

Write the rate that expresses the comparison of dollars to hours. Then find the average rate of pay by finding the unit rate.

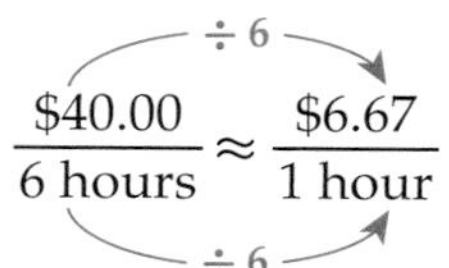

$$\frac{\$40.00}{6 \text{ hours}} \approx \frac{\$6.67}{1 \text{ hour}} \quad (\div 6)$$

Divide the numerator and denominator by 6 to get a denominator of 1.

Lloyd earned an average of about $6.67 per hour.

Reading Math

Math Symbols The symbol ≈ is read *approximately equal to.*

CHECK Your Progress

Express each rate as a unit rate.

c. 24 tickets for 8 rides

d. 4 inches of rain in 5 hours

Real-World Link In the U.S. House of Representatives, the number of representatives from each state is based on a state's population in the preceding census.

Real-World EXAMPLE Compare Unit Rates

4 CIVICS The population of Pennsylvania is about 12,300,000, and the population of Kentucky is about 4,000,000. If there are 19 members of the U.S. House of Representatives from Pennsylvania and 6 from Kentucky, in which state does a member represent more people?

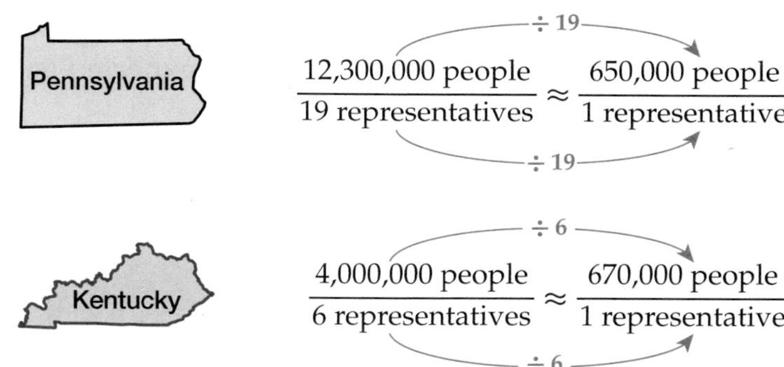

$$\frac{12{,}300{,}000 \text{ people}}{19 \text{ representatives}} \approx \frac{650{,}000 \text{ people}}{1 \text{ representative}} \quad (\div 19)$$

$$\frac{4{,}000{,}000 \text{ people}}{6 \text{ representatives}} \approx \frac{670{,}000 \text{ people}}{1 \text{ representative}} \quad (\div 6)$$

A member represents more people in Kentucky than in Pennsylvania.

CHECK Your Progress

SHOPPING Decide which is the better buy. Explain your reasoning.

e. a 17-ounce box of cereal for $4.89 or a 21-ounce box for $5.69

f. 6 cans of green beans for $1 or 10 cans for $1.95

CHECK Your Understanding

Examples 1, 2 (p. 190) **Express each ratio in simplest form.**

1. 12 missed days out of 180 days
2. 12 wins to 18 losses
3. 6 inches of water for 7 feet of snow
4. 3 quarts of soda : 1 gallon of juice

Example 3 (p. 191) **Express each rate as a unit rate.**

5. \$50 for 4 days of work
6. 3 pounds of dog food in 5 days

Example 4 (p. 191)

7. **SHOPPING** The Beauty Mart offers a 9-ounce bottle of shampoo for \$9.79. It is advertising a 34-ounce bottle of the same brand at a special price of \$36.36. Which bottle is the better buy? Explain your reasoning.

Practice and Problem Solving

HOMEWORK HELP

For Exercises	See Examples
8–11	1
12–15	2
16–21	3
22–23	4

Express each ratio in simplest form.

8. 14 chosen out of 70 who applied
9. 28 out of 100 doctors disagree
10. 33 stores open to 18 closed
11. 56 boys to 64 girls participated
12. 1 cup vinegar in 8 pints of water
13. 2 yards wide : 10 feet long
14. 20 centimeters out of 1 meter cut
15. 2,500 pounds for 1 ton of steel

16. **BASEBALL** As of 2005, Hank Aaron was the MLB career all-time hitter, with 3,771 hits in 3,298 games. What was Aaron's average number of hits per game?

17. **FUEL MILEAGE** Manufacturers must publish a car's gas mileage or the average number of miles one can expect to drive per gallon of gasoline. The test of a new hybrid car resulted in 4,840 miles being driven using 88 gallons of gas. Find the car's expected gas mileage.

Real-World Link . . . Gas mileage can be improved by as much as 3.3% by keeping tires inflated to the proper pressure.
Source: U.S. Government

Express each rate as a unit rate.

18. 153 points in 18 games
19. 350 miles on 15 gallons
20. 100 meters in 12 seconds
21. 1,473 people entered in 3 hours

22. **MUSIC** A 20-gigabyte digital music player sells for \$249. A similar 30-gigabyte player sells for \$349. Which player offers the better price per gigabyte of storage? Explain.

23. **MEASUREMENT** Logan ran a 200-meter race in 25.24 seconds, and Scott ran 0.4 kilometer in 52.77 seconds. Who ran faster, Logan or Scott? Explain.

24. **MAGAZINES** Which costs more per issue, an 18-issue subscription for \$40.50 or a 12-issue subscription for \$33.60? Explain.

25. **RACES** Jill, Leon, and Emily participated in a bike race. Jill biked the first half at 6 miles per hour and the second half at 12 miles per hour. Leon biked the first third at 12 miles per hour, then dropped down to 8 miles per hour for the 2nd third, and finished the last third at 7 miles per hour. Emily paced out the entire race at 8.5 miles per hour. Who finished first? Explain.

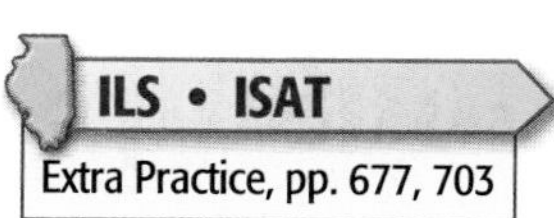

Extra Practice, pp. 677, 703

H.O.T. Problems

26. **Which One Doesn't Belong?** Identify the phrase that does not represent the same rate as the other two. Explain your reasoning.

36 miles per hour	3,168 miles per minute	52.8 feet per second

27. **CHALLENGE** Maria has dimes and nickels in the ratio of 5:1. If she trades 2 of her dimes for 4 nickels, the ratio of coins is 9:4. How many dimes did she have at the beginning? Explain.

28. **WRITING IN MATH** Explain how to write a rate as a unit rate.

ISAT PRACTICE 6.D.3

29. Lucy typed 210 words in 5 minutes, and Yvonne typed 336 words in 8 minutes. Based on these rates, which statement is true?

    A Lucy's rate was 3-words-per-minute slower than Yvonne's.

    B Lucy's rate was 25.2-words-per-minute faster than Yvonne's.

    C Lucy's rate was about 15.8-words-per-minute faster than Yvonne's.

    D Lucy's rate was equal to Yvonne's.

30. Jackson drove 70 miles per hour for 4 hours and then 55 miles per hour for 2 hours to go to a conference. How far did Jackson drive in all?

    F 390 miles

    G 360 miles

    H 320 miles

    J 280 miles

Spiral Review

GEOMETRY Graph each pair of ordered pairs. Then find the distance between the points. Round to the nearest tenth. (Lesson 3-7)

31. $(1, 4), (6, -3)$
32. $(-1, 5), (3, -2)$
33. $(-5, -2), (-1, 0)$
34. $(-2, -3), (3, 1)$

35. **MEASUREMENT** A square floor exercise mat measures 40 feet on each side. Find the length of the mat's diagonal. (Lesson 3-6)

GET READY for the Next Lesson

PREREQUISITE SKILL Write each expression as a decimal. (Lesson 2-1)

36. $\frac{19}{5}$
37. $\frac{3}{8}$
38. $\frac{12.4}{4}$
39. $\frac{2.5}{5}$

4-2 Proportional and Nonproportional Relationships

MAIN IDEA

Identify proportional and nonproportional relationships.

IL Learning Standards

6.D.3 Apply ratios and proportions **to solve practical problems.**
8.D.3b Propose and solve problems using proportions, formulas and linear functions.

New Vocabulary

proportional
nonproportional

IL Math Online

glencoe.com

- Extra Examples
- Personal Tutor
- Self-Check Quiz
- Reading in the Content Area

GET READY for the Lesson

PIZZA Ms. Cochran is planning a year-end pizza party for her students. Ace Pizza offers free delivery and charges $8 for each medium pizza.

1. Copy and complete the table to determine the cost for different numbers of pizzas ordered.

Cost ($)	8			
Pizzas Ordered	1	2	3	4

2. For each number of pizzas, write the relationship of the cost and number of pizzas as a ratio in simplest form. What do you notice?

In the example above, notice that while the number of pizzas ordered and the cost both change or vary, the ratio of these quantities remains the same, a constant $8 per pizza.

$$\frac{\text{cost of order}}{\text{pizzas ordered}} = \frac{8}{1} = \frac{16}{2} = \frac{24}{3} = \frac{32}{4} \text{ or \$8 per pizza}$$

This relationship is expressed by saying that the cost of an order is *proportional* to the number of pizzas ordered.

If two quantities are **proportional**, then they have a constant ratio. For relationships in which this ratio is not constant, the two quantities are said to be **nonproportional**.

EXAMPLES Identify Proportional Relationships

1 **PIZZA Uptown Pizzeria sells medium pizzas for $7 each but charges a $3 delivery fee per order. Is the cost of an order proportional to the number of pizzas ordered?**

Find the cost for 1, 2, 3, and 4 pizzas and make a table to display numbers and cost.

Cost ($)	10	17	24	31
Pizzas Ordered	1	2	3	4

For each number of pizzas, write the relationship of the cost and number of pizzas as a ratio in simplest form.

$$\frac{\text{cost of order}}{\text{pizzas ordered}} \rightarrow \quad \frac{10}{1} \text{ or } 10 \quad \frac{17}{2} \text{ or } 8.5 \quad \frac{24}{3} \text{ or } 8 \quad \frac{31}{4} \text{ or } 7.75$$

Since the ratios of the two quantities are not the same, the cost of an order is *not* proportional to the number of pizzas ordered. The relationship is nonproportional.

2 **BEVERAGES You can use the recipe shown to make a healthier version of a popular beverage. Is the amount of mix used proportional to the amount of sugar used?**

Find the amount of mix and sugar needed for different numbers of batches and make a table to show these mix and sugar measures.

Cups of Sugar	$\frac{1}{2}$	1	$1\frac{1}{2}$	2
Envelopes of Mix	1	2	3	4
Quarts of Water	2	4	6	8

For each number of cups of sugar, write the relationship of the cups and number of envelopes of mix as a ratio in simplest form.

$$\frac{\text{cups of sugar}}{\text{envelopes of mix}} \rightarrow \frac{\frac{1}{2}}{1}, \frac{1}{2}, \frac{1\frac{1}{2}}{3}, \frac{2}{4}$$

All of the ratios between the two quantities can be simplified to 0.5. The amount of mix used is proportional to the amount of sugar used.

CHECK Your Progress

a. **BEVERAGES** In Example 2, is the amount of sugar used proportional to the amount of water used?

b. **MONEY** At the beginning of the school year, Isabel had $120 in the bank. Each week, she deposits another $20. Is her account balance proportional to the number of weeks since she started school?

CHECK Your Understanding

Examples 1, 2 (pp. 194–195)

1. **ELEPHANTS** An adult elephant drinks about 225 liters of water each day. Is the number of days that an elephant's water supply lasts proportional to the number of liters of water the elephant drinks?

2. **PACKAGES** A package shipping company charges $5.25 to deliver a package. In addition, they charge $0.45 for each pound over one pound. Is the cost to ship a package proportional to the weight of the package?

3. **SCHOOL** At a certain middle school, every homeroom teacher is assigned 28 students. There are 3 teachers who do not have a homeroom. Is the number of students at this school proportional to the number of teachers?

4. **JOBS** Andrew earns $18 per hour for mowing lawns. Is the amount of money he earns proportional to the number of hours he spends mowing?

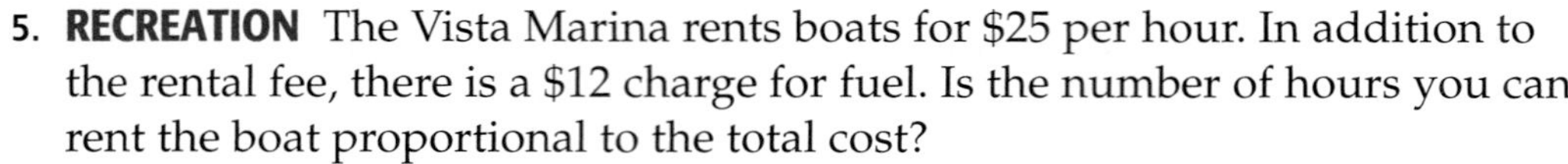

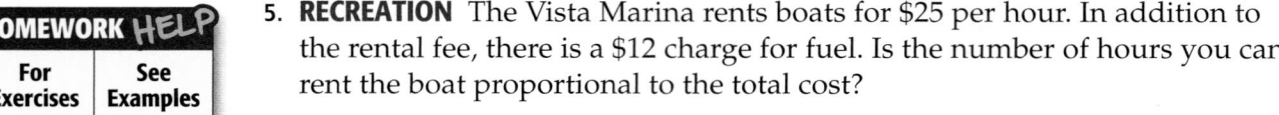

HOMEWORK HELP	
For Exercises	See Examples
5–12	1, 2

5. **RECREATION** The Vista Marina rents boats for $25 per hour. In addition to the rental fee, there is a $12 charge for fuel. Is the number of hours you can rent the boat proportional to the total cost?

6. **ELEVATORS** An elevator *ascends* or goes up at a rate of 750 feet per minute. Is the height to which the elevator ascends proportional to the number of minutes it takes to get there?

7. **PLANTS** Kudzu is a vine that grows an average of 7.5 feet every 5 days. Is the number of days of growth proportional to the length of the vine as measured on the last day?

8. **TEMPERATURE** To convert a temperature in degrees Celsius to degrees Fahrenheit, multiply the Celsius temperature by $\frac{9}{5}$ and then add 32°. Is a temperature in degrees Celsius proportional to its equivalent temperature in degrees Fahrenheit?

Real-World Link Ascending at a speed of 1,000 feet per minute, the five outside elevators of the Westin St. Francis are the fastest glass elevators in San Francisco.

Source: City of San Francisco

ADVERTISING For Exercises 9 and 10, use the following information.
On Saturday, Querida gave away 416 coupons for a free appetizer at a local restaurant. The next day, she gave away about 52 coupons an hour.

9. Is the number of coupons Querida gave away on Sunday proportional to the number of hours she worked that day?
10. Is the total number of coupons Querida gave away on Saturday and Sunday proportional to the number of hours she worked on Sunday?

SHOPPING For Exercises 11 and 12, use the following information.
MegaMart collects a sales tax equal to $\frac{1}{16}$ of the retail price of each purchase and sends this money to the state government.

11. Is the amount of tax collected proportional to the cost of an item before tax is added?
12. Is the amount of tax collected proportional to the cost of an item after tax has been added?

MEASUREMENT For Exercises 13 and 14, determine whether the measures for the figure shown are proportional.

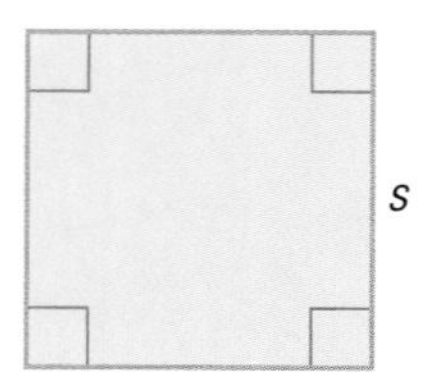

13. the length of a side and the perimeter
14. the length of a side and the area

POSTAGE For Exercises 15 and 16, use the table below that shows the price to mail a first-class letter for various weights.

15. Is the cost to mail a letter proportional to its weight? Explain your reasoning.
16. How can you determine the cost of a letter that weighs 5 ounces?

Cost ($)	0.41	0.58	0.75	1.31	■
Weight (oz)	1	2	3	4	5

Extra Practice, pp. 677, 703

H.O.T. Problems

17. **OPEN ENDED** Give one example of a proportional relationship and one example of a nonproportional relationship. Justify your examples.

18. **CHALLENGE** This year Andrea celebrated her 10th birthday, and her brother Carlos celebrated his 5th birthday. Andrea noted that she was now twice as old as her brother was. Is the relationship between their ages proportional? Explain your reasoning using a table of values.

19. **WRITING IN MATH** Luke uses $200 in birthday money to purchase some $20 DVDs. He claims that the amount of money remaining after his purchase is proportional to the number of DVDs he decides to buy, because the DVDs are each sold at the same price. Is his claim valid? If his claim is false, name two quantities in this situation that are proportional.

ISAT PRACTICE 6.D.3, 8.D.3b

20. Mr. Martinez is comparing the price of oranges from several different markets. Which market's pricing guide is based on a constant unit price?

A

Farmer's Market	
Number of Oranges	Total Cost ($)
5	3.50
10	6.00
15	8.50
20	11.00

B

The Fruit Place	
Number of Oranges	Total Cost ($)
5	3.50
10	6.50
15	9.50
20	12.50

C

Central Produce	
Number of Oranges	Total Cost ($)
5	3.00
10	6.00
15	9.00
20	12.00

D

Green Grocer	
Number of Oranges	Total Cost ($)
5	3.00
10	5.00
15	7.00
20	9.00

Spiral Review

Express each ratio in simplest form. (Lesson 4-1)

21. 40 working hours out of 168 hours

22. 2 inches of shrinkage to 1 yard of material

23. **GEOMETRY** The vertices of right triangle ABC are $A(-2, -5)$, $B(-2, 8)$, and $C(1, 4)$. Find the perimeter of the triangle. (Lesson 3-7)

ALGEBRA Write and solve an equation to find each number. (Lesson 1-10)

24. The product of -9 and a number is 45.

25. A number divided by 4 is -16.

GET READY for the Next Lesson

PREREQUISITE SKILL Evaluate each expression. (Lesson 1-2)

26. $\frac{45 - 33}{10 - 8}$

27. $\frac{85 - 67}{2001 - 1995}$

28. $\frac{29 - 44}{55 - 50}$

29. $\frac{18 - 19}{25 - 30}$

4-3 Rate of Change

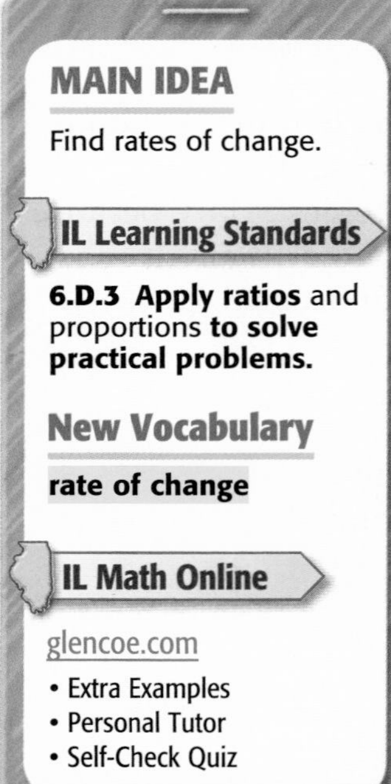

GET READY for the Lesson

E-MAIL The table shows the number of entries in Alicia's e-mail contact list at the end of 2004 and 2006.

Alicia's E-mail Contact List		
Entries	10	38
Year	2004	2006

1. What is the change in the number of entries from 2004 to 2006?
2. Over what number of years did this change take place?
3. Write a rate that compares the change in the number of entries to the change in the number of years. Express your answer as a unit rate and explain its meaning.

A **rate of change** is a rate that describes how one quantity changes in relation to another.

EXAMPLE Find a Positive Rate of Change

1 **E-MAIL Alicia had 62 entries in her e-mail contact list at the end of 2007. Use the information above to find the rate of change in the number of entries in her e-mail contact list between 2004 and 2007.**

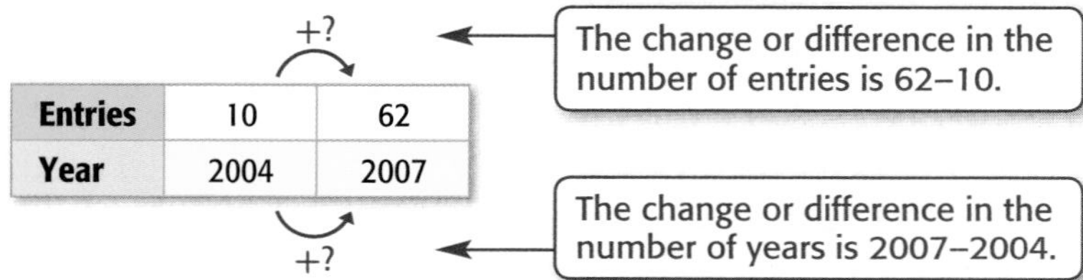

Entries	10	62
Year	2004	2007

+?
The change or difference in the number of entries is 62–10.
+?
The change or difference in the number of years is 2007–2004.

Write a rate that compares the change in each quantity.

$$\frac{\text{change in entries}}{\text{change in years}} = \frac{(62 - 10)\text{ entries}}{(2007 - 2004)\text{ years}}$$ Her contact list changed from 10 to 62 entries from 2004 to 2007.

$$= \frac{52\text{ entries}}{3\text{ years}}$$ Subtract to find the change in the number of entries and years.

$$\approx \frac{17\text{ entries}}{1\text{ year}}$$ Express this rate as a unit rate.

Since this rate is positive, Alicia's e-mail contact list *increased* or grew at an average rate of about 17 entries per year between 2004 and 2007.

CHECK Your Progress

a. **HEIGHTS** The table shows Ramon's height at ages 8 and 11. Find the rate of change in his height between these ages.

Height (in.)	51	58
Age (yr)	8	11

Study Tip

Broken Line Graph In these two line graphs, the lines are broken because there are no data points between the points on the graph.

A graph of the data in Example 1 is shown at the right. The data points are connected by a broken line segment to show the rate of change.

A positive rate of change is shown by a segment slanting *upward* from left to right. A negative rate of change is shown by a segment slanting *downward* from left to right.

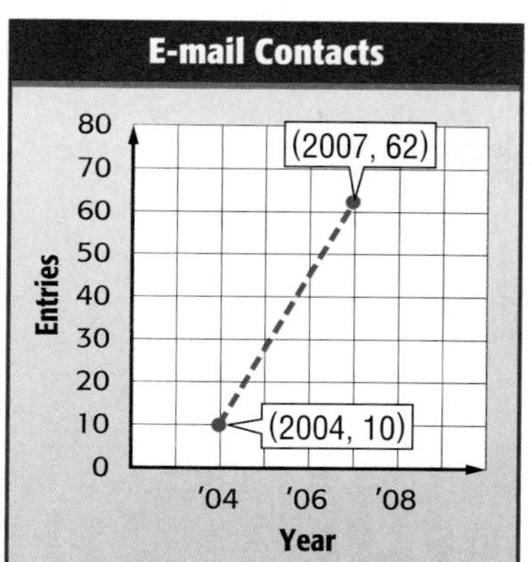

EXAMPLE Find a Negative Rate of Change

2 COMPUTERS The graph shows the average cost of personal computers for the years 1997–2002. Find the rate of change in cost between 1998 and 2000. Describe how this rate is shown on the graph.

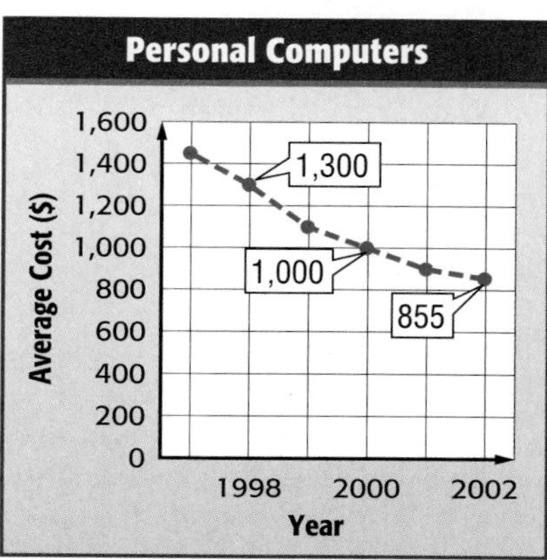

Source: *New York Times Almanac*

Make a table of the data using the coordinates of the points listed on the graph.

Year	Cost (dollars)
1998	1,300
2000	1,000

Use the data to write a rate comparing the change in cost to the change in years.

$\dfrac{\text{change in cost}}{\text{change in years}} = \dfrac{1{,}000 - 1{,}300}{2000 - 1998}$ Cost changed from \$1,300 to \$1,000 from 1998 to 2000.

$= \dfrac{-300}{2}$ Subtract to find the change in cost amounts and years.

$= \dfrac{-150}{1}$ Express the answer as a unit rate.

The rate of change was −\$150 per year. The rate is negative because the average cost of a personal computer *decreased* between 1998 and 2000. This is shown on the graph by a line segment slanting downward from left to right.

CHECK Your Progress

b. In the graph above, find the rate of change between 2000 and 2002.

c. Describe how this rate of change is shown on the graph.

On a graph, rates of change can be compared by measuring how fast segments rise or fall when the graph is read from left to right.

EXAMPLE Compare Rates of Change

Real-World Career. **How Does a Webmaster Use Math?** *Webmasters* are responsible for designing and creating Web sites. They often create their own programs using specific computer language. This requires strong logical reasoning skills.

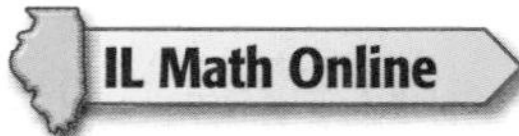

For more information, go to glencoe.com.

3 INTERNET The graph shows the number of Internet users in the United States. Compare the rate of change between 2002 and 2003 to the rate of change between 2003 and 2004.

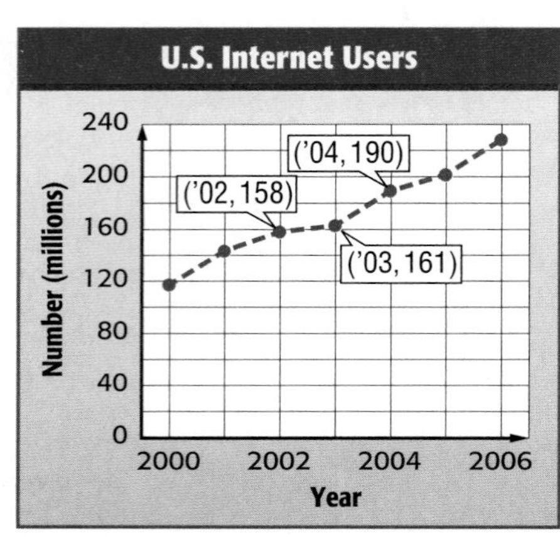

Source: *New York Times Almanac*

The segment from 2003 to 2004 appears steeper than the segment from 2002 to 2003. So, it appears the rate of change between 2003 and 2004 was greater than the rate of change between 2002 and 2003.

Check Find and compare the rates of change.

From 2002 to 2003

$$\frac{\text{change in number}}{\text{change in years}} = \frac{161 - 158}{2003 - 2002} = \frac{3}{1} \text{ or } 3$$

From 2003 to 2004

$$\frac{\text{change in number}}{\text{change in years}} = \frac{190 - 161}{2004 - 2003} = \frac{29}{1} \text{ or } 29$$

Since $29 > 3$, the rate of change between 2003 and 2004 is greater than the rate of change between 2002 and 2003. ✓

CHECK Your Progress

d. **NATURAL RESOURCES** Use the table to make a graph of the data. During which 2-year period was the rate of change in oil production the greatest? Explain your reasoning.

Texas Oil Production						
Barrels (millions)	478.1	440.6	348.9	329.8	398.5	385.1
Year	1996	1998	2000	2002	2004	2006

Study Tip

Absolute Values
When comparing negative rates of change, compare the absolute values of the numbers.

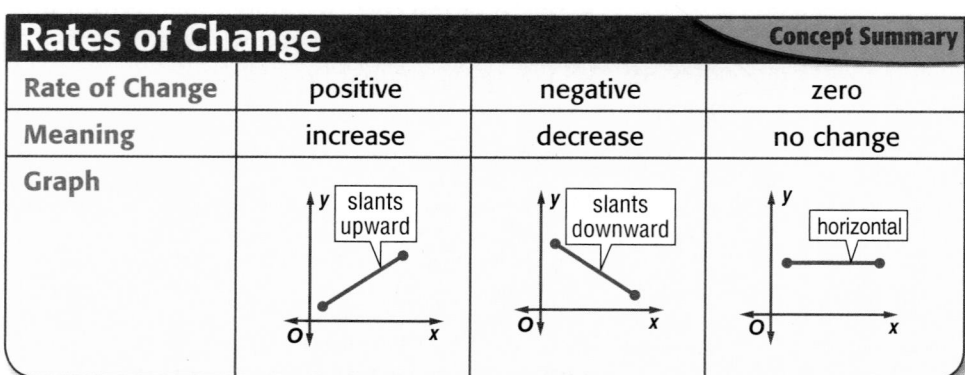

Rates of Change

Concept Summary

Rate of Change	positive	negative	zero
Meaning	increase	decrease	no change
Graph	slants upward	slants downward	horizontal

CHECK Your Understanding

TEST SCORES For Exercises 1–3, use the information in the table at the right that shows Jared's math test scores for the first semester.

Test	Score
1	67
2	75
3	77
4	83
5	83
6	79

Example 1 (p. 198)
1. Find the rate of change in test scores from Test 2 to Test 4.

Example 2 (p. 199)
2. Find the rate of change in test scores from Test 5 to Test 6.

Example 3 (p. 200)
3. Make a graph of the data. Between what two tests is the rate of increase the greatest? Explain.

Practice and Problem Solving

HOMEWORK HELP

For Exercises	See Examples
4, 5, 13, 14	1
7, 8, 10, 11	2
6, 9, 12, 15	3

TICKET SALES For Exercises 4–6, use the information in the table at the right that shows the number of Spring Fling tickets Imani sold at different times during the school day.

Time	Tickets Sold
9:00	4
10:30	2
11:00	10
11:30	10
12:00	15
2:30	6

4. Find the rate of change in tickets sold per half hour between 10:30 and 11:00.
5. Find the rate of change in tickets sold per half hour between 12:00 and 2:30.
6. Make a graph of the data. During which time period was Imani's selling rate the greatest? Explain.

INVESTMENTS For Exercises 7–9, use the following information.
The value of a company's stock over a 5-day period is shown in the table.

Value ($)	57.48	53.92	50.25	49.74	44.13
Day	1	2	3	4	5

7. Determine the rate of change in value between Day 1 and Day 3.
8. What was the rate of change in value between Day 2 and Day 5?
9. Make a graph of the data. During which 2-day period was the rate of change in the stock value greatest?

TELEVISION For Exercises 10–12, use the information below and at the right.
The graph shows the number of viewers who watched new episodes of a show.

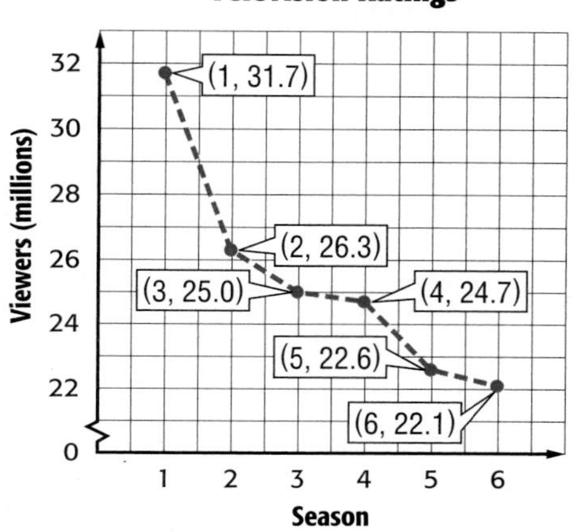

10. Find the rate of change in viewership between season 1 and season 3.
11. Find the rate of change in viewership between season 2 and season 6.
12. Between which two seasons was the rate of change in viewership greatest?

RADIO **For Exercises 13–15, use the graph at the right.**

13. Find the rate of change in the number of U.S. sports radio stations from 2002 to 2004.

14. Find the rate of change in the number of U.S. sports radio stations from 2003 to 2005.

15. During which time period did the number of U.S. sports radio stations increase at the fastest rate?

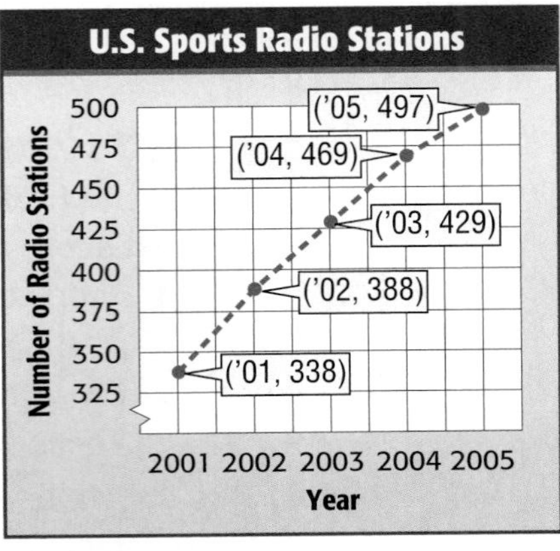

Source: *The World Almanac*

FAST FOOD **For Exercises 16 and 17, use the information below.**

The graph shows the estimated total of U.S. food and drink sales in billions of dollars from 1980 to 2005.

16. During which time period was the rate of change in food and drink sales greatest? Explain your reasoning.

17. Find the rate of change during that period.

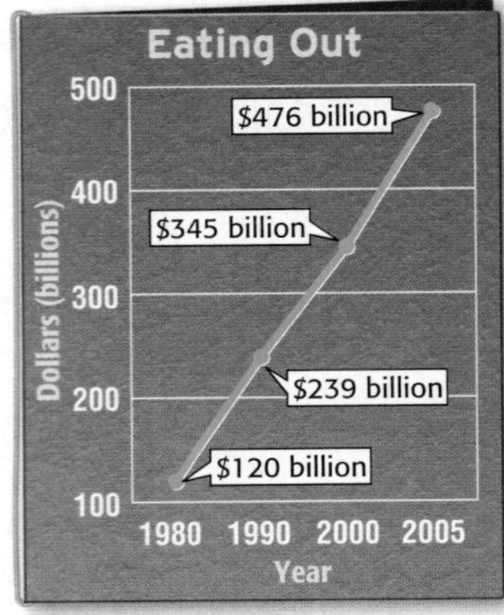

Source: National Restaurant Association

SALES **For Exercises 18 and 19, use the following information.**

The Recording Industry Association of America reported 938.9 million CDs were shipped to retailers in 1999. In 2004, this figure was 767 million.

18. Find the rate of change from 1999 to 2004.

19. If this rate of change were to continue, what would be the total number of CDs shipped in 2012? Explain your reasoning.

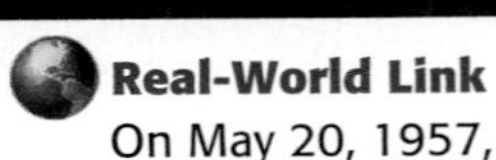
Real-World Link

On May 20, 1957, an F5 tornado touched down in Jackson, Missouri. It was the deadliest recorded tornado in Missouri's history.

Source: University of Missouri

20. **PUPPIES** An eight-week-old puppy weighed 9 pounds. After 3 weeks, she weighed 14 pounds. Find the rate of change in the puppy's weight.

TORNADOES **For Exercises 21 and 22, refer to the table at the right.**

21. Graph the data. During which interval was the rate of change in the number of tornadoes the greatest? the least?

22. Is it reasonable to state that between 2001 and 2006, the number of tornadoes in a given year changed very little? Explain.

Missouri Tornadoes

Year	Number of Tornadoes
2001	39
2002	29
2003	84
2004	69
2005	32
2006	102

Source: NOAA's National Weather Service

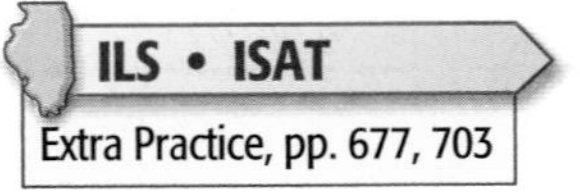

Extra Practice, pp. 677, 703

H.O.T. Problems

23. **OPEN ENDED** Create a set of gasoline price data that has a rate of change of $0.08 per gallon over a period of 4 days.

24. **NUMBER SENSE** Does the height of a candle as it burns over time show a *positive* or *negative* rate of change? Explain your reasoning.

25. **CHALLENGE** Liquid is poured at a constant rate into a beaker that is shaped like the one at the right. Draw a graph of the level of liquid in the beaker as a function of time.

26. **WRITING IN MATH** Explain the difference between the *rate of change* between a set of data values and the *change* between data values.

ISAT PRACTICE 6.D.3

27. The graph shows the altitude of a falcon over time.

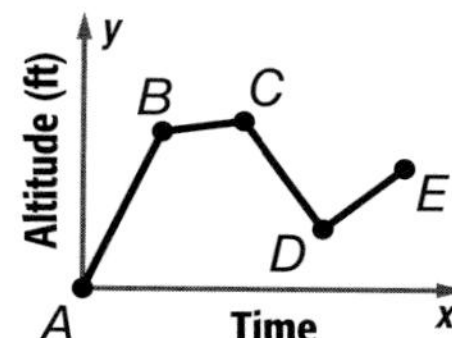

Between which two points on the graph was the bird's rate of change in altitude negative?

A *A* and *B*

B *B* and *C*

C *C* and *D*

D *D* and *E*

28. Sarah earns $52 for 4 hours of work. At this rate, how many hours would she need to work to earn $975?

F 13 h

G 18.75 h

H 75 h

J 243.75 h

29. Ralph rode his bike an average speed of 16 miles per hour for two hours on Saturday and then an average speed of 13 miles per hour for three hours. How many miles did Ralph ride in all?

A 29 miles

B 34 miles

C 71 miles

D 74 miles

Spiral Review

30. **MONEY** Cassie deposits $40 in a savings account. The money earns $1.40 per month in simple interest, and she makes no further deposits. Is her account balance proportional to the number of months since her initial deposit? (Lesson 4-2)

31. **SHOPPING** Which is the better buy: 1 pound 4 ounces of cheese for $4.99 or 2 pounds 6 ounces for $9.75? Explain your reasoning. (Lesson 4-1)

GET READY for the Next Lesson

32. **PREREQUISITE SKILL** Michael tutors elementary school students in math 1.5 hours each week. Is the total number of hours that he spends tutoring proportional to the number of weeks he tutors during the year? Explain your reasoning. (Lesson 4-1)

4-4 Constant Rate of Change

MAIN IDEA

Identify proportional and nonproportional linear relationships by finding a constant rate of change.

IL Learning Standards

6.D.3 Apply ratios and proportions **to solve practical problems.**

New Vocabulary

linear relationship
constant rate of change

IL Math Online

glencoe.com

- Extra Examples
- Personal Tutor
- Self-Check Quiz

GET READY for the Lesson

MUSIC Vineeta can download two songs from the Internet each minute. This is shown in the table and in the graph.

Number of Songs	0	2	4	6	8
Time (minutes)	0	1	2	3	4

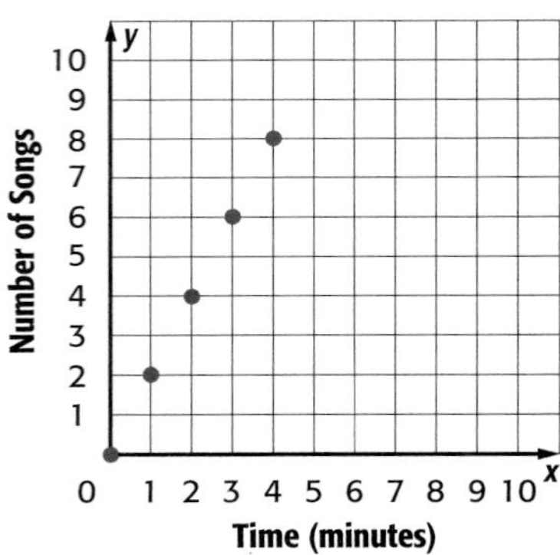

1. Pick several pairs of points and find the rate of change between them. What is true of these rates?

Relationships that have straight-line graphs, like the one in the example above, are called **linear relationships**. Notice that as the time in minutes increases by 1, the number of songs increases by 2.

+2 +2 +2 +2

Number of Songs	0	2	4	6	8
Time (minutes)	0	1	2	3	4

+1 +1 +1 +1

Rate of Change

$\frac{2}{1}$ = 2 songs per minute

The rate of change between any two points in a linear relationship is the same or *constant*. A linear relationship has a **constant rate of change**.

EXAMPLE Identify Linear Relationships

1 **MONEY The balance in an account after several transactions is shown. Is the relationship between the balance and number of transactions linear? If so, find the constant rate of change. If not, explain your reasoning.**

Number of Transactions	Balance ($)
3	170
6	140
9	110
12	80

	Number of Transactions	Balance ($)	
	3	170	
+3	6	140	−30
+3	9	110	−30
+3	12	80	−30

As the number of transactions increases by 3, the balance in the account decreases by $30.

Since the rate of change is constant, this is a linear relationship. The constant rate of change is $\frac{-30}{3}$ or $-\$10$ per transaction. This means that, on average, each transaction involved a $10 *withdrawal*.

CHECK Your Progress

Determine whether the relationship between the two quantities described in each table is linear. If so, find the constant rate of change. If not, explain your reasoning.

a.

Cooling Water	
Time (min)	**Temperature (°F)**
5	95
10	90
15	86
20	82

b.

Wrapping Paper	
Number of Rolls	**Total Cost ($)**
2	8.50
4	17.00
6	25.50
8	34.00

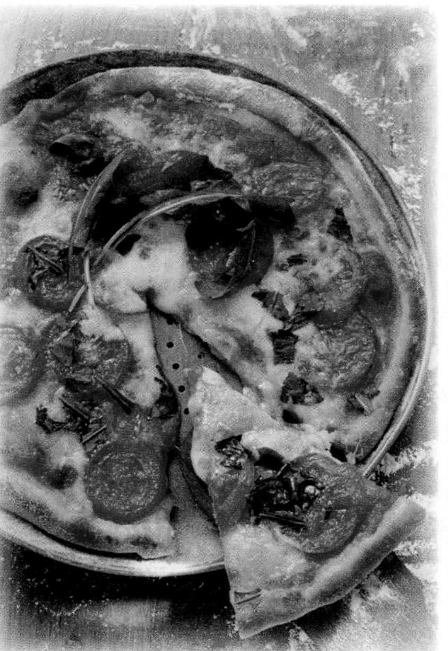

Real-World Link Pizza Margherita, made with fresh tomatoes, basil, garlic, and fresh mozzarella cheese, was actually named after Queen Margherita of Italy in 1889. Very simple pizzas may have been eaten as early as 500 B.C.

EXAMPLE Find a Constant Rate of Change

2 FOOD Find the constant rate of change for the cost of each personal pizza ordered. Interpret its meaning.

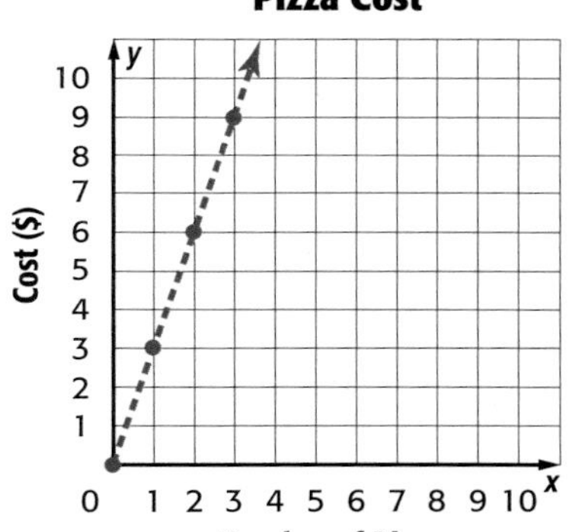

Choose any two points on the line and find the rate of change between them.

(1, 3) ⟶ 1 pizza, $3

(3, 9) ⟶ 3 pizzas, $9

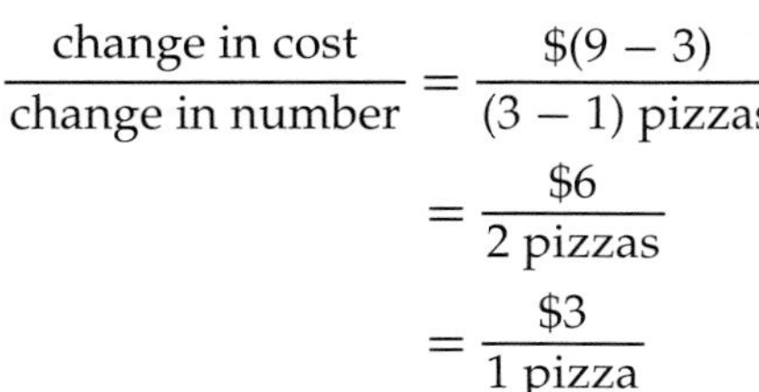

$\frac{\text{change in cost}}{\text{change in number}} = \frac{\$(9-3)}{(3-1)\text{ pizzas}}$ The cost changed from $9 to $3 while the number changed from 3 pizzas to 1 pizza.

$= \frac{\$6}{2\text{ pizzas}}$ Subtract to find the change in the cost and number of pizzas.

$= \frac{\$3}{1\text{ pizza}}$ Express this rate as a unit rate.

The pizza cost is $3 for every 1 pizza ordered.

CHECK Your Progress

c. **SERVICE PROJECT** Find the constant rate of change for the time it takes to complete a highway trash pickup project for each number of volunteers in the graph shown. Interpret its meaning.

Some, but not all, linear relationships are also proportional.

Study Tip

Look Back To review **identifying proportional relationships**, see Lesson 4-2.

EXAMPLE Identify Proportional Relationships

3 **TEMPERATURE Use the graph to determine if there is a proportional linear relationship between a temperature on the Fahrenheit scale and a temperature on the Celsius scale. Explain your reasoning.**

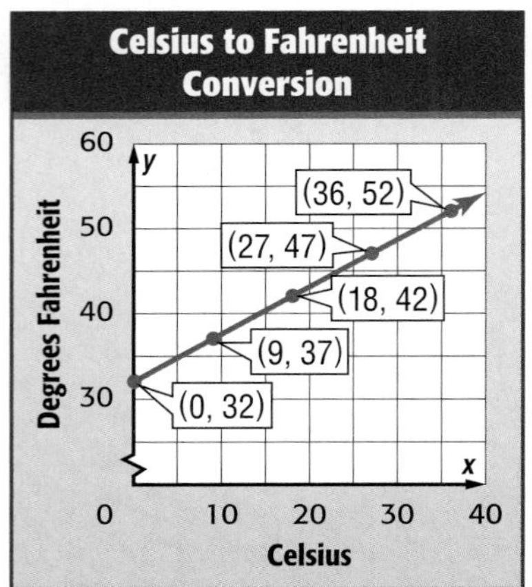

Since the graph of the data forms a line, the relationship between the two scales is linear. This can also be seen in the table of values created using the points on the graph.

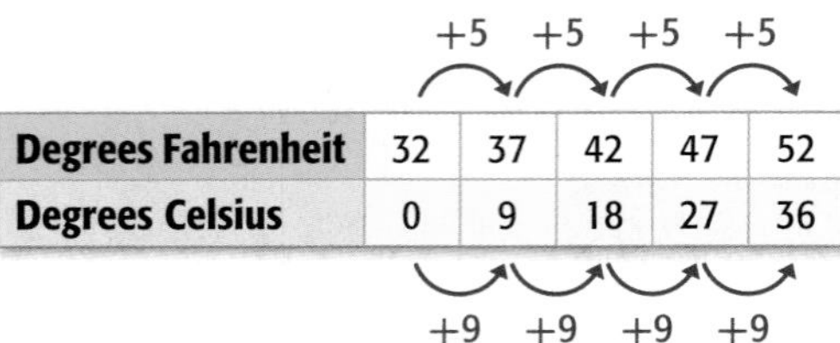

	+5	+5	+5	+5	
Degrees Fahrenheit	32	37	42	47	52
Degrees Celsius	0	9	18	27	36
	+9	+9	+9	+9	

Constant Rate of Change

$$\frac{\text{change in °F}}{\text{change in °C}} = \frac{5}{9}$$

To determine if the two scales are proportional, express the relationship between the degrees for several columns as a ratio.

$$\frac{\text{degrees Fahrenheit}}{\text{degrees Celsius}} \longrightarrow \quad \frac{37}{9} \approx 4.11 \quad \frac{42}{18} \approx 2.33 \quad \frac{47}{27} \approx 1.74 \quad \frac{52}{36} \approx 1.44$$

Since the ratios are not all the same, a temperature in degrees Celsius is *not* proportional to the same temperature in degrees Fahrenheit.

CHECK Your Progress

d. **MEASUREMENT** Use the graph to determine if there is a proportional linear relationship between the weight of an object measured in pounds and the mass of the same object measured in kilograms. Explain your reasoning.

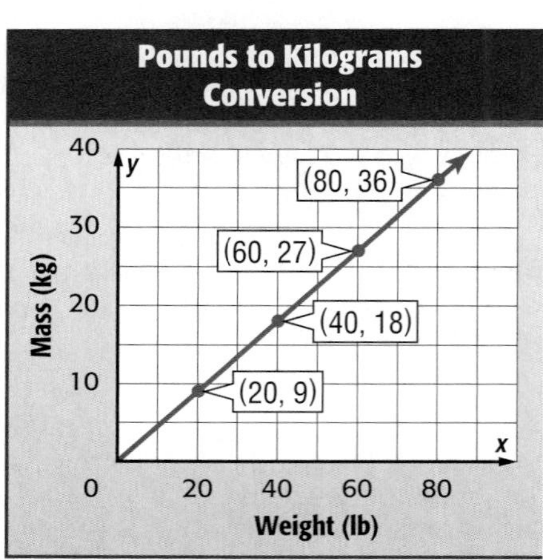

Proportional Linear Relationships

Concept Summary

Words Two quantities a and b have a proportional linear relationship if they have a constant ratio and a constant rate of change.

Symbols $\frac{b}{a}$ is constant and $\frac{\text{change in } b}{\text{change in } a}$ is constant.

CHECK Your Understanding

Example 1 (p. 204)

Determine whether the relationship between the two quantities described in each table is linear. If so, find the constant rate of change. If not, explain your reasoning.

1\.

Volume of Cube	
Side Length (cm)	**Volume (cm^3)**
2	8
3	27
4	64
5	125

2\.

Paint Needed for Chairs	
Number of Chairs	**Cans of Paint**
5	6
10	12
15	18
20	24

Example 2 (p. 205)

Find the constant rate of change for each graph and interpret its meaning.

3\. **Distances on Map**

Actual Distance (mi): 0, 30, 60, 90 — Map Distance (in.): 0, 2, 4, 6

4\.

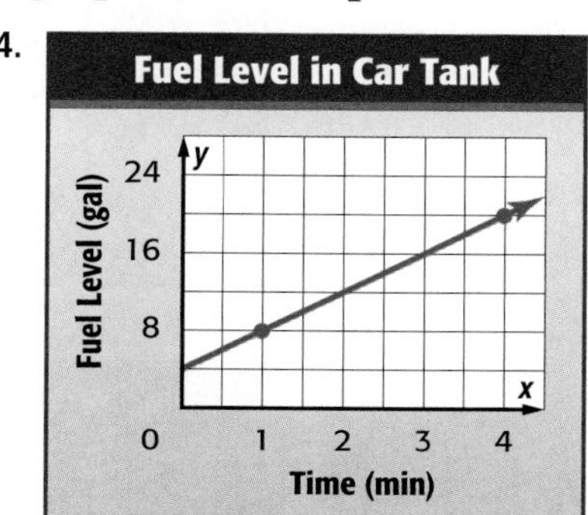

Example 3 (p. 206)

Determine whether a proportional linear relationship exists between the two quantities shown in each of the indicated graphs. Explain your reasoning.

5\. Exercise 3

6\. Exercise 4

Practice and Problem Solving

HOMEWORK HELP	
For Exercises	**See Examples**
7–10	1
11–16	2
17–22	3

Determine whether the relationship between the two quantities described in each table is linear. If so, find the constant rate of change. If not, explain your reasoning.

7\.

Cost of Electricity to Run Personal Computer	
Time (h)	**Cost (¢)**
5	15
8	24
12	36
24	72

8\.

Total Number of Customers Helped at Jewelry Store	
Time (h)	**Total Helped**
1	12
2	24
3	36
4	60

9\.

Distance Traveled by Falling Object				
Distance (m)	4.9	19.6	44.1	78.4
Time (s)	1	2	3	4

10\.

Italian Dressing Recipe				
Oil (c)	2	4	6	8
Vinegar (c)	$\frac{3}{4}$	$1\frac{1}{2}$	$2\frac{1}{4}$	3

Find the constant rate of change for each graph and interpret its meaning.

11.

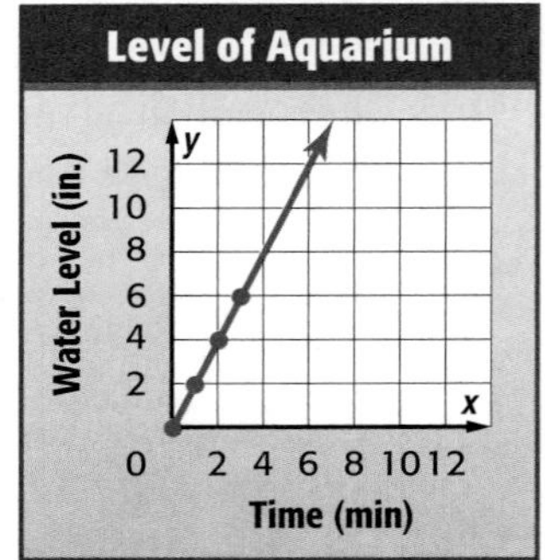

12.

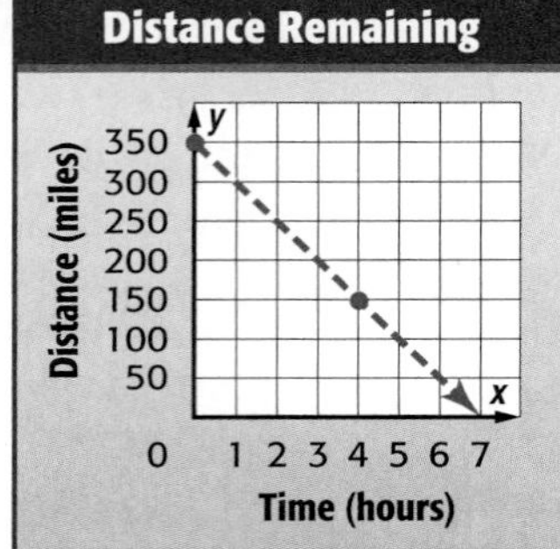

13.

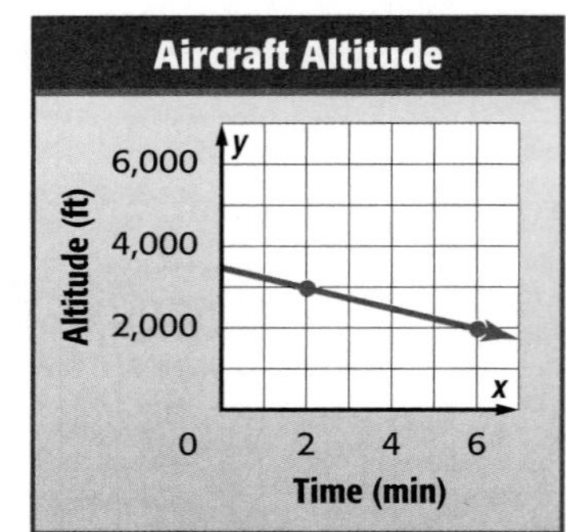

14.

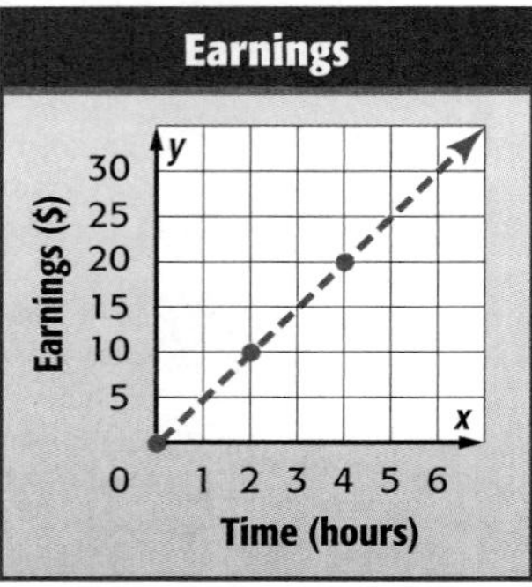

15.

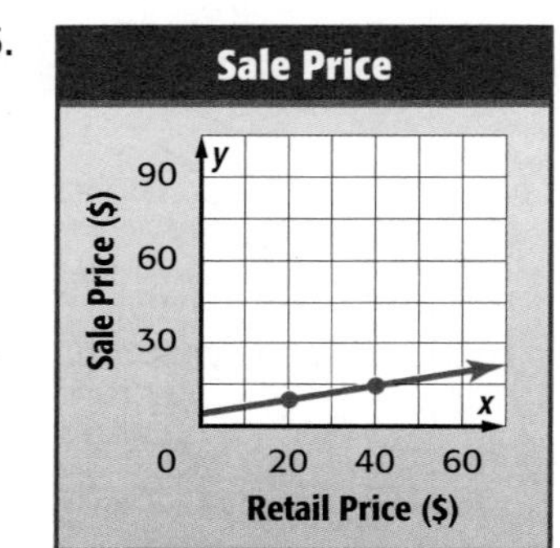

16.

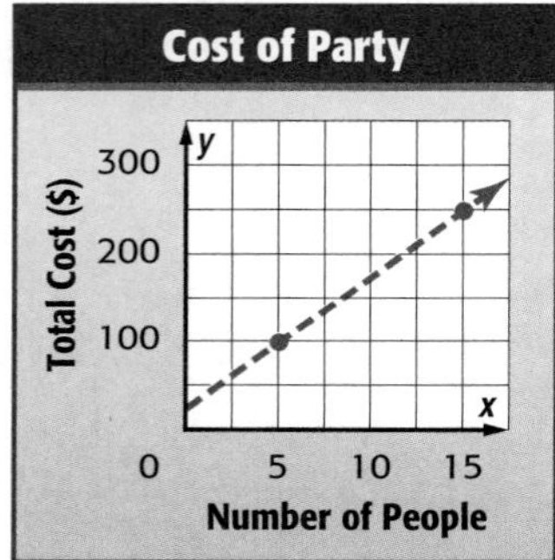

Determine whether a proportional relationship exists between the two quantities shown in each of the indicated graphs. Explain your reasoning.

17. Exercise 11 **18.** Exercise 12 **19.** Exercise 13

20. Exercise 14 **21.** Exercise 15 **22.** Exercise 16

CELL PHONES For Exercises 23 and 24, use the following information. Both Luis and Miriam have cell phone plans. Their costs for several minutes are shown.

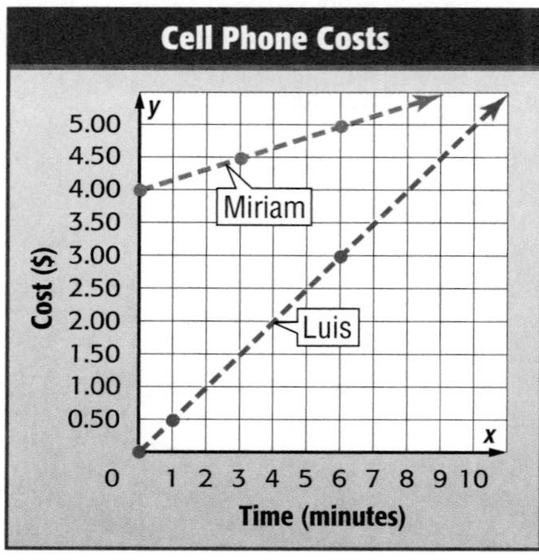

23. Who is spending more money each minute? Explain your reasoning.

24. Whose plan is proportional to the number of minutes the phone is used? Explain.

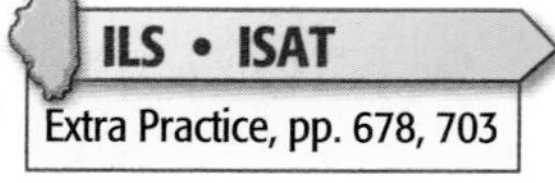

H.O.T. Problems

25. **OPEN ENDED** Graph two quantities that have a proportional linear relationship. Justify your answer.

26. **CHALLENGE** Examine the graphs in Exercises 3, 4, and 11–16, as well as your corresponding answers in Exercises 5 and 17–22. What point do all of the graphs that represent proportional linear relationships have in common?

27. **WRITING IN MATH** Write a real-world problem in which you would need to find a constant rate of change. Then solve your problem. Is the relationship described in your problem proportional? Explain.

ISAT PRACTICE 6.D.3

28. Tickets to the school play are \$2.50 each. Which table contains values that fit this situation, if c represents the total cost for t tickets?

A

Cost of Play Tickets				
c	\$2.50	\$3.25	\$4.00	\$4.75
t	1	2	3	4

B

Cost of Play Tickets				
c	\$3.50	\$6.00	\$8.50	\$11.00
t	1	2	3	4

C

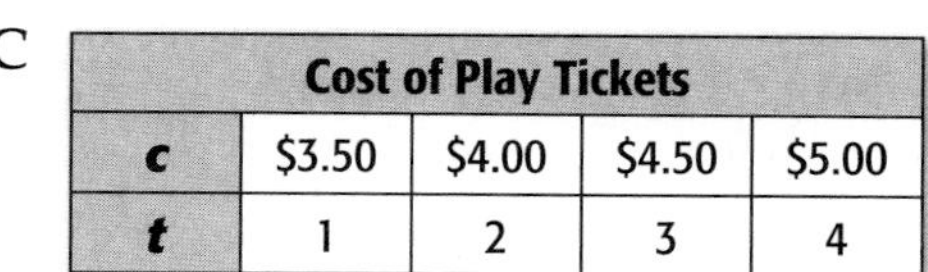

Cost of Play Tickets				
c	\$3.50	\$4.00	\$4.50	\$5.00
t	1	2	3	4

D

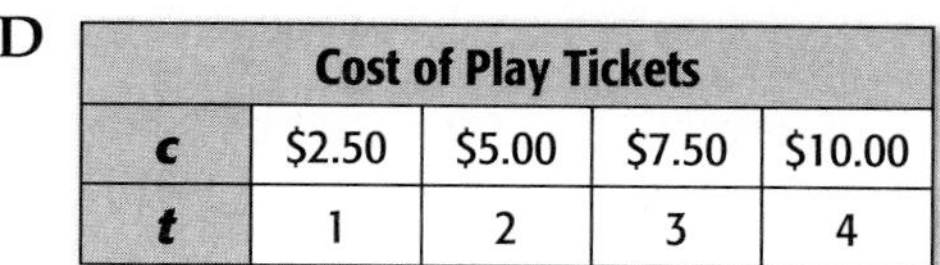

Cost of Play Tickets				
c	\$2.50	\$5.00	\$7.50	\$10.00
t	1	2	3	4

29. The graph shows the distance Bianca traveled over her 2-hour bike ride.

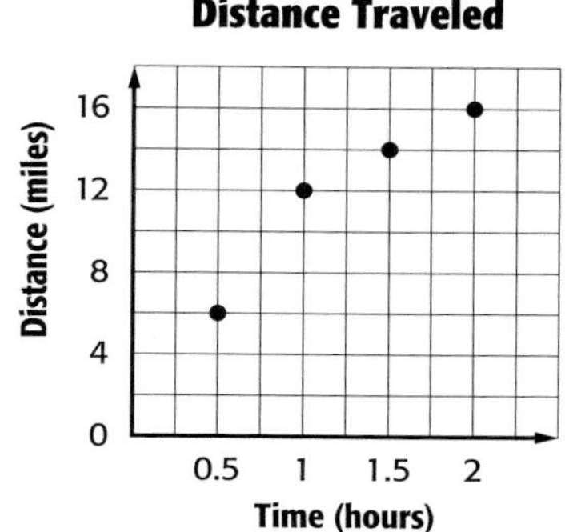

Which of the following is true?

F She traveled at a constant speed of 12 miles per hour for the entire ride.

G She traveled at a constant speed of 8 miles per hour for the last hour.

H She traveled at a constant speed of 4 miles per hour for the last hour.

J She traveled at a constant speed of 8 miles per hour for the entire ride.

Spiral Review

30. **TEMPERATURE** At 6 A.M., the temperature was 33°F, and at 8 A.M. it was 45°F. Find the rate of temperature change in degrees per hour. (Lesson 4-3)

31. **MONEY** Olivia earns an allowance of \$20 per week. Is the amount of money she receives proportional to the number of weeks? (Lesson 4-2)

GET READY for the Next Lesson

PREREQUISITE SKILL **Solve each equation. Check your solution.** (Lesson 1-10)

32. $5 \cdot x = 6 \cdot 10$

33. $8 \cdot 3 = 4 \cdot y$

34. $2 \cdot d = 3 \cdot 5$

35. $2.1 \cdot 7 = 3 \cdot a$

4-5 Solving Proportions

MAIN IDEA

Use proportions to solve problems.

IL Learning Standards

6.D.3 Apply ratios and proportions to solve practical problems.
8.D.3b Propose and solve problems using proportions, formulas and linear functions.
Also addresses 6.C.3a, 6.C.3b, 8.A.3b, 8.D.3a.

New Vocabulary

equivalent ratios
proportion
cross products
constant of proportionality

IL Math Online

glencoe.com

- Concepts in Motion
- Extra Examples
- Personal Tutor
- Self-Check Quiz

GET READY for the Lesson

SHOPPING A local department store advertised a sale as shown at the right.

1. Write a ratio in simplest form that compares the cost to the number of bottles of nail polish.
2. Suppose you and some friends wanted to buy 6 bottles of polish. Write a ratio comparing the cost to the number of bottles of polish.
3. Is the cost proportional to the number of bottles of polish purchased? Explain.

In the example above, the ratios of the cost to the number of bottles of polish for two or six bottles are equal or **equivalent ratios** because they simplify to the same ratio, $\frac{5}{2}$.

$$\frac{\$5}{\text{2 bottles of polish}} = \frac{\$15}{\text{6 bottles of polish}}$$

Proportion — Key Concept

Words A **proportion** is an equation stating that two ratios or rates are equivalent.

Symbols

Numbers	Algebra
$\frac{6}{8} = \frac{3}{4}$	$\frac{a}{b} = \frac{c}{d}, b \neq 0, d \neq 0$

Consider the following proportion.

$$\frac{a}{b} = \frac{c}{d}$$

$\frac{a}{\cancel{b}_1} \cdot \overset{1}{\cancel{b}}d = \frac{c}{\cancel{d}_1} \cdot b\overset{1}{\cancel{d}}$ Multiply each side by bd and divide out common factors.

$ad = bc$ Simplify.

The products ad and bc are called the **cross products** of this proportion. The cross products of any proportion are equal. You can use cross products to *solve proportions* in which one of the quantities is not known.

$\frac{6}{8} = \frac{3}{4}$ → $8 \cdot 3 = 24$, → $6 \cdot 4 = 24$ — The cross products are equal.

EXAMPLE Write and Solve a Proportion

1 TEMPERATURE After 2 hours, the air temperature had risen 7°F. Write and solve a proportion to find the amount of time it will take at this rate for the temperature to rise an additional 13°F.

Write a proportion. Let t represent the time in hours.

temperature → $\frac{7}{2} = \frac{13}{t}$ ← temperature
time → ← time

$\frac{7}{2} = \frac{13}{t}$	Write the proportion.
$7 \cdot t = 2 \cdot 13$	Find the cross products.
$7t = 26$	Multiply.
$\frac{7t}{7} = \frac{26}{7}$	Divide each side by 7.
$t \approx 3.7$	Simplify.

It will take about 3.7 hours to rise an additional 13°F.

CHECK Your Progress

Solve each proportion.

a. $\frac{x}{4} = \frac{9}{10}$ b. $\frac{2}{34} = \frac{5}{y}$ c. $\frac{7}{3} = \frac{n}{2.1}$

Real-World Link
There are four different blood types: A, B, AB, and O. People with Type O blood are considered *universal donors.* Their blood can be transfused into people with any blood type.
Source: The American Red Cross

Real-World EXAMPLE Make Predictions

2 BLOOD During a blood drive, the ratio of Type O donors to non-Type O donors was 37:43. About how many Type O donors would you expect in a group of 300 donors?

Write the ratio for the given information.

Type O donors → total donors → $\frac{37}{37 + 43}$ or $\frac{37}{80}$

Write and solve a proportion. Let t represent the number of Type O donors you would expect to see in the larger population.

Type O donors → $\frac{37}{80} = \frac{t}{300}$ ← Type O donors
total donors → ← total donors

$37 \cdot 300 = 80t$	Find the cross products.
$11{,}100 = 80t$	Multiply.
$\frac{11{,}100}{80} = \frac{80t}{80}$	Divide each side by 80.
$t = 138.75$	Simplify.

You would expect to find about 139 people with Type O blood in a group of 300 donors.

CHECK Your Progress

d. **RECYCLING** Recycling 2,000 pounds of paper saves about 17 trees. Write and solve a proportion to determine how many trees you would expect to save by recycling 5,000 pounds of paper.

You can also use the constant ratio to write an equation expressing the relationship between two proportional quantities. The constant ratio is also called the **constant of proportionality**.

EXAMPLE Write and Use an Equation

3 GASOLINE Jaycee bought 8 gallons of gasoline for $22.32. Write an equation relating the cost to the number of gallons of gasoline. How much would Jaycee pay for 11 gallons at this same rate?

Find the constant of proportionality between cost and gallons.

$$\frac{\text{cost in dollars}}{\text{gasoline in gallons}} = \frac{22.32}{8} \text{ or } 2.79$$

Words	The cost is $2.79 times the number of gallons.
Variable	Let c represent the cost. Let g represent the number of gallons.
Equation	$c = 2.79 \cdot g$

Study Tip

Checking Your Equation You can check to see if the equation you wrote is accurate by testing the two known quantities.

$c = 2.79g$

$22.32 = 2.79(8)$

$22.32 = 22.32$

Find the cost for 11 gallons sold at the same rate.

$c = 2.79g$ Write the equation.

$c = 2.79(11)$ Replace g with the number of gallons.

$c = 30.69$ Multiply.

The cost for 11 gallons is $30.69.

CHECK Your Progress

e. **TYPING** Olivia typed 2 pages in 15 minutes. Write an equation relating the number of minutes m to the number of pages p typed. If she continues typing at this rate, how many minutes will it take her to type 10 pages? to type 25 pages?

CHECK Your Understanding

Example 1 (p. 211)

Solve each proportion.

1. $\frac{1.5}{6} = \frac{10}{p}$
2. $\frac{3.2}{9} = \frac{n}{36}$
3. $\frac{41}{x} = \frac{5}{2}$

For Exercises 4 and 5, assume all situations are proportional.

Example 2 (p. 211)

4. **TEETH** For every 7 people who say they floss daily, there are 18 people who say they do not. Write and solve a proportion to determine out of 65 people how many you would expect to say they floss daily.

Example 3 (p. 212)

5. **TUTORING** Amanda earns $28.50 tutoring for 3 hours. Write an equation relating her earnings m to the number of hours h she tutors. How much would Amanda earn tutoring for 2 hours? for 4.5 hours?

Practice and Problem Solving

HOMEWORK HELP	
For Exercises	See Examples
6–13	1
14–19	2
20–25	3

Solve each proportion.

6. $\frac{k}{7} = \frac{32}{56}$
7. $\frac{x}{13} = \frac{18}{39}$
8. $\frac{44}{p} = \frac{11}{5}$
9. $\frac{2}{w} = \frac{0.4}{0.7}$
10. $\frac{6}{25} = \frac{d}{30}$
11. $\frac{2.5}{6} = \frac{h}{9}$
12. $\frac{3.5}{8} = \frac{a}{3.2}$
13. $\frac{48}{9} = \frac{72}{n}$

For Exercises 14–21, assume all situations are proportional.

14. **COOKING** Evarado paid \$1.12 for a dozen eggs. Write and solve a proportion to determine the cost of 3 eggs.
15. **TRAVEL** A certain vehicle can travel 483 miles on 14 gallons of gasoline. Write and solve a proportion to determine how many gallons of gasoline this vehicle will need to travel 600 miles.
16. **ILLNESS** For every person who actually has the flu, there are 6 people who have flu-like symptoms resulting from a cold. If a doctor sees 40 patients, write and solve a proportion to determine how many of these you would expect to have a cold.
17. **LIFE SCIENCE** For every left-handed person, there are about 4 right-handed people. If there are 30 students in a class, write and solve a proportion to predict the number of students who are right-handed.

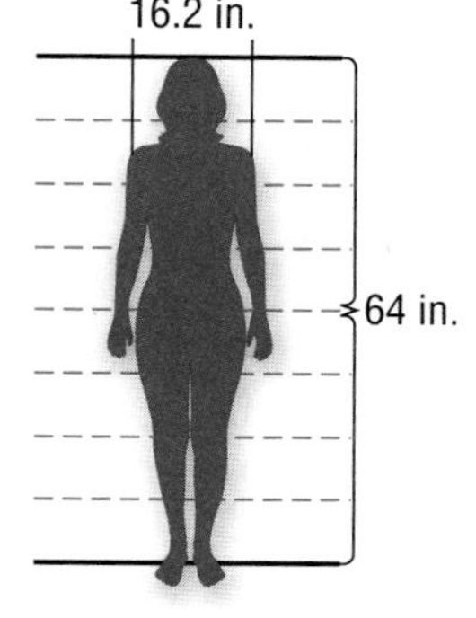

Real-World Link Although people vary in size and shape, in general, people do not vary in proportion. **Source:** *Art Talk*

TRAVEL For Exercises 18 and 19, use the following information.
A speed limit of 100 kilometers per hour (kph) is approximately equal to 62 miles per hour (mph). Write and solve a proportion to predict the following measures. Round your answers to the nearest whole number.

18. a speed limit in mph for a speed limit of 75 kph
19. a speed limit in kph for a speed limit of 20 mph
20. **PHOTOGRAPHY** It takes 2 minutes to print out 3 digital photos. Write an equation relating the number of photos n to the number of minutes m. At this rate, how long will it take to print 10 photos? 14 photos?
21. **MEASUREMENT** The width of a woman's shoulders is proportional to her height. A woman who is 64 inches tall has a shoulder width of 16.2 inches. Find the height of a woman who has a shoulder width of 18.5 inches.

PLANETS For Exercises 22–25, use the table to write a proportion relating the weights on two planets. Then find the missing weight. Round to the nearest tenth.

Weights on Different Planets Earth Weight = 120 pounds	
Mercury	45.6 pounds
Venus	109.2 pounds
Uranus	96 pounds
Jupiter	304.8 pounds

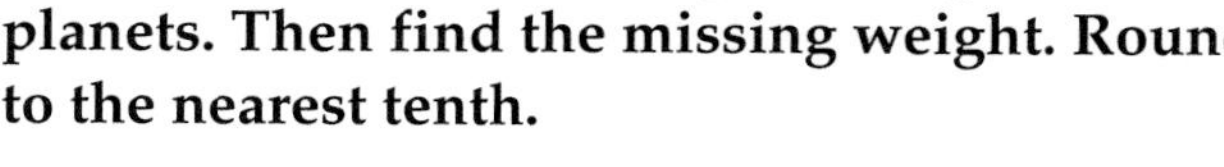

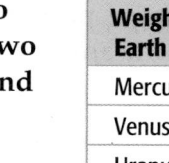

22. Earth: 90 pounds; Venus: ■ pounds
23. Mercury: 55 pounds; Earth ■ pounds
24. Jupiter: 350 pounds; Uranus: ■ pounds
25. Venus: 115 pounds; Mercury: ■ pounds

ILS • ISAT
Extra Practice, pp. 678, 703

26. **FIND THE DATA** Refer to the Data File on pages 16–19. Choose some data and write a real-world problem that could be solved by using a proportion.

27. **MEASUREMENT** A 5-pound bag of grass seed covers 2,000 square feet. An opened bag has 3 pounds of seed remaining in it. Will this be enough to seed a 14-yard by 8-yard piece of land? Explain your reasoning.

H.O.T. Problems

28. **OPEN ENDED** List two other amounts of cinnamon and sugar, one larger and one smaller, that are proportional to $1\frac{1}{2}$ tablespoons of cinnamon for every 3 tablespoons of sugar. Justify your answers.

CHALLENGE **Solve each equation.**

29. $\frac{2}{3} = \frac{18}{x+5}$

30. $\frac{x-4}{10} = \frac{7}{5}$

31. $\frac{4.5}{17-x} = \frac{3}{8}$

32. **WRITING IN MATH** Explain why it might be easier to write an equation to represent a proportional relationship rather than using a proportion.

ISAT PRACTICE 6.D.3, 8.D.3b

33. Michael paid $24 for 3 previously viewed DVDs at Play-It-Again Movies. Which equation can he use to find the cost c of purchasing 12 previously viewed DVDs from this same store?

A $c = 12 \cdot 24$ C $c = 12 \cdot 8$

B $c = 24 \cdot 4$ D $c = 72 \cdot 36$

34. An amusement park line is moving about 4 feet every 15 minutes. At this rate, approximately how long will it take for a person at the back of the 50-foot line to reach the front of the line?

F 1 hour H 5 hours

G 3 hours J 13 hours

35. **SHORT RESPONSE** The graph shows the results of a class survey. Write a proportion to predict how many students out of 515 in the entire middle school think recycling is the best way to take care of resources.

Spiral Review

36. **BABYSITTING** Brenna charges $15, $30, $45, and $60 for babysitting 1, 2, 3, and 4 hours, respectively. Is the relationship between the number of hours and the amount charged linear? If so, find the constant rate of change. If not, explain why not. (Lesson 4-4)

37. **GASOLINE** A truck can go 81 miles on 4.5 gallons of gasoline. At that rate, how much will it cost to travel 207 miles if gasoline costs $2.69 per gallon? (Lesson 4-3)

GET READY for the Next Lesson

38. **PREREQUISITE SKILL** Jacquelyn pays $8 for fair admission but then must pay $0.75 for each ride. If she rides five rides, what is the total cost at the fair? (Lesson 1-1)

CHAPTER 4

Mid-Chapter Quiz

Lessons 4-1 through 4-5

IL Learning Standards
6.D.3, 8.D.3b

Express each ratio in simplest form. (Lesson 4-1)

1. 32 out of 100 dentists
2. 12 tickets chosen out of 60 tickets
3. 300 points in 20 games

Express each rate as a unit rate. (Lesson 4-1)

4. 750 yards in 25 minutes
5. $420 for 15 tickets
6. 40 laps in 6 races

7. **MULTIPLE CHOICE** In her last race, Bergen swam 1,500 meters in 30 minutes. On average, how many meters did she swim per minute? (Lesson 4-1)

   A 25

   B 30

   C 40

   D 50

8. **ICE CREAM** In one 8-hour day, Bella's Ice Cream Shop sold 72 cones of vanilla ice cream. In one hour, they sold 9 cones of vanilla ice cream. Is the total number of cones sold in one hour proportional to the number of cones sold during the day? (Lesson 4-2)

9. **DISHES** Jack washed 60 plates in 30 minutes. It took him 3 minutes to wash 6 plates. Is the number of plates washed in 3 minutes proportional to the total number of plates he washed in 30 minutes? (Lesson 4-2)

10. **TEMPERATURE** At 6 P.M., it was 84°F. At 11 P.M., it was 67°F. Find the rate of temperature change in degrees per hour. (Lesson 4-3)

11. **ANIMALS** In 1999, the number of endangered animal species was 358. By 2005, the number was 389. Find the rate of change of endangered species per year. (Lesson 4-3)

12. Is the relationship between the amount of money owed on a CD player and the number of payments linear? If so, find the constant rate of change. (Lesson 4-4)

Amount Owed ($)	180	150	120	90
Number of Payments	1	2	3	4

13. Is the relationship between the time and the distance covered linear? If so, find the constant rate of change. (Lesson 4-4)

Distance (ft)	0	13	26	39
Time (s)	0	2	4	6

Solve each proportion. (Lesson 4-5)

14. $\frac{33}{r} = \frac{11}{2}$
15. $\frac{x}{36} = \frac{15}{24}$
16. $\frac{5}{9} = \frac{4.5}{a}$

17. **MULTIPLE CHOICE** A bread recipe uses 4 cups of flour and $2\frac{1}{2}$ cups of water. If a baker puts 24 cups of flour into the mixer, how many cups of water will he need? (Lesson 4-5)

    F 15 G 12 H 8 J 6

18. **WORLD RECORDS** In 2006, Timothy Janus set a world record by eating 51 tamales in 12 minutes. At this rate, how many tamales could he consume in 16 minutes? (Lesson 4-5)

19. **MEASUREMENT** Light travels approximately 1,860,000 miles in 10 seconds. How long will it take light to travel 93,000,000 miles from the Sun to Earth? (Lesson 4-5)

4-6 Problem-Solving Investigation

MAIN IDEA: Solve problems by drawing a diagram.

ILS **6.B.3a Solve practical computation problems involving whole numbers, integers and rational numbers. 6.C.3a Select computational procedures and solve problems with whole numbers, fractions, decimals,** percents and proportions.

P.S.I. TEAM +

e-Mail: DRAW A DIAGRAM

GABRIELLA: The school theater is arranged in sections so that each row has the same number of seats. I am seated in the 5th row from the front and the 3rd row from the back. My seat is 6th from the left and 2nd from the right.

YOUR MISSION: Draw a diagram to find how many seats are in Gabriella's section of the theater.

Understand	Her seat is in the 5th row from the front and 3rd row from the back. It is 6th from the left and 2nd from the right. You want to find how many seats are in her section of the theater.
Plan	Draw a diagram showing the rows of the theater based on the location of Gabriella's seat.
Solve	There are 7 rows in Gabriella's section of the theater and 7 seats in each row. So there are 7 × 7 or 49 seats in her section. 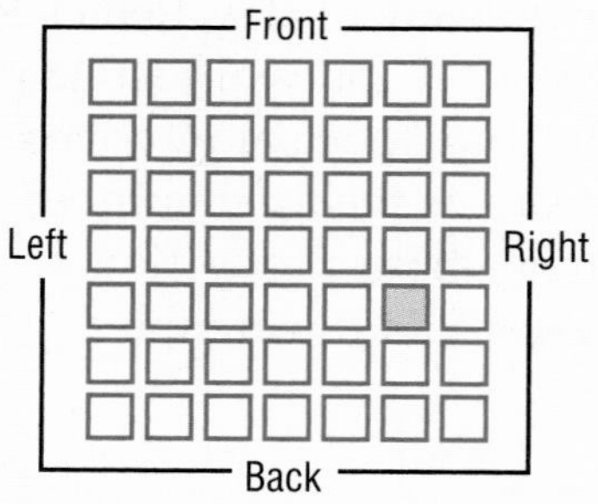
Check	Count the number of seats on your diagram. There are 49 seats. ✓

Analyze The Strategy

1. Describe another way to find the number of seats in Gabriella's section without drawing a diagram.
2. **WRITING IN MATH** Write a problem that is more easily solved by drawing a diagram. Then draw a diagram and solve the problem.

Mixed Problem Solving

ILS • ISAT

Extra Practice, pp. 678, 703

For Exercises 3–5, use the *draw a diagram* strategy to solve the problem.

3. **SEATING** Refer to the problem at the beginning of the lesson. Elena is sitting in the 4th row from the front and the 6th row from the back in a different section. Her seat is 2nd from the left and 6th from the right. How many seats are in her section of the theater?

4. **WATER** A 500-gallon water tank is being filled. Eighty gallons are in the tank after 6 minutes. How many minutes will it take to fill the tank?

5. **GEOMETRY** A stock clerk is piling baseballs in the shape of a square-based pyramid, as shown. If the pyramid is to have five layers, how many baseballs will he need?

Use any strategy to solve Exercises 6–14. Some strategies are shown below.

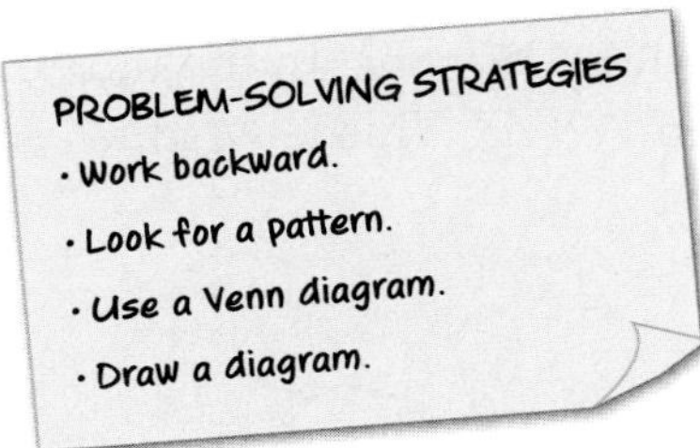

PROBLEM-SOLVING STRATEGIES
• Work backward.
• Look for a pattern.
• Use a Venn diagram.
• Draw a diagram.

6. **AGES** Nick, Sanchez, Hao, Dion, and Toshio are friends. Nick is not the youngest. Dion is younger than Nick but older than Hao. Hao is older than Sanchez and Toshio. Sanchez is not the youngest. Write the boys' names in order from youngest to oldest.

7. **MAPS** On a coordinate map, Jerome's house is located at (9, 7) and his school is located at (6, 2). If a path connects the two and each block is 0.1 mile, how far apart are they?

8. **SCRAPBOOKS** A scrapbook page measures 12 inches long by 12 inches wide. How many 3-inch by 5-inch horizontal photographs can be placed on the page if $\frac{1}{2}$ inch is placed between each photo and at least 1 inch is left as a margin on all four sides?

12 in.
1 in.
1 in.

9. **DESSERTS** At a birthday party, 12 people chose cake for dessert and 8 people chose ice cream. Five people chose both cake and ice cream. How many people had dessert?

10. **SCHOOL** Of the 30 students in a science class, 19 like to do chemistry labs, 15 prefer physical science labs, and 7 like to do both. How many students like chemistry labs but not physical science labs?

11. **PARKS** The Morris family is driving to an amusement park. They drive 162 miles on the highway and 63 miles through towns. If the car can go 21 miles on 1 gallon of gas in town and 36 miles on 1 gallon of gas on the highway, how many gallons of gas will the Morris family use?

12. **MONEY** Junco has 9 coins in her pocket that total $1. The coins are nickels, dimes, and quarters. She has 2 more nickels than quarters. How many of each coin does she have?

13. **MEASUREMENT** It takes 20 minutes to cut a log into 5 equal-size pieces. How long will it take to cut a similar log into 3 equal-size pieces?

14. **FLIGHTS** A DC-11 jumbo jet carries 345 passengers with 38 in first-class and the rest in coach. For a day flight, a first-class ticket from Los Angeles to Chicago costs $650, and a coach ticket costs $230. What will be the ticket sales if the flight is full?

4-7 Similar Polygons

MAIN IDEA

Identify similar polygons and find missing measures of similar polygons.

IL Learning Standards

6.D.3 Apply ratios and proportions to solve practical problems.
9.A.3c Use concepts of symmetry, congruency, **similarity,** scale, perspective, and angles **to describe and analyze two-** and three-**dimensional shapes found in practical applications** (e.g., geodesic domes, A-frame houses, basketball courts, inclined planes, art forms, blueprints).

New Vocabulary

polygon
similar
corresponding parts
congruent
scale factor

IL Math Online

glencoe.com

- Extra Examples
- Personal Tutor
- Self-Check Quiz

MINI Lab

Follow the steps below to discover how the triangles at the right are related.

STEP 1 Copy both triangles onto tracing paper.

STEP 2 Measure and record the sides of each triangle.

STEP 3 Cut out both triangles.

1. Compare the angles of the triangles by matching them up. Identify the angle pairs that have equal measure.
2. Express the ratios $\frac{DF}{LK}$, $\frac{EF}{JK}$, and $\frac{DE}{LJ}$ as decimals to the nearest tenth.
3. What do you notice about the ratios of these sides of matching triangles?

A **polygon** consists of a sequence of consecutive line segments in a plane, placed end to end to form a simple closed figure. Polygons that have the same shape are called **similar** polygons. In the figure below, polygon *ABCD* is similar to polygon *WXYZ*. This is written as polygon *ABCD* ~ polygon *WXYZ*.

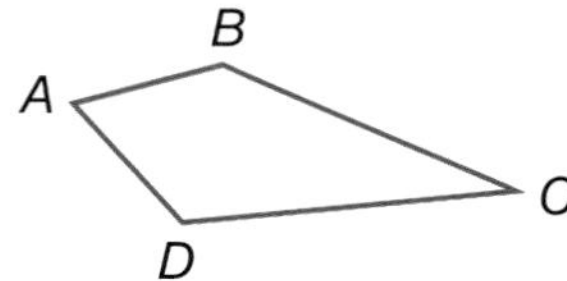

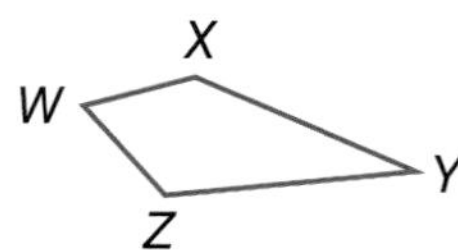

The parts of similar figures that "match" are called **corresponding parts**.

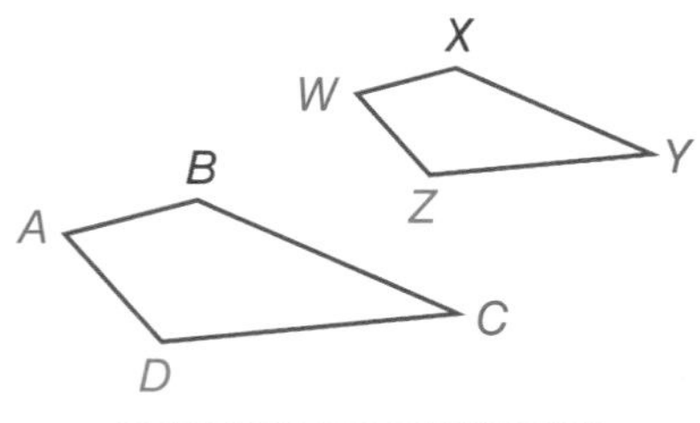

Corresponding Angles

$\angle A \leftrightarrow \angle W$, $\angle B \leftrightarrow \angle X$,
$\angle C \leftrightarrow \angle Y$, $\angle D \leftrightarrow \angle Z$

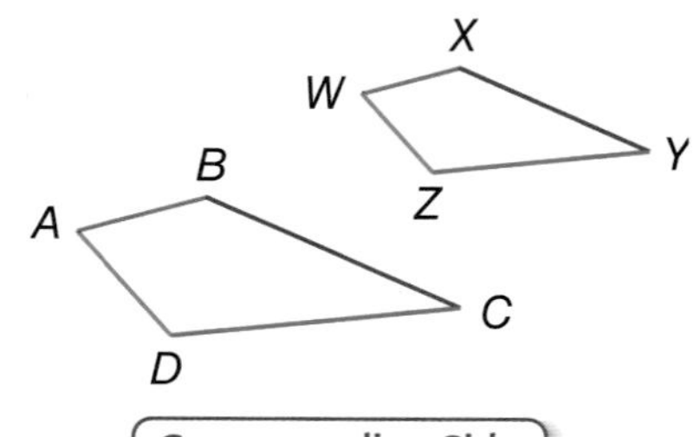

Corresponding Sides

$\overline{AB} \leftrightarrow \overline{WX}$, $\overline{BC} \leftrightarrow \overline{XY}$,
$\overline{CD} \leftrightarrow \overline{YZ}$, $\overline{DA} \leftrightarrow \overline{ZW}$

The similar triangles in the Mini Lab suggest the following.

Similar Polygons

Key Concept

Words If two polygons are similar, then
- their corresponding angles are **congruent**, or have the same measure, and
- the measures of their corresponding sides are proportional.

Model

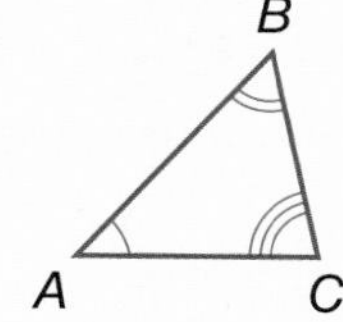

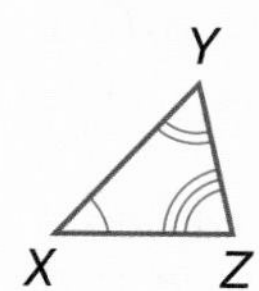

$\triangle ABC \sim \triangle XYZ$

Symbols $\angle A \cong \angle X$, $\angle B \cong \angle Y$, $\angle C \cong \angle Z$, and $\frac{AB}{XY} = \frac{BC}{YZ} = \frac{AC}{XZ}$

Reading Math

Congruence The symbol $\cong$ is read *is congruent to.* Arcs are used to show congruent angles.

EXAMPLE Identify Similar Polygons

1 Determine whether rectangle *HJKL* is similar to rectangle *MNPQ*. Explain.

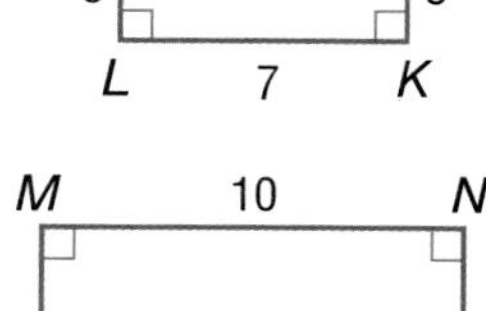

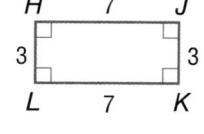

First, check to see if corresponding angles are congruent.

Since the two polygons are rectangles, all of their angles are right angles. Therefore, all corresponding angles are congruent.

M 10 N
6 6
Q 10 P

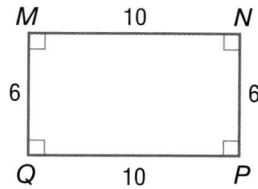

Next, check to see if corresponding sides are proportional.

$\frac{HJ}{MN} = \frac{7}{10}$ $\frac{JK}{NP} = \frac{3}{6}$ or $\frac{1}{2}$ $\frac{KL}{PQ} = \frac{7}{10}$ $\frac{LH}{QM} = \frac{3}{6}$ or $\frac{1}{2}$

Since $\frac{7}{10}$ and $\frac{1}{2}$ are not equivalent ratios, rectangle *HJKL* is *not* similar to rectangle *MNPQ*.

Study Tip

Common Error
Do not assume that two rectangles are similar just because their corresponding angles are congruent. Their corresponding sides must also be proportional.

CHECK Your Progress

Determine whether these polygons are similar. Explain.

a.

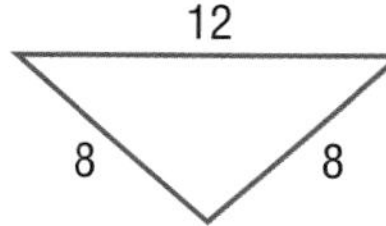

12
8 8

b.

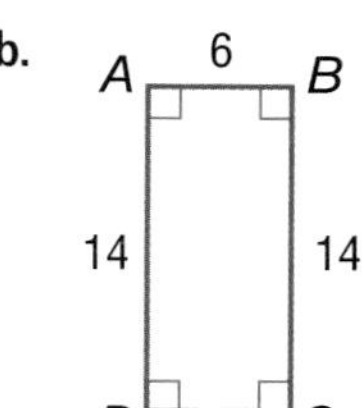

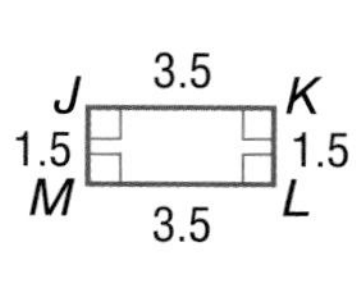

The ratio of the lengths of two corresponding sides of two similar polygons is called the **scale factor**. You can use the scale factor of similar figures or a proportion to find missing measures.

EXAMPLE Find Missing Measures

2 **GEOMETRY** **Given that polygon $WXYZ \sim$ polygon $ABCD$, find the missing measure.**

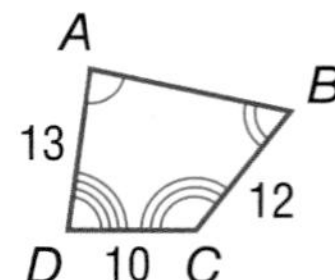

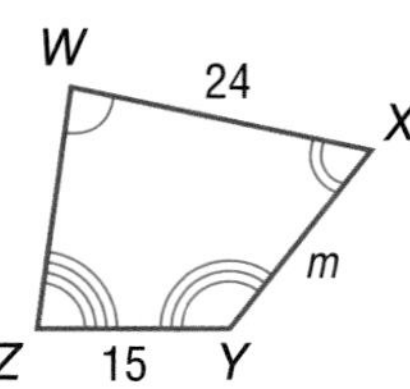

METHOD 1 **Write a proportion.**

The missing measure m is the length of $\overline{XY}$. Write a proportion.

polygon *WXYZ* → $\frac{XY}{BC} = \frac{YZ}{CD}$ ← polygon *WXYZ*
polygon *ABCD* → ← polygon *ABCD*

$\frac{m}{12} = \frac{15}{10}$ — $XY = m$, $BC = 12$, $YZ = 15$, and $CD = 10$.

$m \cdot 10 = 12 \cdot 15$ — Find the cross products.

$10m = 180$ — Multiply.

$m = 18$ — Divide each side by 10.

Reading Math

Segment Measure The *measure* of $\overline{XY}$ is written as *XY*. It represents a number.

METHOD 2 **Use the scale factor to write an equation.**

Find the scale factor from polygon *WXYZ* to polygon *ABCD*.

scale factor: $\frac{YZ}{CD} = \frac{15}{10}$ or $\frac{3}{2}$ — The scale factor is the constant of proportionality.

Words	A length on polygon *WXYZ*	is $\frac{3}{2}$ times as long as	a corresponding length on polygon *ABCD*.
Variable	Let m represent the measure of $\overline{XY}$.		
Equation	$m = \frac{3}{2} \cdot 12$		

$m = \frac{3}{2}(12)$ — Write the equation.

$m = 18$ — Multiply.

Study Tip

Scale Factor
In Example 2, the scale factor from polygon *ABCD* to polygon *WXYZ* is $\frac{2}{3}$, which means that a length on polygon *ABCD* is $\frac{2}{3}$ as long as a length on polygon *WXYZ*.

CHOOSE Your Method

Find each missing measure above.

c. WZ

d. AB

Square A ~ square B with a scale factor of 3:2. Notice that the ratio of their perimeters is 12:8 or 3:2.

3 m — Square A

2 m — Square B

Square	Perimeter
A	12 m
B	8 m

This and other related examples suggest the following.

Ratios of Similar Figures

Key Concept

Words If two figures are similar with a scale factor of $\frac{a}{b}$, then the perimeters of the figures have a ratio of $\frac{a}{b}$.

Model

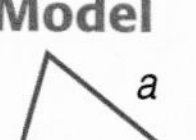

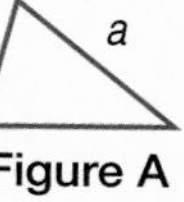

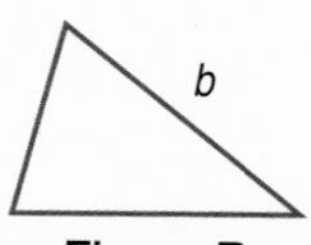

ISAT EXAMPLE 6.D.3, 9.A.3c

3 Triangle LMN is similar to triangle PQR. If the perimeter of $\triangle LMN$ is 64 units, what is the perimeter of $\triangle PQR$?

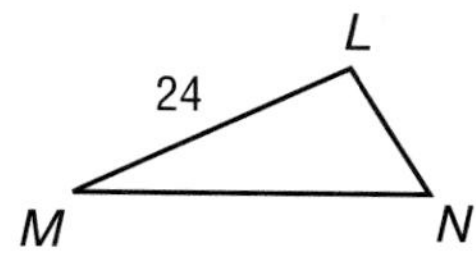

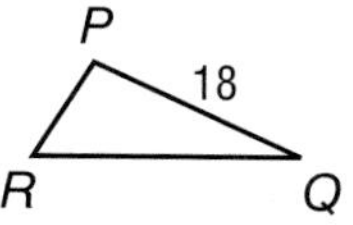

A 108 units

B 96 units

C 48 units

D 36 units

Test-Taking Tip

Similarity Statements In naming similar triangles, the order of the vertices indicates the corresponding parts. Read the similarity statement carefully to be sure that you compare corresponding parts.

Read the Item

You know the measures of two corresponding sides and the perimeter of $\triangle LMN$. You need to find the perimeter of $\triangle PQR$.

Solve the Item

Triangle $LMN \sim$ triangle PQR with a scale factor of $\frac{24}{18}$ or $\frac{4}{3}$. The ratio of the perimeters of $\triangle LMN$ to $\triangle PQR$ is also $\frac{4}{3}$.

perimeter of $\triangle LMN \rightarrow$ / perimeter of $\triangle PQR \rightarrow$ $\frac{64}{x} = \frac{4}{3}$	Scale factor relating $\triangle LMN$ to $\triangle PQR$
$64 \cdot 3 = 4 \cdot x$	Find the cross products.
$192 = 4x$	Multiply.
$\frac{192}{4} = \frac{4x}{4}$	Divide each side by 4.
$48 = x$	Simplify.

The answer is C.

CHECK Your Progress

e. Square $KLMN$ is similar to square $TUVW$. If the perimeter of square $KLMN$ is 32 units, what is the perimeter of square $TUVW$?

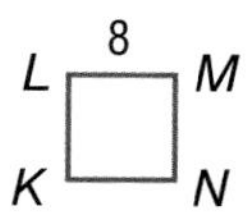

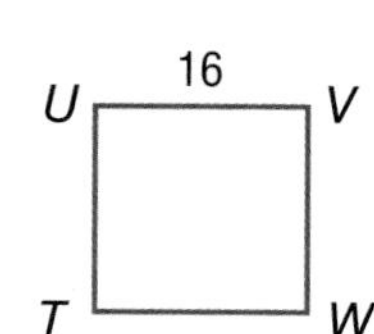

F 128 units

G 96 units

H 64 units

J 40 units

CHECK Your Understanding

Example 1 (p. 219)

Determine whether each pair of polygons is similar. Explain.

1. 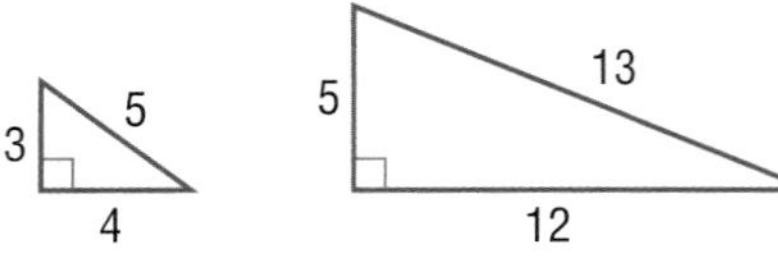

2. 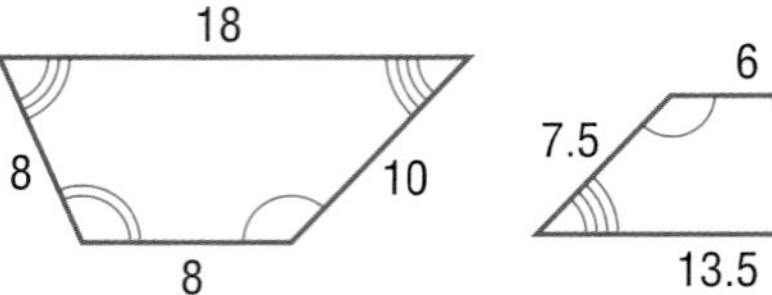

Example 2 (p. 220)

3. In the figure at the right, $\triangle FGH \sim \triangle KLJ$. Write and solve a proportion to find each missing side measure.

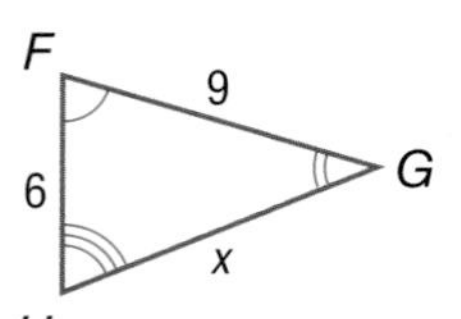

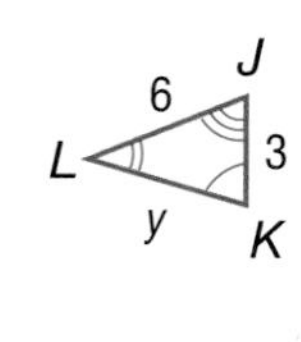

Example 3 (p. 221)

4. **MULTIPLE CHOICE** $\triangle ABC$ is similar to $\triangle XYZ$. If the perimeter of $\triangle ABC$ is 40 units, what is the perimeter of $\triangle XYZ$?

A 10 units **C** 40 units

B 20 units **D** 80 units

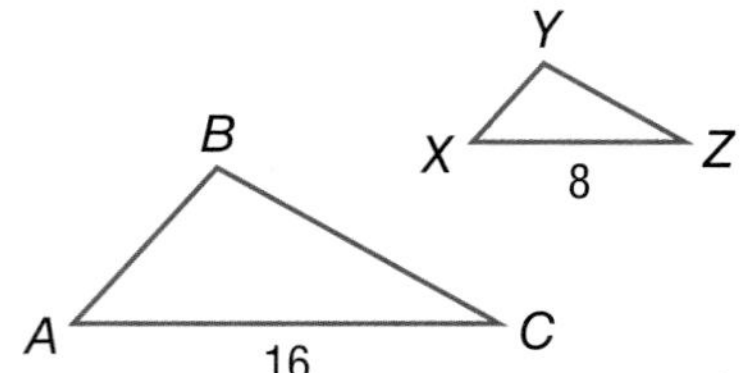

Practice and Problem Solving

HOMEWORK HELP	
For Exercises	See Examples
5–8	1
9–12	2
18, 19	3

Determine whether each pair of polygons is similar. Explain.

5. 3, 4, 7, 8

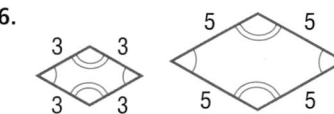

6. 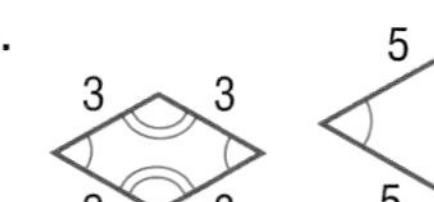

7. 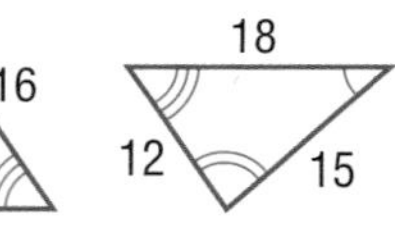

18, 12, 15

8. 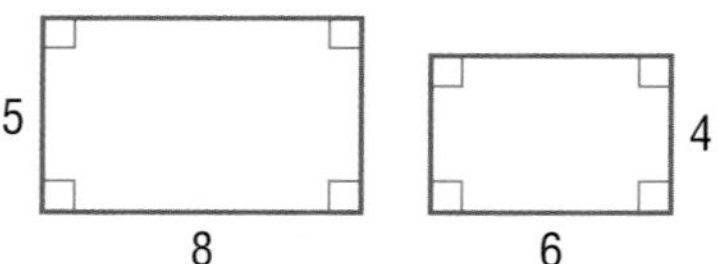

Each pair of polygons is similar. Write and solve a proportion to find each missing side measure.

9. 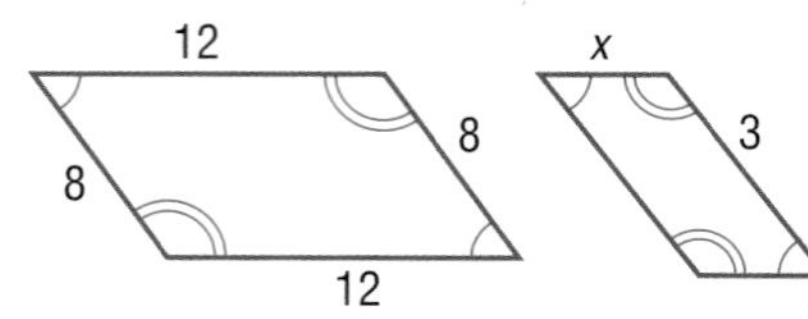

10. 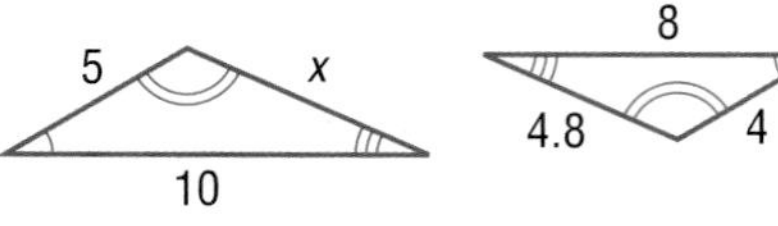

11. 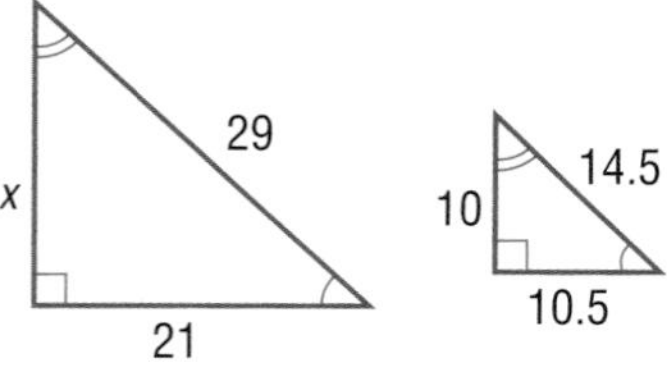

12. 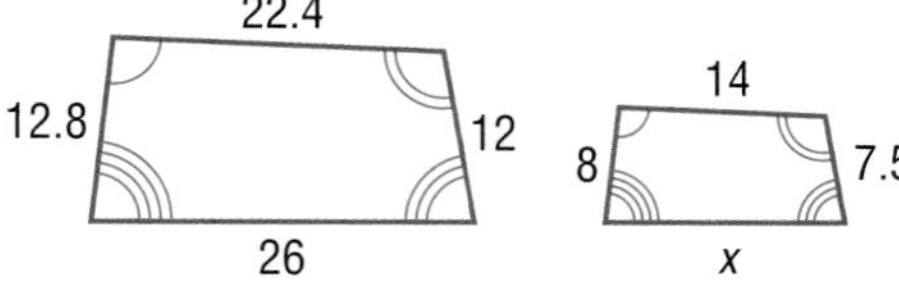

13. **LIFE SCIENCE** The scale factor from the model of a human inner ear to the actual ear is 55:2. If one of the bones of the model is 8.25 centimeters long, how long is the actual bone in a human ear?

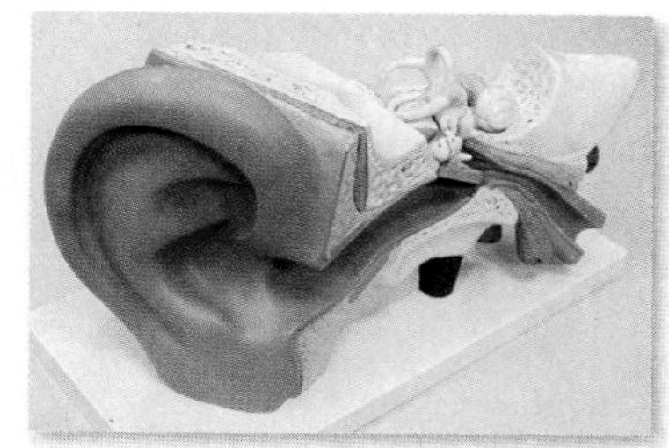

ILS • ISAT
Extra Practice, pp. 679, 703

14. **TELEVISION** The ratio of the length of a wide-screen TV to its width is 16:9. Find the width of a wide-screen TV if the length measures 28 inches. Round to the nearest tenth.

H.O.T. Problems

15. **CHALLENGE** Suppose two rectangles are similar with a scale factor of 2. What is the ratio of their areas? Explain.

WRITING IN MATH Determine whether each statement is *always, sometimes,* or *never* true. Explain your reasoning.

16. Any two rectangles are similar.

17. Any two squares are similar.

ISAT PRACTICE 6.D.3, 9.A.3c

18. Triangle FGH is similar to triangle RST.

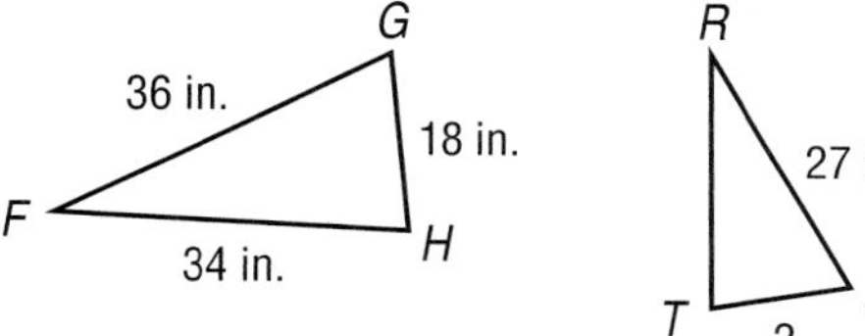

What is the length of $\overline{TS}$?

A $13\frac{1}{2}$ inches

B $22\frac{2}{3}$ inches

C 24 inches

D $25\frac{1}{2}$ inches

19. Quadrilateral $ABCD$ is similar to quadrilateral $WXYZ$.

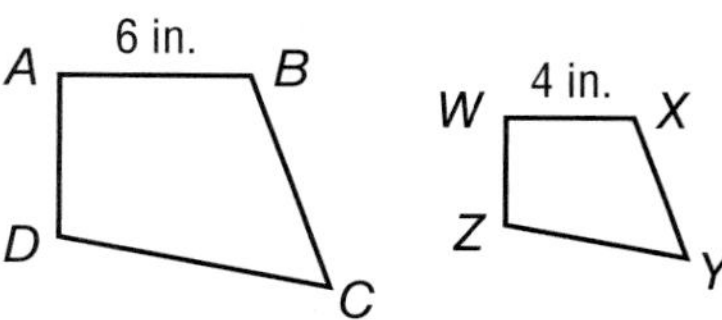

If the perimeter of quadrilateral $ABCD$ is 54 units, what is the perimeter of quadrilateral $WXYZ$?

F 13.5 inches

G 24 inches

H 27 inches

J 36 inches

Spiral Review

20. **ROCK CLIMBING** Grace is working her way up a climbing wall. Every 5 minutes she is able to climb 6 feet, but then loses her footing, slips back 1 foot, and decides to rest for 1 minute. If the rock wall is 30 feet tall, how long will it take her to reach the top? Use the *draw a diagram* strategy. (Lesson 4-6)

Solve each proportion. (Lesson 4-5)

21. $\frac{5}{4} = \frac{y}{12}$

22. $\frac{120}{b} = \frac{24}{60}$

23. $\frac{0.6}{5} = \frac{1.5}{n}$

GET READY for the Next Lesson

PREREQUISITE SKILL Graph and connect each pair of ordered pairs. (Lesson 3-6)

24. $(-2.5, 1.5), (1.5, -3.5)$

25. $\left(-2, -1\frac{1}{2}\right), \left(4, 3\frac{1}{2}\right)$

26. $\left(-2\frac{1}{3}, 1\right), \left(2, 3\frac{2}{3}\right)$

Extend 4-7

Geometry Lab
The Golden Rectangle

MAIN IDEA

Find the value of the golden ratio.

IL Learning Standards

6.D.3 Apply ratios and proportions to solve practical problems. *Also addresses 9.A.3c.*

ACTIVITY

STEP 1 Cut out a rectangle that measures 34 units long by 21 units wide. Using your calculator, find the ratio of the length to the width. Express it as a decimal to the nearest hundredth. Record your data in a table like the one below.

length	34	21			
width	21	13			
ratio					
decimal					

STEP 2 Cut this rectangle into two parts, in which one part is the largest possible square and the other part is a rectangle. Record the rectangle's length and width. Write the ratio of length to width. Express it as a decimal to the nearest hundredth and record in the table.

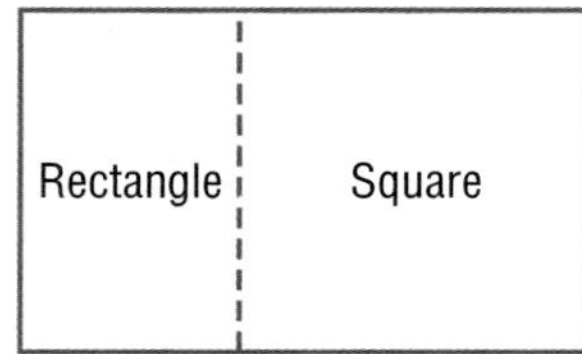

STEP 3 Repeat the procedure described in Step 2 until the remaining rectangle measures 3 units by 5 units.

Analyze the Results

1. Describe the pattern in the ratios you recorded.
2. **MAKE A CONJECTURE** If the rectangles you cut out are described as *golden rectangles,* what is the value of the *golden ratio?*
3. Write a definition of golden rectangle. Use the word *ratio* in your definition. Then describe the shape of a golden rectangle.
4. Determine whether all golden rectangles are similar. Explain your reasoning.
5. **RESEARCH** There are many examples of the golden rectangle in architecture. Two are shown at the right. Use the Internet or another resource to find three places where the golden rectangle is used in architecture.

4-8 Dilations

MAIN IDEA

Graph dilations on a coordinate plane.

IL Learning Standards

6.D.3 Apply ratios and proportions to solve practical problems.
9.A.3b Draw transformation images of figures, with and **without the use of technology.** *Also addresses 9.A.3c.*

New Vocabulary

dilation
center
enlargement
reduction

IL Math Online

glencoe.com

- Concepts in Motion
- Extra Examples
- Personal Tutor
- Self-Check Quiz

MINI Lab

The figure shown is drawn on 0.5-centimeter grid paper, so each square is 0.5-by-0.5 centimeter. Redraw the figure using squares that are 1-by-1 centimeter. Use point A as your starting point.

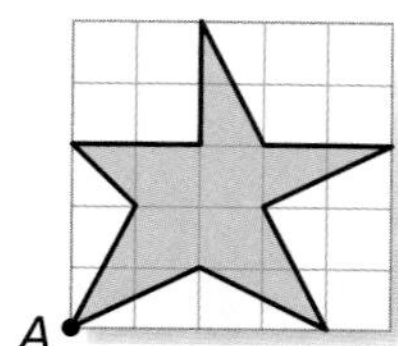

1. Measure and compare corresponding lengths on the original and new figure. Describe the relationship between these measurements. How does this relate to the change in grid size?
2. **MAKE A CONJECTURE** What size squares should you use to create a version of the original figure with dimensions that are four times the corresponding lengths on the original? Explain.

The image produced by enlarging or reducing a figure is called a **dilation**. A dilation image is similar to the original figure. This means that corresponding lengths on the two figures are proportional.

The **center** of the dilation is a fixed point used for measurement when altering the size of the figure. The ratio of a length on the image to a length on the original figure is the scale factor of the dilation.

EXAMPLE Draw a Dilation

1 Copy polygon $ABCD$ shown on graph paper. Then draw the image of the figure after a dilation with center A by a scale factor of 2.

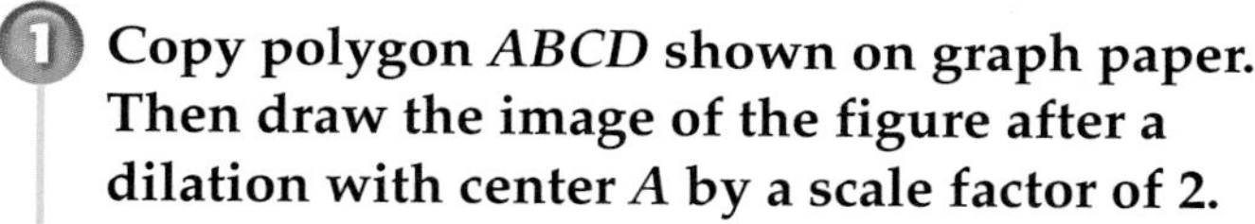

Step 1 Draw ray AB, or $\overrightarrow{AB}$, extending it to the edges of the grid.

Step 2 Use a ruler to locate point B' on $\overrightarrow{AB}$ such that $AB' = 2(AB)$.

Step 3 Repeat Steps 1 and 2 for points C' and D'. Then draw polygon $A'B'C'D'$ where $A = A'$.

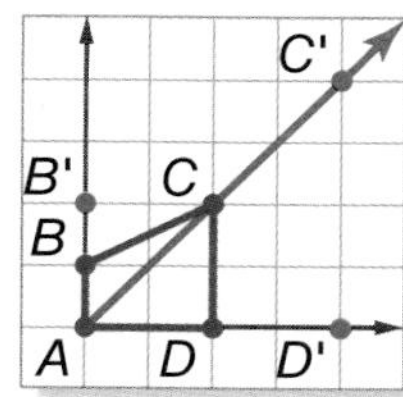

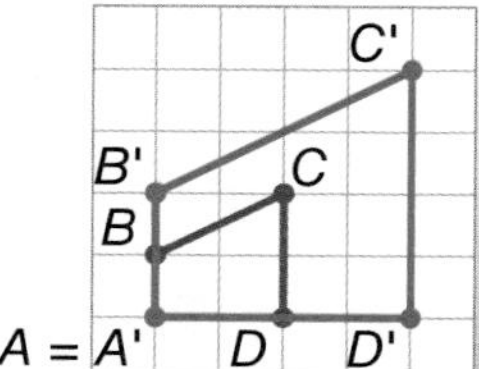

CHECK Your Progress

a. Draw and label a large triangle XYZ on grid paper. Then draw the image of $\triangle XYZ$ after a dilation with center X and scale factor $\frac{1}{4}$.

In Example 1, if point A has coordinates (0, 0), then the table below lists the coordinates of corresponding points on the original figure and its image. Notice that the coordinates of the image are (ax, ay), where a is the scale factor.

Original Coordinates	Relationship	Image Coordinates
$D(2, 0)$	$(2 \cdot 2, 0 \cdot 2)$	$D'(4, 0)$
$C(2, 2)$	$(2 \cdot 2, 2 \cdot 2)$	$C'(4, 4)$
$B(0, 1)$	$(0 \cdot 2, 1 \cdot 2)$	$B'(0, 2)$
$A(0, 0)$	$(0 \cdot 2, 0 \cdot 2)$	$A'(0, 0)$

Study Tip

Dilations on a Coordinate Plane
The ratio of the x- and y-coordinates of the vertices of an image to the corresponding values of the coordinates of the vertices of the original figure is the same as the scale factor of the dilation.

To find the coordinates of the vertices of an image after a dilation with center (0, 0), multiply the x- and y-coordinates by the scale factor.

EXAMPLE Graph a Dilation

2 **Graph $\triangle JKL$ with vertices $J(3, 8)$, $K(10, 6)$, and $L(8, 2)$. Then graph its image $\triangle J'K'L'$ after a dilation with a scale factor of $\frac{1}{2}$.**

To find the vertices of the dilation, multiply each coordinate in the ordered pairs by $\frac{1}{2}$. Then graph both images on the same axes.

$$J(3, 8) \rightarrow \left(3 \cdot \frac{1}{2}, 8 \cdot \frac{1}{2}\right) \rightarrow J'\left(\frac{3}{2}, 4\right)$$
$$K(10, 6) \rightarrow \left(10 \cdot \frac{1}{2}, 6 \cdot \frac{1}{2}\right) \rightarrow K'(5, 3)$$
$$L(8, 2) \rightarrow \left(8 \cdot \frac{1}{2}, 2 \cdot \frac{1}{2}\right) \rightarrow L'(4, 1)$$

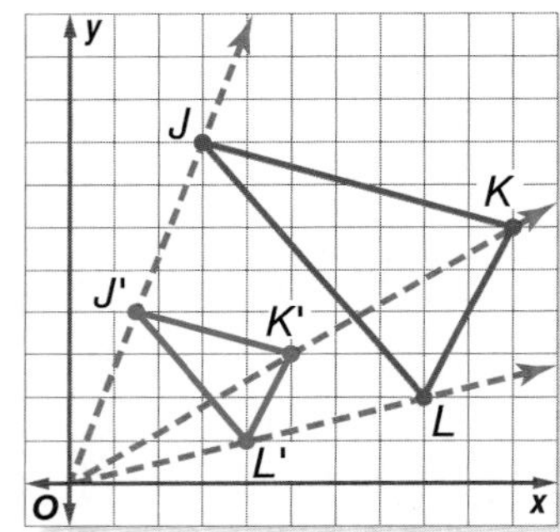

Check for Reasonableness
Draw lines through the origin and each of the vertices of the original figure. The vertices of the dilation should lie on those same lines.

CHECK Your Progress

Find the coordinates of the image of $\triangle JKL$ after a dilation with each scale factor. Then graph $\triangle JKL$ and $\triangle J'K'L'$.

b. scale factor: 3

c. scale factor: $\frac{1}{3}$

Examine the scale factors and the images produced after the dilations in Examples 1 and 2. These and other examples suggest the following.

- A dilation with a scale factor greater than 1 produces an **enlargement**, an image that is larger than the original figure.
- A dilation with a scale factor between 0 and 1 produces a **reduction**, an image that is smaller than the original figure.

EXAMPLE Find and Classify a Scale Factor

Study Tip

Alternate Form
Scale factors can also be written as decimals.

3 **Quadrilateral $V'Z'X'W'$ is a dilation of quadrilateral $VZXW$. Find the scale factor of the dilation, and classify it as an *enlargement* or a *reduction*.**

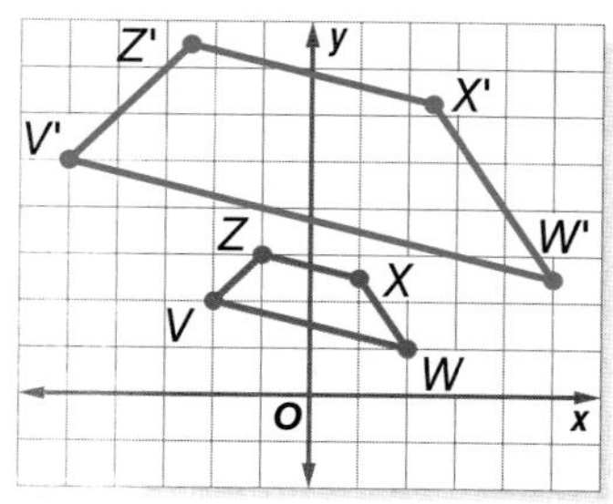

Write a ratio of the x- or y-coordinate of one vertex of the dilation to the x- or y-coordinate of the corresponding vertex of the original figure. Use the y-coordinates of $V(-2, 2)$ and $V'(-5, 5)$.

$\frac{y\text{-coordinate of point } V'}{y\text{-coordinate of point } V} = \frac{5}{2}$ Verify by using other coordinates.

The scale factor is $\frac{5}{2}$. Since $\frac{5}{2} > 1$, the dilation is an enlargement.

Before Dilation

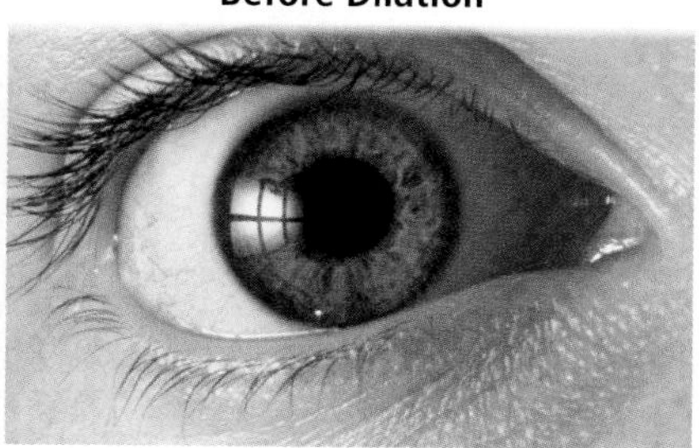

CHECK Your Progress

d. Triangle $A'B'C'$ is a dilation of $\triangle ABC$. Find the scale factor of the dilation, and classify it as an *enlargement* or a *reduction*.

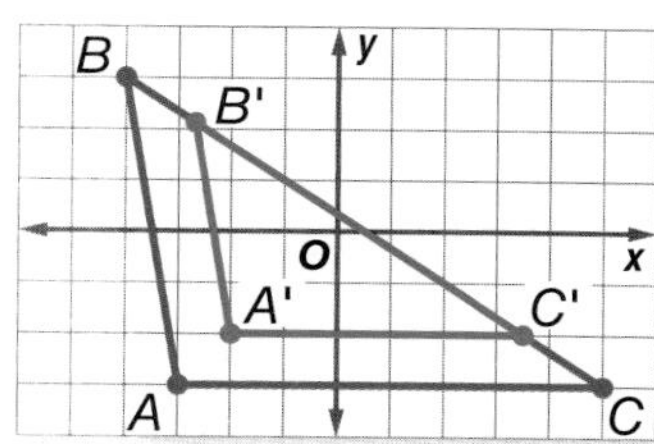

After Dilation

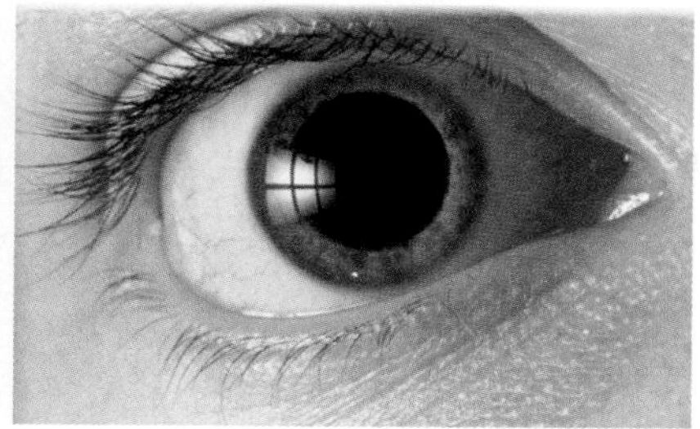

Real-World Link . . . .
An optometrist will often dilate the pupils to better examine a patient's retina, the layer of nerve tissue that receives and transmits images to the brain.

Real-World EXAMPLE

4 **EYES** **An optometrist dilates a patient's pupils by a factor of $\frac{5}{3}$. If the pupil before dilation has a diameter of 5 millimeters, find the new diameter after the pupil is dilated.**

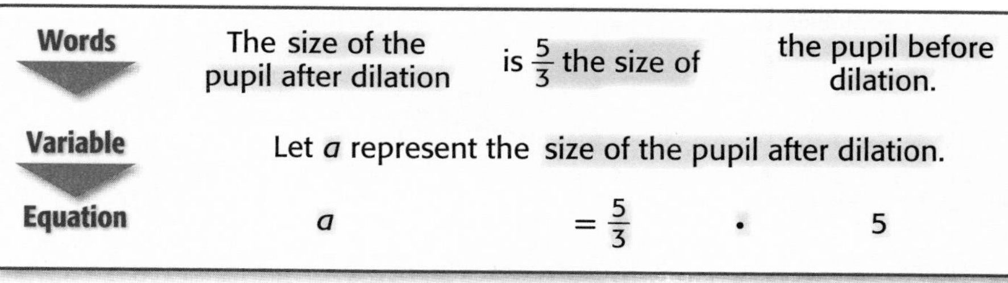

Words	The size of the pupil after dilation	is $\frac{5}{3}$ the size of	the pupil before dilation.
Variable	Let a represent the size of the pupil after dilation.		
Equation	a	$= \frac{5}{3} \cdot$	5

$a = \frac{5}{3}(5)$ Write the equation.

$a \approx 8.33$ Multiply.

The pupil will be about 8.3 millimeters in diameter after dilation.

CHECK Your Progress

e. **COMPUTERS** Dante uses an image of his dog as the wallpaper on his computer desktop. The original image is 5 inches high and 7 inches wide. If his computer scales the image by a factor of $\frac{5}{4}$, what are the dimensions of the dilated image?

CHECK Your Understanding

Example 1 (p. 225)

Copy $\triangle ABC$ on graph paper. Then draw the image of the figure after the dilation with the given center and scale factor.

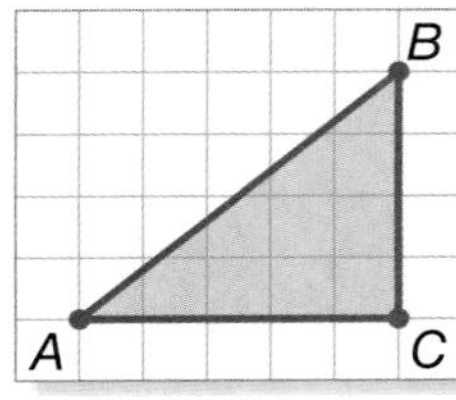

1. center: A, scale factor: $\frac{1}{2}$
2. center: C, scale factor: $\frac{3}{2}$

Example 2 (p. 226)

Triangle JKL has vertices $J(-4, 2)$, $K(-2, -4)$, and $L(3, 6)$. Find the vertices of $\triangle J'K'L'$ after a dilation with the given scale factor. Then graph $\triangle JKL$ and $\triangle J'K'L'$.

3. scale factor: 3
4. scale factor: $\frac{1}{4}$

Example 3 (p. 227)

5. On the graph, $\overline{A'B'}$ is a dilation of $\overline{AB}$. Find the scale factor of the dilation, and classify it as an *enlargement* or as a *reduction*.

Example 4 (p. 227)

6. **GRAPHIC DESIGN** Jacqui designed a 6-inch by $7\frac{1}{2}$-inch logo for her school. The logo is to be reduced by a scale factor of $\frac{1}{3}$ and used to make face paintings. What are the dimensions of the dilated image?

Practice and Problem Solving

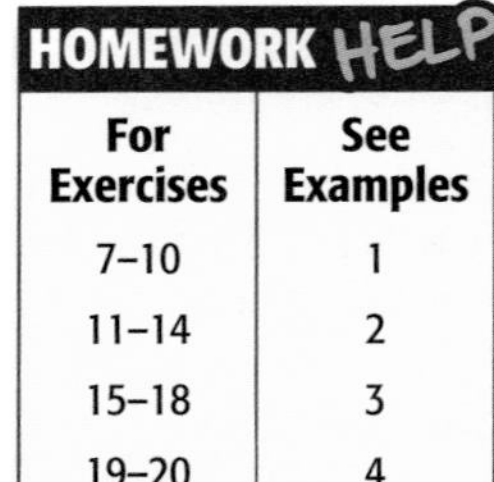

HOMEWORK HELP

For Exercises	See Examples
7–10	1
11–14	2
15–18	3
19–20	4

Copy each figure on graph paper. Then draw the image of the figure after the dilation with the given center and scale factor.

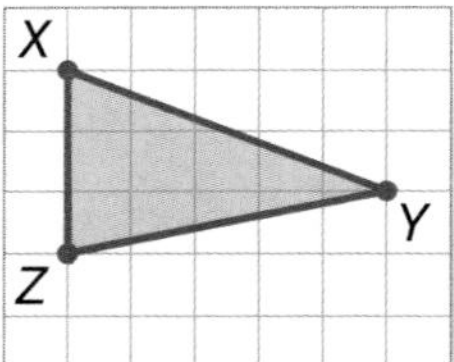

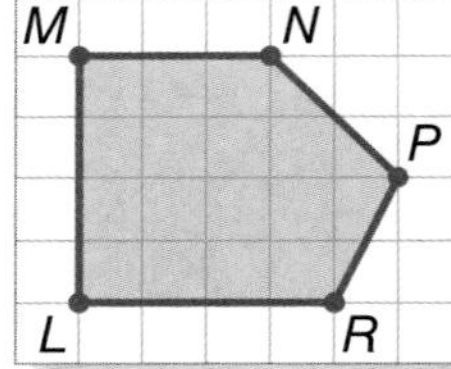

7. center: X, scale factor: $\frac{7}{3}$
8. center: Z, scale factor: $\frac{2}{3}$
9. center: L, scale factor: $\frac{3}{4}$
10. center: N, scale factor: 2

Find the vertices of polygon $H'J'K'L'$ after polygon $HJKL$ is dilated using the given scale factor. Then graph polygon $HJKL$ and polygon $H'J'K'L'$.

11. $H(-1, 3)$, $J(3, 2)$, $K(2, -3)$, $L(-2, -2)$; scale factor 2
12. $H(0, 2)$, $J(3, 1)$, $K(0, -4)$, $L(-2, -3)$; scale factor 3
13. $H(-6, 2)$, $J(4, 4)$, $K(7, -2)$, $L(-2, -4)$; scale factor $\frac{1}{2}$
14. $H(-8, 4)$, $J(6, 4)$, $K(6, -4)$, $L(-8, -4)$; scale factor $\frac{3}{4}$

On each graph, one figure is a dilation of the other. Find the scale factor of each dilation and classify it as an enlargement or as a reduction.

15. 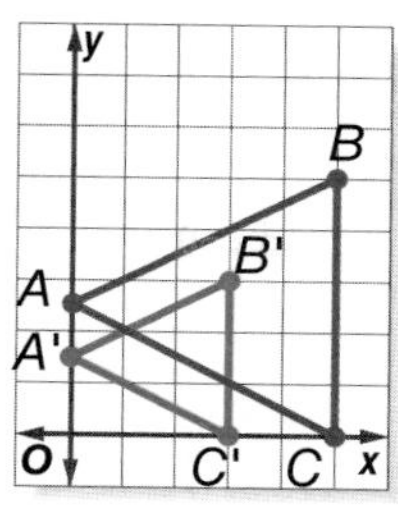

16. 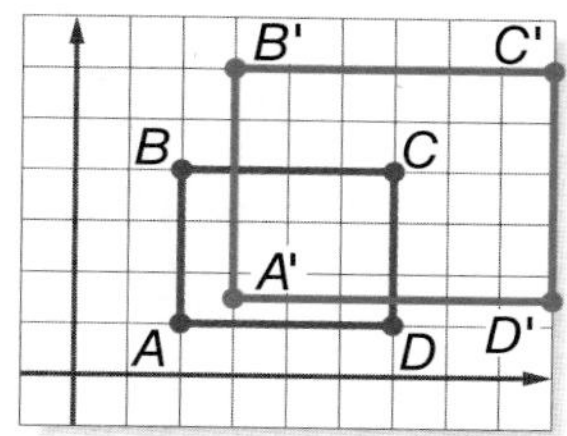

17. 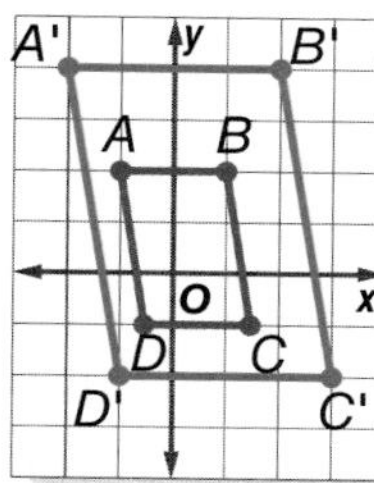

18. 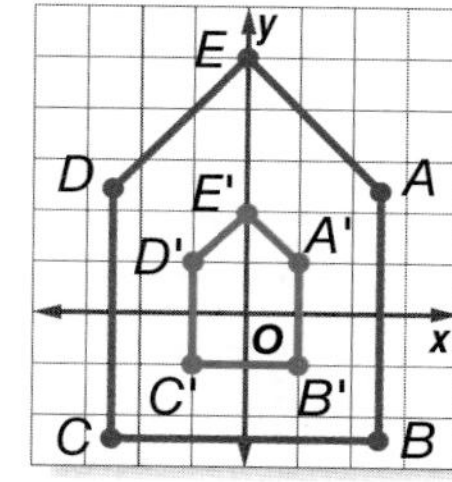

Real-World Link
Each Ohio Bicentennial Barn painted by Scott Hagan took approximately 18 hours and 7 gallons of paint to complete.
Source: Ohio Farm Bureau Federation

19. **PUBLISHING** To place a picture in his class newsletter, Joquin must reduce the picture by a scale factor of $\frac{3}{10}$. Find the dimensions of the reduced picture if the original is 15 centimeters wide and 10 centimeters high.

20. **PROJECTION** An overhead projector transforms the image on a transparency so that it is shown enlarged by a scale factor of 3.5 on a screen. If the original image is 3 inches long by 4 inches wide, find the dimensions of the projected image.

21. **BARN ART** Scott Hagan painted the Ohio bicentennial logo on one barn in each of Ohio's 88 counties. Each logo measured about 20 feet by 20 feet. Although Hagan drew each logo freehand, they are amazingly similar. If the original logo on which each painting was based measured 5 inches by 5 inches, what is the scale factor from the original logo to one of Hagan's paintings? Justify your answer.

DRAWING For Exercises 22 and 23, use the following information.

Artists use dilations to create the illusion of distance and depth. If you stand on a sidewalk and look in the distance, the parallel sides appear to converge and meet at a point. This is called the vanishing point.

22. Which figure appears to be closer? Explain your reasoning.

23. Draw a figure similar to the one shown at the right. Measure the larger rectangle. Above the horizon, draw a similar figure that is $\frac{7}{5}$ the size of that rectangle.

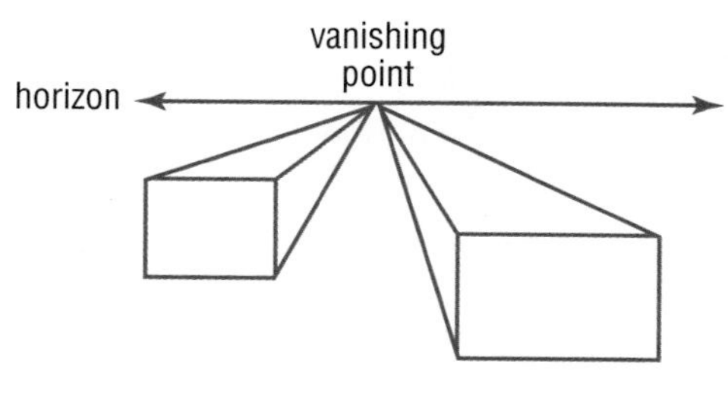

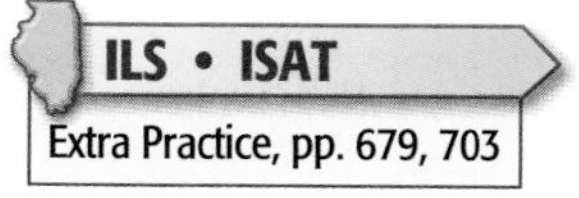

H.O.T. Problems

24. **OPEN ENDED** Graph a triangle and its image after a dilation with a scale factor greater than 1. Graph the resulting image after a dilation with a scale factor between 0 and 1. Predict the scale factor from the original to the final image. Explain your reasoning and verify your prediction.

25. **CHALLENGE** Describe the image of a figure after a dilation with a scale factor of −2.

26. **WRITING IN MATH** Write a general rule for finding the new coordinates of any ordered pair (x, y) after a dilation with a scale factor of k.

ISAT PRACTICE 6.D.3, 9.A.3b

27. Square A is similar to square B.

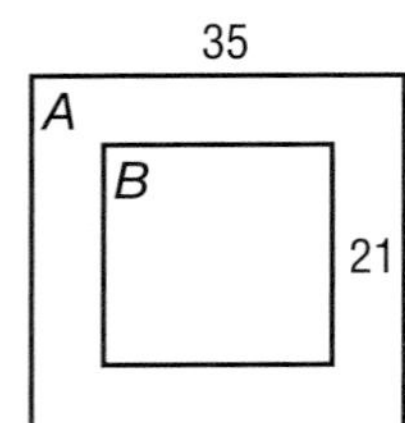

What scale factor was used to dilate square A to square B?

A $\frac{1}{7}$

B $\frac{3}{5}$

C $\frac{5}{3}$

D 7

28. Quadrilateral $LMNP$ was dilated to form quadrilateral $WXYZ$.

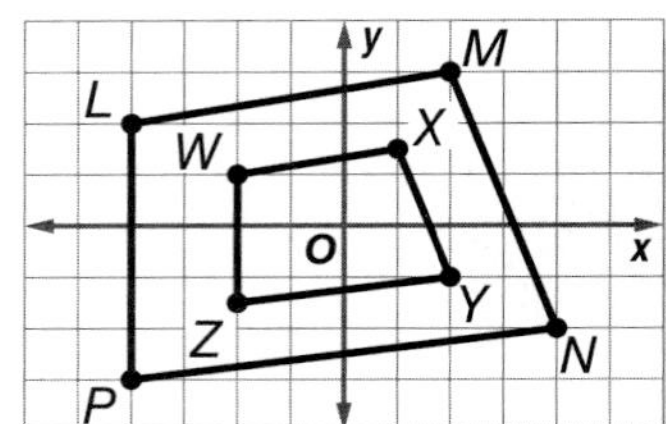

Which number best represents the scale factor used to change quadrilateral $LMNP$ into quadrilateral $WXYZ$?

F 3 **H** 2

G $\frac{1}{2}$ **J** $\frac{1}{3}$

Spiral Review

29. The triangles at the right are similar. Write and solve a proportion to find the missing measure. (Lesson 4-7)

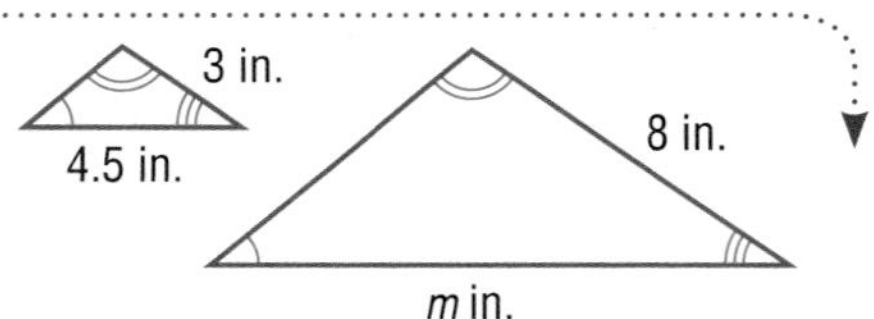

30. **GEOMETRY** A rectangle is 12 meters by 7 meters. To the nearest tenth, what is the length of one of its diagonals? (Lesson 3-6)

31. **TECHNOLOGY** A backpacker uses her GPS (Global Positioning System) receiver to find how much farther she needs to go to get to her stopping point. She is at the red dot on her GPS receiver screen, and the blue dot shows her destination. How much farther does she need to go? (Lesson 3-7)

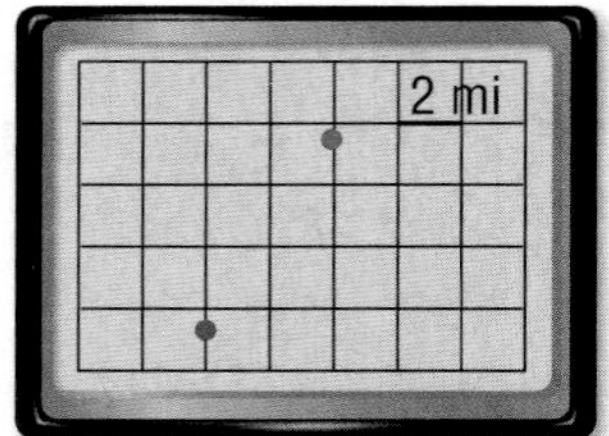

GET READY for the Next Lesson

PREREQUISITE SKILL Write a proportion and solve for x. (Lesson 4-5)

32. 3 cm is to 5 ft as x cm is to 9 ft

33. 4 in. is to 5 mi as 5 in. is to x mi

Spreadsheet Lab
Dilations

MAIN IDEA

Use a spreadsheet to enlarge and reduce polygons.

IL Learning Standards

6.D.3 Apply ratios and proportions to solve practical problems.
9.A.3b Draw transformation images of figures, with and without **the use of technology.** *Also addresses 9.A.3c.*

A computer spreadsheet is a useful tool for calculating the vertices of polygons. You can enlarge or reduce polygons by using a spreadsheet to automatically calculate the new coordinates of the vertices of the dilation.

ACTIVITY

Emma has plotted a pentagon on graph paper. The coordinates of the vertices of the pentagon are (2, 2), (4, 2), (5, 4), (3, 6), and (1, 4). She wants to multiply the coordinates by 3 to enlarge the pentagon. She enters the coordinates on a spreadsheet as shown below.

Set up the spreadsheet like the one shown below.

Pentagon Dilation.xls

◇	A	B	C	D
1	original		dilation	
2	x-coordinate	y-coordinate	x-coordinate	y-coordinate
3	2	2	=A3*3	=B3*3
4	4	2	=A4*3	=B4*3
5	5	4		
6	3	6		
7	1	4		

Sheet 1 / Sheet 2 / Sheet 3

Enter the formulas in columns C and D to complete the dilation.

ANALYZE THE RESULTS

1. How will the formulas in columns C and D change the original pentagon? How do you know?
2. Graph the original pentagon and its dilation on graph paper.
3. What is the percent of increase of the original pentagon to its dilation?
4. Find the coordinates of the pentagon enlarged 5 times.
5. Find the coordinates of the pentagon reduced by one half.
6. **MAKE A CONJECTURE** What type of dilation occurred if the new coordinates of the pentagon are (5, 5), (10, 5), (12.5, 10), (7.5, 15), and (2.5, 10)? What is the scale factor?
7. Select another geometric figure and plot its points on graph paper. Set up a spreadsheet to find two dilations, one enlargement and one reduction of the same figure.

4-9 Indirect Measurement

MAIN IDEA

Solve problems involving similar triangles.

IL Learning Standards

6.D.3 Apply ratios and proportions to solve practical problems.
8.D.3b Propose and solve problems using proportions, formulas and linear functions.
Also addresses 9.A.3c.

New Vocabulary

indirect measurement

IL Math Online

glencoe.com

- Extra Examples
- Personal Tutor
- Self-Check Quiz

GET READY for the Lesson

HISTORY Thales is known as the first Greek scientist, engineer, and mathematician. Legend says that he was the first to determine the height of the pyramids in Egypt by examining the shadows made by the Sun. He considered three points: the top of the objects, the lengths of the shadows, and the bases.

1. What appears to be true about the corresponding angles in the two triangles?
2. If the corresponding sides are proportional, what could you conclude about the triangles?

Indirect measurement allows you to use properties of similar polygons to find distances or lengths that are difficult to measure directly. The type of indirect measurement Thales used is called *shadow reckoning.* He measured his height and the length of his shadow then compared it with the length of the shadow cast by the pyramid.

$$\frac{\text{Thales' shadow}}{\text{pyramid's shadow}} = \frac{\text{Thales' height}}{\text{pyramid height}}$$

EXAMPLE Use Shadow Reckoning

1 **CITY PROPERTY A fire hydrant 2.5 feet high casts a 5-foot shadow. How tall is a street light that casts a 26-foot shadow at the same time? Let h represent the height of the street light.**

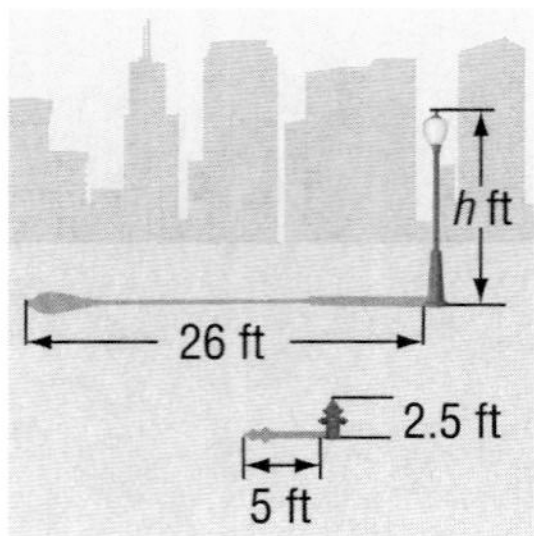

Shadow		Height
hydrant → street light →	$\frac{5}{26} = \frac{2.5}{h}$	← hydrant ← street light
	$5h = 2.5 \cdot 26$	Find the cross products.
	$5h = 65$	Multiply.
	$\frac{5h}{5} = \frac{65}{5}$	Divide each side by 5.
	$h = 13$	

The street light is 13 feet tall.

Your Progress

a. **STREETS** At the same time a 2-meter street sign casts a 3-meter shadow, a telephone pole casts a 12.3-meter shadow. How tall is the telephone pole?

You can also use similar triangles that do not involve shadows to find missing measurements.

EXAMPLE Use Indirect Measurement

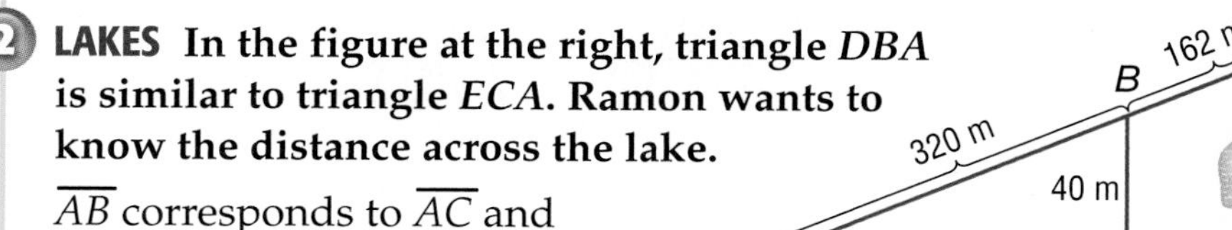

2 **LAKES In the figure at the right, triangle *DBA* is similar to triangle *ECA*. Ramon wants to know the distance across the lake.**

$\overline{AB}$ corresponds to $\overline{AC}$ and $\overline{BD}$ corresponds to $\overline{CE}$.

$\frac{AB}{AC} = \frac{BD}{CE}$	Write a proportion.
$\frac{320}{482} = \frac{40}{d}$	Replace *AB* with 320, *AC* with 482, and *BD* with 40.
$40 \cdot 482 = 320d$	Find the cross products.
$\frac{19{,}280}{320} = \frac{320d}{320}$	Multiply. Then divide each side by 320.
$x = 60.25$	

The distance across the lake is 60.25 meters.

Your Progress

b. **STREETS** Find the length of Kentucky Lane.

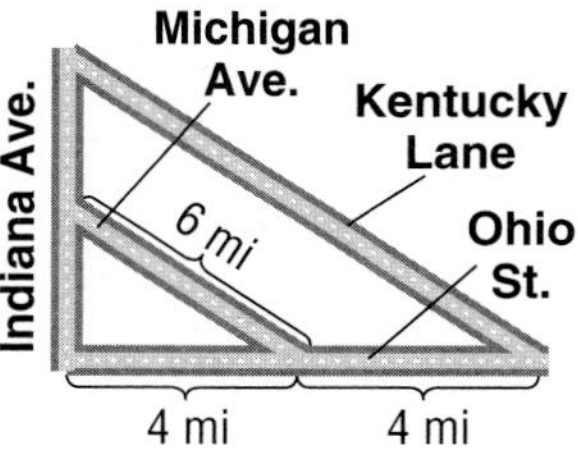

CHECK Your Understanding

Examples 1 and 2 (pp. 232–233)

In Exercises 1 and 2, the triangles are similar.

1. **TREES** How tall is the tree?

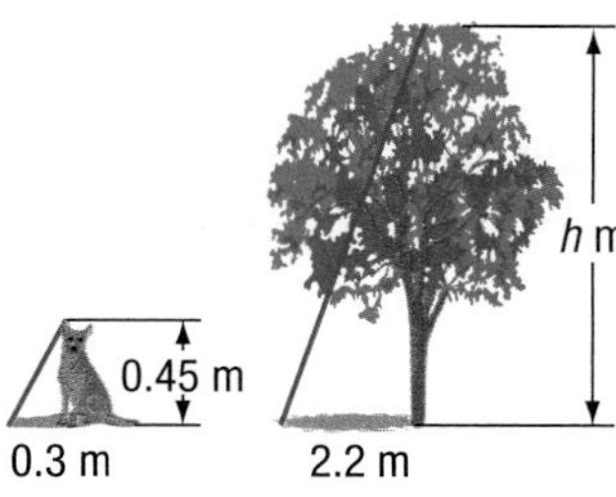

2. **WALKING** Find the distance from the park to the house.

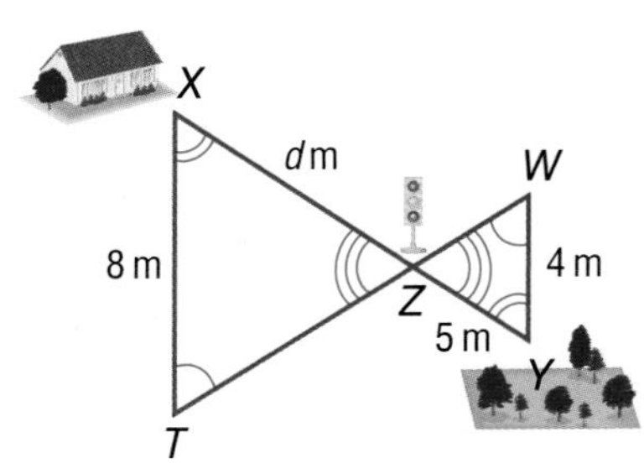

Practice and Problem Solving

HOMEWORK HELP	
For Exercises	See Examples
3–4	1
5–6	2

In Exercises 3–8, the triangles are similar. Write a proportion and solve the problem.

3. **BUILDING** How tall is the building?

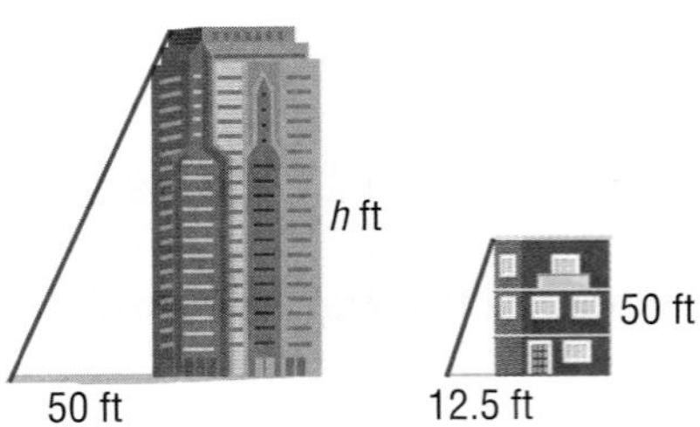

4. **FLAGS** How tall is the taller flagpole?

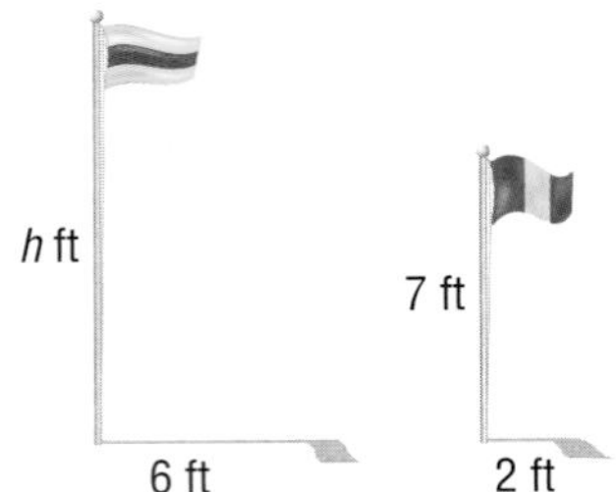

5. **PARKS** How far is it from the log ride to the pirate ship?

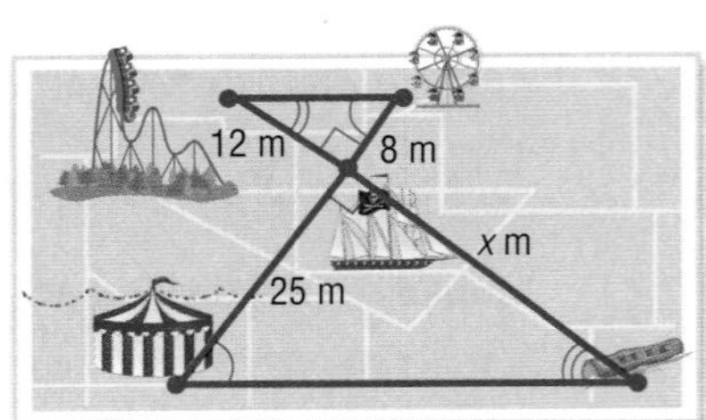

6. **CREEKS** About how long is the log that goes across the creeks?

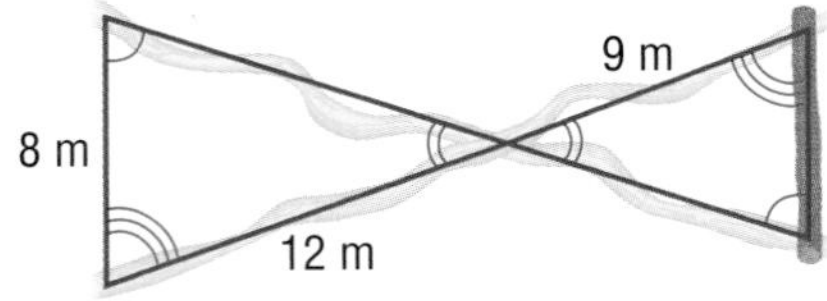

7. **CONSTRUCTION** Find the height of the brace.

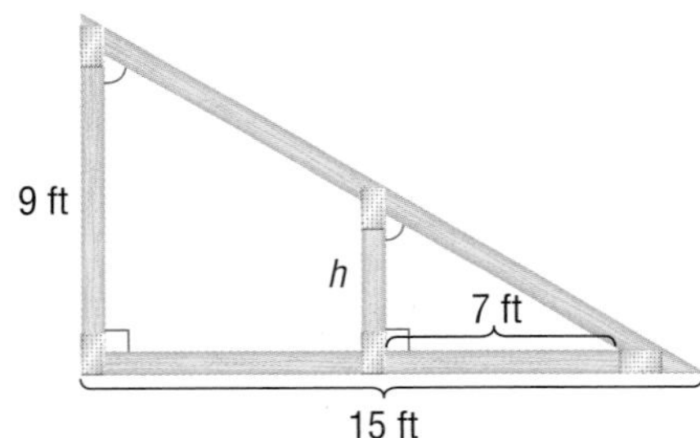

8. **LAKES** How deep is the water 62 meters from the shore?

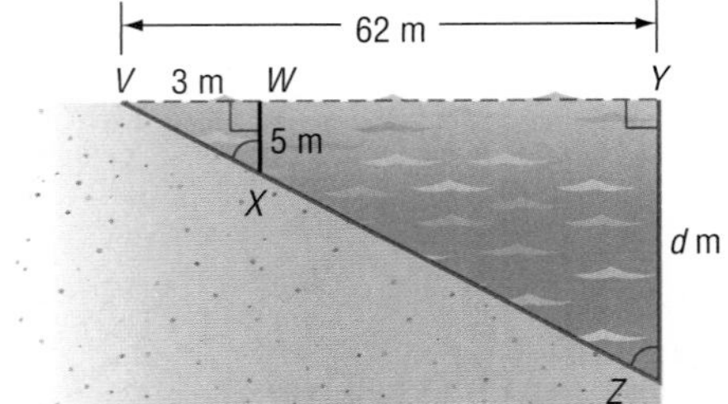

For Exercises 9 and 10, draw a diagram.

9. **FERRIS WHEELS** The Giant Wheel at Cedar Point in Ohio is one of the tallest Ferris wheels in the country at 136 feet tall. If the Giant Wheel casts a 34-foot shadow, write and solve a proportion to find the height of a nearby man who casts a $1\frac{1}{2}$-foot shadow.

10. **BASKETBALL** At 7 feet 2 inches, Margo Dydek is one of the tallest women to play professional basketball. Her coach, Carolyn Peck, is 6 feet 4 inches tall. If Ms. Peck casts a shadow that is 4 feet long, about how long would Ms. Dydek's shadow be? Round to the nearest tenth.

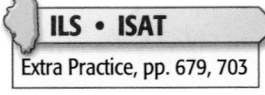

ILS • ISAT
Extra Practice, pp. 679, 703

H.O.T. Problems

11. **OPEN ENDED** Describe a situation that requires indirect measurement. Explain how to solve the problem.

12. **CHALLENGE** You cut a square hole $\frac{1}{4}$-inch wide in a piece of cardboard. With the cardboard 30 inches from your face, the moon fits exactly into the square hole. The moon is about 240,000 miles from Earth. Estimate the moon's diameter. Draw a diagram of the situation. Then write a proportion and solve the problem.

13. **WRITING IN MATH** What measures must be known in order to calculate the height of tall objects using shadow reckoning?

ISAT PRACTICE 6.D.3, 9.A.3c

14. A child $4\frac{1}{2}$ feet tall casts a 6-foot shadow. A nearby statue casts a 12-foot shadow.

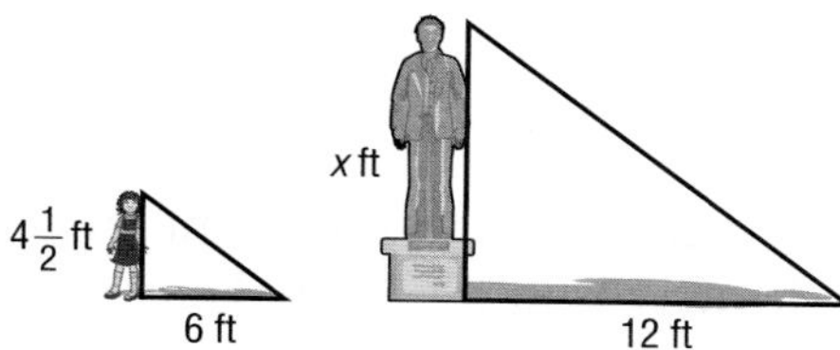

What is the height of the statue?

A $8\frac{1}{4}$ ft　　**C** $13\frac{1}{2}$ ft

B 9 ft　　**D** 24 ft

15. A telephone pole casts a 24-foot shadow. Belinda, who is 5 feet 8 inches tall, casts a 7-foot shadow.

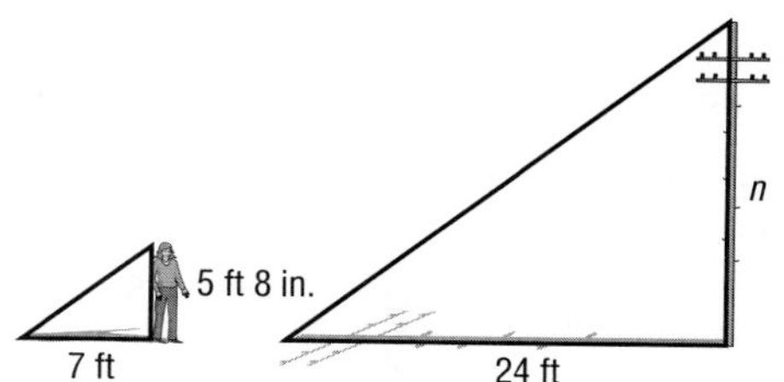

Which is closest to the height of the telephone pole?

F 50 ft　　**H** 20 ft

G 40 ft　　**J** 10 ft

Spiral Review

16. **WATER SAFETY** A Coast Guard boat was patrolling a region of ocean shown on the grid. If their search region was reduced to 60% of its original size, what are the coordinates of region's boundary? (Lesson 4-8)

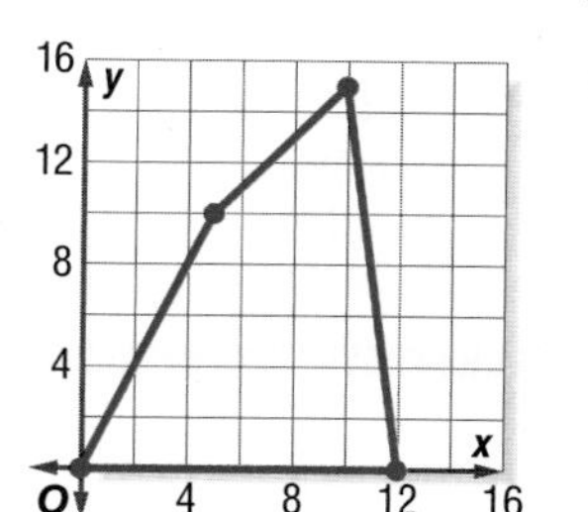

17. **PARTIES** For your birthday party, you make a map to your house on a 3-inch wide by 5-inch long index card. How long will your map be if you use a copier to enlarge it so it is 8 inches wide? (Lesson 4-7)

Estimate each square root to the nearest whole number. (Lessons 3-2)

18. $\sqrt{11}$　　19. $\sqrt{48}$　　20. $-\sqrt{118}$

GET READY for the Next Lesson

PREREQUISITE SKILL **Solve each proportion.** (Lesson 4-5)

21. $\frac{1 \text{ in.}}{12 \text{ ft}} = \frac{x \text{ in.}}{50 \text{ ft}}$　　22. $\frac{8 \text{ cm}}{x \text{ km}} = \frac{1 \text{ cm}}{100 \text{ km}}$　　23. $\frac{1 \text{ cm}}{3 \text{ m}} = \frac{x \text{ cm}}{62 \text{ m}}$　　24. $\frac{1 \text{ in.}}{50 \text{ mi}} = \frac{2 \text{ in.}}{x \text{ mi}}$

4-10 Scale Drawings and Models

MAIN IDEA

Solve problems involving scale drawings.

IL Learning Standards

7.C.3a Construct a simple scale drawing for a given situation.
9.A.3c Use concepts of symmetry, congruency, similarity, **scale,** perspective, and angles **to describe and analyze two-** and three-**dimensional shapes found in practical applications** (e.g., geodesic domes, A-frame houses, basketball courts, inclined planes, art forms, blueprints).

New Vocabulary

scale drawing
scale model
scale

IL Math Online

glencoe.com

- Extra Examples
- Personal Tutor
- Self-Check Quiz

GET READY for the Lesson

STATUES The statue in the Lincoln Memorial is shown at the right.

1. How many inches tall is the photo of the statue?
2. The actual height of the statue is 19 feet. Write a ratio comparing the photo height to the actual height.
3. Simplify the ratio and compare it to the scale shown below the photo.

1 inch = 9.5 feet

A **scale drawing** or a **scale model** is used to represent an object that is too large or too small to be drawn or built at actual size. The **scale** is the ratio of a length on a drawing or model to its actual length.

1 inch = 4 feet	1 inch represents an actual distance of 4 feet.
1:30	1 unit represents an actual distance of 30 units.

Distances on a scale drawing are proportional to distances in real life.

Real-World EXAMPLE Use a Scale Drawing

1 **GEOGRAPHY Use the map to find the actual distance between Grenada, Mississippi, and Little Rock, Arkansas.**

The distance on the map is about 5.2 centimeters.

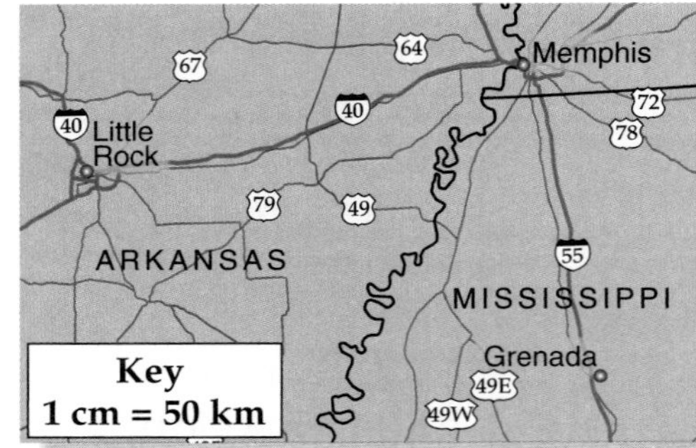

METHOD 1 **Write and solve a proportion.**

Let x represent the actual distance to Little Rock.

Scale **Distance**

$$\text{map} \rightarrow \frac{1 \text{ cm}}{50 \text{ km}} = \frac{5.2 \text{ cm}}{x \text{ km}} \leftarrow \text{map} \quad (\text{actual} \rightarrow, \leftarrow \text{actual})$$

$1 \cdot x = 50 \cdot 5.2$ Find the cross products.

$x = 260$ Simplify.

METHOD 2 **Write and solve an equation.**

Write the scale as $\frac{50 \text{ km}}{1 \text{ cm}}$, which means 50 kilometers per centimeter.

Words	The actual distance	is	50 kilometers per centimeter	of	map distance.
Variables	Let a represent the actual distance in kilometers. Let m represent the map distance in centimeters.				
Equation	a	$=$	50	$\cdot$	m

$a = 50m$ — Write the equation.

$a = 50(5.2)$ or 260 — Replace m with 5.2 and multiply.

The actual distance between the two cities is about 260 kilometers.

CHOOSE Your Method

a. **GEOGRAPHY** Use an inch ruler and the map shown to find the actual distance between Charlotte and Spartanburg. Measure to the nearest quarter inch.

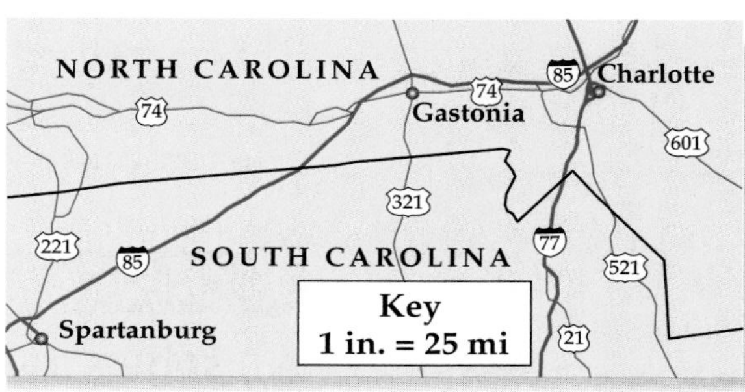

Real-World Link Scientists estimate that the Tyrannosaurus rex was 40 feet long, 18 feet high, and weighed 6 tons.

Real-World EXAMPLE Find the Scale

2 **MOVIES One of the models of a dinosaur used in the filming of a movie was only 15 inches tall. In the movie, the dinosaur appeared to have an actual height of 20 feet. What was the scale of the model?**

Let x represent the actual length of the dinosaur in feet.

Study Tip

Scales Scales and scale factors are always written so that the drawing or model length comes first in the ratio.

Length / Scale

model → / actual →

$$\frac{15 \text{ in.}}{20 \text{ ft}} = \frac{1 \text{ in.}}{x \text{ ft}}$$ ← model / ← actual

$$15 \cdot x = 20 \cdot 1$$ Find the cross products.

$$\frac{15x}{15} = \frac{20}{15}$$ Multiply. Then divide each side by 15.

$$x = 1\frac{5}{15} \text{ or } 1\frac{1}{3}$$ Simplify.

So, the scale is 1 inch = $1\frac{1}{3}$ feet.

CHECK Your Progress

b. **ARCHITECTURE** The model Mr. Vicario made of the building he designed is 25.6 centimeters tall. If the actual building is to be 64 meters tall, what is the scale of his model?

The scale factor for scale drawings and models is the scale written as a unitless ratio in simplest form. The scale should be converted to the same unit of measure before dropping the unit.

Study Tip

Scale Factors
A scale factor between 0 and 1 means that the model is smaller than the actual object. A scale factor greater than 1 means that the model is larger than the actual object.

EXAMPLE Find the Scale Factor

3 Find the scale factor for the dinosaur model in Example 2.

$\frac{1 \text{ in.}}{1\frac{1}{3} \text{ ft}} = \frac{1 \text{ in.}}{16 \text{ in.}}$ Convert $1\frac{1}{3}$ feet to inches by multiplying by 12.

The scale factor is $\frac{1}{16}$ or 1:16. This means that the dinosaur model is $\frac{1}{16}$ the size of the dinosaur's appearance in the movie.

CHECK Your Progress

Find the scale factor for each scale.

c. 1 inch = 15 feet

d. 10 cm = 2.5 m

To construct a scale drawing of an object, find an appropriate scale.

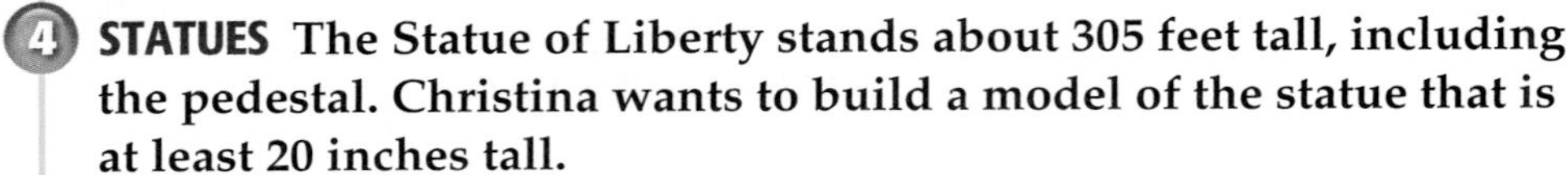

Real-World EXAMPLE Construct a Scale Model

4 STATUES The Statue of Liberty stands about 305 feet tall, including the pedestal. Christina wants to build a model of the statue that is at least 20 inches tall.

Find the scale if the model is 20 inches tall.

model → / actual → $\frac{20 \text{ inches}}{305 \text{ feet}} = \frac{1 \text{ in.}}{15.25 \text{ ft}}$ Divide the numerator and denominator by 20 so the numerator equals 1.

The scale is 1 in. = 15.25 ft. Using this scale, find the height of the pedestal on the model if the actual height of the pedestal is 154 feet.

model → / actual → $\frac{1 \text{ in.}}{15.25 \text{ ft}} = \frac{x \text{ in.}}{154 \text{ ft}}$

$1 \cdot 154 = 15.25 \cdot x$ Find the cross products.

$154 = 15.25x$ Multiply.

$10.1 \approx x$ Divide by 15.25.

The height of the pedestal in the model should be at least 10.1 inches tall.

CHECK Your Progress

e. **EARTH SCIENCE** Kaliah is making a model of a cross-section of Earth. He wants the core to be less than 10 inches in diameter. The actual Earth core is about 1,500 miles in diameter. Choose an appropriate scale and use it to determine the diameter of his model if the diameter of Earth is 7,926 miles.

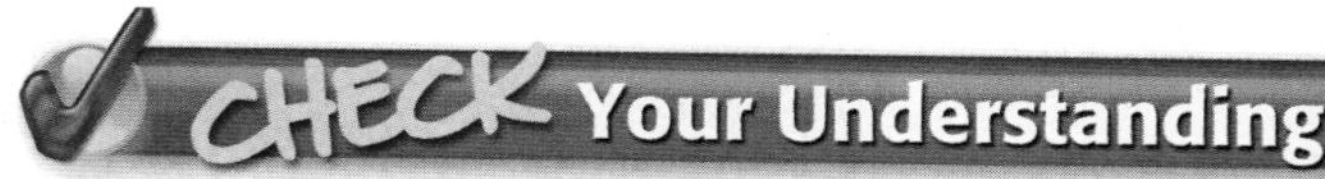

Example 1 (p. 236)

GEOGRAPHY **Use the map and an inch ruler to find the actual distance between each pair of cities.**

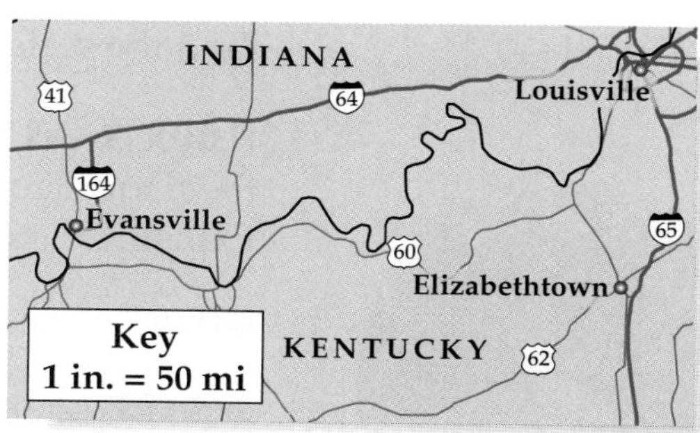

1. Evansville and Louisville
2. Louisville and Elizabethtown

BUILDINGS **For Exercises 3 and 4, use the following information.**

Examples 2 and 3 (pp. 237–238)

At 1,450 feet, the Sears Tower in Chicago is the tallest building in the United States.

3. If a scale model of the building is 29 inches tall, what is the scale?
4. What is the scale factor for the model?

Example 4 (p. 238)

5. **DECORATING** Before redecorating, Nichelle makes a scale drawing of her bedroom on an 8.5- by 11-inch piece of paper. If the room is 10 feet wide by 12 feet long, choose an appropriate scale for her drawing and find the dimensions of the room on the drawing.

Practice and Problem Solving

HOMEWORK HELP

For Exercises	See Examples
6–11	1
12–13	2
14–15	3
16–17	4

FLOOR PLANS **For Exercises 6–11, use the portion of the architectural drawing shown and an inch ruler.**

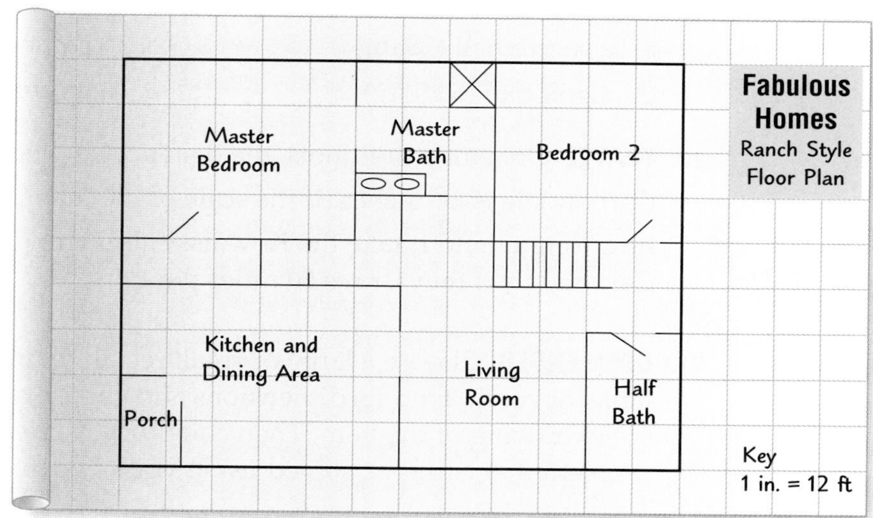

Find the actual length and width of each room. Measure to the nearest eighth of an inch.

6. half bath
7. master bath
8. porch
9. bedroom 2
10. master bedroom
11. living room

12. **ARCHITECTURE** An architect uses a special ruler to help draw designs and blueprints. A wall in a room on the blueprint is $22\frac{1}{2}$ inches long. When the house is built, the actual wall is 30 feet long. What is the scale of the blueprint?

13. **BIOLOGY** One of the smallest fish is the female stout infantfish. The actual length of the fish is about 8 millimeters long. Find the scale of the drawing.

14. **FLOOR PLANS** What is the scale factor of the floor plan used in Exercises 6–11? Explain its meaning.

15. **MOVIES** What is the scale factor of the model used in Exercise 12?

16. **SPIDERS** A tarantula's body length is 5 centimeters. Choose an appropriate scale for a model of the spider that is to be just over 6 meters long. Then use it to determine how long the tarantula's 9-centimeter legs should be.

Real-World Link Earth has an approximate circumference of 40,000 kilometers, while the Moon has an approximate circumference of 11,000 kilometers.
Source: *World Almanac for Kids*

17. **AIRPLANES** Dorie is building a model of a DC-10 aircraft. The actual aircraft is 182 feet long and has a wingspan of 155 feet. If Dorie wants her model to be no more than 2 feet long, choose an appropriate scale for her model. Then use it to find the length and wingspan of her model.

SPACE SCIENCE For Exercises 18 and 19, use the information at the left.

18. Suppose you are making a scale model of Earth and the Moon. You decide to use a basketball to represent Earth. A basketball's circumference is about 30 inches. What is the scale of your model?

19. Which of the following should you use to represent the Moon in your model so it is proportional to the model of Earth in Exercise 18? (The number in parentheses is the object's circumference.) Explain.

 a. a soccer ball (28 in.)
 b. a tennis ball (8.25 in.)
 c. a golf ball (5.25 in.)
 d. a marble (4 in.)

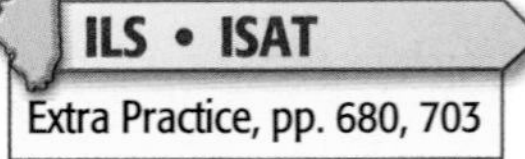

20. **TRAVEL** On a map of Illinois, the distance between Champaign and Carbondale is $6\frac{3}{4}$ inches. If the scale of the map is $\frac{1}{2}$ inch = 15 miles, about how long would it take the Kowalski family to drive from Champaign to Carbondale if they drove 60 miles per hour?

H.O.T. Problems

21. **OPEN ENDED** Choose a large or small rectangular item such as a calculator, table, or room. Find its dimensions and choose an appropriate scale for a scale drawing of the item. Then construct a scale drawing and write a problem that could be solved using your drawing.

22. **FIND THE ERROR** On a map, 1 inch represents 4 feet. Aaron and Melisa are finding the scale factor of the map. Who is correct? Explain.

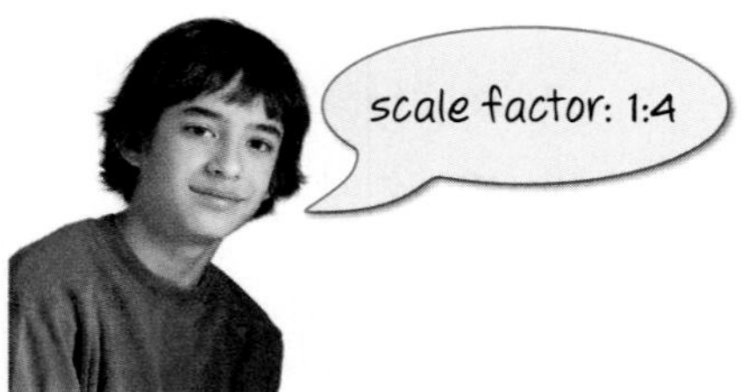

Aaron

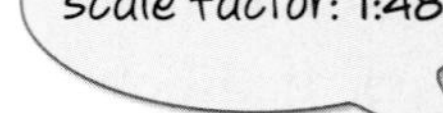

Melisa

23. **CHALLENGE** Describe how you could find the scale on a map that did not have a scale printed on it.

24. **WRITING IN MATH** One model is built on a 1:75 scale. Another model of the same object is built on a 1:100 scale. Which model is larger? Explain.

ISAT PRACTICE 7.C.3a, 9.A.3c

25. Jevonte is building a model of a ship with an actual length of 15 meters.

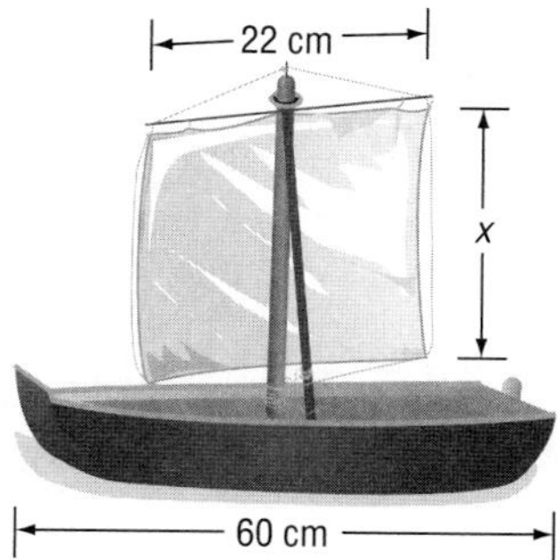

What other information is needed to find x, the height of the model's mast?

A the overall width of the actual ship

B the scale factor used

C the overall height of the actual mast

D the speed of the ship in the water

26. The actual width w of a garden is 18 feet. Use the scale drawing of the garden to find the actual length ℓ.

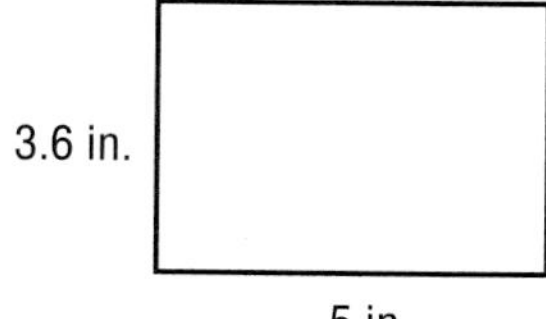

F 17.2 ft

G 18 ft

H 20 ft

J 25 ft

Spiral Review

27. **TREES** A tree casts a shadow of 24 feet while Rishi casts a shadow of 8 feet. If Rishi is 6 feet tall, how tall is the tree? (Lesson 4-9)

For Excercises 28 and 29, find the vertices of polygon $A'B'C'$ after polygon ABC is dilated using the given scale factor. (Lesson 4-8)

28. (1, 1), (2, 2), (5, 5); scale factor 4

29. (0, 0), (3, −2), (−6, −3); scale factor $\frac{2}{3}$

Estimate each square root to the nearest whole number. (Lesson 3-2)

30. $\sqrt{11}$

31. $\sqrt{48}$

32. $-\sqrt{118}$

33. **BAKING** A recipe calls for 2 cups of raisins for 84 cookies. How many cups of raisins are needed for 126 cookies? (Lesson 4-1)

ALGEBRA Solve each equation. Check your solution(s). (Lesson 3-1)

34. $p^2 = 0.49$

35. $t^2 = \frac{1}{144}$

36. $6{,}400 = r^2$

CHAPTER 4 Study Guide and Review

IL Math Online glencoe.com
- STUDY TO GO
- Vocabulary Review

FOLDABLES® Study Organizer ▷ GET READY to Study

Be sure the following Big Ideas are noted in your Foldable.

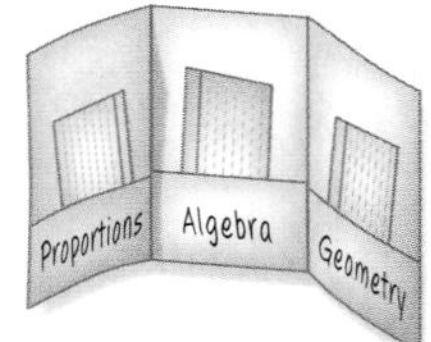

BIG Ideas

Rates (Lessons 4-1, 4-3, and 4-4)
- A rate is a comparison of two quantities with different types of units.
- To find the rate of change, divide the difference in the y-coordinates by the difference in the x-coordinates.
- Two quantities a and b have a proportional linear relationship if they have a constant ratio and a constant rate of change.

Proportions (Lessons 4-2 and 4-5)
- If two related quantities are proportional, then they have a constant ratio.
- A proportion is an equation stating that two ratios or rates are equivalent.
- The cross products of a proportion are equal.

Similar Polygons (Lesson 4-7)
- If two figures are similar with a scale factor of $\frac{a}{b}$, then the perimeters of the figures have a ratio of $\frac{a}{b}$.

Dilations (Lesson 4-8)
- The image produced by enlarging or reducing a figure is called a dilation.

Measurement (Lessons 4-9 and 4-10)
- A scale is determined by the ratio of a given length on a drawing or model to its corresponding actual length.
- Indirect measurement is a technique using proportions to find a measurement.

Key Vocabulary

center (p. 225)
congruent (p. 219)
constant of proportionality (p. 212)
constant rate of change (p. 204)
corresponding parts (p. 218)
cross products (p. 210)
dilation (p. 225)
enlargement (p. 226)
equivalent ratios (p. 210)
indirect measurement (p. 232)
linear relationship (p. 204)
nonproportional (p. 194)
polygon (p. 218)
proportion (p. 210)
proportional (p. 194)
rate (p. 191)
rate of change (p. 198)
ratio (p. 190)
reduction (p. 226)
scale (p. 236)
scale drawing (p. 219, 236)
scale factor (p. 219)
scale model (p. 236)
similar (p. 218)
unit rate (p. 191)

Vocabulary Check

State whether each sentence is *true* or *false*. If *false*, replace the underlined word to make a true sentence.

1. Polygons that have the same <u>size</u> are called similar polygons.
2. A <u>unit rate</u> is one in which the denominator is 1 unit.
3. A ratio of two measurements having <u>similar</u> units is called a rate.
4. In a relationship in which the ratio is not constant, the two quantities are said to be <u>nonproportional</u>.
5. A <u>scale</u> is the ratio of a length on a drawing or model to its corresponding actual length.
6. Comparing two numbers by <u>multiplication</u> is called a proportion.

Lesson-by-Lesson Review

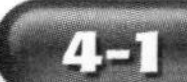

4-1 Ratios and Rates (pp. 190–193)

6.D.3

Express each ratio in simplest form.

7. 5 teachers for 140 students
8. 16 dogs:10 cats
9. 2 feet out of 2 yards
10. **SHOPPING** An 8-pound bag of cat food sells for $13.89. A 20-pound bag of the same brand sells for $24.79. Which is the better buy? Explain your reasoning.

Example 1 **Express the ratio *10 milliliters to 8 liters* in simplest form.**

$\frac{10 \text{ milliliters}}{8 \text{ liters}}$

$= \frac{10 \text{ milliliters}}{8{,}000 \text{ milliliters}}$ 8 liters = 8 × 1,000 or 8,000 milliliters.

$= \frac{1}{800}$ Divide numerator and denominator by 10.

The ratio in simplest form is $\frac{1}{800}$ or 1:800.

4-2 Proportional and Nonproportional Relationships (pp. 194–197)

6.D.3, 8.D.3b

11. **INTERNET** An Internet company charges $30 a month. There is also a $30 installation fee. Is the number of months you can have Internet proportional to the total cost?
12. **WORK** On Friday, Jade washed 9 vehicles in 4 hours. The next day she washed 15 vehicles in 6 hours. Is the number of vehicles she washed proportional to the time it took her to wash them?

Example 2 **Is the amount of money earned proportional to the number of haircuts?**

Earnings ($)	28	56	84	112
Haircuts	1	2	3	4

$\frac{\text{earnings}}{\text{haircuts}} \rightarrow \frac{28}{1}, \frac{56}{2}, \frac{84}{3}, \frac{112}{4}$

Since these ratios are all equal to 28, the amount of money earned is proportional to the number of haircuts.

4-3 Rate of Change (pp. 198–203)

6.D.3

MONEY **For Exercises 13 and 14, use the following information.**

The table below shows Victor's weekly allowance between the ages of 6 and 15.

$ per week	1.00	2.00	2.00	3.00	5.00
Age (yr)	6	8	10	12	15

13. Find the rate of change in his allowance between ages 12 and 15.
14. Was the rate of change between ages 8 and 10 positive, negative, or zero?

Example 3 **Kira's savings account balance at the beginning of the month was $242. Fifteen days later, the balance was $260.75. Find the rate of change in her savings account per day.**

$$\frac{\text{change in account balance}}{\text{change in time}} = \frac{(\$260.75 - \$242)}{15 - 0 \text{ days}}$$

$$= \frac{\$18.75}{15 \text{ days}} \text{ or } \frac{\$1.25}{1 \text{ day}}$$

Kira's savings account increased on average $1.25 per day.

4-4 Constant Rate of Change (pp. 204–209)

6.D.3

15. **RAINFALL** The amount of rainfall after several hours is shown. Is the relationship between the amount of rainfall and number of hours linear? If so, find the constant rate of change. If not, explain your reasoning.

Number of Hours	Rainfall (inches)
1	2
2	4
3	7
4	9

16. **PHONE CALL** The cost of a long-distance phone call after several minutes is shown. Is the relationship between the cost and number of minutes linear? If so, find the constant rate of change. If not, explain your reasoning.

Number of Minutes	Cost (¢)
3	7
6	14
9	21
12	28

Example 4 The distance traveled in a car trip is shown. Is the relationship between the distance traveled and number of hours spent in the car linear? If so, find the constant rate of change. If not, explain your reasoning.

	Number of Hours	Distance (miles)	
	2	120	
+2	4	240	×2
+2	6	360	×2
+2	8	480	×2

As the number of hours increases by two, the distance doubles. Since the rate of change is constant, this is a linear relationship. So, the constant rate of change is $\frac{120}{2}$ or 60 miles per hour. This means that for every hour they are in the car, they travel 60 miles.

4-5 Solving Proportions (pp. 210–214)

6.D.3, 8.D.3b

Solve each proportion.

17. $\frac{3}{r} = \frac{6}{8}$

18. $\frac{30}{0.5} = \frac{y}{0.25}$

19. $\frac{7}{4} = \frac{n}{2}$

20. $\frac{k}{5} = \frac{72}{8}$

21. **SPEED** A squirrel can run 1 mile in 5 minutes. How far can it travel in 16 minutes?

Example 5 **Solve $\frac{9}{x} = \frac{4}{18}$.**

$\frac{9}{x} = \frac{4}{18}$	Write the equation.
$9 \cdot 18 = x \cdot 4$	Find the cross products.
$162 = 4x$	Multiply.
$\frac{162}{4} = \frac{4x}{4}$	Divide each side by 4.
$40.5 = x$	Simplify.

Mixed Problem Solving
For mixed problem-solving practice, see page 703.

4-6 PSI: Draw a Diagram (pp. 216–217)

6.B.3a, 6.C.3a

Solve. Use the *draw a diagram* strategy.

22. **CONCERTS** Nina, Tyrese, Leslie, and Ethan are going to a rock concert. In how many different orders can they enter the concert?

23. **PHYSICAL SCIENCE** A tennis ball is dropped from 12 feet above the ground. It hits the ground and bounces up half as high as it fell. This is true for each successive bounce. What height does the ball reach on the fourth bounce?

24. **MEASUREMENT** Jasmine unrolled 48 feet of carpet. This is $\frac{3}{4}$ of the total amount of carpet needed for the library. What is the total amount of carpet needed for the library?

Example 6 **A photographer is taking the eighth grade class picture. She places 8 students in the first row. Each additional row has 4 more students in it. If there are a total 80 students, how many rows will there be?**

Draw a diagram with 8 students in row one and then add 4 more students to each additional row.

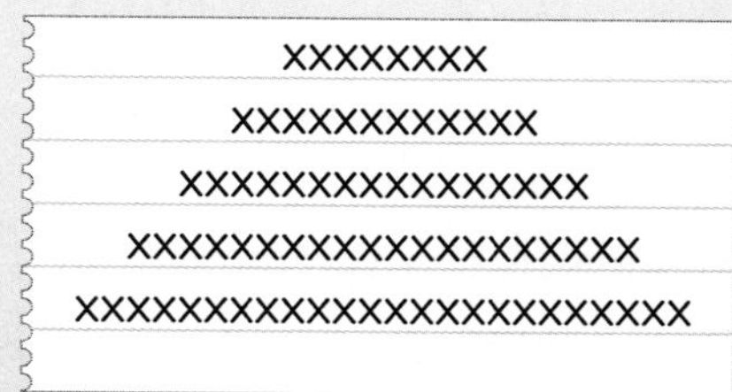

There are a total of 5 rows.

4-7 Similar Polygons (pp. 218–223)

6.D.3, 9.A.3c

Each pair of polygons is similar. Write a proportion to find each missing measure. Then solve.

25.

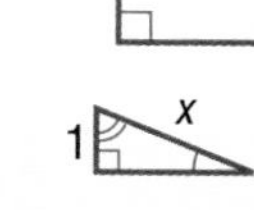

26.

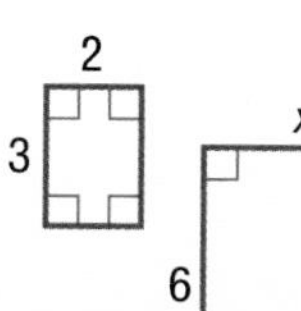

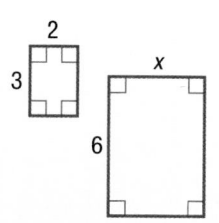

27. **MEASUREMENT** If square D has a perimeter of 49 feet and square F has a perimeter of 64 feet, what is the scale factor of the two squares?

28. **PHOTOGRAPHS** Your family has digital pictures of your vacation that are 3 inches by 5 inches. You are taking them to be enlarged so that the width of the new picture is 8 inches. What will the new length be?

Example 7 **Rectangle *GHJK* is similar to rectangle *PQRS*. Find the value of *x*.**

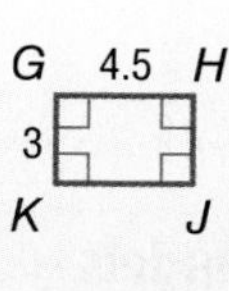

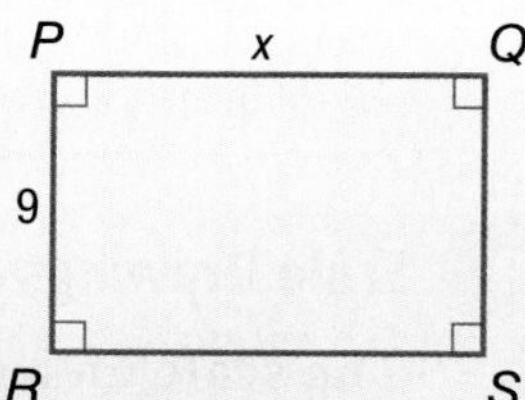

The scale factor from *GHJK* to *PQRS* is $\frac{GK}{PR}$, which is $\frac{3}{9}$ or $\frac{1}{3}$.

$\frac{GH}{PQ} = \frac{1}{3}$ Write a proportion.

$\frac{4.5}{x} = \frac{1}{3}$ $GH = 4.5$ and $PQ = x$

$4.5 \cdot 3 = 1 \cdot x$ Find the cross products.

$13.5 = x$ Multiply.

4-8 Dilations (pp. 225–230)

6.D.3, 9.A.3b

29. Segment $C'D'$ with endpoints $C'(-8, 20)$ and $D'(4, 16)$ is a dilation of segment CD with endpoints $C(-2, 5)$ and $D(1, 4)$. Find the scale factor of the dilation, and classify it as an *enlargement* or as a *reduction*.

30. **GEOMETRY** Triangle ABC has vertices $A(-3, -6)$, $B(6, 3)$, and $C(9, -3)$. Find the vertices of its image for a dilation with a scale factor of $\frac{1}{3}$. Then graph $\triangle ABC$ and its dilation.

Example 8 **Segment XY has endpoints $X(-4, 1)$ and $Y(8, -2)$. Find the endpoints of its image for a dilation with a scale factor of $\frac{3}{4}$.**

Multiply each coordinate in the ordered pair by $\frac{3}{4}$.

$X(-4, 1) \rightarrow \left(-4 \cdot \frac{3}{4}, 1 \cdot \frac{3}{4}\right) \rightarrow X'\left(-3, \frac{3}{4}\right)$

$Y(8, -2) \rightarrow \left(8 \cdot \frac{3}{4}, -2 \cdot \frac{3}{4}\right) \rightarrow Y'\left(6, -1\frac{1}{2}\right)$

4-9 Indirect Measurement (pp. 232–235)

6.D.3, 9.A.3c

31. **TREES** A 36-foot tree casts a 9-foot shadow at the same time a building casts a 15-foot shadow. How tall is the building?

32. **BUILDINGS** A building casts an 18.5-foot shadow. How tall is the building if a 10-foot tall sculpture nearby casts a 7-foot shadow?

Example 9 **A flagpole casts a shadow that is 6 meters long. A boy casts a shadow that is 1.2 meters long. If the flagpole is 7.5 meters tall, how tall is the boy?**

$$\begin{matrix}\text{flagpole} \rightarrow \\ \text{boy} \rightarrow\end{matrix} \quad \frac{6}{1.2} = \frac{7.5}{x} \quad \begin{matrix}\leftarrow \text{flagpole} \\ \leftarrow \text{boy}\end{matrix}$$

$$1.2 \cdot 7.5 = 6 \cdot x$$
$$9 = 6x$$
$$1.5 = x$$

The boy is 1.5 meters tall.

4-10 Scale Drawings and Models (pp. 236–241)

7.C.3a, 9.A.3c

The scale on a map is 3 centimeters = 7 kilometers. Find the actual distance for each map distance.

33. 9 cm

34. 21 cm

35. **ARCHITECTS** On an architect's blueprint, the dimensions of a room are 5 inches by 8 inches. If the actual dimensions of the room are 10 feet by 16 feet, what is the scale of the blueprint?

Example 10 **The scale on a model of a bullfrog is 2 centimeters = 25 millimeters. Find the actual length of a bullfrog if the model length is 11 centimeters.**

$$\frac{2 \text{ cm}}{25 \text{ mm}} = \frac{11 \text{ cm}}{x \text{ mm}} \quad \begin{matrix}\leftarrow \text{model length} \\ \leftarrow \text{actual length}\end{matrix}$$

$2 \cdot x = 25 \cdot 11$ Find the cross products.

$2x = 275$ Multiply.

$x = 137.5$ Divide each side by 2.

The actual length is 137.5 millimeters.

Practice Test

IL Math Online glencoe.com
• Chapter Test

1. Express the ratio 15 inches to 1 foot in simplest form.

2. Express 112 feet in 2.8 seconds as a unit rate.

3. **MULTIPLE CHOICE** At Flynn's Apple Orchard, 16 acres of land produced 368 bushels of apples. Which rate represents the number of bushels per acre?

   A 16:1   **C** 23:2
   B 23:1   **D** 46:1

4. **MEASUREMENT** Nick rides his bike 20 miles every two days. Is the distance Nick rides proportional to the number of days?

Solve each proportion.

5. $\frac{3}{a} = \frac{9}{12}$

6. $\frac{5}{3} = \frac{20}{y}$

7. **NUTRITION** An 8-ounce serving of milk provides 30% of the daily value of calcium. How much milk provides 50% of the daily value of calcium?

8. **FOOD** Of the 30 students in a life skills class, 19 like to cook main dishes, 15 prefer baking desserts, and 7 like to do both. How many students like to cook main dishes, but not bake desserts? Use the *draw a diagram* strategy.

Each pair of polygons is similar. Write a proportion to find each missing measure. Then solve.

9. 

10. 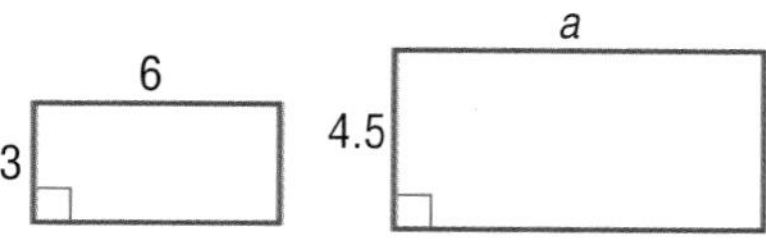

11. **GEOMETRY** Triangle ABC has vertices $A(1, 1)$, $B(-2, 4)$, and $C(3, -2)$. Find the vertices of its image for a dilation with a scale factor of 2. Then graph $\triangle ABC$ and its dilation.

12. **TRAVEL** On a map, 1 inch = 7.5 miles. How many miles does 2.5 inches represent?

LIBRARIES For Exercises 13 and 14, use the table that shows the number of teens that use the school library during the week.

Day	Number of Teens
Monday	110
Tuesday	123
Wednesday	155
Thursday	150
Friday	75

13. Find the rate of change in the number of teens per day from Monday to Tuesday.

14. Find the rate of change in the number of teens per day from Wednesday to Friday. Then interpret its meaning.

15. **MULTIPLE CHOICE** A child $4\frac{1}{2}$ feet tall casts a 6-foot shadow. A nearby statue casts a 12-foot shadow. How tall is the statue?

   F $8\frac{1}{4}$ ft   **H** $13\frac{1}{2}$ ft
   G 9 ft   **J** 24 ft

16. **MEASUREMENT** Is the relationship between the weight and number of months linear? If so, find the constant rate of change. If not, explain your reasoning.

Number of Months	Weight (lb)
4	14
6	18
8	20
10	22

CHAPTER 4 ISAT Practice

Cumulative, Chapters 1–4

IL Math Online glencoe.com
• Test Practice

PART 1 Multiple Choice

Read each question. Then fill in the correct answer on the answer sheet provided by your teacher or on a sheet of paper.

1. A jar contains 25% green buttons, 32% yellow buttons, 20% brown buttons, and 23% white buttons. There are 300 buttons in the jar altogether. Which proportion can be used to find w, the total number of white buttons in the jar?

   A $\frac{23}{100} = \frac{300}{w}$

   B $\frac{23}{w} = \frac{300}{100}$

   C $\frac{23}{100} = \frac{w}{300}$

   D $\frac{23}{300} = \frac{w}{100}$

2. Trapezoid $ABCD$ is similar to trapezoid $WXYZ$. Find the length of $\overline{XY}$.

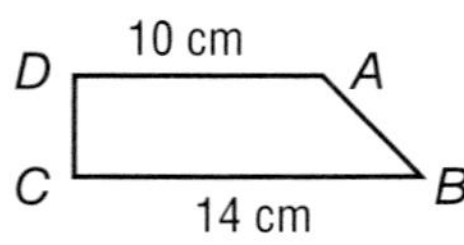

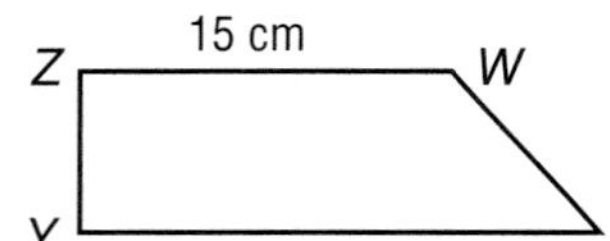

   F 20 cm

   G 21 cm

   H 24 cm

   J 27 cm

TEST-TAKING TIP

Question 2 This problem involves similar figures. If two polygons are similar, then you can use a scale factor or a proportion to find the missing measure(s).

3. How many seconds are in $1\frac{1}{2}$ hours?

   A 90

   B 540

   C 3,600

   D 5,400

4. The scale drawing of a football field was made using a scale of 1 inch = 20 yards.

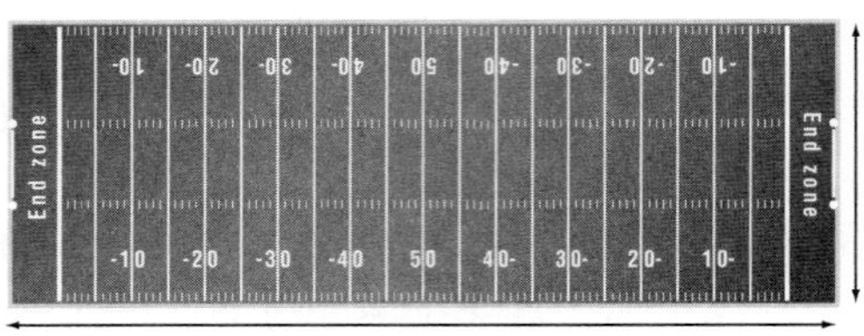

   What is the length, in yards, of the football field, including the end zones?

   F 100 yd

   G 120 yd

   H 130 yd

   J 150 yd

5. Which expression is equivalent to $x(2 + y)$?

   A $2x + y$

   B $2xy$

   C $2x + 2y$

   D $2x + xy$

6. Between which two whole numbers is $\sqrt{66}$ located on a number line?

   F 6 and 7

   G 7 and 8

   H 8 and 9

   J 9 and 10

7. Which of the following operations performed on −5 does not result in the same answer?

   A divide by one

   B multiply by one

   C add zero

   D multiply by zero

Preparing for ISAT
For test-taking strategies and practice, see pages 712–729.

8. Rebekah is $1\frac{1}{2}$ meters tall. About how tall is she in feet and inches?
(1 meter ≈ 39 inches)

F 3 feet 3 inches
G 4 feet 0 inches
H 4 feet 9 inches
J 4 feet 8 inches

9. During a 3-hour period, 2,292 people rode the roller coaster at an amusement park. Which proportion can be used to find x, the number of people who rode the coaster during a 12-hour period if the rate is the same?

A $\frac{3}{2{,}292} = \frac{x}{12}$
B $\frac{3}{2{,}292} = \frac{12}{x}$
C $\frac{3}{x} = \frac{12}{2{,}292}$
D $\frac{x}{3} = \frac{12}{2{,}292}$

10. A park is shaped like a rectangle with the dimensions shown below. Which of the following is closest to the length of a diagonal of the park?

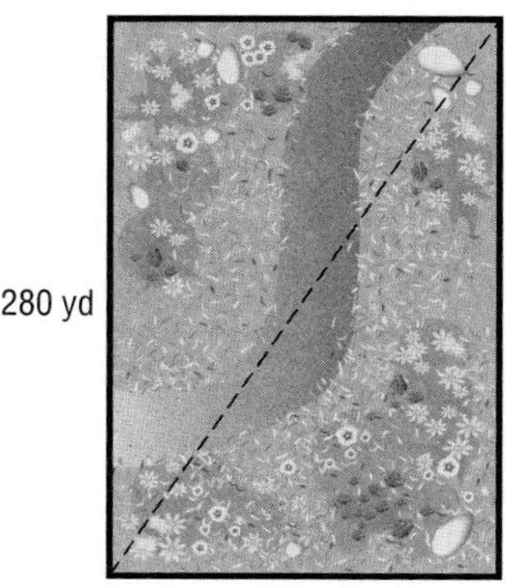

F 165 yd
G 290 yd
H 340 yd
J 405 yd

PART 2 Short Response/Grid In

Record your answers on the answer sheet provided by your teacher or on a sheet of paper.

11. A teacher plans to buy 5 pencils for each student in her class. If pencils come in packages of 18 and cost \$1.99 per package, what other information is needed to find the cost of the pencils?

12. What is the length of the missing side of the right triangle?

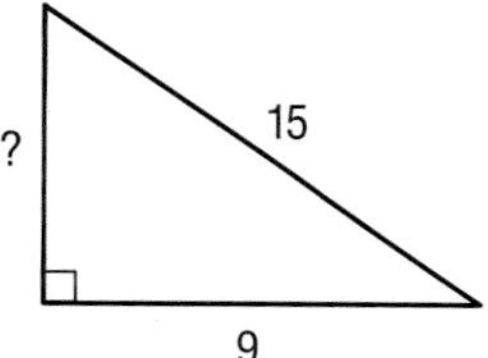

13. Write a fraction that is between $\frac{2}{3}$ and $\frac{9}{10}$.

PART 3 Extended Response

Record your answers on the answer sheet provided by your teacher or on a sheet of paper. Show your work.

14. The table shows how much Heather pays to rent videos.

Number of Videos	Cost (\$)
2	5
4	10
6	15
8	20

a. Graph the data from the table and connect the points with a line.
b. Find the slope of the line.
c. What is the cost per video?
d. How much money will Heather pay to rent 10 videos?

NEED EXTRA HELP?														
If You Missed Question...	1	2	3	4	5	6	7	8	9	10	11	12	13	14
Go to Lesson...	4-5	4-7	4-5	4-10	1-2	3-2	1-2	4-5	4-5	3-6	1-1	3-5	2-2	4-4
IL Learning Standards	6.D.3	6.D.3	6.D.3	6.D.3	8.A.3a	8.D.3c	8.A.3a	6.D.3	6.D.3	9.D.3	6.B.3a	9.D.3	6.A.3	7.C.3a

Percent

Illinois Learning Standards

6.A.3 Represent fractions, decimals, percentages, exponents and scientific notation in equivalent forms.
8.A.3b Solve problems using linear expressions, equations and inequalities.

Key Vocabulary

percent (p. 252)
percent equation (p. 279)
percent of change (p. 284)
percent proportion (p. 263)

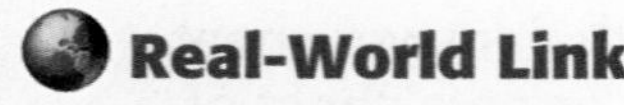

Real-World Link

Cherries Michigan is the leading tart cherry producing state. It accounts for about 70% of the national production of approximately 103,000 tons of cherries. You can use percents to determine the amount of cherries produced in Michigan.

FOLDABLES® Study Organizer

Percent Make this Foldable to help you organize your notes. Begin with five sheets of $8\frac{1}{2}'' \times 11''$ paper.

1. **Draw** a large circle on one of the sheets of paper.

2. **Stack** the sheets of paper. Place the one with the circle on top. Cut all five sheets in the shape of a circle.

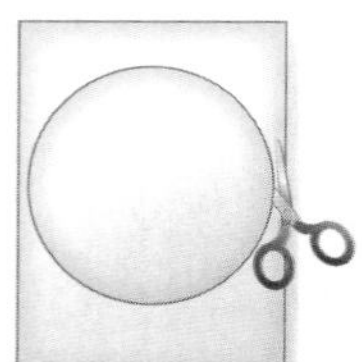

3. **Staple** the circles on the left side. Write the chapter title on the front and the four lesson titles on the inside right pages.

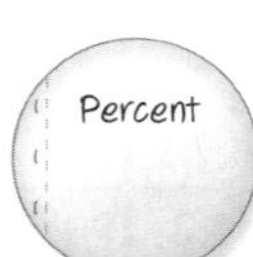

4. **Turn** the circle to the back side so that the staples are still on the left. Write the last four lesson titles on the front and right pages of the journal.

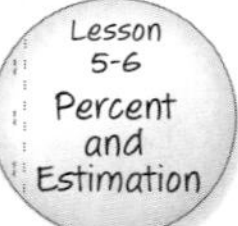

GET READY for Chapter 5

Diagnose Readiness You have two options for checking Prerequisite Skills.

Option 2

IL Math Online Take the Online Readiness Quiz at glencoe.com.

Option 1

Take the Quick Check below. Refer to the Quick Review for help.

QUICK Quiz

Compute each product mentally.
(Lesson 2-3)

1. $\frac{1}{3} \cdot 303$
2. $644 \cdot \frac{1}{2}$
3. $0.1 \cdot 550$
4. $64 \cdot 0.5$

Write each fraction as a decimal.
(Lesson 2-1)

5. $\frac{2}{5}$
6. $\frac{7}{8}$
7. $\frac{3}{4}$
8. $\frac{3}{8}$
9. **SCHOOL** Andrea answered 18 out of 20 questions correctly on a math quiz. Write her score as a decimal. (Lesson 2-1)

Solve each equation or proportion.
(Lessons 2-7 and 4-5)

10. $0.25d = 130$
11. $48r = 12$
12. $0.4m = 22$
13. $0.02n = 9$
14. $\frac{x}{10} = \frac{3}{5}$
15. $\frac{4}{9} = \frac{14}{b}$
16. **RECIPES** Ruben's chocolate chip cookie recipe uses 2 eggs for 2 dozen cookies. How many eggs does Ruben need to make 72 cookies? (Lesson 4-5)

QUICK Review

Example 1

Compute $\frac{1}{4} \cdot 820$ mentally.

$\frac{1}{4} \cdot 820$ is one fourth of 820, or 205.

Example 2

Write $\frac{5}{8}$ as a decimal.

To change $\frac{5}{8}$ to a decimal, divide 5 by 8.

$$\begin{array}{r} 0.625 \\ 8\overline{)5.000} \\ -4\,8 \\ \hline 20 \\ -16 \\ \hline 40 \\ -40 \\ \hline 0 \end{array}$$

So, $\frac{5}{8} = 0.625$.

Example 3

Solve $\frac{w}{12} = \frac{5}{6}$.

$\frac{w}{12} = \frac{5}{6}$	Write the proportion.
$6 \cdot w = 12 \cdot 5$	Find cross products.
$6w = 60$	Simplify.
$\frac{6w}{6} = \frac{60}{6}$	Divide each side by 6.
$w = 10$	Simplify.

5-1 Ratios and Percents

MAIN IDEA

Write ratios as percents and vice versa.

IL Learning Standards

6.A.3 Represent fractions, decimals, **percentages,** exponents and scientific notation **in equivalent forms. 6.D.3 Apply ratios** and proportions **to solve practical problems.** *Also addresses 8.D.3b, 8.C.3.*

New Vocabulary

percent

IL Math Online

glencoe.com

- Extra Examples
- Personal Tutor
- Self-Check Quiz

GET READY for the Lesson

ENDANGERED SPECIES The table shows the approximate number of endangered species in the world in a recent year.

Group	Ratio of Endangered Species to Total Number of Species
Birds	250 to 9,000
Mammals	320 to 9,000
Fish	80 to 24,500
Reptiles	80 to 8,000
Amphibians	20 to 5,000

Source: *The New York Times Almanac*

1. Name two groups that have ratios in which the total number of species are the same.
2. Describe how to determine which group has the greatest ratio of endangered species to total number of species.

Ratios such as 250 out of 9,000 or 80 out of 8,000 can be written as percents.

Percent — Key Concept

Words A **percent** is a ratio that compares a number to 100.

	Percent	Ratio	Fraction
Numbers	27%	27 out of 100	$\frac{27}{100}$
Algebra	x%	x out of 100	$\frac{x}{100}$

EXAMPLES Write Ratios as Percents

Write each ratio as a percent.

1 POPULATION In a recent census, 26 out of every 100 people living in Illinois were younger than 18.

26 out of 100 = 26%   Definition of percent

2 SCHOOL At a local middle school, 140 students take Spanish for every 100 students who take French.

140 per 100 = 140%   Definition of percent

Study Tip

Large Percents
Notice that some percents, such as 140%, are greater than 100%. Since percent means hundredths or per 100, a percent like 140% means 140 per 100.

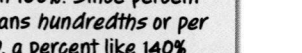

CHECK Your Progress

a. **FOOTBALL** During his football career, Dan Marino completed a pass about 59 times out of every 100 passes he threw.

b. **TECHNOLOGY** In a recent year, 50.5 out of 100 households in the United States had access to the Internet.

To write a fraction as a percent, find an equivalent fraction with a denominator of 100.

Real-World Link
Up until the early 1800s, the Cherokee lived in Georgia, Alabama, North Carolina, South Carolina, Tennessee, Kentucky, and West Virginia. In the 1830s, 17,000 were forced to move to what is now Oklahoma.
Source: The Cherokee Nation

Real-World EXAMPLES Write Fractions as Percents

Write each ratio or fraction as a percent.

3 NATIVE AMERICANS About 1 out of every 10 Native Americans in the United States are part of the Cherokee Nation.

$\frac{1}{10} = \frac{x}{100}$

$\frac{1}{10} = \frac{10}{100}$ (× 10 numerator and denominator)

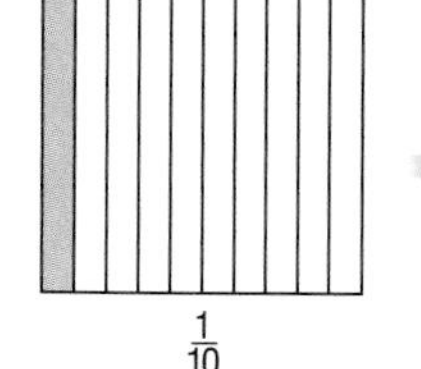

$\frac{1}{10}$

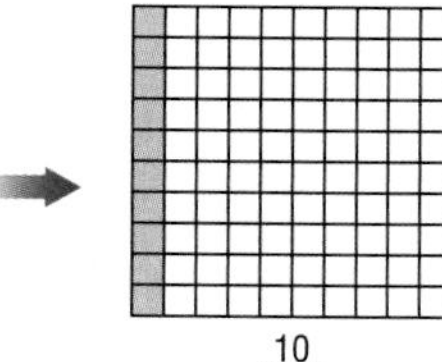

$\frac{10}{100}$

So, 1 out of 10 equals 10%.

4 BUSINESS About $\frac{1}{200}$ of the toys were defective.

$\frac{1}{200} = \frac{x}{100}$

$\frac{1}{200} = \frac{0.5}{100}$ (÷ 2 numerator and denominator)

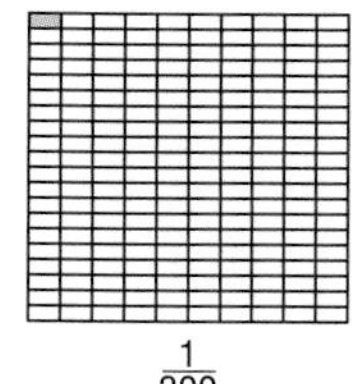

$\frac{1}{200}$

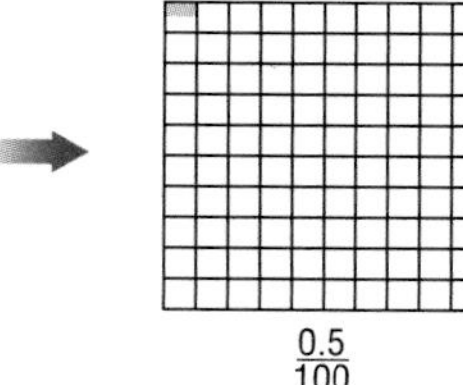

$\frac{0.5}{100}$

So, 1 out of 200 equals 0.5%.

Study Tip
Small Percents
In Example 4, notice that 0.5% is less than 1%. Percents can be even smaller, such as 0.001%, which is equal to $\frac{1}{100{,}000}$.

CHECK Your Progress

c. **TRAVEL** Almost $\frac{3}{4}$ of people who travel buy tickets online.

d. **ECOLOGY** About $\frac{2}{25}$ of the trash in landfills is metal.

Real-World EXAMPLE Write Percents as Fractions

5 MOVIES The circle graph shows the favorite movie treats of a group of students. Write the percent for popcorn as a fraction in simplest form.

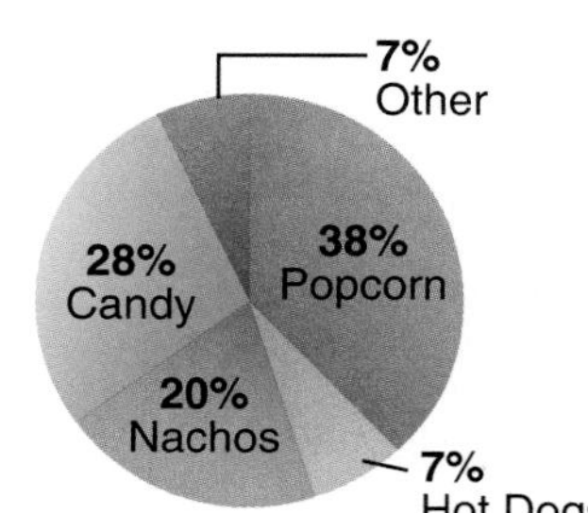

$38\% = \frac{38}{100}$ Definition of percent

$= \frac{19}{50}$ Simplify.

CHECK Your Progress

Write as a fraction in simplest form.

e. candy

f. nachos

g. hot dogs

Check Your Understanding

Examples 1, 2 (p. 252) **Write each ratio as a percent.**

1. 17 out of 100
2. 237 per 100
3. **TAXES** In Illinois, the sales tax rate is 6.25 cents for every 100 cents spent.

Examples 3, 4 (p. 253) **Write each ratio or fraction as a percent.**

4. 7:10
5. $\frac{9}{20}$
6. 1 out of 500

Example 5 (p. 253) **Write each percent as a fraction in simplest form.**

7. 19%
8. 50%
9. 18%

Practice and Problem Solving

HOMEWORK HELP	
For Exercises	See Examples
10, 11	1, 2
12–19	3, 4
20–27	5

Write each ratio or fraction as a percent.

10. 23 out of 100
11. 110 per 100
12. $\frac{17}{50}$
13. $\frac{7}{20}$
14. 8 out of 25
15. 54 out of 300
16. 2:5
17. 9:10
18. **WATER** About $\frac{2}{5}$ of Michigan's area is water. Write this ratio as a percent.
19. **AIRLINES** One in 50 flights in a recent year was cancelled. Write this ratio as a percent.

Write each percent as a fraction in simplest form.

20. 29%
21. 43%
22. 40%
23. 70%
24. 45%
25. 28%
26. 64%
27. 65%
28. **LIFE SCIENCE** Sixty percent of a human body is made up of water. Write this percent as a fraction in simplest form.
29. **MUSIC** The influences in the purchase of CDs by buyers ages 12–44 are shown in the graphic. Write each percent as a fraction in simplest form.
30. **POPULATION** According to a recent census, the population of Houston, Texas, is about $\frac{7}{1{,}000}$ of the United States population. Write this fraction as a percent.
31. **TEETH** Humans have $\frac{8}{5}$ more teeth as adults than when they are children. Write this fraction as a percent.

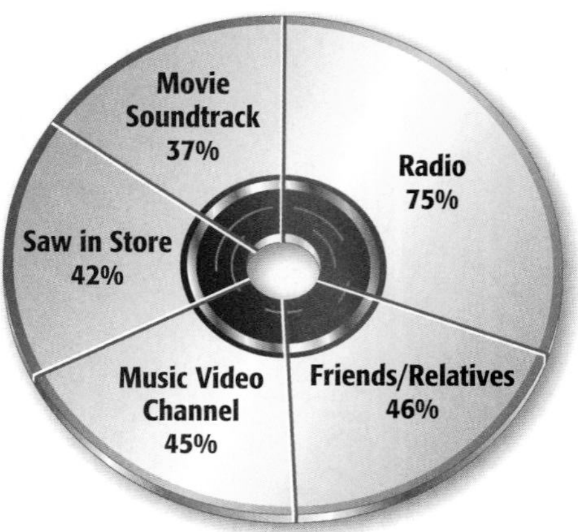

Source: Edison Media Research

Extra Practice, pp. 680, 704

H.O.T. Problems

32. **CHALLENGE** Explain how to find the percent of heads on a coin toss if 28 out of 50 tosses landed on tails.

33. **OPEN ENDED** Find a percent that is between $\frac{1}{2}$ and $\frac{3}{4}$. Justify your answer.

34. **Which One Doesn't Belong?** Identify the ratio that does not belong with the other three. Explain your reasoning.

1 out of 4	2:8	4:12	25%

35. **WRITING IN MATH** Refer to the information on page 252 on endangered species. Express all of the ratios as percents. Explain how doing so helps compare the groups.

ISAT PRACTICE 6.A.3, 6.D.3

36. What percent of the grid is not shaded?

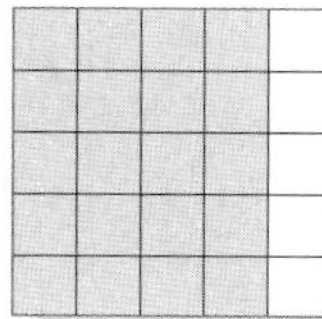

A 65%   C 80%

B 50%   D 20%

37. A soccer team played twenty games, of which they won fourteen. What percent of the games did they win?

F 30%

G 60%

H 70%

J 80%

Spiral Review

38. **HOBBIES** Mia's dollhouse is a replica of her family's townhouse. The outside dimensions of the dollhouse are 25 inches by 35 inches. If the actual outside dimensions of the townhouse are 25 feet by 35 feet, what is the scale of the dollhouse? (Lesson 4-10)

39. **MAILBOXES** A mailbox casts an 18-inch shadow. A tree casts a 234-inch shadow. If the mailbox is 4 feet tall, how tall is the tree? (Lesson 4-9)

40. **CARS** After driving 150 miles, Mr. Ruiz has used 5 gallons of gasoline. He uses 3 gallons of gas driving another 100 miles. Find the rate of change in miles per gallon for the given distances. (Lesson 4-3)

41. Write 1.8, 1.07, $1\frac{8}{9}$, and $1\frac{1}{2}$ in order from least to greatest. (Lesson 2-2)

GET READY for the Next Lesson

PREREQUISITE SKILL Write each fraction as a decimal. (Lesson 2-1)

42. $\frac{3}{5}$ 43. $\frac{3}{4}$ 44. $\frac{5}{8}$ 45. $\frac{1}{3}$

5-2 Comparing Fractions, Decimals, and Percents

MAIN IDEA

Write percents as fractions and decimals and vice versa.

IL Learning Standards

6.A.3 Represent fractions, decimals, percentages, exponents and scientific notation **in equivalent forms.**

IL Math Online

glencoe.com

- Extra Examples
- Personal Tutor
- Self-Check Quiz

GET READY for the Lesson

GAMES Taino surveyed his classmates about their favorite type of game. The results are shown in the table.

Favorite Types of Games	
Type of Game	**Percent of Favorite**
Board Game	11%
Card Game	9%
Computer or Video Game	45%
Sports Game	17%
None of the above	18%

1. Write each percent as a fraction. Do not simplify the fractions.
2. Write each fraction in Exercise 1 as a decimal.
3. How could you write a percent as a decimal without writing the fraction first?

Fractions, percents, and decimals are all different ways to represent the same ratio.

Remember that *percent* means *per hundred*. In Lesson 5-1, you wrote percents as fractions with 100 in the denominator. Similarly, you can write percents as decimals by dividing by 100.

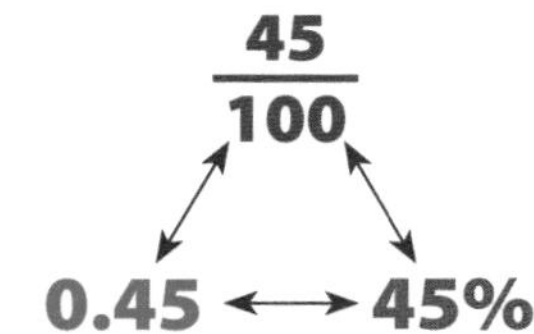

Percents and Decimals

Concept Summary

Percent ⟶ Decimal	**Decimal ⟶ Percent**
To write a percent as a decimal, divide by 100 and remove the percent symbol. $45\% = 45\% = 0.45$	To write a decimal as a percent, multiply by 100 and add the percent symbol. $0.45 = 0.45 = 45\%$

EXAMPLES Percents as Decimals

Write each percent as a decimal.

1 35%

$35\% = 35\%$ Divide by 100.

$= 0.35$ Remove the percent symbol.

2 115%

$115\% = 115\%$ Divide by 100.

$= 1.15$ Remove the percent symbol.

Study Tip

Percents and Decimals To divide by 100, move the decimal point two places to the left.

CHECK Your Progress

a. 27%

b. 145%

c. 0.2%

EXAMPLES Decimals as Percents

Study Tip

Decimals Greater Than One Notice that decimals like 1.66 that are greater than 1 are equivalent to percents greater than 100.

Write each decimal as a percent.

3 **0.2**

$0.2 = 0.20$ Multiply by 100.

$= 20\%$ Add the percent symbol.

4 **1.66**

$1.66 = 1.66$ Multiply by 100.

$= 166\%$ Add the percent symbol.

CHECK Your Progress

d. 0.83 **e.** 1.764 **f.** 0.005

You have learned to write a fraction as a percent by finding an equivalent fraction with a denominator of 100. This method works well if the denominator is a factor of 100. If the denominator is *not* a factor of 100, you can solve a proportion or you can write the fraction as a decimal and then write the decimal as a percent.

EXAMPLES Fractions as Percents

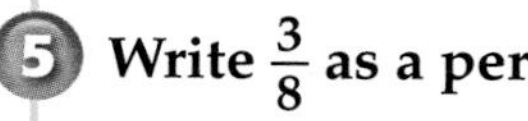

5 **Write $\frac{3}{8}$ as a percent.**

METHOD 1 **Use a proportion.**

$$\frac{3}{8} = \frac{x}{100}$$
$$3 \cdot 100 = 8 \cdot x$$
$$300 = 8x$$
$$\frac{300}{8} = \frac{8x}{8}$$
$$37.5 = x$$

METHOD 2 **Write as decimal.**

First write as a decimal.
Then write as a percent.

$\frac{3}{8} = 0.375$

$= 37.5\%$

$$\begin{array}{r} 0.375 \\ 8\overline{)3.000} \\ -2\,4 \\ \hline 60 \\ -56 \\ \hline 40 \\ -40 \\ \hline 0 \end{array}$$

So, $\frac{3}{8} = \frac{37.5}{100}$ or 37.5%.

6 **Write $\frac{2}{3}$ as a percent.**

$\frac{2}{3} = 0.66\overline{6}$

$= 66.\overline{6}\%$

$$\begin{array}{r} 0.66\ldots \\ 3\overline{)2.0} \\ -1\,8 \\ \hline 20 \\ -18 \\ \hline 2 \end{array}$$

So, $\frac{2}{3} = 66.\overline{6}\%$.

Study Tip

Percents In real-world situations, $66.\overline{6}\%$ will usually be rounded to 67% or 66.7%.

CHOOSE Your Method

Write each fraction as a percent.

g. $\frac{7}{25}$ **h.** $\frac{3}{16}$ **i.** $\frac{1}{9}$

Real-World Link The average tax refund in 2006 was $2,423.
Source: IRS

Real-World EXAMPLE Compare Numbers

7 TAXES In a recent survey, 0.6 of the people said they will use their tax refund to pay bills, and 7% said they will just spend it. Do more people pay bills or spend their refund?

Since $0.6 = 60\%$ and $60\% > 7\%$, more people plan on using their tax refund to pay bills than for spending.

CHECK Your Progress

j. **VACATION** In a survey, 14% of students said they would travel over spring break, and 3 out of 25 said they would watch videos. Is a bigger part of students traveling or watching videos?

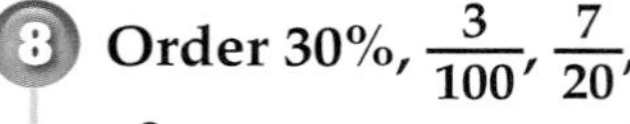

EXAMPLE Order Numbers

8 Order 30%, $\frac{3}{100}$, $\frac{7}{20}$, and 0.33 from least to greatest.

$\frac{3}{100} = 3\%$ $\qquad$ $\frac{7}{20} = \frac{35}{100}$ or 35% $\qquad$ $0.33 = 33\%$

From least to greatest, the percents are 3%, 30%, 33%, and 35%.

So, from least to greatest, the numbers are $\frac{3}{100}$, 30%, 0.33, and $\frac{7}{20}$.

CHECK Your Progress

Order each set of numbers from least to greatest.

k. 22%, $\frac{1}{10}$, $\frac{3}{25}$, 0.25

l. $\frac{1}{5}$, 40%, 0.401, $\frac{4}{25}$

CHECK Your Understanding

Examples 1, 2 (p. 256)

Write each percent as a decimal.

1. 40%
2. 18%
3. 0.3%

Examples 3, 4 (p. 257)

Write each decimal as a percent.

4. 0.725
5. 1.23
6. 0.3

Examples 5, 6 (p. 257)

Write each fraction as a percent.

7. $\frac{11}{25}$
8. $\frac{13}{40}$
9. $\frac{5}{6}$

Example 7 (p. 258)

10. **HOMEWORK** At Hancock Middle School, 57% of the eighth-grade students spend at least 30 minutes a day on math homework. Of the seventh-grade students, 0.5 study this long. In which grade do a greater percent of students spend at least 30 minutes a day on math homework?

Example 8 (p. 258)

Order each set of numbers from least to greatest.

11. $\frac{17}{25}$, 60%, 0.062, $\frac{13}{20}$
12. 0.99, $\frac{9}{10}$, 9%, $\frac{19}{20}$

Practice and Problem Solving

HOMEWORK HELP

For Exercises	See Examples
13–22	1,2
23–32	3,4
33–42	5,6
43–46	7
47–52	8

Write each percent as a decimal.

13. 90%
14. 80%
15. 172%
16. 245%
17. 0.4%
18. 84.2%
19. 7%
20. 5%

21. **ENERGY** A recent study indicated that 11% of the United States' energy comes from nuclear power. Write this number as a decimal.

22. **WATER** Only about 0.5% of the world's water resources are drinkable by humans, animals, and plants. Write this number as a decimal.

Write each decimal as a percent.

23. 0.62
24. 0.94
25. 0.475
26. 0.832
27. 0.007
28. 0.009
29. 2.75
30. 1.38

31. **PETS** If 0.21 of adults own a dog, what percent of adults own a dog?

32. **SURVEYS** In a survey, 0.312 of teens said that their favorite sport was soccer or basketball. What percent of the teens chose soccer or basketball as their favorite sport?

Write each fraction as a percent.

33. $\frac{17}{20}$
34. $\frac{12}{25}$
35. $\frac{8}{5}$
36. $\frac{7}{4}$
37. $\frac{1}{40}$
38. $\frac{1}{125}$
39. $\frac{4}{9}$
40. $\frac{2}{3}$

41. **HOT DOGS** About 6 in 30 people prefer mustard on their hot dogs. What percent of people prefer mustard on their hot dogs?

42. **CATS** About $\frac{17}{45}$ of American households own at least one cat. What percent of American households own at least one cat?

SCHEDULE The graph shows how many hours Jack spends on daily activities.

43. What percent of the day does Jack attend school?

44. What percent of Jack's day is for other activities? Round your answer to the nearest whole percent.

45. **CAMPING** About 17% of kids will attend an overnight summer camp, $\frac{11}{50}$ will attend a day camp, and 0.59 will attend no summer camp at all. Which group of kids is the greatest?

46. **BAND** At Jeremy's high school, about $\frac{3}{16}$ of the students are in the band, 0.31 of high school students play at least one sport, and 13% are in the drama club. Of these three, which type of extra-curricular activity is most popular among students at Jeremy's high school?

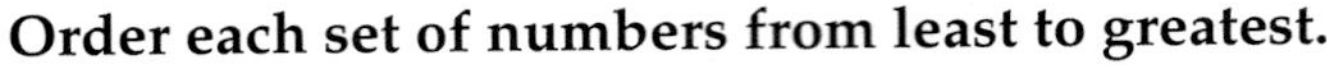

Order each set of numbers from least to greatest.

47. $\frac{3}{4}$, 0.8, 8%, $\frac{7}{10}$

48. 0.2, $\frac{1}{4}$, 2%, $\frac{3}{20}$

49. $\frac{1}{20}$, 7%, 0.09, $\frac{2}{25}$

50. 84%, 0.88, $\frac{41}{50}$, $\frac{4}{5}$

51. 31%, $\frac{3}{10}$, $\frac{3}{13}$, 0.305

52. 6.5%, $\frac{3}{5}$, 0.556, $\frac{1}{6}$

53. **BASEBALL** In a recent year, Major League Baseball player Jack Wilson's batting average was 0.308. Melvin Mora hit safely 17 out of every 50 at-bats and Bobby Abreu hit safely 30.1% of the time. Find Mora's and Abreu's batting averages and order all three averages from least to greatest.

Real-World Link

A batting average is found by dividing the number of hits a batter has by the number of times the batter is at bat, not including times when a batter is walked or hit by a pitch.

Replace each ● with <, >, or = to make a true sentence.

54. 0.035 ● $3\frac{1}{2}$%

55. $\frac{1}{250}$ ● $\frac{3}{4}$%

56. $\frac{7}{4}$ ● $1\frac{1}{4}$%

57. **ANALYZE TABLES** A nutrition label from a popular brand of soda is shown at the right. Would more or less than $\frac{1}{5}$ of a person's daily value of carbohydrates come from this can of soda? Explain your reasoning.

Nutrition Facts
Serving Size 1 can (360mL)

Amount Per Serving	
Calories 140	
	% Daily Value*
Total Fat 0g	0%
Sodium 20mg	1%
Total Carbohydrate 36g	12%
Sugars 36g	
Protein 0g	0%

* Percent Daily Values are based on a 2,000 calorie diet.

58. **TRAVEL** The projected number of household trips in 2010 is 50,000,000. About 14,000,000 of these trips will involve air travel. What percent of the trips will involve air travel?

SELECT A FORM For Exercises 59 and 60, use the following information.

Lisa ate $\frac{1}{8}$ of the cookies, gave 0.25 to her friend Kaitlyn, and gave 37.5% to her sister. To solve each problem below, select the form of number (fraction, decimal, or percent) that would be easiest to use. Explain your reasoning. Then use that form to solve the problem.

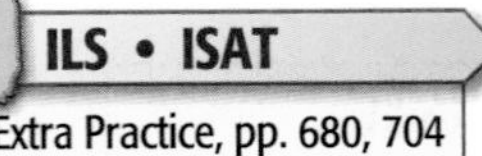

Extra Practice, pp. 680, 704

59. Did Lisa eat more cookies than she gave to Kaitlyn?

60. Who was given more cookies, Kaitlyn or Lisa's sister?

H.O.T. Problems

61. **FIND THE ERROR** Michela and Toni are changing 0.9 to a percent. Who is correct? Explain your reasoning.

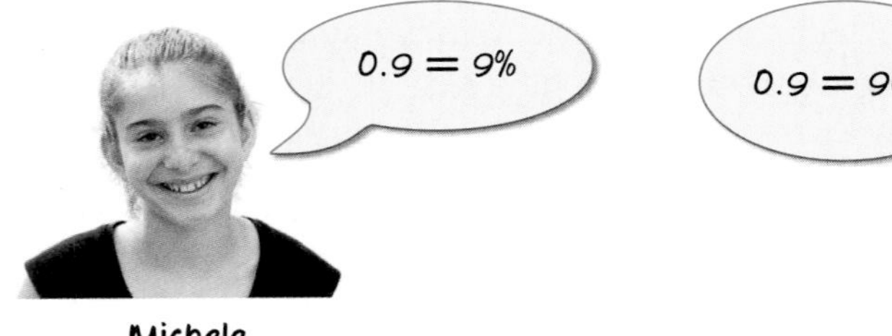

Michela

Toni

62. **CHALLENGE** Write $1\frac{3}{5}$ as a percent. Justify your answer.

63. **OPEN ENDED** Write a percent that is between $\frac{3}{5}$ and $\frac{2}{3}$.

64. **WRITING IN MATH** Is 0.04 less than or greater than 40%? Explain your reasoning.

ISAT PRACTICE 6.A.3

65. Mr. Lee asked his students how many hours they watched public television last week. The responses are shown in the table. Which number represents the portion of students who said they watched more than 1 hour?

Number of Hours Watched	% of Students
Less than or equal to 1 hour	92.5%
Between 1 and 2 hours	5%
More than 2 hours	2.5%

A 0.75

B $\frac{75}{100}$

C $\frac{5}{100}$

D 0.075

66. Between which two percents is $\frac{7}{40}$?

F 15% and 16%

G 16% and 17%

H 17% and 18%

J 19% and 20%

67. **SHORT RESPONSE** What percent of the square is shaded?

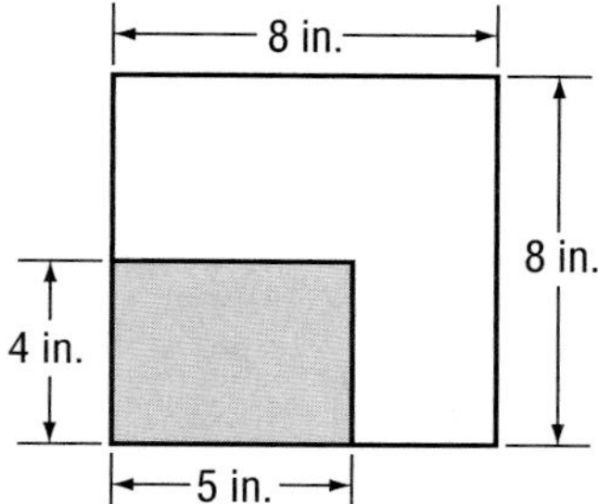

Spiral Review

Write each ratio as a percent. (Lesson 5-1)

68. 27 out of 100

69. 0.6 out of 100

70. 9:20

71. 33:50

72. **BUILDINGS** The scale on a model of an office building is 3 centimeters = 45 meters. Find the actual length of the building for a model distance of 5 centimeters. (Lesson 4-10)

73. **FOOD** Three fourths of a pan of lasagna is to be divided equally among 6 people. What part of the lasagna will each person receive? (Lesson 2-4)

Order the integers in each set from least to greatest. (Lesson 1-3)

74. {–12, 5, –5, 13, –1}

75. {42, –56, –13, 101, 13}

76. {64, –58, –65, 57, –61}

GET READY for the Next Lesson

PREREQUISITE SKILL Solve each proportion. (Lesson 4-5)

77. $\frac{5}{6} = \frac{x}{24}$

78. $\frac{a}{12} = \frac{2}{15}$

79. $\frac{2}{7} = \frac{5}{t}$

80. $\frac{3}{n} = \frac{10}{8}$

READING to SOLVE PROBLEMS

Comparing Data

When you are solving a word problem that involves comparing data, look for words such as *more than, times*, or *percent*. They give you a clue about what operation to use.

For example, the table shows the final standings for the Western Conference of the United Soccer League's W-League for the 2005 season.

W-League Western Conference					
Team	**Games**	**Wins**	**Losses**	**Ties**	**Points**
Vancouver	14	13	1	0	39
Arizona	14	10	3	1	31
Mile High	14	10	4	0	30
Denver	14	7	6	1	22
Seattle	14	5	8	1	16
Fort Collins	14	2	11	1	7
San Diego	14	0	14	0	0

Source: United Soccer Leagues

You can compare the data in several ways.

Difference Vancouver had *17 more points* than Denver.
$39 - 22 = 17$

Ratio Mile High won *5 times as many games* as Fort Collins.
$10 \div 2 = 5$

Percent Arizona lost about *21% of the games* they played.
$(3 \div 14) \times 100 \approx 21$

PRACTICE

Determine whether each problem asks for a *difference, ratio*, or *percent*. Write out the key words in each problem. Then solve each problem.

1. How many more games did Arizona win than lose or tie?
2. What percent of the time did Vancouver win its games?
3. How many times as many games did Mile High win than Seattle?
4. **WRITING IN MATH** Write three statements comparing the data in the table. One comparison should be a difference, one should be a ratio, and one should be a percent.

5-3 Algebra: The Percent Proportion

MAIN IDEA

Solve problems using the percent proportion.

IL Learning Standards

6.A.3 Represent fractions, decimals, percentages, exponents and scientific notation **in equivalent forms.**
6.D.3 Apply ratios and proportions to solve practical problems.
Also addresses 8.D.3b, 8.C.3.

New Vocabulary

percent proportion

IL Math Online

glencoe.com
- Extra Examples
- Personal Tutor
- Self-Check Quiz
- Reading in the Content Area

MINI Lab

You can use a proportion model to determine the percent represented by 3 out of 5.

STEP 1 Draw a 10-by-1 rectangle on grid paper. Label the units on the right from 0 to 100.

STEP 2 On the left side, mark equal units from 0 to 5, because 5 represents the whole quantity.

STEP 3 Draw a horizontal line from 3 on the left side of the model. The number on the right side is the percent.

For Exercises 1–3, use the model above.

1. What is 40% of 5?
2. 4 is 80% of what number?
3. Draw a model and find what percent 7 is of 20.

In a **percent proportion**, one ratio compares a part to the whole. The other ratio is the equivalent percent written as a fraction with a denominator of 100.

3 out of 5 is 60%.

$$\text{part} \rightarrow \frac{3}{5} = \frac{60}{100} \Big\} \text{percent} \quad \text{whole} \rightarrow$$

EXAMPLE Find the Percent

22 is what percent of 110?

Since 22 is being compared to 110, 22 is the part and 110 is the whole. You need to find the percent. Let n represent the percent.

part → whole → $\frac{22}{110} = \frac{n}{100}$ } percent	Write the percent proportion.
$22 \cdot 100 = 110 \cdot n$	Find the cross products.
$2{,}200 = 110n$	Multiply.
$\frac{2{,}200}{110} = \frac{110n}{110}$	Divide each side by 110.
$20 = n$	Simplify.

22 is 20% of 110.

CHECK Your Progress

a. 17 is what percent of 68?

b. 41.4 is what percent of 92?

EXAMPLE Find the Part

Reading Math

Percents The whole usually follows the word *of*.

2 What number is 80% of 500?

The percent is 80% and the whole is 500. You need to find the part. Let p represent the part.

part → / whole →	$\frac{p}{500} = \frac{80}{100}$ } percent	Write the percent proportion.
	$p \cdot 100 = 500 \cdot 80$	Find the cross products.
	$100p = 40{,}000$	Multiply.
	$\frac{100p}{100} = \frac{40{,}000}{100}$	Divide each side by 100.
	$p = 400$	Simplify.

400 is 80% of 500.

CHECK Your Progress

c. What number is 35% of 48?

d. Find 12.5% of 88.

EXAMPLE Find the Whole

3 14.4 is 32% of what number?

The percent is 32% and the part is 14.4. You need to find the whole. Let w represent the whole.

part → / whole →	$\frac{14.4}{w} = \frac{32}{100}$ } percent	Write the percent proportion.
	$14.4 \cdot 100 = 32 \cdot w$	Find the cross products.
	$1{,}440 = 32w$	Multiply.
	$\frac{1{,}440}{32} = \frac{32w}{32}$	Divide each side by 32.
	$45 = w$	Simplify.

14.4 is 32% of 45.

CHECK Your Progress

e. 23.4 is 30% of what number?

f. 19 is 62.5% of what number?

Types of Percent Problems — Concept Summary

Type	Example	Proportion
Find the Percent	7 is what percent of 10?	$\frac{7}{10} = \frac{n}{100}$
Find the Part	What number is 70% of 10?	$\frac{p}{10} = \frac{70}{100}$
Find the Whole	7 is 70% of what number?	$\frac{7}{w} = \frac{70}{100}$

EXAMPLE Percents Greater than 100

4 **6 is what percent of 5?**

6 is being compared to 5, so 5 is the whole, and 6 is the part. You need to find the percent. Let n represent the percent.

Study Tip

Check for Reasonableness Since the part is greater than the whole, $6 > 5$, it makes sense that the percent would be greater than 100.

part → whole → $\frac{6}{5} = \frac{n}{100}$ } percent	Write the percent proportion.
$6 \cdot 100 = 5 \cdot n$	Find the cross products.
$600 = 5n$	Multiply.
$\frac{600}{5} = \frac{5n}{5}$	Divide each side by 5.
$120 = n$	Simplify.

6 is 120% of 5.

CHECK Your Progress

g. 12 is what percent of 6?

h. Find 175% of 18.

Real-World EXAMPLE

5 **JEWELRY** **Silver jewelry that is stamped with the numbers 925 means that 92.5% of the metal used is pure silver and the rest is made up of other metals. If a bracelet has 11 grams of silver in it, how much does the bracelet weigh?**

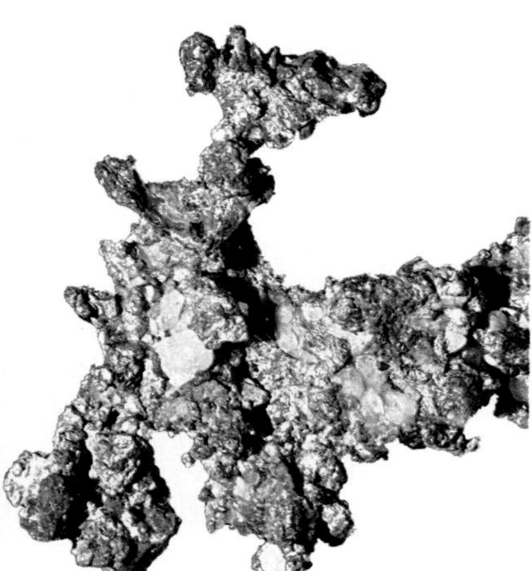

Real-World Link The United States produces about 6.5% of the world's silver. Mexico and Peru top the list with about 16% each of the world's silver production.

Source: The Silver Users Association

The percent is 92.5%, and the part is 11 grams. You need to find the total weight of the bracelet.

Words	11 grams is 92.5% of what number of grams?
Variable	Let w represent the whole.
Proportion	part → whole → $\frac{11}{w} = \frac{92.5}{100}$ } percent

$\frac{11}{w} = \frac{92.5}{100}$	Write the percent proportion.
$11 \cdot 100 = w \cdot 92.5$	Find the cross products.
$1{,}100 = 92.5w$	Multiply.
$\frac{1{,}100}{92.5} = \frac{92.5w}{92.5}$	Divide each side by 92.5.
$11.9 \approx w$	Simplify.

The bracelet weighs about 11.9 grams.

CHECK Your Progress

i. **SCHOOL** Carmila answered 23 questions correctly on her science test and received a grade of 92%. How many questions were on the test?

Write a percent proportion and solve each problem. Round to the nearest tenth if necessary.

Examples 1, 2 (pp. 263–264)

1. 70 is what percent of 280?
2. What percent of 49 is 7?
3. What number is 60% of 90?
4. Find 72% of 200.

Examples 3, 4 (pp. 264–265)

5. 151.5 is 75% of what number?
6. 126 is 30% of what number?
7. 48 is what percent of 30?
8. Find 118% of 19.

Example 5 (p. 265)

9. **ANIMALS** A tiger can eat food that weighs up to about 15% of its body weight. If a tiger can eat 75 pounds of food, how much does a tiger weigh?

Practice and Problem Solving

HOMEWORK HELP

For Exercises	See Examples
10, 11	1
12, 13	2
14, 15	3
16, 17	4
18, 19	5

Write a percent proportion and solve each problem. Round to the nearest tenth if necessary.

10. 3 is what percent of 15?
11. 120 is what percent of 360?
12. What is 15% of 60?
13. What is 17% of 350?
14. 18 is 45% of what number?
15. 95 is 95% of what number?
16. 15.12 is what percent of 12?
17. Find 250% of 57.
18. **BRACES** In a recent survey, 34% of kids said they will get dental braces. If nearly 28,800 kids were surveyed, about how many will get braces?
19. **PETS** There are about 68 million owned dogs in the United States. Of these, 13.6 million were adopted from an animal shelter. About what percent of owned dogs were adopted from an animal shelter?

Write a percent proportion to solve each problem. Then solve. Round to the nearest tenth if necessary.

20. What is 2.5% of 95?
21. 4 is what percent of 550?
22. 98 is 22.5% of what number?
23. Find 5.8% of 42.
24. What percent of 110 is 1?
25. 57 is 13.5% of what number?

SNACKS For Exercises 26–28, use the snack recipe at the right.

26. Chocolate chips make up what percent of the recipe?
27. The amount of powdered sugar used is what percent of the amount of cereal used?
28. Which ingredient is 67% of the total recipe?

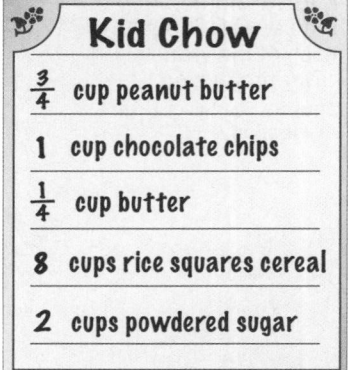

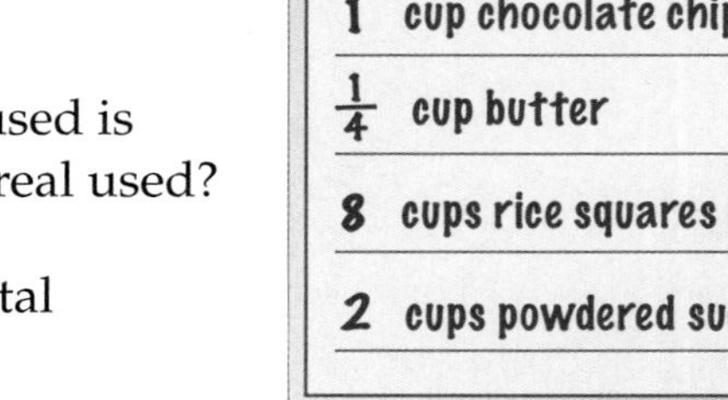

Kid Chow
$\frac{3}{4}$ cup peanut butter
1 cup chocolate chips
$\frac{1}{4}$ cup butter
8 cups rice squares cereal
2 cups powdered sugar

Extra Practice, pp. 681, 704

H.O.T. Problems

29. **CHALLENGE** Choose any two numbers, x and y. Find $x\%$ of y and $y\%$ of x. Will the results always be the same? Explain.

30. **WRITING IN MATH** Alonzo scored a 79% on his first test of the quarter. Will a score of 38 out of 45 on the next test help or hurt his grade? Explain your reasoning.

ISAT PRACTICE 6.A.3, 6.D.3

31. A baseball stadium manager expects that 60% of the fans at a game will buy at least \$3.00 in concessions. If there are 5,600 fans at a game, which statement does *not* represent the manager's expectation?

A 3,360 fans each will buy at least \$3.00 in concessions.

B 2,240 fans each will buy fewer than \$3.00 in concessions.

C More than $\frac{1}{2}$ of the fans each will buy at least \$3.00 in concessions.

D Less than $\frac{2}{5}$ of the fans each will buy fewer than \$3.00 in concessions.

32. A pattern of equations is shown below.

1% of 100 = 1
2% of 50 = 1
4% of 25 = 1
8% of 12.5 = 1
16% of 6.25 = 1

Which statement best describes this pattern?

F If the percent is doubled and the whole is doubled, the answer is 1.

G If the percent is doubled and the whole is halved, the answer is 1.

H If the percent is increased by 2 and the whole is halved, the answer is 1.

J If the percent remains the same and the whole is halved, the answer is 1.

Spiral Review

33. Order the set of numbers $\frac{1}{6}$, 16%, and 0.016 from least to greatest. (Lesson 5-2)

34. **LUNCH** Forty-eight percent of first period class buys a school lunch. Write this percent as a fraction in simplest form. (Lesson 5-1)

NUMBER SENSE **Name all sets of numbers to which each real number belongs.** (Lesson 3-4)

35. $\sqrt{21}$

36. 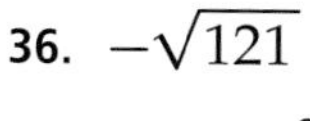
$-\sqrt{121}$

37. **GEOMETRY** Find the perimeter of the right triangle. (Lesson 3-5)

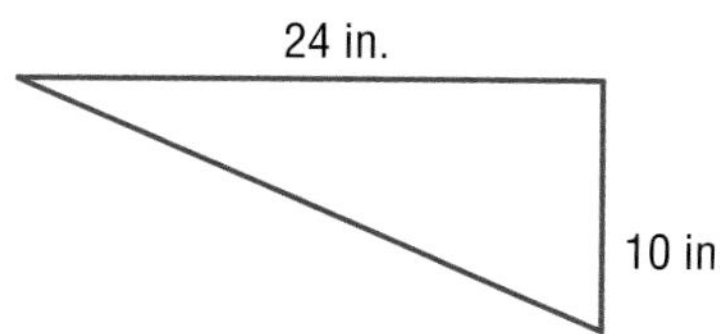

GET READY for the Next Lesson

PREREQUISITE SKILL **Compute each product mentally.** (Lesson 2-3)

38. $\frac{1}{2} \cdot 422$

39. $639 \cdot \frac{1}{3}$

40. $0.1 \cdot 722$

41. $0.5 \cdot 680$

5-4 Finding Percents Mentally

MAIN IDEA

Compute mentally with percents.

IL Learning Standards

6.C.3b Show evidence that computational results using whole numbers, fractions, decimals, **percents** and proportions **are correct and/or that estimates are reasonable.** *Also addresses 6.A.3.*

IL Math Online

glencoe.com

- Extra Examples
- Personal Tutor
- Self-Check Quiz

GET READY for the Lesson

COINS Paloma saves money by putting all her spare change in a large jar. She emptied the jar and made a table listing the types of coins she had saved.

Type of Coin	Number
penny	410
nickel	90
dime	120
quarter	36
half-dollar	4
dollar	8

1. Seventy-five percent of the dimes she collected were minted after the year 2000. How could you find 75% of 120 mentally?
2. Use mental math to find the number of dimes minted after the year 2000.
3. If 25% of the dollars she collected were Sacagawea dollars, use mental math to find the number of Sacagawea dollars she collected.

When you compute with common percents like 75% or 25%, it may be easier to use the fraction form of the percent. This number line shows some fraction-percent equivalents.

0%	12.5%	25%	37.5%	50%	62.5%	75%	87.5%	100%
0	$\frac{1}{8}$	$\frac{1}{4}$	$\frac{3}{8}$	$\frac{1}{2}$	$\frac{5}{8}$	$\frac{3}{4}$	$\frac{7}{8}$	1

Since some percents are used more frequently than others, it is helpful to be familiar with the percent-fraction equivalencies shown below.

Percent-Fraction Equivalents — Key Concept

$25\% = \frac{1}{4}$	$20\% = \frac{1}{5}$	$16\frac{2}{3}\% = \frac{1}{6}$	$12\frac{1}{2}\% = \frac{1}{8}$	$10\% = \frac{1}{10}$
$50\% = \frac{1}{2}$	$40\% = \frac{2}{5}$	$33\frac{1}{3}\% = \frac{1}{3}$	$37\frac{1}{2}\% = \frac{3}{8}$	$30\% = \frac{3}{10}$
$75\% = \frac{3}{4}$	$60\% = \frac{3}{5}$	$66\frac{2}{3}\% = \frac{2}{3}$	$62\frac{1}{2}\% = \frac{5}{8}$	$70\% = \frac{7}{10}$
$100\% = 1$	$80\% = \frac{4}{5}$	$83\frac{1}{3}\% = \frac{5}{6}$	$87\frac{1}{2}\% = \frac{7}{8}$	$90\% = \frac{9}{10}$

EXAMPLES Use Fractions to Compute Mentally

1 Compute 20% of 45 mentally.

20% of $45 = \frac{1}{5} \cdot 45$ or 9 — Use the fraction form of 20%, which is $\frac{1}{5}$.

2 **Compute $33\frac{1}{3}\%$ of 93 mentally.**

$33\frac{1}{3}\%$ of $93 = \frac{1}{3} \cdot 93$ or 31 — Use the fraction form of $33\frac{1}{3}\%$, which is $\frac{1}{3}$.

CHECK Your Progress

Compute mentally.

a. 25% of 32

b. $12\frac{1}{2}\%$ of 160

c. 80% of 45

You can also use decimals to find percents mentally. Remember that 10% = 0.1 and 1% = 0.01.

EXAMPLES Use Decimals to Compute Mentally

Study Tip

Multiplying by Decimals To multiply by 0.1, move the decimal point one place to the left. To multiply by 0.01, move the decimal point two places to the left.

Compute mentally.

3 **10% of 98**

10% of 98 = $0.1 \cdot 98$ or 9.8

4 **1% of 235**

1% of 235 = $0.01 \cdot 235$ or 2.35

CHECK Your Progress

d. 10% of 65

e. 1% of 450

f. 3% of 22

Real-World EXAMPLE

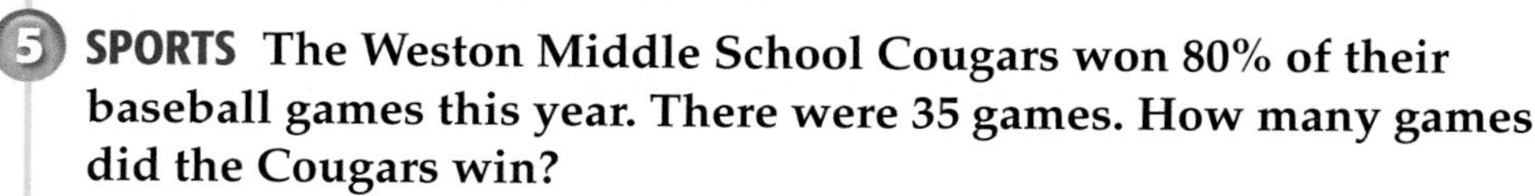

5 **SPORTS** **The Weston Middle School Cougars won 80% of their baseball games this year. There were 35 games. How many games did the Cougars win?**

METHOD 1 **Use a fraction.**

80% of 35 = $\frac{4}{5}$ of 35

80% of 35 is 28.

THINK $\frac{1}{5}$ of 35 is 7. So, $\frac{4}{5}$ of 35 is $4 \cdot 7$ or 28.

METHOD 2 **Use a decimal.**

80% of 35 = 0.8 of 35

80% of 35 is 28.

THINK 0.1 of 35 is 3.5. So, 0.8 of 35 is $8 \cdot 3.5$ or 28.

The Cougars won 28 baseball games.

Real-World Link The Baseball Hall of Fame is located in Cooperstown, New York. It was dedicated in 1939, 100 years after Abner Doubleday started the game of baseball.

Source: National Baseball Hall of Fame and Museum

CHOOSE Your Method

g. **TIPPING** Alan and his brother ate lunch at the local café. They left a tip that was 20% of the bill. If the bill was \$15.50, how much did Alan and his brother leave for the tip?

Check Your Understanding

Examples 1–4 (pp. 268–269)

Compute mentally.

1. 50% of 120
2. $33\frac{1}{3}$% of 60
3. $37\frac{1}{2}$% of 72
4. 1% of 52
5. 10% of 350
6. 2% of 630

Example 5 (p. 269)

7. **BOOKS** An author receives a payment, or commission, equal to 25% of the total sales of her book. Determine the amount of money she will receive if the total sales are $48,000.

Practice and Problem Solving

HOMEWORK HELP

For Exercises	See Examples
8–15	1–2
16–23	3–4
24, 25	5

Compute mentally.

8. 25% of 44
9. 50% of 62
10. $12\frac{1}{2}$% of 64
11. $16\frac{2}{3}$% of 54
12. 40% of 35
13. 60% of 15
14. $66\frac{2}{3}$% of 120
15. $62\frac{1}{2}$% of 160
16. 10% of 57
17. 10% of 125
18. 1% of 81
19. 1% of 28.3
20. 3% of 130
21. 7% of 210
22. 10% of 17.1
23. 10% of 10.2

24. **HAIR** A blonde or brunette has about 100,000 hairs on her head. However, a redhead averages only 90% of this number. What is the average number of hairs on the head of a redhead?

25. **TRAVEL** About 10% of travel trips in the United States include a visit to an amusement park. If there were 920 million travel trips in the United States, how many of those included a visit to an amusement park?

Replace each ● with <, >, or = to make a true statement.

26. $66\frac{2}{3}$% of 18 ● 60% of 15
27. 1% of 150 ● 10% of 15

28. **MEASUREMENT** The Amazon is the second longest river in the world with a length of about 4,000 miles. If the longest river in the world, the Nile, is about 104% of the length of the Amazon, find the length of the Nile River.

MONEY For Exercises 29 and 30, use the following information.

The graphic shows the results of a survey asking teens about their allowances. Suppose 1,000 teens were surveyed.

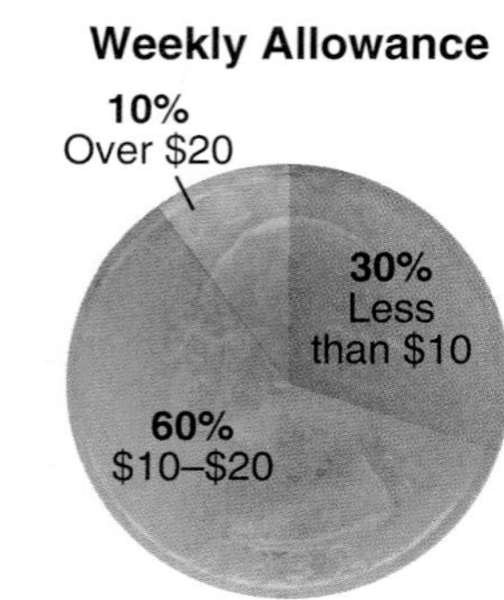

29. How many teens receive at most $20 weekly allowance?

30. How many teens receive less than a $10 weekly allowance?

31. **FIND THE DATA** Refer to the Data File on pages 16–19. Choose some data and write a real-world problem in which you could mentally compute a percent.

ILS • ISAT

Extra Practice, pp. 681, 704

H.O.T. Problems

32. **CHALLENGE** The sum of two whole numbers, x and y, is 90. Twenty percent of x is equal to 80% of y. Find the two numbers. Explain your reasoning.

33. **OPEN ENDED** Find two values of x for which you could mentally find $66\frac{2}{3}\%$ of x. Explain your reasoning.

34. **FIND THE ERROR** Camille and Manuel are finding 10% of 95. Who is correct? Justify your choice.

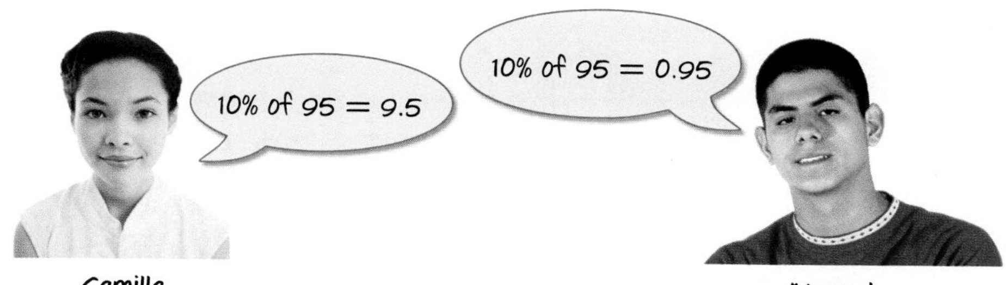

10% of 95 = 9.5
10% of 95 = 0.95
Camille
Manuel

35. **WRITING IN MATH** Explain how to find 75% of 40 mentally.

ISAT PRACTICE 6.C.3b

36. Allison, Raul, and Theo drove from Austin, Texas, to Los Angeles, California, a distance of 1,224 miles. Allison drove $\frac{1}{3}$ of the total distance, Raul drove 40%, and Theo drove the remainder. How many miles were driven by the person who drove the greatest distance?

A 330.5 C 489.6

B 408 D 734.4

37. Etu bought the items listed below. How much money did he save if each item was 20% off the regular price?

Item	Regular Price ($)
Shirt	19
Ties	9
Belt	8
Shoes	29

F $52 H $24

G $36 J $13

Spiral Review

38. **TESTS** Alicia got 41 out of 52 questions correct on a test. What was her percent correct? (Lesson 5-3)

Write each fraction as a percent. (Lesson 5-2)

39. $\frac{9}{20}$ 40. $\frac{7}{8}$ 41. $\frac{3}{500}$ 42. $\frac{2}{9}$

43. **MEASUREMENT** A snail travels one mile in about 30 hours. At this rate, how far can a snail travel in 1 day? (Lesson 2-4)

GET READY for the Next Lesson

PREREQUISITE SKILL Draw the next three figures in the pattern. (Lesson 2-8)

44.

5-5 Problem-Solving Investigation

MAIN IDEA: Determine a reasonable answer.

6.C.3b Show evidence that computational results using whole numbers, fractions, decimals, percents and proportions **are correct and/or that estimates are reasonable.**

P.S.I. TEAM +

e-Mail: REASONABLE ANSWERS

LINA: Student Council hopes to donate \$800 to a local food bank. One way that we raise money is by having a student-teacher basketball game. Over the weekend, we raised \$1,550 at the basketball game, and plan to donate 40% of the money to the food bank and keep the remaining 60% for other Student Council projects.

YOUR MISSION: Is it reasonable to expect that Student Council can donate \$800 to the food bank?

Understand	You know how much money Student Council raised. They will donate 40% to the food bank. You want to know if the donation will be at least \$800.
Plan	Use mental math to determine a reasonable answer.
Solve	THINK 40% is close to 50% or $\frac{1}{2}$, and $\frac{1}{2}$ of \$1,550 is \$775. Since 40% is less than 50%, Student Council will donate less than \$775.
Check	Find 40% of \$1,550. 40% of 1,550 $= \frac{4}{10}$ of 1,550. Since $\frac{1}{10}$ of 1,550 is 155, $\frac{4}{10}$ of 1,550 is 4×155 or 620. Student Council will donate \$620 which is less than the goal of \$800. ✓

Analyze The Strategy

1. Explain why determining a reasonable answer was an appropriate strategy for solving the above problem.
2. **WRITING IN MATH** Explain why mental math skills are important when finding the reasonable answers.

Mixed Problem Solving

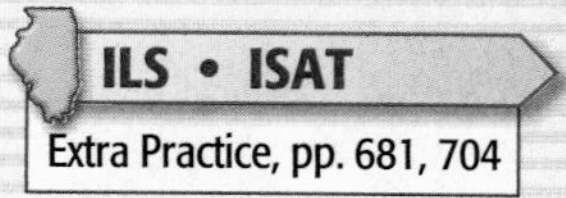
ILS • ISAT
Extra Practice, pp. 681, 704

For Exercises 3–5, determine a reasonable answer.

3. **MONEY** Suki wants to buy an MP3 player that costs $129. She found it on sale for 75% of the original price. Would the sale price be about $30, $60, or $90? Explain.

4. **CLOTHES** Jason received a $100 gift card from a local store. He found a shirt for $24 and a pair of pants for $43.99. Does he have enough money to buy a pair of shoes for $35.99? Explain.

5. **BABYSITTING** Cameron is paid $8.50 an hour to watch his nephew. If he is saving to buy a new skateboard that costs $325, should he babysit for about 20, 30, or 40 hours? Explain.

Use any strategy to solve Exercises 6–13. Some strategies are shown below.

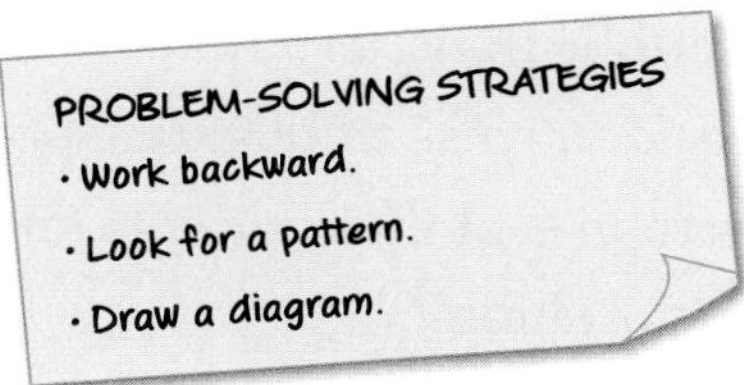
PROBLEM-SOLVING STRATEGIES
• Work backward.
• Look for a pattern.
• Draw a diagram.

6. **TRAVEL** Alex is saving money for a camping trip. He needs $54 for food and $320 for equipment. He has saved $150. If he can save $40 each week, in how many weeks will he have enough money?

7. **NUMBER THEORY** Study the pattern.

$$1 \times 1 = 1$$
$$11 \times 11 = 121$$
$$111 \times 111 = 12{,}321$$
$$1111 \times 1111 = 1{,}234{,}321$$

Without doing the multiplication, find 1111111×1111111.

8. **JEWELRY** Bethany is making a necklace with a pattern of blue, green, and white beads as shown below. What percent of the necklace will be white beads?

9. **PARTY PLANNING** Jasmine is preparing for a surprise party. She bought invitations which cost $\frac{1}{4}$ of the money she had. Then she bought decorations, which cost $\frac{1}{2}$ of what remained. She had $15 left for a cake. How much money did she have at the beginning of the shopping trip?

10. **PETS** In a recent survey, 44% of students at Davison High School own a cat. If there are 1,532 students in the school, is 600, 675, or 715 a reasonable estimate for the number of students who own a cat? Explain.

11. **POPULATION** About 12.25% of the people in the U.S. live in California. If the U.S. population is about 297,000,000, estimate the population of California.

12. **TRUCKS** The five most popular colors for an SUV/Truck are listed in the table shown. If a plant manufactured 1,500 trucks one month, how many were *not* white?

Color	Percent Manufactured
White	26
Other	21
Silver	16
Gray	13
Black	13
Red	11

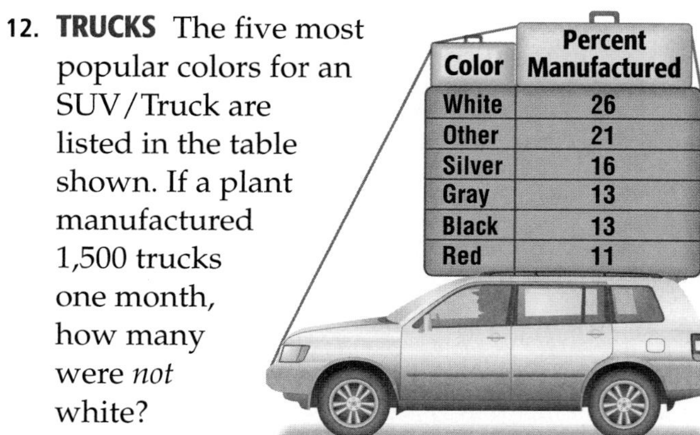

13. **MEASUREMENT** The entrance of a new convention center will need 1.8×10^5 square feet of ceramic tile. The tiles measure 1 foot by 2 feet and are sold in boxes of 48. How many boxes of tiles are needed to tile the entrance?

CHAPTER 5

Mid-Chapter Quiz

Lessons 5-1 through 5-5

IL Learning Standards
6.A.3, 6.D.3

Write each ratio or fraction as a percent. (Lesson 5-1)

1. 3 out of 16
2. 8:10
3. $\frac{13}{25}$
4. $\frac{7}{20}$

5. **MULTIPLE CHOICE** Fifteen percent of the dogs at a show were Labrador retrievers. Which is *not* true? (Lesson 5-1)
   A $\frac{3}{20}$ of the dogs were Labrador retrievers.
   B 15 out of every 100 dogs were Labrador retrievers.
   C 85% of the dogs were not Labrador retrievers.
   D 1 out of every 15 dogs was a Labrador retriever.

Write each decimal or fraction as a percent. (Lesson 5-2)

6. 0.325
7. $\frac{3}{200}$
8. $\frac{4}{15}$
9. 1.72

10. **SCHOOL** Santos answered 37 out of 40 questions correctly on an English exam. On the same exam, Chantal scored 87.5% and David correctly answered $\frac{9}{10}$ of the questions. Which student correctly answered the most questions? (Lesson 5-2)

11. **TIME** Use the graph below. Does Leah spend more of her day sleeping or at school? Explain your reasoning. (Lesson 5-2)

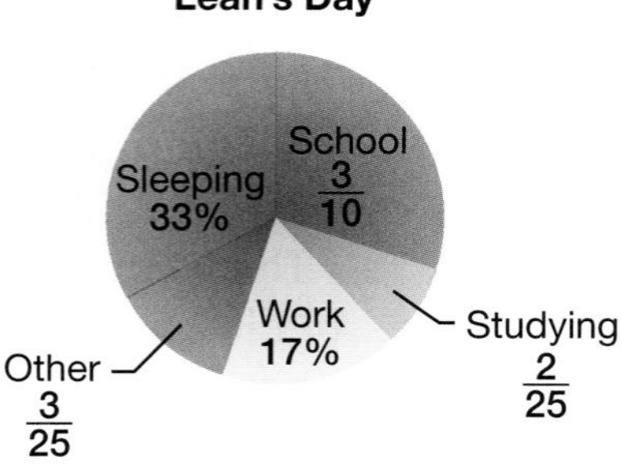

Write a percent proportion to solve each problem. Then solve. Round to the nearest tenth if necessary. (Lesson 5-3)

12. 63 is what percent of 84?
13. Find 41% of 700.
14. 294 is 35% of what number?
15. What number is 134% of 62?

16. **MULTIPLE CHOICE** A study showed that 37.5% of residents in a certain neighborhood use public transportation. If there are 168 residents in the neighborhood, which statement is *not* supported by this study? (Lesson 5-3)
   F More than half the residents do not use public transportation.
   G Less than 62.5% of the residents do not use public transportation.
   H 63 residents use public transportation.
   J Less than $\frac{2}{5}$ of the residents use public transportation.

Compute mentally. (Lesson 5-4)

17. 25% of 64
18. 1% of 58.5
19. $66\frac{2}{3}$% of 45
20. 3% of 600

21. **HOMEWORK** Sean has 192 pages of reading to do in the next three days. He wants to complete $33\frac{1}{3}$% of the reading tonight. Compute mentally how many pages Sean should read tonight. Explain your reasoning. (Lesson 5-4)

22. **FOOD** In one month, the Schaffer family spent \$121.59, \$168.54, \$98.67, and \$141.78 on groceries. If their grocery budget is \$500 per month, did they stay within their budget? Explain. (Lesson 5-5)

5-6 Percent and Estimation

MAIN IDEA

Estimate by using equivalent fractions and percents.

IL Learning Standards

6.C.3b Show evidence that computational results using whole numbers, fractions, decimals, **percents** and proportions **are correct and/or that estimates are reasonable.**

New Vocabulary

compatible numbers

IL Math Online

glencoe.com

- Concepts in Motion
- Extra Examples
- Personal Tutor
- Self-Check Quiz

GET READY for the Lesson

PLANETS The distance from Earth to the Sun is about 19% of the distance from Jupiter to the Sun.

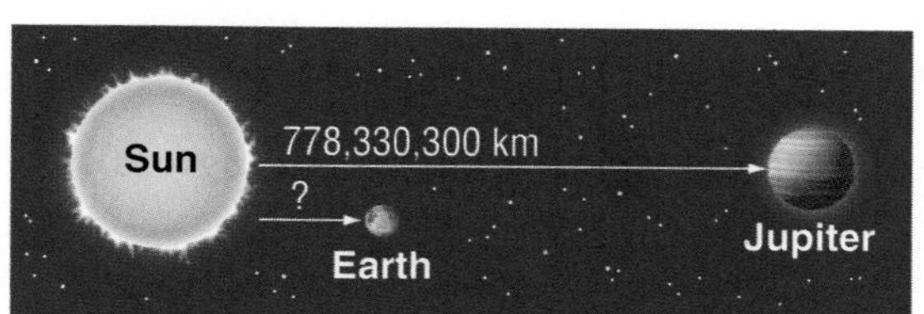

1. Round the distance from Jupiter to the Sun to the nearest hundred million kilometers.
2. Round 19% to the nearest ten percent.
3. Use mental math to estimate the distance from Earth to the Sun.

When an exact answer is not needed, you can estimate a percent of a number by using compatible numbers. **Compatible numbers** are two numbers that are easy to divide mentally.

EXAMPLES Estimate Percents of Numbers

1 **Estimate 19% of 30.**

$19\% \approx 20\%$ or $\frac{1}{5}$. 5 and 30 are compatible numbers.

$\frac{1}{5}$ of 30 is 6. So, 19% of 30 is about 6.

2 **25% of 41**

25% is $\frac{1}{4}$, and 41 is about 40. $\frac{1}{4}$ and 40 are compatible numbers.

$\frac{1}{4}$ of 40 is 10. So, 25% of 41 is about 10.

3 **Estimate 65% of 76.**

$65\% \approx 66\frac{2}{3}\%$ or $\frac{2}{3}$, and 76 is about 75. 3 and 75 are compatible numbers.

$\frac{1}{3}$ of 75 is 25, and $\frac{2}{3}$ of 75 is $2 \cdot 25$ or 50. So, 65% of 76 is about 50.

CHECK Your Progress

Estimate. Justify your answer.

a. 24% of 44 b. 40% of 49 c. 13% of 65

Sometimes estimation provides the best answer to a real-world problem.

4 **LEFT–HANDEDNESS About 11% of the population is left-handed. If there are about 13 million people in Illinois, about how many residents of Illinois are left-handed?**

11% of 13 million ≈ 10% or $\frac{1}{10}$ of 13 million — 11% is about 10%.

= 1.3 million — $\frac{1}{10} \times 13 = 1.3$

So, about 1.3 million residents of Illinois are left-handed.

CHECK Your Progress

d. **MONEY** A circulating $5 bill in the United States lasts about 22% as long as a $100 bill. If a $100 bill lasts nine years, estimate how long a $5 bill lasts.

You can use similar techniques to estimate a percent.

EXAMPLES Estimate Percents

Estimate each percent.

5 **8 out of 25**

$\frac{8}{25} \approx \frac{8}{24}$ or $\frac{1}{3}$ — 25 is close to 24.

$\frac{1}{3} = 33\frac{1}{3}\%$

So, 8 out of 25 is about $33\frac{1}{3}\%$.

> **Study Tip**
> **Estimation**
> When estimating, estimate so that you change the ratio the least.

6 **14 out of 25**

$\frac{14}{25} \approx \frac{15}{25}$ or $\frac{3}{5}$ — 14 is close to 15.

$\frac{3}{5} = 60\%$

So, 14 out of 25 is about 60%.

7 **89 out of 121**

$\frac{89}{121} \approx \frac{90}{120}$ or $\frac{3}{4}$ — 89 is close to 90, and 121 is close to 120.

$\frac{3}{4} = 75\%$

So, 89 out of 121 is about 75%.

CHECK Your Progress

Estimate each percent. Justify your answer.

e. 7 out of 57 f. 9 out of 25 g. 7 out of 79

Examples 1–3 (p. 275)

Estimate.

1. 49% of 160
2. $66\frac{2}{3}$% of 20
3. 73% of 65

Example 4 (p. 276)

4. **SCHOOL** Math is the favorite subject of about 28% of students, according to a recent study. If there are 30 students in your class, estimate the number of students who would pick math as their favorite subject.

Examples 5–7 (p. 276)

Estimate each percent.

5. 6 out of 35
6. 8 out of 79
7. 14 out of 19

Practice and Problem Solving

HOMEWORK HELP

For Exercises	See Examples
8–15	1–3
16–23	5–7
24–25	4

Estimate.

8. 29% of 50
9. 67% of 93
10. 20% of 76
11. 25% of 63
12. 21% of 71
13. 92% of 41
14. 48% of 159
15. 73% of 81

Estimate each percent.

16. 7 out of 29
17. 6 out of 59
18. 2 out of 15
19. 5 out of 36
20. 8 out of 23
21. 7 out of 11
22. 4 out of 21
23. 9 out of 55

24. **MEASUREMENT** The length of an object, in inches, is about 39% of its length in centimeters. Estimate the length, in inches, of an object 50 centimeters long.

25. **SPORTS** A place kicker made 73% of his field goal attempts last season. If he had 46 attempts, estimate the number of field goals that he made.

26. **BASEBALL** Ty Cobb played baseball from 1905 to 1928 and has the highest career batting average of all Major League players. He had 11,434 at bats and 4,189 hits. Estimate what percent of the time he had a hit.

27. **ANALYZE TABLES** Estimate the percent of the population of each state that lives in each city. Then determine which city has the greatest percent of its state's population.

2005 Population

City	City Population	Entire State Population
New York, NY	8,143,197	19,254,630
Los Angeles, CA	3,844,829	36,132,147
Chicago, IL	2,842,518	12,763,371

Source: U.S. Beacon and U.S. Census Bureau

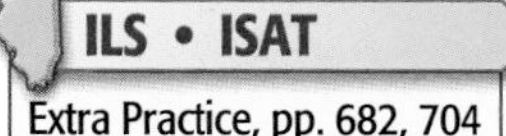

Extra Practice, pp. 682, 704

Estimate.

28. 26.5% of 123
29. 124% of 41
30. 249% of 119

H.O.T. Problems

31. **NUMBER SENSE** Use mental math to determine which is greater: 24% of 480 or 51% of 240. Explain your reasoning.

CHALLENGE Determine whether each statement about estimating percents of numbers is *sometimes, always,* or *never* true. Explain.

32. If both the percent and the number are rounded up, the estimate will be greater than the actual answer.

33. If the percent is rounded up and the number is rounded down, the estimate will be greater than the actual answer.

34. **WRITING IN MATH** Write a real-world problem that you would solve using a fraction and compatible numbers. Then solve the problem.

ISAT PRACTICE 6.C.3b

35. Tay took his father to dinner for his birthday. When the bill came, Tay's father reminded him that it is customary to tip the server 15% of the bill. If the bill was \$19.60 and Tay estimated the tip to be \$3, which of the following shows his method of estimation?

A 15% of \$19.60 ≈ 15% of \$15

B 15% of \$19.60 ≈ 10% of \$20

C 15% of \$19.60 ≈ 20% of \$20

D 15% of \$19.60 ≈ 15% of \$20

36. There are 150 students who participate in athletics at Southland High School. If there are 325 total students, about what part of the student body participates in athletics?

F 40%

G 45%

H 55%

J 60%

Spiral Review

37. **LIFE EXPECTANCY** The average life expectancy in the United States is about 77 years of age. In 1901, the average life expectancy was about 63% of this number. Would 30, 48, or 60 years of age be a reasonable life expectancy for the year 1901? Explain. (Lesson 5-5)

38. **BUSES** Of the 840 students at Moyer Middle School, 75% ride the bus. Use mental math to find the number of students who ride the bus. (Lesson 5-4)

39. **SEATING** A teacher would like to make a square seating chart. If there are 25 students in the class, how many students should be in each row? (Lesson 3-1)

GET READY for the Next Lesson

PREREQUISITE SKILL Solve each equation. (Lesson 2-7)

40. $0.2a = 7$

41. $20s = 8$

42. $0.35t = 140$

43. $30n = 3$

Algebra: The Percent Equation

MAIN IDEA

Solve problems using a percent equation.

IL Learning Standards

8.A.3b Solve problems using linear expressions, **equations** and inequalities.

New Vocabulary

percent equation

IL Math Online

glencoe.com

- Extra Examples
- Personal Tutor
- Self-Check Quiz

GET READY for the Lesson

GEOGRAPHY The approximate area of New York is 55,000 square miles. Of this area, about 13% is water.

Total Area (sq mi)	Percent of Area Occupied by Water
55,000	13%

Source: *New York Times Almanac*

1. Use a percent proportion to find the area of water in New York.
2. Express the percent for New York as a decimal. Multiply the total area of New York by this decimal.
3. How are the answers for Exercises 1 and 2 related?

A **percent equation** is an equivalent form of a percent proportion in which the percent is written as a decimal.

$$\frac{\text{part}}{\text{whole}} = \text{percent}$$ The percent is written as a decimal.

$$\frac{\text{part}}{\text{whole}} \cdot \textbf{whole} = \text{percent} \cdot \textbf{whole}$$ Multiply each side by the whole.

$$\text{part} = \text{percent} \cdot \text{whole}$$ This form is called the percent equation.

EXAMPLE Find the Part

1 Find 6% of 525.

Estimate 1% of 500 is 5. So, 6% of 500 is 6 • 5 or 30.

The percent is 6%. The whole is 525. You need to find the part. Let p represent the part.

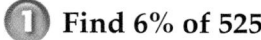

part = percent • whole

$p = 0.06 \cdot 525$ Write the percent equation. Note that the percent has been written as a decimal.

$p = 31.5$ Multiply.

Check for Reasonableness $31.5 \approx 30$ ✓

CHECK Your Progress

Write a percent equation to solve each problem. Then solve. Round to the nearest tenth if necessary.

a. What number is 35% of 88?

b. Find 15% of 275.

In some instances the percent or the whole are unknown. Solve the percent equation for the missing value.

EXAMPLE Find the Percent

2 **420 is what percent of 600?**

Estimate $\frac{420}{600} \approx \frac{400}{600}$ or $66\frac{2}{3}\%$

The part is 420. The whole is 600. You need to find the percent. Let n represent the percent.

$\underbrace{\text{part}} = \underbrace{\text{percent}} \cdot \underbrace{\text{whole}}$

$420 = n \cdot 600$	Write the percent equation.
$\frac{420}{600} = \frac{n \cdot 600}{600}$	Divide each side by 600.
$0.7 = n$	Simplify.

Since $0.7 = 70\%$, 420 is 70% of 600. Note that the answer, a decimal, must be converted to a percent.

Check for Reasonableness $70\% \approx 66\frac{2}{3}\%$ ✓

Study Tip

Decimals and Percents When finding the percent, be sure to place the decimal point correctly when writing your answer.

CHECK Your Progress

Write a percent equation to solve each problem. Then solve. Round to the nearest tenth if necessary.

c. 62 is what percent of 186?

d. What percent of 750 is 6?

EXAMPLE Find the Whole

3 **65 is 52% of what number?**

Estimate 65 is 50% of 130.

The part is 65. The percent is 52%. You need to find the whole. Let w represent the whole.

$\underbrace{\text{part}} = \underbrace{\text{percent}} \cdot \underbrace{\text{whole}}$

$65 = 0.52 \cdot w$	Write the percent equation. Note that the percent has been written as a decimal.
$\frac{65}{0.52} = \frac{0.52w}{0.52}$	Divide each side by 0.52.
$125 = w$	Simplify.

So, 65 is 52% of 125.

Check for Reasonableness $125 \approx 130$ ✓

CHECK Your Progress

Write a percent equation to solve each problem. Then solve. Round to the nearest tenth if necessary.

e. 210 is 75% of what number?

f. 54 is 18% of what number?

The Percent Equation

Concept Summary

Type	Example	Equation
Find the Part	What number is 25% of 60?	$p = 0.25(60)$
Find the Percent	15 is what percent of 60?	$15 = n(60)$
Find the Whole	15 is 25% of what number?	$15 = 0.25w$

Real-World Link State sales tax rates range from 0% in Alaska, Delaware, Montana, New Hampshire, and Oregon, to 7.25% in California.
Source: Federation of Tax Administrators

Real-World EXAMPLE

4 **SCOOTERS** **Margarite's parents are buying her a motor scooter. The scooter costs $244. If a 6% sales tax is added, what is the total cost of the scooter?**

METHOD 1 **Find the amount of tax first.**

The whole is $244. The percent is 6%. You need to find the amount of the tax, or the part. Let t represent the amount of tax.

part = percent • whole

$t = 0.06 \cdot 244$ Write the percent equation, writing 6% as a decimal.

$t = 14.64$ Multiply.

The tax is $14.64. The total cost of the scooter is $244.00 + $14.64 or $258.64.

METHOD 2 **Find the total percent first.**

Find 100% + 6% or 106% of $244 to find the total cost, including tax. Let t represent the total cost.

part = percent • whole

$t = 1.06 \cdot 244$ Write the percent equation, writing 106% as a decimal.

$t = 258.64$ Multiply.

The total cost of the scooter is $258.64.

CHOOSE Your Method

g. **SALES TAX** Zach bought a television that costs $350. Since he lives in Rhode Island, a 7% sales tax was added. What was the total cost of the television?

h. **PAYCHECKS** Paige earned $250 before taxes working at a movie theater. If 23% of her pay is withheld for taxes, how much is her take-home pay?

CHECK Your Understanding

Examples 1–3 (pp. 279–280)

Solve each problem using a percent equation.

1. Find 85% of 920.
2. What number is 4% of 30?
3. 25 is what percent of 625?
4. What percent of 800 is 2?
5. 680 is 34% of what number?
6. 25% of what number is 10?

Example 4 (p. 281)

7. **PROFIT** A dealership sets car prices so that there is a 40% profit. If the dealership paid $5,300 for a car, for how much should they sell the car?

Practice and Problem Solving

HOMEWORK HELP

For Exercises	See Examples
8, 9, 14, 15	1
10, 11, 16, 17	2
12, 13, 18, 19	3
20–23	4

Solve each problem using a percent equation.

8. Find 60% of 30.
9. What is 40% of 90?
10. What percent of 90 is 36?
11. 45 is what percent of 150?
12. 75 is 50% of what number?
13. 15% of what number is 30?
14. What number is 13% of 52?
15. Find 24% of 84.
16. 6 is what percent of 3,000?
17. What percent of 5,000 is 6?
18. 3% of what number is 9?
19. 50 is 10% of what number?
20. **CLOTHING** A jacket costs $75. If a 7.25% sales tax is added, what is the total cost of the jacket?
21. **FUEL MILEAGE** A car can travel 32 miles per gallon of gasoline. When the tires are under-inflated, the car gets 15% fewer miles per gallon. What is the fuel mileage of the car with under-inflated tires?
22. **SNOWBOARDS** Jerome is buying a snowboard on sale. The total cost, including a 7% sales tax, is $256.80. Find the cost of the snowboard before tax.
23. **SPORTS** The University of Maryland won the 2006 Women's NCAA basketball championship. During the regular season, they won 87.5% of their games. If they played 32 games, how many did they win?
24. **FOOTBALL** Which quarterback has the greatest percent of completed passes?

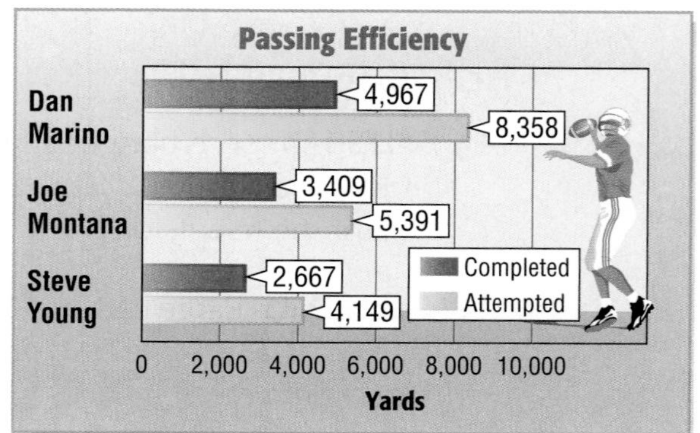

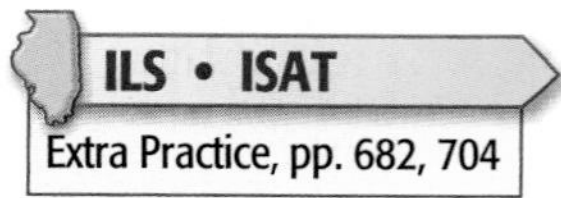

Extra Practice, pp. 682, 704

Solve each problem using a percent equation.

25. Find $6\frac{1}{4}\%$ of 150.

26. 360 is what percent of 270?

H.O.T. Problems

27. **CHALLENGE** Determine whether $a\%$ of b is *sometimes*, *always*, or *never* equal to $b\%$ of a. Explain your reasoning.

28. **CHALLENGE** Mrs. McGary budgeted a certain amount of money for new shoes. Before she could buy them, there was a 20% increase in price. She waited for a month, and the store discounted the shoes 20%. She bought the shoes, thinking that they would cost less than the original price. Was she correct? Explain your reasoning.

29. **WRITING IN MATH** Explain, using an example, how a 5% discount plus 5% sales tax on an item does *not* result in the original price of the item.

ISAT PRACTICE 8.A.3b

30. Mr. Dempsey receives a 7% commission for every appliance he sells. If he sells a refrigerator for $1,299, what is his commission?

    A $9.09 **C** $92.93

    B $90.93 **D** $909.30

31. Shirley purchased an antique dresser for $350. She restored the dresser and sold it for a 50% profit. For how much did Shirley sell the dresser?

    F $175 **H** $525

    G $367.50 **J** $700

Spiral Review

32. **ELECTIONS** Thirteen out of 34 students voted for Emil for Student Council representative. Estimate the percent of voters who voted for Emil. (Lesson 5-5)

Compute mentally. (Lesson 5-4)

33. 20% of $200

34. 62.5% of 96

35. 75% of 84

36. 6% of 150

GEOMETRY Find the distance between each pair of points. Round to the nearest tenth, if necessary. (Lesson 3-7)

37. $S(2, 3), T(0, 6)$

38. $E(-1, 1), F(3, -2)$

39. $W(4, -6), V(-3, -5)$

40. **WEATHER** Ruben read that the low temperature for the day was expected to be −5°F and the high temperature was expected to be 8°F. What was the difference in the expected high and low temperatures? (Lesson 1-5)

ALGEBRA Evaluate each expression if $f = -9$, $g = -6$, and $h = 8$. (Lesson 1-2)

41. $-5fg$

42. $2gh$

43. $-10fh$

GET READY for the Next Lesson

PREREQUISITE SKILL Evaluate each expression. (Lesson 1-3)

44. $|17 - 24|$

45. $|340 - 253|$

46. $|531 - 487|$

47. $|352 - 581|$

5-8 Percent of Change

MAIN IDEA

Find and use the percent of increase or decrease.

IL Learning Standards

6.D.3 Apply ratios and proportions **to solve practical problems.**
8.A.3b Solve problems using linear expressions, **equations** and inequalities.

New Vocabulary

percent of change
percent of increase
percent of decrease
markup
selling price
discount

IL Math Online

glencoe.com

- Extra Examples
- Personal Tutor
- Self-Check Quiz

GET READY for the Lesson

STAMPS Over the years, the price of stamps has increased. Refer to the table below that shows the change in stamp prices from 1963 to 1981.

Price of a Stamp	
Effective Date	**Price for the First Ounce (¢)**
January 7, 1963	5
March 2, 1974	10
May 29, 1978	15
November 1, 1981	20

1. How much did the price increase from 1963 to 1974?
2. Write the ratio $\frac{\text{amount of increase}}{\text{price in 1963}}$. Then write the ratio as a percent.
3. How much did the price increase from 1974 to 1978? Write the ratio $\frac{\text{amount of increase}}{\text{price in 1974}}$. Then write the ratio as a percent.
4. How much did the price increase from 1978 to 1981? Write the ratio $\frac{\text{amount of increase}}{\text{price in 1978}}$. Then write the ratio as a percent.
5. **MAKE A CONJECTURE** Why are the amounts of increase the same but the percents different?

The percent that an amount changes from its original amount is called the **percent of change**.

Percent of Change — Key Concept

Words A percent of change is a ratio that compares the change in quantity to the original amount.

Symbols $\text{percent of change} = \frac{\text{amount of change}}{\text{original amount}}$

To find the percent of change, do the following:

Step 1 Subtract to find the amount of change.

Step 2 Write the ratio $\frac{\text{amount of change}}{\text{original amount}}$ as a decimal.

Step 3 Write the decimal as a percent.

When the new amount is greater than the original, the percent of change is a **percent of increase**. When the new amount is less than the original, the percent of change is called a **percent of decrease**.

Study Tip

Percent of Change When finding percent of change, always use the original amount as the whole.

Real-World EXAMPLES Find Percent of Change

1 YEARBOOKS Last year the Yearbook Club at Wesley Middle School sold 174 yearbooks. This year they sold 200 yearbooks. Find the percent of change. Round to the nearest tenth if necessary. State whether the change is an *increase* or *decrease*.

Step 1 The amount of change is 200 − 174 or 26.

Step 2

$\text{percent of change} = \dfrac{\text{amount of change}}{\text{original amount}}$	Definition of percent of change
$= \dfrac{26}{174}$	The amount of change is 26. The original amount is 174.
≈ 0.1494252	Divide. Use a calculator.

Step 3 The decimal 0.1494252 written as a percent is 14.94252%. To the nearest tenth, the percent of change is 14.9%.

Since the new number of yearbooks is greater than the original, it is a percent of increase.

Real-World Link The National Oceanic and Atmospheric Administration or NOAA is the government agency responsible for monitoring the weather in the United States. The agency is able to monitor storms such as hurricanes from the sky.

2 WEATHER On average, Kentucky has 45 inches of rainfall per year, but in 2006, it had almost 54 inches. Find the percent of change. State whether the change is an *increase* or *decrease*.

Step 1 The amount of change is 54 − 45 or 9.

Step 2

$\text{percent of change} = \dfrac{\text{amount of change}}{\text{original amount}}$	Definition of percent of change
$= \dfrac{9}{45}$	The amount of change is 9. The original amount is 45.
$= 0.20$	Divide.

Step 3 The decimal 0.20 written as a percent is 20%. So, the percent of change is 20%.

The new amount is greater than the original. It is a percent of increase.

CHECK Your Progress

Find each percent of change. Round to the nearest tenth if necessary. State whether the percent of change is an *increase* or a *decrease*.

a. original: 6 hours
new: 10 hours

b. original: 80 water bottles
new: 55 water bottles

c. original: 15 meters
new: 6 meters

d. original: 1.25 hours
new: 3.5 hours

A store sells an item for more than it paid for that item. The extra money is used to cover the expenses and to make a profit. The increase in the price is called the **markup**. The percent of markup is a percent of increase. The amount the customer pays is called the **selling price**.

EXAMPLE Find the Selling Price

3 **BUSINESS A bead store buys beads at wholesale prices and then prices them to sell at a 75% markup. If a strand of beads costs the store $9.14, what is the selling price for the strand?**

Study Tip

Check for Reasonableness To estimate the selling price, think 75% of 9.14 is about $\frac{3}{4}$ of 10 or 7.50. The selling price should be about \$9 + \$7.50, or \$16.50.

METHOD 1 **Find the amount of the markup first.**

The whole is \$9.14. The percent is 75%. You need to find the amount of the markup, or the part. Let m represent the amount of the markup.

part = percent • whole

$m = 0.75 \cdot 9.14$ Write the percent equation.

$m \approx 6.86$ Multiply.

Add the markup \$6.86 to the store's cost \$9.14 to find the selling price. \$9.14 + \$6.86 = \$16.00

METHOD 2 **Find the total percent first.**

The customer will pay 100% of the store's cost plus an extra 75% of the cost. Find 100% + 75% or 175% of the store's cost. Let p represent the price.

part = percent • whole

$p = 1.75 \cdot 9.14$ Write the percent equation.

$p \approx 16.00$ Multiply.

The selling price of the beads is \$16.00.

CHOOSE Your Method

Find the selling price for each item given the percent of markup.

e. digital camera: \$120, 55% markup

f. sunglasses: \$7, 30% markup

g. **SHIPPING** Cheng-Yu ordered a book that cost \$24 from an online store. Her total with the shipping charge was \$27. What was the percent of markup charged for shipping?

The amount by which a regular price is reduced is called the **discount**. The percent of change is a percent of decrease.

Real-World Link . . . .
How Does a Music Producer Use Math?
Music producers are responsible for planning and organizing the budget for recordings. They also use statistics to help predict songs that will be hits.

IL Math Online

For more information, go to glencoe.com.

EXAMPLE Find the Sale Price

4 **MUSIC The CD Discount Superstore is advertising a 20% off sale. Jonas wants to buy a CD that originally costs $18.50. Find the sale price of the CD.**

METHOD 1 Find the amount of the discount first.

The percent is 20%, and the whole is 18.50. We need to find the amount of the discount, or the part. Let d represent the amount of discount.

part = percent • whole

$d = 0.20 \cdot 18.50$ Write the percent equation.

$d = 3.70$ Multiply.

Subtract the amount of the discount from the original price to find the sale price. $18.50 – $3.70 = $14.80.

METHOD 2 Find the percent paid first.

If the amount of the discount is 20%, the percent paid is 100% – 20% or 80%. Find 80% of $18.50. Let s represent the sale price.

part = percent • whole

$s = 0.80 \cdot 18.50$ Write the percent equation.

$s = 14.80$ Multiply.

The sale price of the CD is $14.80.

CHOOSE Your Method

Find the sale price of each item to the nearest cent.

h. CD: $14.50, 10% off **i.** sweater: $39.95, 25% off

CHECK Your Understanding

Examples 1, 2 (p. 285)

Find each percent of change. Round to the nearest tenth if necessary. State whether the percent of change is an *increase* or a *decrease*.

1. original: $40 new: $32

2. original: 25 CDs new: 32 CDs

3. original: 325 miles new: 400 miles

Example 3 (p. 286)

Find the selling price for each item given the percent of markup.

4. roller blades: $60, 35% markup

5. coat: $87, 33% markup

Example 4 (p. 287)

6. **BICYCLES** Find the sale price of a bicycle that is regularly $140 and is on sale for 40% off the original price.

Practice and Problem Solving

HOMEWORK HELP	
For Exercises	**See Examples**
7–14	1, 2
15–18	3
19–22	4

Find each percent of change. Round to the nearest tenth if necessary. State whether the percent of change is an *increase* or a *decrease*.

7. original: 6 tickets
new: 9 tickets

8. original: 27 guests
new: 39 guests

9. original: $80
new: $64

10. original: $560
new: $420

11. original: 68°F
new: 51°F

12. original: 150 e-mails
new: 98 e-mails

13. **TELEVISION** On Tuesday night, 17.8 million households watched a popular television show. On Wednesday night, 16.6 million households watched the same show. Find the percent of decrease in the number of households watching the show from Tuesday to Wednesday.

14. **STOCK** Patrice invested $300 into a particular stock. The amount doubled within a few weeks. Find the percent of increase.

Find the selling price for each item given the cost to the store and the markup.

15. computer: $700, 30% markup
16. CD player: $120, 20% markup
17. jeans: $25, 45% markup
18. baseball cap: $12, 48% markup

Find the sale price of each item to the nearest cent.

19. video game: $75, 25% off
20. trampoline: $399, 15% off
21. skateboard: $119.95, 30% off
22. earrings: $19.50, 35% off

23. **INTERNET** An Internet service provider offers connection speed that is 35% faster than dial-up. If it takes Brad 8 seconds to connect to the Internet using dial-up, how long would it take using this provider?

24. **ADVERTISING** A box of cereal advertised that the new box contained 30% more cereal than the previous box. If the new box contains 26 ounces of cereal, how many ounces of cereal were in the previous box?

25. **FIND THE DATA** Refer to the Data File on pages 16–19. Choose some data and write a real-world problem in which you would need to find the percent of change.

26. **GASOLINE** The table gives the average price of gasoline in the United States at the end of April for several years. What was the greatest percent of increase? During which year(s) did it occur?

Price of a Gallon of Gasoline

Year	Price ($)
2004	1.77
2005	2.19
2006	2.88
2007	2.92

Source: Energy Information Administration

27. **ALGEBRA** Students receive a 20% discount off the price of an adult ticket at the theater. If a student ticket is $6.80, find the price of an adult ticket. (*Hint*: Let p represent the part and $p + 6.80$ represent the whole.)

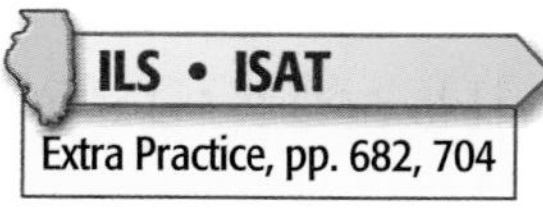

Extra Practice, pp. 682, 704

H.O.T. Problems

28. **CHALLENGE** Jordyn purchased a sweater which originally cost $\$x$. The sale price was 20% off the retail, and she had a coupon which took an additional 15% off the sale price. Sales tax of 6.5% was added to the cost at the end. Write the final cost of the sweater in terms of x.

29. **FIND THE ERROR** Chris and Samuel are solving the following problem: *The price of a school play ticket rose from $5.75 to $6.25. What is the percent of increase for the price of a ticket?* Who is correct? Explain your reasoning.

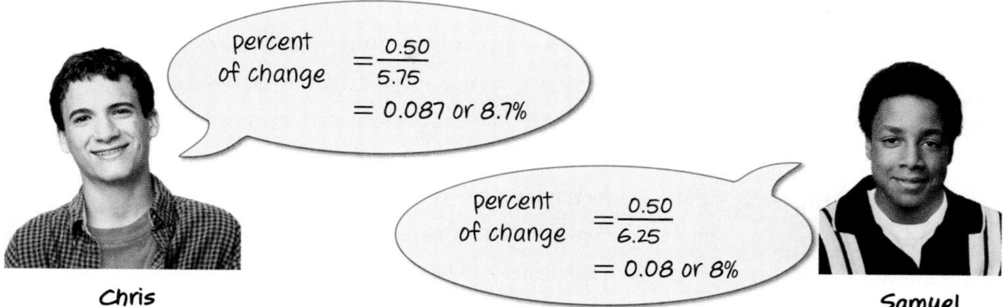

30. **WRITING IN MATH** Write and solve a real-world problem involving a 25% increase or decrease in some quantity.

ISAT PRACTICE 6.D.3, 8.A.3b

31. A television originally cost $1,250. Samuel bought it at 30% off. How much was deducted from the original amount?

    A $875

    B $675

    C $425

    D $375

32. Grace and her two brothers shared the cost of a new video game system equally. The original price of the system was $179. They received a 15% discount off the original price and paid 7.5% sales tax on the discounted price. Find the approximate amount that each paid for the video game system.

    F $51 **H** $60

    G $55 **J** $66

Spiral Review

33. **PETS** About 16% of all dogs and cats that are pets were adopted from an animal shelter. If a community has licensed 245 dogs and cats as pets, about how many came from a shelter? (Lesson 5-7)

Estimate. (Lesson 5-6)

34. 21% of 60
35. 25% of 83
36. 12% of 31
37. 34% of 95

Express each rate as a unit rate. (Lesson 4-1)

38. $36 in 3 hours
39. 1.5 inches of rain in 5 months

GET READY for the Next Lesson

PREREQUISITE SKILL **Solve each equation.** (Lesson 2-7)

40. $45 = 300 \cdot a \cdot 3$
41. $24 = 200 \cdot 0.04 \cdot y$
42. $21 = 60 \cdot m \cdot 5$

5-9 Simple Interest

MAIN IDEA

Solve problems involving simple interest.

IL Learning Standards

8.A.3b Solve problems using linear expressions, **equations** and inequalities.

New Vocabulary

interest
principal

IL Math Online

glencoe.com

- Extra Examples
- Personal Tutor
- Self-Check Quiz

GET READY for the Lesson

CARS Have you ever dreamed of buying your first car? Suppose you want to buy a used car that costs \$4,000. You can pay \$400 now and borrow the remaining \$3,600. To pay off the loan, you will pay \$131.50 each month for the next 36 months.

1. How much money will you pay in all for the car?
2. How much will it cost you to borrow the money for the car?

Interest is the amount of money paid or earned for the use of money. For a savings account, you earn interest from the bank. For a credit card or a loan, you pay interest to the bank. To solve problems involving simple interest, use the following formula.

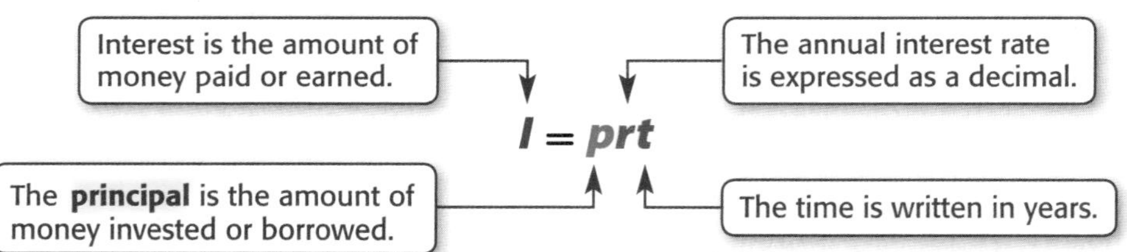

Interest is the amount of money paid or earned.
The annual interest rate is expressed as a decimal.
I = prt
The principal is the amount of money invested or borrowed.
The time is written in years.

EXAMPLE Find Simple Interest

1 Find the simple interest for \$500 invested in a savings account at 3.25% for 3 years.

$I = prt$ Write the simple interest formula.

$I = 500 \cdot 0.0325 \cdot 3$ Replace p with 500, r with 0.0325, and t with 3.

$I = 48.75$

The simple interest is \$48.75.

CHECK Your Progress **Find the simple interest to the nearest cent.**

a. \$400 at 3.67% for 2 years

b. \$770 at 16% for 6 months

ISAT EXAMPLE Find the Total Amount 8.A.3b

2 **What is the total amount of money owed on a credit card with a balance of $1,500 at a simple interest rate of 22% after 1 month?**

A $1,502.75 **B** $1,527.50 **C** $1,533 **D** $1,830

Test-Taking Tip

Converting Units When using the formula $I = prt$, remember that time is in years. One month is $\frac{1}{12}$ year.

Read the Item

You need to find the total amount in an account.

Solve the Item

$I = prt$	Simple interest formula
$I = 1{,}500 \cdot 0.22 \cdot \frac{1}{12}$	$p = 1{,}500$, $r = 0.22$, $t = \frac{1}{12}$
$I = 27.5$	Simplify.

The amount of money owed is 1,500 + 27.50 or $1,527.50. The answer is B.

CHECK Your Progress

c. What is the total amount of money in dollars in an account where $95 is invested at a simple interest rate of 7.5% for 8 months?

F $152.50 **G** $152 **H** $142.50 **J** $99.75

Real-World Link The average cost of one year at a public university is over $11,000. Financial aid such as scholarships, grants, loans, and work study can help students pay for this.

Real-World EXAMPLE Find the Interest Rate

3 **STUDENT LOANS José's brother, Luis, makes monthly payments of $290.28 on his student loan of $5,000. He will pay off his loan in $1\frac{1}{2}$ years. Find the simple interest rate of his loan.**

First find the total that Luis will pay.

$290.28 · 18 = $5,225.04 $1\frac{1}{2}$ years = 18 months

He will pay $5,225.04 − $5,000 or $225.04 in interest. So, $I = 225.04$.

The principal is $5,000. So, $p = 5{,}000$.

The loan will be for $1\frac{1}{2}$ or 1.5 years. So, $t = 1.5$.

$I = prt$	Write the simple interest formula.
$225.04 = 5{,}000 \cdot r \cdot 1.5$	Replace I with 225.04, p with 5,000, and t with 1.5.
$225.04 = 7{,}500r$	Simplify.
$\frac{225.04}{7{,}500} = \frac{7{,}500r}{7{,}500}$	Divide each side by 7,500.
$0.03 = r$	

The simple interest rate is 0.03 or 3%.

CHECK Your Progress

d. **SAVINGS BOND** Louie purchased a $200 savings bond. After 5 years, it is worth $232.50. Find the simple interest rate for his bond.

CHECK Your Understanding

Example 1 (p. 290)

Find the simple interest to the nearest cent.

1. \$300 at 7.5% for 5 years
2. \$230 at 12% for 8 months

Example 2 (p. 291)

Find the total amount in each account to the nearest cent.

3. \$660 at 5.25% for 2 years
4. \$385 at 12.6% for 9 months
5. **MULTIPLE CHOICE** Nina invested \$100 in a savings account for 4 years. Find the total amount in her account if it earns a simple interest of 2.75%.

   A \$109 **B** \$110 **C** \$111 **D** \$112

Example 3 (p. 291)

6. **CAR SALES** Keisha borrowed \$4,000 to buy a car. If her monthly payments are \$184.17 for 2 years, what is the simple interest rate for her loan?

Practice and Problem Solving

HOMEWORK HELP

For Exercises	See Examples
7–10	1
11–14	2
15, 16	3

Find the simple interest to the nearest cent.

7. \$250 at 6% for 3 years
8. \$725 at 4.5% for 4 years
9. \$834 at 7.25% for 2 months
10. \$3,070 at 8.65% for 24 months

Find the total amount in each account to the nearest cent.

11. \$2,250 at 5% for 3 years
12. \$5,060 at 7.2% for 5 years
13. \$575 at 4.25% for 6 months
14. \$950 at 7.85% for 10 months
15. **BASEBALL CARDS** The prices for a vintage baseball card are given at the right. Determine the simple interest rate for a card purchased as an investment in 1968 and sold in 2006.

Year	Price for Baseball Card
1968	\$18.00
2006	\$325.80

16. **SAVINGS** Colin is borrowing money from his parents to purchase a \$700 computer. He will pay them \$35 per month for two years. Determine the simple interest rate on Colin's loan.
17. **CARS** Felicia took out a 5-year loan for \$15,000 to buy a car. If the simple interest rate was 11%, how much total will she pay including interest?

Find the simple interest to the nearest cent.

18. \$1,000 at $7\frac{1}{2}$% for 30 months
19. \$5,200 at $13\frac{1}{5}$% for $1\frac{1}{2}$ years
20. **CREDIT CARDS** The balance on a credit card was \$500. Mr. Cook paid the minimum monthly payment of \$25. The remaining balance was charged a simple interest rate of 18%. If no additional purchases were made, what was the balance the next month?
21. **HOUSING** The Turners need to borrow \$100,000 to purchase a home. The credit union is offering a 30-year mortgage loan at 5.38% interest while the community bank has a 25-year mortgage loan at 6.12% interest. Assuming simple interest, which loan will result in less total interest?

ILS • ISAT

Extra Practice, pp. 683, 704

H.O.T. Problems

22. **CHALLENGE** What will be the monthly payments on a loan of $25,000 at 9% simple interest so that it will be paid off in 15 years? How much will the total interest be?

23. **OPEN ENDED** Give a principal and interest rate where the amount of simple interest earned in 6 months is more than $100.

24. **WRITING IN MATH** If you have money in a savings account for 8 months, what value for t would you use to find the interest you have earned? Explain.

ISAT PRACTICE 8.A.3b

25. Mr. and Mrs. Owens placed $1,500 in a college savings account with a simple interest rate of 4% when Lauren was born. How much will be in the account in 18 years when Lauren is ready to go to college? Assume no more deposits or withdrawals were made.

A $1,080

B $2,580

C $10,800

D $12,300

26. Dave borrowed $4,000 at 9% simple interest for one year. He made no payments during that year. How much interest is owed at the end of the year?

F $90

G $180

H $270

J $360

Spiral Review

27. **SALES** What is the sale price of a $200 cell phone on sale at 10% off the regular price? (Lesson 5-8)

Solve each problem using a percent equation. (Lesson 5-7)

28. What percent of 70 is 17.5?

29. 18 is 30% of what number?

30. **HEALTH** Shashawn's heart beats 18 times in 15 seconds. Write and solve a proportion to determine how many times her heart beats in 1 minute or 60 seconds. (Lesson 4-5)

31. Express 0.000084 in scientific notation. (Lesson 2-10)

Problem Solving in Language Arts

Real-World Unit Project

Are We Similar? It's time to complete your project. Use the information you have gathered about similarity and your profession to prepare a poster. Be sure to include diagrams and calculations with your project.

IL Math Online **Unit Project at** glencoe.com

Extend 5-9

Spreadsheet Lab
Compound Interest

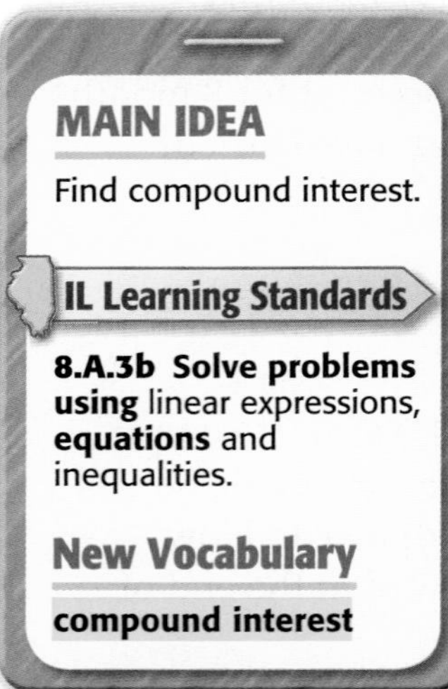
MAIN IDEA
Find compound interest.
IL Learning Standards
8.A.3b Solve problems using linear expressions, **equations** and inequalities.
New Vocabulary
compound interest

Simple interest, which you studied in Lesson 5-9, is paid only on the initial principal of a savings account or a loan. **Compound interest** is paid on the initial principal and on interest earned in the past. You can use a spreadsheet to investigate the growth of compound interest.

ACTIVITY

SAVINGS Find the value of a $2,000 savings account after four years if the account pays 8% interest compounded semiannually.

8% interest compounded semiannually means that the interest is paid twice a year. The interest rate is 8% ÷ 2 or 4% for each 6 months.

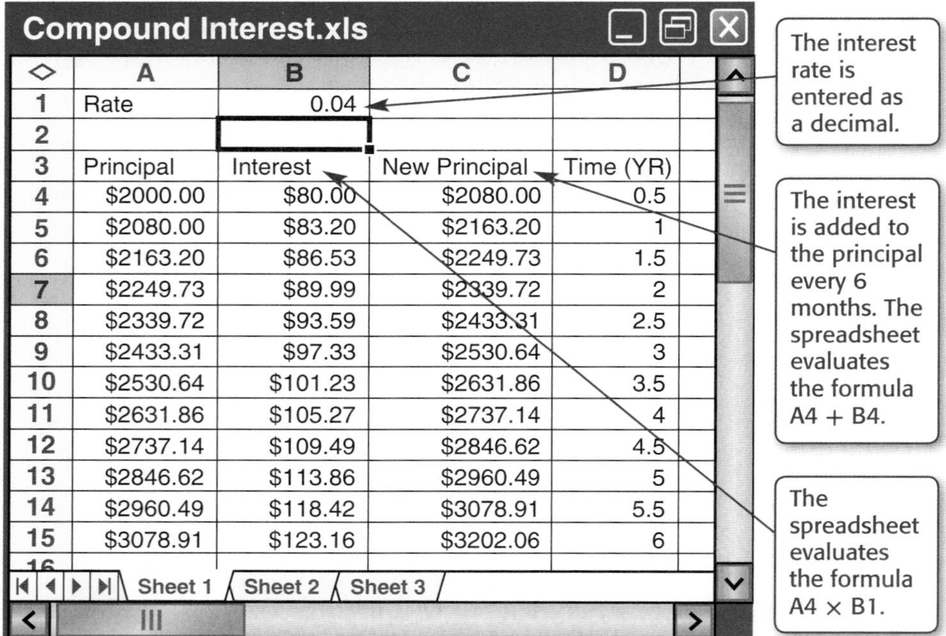
Compound Interest.xls

	A	B	C	D
1	Rate	0.04		
2				
3	Principal	Interest	New Principal	Time (YR)
4	$2000.00	$80.00	$2080.00	0.5
5	$2080.00	$83.20	$2163.20	1
6	$2163.20	$86.53	$2249.73	1.5
7	$2249.73	$89.99	$2339.72	2
8	$2339.72	$93.59	$2433.31	2.5
9	$2433.31	$97.33	$2530.64	3
10	$2530.64	$101.23	$2631.86	3.5
11	$2631.86	$105.27	$2737.14	4
12	$2737.14	$109.49	$2846.62	4.5
13	$2846.62	$113.86	$2960.49	5
14	$2960.49	$118.42	$3078.91	5.5
15	$3078.91	$123.16	$3202.06	6

Sheet 1
Sheet 2
Sheet 3
The interest rate is entered as a decimal.
The interest is added to the principal every 6 months. The spreadsheet evaluates the formula A4 + B4.
The spreadsheet evaluates the formula A4 × B1.

The value of the savings account after four years is $2,737.14.

EXERCISES

1. Use a spreadsheet to find the value of a savings account if $2,000 is invested for four years at 8% interest compounded quarterly.
2. Suppose you leave $1,000 in each of three bank accounts paying 6% interest per year. One account pays simple interest, one pays interest compounded semiannually, and one pays interest compounded quarterly. Use a spreadsheet to find the amount of money in each account after three years.
3. **MAKE A CONJECTURE** How does the amount of interest change if the compounding occurs more frequently? Explain your reasoning.

CHAPTER 5 Study Guide and Review

IL Math Online glencoe.com
- STUDY TO GO
- Vocabulary Review

FOLDABLES Study Organizer — GET READY to Study

Be sure the following Big Ideas are noted in your Foldable.

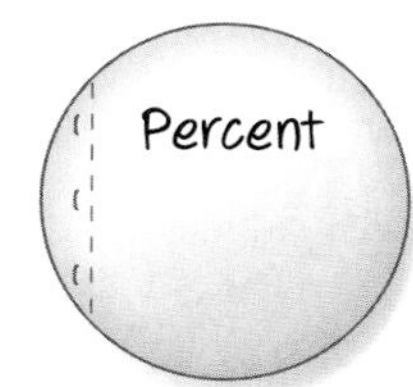

BIG Ideas

Percent (Lessons 5-1 and 5-2)
- A percent is a ratio that compares a number to 100.
- To write a percent as a decimal, divide by 100 and remove the percent symbol.
- To write a decimal as a percent, multiply by 100 and add the percent symbol.

Percent Proportion (Lesson 5-3)
- A percent proportion is $\frac{\text{part}}{\text{whole}}$ = percent, where the percent is written as a fraction.

Percent–Fraction Equivalents			
$25\% = \frac{1}{4}$	$50\% = \frac{1}{2}$	$75\% = \frac{3}{4}$	$100\% = 1$
$20\% = \frac{1}{5}$	$40\% = \frac{2}{5}$	$60\% = \frac{3}{5}$	$80\% = \frac{4}{5}$
$16\frac{2}{3}\% = \frac{1}{6}$	$33\frac{1}{3}\% = \frac{1}{3}$	$66\frac{2}{3}\% = \frac{2}{3}$	$83\frac{1}{3}\% = \frac{5}{6}$
$12\frac{1}{2}\% = \frac{1}{8}$	$37\frac{1}{2}\% = \frac{3}{8}$	$62\frac{1}{2}\% = \frac{5}{8}$	$87\frac{1}{2}\% = \frac{7}{8}$
$10\% = \frac{1}{10}$	$30\% = \frac{3}{10}$	$70\% = \frac{7}{10}$	$90\% = \frac{9}{10}$

Percent Equation (Lesson 5-7)
- A percent equation is part = percent • whole, where the percent is written as a decimal.

Percent of Change (Lesson 5-8)
- A percent of change is a ratio that compares the change in quantity to the original amount.

Key Vocabulary

compatible numbers (p. 275)
compound interest (p. 294)
discount (p. 286)
interest (p. 290)
markup (p. 286)
percent (p. 252)
percent of change (p. 284)
percent of decrease (p. 285)
percent equation (p. 279)
percent of increase (p. 285)
percent proportion (p. 263)
principal (p. 290)
selling price (p. 286)

Vocabulary Check

Choose the correct term or numbers to complete each sentence.

1. A (proportion, percent) is a ratio that compares a number to 100.
2. (Percents, Compatible numbers) are numbers that are easy to divide mentally.
3. A (markup, discount) is an increase in price.
4. 25% of 16 is (4, 40).
5. The (interest, principal) is the amount borrowed.
6. In the proportion $\frac{6}{5} = \frac{120}{100}$, the (part, whole) is 6.
7. A (markup, discount) is a decrease in price.
8. The interest formula is ($I = prt$, $p = Irt$).
9. The number 0.015 written as a percent is (0.15%, 1.5%).
10. The (interest, principal) is the money paid for the use of money.

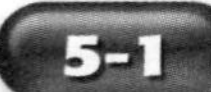

Chapter 5 Study Guide and Review

Lesson-by-Lesson Review

5-1 Ratios and Percents (pp. 252–255)

6.A.3, 6.D.3

Write each ratio or fraction as a percent.

11. $\frac{4}{5}$
12. 16.5 out of 100
13. **WEATHER** There is a 1 in 5 chance of rain tomorrow. Write this as a percent.

Write each percent as a fraction in simplest form.

14. 90%
15. 120%

Example 1 Write $\frac{1}{4}$ as a percent.

$\frac{1}{4} = \frac{25}{100}$ (× 25) So, $\frac{1}{4} = 25\%$.

Example 2 Write 35% as a fraction in simplest form.

$35\% = \frac{35}{100}$ or $\frac{7}{20}$

5-2 Comparing Fractions, Decimals, and Percents (pp. 256–261)

6.A.3

Write each percent as a decimal.

16. 4.3%
17. 147%
18. 0.7%

Write each decimal as a percent.

19. 0.7
20. 0.015
21. 2.55

Write each fraction as a percent.

22. $\frac{3}{40}$
23. $\frac{24}{25}$
24. $\frac{1}{6}$
25. **CELL PHONES** Adam used $\frac{7}{8}$ of his total monthly minutes while Andrea used 88%. Which friend used the greater part of his or her minutes?

Example 3 Write 24% as a decimal.

$24\% = 24\%$ Divide by 100 and remove
$= 0.24$ the percent symbol.

Example 4 Write 0.04 as a percent.

$0.04 = 0.04$ Multiply by 100 and add the
$= 4\%$ percent symbol.

Example 5 Write $\frac{9}{25}$ as a percent.

$\frac{9}{25} = 0.36$ Write as a decimal.
$= 36\%$ Change the decimal to percent.

5-3 Algebra: The Percent Proportion (pp. 263–267)

6.A.3, 6.D.3

Write a percent proportion and solve each problem. Round to the nearest tenth if necessary.

26. 15 is 30% of what number?
27. Find 45% of 18.
28. 75 is what percent of 250?
29. **SPORTS** Inali made about 81% of his free throws in the game. If he made 13 free throws, how many attempts did he make?

Example 6 18 is what percent of 27?

The whole is 27, and the part is 18. Let n represent the percent.

$\frac{18}{27} = \frac{n}{100}$ Percent proportion
$18 \cdot 100 = 27 \cdot n$ Find the cross products.
$1,800 = 27n$ Multiply.
$\frac{1,800}{27} = \frac{27n}{27}$ Divide each side by 27.
$66.7 \approx n$ Simplify.

So, 18 is 66.7% of 27.

Mixed Problem Solving
For mixed problem-solving practice, see page 704.

5-4 Finding Percents Mentally (pp. 268–271)

6.C.3b

Compute mentally.

30. 90% of 100
31. 10% of 18.3
32. $66\frac{2}{3}$% of 24
33. 6% of 200
34. **ANIMALS** Compute mentally the number of hours a day a Koala bear sleeps if it spends $83\frac{1}{3}$% of a day asleep.

Example 7 **Compute 50% of 42 mentally.**

50% of 42 = $\frac{1}{2}$ of 42 or 21   50% = $\frac{1}{2}$

5-5 PSI: Reasonable Answers (pp. 272–273)

6.C.3b

Determine a reasonable answer.

35. **ECOLOGY** In a survey of 1,413 consumers, 6% said they would be willing to pay more for recycled products in order to protect the environment. Is 8.4, 84, or 841 a reasonable estimate for the number of consumers willing to pay more? Explain.
36. **PIZZA** Twelve friends share three large pizzas. If they split the cost evenly among themselves, and each pizza cost $11.95, will each person pay about $2, $3, or $4? Explain.

Example 8 **Philip's flight departed at 9:10 A.M. and arrived at 3:15 P.M., Eastern Standard Time. While in flight, Philip checked his watch and estimated that he had completed about 63% of the trip. Is 11 A.M., 12 P.M., or 1 P.M. a reasonable estimate for the time that Philip checked his watch?**

The total duration of the trip is 365 minutes, or 6 hours and 5 minutes. One half, or 50%, of the trip would be 3 hours and $2\frac{1}{2}$ minutes after departure, or about 12:12 P.M. Since 63% is greater than 50%, 1 P.M. is the only reasonable answer.

5-6 Percent and Estimation (pp. 275–278)

6.C.3b

Estimate.

37. 67% of 60
38. 41% of 39

Estimate each percent.

39. 33 out of 98
40. 19 out of 52
41. **MEASUREMENT** The average temperature of Earth is about 8% of Venus' average temperature of 850°F. Estimate Earth's average temperature.

Example 9 **Estimate 8% of 104.**

104 is about 100.
8% of 100 is 8.
So, 8% of 104 is about 8.

CHAPTER 5 Study Guide and Review

5-7 Alegebra: The Percent Equation (pp. 279–283)

Solve each problem using the percent equation.

8.A.3b

42. 4,620 is 66% of what number?
43. Find 15% of 82.
44. 25 is what percent of 125?
45. **MOVIES** India makes about 1,000 movies yearly. If the U.S. averages 63.3% of this amount, how many movies does the U.S. make yearly?

Example 10 **70 is 25% of what number?**

The part is 70, and the percent is 25. You need to find the whole. Let n represent the whole.

$70 = 0.25n$	Write the percent equation.
$\frac{70}{0.25} = \frac{0.25n}{0.25}$	Divide each side by 0.25.
$280 = n$	Simplify.

So, 70 is 25% of 280.

5-8 Percent of Change (pp. 284–289)

Find each percent of change. Round to the nearest tenth if necessary. State whether the percent of change is an *increase* or a *decrease*.

6.D.3, 8.A.3b

46. original: 10
new: 15
47. original: 8
new: 10
48. original: 37.5
new: 30
49. original: 18
new: 12
50. **ANIMALS** At birth, a giraffe was 62 inches tall and grew at the highly unusual rate of 0.5 inch per hour. By what percent did the height of the giraffe increase in the first 24 hours?

Example 11 **Find the percent of change if the original amount is 900 and the new amount is 725. Round to the nearest tenth. State whether the change is an *increase* or *decrease*.**

The amount of change is 900 − 725 or 175.

$$\text{percent of change} = \frac{\text{amount of change}}{\text{original amount}}$$
$$= \frac{175}{900}$$
$$\approx 0.194 \text{ or } 19.4\%$$

Since the new amount is less than the original, it is a percent of decrease.

5-9 Simple Interest (pp. 290–293)

Find the simple interest to the nearest cent.

8.A.3b

51. $100 at 8.5% for 2 years
52. $350 at 5% for 3 years
53. $260 at 17.5% for 18 months
54. **RETIREMENT** At age 20, Mark invested $500 into a retirement account with a simple interest rate of 6.5%. He makes no more deposits or withdrawals. Find the account value at age 65.

Example 12 **Find the simple interest for $250 invested at 5.5% for 2 years.**

$I = prt$	Simple interest formula
$I = 250 \cdot 0.055 \cdot 2$	Write 5.5% as 0.055.
$I = 27.50$	Simplify.

The simple interest is $27.50.

CHAPTER 5 Practice Test

IL Math Online glencoe.com
• Chapter Test

Write each ratio or fraction as a decimal and as a percent.

1. 74 per 100 2. 3:50 3. $\frac{4}{22}$

4. **FIELD TRIPS** Seventeen students brought their permission slips to go to the zoo. If there are 18 students in the class, what percent of the class brought their permission slip? Round to the nearest tenth.

Express each percent as a decimal.

5. 135% 6. 14.6% 7. 0.97%

8. Order the set of numbers 38%, $\frac{3}{8}$, and 0.038 from least to greatest.

Compute mentally.

9. 30% of 60 10. 1% of 99

11. $33\frac{1}{3}$% of 90 12. $62\frac{1}{2}$% of 48

13. **MULTIPLE CHOICE** The figure below shows 8 shaded isosceles triangles formed by the diagonals of three adjacent squares.

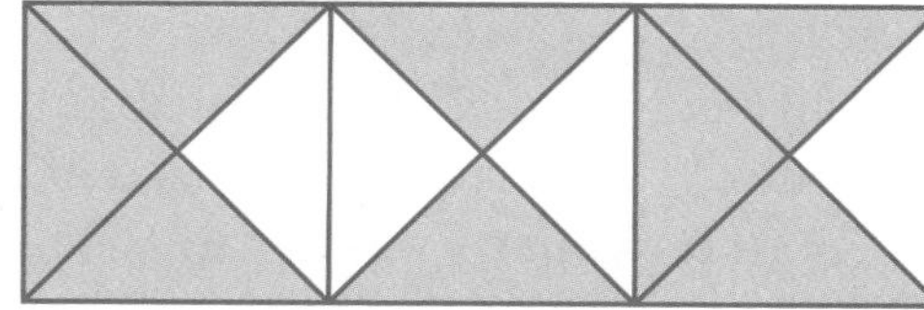

If the total area of the figure is 12 square feet, which statement is true?

A The shaded area is more than 75% of the area of the figure.
B The unshaded area is $\frac{2}{3}$ of the area of the figure.
C The shaded area is 6 square feet.
D The unshaded area is 4 square feet.

Estimate.

14. 23% of 16 15. 9% of 81

16. **TAXES** Sandra estimated that about 35% of her $420 paycheck was deducted for taxes and insurance. Did about $100, $150, or $200 get deducted from her pay?

Write a percent proportion and solve each problem. Round to the nearest tenth.

17. What is 2% of 3,600?

18. 62 is 90% of what number?

Solve using the percent equation.

19. Find 45% of 600.

20. 75 is what percent of 30?

21. **MEDICINE** About 37% of the people in the United States have type O^+ blood. If there are 250 million people in the United States, how many have type O^+ blood?

Find each percent of change and state whether it is an *increase* or *decrease*. Round to the nearest tenth if necessary.

22. original: $15
new: $12

23. original: 40 cars
new: 55 cars

24. **BUSINESS** A shoe store prices items at a 45% markup rate. If the store purchases an athletic shoe for $40, find the selling price of the shoe.

25. **MULTIPLE CHOICE** Geoff saved $75 in an account that earns 4.9% simple interest annually. If he does not deposit or withdraw any money for 18 months, which statement is *not* supported by this information?

F The interest earned will be $18.92.
G The interest earned will be $5.51.
H The total amount will be $80.51.
J The interest earned in this time will be greater than 4.9% of the principal.

CHAPTER 5

ISAT Practice

Cumulative, Chapters 1–5

IL Math Online glencoe.com
- Test Practice

PART 1 Multiple Choice

Read each question. Then fill in the correct answer on the answer sheet provided by your teacher or on a sheet of paper.

1. If a pair of inline skates is on sale for 35% off the regular price of $120, what is the sale price of the skates?

   A $48

   B $78

   C $94

   D $140

2. Alan is buying a television that is regularly priced at $149.99. It is on sale for $\frac{1}{5}$ off the original price. Which expression can he use to estimate the discount on the television?

   F $0.02 \times \$150$

   G $0.05 \times \$150$

   H $0.2 \times \$150$

   J $0.5 \times \$150$

3. Andrew purchased a coat for $67.20 that regularly sells for $84.00. What was the percent discount that Andrew received?

   A 16.8%

   B 20%

   C 25%

   D 80%

TEST-TAKING TIP

Question 3 To find the percent of discount, you can use the proportion $\frac{\text{percent discount}}{100\%} = \frac{\text{amount of discount}}{\text{regular price}}$.

4. Find $-17 - (5)$.

   F -22

   G -12

   H 22

   J 85

5. Jeanne's grandfather gave her money for her birthday. She bought 4 CDs at $12.99 each and a sweater for $25.99. Then she spent $2.70 on an ice cream cone. She had $4.35 left over. Which expression can be used to find how much money Jeanne received from her grandfather?

   A $4(12.99 + 25.99 + 2.70 + 4.35)$

   B $12.99 + 25.99 + 2.70 + 4.35$

   C $4(12.99) + 25.99 + 2.70 + 4.35$

   D $4(12.99) + 4(25.99) + 4(2.70) + 4(4.35)$

6. Find the height, in feet, of the skateboarding ramp shown below.

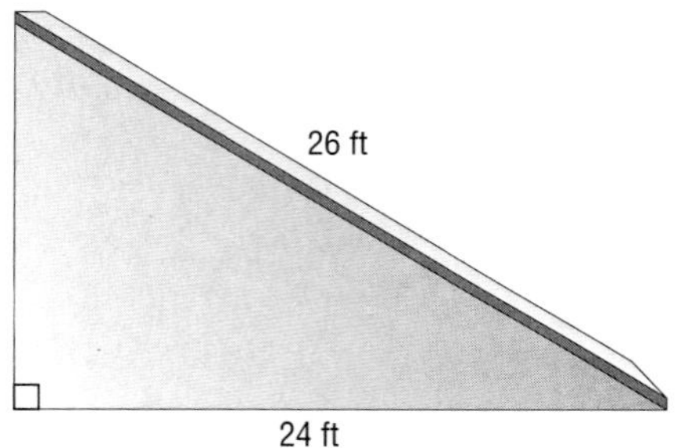

   F 10 ft

   G 22 ft

   H 25 ft

   J 34 ft

7. Rosa can read about 21 pages in about 20 minutes. If she continues to read at this rate, about how many pages can she read in 4 hours?

   A 220

   B 230

   C 240

   D 250

8. Eliza purchased a dress off the clearance rack. The original cost for the dress was $35. The dress was marked down 50%, and the sign on the rack said to take an additional 20% off the discounted price. What was the final sale price Eliza paid for the dress?

   F $3.50

   G $10.50

   H $14.00

   J $17.50

Preparing for ISAT
For test-taking strategies and practice, see pages 712–729.

9. Adrian swam 75 meters in 45 seconds, and Carlos swam 125 meters in 75 seconds. Based on these rates, which statement is true?

   A Adrian's average speed was 2 meters per second faster than Carlos's average speed.

   B Carlos's average speed was equal to Adrian's average speed.

   C Carlos's average speed was 2 meters per second faster than Adrian's average speed.

   D Adrian's average speed was 3 meters per second faster than Carlos's average speed.

10. In 2003, a new planet was discovered. This new planet is 10^{10} miles from the sun. Which of the following represents this number in standard notation?

   F 10,000,000,000 mi

   G 10,000,000 mi

   H 10,000 mi

   J 100 mi

11. Martin and his sister agreed to split the cost of a new board game. They received a 25% discount on the board game and paid 5.5% sales tax on the discounted price. If the original price of the board game was $30, how much did Martin and his sister each put toward the cost of the board game?

   A $20.57

   B $11.87

   C $10.29

   D $9.77

PART 2 Short Response/Grid In

Record your answers on the answer sheet provided by your teacher or on a sheet of paper.

12. The widths of a race track are shown below. What is the percent of increase in the track width from the straightaway to the turn?

Part of Track	Width (feet)
straightaway	50
turn	60

13. If $m = 7$ and $n = 4$, then find the value of $3(2m - 3n)$.

PART 3 Extended Response

Record your answers on the answer sheet provided by your teacher or on a sheet of paper. Show your work.

14. Refer to the figures below.

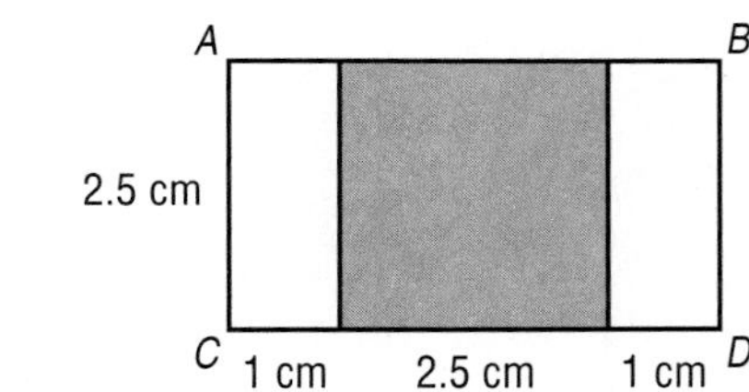

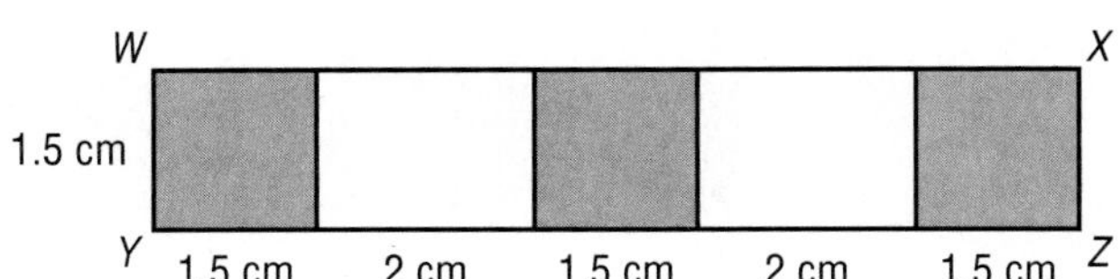

   a. Find the percent of area that is shaded for each rectangle.

   b. Which rectangle has the greater percent of area that is shaded? Explain.

NEED EXTRA HELP?														
If You Missed Question...	1	2	3	4	5	6	7	8	9	10	11	12	13	14
Go to Lesson...	5-8	5-6	5-3	1-5	1-2	3-5	4-1	5-8	4-1	2-10	5-8	5-8	1-2	5-8
IL Learning Standards	8.A.3b	6.C.3b	6.A.3	6.B.3a	8.A.3a	9.D.3	6.D.3	8.A.3b	6.D.3	6.A.3	8.A.3b	8.A.3b	8.A.3a	8.A.3b

Unit 3

Geometry and Measurement

Focus

Investigate the geometry and measurement of two- and three-dimensional figures.

CHAPTER 6
Geometry and Spatial Reasoning

BIG Idea Use relationships among lines and angles and apply transformational geometry.

CHAPTER 7
Measurement: Area and Volume

BIG Idea Determine the area, surface area, and volume of geometric figures.

Problem Solving in Science
Real-World Unit Project
Turn Over a New Leaf You have been selected to join a team of botanists that will be studying leaves. In this project, you will be collecting and analyzing leaves to find out why they are all flat. You'll investigate the relationship between the volume and surface area of a leaf. So, put on your hiking shoes, and don't forget to bring along your geometry and measurement tools. You're about to go on a nature hike!
IL Math Online Log on to glencoe.com to begin.

Geometry and Spatial Reasoning

Illinois Learning Standards

9.A.3b Draw transformation images of figures, with and without the use of technology.
9.A.3c Use concepts of symmetry, congruency, similarity, scale, perspective, and angles to describe and analyze two- and three-dimensional shapes found in practical applications (e.g., geodesic domes, A-frame houses, basketball courts, inclined planes, art forms, blueprints).

Key Vocabulary

congruent polygons (p. 320)
reflection (p. 332)
transformation (p. 332)
translation (p. 337)

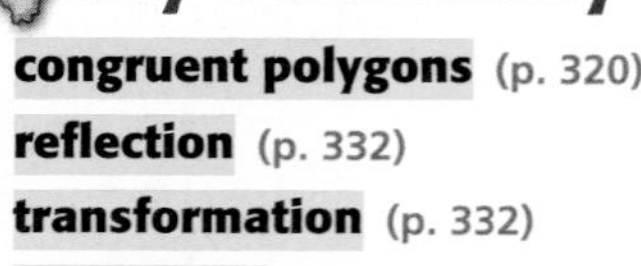

Real-World Link

Architecture Fallingwater, located in Ohiopyle, Pennsylvania, was designed by famous architect Frank Lloyd Wright. Notice the geometric shapes and parallel lines in the design.

FOLDABLES® Study Organizer

Geometry and Spatial Reasoning Make this Foldable to help you organize your notes. Begin with 7 sheets of plain $8\frac{1}{2}'' \times 11''$ paper.

1. **Fold** a sheet of paper in half lengthwise. Cut a 1″ tab along the left edge through one thickness.

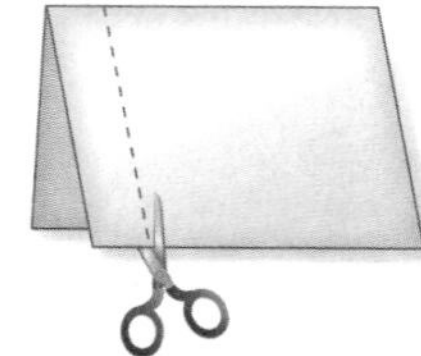

2. **Glue** the 1″ tab down. Write the title of the lesson on the front tab.

3. **Repeat** Steps 1 and 2 for the remaining sheets of paper. Staple together to form a booklet.

GET READY for Chapter 6

Diagnose Readiness You have two options for checking Prerequisite Skills.

Option 2

IL Math Online Take the Online Readiness Quiz at glencoe.com.

Option 1

Take the Quick Check below. Refer to the Quick Review for help.

QUICK Quiz

Solve each equation. (Lesson 1-9)

1. $49 + b + 45 = 180$
2. $t + 98 + 55 = 180$
3. $15 + 67 + k = 180$
4. **LAWNS** Lawrence made $60 on Monday and $48 on Tuesday mowing lawns. How much did he make on Wednesday if his three-day total was $180? (Lesson 1-9)

QUICK Review

Example 1

Solve $82 + g + 41 = 180$.

$82 + g + 41 = 180$	Write the equation.
$123 + g = 180$	Add 82 and 41.
$-123 \quad -123$	Subtract 123 from each side.
$g = 57$	

Evaluate each expression. (Lesson 1-2)

5. $(3 - 2)180$
6. $(7 - 2)180$
7. $(9 - 2)180$
8. $(11 - 2)180$
9. **NUMBER SENSE** Find the product of the difference of 5 and 2 and 180. (Lesson 1-2)

Example 2

Evaluate $(8 - 2)180$.

$(8 - 2)180 = (6)180$	Subtract 2 from 8.
$= 1{,}080$	Multiply.

Find the value of x in each triangle. (Lesson 1-9)

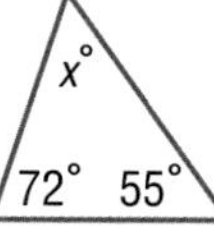

11.

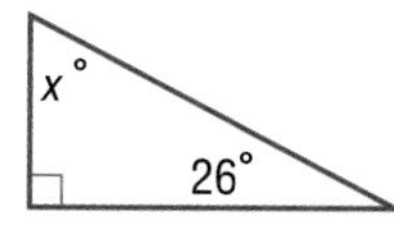

12.

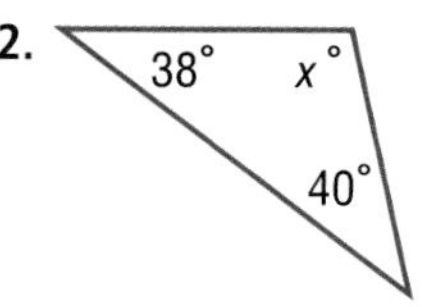

13.

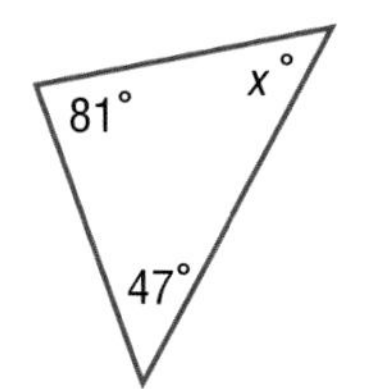

Example 3

Find the value of x in $\triangle ABC$.

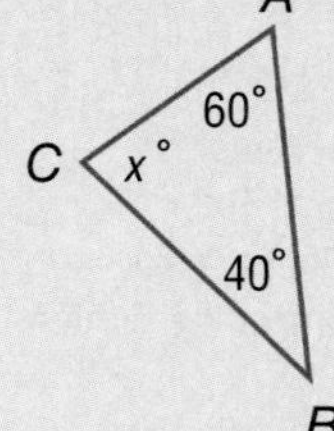

The sum of the measures of the angles of a triangle is 180°.

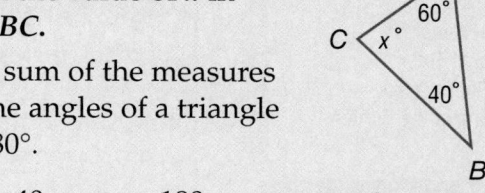

$60 + 40 + x = 180$	$m\angle A = 60°, m\angle B = 40°$
$100 + x = 180$	Add.
$-100 \quad = -100$	Subtract 100 from each side.
$x = 80$	

6-1 Line and Angle Relationships

MAIN IDEA

Identify special pairs of angles and relationships of angles formed by two parallel lines cut by a transversal.

IL Learning Standards

7.A.3b Apply the concepts and attributes of length, capacity, weight/mass, perimeter, area, volume, time, temperature and **angle measures in practical situations.** *Also addresses 9.A.3c, 9.B.3, 9.C.3a, 9.C.3b.*

New Vocabulary

vertical angles
complementary angles
supplementary angles
perpendicular lines
parallel lines
transversal
interior angles
exterior angles
alternate interior angles
alternate exterior angles
corresponding angles

IL Math Online

glencoe.com

- Extra Examples
- Personal Tutor
- Self-Check Quiz
- Reading in the Content Area

MINI Lab

STEP 1 Draw two horizontal lines on notebook paper and a line that intersects both of those lines as shown.

STEP 2 Label the angles formed as shown.

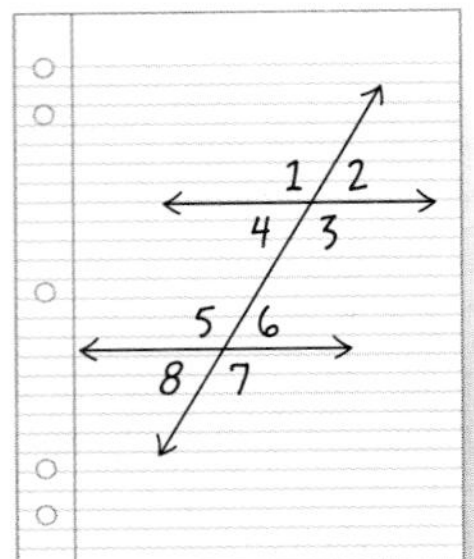

1. Suppose that the measures of angles 4 and 6 are each 60°. Using angle relationships you have previously learned or a protractor, find and record the measure of each numbered angle. Explain your reasoning.
2. What is the relationship between the two horizontal lines?
3. *Congruent angles* are angles that have the same measure. Describe the pairs of angles that appear to be congruent.
4. What do you notice about the measures of angles that are side by side?

In previous courses, you have learned that pairs of angles can be classified by their relationship to each other.

Special Pairs of Angles — Concept Summary

Vertical angles are opposite angles formed by intersecting lines.

∠1 and ∠2 are vertical angles.
∠3 and ∠4 are vertical angles.

Vertical angles are congruent.

The sum of the measures of **complementary angles** is 90°.

∠*ABD* and ∠*DBC* are complementary angles.

The sum of the measures of **supplementary angles** is 180°.

∠*C* and ∠*D* are supplementary angles.

You can use the relationships between pairs of angles to find missing measures. Recall that angles can be named by three points.

EXAMPLES Find a Missing Angle Measure

Reading Math

Angle Measure Read *m∠ABC* as *the measure of angle ABC.*

1 **In the figure, $m\angle ABC = 90°$. Find the value of x.**

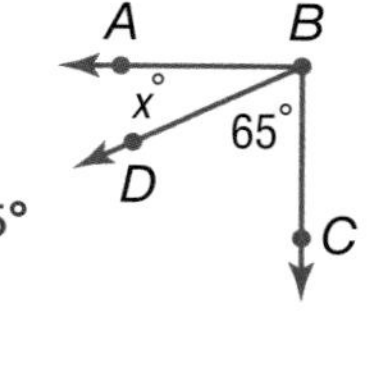

$m\angle ABD + m\angle DBC = 90$	Write an equation.
$x + 65 = 90$	$m\angle ABD = x$ and $m\angle DBC = 65°$
$-65 = -65$	Subtract 65 from each side.
$x = 25$	Simplify.

2 **Find the value of x in the figure.**

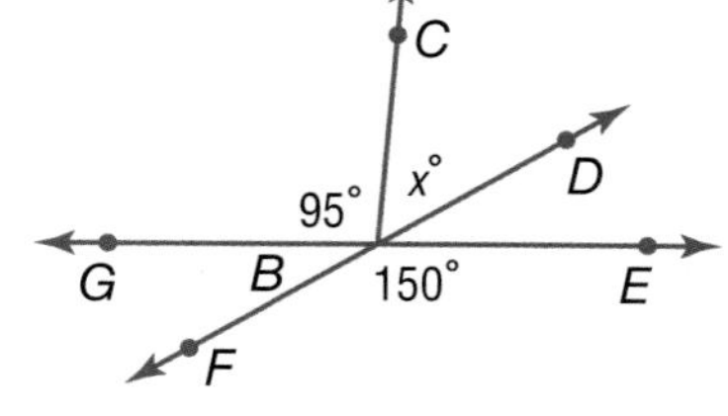

Angles *GBD* and *FBE* are vertical angles and thus are congruent.

$m\angle GBD = m\angle FBE$

$95 + x = 150$	Write an equation.
$-95 = -95$	Subtract 95 from each side.
$x = 55$	Simplify.

Reading Math

Congruent and Equals The ≅ symbol is used to show that two angles are congruent. So, $\angle GBD \cong \angle FBE$. The = symbol is used to show that two measures are equal. So, $m\angle GBD = m\angle FBE$.

CHECK Your Progress

Find the value of x in each figure.

a. b.

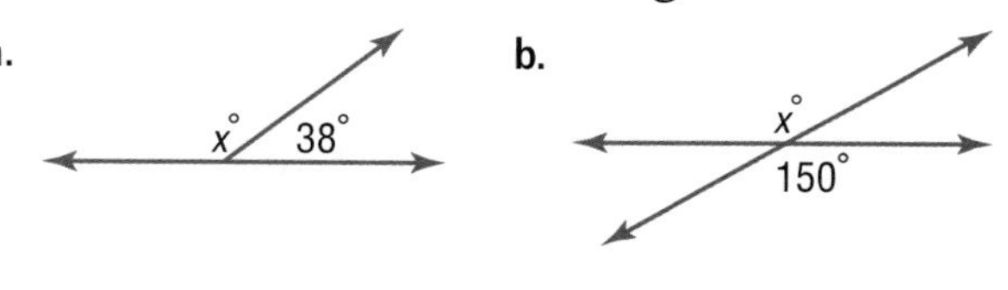

c.

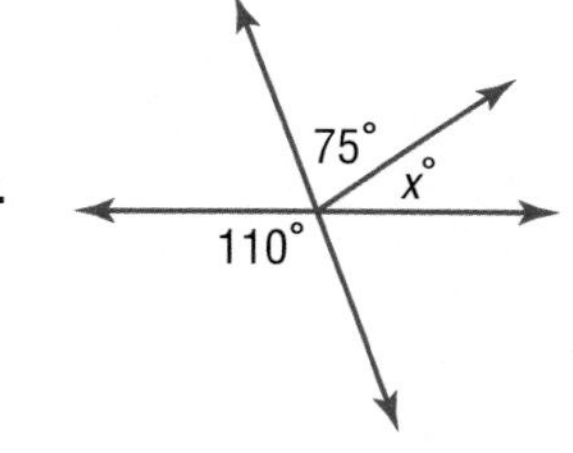

Lines that intersect at right angles are called **perpendicular lines**. Two lines in a plane that never intersect or cross are called **parallel lines**.

A red right angle symbol indicates that lines *m* and *n* are perpendicular.

m

n

$m \perp n$

p *q*

$p \parallel q$

Red arrowheads indicate that lines *p* and *q* are parallel.

Reading Math

Parallel and Perpendicular Lines Read $m \perp n$ as *m is perpendicular to n.* Read $p \parallel q$ as *p is parallel to q.*

A line that intersects two or more other lines is called a **transversal**. Eight angles are formed that have special names. Four **interior angles** lie inside the two lines, and four **exterior angles** lie outside the two lines.

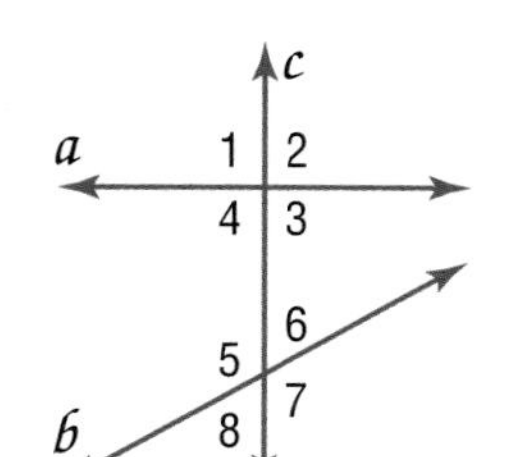

Line *c* is a transversal of lines *a* and *b*.

∠3, ∠4, ∠5, and ∠6 are interior angles.

∠1, ∠2, ∠7, and ∠8 are exterior angles.

If the two lines cut by a transversal are parallel, then these special pairs of angles are congruent.

Transversals and Angles

Key Concept

Alternate interior angles are interior angles that lie on opposite sides of the transversal.

Examples:
$\angle 4 \cong \angle 6$,
$\angle 3 \cong \angle 5$

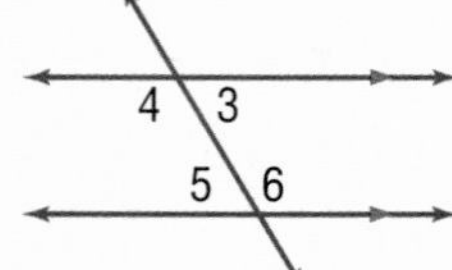

Alternate exterior angles are exterior angles that lie on opposite sides of the transversal.

Examples:
$\angle 1 \cong \angle 7$,
$\angle 2 \cong \angle 8$

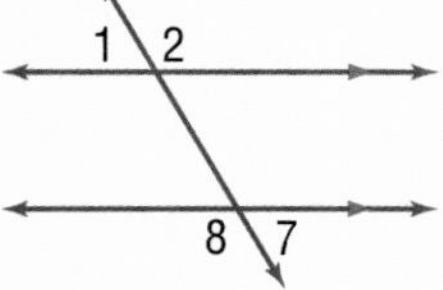

Corresponding angles are those angles that are in the same position on the two lines in relation to the transversal.

Examples:
$\angle 1 \cong \angle 5$,
$\angle 3 \cong \angle 7$

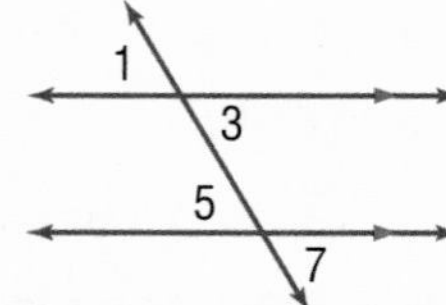

Examples:
$\angle 2 \cong \angle 6$,
$\angle 4 \cong \angle 8$,

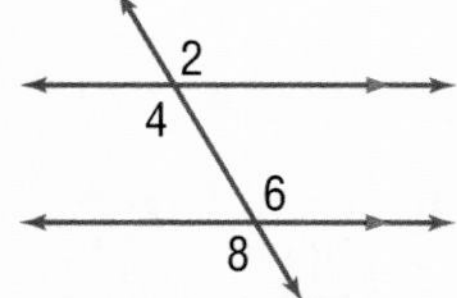

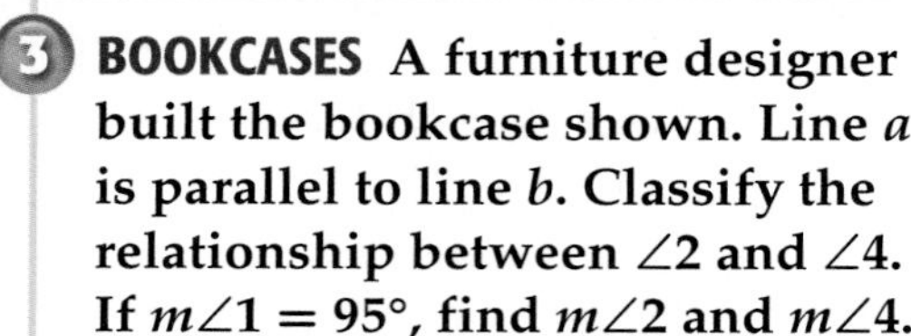

Real-World EXAMPLE Find an Angle Measure

3 BOOKCASES A furniture designer built the bookcase shown. Line *a* is parallel to line *b*. Classify the relationship between $\angle 2$ and $\angle 4$. If $m\angle 1 = 95°$, find $m\angle 2$ and $m\angle 4$.

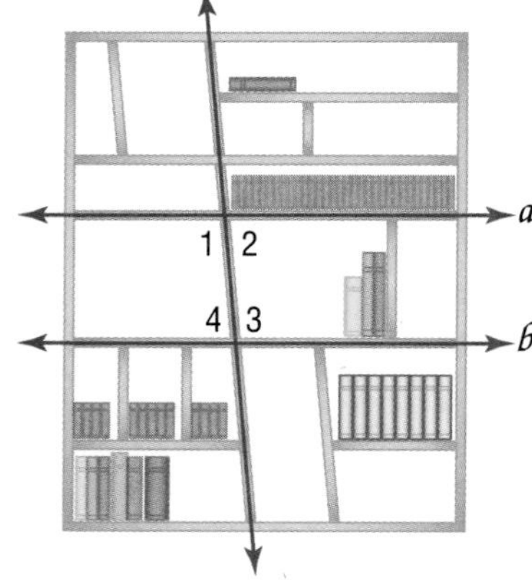

Since $\angle 1$ and $\angle 2$ are supplementary, the sum of their measures is 180°. Therefore, $m\angle 2 = 180° - 95°$ or 85°.

Since $\angle 2$ and $\angle 4$ are interior angles that lie on opposite sides of the transversal, they are alternate interior angles.

Since $\angle 2$ and $\angle 4$ are alternate interior angles, they are congruent. So, $m\angle 4 = 85°$.

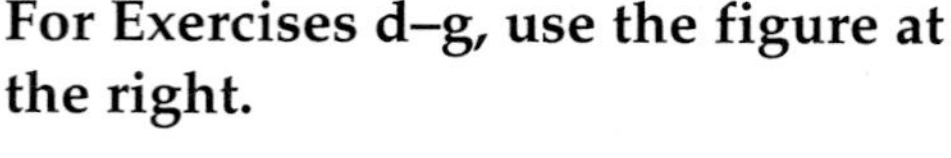

CHECK Your Progress

For Exercises d–g, use the figure at the right.

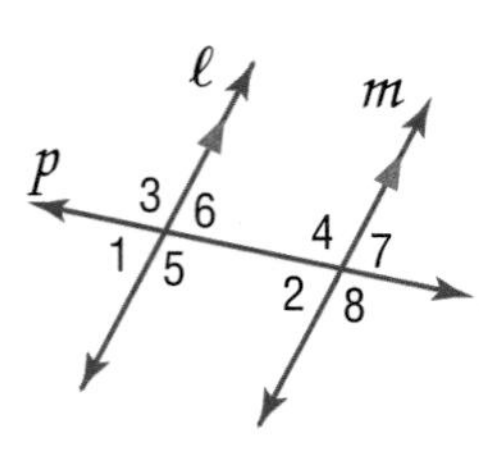

d. Classify the relationship between $\angle 6$ and $\angle 7$.

e. Classify the relationship between $\angle 3$ and $\angle 8$.

f. If $m\angle 1 = 63°$, find $m\angle 7$ and $m\angle 4$. Justify your method.

g. If $m\angle 8 = 122°$, find $m\angle 6$ and $m\angle 1$. Justify your method.

Real-World Career . . .
How Does a Furniture Designer Use Math? Furniture designers use line and angle relationships when they create drawings of furniture items such as bookcases.

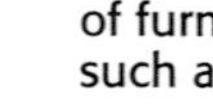

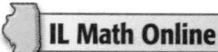

IL Math Online

For more information, go to glencoe.com.

Examples 1, 2 (p. 307)

Find the value of x in each figure.

1.
2. 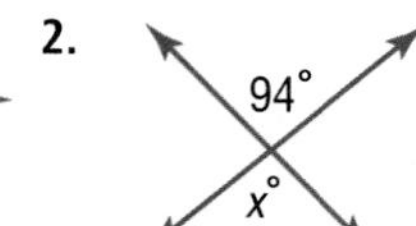

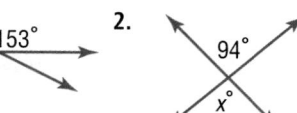

3. 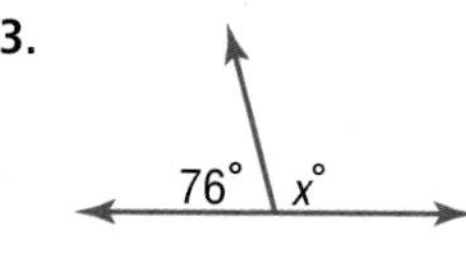

4. 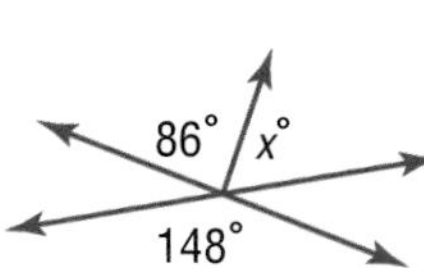

Example 3 (p. 308)

Classify each pair of angles as ***alternate interior, alternate exterior,*** **or** ***corresponding.***

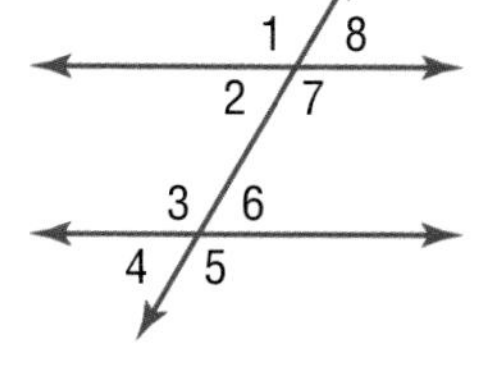

5. ∠4 and ∠8
6. ∠5 and ∠7
7. ∠3 and ∠7
8. ∠6 and ∠8

9. **STAIRS** Refer to the porch stairs shown. Line m is parallel to line n. Classify the relationship between ∠1 and ∠2. If $m\angle 3 = 40°$, find $m\angle 1$ and $m\angle 2$. Explain your reasoning.

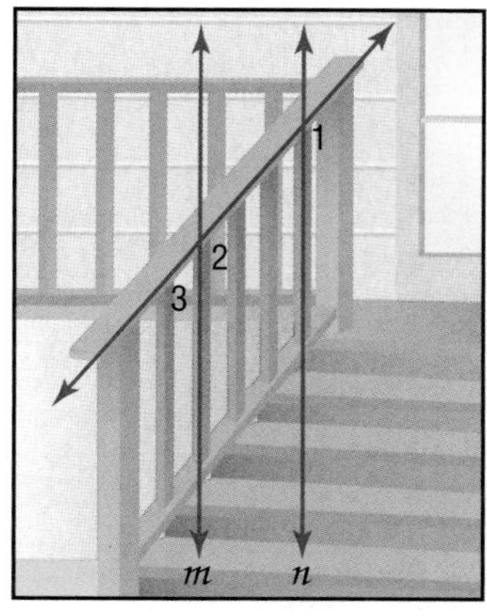

Practice and Problem Solving

HOMEWORK HELP	
For Exercises	See Examples
10–17	1, 2
18–27	3

Find the value of x in each figure.

10. 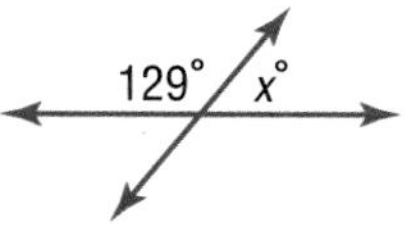

11. 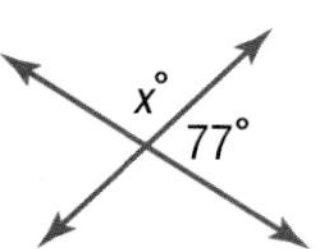

12. 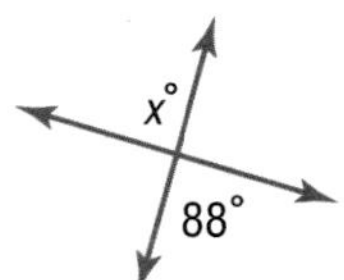

13. 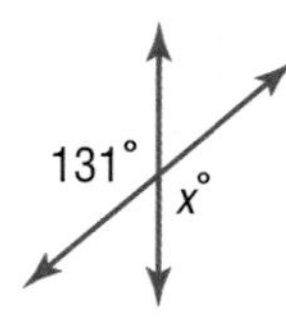

14. 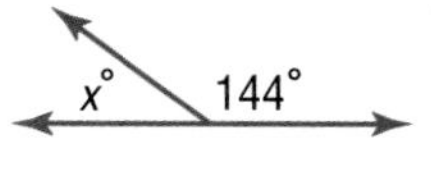

15. 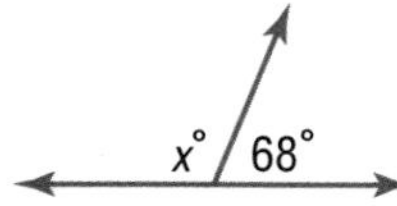

16. 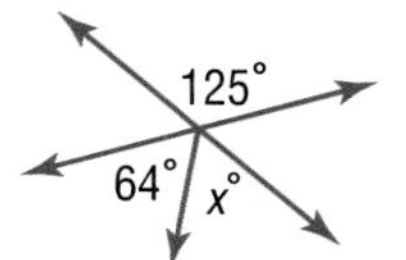

17. 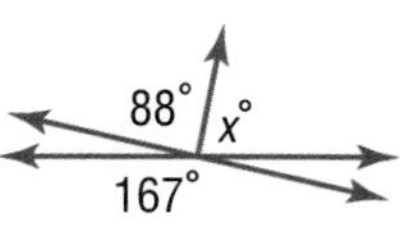

Classify each pair of angles as ***alternate interior, alternate exterior,*** **or** ***corresponding.***

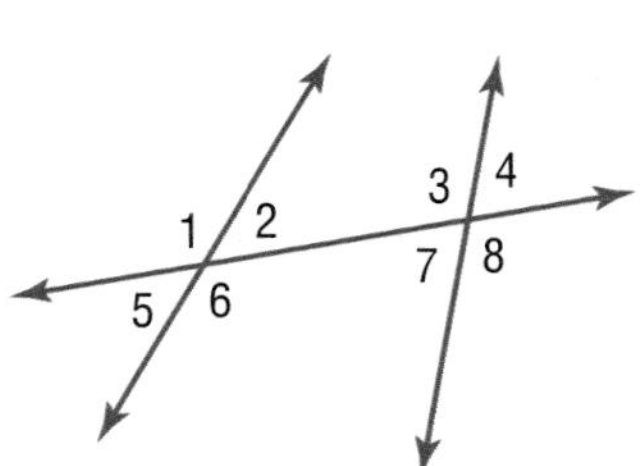

18. ∠2 and ∠4
19. ∠3 and ∠6
20. ∠1 and ∠3
21. ∠2 and ∠7
22. ∠1 and ∠8
23. ∠4 and ∠5

24. **ART** Classify the relationship between $\angle 1$ and $\angle 2$ on the quilt design on the barn below.

25. **RAILROADS** Classify the relationship between $\angle 3$ and $\angle 4$ on the railroad tracks below.

26. **CITY PLANNING** Refer to the street map of Washington, D.C. If K Street and Constitution Avenue are parallel and $m\angle 1 = 22°$, classify the relationship between $\angle 1$ and $\angle 2$. Then find $m\angle 2$. Explain your reasoning.

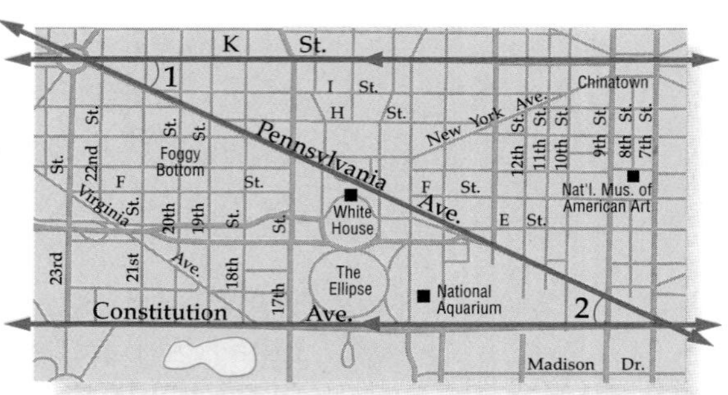

27. **ARCHITECTURE** The Leaning Tower of Pisa located in the town of Pisa, Italy, is one of the most famous architectural wonders in the world. Refer to the image at the left. If $m\angle 1 = 84.5°$, classify the relationship between $\angle 1$ and $\angle 3$. Then find $m\angle 2$. Explain your reasoning.

Real-World Link
Since construction began on the Leaning Tower of Pisa in 1173, engineers have tried to stop the progression of its lean.
Source: NOVA

ALGEBRA For Exercises 28 and 29, parallel lines are cut by a transversal. Find the value of x.

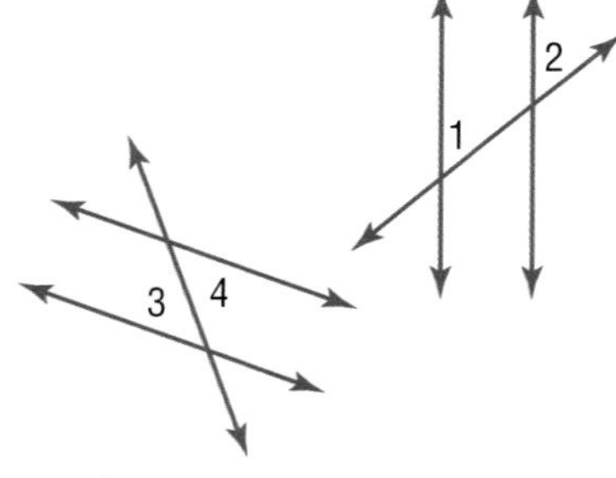

28. Angles 1 and 2 are corresponding angles, $m\angle 1 = 45°$, and $m\angle 2 = (x + 25)°$.

29. Angles 3 and 4 are alternate interior angles, $m\angle 3 = 2x°$, and $m\angle 4 = 80°$.

For Exercises 30–35, use the figure below. Justify each answer.

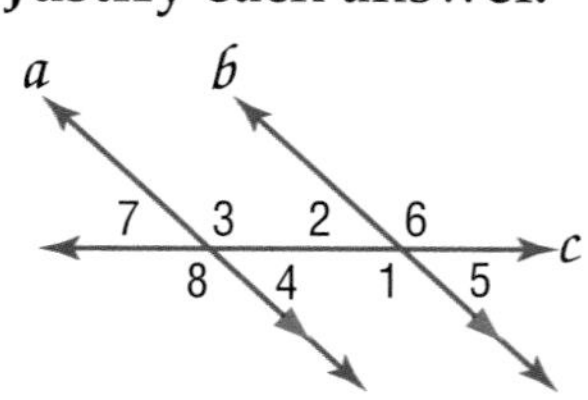

30. Find $m\angle 4$ if $m\angle 5 = 43°$.
31. Find $m\angle 1$ if $m\angle 3 = 135°$.
32. Find $m\angle 6$ if $m\angle 8 = 126°$.
33. Find $m\angle 5$ if $m\angle 7 = 38°$.
34. Find $m\angle 2$ if $m\angle 4 = 62°$.
35. Find $m\angle 8$ if $m\angle 1 = 150°$.

ILS • ISAT
Extra Practice, pp. 683, 705

H.O.T. Problems

36. **OPEN ENDED** Draw a pair of parallel lines cut by a transversal. Estimate the measure of one angle and label it. Without using a protractor, label all the other angles with their approximate measure.

37. **REASONING** If a transversal is perpendicular to one of two parallel lines, is it *always, sometimes,* or *never* perpendicular to the other parallel line? Explain your reasoning.

38. **CHALLENGE** In the figure at the right, quadrilateral *ABCD* is a parallelogram. Side *CD* has been extended to include point *E*. Make a conjecture about the relationship of $\angle DAB$ and $\angle ADC$. Justify your reasoning.

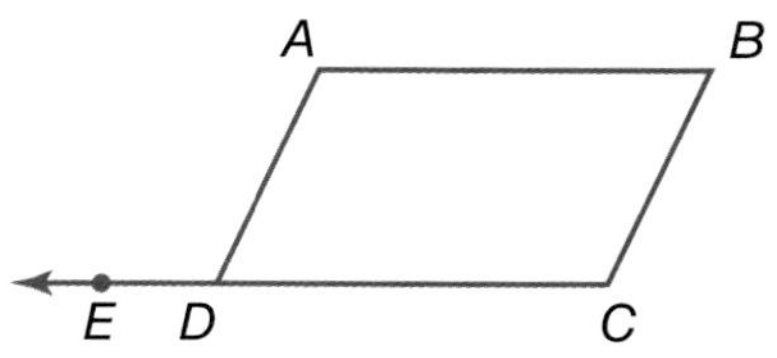

39. **WRITING IN MATH** If two parallel lines are cut by a transversal, what relationship exists between interior angles that are on the same side of the transversal? Explain your reasoning.

ISAT PRACTICE 7.A.3b

40. Lines *a* and *b* are parallel in the figure below. Find the value of *x*.

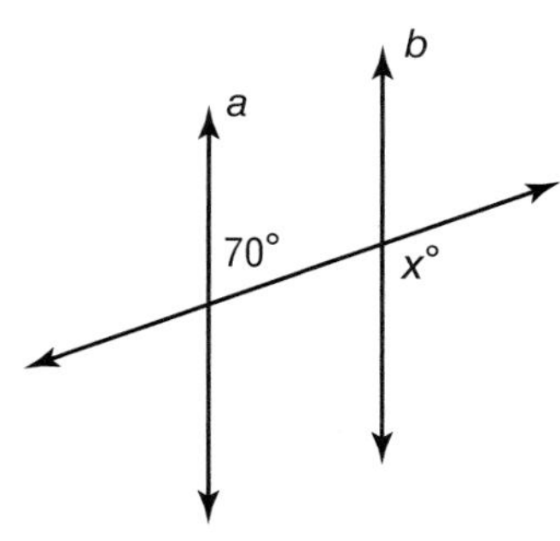

A 70
B 80
C 100
D 110

41. Which of the following statements is *not* true concerning $\angle A$, $\angle B$, and $\angle C$ labeled on the glass pyramid structure at the Louvre in Paris, France?

F $\angle B$ and $\angle C$ are obtuse angles.
G $\angle A$ and $\angle C$ are vertical angles.
H $\angle A$ and $\angle B$ are alternate interior angles.
J $\angle A$ and $\angle C$ are congruent.

Spiral Review

42. **SAVINGS** The Millers open a savings account for their newborn son with \$430. Find the total amount in the account after 3 years if the simple interest rate is 2.5%. (Lesson 5-9)

Find each percent of change. Round to the nearest tenth if necessary. State whether the percent of change is an *increase* or a *decrease*. (Lesson 5-8)

43. original: 20 members
new: 27 members

44. original: \$45
new: \$18

45. original: 620 pages
new: 31 pages

GET READY for the Next Lesson

46. **PREREQUISITE SKILL** After a trip to the mall, Alex and Marcus counted their money to see how much they had left. Alex said, "If I had \$4 more, I would have as much as you." Marcus replied, "If I had \$4 more, I would have twice as much as you." How much does each boy have? (Lesson 1-1)

Extend 6-1

Geometry Lab
Triangles

MAIN IDEA

Use parallel lines to investigate the sum of the measures of the angles in a triangle and similar triangles.

IL Learning Standards

9.B.3 Identify, describe, classify and compare two- and three-**dimensional geometric figures and models according to their properties.**
9.C.3b Develop and solve problems using geometric relationships and models, with and **without the use of technology.** *Also addresses 9.A.3a, 9.A.3c, 9.C.3a.*

In the previous lesson, you identified special pairs of angles that are formed when parallel lines are cut by a transversal. In this lab, you will use those angle relationships to discover the sum of the measures of the angles of a triangle. You will also extend your work with similar triangles.

ACTIVITY Angles in a Triangle

1 **STEP 1** Draw a pair of parallel lines.

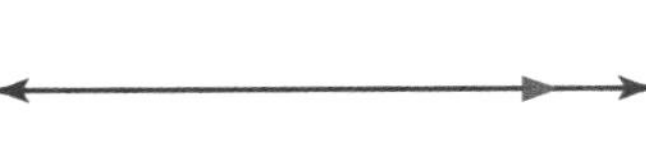

STEP 2 Draw a transversal as shown. Label ∠1 and ∠2.

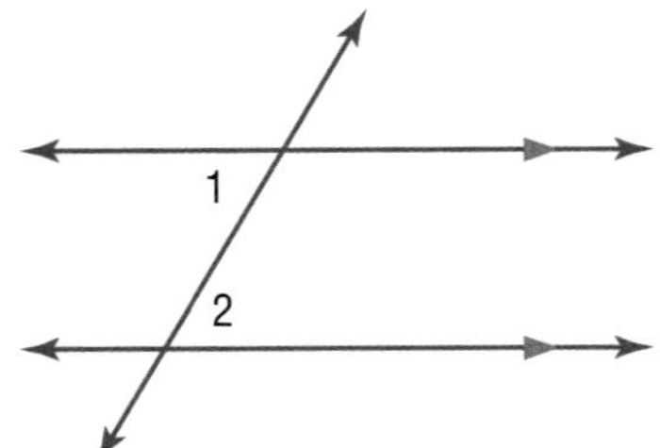

STEP 3 Draw a second transversal as shown. Label ∠3 and ∠4. Label the triangle formed by these lines *ABC.*

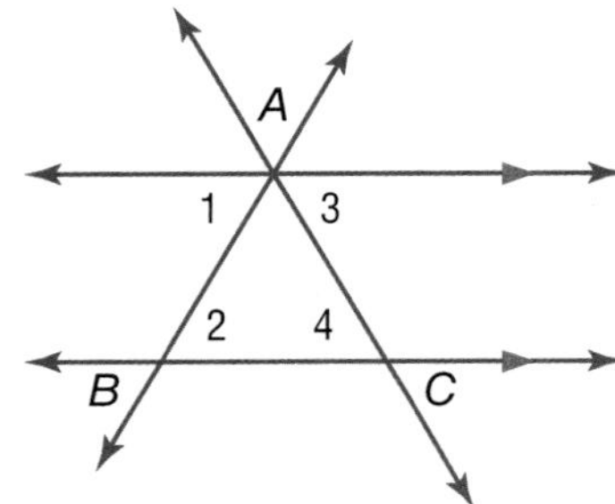

Analyze the Results

1. Classify the relationship between ∠1 and ∠2. What is true about this pair of angles?
2. Classify the relationship between ∠3 and ∠4. What is true about this pair of angles?
3. What type of angle is formed by ∠1, ∠3, and ∠*BAC*? What is the sum of the measures of ∠1, ∠3, and ∠*BAC*?
4. What can you conclude about the sum of the measures of the angles in △*ABC*? Explain your reasoning?
5. **MAKE A CONJECTURE** Based on this activity, what is the sum of the measures of the angles of any triangle?

Review Vocabulary

similar polygons polygons that have the same shape (p. 218)

In Lesson 4-7, you learned that if two triangles are similar, then their corresponding angles are congruent. In addition, if two angles of one triangle are congruent to two angles of another triangle, then the triangles are similar. In the figures below, $\triangle ABC \sim \triangle XYZ$.

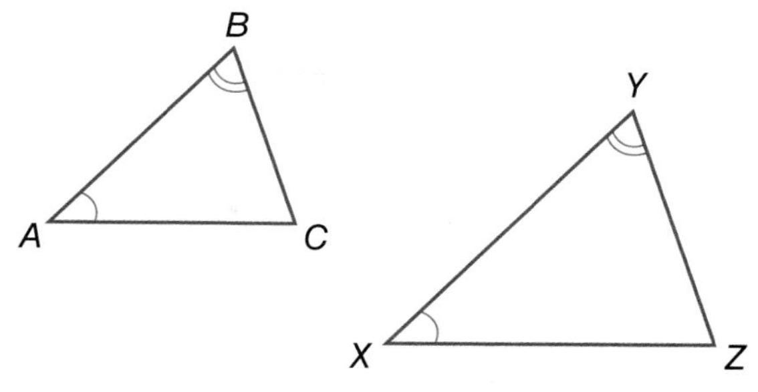

ACTIVITY Similar Triangles

2 **STEP 1** Draw a pair of parallel lines.

STEP 2 Draw two transversals as shown. Label ∠1, ∠2, ∠3, and ∠4. Label the triangles *RST* and *USV*.

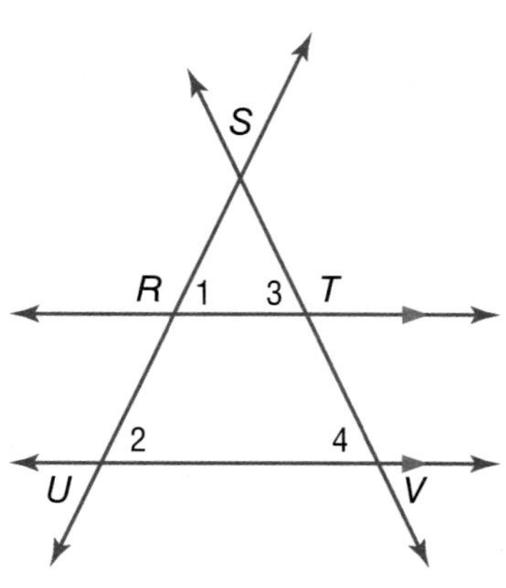

Analyze the Results

6. What type of angles are ∠1 and ∠2? What is true about this pair of angles?
7. What type of angles are ∠3 and ∠4? What is true about this pair of angles?
8. What can you conclude about $\triangle RST$ and $\triangle USV$? Explain your reasoning.
9. Determine whether $\triangle ABC$ is similar to $\triangle CDE$ in the figure shown below. Justify your answer.

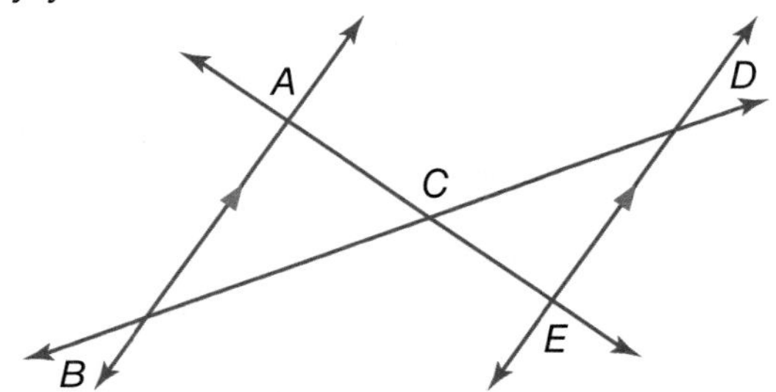

Problem-Solving Investigation

MAIN IDEA: Solve problems by using the logical reasoning strategy.

9.C.3a Construct, develop and communicate logical arguments (informal proofs) about geometric figures and patterns.

P.S.I. TEAM +

e-Mail: USE LOGICAL REASONING

CHRIS: I know that the sum of the measures of the angles in a triangle is 180°, and that an acute angle measures less than 90°.

YOUR MISSION: Given a right triangle, use logical reasoning to make a conjecture about the sum of the measures of the two acute angles of any right triangle.

Understand	Investigate the angle measures of right triangles to see whether there is a pattern.
Plan	Draw several right triangles, measure each angle, and look for a pattern.
Solve	Triangle 1 (A, B, C): $m\angle A = 45°$, $m\angle B = 45°$, $m\angle C = 90°$ Triangle 2 (A, B, C): $m\angle A = 90°$, $m\angle B = 35°$, $m\angle C = 55°$ Triangle 3 (A, B, C): $m\angle A = 50°$, $m\angle B = 90°$, $m\angle C = 40°$ It appears that the sum of the measures of the acute angles of a right triangle is 90°. So, the acute angles are complementary.
Check	You can try several more examples to see whether your conjecture appears to be true. But at this point, it is just a conjecture, not an actual proof.

Analyze The Strategy

1. **Inductive reasoning** is the process of making a conjecture after observing several examples. Determine where Chris used inductive reasoning. Explain.
2. **WRITING IN MATH** Write about a situation in which you use inductive reasoning.

Mixed Problem Solving

ILS • ISAT

Extra Practice, pp. 683, 705

For Exercises 3–5, solve each problem using logical reasoning.

3. **GEOMETRY** Draw several rectangles and their diagonals. Measure the lengths of their diagonals. What seems to be true about the measures of the lengths of the diagonals of a rectangle?

4. **JOBS** Anne, Roberto, Karina, and Josh all have summer jobs. One mows lawns, one lifeguards at the city pool, one delivers newspapers, and one babysits. From the clues below, list each person and their job.
   - Josh does not wear a swimming suit for his job.
   - Karina's wage depends on the number of children she watches.
   - Roberto lives next door to the person who delivers newspapers.
   - Anne is an excellent swimmer.

5. **NUMBER SENSE** Write each fraction in the table as a decimal. Then use logical reasoning to write the decimal equivalents for the fractions $\frac{3}{11}$, $\frac{6}{11}$, and $\frac{9}{11}$.

Fraction	Decimal
$\frac{1}{11}$	
$\frac{4}{11}$	
$\frac{8}{11}$	

Use any strategy to solve Exercises 6–11. Some strategies are shown below.

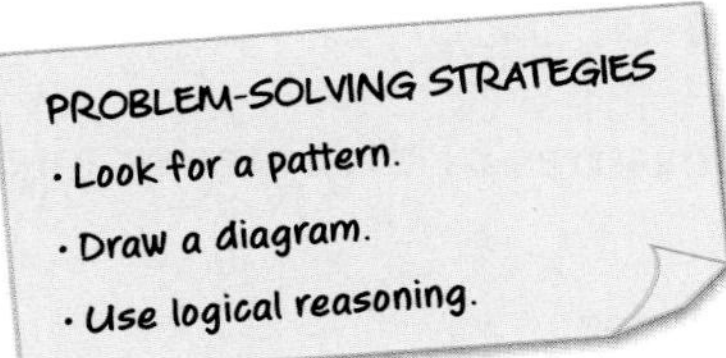

PROBLEM-SOLVING STRATEGIES
• Look for a pattern.
• Draw a diagram.
• Use logical reasoning.

6. **GEOMETRY** Right triangles are arranged according to the pattern below. If each triangle has an area of 12 square inches, find the area of the pattern formed by the fifth figure.

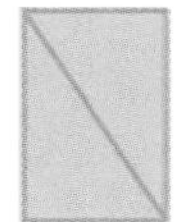  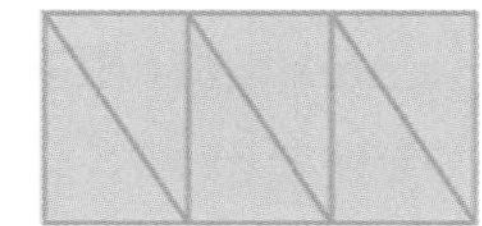

7. **PHONES** Ajay and his sister are each looking over their phone bill and at the number of hours they spent on the phone. Ajay said, "If I was on the phone twice as long, I would have been on the phone as long as you." His sister replied, "If I was on the phone twice as long, I would have been on the phone four times as long as you." How much time did each person spend on the phone?

8. **BALLET** A group of ballet dancers are practicing a formation on stage. The first row has one dancer and each additional row has two more dancers than the previous row. If there are 25 dancers, how many rows can they form?

9. **SHOPPING** Lakisha needs $8\frac{1}{4}$ pounds of ground beef for a party. She can buy ground beef in 1-pound, $2\frac{1}{2}$-pound, or 3-pound packages. If Lakisha wants to spend the least amount of money, which packages should she buy and how many?

10. **MEASUREMENT** The circumference of Earth around the equator is 24,901.55 miles. The circumference through the North and South Poles is 24,859.82 miles. How much greater is the circumference of Earth around the equator than through the poles?

11. **BIRDS** The arctic tern has the longest migration of any bird. Each year, it flies over 21,750 miles. If the average lifespan of an arctic tern is 20 years, how many miles, on average, will it have flown in the course of its life?

6-3 Polygons and Angles

MAIN IDEA

Find the sum of the angle measures of a polygon and the measure of an interior angle of a regular polygon.

IL Learning Standards

9.B.3 Identify, describe, classify and compare two- and three-**dimensional geometric figures and models according to their properties.** **9.C.3b Develop and solve problems using geometric relationships and models,** with and **without the use of technology.** *Also addresses 7.A.3b, 9.A.3c, 9.C.3a.*

New Vocabulary

interior angle
equilateral
equiangular
regular polygon

IL Math Online

glencoe.com

- Extra Examples
- Personal Tutor
- Self-Check Quiz

MINI Lab

Copy and complete the table. The sum of the angle measures of a triangle is 180°.

Number of Sides	Sketch of Figure	Number of Triangles	Sum of Angle Measures
3		1	1(180°)=180°
4		2	2(180°)=360°
5			
6			

1. Predict the number of triangles and the sum of the angle measures in a polygon with 8 sides.
2. Write an algebraic expression that could represent the number of triangles in an n-sided polygon. Then write an expression to represent the sum of the angle measures in an n-sided polygon.

In the Mini Lab, you used the sum of the angle measures of a triangle to find the sum of the interior angle measures of various polygons. An **interior angle** is an angle that lies inside a polygon.

Interior Angle Sum of a Polygon — Key Concept

Words The sum of the measures of the interior angles of a polygon is $(n - 2)180$, where n represents the number of sides.

Symbols $S = (n - 2)180$.

EXAMPLE Find the Sum of Interior Angle Measures

1 **ALGEBRA Find the sum of the measures of the interior angles of a decagon.**

$S = (n - 2)180$ Write an equation.

$S = (10 - 2)180$ A decagon has 10 sides. Replace n with 10.

$S = (8)180$ or 1,440 Simplify.

The sum of the measures of the interior angles of a decagon is 1,440°.

CHECK Your Progress

Find the sum of the angle measures of each polygon.

a. hexagon b. octagon c. 15-gon

A polygon that is **equilateral** (all sides congruent) and **equiangular** (all angles congruent) is called a **regular polygon**. Since all the angles of a regular polygon are congruent, their measures are equal.

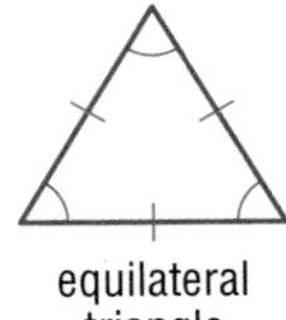
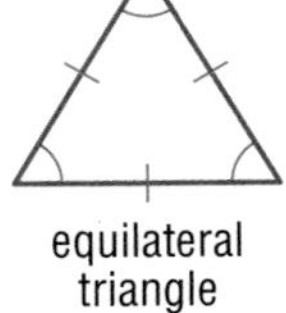

equilateral triangle

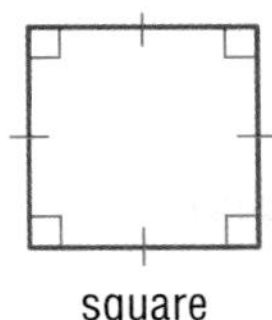
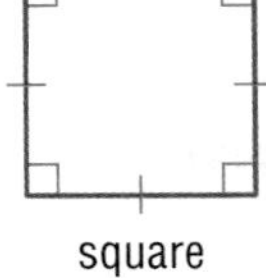

square

regular pentagon

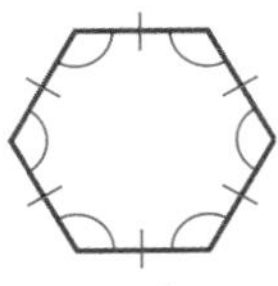

regular hexagon

Real-World EXAMPLE

2 ARCHITECTURE The Ennis-Brown House in Los Angeles, California, shown at the right was designed by architect Frank Lloyd Wright. The exterior of the house consists of repeating regular quadrilaterals. Find the measure of an interior angle of a regular quadrilateral.

Real-World Link

Frank Lloyd Wright designed 1,141 buildings during his 70-year career. He used obtuse angles and circles, creating unusually shaped structures such as the spiral Guggenheim Museum in New York City.

Step 1 Find the sum of the measures of the angles.

$S = (n - 2)180$	Write an equation.
$S = (4 - 2)180$	Replace n with 4.
$S = (2)180$ or 360	Simplify.

The sum of the measures of the interior angles is 360°.

Step 2 Divide 360 by 4, the number of interior angles, to find the measure of one interior angle. So, the measure of one interior angle of a regular quadrilateral is $360° \div 4$ or $90°$.

CHECK Your Progress

Find the measure of one interior angle in each regular polygon. Round to the nearest tenth if necessary.

d. octagon **e.** heptagon **f.** 20-gon

CHECK Your Understanding

Example 1 (p. 316)

Find the sum of the angle measures of each polygon.

1. quadrilateral
2. nonagon
3. 12-gon

Example 2 (p. 317)

4. **QUILTING** The quilt pattern shown is made of repeating equilateral triangles. What is the measure of one interior angle of a triangle?

Practice and Problem Solving

HOMEWORK HELP	
For Exercises	See Examples
5–10	1
11–16	2

Find the sum of the measures of the interior angles of each polygon.

5. pentagon
6. heptagon
7. 11-gon
8. 14-gon
9. 19-gon
10. 24-gon

11. **ART** The sculpture below consists of repeating regular pentagons and hexagons. Find the measure of one interior angle of a pentagon.

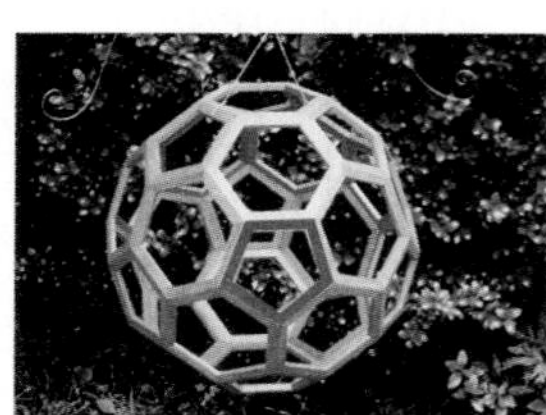

12. **NATURE** Each chamber of a bee honeycomb is a regular hexagon. What is the measure of an interior angle in the honeycomb?

Find the measure of one interior angle in each regular polygon. Round to the nearest tenth if necessary.

13. nonagon
14. decagon
15. 13-gon
16. 16-gon

ART For Exercises 17 and 18, use the following information.
A tessellation is a repetitive pattern of polygons that fit together without overlapping and without gaps between them. For each tessellation, find the measure of each angle at the circled vertex. Then find the sum of the angles.

17.

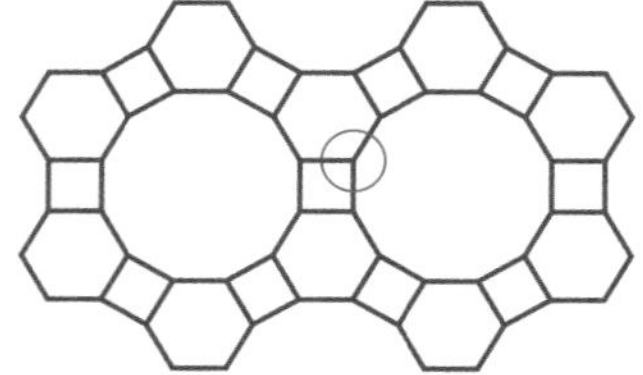

18.

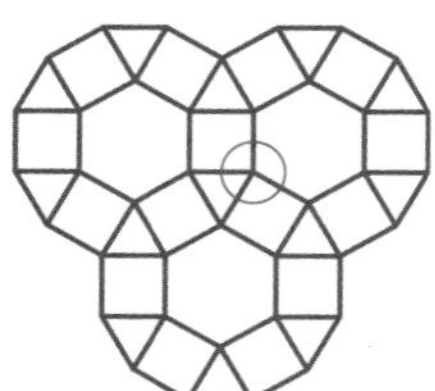

19. **ARCHITECTURE** The surface of the dome of Spaceship Earth in Orlando, Florida, consists of repeating equilateral triangles as shown. Find the measure of each angle in each outlined triangle. Then make a conjecture about the interior angle measures in equilateral triangles of different sizes.

ILS • ISAT
Extra Practice, pp. 684, 705

H.O.T. Problems

20. **CHALLENGE** How many sides does a regular polygon have if the measure of an interior angle is 160°? Justify your answer.

21. **WRITING IN MATH** Explain the relationship between the number of sides of a regular polygon and the measure of each interior angle.

ISAT PRACTICE 9.B.3, 9.C.3b

22. The following statements are true about $\triangle GHK$.

- $m\angle G = m\angle H + m\angle K$.
- $m\angle H$ and $m\angle K$ are complementary.
- The measure of each angle is evenly divisible by 15.

Which choice does *not* fit all three statements for angles G, H, and K?

A $m\angle G = 90°$
$m\angle H = 45°$
$m\angle K = 45°$

B $m\angle G = 90°$
$m\angle H = 75°$
$m\angle K = 15°$

C $m\angle G = 90°$
$m\angle H = 50°$
$m\angle K = 40°$

D $m\angle G = 90°$
$m\angle H = 60°$
$m\angle K = 30°$

23. Which statement is *not* true about the pattern of repeating regular octagons and rectangles?

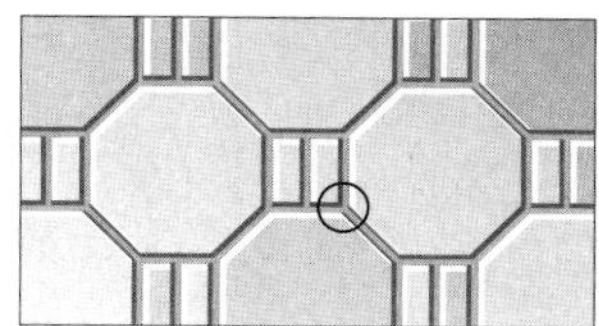

F The sum of the angles in each rectangle is 360°.

G The sum of the angles in each octagon is 1,080°.

H The sum of the angles at the circled vertex is 270°.

J The measure of each interior angle of an octagon is 135°.

Spiral Review

24. **JUICE** You have a large container of pineapple juice, an empty 5-pint container, and an empty 4-pint container. Explain how you can use only these containers to measure 2 pints of juice. (Lesson 6-2)

25. Find the value of x in the figure. (Lesson 6-1)

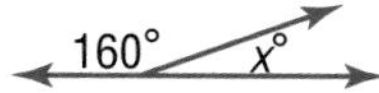

SCHOOL For Exercises 26 and 27, use the following information.
A recent survey asked parents to grade themselves based on their involvement in their children's education. The results are shown at the right. (Lesson 5-2)

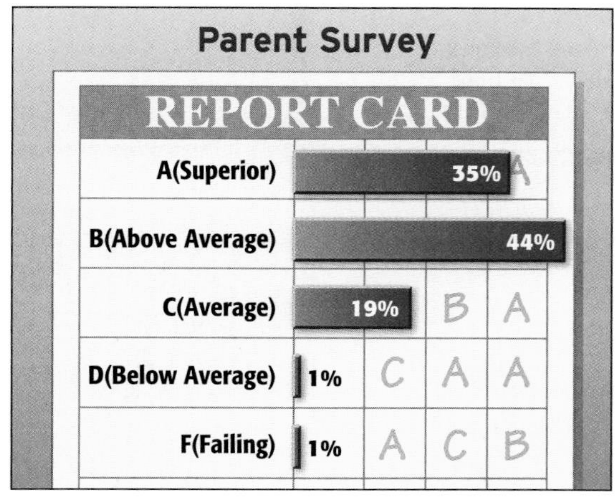

26. Write the percent of parents who gave themselves an A as a decimal and as a fraction in simplest form.

27. Did more or less than $\frac{2}{5}$ of the parents give themselves a B?

GET READY for the Next Lesson

PREREQUISITE SKILL Decide whether the figures are congruent. Write *yes* or *no* and explain your reasoning.

28. 

29. 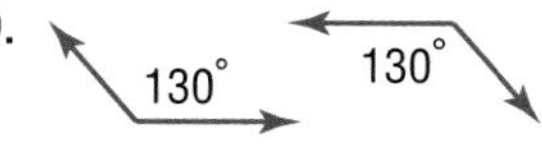

30. 8 mm 4 mm

6-4 Congruent Polygons

MAIN IDEA

Identify congruent polygons.

IL Learning Standards

9.A.3c Use concepts of symmetry, **congruency,** similarity, scale, perspective, and angles **to describe and analyze two-** and three-**dimensional shapes found in practical applications** (e.g., geodesic domes, A-frame houses, basketball courts, inclined planes, art forms, blueprints). *Also addresses 9.B.3, 9.C.3a, 9.C.3b.*

New Vocabulary

congruent polygon

IL Math Online

glencoe.com

- Extra Examples
- Personal Tutor
- Self-Check Quiz

GET READY for the Lesson

PROJECTS Leticia's art class is studying abstract art. She is painting a piece as part of her project.

1. How many different rectangles are used in the painting? Draw each rectangle.
2. Copy the painting and label all matching rectangles with the same number, starting with 1.

Polygons that have the same size and shape are called **congruent polygons**.

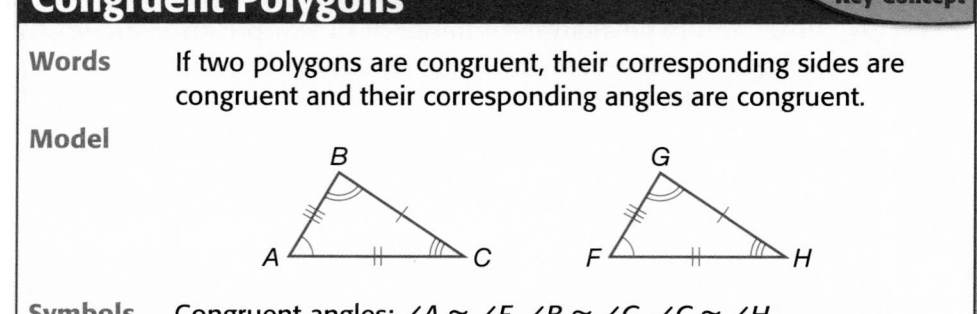

Congruent Polygons — Key Concept

Words If two polygons are congruent, their corresponding sides are congruent and their corresponding angles are congruent.

Model

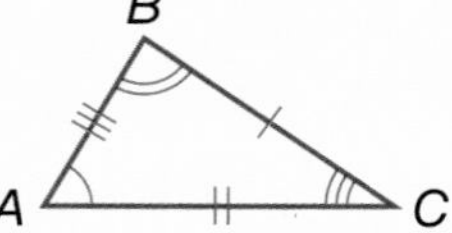

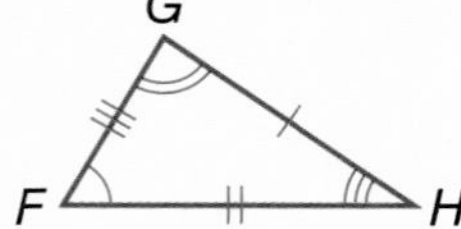

Symbols Congruent angles: $\angle A \cong \angle F$, $\angle B \cong \angle G$, $\angle C \cong \angle H$

Congruent sides: $\overline{BC} \cong \overline{GH}$, $\overline{AC} \cong \overline{FH}$, $\overline{AB} \cong \overline{FG}$

In a congruence statement, the letters identifying each polygon are written so that corresponding vertices appear in the same order. For example, for the diagram below, write $\triangle CBD \cong \triangle PQR$.

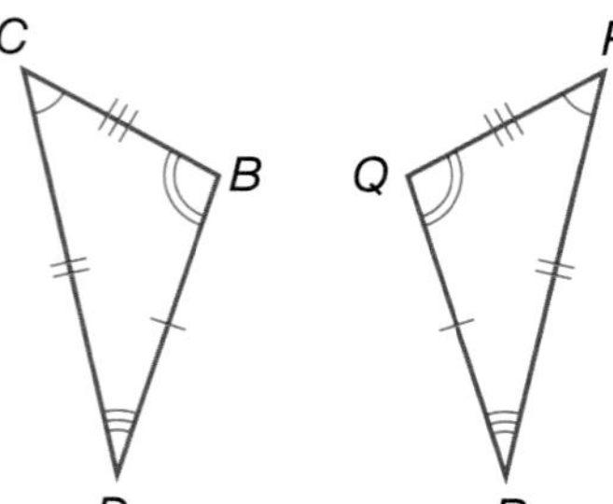

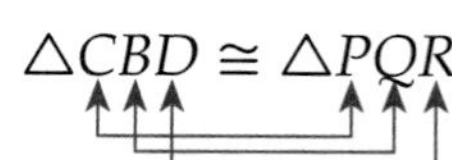

Vertex *C* corresponds to vertex *P*.
Vertex *B* corresponds to vertex *Q*.
Vertex *D* corresponds to vertex *R*.

Two polygons are congruent if all pairs of corresponding angles are congruent and all pairs of corresponding sides are congruent.

EXAMPLE Identify Congruent Polygons

1 Determine whether the triangles shown are congruent. If so, name the corresponding parts and write a congruence statement.

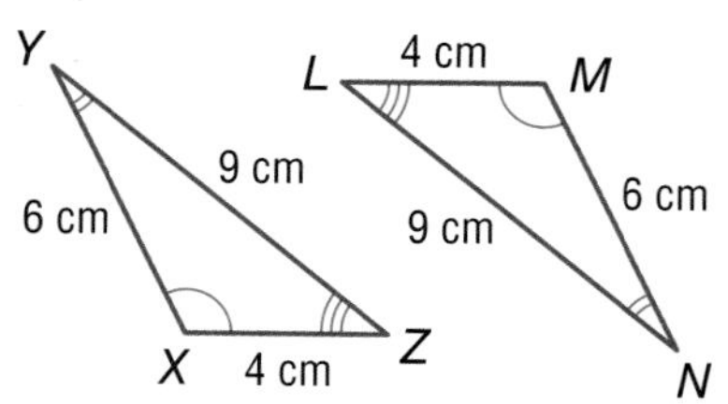

The arcs indicate that $\angle X \cong \angle M$, $\angle Y \cong \angle N$, and $\angle Z \cong \angle L$.

The side measures indicate that $\overline{XY} \cong \overline{MN}$, $\overline{YZ} \cong \overline{NL}$, and $\overline{XZ} \cong \overline{ML}$.

Since all pairs of corresponding angles and sides are congruent, the two triangles are congruent. One congruence statement is $\triangle XYZ \cong \triangle MNL$.

Study Tip

Congruence Statements Other possible congruence statements for Example 1 are $\triangle YZX \cong \triangle NLM$, $\triangle ZXY \cong \triangle LMN$, $\triangle YXZ \cong \triangle NML$, $\triangle XZY \cong \triangle MLN$, and $\triangle ZYX \cong \triangle LNM$.

CHECK Your Progress

Determine whether the polygons shown are congruent. If so, name the corresponding parts and write a congruence statement.

a.

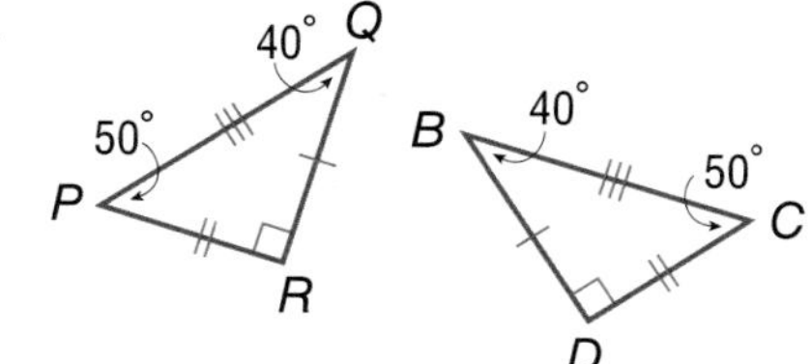

b.

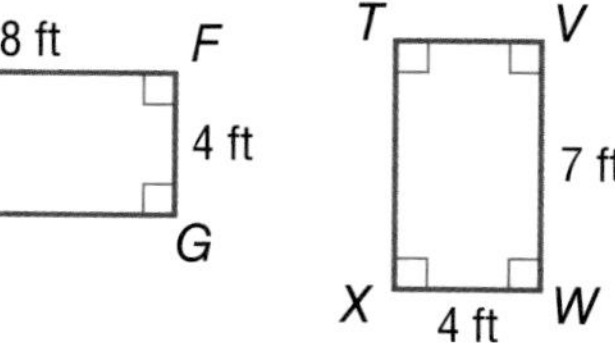

EXAMPLES Find Missing Measures

In the figure, $\triangle AFH \cong \triangle QRN$.

2 Find $m\angle Q$.

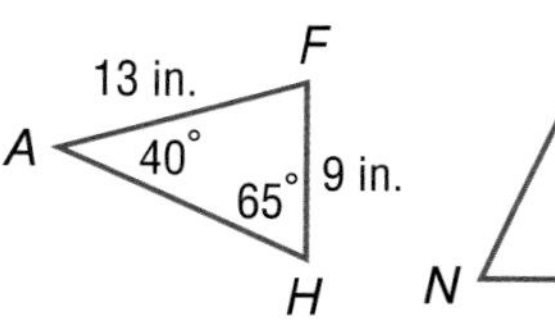

According to the congruence statement, $\angle A$ and $\angle Q$ are corresponding angles. So, $\angle A \cong \angle Q$. Since $m\angle A = 40°$, $m\angle Q = 40°$.

3 Find RN.

$\overline{FH}$ corresponds to $\overline{RN}$. So, $\overline{FH} \cong \overline{RN}$. Since $FH = 9$ inches, $RN = 9$ inches.

Reading Math

Recall that symbols like *RN* refer to the measure of the segment with those endpoints.

CHECK Your Progress

In the figure, quadrilateral *ABCD* is congruent to quadrilateral *WXYZ*. Find each measure.

c. $m\angle X$

d. YX

e. $m\angle Y$

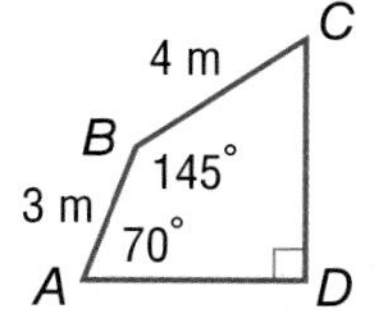

CHECK Your Understanding

Example 1 (p. 321)

Determine whether the polygons shown are congruent. If so, name the corresponding parts and write a congruence statement.

1\.

2\.

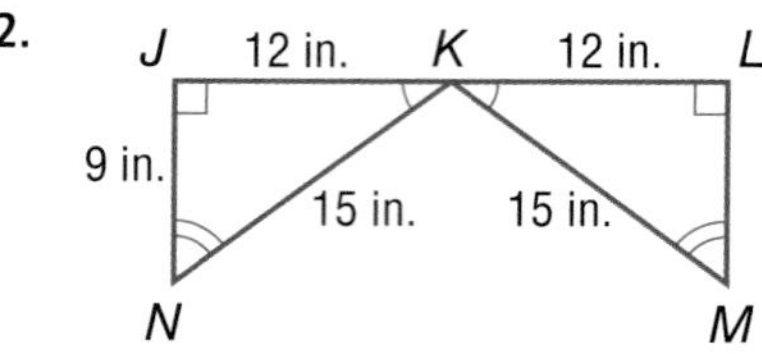

Examples 2, 3 (p. 321)

In the figure, $\triangle PQR \cong \triangle YWX$. Find each measure.

3\. $m\angle X$

4\. YW

5\. XY

6\. $m\angle W$

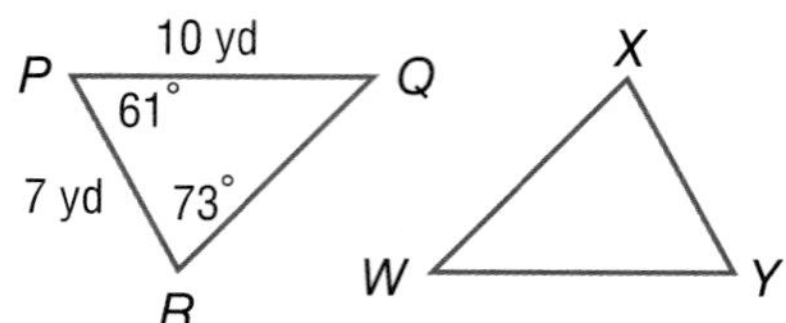

Practice and Problem Solving

HOMEWORK HELP	
For Exercises	See Examples
7–8	1
9–12	2, 3

Determine whether the polygons shown are congruent. If so, name the corresponding parts and write a congruence statement.

7\.

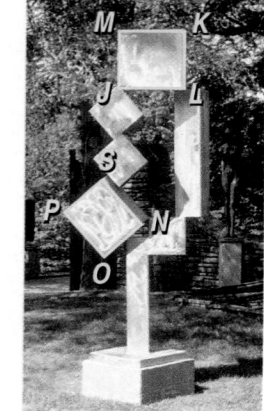

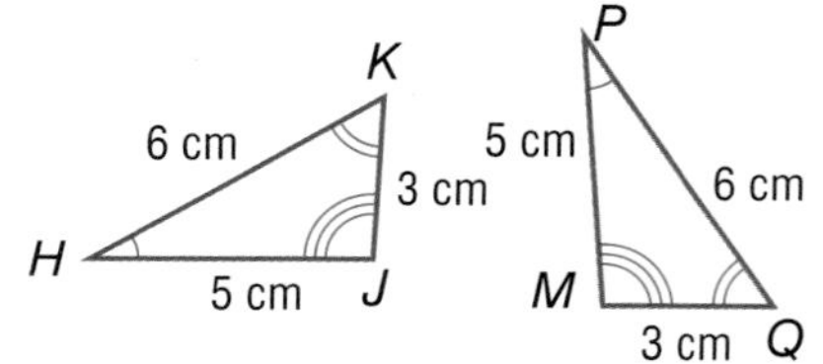

8\.

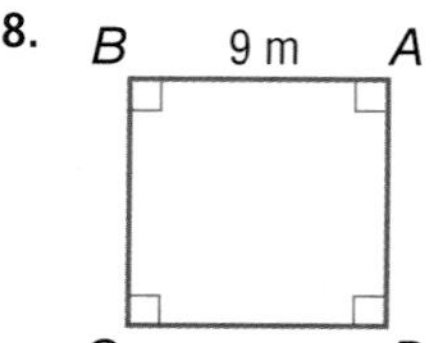

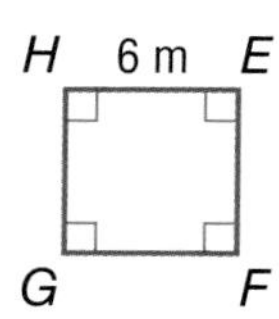

In the figure, quadrilateral *ABCD* is congruent to quadrilateral *HEFG*. Find each measure.

9\. AD

10\. DC

11\. $m\angle G$

12\. $m\angle H$

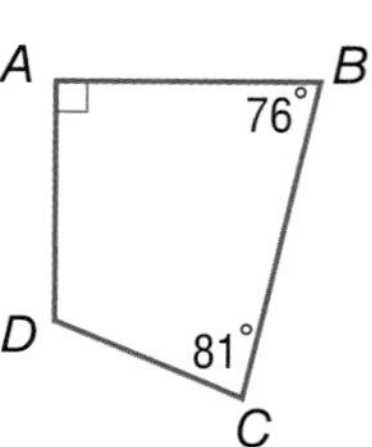

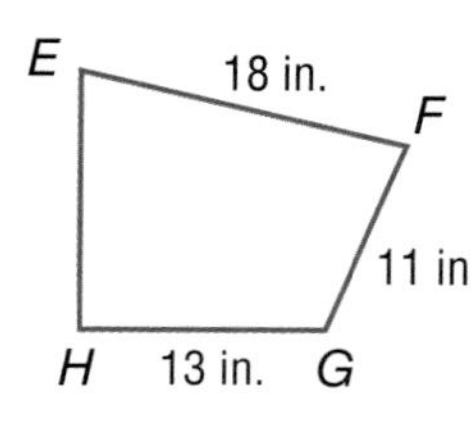

13\. **ART** The structure shown at the right, *Cubi XII*, created by David Smith, is located at the Hirshhorn Museum and Sculpture Garden in Washington, D.C. If quadrilaterals *JMKL* and *PSNO* are both squares, write one statement you would need to know in order to show that the quadrilaterals are congruent. Explain your reasoning.

Real-World Link

The Bank of China Tower uses triangular bracing as protection against high winds caused by typhoons.

Source: Great Buildings

14\. **ARCHITECTURE** The Bank of China Tower shown at the left was designed by architect I.M. Pei and consists of congruent glass triangles. If $\triangle WXY \cong \triangle VWZ$, and $m\angle V = 60°$, and $m\angle VWZ = 50°$, find $m\angle Y$.

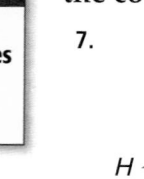

15. **INSECTS** The wings of a monarch butterfly are shaped as congruent quadrilaterals. Write a congruence statement. Then find $m\angle A$ if $m\angle Z = 45°$, $m\angle Y = 145°$, and $m\angle X = 90°$.

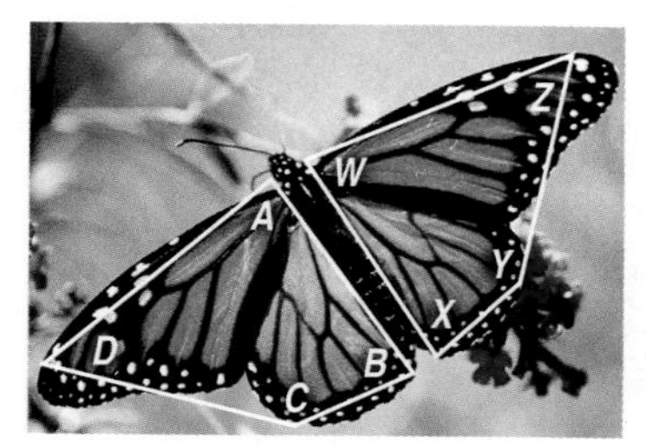

H.O.T. Problems

16. **CHALLENGE** State whether the following statement is *sometimes, always* or *never* true. Explain your reasoning.

If the areas of two rectangles are equal, then the rectangles are congruent.

17. **WRITING IN MATH** Explain how you could determine whether two similar polygons were also congruent.

ISAT PRACTICE 9.A.3c

18. Which statement must be true if $\triangle PQR \cong \triangle TUV$?

A $\overline{PQ} \cong \overline{UV}$

B $\overline{QR} \cong \overline{TV}$

C $\angle P \cong \angle T$

D $\angle R \cong \angle U$

19. **SHORT RESPONSE** In the bridge below, $\triangle ABD \cong \triangle CBD$, $\overline{AD}$ is 300 feet long, $\overline{BD}$ is 149 feet long, and $\overline{AB}$ is about 335 feet long. What is the length of $\overline{CD}$?

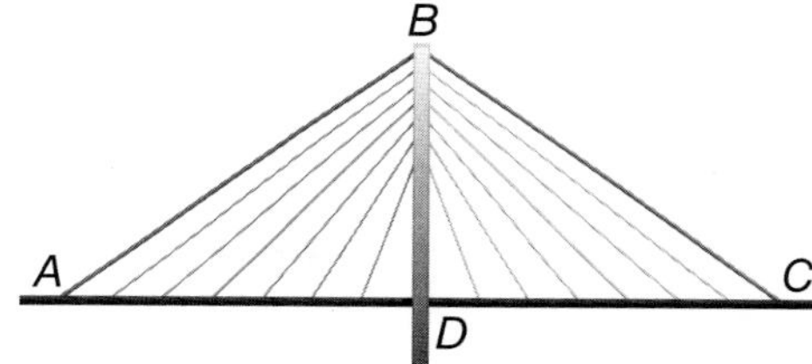

Spiral Review

ALGEBRA Find the measure of one interior angle in each regular polygon. Round to the nearest tenth if necessary. (Lesson 6-3)

20. triangle
21. pentagon
22. heptagon
23. nonagon

24. **CITY SERVICES** The street maintenance vehicles for the city of Centerburg cannot safely make turns less than 70°. Should the proposed site of the new maintenance garage at the northeast corner of Park and Main be approved? Explain. (Lesson 6-1)

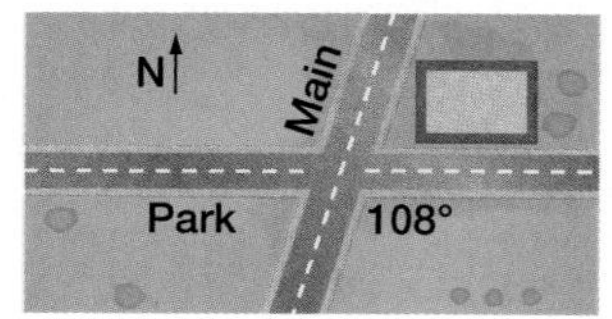

GET READY for the Next Lesson

PREREQUISITE SKILL Which figure *cannot* be folded so one half matches the other half?

25.

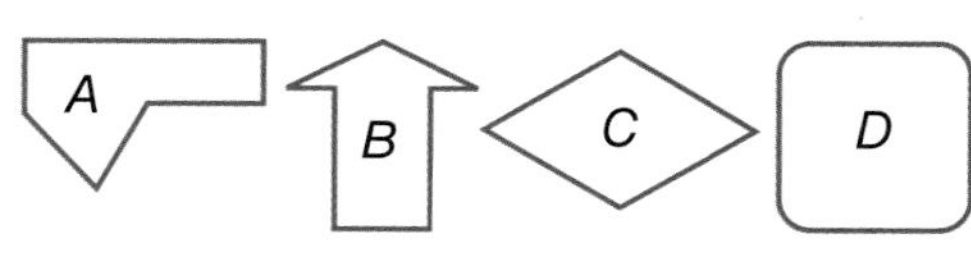

26.

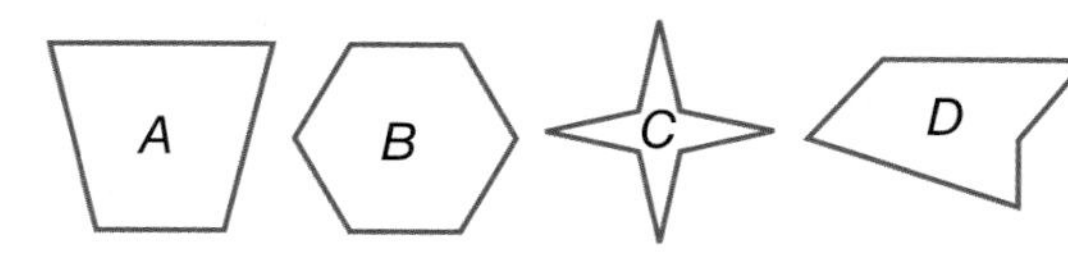

Extend 6-4

Geometry Lab
Investigating Congruent Triangles

In this lab, you will investigate whether it is possible to show that two triangles are congruent without showing that all six pairs of corresponding parts are congruent.

MAIN IDEA

Investigate which three pairs of corresponding parts can be used to show that two triangles are congruent.

IL Learning Standards

9.A.3a Draw or construct **two-** and three-**dimensional geometric figures** including prisms, pyramids, cylinders and cones.
9.A.3c Use concepts of symmetry, **congruency,** similarity, scale, perspective, and angles **to describe and analyze two-** and three-dimensional **shapes** found in practical applications (e.g., geodesic domes, A-frame houses, basketball courts, inclined planes, art forms, blueprints).
Also addresses 9.B.3, 9.C.3a, 9.C.3b.

IL Math Online

glencoe.com
• Concepts in Motion

ACTIVITY 1

STEP 1 Draw a triangle on a piece of patty paper. Copy the sides onto another piece of patty paper and cut them out.

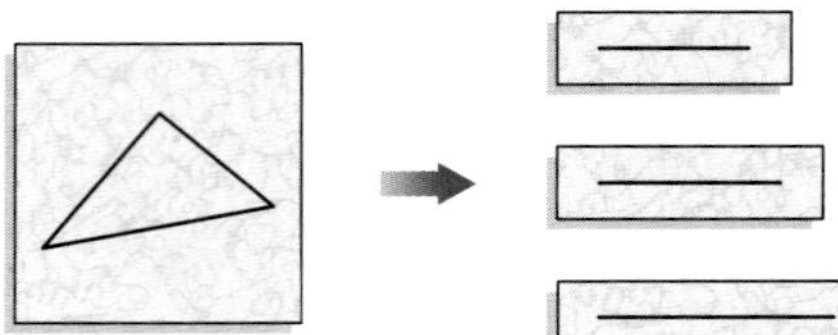

STEP 2 Arrange and tape the pieces together so that they form a triangle.

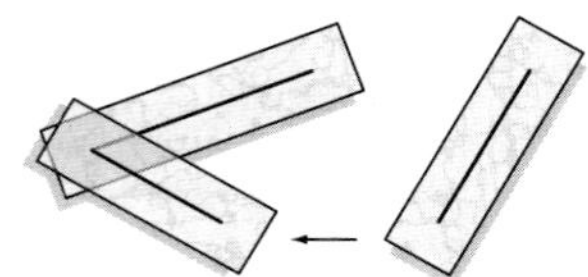

Analyze the Results

1. Is the triangle you formed congruent to the original triangle? Explain.
2. Try to form another triangle with the given sides. Is it congruent to the original triangle?
3. **MAKE A CONJECTURE** Based on this activity, can three pairs of congruent sides be used to show that two triangles are congruent?

ACTIVITY 2

STEP 1 Draw a triangle on a piece of patty paper. Copy each angle of the triangle onto separate pieces of patty paper. Extend each ray of each angle to the edge of the patty paper.

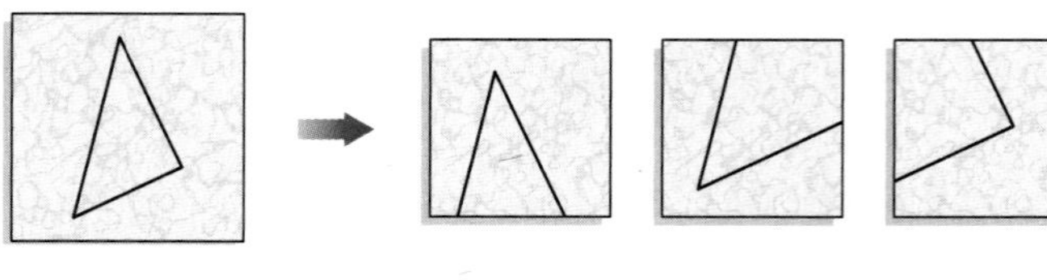

STEP 2 Arrange and tape the pieces together so that they form a triangle.

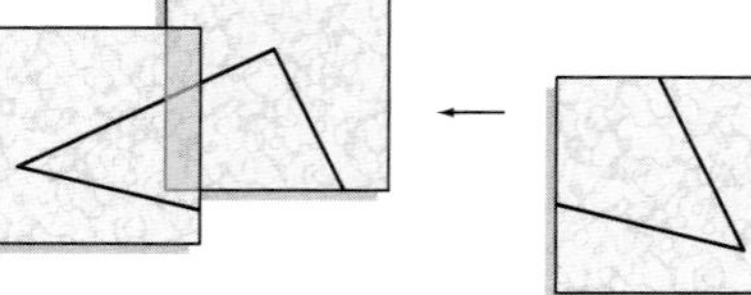

ANALYZE THE RESULTS

4. Is the triangle you formed congruent to the original triangle? Explain.
5. Try to form another triangle with the given angles. Is it congruent to the original triangle?
6. **MAKE A CONJECTURE** Based on this activity, can three pairs of congruent angles be used to show that two triangles are congruent?

ACTIVITY

3 **STEP 1** Draw a triangle on a piece of patty paper. Copy two sides of the triangle and the angle between them onto separate pieces of patty paper and cut them out.

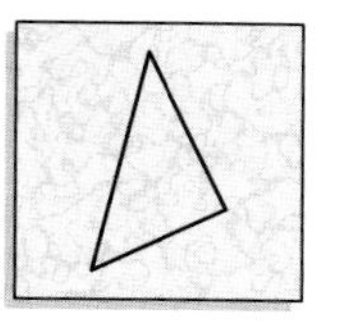

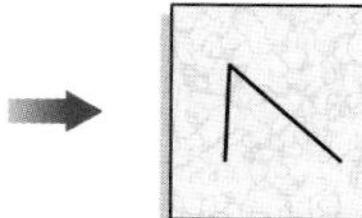

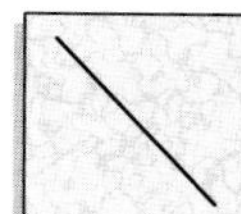

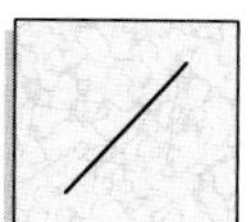

STEP 2 Arrange and tape the pieces together so that the two sides are joined to form the rays of the angle. Then tape these joined pieces onto a piece of construction paper and connect the two rays to form a triangle.

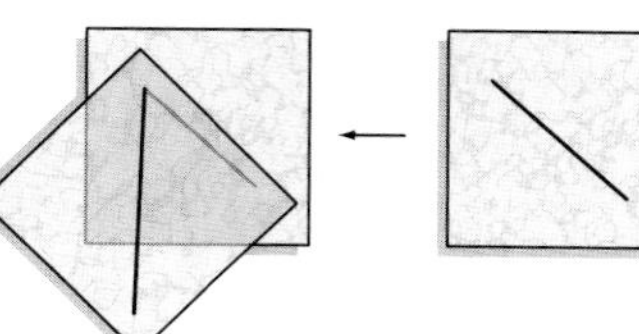

ANALYZE THE RESULTS

7. Is the triangle you formed congruent to the original triangle? Explain.
8. Try to form another triangle with the given sides and included angle. Is it congruent to the original triangle?
9. **MAKE A CONJECTURE** Based on this activity, can two pairs of congruent sides and the pair of congruent angles between them be used to show that two triangles are congruent?
10. **EXTENSION** Use patty paper to investigate and make a conjecture about whether each of these additional cases can be used to show that two triangles are congruent.

Case 4 two pairs of congruent sides and a pair of congruent angles *not* between them

Case 5 two pairs of congruent angles and the pair of congruent sides between them

Case 6 two pairs of congruent angles and a pair of congruent sides *not* between them

Conjectures
In this lab, you used inductive reasoning to make conjectures. You will learn actual proofs in later courses.

Mid-Chapter Quiz

Lessons 6-1 through 6-4

IL Learning Standards
9.A.3c, 9.B.3

Find the value of x in each figure. (Lesson 6-1)

1. 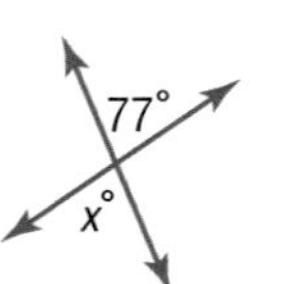

2. 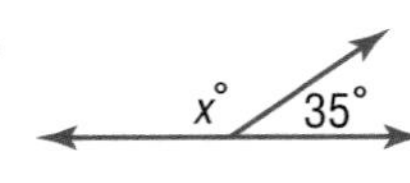

3. 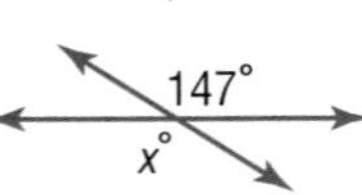

4. 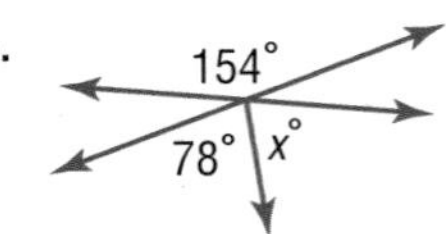

For Exercises 5–8, use the figure. Classify each pair of angles as *alternate interior, alternate exterior,* or *corresponding.* (Lesson 6-1)

5. $\angle 7$ and $\angle 1$
6. $\angle 2$ and $\angle 6$
7. $\angle 6$ and $\angle 4$
8. $\angle 2$ and $\angle 8$

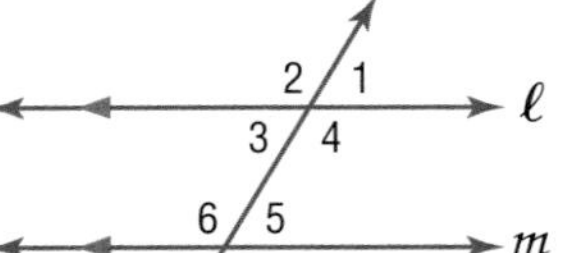

9. **LINES** Refer to the figure below. Classify the relationship between $\angle R$ and $\angle S$. Then find $m\angle R$. (Lesson 6-4)

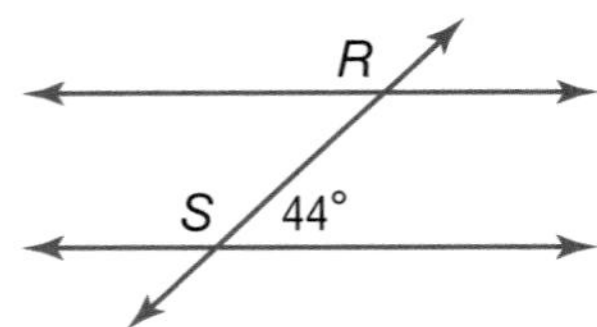

10. **NUMBERS** Consider the following pattern.

$$1^2 = 1$$
$$11^2 = 121$$
$$111^2 = 12{,}321$$

Use logical reasoning to find the next equation. Explain your reasoning. (Lesson 6-2)

ALGEBRA Find the sum of the measures of the interior angles of each polygon. (Lesson 6-3)

11. pentagon
12. 20-gon
13. 15-gon

14. **MULTIPLE CHOICE** Mrs. Lytle's kitchen tile is made up of a pattern of repeating regular octagons and squares. Which statement is true concerning the pattern? (Lesson 6-3)

A The sum of the angle measures in each square is 180°.

B The sum of the angle measures at each vertex is 1,080°.

C The measure of the angle at each vertex is 90°.

D The measure of each interior angle of an octagon is 135°.

15. **KITES** Determine whether the indicated triangles in the kite below are congruent. If so, name the corresponding parts and write a congruence statement. (Lesson 6-4)

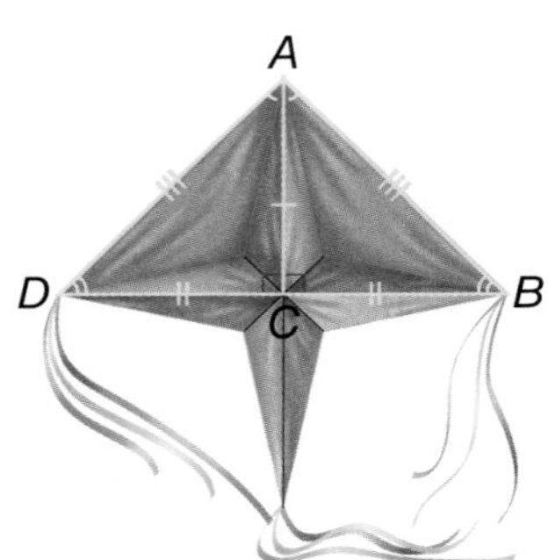

In the figure, quadrilateral $QRST$ is congruent to quadrilateral $JKLM$. Find each measure. (Lesson 6-4)

16. QT

17. QR

18. $m\angle M$
19. $m\angle K$

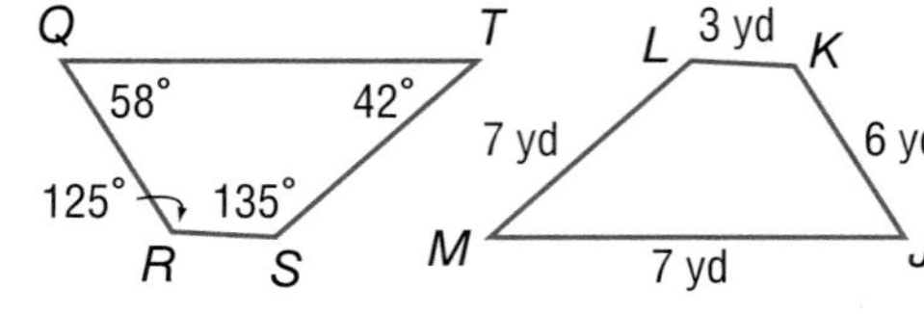

20. **MULTIPLE CHOICE** Which statement is *not* true if $\triangle ABC \cong \triangle DEF$? (Lesson 6-4)

F $\overline{BC} \cong \overline{EF}$

G $\overline{AB} \cong \overline{DE}$

H $\angle F \cong \angle B$

J $\angle A \cong \angle D$

6-5 Symmetry

MAIN IDEA

Identify line symmetry and rotational symmetry.

IL Learning Standards

9.A.3c Use concepts of symmetry, congruency, similarity, scale, perspective, and angles **to describe and analyze two-** and three-**dimensional shapes found in practical applications (e.g.,** geodesic domes, A-frame houses, basketball courts, inclined planes, **art forms**, blueprints). *Also addresses 9.C.3a, 9.C.3b.*

New Vocabulary

line symmetry
line of symmetry
rotational symmetry
angle of rotation

IL Math Online

glencoe.com

- Extra Examples
- Personal Tutor
- Self-Check Quiz

MINI Lab

ARCHITECTURE The Pentagon is the headquarters of the United States Department of Defense and is located near Washington, D.C. Trace the outline of the Pentagon onto both a piece of tracing paper and a transparency.

1. Draw a line through the center and one vertex of the Pentagon. Then fold your paper across this line. What do you notice about the two halves?
2. Are there other lines you can draw that will produce the same result? If so, how many?
3. Place the transparency over the outline on your tracing paper. Use your pencil point at the center of the Pentagon to hold the transparency in place. How many times can you rotate the transparency from its original position so that the two figures match?
4. Find the first angle of rotation by dividing 360° by the total number of times the figures matched.
5. List the other angles of rotation by adding the measure of the first angle of rotation to the previous angle measure. Stop when you reach 360°.

A figure has **line symmetry** if it can be folded over a line so that one half of the figure matches the other half. This fold line is called the **line of symmetry**.

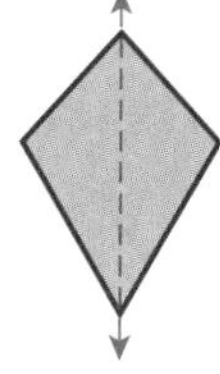
vertical line of symmetry

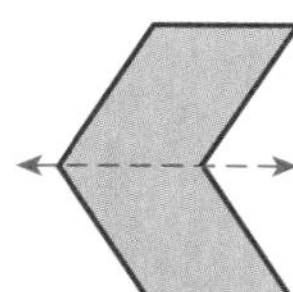
horizontal line of symmetry

no line of symmetry

Some figures, such as the Pentagon in the Mini Lab above, have more than one line of symmetry. The figure at the right has multiple lines of symmetry: one vertical, one horizontal, and two diagonal.

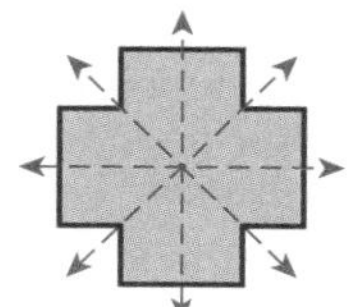

EXAMPLE Identify Line Symmetry

1 FLAGS Determine whether the figure has line symmetry. If it does, trace the figure and draw all lines of symmetry. If not, write *none*.

The state flag of Arizona has one vertical line of symmetry.

a. 

b. 

c. 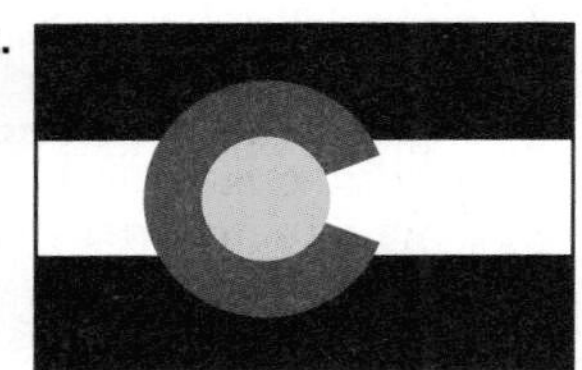

A figure has **rotational symmetry** if it can be rotated or turned less than 360° about its center so that the figure looks exactly as it does in its original position. The degree measure of the angle through which the figure is rotated is called the **angle of rotation**. Some figures have just one angle of rotation, while others, like the Pentagon, have several.

Many companies and nonprofit groups, such as the American Red Cross, use a logo so people can easily identify their products or services. They often design their logo to have line or rotational symmetry.

EXAMPLE Identify Rotational Symmetry

2 DESIGNS Determine whether the figure has rotational symmetry. Write *yes* or *no*. If *yes*, name its angle(s) of rotation.

Yes, this figure has rotational symmetry. It will match itself after being rotated 180°.

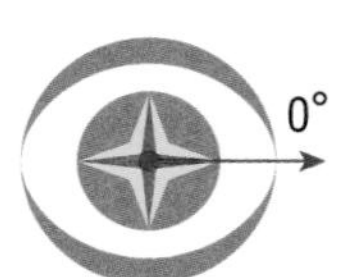

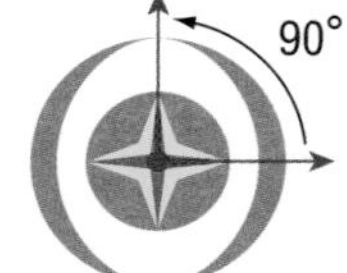

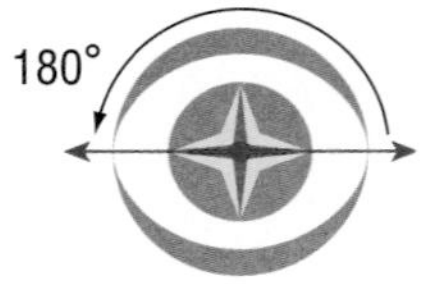

CHECK Your Progress

d. 

e. 

f. 

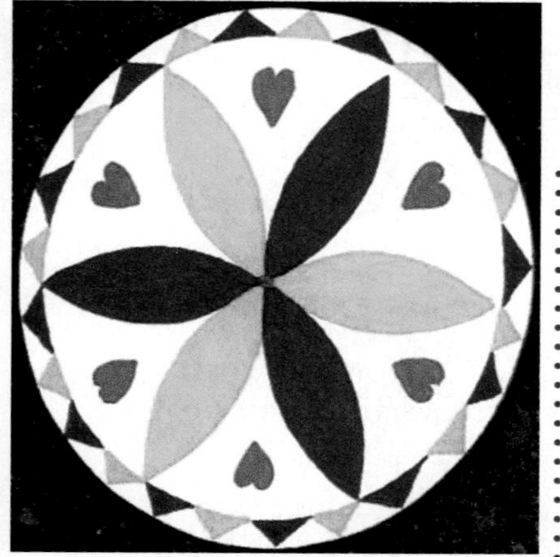

Real-World Link The Pennsylvania Dutch, or Pennsylvania Germans, created signs that were painted on the sides of barns or houses. Many feature designs that have rotational symmetry.

EXAMPLE Use a Rotation

3 FOLK ART Copy and complete the barn sign shown so that the completed figure has rotational symmetry with 90°, 180°, and 270° as its angles of rotation.

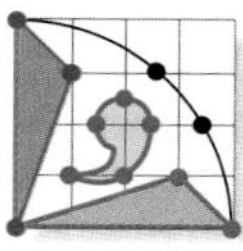

Use the procedure described above and the points indicated to rotate the figure 90°, 180°, and 270° counterclockwise. A 90° rotation clockwise produces the same rotation as a 270° rotation counterclockwise.

90° counterclockwise

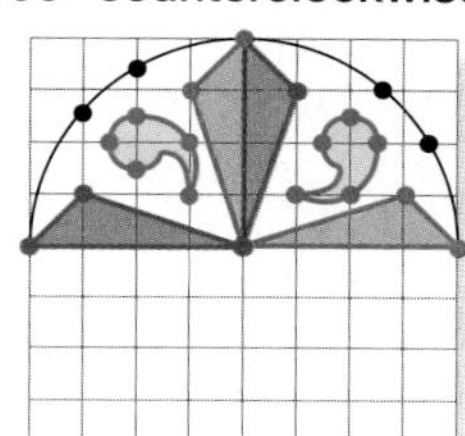

180° counterclockwise

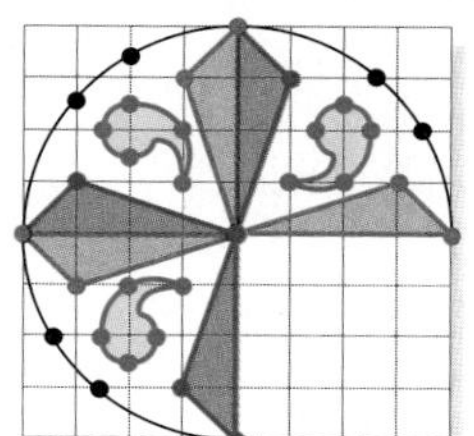

90° clockwise

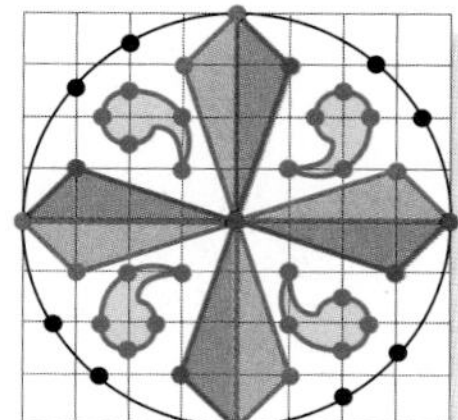

CHECK Your Progress

g. **SYMBOLS** Copy and complete the symbol for recycling shown so that the completed figure has rotational symmetry with 120° and 240° as its angles of rotation.

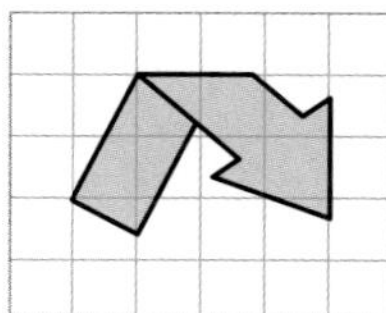

CHECK Your Understanding

SPORTS For Exercises 1 and 2, complete parts a and b for each figure.

Example 1 (p. 328) a. **Determine whether the logo has line symmetry. If it does, trace the figure and draw all lines of symmetry. If not, write *none*.**

Example 2 (p. 328) b. **Determine whether the logo has rotational symmetry. Write *yes* or *no*. If *yes*, name its angle(s) of rotation.**

1. 

2. 

Example 3 (p. 329)

3. **ARCHITECTURE** Copy and complete the window so that the completed figure has rotational symmetry with 45°, 90°, 135°, 180°, 225°, 270°, and 315° as its angles of rotation.

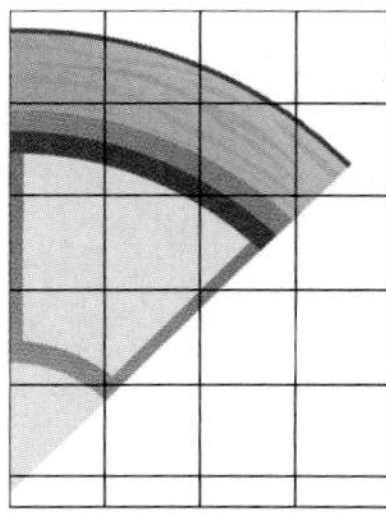

Practice and Problem Solving

For Exercises	See Examples
4a–7a, 8	1
4b–7b, 9	2
10, 11	3

HOMEWORK HELP

STAINED GLASS For Exercises 4–7, complete parts a and b for each stained glass pattern.

a. Determine whether the pattern has line symmetry. If it does, trace the pattern and draw all lines of symmetry. If not, write *none*.

b. Determine whether the pattern has rotational symmetry. Write *yes* or *no*. If *yes*, name its angle(s) of rotation.

4. 

5. 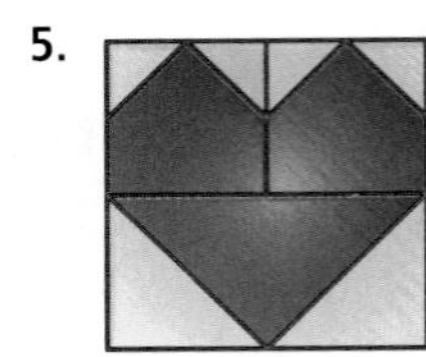

6. 

7. 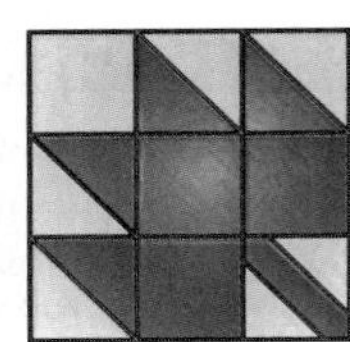

MUSIC For Exercises 8 and 9, use the diagrams below.

a. 

b.

c. 

d. 

8. Determine whether each instrument has line symmetry. If it does, trace the instrument and draw all lines of symmetry. If not, write *none*.

9. Which of the instruments above could be rotated and still look the same? If any, name the angle(s) of rotation.

10. **HUBCAPS** A partial hubcap is shown. Copy and complete the figure so that the completed hubcap has rotational symmetry of 90°, 180°, and 270°.

11. **PIZZA** A piece of pizza is shown. Copy and complete the figure so that the entire pizza has rotational symmetry of 60°, 120°, 180°, 240°, and 300°. How many slices are needed to complete the pizza?

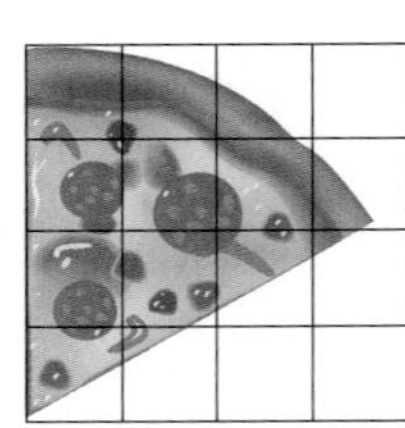

12. **ARCHITECTURE** Determine whether the Taj Mahal in Agra, India, has line symmetry. If it does, state the number of lines of symmetry and describe each one. If not, write *none*.

Taj Mahal

Real-World Link
The stained glass window of the Notre Dame Cathedral in Paris, France, has a diameter of 10 meters. The Cathedral itself is 35 meters high, 48 meters wide, and 130 meters long.
Source: Paris Digest

13. **ART** Describe the kind(s) of symmetry shown in the stained glass window at the left.

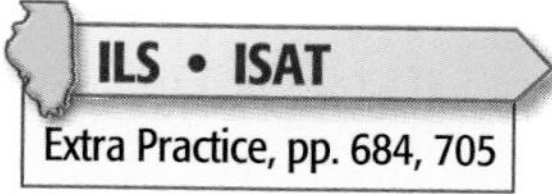

14. **STATES** Which capital letters in SOUTH CAROLINA produce the same letter after being rotated 180°?

15. **QUADRILATERALS** Which types of quadrilaterals have line symmetry? Which have rotational symmetry?

H.O.T. Problems

CHALLENGE For Exercises 16 and 17, determine whether each statement is *true* or *false*. If *false*, give a counterexample.

16. If a figure has one horizontal and one vertical line of symmetry, then it also has rotational symmetry.

17. If a figure has rotational symmetry, it also has line symmetry.

18. **WRITING IN MATH** Explain the difference between line symmetry and rotational symmetry.

ISAT PRACTICE 9.A.3c

19. The figures below have a repeating pattern.

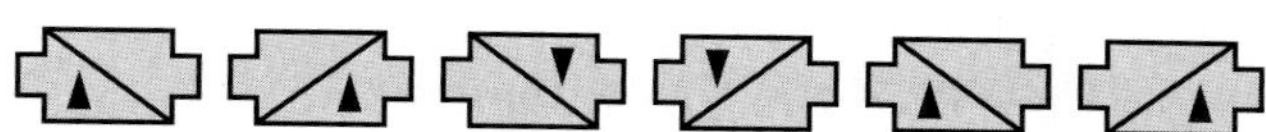

Which shows a 180° rotation of the 17th figure in the pattern?

A  B  C  D 

Spiral Review

20. **ALGEBRA** Find the value of x in the two congruent triangles. (Lesson 6-4)

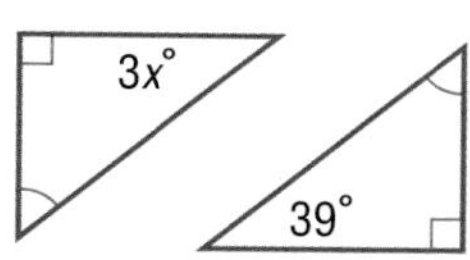

ALGEBRA Find the sum of the measures of the interior angles of each polygon. (Lesson 6-3)

21. hexagon
22. octagon
23. 14-gon
24. 20-gon

25. **SHOPPING** A pair of boots costs \$130 and is on sale for 15% off this price. Find the amount of the discount. (Lesson 5-8)

GET READY for the Next Lesson

PREREQUISITE SKILL Find the coordinates of the vertices of polygon $H'J'K'L'$ after polygon $HJKL$ is dilated using the given scale factor. Then graph polygon $HJKL$ and its dilation. (Lesson 4-8)

26. $H(-6, 2)$, $J(4, 4)$, $K(7, -2)$, $L(-2, -4)$; scale factor $\frac{1}{2}$

6-6 Reflections

MAIN IDEA

Graph reflections on a coordinate plane.

IL Learning Standards

9.A.3b Draw transformation images of figures, with and **without the use of technology.**
9.C.3b Develop and solve problems using geometric relationships and models, with and **without the use of technology.**

New Vocabulary

reflection
line of reflection
transformation
image

IL Math Online

glencoe.com
- Extra Examples
- Personal Tutor
- Self-Check Quiz

GET READY for the Lesson

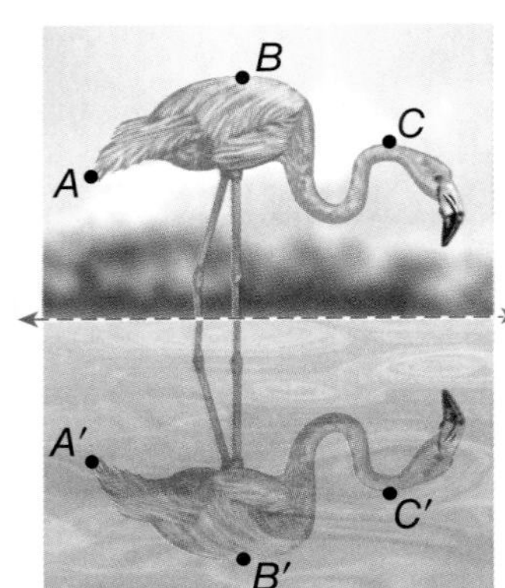

NATURE The surface of the water in the art shown acts like a mirror by producing an image of the flamingo.

1. Compare the shape and size of the bird on either side of the line of symmetry.
2. Compare the perpendicular distance from the line of symmetry to each of the points shown. What do you observe?
3. The points *A*, *B*, and *C* appear *clockwise* on the bird. How are these points oriented on the other side of the line of symmetry?

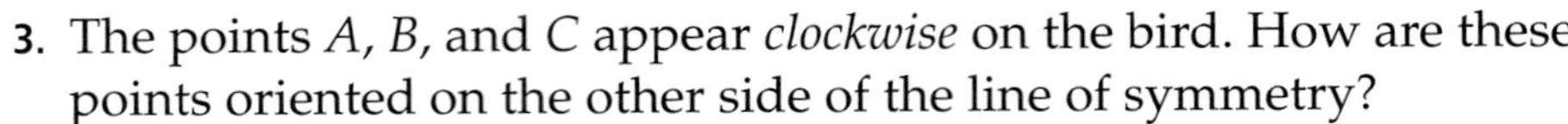

The mirror image produced by flipping a figure over a line is called a **reflection**. This line is called the **line of reflection**. A reflection is one type of **transformation** or mapping of a geometric figure. In mathematics, an **image** is the position of a figure after a transformation. The image of point *A* is written as *A*′. *A*′ is read as *A prime*.

EXAMPLE Draw a Reflection

1 **Copy △*JKL* at the right on graph paper. Then draw the image of the figure after a reflection over the given line.**

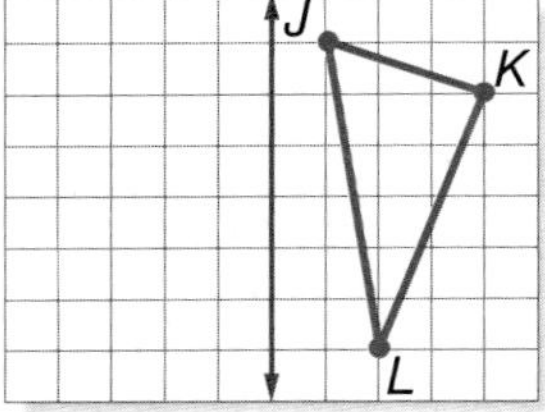

Step 1 Count the number of units between each vertex and the line of reflection.

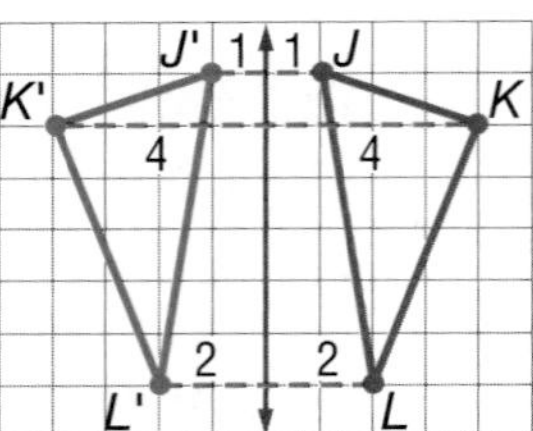

Step 2 For each vertex, plot a point the same distance away from the line on the other side.

Step 3 Connect the new vertices to form the image of △*JKL*, △*J*′*K*′*L*′.

CHECK Your Progress

a. Copy the figure on a piece of graph paper. Then draw the image of the figure after a reflection over the given line.

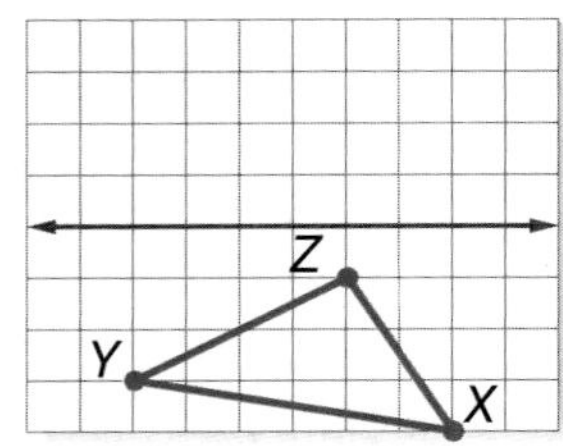

EXAMPLES Reflect a Figure Over an Axis

Review Vocabulary

vertex the point where two sides of a figure intersect; *Example:* point P in $\triangle PQR$ is formed by the intersection of $\overline{PQ}$ and $\overline{PR}$.

2 **Graph $\triangle PQR$ with vertices $P(-3, 4)$, $Q(4, 2)$, and $R(-1, 1)$. Then graph the image of $\triangle PQR$ after a reflection over the x-axis, and write the coordinates of its vertices.**

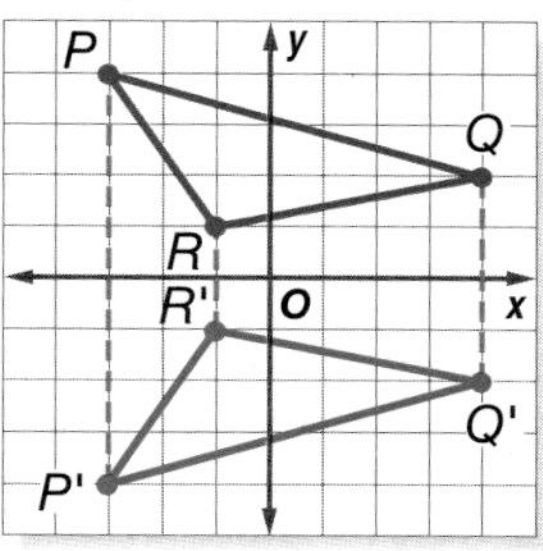

The coordinates of the vertices of the image are $P'(-3, -4)$, $Q'(4, -2)$, and $R'(-1, -1)$. Examine the relationship between the coordinates of each figure.

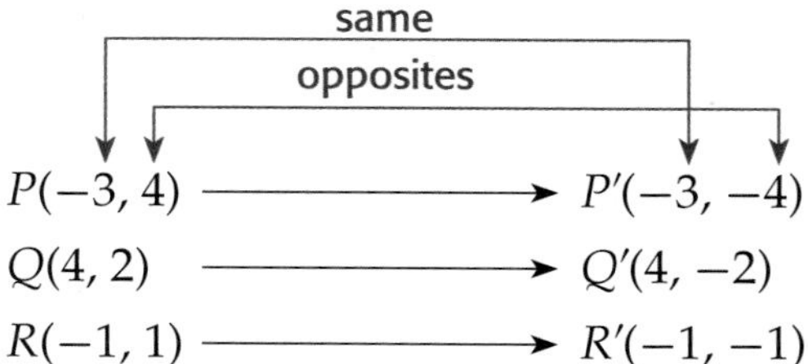

$P(-3, 4) \longrightarrow P'(-3, -4)$

$Q(4, 2) \longrightarrow Q'(4, -2)$

$R(-1, 1) \longrightarrow R'(-1, -1)$

Notice that the y-coordinate of a point reflected over the x-axis is the opposite of the y-coordinate of the original point.

3 **Graph quadrilateral $ABCD$ with vertices $A(-4, 1)$, $B(-2, 3)$, $C(0, -3)$, and $D(-3, -2)$. Then graph the image of $ABCD$ after a reflection over the y-axis, and write the coordinates of its vertices.**

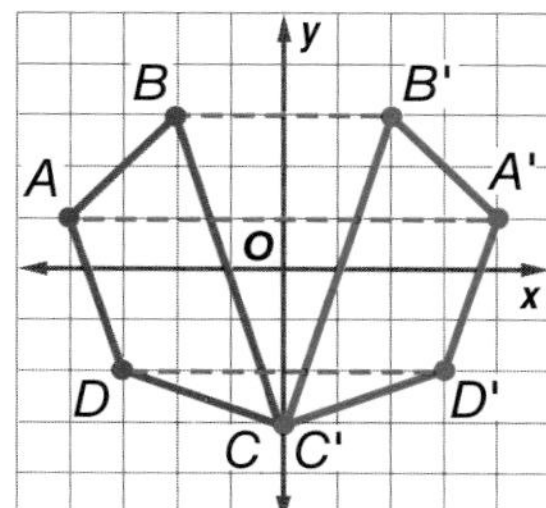

The coordinates of the vertices of the image are $A'(4, 1)$, $B'(2, 3)$, $C'(0, -3)$, and $D'(3, -2)$. Examine the relationship between the coordinates of each figure.

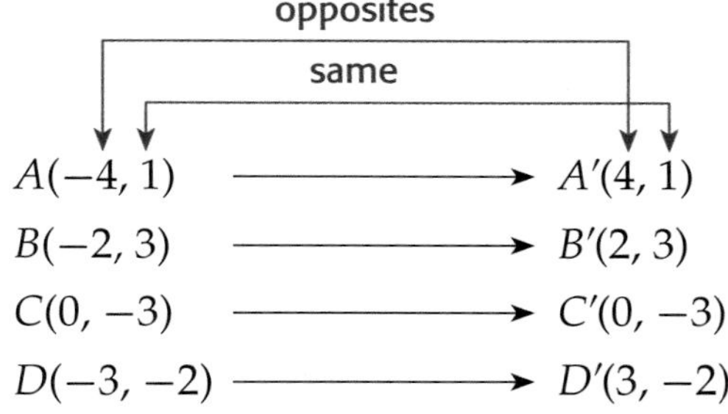

$A(-4, 1) \longrightarrow A'(4, 1)$

$B(-2, 3) \longrightarrow B'(2, 3)$

$C(0, -3) \longrightarrow C'(0, -3)$

$D(-3, -2) \longrightarrow D'(3, -2)$

Notice that the x-coordinate of a point reflected over the y-axis is the opposite of the x-coordinate of the original point.

Study Tip

Points on Line of Reflection Notice that if a point lies on the line of reflection, the image of that point has the same coordinates as those of the point on the original figure.

CHECK Your Progress

Graph $\triangle FGH$ with vertices $F(1, -1)$, $G(5, -3)$, and $H(2, -4)$. Then graph the image of $\triangle FGH$ after a reflection over the given axis, and write the coordinates of its vertices.

b. x-axis

c. y-axis

If a figure touches the line of reflection as it does in Example 3, then the figure and its image together form a new figure that has line symmetry. The line of reflection is then also a line of symmetry.

EXAMPLE Use a Reflection

Real-World Link Approximately 50 million kites are sold in the United States each year.

4 KITES Copy and complete the kite shown so that the completed figure has a vertical line of symmetry.

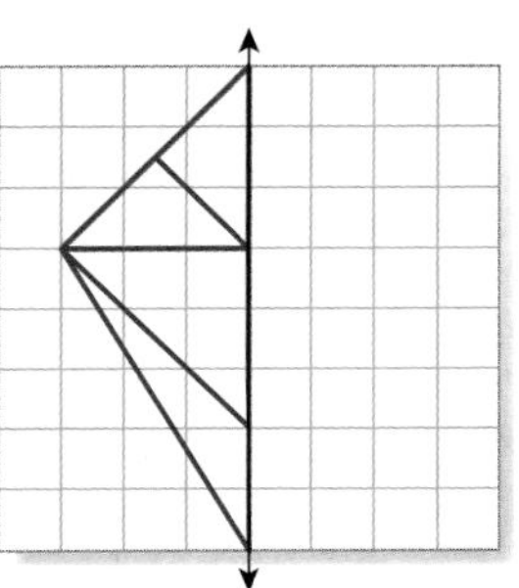

You can reflect the half of the kite shown over the indicated vertical line.

Find the distance from each vertex on the figure to the line of reflection.

Then plot a point that same distance away on the opposite side of the line. Connect vertices as appropriate.

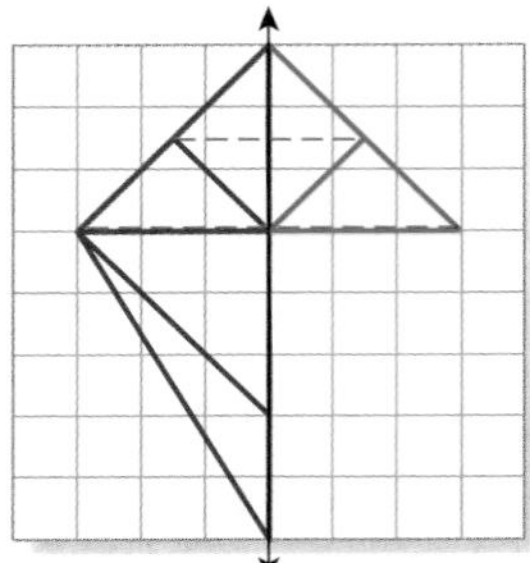

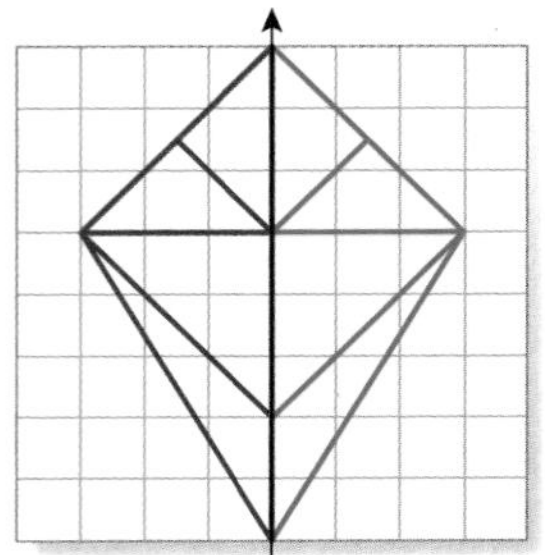

 CHECK Your Progress

d. **ART** Copy and complete the portion of the animal shown so that the completed picture has horizontal line symmetry. What is the animal?

CHECK Your Understanding

Examples 1–3 (pp. 332–333)

Graph the figure with the given vertices. Then graph the image of the figure after a reflection over the *x*-axis and *y*-axis and write the coordinates of the image's vertices.

1. $\triangle ABC$ with vertices $A(3, 5)$, $B(4, 1)$, and $C(1, 2)$
2. $\triangle WXY$ with vertices $W(-1, -2)$, $X(0, -4)$, and $Y(-3, -5)$

Example 4 (p. 334)

3. **HOT TUBS** Copy and complete the hot tub design shown so that the completed design has vertical line symmetry.

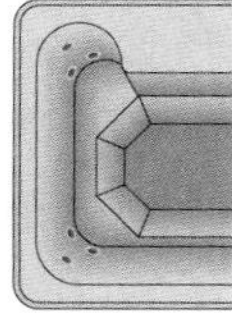

Practice and Problem Solving

HOMEWORK HELP	
For Exercises	**See Examples**
4, 5	1
6–9	2, 3
10, 11	4

Copy each figure onto graph paper. Then draw the image of the figure after a reflection over the given line.

4. 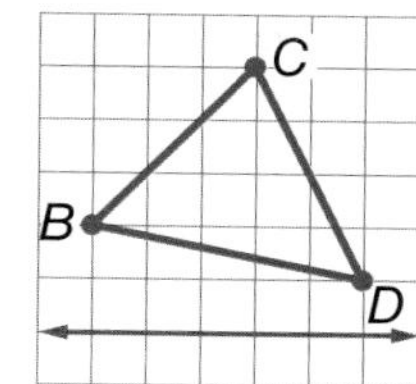

5. 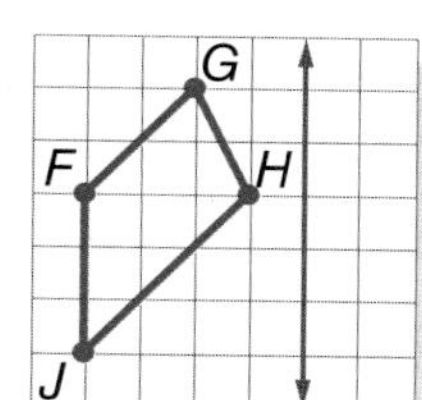

Graph the figure with the given vertices. Then graph the image of the figure after a reflection over the given axis, and write the coordinates of the image's vertices.

6. triangle ABC with vertices $A(-1, -1)$, $B(-2, -4)$, and $C(-4, -1)$; x-axis
7. triangle FGH with vertices $F(3, 3)$, $G(4, -3)$, and $H(2, 1)$; y-axis
8. square $JKLM$ with vertices $J(-2, 0)$, $K(-1, -2)$, $L(-3, -3)$, and $M(-4, -1)$; y-axis
9. quadrilateral $PQRS$ with vertices $P(1, 3)$, $Q(3, 5)$, $R(5, 2)$, and $S(3, 1)$; x-axis

10. **CARS** The drawing shows the left half of a car. Copy the drawing onto grid paper. Then draw the right side of the car so that the completed drawing has a vertical line of symmetry.

11. **ART** The top half of a Ukranian decorative egg is shown. Copy the figure onto a piece of paper. Then draw the egg design after it has been reflected over a horizontal line.

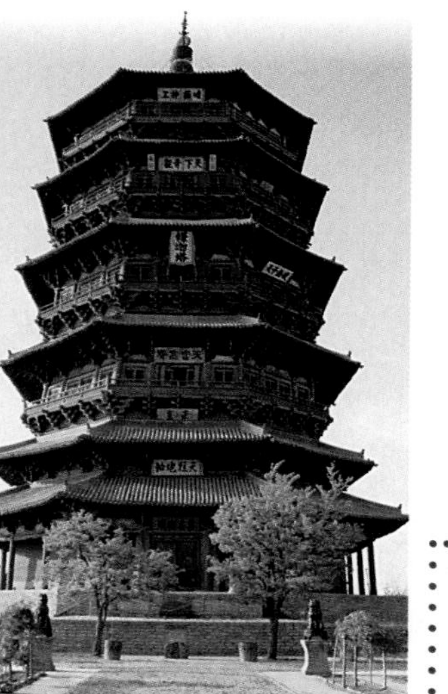

12. **ARCHITECTURE** Describe in what ways the symmetry of the Fogong Monastery, shown at the left, is similar to that of the Eiffel Tower in Paris, France, shown at the right.

Real-World Link
The Fogong Monastery in Yingxian, China, is an example of a *pagoda*, a popular style of traditional Chinese architecture. The monastery has five stories and each story is octagonal.

13. Triangle XYZ has vertices $X(-1, 3)$, $Y(2, 5)$, and $Z(3, -2)$. Find the coordinates of the image after a reflection over the x-axis and then the y-axis.

14. **FIND THE DATA** Refer to the Data File on pages 16–19. Choose an image that illustrates a reflection.

Copy each figure onto graph paper. Then draw the image of the figure after a reflection over the given line.

15. 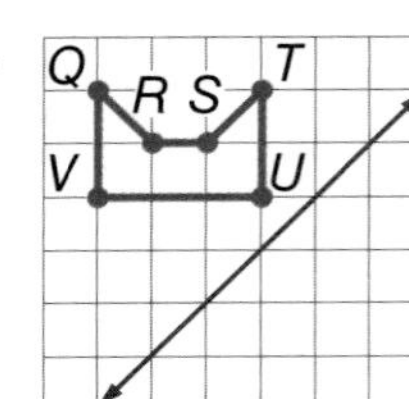

16. 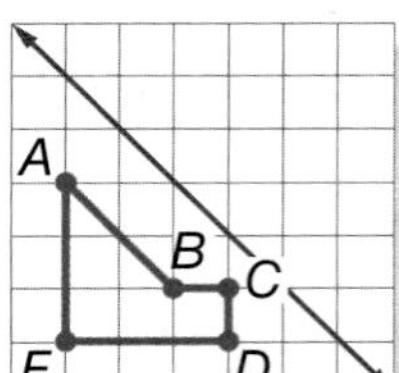

ILS • ISAT
Extra Practice, pp. 685, 705

H.O.T. Problems

17. **OPEN ENDED** Draw a right triangle ABC in the first quadrant of a coordinate plane. Then draw the image after a reflection over the x-axis.

18. **CHALLENGE** Suppose point K with coordinates $(7, -2)$ is reflected so that the coordinates of its image are $(7, 2)$. Without graphing, which axis was this point reflected over? Explain your reasoning.

19. **WRITING IN MATH** Find the coordinates of the point (x, y) after it has been reflected over the x-axis. Then find the coordinates of the point (x, y) after it has been reflected over the y-axis. Explain your reasoning.

ISAT PRACTICE 9.A.3b, 9.C.3b

20. Which of the following is the reflection of $\triangle ABC$ with vertices $A(1, -1)$, $B(4, -1)$, and $C(2, -4)$ over the x-axis?

A 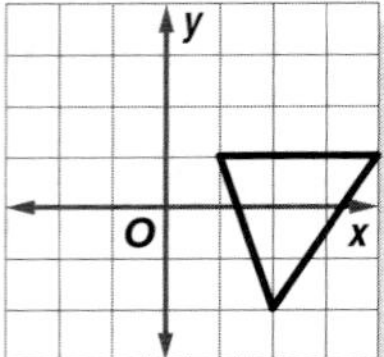

B 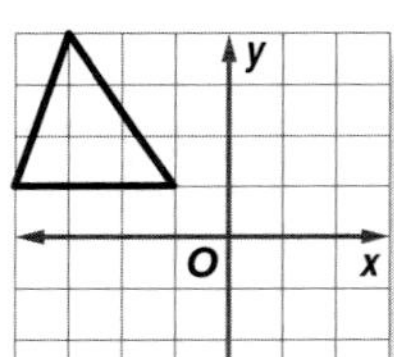

C 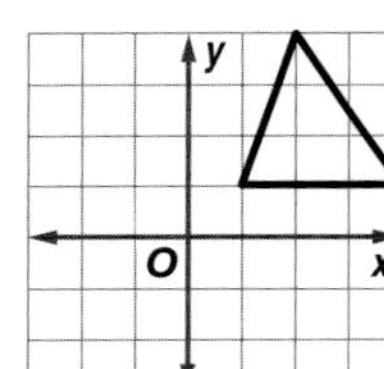

D 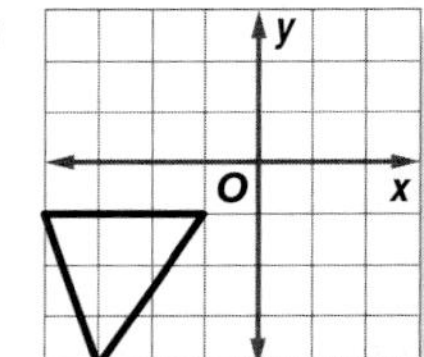

Spiral Review

Determine whether each regular polygon has rotational symmetry. Write *yes* or *no*. If *yes*, name its angle(s) of rotation. (Lesson 6-5)

21. 

22. 

23. 

24. **ALGEBRA** Find the value of x if the triangles at the right are congruent. (Lesson 6-4)

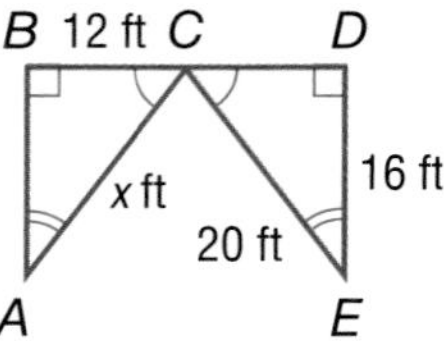

GET READY for the Next Lesson

PREREQUISITE SKILL Add. (Lesson 1-4)

25. $-4 + (-1)$

26. $-5 + 3$

27. $-1 + 4$

6-7 Translations

MAIN IDEA

Graph reflections on a coordinate plane.

IL Learning Standards

9.A.3b Draw transformation images of figures, with and **without the use of technology.**
9.C.3b Develop and solve problems using geometric relationships and models, with and **without the use of technology.**

New Vocabulary

translation

IL Math Online

glencoe.com

- Extra Examples
- Personal Tutor
- Self-Check Quiz

GET READY for the Lesson

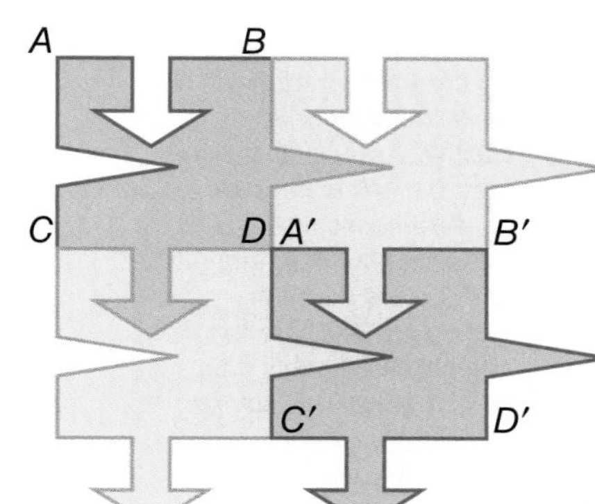

DESIGN Carmen created the design at the right on her computer. It was formed by making a template and repeating it horizontally and vertically.

1. Describe the motion involved in moving the design from one position to another.
2. Compare the size, shape, and orientation of the design piece in its original position to that of the piece in its new position.

A **translation** (sometimes called a *slide*) is the movement of a figure from one position to another without turning it.

EXAMPLE Draw a Translation

1 **Copy trapezoid *WXYZ* at the right on graph paper. Then draw the image of the figure after a translation 4 units left and 2 units down.**

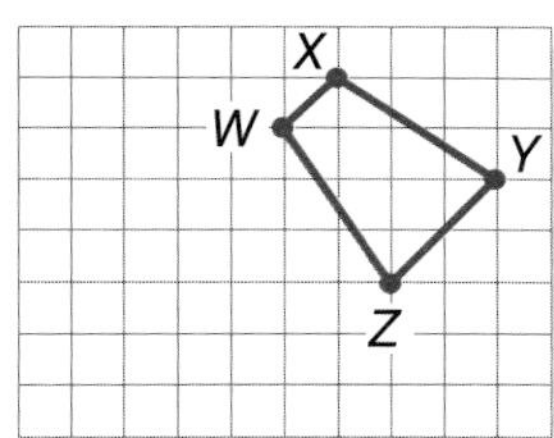

Step 1 Move each vertex of the trapezoid 4 units left and 2 units down.

Step 2 Connect the new vertices to form the image.

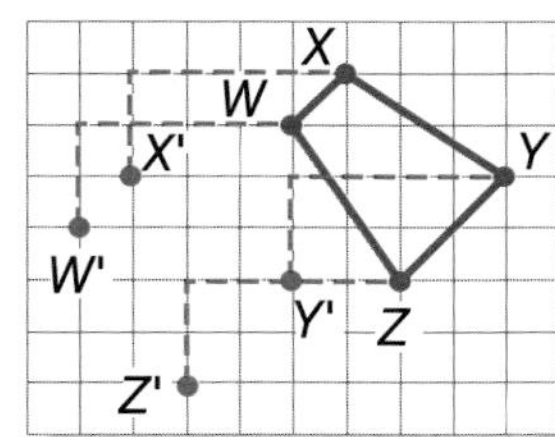

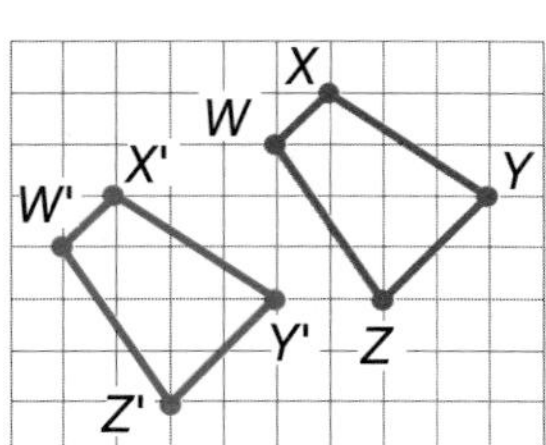

CHECK Your Progress

a. Copy square *EFGH* at the right on graph paper. Then draw the image of the figure after a translation 5 units right and 3 units up.

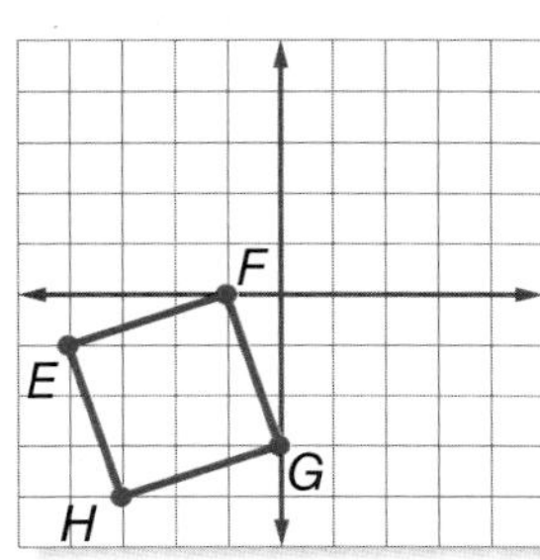

EXAMPLE Translation in the Coordinate Plane

2 **Graph $\triangle JKL$ with vertices $J(-3, 4)$, $K(1, 3)$, and $L(-4, 1)$. Then graph the image of $\triangle JKL$ after a translation 2 units right and 5 units down. Write the coordinates of its vertices.**

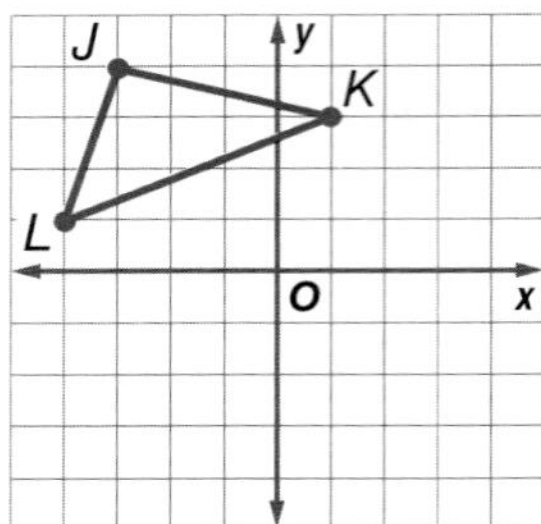

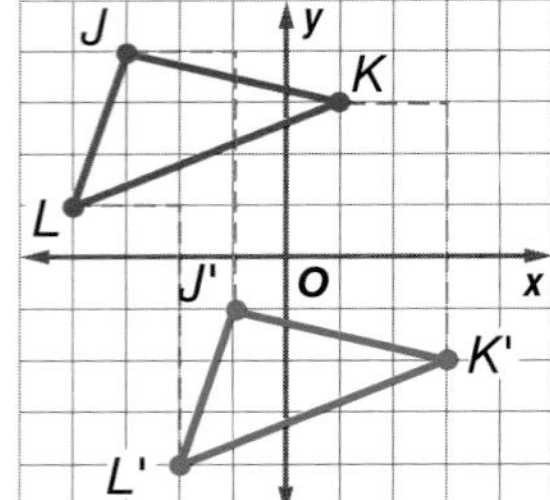

The coordinates of the vertices of the image are $J'(-1, -1)$, $K'(3, -2)$, and $L'(-2, -4)$. Notice that these vertices can also be found by adding 2 to the x-coordinates and -5 to the y-coordinates, or $(2, -5)$.

Original		Add (2, –5).		Image
$J(-3, 4)$	→	$(-3 + 2, 4 + (-5))$	→	$J'(-1, -1)$
$K(1, 3)$	→	$(1 + 2, 3 + (-5))$	→	$K'(3, -2)$
$L(-4, 1)$	→	$(-4 + 2, 1 + (-5))$	→	$L'(-2, -4)$

Study Tip

Translations
In the coordinate plane, a translation can be described using an ordered pair. A translation *up* or to the *right* is positive. A translation *down* or to the *left* is negative. $(2, -5)$ means a translation 2 units right and 5 units down. In general, if (x, y) are the original coordinates, then $(x + a, y + b)$ moves the point (x, y) a units horizontally and b units vertically.

CHECK Your Progress

Graph $\triangle ABC$ with vertices $A(4, -3)$, $B(0, 2)$, and $C(5, 1)$. Then graph its image after each translation, and write the coordinates of its vertices.

b. 2 units down

c. 4 units left and 3 units up

ISAT EXAMPLE 9.A.3b, 9.C.3b

3 **If triangle PQR is translated 2 units left and 3 units down, what are the coordinates of point R'?**

A (2, 2) **C** (4, 2)

B (4, –1) **D** (2, –1)

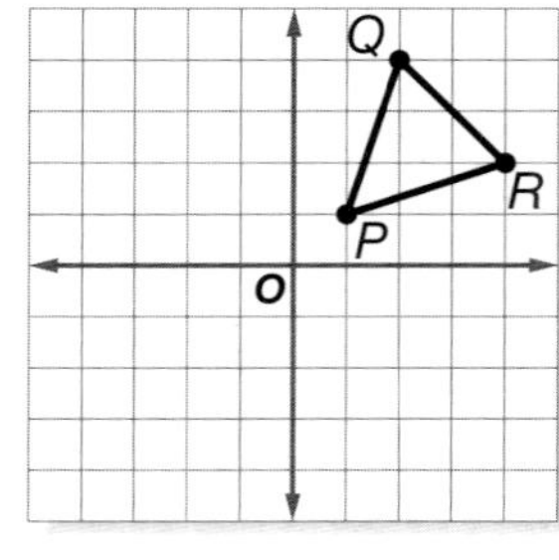

Read the Item

You are asked to determine the coordinates of point R' after the original figure has been translated 2 units left and 3 units down.

Solve the Item

You can answer this question without translating the entire triangle.

Test-Taking Tip

Eliminate the Possibilities Since point R was translated 2 units left, the x-coordinate of point R' is $4 - 2$ or 2. This eliminates choices B and C.

The coordinates of point R are (4, 2).	Original Figure
The x-coordinate of R is 4, so the x-coordinate of R' is $4 - 2$ or 2.	Translating 2 units left is the same as subtracting 2 from the x-coordinate.
The y-coordinate of R is 2, so the y-coordinate of R' is $2 - 3$ or -1.	Translating 3 units down is the same as subtracting 3 from the y-coordinate.

The coordinates of R' are (2, −1).

The answer is D.

CHECK Your Progress

d. If $\triangle ABC$ with vertices $A(-3, -4)$, $B(-1, -3)$, and $C(-3, 1)$ is translated 3 units to the right and 4 units up, what are the coordinates of B'?

F (2, 1) H (−4, 1)
G (−4, −7) J (2, −7)

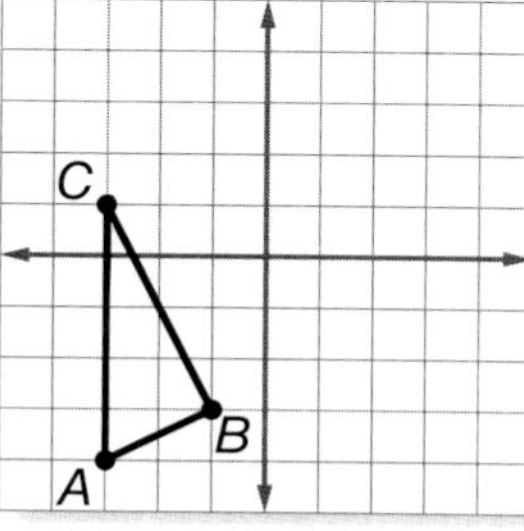

CHECK Your Understanding

Example 1 (p. 337)

For Exercises 1 and 2, copy the figure at the right.

1. Draw the image of $\triangle ABC$ after a translation 4 units left and 1 unit up.
2. Draw the image of $\triangle ABC$ after a translation 2 units right and 3 units down.

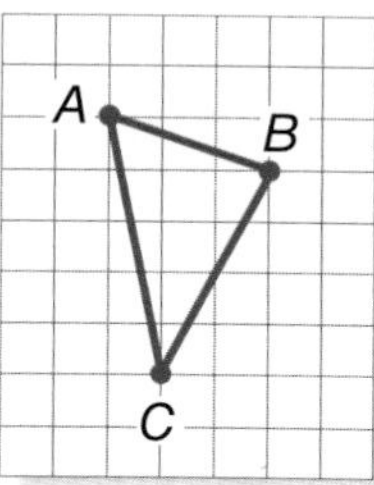

Example 2 (p. 338)

Graph $\triangle XYZ$ with vertices $X(-4, -4)$, $Y(-3, -1)$, and $Z(2, -2)$. Then graph the image of $\triangle XYZ$ after each translation, and write the coordinates of its vertices.

3. 3 units right and 4 units up
4. 2 units left and 3 units down

Example 3 (p. 338)

5. **MULTIPLE CHOICE** Triangle PQR is translated 5 units left and 3 units down. If the coordinates of P' are (−3, 8), find the coordinates of P.

A (−8, 11) C (2, 11)
B (−6, 3) D (2, 5)

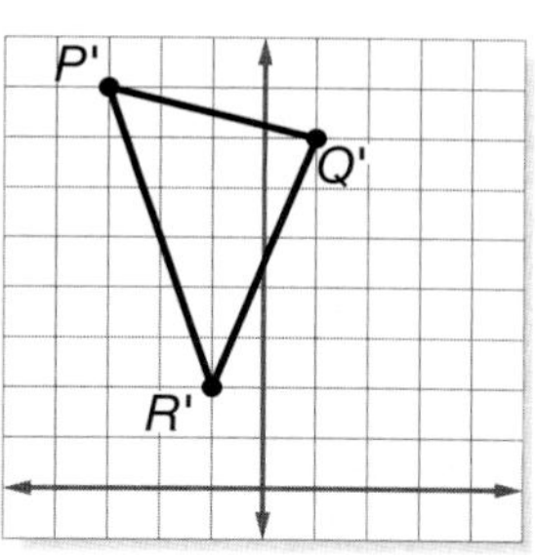

Practice and Problem Solving

HOMEWORK HELP

For Exercises	See Examples
6–9	1
10–11	2
19, 20	3

Copy each figure onto graph paper. Then draw the image of the figure after the indicated translation.

6. 5 units right and 3 units up

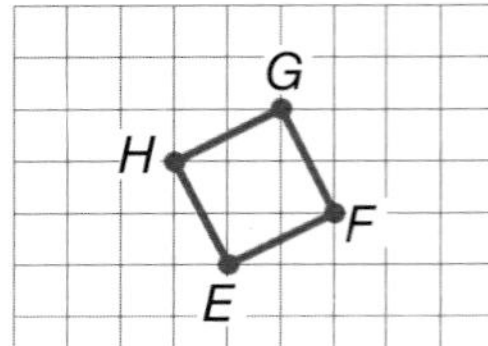

7. 3 units right and 4 units down

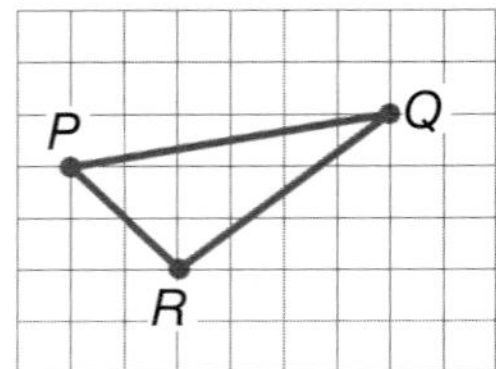

8. 2 units left and 5 units down

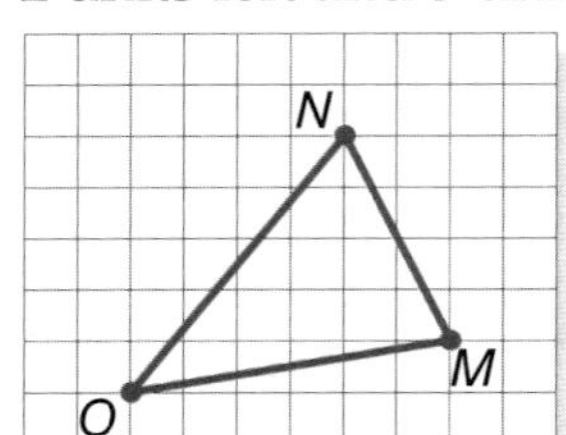

9. 1 unit left and 2 units up

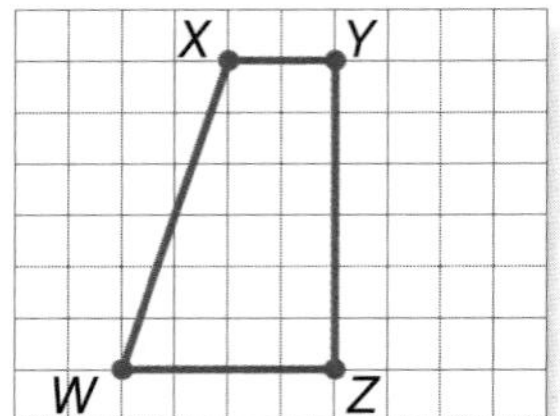

Graph the figure with the given vertices. Then graph the image of the figure after the indicated translation, and write the coordinates of its vertices.

10. $\triangle ABC$ with vertices $A(1, 2)$, $B(3, 1)$, and $C(3, 4)$ translated 2 units left and 1 unit up

11. rectangle $JKLM$ with vertices $J(-3, 2)$, $K(3, 5)$, $L(4, 3)$, and $M(-2, 0)$ translated 1 unit right and 4 units down

12. **ARCHITECTURE** The arches in the first three stories of the Colosseum in Rome, Italy, are translations of one another. Describe the translations needed to move arch *A* to arch *B* in the photo at the right.

13. **SCIENCE** A diagram of a DNA double helix is shown below. Look for a pattern. Copy the double helix and indicate where this pattern repeats or is translated. Find how many translations of the original pattern are shown in the diagram.

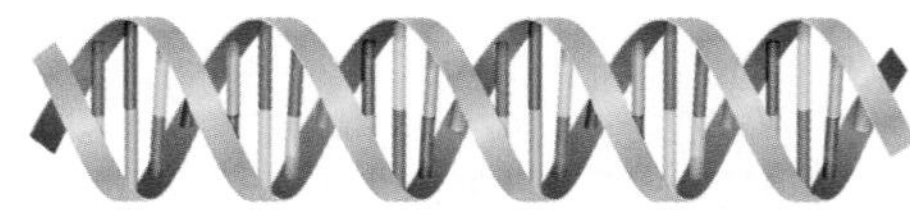

14. **WALLPAPER** The wallpaper design at the right is a traditional Japanese design. Describe the minimum number of translations of the original pattern, *A*, needed to create the section shown.

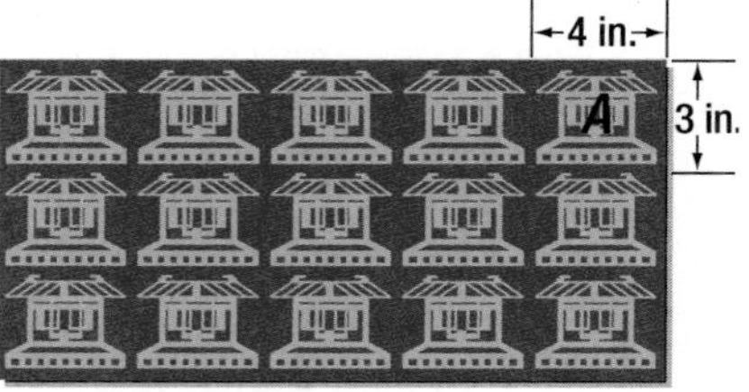

ILS • ISAT
Extra Practice, pp. 685, 705

15. **GEOMETRY** Triangle ABC has vertices $A(4, 3)$, $B(-7, 0)$, and $C(6, 5)$. When translated, A' has coordinates $(-1, 3)$. Find the coordinates of B' and C'. Then describe the translation of triangle ABC.

H.O.T. Problems

16. **REASONING** A figure is translated by $(-5, 7)$. Then the result is translated by $(5, -7)$. Without graphing, what is the final position of the figure? Explain your reasoning.

17. **CHALLENGE** What are the coordinates of the point (x, y) after being translated m units left and n units up?

18. **WRITING IN MATH** Write a real-world problem in which you would need to translate a figure. Then solve your problem.

ISAT PRACTICE 9.A.3b, 9.C.3b

19. If $\triangle PQR$ is translated 4 units right and 3 units up, what are the coordinates of R'?

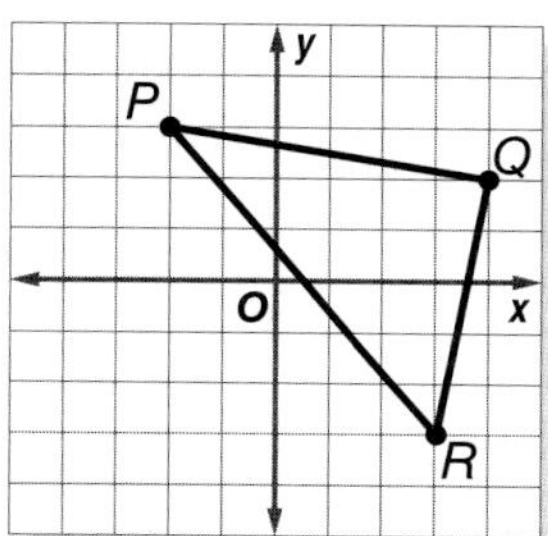

A $(-1, -6)$ C $(-1, 0)$
B $(7, 0)$ D $(7, -6)$

20. Find the coordinates of C' of trapezoid $ABCD$ after a translation 3 units right and 7 units down.

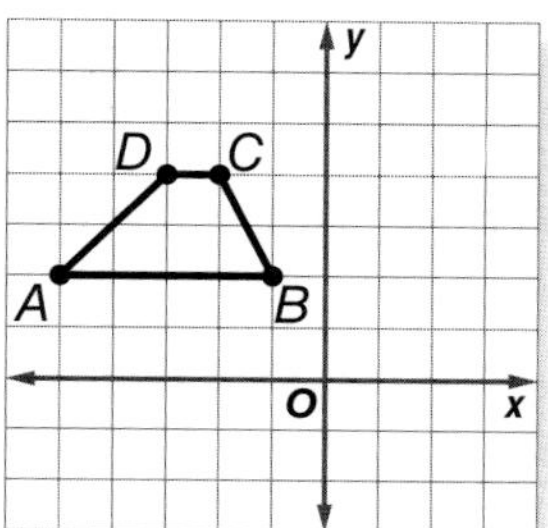

F $(1, 3)$ H $(1, -3)$
G $(5, 7)$ J $(-9, 1)$

Spiral Review

21. Graph polygon $ABCDE$ with vertices $A(-5, -3)$, $B(-2, 1)$, $C(-3, 4)$, $D(0, 2)$, and $E(0, -3)$. Then graph the image of the figure after a reflection over the y-axis, and write the coordinates of its vertices. (Lesson 6-6)

CATS For Exercises 22 and 23, use the photo of the cat at the right. (Lesson 6-5)

22. Does the face of the cat have line symmetry? If so, indicate how many. If not, write *none*.

23. Does the cat's face have rotational symmetry? If *yes*, name its angle(s) of rotation.

Order each set of numbers from least to greatest. (Lesson 5-2)

24. $16\%, \frac{1}{6}, 1.6, \frac{1}{16}$

25. $\frac{3}{8}, 0.65, 38\%, \frac{5}{8}$

26. $0.44, \frac{4}{5}, \frac{4}{9}, 88\%$

CHAPTER 6 Study Guide and Review

IL Math Online glencoe.com
• STUDY TO GO
• Vocabulary Review

FOLDABLES® Study Organizer GET READY to Study

Be sure the following Big Ideas are noted in your Foldable.

BIG Ideas

Angle Relationships (Lesson 6-1)
- When two parallel lines are cut by a transversal, congruent angle pairs are formed: alternate interior angles, alternate exterior angles, and corresponding angles.

Polygons (Lessons 6-3 and 6-4)
- The sum of the measures of the interior angles of a polygon is $(n - 2)(180)$.
- In congruent polygons, corresponding sides and angles are congruent.

Symmetry (Lesson 6-5)
- A figure with line symmetry can be folded over a line so that the two halves match.
- A figure with rotational symmetry can be rotated about its center so that it looks exactly as it does in its original position.

Transformations (Lessons 6-6 and 6-7)
- In a reflection, the image is congruent to the original figure, but the orientation of the image is different from that of the original figure.
- In a translation, the image is congruent to the original figure, and the orientation of the image is the same as that of the original figure.

Key Vocabulary

alternate exterior angles (p. 308)
alternate interior angles (p. 308)
complementary angles (p. 306)
corresponding angles (p. 308)
exterior angles (p. 307)
image (p. 332)
inductive reasoning (p. 314)
interior angles (p. 307)
line of reflection (p. 332)
line of symmetry (p. 327)
line symmetry (p. 327)
reflection (p. 332)
rotational symmetry (p. 328)
supplementary angles (p. 306)
transformation (p. 332)
translation (p. 337)
transversal (p. 307)
vertical angles (p. 306)

Vocabulary Check

State whether each sentence is *true* or *false*. If *false*, replace the underlined word or number to make a true sentence.

1. $m\angle 1$ is read as the <u>*measure*</u> of $\angle 1$.
2. A translation of (3, −2) means a translation 3 units <u>left</u> and 2 units down.
3. If $\triangle ABC \cong \triangle DEF$, then <u>$\angle C$</u> $\cong \angle E$.
4. <u>Inductive</u> reasoning is the process of making a rule after observing several examples and using that rule to make a decision.
5. A polygon whose angles are all congruent is said to be <u>equilateral</u>.
6. A rectangle will match itself after being rotated <u>90°, 180°, and 270°</u>.
7. P', the image of point P, is read as <u>*P prime*</u>.
8. When a transformation occurs, the resulting figure is called a <u>line of reflection</u>.

Lesson-by-Lesson Review

6-1 Line and Angle Relationships (pp. 306–311)

7.A.3b

Find the value of x in each figure.

9. 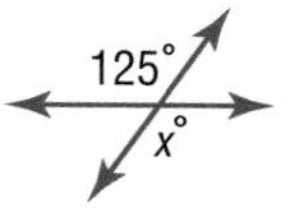

10. 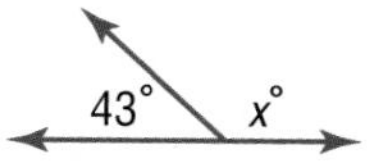

11. 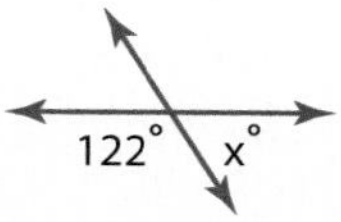

12. 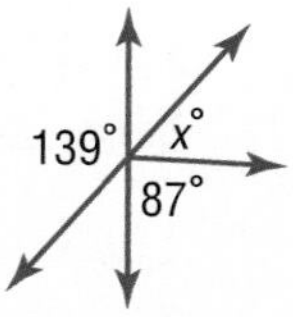

Refer to the figure below. Classify each pair of angles as *alternate interior, alternate exterior,* or *corresponding*.

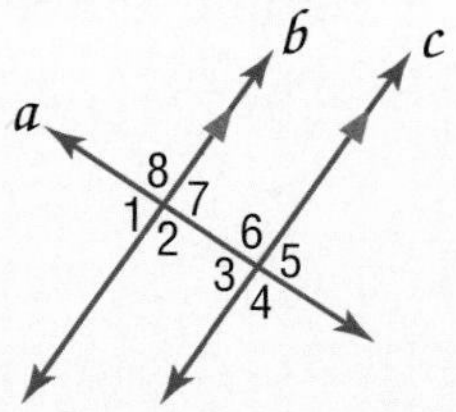

13. $\angle 8$ and $\angle 6$
14. $\angle 1$ and $\angle 5$
15. $\angle 4$ and $\angle 2$
16. $\angle 3$ and $\angle 7$

17. **ARCHITECTURE** Parallel lines are cut by a transversal. If $m\angle 1 = 86°$, classify the relationship between $\angle 2$ and $\angle 3$. Then find $m\angle 2$.

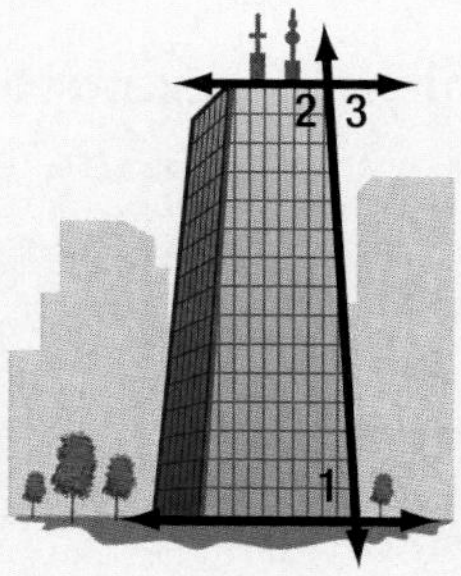

Example 1 **Find the value of x in the figure.**

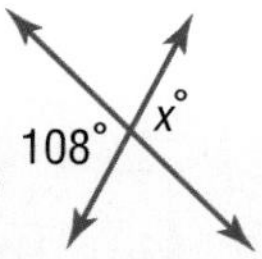

Since the angle labeled $x°$ and the angle labeled 108° are vertical angles, they are congruent.

Therefore, $x = 108$.

Example 2 **Classify $\angle 3$ and $\angle 5$ as *alternate interior, alternate exterior,* or *corresponding angles.* If $m\angle 3 = 65°$, find $m\angle 5$.**

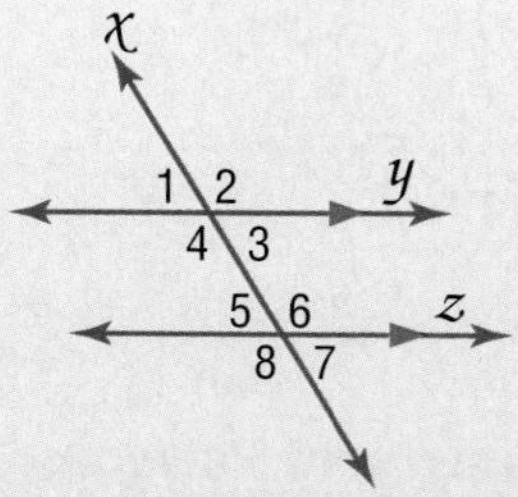

Since $\angle 3$ and $\angle 5$ are interior angles that lie on opposite sides of the transversal, they are alternate interior angles. Since $\angle 3$ and $\angle 5$ are alternate interior angles, they are congruent. So, $m\angle 5 = 65°$.

6-2 PSI: Use Logical Reasoning (pp. 314–315)

9.C.3a

Solve each problem using logical reasoning.

18. **GEOMETRY** Draw several squares and connect the opposite vertices. Then measure the four angles that are formed by the intersecting diagonals on each square. What seems to be true about the diagonals of a square?

Example 3

Use logical reasoning to find the next number.

3, 5, 8, 12, 17, …

3 → +2 → 5 → +3 → 8 → +4 → 12 → +5 → 17

Since the numbers increase by 2, 3, 4, and 5, the next number will increase by 6. The next number is 23.

CHAPTER 6 Study Guide and Review

6-3 Polygons and Angles (pp. 316–319)

9.B.3, 9.C.3b

Find the sum of the measures of the interior angles of each polygon.

19. decagon
20. 32-gon

Find the measure of one interior angle in each regular polygon. Round to the nearest tenth if necessary.

21. heptagon
22. pentagon

23. **RUGS** Find the measure of an interior angle of a rug shaped like a regular octagon.

Example 4 **Find the measure of one interior angle of a regular hexagon.**

Find the sum of the measures of the angles.

$S = (n - 2)180$	Write an equation.
$S = (6 - 2)180$	Replace n with 6.
$S = (4)180$	Subtract.
$S = 720$	Multiply.

The sum of the measures of the interior angles is 720°.

Divide 720° by 6, the number of interior angles. So, the measure of one interior angle of a regular hexagon is 720° ÷ 6 or 120°.

6-4 Congruent Polygons (pp. 320–323)

9.A.3c

Determine whether the polygons shown are congruent. If so, name the corresponding parts and write a congruence statement.

24.

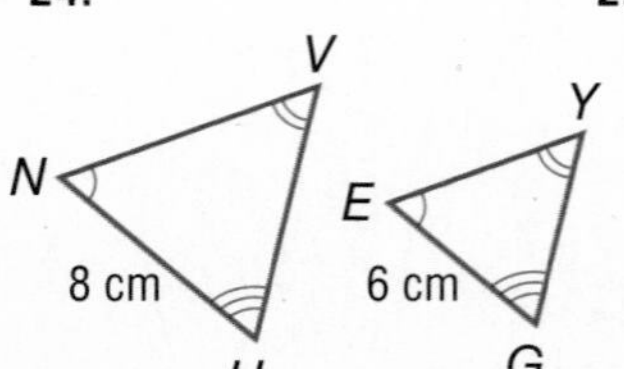

25.

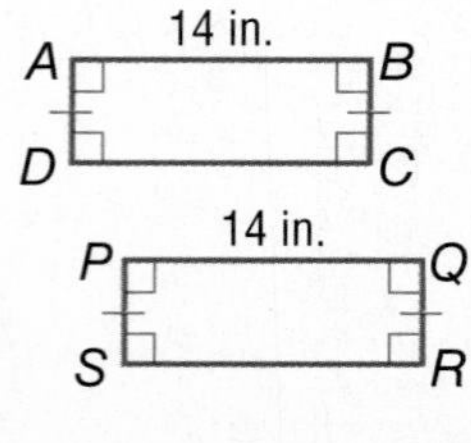

26. **ART** $\triangle BGY \cong \triangle MGK$ in the art design below. If $m\angle Y = 55°$, find $m\angle K$.

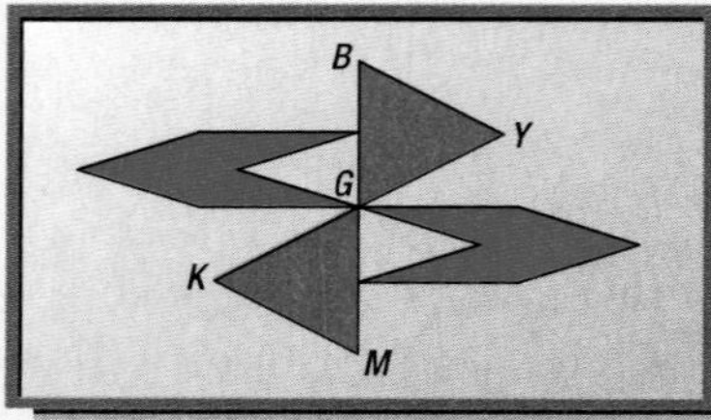

Example 5 **In the figure below, $\triangle ABC \cong \triangle RPQ$. Find PQ.**

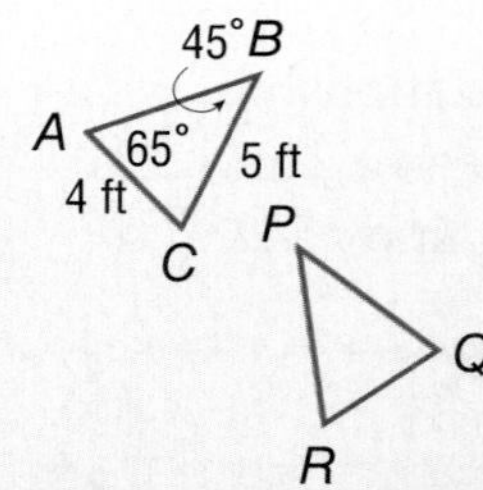

$\overline{PQ}$ corresponds to $\overline{BC}$.
Since $BC = 5$ feet, $PQ = 5$ feet.

Mixed Problem Solving
For mixed problem-solving practice, see page 705.

6-5 Symmetry (pp. 327–331)

9.A.3c

BLOCKS Determine whether each pattern block has line symmetry. If it does, trace the figure and draw all lines of symmetry. If not, write *none*.

27. 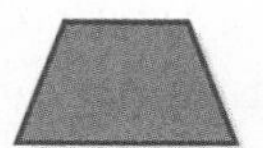

28. 

29. 

30. Which of the figures above has rotational symmetry? Name the angle(s) of rotation.

31. **ART** Determine whether the plate design below has rotational symmetry. If it does, name the angle(s) of rotation.

Example 6 **Determine whether the figure below has line symmetry. If it does, trace the figure and draw all lines of symmetry. If not, write *none*.**

The figure has line symmetry.

Example 7 **Determine whether the figure above has rotational symmetry. If it does, name its angle(s) of rotation.**

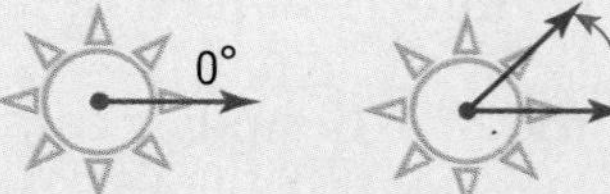

The figure has rotational symmetry. Its angles of rotation are 45°, 90°, 135°, 180°, 225°, 270°, and 315°.

6-6 Reflections (pp. 332–336)

9.A.3b, 9.C.3b

Graph parallelogram *QRST* with vertices *Q*(2, 5), *R*(4, 5), *S*(3, 1), and *T*(1, 1). Then graph its image after a reflection over the given axis, and write the coordinates of its vertices.

32. x-axis

33. y-axis

34. **ANIMALS** Copy and complete the starfish shown so that the completed figure has a vertical line of symmetry.

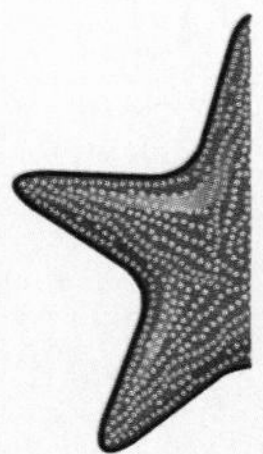

Example 8 **Graph $\triangle FGH$ with vertices $F(1, -1)$, $G(3, 1)$, and $H(2, -3)$ and its image after a reflection over the y-axis.**

The x-coordinate of a point reflected over the y-axis is the opposite of the x-coordinate of the original point. So, the coordinates of the vertices of the image are $F'(-1, -1)$, $G'(-3, 1)$, and $H'(-2, -3)$.

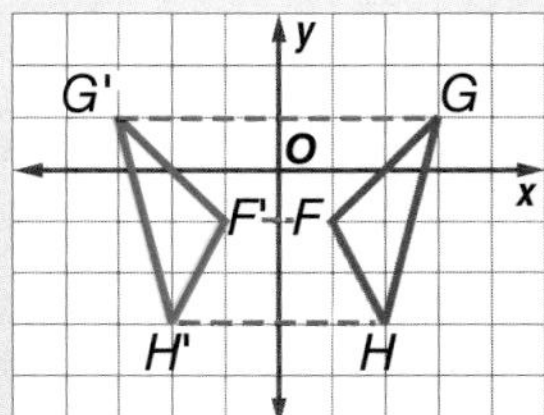

6-7 Translations (pp. 337–341)

9.A.3b, 9.C.3b

Copy the figure at the right onto graph paper. Then draw the image of the figure after the indicated translation.

35. 4 units left and 2 units up
36. 3 units right and 1 unit down

Graph $\triangle ABC$ with vertices $A(2, 2)$, $B(3, 5)$, and $C(5, 3)$. Then graph its image after the indicated translation, and write the coordinates of its vertices.

37. 1 unit right and 4 units down
38. 2 units left and 3 units up
39. **HIKING** From her car, Marjorie hiked 2 miles north and 3 miles west before she decided to stop and rest. If her starting point can be represented by the point $P(1, 4)$, what are the coordinates of her resting point? Assume that each unit in the coordinate plane is equal to one mile.

Example 9 **Graph $\triangle XYZ$ with vertices $X(-3, -1)$, $Y(-1, 0)$, and $Z(-2, -3)$ and its image after a translation 4 units right and 1 unit up.**

The coordinates of the vertices of the image can be found by adding 4 to the x-coordinates and 1 to the y-coordinates. The coordinates of the image are $X'(1, 0)$, $Y'(3, 1)$, and $Z'(2, -2)$.

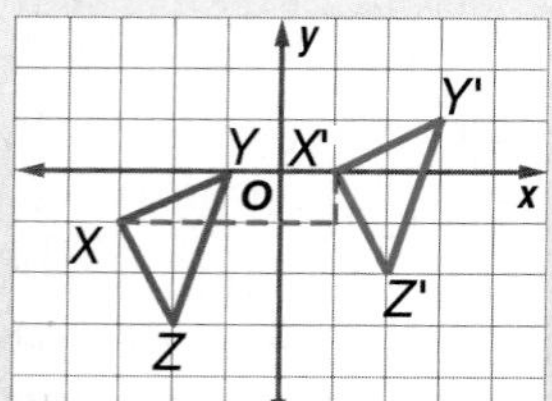

Practice Test

IL Math Online glencoe.com
• Chapter Test

1. **ALGEBRA** Find the value of x.

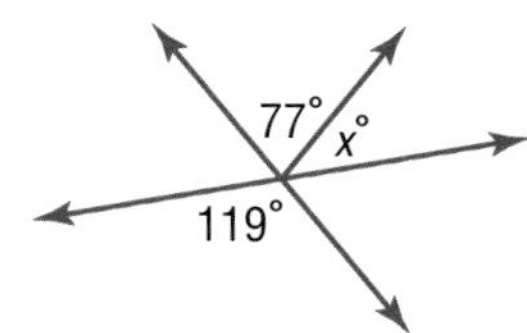

2. **ALGEBRA** Angles P and Q are supplementary. Find $m\angle P$ if $m\angle Q = 139°$.

ALGEBRA Find the sum of the measures of the interior angles of each regular polygon. Then, find the measure of one interior angle.

3. octagon
4. 15-gon

5. **MULTIPLE CHOICE** Which of the following statements is *not* true concerning the quadrilaterals in the quilt pattern?

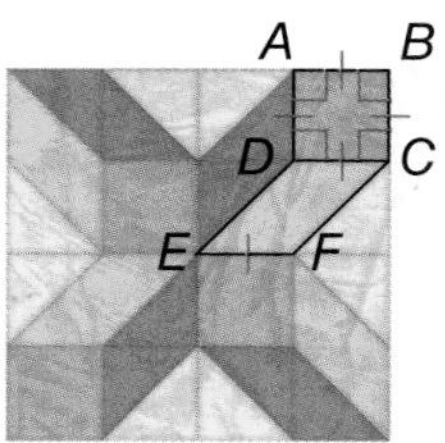

A The sum of the angle measures in quadrilateral $CDEF$ is 360°.

B Quadrilateral $ABCD$ is a regular polygon.

C The quadrilaterals are congruent.

D The sum of the angle measures in quadrilateral $ABCD$ is 360°.

In the figure below, $\triangle MNP \cong \triangle ZYX$. Find each measure.

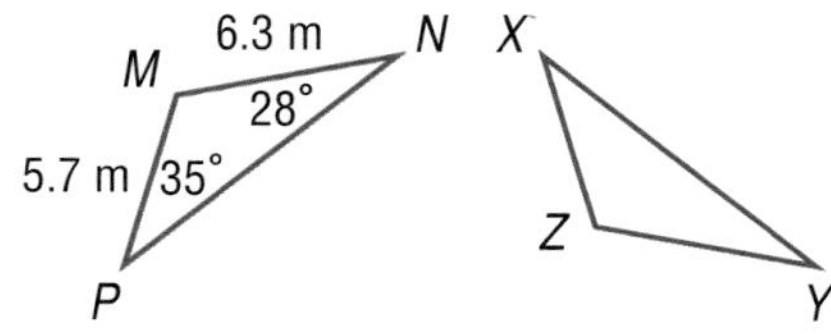

6. ZY
7. $\angle X$
8. $\angle Z$

NATURE Determine whether each figure has line symmetry. If it does, trace the figure and draw all lines of symmetry. If not, write *none*.

9. 

10.

11. 

12. **NATURE** Which figure above has rotational symmetry? Name its angle(s) of rotation.

13. **MULTIPLE CHOICE** A portion of an archway is shown. Which of the following shows the completed archway with vertical line symmetry?

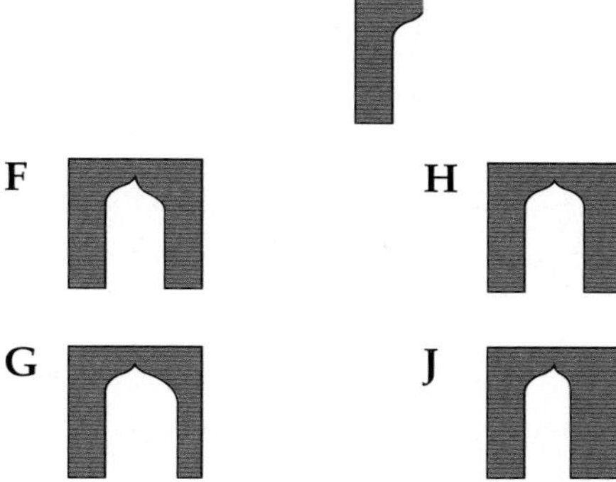

Graph $\triangle JKL$ with vertices $J(2, 3)$, $K(-1, 4)$, and $L(-3, -5)$. Then graph its image and write the coordinates of its vertices after each transformation.

14. reflection over the x-axis
15. translation 2 units left and 5 units up

16. **CHESS** Describe the minimum number of translations needed to create the pattern of the chess board shown from the original square B if each square has a side length of 1 inch.

CHAPTER 6 ISAT Practice

Cumulative, Chapter 1–6

IL Math Online glencoe.com

• Test Practice

PART 1 Multiple Choice

Read each question. Then fill in the correct answer on the answer sheet provided by your teacher or on a sheet of paper.

1. If $\triangle LMN$ is translated 5 units up and 7 units to the right, what are the coordinates of point L'?

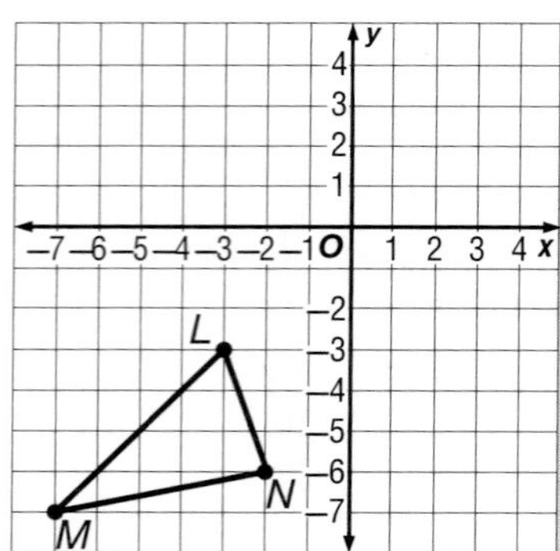

A $(-10, 2)$ C $(2, 5)$

B $(4, 2)$ D $(4, -3)$

2. A refrigerator costs \$560. If the refrigerator is on sale for 30% off the regular price, how much is the discount?

F \$392 H \$175

G \$260 J \$168

3. A microscope slide shows 35 red blood cells out of 60 blood cells. How many red blood cells would be expected in a sample of the same blood that has 840 blood cells?

A 2.5 C 510

B 490 D 1,440

TEST-TAKING TIP

Question 3 The ratio of the number of red blood cells to the total blood cells on the first slide is the same as the ratio on the second slide. Use a proportion.

4. The graph of rectangle *LMNP* is shown below.

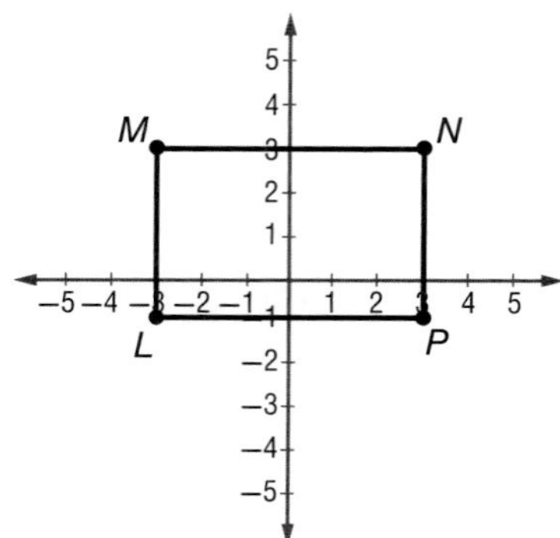

What is the area, in square units, of rectangle *LMNP*?

F 24 H 12

G 18 J 9

5. Find $-18 - (-7)$.

A -25 C -9

B -11 D 25

6. A circle with a radius of 4 units has its center at $(1, -2)$ on a coordinate grid. If the circle is translated 5 units up and 4 units left, what will be the coordinates of the new center?

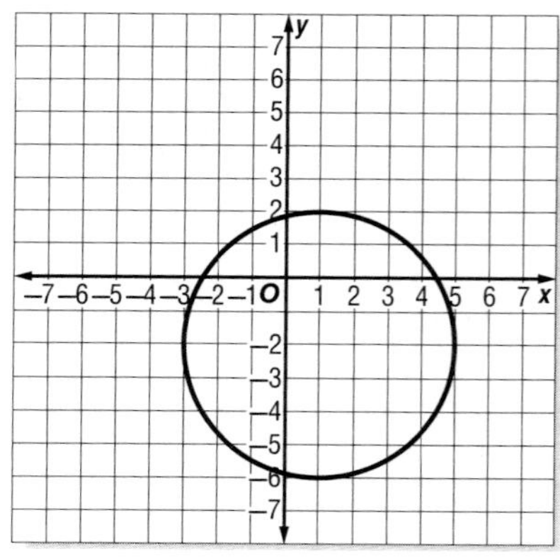

F $(-5, 2)$ H $(-3, 3)$

G $(-4, 2)$ J $(5, 3)$

Preparing for ISAT
For test-taking strategies and practice, see pages 712–729.

7. Which figure is congruent to the figure below?

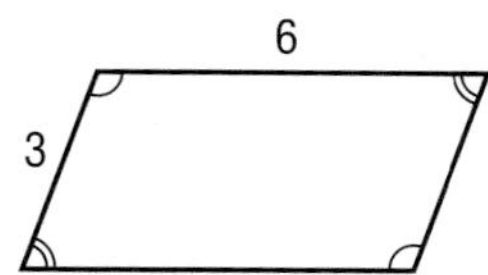

A 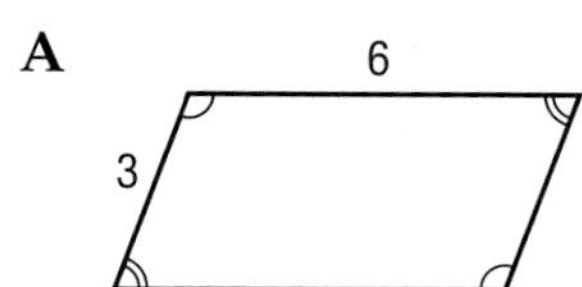

B 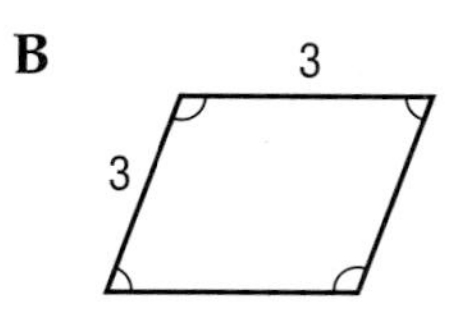

C 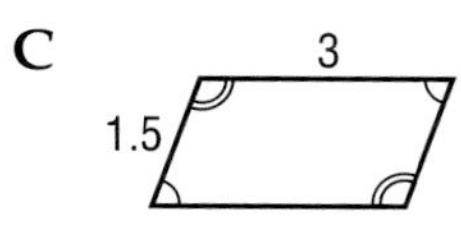

D 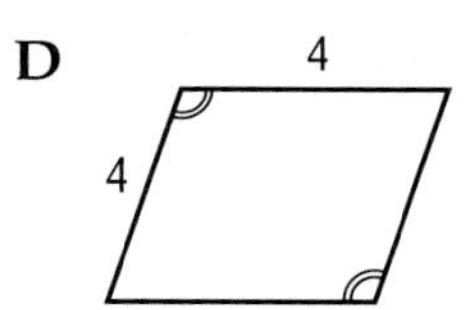

8. Jesse purchased a new digital camera for \$499 and a printer for \$299 including tax. If he plans to pay the total amount in 6 equal monthly payments, what is a reasonable estimate of the amount he will pay each month?

F \$66.50

G \$133.00

H \$155.00

J \$165.00

PART 2 Short Response/Grid In

Record your answers on the answer sheet provided by your teacher or on a sheet of paper.

9. Dannie can make 3 bracelets in 55 minutes. At this rate, how many hours will it take her to make 18 bracelets?

10. Stu saved \$19.75 when he purchased shoes. If the sale price was 25% off the regular price, what was the original price?

PART 3 Extended Response

Record your answers on the answer sheet provided by your teacher or on a sheet of paper. Show your work.

11. Use the figure in the coordinate grid.

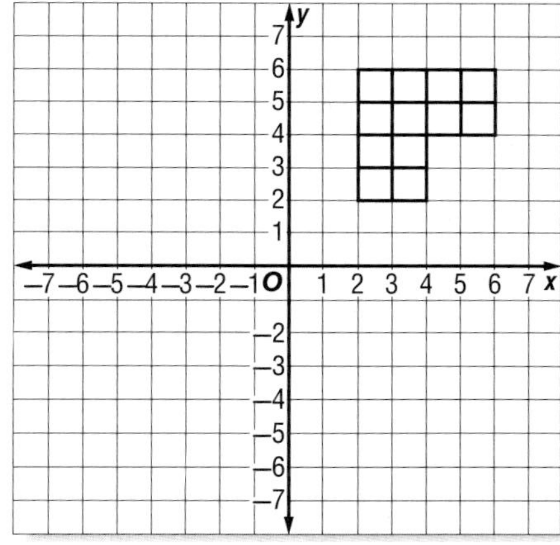

a. Graph the figure after a reflection over the x-axis.

b. Graph the figure after a reflection over the y-axis.

c. Graph the figure if it is reflected over the line $y = 2$ and then over the line $y = -2$. What transformation is this the same as?

NEED EXTRA HELP?											
If You Missed Question...	1	2	3	4	5	6	7	8	9	10	11
Go to Lesson...	6-7	5-8	4-5	3-7	1-5	6-7	6-4	1-1	4-1	5-8	6-6
IL Learning Standards	9.A.3b	8.A.3b	6.D.3	8.D.3c	6.B.3a	9.A.3b	9.A.3c	6.B.3a	6.D.3	8.A.3b	9.A.3b

Measurement: Area and Volume

Illinois Learning Standards

7.A.3b Apply the concepts and attributes of length, capacity, weight/mass, perimeter, area, volume, time, temperature and angle measures in practical situations.
7.C.3b Use concrete and graphic models and appropriate formulas to find perimeters, areas, surface areas and volumes of two- and three-dimensional regions.

Key Vocabulary

cone (p. 381)
cylinder (p. 374)
pyramid (p. 369)
prism (p. 369)

Real-World Link

Caves Stalactites and stalagmites are cone-shaped formations found in caves such as Mammoth Cave National Park in Kentucky. If you know the diameter of the base and the height of the formation, you can determine the volume of rocks and minerals in the formation.

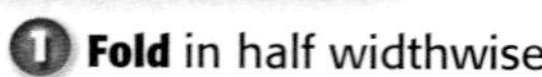

Measurement: Area and Volume Make this Foldable to help you organize your notes. Begin with a piece of 11″ × 17″ paper.

1. **Fold** in half widthwise.

2. **Open** and fold the bottom to form a pocket. Glue edges.

3. **Label** each pocket. Place several index cards in each pocket.

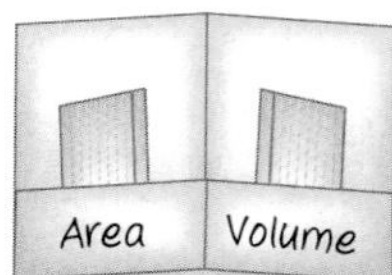

GET READY for Chapter 7

Diagnose Readiness You have two options for checking Prerequisite Skills.

Option 2

IL Math Online Take the Online Readiness Quiz at glencoe.com.

Option 1

Take the Quick Check below. Refer to the Quick Review for help.

QUICK Quiz

Multiply. (Lessons 2-3 and 2-9)

1. $\frac{1}{3} \cdot 8 \cdot 12$
2. $\frac{1}{3} \cdot 4 \cdot 9^2$
3. **RUNNING** Julian runs 4 miles a day for 6 days each week. If he decides to run $\frac{1}{3}$ of this distance, how many miles will he run in one week? (Lesson 2-3)

Evaluate $2ab + 2bc + 2ac$ for the values of the variables indicated. (Lesson 1-2)

4. $a = 5, b = 4, c = 8$
5. $a = 2, b = 3, c = 9$
6. $a = 5.4, b = 2.9, c = 7.1$
7. $a = 2.6, b = 6.4, c = 10.8$

Find the value of each expression. Use $\pi \approx 3.14$. Round to the nearest tenth. (Prior Grade)

8. $\pi \cdot 15$
9. $2 \cdot \pi \cdot 3.2$
10. $\pi \cdot 7^2$
11. $\pi \cdot (19 \div 2)^2$
12. **PIZZA** The distance, in inches, around a circular pizza with diameter 14 inches is given by the expression $\pi \cdot 14$. Evaluate this expression. Round to the nearest tenth. (Prior Grade)

QUICK Review

Example 1

Multiply $\frac{1}{3} \cdot 5 \cdot 6^2$.

$\frac{1}{3} \cdot 5 \cdot 6^2 = \frac{1}{3} \cdot 5 \cdot 36$ Evaluate 6^2.

$= \frac{1}{3} \cdot 180$ Multiply 5 by 36.

$= 60$ Multiply $\frac{1}{3}$ by 180.

Example 2

Evaluate $2ab + 2bc + 2ac$ if $a = 7$, $b = 4$, and $c = 2$.

$2ab + 2bc + 2ac$

$= 2(7)(4) + 2(4)(2) + 2(7)(2)$ $a = 7, b = 4,$ and $c = 2$

$= 56 + 16 + 28$ Multiply.

$= 100$ Add.

Example 3

Evaluate $\pi \cdot 16^2$. Use $\pi \approx 3.14$. Round to the nearest tenth.

$\pi \cdot 16^2 \approx 3.14 \cdot 256$ Evaluate 16^2.

≈ 803.8 Multiply 3.14 by 256.

Circumference and Area of Circles

MAIN IDEA

Find the circumference and area of circles.

IL Learning Standards

7.A.3b Apply the concepts and attributes of length, capacity, weight/mass, perimeter, **area,** volume, time, temperature and angle measures **in practical situations.**
7.C.3b Use concrete and graphic models and appropriate formulas to find perimeters, **areas,** surface areas and volumes **of two-** and three-**dimensional regions.** *Also addresses 9.C.3a.*

New Vocabulary

circle
center
radius
chord
diameter
circumference
pi

IL Math Online

glencoe.com

- Extra Examples
- Personal Tutor
- Self-Check Quiz

MINI Lab

STEP 1 Measure and record the distance *d* across the circular part of an object, such as a battery or a can, through its center.

STEP 2 Place the object on a piece of paper. Mark the point where the object touches the paper on both the object and on the paper.

STEP 3 Carefully roll the object so that it makes one complete rotation. Then mark the paper again.

STEP 4 Finally, measure the distance *C* between the marks.

1. What distance does C represent?
2. Find the ratio $\frac{C}{d}$ for this object.
3. Repeat the steps above for at least two other circular objects and compare the ratios of C to d. What do you observe?
4. Graph the data you collected as ordered pairs, (d, C). Then describe the graph.

A **circle** is a set of points in a plane that are the same distance from a given point in the plane, called the **center**. The segment from the center to any point on the circle is called the **radius**. A **chord** is any segment with both endpoints on the circle. A **diameter** is a chord that passes through the center. It is the longest chord.

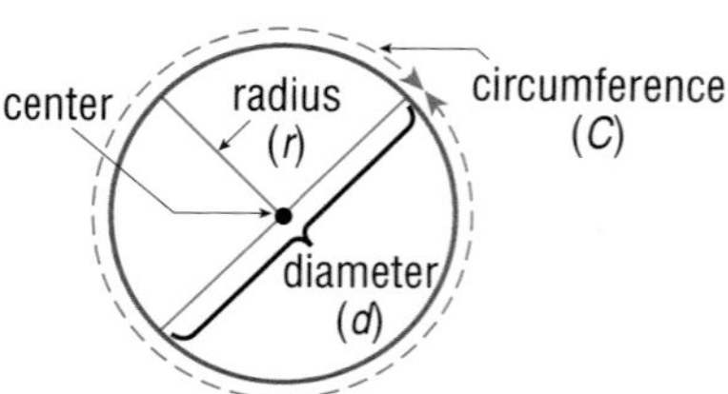

The diameter of a circle is twice its radius or $d = 2r$.

The distance around the circle is called the **circumference**. The ratio of the circumference of a circle to its diameter is always 3.1415926…. It is represented by the Greek letter **π (pi)**. The numbers 3.14 and $\frac{22}{7}$ are often used as approximations for π. So, $\frac{C}{d} = \pi$. This can also be written as $C = \pi d$ or $C \approx 3.14d$.

Circumference of a Circle

Key Concept

Words The circumference C of a circle is equal to its diameter d times π, or 2 times its radius r times π.

Symbols $C = \pi d$ or $C = 2\pi r$

Model

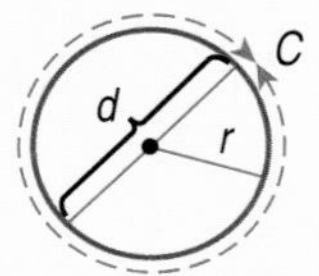

Study Tip

Calculating with π When evaluating expressions involving π, use the π key on a calculator to obtain the most accurate result. However, using 3.14 for π will result in a close approximation.

EXAMPLES Find the Circumferences of Circles

Find the circumference of each circle. Round to the nearest tenth.

1

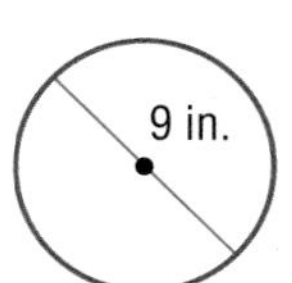

$C = \pi d$	Circumference of a circle
$C = \pi \cdot 9$	Replace d with 9.
$C = 9\pi$	This is the *exact* circumference.

Use a calculator to find 9π. 9 [×] [2nd] [π] [ENTER] 28.27433388

The circumference is about 28.3 inches.

2

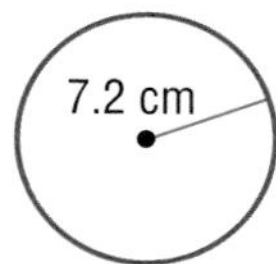

$C = 2\pi r$	Circumference of a circle
$C = 2 \cdot \pi \cdot 7.2$	Replace r with 7.2.
$C \approx 45.2$	Use a calculator.

The circumference is about 45.2 centimeters.

CHECK Your Progress

a. 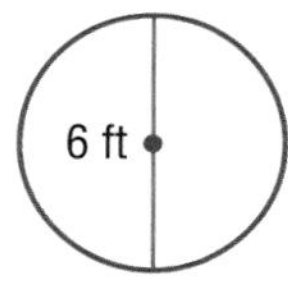

b. 

c. 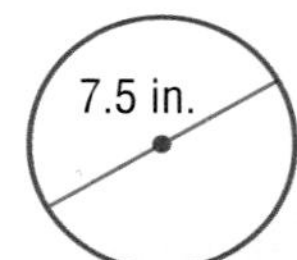

A circle can be decomposed into congruent wedge-like pieces. Then the pieces can be rearranged to form a figure that resembles a parallelogram.

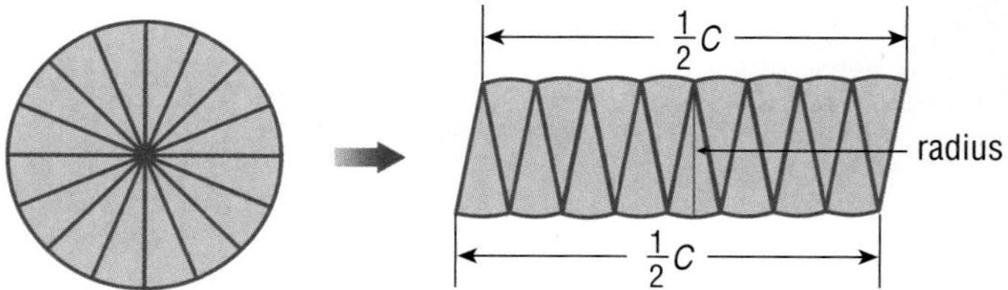

Since the circle has an area that is relatively close to the area of the parallelogram-shaped figure, you can use the formula for the area of a parallelogram to find the formula for the area of a circle.

$A = bh$	Area of a parallelogram
$A = \left(\frac{1}{2} \cdot C\right)r$	The base of the parallelogram is one-half the circumference and the height is the radius.
$A = \left(\frac{1}{2} \cdot 2\pi r\right)r$	Replace C with $2\pi r$.
$A = \pi \cdot r \cdot r$ or πr^2	Simplify.

Area of a Circle

Key Concept

Words The area A of a circle is equal to π times the square of the radius r.

Symbols $A = \pi r^2$

Model

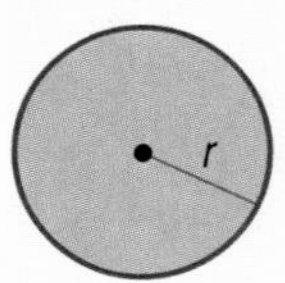

EXAMPLES Find the Areas of Circles

Find the area of each circle. Round to the nearest tenth.

3

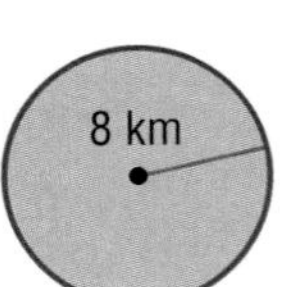

$A = \pi r^2$	Area of a circle
$A = \pi \cdot 8^2$	Replace r with 8.
$A = \pi \cdot 64$	Evaluate 8^2. This is the *exact* area.
$A \approx 201.1$	Use a calculator.

The area is about 201.1 square kilometers.

4

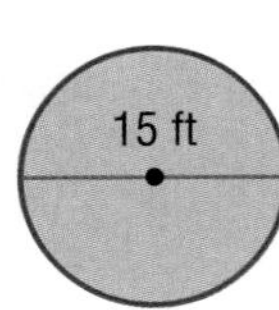

$A = \pi r^2$	Area of a circle
$A = \pi (7.5)^2$	Replace r with half of 15 or 7.5.
$A = \pi \cdot 56.25$	Evaluate 7.5^2. This is the *exact* area.
$A \approx 176.7$	Use a calculator.

The area is about 176.7 square feet.

CHECK Your Progress

Find the area of each circle. Round to the nearest tenth.

d. The radius is 11 inches.

e. The diameter is 5 meters.

Real-World Link . . . . Point State Park in Pittsburgh, Pennsylvania, is located where the Allegheny and Monongahela rivers meet to form the Ohio River.

Source: Pennsylvania Department of Conservation

Real-World EXAMPLE

5 **STATE PARKS Suppose you walk around the edge of the circular Point State Park fountain and estimate its circumference to be 470 feet. Based on your estimate, what is the approximate diameter of the fountain?**

$C = \pi d$	Circumference of a circle
$470 = \pi d$	Replace C with 470.
$\frac{470}{\pi} = d$	Divide each side by π.
$149.6 \approx d$	Use a calculator.

The diameter of the fountain is about 150 feet.

CHECK Your Progress

f. **HOME DECOR** A catalog states that a circular area rug covers 19.5 square feet. What is the approximate diameter of the rug?

CHECK Your Understanding

Find the circumference of each circle. Round to the nearest tenth.

Examples 1, 2 (p. 353)

1. 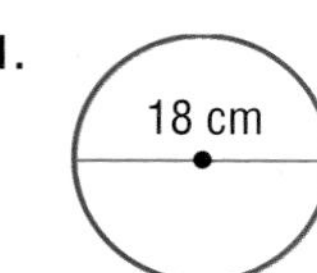

2. 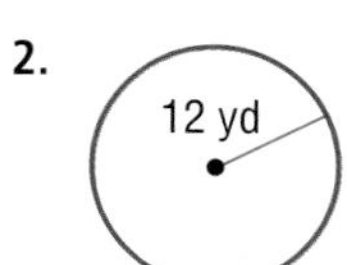

3. 2.5 mi

Find the area of each circle. Round to the nearest tenth.

Examples 3, 4 (p. 354)

4. 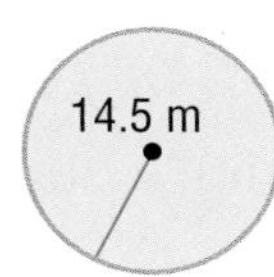

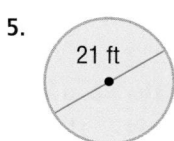

5. 21 ft

6. 18.25 in.

Example 5 (p. 354)

7. **BRACELETS** When Cammie finished making a friendship bracelet, it was 7.9 inches long. What was the diameter of the bracelet?

Practice and Problem Solving

HOMEWORK HELP	
For Exercises	See Examples
8–11	1, 2
12–15	3, 4
16–19	5

Find the circumference of each circle. Round to the nearest tenth.

8. 24 mm

9. 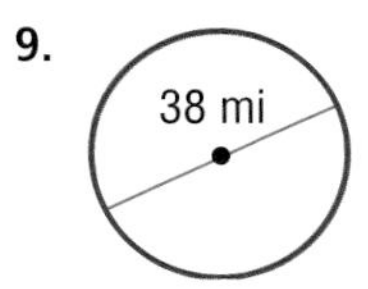

10. 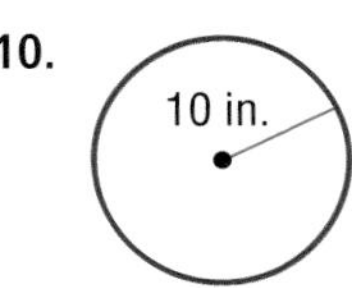

11. 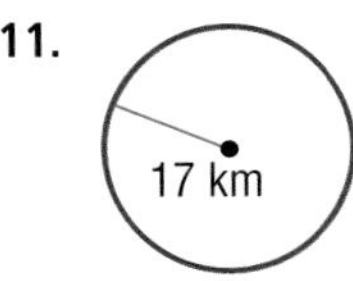

Find the area of each circle. Round to the nearest tenth.

12. 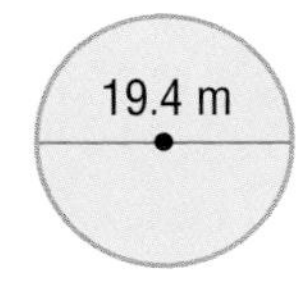

13. 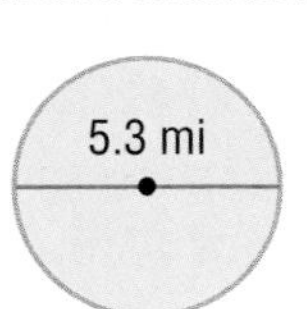

14. 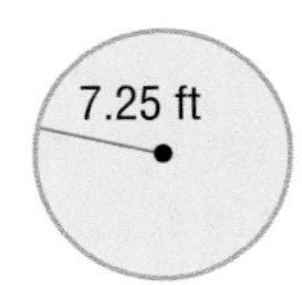

15. 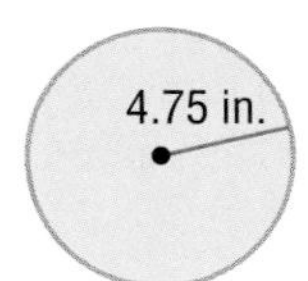

16. **PETS** Simone purchased a circular exercise pen with a radius of 2.5 feet to keep her new puppy safe. Find the area inside the pen.

17. **MEASUREMENT** A circular table top has a radius of $2\frac{1}{4}$ feet. A decorative trim is placed along the outside edge of the table. How long is the trim?

18. **SAFETY** A light in a parking lot illuminates a circular area 15 meters across. What is the area of the parking lot covered by the light?

19. **BICYCLES** Jerrod's mountain bike has a tire diameter of 26 inches. How far will the bike travel in 100 rotations of its tires?

Find the exact circumference and area of each circle.

20. The radius is 3.5 centimeters.

21. The diameter is 8.6 kilometers.

22. The diameter is 9 inches.

23. The radius is 0.6 mile.

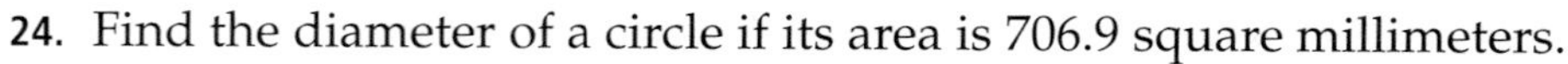

24. Find the diameter of a circle if its area is 706.9 square millimeters.

25. **GARDENING** Mr. Townes created a 2-foot wide garden path around a circular garden. The radius of the garden is 7 feet. He wants to cover the path in stones. If Mr. Townes needs 1 bag of stones for every 5 square feet of path, how many bags of stones will he need to cover his garden path?

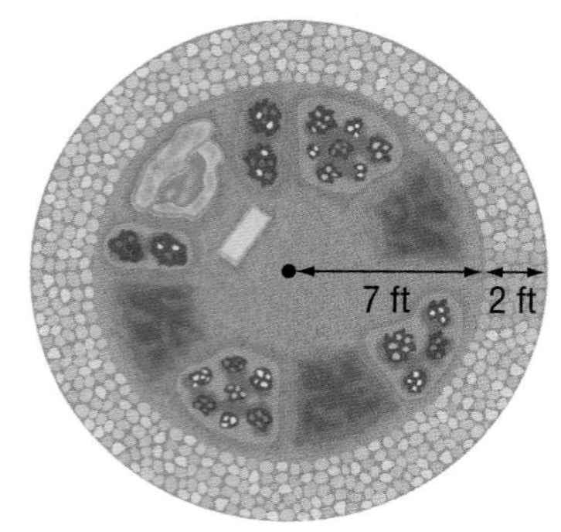

Real-World Link . . . . Trees should be planted so that they have plenty of room to grow. The planting site should have an area of at least 2 to 3 times the diameter of the circle the spreading roots of the maturing tree are expected to occupy.

Source: University of Georgia

Another approximate value for π is $\frac{22}{7}$. Use this value to find the circumference and area of each circle.

26. The diameter is 7 feet.

27. The radius is $2\frac{1}{3}$ inches.

28. **BAKING** Joaquim is baking giant cookies for the school bake sale. They will be sold for $20 for one large cookie or $20 for three smaller cookies. Which offer is the better buy? Explain your reasoning.

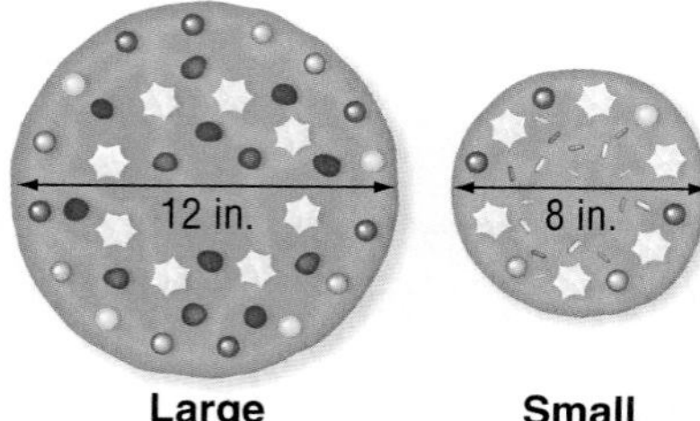

29. **SPORTS** Three tennis balls are packaged one on top of the other in a can. Which measure is greater, the can's height or circumference? Explain.

30. **TREES** During a construction project, barriers are placed around trees. For each inch of trunk diameter, the protection zone should have a radius of $1\frac{1}{2}$ feet. Find the area of this zone for a tree with a trunk circumference of 63 inches.

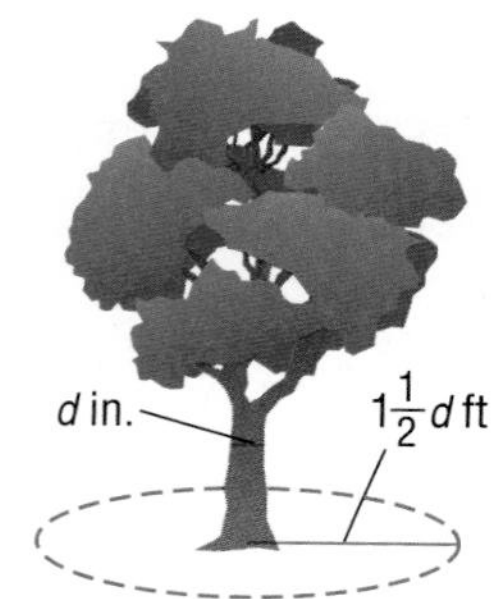

31. **GRAPHIC ARTS** Michael is painting a sign for a new coffee shop. On the sign, he drew a circle with a radius of 2 feet. He then drew another circle with a radius 1.5 times larger. How much greater is the area of the larger circle?

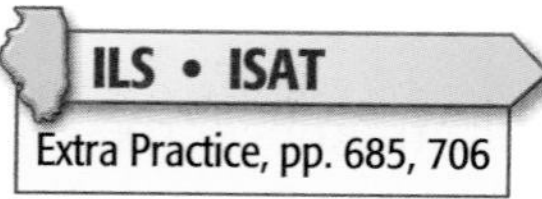

Extra Practice, pp. 685, 706

32. **FIND THE DATA** Refer to the Data File on pages 16–19. Choose some data and write a real-world problem in which you would determine the area of a circle.

H.O.T. Problems

33. **OPEN ENDED** Draw and label a circle that has a circumference between 5 and 10 centimeters. Justify your answer.

34. **NUMBER SENSE** If the radius of a circle is halved, how will this affect its circumference and its area? What happens to the circumference and area if the radius is doubled or tripled? Explain your reasoning. (*Hint*: Find the circumference and area for each circle and organize the data in a table.)

CHALLENGE Find the area of each shaded region.

35. 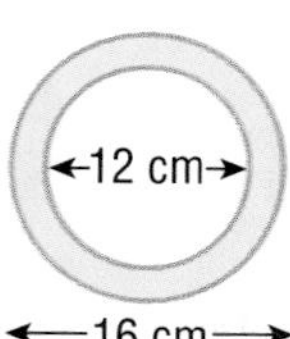

36. 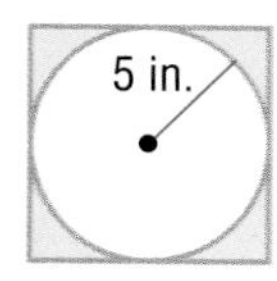

37. 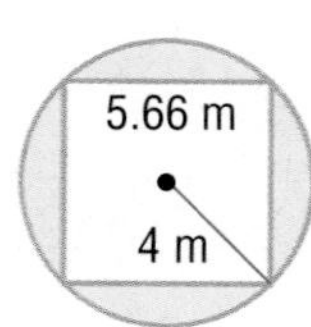

38. **WRITING IN MATH** Explain how the circumference and area of a circle are related or different.

ISAT PRACTICE 7.A.3b, 7.C.3b

39. In the figure below, the radius of the inscribed circle is 8 inches. What is the perimeter of square $WXYZ$?

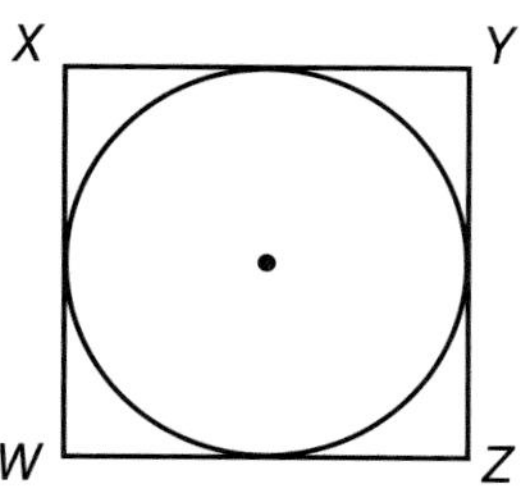

A 16π in.

B 64 in.

C 32 in.

D 64π in.

40. Using the two circles shown below, what is $\frac{\text{circumference of circle } x}{\text{circumference of circle } y}$?

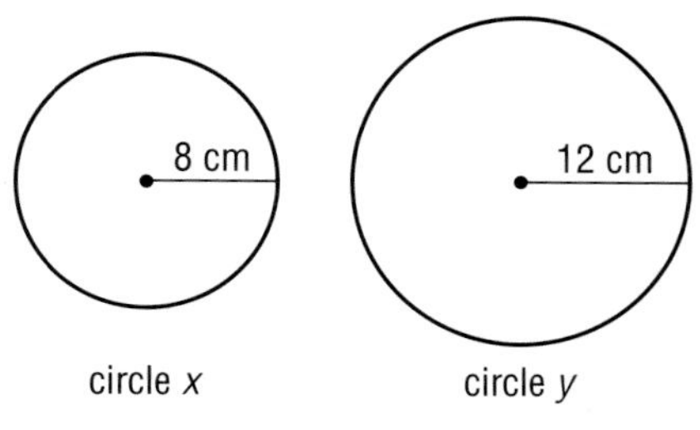

F $\frac{3\pi}{4}$

G $\frac{4\pi}{3}$

H $\frac{2}{3}$

J $\frac{4}{3}$

Spiral Review

GEOMETRY For Exercises 41 and 42, use $\triangle ABC$ with vertices $A(-2, -2)$, $B(-1, 2)$, and $C(1, 0)$.

41. **GEOMETRY** Graph $\triangle ABC$ and its image after it is translated 2 units right and 1 unit up. (Lesson 6-7)

42. **GEOMETRY** What are the coordinates of $\triangle A'B'C'$ when $\triangle ABC$ is reflected over the x-axis? (Lesson 6-6)

43. **ART** At an auction in New York City, a 2.55-square inch portrait of George Washington sold for $1.2 million. About how much did the buyer pay per square inch for the portrait? (Lesson 4-1)

GET READY for the Next Lesson

44. **PREREQUISITE SKILL** The price of calculators has been decreasing. A calculator sold for $125 in 1995, $107 in 2000, and $89 in 2005. Use the *look for a pattern* strategy to determine the price of a similar calculator in 2015 if the price decrease continues at the same rate.

Extend 7-1

Geometry Lab
Investigating Arcs and Angles

MAIN IDEA

Find measures of arcs and inscribed angles.

IL Learning Standards

7.A.3a Measure length, capacity, weight/mass and **angles using sophisticated instruments (e.g., compass,** protractor, trundle wheel). **9.A.3a Draw or construct two-** and three-**dimensional geometric figures** including prisms, pyramids, cylinders and cones. *Also addresses 7.B.3.*

New Vocabulary

central angle
arc
minor arc
major arc
semicircle
inscribed angle

In Lesson 6-1, you learned about angle relationships. Angles can also be placed in circles. A **central angle** is an angle that intersects a circle in two points and has its vertex at the center of the circle. It separates the circle into two parts, each of which is an **arc**.

The measure of a central angle is equivalent to the measure of its corresponding arc. There are three types of arcs.

A **minor arc** measures less than 180°.	A **major arc** measures more than 180°.	A **semicircle** measures 180°.
A, $\widehat{AC}$, 110°, B, C	D, $\widehat{DFE}$, E, 60°, G, F	J, $\widehat{JKL}$, K, N, L, M, $\widehat{JML}$

An **inscribed angle** is an angle that has its vertex on the circle, and its sides contain chords of the circle.

ACTIVITY Measure of Inscribed Angles

STEP 1 Use a compass to draw a circle and label the center *C*.

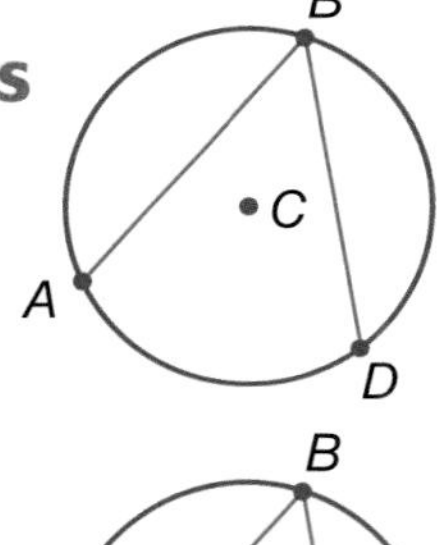

STEP 2 Use a straightedge to draw chords *BA* and *BD* that do not go through the center of the circle.

STEP 3 Use a straightedge to draw $\overline{AC}$ and $\overline{CD}$.

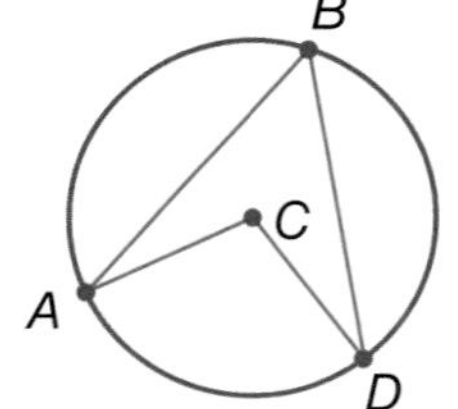

STEP 4 Measure $\angle ABD$ and $\angle ACD$.

Analyze the Results

1. What seems to be the relationship between $m\angle ABD$ and $m\angle ACD$?
2. Repeat Steps 1–4 with several different inscribed angles.
3. **MAKE A PREDICTION** Draw a circle with a radius of 3 inches. Then draw a central angle that measures 60° and an inscribed angle that intercepts the same arc. Without measuring, predict the measure of the inscribed angle. Then check your prediction by measuring.

Reading Math

Arcs and Segments

The symbol $\widehat{AC}$ is read *arc AC.* The symbol $\overline{AC}$ is read *segment AC.*

ACTIVITY Angles Inscribed in a Semicircle

2 STEP 1 Use a compass to draw a circle with center *X* and diameter $\overline{YZ}$.

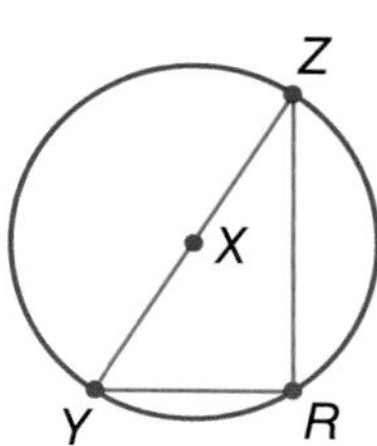

STEP 2 Draw and label any point *R* on $\widehat{YZ}$. Use a straightedge to draw $\overline{RY}$ and $\overline{RZ}$.

Vocabulary Link

Inscribe

Everyday Use to write, engrave, or print characters on

Math Use to have its vertex (or vertices) on a circle and its sides containing chords of the circle.

Analyze the Results

4. What shape is formed by $\overline{RY}$, $\overline{RZ}$, and $\overline{YZ}$?
5. Find $m\angle YRZ$. What kind of triangle is triangle *YRZ*?
6. Draw and label another point *T* on $\widehat{YZ}$. Draw $\overline{TY}$ and $\overline{TZ}$. Find $m\angle YTZ$.
7. **MAKE A CONJECTURE** What is true about inscribed angles that intercept a semicircle?
8. Find the measures of the missing angles and arcs in the figure at the right.

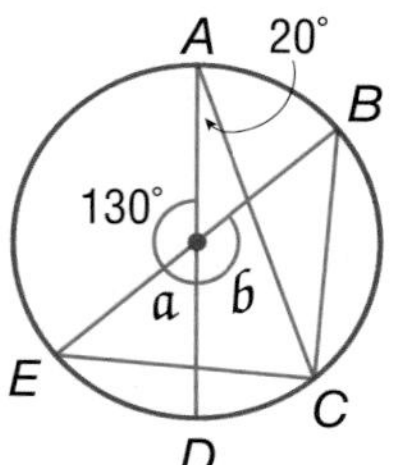

a. $\widehat{DB}$ b. $\angle a$ c. $\widehat{ECA}$ d. $\angle b$

e. $\angle ECB$ f. $\widehat{BA}$ g. $\widehat{DC}$ h. $\widehat{CB}$

ACTIVITY Chords and Diameters

3 STEP 1 Use a compass to draw a circle and label the center *P*. Draw a chord that is not a diameter. Label it $\overline{EF}$.

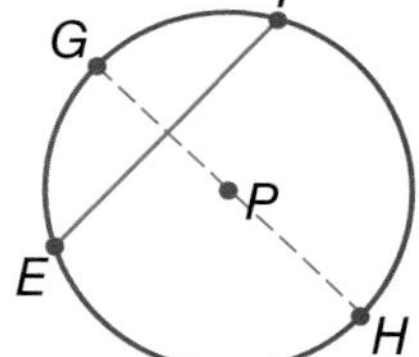

STEP 2 Construct a line segment through *P* that is perpendicular to $\overline{EF}$ with endpoints on the circle. Label this as diameter $\overline{GH}$.

Analyze the Results

9. Compare the lengths of $\widehat{EG}$ and $\widehat{FG}$. Then compare the lengths of $\widehat{EH}$ and $\widehat{FH}$.
10. What is the relationship between diameter $\overline{GH}$ and chord $\overline{EF}$?
11. **MAKE A CONJECTURE** What is the relationship among a diameter, a chord, and its arc if the diameter is perpendicular to the chord?

7-2 Problem-Solving Investigation

MAIN IDEA: Solve a simpler problem.

ILS **6.B.3a Solve practical computation problems involving whole numbers, integers and rational numbers. 6.C.3a Select computational procedures and solve problems with whole numbers,** fractions, **decimals, percents** and proportions.

P.S.I. TEAM +

e-Mail: SOLVE A SIMPLER PROBLEM

GINA: It looks like the figure is made of 25 squares. But, I think there are more squares than that.

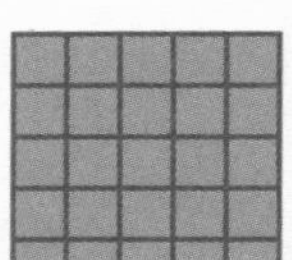

YOUR MISSION: Solve a simpler problem to find how many squares of any size are in the figure.

Understand	You know that the figure is a 5 × 5 grid, so the possible sizes for squares are 1 × 1, 2 × 2, 3 × 3, 4 × 4, and 5 × 5. You want to find the total number of squares.
Plan	Solve the simpler problem by counting the number of squares when the figure is a 2 × 2 grid and a 3 × 3 grid. Then look for a pattern.
Solve	For a 2 × 2 grid, the possible sizes are 1 × 1 and 2 × 2. There are four 1 × 1 squares, and one 2 × 2 square. So, there are 4 + 1 or 5 different squares. For a 3 × 3 grid, the possible sizes are 1 × 1, 2 × 2, and 3 × 3. There are nine 1 × 1 squares, there are four 2 × 2 squares, and one 3 × 3 square. So, there are 9 + 4 + 1 or 14 different squares. Make a conjecture with a 4 × 4 grid, then look for a pattern. (see table below) So, a 5 × 5 grid has 55 squares.
Check	Check your pattern carefully to make sure the answer is correct.

Number of Small Squares	1	4	9	16	25
Number of Squares of Any Size	1	5	14	30	55

+4 +9 +16 +25

Analyze The Strategy

1. Explain why it was helpful for Gina to solve a simpler problem.
2. **WRITING IN MATH** Write about a situation in which you might need to solve a simpler problem in order to solve a more complicated problem. Then solve the problem.

Mixed Problem Solving

Use the *solve a simpler problem* strategy to solve Exercises 3–6.

3. **CARPENTRY** Working separately, three carpenters can make three chairs in three days. How many chairs can 7 carpenters working at the same rate make in 30 days?

4. **TABLES** The school cafeteria has 15 square tables that can be pushed together to form one long table for class parties. Each square table can seat only one person on each side. How many people can be seated at the combined tables?

5. **PROGRAMS** The school needs 250 programs for the band concert. They can purchase them in packages of 30 or 80 from the printer. How many of each package should they buy?

6. **CRAFTS** Levon needs to cut a long straw into 25 smaller pieces. How many cuts will he need to make?

Use any strategy to solve Exercises 7–16. Some strategies are shown below.

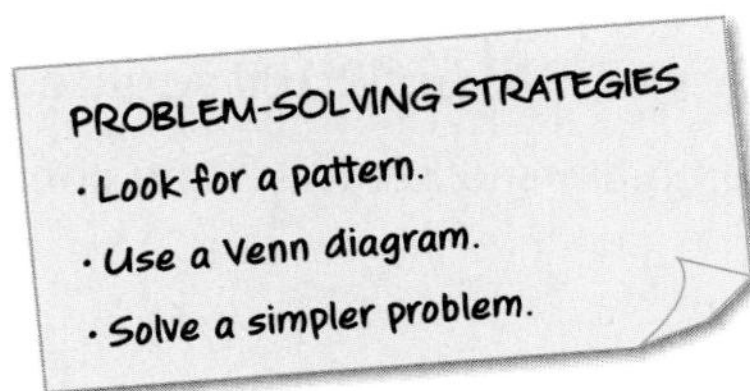

PROBLEM-SOLVING STRATEGIES
• Look for a pattern.
• Use a Venn diagram.
• Solve a simpler problem.

7. **VOLUNTEER** Five students can each volunteer for five hours in five days. At this rate, how many hours can 11 students volunteer in 15 days?

CLUBS For Exercises 8 and 9, use the following information.
In a recent survey, 35 eighth graders said they wanted to join the band and 32 eighth graders said they wanted to join the choir. Of those, 15 wanted to belong to both groups.

8. Draw a Venn diagram of the situation.

9. How many students responded to this survey?

10. **ANALYZE GRAPHS** The graph represents a survey of students about their chocolate preferences. About what percent of students preferred dark chocolate?

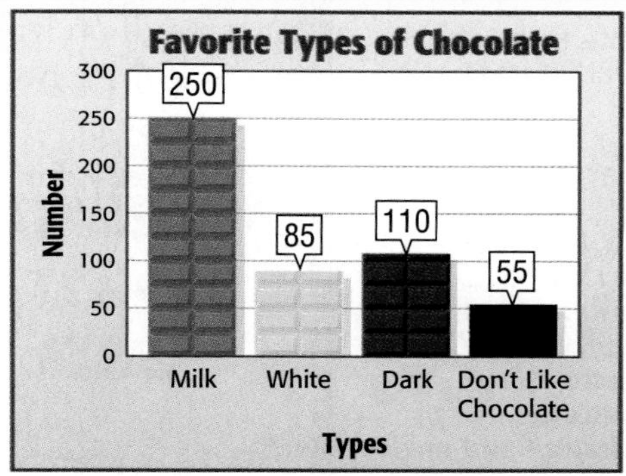

11. **RESTAURANTS** Consuelo had dinner with some friends and ordered a meal for $9.95, a drink for $1.25, and dessert for $2.75. A sales tax of 6.5% is added to her bill. If she leaves a tip of 18% after the sales tax, what is the total cost of her meal?

12. **PIZZA** What is the largest number of pieces that can be cut from one pizza using five straight cuts?

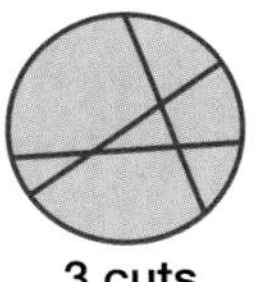
3 cuts

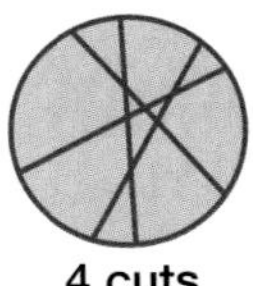
4 cuts

13. **SCHOOL SUPPLIES** Ethan wishes to buy 4 pens, 1 ruler, and 8 folders at the school store. The prices are shown in the table below. If there is no tax, is $11 enough to pay for Ethan's school supplies? Explain.

Item	Cost
Pens	$1.75
Ruler	$1.09
Folder	$0.55

14. **PHONES** A cellular phone company charges $25 per month plus $0.03 per minute. If Clay's monthly bill is $35.38, how many minutes did he use the phone?

Explore 7-3

Measurement Lab
Area of Irregular Figures

MAIN IDEA

Estimate areas of irregular figures.

IL Learning Standards

7.A.3b Apply the concepts and attributes of length, capacity, weight/mass, perimeter, **area,** volume, time, temperature and angle measures **in practical situations.**
7.C.3b Use concrete and **graphic models and appropriate formulas to find** perimeters, **areas,** surface areas and volumes **of two-** and three-**dimensional regions.**

An irregular figure has sides that are not line segments. To estimate the area of an irregular figure, separate the figure into simpler shapes. Then find the sum of these areas.

ACTIVITY

Estimate the area of Idaho.

STEP 1 First, separate the figure into a triangle and a rectangle.

triangle
481 mi
100 mi
170 mi
IDAHO
300 mi
rectangle

STEP 2 **Area of triangle**

$A = \frac{1}{2}bh$

$= \frac{1}{2} \cdot 200 \cdot 311$ $\quad b = 300 - 100$ or 200, $h = 481 - 170$ or 311

$= 31{,}100$ $\quad$ Simplify.

Area of rectangle

$A = \ell w$

$= 300 \cdot 170$ or $51{,}000$ $\quad \ell = 300$ and $w = 170$

The area of Idaho is about 31,100 + 51,000 or 82,100 square miles.

Check for Reasonableness Solve the problem another way. How does it compare to the answer in the activity?

Analyze the Results

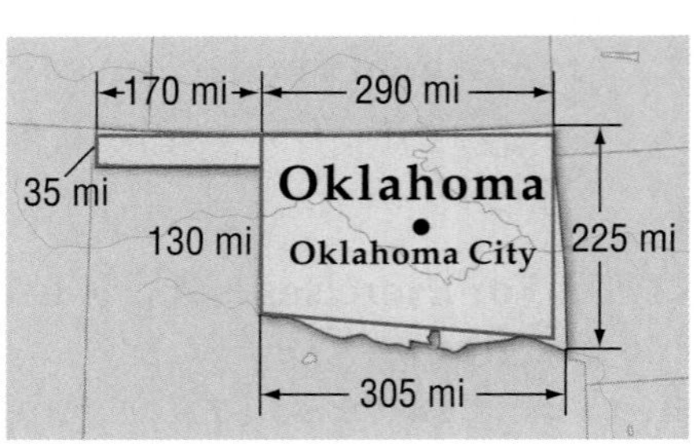

1. In the figure at the right, the area of Oklahoma is separated into polygons. Explain how polygons can be used to estimate the total land area.
2. Estimate the area of each region.
3. Estimate the total area of Oklahoma.

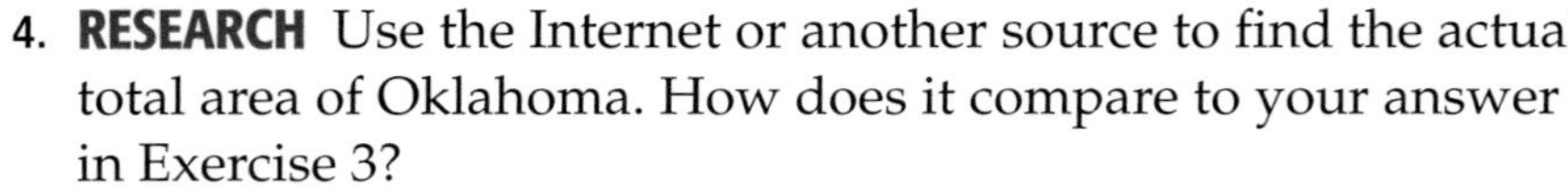

4. **RESEARCH** Use the Internet or another source to find the actual total area of Oklahoma. How does it compare to your answer in Exercise 3?
5. **RESEARCH** Estimate the area of another state. Use the Internet or another source to compare your estimate with the actual area.

7-3 Area of Composite Figures

MAIN IDEA

Find the area of composite figures.

IL Learning Standards

7.A.3b Apply the concepts and attributes of length, capacity, weight/mass, perimeter, **area,** volume, time, temperature and angle measures **in practical situations.**
7.C.3b Use concrete and **graphic models and appropriate formulas to find** perimeters, **areas,** surface areas and volumes **of two-** and three-**dimensional regions.**

New Vocabulary

composite figure

IL Math Online

glencoe.com

- Extra Examples
- Personal Tutor
- Self-Check Quiz
- Reading in the Content Area

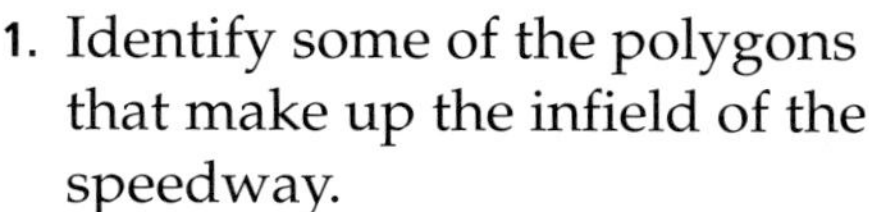

GET READY for the Lesson

SPEEDWAY A diagram of the Indianapolis Motor Speedway is shown.

1. Identify some of the polygons that make up the infield of the speedway.
2. How can the polygons be used to find the total area of the infield?

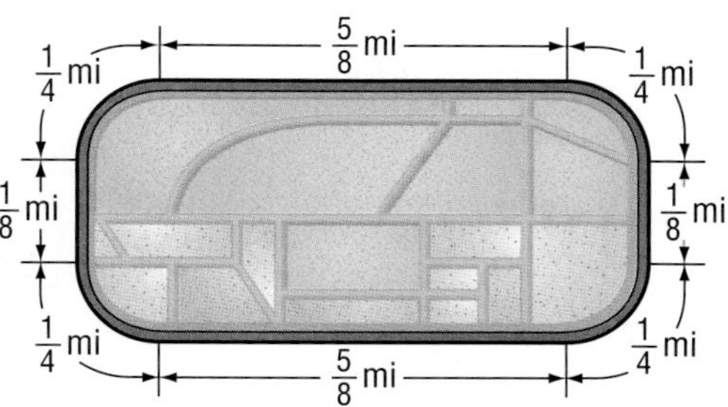

A **composite figure** is made up of two or more shapes.

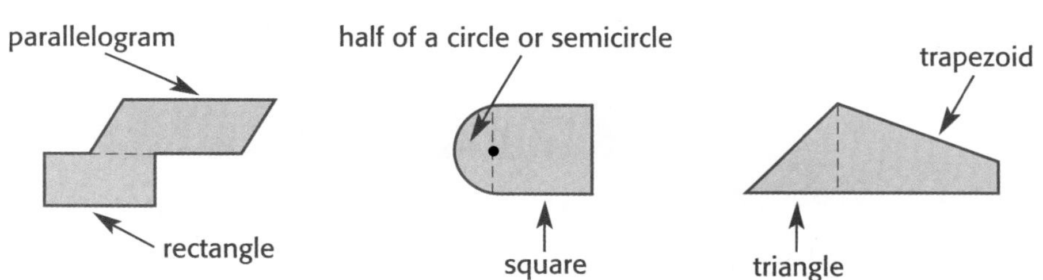

To find the area of a composite figure, decompose the figure into shapes with areas you know how to find. Then find the sum of these areas.

The following is a review of area formulas.

Area Formulas — Key Concept

Shape	Words	Formula
Parallelogram	The area A of a parallelogram is the product of any base b and its height h.	$A = bh$
Triangle	The area A of a triangle is half the product of any base b and its height h.	$A = \frac{1}{2}bh$
Trapezoid	The area A of a trapezoid is half the product of the height h and the sum of the bases, b_1 and b_2.	$A = \frac{1}{2}h(b_1 + b_2)$
Circle	The area A of a circle is equal to π times the square of the radius r.	$A = \pi r^2$

EXAMPLE Find the Area of a Composite Figure

Study Tip

Semicircle
Since a semicircle is half a circle, its area is $\frac{1}{2}\pi r^2$.

1 **Find the area of the composite figure.**

The figure can be separated into a semicircle and a triangle.

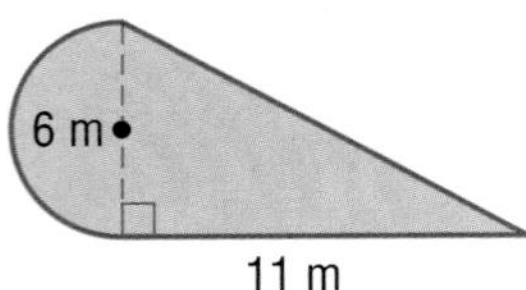

Area of semicircle

$A = \frac{1}{2}\pi r^2$

$A = \frac{1}{2} \cdot \pi \cdot 3^2$

$A \approx 14.1$

Area of triangle

$A = \frac{1}{2}bh$

$A = \frac{1}{2} \cdot 6 \cdot 11$

$A = 33$

The area of the figure is about 14.1 + 33 or 47.1 square meters.

CHECK Your Progress

Find the area of each figure. Round to the nearest tenth if necessary.

a. 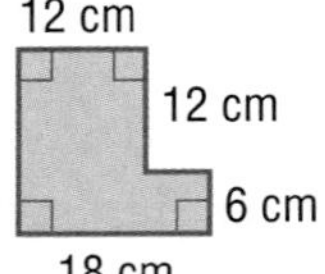

b. 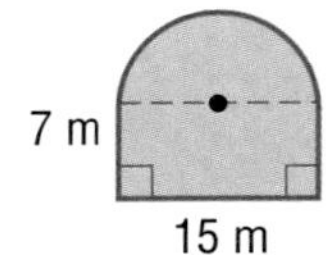

c. 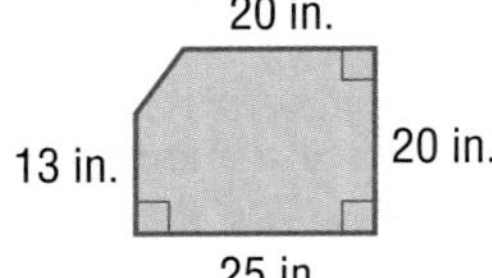

Real-World Link
There are 336 dimples on a regulation golf ball.
Source: Scigolf

Real-World EXAMPLE

2 **GOLF The plan for one hole of a miniature golf course is shown. It is composed of a trapezoid and a parallelogram. How many square feet of turf will be needed for this plan?**

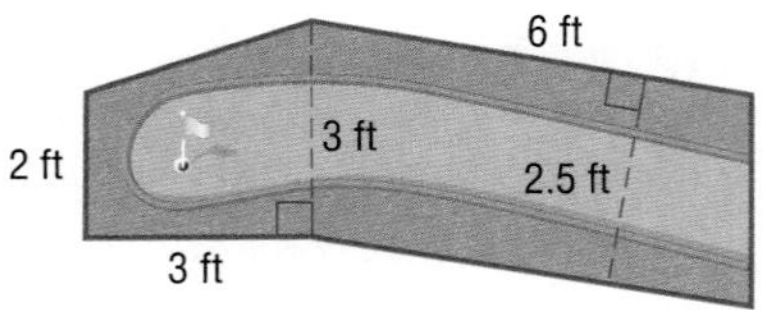

Area of trapezoid

$A = \frac{1}{2}h(b_1 + b_2)$

$A = \frac{1}{2}(3)(2 + 3)$

$A = 7.5$

Area of parallelogram

$A = bh$

$A = 6 \cdot 2.5$

$A = 15$

So, 7.5 + 15 or 22.5 square feet of turf will be needed.

CHECK Your Progress

d. **SHEDS** Chloe's father is building a shed. How many square feet of wood are needed to build the back of the shed shown at the right?

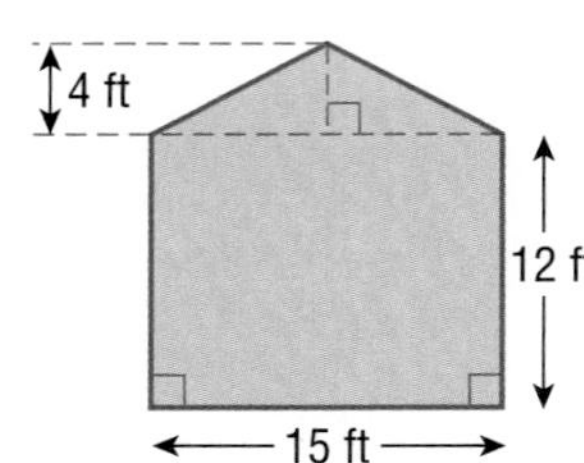

Study Tip

Congruent Triangles Congruent triangles have corresponding sides and angles that are congruent.

EXAMPLE Find the Area of a Shaded Region

3 **In the figure at the right, four congruent triangles are cut from a rectangle. Find the area of the shaded region. Round to the nearest tenth if necessary.**

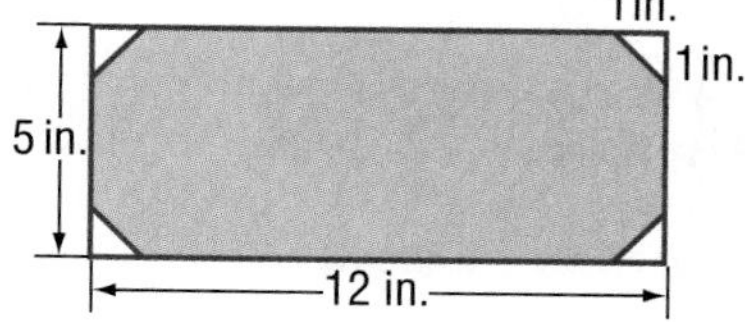

Find the area of the rectangle and subtract the area of the four triangles.

Area of rectangle		**Area of triangles**	
$A = \ell w$		$A = 4 \cdot \left(\frac{1}{2}bh\right)$	
$A = 12 \cdot 5$	$\ell = 12, w = 5$	$A = 4 \cdot \frac{1}{2} \cdot 1 \cdot 1$	$b = 1, h = 1$
$A = 60$	Simplify.	$A = 2$	Simplify.

The area of the shaded region is 60 – 2 or 58 square inches.

CHECK Your Progress

e. Two rectangles are cut from a larger rectangle. Find the area of the shaded region. Round to the nearest tenth if necessary.

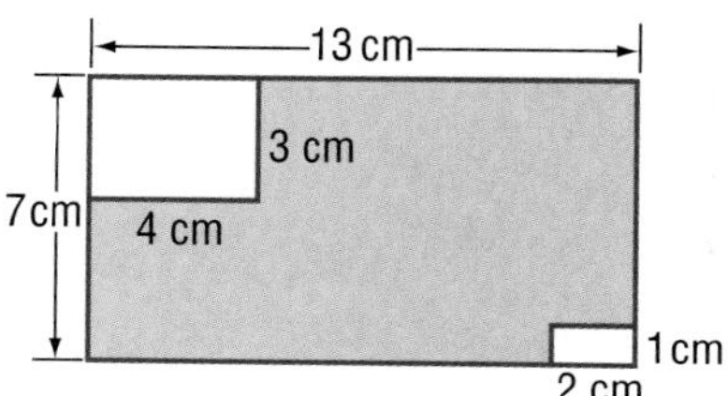

CHECK Your Understanding

Example 1 (p. 364)

Find the area of each figure. Round to the nearest tenth if necessary.

1.

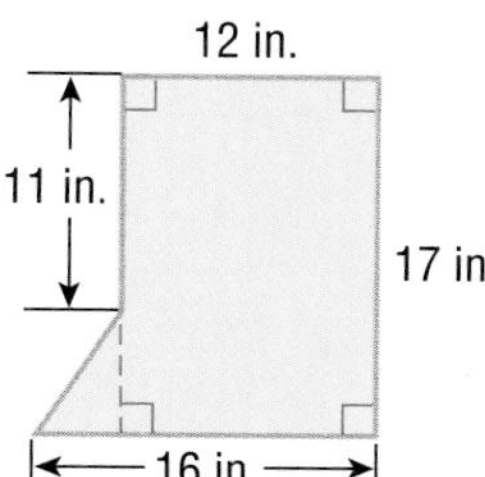

2.

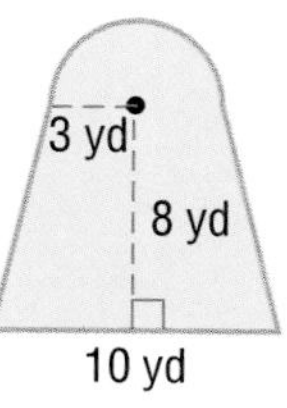

Examples 2, 3 (pp. 364, 365)

3. **WINDOWS** The Lunas installed the window shown below. How many square feet is the window?

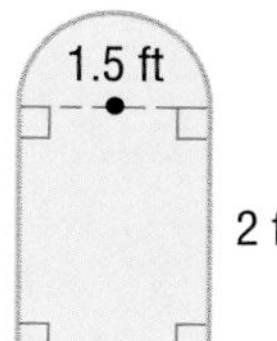

4. A triangle is cut from a rectangle. Find the area of the shaded region.

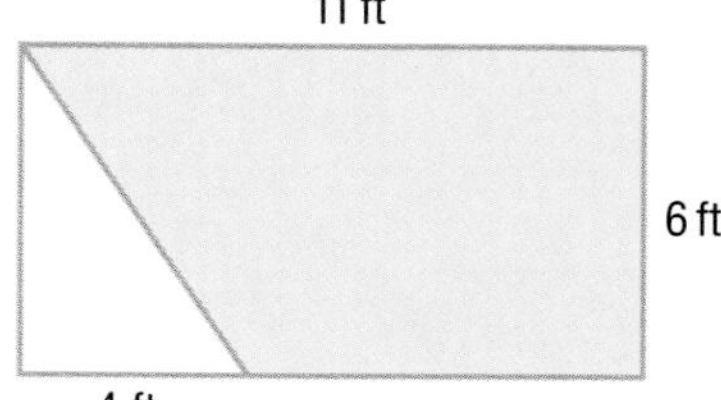

Practice and Problem Solving

HOMEWORK HELP	
For Exercises	See Examples
5–10	1
11, 12	2
13–16	3

Find the area of each figure. Round to the nearest tenth if necessary.

5.
12 cm
4.5 cm
2 cm
5 cm

6. 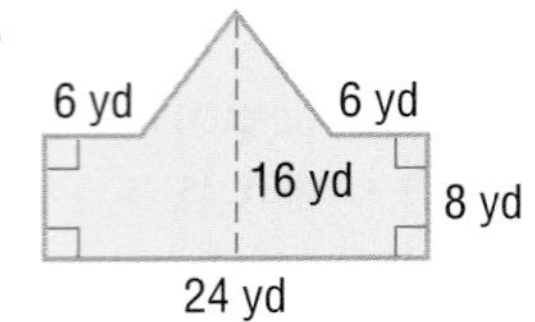

7. 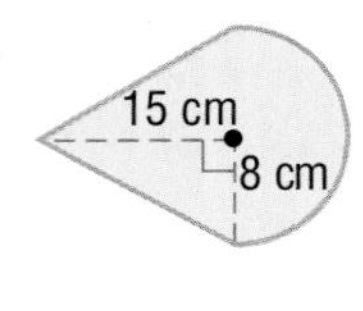

8. 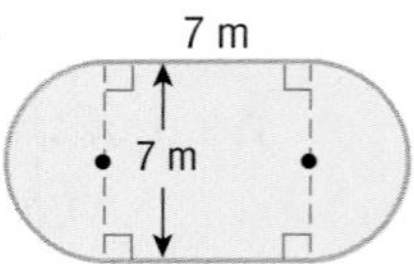

9. 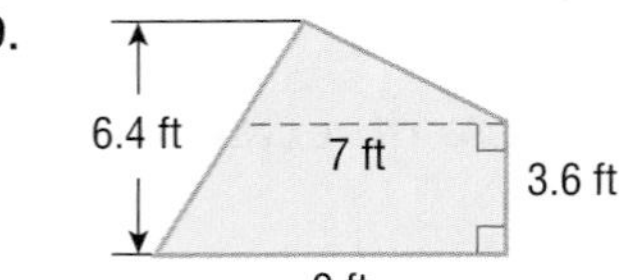

10. 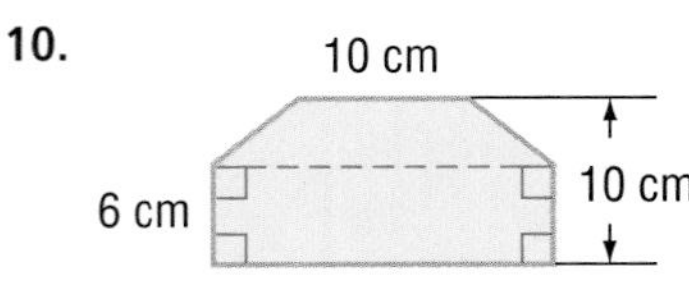

11. **CARPENTRY** Scott is constructing a deck like the one shown. What is the area of the deck?

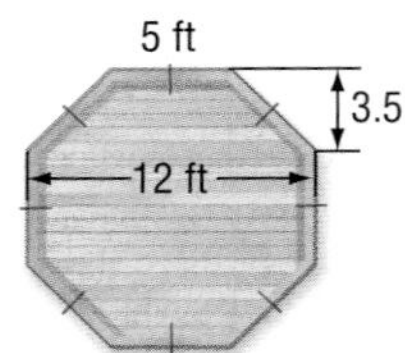

12. **JEWELRY** A necklace comes with a gold pendant. What is the area of the pendant in square centimeters?

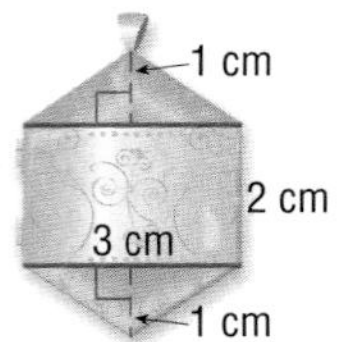

Find the area of the shaded region. Round to the nearest tenth if necessary.

13. 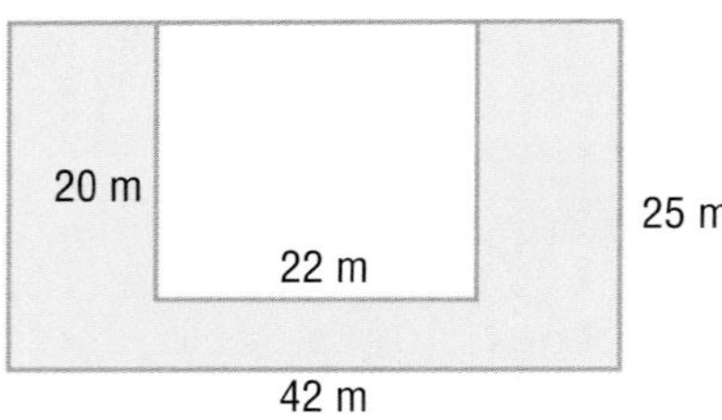

14. 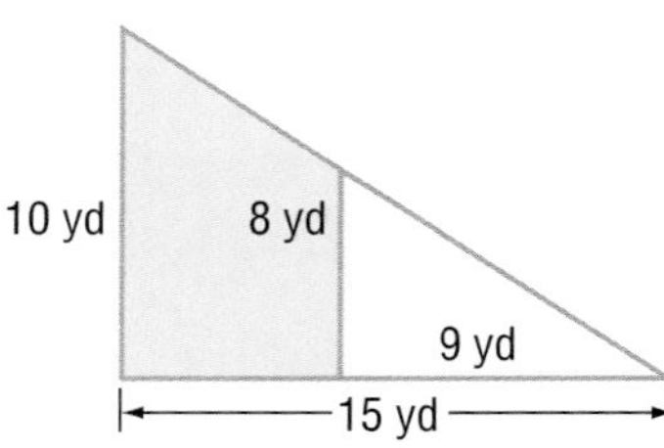

15. 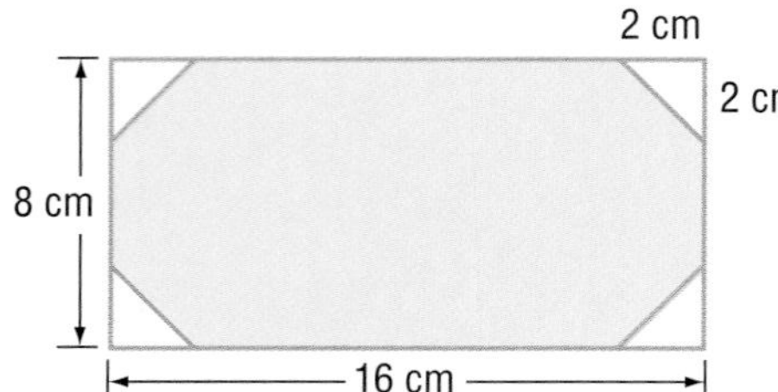

16. 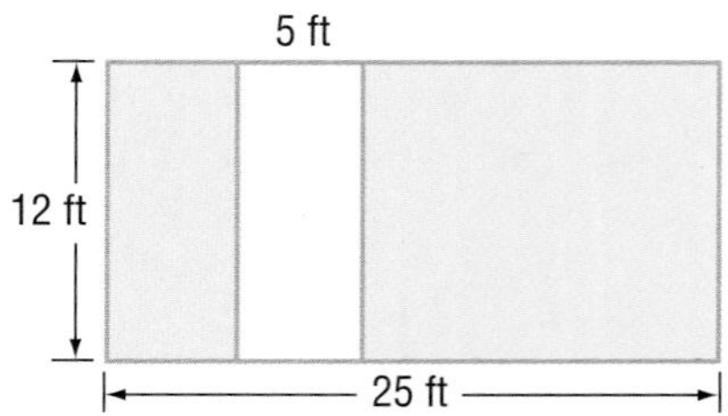

17. **CARPETING** Zoe's mom is carpeting her bedroom and needs to know the amount of floor space. How many square feet of carpeting are needed for the room?

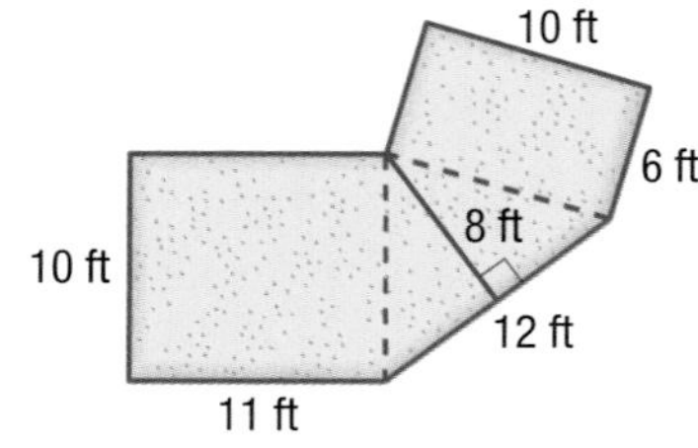

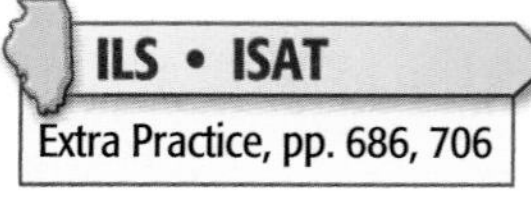

Extra Practice, pp. 686, 706

H.O.T. Problems

18. **CHALLENGE** In the diagram at the right, a 2-foot wide flower border surrounds the pond. What is the area of the border?

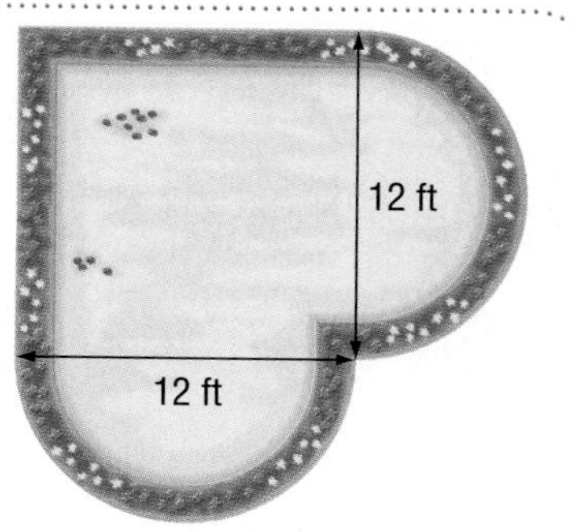

19. **WRITING IN MATH** Explain at least two different ways of finding the area of a hexagon. Include a drawing with your answer.

ISAT PRACTICE 7.A.3b, 7.C.3b

20. What is the total area of the figure shown?

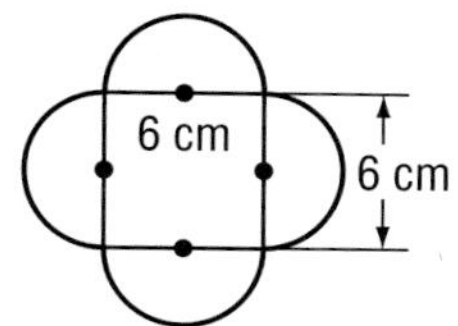

A 92.5 cm^2

B 64.3 cm^2

C 56.5 cm^2

D 36.0 cm^2

21. A rectangular vegetable garden that is 32 feet long and 21 feet wide is on a rectangular lot that is 181 feet long and 48 feet wide. The rest of the lot is grass. Approximately how many square feet is grass?

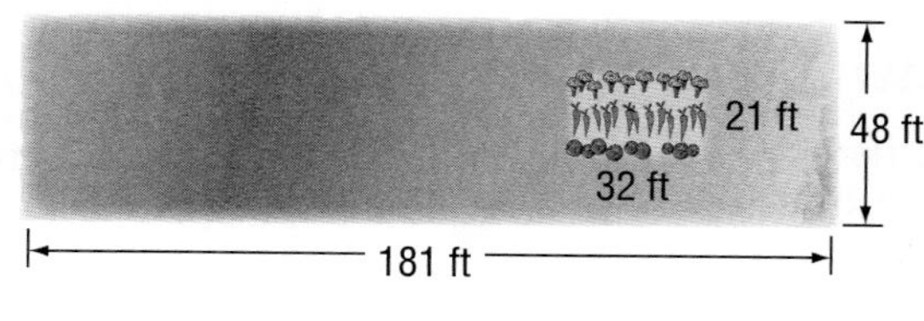

F 8,688 ft^2

G 8,635 ft^2

H 8,016 ft^2

J 282 ft^2

Spiral Review

22. **MODELS** Suppose you had 100 cubes. Use the *solve a simpler problem* strategy to determine the largest cube you could build with the cubes. (Lesson 7-2)

23. **ANIMALS** A dog is wearing a 10-foot long leash. If the leash is tied to a stake in the middle of a yard, how much space does the dog have to play? Round to the nearest tenth. (Lesson 7-1)

24. **GEOMETRY** Graph rectangle *ABCD* with vertices $A(-1, 3)$, $B(5, 3)$, $C(5, -2)$, and $D(-1, -2)$. Then graph its image after a translation 2 units right and 4 units down. (Lesson 6-7)

GET READY for the Next Lesson

PREREQUISITE SKILL **Classify each polygon according to its number of sides.**

25. 

26. 

27. 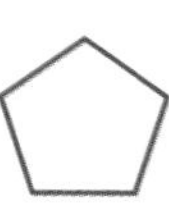

28. 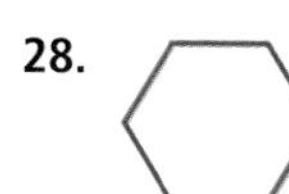

7-4 Three-Dimensional Figures

MAIN IDEA

Identify and draw three-dimensional figures.

IL Learning Standards

9.B.3 Identify, describe, classify and compare two- and **three-dimensional geometric figures and models according to their properties.**

New Vocabulary

coplanar
parallel
solid
polyhedron
edge
face
vertex
diagonal
skew lines
prism
base
pyramid

IL Math Online

glencoe.com

- Extra Examples
- Personal Tutor
- Self-Check Quiz

GET READY for the Lesson

MONUMENTS A two-dimensional figure has two dimensions, length and width. A three-dimensional figure, like the Washington Monument, has three dimensions, length, width, and height.

1. Name the two-dimensional shapes that make up the sides of the building.
2. If you observed the building from directly above, what two-dimensional figure would you see?
3. How are two- and three-dimensional figures related?

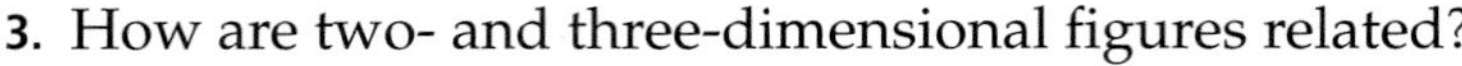

The figure at the right shows rectangle *ABCD*. Lines *AB* and *DC* are **coplanar** because they lie in the same plane. They are also **parallel** because they will never intersect, no matter how far they are extended.

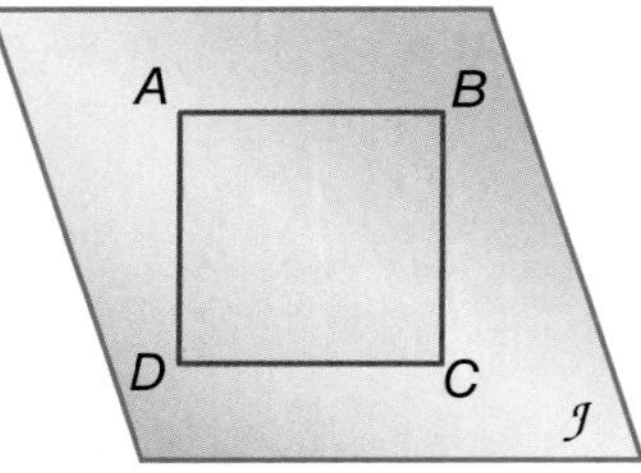

A
B
D
C
J

Just as two lines in a plane can intersect or be parallel, there are different ways that planes may be related in space.

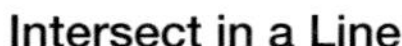

Intersect in a Line

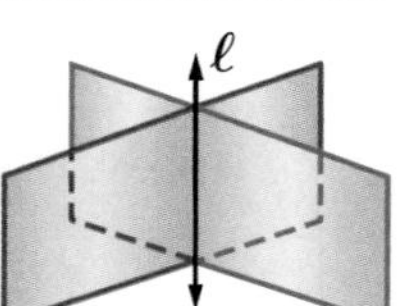

ℓ

Intersect at a Point

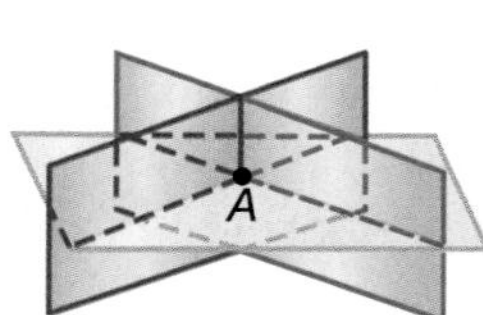

A

No Intersection

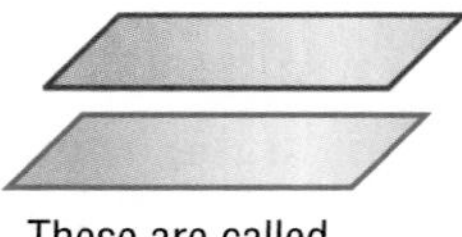

These are called *parallel planes.*

Intersecting planes can also form three-dimensional figures or **solids**. A **polyhedron** is a solid with flat surfaces that are polygons. Some terms associated with three-dimensional figures are *edge, face, vertex,* and *diagonal.*

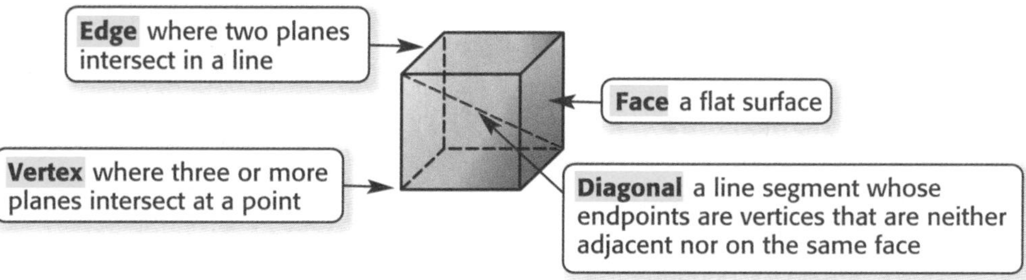

Edge where two planes intersect in a line
Face a flat surface
Vertex where three or more planes intersect at a point
Diagonal a line segment whose endpoints are vertices that are neither adjacent nor on the same face

Notice that in the figure at the right, $\overline{WX}$ and $\overline{KL}$ do not intersect. These segments are not parallel because they do not lie in the same plane. Lines that do not intersect and are not coplanar are called **skew lines**.

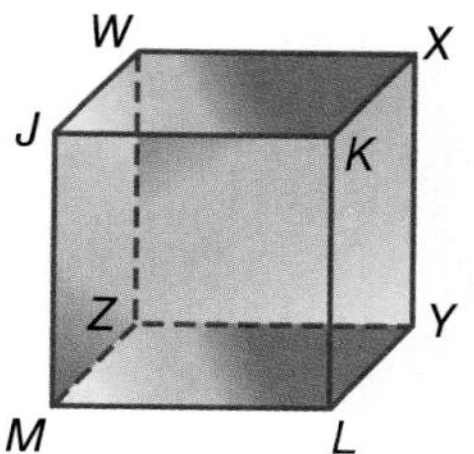

Vocabulary Link

Intersection

Everyday Use the place where two roads cross

Math Use any point or points that figures have in common

EXAMPLES Identify Relationships

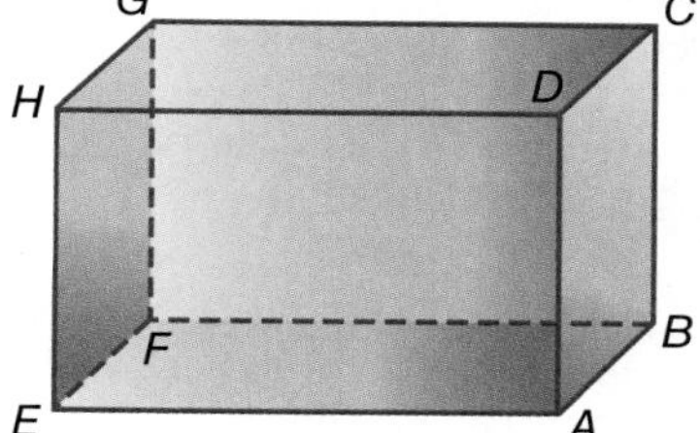

1 **Name a plane that is parallel to plane *ABC*.**

Plane *EFG* is parallel to plane *ABC*.

2 **Identify a segment that is skew to $\overline{CG}$.**

$\overline{CG}$ and $\overline{EH}$ are skew.

3 **Identify a pair of points between which a diagonal can be drawn.**

A segment between points *A* and *G* forms a diagonal.

CHECK Your Progress

a. Identify the intersection of planes *ABC* and *CDH*.

Prisms and pyramids are common solids. Their names are based on the shape of their bases.

A **prism** is a polyhedron with two parallel, congruent faces called **bases**. A **pyramid** is a polyhedron with one base that is a polygon and faces that are triangles.

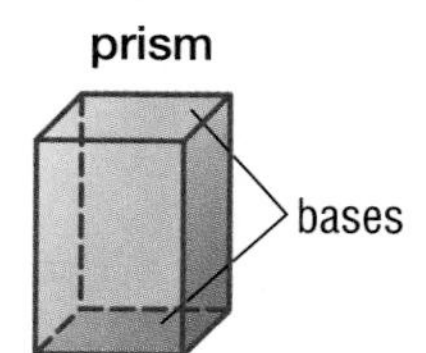

Study Tip

Common Error In the drawing of a rectangular prism, the bases do not have to be on the top and bottom. Any two parallel rectangles are bases. In a triangular pyramid, any face is a base.

EXAMPLES Identify Prisms and Pyramids

Identify each solid. Name the number and shapes of the faces. Then name the number of edges and vertices.

4

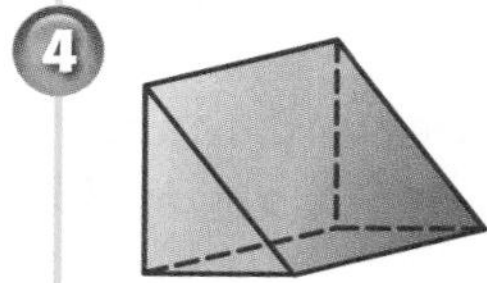

The figure has two parallel congruent bases that are triangles, so it is a triangular prism. The other three faces are rectangles. It has a total of 5 faces, 9 edges, and 6 vertices.

5

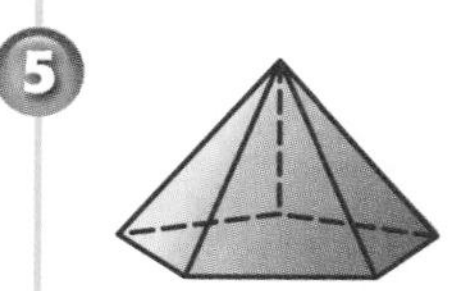

The figure has one base that is a pentagon, so it is a pentagonal pyramid. The other faces are triangles. It has a total of 6 faces, 10 edges, and 6 vertices.

CHECK Your Progress

b.

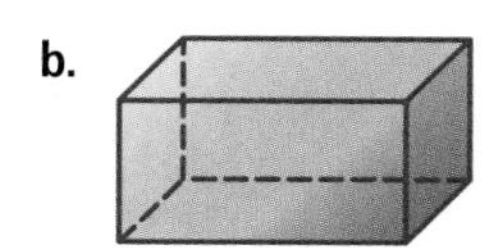

c.

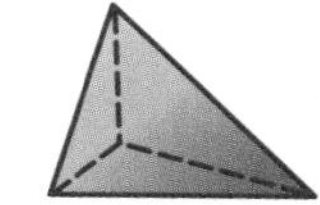

d.

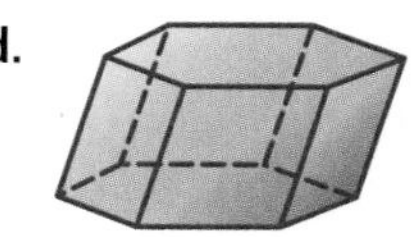

You can use three-dimensional drawings of objects to describe how different parts of the objects are related in space.

EXAMPLE Analyze Drawings

6 **FURNITURE The photo shows a garden bench. Draw and label the top, front, and side views of the bench.**

CHECK Your Progress

e. **TOOLBOX** Draw and label the top, front, and side views of the toolbox shown.

Real-World Career. . .
How Does a Landscape Architect Use Math?
Landscape architects use geometry when creating their designs. They begin with simple geometric shapes, then add lines and angles to make the space more interesting.

IL Math Online
For more information, go to glencoe.com.

CHECK Your Understanding

Examples 1–3 (p. 369)

Use the figure at the right to identify the following points, lines, or planes.

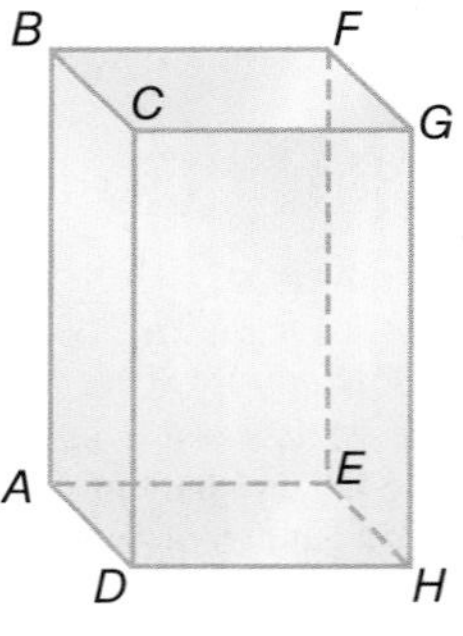

1. parallel planes
2. skew lines
3. two points that form a diagonal when connected
4. intersecting planes

Examples 4, 5 (p. 369)

Identify each solid. Name the number and shapes of the faces. Then name the number of edges and vertices.

5. 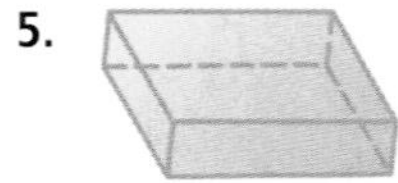

6. 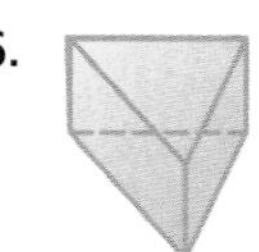

7. 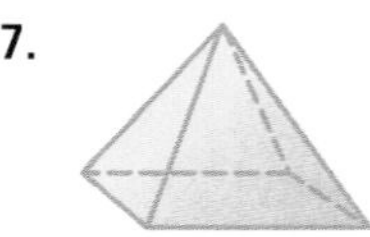

Example 6 (p. 370)

8. **AQUARIUMS** Draw and label the top, front, and side views of the aquarium shown.

Practice and Problem Solving

HOMEWORK HELP

For Exercises	See Examples
9–12	1–3
13–16	4, 5
17–18	6

Use the figure at the right to identify the following points, lines, or planes.

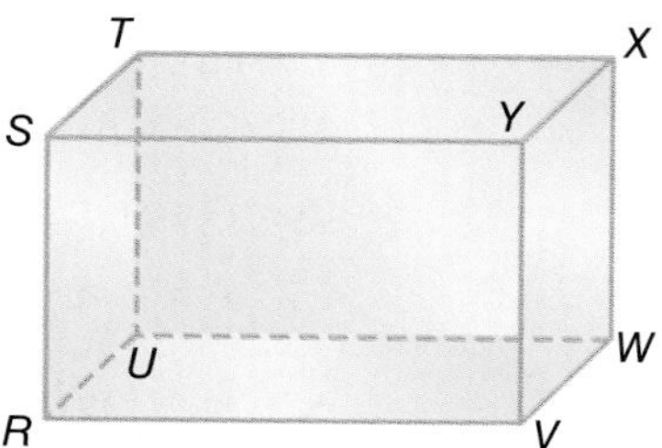

9. parallel planes
10. skew lines
11. two points that form a diagonal when connected
12. intersecting planes

Identify each solid. Name the number and shapes of the faces. Then name the number of edges and vertices.

13. 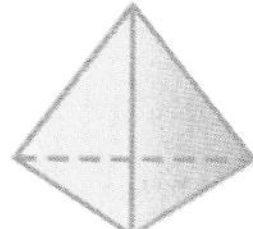
14. 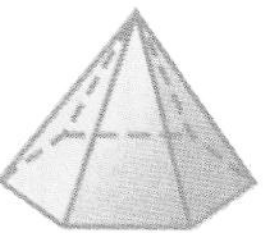
15. 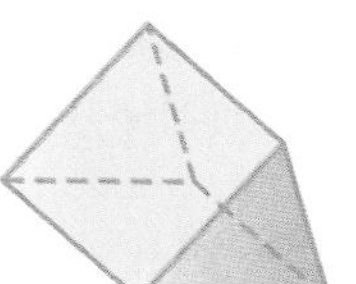
16. 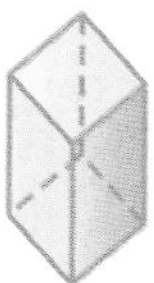

17. **BUILDINGS** Draw and label the top, front, and side views of the building shown.

18. **CABINET** A wood file cabinet is shown. Draw and label the top, front, and side views of the cabinet.

CHEMISTRY For Exercises 19–21, complete parts a and b for each atomic model.

a. **Identify the solid or solids that form each model.**

b. **Draw and label the top and one side view of the model.**

19.

Methane

20.

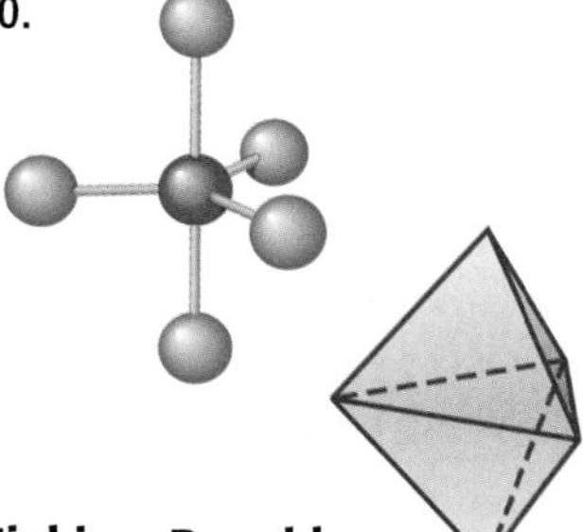

Niobium Bromide

21.

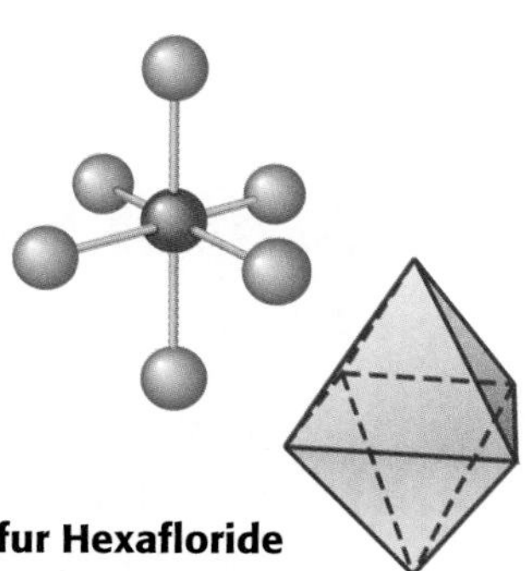

Sulfur Hexafloride

22. State whether the following conjecture is *true* or *false*. If *false*, provide a counterexample.

Two planes in three-dimensional space can intersect at one point.

ILS • ISAT

Extra Practice, pp. 686, 706

H.O.T. Problems

23. **OPEN ENDED** Choose a real-world object such as a chair or a desk. Draw the top, front, and side views of your object.

CHALLENGE Determine whether each statement is *always*, *sometimes*, or *never* true. Explain your reasoning.

24. A prism has 2 bases and 4 sides.
25. A pyramid has parallel sides.

26. **WRITING IN MATH** Explain whether a top-front-side view diagram *always* provides enough information to draw a figure. If not, provide a counterexample.

ISAT PRACTICE 9.B.3

27. Benita received the gift box shown.

Which drawing best represents the top view of the gift box?

A

B

C

D

28. Which of the following represents a side view of the figure below?

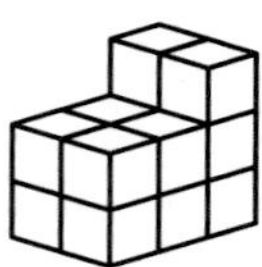

F

G

H

J

Spiral Review

29. Find the area of the figure. Round to the nearest tenth. (Lesson 7-3)

$7\frac{1}{2}$ in.
$8\frac{1}{4}$ in.
$8\frac{1}{4}$ in.
16 in.

30. **BICYCLES** The tires on a bicycle are 26 inches in diameter. How far will the bicycle travel in 150 rotations of its tires? Round to the nearest tenth. (Lesson 7-1)

GET READY for the Next Lesson

PREREQUISITE SKILL Find the area of each triangle described.

31. base, 3 in.; height, 10 in.
32. base, 8 ft; height, 7 ft
33. base, 5 cm; height, 11 cm

7-5 Volume of Prisms and Cylinders

MAIN IDEA

Find the volumes of prisms and cylinders.

IL Learning Standards

7.A.3b Apply the concepts and attributes of length, capacity, weight/mass, perimeter, area, **volume,** time, temperature and angle measures **in practical situations.**
7.C.3b Use concrete and graphic models and appropriate formulas to find perimeters, areas, surface areas and **volumes of** two- and **three-dimensional regions.**

New Vocabulary

volume
cylinder
composite solid

IL Math Online

glencoe.com
- Extra Examples
- Personal Tutor
- Self-Check Quiz

MINI Lab

The rectangular prism at the right has a volume of 12 cubic units.

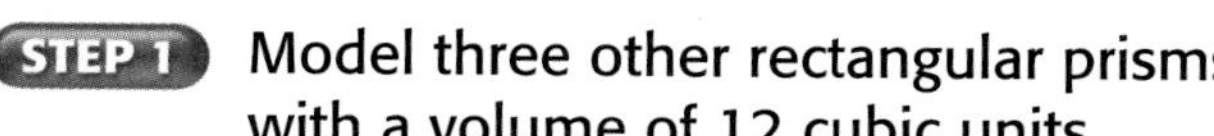

STEP 1 Model three other rectangular prisms with a volume of 12 cubic units.

STEP 2 Copy and complete the following table.

Prism	Length (units)	Width (units)	Height (units)	Area of Base (units^2)
A	4	1	3	4
B				
C				
D				

1. Describe how the volume V of each prism is related to its length ℓ, width w, and height h.
2. Describe how the area of the base B and the height h of each prism is related to its volume V.

Volume is the measure of the space occupied by a solid. Standard measures of volume are cubic units such as cubic inches (in^3) or cubic feet (ft^3).

Volume of a Prism — Key Concept

Words The volume V of a prism is the area of the base B times the height h.

Symbols $V = Bh$

Models

EXAMPLES Find the Volumes of Prisms

1 Find the volume of the rectangular prism.

$V = Bh$ Volume of a prism

$V = (\ell \cdot w)h$ The base is a rectangle, so $B = \ell \cdot w$.

$V = (9 \cdot 5)6.5$ $\ell = 9, w = 5, h = 6.5$

$V = 292.5$ Simplify.

The volume is 292.5 cubic centimeters.

Study Tip

Common Error Remember that the bases of a triangular prism are triangles. In Example 2, these bases are not on the top and bottom of the figure, but on its sides.

 **Find the volume of the triangular prism.**

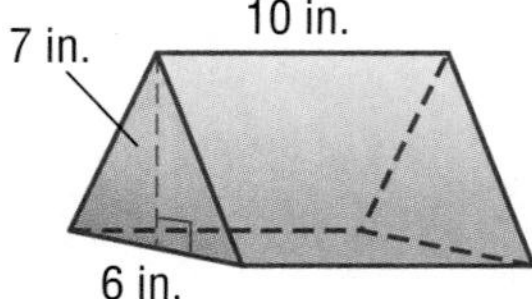

$V = Bh$ Volume of a prism

$V = \left(\frac{1}{2} \cdot 6 \cdot 7\right)h$ The base is a triangle, so $B = \frac{1}{2} \cdot 6 \cdot 7$.

$V = \left(\frac{1}{2} \cdot 6 \cdot 7\right)10$ The height of the prism is 10.

$V = 210$ Simplify.

The volume is 210 cubic inches.

CHECK Your Progress **Find the volume of each prism.**

a. 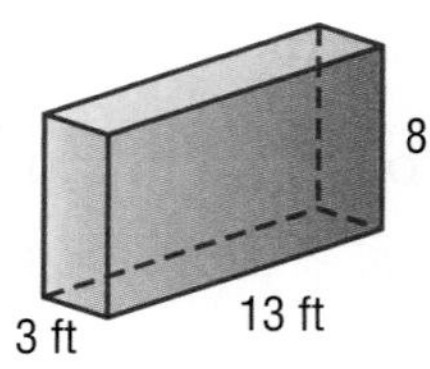

b. 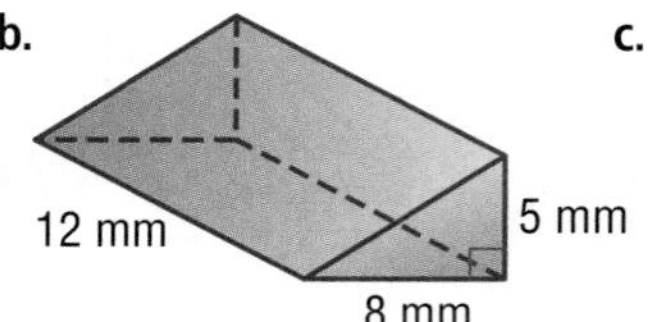

c. 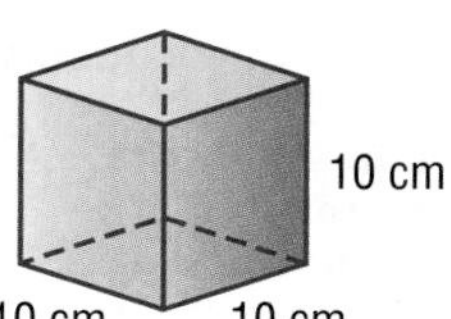

A **cylinder** is a solid with bases that are congruent, parallel circles connected with a curved side. You can use the formula $V = Bh$ to find the volume of a cylinder, where the base is a circle.

Volume of a Cylinder

Key Concept

Words The volume V of a cylinder with the area of the base B times the height h.

Model

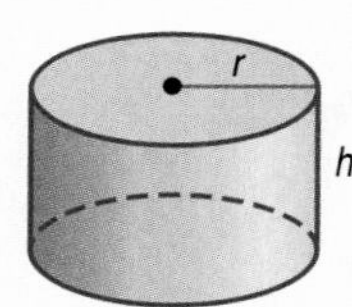

Symbols $V = Bh$

Study Tip

Estimation You can estimate the volume of the cylinder in Example 3 to be about $3 \cdot 7^2 \cdot 20$ or 2,940 ft^3 to check the reasonableness of your result.

EXAMPLE Find the Volume of a Cylinder

 **Find the volume of the cylinder. Round to the nearest tenth.**

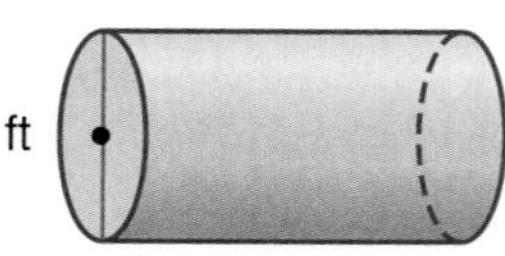

Since the diameter is 13 feet, the radius is 6.5 feet.

$V = \pi r^2 h$ Volume of a cylinder

$V = \pi \cdot 6.5^2 \cdot 20$ Replace r with 6.5 and h with 20.

$V \approx 2{,}654.6$ Simplify. Use a calculator.

The volume is about 2,654.6 cubic feet.

 **CHECK Your Progress**

Find the volume of each cylinder. Round to the nearest tenth.

d. radius, 2 in.; height 7 in.

e. diameter, 18 cm; height 5 cm

Objects that are made up of more than one type of solid are called **composite solids.** To find the volume of a composite solid, decompose the figure into solids whose volumes you know how to find.

Study Tip

Estimation
You can check the reasonableness of your result in Example 4 by estimating the volume. The volume should be slightly less than 12 • 12 • 12 or 1,728 mm³.

EXAMPLE Find the Volume of a Composite Solid

4 CRAFTS Tanya uses beads shaped like cubes to make jewelry. Each bead has a circular hole through the middle. Find the volume of the bead.

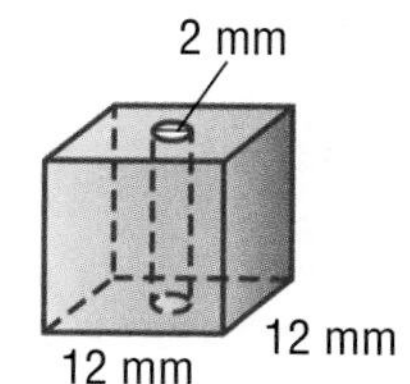

The bead is made of one rectangular prism and one cylinder. Find the volume of each solid.

Rectangular Prism

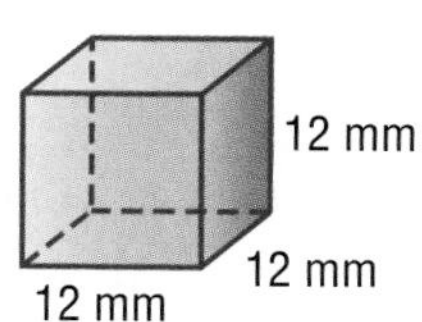

$V = Bh$

$V = (12 \cdot 12)12$ or 1,728

Cylinder

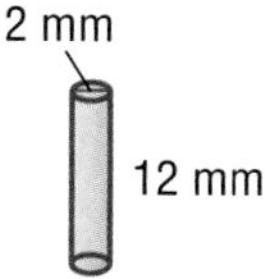

$V = Bh$

$V = (\pi \cdot 1^2)12$ or 37.7

The volume of the bead is 1,728 − 37.7 or 1,690.3 cubic millimeters.

CHECK Your Progress

f. **BIRDS** The Ecology Club is building birdhouses, similar to the one shown at the right, to put in a nature preserve. Find the volume of the birdhouse.

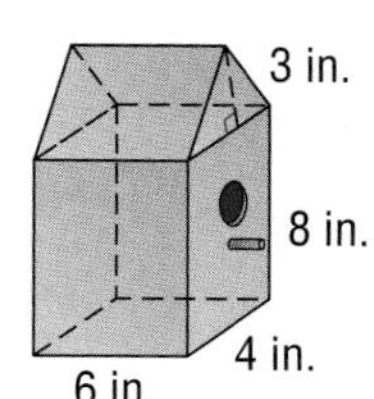

CHECK Your Understanding

Examples 1, 2 (pp. 373–374)

Find the volume of each prism. Round to the nearest tenth if necessary.

1.

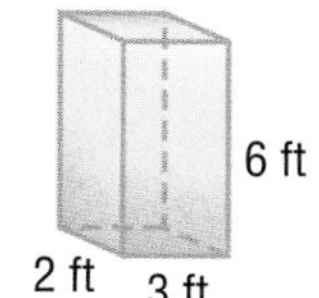

2.

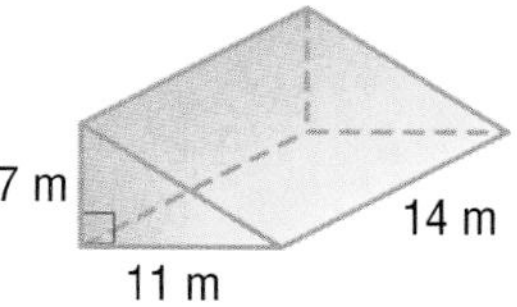

Example 3 (p. 374)

Find the volume of each cylinder. Round to the nearest tenth.

3.

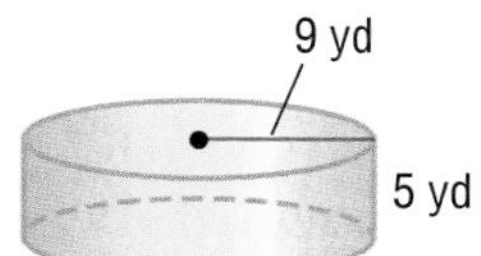

4.

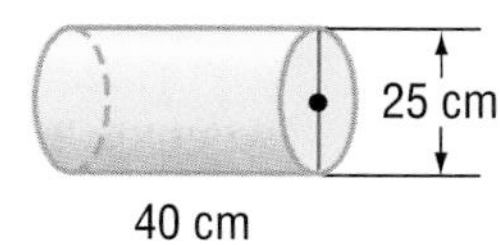

Example 4 (p. 375)

5. **TOYS** Gloria's younger sister received the toy house shown as a gift. What is the volume of the toy house?

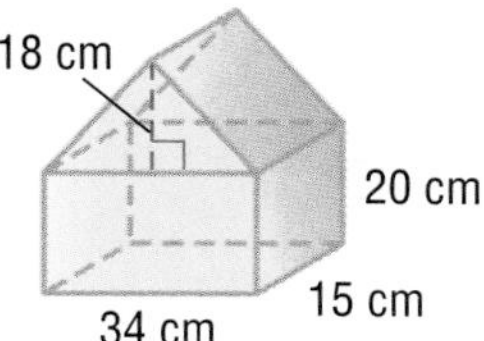

Practice and Problem Solving

HOMEWORK HELP

For Exercises	See Examples
6–9, 12, 13	1, 2
10, 11, 14, 15	3
16, 17	4

Find the volume of each solid. Round to the nearest tenth if necessary.

6.

4 in.
$1\frac{1}{2}$ in.
5 in.

7.

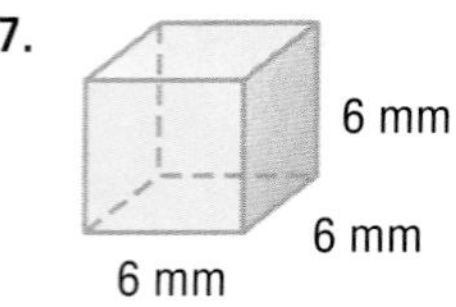

8.

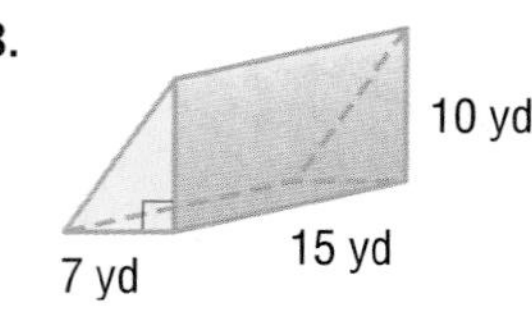

9.

8 m
12 m
16 m

10.

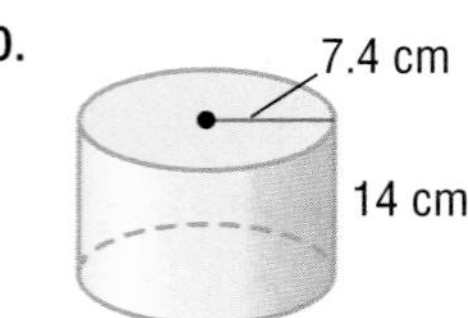

11.

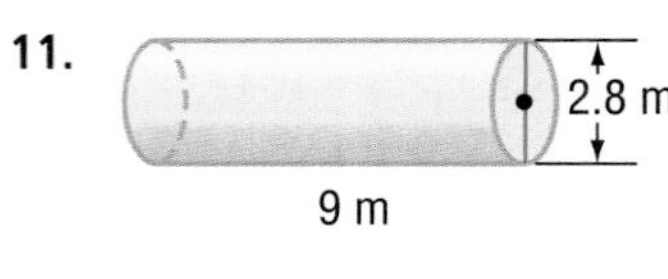

12. rectangular prism: length, 4 in.; width, 6 in.; height, 17 in.
13. triangular prism: base of triangle, 5 ft; altitude, 14 ft; height of prism, $8\frac{1}{2}$ ft
14. cylinder: radius, 25 m; height, 20 m
15. cylinder: diameter, 7.2 cm; height, 5.8 cm

16. **MAILBOXES** The Francos have the mailbox shown below. Find the volume of the mailbox.

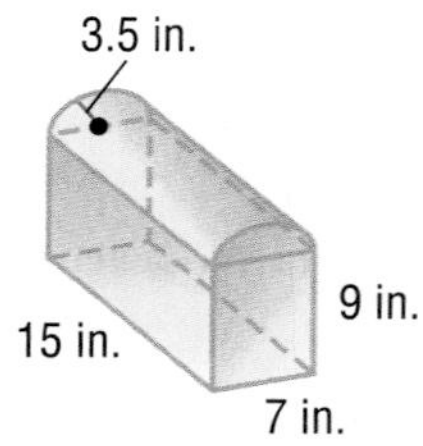

17. **TOWELS** An unused roll of paper towels has the dimensions shown. What is the volume of the unused roll?

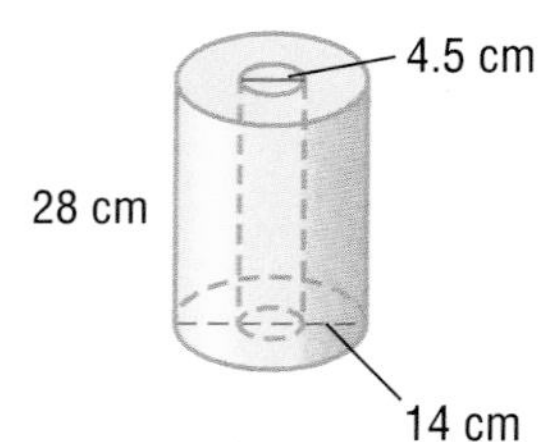

18. Find the height of a rectangular prism with a length of 6.8 meters, a width of 1.5 meters, and a volume of 91.8 cubic meters.

19. Find the height of a cylinder with a radius of 4 inches and a volume of 301.6 cubic inches.

20. **BAND** The Band Boosters buy popcorn in large bags that have a volume of 2,500 cubic inches. They make individual boxes to sell that are 2 inches by 6 inches by 8 inches. If they sold 20 boxes, how much of the original bag is left?

21. **BUSINESS** The original package for the Crackle Cereal Company's cereal is shown at the right. They want to design a new package with the same volume but in the shape of a cylinder. If the height remains the same as the original, what is the least value they should use for the diameter of the new package? Explain your reasoning.

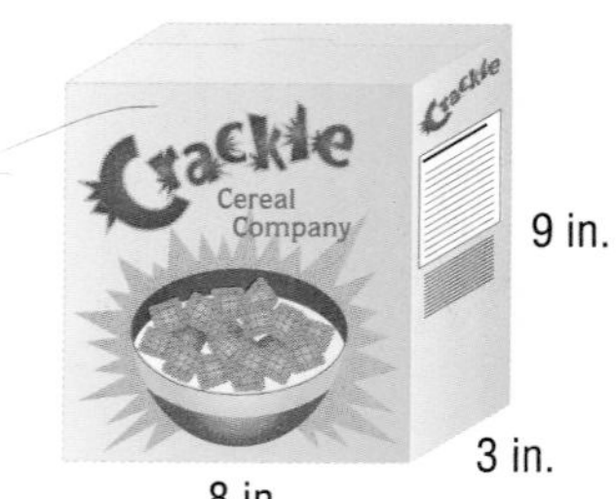

22. **POOLS** A wading pool is to be 20 feet long, 11 feet wide, and 1.5 feet deep. The excavated dirt is to be hauled away by wheelbarrow. If the wheelbarrow holds 9 cubic feet of dirt, how many wheelbarrows of dirt must be hauled away from the site?

CONVERTING UNITS OF MEASURE For Exercises 23–25, use the cubes and the information below.

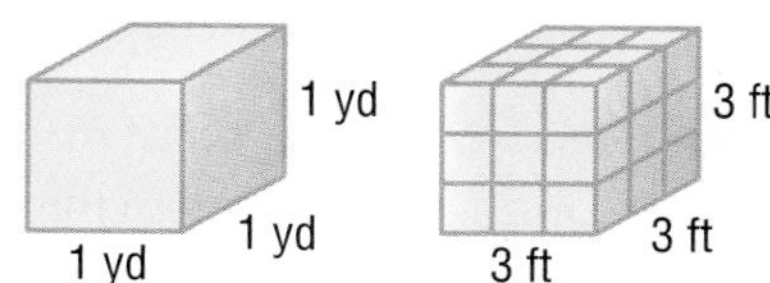

The volume of the left cube is 1 cubic yard. The right cube is the same size, but the unit of measure has been changed. So, 1 cubic yard = (3)(3)(3) or 27 cubic feet. Use a similar process to convert each measurement.

23. $1 \text{ ft}^3 = \blacksquare \text{ in}^3$ 24. $1 \text{ cm}^3 = \blacksquare \text{ mm}^3$ 25. $1 \text{ m}^3 = \blacksquare \text{ cm}^3$

26. **GARDENING** Candice is making a raised vegetable garden with the dimensions shown. Each bag of potting soil she plans to use has 0.5 cubic yard of soil. How many bags of soil will she need to fill her garden?

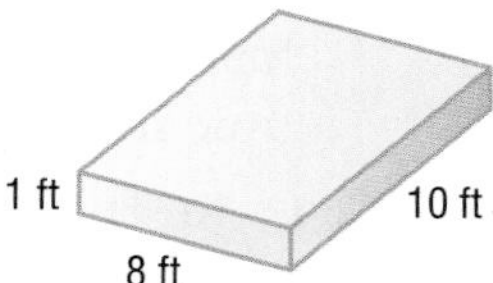

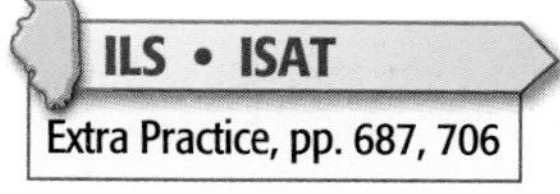

27. **GEOMETRY** Explain how you would find the volume of the hexagonal prism shown at the right. Then find its volume.

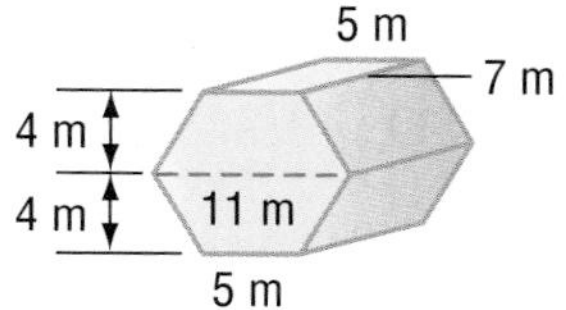

H.O.T. Problems

CHALLENGE For Exercises 28–31, describe how the volume of each solid is affected after the indicated change in its dimension(s).

28. You double one dimension of a rectangular prism.
29. You double two dimensions of a rectangular prism.
30. You double all three dimensions of a rectangular prism.
31. You double the radius of a cylinder.

32. **OPEN ENDED** Find the volume of a can or other cylindrical object, making sure to include appropriate units. Explain your method.

33. **FIND THE ERROR** Megan and Ana are finding the volume of the prism shown at the right. Who is correct? Explain your reasoning.

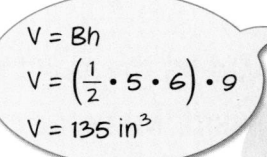

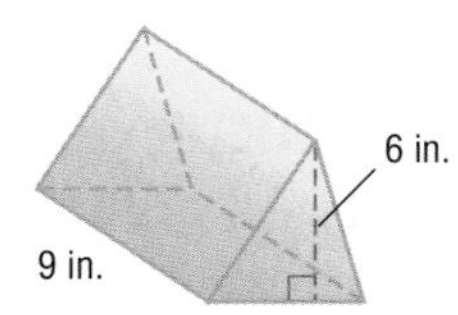

34. **SELECT A TOOL** Tyree needs to find the volume of the figure at the right. Which of the following tools might Tyree use to find the volume of the figure? Justify your selection(s). Then, use the tool(s) to solve the problem.

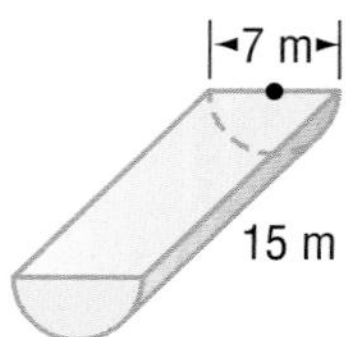

make a model | calculator | paper/pencil

35. **WRITING IN MATH** Write two formulas that you can use to find the volume of a rectangular prism. State the formula that you prefer to use and explain why.

ISAT PRACTICE 7.A.3b, 7.C.3b

36. A cylinder is 30 inches tall and has a diameter of 12 inches. Which is the closest to the volume of the cylinder in cubic feet?

A $1\ ft^3$

B $2\ ft^3$

C $3\ ft^3$

D $4\ ft^3$

37. **SHORT RESPONSE** A cardboard box has the dimensions shown below. What is the volume of the cardboard box in cubic feet?

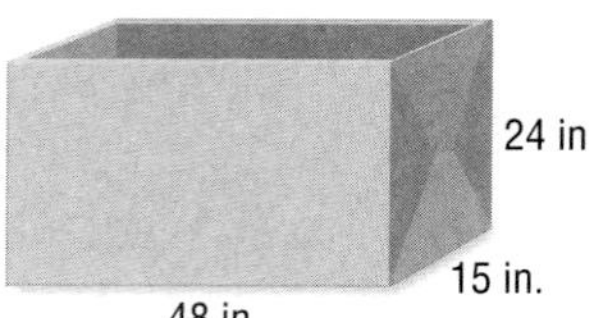

Spiral Review

38. How many edges does an octagonal pyramid have? (Lesson 7-4)

39. **SPORTS** The rectangular area under the basket is known as the key. The key and the free-throw circle of a high school basketball court is shown. Find the area of the floor taken up by these elements. (Lesson 7-3)

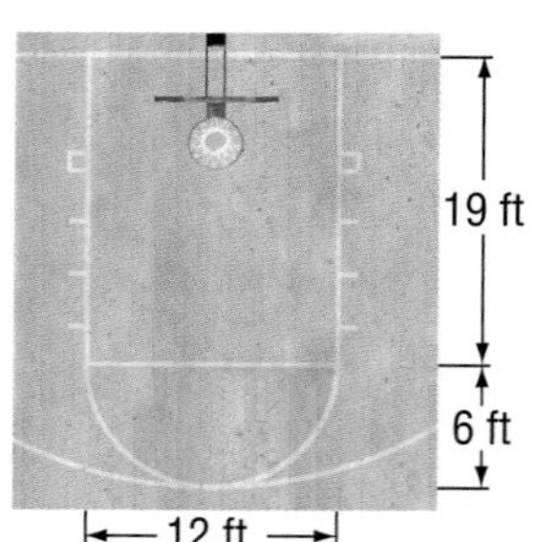

40. **MEASUREMENT** The circumference of a circle is 16.5 feet. What is its area to the nearest tenth of a square foot? (Lesson 7-1)

41. **WOOL** Texas ranchers produce about 20% of U.S. wool. If 27.5 million pounds of wool are produced each year, how many pounds of wool are *not* produced in Texas? (Lesson 5-7)

Write each percent as a fraction or mixed number in simplest form. (Lesson 5-1)

42. 0.12%
43. 225%
44. 135%
45. $\frac{3}{8}\%$

GET READY for the Next Lesson

PREREQUISITE SKILL **Multiply.**

46. $\frac{1}{3} \cdot 6 \cdot 10$
47. $\frac{1}{3} \cdot 7 \cdot 15$
48. $\frac{1}{3} \cdot 4^2 \cdot 9$
49. $\frac{1}{3} \cdot 6^2 \cdot 20$

CHAPTER 7

Mid-Chapter Quiz

Lessons 7-1 through 7-5

IL Learning Standards
7.A.3b, 7.C.3b

Find the circumference and area of each circle. Round to the nearest tenth. (Lesson 7-1)

1. 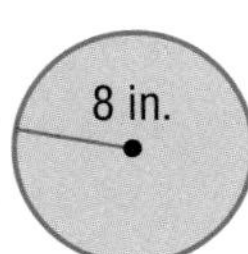

2. 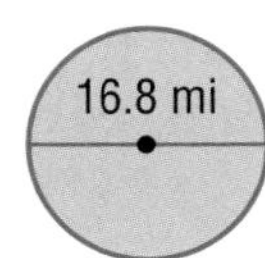

MEASUREMENT For Exercises 3 and 4, use the following information. Round to the nearest tenth. (Lesson 7-1)
A shot-putter must stay inside the circle shown.

3. What is the area of the region in which the athlete is able to move?

4. What is the circumference of the circular region?

5. **DANCE** Balloons come in packages of 15 or 35. Julie needs 195 balloons for the spring dance. How many packages of each size should she buy? Use the *solve a simpler problem* strategy. (Lesson 7-2)

Find the area of each figure. Round to the nearest tenth if necessary. (Lesson 7-3)

6. 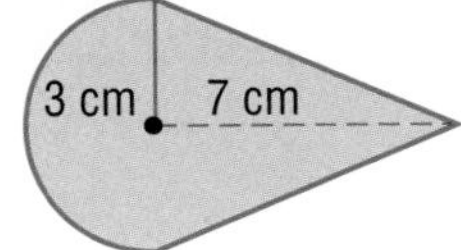

7. 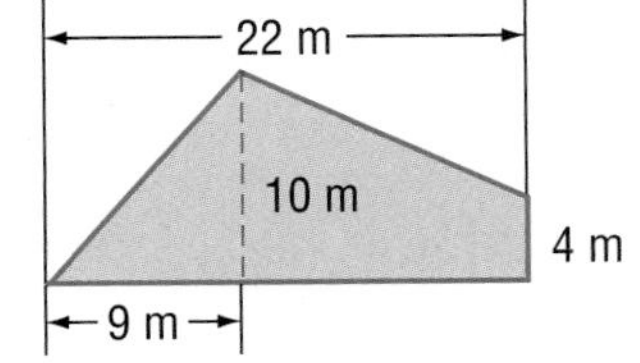

8. **GAMES** Draw and label the top, front, and side views of the puzzle cube. (Lesson 7-4)

9. **MULTIPLE CHOICE** Juanita wants to sketch all of the faces of a triangular prism. What shapes will appear on her paper? (Lesson 7-4)

   A 2 squares, 2 triangles
   B 2 triangles, 3 rectangles
   C 3 triangles
   D 1 triangle, 3 rectangles

Find the volume of each solid. Round to the nearest tenth if necessary. (Lesson 7-5)

10. 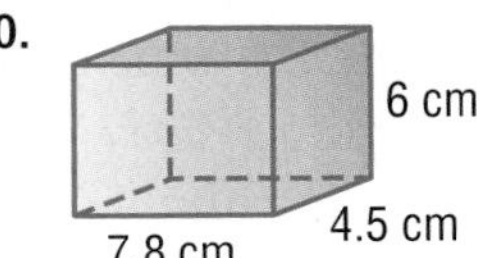

11. 14 yd, 30 yd (cylinder)

12. **MULTIPLE CHOICE** Find the volume of a cube-shaped box with edges 15 inches in length. (Lesson 7-5)

   F 225 in^3 **H** 1,350 in^3
   G 900 in^3 **J** 3,375 in^3

13. Find the width of a rectangular prism with a length of 7.6 meters, a height of 8 meters, and a volume of 88.4 cubic meters. Round to the nearest tenth. (Lesson 7-5)

7-6 Volume of Pyramids and Cones

MAIN IDEA

Find the volumes of pyramids and cones.

IL Learning Standards

7.C.3b Use concrete and graphic models and appropriate formulas to find perimeters, areas, surface areas and **volumes of** two- and **three-dimensional regions.**
9.A.3a Draw or **construct** two- and **three-dimensional geometric figures including prisms, pyramids,** cylinders and cones. *Also addresses 7.A.3b.*

New Vocabulary

cone

IL Math Online

glencoe.com

- Extra Examples
- Personal Tutor
- Self-Check Quiz

MINI Lab

In this Mini Lab, you will investigate the relationship between the volume of a pyramid and the volume of a prism with the same base area and height.

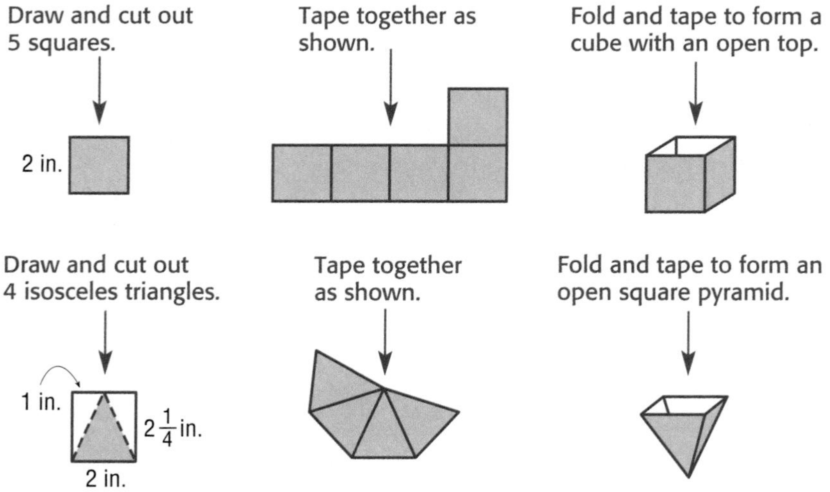

Draw and cut out 5 squares.
2 in.
Tape together as shown.
Fold and tape to form a cube with an open top.
Draw and cut out 4 isosceles triangles.
1 in.
$2\frac{1}{4}$ in.
2 in.
Tape together as shown.
Fold and tape to form an open square pyramid.

1. Compare the base areas and the heights of the two solids.
2. Fill the pyramid with rice, sliding a ruler across the top to level the amount. Pour the rice into the cube. Repeat until the prism is filled. How many times did you fill the pyramid in order to fill the cube?
3. What fraction of the cube's volume does one pyramid fill?

The volume of a pyramid is one-third the volume of a prism with the same base area and height.

Volume of a Pyramid — Key Concept

Words The volume V of a pyramid is one-third the area of the base B times the height h.

Symbols $V = \frac{1}{3}Bh$

Model

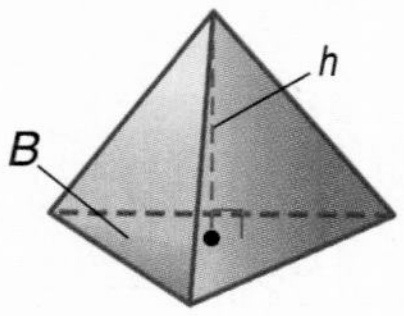

The height of a pyramid or cone is the distance from the vertex, perpendicular to the base.

Study Tip

Estimation
You can estimate the volume of the pyramid in Example 1 to be about $\frac{1}{3}\left(\frac{1}{2} \cdot 8 \cdot 6\right)(11)$ or 88 m^3. Since 95.04 m^3 is close to 88 m^3, the answer is reasonable.

EXAMPLE Find the Volume of a Pyramid

1 **Find the volume of the pyramid. Round to the nearest tenth.**

$V = \frac{1}{3}Bh$ — Volume of a pyramid

$V = \frac{1}{3}\left(\frac{1}{2} \cdot 8.1 \cdot 6.4\right)11$ — $B = \frac{1}{2} \cdot 8.1 \cdot 6.4$, $h = 11$

$V = 95.04$ — Simplify.

The volume is about 95.0 cubic meters.

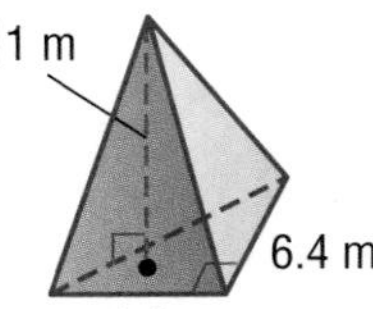

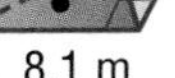

CHECK Your Progress

a. Find the volume of a pyramid that has a height of 5 yards and a square base with sides 2 yards long.

Real-World EXAMPLE

2 **ARCHITECTURE The Louvre Pyramid in Paris has a square base with sides 112 feet long. If the volume is 296,875 cubic feet, find the height of the pyramid.**

$V = \frac{1}{3}Bh$ — Volume of a pyramid

$296{,}875 = \frac{1}{3} \cdot 12{,}544 \cdot h$ — Replace V with 296,875 and B with $112 \cdot 112$ or 12,544.

$296{,}875 = \frac{12{,}544}{3}h$ — Multiply.

$\frac{3}{12{,}544} \cdot 296{,}875 = \frac{3}{12{,}544} \cdot \frac{12{,}544}{3}h$ — Multiply each side by $\frac{3}{12{,}544}$.

$71 \approx h$ — Simplify.

The height of the pyramid is about 71 feet.

Real-World Link
American architect I.M. Pei designed the glass pyramid which serves as an entrance to the Louvre. It was dedicated in 1989.
Source: The Louvre Museum

CHECK Your Progress

b. **CRAFTS** Nicco made a pyramid-shaped candle. The volume of the candle is 864 cubic centimeters and its base has an area of 144 square centimeters. How high is the candle?

A **cone** is a three-dimensional figure with one circular base. A curved surface connects the base and the vertex. The volumes of a cone and a cylinder are related in the same way as those of a pyramid and prism.

Volume of a Cone — Key Concept

Words The volume V of a cone with radius r is one-third the area of the base B times the height h.

Model

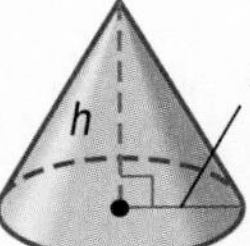

Symbols $V = \frac{1}{3}Bh$ or $V = \frac{1}{3}\pi r^2h$

 Find the Volume of a Cone

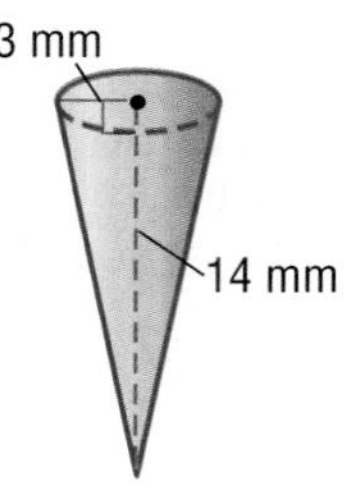

3 Find the volume of the cone.

$V = \frac{1}{3}\pi r^2 h$ Volume of a cone

$V = \frac{1}{3} \cdot \pi \cdot 3^2 \cdot 14$ Replace *r* with 3 and *h* with 14.

$V \approx 131.9$ Simplify. Use a calculator.

The volume is about 131.9 cubic millimeters.

 Your Progress

Find the volume of each cone. Round to the nearest tenth.

c. 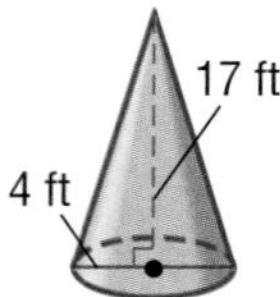

d. 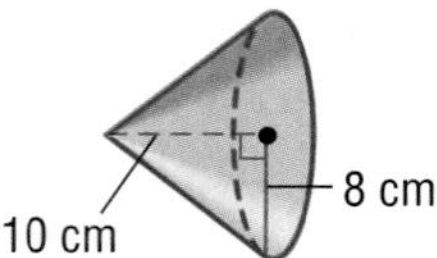

CHECK Your Understanding

Example 1 (p. 381) **Find the volume of each pyramid. Round to the nearest tenth.**

1. 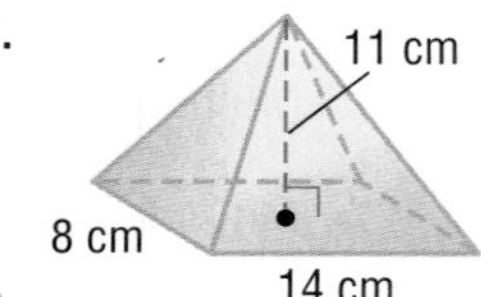

2. 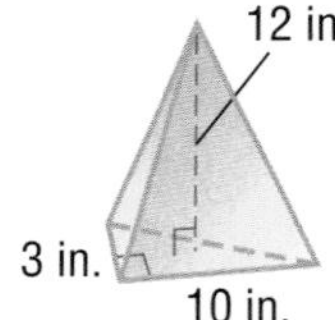

3. Find the volume of a pyramid that has a height of 125 centimeters and a square base with sides 95 centimeters long.

4. Find the volume of a pyramid that has a height of 17 feet and a square base with sides 22 feet long.

Example 2 (p. 381)

5. **ARCHAEOLOGY** El Castillo, the pyramid at Chichen Itza in Mexico is 30 meters tall with a volume of about 30,580 cubic meters. What is the length of each side of the square base?

Example 3 (p. 382) **Find the volume of each cone. Round to the nearest tenth.**

6. 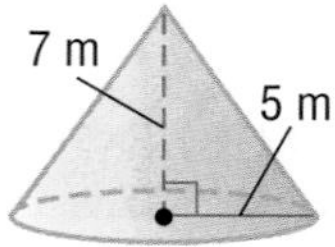

7. 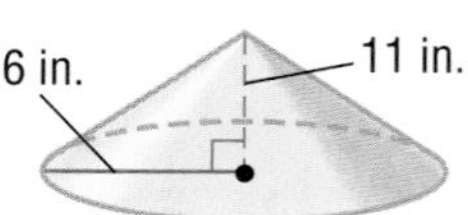

8. 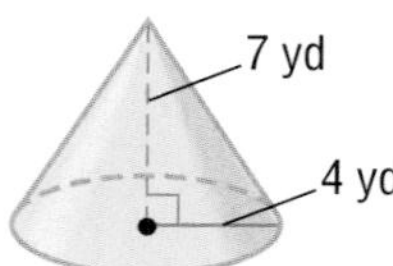

9. 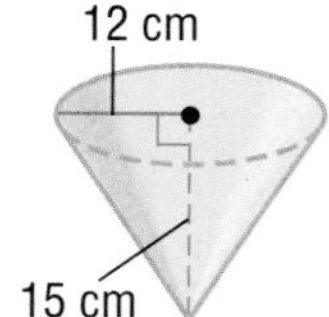

Practice and Problem Solving

HOMEWORK HELP	
For Exercises	See Examples
10–13	1
18	2
14–17	3

Find the volume of each pyramid. Round to the nearest tenth.

10. 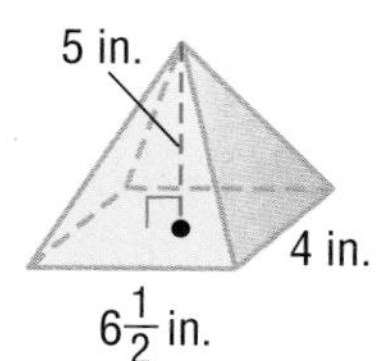

11. 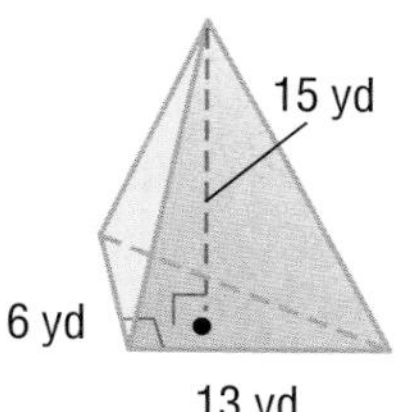

12. 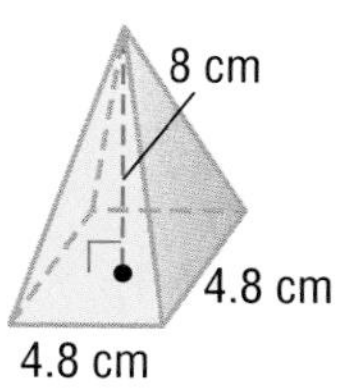

13. triangular pyramid: triangle base, 10 cm; triangle height, 7 cm; pyramid height, 15 cm

Find the volume of each cone. Round to the nearest tenth.

14. 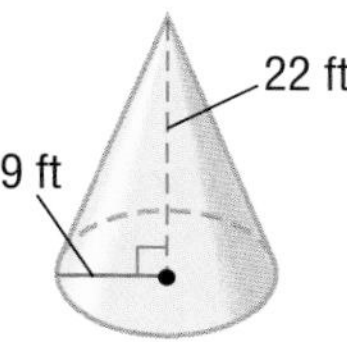

15. 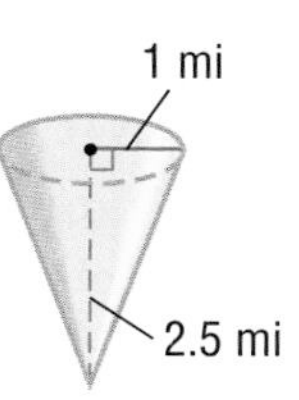

16. 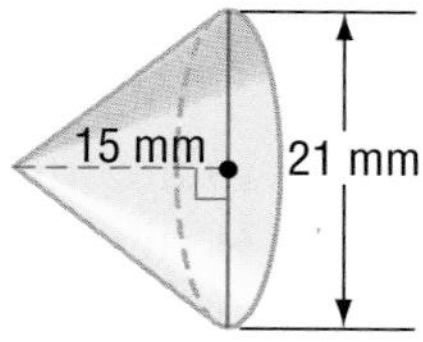

17. cone: diameter, 12 m; height, 5 m

18. **SCIENCE** A model of a volcano constructed for a science project is cone-shaped with a diameter of 8 inches. If the volume of the model is about 201 cubic inches, how tall is the model?

Find the volume of each solid. Round to the nearest tenth if necessary.

19. 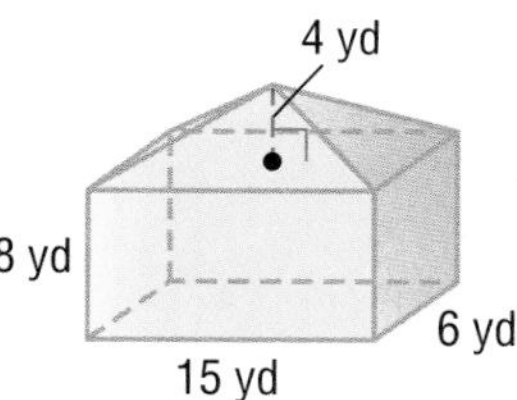

20. 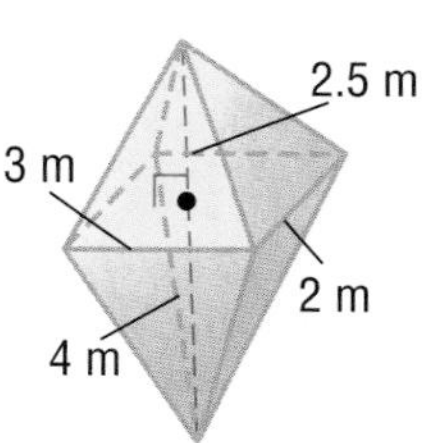

21. 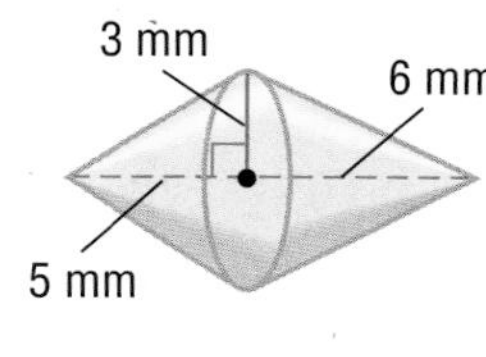

22. **HATS** A clown wants to fill his party hat with confetti. Use the drawing at the right to determine how much confetti his hat will hold.

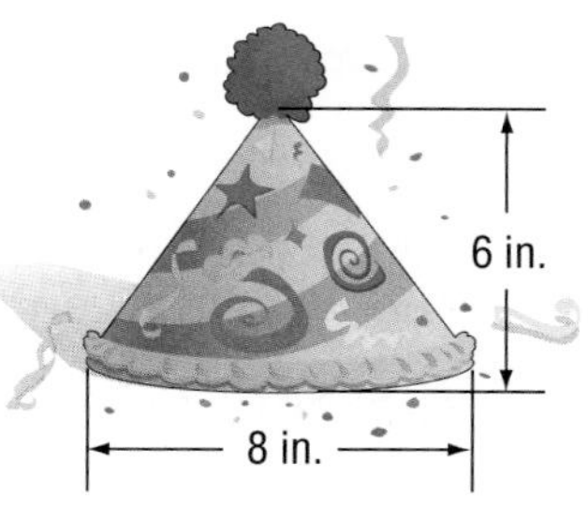

23. **IRRIGATION** A water tank like the one at the right is used to water flowers at a park. Water can be pumped from the tank at a rate of 25 liters per minute. How long will it take to use all of the water in a full tank? Round to the nearest minute. (*Hint*: 1 liter = 1,000 cm^3)

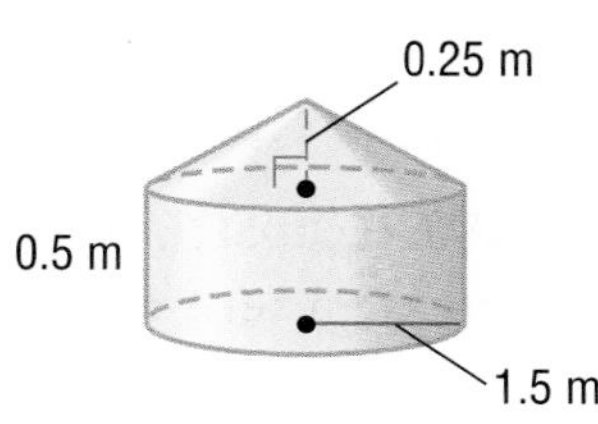

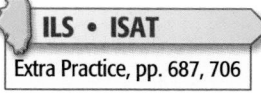

ILS • ISAT
Extra Practice, pp. 687, 706

H.O.T. Problems

24. **CHALLENGE** How could you change the height of a cone so that its volume would remain the same when its radius was tripled?

25. **OPEN ENDED** Draw and label a triangular pyramid with a volume of 36 cubic centimeters.

26. **NUMBER SENSE** Which would have a greater effect on the volume of a cone, doubling its radius or doubling its height? Explain your reasoning.

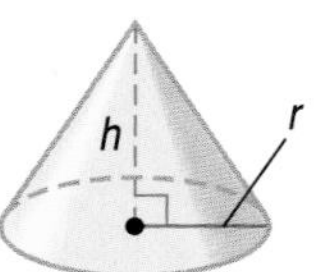

27. **WRITING IN MATH** Write about a real-world situation that can be solved by finding the volume of a cone.

ISAT PRACTICE 7.C.3b, 9.A.3a

28. A rectangular pyramid has a base 18 inches by 30 inches and a height of 36 inches. Which is closest to the volume of the pyramid in cubic feet?

A 2.5 ft^3

B 3 ft^3

C 4 ft^3

D 5.5 ft^3

29. Find the volume of the cylinder. Round to the nearest tenth if necessary.

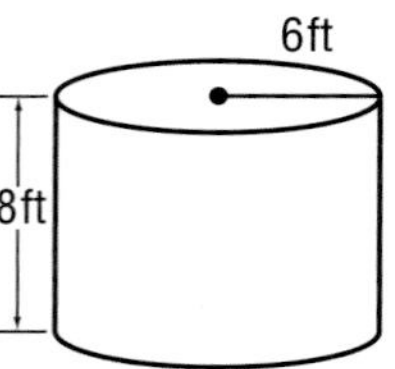

F 48 ft^3 **H** 288 ft^3

G 150.3 ft^3 **J** 904.8 ft^3

Spiral Review

30. **DISPENSER** Find the volume of the soap dispenser at the right. (Lesson 7-5)

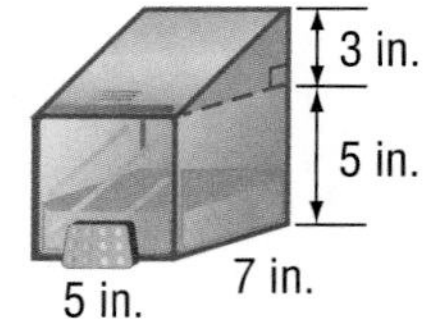

31. Name the number and shapes of the faces of a trapezoidal prism. Then name the number of edges and vertices. (Lesson 7-4)

32. **GEOMETRY** Graph triangle ABC with vertices $A(1, 2)$, $B(4, -1)$, and $C(2, -4)$. Then graph its image after a reflection over the y-axis, and write the coordinates of the image's vertices. (Lesson 6-6)

33. **SHOPPING** Etu saved $90 when he purchased a DVD recorder on sale. If the sale price was 37.5% off the regular price, what was the regular price of the DVD recorder? (Lesson 5-7)

GET READY for the Next Lesson

PREREQUISITE SKILL Find the circumference of each circle. Round to the nearest tenth. (Lesson 7-1)

34. diameter, 9 in. 35. diameter, 5.5 ft 36. radius, 2 m 37. radius, 3.8 cm

Explore 7-7

Measurement Lab
Surface Area of Cylinders

MAIN IDEA

Find the surface area of cylinders using models and nets.

IL Learning Standards

7.C.3b Use concrete and graphic models and appropriate formulas to find perimeters, areas, **surface areas** and volumes **of** two- and **three-dimensional regions.** *Also addresses 7.A.3b.*

New Vocabulary

net

Nets are two-dimensional patterns of three-dimensional figures. When you construct a net, you are decomposing the three-dimensional figure into separate shapes. You can use a net to find the area of each surface of a three-dimensional figure such as a cylinder.

ACTIVITY

STEP 1 Use an empty cylinder-shaped container that has a lid. Measure and record the height of the container.

STEP 2 Then label the lid and bottom face using a blue marker. Label the curved side using a red marker.

STEP 3 Take off the lid of the container and make 2 cuts as shown. Next, cut off the sides of the lid. Finally, lay the lid, the curved side, and the bottom flat to form the net of the container.

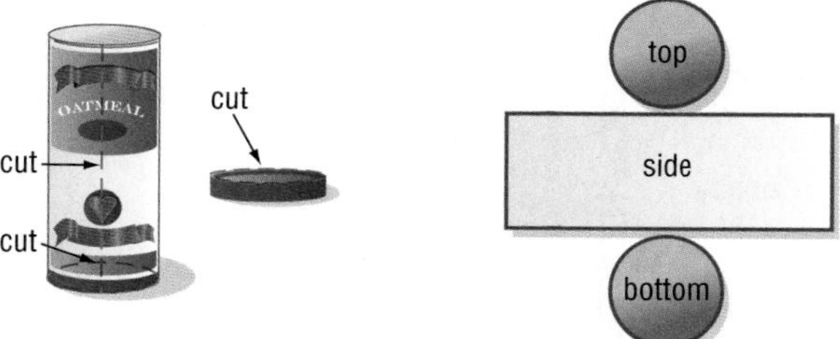

Analyze the Results

1. Classify the two-dimensional shapes that make up the net of the container.
2. Find the area of each shape. Then find the sum of these areas.
3. Find the diameter of the top of the container and use it to find the perimeter or circumference of that face.
4. Multiply the circumference by the height of the container. What does this product represent?
5. Add the product from Exercise 4 to the sum of the areas of the two circular bases.
6. Compare your answers from Exercises 2 and 5.
7. **MAKE A CONJECTURE** Write a method for finding the area of all the surfaces of a cylinder given the measures of its height and the diameter of one of its bases.

Surface Area of Prisms and Cylinders

MAIN IDEA

Find the lateral and total surface area of prisms and cylinders.

IL Learning Standards

7.C.3b Use concrete and graphic models and appropriate formulas to find perimeters, areas, **surface areas** and volumes **of** two- and **three-dimensional regions.**
9.A.3a Draw or construct two- and **three-dimensional geometric figures including prisms,** pyramids, **cylinders** and cones. *Also addresses 7.A.3b.*

New Vocabulary

lateral face
lateral surface area
total surface area

IL Math Online

glencoe.com

- Extra Examples
- Personal Tutor
- Self-Check Quiz

MINI Lab

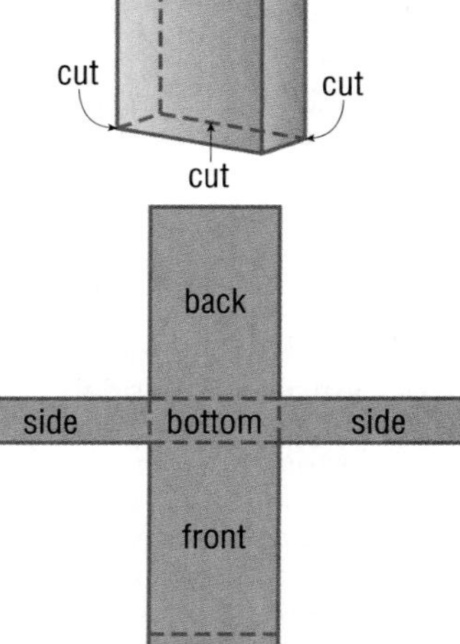

STEP 1 Use an empty box with a tuck-in lid. Measure and record the height of the box and the perimeter of the top or bottom face.

STEP 2 Label the top, bottom, front, back, and side faces using a marker.

STEP 3 Open the lid and make 5 cuts as shown. Then open the box and lay it flat to form a net of the box. Measure and record the dimensions of each face.

1. Find the area of each face. Then find the sum of these areas.
2. Multiply the perimeter of a base by the height of the box. What does this product represent?
3. Add the product from Exercise 2 to the sum of the areas of the two bases.
4. Compare your answers from Exercises 1 and 3.

In the Mini Lab, you found the area of each surface, or face, of a box. A **lateral face** of a solid is any flat surface that is *not* a base. The **lateral surface area** of a solid is the sum of the areas of its lateral faces. The **total surface area** of a solid is the sum of the areas of all its surfaces.

Lateral Surface Area of a Prism

Key Concept

Words The lateral area L of a prism is the perimeter P of the base times the height h of the prism.

Symbols $L = Ph$

Model

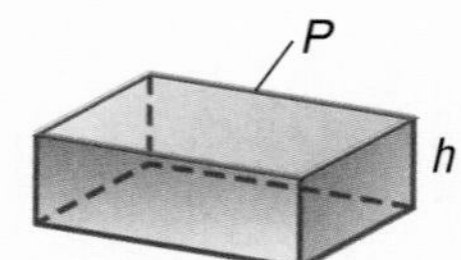

Total Surface Area of a Prism

Words The total surface area S of a prism is the lateral surface area L plus the area of the two bases $2B$.

Symbols $S = L + 2B$ or $S = Ph + 2B$

Model

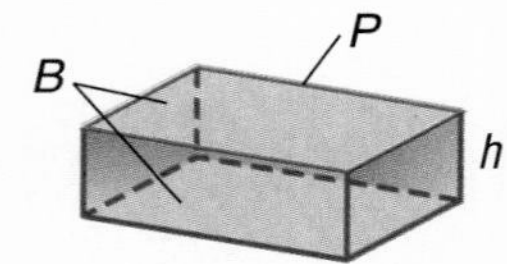

EXAMPLES Surface Areas of a Prism

Study Tip

Bases of Rectangular Prisms
For the examples and exercises in this book, assume that the top and the bottom faces of a rectangular prism are its bases.

1 **Find the lateral and total surface areas of the rectangular prism.**

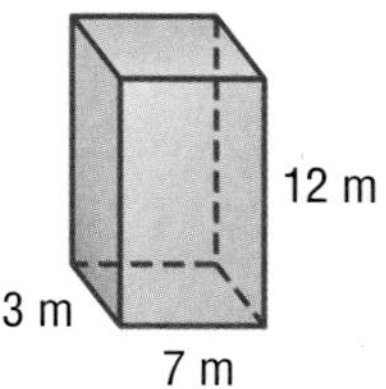

The bases of this prism are rectangles that are 3 meters wide and 7 meters long. Begin by finding the perimeter and area of one base.

Perimeter of Base

$P = 2\ell + 2w$

$P = 2(7) + 2(3)$ or 20

Area of Base

$B = \ell w$

$B = 7(3)$ or 21

Use this information to find the lateral and total surface areas.

Lateral Surface Area

$L = Ph$

$L = 20(12)$ or 240

Total Surface Area

$S = L + 2B$

$S = 240 + 2(21)$ or 282

The lateral surface area is 240 square meters, and the total surface area of the prism is 282 square meters.

Real-World Link
Competitive water skiing consists of 3 events—slalom, jumping, and tricks—and has divisions ranging from under 12 years of age to 85 years of age and older.
Source: USA Water Ski

2 **WATER SKIING** **The ramp for competitive water skiing is a wedge-shaped ramp that is covered in wax or fiberglass. Find the total surface area of the ramp.**

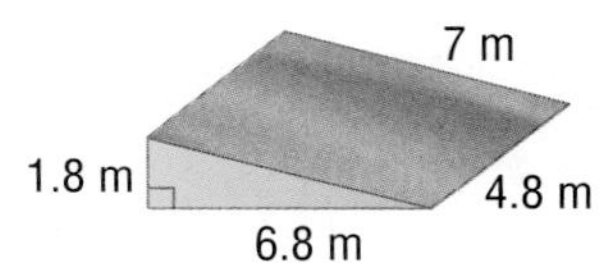

Estimate $S = (2 + 7 + 7)5 + 7(2)$ or 94m^2

The bases of the prism are triangles with side lengths of 1.8 meters, 6.8 meters, and 7 meters. Find the perimeter and area of one base.

Perimeter of Base

$P = 1.8 + 6.8 + 7$

$P = 15.6$

Area of Base

$B = \frac{1}{2}bh$

$B = \frac{1}{2}(6.8)(1.8)$ or 6.12

Use this information to find the total surface area.

$S = Ph + 2B$ Total surface area of prism

$S = 15.6(4.8) + 2(6.12)$ $P = 15.6$, $h = 4.8$, and $B = 6.12$.

$S = 87.12$ Simplify.

The surface area is 87.12 square meters. Compare to the estimate.

CHECK Your Progress

Find the lateral and total surface areas of each prism.

a. 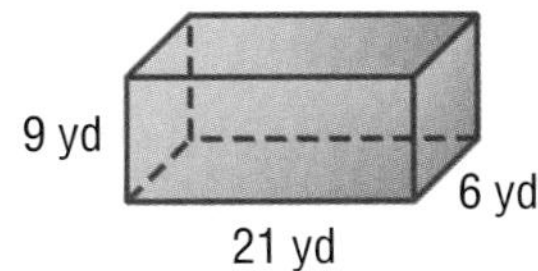

b. 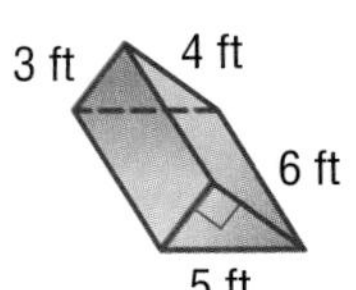

You can find the total surface area of a cylinder by finding the area of its two bases and adding the area of the curved surface. The lateral area of a cylinder is the area of the curved surface. If you unfold a cylinder, its net is two circles and a rectangle.

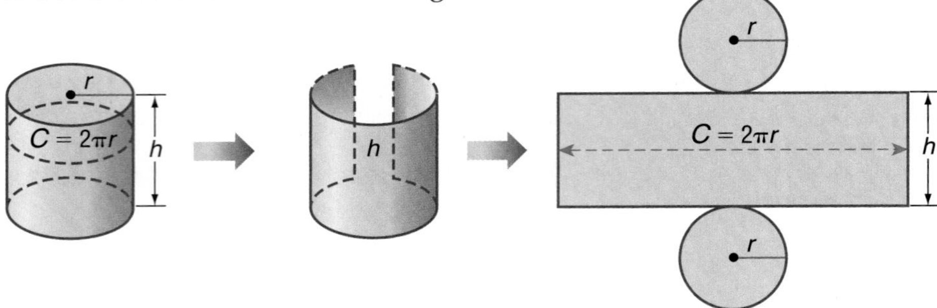

Model	Net	Area
2 circular bases	2 congruent circles with radius r	$2(\pi r^2)$ or $2\pi r^2$
1 curved surface	1 rectangle with width h and length $2\pi r$	$2\pi r \cdot h$ or $2\pi rh$

Study Tip

Cylinders
The formulas for the lateral and total surface areas of cylinders are similar to those of prisms.

Prism: $L = Ph$
For cylinders, the base is a circle, so its perimeter is the circumference.

Prism: $S = L + 2B$
For cylinders, the base B is a circle with area πr^2.

Just as with prisms, you can use the measures of a cylinder to find the lateral and total surface areas of a cylinder.

Lateral Surface Area of a Cylinder

Key Concept

Words The lateral area L of a cylinder with height h and radius r is the circumference of the base times the height.

Symbols $L = 2\pi rh$

Model

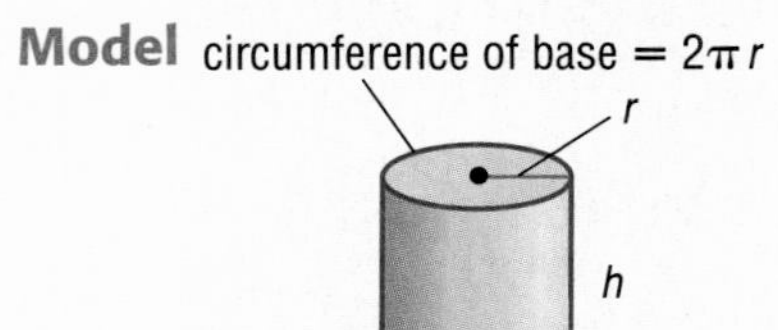

Total Surface Area of a Cylinder

Words The surface area S of a cylinder with height h and radius r is the lateral area plus the area of the two bases.

Symbols $S = L + 2\pi r^2$ or $S = 2\pi rh + 2\pi r^2$

Model

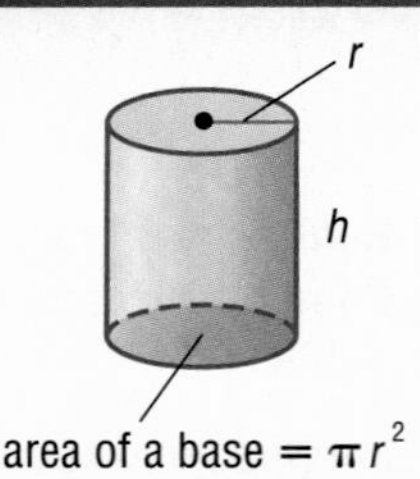

area of a base = πr^2

EXAMPLES Surface Areas of Cylinders

3 **Find the lateral area and the total surface area of the cylinder. Round to the nearest tenth.**

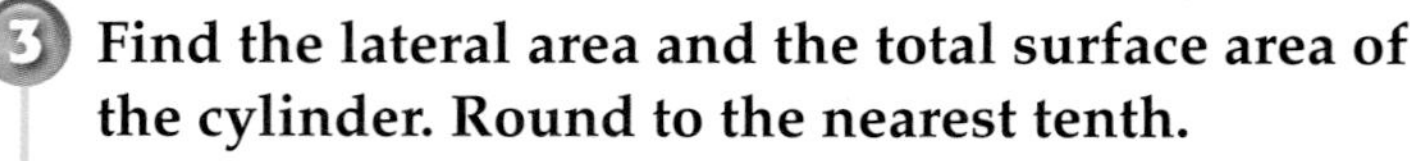

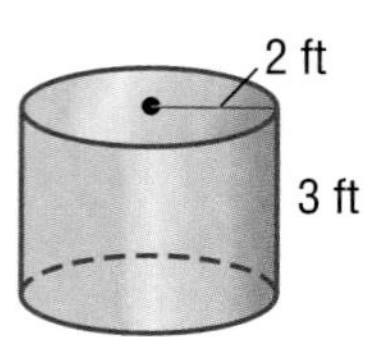

Lateral Surface Area	**Total Surface Area**
$L = 2\pi rh$	$S = L + 2\pi r^2$
$L = 2\pi(2)(3)$	$S = 37.7 + 2\pi(2)^2$
$L \approx 37.7$	$S \approx 62.8$

The lateral area is about 37.7 square feet, and the surface area of the cylinder is about 62.8 square feet.

4 LABELS Find the area of the label on the can of vegetables shown at the right.

Since the label covers the lateral surface of the can, you only need to find the can's lateral surface area.

Estimate $L = 2\pi rh$

$L \approx 2(3)(2)(5)$ $\quad \pi \approx 3, r = 1.75 \approx 2, h = 5$

$L \approx 60 \text{ in}^2$

$L = 2\pi rh$	Lateral surface area of cylinder
$L = 2\pi(1.75)(5)$	$r = 1.75, h = 5$
$L \approx 55.0$	Simplify.

The area of the label is about 55 square inches. Compare to the estimate.

CHECK Your Progress

Find the lateral and total surface areas of each cylinder. Round to the nearest tenth.

c. 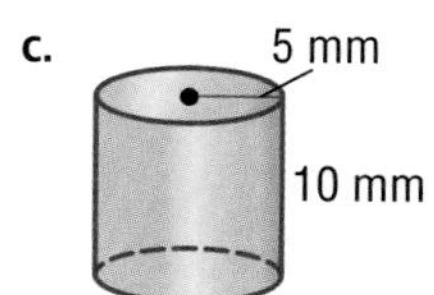

d. 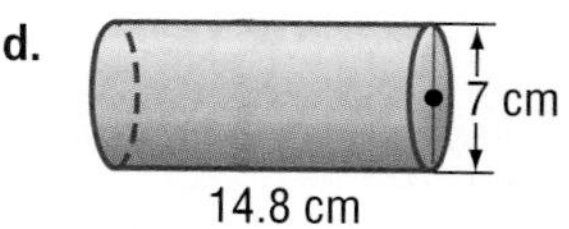

CHECK Your Understanding

Examples 1, 2 (p. 387) **Find the lateral and total surface areas of each solid. Round to the nearest tenth if necessary.**

1. 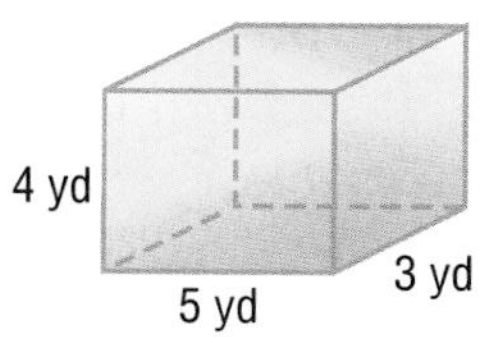

2. 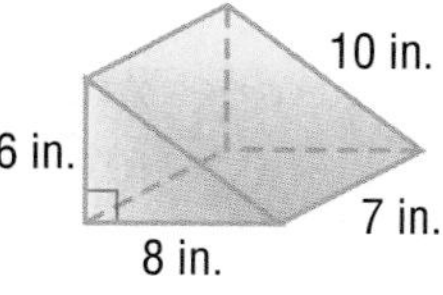

Example 3 (p. 388)

3. 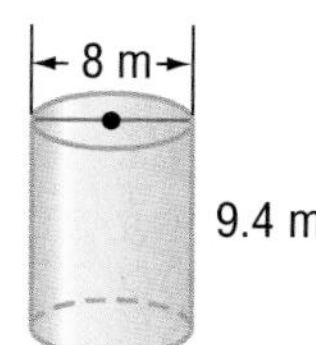

4. 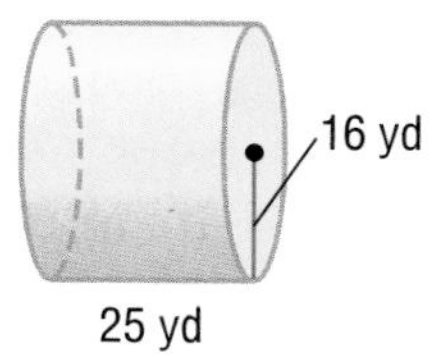

Example 4 (p. 389)

5. **CONTAINERS** Frozen orange juice often comes in cylindrical cardboard containers with metal lids. Find the area of the cardboard portion of the orange juice container shown.

Practice and Problem Solving

HOMEWORK HELP	
For Exercises	See Examples
6, 7	1
8, 9, 12	2
10, 11	3
13	4

Find the lateral and total surface areas of each solid. Round to the nearest tenth if necessary.

6.
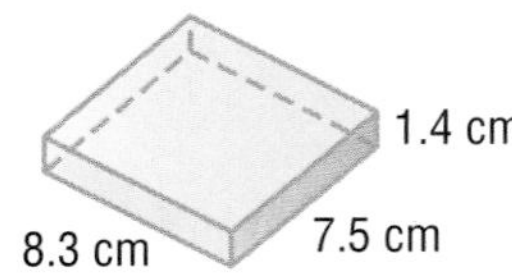

7.
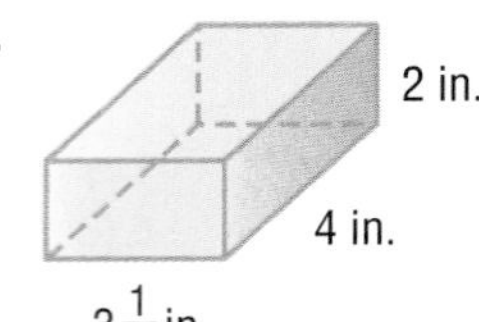

8.
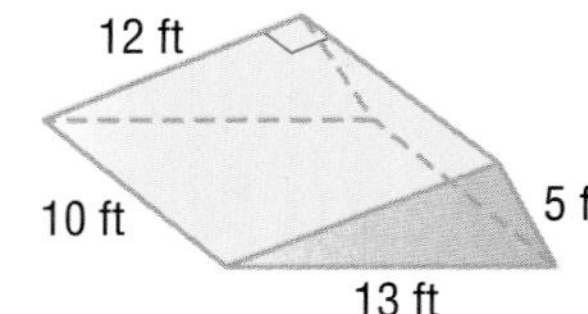

9.
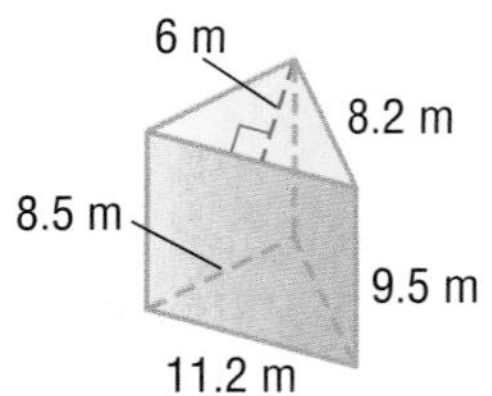

10.
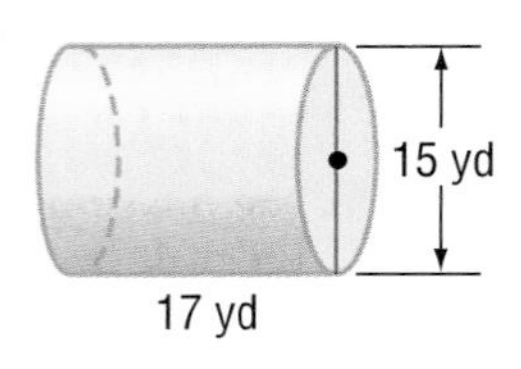

11.
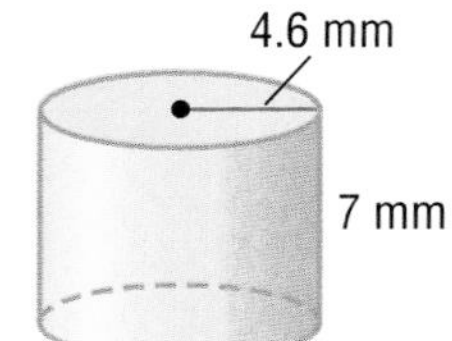

12. **CAMPING** A manufacturer makes nylon tents like the one shown. How much material is needed to make the tent?

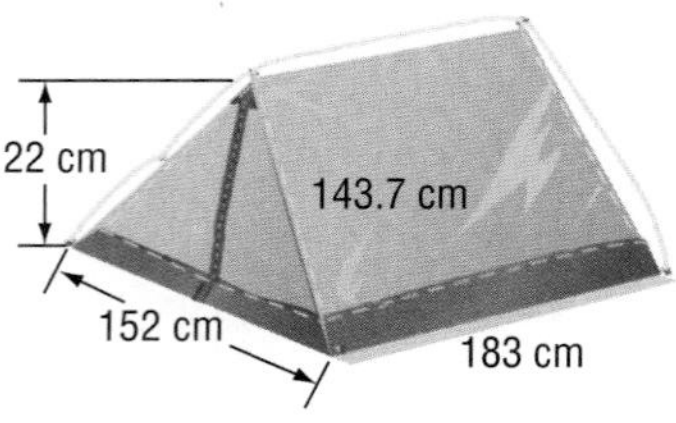

13. **ART** Sabrina made a plant pot in ceramics class. A glaze will go on the outside, the bottom, and the inside of the pot. If the walls of the pot are $\frac{1}{2}$ inch thick, how many square inches of surface will be glazed?

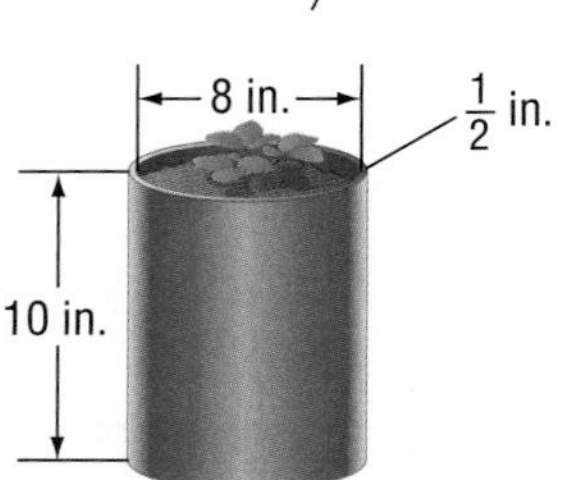

14. A rectangular prism has length 12 centimeters and width 4 centimeters. If its surface area is 467 square centimeters, what is the height of the prism?

15. **TOYS** The windows and doors of the dollhouse have an area of 36 square inches. The dollhouse does not have a bottom nor a back. If you want to paint the dollhouse, how many square inches of surface would you paint?

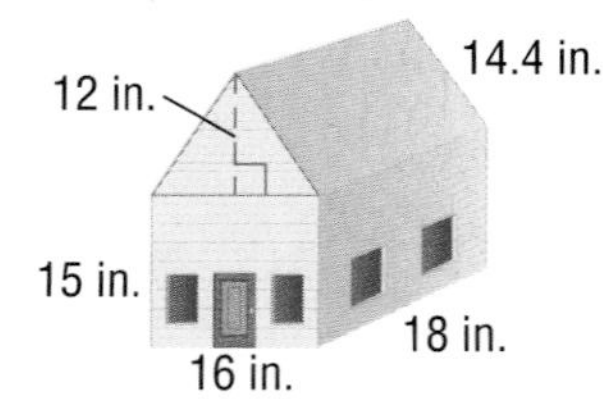

16. **PACKAGING** Two possible designs for a new cereal are shown below. The volumes are approximately equal. Which design would use less material to produce? Explain.

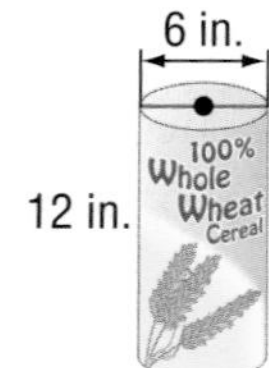

17. **PLUMBING** A hollow piece of a cylindrical pipe is shown. Find the total surface area of the pipe, including the interior.

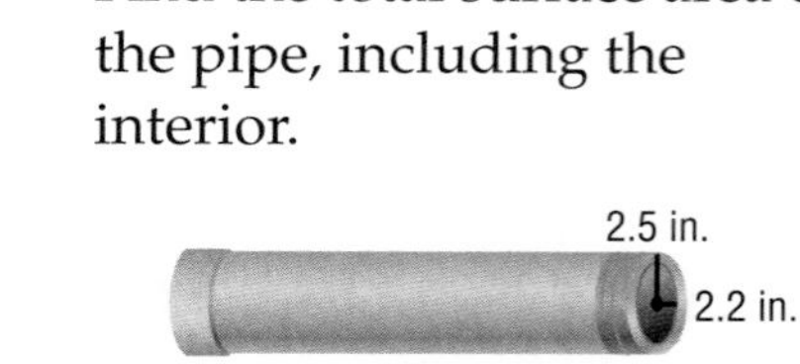

H.O.T. Problems

18. **REASONING** Determine whether the following statement is *true* or *false*. If *false*, give a counterexample.

If two rectangular prisms have the same volume, then they also have the same surface area.

19. **CHALLENGE** Will the surface area of a cylinder increase more if you double the height or double the radius? Explain your reasoning.

20. **NUMBER SENSE** If you triple the radius of a cylinder, explain how this affects the lateral area of the cylinder.

21. **WRITING IN MATH** Explain the difference between lateral area and surface area.

ISAT PRACTICE 7.C.3b, 9.A.3a

22. Molly is painting the rectangular toy chest shown in the diagram below.

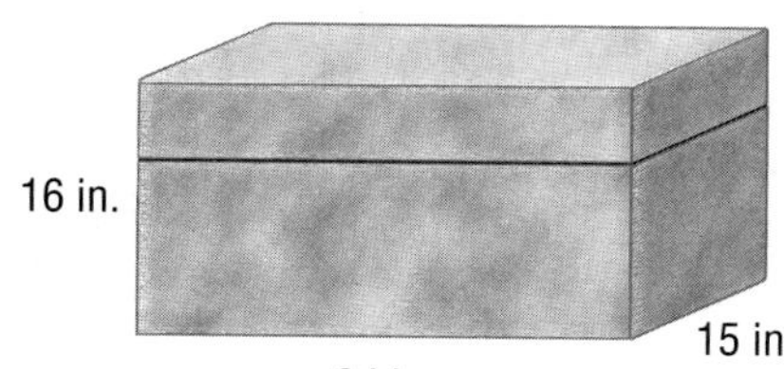

If Molly paints only the outside of the toy chest, what is the total surface area, in square inches, she will paint?

A 330 in^2 **C** 1,968 in^2

B 399 in^2 **D** 5,760 in^2

23. A roller like the one shown is used for painting.

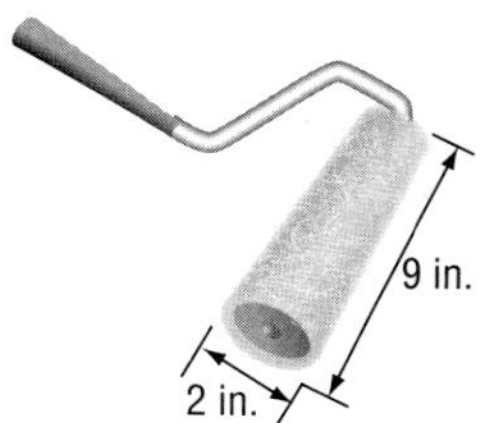

To the nearest tenth, how many square inches does a single rotation of the paint roller cover?

F 18.0 **H** 56.5

G 28.3 **J** 113.1

Spiral Review

Find the volume of each solid. Round to the nearest tenth if necessary. (Lesson 7-6)

24. rectangular pyramid: length, 14 m; width, 12 m; height, 7 m

25. cone: diameter, 22 cm; height, 24 cm

26. **HEALTH** The inside of a refrigerator in a medical laboratory measures 17 inches by 18 inches by 42 inches. You need at least 8 cubic feet to refrigerate some samples from the lab. Is the refrigerator large enough for the samples? Explain your reasoning. (Lesson 7-5)

GET READY for the Next Lesson

PREREQUISITE SKILL Multiply. (Lesson 2-3)

27. $\frac{1}{2} \cdot 2.8$

28. $\frac{1}{2} \cdot 10 \cdot 23$

29. $\frac{1}{2} \cdot 2.5 \cdot 16$

30. $\frac{1}{2}\left(3\frac{1}{2}\right)(20)$

Extend 7-7

Measurement Lab
Net of a Cone

MAIN IDEA

Make a net of a cone.

IL Learning Standards

9.A.3a Draw or construct two- and **three-dimensional geometric figures including** prisms, pyramids, cylinders and **cones.** *Also addresses 7.A.3b.*

A cone is a three-dimensional figure with one circular base. The lateral surface is part of a larger circle. So that the edges match, the circumference of the base is equal to *part* of the circumference of the larger circle.

ACTIVITY Make a Net of a Cone

STEP 1 Use a compass to draw two circles slightly touching, one with a radius of 17 centimeters and one with a radius of 8 centimeters.

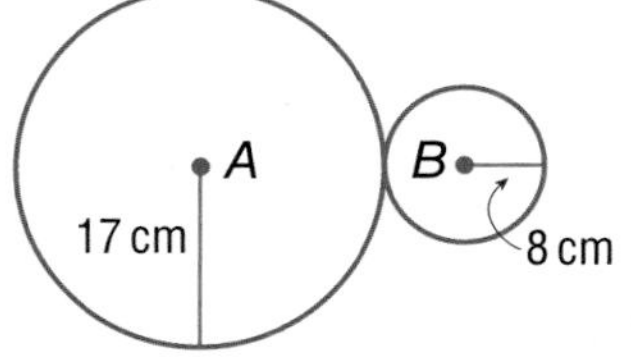

STEP 2 Think: What part of the circumference of A is equal to the circumference of B? Let x represent the part.

$x(34\pi) = 16\pi$ The circumference of A is 34π. The circumference of B is 16π.

$x \cdot \frac{34\pi}{34\pi} = \frac{16\pi}{34\pi}$ Divide each side by 34π.

$x \approx 0.47$ Simplify.

You need 0.47 of the circumference of A.

STEP 3 Find the size of the central angle to be cut from A.

$0.47 \cdot 360° \approx 170°$

Cut a central angle of 170° from circle A and make a cone.

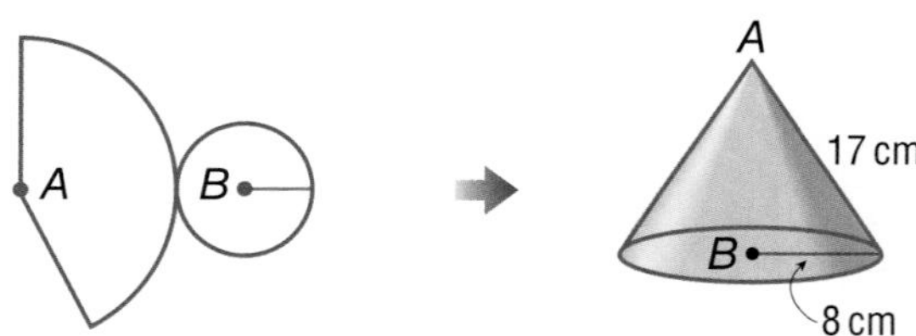

Analyze the Results

Find the central angle of each cone and then make a net and the cone.

1.

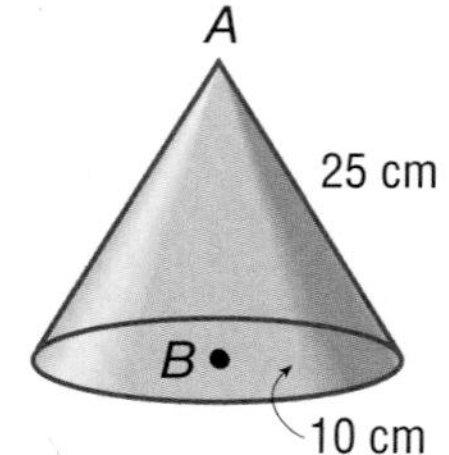

2.

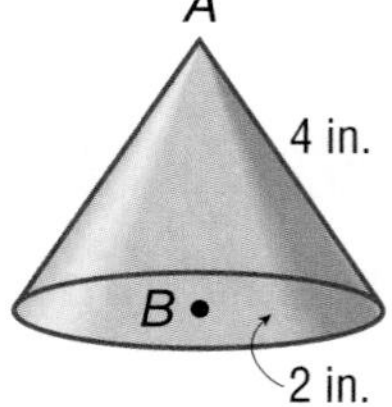

7-8 Surface Area of Pyramids

MAIN IDEA

Find the lateral and total surface areas of pyramids.

IL Learning Standards

7.A.3b Apply the concepts and attributes of length, capacity, weight/mass, perimeter, **area,** volume, time, temperature and angle measures **in practical situations.**
7.C.3b Use concrete and **graphic models and appropriate formulas to find** perimeters, areas, **surface areas** and volumes **of** two- and **three-dimensional regions.**

New Vocabulary

regular pyramid
slant height

IL Math Online

glencoe.com

- Extra Examples
- Personal Tutor
- Self-Check Quiz

GET READY for the Lesson

MUSEUMS The Rock and Roll Hall of Fame and Museum opened in Cleveland, Ohio, in 1995.

1. Not including the base, how many faces does this pyramid have? What shape are they?
2. How could you find the total area of the glass used for the building?

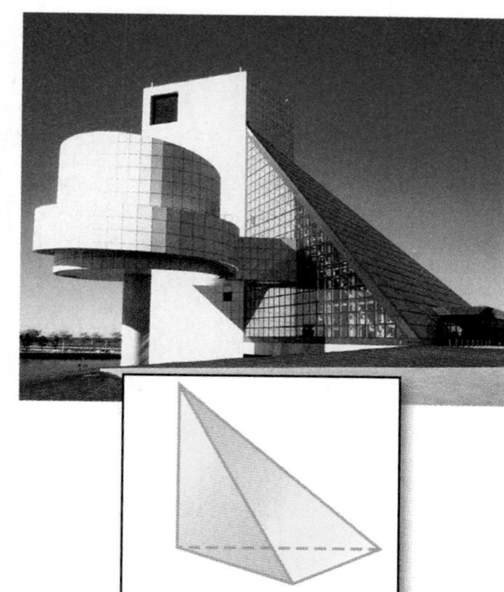

A **regular pyramid** is a pyramid with a base that is a regular polygon. The lateral faces of a regular pyramid are congruent isosceles triangles. At the top of the pyramid, these triangles meet at a common point called the vertex. The altitude or height of each lateral face is called the **slant height** of the pyramid.

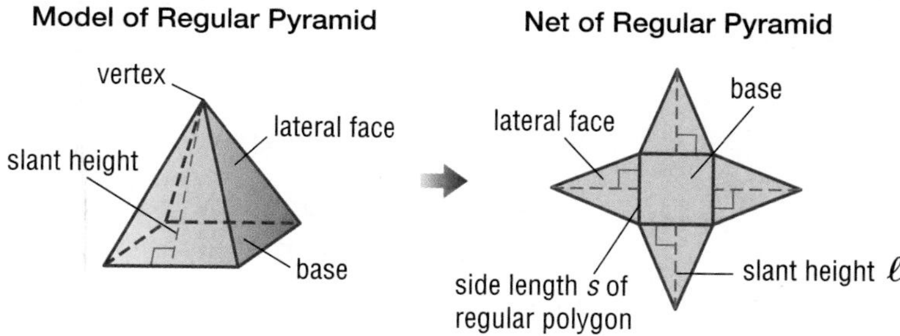

To find the lateral area L of a regular pyramid, look at its net. The lateral area of a pyramid is the sum of the areas of its lateral faces, which are all triangles.

The net of a square pyramid is a square and four triangles as shown above.

$L = 4\left(\frac{1}{2}s\ell\right)$ Area of the lateral faces

$L = \frac{1}{2}(4s)\ell$ Commutative Property of Multiplication

$L = \frac{1}{2}P\ell$ The perimeter of the base P is $4s$.

The total surface area of a regular pyramid is the lateral surface area plus the area of the base.

Lateral Surface Area of a Pyramid

Key Concept

Words The lateral surface area L of a regular pyramid is half the perimeter P of the base times the slant height ℓ.

Symbols $L = \frac{1}{2}P\ell$

Model

Total Surface Area of a Pyramid

Words The total surface area S of a regular pyramid is the lateral area L plus the area of the base B.

Symbols $S = L + B$ or $S = \frac{1}{2}P\ell + B$

Model

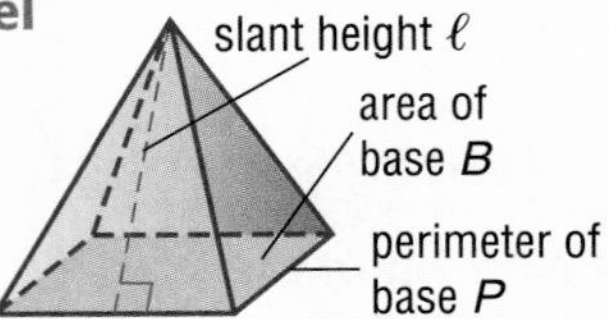

EXAMPLE Surface Areas of a Pyramid

1 Find the lateral and total surface areas of the triangular pyramid.

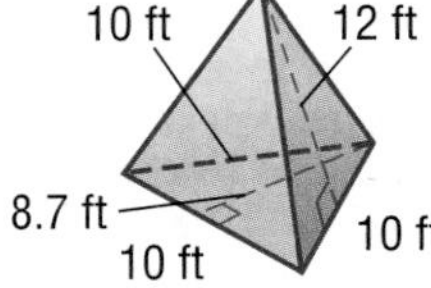

$L = \frac{1}{2}P\ell$ $\qquad S = L + B$

$L = \frac{1}{2} \cdot 30 \cdot 12$ $\qquad S = 180 + 43.5$ $\qquad B = \frac{1}{2} \cdot 10 \cdot 8.7$

$L = 180$ $\qquad S = 223.5$

The lateral and total surface areas are 180 and 223.5 square feet.

CHECK Your Progress

a. Find the lateral and total surface areas of a pyramid with a slant height of 18 meters and a square base with 11-meter sides.

Real-World EXAMPLE

Real-World Link The Pyramid of the Sun in Teotihuacán, Mexico, was built in the second century, A.D. It is about 71 meters tall, and its square base has side lengths of 223.5 meters.

2 ARCHITECTURE Use the information at the left to find the lateral surface area of the Pyramid of the Sun if it has a slant height of 132.5 meters.

$L = \frac{1}{2}P\ell$	Lateral surface area of a pyramid
$L = \frac{1}{2} \cdot 894 \cdot 132.5$	$P = 223.5(4)$ or 894 and $\ell = 132.5$
$L = 59{,}227.5$	Simplify.

The lateral area of the pyramid is 59,227.5 square meters.

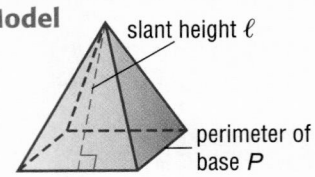

CHECK Your Progress

b. **AWARDS** A music award is a square pyramid with a 6-inch-long base and a 13-inch slant height. Find the award's total surface area.

CHECK Your Understanding

Example 1 (p. 394)

Find the lateral and total surface areas of each regular pyramid. Round to the nearest tenth if necessary.

1. 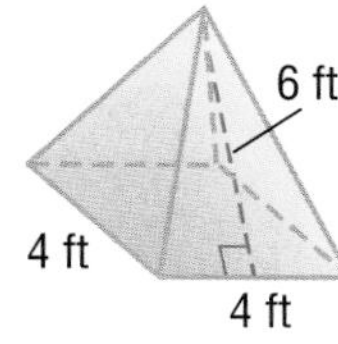

2. 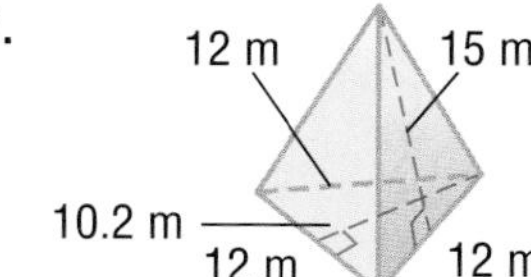

Example 2 (p. 394)

3. **EVENTS** The Pyramid Arena in Memphis is a regular square pyramid. Each face of the arena has a base of 600 feet and a height of about 477 feet. Find the lateral surface area of the pyramid.

Practice and Problem Solving

HOMEWORK HELP	
For Exercises	See Examples
4–9	1
10, 11	2

Find the lateral and total surface area of each regular pyramid. Round to the nearest tenth if necessary.

4. 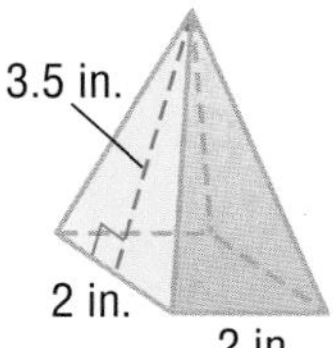

5. 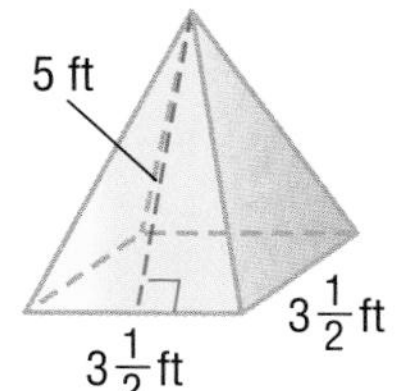

6. 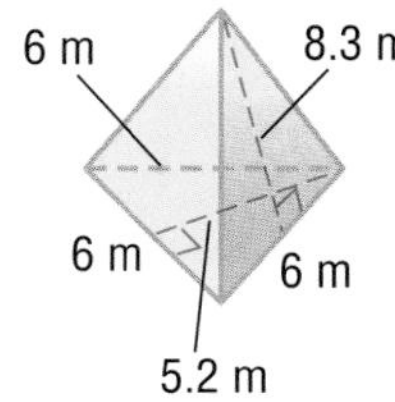

7. 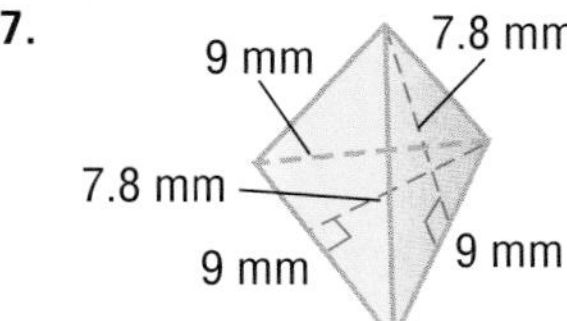

8. 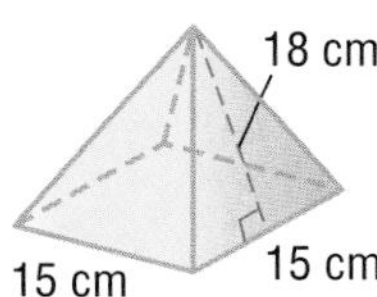

9. 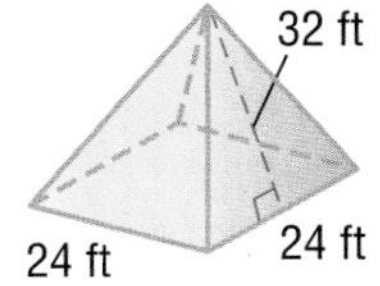

10. **ARCHITECTURE** The Transamerica Pyramid in San Francisco is shaped like a square pyramid. It has a slant height of 856.1 feet and each side of its base is 145 feet. Find the lateral area of the building.

11. **ROOFS** A pyramid-shaped roof has a slant height of 16 feet and its square base is 40 feet wide. How much roofing material is needed to cover the roof?

12. A square pyramid has a lateral area of 107.25 square centimeters and a slant height of 8.25 centimeters. Find the length of each side of its base.

13. **ARCHAEOLOGY** The Pyramid of Khafre in Egypt stands 471 feet tall. The sides of its square base are 705 feet in length. Find the lateral surface area of the Pyramid of Khafre. (*Hint*: Use the Pythagorean Theorem to find the pyramid's slant height ℓ.)

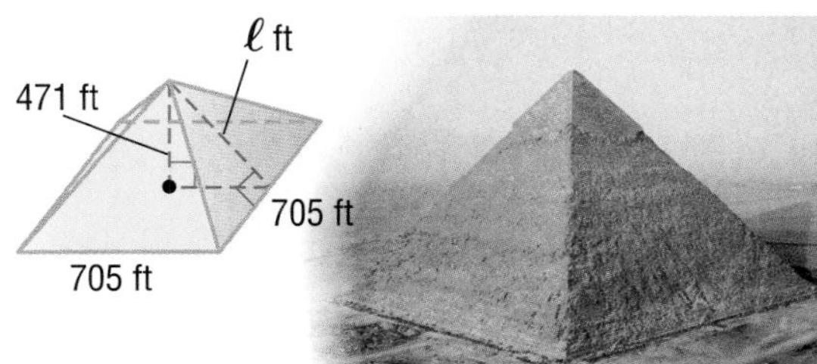

ILS • ISAT

Extra Practice, pp. 688, 706

H.O.T. Problems

CHALLENGE For Exercises 14–16, use the drawings of the figure shown. The total height of the figure is 20 inches.

14. Find the height h of the pyramid.
15. Use the height of the pyramid to find the slant height, l.
16. Which has a greater surface area, the prism or the pyramid? Explain your reasoning.

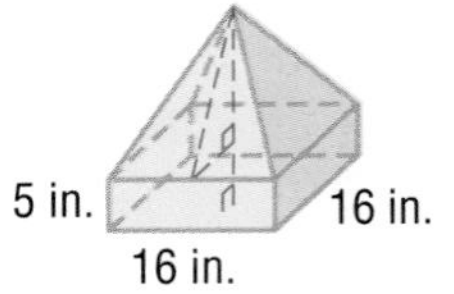

Side View of Pyramid

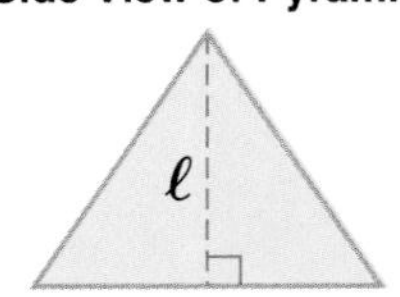

17. **OPEN ENDED** A pyramid has a base that is 3 inches square and a slant height of 4 inches. A rectangular prism has the same surface area. Give possible side lengths of the prism.
18. **WRITING IN MATH** Explain how you can use the height of a pyramid to find the slant height.

ISAT PRACTICE 7.A.3b, 7.C.3b

19. Which is the best estimate for the surface area of the pyramid?

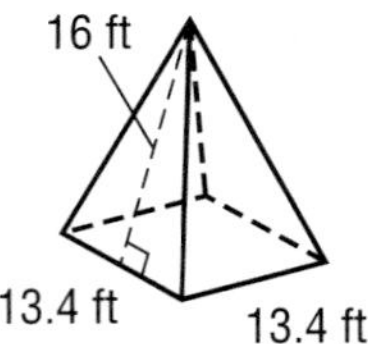

A 107 ft^2

B 180 ft^2

C 429 ft^2

D 608 ft^2

20. The net of a paperweight is shown below. Which is closest to the lateral surface area of the paperweight?

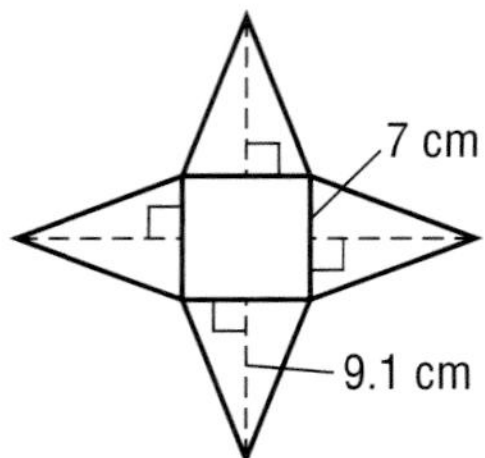

F 32 cm^2 **H** 127 cm^2

G 49 cm^2 **J** 176 cm^2

Spiral Review

21. **PACKAGING** Find the surface area of a can that has a diameter of 3 inches and a height of 5 inches. (Lesson 7-7)
22. **MOUNTAINS** A student is creating a clay model of a mountain shaped like a cone. If the mountain is 4 feet tall and the radius of the base is 2 feet, what is the volume of clay needed to make the mountain? Round to the nearest tenth if necessary. (Lesson 7-6)

GET READY for the Next Lesson

PREREQUISITE SKILL Solve each proportion. (Lesson 4-2)

23. $\frac{16}{n} = \frac{12}{40}$
24. $\frac{3}{5} = \frac{x}{8}$
25. $\frac{a}{13} = \frac{7}{39}$
26. $\frac{10}{26} = \frac{30}{w}$

Explore 7-9

Spreadsheet Lab
Similar Solids

MAIN IDEA

Investigate the relationships between the surface areas and volumes of similar solids.

IL Learning Standards

9.A.3c Use concepts of symmetry, congruency, **similarity,** scale, perspective, and angles **to describe and analyze** two- and **three-dimensional shapes** found in practical applications (e.g., geodesic domes, A-frame houses, basketball courts, inclined planes, art forms, blueprints). **9.C.3b Develop and solve problems using geometric relationships and models, with** and without **the use of technology.** *Also addresses 6.D.3, 9.C.3a.*

In this activity you will use a spreadsheet to investigate the relationship between surface areas and volumes of similar solids, solids that have the same shape and whose linear measures are proportional.

ACTIVITY

1 Find the surface area and volume of the prism at the right. Then find the surface areas and volumes of similar prisms with scale factors of 2, 3, and 4.

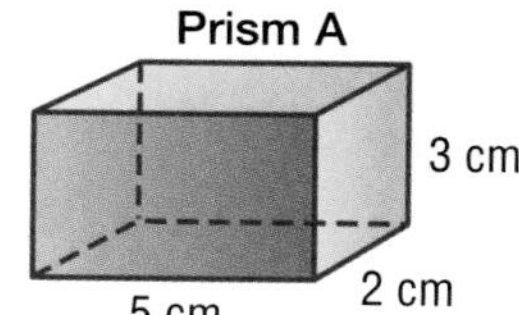

Similar Prisms.xls

◇	A	B	C	D	E	F	G
1	Prism	Scale Factor	Length	Width	Height	Surface Area	Volume
2	A	1	5	2	3	62	30
3	B	2	10	4	6	248	240
4	C	3	15	6	9	558	810
5	D	4	20	8	12	992	1920

Sheet 1 / Sheet 2 / Sheet 3

The spreadsheet evaluates the formula 2*C3*D3+2*C3*E3+2*D3*E3.

The spreadsheet evaluates the formula C5*D5*E5.

ANALYZE THE RESULTS

1. What is the ratio of the surface area of prism B to the surface area of prism A? of prism C to prism A? of prism D to prism A?
2. How are the answers to Exercise 1 related to the scale factors?
3. What is the ratio of the volume of prism B to the volume of prism A? of prism C to prism A? of prism D to prism A?
4. How are the answers to Exercise 3 related to the scale factors?
5. **MAKE A PREDICTION** If the dimensions of prism E are 5 times that of prism A, predict the ratio of the surface areas of prism E to prism A.
6. Explain how you can use the ratio in Exercise 5 to predict the surface area of prism E. Find the surface area using the spreadsheet.
7. **MAKE A PREDICTION** If the dimensions of prism E are 5 times that of prism A, predict the ratio of the volumes of prism E to prism A.
8. Explain how you can use the ratio in Exercise 6 to predict the volume of prism E. Find the volume using the spreadsheet.

ACTIVITY

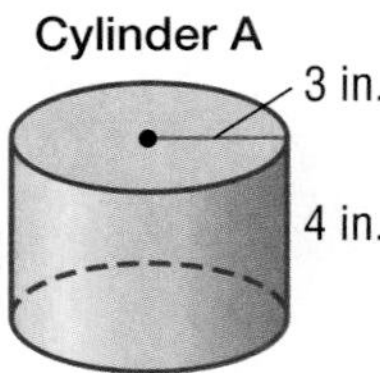

2 **Find the surface area and volume of the cylinder at the right. Then find the surface areas and volumes of similar cylinders with scale factors of 2, 3, and 4.**

Similar Cylinders.xls

	A	B	C	D	E	F	G
1	Cylinder	Scale Factor	Radius	Height	Surface Area	Volume	
2	A	1	3	4	131.9	113.1	
3	B	2	6	8	527.8	904.78	
4	C	3	9	12	1,187.5	3053.6	
5	D	4	12	16	2,111.2	7238.2	

Sheet 1 / Sheet 2 / Sheet 3

The spreadsheet evaluates the formula 2*PI()*C3^2+2*PI()*C3*D3.

The spreadsheet evaluates the formula PI()*C5^2*D5.

Study Tip

Spreadsheet Notation In Microsoft® Excel®, the expression PI() gives the value for π. The expression C5^2 squares the value in cell C5.

Analyze the Results

9. What is the ratio of the surface areas of cylinder B to cylinder A? of cylinder C to cylinder A? of cylinder D to cylinder A?

10. How are the answers to Exercise 9 related to the scale factors of each cylinder?

11. What is the ratio of the volume of cylinder B to the volume of cylinder A? of cylinder C to cylinder A? of cylinder D to cylinder A?

12. How are the answers to Exercise 11 related to the scale factors of each cylinder?

13. **MAKE A PREDICTION** If the dimensions of cylinder F are 6 times that of cylinder A, predict the ratio of the surface areas of cylinder F to cylinder A.

14. Explain how you can use the ratio to predict the surface area of cylinder F. Find the surface area using the spreadsheet.

15. **MAKE A PREDICTION** If the dimensions of cylinder F are 5 times that of cylinder A, predict the ratio of the volumes of cylinder F to cylinder A.

16. **MAKE A CONJECTURE** If two solids A and B are similar and the scale factor relating solid A to solid B is $\frac{a}{b}$, write expressions for the ratios of their surface areas and volumes.

7-9 Similar Solids

MAIN IDEA

Find dimensions, surface area, and volume of similar solids.

IL Learning Standards

9.A.3c Use concepts of symmetry, congruency, **similarity,** scale, perspective, and angles **to describe and analyze** two- and **three-dimensional shapes** found in practical applications (e.g., geodesic domes, A-frame houses, basketball courts, inclined planes, art forms, blueprints). **9.C.3b Develop and solve problems using geometric relationships and models, with** and without **the use of technology.** *Also addresses 6.D.3, 9.C.3a.*

New Vocabulary

similar solids

IL Math Online

glencoe.com

- Extra Examples
- Personal Tutor
- Self-Check Quiz

GET READY for the Lesson

The model car at the right is $\frac{1}{43}$ the size of the original car.

1. If the model car is 4.2 inches long, 1.6 inches wide, and 1.3 inches tall, what are the dimensions of the original car?
2. Make a conjecture about the radius of the wheel of the original car compared to the model.

The pyramids at the right have the same shape. The ratios of their corresponding linear measures, such as length, width, or height, are $\frac{6}{2}$ or 3 and $\frac{12}{4}$ or 3. We say that 3 is the scale factor.

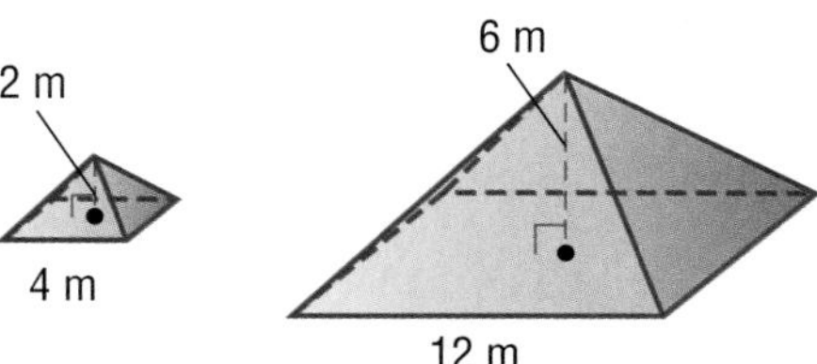

These pyramids are called **similar solids** because they have the same shape, their corresponding linear measures are proportional, and their corresponding faces are similar polygons. If you know two solids are similar, you can use a proportion to find a missing measure.

EXAMPLE Find Missing Linear Measures

1 **The cylinders at the right are similar. Find the height of cylinder A.**

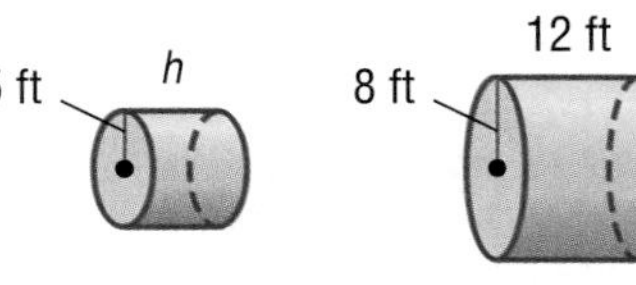

Since the two cylinders are similar, the ratios of their corresponding linear measures are proportional.

Words	$\frac{\text{radius cylinder A}}{\text{radius cylinder B}}$ is proportional to $\frac{\text{height cylinder A}}{\text{height cylinder B}}$
Variable	Let h represent the height of cylinder A.
Equation	$\frac{5}{8} = \frac{h}{12}$

$\frac{5}{8} = \frac{h}{12}$ Write the proportion.

$5 \cdot 12 = 8 \cdot h$ Find the cross products.

$\frac{5 \cdot 12}{8} = \frac{8 \cdot h}{8}$ Divide each side by 8.

$7.5 = h$ Simplify.

The height of cylinder A is 7.5 feet.

CHECK Your Progress

Find the missing measure for each pair of similar solids.

a.

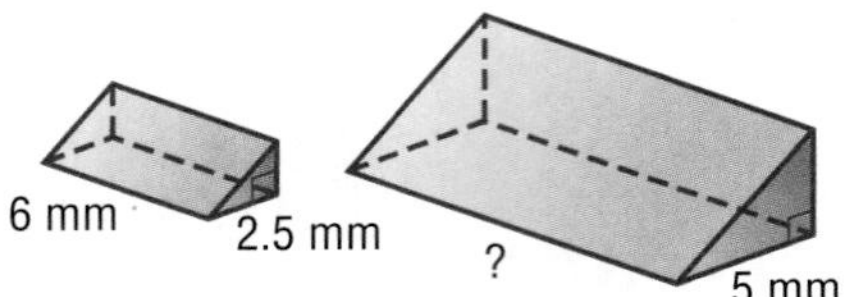

b.

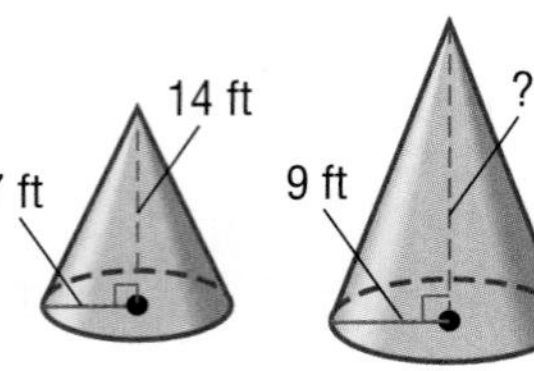

As you discovered in the Geometry Lab prior to this lesson, the surface areas and volumes of similar solids are proportional.

Ratios of Similar Solids

Key Concept

Ratios of Surface Area

Words If two solids are similar, the ratio of their surface areas is proportional to the square of the scale factor between them.

Symbols $\frac{\text{surface area of solid A}}{\text{surface area of solid B}} = \left(\frac{a}{b}\right)^2$

Ratios of Volumes

Words If two solids are similar, the ratio of their volumes is proportional to the cube of the scale factor between them.

Symbols $\frac{\text{volume of solid A}}{\text{volume of solid B}} = \left(\frac{a}{b}\right)^3$

Model

Solid A

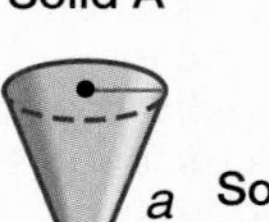

Solid B

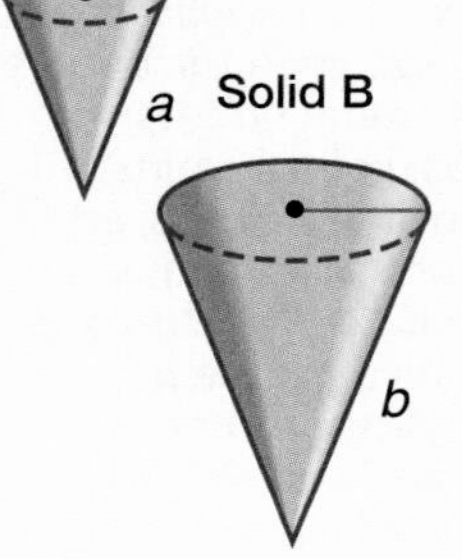

> **Study Tip**
>
> **Scale Factor** Remembering that area is expressed in *square* units can help you remember to *square* the scale factor when working with surface areas of similar solids.

EXAMPLE Find the Surface Area of a Similar Solid

2 **The pyramids at the right are similar. Find the total surface area of pyramid B.**

Pyramid A $S = 224 \text{ in}^2$

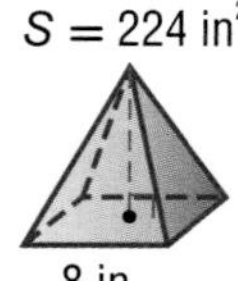

Pyramid B

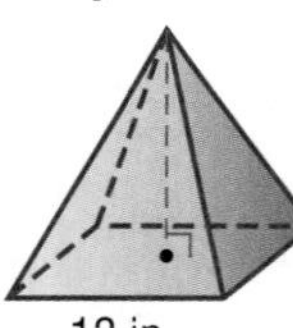

The ratio of the measures of pyramid A to pyramid B is $\frac{a}{b} = \frac{8}{12}$ or $\frac{2}{3}$.

$$\frac{\text{surface area of pyramid A}}{\text{surface area of pyramid B}} = \left(\frac{a}{b}\right)^2$$ Write a proportion.

$$\frac{224}{S} = \left(\frac{2}{3}\right)^2$$ Substitute the known values. Let S = the surface area of pyramid B.

$$\frac{224}{S} = \frac{4}{9}$$ $\left(\frac{2}{3}\right)^2 = \frac{2}{3} \cdot \frac{2}{3}$ or $\frac{4}{9}$

$$224 \cdot 9 = 4S$$ Find the cross products.

$$\frac{224 \cdot 9}{4} = \frac{4S}{4}$$ Divide each side by 4.

$$504 = S$$ Simplify.

The surface area of pyramid B is 504 square inches.

Find the missing measure for each pair of similar solids. Round to the nearest tenth if necessary.

c. $S = ?$ 10 m; 15 m $S = 5{,}654.9 \text{ m}^2$

d. 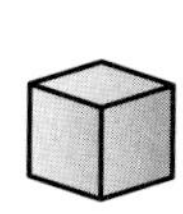
3 yd
$S = 132 \text{ yd}^2$

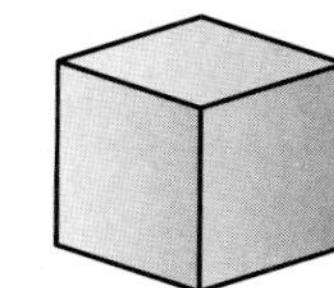
18 yd
$S = ?$

9.A.3c, 9.C.3b

ISAT EXAMPLE Find Volume of a Similar Solid

3 **A cube has a volume of 27 cubic feet. Suppose the dimensions are doubled. What is the volume of the new cube?**

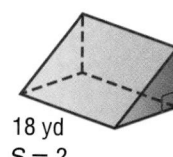

A 13.5 ft^3 **B** 54 ft^3 **C** 108 ft^3 **D** 216 ft^3

Test-Taking Tip

Scale Factors
When the lengths of all dimensions of a solid are multiplied by a scale factor x, then the surface area is multiplied by x^2 and the volume is multiplied by x^3.

Read the Item

You know that the cubes are similar, the ratio of the side lengths $\frac{a}{b}$ is $\frac{1}{2}$, and the volume of the smaller cube is 27 cubic feet.

Solve the Item

Since the volumes of similar solids have a ratio of $\left(\frac{a}{b}\right)^3$ and $\frac{a}{b} = \frac{1}{2}$, replace a with 1 and b with 2 in $\left(\frac{a}{b}\right)^3$.

$\frac{\text{volume of smaller cube}}{\text{volume of larger cube}} = \left(\frac{a}{b}\right)^3$ Write a proportion.

$\frac{27}{V} = \left(\frac{1}{2}\right)^3$ Substitute the known values. Let V represent the volume of the larger cube.

$\frac{27}{V} = \frac{1}{8}$ $\left(\frac{1}{2}\right)^3 = \frac{1}{2} \cdot \frac{1}{2} \cdot \frac{1}{2}$

$27 \cdot 8 = V \cdot 1$ Find the cross products.

$216 = V$ Multiply.

So, the volume of the larger cube is 216 cubic feet. The answer is D.

CHECK Your Progress

e. A triangular prism has a volume of 896 cubic meters. If the prism is reduced to one-fourth its original size, what is the volume of the new prism?

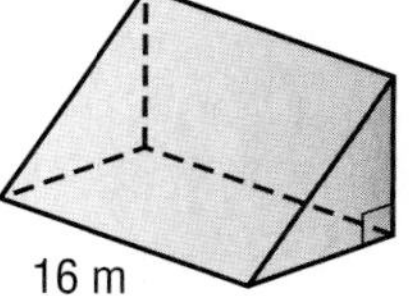
16 m

4 m

F 14 m^3 **H** 64 m^3

G 56 m^3 **J** 224 m^3

Examples 1, 2 (pp. 399–400)

For Exercises 1 and 2, use the two similar pyramids shown. Round to the nearest tenth if necessary.

1. Find the missing side length.
2. Find the missing surface area.

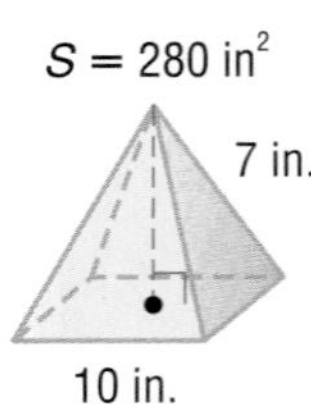

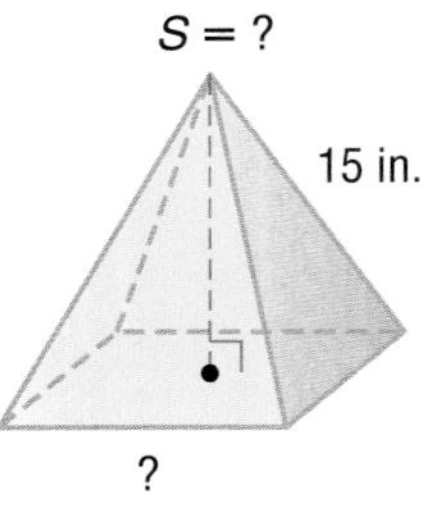

Example 3 (p. 401)

3. **MULTIPLE CHOICE** A cone has a volume of 134.4 cubic centimeters. Suppose that the dimensions are reduced to half their current value. What is the volume of the resulting cone?

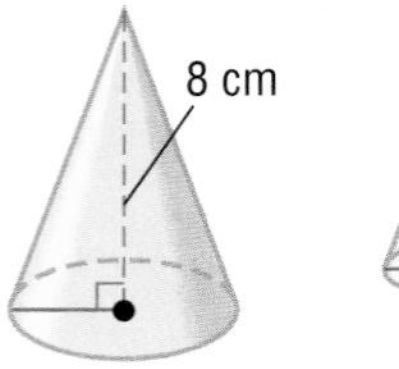

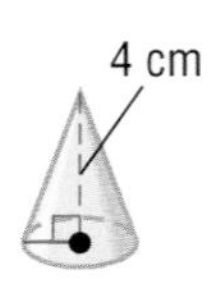

A 8.4 cm^3 **B** 16.8 cm^3 **C** 33.6 cm^3 **D** 67.2 cm^3

Practice and Problem Solving

HOMEWORK HELP

For Exercises	See Examples
4, 5, 10	1
6, 7	2
8, 9, 11, 23, 24	3

Find the missing measure for each pair of similar solids. Round to the nearest tenth if necessary.

4. 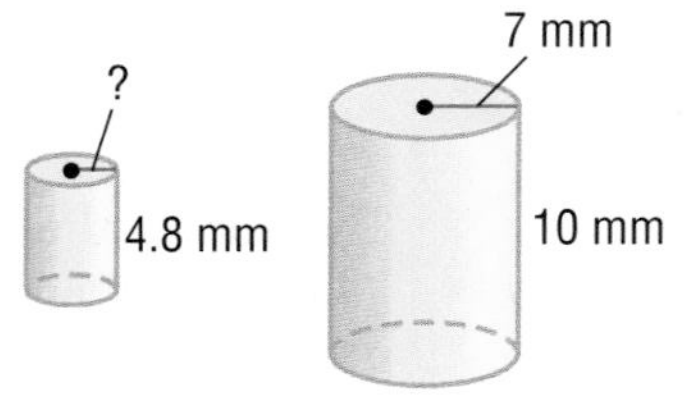

5. 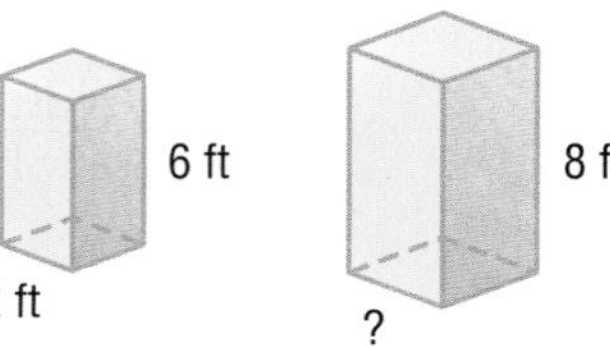

6. 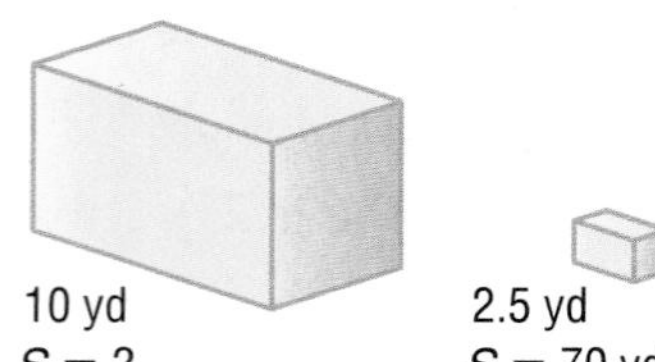

7. 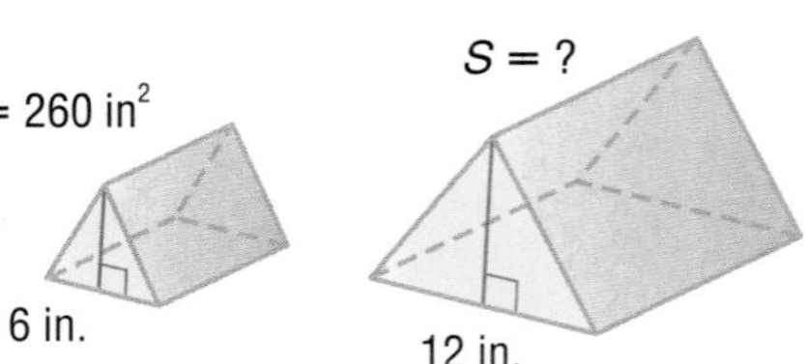

8. 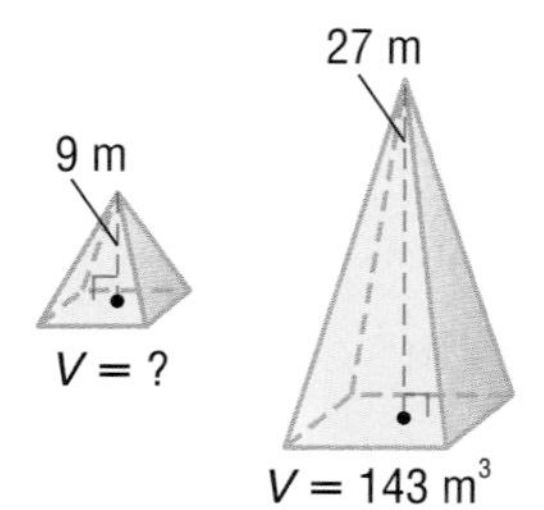

9. 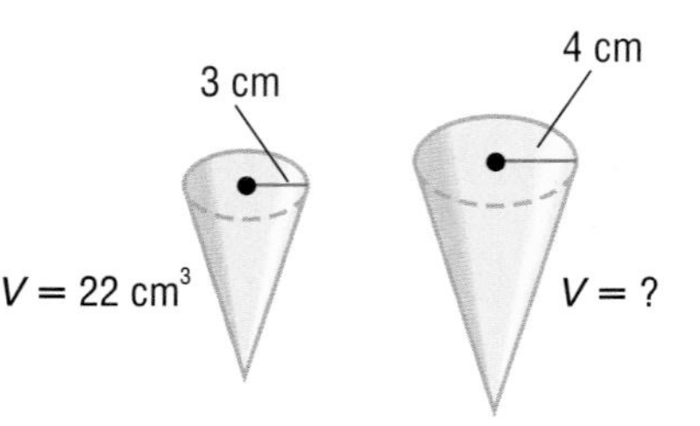

10. **ARCHITECTURE** The model of a high-rise apartment building is 25.2 inches tall. On the model, 2 inches represents 45 feet. What is the height of the building?

11. **ART** In art class, Rueben made two similar cylindrical containers. One was 4 inches tall, and the other was 8 inches tall. If the volume of the smaller container is 16.7 cubic inches, find the volume of the larger container.

For Exercises 12–14, use the two similar prisms at the right.

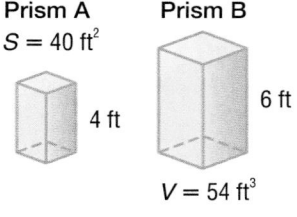

12. Write the ratio of the surface areas and the ratio of the volumes.

13. Find the surface area of prism B.

14. Find the volume of prism A.

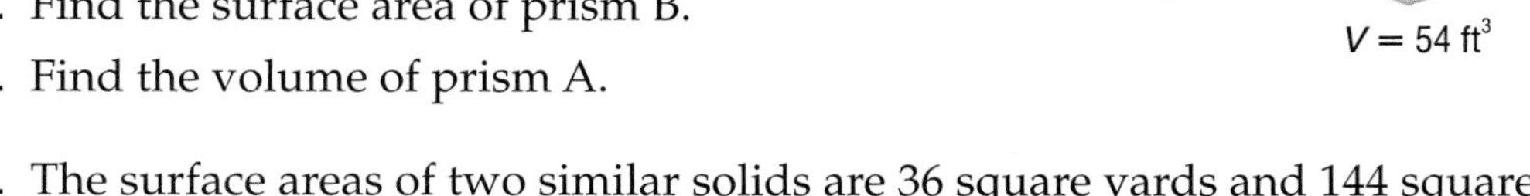

15. The surface areas of two similar solids are 36 square yards and 144 square yards. Find the ratio of their linear measures.

16. **HOBBIES** Darcy is building a doll house similar to her family's house. If the doll house will be $\frac{1}{20}$ the size of her actual house, what will be the lateral surface area of her doll house, not including the roof? Round to the nearest tenth.

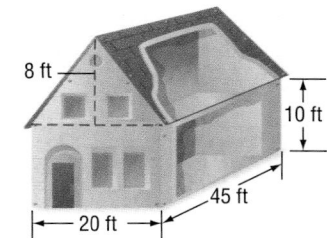

17. **AQUARIUMS** A zoo has three cylindrical aquariums. The smallest is $\frac{3}{4}$ the size of the one shown, while the largest is $1\frac{1}{2}$ times larger. Determine the volumes of the three aquariums. Round to the nearest tenth.

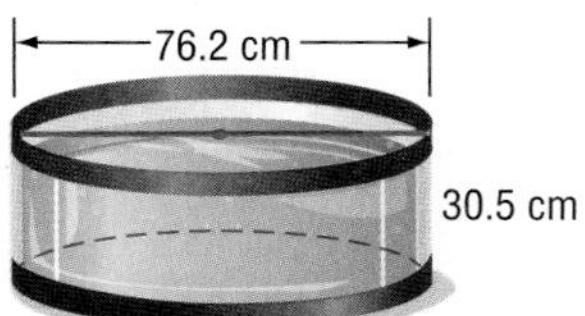

ILS • ISAT
Extra Practice, pp. 688, 706

H.O.T. Problems

18. **CHALLENGE** The ratio of the surface areas of two similar pyramids is $\frac{1}{25}$. What is the ratio of the volumes of the pyramids? Explain your reasoning.

19. **OPEN ENDED** Draw and label two cones that are similar. Explain why they are similar.

20. **SELECT A TECHNIQUE** Ruby is packing two similar boxes. The smaller box is 9 inches long and 12 inches tall, and the larger box is 18 inches long and 24 inches tall. Which of the following techniques might Ruby use to determine how much greater the volume of the larger box is? Justify your selection(s). Then use the technique(s) to solve the problem.

mental math | number sense | estimation

21. **REASONING** *True* or *False*? All spheres are similar. Explain your reasoning.

22. **WRITING IN MATH** Refer to the application at the beginning of the lesson. Write a real-world problem involving a model car. Then solve your problem.

ISAT PRACTICE 9.A.3c, 9.C.3b

23. The triangular prisms shown are similar.

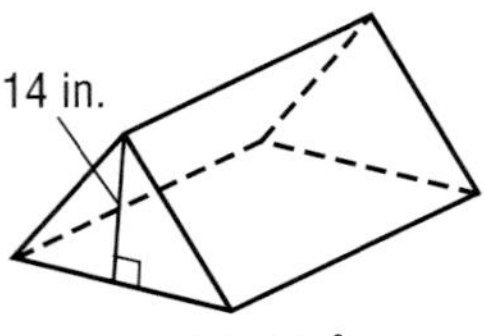

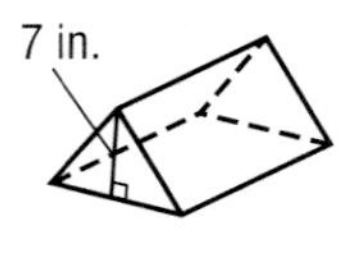

Find the volume of the smaller prism.

A 211 in^3

B 844 in^3

C $3{,}376 \text{ in}^3$

D $6{,}752 \text{ in}^3$

24. The dimensions of two cubes are shown below.

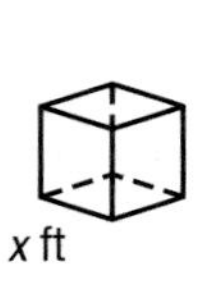

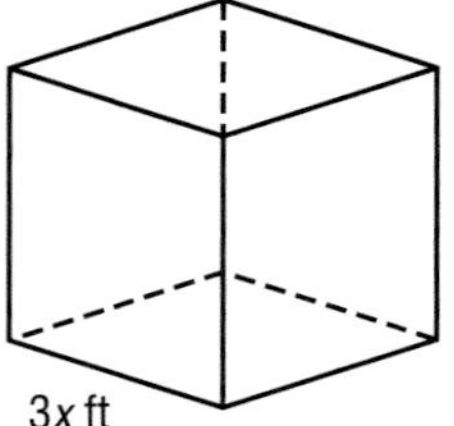

The volume of the smaller cube is 125 cubic feet. Find the volume of the larger cube.

F 375 ft^3

G $3{,}375 \text{ ft}^3$

H $5{,}125 \text{ ft}^3$

J $15{,}625 \text{ ft}^3$

Spiral Review

25. **HISTORY** The great pyramid of Khufu in Egypt was originally 481 feet high, and had a square base measuring 756 feet on a side and slant height of about 611.8 feet. What was its lateral surface area? Round to the nearest tenth. (Lesson 7-8)

26. **MEASUREMENT** Find the lateral surface and total surface area of the rectangular prism at the right. (Lesson 7-7)

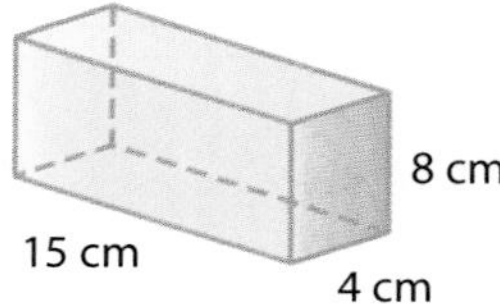

27. **GEOMETRY** Graph parallelogram $QRST$ with vertices $Q(-3, 3)$, $R(2, 4)$, $S(3, 2)$, and $T(-2, 1)$. Then graph the image of the figure after a reflection over the x-axis, and write the coordinates of its vertices. (Lesson 6-6)

28. **ALGEBRA** Find the value of x in the two congruent triangles. (Lesson 6-4)

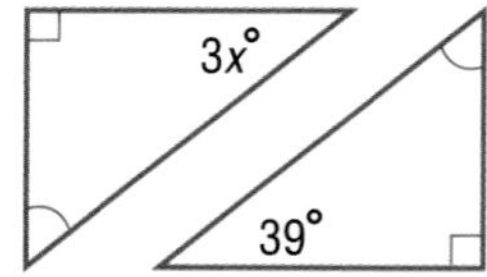

29. **MONEY** A \$750 investment earned \$540 in 6 years. Find the simple interest rate. (Lesson 5-9)

Problem Solving in Science

Real-World Unit Project

Turn Over a New Leaf It's time to complete your project. Use the information and data you have gathered about leaves to prepare a graphic organizer. Be sure to include leaf samples and the necessary calculations with your project.

IL Math Online **Unit Project at** glencoe.com

CHAPTER 7 Study Guide and Review

IL Math Online glencoe.com
- STUDY TO GO
- Vocabulary Review

FOLDABLES Study Organizer — GET READY to Study

Be sure the following Big Ideas are noted in your Foldable.

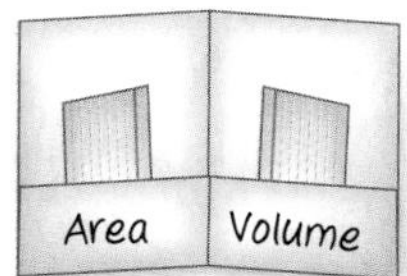

BIG Ideas

Circles (Lesson 7-1)
- Circumference: $C = \pi d$ or $C = 2\pi r$
- Area: $A = \pi r^2$

Volume (Lessons 7-5 and 7-6)
- Prism: $V = Bh$
- Cylinder: $V = Bh$ or $V = \pi r^2 h$
- Pyramid: $V = \frac{1}{3}Bh$
- Cone: $V = \frac{1}{3}Bh$ or $V = \frac{1}{3}\pi r^2 h$

Surface Area (Lessons 7-7 and 7-8)
- Prism
  Lateral Surface Area: $L = Ph$
  Total Surface Area: $S = L + 2B$
- Pyramid
  Lateral Surface Area: $L = P\ell$
  Total Surface Area: $S = L + B$
- Cylinder
  Lateral Surface Area: $L = 2\pi rh$
  Total Surface Area: $S = L + 2B$

Similar Solids (Lesson 7-9)
- If two solids are similar with a scale factor of $\frac{a}{b}$, then the surface areas have a ratio of $\left(\frac{a}{b}\right)^2$ and the volumes have a ratio of $\left(\frac{a}{b}\right)^3$.

Key Vocabulary

base (p. 369)	lateral surface area (p. 386)
center (p. 352)	net (p. 385)
chord (p. 352)	pi (p. 352)
circle (p. 352)	polyhedron (p. 368)
circumference (p. 352)	prism (p. 369)
composite figure (p. 363)	pyramid (p. 369)
composite solid (p. 375)	radius (p. 352)
cone (p. 381)	regular pyramid (p. 393)
coplanar (p. 368)	similar solids (p. 399)
cylinder (p. 374)	slant height (p. 393)
diameter (p. 352)	solid (p. 368)
edge (p. 368)	total surface area (p. 386)
face (p. 368)	vertex (p. 368)
lateral face (p. 386)	volume (p. 373)

Vocabulary Check

State whether each sentence is *true* or *false*. If *false*, replace the underlined word or number to make a true sentence.

1. The flat surface of a prism is called a face.
2. Circumference is the distance around a circle.
3. The measure of the space occupied by a solid is called the total surface area.
4. A cylinder is a figure that has two parallel, congruent circular bases.
5. A solid is any two-dimensional figure.
6. The side of a prism is called a vertex.
7. The radius is the distance across a circle through its center.

Lesson-by-Lesson Review

7-1 Circumference and Area of Circles (pp. 352–357)

7.A.3b, 7.C.3b

Find the circumference and area of each circle. Round to the nearest tenth.

8. radius: 18 in.
9. diameter: 6 cm
10. **LANDSCAPING** Bill is planting a circular flower bed. What is the area of the flower bed if the diameter is 30 feet?

Example 1 **Find the circumference and area of the circle.**

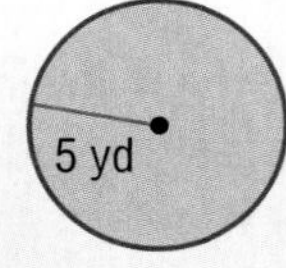

The radius is 5 yards.

$C = 2\pi r$ $\quad A = \pi r^2$

$C = 2 \cdot \pi \cdot 5$ $\quad A = \pi \cdot 5^2$

$C \approx 31.4$ yd $\quad A \approx 78.5$ yd^2

7-2 PSI: Solve a Simpler Problem (pp. 360–361)

6.B.3a, 6.C.3a

Solve. Use the *solve a simpler problem* strategy.

11. **GEOGRAPHY** The total area of Arizona is 114,006 square miles. Of that, about 42% of the land is desert. About how many square miles of Arizona's land is *not* covered by desert?

Example 2 **A total of 450 students were surveyed. If 60% of the students voted to hold a carnival, find the number of students who voted for the carnival.**

Find 10% of 450 and use the result to find 60% of 450.

10% of 450 = 45; so 60% is 6 × 45 or 270.

So, 270 students voted for the carnival.

7-3 Area of Composite Figures (pp. 363–367)

7.A.3b, 7.C.3b

Find the area of each figure. Round to the nearest tenth if necessary.

12. 13.

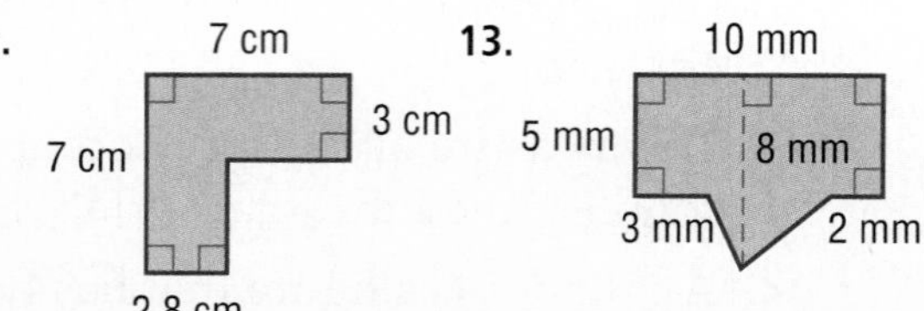

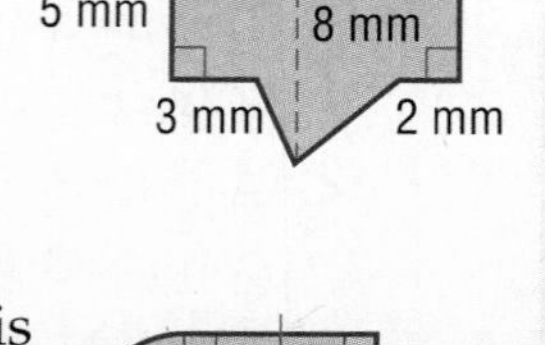

14. **BASKETBALL** Travis is going to paint part of a basketball court as shown. What is the area of the court?

12 ft

Example 3 **Find the area of the composite figure.**

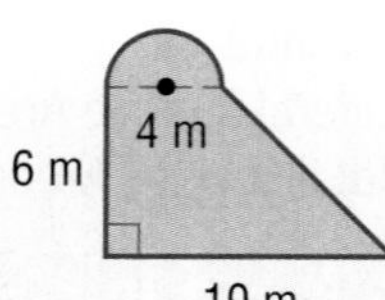

Area of semicircle

$A = \frac{1}{2} \cdot \pi \cdot 2^2$

$A \approx 6.3$

Area of trapezoid

$A = \frac{1}{2}(6)(4 + 10)$

$A = 42$

The area is about 6.3 + 42 or 48.3 square meters.

Mixed Problem Solving
For mixed problem-solving practice, see page 706.

7-4 Three-Dimensional Figures (pp. 368–372)

9.B.3

Identify each solid. Name the number and shapes of the faces. Then name the number of edges and vertices.

15. 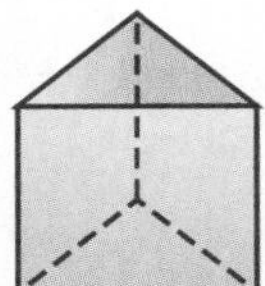

16. 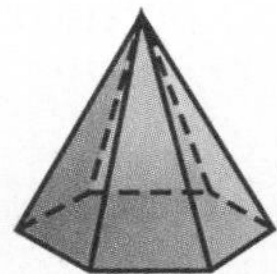

17. **CRYSTALS** Kelli found a crystal in the shape of a pentagonal pyramid. How many faces, edges, and vertices does the crystal have?

Example 4 **Name the number and shapes of the faces of a rectangular prism. Then name the number of edges and vertices.**

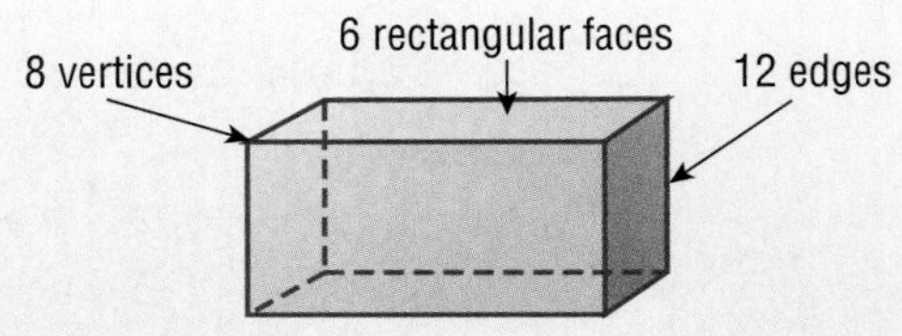

7-5 Volume of Prisms and Cylinders (pp. 373–378)

7.A.3b, 7.C.3b

Find the volume of each solid.

18. 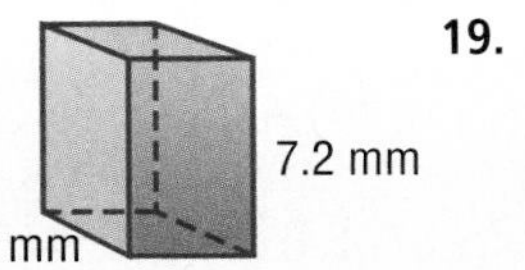

19. 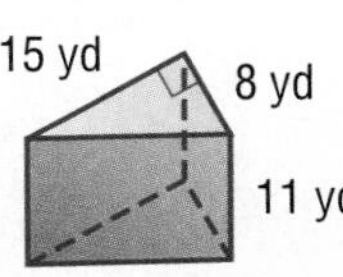

20. **MUSIC** A drum is 15 inches in diameter and 10 inches tall. Find its volume.

Example 5 **Find the volume of the solid.**

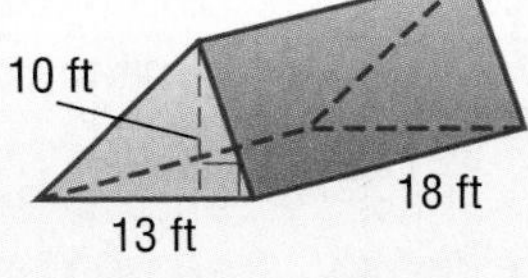

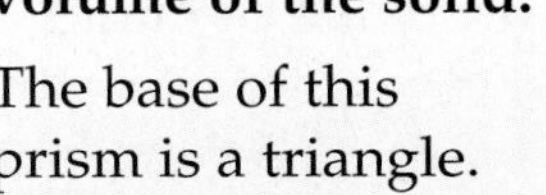

The base of this prism is a triangle.

$V = Bh$

$V = \left(\frac{1}{2} \cdot 13 \cdot 10\right)18$

$V = 1{,}170 \text{ ft}^3$

7-6 Volume of Pyramids and Cones (pp. 380–384)

7.C.3b, 9.A.3a

Find the volume of each solid. Round to the nearest tenth if necessary.

21. 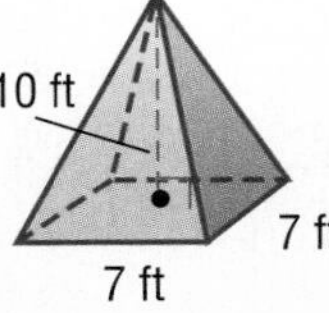

22. 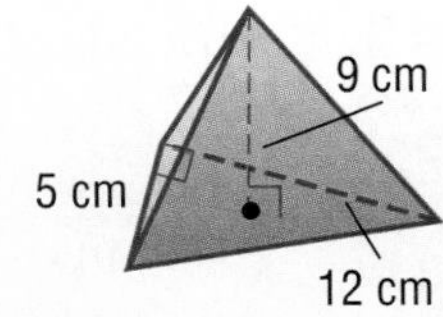

23. cone: diameter, 9 yd; height, 21 yd

24. **ICE CREAM** A waffle cone is five inches tall. The opening of the cone has a radius of 1.5 inches. What is the volume of ice cream that the cone can hold?

Example 6 **Find the volume of the pyramid.**

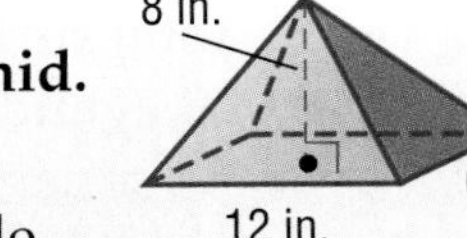

The base B of the pyramid is a rectangle.

$V = \frac{1}{3}Bh$

$V = \frac{1}{3}(12 \cdot 6)8$

$V = 192 \text{ in}^3$

7-7 Surface Area of Prisms and Cylinders (pp. 386–391)

7.C.3b, 9.A.3a

Find the surface area of each solid. Round to the nearest tenth if necessary.

25. 26.

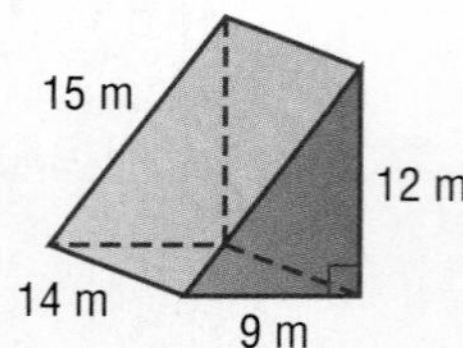

Example 7 **Find the surface area of the cylinder.**

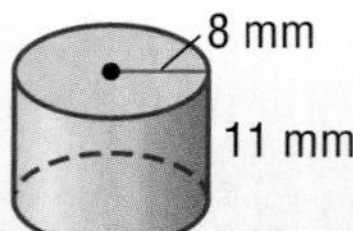

$S = 2\pi r^2 + 2\pi rh$ Surface area of a cylinder

$S = 2\pi(8)^2 + 2\pi(8)(11)$ $r = 8$ and $h = 11$

$S \approx 955.0 \text{ mm}^2$ Simplify.

7-8 Surface Area of Pyramids (pp. 393–396)

7.A.3b, 7.C.3b

27. **ARCHITECTURE** A hotel shaped like a square pyramid has a slant height of 92.5 meters and each side of its base is 183.5 meters long. What is the lateral surface area of the pyramid?

Example 8 **Find the total surface area of the square pyramid.**

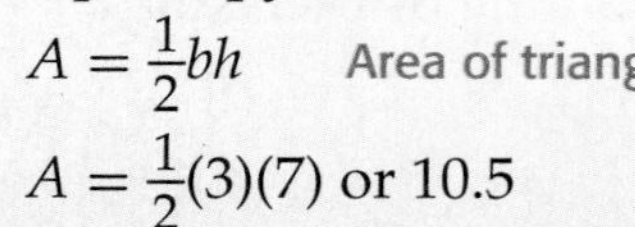

$A = \frac{1}{2}bh$ Area of triangle

$A = \frac{1}{2}(3)(7)$ or 10.5

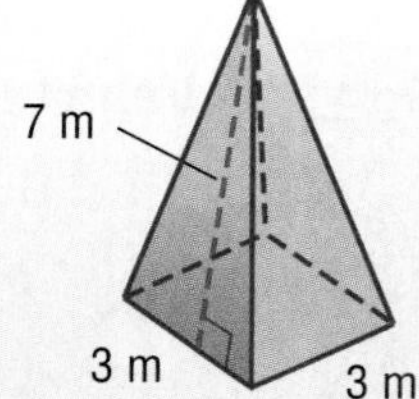

The total lateral area is 4(10.5) or 42 square meters. The area of the base is 3(3) or 9 square meters. So, the total surface area is 42 + 9 or 51 square meters.

7-9 Similar Solids (pp. 399–404)

9.A.3c, 9.C.3b

28. Cylinders A and B are similar. If the total surface area of cylinder A is 84 square feet, what is the total surface area of cylinder B?

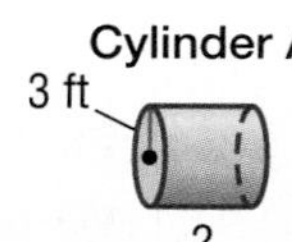

Example 9 **Two similar cones are shown at the right. Find the volume of the smaller cone.**

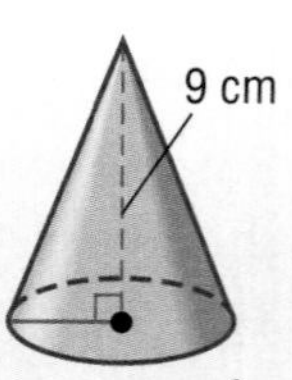

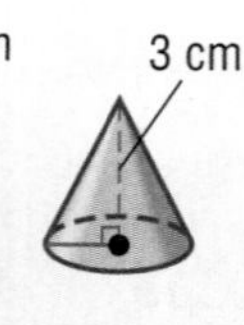

$\frac{\text{volume of smaller cone}}{\text{volume of larger cone}} = \left(\frac{a}{b}\right)^3$ Write a proportion.

$\frac{V}{184} = \frac{1}{27}$ $\quad \frac{1}{27} = \left(\frac{1}{3}\right)^3$

$V \cdot 27 = 184 \cdot 1$ Find the cross products.

$\frac{27V}{27} = \frac{184}{27}$ Divide each side by 27.

$V = 6.8 \text{ cm}^3$ Simplify.

Chapter 7 Practice Test

IL Math Online glencoe.com
• Chapter Test

Find the circumference and area of each figure. Round to the nearest tenth if necessary.

1. 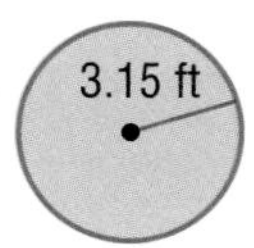

2. 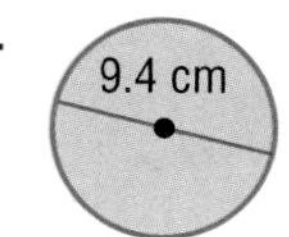

3. **MULTIPLE CHOICE** A jogger ran around a circular track two times. If the track has a radius of 25 yards, about how far did the jogger run?

   A 314 yd
   B 157 yd
   C 78.5 yd
   D 50 yd

Find the area of each figure. Round to the nearest tenth if necessary.

4. 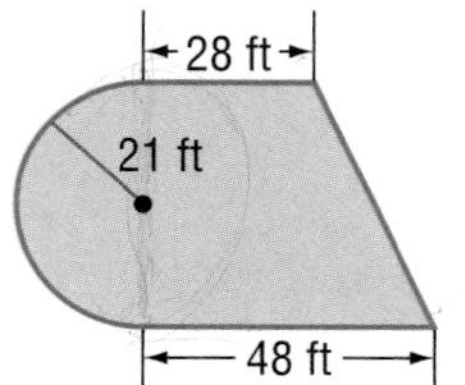

5. 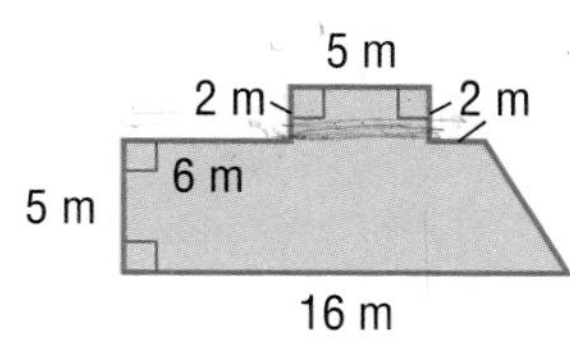

6. **GEOMETRY** Identify the solid. Name the number and shapes of its faces. Then name its number of edges and vertices.

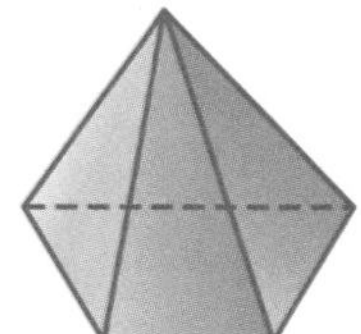

7. **CAKE DECORATION** Mrs. Lee designed the flashlight birthday cake shown below. If one container of frosting covers 250 square inches of cake, how many containers will she need to frost the top of this cake? Explain.

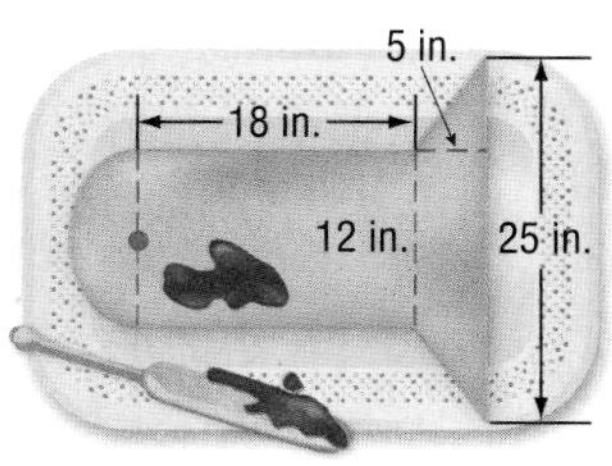

Find the volume of each solid. Round to the nearest tenth.

8. 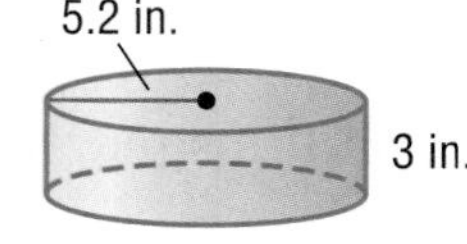

9. 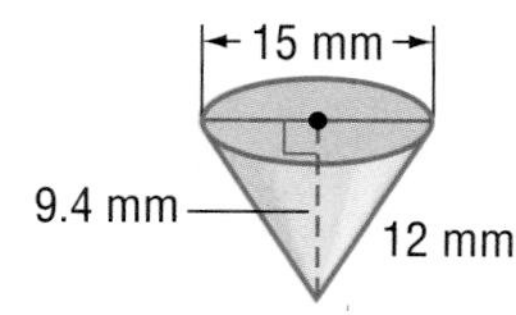

10. **FUEL** The fuel tank is made up of a cylinder. What is the volume of the tank? Round to the nearest tenth.

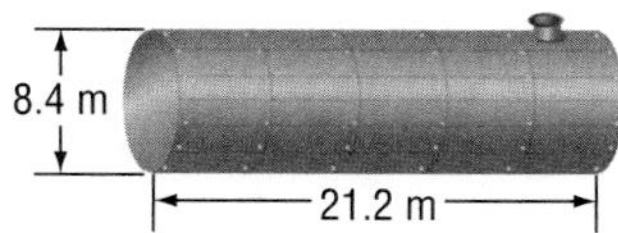

Find the volume and the total surface area of each solid. Round to the nearest tenth if necessary.

11. 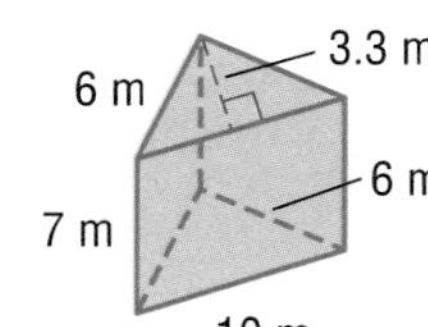

12. 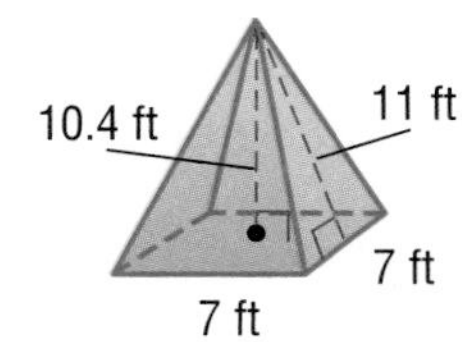

13. **MULTIPLE CHOICE** Find the volume of the solid.

   F 2,160 ft^3
   G 2,520 ft^3
   H 3,600 ft^3
   J 7,200 ft^3

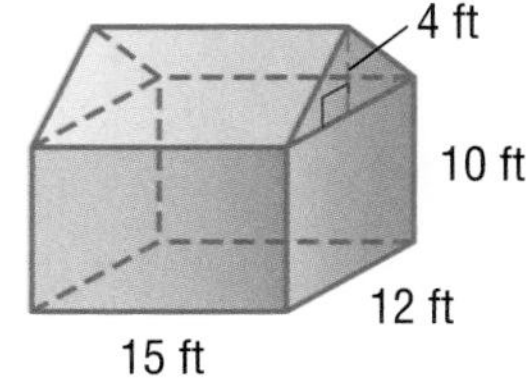

For Exercises 14–16, use the two similar prisms.

14. Write the ratio of the surface areas.

15. Find the total surface area of prism B.

16. Find the volume of prism A.

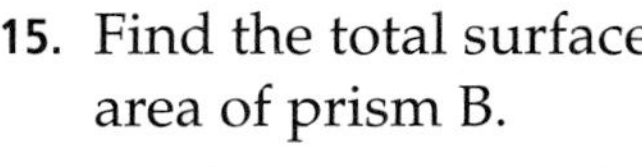
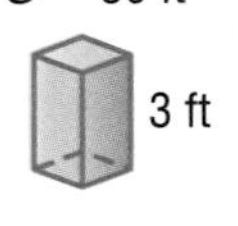

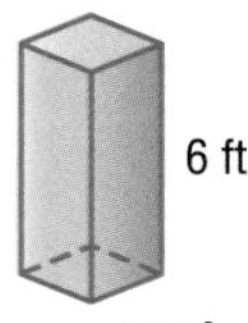

ISAT Practice

Cumulative, Chapters 1–7

IL Math Online glencoe.com
• Test Practice

PART 1 Multiple Choice

Read each question. Then fill in the correct answer on the answer sheet provided by your teacher or on a sheet of paper.

1. The figure shows a circle inside a square.

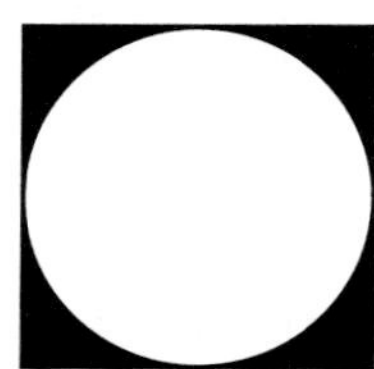

Which procedure should be used to find the area of the shaded region?

A Find the area of the square and then subtract the area of the circle.

B Find the area of the circle and then subtract the area of the square.

C Find the perimeter of the square and then subtract the circumference of the circle.

D Find the circumference of the circle and then subtract the perimeter of the square.

2. If $\triangle LMN$ is translated 7 units up and 2 units to the right, what are the coordinates of point L'?

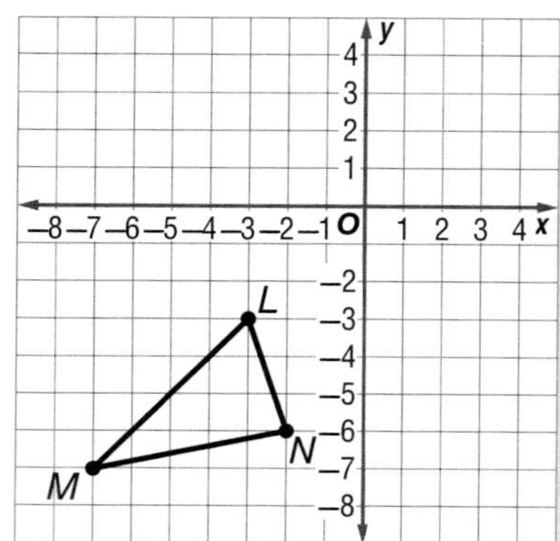

F (−1, 4)

G (7, 2)

H (2, 7)

J (4, −1)

3. What is the surface area of the shoe box?

A 200 in^2

B 224 in^2

C 400 in^2

D 448 in^2

TEST-TAKING TIP

Question 3 Most standardized tests will include any commonly used formulas at the front of the test booklet, but it will save you time to memorize many of these formulas. For example, you should memorize that the surface area of a prism is $2\ell h + 2\ell w + 2hw$.

4. What is the area of the shaded region in the figure below?

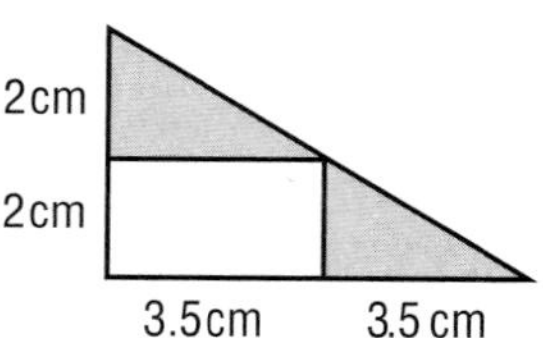

F 6.5 cm

G 7 cm

H 13 cm

J 26 cm

5. Martin and his two brothers equally shared the cost of a new computer game with a list price of \$35. They received a 25% discount on the video game and paid 5.5% sales tax on the discounted price. Find the approximate amount that each of the brothers paid toward the cost of the game.

A \$14.77

B \$11.73

C \$9.23

D \$8.42

Preparing for ISAT
For test-taking strategies and practice, see pages 712–729.

6. Suppose you know the side lengths of each figure below. Which one would contain enough information to let you find the length of diagonal d?

F 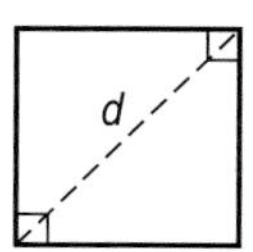

H 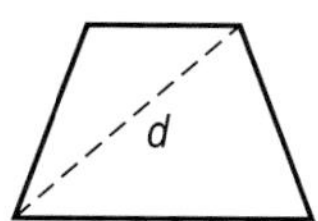

G 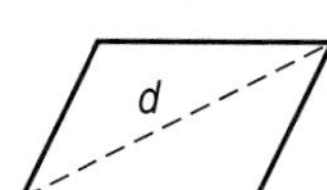

J 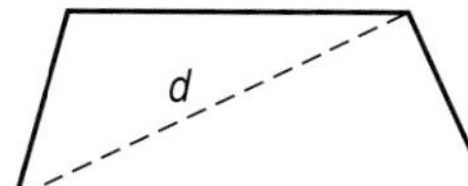

7. An isosceles triangle is removed from a rectangle as shown in the figure below. Find the area of the remaining part of the rectangle.

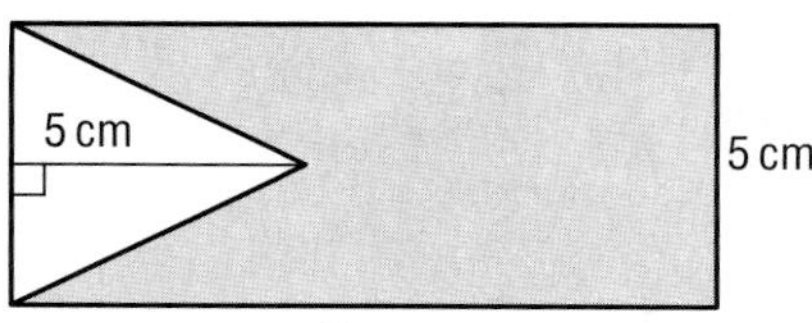

A 60 cm^2 **C** 47.5 cm^2

B 55 cm^2 **D** 35 cm^2

8. Susan has two similar rectangular packages. The dimensions of the first box is three times that of the second package. How many times greater is the volume of the first package than of the second package?

F 81 **H** 9

G 27 **J** 3

PART 2 Short Response/Grid In

Record your answers on the answer sheet provided by your teacher or on a sheet of paper.

9. A stackable block shown below is made of wood. The height and width of each section is 6 cm. The length is 12 cm.

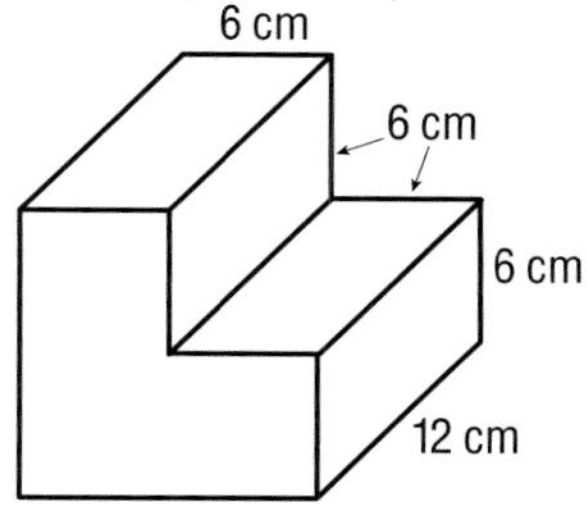

What is the volume, in cubic centimeters, of the wood used to create this block?

10. Find $a - 2b$ if $a = 2$ and $b = 5$.

PART 3 Extended Response

Record your answers on the answer sheet provided by your teacher or on a sheet of paper. Show your work.

11. The Films Committee is selling popcorn. They can choose from the two containers shown to sell the popcorn.

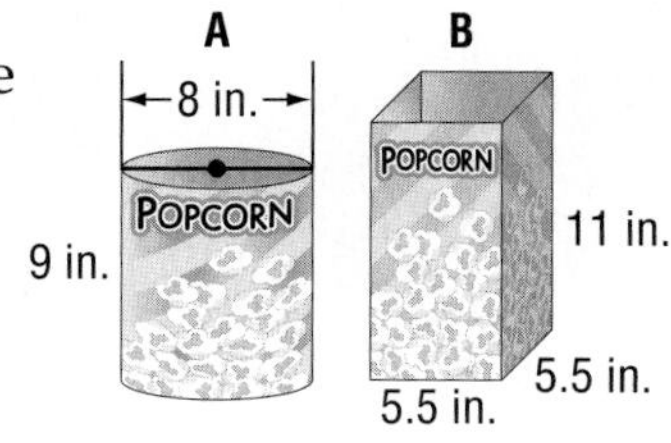

a. Which container will hold more popcorn? Justify your selection.

b. Which container requires less packaging to construct? Explain your reasoning.

NEED EXTRA HELP?											
If You Missed Question...	1	2	3	4	5	6	7	8	9	10	11
Go to Lesson...	7-1	6-7	7-7	7-3	5-8	3-5	7-3	7-9	7-5	1-2	7-7
IL Learning Standards	7.A.3b	9.A.3b	7.C.3b	7.A.3b	6.D.3	9.D.3	7.A.3b	9.A.3c	7.A.3b	8.A.3a	7.C.3b

Unit 4

Algebraic Thinking: Linear and Nonlinear Functions

Focus

Analyze and represent linear and nonlinear functions and solve linear equations.

Chapter 8
Algebra: More Equations and Inequalities

BIG Idea Solve simple linear equations and inequalities over the rational numbers.

Chapter 9
Algebra: Linear Functions

BIG Idea Use linear functions, systems of linear equations, and understanding of slope to represent, analyze, and solve problems.

Chapter 10
Algebra: Nonlinear Functions and Polynomials

BIG Idea Analyze and represent nonlinear functions.

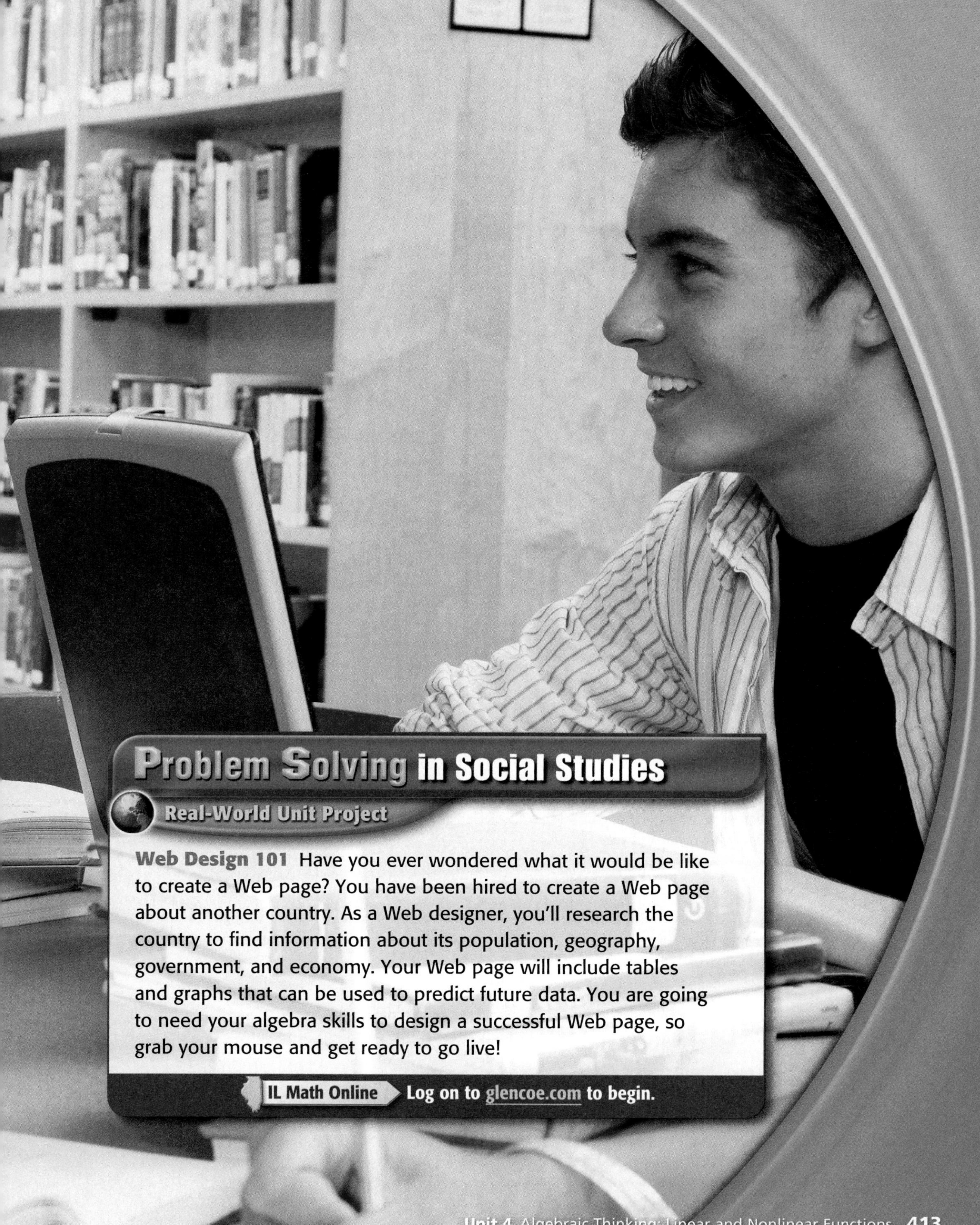

Problem Solving in Social Studies

Real-World Unit Project

Web Design 101 Have you ever wondered what it would be like to create a Web page? You have been hired to create a Web page about another country. As a Web designer, you'll research the country to find information about its population, geography, government, and economy. Your Web page will include tables and graphs that can be used to predict future data. You are going to need your algebra skills to design a successful Web page, so grab your mouse and get ready to go live!

IL Math Online Log on to glencoe.com to begin.

Algebra: More Equations and Inequalities

Illinois Learning Standards

8.A.3b Solve problems using linear expressions, equations and inequalities.
8.D.3a Solve problems using numeric, graphic or symbolic representations of variables, expressions, equations and inequalities.

Key Vocabulary

equivalent expressions (p. 416)
like terms (p. 417)
two-step equation (p. 422)

Real-World Link

Beaches The North Carolina shoreline has been decreasing at an average rate of about 18 inches per year. You can write an equation to describe the change in the amount of shoreline for a given number of years.

Algebra: More Equations and Inequalities Make this Foldable to help you organize your notes. Begin with a plain sheet of 11″ × 17″ paper.

1. **Fold** in half lengthwise.

2. **Fold** again from top to bottom.

3. **Open** and cut along the second fold to make two tabs.

4. **Label** each tab as shown.

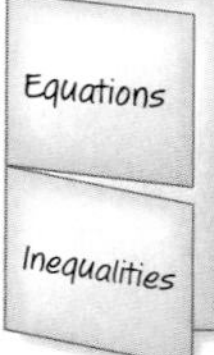

GET READY for Chapter 8

Diagnose Readiness You have two options for checking Prerequisite Skills.

Option 2

IL Math Online Take the Online Readiness Quiz at glencoe.com.

Option 1

Take the Quick Check below. Refer to the Quick Review for help.

QUICK Quiz

Determine whether each statement is true or false. (Lesson 1-3)

1. $10 > 4$
2. $3 < -3$
3. $-8 < -7$
4. $-1 > 0$
5. **WEATHER** The temperature in Sioux City, Iowa, was $-7°$F while the temperature in Des Moines, Iowa, was $-5°$F. Which city was warmer? Explain. (Lesson 1-3)

Write an algebraic equation for each verbal sentence. (Lesson 1-7)

6. Ten increased by a number is -8.
7. The difference of -5 and $3x$ is 32.
8. Twice a number decreased by 4 is 26.
9. **MONEY** Bianca has $1 less than twice as much as her brother. If her brother had $15, how much money did Bianca have? (Lesson 1-9)

Solve each equation. Check your solution. (Lessons 1-9 and 1-10)

10. $n + 8 = -9$
11. $4 = m + 19$
12. $-4 + a = 15$
13. $z - 6 = -10$
14. $3c = -18$
15. $-42 = -6b$
16. $\frac{w}{4} = -8$
17. $12 = \frac{r}{-7}$

QUICK Review

Example 1

Determine whether the statement $-2 > 1$ is *true* or *false*.

Plot the points on a number line.

Since -2 is to the left of 1, $-2 < 1$. The statement is false.

Example 2

Write an algebraic equation for the verbal sentence *twice a number increased by 3 is –5*.

Let x represent the number.

Twice a number	increased by	3	is	–5.
$2x$	$+$	3	$=$	-5

So, the equation is $2x + 3 = -5$.

Example 3

Solve $44 = k - 7$.

$44 = k - 7$	Write the equation.
$+7 = \quad +7$	Add 7 to each side.
$51 = k$	Simplify.

8-1 Simplifying Algebraic Expressions

MAIN IDEA

Use the Distributive Property to simplify algebraic expressions.

IL Learning Standards

8.A.3a Apply the basic properties of commutative, associative, **distributive,** transitive, inverse, identity, zero, equality and order of operations **to solve problems.**
8.A.3b Solve problems using linear expressions, equations and inequalities. *Also addresses 8.D.3a.*

New Vocabulary

equivalent expressions
term
coefficient
like terms
constant
simplest form
simplifying the expression

IL Math Online

glencoe.com

- Extra Examples
- Personal Tutor
- Self-Check Quiz
- Reading in the Content Area

MINI Lab

You can use algebra tiles to rewrite the algebraic expression $2(x + 3)$.

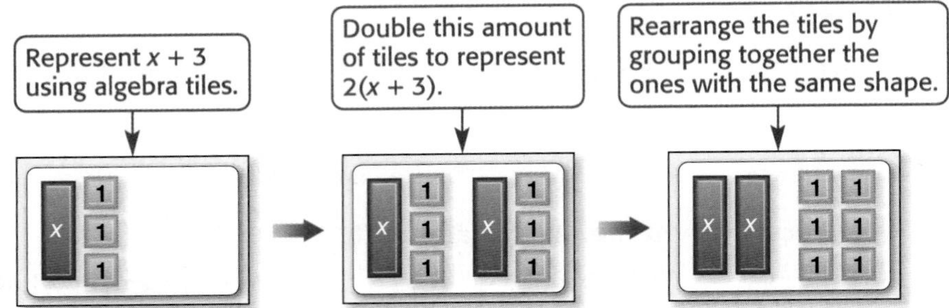

Represent x + 3 using algebra tiles.
Double this amount of tiles to represent 2(x + 3).
Rearrange the tiles by grouping together the ones with the same shape.

1. Choose two positive and one negative value for x. Then evaluate $2(x + 3)$ and $2x + 6$ for each of these values. What do you notice?
2. Use algebra tiles to rewrite the expression $3(x - 2)$. (*Hint*: Use one green x-tile and 2 red –1-tiles to represent $x - 2$.)

In Chapter 1, you learned that expressions like $3(2 + 7)$ can be rewritten using the Distributive Property and then simplified.

$$3(2 + 7) = 3(2) + 3(7) \quad \text{Distributive Property}$$
$$= 6 + 21 \text{ or } 27 \quad \text{Multiply. Then add.}$$

The Distributive Property can also be used to simplify an algebraic expression like $2(x + 3)$.

$$2(x + 3) = 2(x) + 2(3) \quad \text{Distributive Property}$$
$$= 2x + 6 \quad \text{Multiply.}$$

The expressions $2(x + 3)$ and $2x + 6$ are **equivalent expressions**, because no matter what x is, these expressions have the same value.

EXAMPLES Write Expressions With Addition

Use the Distributive Property to rewrite each expression.

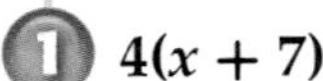

1 **$4(x + 7)$**

$$4(x + 7) = 4(x) + 4(7)$$
$$= 4x + 28 \quad \text{Simplify.}$$

2 **$(y + 2)5$**

$$(y + 2)5 = y \cdot 5 + 2 \cdot 5$$
$$= 5y + 10 \quad \text{Commutative Property}$$

CHECK Your Progress

a. $6(a + 4)$ b. $(n + 3)8$ c. $-2(x + 1)$

EXAMPLES Write Expressions with Subtraction

Use the Distributive Property to rewrite each expression.

3 $6(p - 5)$

$6(p - 5) = 6[p + (-5)]$	Rewrite $p - 5$ as $p + (-5)$.
$= 6(p) + 6(-5)$	Distributive Property
$= 6p + (-30)$	Simplify.
$= 6p - 30$	Definition of subtraction

Study Tip

Look Back
You can review multiplying integers in Lesson 1-6.

4 $-2(x - 8)$

$-2(x - 8) = -2[x + (-8)]$	Rewrite $x - 8$ as $x + (-8)$.
$= -2(x) + (-2)(-8)$	Distributive Property
$= -2x + 16$	Simplify.

CHECK Your Progress

d. $3(y - 10)$ **e.** $-7(w - 4)$ **f.** $(n - 2)(-9)$

When plus or minus signs separate an algebraic expression into parts, each part is called a **term**. The numerical factor of a term that contains a variable is called the **coefficient** of the variable.

Reading Math

Coefficients In $-4x$, the coefficient is -4. In x, the coefficient is 1.

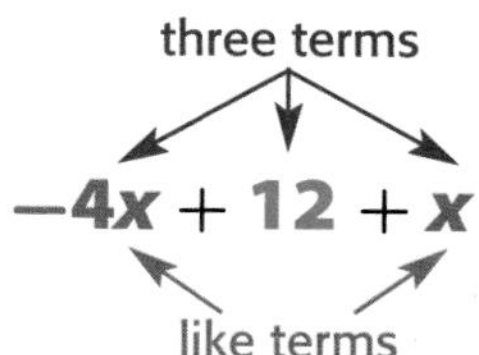

Like terms contain the same variables to the same powers. For example, $3x^2$ and $-7x^2$ are like terms. So are $8xy^2$ and $12xy^2$. But $10x^2z$ and $22xz^2$ are *not* like terms. A term without a variable is called a **constant**. Constant terms are also like terms.

EXAMPLE Identify Parts of an Expression

5 **Identify the terms, like terms, coefficients, and constants in the expression $6n - 7n - 4 + n$.**

$6n - 7n - 4 + n = 6n + (-7n) + (-4) + n$	Definition of subtraction
$= 6n + (-7n) + (-4) + 1n$	Identity Property; $n = 1n$

- Terms: $6n, -7n, -4, n$
- Coefficients: 6, −7, 1
- Like terms: $6n, -7n, n$
- Constants: −4.

CHECK Your Progress **Identify the terms, like terms, coefficients, and constants in each expression.**

g. $9y - 4 - 11y + 7$ **h.** $3x + 2 - 10 - 3x$

An algebraic expression is in **simplest form** if it has no like terms and no parentheses. You can use the Distributive Property to combine like terms. This is called **simplifying the expression**.

EXAMPLES Simplify Algebraic Expressions

6 **Simplify the expression $4y + y$.**

$4y$ and y are like terms.

$4y + y = 4y + 1y$	Identity Property; $y = 1y$
$= (4 + 1)y$ or $5y$	Distributive Property; simplify.

Study Tip

Equivalent Expressions To check whether $4y + y$ and $5y$ are equivalent expressions, substitute any value for y and see whether the expressions have the same value.

7 **Simplify the expression $7x - 2 - 7x + 6$.**

$7x$ and $-7x$ are like terms. -2 and 6 are also like terms.

$7x - 2 - 7x + 6 = 7x + (-2) + (-7x) + 6$	Definition of subtraction
$= 7x + (-7x) + (-2) + 6$	Commutative Property
$= [7 + (-7)]x + (-2) + 6$	Distributive Property
$= 0x + 4$	Simplify.
$= 0 + 4$ or 4	$0x = 0 \cdot x$ or 0

CHECK Your Progress

Simplify each expression.

i. $4z - z$

j. $6 - 3n + 3n$

k. $2g - 3 + 11 - 8g$

Real-World Link In 2006, the top 10 music moneymakers made a collective $973 million. The majority of this money comes from concert sales.
Source: *Forbes*

Real-World EXAMPLE

8 **CONCERTS** **At a concert, you buy some souvenir T-shirts for $12.00 each and the same number of CDs for $7.50 each. Write an expression in simplest form that represents the total amount spent.**

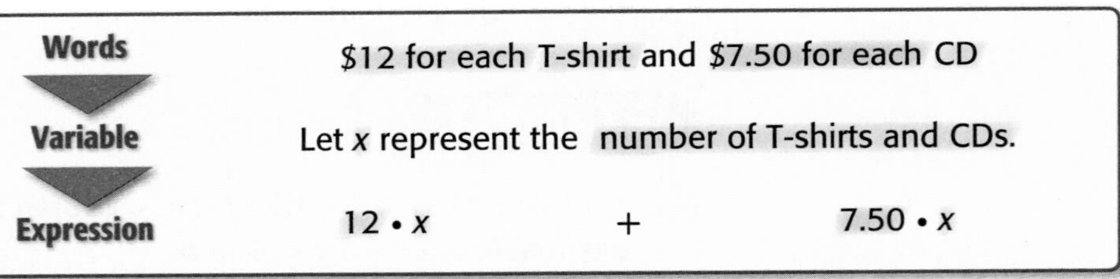

Words	$12 for each T-shirt and $7.50 for each CD		
Variable	Let x represent the number of T-shirts and CDs.		
Expression	$12 \cdot x$	$+$	$7.50 \cdot x$

$12x + 7.50x = (12 + 7.50)x$	Distributive Property
$= 19.50x$	Simplify.

The expression $19.50x$ represents the total amount spent.

CHECK Your Progress

l. **MONEY** You have saved some money. Your friend has saved $50 less than you. Write an expression in simplest form that represents the total amount of money you and your friend have saved.

CHECK Your Understanding

Examples 1–4 (pp. 416–417)

Use the Distributive Property to rewrite each expression.

1. $5(x + 4)$
2. $2(n + 7)$
3. $(y + 6)3$
4. $(a + 9)4$
5. $2(p - 3)$
6. $6(4 - k)$
7. $-6(g - 2)$
8. $-3(a + 9)$

Example 5 (p. 417)

Identify the terms, like terms, coefficients, and constants in each expression.

9. $5n - 2n - 3 + n$
10. $8a + 4 - 6a - 5a$
11. $7 - 3d - 8 + d$

Examples 6, 7 (p. 418)

Simplify each expression.

12. $8n + n$
13. $7n + 5 - 7n$
14. $4p - 7 + 6p + 10$

Example 8 (p. 418)

15. **BASKETBALL** You go to watch a basketball game and buy 3 bottles of water that each cost x dollars and a large bag of peanuts for \$4.50. Write an expression in simplest form that represents the total amount of money you spent.

Practice and Problem Solving

HOMEWORK HELP

For Exercises	See Examples
16–27	1–4
28–33	5
34–39	6, 7
40–43	8

Use the Distributive Property to rewrite each expression.

16. $3(x + 8)$
17. $-8(a + 1)$
18. $(b + 8)5$
19. $(p + 7)(-2)$
20. $4(x - 6)$
21. $6(5 - q)$
22. $-8(c - 8)$
23. $-3(5 - b)$
24. $(d + 2)(-7)$
25. $-4(n - 3)$
26. $(10 - y)(-9)$
27. $(6 + z)3$

Identify the terms, like terms, coefficients, and constants in each expression.

28. $2 + 3a + 9a$
29. $7 - 5x + 1$
30. $4 + 5y - 6y + y$
31. $n + 4n - 7n - 1$
32. $-3d + 8 - d - 2$
33. $9 - z + 3 - 2z$

Simplify each expression.

34. $n + 5n$
35. $12c - c$
36. $5x + 4 + 9x$
37. $2 + 3d + d$
38. $-3r + 7 - 3r - 12$
39. $-4j - 1 - 4j + 6$

Write an expression in simplest form that represents the total amount in each situation.

40. **BOWLING** You rent x pairs of shoes for \$2 each. You buy the same number of drinks for \$1.50 each. You also pay \$9 for a bowling lane.

41. **TELEVISION** You watch x minutes of television on Monday, the same amount on Wednesday, and 30 minutes on Friday.

42. **MAGAZINES** You subscribe to m different magazines. Your friend subscribes to 2 fewer than you.

43. **BIRTHDAYS** Today is your friend's birthday. She is y years old. Her brother is 5 years younger.

44. **GOVERNMENT** In 2007, in the Texas Legislature, there were 119 more members in the House of Representatives than in the Senate. If there were m members in the Senate, write an expression in simplest form to represent the total number of members in the Texas Legislature.

45. **FIND THE DATA** Refer to the Data File on pages 16–19. Choose some data and write a real-world problem for which you could write and simplify an algebraic expression.

Use the Distributive Property to rewrite each expression.

46. $3(2y + 1)$ 47. $-4(3x + 5)$ 48. $-6(12 - 8n)$ 49. $4(x - y)$

50. $-2(3a - 2b)$ 51. $(-2 - n)(-7)$ 52. $5x(y - z)$ 53. $-6a(2b + 5c)$

ALGEBRA Write a real-world verbal expression for each algebraic expression.

54. $3x + 15$ 55. $6a - 14$ 56. $7.50y + 9$

57. **SCHOOL** You are ordering T-shirts with your school's mascot printed on them. Each T-shirt costs $4.75. The printer charges a set-up fee of $30 and $2.50 to print each shirt. Write two expressions that you could use to represent the total cost of printing n T-shirts.

MEASUREMENT Write two equivalent expressions for the area of each figure.

58.

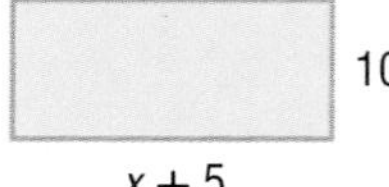

59.

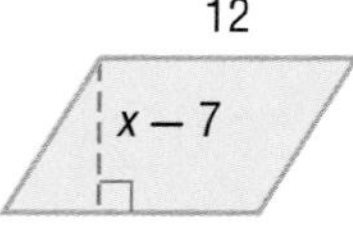

60.

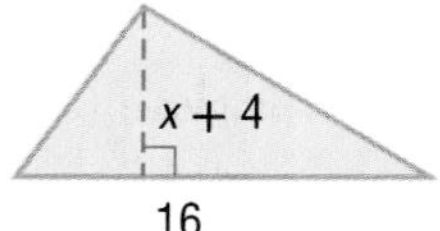

61. **SCHOOL** You spent m minutes studying on Monday. On Tuesday, you studied 15 more minutes than you did on Monday. Wednesday, you studied 30 minutes less than you did on Tuesday. You studied twice as long on Thursday as you did on Monday. On Friday, you studied 20 minutes less than you did on Thursday. Write an expression in simplest form to represent the number of minutes you studied for these five days.

ILS • ISAT
Extra Practice, pp. 688, 707

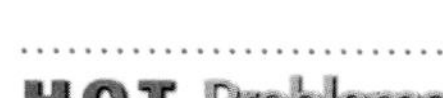

62. **OPEN ENDED** Write an expression that has three terms and simplifies to $4x - 7$. Identify the coefficient(s) and constant(s) in your expression.

63. **Which One Doesn't Belong?** Identify the expression that is not equivalent to the other three. Explain your reasoning.

$x - 2 + 3x$	$4(x - 2)$	$7 + 4x - 9$	$4x - 2$

64. **CHALLENGE** Simplify the expression $8x^2 - 2x + 12x - 3$. Show that your answer is true for $x = 2$.

65. **WRITING IN MATH** Is $2(x - 1) + 3(x - 1) = 5(x - 1)$ a true statement? If so, justify your answer using mathematical properties. If not, give a counterexample.

ISAT PRACTICE 8.A.3a, 8.A.3b

66. Which property is used in the equation below?

$$4x + 32 = 4(x + 8)$$

A Associative Property of Addition
B Commutative Property of Addition
C Distributive Property
D Reflexive Property

67. Which expression is equivalent to $5a + 5b$?

F $5ab$
G $5(a + b)$
H $5a + b$
J $a + 5b$

Spiral Review

68. **MEASUREMENT** The prisms at the right are similar. Find the volume of the smaller prism. Round to the nearest tenth. (Lesson 7-9)

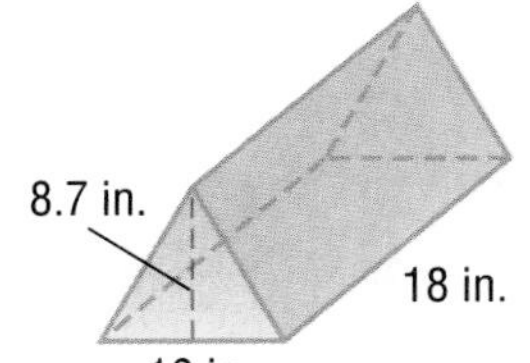

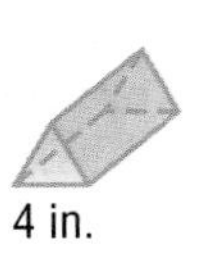

MEASUREMENT Find the lateral area and the surface area of each regular pyramid. Round to the nearest tenth if necessary. (Lesson 7-8)

69. 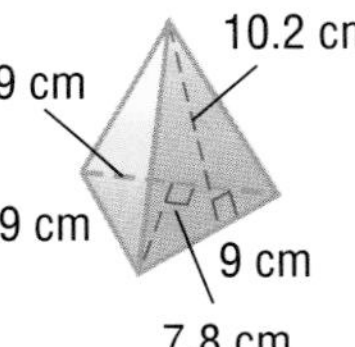

70. 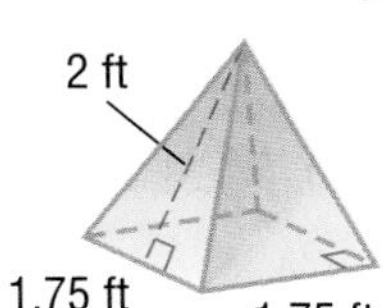

71. 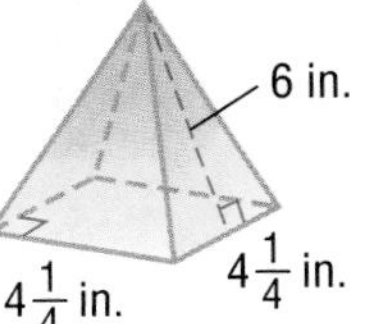

72. **INTERNET** The number of U.S. households with high-speed Internet access increased 66% from 2003 to 2004. If 63 million households had high-speed Internet access in 2004, how many households had high-speed Internet access in 2003? (Lesson 5-8)

73. Determine whether the set of numbers in the table is proportional. (Lesson 4-2)

Time (hours)	1	2	3	4	5	6
Rental Charge	$13	$23	$33	$43	$53	$63

Express each rate as a unit rate. Round to the nearest tenth if necessary. (Lesson 4-1)

74. $5 for 4 loaves of bread

75. 183.4 miles in 3.2 hours

GET READY for the Next Lesson

PREREQUISITE SKILL Solve each equation. Check your solution.
(Lessons 1-9 and 1-10)

76. $x + 8 = 2$

77. $y - 5 = -9$

78. $32 = -4n$

79. $\frac{a}{3} = -15$

8-2 Solving Two-Step Equations

MAIN IDEA

Solve two-step equations.

IL Learning Standards

8.A.3b Solve problems using linear expressions, **equations** and inequalities.
8.D.3a Solve problems using numeric, graphic **or symbolic representations of variables,** expressions, **equations** and inequalities. *Also addresses 8.C.3.*

New Vocabulary

two-step equation

IL Math Online

glencoe.com

- Concepts in Motion
- Extra Examples
- Personal Tutor
- Self-Check Quiz

GET READY for the Lesson

PETS Mario bought 3 small bags of dog treats and one bag of cat food. His total was \$7, but the receipt did not show the individual price of the dog treats.

1. Explain how you could use the work backward strategy to find the cost of each bag of dog treats.
2. Find the cost of each bag.

The solution to this problem can also be found by solving the two-step equation $3x + 1 = 7$, where x is the cost per bag of dog treats.

A **two-step equation** contains two operations. In the equation $3x + 1 = 7$, x is multiplied by 3 and then 1 is added. To solve two-step equations, undo each operation in reverse order.

EXAMPLES Solve Two-Step Equations

1 **Solve $3x + 1 = 7$.**

METHOD 1 **Use a model.**

Remove one 1-tile from each mat.

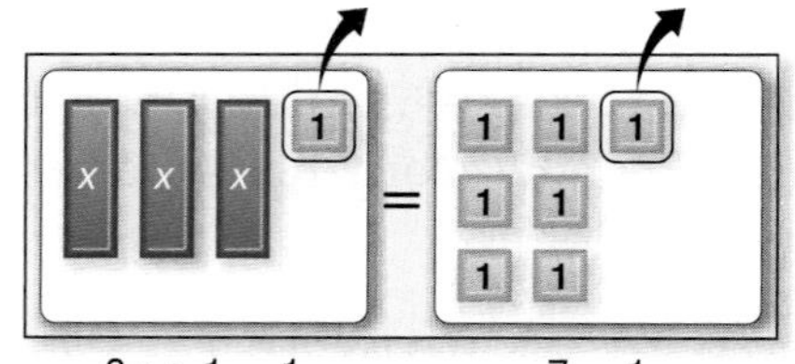

$3x + 1 - 1 = 7 - 1$

Separate the remaining tiles into 3 equal groups.

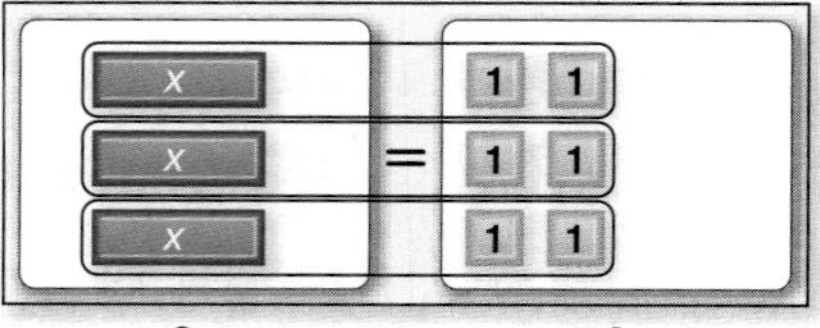

$3x = 6$

There are 2 1-tiles in each group, so $x = 2$.

METHOD 2 **Use symbols.**

Use the Subtraction Property of Equality.

$$\begin{array}{rcrl} 3x + 1 &=& 7 & \text{Write the equation.} \\ -1 &=& -1 & \text{Subtract 1 from each side.} \\ \hline 3x &=& 6 & \end{array}$$

Use the Division Property of Equality.

$3x = 6$

$\frac{3x}{3} = \frac{6}{3}$ Divide each side by 3.

$x = 2$ Simplify.

Using either method, the solution is 2.

2 **Solve $25 = \frac{1}{4}n - 3$.**

METHOD 1 **Vertical method**

$25 = \frac{1}{4}n - 3$	Write the equation.
$+3 = \quad +3$	Add 3 to each side.
$28 = \frac{1}{4}n$	Simplify.
$4 \cdot 28 = 4 \cdot \frac{1}{4}n$	Multiply each side by 4.
$112 = n$	

METHOD 2 **Horizontal method**

$$\frac{1}{4}n - 3 = 25$$
$$\frac{1}{4}n - 3 + 3 = 25 + 3$$
$$\frac{1}{4}n = 28$$
$$4 \cdot \frac{1}{4}n = 4 \cdot 28$$
$$n = 112$$

The solution is 112.

CHOOSE Your Method

Solve each equation. Check your solution.

a. $3x + 2 = 20$ b. $5 + 2n = -1$ c. $-1 = \frac{1}{2}a + 9$

Some two-step equations have a term with a negative coefficient.

Equations with Negative Coefficients

3 **Solve $6 - 3x = 21$.**

$6 - 3x = 21$	Write the equation.
$6 + (-3x) = 21$	Rewrite the left side as addition.
$6 - 6 + (-3x) = 21 - 6$	Subtract 6 from each side.
$-3x = 15$	Simplify.
$\frac{-3x}{-3} = \frac{15}{-3}$	Divide each side by −3.
$x = -5$	Simplify.

The solution is −5.

Check	
$6 - 3x = 21$	Write the equation.
$6 - 3(-5) \stackrel{?}{=} 21$	Replace x with −5.
$6 - (-15) \stackrel{?}{=} 21$	Multiply.
$6 + 15 \stackrel{?}{=} 21$	To subtract a negative number, add its opposite.
$21 = 21$ ✓	The sentence is true.

Study Tip

Common Error
A common mistake when solving the equation in Example 3 is to divide each side by 3 instead of −3. Remember that you are dividing by the coefficient of the variable, which in this instance is a negative number.

CHECK Your Progress

Solve each equation. Check your solution.

d. $10 - \frac{2}{3}p = 52$ e. $-19 = -3x + 2$ f. $\frac{n}{-3} - 2 = -18$

Sometimes it is necessary to combine like terms before solving an equation.

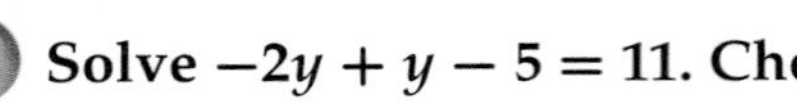

EXAMPLE Combine Like Terms First

4 **Solve $-2y + y - 5 = 11$. Check your solution.**

$-2y + y - 5 = 11$	Write the equation.
$-2y + 1y - 5 = 11$	Identity Property; $y = 1y$
$-y - 5 = 11$	Combine like terms; $-2y + 1y = (-2 + 1)y$ or $-y$.
$-y - 5 + 5 = 11 + 5$	Add 5 to each side.
$-y = 16$	Simplify.
$\frac{-1y}{-1} = \frac{16}{-1}$	$-y = -1y$; divide each side by -1.
$y = -16$	Simplify.

The solution is –16.

Check $-2y + y - 5 = 11$	Write the equation.
$-2(-16) + (-16) - 5 \stackrel{?}{=} 11$	Replace y with -16.
$32 + (-16) - 5 \stackrel{?}{=} 11$	Multiply.
$11 = 11$ ✓	The statement is true.

CHECK Your Progress

Solve each equation. Check your solution.

g. $x + 4x = 45$ **h.** $10 = 2a + 13 - a$ **i.** $-3 = 6 - 5w + \frac{5}{2}w$

CHECK Your Understanding

Examples 1–3 (pp. 422–423)

Solve each equation. Check your solution.

1. $6x + 5 = 29$
2. $-2 = 9m - 11$
3. $10 = \frac{a}{4} + 3$
4. $\frac{2}{3}x - 5 = 7$
5. $3 - 5y = -37$
6. $\frac{c}{-2} - 4 = 3$

Example 3 (p. 423)

7. **ELECTRONICS** Mr. Sampson bought a home theater system. The total cost of the system was \$816, and he pays \$34 a month on the balance. The current balance owed is \$272. Solve the equation $272 = 816 - 34m$ to determine the number of monthly payments Mr. Sampson has made.

Example 4 (p. 424)

Solve each equation. Check your solution.

8. $6k - 10k = 16$
9. $5d + 4 - 6d = 11$
10. $1 = 4\frac{1}{2} - 2p + \frac{10}{3}p$
11. **MOVIES** Cassidy went to the movies with some of her friends. The tickets cost \$6.50 apiece, and each person received a \$1.75 student discount. The total amount paid for all the tickets was \$33.25. Solve the equation $33.25 = 6.50p - 1.75p$ to determine the number of people who went to the movies.

Practice and Problem Solving

HOMEWORK HELP

For Exercises	See Examples
12–19, 24, 25	1, 2
20–23	3
26–33	4

Solve each equation. Check your solution.

12. $2h + 9 = 21$
13. $11 = 2b + 17$
14. $5 = 4a - 7$
15. $-17 = 6p - 5$
16. $2g - 3 = -19$
17. $16 = 5x - 9$
18. $13 = \frac{g}{3} + 4$
19. $5 + \frac{y}{8} = -3$
20. $3 - 8c = 35$
21. $13 - 3d = -8$
22. $-\frac{1}{2}x - 7 = -11$
23. $15 - \frac{w}{4} = 28$

24. **VACATION** Four friends decide to go to the aquarium together. Each person pays $\$x$ a ticket and \$10 each for the shark exhibit. The total cost is \$64. Solve $4x + 4(10) = 64$ to find how much each person pays for a ticket.

25. **GIFTS** Larina received a \$50 gift card to an online store. She wants to purchase some bracelets that cost \$8 each. There will be a \$10 overnight delivery fee. Solve $8n + 10 = 50$ to find the number of bracelets she can purchase.

Solve each equation. Check your solution.

26. $28 = 3m - 7m$
27. $y + 5y = 24$
28. $3 - 6x + 8x = 9$
29. $-21 = 9a - 15 - 3a$
30. $26 = g + 10 - 3g$
31. $8x + 5 - x = -2$

32. **GAMES** Brent had \$26 when he went to the fair. After playing 5 games and then 2 more, he had \$15.50 left. Solve $15.50 = 26 - 5p - 2p$ to find the price for each game.

33. **SPORTS** LaTasha paid \$75 to join a summer golf program. The course where she plays charges \$30 per round, but since she is a student, she receives a \$10 discount per round. If LaTasha spent \$375, use the equation $375 = 30g - 10g + 75$ to find out how many rounds of golf LaTasha played.

Solve each equation. Check your solution.

34. $4(x + 2) = 20$
35. $6(w - 2) = 54$
36. $-4\frac{2}{5} = \frac{6}{5}(t + 1)$
37. $\frac{a - 4}{5} = 12$
38. $\frac{n + 3}{8} = -4$
39. $\frac{6 + z}{10} = -2$

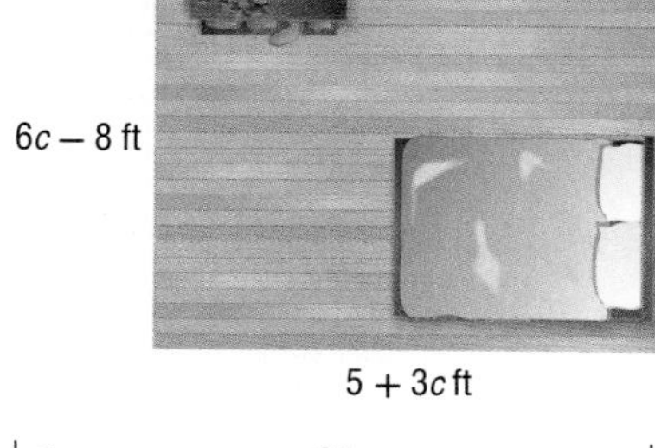

40. **HOME IMPROVEMENT** If Mr. Arenth wants to put new carpeting in the room shown, how many square feet should he order?

41. **ANIMALS** Solve $4x + 12 = 171$. If x stands for the number of animals in a pet store, can it be a solution? Explain.

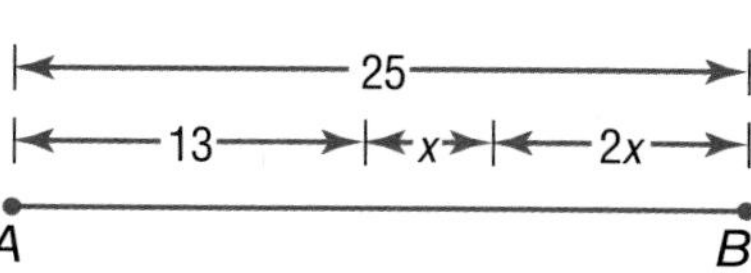

42. **GEOMETRY** Write an equation to represent the length of $\overline{AB}$. Then find the value of x.

ILS • ISAT

Extra Practice, pp. 689, 707

H.O.T. Problems

43. **FIND THE ERROR** Jeanie and Juan are solving the equation $6x + 3 = 18$. Who is correct? Explain.

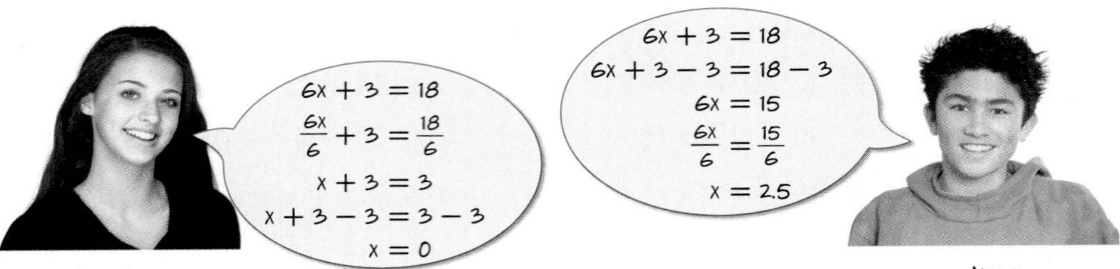

44. **CHALLENGE** Solve $(x + 5)^2 = 49$. (*Hint*: There are two solutions.)

45. **WRITING IN MATH** Explain how you can use the *work backward* problem-solving strategy to solve a two-step equation.

ISAT PRACTICE 8.A.3b, 8.D.3a

46. What value of y makes the equation true?

$$\frac{y}{4} - 7 = 3$$

A 3

B 16

C 40

D 84

47. What is the value of m if $-6m + 4 = -32$?

F 6

G $4\frac{2}{3}$

H $2\frac{1}{3}$

J −6

Spiral Review

Use the Distributive Property to rewrite each expression. (Lesson 8-1)

48. $6(a + 6)$

49. $-3(x + 5)$

50. $(y - 8)4$

51. $-8(p - 7)$

52. **MEASUREMENT** The cylinders at the right are similar. Find the surface area of the larger cylinder. Round to the nearest tenth. (Lesson 7-9)

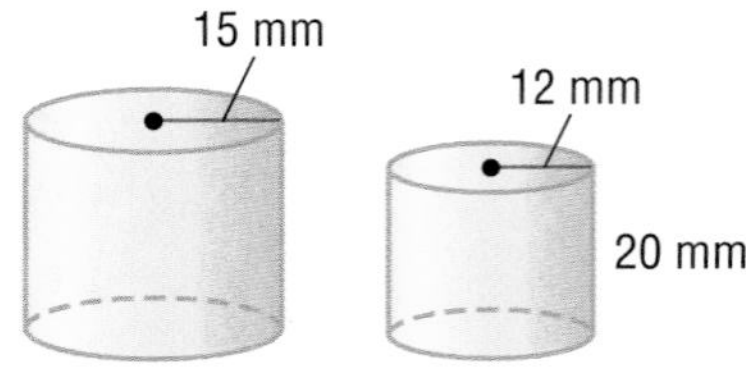

53. **MEASUREMENT** If one leg of a right triangle is 5 feet and its hypotenuse is 13 feet, how long is the other leg? (Lesson 3-5)

54. Write 4.78×10^{-4} in standard form. (Lesson 2-10)

GET READY for the Next Lesson

PREREQUISITE SKILL Write an algebraic equation for each verbal sentence. (Lesson 1-7)

55. A number increased by 5 is 17.

56. The quotient of a number and 2 is −2.

8-3 Writing Two-Step Equations

MAIN IDEA

Write two-step equations that represent real-life situations.

IL Learning Standards

8.A.3b Solve problems using linear expressions, **equations** and inequalities.
8.D.3a Solve problems using numeric, graphic **or symbolic representations of variables,** expressions, **equations** and inequalities.

IL Math Online

glencoe.com

- Extra Examples
- Personal Tutor
- Self-Check Quiz

GET READY for the Lesson

SUMMER CAMP You want to attend a two-week robotics day camp this summer that costs \$700. Your parents have agreed to pay the deposit of \$400 if you pay the rest in weekly payments of \$15.

Payments	Amount Paid
0	$400 + 15(0) = 400$
1	$400 + 15(1) = 415$
2	$400 + 15(2) = 430$
3	$400 + 15(3) = 445$
⋮	⋮

1. Let n represent the number of payments. Write an expression that represents the amount of the camp fee paid after n payments.
2. Write and solve an equation to find the number of payments you will have to make in order to pay off the balance of the camp.
3. What type of equation did you write for Exercise 2? Explain your reasoning.

In Chapter 1, you learned how to write verbal sentences as one-step equations. Some verbal sentences translate to two-step equations.

Words	The sum of 400 and 15 times a number is 700.
Variable	Let n represent the number.
Equation	$400 + 15n = 700$

EXAMPLES Translate Sentences into Equations

Translate each sentence into an equation.

	Sentence	Equation
1	Eight less than three times a number is −23.	$3n - 8 = -23$
2	Thirteen is 7 more than twice a number.	$13 = 2n + 7$
3	The quotient of a number and 4, decreased by 1, is equal to 5.	$\frac{n}{4} - 1 = 5$

CHECK Your Progress

a. Fifteen equals three more than six times a number.

b. If 10 is increased by the quotient of a number and 6, the result is 5.

c. The difference between 12 and twice a number is 18.

Real-World Career . . .
How Does a Personal Trainer Use Math?
Personal trainers use math to help them set training schedules and to track the fitness of their clients.

IL Math Online
For more information, go to glencoe.com.

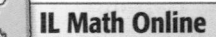

Study Tip
Look Back
You can review **writing equations** in Lesson 1-7.

Real-World EXAMPLES

4 **PERSONAL TRAINING** **A personal trainer buys a weight bench for \$500 and w weights for \$25 each. The total cost of the purchase is \$850. How many weights were purchased?**

Words	Bench	plus	\$25 per weight			equals	\$850.
Variable	Let w represent the number of weights.						
Expression	500	+	25	·	w	=	850

$500 + 25w = 850$ Write the equation.

$500 - 500 + 25w = 850 - 500$ Subtract 500 from each side.

$25w = 350$ Simplify.

$\frac{25w}{25} = \frac{350}{25}$ Divide each side by 25.

$w = 14$

So, 14 weights were purchased.

5 **DINING** **You and your friend's lunch cost \$19. Your lunch cost \$3 more than your friend's. How much was your friend's lunch?**

Words	Your friend's lunch	plus	your lunch	equals	\$19.
Variable	Let f represent the cost of your friend's lunch.				
Equation	f	+	$f + 3$	=	19

$f + f + 3 = 19$ Write the equation.

$2f + 3 = 19$ Combine like terms.

$2f + 3 - 3 = 19 - 3$ Subtract 3 from each side.

$2f = 16$ Simplify.

$\frac{2f}{2} = \frac{16}{2}$ Divide each side by 2.

$f = 8$

Your friend spent \$8.

CHECK Your Progress

d. **METEOROLOGY** Suppose the current temperature is 54°F. It is expected to rise 2°F each hour for the next several hours. In how many hours will the temperature be 78°F?

e. **MEASUREMENT** The perimeter of a rectangle is 40 inches. The width is 8 inches shorter than the length. Write and solve an equation to find the dimensions of the rectangle.

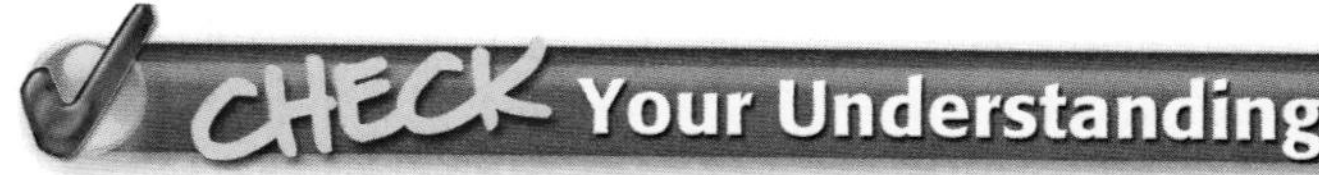

Examples 1–3 (p. 427)

Translate each sentence into an equation.

1. One more than three times a number is 7.
2. Seven less than twice a number is -1.
3. The quotient of a number and 5, less 10, is 3.

For Exercises 4 and 5, write and solve an equation to solve each problem.

Example 4 (p. 428)

4. **MOVIES** You already owe $4.32 in overdue rental fees and are returning a movie that is 4 days late. Now you owe $6.48. How much is a daily fine for an overdue movie?

Example 5 (p. 428)

5. **SHOPPING** Marty paid $121 for shoes and clothes. He paid $45 more for clothes than he did for shoes. How much did Marty pay for the shoes?

Practice and Problem Solving

HOMEWORK HELP

For Exercises	See Examples
6–9	1–3
10–13	4
14, 15	5

Translate each sentence into an equation.

6. Four less than five times a number is equal to 11.
7. Fifteen more than twice a number is 9.
8. Eight more than four times a number is -12.
9. Six less than seven times a number is equal to -20.

For Exercises 10–15, write and solve an equation to solve each problem.

10. **MUSIC** Monica has saved $725 for a new guitar and lessons. Her guitar costs $475, and guitar lessons are $25 per hour. Determine how many hours of lessons she can afford.

11. **BOOKS** You buy 3 books that each cost the same amount and a magazine, all for $55.99. You know that the magazine costs $1.99. How much does each book cost?

12. **CELL PHONES** Use the poster at the right. If your bill for one month was $113.74, find the number of minutes you used.

13. **TICKETS** It costs $13 for admission to an amusement park, plus $1.50 for each ride. If you have a total of $35.50 to spend, what is the greatest number of rides you can go on?

14. **MONUMENTS** From ground level to the tip of the torch, the Statue of Liberty and its pedestal are 92.99 meters high. The pedestal is 0.89 meter higher than the statue. How high is the Statue of Liberty?

Real-World Link When diving, the peregrine falcon can reach speeds of up to 175 miles per hour.
Source: *Time for Kids Almanac*

15. **GEOMETRY** Find the value of x in the parallelogram at the right.

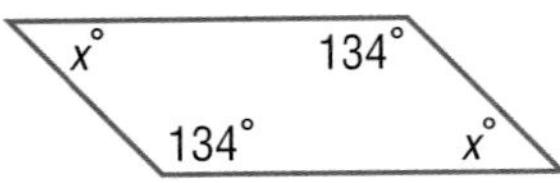

ANIMALS For Exercises 16–18, use the information at the left.

16. The top speed of a peregrine falcon is 20 miles per hour less than three times the top speed of a cheetah. What is the cheetah's top speed?
17. A sailfish can swim up to 1 mile per hour less than one fifth the top speed of a peregrine falcon. Find the top speed that a sailfish can swim.
18. The peregrine falcon can reach speeds about 14 miles per hour more than 7 times the speed of the fastest human. What is the approximate top speed of the fastest human?

19. **BASEBALL** Javier went to the batting cages to practice hitting. He rented a helmet for \$4 and paid \$0.75 for each group of 20 pitches. If he spent a total of \$7 at the batting cages, how many groups of pitches did he pay for?

20. **SNOWBOARDING** Madison would like to take snowboarding lessons at Powder Mountain. She has saved \$550 for lessons and a junior season pass. How many more semi-private lessons than private lessons can she take?

Powder Mountain Ski Resort Snowboarding Lessons	
Semi-Private	\$45/lesson
Private	\$60/lesson
Junior Season Pass	\$315

21. **ALGEBRA** Three consecutive even integers can be represented by n, $n + 2$, and $n + 4$. If the sum of three consecutive even integers is 36, what are the integers?

JOBS For Exercises 22 and 23, use the following information.
Hunter and Amado are each trying to save \$600 for a summer trip. Hunter started with \$150 and earns \$7.50 per hour working at a grocery store. Amado has nothing saved, but he earns \$12 per hour painting houses.

22. Make a conjecture about who will take longer to save enough money for the trip. Justify your reasoning.
23. Write and solve two equations to check your conjecture.

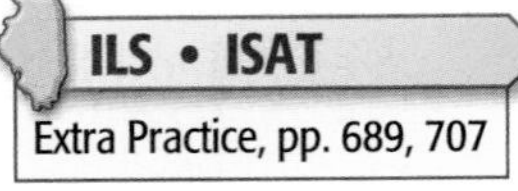

Extra Practice, pp. 689, 707

For Exercises 24 and 25, write a problem that could be solved using each equation.

24. $4x + 20 = 70$
25. $2x - 6 = 25$

H.O.T. Problems

26. **OPEN ENDED** If 12 less than 4 times a number is 8, the number is 5. Write a different sentence where the unknown number is also 5.
27. **CHALLENGE** The ages of three siblings combined is 27. The oldest is twice the age of the youngest. The middle child is 3 years older than the youngest. Write and solve an equation to find the ages of each sibling.

28. **SELECT A TECHNIQUE** Sherrie bought 3 bottles of sports drink for \$6.42. If the sales tax was \$0.42, which technique would you use to determine the cost of each bottle of sports drink? Justify your selection. Then find the cost of each bottle of sports drink.

mental math | estimation | paper/pencil

29. **WRITING IN MATH** Write about a real-world situation that can be solved using a two-step equation. Then write the equation and solve the problem.

ISAT PRACTICE 8.A.3b, 8.D.3a

30. A company employs 72 workers. It plans to increase the number of employees by 6 per month until it has twice its current workforce. Which equation can be used to determine m, the number of months it will take for the number of employees to double?

A $6m + 72m = 144$

B $2m + 72 = 144$

C $2(6m + 72) = 144$

D $6m + 72 = 144$

31. Kimberly needs \$45 to go to the amusement park. She has \$13. She earns \$8 per hour working at her job. The equation $8h + 13 = 45$ shows this relationship. How many hours does Kimberly need to work to earn enough money to go to the park?

F 8

G 7

H 6

J 4

Spiral Review

Solve each equation. Check your solution. (Lesson 8-2)

32. $5x + 2 = 17$

33. $-7b + 13 = 27$

34. $-6 = \frac{n}{8} + 1$

35. $-15 = -4p + 9$

Simplify each expression. (Lesson 8-1)

36. $5x + 6 - x$

37. $8 - 3n + 3n$

38. $7a - 7a - 9$

39. $3 - 4y + 9y$

40. **GEOMETRY** Copy the figure at the right onto graph paper. Then draw the image of the figure after it is translated 4 units left and 2 units up. (Lesson 6-7)

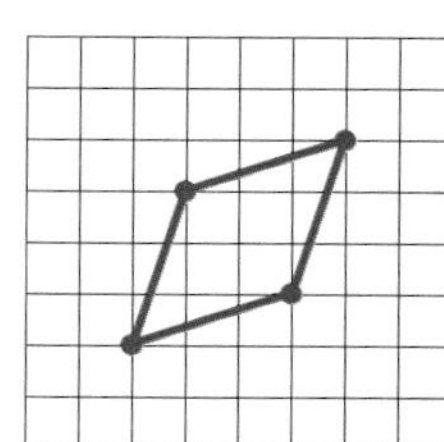

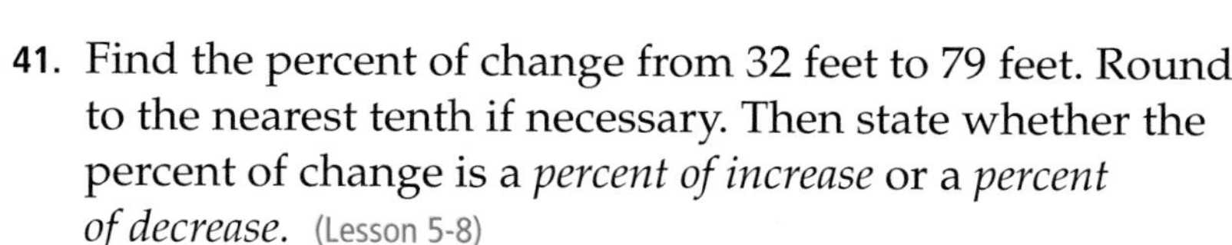

41. Find the percent of change from 32 feet to 79 feet. Round to the nearest tenth if necessary. Then state whether the percent of change is a *percent of increase* or a *percent of decrease.* (Lesson 5-8)

GET READY for the Next Lesson

PREREQUISITE SKILL **Simplify each expression.** (Lesson 8-1)

42. $2x - 8 + 2x$

43. $-5n + 7 + 5n$

44. $8p - 3 + 3$

45. $-6 - 15a + 6$

Explore 8-4

Algebra Lab
Equations with Variables on Each Side

MAIN IDEA

Solve equations with variables on each side using algebra tiles.

IL Learning Standards

8.A.3b Solve problems using linear expressions, **equations** and inequalities.
8.D.3a Solve problems using numeric, graphic **or symbolic representations of variables,** expressions, **equations** and inequalities.

You can use algebra tiles to solve equations that have variables on each side of the equation.

ACTIVITY

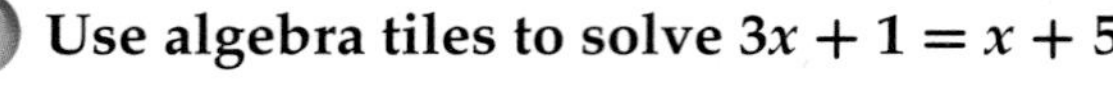

1 Use algebra tiles to solve $3x + 1 = x + 5$.

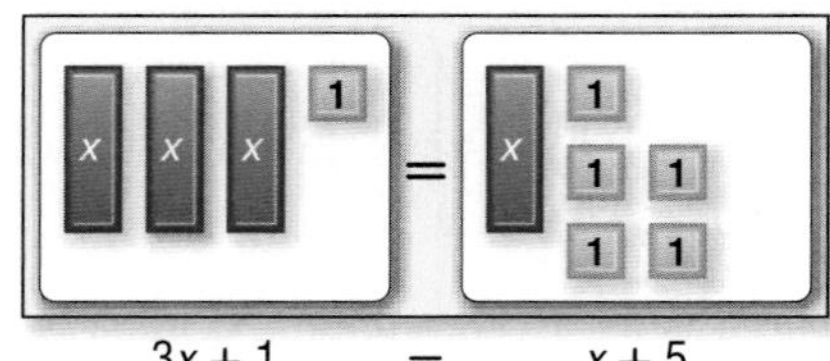

Model the equation.

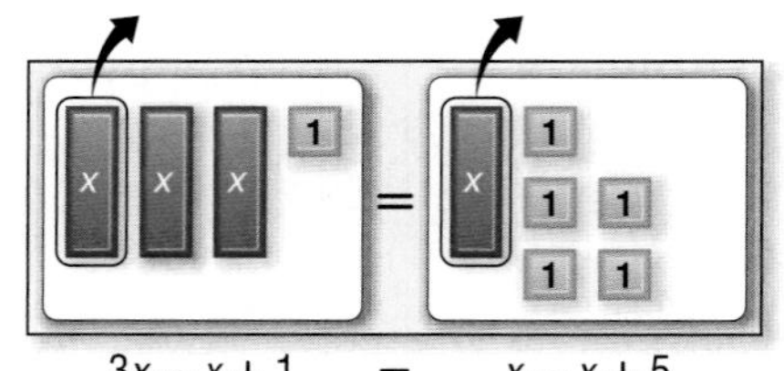

Remove the same number of x-tiles from each side of the mat until there are x-tiles on only one side.

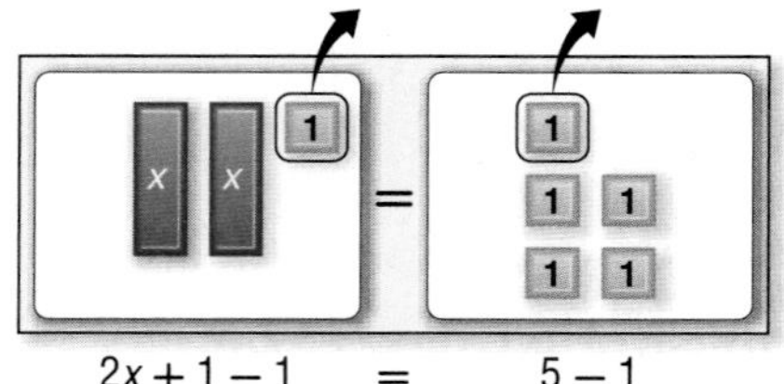

Remove the same number of 1-tiles from each side of the mat until the x-tiles are by themselves on one side.

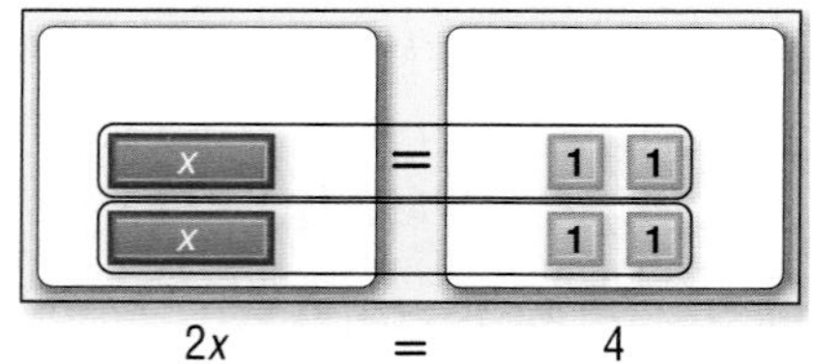

Separate the tiles into two equal groups.

Therefore, $x = 2$. Since $3(2) + 1 = 2 + 5$, the solution is correct.

CHECK Your Progress

Use algebra tiles to solve each equation.

a. $x + 2 = 2x + 1$
b. $2x + 7 = 3x + 4$
c. $2x - 5 = x - 7$
d. $8 + x = 3x$
e. $4x = x - 6$
f. $2x - 8 = 4x - 2$

Analyze the Results

1. Identify the property of equality that allows you to remove a 1-tile or -1-tile from each side of an equation mat.

ACTIVITY

2 **Use algebra tiles to solve $x - 4 = 2x + 2$.**

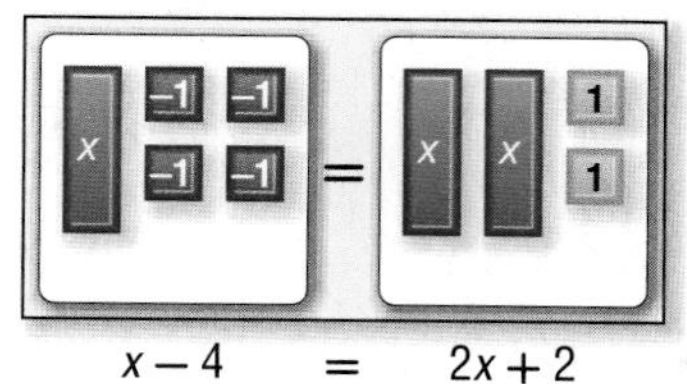

Model the equation.

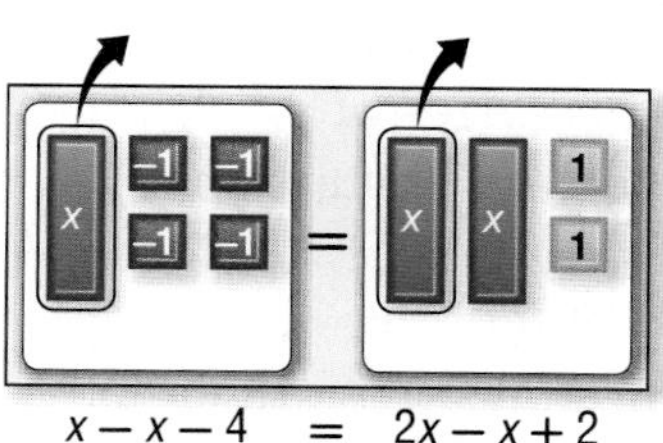

Remove the same number of x-tiles from each side of the mat until there is an x-tile by itself on one side.

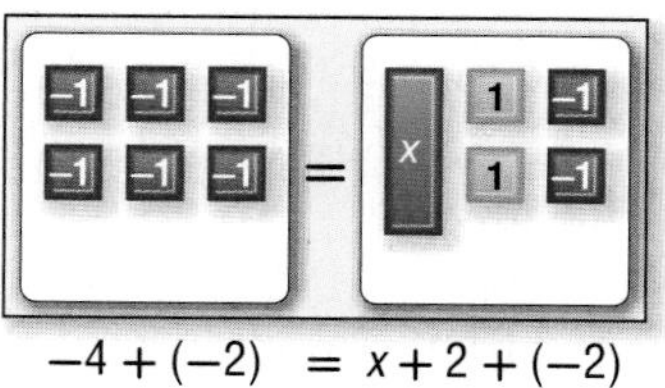

To isolate the x-tile, it is not possible to remove the same number of 1-tiles from each side of the mat. Add two -1-tiles to each side of the mat.

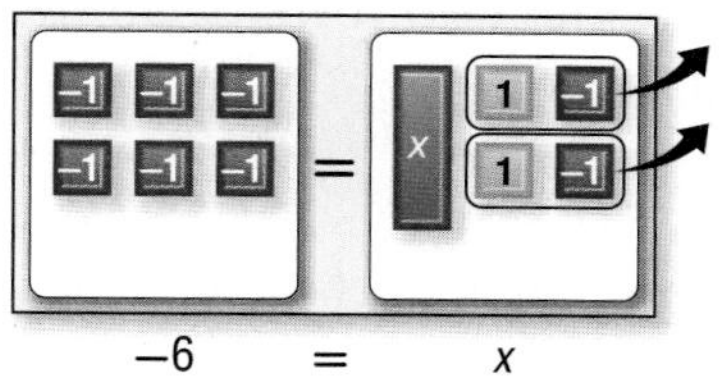

Remove the zero pairs from the right side. There are six -1-tiles on the left side of the mat. The x-tile is isolated on the right side of the mat.

Therefore, $x = -6$. Since $-6 - 4 = 2(-6) + 2$, the solution is correct.

CHECK Your Progress

Use algebra tiles to solve each equation.

g. $x + 6 = 3x - 2$ **h.** $3x + 3 = x - 5$ **i.** $2x + 1 = x - 7$

j. $x - 4 = 2x + 5$ **k.** $3x - 2 = 2x + 3$ **l.** $2x + 5 = 4x - 1$

Analyze the Results

2. Explain why you can remove an x-tile from each side of the mat.
3. Solve $x + 4 = 3x - 4$ by removing 1-tiles first. Then solve the equation by removing x-tiles first. Does it matter whether you remove x-tiles or 1-tiles first? Is one way more convenient? Explain.
4. **MAKE A CONJECTURE** In the set of algebra tiles, $-x$ is represented by [–x tile]. Explain how you could use $-x$-tiles and other algebra tiles to solve $-3x + 4 = -2x - 1$.

8-4 Solving Equations with Variables on Each Side

MAIN IDEA

Solve equations with variables on each side.

IL Learning Standards

8.A.3b Solve problems using linear expressions, **equations** and inequalities.
8.D.3a Solve problems using numeric, graphic or **symbolic representations of variables,** expressions, **equations** and inequalities.

IL Math Online

glencoe.com
- Extra Examples
- Personal Tutor
- Self-Check Quiz

GET READY for the Lesson

FUNDRAISING Jordan and Tanner are both selling gift wrap for a school fundraiser. Jordan has already sold 8 packages of gift wrap before Tanner starts. Tanner sells an average of 5 packages of gift wrap per day, and Jordan sells an average of 4 packages per day.

Time (days)	Jordan's Sales	Tanner's Sales
0	$8 + 4(0) = 8$	$5(0) = 0$
1	$8 + 4(1) = 12$	$5(1) = 5$
2	$8 + 4(2) = 16$	$5(2) = 10$
3	$8 + 4(3) = 20$	$5(3) = 15$
⋮	⋮	⋮

1. Copy the table. Continue filling in rows to find how many days until Tanner and Jordan sell the same number of packages.
2. Write an expression for Jordan's gift wrap sales after d days.
3. Write an expression for Tanner's gift wrap sales after d days.
4. On which day will Tanner's sales pass Jordan's sales?
5. Write an equation that could be used to find how many days it will take until Tanner and Jordan sell the same number of packages.

Some equations, like $8 + 4d = 5d$, have variables on each side of the equals sign. To solve these equations, use the Addition or Subtraction Property of Equality to write an equivalent equation with the variables on one side of the equals sign. Then solve the equation.

EXAMPLES Equations with Variables on Each Side

1 Solve $8 + 4d = 5d$. Check your solution.

$8 + 4d = 5d$	Write the equation.
$8 + 4d - 4d = 5d - 4d$	Subtract $4d$ from each side.
$8 = d$	Simplify by combining like terms.

Subtract $4d$ from the left side of the equation to isolate the variable.

Subtract $4d$ from the right side of the equation to keep it balanced.

To check your solution, replace d with 8 in the original equation.

Check	$8 + 4d = 5d$	Write the original equation.
	$8 + 4(8) \stackrel{?}{=} 5(8)$	Replace d with 8.
	$40 = 40$ ✓	The sentence is true.

The solution is 8.

2 **Solve $6n - 1 = 4n - 5$.**

$6n - 1 = 4n - 5$	Write the equation.
$6n - 4n - 1 = 4n - 4n - 5$	Subtract 4*n* from each side.
$2n - 1 = -5$	Simplify.
$2n - 1 + 1 = -5 + 1$	Add 1 to each side.
$2n = -4$	Simplify.
$n = -2$	Mentally divide each side by 2.

CHECK Your Progress

Solve each equation. Check your solution.

a. $8a = 5a + 21$ b. $3x - 7 = 8x + 23$ c. $7g - 12 = 3 + \frac{7}{3}g$

Real-World EXAMPLE

3 **CELL PHONES A cellular phone provider charges $24.95 per month plus $0.10 per minute for calls. Another cellular provider charges $19.95 per month plus $0.20 per minute for calls. For how many minutes of calls is the monthly cost of both providers the same?**

Words	$24.95 per month plus $0.10 per minute	equals	$19.95 per month plus $0.20 per minute
Variable	Let *m* represent the minutes.		
Equation	$24.95 + 0.10m = 19.95 + 0.20m$		

$24.95 + 0.10m = 19.95 + 0.20m$	Write the equation.
$24.95 + 0.10m - 0.10m = 19.95 + 0.20m - 0.10m$	Subtract 0.10*m* from each side.
$24.95 = 19.95 + 0.10m$	
$24.95 - 19.95 = 19.95 - 19.95 + 0.10m$	Subtract 19.95 from each side.
$5 = 0.10m$	
$\frac{5}{0.10} = \frac{0.10m}{0.10}$	Divide each side by 0.10.
$50 = m$	

Check for Reasonableness $\$25 + 50(\$0.10) = \$30$
$\$20 + 50(\$0.20) = \$30$

The monthly cost is the same for 50 minutes of calls.

Real-World Link Congress established the first official United States flag on June 14, 1777.
Source: Office of Citizen Services and Communications

CHECK Your Progress

d. **FLAGS** The length of a flag is 0.3 foot less than twice its width. If the perimeter is 14.4 feet longer than the width, find the dimensions of the flag.

CHECK Your Understanding

Examples 1, 2 (pp. 434–435)

Solve each equation. Check your solution.

1. $5n + 9 = 2n$
2. $3k + 14 = k$
3. $10x = 3x - 28$
4. $7y - 8 = 6y + 1$
5. $2a + 21 = 8a - 9$
6. $-4p - 3 = 2 + p$

Example 3 (p. 435)

7. **CAR RENTAL** EZ Car Rental charges $40 a day plus $0.25 per mile. Ace Rent-A-Car charges $25 a day plus $0.45 per mile. What number of miles results in the same cost for one day?

Practice and Problem Solving

HOMEWORK HELP	
For Exercises	See Examples
8–11	1
12–19	2
20–23	3

Solve each equation. Check your solution.

8. $7a + 10 = 2a$
9. $11x = 24 + 8x$
10. $9g - 14 = 2g$
11. $m - 18 = 3m$
12. $5p + 2 = 4p - 1$
13. $8y - 3 = 6y + 17$
14. $15 - 3n = n - 1$
15. $3 - 10b = 2b - 9$
16. $-6f + 13 = 2f - 11$
17. $2z - 31 = -9z + 24$
18. $2.5h - 15 = 4h$
19. $21.6 - d = 5d$

Define a variable, write an equation, and solve to find each number.

20. Eighteen less than three times a number is twice the number.
21. Eleven more than four times a number equals the number less 7.

For Exercises 22 and 23, write and solve an equation to solve each problem.

22. **TICKETS** If you pay a one-time fee of $30, you can purchase gold tickets for your local minor league baseball team for only $3 a game. Regular tickets sell at the stadium for $6. How many gold tickets would you need to buy to equal the cost of regular tickets?

23. **BASKETBALL** Will averages 18 points a game and is the all-time scoring leader on his team with 483 points. Tom averages 21 points a game and is currently second on the all-time scorers list with 462 points. If both players continue to play at the same rate, how many games will it take until Tom and Will have scored the same number of total points?

MEASUREMENT Write an equation to find the value of x so that each pair of polygons has the same perimeter. Then solve.

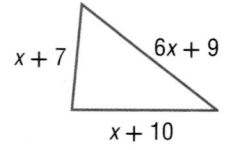

24.

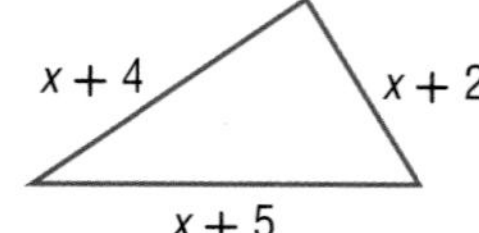

25.

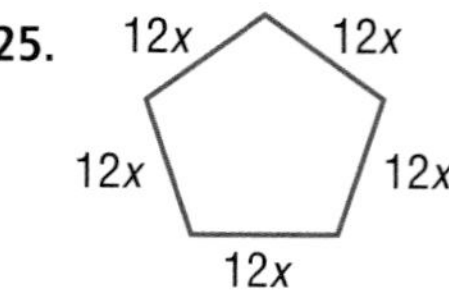

26. **MEASUREMENT** Write and solve an equation to find the perimeter and area of the square at the right.

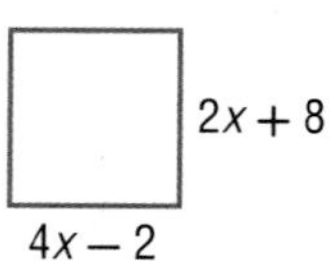

Extra Practice, pp. 689, 707

H.O.T. Problems

27. **CHALLENGE** The cheerleaders are selling school sweatshirts at a local fall festival. The fee for a booth is $10 plus 7% of their sales. The sweatshirts are being sold for $15, and they each cost $9 to make. Write and solve an equation to find how many sweatshirts they must sell to break even.

28. **OPEN ENDED** Write a word problem that can be solved using the equation $5x = 3x + 20$.

29. **CHALLENGE** Find the area of the rectangle at the right.

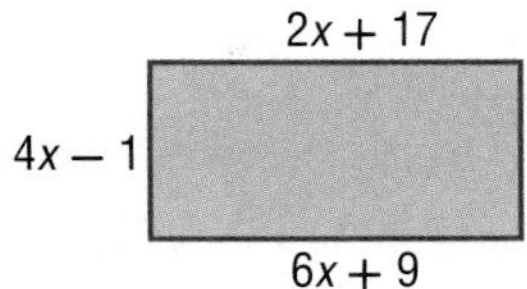

30. **WRITING IN MATH** Explain how to solve the equation $2 - 4x = 6x - 8$.

ISAT PRACTICE 8.A.3b, 8.D.3a

31. Carpet cleaner A charges $28.25 plus $18 a room. Carpet cleaner B charges $19.85 plus $32 a room. Which equation can be used to find the number of rooms for which the total cost of both carpet cleaners is the same?

 A $28.25x + 18 = 19.85x + 32$

 B $28.25 + 32x = 19.85 + 18x$

 C $28.25 + 18x = 19.85 + 32x$

 D $(28.25 + 18)x = (19.85 + 32)x$

32. Find the value of x so that the polygons have the same perimeter.

 x + 4, x + 4, x + 1; 2x, 2x, 2x, 2x, 2x, 2x

 F 4 **H** 2

 G 3 **J** 1

Spiral Review

33. **SHOPPING** Marisa bought 4 paperback books, each at the same price. The tax on her purchase was $2.35, and the total was $34.15. Write and solve an equation to find the price of each book. (Lesson 8-3)

ALGEBRA Solve each equation. (Lesson 8-2)

34. $9 + 5y = 19$
35. $-6 = 4 + 2x$
36. $8 - k = 17$
37. $2 = 18 - 4d$

38. **SAVINGS** Shala's savings account earned $4.57 in 6 months at a simple interest rate of 4.75%. How much was in her account at the beginning of that 6-month period? (Lesson 5-9)

GET READY for the Next Lesson

39. **PREREQUISITE SKILL** Enrique has $37.50 to spend at the cinema. A drink costs $1.75, popcorn costs $2.25, and tickets cost $8.50. Use the *work backward* strategy to determine how many friends he can invite to go with him if he pays for himself and for his friends. (Lesson 1-8)

8-5 Problem-Solving Investigation

MAIN IDEA: Guess and check to solve problems.

6.B.3a Solve practical computation problems involving whole numbers, integers and rational numbers. 6.C.3a Select computational procedures and solve problems with whole numbers, fractions, decimals, percents and proportions.

P.S.I. TEAM +

e-Mail: GUESS AND CHECK

ADRIENNE: My class is going on a field trip to the museum to see an exhibit by a local artist. Admission for students is $2, and adult admission is $4. The total amount of money collected is $66. A total of 30 people are going on the trip.

YOUR MISSION: Guess and check to find the number of students and adults who are going on the field trip.

Understand	The student cost is $2 and the adult cost is $4. There is a total of 30 people going on the trip.
Plan	Make a guess, and check to see if it is correct.
Solve	Find the combination that gives a total of $66. In the list, *s* is the number of students and *a* is the number of adults who went on the trip. (see table below) So, 27 students and 3 adults are going on the field trip.
Check	The sum of 27 students and 3 adults is 30. Since $2(27) + 4(3) = 66$, the guess is correct. ✓

s	a	$2s + 4a$	Check
26	4	$2(26) + 4(4) = 68$	too high
29	1	$2(29) + 4(1) = 62$	too low
28	2	$2(28) + 4(2) = 64$	still too low
27	3	$2(27) + 4(3) = 66$	correct

Analyze The Strategy

1. For the problem above, 23 students and 5 adults would also spend $66 to get into the museum. Explain why this could not be the correct solution.
2. **WRITING IN MATH** Write a problem that could be solved by guessing and checking. Then write the steps you would take to find the solution.

Mixed Problem Solving

ILS • ISAT

Extra Practice, pp. 690, 707

For Exercises 3–5, solve using the *guess and check* strategy.

3. **NUMBER THEORY** A number is squared, and the result is 576. Find the number.

4. **COINS** Max has $2.50 in quarters, dimes, and nickels. If he has 18 coins, how many of each coin does he have?

5. **SHOPPING** Shyla was buying gifts for each of her 8 cousins. She bought everyone either a ring for $6 or a toy for $7. If she spent a total of $53, how many of each did she buy?

Use any strategy to solve Exercises 6–14. Some strategies are shown below.

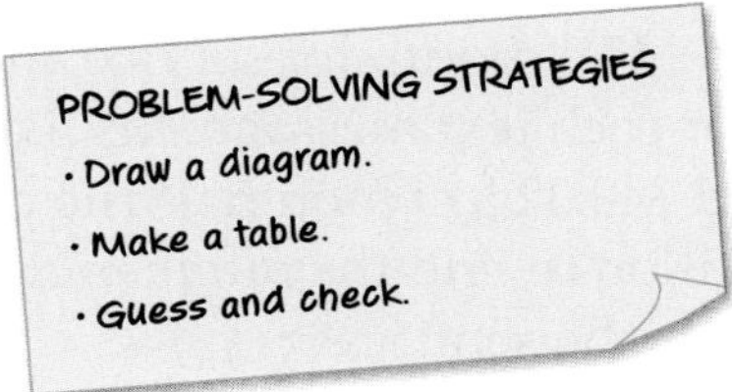

6. **MEASUREMENT** The length ℓ of the rectangle below is longer than its width w. List the possible whole number dimensions for the rectangle, and identify the dimensions that give the greatest perimeter.

$A = 36 \text{ in}^2$ w

ℓ

7. **NUMBERS** Name three numbers that have a sum of 23 if the greatest number is 9 more than the least number.

8. **NEWSPAPERS** The list at the right shows the number of letters in the first 20 words of an article on the front page of a newspaper. What number of letters occurs most often?

The Daily Reader

3	5	7	4
4	7	6	4
5	5	3	6
8	4	5	5
6	5	7	7

9. **MOVING** Marcel is moving and wants to put all of his 20 CD cases in one box. Give two possible dimensions for a box that would hold the cases with no space leftover.

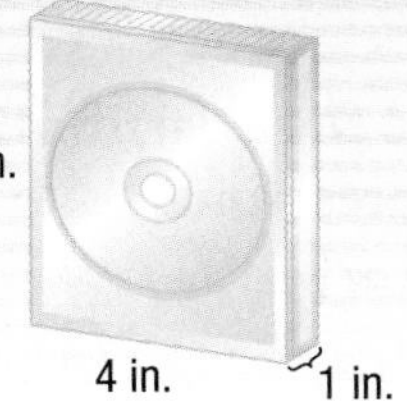

10. **SKATEBOARDS** Ashton wants to save $54 for a new skateboard. He needs to save twice as much money as he has already saved to reach his goal. Write and solve an equation to find how much money he has saved so far.

11. **SIBLINGS** Three siblings have a combined age of 108 years. The oldest is 8 years older than the youngest. What are the ages of the siblings?

ANALYZE TABLES For Exercises 12 and 13, use the following information.

One hundred fifteen students at Blendon Middle School could sign up to hear three different speakers for career day. Seventy students heard the nurse speak, 37 heard the firefighter, and 63 heard the Webmaster. Some students heard more than one speaker. The results are shown below.

Number of Students	Speaker
15	all three
20	nurse or firefighter
30	Webmaster or nurse
12	firefighter only

12. How many students signed up only for Webmaster?

13. How many students did *not* sign up for nurse?

14. **NUMBER SENSE** Find the product of $1 - \frac{1}{2}, 1 - \frac{1}{2}, 1 - \frac{1}{3}, 1 - \frac{1}{4}, \ldots, 1 - \frac{1}{48}, 1 - \frac{1}{49}$, and $1 - \frac{1}{50}$.

CHAPTER 8 Mid-Chapter Quiz

Lessons 8-1 through 8-5

IL Learning Standards

8.A.3b, 8.D.3a

Use the Distributive Property to rewrite each expression. (Lesson 8-1)

1. $3(x + 2)$
2. $-2(a - 3)$
3. $5(3c - 7)$
4. $-4(2n + 3)$

Simplify each expression. (Lesson 8-1)

5. $2a - 13a$
6. $6b + 5 - 6b$
7. $2m + 5 - 8m$
8. $7x + 2 - 8x + 5$

9. Identify the terms, like terms, coefficients, and constants in the expression $5 - 4x + x - 3$. (Lesson 8-1)

Solve each equation. Check your solution. (Lesson 8-2)

10. $3m + 5 = 14$
11. $-2k + 7 = -3$
12. $11 = \frac{1}{3}a + 2$
13. $-15 = -7 - p$

14. **MULTIPLE CHOICE** A diagram of a room is shown below.

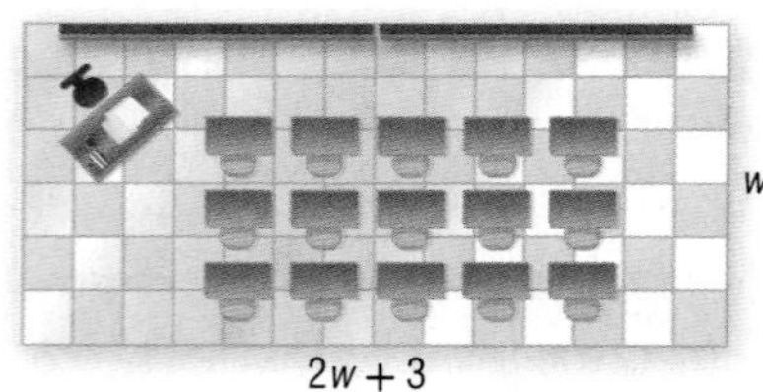

If the perimeter of the room is 78 feet, find its width. (Lesson 8-2)

A 12 ft

B 15 ft

C 25 ft

D 27 ft

15. **EXERCISE** Brandi rode her bike the same distance on Tuesday and Thursday, and 20 miles on Saturday for a total of 50 miles for the week. Solve the equation $2m + 20 = 50$ to find the distance Brandi rode on Tuesday and Thursday. (Lesson 8-2)

Translate each sentence into an equation. Then find each number. (Lesson 8-3)

16. Nine more than the quotient of a number and 3 is 14.
17. The quotient of a number and -7, less 4, is -11.
18. The difference between three times a number and 10 is 17.
19. The difference between twice a number and 13 is -21.

20. **TEXT MESSAGES** A cell phone company charges \$45 a month for service and \$0.12 extra for each text message. Ms. Barnes was charged \$49.32 last month. Write and solve an equation to find the number of text messages she sent. (Lesson 8-3)

Solve each equation. Check your solution. (Lesson 8-4)

21. $3x + 7 = 2x$
22. $7p - 6 = 4p$
23. $3y - 5 = 5y + 7$
24. $4m + 7 = -3m + 49$

25. **MEASUREMENT** Write and solve an equation to find the value of x so that the polygons have the same perimeter. (Lesson 8-4)

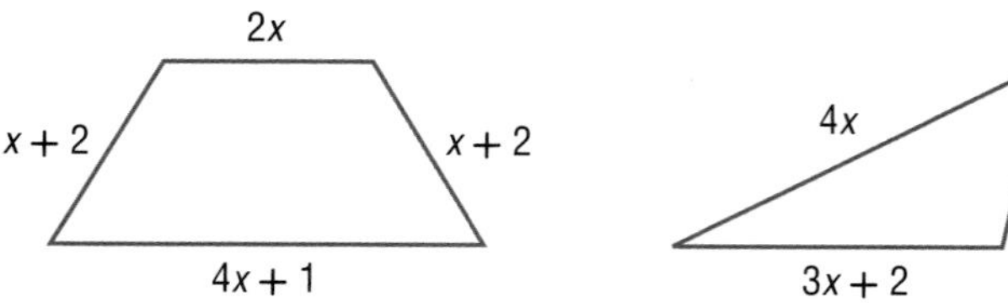

26. **MONEY** Marlisa has exactly \$61 in one-dollar, five-dollar, and ten-dollar bills. If she has 14 bills in all, how many of each bill does she have? (Lesson 8-5)

8-6 Inequalities

First-Class Mail Rates

Weight not over (ounces)	Rate
1	$0.41
2	$0.65
3	$0.89
4	$1.13
5	$1.37

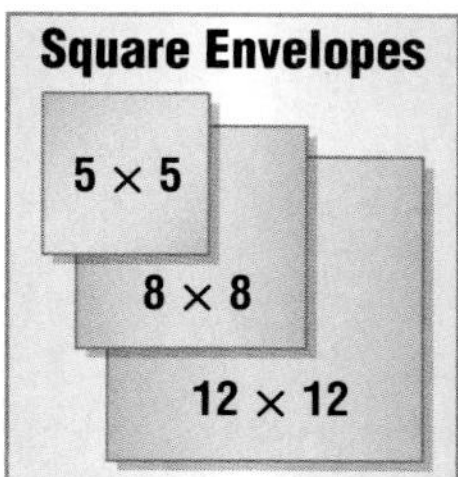

MAIN IDEA

Write and graph inequalities.

IL Learning Standards

8.A.3b Solve problems using linear expressions, equations and **inequalities.**
8.D.3a Solve problems using numeric, graphic or symbolic representations of variables, expressions, equations **and inequalities.** *Also addresses 8.C.3.*

IL Math Online

glencoe.com
- Extra Examples
- Personal Tutor
- Self-Check Quiz

GET READY for the Lesson

POSTAL SERVICE Iko wants to mail square invitations to a birthday party. Square envelopes must be 5 inches by 5 inches or *greater*. She will pay $0.41 in postage for every invitation that weighs 1 ounce or *less*.

1. List three envelope sizes that Iko can use.
2. How much will it cost to mail an invitation that weighs 2.5 ounces?

In Chapter 1, you learned that a mathematical sentence that contains $>$ or $<$ is called an inequality. When used to compare a variable and a number, inequalities can describe a range of values.

EXAMPLES Write Inequalities with $<$ or $>$

Write an inequality for each sentence.

1. **LUGGAGE A suitcase must weigh less than 40 pounds.**

   Let w = suitcase's weight.

   $w < 40$

2. **AGE You must be over 12 years old to play.**

   Let a = person's age.

   $a > 12$

CHECK Your Progress

a. **MOVIES** You must be older than 17 to see the movie.

b. **SPORTS** Members of a swim team must be under 15 years of age.

The symbols $\leq$ and $\geq$ combine $<$ and $>$ with part of the equals sign.

EXAMPLES Write Inequalities with $\leq$ or $\geq$

Write an inequality for each sentence.

3. **ROLLER COASTERS You must beat least 48 inches tall to ride the roller coaster.**

   Let h = person's height.

   $h \geq 48$

4. **MENU You must be 12 years of age or younger to order from the children's menu.**

   Let a = person's age.

   $a \leq 12$

CHECK Your Progress

c. **VOTING** You must be 18 years of age or older to vote.

d. **TRAVEL** A fuel tank holds at most 16 gallons of gasoline.

Reading Math

Inequality Symbols
$\leq$ less than or equal to
$\geq$ greater than or equal to

Inequalities				
Words	• is less than • is fewer than	• is greater than • is more than • exceeds	• is less than or equal to • is no more than • is at most	• is greater than or equal to • is no less than • is at least
Symbols	$<$	$>$	$\leq$	$\geq$

Inequalities with variables are open sentences. When the variable is replaced with a number, the inequality becomes either true or false.

EXAMPLES Determine the Truth of an Inequality

For the given value, state whether each inequality is *true* or *false*.

5 $a + 2 > 8, a = 5$

$a + 2 > 8$ Write the inequality.

$5 + 2 \overset{?}{>} 8$ Replace a with 5.

$7 \not> 8$ Simplify.

Since 7 is not greater than 8, $7 > 8$ is false.

6 $10 \leq 7 - x, x = -3$

$10 \leq 7 - x$ Write the inequality.

$10 \overset{?}{\leq} 7 - (-3)$ Replace x with -3.

$10 \leq 10$ Simplify.

While $10 < 10$ is false, $10 = 10$ is true, so $10 \leq 10$ is true.

Symbols
Read $7 \not> 8$ as *7 is not greater than 8.*

CHECK Your Progress

For the given value, state whether each inequality is *true* or *false*.

e. $n - 6 < 15, n = 18$ **f.** $-3p \geq 24, p = 8$ **g.** $-2 > 5y - 7, y = 1$

Inequalities can be graphed on a number line. Since it is impossible to show all the values that make an inequality true, an open or closed circle is used to indicate where these values begin, and an arrow to the left or to the right is used to show that they continue in the indicated direction.

EXAMPLES Graph an Inequality

Graph each inequality on a number line.

7 $n < 3$

Place an open circle at 3. Then draw a line and an arrow to the left.

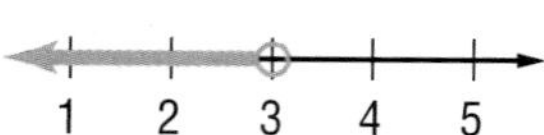

The open circle means the number 3 is not included in the graph.

8 $n \geq 3$

Place a closed circle at 3. Then draw a line and an arrow to the right.

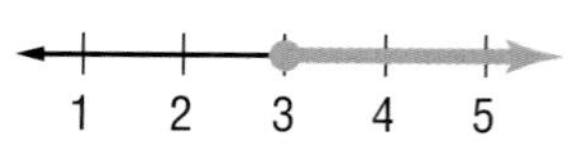

The closed circle means the number 3 is included in the graph.

CHECK Your Progress

Graph each inequality on a number line.

h. $x > 2$ **i.** $x < 1$ **j.** $x \leq 5$ **k.** $x \geq -4$

CHECK Your Understanding

Examples 1–4 (p. 441)

Write an inequality for each sentence.

1. **DRIVING** Your speed must be 55 miles per hour or less.
2. **BOARD GAMES** The game is recommended for ages greater than 6.

Examples 5, 6 (p. 442)

For the given value, state whether each inequality is *true* or *false*.

3. $x - 11 < 9, x = 20$
4. $42 \geq 6a, a = 8$
5. $\frac{n}{3} + 1 \leq 6; n = 15$

Examples 7, 8 (p. 442)

Graph each inequality on a number line.

6. $n > 4$
7. $p \leq 2$
8. $x \geq 0$
9. $a < 7$

Practice and Problem Solving

HOMEWORK HELP

For Exercises	See Examples
10–15	1–4
16–21	5, 6
22–29	7, 8

Write an inequality for each sentence.

10. **GOVERNMENT** To be a U.S. senator, you must be 30 years of age or older.
11. **TIPPING** For a group of 10 or more, an 18% tip is already included.
12. **CAPACITY** The maximum occupancy must be less than 512 people.
13. **PHONES** The phone costs no more than $25.
14. **SHOPPING** You must spend more than $50 to receive a discount.
15. **WRESTLING** The heavyweight division is greater than 200 pounds.

For the given value, state whether each inequality is *true* or *false*.

16. $12 + a < 20, a = 9$
17. $15 - k > 6, k = 8$
18. $-3y < 21; y = 8$
19. $32 \leq 2x, x = 16$
20. $\frac{n}{4} \geq 5, n = 12$
21. $\frac{-18}{x} > 9, x = -2$

Graph each inequality on a number line.

22. $x > 6$
23. $a > 0$
24. $y < 8$
25. $h < 2$
26. $w \leq 3$
27. $p \geq 7$
28. $1 \leq n$
29. $4 \geq d$

SPORTS For Exercises 30–33, use the graph that shows the number of children ages 5–14 treated recently in U.S. emergency rooms.

30. In which sport(s) were more than 150,000 children injured?
31. In which sport(s) were at least 75,000 children injured?
32. Of the sports listed, which have fewer than 100,000 injuries?
33. Write an inequality comparing the number treated for soccer-related injuries with those treated for football-related injuries.

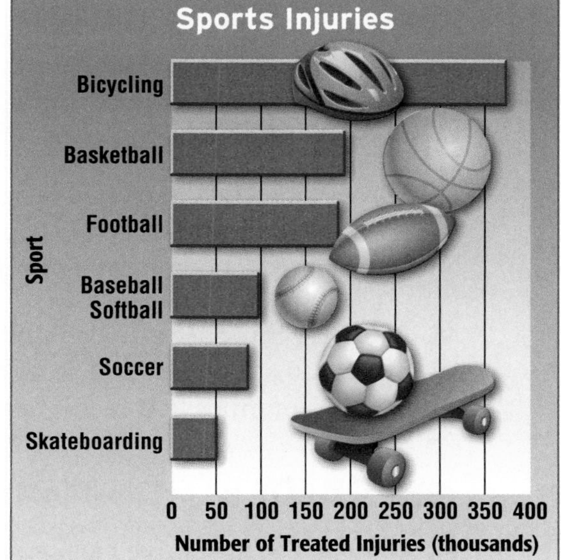

Source: Children's Hospital of Pittsburgh

ILS • ISAT
Extra Practice, pp. 690, 707

H.O.T. Problems

34. **FIND THE ERROR** Isabelle and Marcos are writing an inequality for the expression *at least 2 hours of homework*. Who is correct? Explain.

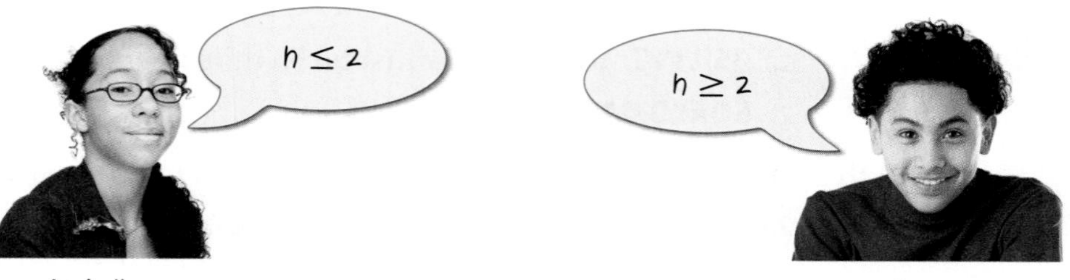

Isabelle

Marcos

35. **CHALLENGE** If $x = 3$, is the following inequality true or false? Explain.

$$\frac{108}{12} + x \geq 15 - 4x + 9$$

36. **WRITING IN MATH** If $a < b$ and $b < c$, what is true about the relationship between a and c? Explain your reasoning and give examples using both positive and negative values for a, b, and c.

ISAT PRACTICE 8.A.3b, 8.D.3a

37. Conner can spend no more than 4 hours at the swimming pool today. Which graph represents the time that Conner can spend at the pool?

A
B
C
D

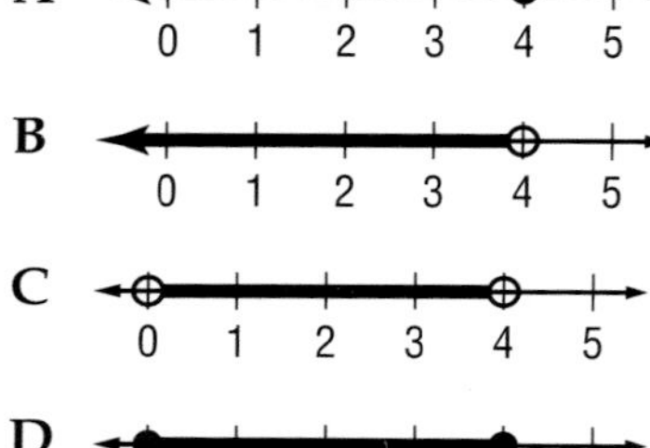

38. Which inequality matches the sentence below?

Members must be 18 years of age or older.

F $m > 18$

G $m \geq 18$

H $m < 18$

J $m \leq 18$

Spiral Review

39. **SOUVENIRS** The Green Gables gift shop sells regular postcards in packages of 5 and large postcards in packages of 3. If Román bought 16 postcards, how many packages of each did he buy? (Lesson 8-5)

40. **ALGEBRA** Suppose you can rent a car for either \$35 a day plus \$0.40 a mile or for \$20 a day plus \$0.55 per mile. Write and solve an equation to find the number of miles that result in the same cost for one day. (Lesson 8-4)

GET READY for the Next Lesson

PREREQUISITE SKILL **Solve each equation.** (Lesson 1-8)

41. $y + 15 = 31$

42. $n + 4 = -7$

43. $a - 8 = 25$

44. $-12 = x - 3$

Solving Inequalities by Adding or Subtracting

MAIN IDEA

Solve inequalities by using the Addition or Subtraction Properties of Inequality.

IL Learning Standards

8.A.3b Solve problems using linear expressions, equations and **inequalities. 8.D.3a Solve problems using numeric,** graphic **or symbolic representations of variables,** expressions, equations **and inequalities.** *Also addresses 8.C.3.*

IL Math Online

glencoe.com

- Extra Examples
- Personal Tutor
- Self-Check Quiz

GET READY for the Lesson

WEATHER The temperature at 7 A.M. in three Pennsylvania cities is shown at the right. The temperature in Pittsburgh is less than the temperature in Philadelphia. If the temperature rises 5° in both cities, will this still be true?

Temperature (°F)	
Erie, PA	26°
Philadelphia, PA	39°
Pittsburgh, PA	27°

1. Add 5 to both sides of the inequality $27 < 39$. Write the resulting inequality and decide whether it is *true* or *false*.
2. Would it be colder in Erie or Philadelphia if the temperature in both cities dropped 10°? Explain.

The examples above demonstrate properties of inequality. These properties are also true for $a \geq b$ and $a \leq b$.

Properties of Inequality — Key Concept

Words When you add or subtract the same number from each side of an inequality, the inequality remains true.

Symbols For all numbers *a*, *b*, and *c*,
1. if $a > b$, then $a + c > b + c$ and $a - c > b - c$.
2. if $a < b$, then $a + c < b + c$ and $a - c < b - c$.

Examples

$$2 > -3 \qquad\qquad 3 < 8$$
$$2 + 5 > -3 + 5 \qquad\qquad 3 - 4 < 8 - 4$$
$$7 > 2 \ ✓ \qquad\qquad -1 < 4 \ ✓$$

Solving an inequality means finding the values of the variable that make the inequality true.

EXAMPLES Solving Inequalities

1 **Solve $n - 8 < 15$. Check your solution.**

$n - 8 < 15$ Write the inequality.

$n - 8 + 8 < 15 + 8$ Add 8 to each side.

$n < 23$ Simplify.

Check $n - 8 < 15$ Write the inequality.

$22 - 8 \stackrel{?}{<} 15$ Replace *n* with a number less than 23, such as 22.

$14 < 15$ ✓ This statement is true.

The solution is $n < 23$.

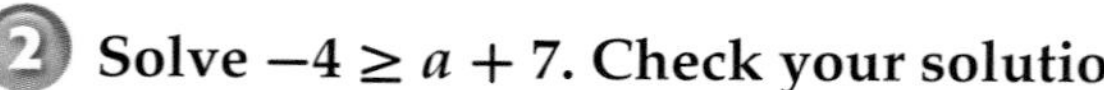

2 Solve $-4 \geq a + 7$. Check your solution.

$-4 \geq a + 7$	Write the inequality.
$-4 - 7 \geq a + 7 - 7$	Subtract 7 from each side.
$-11 \geq a$ or $a \leq -11$	Simplify.

Check Replace a in the original inequality with -11 and then with a number less than -11.

The solution is $a \leq -11$.

Study Tip

Equivalent Inequalities If -11 is greater than or equal to a, then a is less than or equal to -11.

CHECK Your Progress

a. $t + 3 > 12$ b. $n + \frac{1}{2} \geq 4$ c. $y - 1.5 < 2$

ISAT EXAMPLE 8.A.3b, 8.D.3a

3 The Airbus A380 can seat up to 853 passengers. Suppose there are currently 632 passengers boarded on the airplane. Which inequality indicates how many more people are able to board?

A $p < 221$ **B** $p > 221$ **C** $p \leq 221$ **D** $p \geq 221$

Read the Item

The phrase *up to* means *less than or equal to.*

Solve the Item

Let p = the number of passengers left to board.

Estimate $850 - 650 = 200$

Current passengers	plus	passengers left to board	is less than or equal to	853 total passengers.
↓	↓	↓	↓	↓
632	+	p	$\leq$	853

$632 + p \leq 853$	Write the inequality.
$632 - 632 + p \leq 853 - 632$	Subtract 632 from each side.
$p \leq 221$	Simplify.

Check for Reasonableness $200 \approx 221$ ✓

The answer is C.

Real-World Link The Airbus A380 is one of the largest airplanes in the world.

CHECK Your Progress

d. A tornado is classified using the Fujita Tornado Damage Scale, the F-Scale. An F1 tornado has wind speeds that are at least 73 miles per hour. An F2 tornado has wind speeds that are at least 113 miles per hour. Which inequality indicates how much the winds of an F1 tornado need to increase so it becomes at least an F2 tornado?

F $x \geq 40$ **G** $x < 40$ **H** $x \leq 40$ **J** $x > 40$

CHECK Your Understanding

Examples 1–2 (pp. 445–446)

Solve each inequality. Check your solution.

1. $b + 5 > 9$
2. $12 + n \leq 4$
3. $x - 4 < 10$
4. Write an inequality for *three more than a number is at most 15.* Then solve.

Example 3 (p. 446)

5. **MULTIPLE CHOICE** A certain city receives an average of 37 inches of rain per year, and there has been 13 inches of rain so far this year. Which inequality indicates how much more rainfall the city can get and stay at or within the average?

   A $r < 24$ **B** $r > 24$ **C** $r \leq 24$ **D** $r \geq 24$

Practice and Problem Solving

HOMEWORK HELP	
For Exercises	See Examples
6–27	1, 2
28, 29	3

Solve each inequality. Check your solution.

6. $5 + x \leq 18$
7. $10 + n \geq -2$
8. $-4 < k + 6$
9. $3 < y + 8$
10. $c + 10 < 9$
11. $g - 4 \geq 13$
12. $-2 < b - 6$
13. $s - 12 \leq -5$
14. $t - 3 < -9$
15. $-10 \geq x + 6$
16. $a - 3 \leq 5$
17. $-11 > g - 4$
18. $2 + m \geq 3.5$
19. $q + 0.8 \leq -0.5$
20. $v - 6 > 2.7$
21. $p - 4.8 > -6$
22. $d - \frac{2}{3} \leq \frac{1}{2}$
23. $5 > f + 1\frac{1}{4}$

Write an inequality and solve each problem.

24. Five more than a number is at least 13.
25. The difference between a number and 11 is less than 8.
26. Nine less than a number is more than 4.
27. The sum of a number and 17 is no more than 6.
28. **BASKETBALL** Suppose Amos, who is 15 years old, is thinking about joining the City Basketball League. Write and solve an inequality to determine how many years until he is able to join.

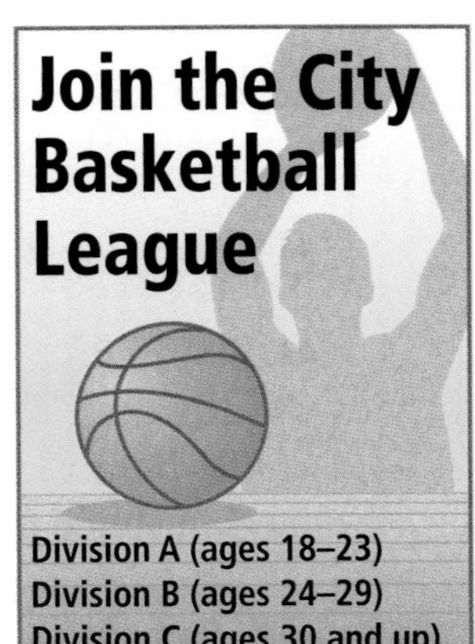

29. **ANIMALS** Hippos usually weigh up to 5,300 pounds. Write and solve an inequality that describes how much weight a young hippo is likely to gain if its current weight is 2,200 pounds.
30. **ART** Suppose an artist had a total of 67 paintings, but sold 34 of them at an auction. Write and solve an inequality that describes how many more paintings, at most, the artist has left to sell.

31. **MEASUREMENT** The height of the parallelogram is greater than its base. Write and solve an inequality to find the possible values of x. Interpret the solution.

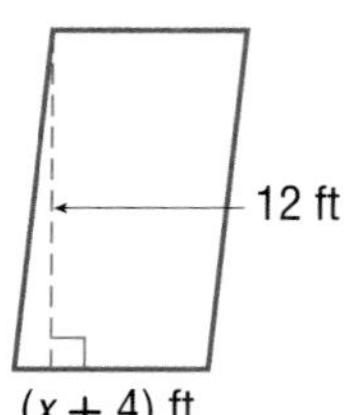

ILS • ISAT
Extra Practice, pp. 690, 707

32. **FIND THE DATA** Refer to the Data File on pages 16–19. Choose some data and write a real-world problem in which you would need to solve an inequality using addition or subtraction.

H.O.T. Problems

CHALLENGE Determine whether each equation or inequality has no solution, one solution, or more than one solution.

33. $y - y = 0$

34. $x + 4 = 9$

35. $x + 4 > 9$

36. $y > y + 1$

37. **OPEN ENDED** Write 2 different inequalities that each have the solution $x < 9$. One inequality should be solved using addition properties, and the other inequality should be solved using subtraction properties.

38. **WRITING IN MATH** Write a word problem that would have the solution $w < 200$.

ISAT PRACTICE 8.A.3b, 8.D.3a

39. **SHORT RESPONSE** Crystal has \$80 to go clothes shopping. She spent \$25 on a new shirt. Write an inequality that represents how much money she has left to spend on clothes.

40. If $w + 4 > 31$, then w could be which of the following values?

A 45

B 18

C 17

D 16

Spiral Review

For the given value, state whether each inequality is *true* or *false*. (Lesson 8-5)

41. $18 - n > 4, n = 11$

42. $13 + x < 21, x = 8$

43. $34 \leq 5p, p = 7$

44. **ALGEBRA** A family membership to the zoo costs \$75 per year and covers admission, but not the \$3 parking fee. Regular admission is \$7 per person. Write and solve an equation to determine how many trips to the zoo a family of four could make for the cost of a membership to equal regular admission. (Lesson 8-4)

GET READY for the Next Lesson

PREREQUISITE SKILL Solve each equation. (Lesson 1-9)

45. $3y = -15$

46. $-18 = -2a$

47. $\frac{w}{4} = 12$

8-8 Solving Inequalities by Multiplying or Dividing

MAIN IDEA

Solve inequalities by using the Multiplication or Division Properties of Inequality.

IL Learning Standards

8.A.3b Solve problems using linear expressions, equations and **inequalities. 8.D.3a Solve problems using numeric, graphic or symbolic representations of variables,** expressions, equations **and inequalities.** *Also addresses 8.C.3.*

IL Math Online

glencoe.com

- Extra Examples
- Personal Tutor
- Self-Check Quiz

GET READY for the Lesson

COINS Lamar, Mario, and Nick put the money from their pockets on the table. Lamar had more money than Nick since \$1.70 > \$1.40. Will this still be true if each boy donates half their money to the school fundraiser?

Name	Amount of Money
Lamar	1 dollar bill, 2 quarters, 2 dimes
Mario	1 dollar bill, 3 quarters, 1 dime, 1 nickel
Nick	5 quarters, 1 dime, 1 nickel

1. Divide each side of the inequality 1.70 > 1.40 by 2. Write the resulting inequality and decide if it is *true* or *false*.
2. Who would have more if Mario and Lamar tripled their money by doing lawn work at home? Explain.

The examples above demonstrate additional properties of inequality. These properties are also true for $a \geq b$ and $a \leq b$.

Properties of Inequality — Key Concept

Words When you multiply or divide each side of an inequality by a positive number, the inequality remains true.

Symbols For all numbers a, b, and c, where $c > 0$,

1. if $a > b$, then $ac > bc$ and $\frac{a}{c} > \frac{b}{c}$.

2. if $a < b$, then $ac < bc$ and $\frac{a}{c} < \frac{b}{c}$.

Examples

$5 < 8$ | $2 > -10$

$4(5) < 4(8)$ | $\frac{2}{2} > \frac{-10}{2}$

$20 < 32$ | $1 > -5$

Study Tip

Checking Solutions You can check the solution in Example 1 by substituting numbers greater than −6 into the inequality and testing it to verify that it holds true.

EXAMPLE Solve Inequalities by Dividing

1 Solve $7y > -42$. Check your solution.

$7y > -42$ Write the inequality.

$\frac{7y}{7} > \frac{-42}{7}$ Divide each side by 7.

$y > -6$ Simplify.

The solution is $y > -6$.

EXAMPLE Solve Inequalities by Multiplying

2 **Solve $\frac{1}{3}x \leq 8$. Check your solution.**

$\frac{1}{3}x \leq 8$ Write the inequality.

$3\left(\frac{1}{3}x\right) \leq 3(8)$ Multiply each side by 3.

$x \leq 24$ Simplify.

The solution is $x \leq 24$. You can check this solution by substituting 24 and a number less than 24 into the inequality.

CHECK Your Progress

Solve each inequality. Check your solution.

a. $3a \geq 45$

b. $\frac{n}{4} < -16$

c. $81 \leq 9p$

What happens when each side of an inequality is multiplied or divided by a negative number?

Graph 3 and 5 on a number line.

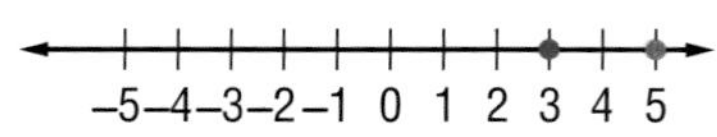

Since 3 is to the left of 5, $3 < 5$.

Multiply each number by -1.

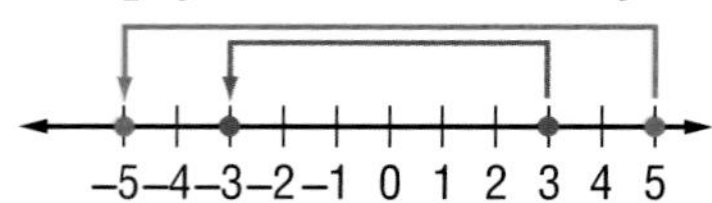

Since -3 is to the right of -5, $-3 > -5$.

Notice that the numbers being compared switched positions as a result of being multiplied by a negative number. In other words, their order reversed.

These and other examples suggest the following properties. These properties also hold true for $a \geq b$ and $a \leq b$.

Properties of Inequality

Key Concept

Words When you multiply or divide each side of an inequality by a negative number, the direction of the inequality symbol must be reversed for the inequality to remain true.

Symbols For all numbers a, b, and c, where $c < 0$,

1. if $a > b$, then $ac < bc$ and $\frac{a}{c} < \frac{b}{c}$.
2. if $a < b$, then $ac > bc$ and $\frac{a}{c} > \frac{b}{c}$.

Examples

$8 > 5$

$-1(8) < -1(5)$ Reverse the inequality symbols.

$-8 < -5$

$-3 < 9$

$\frac{-3}{-3} > \frac{9}{-3}$

$1 > -3$

Study Tip

Common Error Do not reverse the inequality symbol just because there is a negative sign in the inequality, as in $7y < -42$. Only reverse the inequality symbol when you *multiply* or *divide* each side by a negative number.

EXAMPLES Multiply or Divide by a Negative Number

3 **Solve $\frac{a}{-2} \geq 8$. Check your solution.**

$\frac{a}{-2} \geq 8$	Write the inequality.
$-2\left(\frac{a}{-2}\right) \leq -2(8)$	Multiply each side by −2 and reverse the inequality symbol.
$a \leq -16$	Check this result.

4 **Solve $-24 > -6n$. Check your solution.**

$-24 > -6n$	Write the inequality.
$\frac{-24}{-6} < \frac{-6n}{-6}$	Divide each side by −6 and reverse the symbol.
$4 < n$ or $n > 4$	Check this result.

d. $\frac{c}{-7} < -14$ **e.** $-5d \geq 30$ **f.** $-3 \leq \frac{w}{-8}$

Real-World Link Ichiro Suzuki holds the major league record for most hits in a single season. In 2004, he had a total of 262 hits.

Source: Major League Baseball

Some inequalities involve more than one operation. To solve, work backward as you did in solving two-step equations.

Real-World EXAMPLE

5 **BASEBALL Manny was trying to break his school's record by getting 61 hits in one season. Halfway through the season he already had 34 hits. Manny averages 2 hits per game. Write and solve an inequality to find how many more games it will take at that rate for Manny to have at least 61 hits. Interpret the solution.**

The phrase *at least* means *greater than or equal to.* Let g = the number of games he needs to play. Then write an inequality.

$34 + 2g \geq 61$	Write the inequality.
$34 - 34 + 2g \geq 61 - 34$	Subtract 34 from each side.
$2g \geq 27$	Simplify.
$\frac{2g}{2} \geq \frac{27}{2}$	Divide each side by 2.
$g \geq 13.5$	Simplify.

If Manny plays only entire games, he should have 61 hits after 14 more games. Manny should break the record.

CHECK Your Progress

g. **DVDs** Joan has a total of \$250. DVDs cost \$18.95 each. Write and solve an inequality to find how many DVDs she can buy and still have at least \$50. Interpret the solution.

CHECK Your Understanding

Examples 1–2 (pp. 449–450)

Solve each inequality. Check your solution.

1. $3x > 12$
2. $\frac{3}{4} < \frac{7}{9}y$
3. $8x \leq -72$
4. $\frac{h}{4} \geq -6$

Examples 3–4 (p. 451)

5. $-4y > 32$
6. $-56 \leq -7p$
7. $\frac{g}{-2} < -7$
8. $\frac{d}{-3} \geq -3$

Example 5 (p. 451)

9. **RENTAL CARS** A rental car company charges \$45 plus an additional \$0.19 per mile to rent a car. If Lawrence does not want to spend more than \$100 for his rental car, write and solve an inequality to find how many miles he can drive and not spend more than \$100. Interpret the solution.

Practice and Problem Solving

HOMEWORK HELP

For Exercises	See Examples
10–15	1, 2
16–27	3, 4
28–29	5

Solve each inequality. Check your solution.

10. $5x < 15$
11. $9n \leq 45$
12. $14k \geq -84$
13. $-12 > 3g$
14. $-100 \leq 50p$
15. $2y < -22$
16. $-4w \geq 20$
17. $-3r > 9$
18. $-72 < -12h$
19. $-6c \geq -6$
20. $\frac{v}{-4} > 4$
21. $\frac{a}{-3} \geq 5$
22. $\frac{x}{9} \leq -3$
23. $\frac{n}{7} < -14$
24. $\frac{m}{-2} < -7$
25. $\frac{t}{-5} \leq -2$
26. $-8 \leq \frac{y}{0.2}$
27. $\frac{-1}{2}k > -10$

28. **GYM MEMBERSHIP** A local gym charges \$5 each time you enter. They also have yearly memberships for \$190. Write and solve an inequality to find how many times a person should use the gym so that a yearly membership is less expensive than paying each time. Interpret the solution.

29. **WORK** Max charges \$6.25 an hour to rake leaves. He is trying to save enough money for a new pair of shoes that cost \$89. Write and solve an inequality to find how many whole hours Max must work to buy the shoes. Interpret the solution.

Solve each inequality. Graph the solution set on a number line.

30. $6y > 15 + y$
31. $8k + 3 \leq -5$
32. $-5g + 5 \geq -7 - 2g$
33. $7 + \frac{n}{3} < 4$
34. $\frac{w}{8} - 4 \leq -5$
35. $10 - 3x \geq 25 + 2x$

Write an inequality for each sentence. Then solve the inequality.

36. Three times a number increased by four is less than −62.
37. The quotient of a number and −5 increased by one is at most 7.
38. The quotient of a number and 3 minus two is at least −12.
39. The product of −2 and a number minus six is greater than −18.

ILS • ISAT

Extra Practice, pp. 691, 707

H.O.T. Problems

40. **OPEN ENDED** Write an inequality for the following sentence and then solve.

The quotient of a number and −6 increased by 5 is at most 9.

Name three numbers that are possible solutions for x. Explain.

41. **FIND THE ERROR** Sonia and Kendra each solved $7x \leq -49$. Who is correct? Explain.

Sonia	Kendra
$7x \leq -49$	$7x \leq -49$
$\frac{7x}{7} \geq \frac{-49}{7}$	$\frac{7x}{7} \leq \frac{-49}{7}$
$x \geq -7$	$x \leq -7$

42. **CHALLENGE** In five games, you score 16, 12, 15, 13, and 17 points. How many points must you score in the sixth game to have an average of at least 15 points?

43. **WRITING IN MATH** Explain when you should reverse the inequality symbol when solving an inequality.

ISAT PRACTICE 8.A.3b, 8.D.3a

44. Which is a possible value of x if the area of the trapezoid is less than 256 square feet?

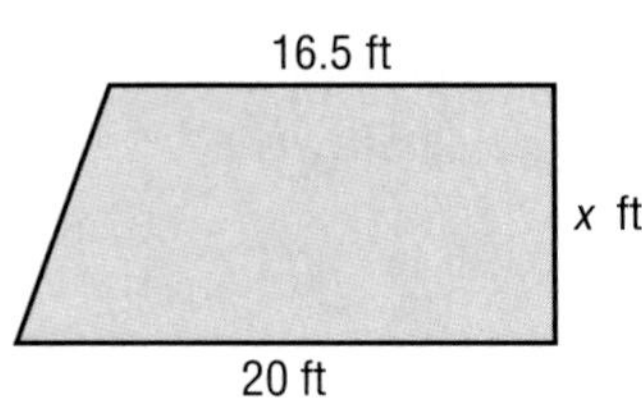

A 14

B 15

C 16

D 17

45. You want to purchase a necklace for \$325. You have already saved \$115 and can set aside \$22 a week. Which inequality can be used to find the number of weeks it will take to save at least \$325?

F $22w + 115 \geq 325$

G $22w + 115 \leq 325$

H $22 + 115w \leq 325$

J $22w + 115 < 325$

Spiral Review

Solve each inequality. Check your solution. (Lesson 8-7)

46. $y + 7 < 9$

47. $a - 5 \leq 2$

48. $j - 8 \geq -12$

49. $-14 > 8 + n$

Write an inequality for each sentence. (Lesson 8-6)

50. **SPEED** A minimum speed on a certain highway is 45 miles per hour.

51. **BIRDS** A hummingbird's wings can beat up to 200 times per second.

52. **MEASUREMENT** Three boxes with height 12 inches, width 10 inches, and length 13 inches are stacked on top of each other. What is the volume of the space that they occupy? (Lesson 7-5)

CHAPTER 8 Study Guide and Review

IL Math Online glencoe.com
- STUDY TO GO
- Vocabulary Review

GET READY to Study

Be sure the following Big Ideas are noted in your Foldable.

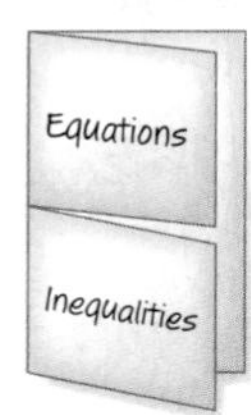

BIG Ideas

Algebraic Expressions (Lesson 8-1)
- Like terms contain the same variables to the same powers.
- A constant is a term without a variable.
- An algebraic expression is in simplest form if it has no like terms and no parentheses.

Equations (Lessons 8-2, 8-3, and 8-4)
- To solve a two-step equation, undo each operation in reverse order.
- To solve equations with variables on each side of the equals sign, use the Addition or Subtraction Property of Equality to write an equivalent equation with the variables on one side of the equals sign. Then solve the equation.

Inequalities (Lesson 8-6)
- When used to compare a variable and a number, inequalities can describe a range of values.

Inequality Properties (Lessons 8-7 and 8-8)
- When you add or subtract the same number from each side of an inequality, the inequality remains true.
- When you multiply or divide each side of an inequality by a positive number, the inequality remains true.
- When you multiply or divide each side of an inequality by a negative number, the direction of the symbol must be reversed for the inequality to be true.

Key Vocabulary

coefficient (p. 417)
constant (p. 417)
equivalent expressions (p. 416)
like terms (p. 417)
simplest form (p. 418)
simplifying the expression (p. 418)
term (p. 417)
two-step equation (p. 422)

Vocabulary Check

State whether each sentence is *true* or *false*. If *false*, replace the underlined word(s) to make a true sentence.

1. Like terms are terms that contain <u>different</u> variables.
2. A <u>two-step equation</u> is an equation that contains two operations.
3. A <u>coefficient</u> is a term without a variable.
4. The numerical factor of a term that contains a variable is called the <u>constant</u> of the variable.
5. When plus or minus signs separate an algebraic expression into parts, each part is called a <u>term</u>.
6. An algebraic expression is in <u>simplest form</u> if it has no like terms and no parentheses.
7. The expressions $4(y + 7)$ and $4y + 28$ are <u>two-step equations</u>.
8. When you use the Distributive Property to combine like terms, you are <u>simplifying the expression</u>.

Lesson-by-Lesson Review

8-1 Simplifying Algebraic Expressions (pp. 416–421)

8.A.3a, 8.A.3b

Use the Distributive Property to rewrite each expression.

9. $4(a + 3)$
10. $(n - 5)(-7)$

Simplify each expression.

11. $p + 6p$
12. $6b - 3 + 7b + 5$
13. **SOCCER** Pam scored n goals. Leo scored 5 fewer than Pam. Write an expression in simplest form to represent the total number of goals scored.

Example 1 Use the Distributive Property to rewrite $-8(x - 9)$.

$-8(x - 9)$	Write the expression.
$= -8[x + (-9)]$	Rewrite $x - 9$ as $x + (-9)$.
$= -8(x) + (-8)(-9)$	Distributive Property
$= -8x + 72$	Simplify.

8-2 Solving Two-Step Equations (pp. 422–426)

8.A.3b, 8.D.3a

Solve each equation. Check your solution.

14. $2x + 5 = 17$
15. $4 = -3y - 2$
16. $\frac{c}{5} + 2 = 9$
17. $39 = a + 6a + 11$
18. **ZOO** Four adults spend \$37 for admission and \$3 for parking at the zoo. Solve the equation $4a + 3 = 40$ to find the cost of admission per person.

Example 2 Solve $5h + 8 = -12$.

$5h + 8 = -12$	Write the equation.
$5h + 8 - 8 = -12 - 8$	Subtract 8 from each side.
$5h = -20$	$-12 - 8 = -12 + (-8)$ or 20
$\frac{5h}{5} = \frac{-20}{5}$	Divide each side by 5.
$h = -4$	Simplify.
The solution is -4.	Check this solution.

8-3 Writing Two-Step Equations (pp. 427–431)

8.A.3b, 8.D.3a

Translate each sentence into an equation.

19. Six more than twice a number is -4.
20. The quotient of a number and 8, less 2, is 5.
21. **MEDICINE** Dr. Miles recommended that Jerome take 8 tablets on the first day and then 4 tablets each day until the prescription was used. The prescription contained 28 tablets. How many days will Jerome be taking tablets after the first day? Write an equation and then solve.

Example 3 Translate the following sentence into an equation. Then solve.

6 less than 4 times a number is equal to 10.

6 less than	4 times a number	is	10.
	$4n - 6$	$=$	10

$4n - 6 = 10$	Write the equation.
$4n - 6 + 6 = 10 + 6$	Add 6 to each side.
$4n = 16$	Simplify.
$\frac{4n}{4} = \frac{16}{4}$	Divide each side by 4.
$n = 4$	Simplify.

8-4 Solving Equations with Variables on Each Side (pp. 434–437)

8.A.3b, 8.D.3a

Solve each equation. Check your solution.

22. $11x = 20x + 18$
23. $4n + 13 = n - 8$
24. $7b - 3 = -2b + 24$
25. $9 - 2y = 8y - 6$
26. **GEOGRAPHY** The coastline of California is 46 miles longer than twice the length of Louisiana's coastline. It is also 443 miles longer than Louisiana's coastline. Find the lengths of the coastlines of California and Louisiana.

Example 4 **Solve $-7x + 5 = x - 19$.**

$-7x + 5 = x - 19$ Write the equation.

$-7x + 7x + 5 = x + 7x - 19$ Add $7x$ to each side.

$5 = 8x - 19$

$5 + 19 = 8x - 19 + 19$ Add 19 to each side.

$24 = 8x$

$\frac{24}{8} = \frac{8x}{8}$ Divide each side by 8.

$3 = x$ Simplify.

The solution is 3.

8-5 PSI: Guess and Check (pp. 438–439)

6.B.3a, 6.C.3a

Solve using the *guess and check* strategy.

27. **FUNDRAISER** The Science Club sold candy bars and pretzels to raise money. They raised a total of \$62.75. If they made \$0.25 on each candy bar and \$0.30 on each pretzel, how many of each did they sell?
28. **FOOD** A store sells apples in 2-pound bags and oranges in 5-pound bags. How many bags of each should you buy if you need exactly 11 pounds of apples and oranges?
29. **BONES** Each hand in the human body has 27 bones. There are 6 more bones in the fingers than in the wrist. There are 3 fewer bones in the palm than in the wrist. How many bones are in each part of the hand?

Example 5 **The product of two consecutive even whole numbers is 1,088. What are the whole numbers?**

The product is close to 1,000.

Make a guess. Try 24 and 26.

$24 \times 26 = 624$ This product is too low.

Adjust the guess upward. Try 30 and 32.

$30 \times 32 = 960$ This product is still too low.

Adjust the guess upward again. Try 34 and 36.

$34 \times 36 = 1,224$ This product is too high.

Try between 30 and 34. Try 32 and 34.

$32 \times 34 = 1,088$ This is the correct product.

The numbers are 32 and 34.

Mixed Problem Solving
For mixed problem-solving practice, see page 707.

8-6 Inequalities (pp. 441–444)

8.A.3b, 8.D.3a

Write an inequality for each sentence.

30. **SPORTS** Participants must be at least 12 years old to play.
31. **PARTY** No more than 15 people at the party.

For the given value, state whether each inequality is *true* or *false*.

32. $19 - a < 20, a = 18$
33. $9 + k > 16, k = 6$

Graph the inequality on a number line.

34. $t < 2$
35. $g \geq 92$
36. **NUTRITION** A food can be labeled low-fat only if it has no more than 3 grams of fat per serving. Write an inequality to describe low-fat foods.

Example 6 **All movie tickets are \$9 and less. Write an inequality for this situation.**

Let t = the cost of a ticket.

$t \leq 9$

Example 7 **Graph the inequality $a < -4$ on a number line.**

Place an open circle at −4.

Then draw a line and an arrow to the left.

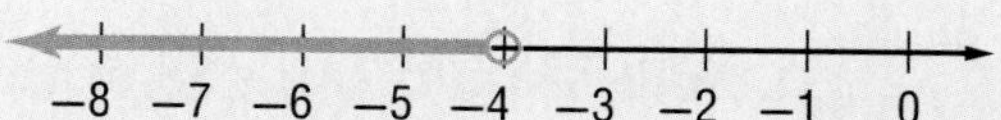

8-7 Solving Inequalities by Adding or Subtracting (pp. 445-448)

8.A.3b, 8.D.3a

Solve each inequality. Check your solution.

37. $b - 9 \geq 8$
38. $15 > 3 + n$
39. $x + 4.8 \leq 2$
40. $r + 5.7 \leq 6.1$
41. $t + \frac{1}{2} < 4$
42. $-1\frac{2}{5} < k - 3$
43. **MOVING** A moving company is loading a 920-pound piano into a service elevator. The elevator can carry a maximum of 1,800 pounds. Write and solve an inequality to determine how much additional weight the elevator can carry.

Example 8 **Solve $x - 7 < 3$. Check your solution.**

	$x - 7 < 3$	Write the inequality.
	$x - 7 + 7 < 3 + 7$	Add 7 to each side.
	$x < 10$	Simplify.
Check	$x - 7 < 3$	Write the inequality.
	$9 - 7 \stackrel{?}{<} 3$	Replace x with a number less than 10, such as 9.
	$2 < 3$ ✓	This statement is true.

8-8 Solving Inequalities by Multiplying and Dividing (pp. 449-453)

8.A.3b, 8.D.3a

Solve each inequality.

44. $\frac{n}{4} < 6$

45. $\frac{k}{1.7} \leq 3$

46. $0.5x > 3.2$

47. $-56 \geq 8y$

48. $9 > \frac{x}{-4}$

49. $-\frac{5}{6}a \leq 2$

50. **GOLF** Aubrey wants to spend less than $38.50 on new golf balls. If each box costs $11, what is the maximum number of boxes of golf balls that she can buy?

51. **JOBS** Dakota earns $8 per hour working at a landscaping company and wants to earn at least $1,200 this summer.
    a. Write an inequality to represent this situation.
    b. Solve the inequality that you found in part a.
    c. What is the minimum number of hours Dakota will have to work?

Example 9 **Solve $-2n \geq 26$. Check your solution.**

$-2n \geq 26$	Write the inequality.
$\frac{-2n}{-2} \leq \frac{26}{-2}$	Divide each side by −2 and reverse the symbol.
$n \leq -13$	Simplify.

The solution is $n \leq -13$. You can check this solution by substituting −13 and a number less than −13 into the inequality.

Practice Test

IL Math Online glencoe.com
• Chapter Test

Use the Distributive Property to rewrite each expression.

1. $-7(x - 10)$
2. $8(2y + 5)$

Simplify each expression.

3. $9a - a + 15 - 10a - 6$
4. $2x + 17x$

Solve each equation. Check your solution.

5. $3n + 18 = 6$
6. $\frac{k}{2} - 11 = 5$
7. $-23 = 3p + 5 + p$
8. $4x - 6 = 5x$
9. $-3a - 2 = 2a + 3$
10. $-2y + 5 = y - 1$

11. **SKATEBOARDING** A skate park charges $6 each time you skate. They also offer a membership for a one-time fee of $24 plus $2 for each time you skate. Write and solve an equation to determine how many times you would have to skate to break even when purchasing the membership.

Translate each sentence into an equation.

12. Three more than twice a number is 15.
13. The quotient of a number and 6 plus 3 is 11.
14. The product of a number and 5 less 7 is 18.

15. **MULTIPLE CHOICE** In the inequality $3x + \$5{,}000 \leq \$80{,}000$, x represents the salary of an employee at a factory. Which phrase most accurately describes the employee's salary?

    A less than $25,000
    B more than $25,000
    C at least $25,000
    D at most $25,000

Solve each equation. Check your solution.

16. $x + 5 = 4x + 26$
17. $3d = 18 - 3d$
18. $-2g + 15 = 45 - 8g$

19. **MUSICAL** Joseph sold tickets to the school musical. He had 12 bills worth $175 for the tickets sold. If all the money was in $5 bills, $10 bills, and $20 bills, how many of each bill did he have?

20. **BANKING** First Bank charges $4.50 per month for a basic checking account plus $0.15 for each check written. Citizen's Bank charges a flat fee of $9. How many checks would you have to write each month in order for the cost to be the same at both banks?

21. **MULTIPLE CHOICE** The perimeter of the rectangle is 44 inches.

    $x + 7$ in.
    $4x$ in.

    What is the area of the rectangle?

    F 22 in^2
    G 120 in^2
    H 392 in^2
    J 440 in^2

For Exercises 22 and 23, write an inequality and then graph the inequality on a number line.

22. **COMPUTERS** A recordable DVD can hold at most 4.7 gigabytes of data.

23. **GAMES** Your score must be over 55,400 to have the new high score.

Solve each inequality. Check your solution.

24. $-4 > \frac{c}{9}$
25. $-2g + 15 > 45$

CHAPTER 8

ISAT Practice

Cumulative, Chapters 1–8

IL Math Online glencoe.com

• Test Practice

PART 1 Multiple Choice

Read each question. Then fill in the correct answer on the answer sheet provided by your teacher or on a sheet of paper.

1. Which property is used in the equation below?

$$5(x - 2) = 5x - 10$$

A Associative Property of Addition

B Commutative Property of Addition

C Distributive Property

D Reflexive Property

2. A farmer packs tomatoes in boxes that weigh 1.4 kilograms when empty. The average tomato weighs 0.2 kilogram and the total weight of a box filled with tomatoes is 11 kilograms. How many tomatoes are packed in each box?

F 62

G 55

H 48

J 13.6

3. There are 4 children in the Owens family. Jamie is $1\frac{1}{2}$ times as tall as Kelly, and he is 6 inches taller than Olivia. Sammy is 56 inches tall, which is 2 inches taller than Olivia. Find Jamie's height.

A 52 inches

B 56 inches

C 58 inches

D 60 inches

4. The sum of a number n and 6 is 23. Which equation shows this relationship?

F $23 + n = 6$

G $6n = 23$

H $n + 6 = 23$

J $n - 6 = 23$

5. Orlando, Eddie, and Dante scored a total of 108 touchdowns this season. Eddie scored 8 more touchdowns than Dante, and Orlando scored twice as many touchdowns as Dante. Which is a reasonable conclusion about the number of touchdowns scored by the players?

A Eddie scored the most touchdowns.

B Orlando scored the most touchdowns.

C Dante scored exactly half of the total number of touchdowns.

D Dante scored the most touchdowns.

6. The largest possible circle is to be cut from a 2 meter board. What will be the approximate area, in square meters, of the remaining board (shaded region)? ($A = \pi r^2$ and $\pi \approx 3.14$)

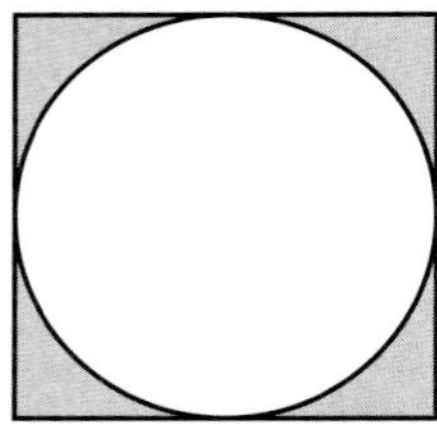

2 meters

F 8.56

G 0.86

H 2.28

J 3.14

7. A rectangular prism has a length of 7.5 inches, a width of 1.4 inches, and a volume of 86.4 cubic inches. What is the height of the rectangular prism? Round to the nearest tenth.

A 0.1

B 8.2

C 462.9

D 907.2

Preparing for ISAT

For test-taking strategies and practice, see pages 712–729.

8. Which expression is equivalent to $2ab + 4ac$?

   F $6abc$
   G $ab + ac$
   H $2a(b + c)$
   J $2a(b + 2c)$

9. About how much paper is needed to make a label that covers only the sides of the soup can shown below? Use 3.14 for π and round to the nearest square inch.

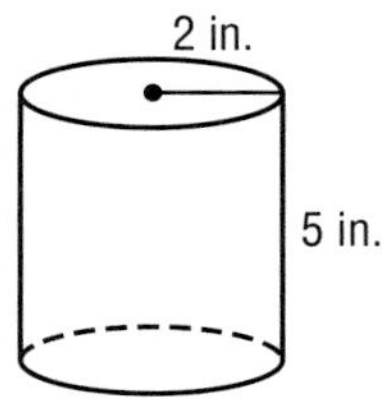

   A 31 in^2
   B 62 in^2
   C 63 in^2
   D 72 in^2

TEST-TAKING TIP

Question 9 When answering a test question involving a 3-dimensional shape, always study the shape and its labels carefully. Ask yourself, "Am I finding surface area or volume?"

10. What is the value of x if $-5x - 4 = -34$?

   F -7
   G -6
   H 6
   J 7

11. $\sqrt{625} =$

   A 15
   B 25
   C 30
   D 35

PART 2 Short Response/Grid In

Record your answers on the answer sheet provided by your teacher or on a sheet of paper.

12. In the figure below, every angle is a right angle. What is the area in square units?

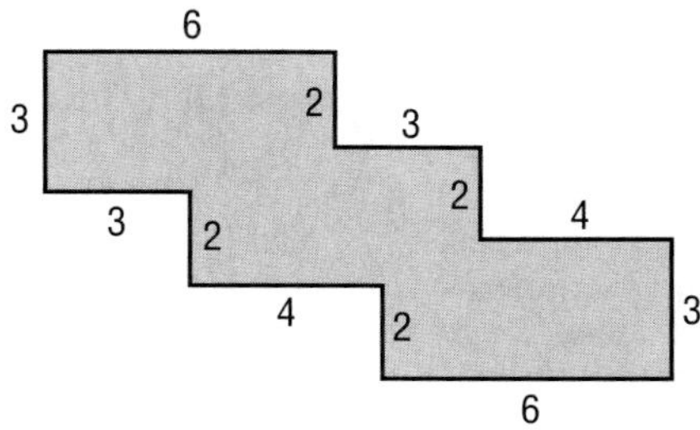

13. During the annual food drive, 60% of the students at Blackfoot Middle School donated at least one canned food item. If there are 600 students at Blackfoot Middle School, how many students did *not* participate in the food drive?

PART 3 Extended Response

Record your answers on the answer sheet provided by your teacher or on a sheet of paper. Show your work.

14. Emily and Shawn are saving money to go to the amusement park. Emily's parents gave her \$10 and then she saves \$7 dollars a week. Shawn saves \$12 a week.

   a. Write an equation to find the number of weeks it will take before Emily and Shawn have saved the same amount.

   b. How many weeks will pass until they have saved the same amount?

NEED EXTRA HELP?														
If You Missed Question...	1	2	3	4	5	6	7	8	9	10	11	12	13	14
Go to Lesson...	8-1	8-2	1-9	1-7	1-1	7-1	7-5	8-1	7-7	8-2	3-1	7-3	5-7	8-4
IL Learning Standards	8.A.3a	8.A.3b	8.A.3b	8.A.3a	6.B.3a	7.A.3b	7.A.3b	8.A.3a	7.C.3b	8.A.3b	6.B.3c	7.A.3b	8.A.3b	8.A.3b

CHAPTER 9

Algebra: Linear Functions

Illinois Learning Standards

8.B.3 Use graphing technology and algebraic methods to analyze and predict linear relationships and make generalizations from linear patterns.
8.D.3b Propose and solve problems using proportions, formulas and linear functions.

Key Vocabulary

constant of variation (p. 487)
linear function (p. 476)
line of fit (p. 511)
slope (p. 481)

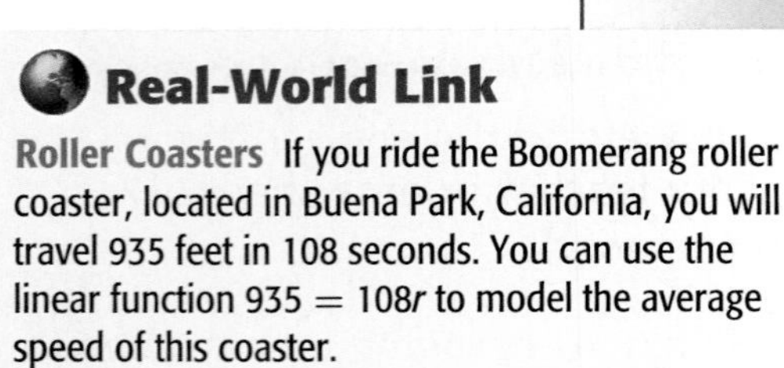

Real-World Link

Roller Coasters If you ride the Boomerang roller coaster, located in Buena Park, California, you will travel 935 feet in 108 seconds. You can use the linear function $935 = 108r$ to model the average speed of this coaster.

Algebra: Linear Functions Make this Foldable to help you organize your notes. Begin with seven sheets of $8\frac{1}{2}'' \times 11''$ paper.

1. **Fold** a sheet of paper in half lengthwise. Cut a 1″ tab along the left edge through one thickness.

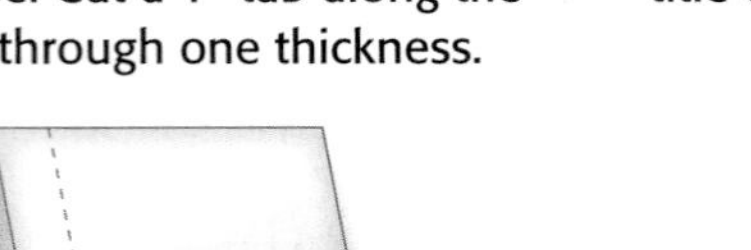

2. **Glue** the 1″ tab down. Write the title of the lesson on the front tab.

3. **Repeat** Steps 1–2 for the remaining sheets of paper. Staple together to form a booklet.

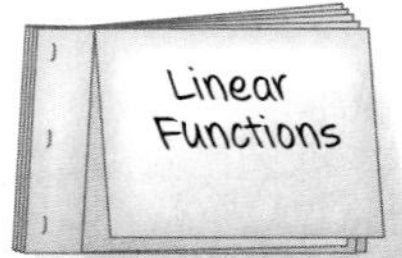

GET READY for Chapter 9

Diagnose Readiness You have two options for checking Prerequisite Skills.

Option 2

IL Math Online Take the Online Readiness Quiz at glencoe.com.

Option 1

Take the Quick Check below. Refer to the Quick Review for help.

QUICK Check

Graph each point on the same coordinate grid. (Prior Grade)

1. $A(-3, -4)$
2. $B(2, -1)$
3. $C(0, -2)$
4. $D(-4, 3)$
5. **WALKING** From his cabin, Derek walked 4 miles south and 2 miles west, where he rested. If the origin represents the cabin, graph the point representing Derek's resting point. (Prior Grade)

Evaluate each expression if $x = 6$. (Lesson 1-2)

6. $3x$
7. $4x - 9$
8. $2x + 8$
9. $5 + x$
10. **PROFIT** The weekly profit of a certain company is $48x - 875$, where x represents the number of units sold. Find the weekly profit, if the company sells 37 units. (Lesson 1-2)

Solve each equation. (Lesson 1-9)

11. $14 = n + 9$
12. $z - 3 = 8$
13. $-17 = b - 21$
14. $23 + r = 15$

QUICK Review

Example 1

Graph $P(-1, 2)$, $Q(3, -1)$, and $R(-4, 0)$ on a coordinate grid.

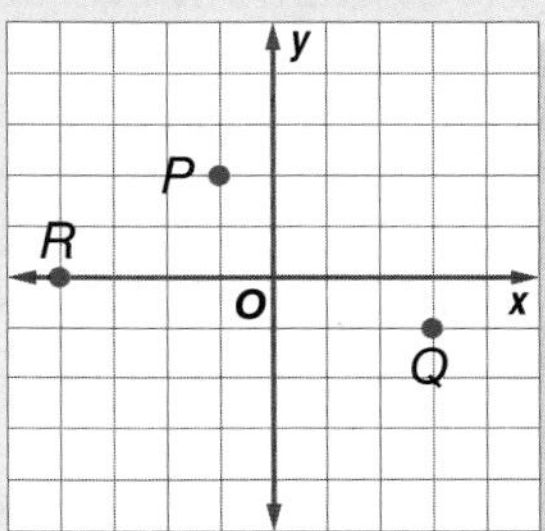

Start at the origin. The first number in each ordered pair is the x-coordinate. The second number in each ordered pair is the y-coordinate.

Example 2

Evaluate $6x - 1$ if $x = 4$.

$$6x - 1 = 6(4) - 1$$ Replace x with 4.

$$= 24 - 1$$ Multiply 6 by 4.

$$= 23$$ Subtract.

Example 3

Solve $18 + m = 7$.

$$18 + m = 7$$ Write the equation.

$$\underline{-18 \quad = -18}$$ Subtract 18 from each side.

$$m = -11$$

9-1 Sequences

MAIN IDEA

Write algebraic expressions to determine any term in an arithmetic sequence.

IL Learning Standards

8.B.3 Use graphing technology and **algebraic methods to analyze and predict linear relationships and make generalizations from linear patterns.**

New Vocabulary

sequence
term
arithmethic sequence
common difference

IL Math Online

glencoe.com

- Extra Examples
- Personal Tutor
- Self-Check Quiz

MINI Lab

Consider the following pattern.

Number of Triangles	1 triangle	2 triangles	3 triangles
Number of Toothpicks	3 toothpicks	5 toothpicks	7 toothpicks

1. Continue the pattern for 4, 5, and 6 triangles. How many toothpicks are needed for each case?
2. How many additional toothpicks are needed for 4 triangles? How many total toothpicks will you need for 7 triangles?

The number of toothpicks needed for each pattern form a sequence. A **sequence** is an ordered list of numbers. Each number in the list is called a **term**. An **arithmetic sequence** is a sequence in which the difference between any two consecutive terms is the same.

3, 5, 7, 9, 11, …
+2 +2 +2 +2

The difference is called the **common difference**.

To find the next number in an arithmetic sequence, add the common difference to the last term.

EXAMPLE Identify Arithmetic Sequences

1 State whether the sequence 17, 12, 7, 2, −3, ... is arithmetic. If it is, state the common difference and write the next three terms.

17, 12, 7, 2, −3
−5 −5 −5 −5

Notice that 12 − 17 = −5, 7 − 12 = −5, and so on.

The terms have a common difference of −5, so the sequence is arithmetic. Continue the pattern to find the next three terms.

−3, −8, −13, −18
−5 −5 −5

The next three terms are −8, −13, and −18.

CHECK Your Progress

State whether each sequence is arithmetic. Write *yes* or *no*. If it is, state the common difference and write the next three terms.

a. 2, 6, 10, 14, 18, …

b. −4, −8, −16, −32, …

Arithmetic sequences can be described by writing algebraic expressions that pair counting numbers with each output.

EXAMPLE Describe an Arithmetic Sequence

Reading Math

And So On Three dots following a list of numbers are read as *and so on*.

2 **Write an expression that can be used to find the nth term of the sequence of the perimeter of squares 4, 8, 12, 16, … . Then write the next three terms.**

Use a table to examine the sequence.

Term Number (n)	1	2	3	4
Perimeter	4	8	12	16

(+1 +1 +1 across term numbers; +4 +4 +4 across perimeters)

The terms have a common difference of 4. Also, each term is 4 times its term number. An expression that can be used to find the nth term is $4n$.

The next three terms are 4(5) or 20, 4(6) or 24, and 4(7) or 28.

CHECK Your Progress **Write an expression that can be used to find the nth term of each sequence. Then find the next three terms.**

c. $-2, -4, -6, -8, \ldots$
d. $\frac{1}{6}, \frac{1}{3}, \frac{1}{2}, \frac{2}{3}, \ldots$
e. $0.5, 1, 1.5, 2, \ldots$

Real-World EXAMPLE

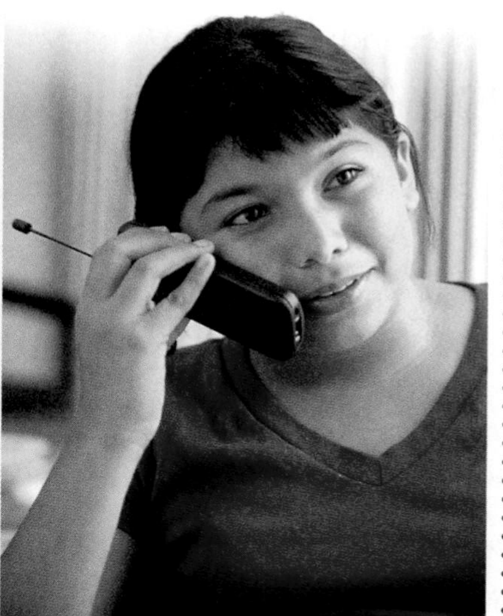

Real-World Link
Approximately 45% of teens use a cell phone and 33% use text messaging.
Source: The Pew Internet & American Life Project

3 **TEXT MESSAGING** **The table shows the monthly cost of sending text messages. How much would it cost to send 60 text messages?**

The common difference between the costs is 0.10. This implies that the expression for the nth message sent is $0.10n$. Compare each cost to the value of $0.10n$ for each number of messages.

Messages	Cost ($)
51	15.10
52	15.20
53	15.30
54	15.40

(+1 +1 +1 across messages; +0.10 +0.10 +0.10 across costs)

Each cost is \$10 more than $0.10n$. So, the expression $0.10n + 10$ is the cost of n messages. To find the cost of sending 60 messages, let c represent the cost. Then write and solve an equation for $n = 60$.

Messages	Cost ($)	$0.10n$
51	15.10	5.10
52	15.20	5.20
53	15.30	5.30
54	15.40	5.40

$c = 0.10n + 10$ Write the equation.

$c = 0.10(60) + 10$ Replace n with 60.

$c = 6 + 10$ or 16 Simplify.

It would cost \$16 to send 60 text messages.

CHECK Your Progress **Write and solve an expression to find the nth term of each arithmetic sequence.**

f. $4, 9, 14, 19, \ldots; n = 12$
g. $-20, -16, -12, -8, \ldots; n = 20$

ISAT EXAMPLE

4 **Which expression can be used to find the nth term in the following sequence, where n represents a number's position in the sequence?**

Position in Sequence	1	2	3	4	n
Term	3	5	7	9	?

A $n + 2$ **B** $2n$ **C** $2n + 1$ **D** $3n$

Read the Item

You need to find an expression to describe any term.

Solve the Item

The terms have a common difference of 2 for every 1 increase in positive number. So, the expression contains $2n$.

- Eliminate choices A and D because they do not contain $2n$.
- Eliminate choice B because $2(1) \neq 3$.
- The expression in choice C is correct for all the listed terms. So, the correct answer is C.

Test-Taking Tip

Eliminate Possibilities
Test $n = 1$ in each expression. Since $2(1) \neq 3$, choice B is eliminated. Next, test $n = 2$. Since $2 + 2 \neq 5$ and $3(2) \neq 5$, choices A and D are eliminated. So, the answer is choice C.

CHECK Your Progress

h. Let n represent the position of a number in the sequence $\frac{1}{4}, \frac{1}{2}, \frac{3}{4}$, 1, … . Which expression can be used to find any term in the sequence?

F $n + \frac{1}{4}$ **G** $2n$ **H** $\frac{1}{4}n$ **J** $4n$

CHECK Your Understanding

Example 1 (p. 464) **State whether each sequence is arithmetic. Write *yes* or *no*. If it is, state the common difference. Write the next three terms of the sequence.**

1. 2, 4, 6, 8, 10, ...
2. 11, 4, −2, −7, −11, ...
3. 8, 2, −4, −10,−16, ...

Example 2 (p. 465) **Write an expression that can be used to find the nth term of each sequence. Then write the next three terms of the sequence.**

4. 3, 6, 9, 12, …
5. −5, −10, −15, −20, …
6. $\frac{1}{10}, \frac{1}{5}, \frac{3}{10}, \frac{2}{5}, \ldots$

Example 3 (p. 465) **Write and solve an expression to find the nth term of each arithmetic sequence.**

7. 25, 23, 21, 19, ... ; $n = 8$
8. 3, 10, 17, 24, ... ; $n = 25$

Example 4 (p. 466)

9. **MULTIPLE CHOICE** In the sequence below, which expression can be used to find the value of the term in the nth position?

Position	1	2	3	4	5	n
Value of Term	6	7	8	9	10	?

A $n + 1$ **B** $n + 5$ **C** $2n$ **D** $6n$

Practice and Problem Solving

HOMEWORK HELP	
For Exercises	See Examples
10–15	1
16–21	2
22–29	3
39, 40	4

State whether each sequence is arithmetic. Write *yes* or *no*. If it is, state the common difference. Write the next three terms of the sequence.

10. 20, 24, 28, 32, 36, ...
11. 1, 10, 100, 1,000, 10,000, ...
12. 189, 63, 21, 7, $2\frac{1}{3}$, ...
13. −6, −4, −2, 0, 2, ...
14. 1, 2, 5, 10, 17, ...
15. 4, $6\frac{1}{2}$, 9, $11\frac{1}{2}$, 14, ...

Write an expression that can be used to find the *n*th term in each sequence. Then write the next three terms of the sequence.

16. 2, 4, 6, 8, ...
17. 12, 24, 36, 48, ...
18. $\frac{1}{3}, \frac{2}{3}, 1, 1\frac{1}{3}, \ldots$
19. $\frac{2}{5}, \frac{4}{5}, 1\frac{1}{5}, 1\frac{3}{5}, \ldots$
20. 5, 9, 13, 17, ...
21. 1, 4, 7, 10, ...

Write and solve an expression to find the *n*th term of each arithmetic sequence.

22. 3, 7, 11, 15, ... ; $n = 8$
23. 23, 25, 27, 29, ... ; $n = 12$
24. 10, 5, 0, −5, ... ; $n = 21$
25. 27, 19, 11, 3, ... ; $n = 17$
26. 34, 49, 64, 79, ... ; $n = 200$
27. 52, 64, 76, 88, ... ; $n = 102$

FITNESS **For Exercises 28 and 29, use the table.**

Week	Time Jogging (min)
1	8
2	16
3	24
4	32
5	?

28. If Luther continues the pattern shown in the table, how many minutes will he spend jogging each day during his fifth week of jogging?
29. Is the amount of time Luther jogs proportional to the number of weeks he has jogged? Explain.

GEOMETRY **For Exercises 30 and 31, use the figure at the right.**

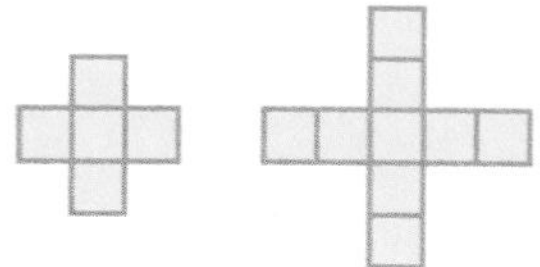
Figure 1 Figure 2 Figure 3

30. How many squares will be in Figure 18?
31. Is the number of squares in each figure proportional to the number of the figure? Explain.

SKIING **For Exercises 32–34, use the following information.**

A ski resort offers a one-day lift pass for \$40 and a yearly lift pass for \$400.

Number of Visits	1	2	3	4	5
Total Cost with One Day Passes (\$)	40	80			
Total Cost with Yearly Pass (\$)	400	400			

32. Is the sequence formed by the total cost with one day passes arithmetic? Explain.
33. Is the sequence formed by the total cost with a yearly pass arithmetic? Explain.
34. How many times would a person have to go skiing to make the yearly pass a better buy?

ILS • ISAT
Extra Practice, pp. 691, 708

H.O.T. Problems

35. **OPEN ENDED** Write an arithmetic sequence in which the common difference is $-\frac{1}{3}$.

36. **REASONING** Determine whether the following statement is *always, sometimes,* or *never* true. Explain.

    A sequence in which a number is added to a term in order to find the next term is an arithmetic sequence.

37. **CHALLENGE** Write an expression that can be used to find the nth term of sequence.

Position	1	3	5	7
Term	8	14	20	26

38. **WRITING IN MATH** Write a real-world problem which uses an arithmetic sequence. Then solve your problem.

ISAT PRACTICE 8.B.3

39. In the sequence below, which expression can be used to find the value of the term in the nth position?

Position	Value of Term
1	0.6
2	1.2
3	1.8
4	2.4
5	3.0
n	?

A $n - 0.4$

B $\frac{n}{5}$

C $\frac{3}{5}n$

D $n + 0.6$

40. The expression below describes a pattern of numbers.

$$-12 - 4(n - 1)$$

If n represents a number's position in the sequence, which pattern of numbers does the expression describe?

F $-12, -16, -20, -24, -28, \ldots$

G $-12, -8, -4, 0, 4, \ldots$

H $12, 8, 4, 0, -4, \ldots$

J $12, 16, 20, 24, 28, \ldots$

Spiral Review

41. **BABYSITTING** You want to buy a pair of \$42 skates with the money you make babysitting. If you charge \$5.25 an hour, write and solve an inequality to find how many whole hours you must babysit to buy the skates. (Lesson 8-8)

Solve each inequality. Check your solution. (Lesson 8-7)

42. $6 + x \leq 16$

43. $5 + n \geq -4$

44. $-3 < k + 8$

45. $9 < y + 12$

46. **PARTY SUPPLIES** Paper cups come in packages of 40 or 75. Monica needs 350 paper cups for the school party. How many packages of each size should she buy? (Lesson 7-2)

GET READY for the Next Lesson

PREREQUISITE SKILL Evaluate each expression if $x = 9$. (Lesson 1-2)

47. $2x - 8$

48. $-5x + 7$

49. $8x - 3$

50. $-15x + 6$

9-2 Functions

MAIN IDEA

Complete function tables.

IL Learning Standards

8.B.3 Use graphing technology and **algebraic methods to analyze and predict linear relationships and make generalizations from linear patterns.**
8.D.3b Propose and solve problems using proportions, formulas and **linear functions.**

New Vocabulary

function
domain
range
function table

IL Math Online

glencoe.com

- Extra Examples
- Personal Tutor
- Self-Check Quiz
- Reading in the Content Area

GET READY for the Lesson

ENTERTAINMENT Suppose you can buy DVDs for $15 each.

1. Copy and complete the table at the right.
2. If 6 DVDs are purchased, what is the total cost?
3. Explain how to find the total cost of 9 DVDs.

DVDs	Cost ($)
1	15
2	30
3	
4	
5	

The total cost depends on, or is a function of, the number of DVDs purchased. A relationship that assigns exactly one output value for each input value is called a **function**. Functions are often written as equations.

$$f(x) = 15x$$

The *input* x is any real number.

$f(x)$ is read *the function of x*, or more simply, *f of x*. It is the *output*.

To find the value of a function for a certain number, substitute the number for the variable x.

EXAMPLES Find a Function Value

Find each function value.

1 $f(9)$ **if** $f(x) = x - 5$

$f(x) = x - 5$ Write the function.

$f(9) = 9 - 5$ or 4 Substitute 9 for x into the function rule.

So, $f(9) = 4$.

2 $f(-3)$ **if** $f(x) = 2x + 1$

$f(x) = 2x + 1$ Write the function.

$f(-3) = 2(-3) + 1$ Substitute -3 for x into the function rule.

$f(-3) = -6 + 1$ or -5 Simplify.

So, $f(-3) = -5$.

CHECK Your Progress

a. $f(2)$ if $f(x) = x - 4$

b. $f(6)$ if $f(x) = 2x - 8$

Study Tip

Input and Output The variable for the input is called the *independent variable* because it can be any number. The variable for the output is called the *dependent variable* because it depends on the input value.

The set of input values in a function is called the **domain**. The set of output values is called the **range**. You can organize the input, rule, and output into a **function table**.

EXAMPLE Make a Function Table

3 **Complete the function table for $f(x) = x + 5$. Then state the domain and range of the function.**

Input	Rule	Output
x	$f(x) = x + 5$	$f(x)$
−2		
−1		
0		
1		

Substitute each value of x, or input, into the function rule. Then simplify to find the output.

Input	Rule	Output
x	$f(x) = x + 5$	$f(x)$
−2	−2 + 5	$f(-2) = 3$
−1	−1 + 5	$f(-1) = 4$
0	0 + 5	$f(0) = 5$
1	1 + 5	$f(1) = 6$

The domain is $\{-2, -1, 0, 1\}$.

The range is $\{3, 4, 5, 6\}$.

CHECK Your Progress

Copy and complete each function table. Then state the domain and range of the function.

c. $f(x) = x - 7$

x	$x - 7$	$f(x)$
−3		
−2		
−1		
0		

d. $f(x) = 4x$

x	$4x$	$f(x)$
−5		
−3		
2		
5		

e. $f(x) = 2x + 3$

x	$2x + 3$	$f(x)$
−1		
2		
3		
5		

Sometimes functions are written using two variables. One variable, usually x, represents the input and the other, usually y, represents the output. The function in Example 3 can also be written as $y = x + 5$.

Real-World Career
How Does a Veterinary Technician Use Math?
A veterinary technician must be able to administer medication and vaccines based on the body weight of the animal.

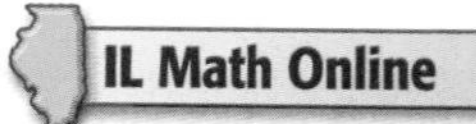
IL Math Online

For more information, go to glencoe.com.

EXAMPLE Functions with Two Variables

4 **DOGS A veterinary technician needs to administer medication to a dog. The dosage is 5 milligrams of medication for every 1 pound of weight. Write a function to represent the amount of medication m needed for p pounds of weight. Then determine how much medication to give to a dog that weighs 33 pounds.**

Words	Amount of medication	equals	5 times	the number of pounds.
Function	m	$=$	$5 \cdot$	p

The function $m = 5p$ represents the situation.

To find the amount of medication needed for 33 pounds, substitute 33 for p.

$m = 5p$ Write the function.

$m = 5(33)$ or 165 Substitute 33 for p.

The technician should give the dog 165 milligrams of medication.

CHECK Your Progress

f. **HOME REPAIR** An air conditioner repair service charges $60 for a service call plus $30 per hour for labor. Write a function to represent the charge c for a service call with h hours of labor. How much would the charge be if there are 3 hours of labor?

CHECK Your Understanding

Examples 1, 2 (p. 469)

Find each function value.

1. $f(4)$ if $f(x) = x - 6$
2. $f(-2)$ if $f(x) = 4x + 1$

Example 3 (p. 470)

Copy and complete each function table. Then state the domain and range of the function.

3. $f(x) = 8 - x$

x	8 − x	f(x)
−3		
−1		
2		
4		

4. $f(x) = 5x + 1$

x	5x + 1	f(x)
−2		
0		
1		
3		

5. $f(x) = 3x - 2$

x	3x − 2	f(x)
−5		
−2		
2		
5		

Example 4 (pp. 470–471)

6. **TRAVEL** On a highway, a car travels an average of 55 miles in one hour. Write a function to represent the distance d a car can travel in t hours. At this rate, how far can the car travel in 5 hours?

Practice and Problem Solving

HOMEWORK HELP

For Exercises	See Examples
7–12	1, 2
13–18	3
19–20	4

Find each function value.

7. $f(7)$ if $f(x) = 5x$
8. $f(9)$ if $f(x) = x + 13$
9. $f(4)$ if $f(x) = 3x - 1$
10. $f(5)$ if $f(x) = 2x + 5$
11. $f(-5)$ if $f(x) = 4x - 1$
12. $f(-12)$ if $f(x) = 2x + 15$

Copy and complete each function table. Then state the domain and range of the function.

13. $f(x) = 6x - 4$

x	6x − 4	f(x)
−5		
−1		
2		
7		

14. $f(x) = 5 - 2x$

x	5 − 2x	f(x)
−2		
0		
3		
5		

15. $f(x) = 7 + 3x$

x	7 + 3x	f(x)
−3		
−2		
1		
6		

Copy and complete each function table. Then state the domain and range of the function.

16. $f(x) = x - 9$

x	$x - 9$	$f(x)$
−2		
−1		
7		
12		

17. $f(x) = 7x$

x	$7x$	$f(x)$
−5		
−3		
2		
6		

18. $f(x) = 4x + 3$

x	$4x + 3$	$f(x)$
−4		
−2		
3		
5		

19. **SPORTS** Tyree's bowling score is handicapped by 30 points, meaning that he receives an additional 30 points on his final score. Write a function that can be used to represent Tyree's final score s given his base score b. What is his adjusted score if he bowled 185?

20. **MUSIC** Leon belongs to a music club that charges a monthly fee of $5, plus $0.50 per song that he downloads. Write a function to represent the amount of money m he would pay in one month to download s songs. What is the cost if he downloads 30 songs?

Find each function value.

21. $f\left(\frac{5}{6}\right)$ if $f(x) = 2x + \frac{1}{3}$

22. $f\left(\frac{5}{8}\right)$ if $f(x) = 4x - \frac{1}{4}$

23. **BIKING** After 1 hour, a cyclist had ridden 12 miles. If she then continued riding at an average rate of 8 miles per hour, how long did it take her to ride 60 miles?

24. **SCUBA DIVING** The table shows the water pressure encountered by a diver. Write a function to represent the pressure p encountered at a depth of d feet. What would the pressure be at a depth of 175 feet? Round to the nearest tenth.

Depth (ft)	Pressure (lb/in^2)
0	14.7
33	29.4
66	44.1
99	58.8
132	73.5

ILS • ISAT
Extra Practice, pp. 691, 708

H.O.T. Problems

25. **OPEN ENDED** If $f(-3) = -8$, write a function rule and find the function values for zero, a negative, and a positive value of x.

26. **CHALLENGE** Write the function rule for each function table.

a.

x	$f(x)$
−3	−30
−1	−10
2	20
6	60

b.

x	$f(x)$
−5	−9
−1	−5
3	−1
7	3

c.

x	y
−2	−3
1	3
3	7
5	11

d.

x	y
−2	−5
1	1
3	5
5	9

27. **WRITING IN MATH** The distance d an object travels after a time t and rate of speed r is given by the function $d = rt$. Explain how a change in the input affects change in the output.

ISAT PRACTICE 8.B.3, 8.D.3b

28. The equation $c = 6.50t$ represents c, the total cost of t tickets for a movie. Which table contains values that satisfy this equation?

A

Cost of Movie Tickets				
t	1	2	3	4
c	\$6.50	\$13.00	\$19.50	\$26.00

B

Cost of Movie Tickets				
t	1	2	3	4
c	\$6.50	\$12.00	\$18.00	\$24.50

C

Cost of Movie Tickets				
t	1	2	3	4
c	\$13.00	\$19.50	\$26.00	\$32.50

D

Cost of Movie Tickets				
t	1	2	3	4
c	\$6.50	\$8.50	\$9.50	\$10.50

29. Stephanie received a \$25 gift certificate to an online music store. If the cost of purchasing a song is \$0.95, which table best describes b, the balance remaining after she buys s songs?

F

s	b
1	\$24.10
2	\$23.20
4	\$21.40
6	\$19.60
8	\$17.80

H

s	b
2	\$23.10
4	\$21.20
5	\$20.25
8	\$17.40
10	\$15.50

G

s	b
0	\$25.00
3	\$22.00
6	\$19.00
9	\$16.00
12	\$13.00

J

s	b
5	\$20.05
10	\$15.10
15	\$10.15
20	\$5.20
25	\$0.25

Spiral Review

30. SAVINGS Orlando has \$20 in his savings account. Each week he adds \$5 and does not take out any money. How much will he have after 7 weeks? (Lesson 9-1)

Solve each inequality. Check your solution. (Lesson 8-8)

31. $6x \leq 36$ **32.** $15n \geq -30$ **33.** $-33 > 11g$ **34.** $-9 < -9x$

35. UTILITIES An airport has changed the booths used for public telephones. The old booths consisted of four sides of a rectangular prism. The new booths are half of a cylinder with an open top. How much less material is needed to construct a new booth than an old booth? (Lesson 7-7)

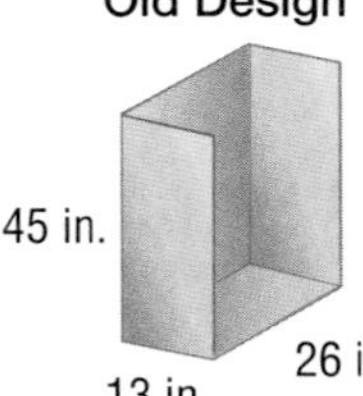

New Design
45 in.
26 in.

36. MEASUREMENT A block of cheese in the shape of a rectangular prism has a volume of 305 cubic centimeters. After several slices are cut from the block, it measures 10.25 centimeters by 6.5 centimeters by 2 centimeters. How much cheese was used? (Lesson 7-5)

37. Find the distance between the points $(-1, 1)$ and $(3, -2)$. (Lesson 3-7)

GET READY for the Next Lesson

PREREQUISITE SKILL Graph each point on the same coordinate plane.

38. $A(-4, 2)$ **39.** $B(3, -1)$ **40.** $C(0, -3)$ **41.** $D(1, 4)$

Extend 9-2

Algebra Lab
Relations and Functions

MAIN IDEA

Determine whether a relation is a function.

IL Learning Standards

8.B.3 Use graphing technology and **algebraic methods to analyze and predict linear relationships and make generalizations from linear patterns.**
8.D.3b Propose and solve problems using proportions, formulas and **linear functions.**

A *relation* expresses how objects in one group, inputs, are assigned or related to objects in another group, outputs. Suppose three students select a favorite color from the colors blue, red, or green. The relation diagrams below show two of several possible results.

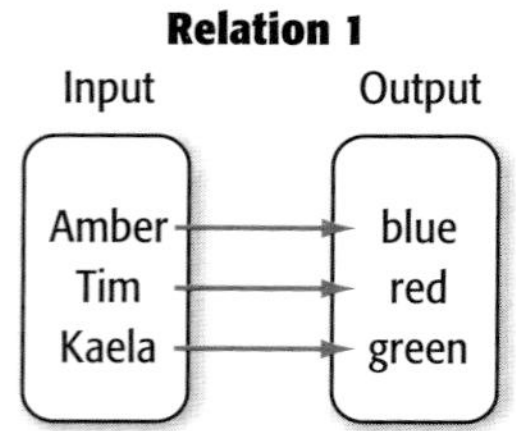

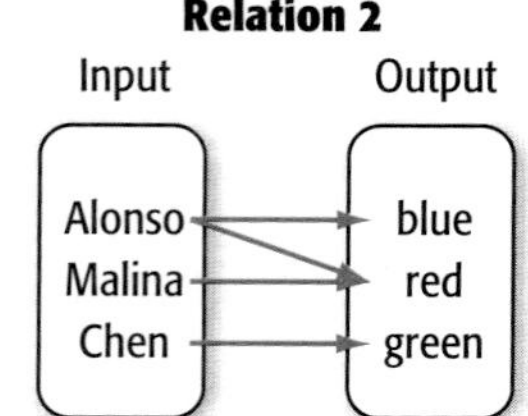

Recall from the previous lesson that a function is a relation in which exactly one output is assigned to each input. In the example above, the first relation is a function, since each person chose one favorite color. The second relation is not a function, since Alonso chose two colors as his favorite.

ACTIVITY

STEP 1 Copy the relation diagram below. Draw lines from the input values to the output values so that the relation is a function.

Input	Output
1	2
3	5
6	7
8	10

STEP 2 Copy the relation diagram from Step 1. Draw lines from the input values to the output values so that the relation is *not* a function.

Analyze the Results

1. A relation can be written as a set of ordered pairs, with the input as the x-coordinate and the output as the y-coordinate. For each relation diagram you drew in the Activity above, write the relation as a set of ordered pairs.
2. Describe why each relation is or is not a function. Explain your reasoning in terms of the ordered pairs.

Determine whether each relation is a function. Explain.

3. $\{(1, 18), (9, 15), (6, 3), (9, 10)\}$
4. $\{(5, 6), (10, 11), (8, 13), (0, 7)\}$

9-3 Representing Linear Functions

MAIN IDEA

Represent linear functions using function tables and graphs.

IL Learning Standards

8.D.3a Solve problems using numeric, graphic or symbolic representations of variables, expressions, **equations** and inequalities.
8.D.3b Propose and solve problems using proportions, formulas and **linear functions.**
Also addresses 8.A.3b, 8.B.3.

New Vocabulary

linear function

IL Math Online

glencoe.com

- Extra Examples
- Personal Tutor
- Self-Check Quiz

GET READY for the Lesson

AVIATION The Lockheed SR-71 Blackbird has a top speed of 36.6 miles per minute. If x represents the minutes traveled at this speed, the function rule for the distance traveled is $y = 36.6x$.

1. Copy and complete the function table.
2. Graph the ordered pairs (x, y) on a coordinate plane. What do you notice?

Input	Rule	Output	(Input, Output)
x	$36.6x$	y	(x, y)
1	36.6(1)	36.6	(1, 36.6)
2	36.6(2)		
3			
4			

Functions can be represented in words, in a table, with a graph, and as ordered pairs.

Real-World EXAMPLE Graph a Function

1 **SCHOOL SUPPLIES The school store sells book covers for \$2 each and notebooks for \$1. Toni wants to buy some of each. The cost of x book covers and y notebooks is $2x + y$. Toni has \$5 to spend, so $2x + y = 5$. Graph $2x + y = 5$ to find how many covers and notebooks Toni can buy.**

$2x + y = 5$ Write the equation.

$2x - 2x + y = 5 - 2x$ Subtract $2x$ from each side to solve for y.

$y = 5 - 2x$ Simplify.

The equation $y = 5 - 2x$ represents a function. Choose values for x and substitute them to find y. Then graph the ordered pairs (x, y).

x	$5 - 2x$	y	(x, y)
0	5 − 2(0)	5	(0, 5)
1	5 − 2(1)	3	(1, 3)
2	5 − 2(2)	1	(2, 1)
3	5 − 2(3)	−1	(3, −1)

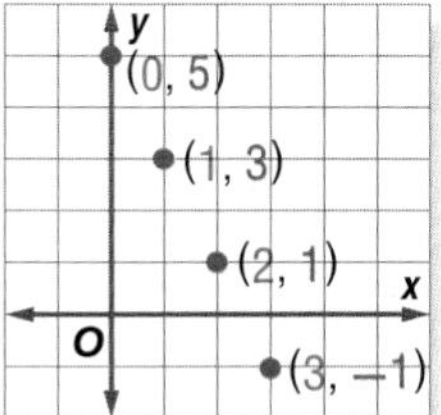

She cannot buy negative amounts, so she can buy 0 covers and 5 notebooks, 1 cover and 3 notebooks, or 2 covers and 1 notebook.

CHECK Your Progress

a. **DECORATING** A repeating pattern is made using 6 triangular tiles x and 1 hexagonal tile y. Graph the function $6x + y = 35$ to find the number of each tile needed if 35 tiles are used.

EXAMPLE Graph a Function

2 **Graph $y = x + 2$.**

- Select any four values for the input x. Substitute these values for x to find the output y.
- Graph each ordered pair. Draw a line that passes through each point.

x	$x + 2$	y	(x, y)
0	$0 + 2$	2	(0, 2)
1	$1 + 2$	3	(1, 3)
2	$2 + 2$	4	(2, 4)
3	$3 + 2$	5	(3, 5)

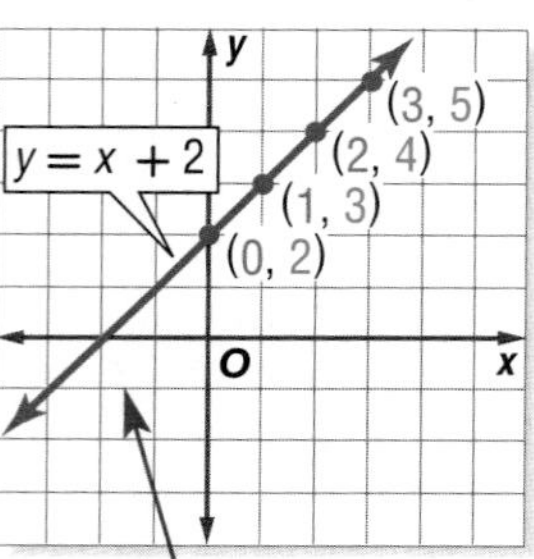

The point where the line crosses the x-axis is the solution to the equation $0 = x + 2$.

Study Tip

Solutions The solutions of an equation are ordered pairs that make an equation representing the function true.

The line is the complete graph of the function. The ordered pair corresponding to any point on the line is a solution of the equation $y = x + 2$.

Check It appears that $(-2, 0)$ is also a solution. Check this by substitution.

$y = x + 2$ Write the function.

$0 \stackrel{?}{=} -2 + 2$ Replace x with -2 and y with 0.

$0 = 0$ ✓ Simplify.

CHECK Your Progress

Graph each function.

b. $y = x - 5$

c. $y = -2x$

d. $y = 2x + 1$

Review Vocabulary

linear relationship relationships that have straight-line graphs (Lesson 4-4)

A function in which the graph of the solutions forms a line is called a **linear function**. Therefore, $y = x + 2$ is a *linear equation*.

Representing Functions — Concept Summary

Words The value of y is one less than the corresponding value of x.

Equation $y = x - 1$

Ordered Pairs $(0, -1), (1, 0), (2, 1), (3, 2)$

Table

x	y
0	−1
1	0
2	1
3	2

Graph

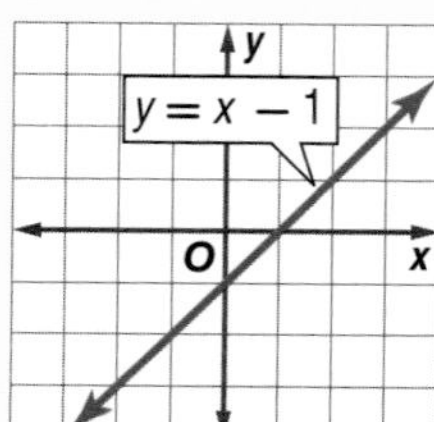

ISAT EXAMPLE 8.D.3a, 8.D.3b

3 **Which line graphed below best represents the table of values for the ordered pairs (x, y)?**

x	−2	−1	0	1
y	−3	−1	1	3

A
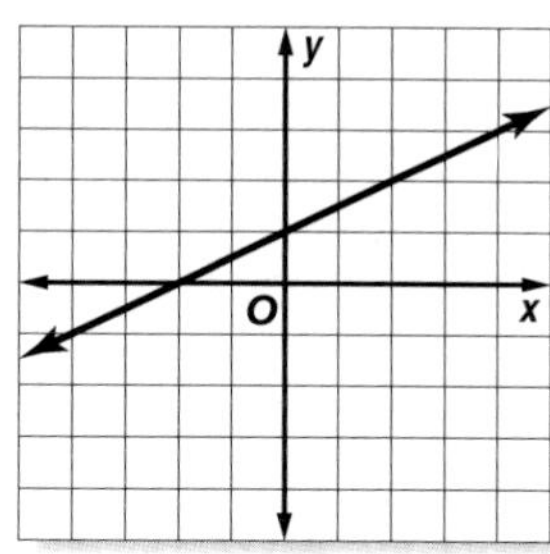

C
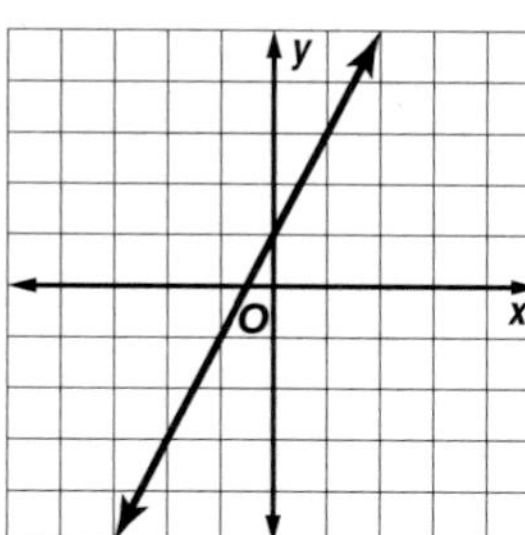

B
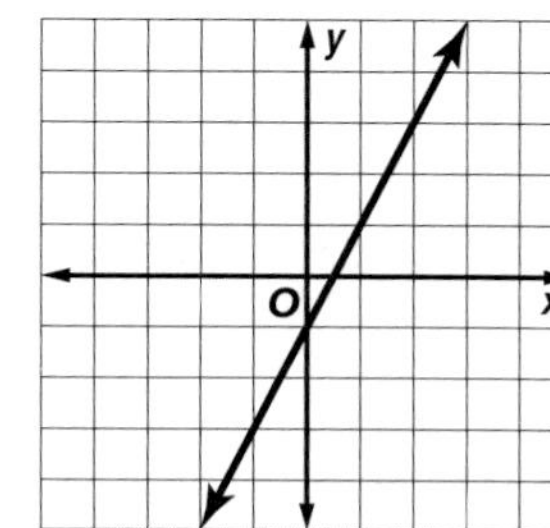

D
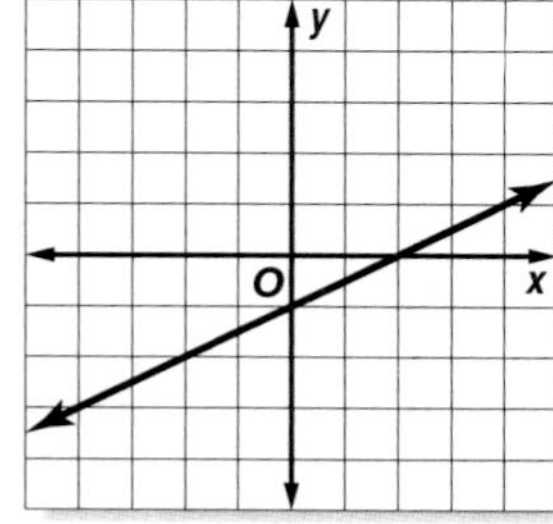

Read the Item

You need to decide which of the four graphs represents the data.

Solve the Item

The values in the table represent the ordered pairs (−2, −3), (−1, −1), (0, 1), and (1, 3). Test the ordered pairs. Graph C is the only graph that contains all these ordered pairs. The answer is C.

Test-Taking Tip

Eliminate the Possibilities By testing the ordered pair (0, 1) first, choices B and D can be eliminated.

CHECK Your Progress

e. The graph of the line $y = 3x + 2$ is drawn on the coordinate grid. Which table of ordered pairs contains only points on this line?

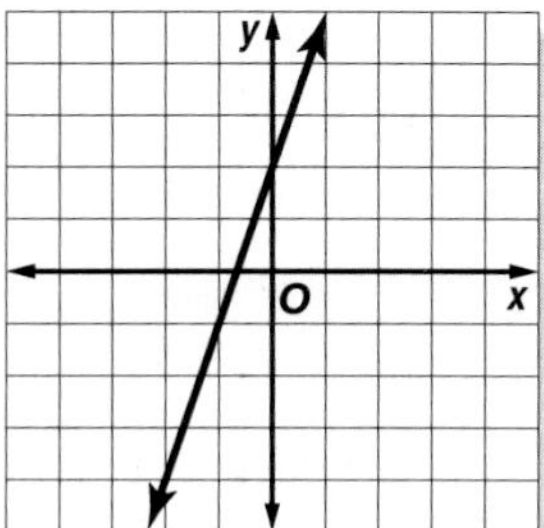

F

x	−1	0	2	3
y	−5	−2	4	7

H

x	−6	−3	0	3
y	0	−1	2	3

G

x	−1	5	7	8
y	−1	1	−3	2

J

x	−3	−1	1	2
y	−7	−1	5	8

CHECK Your Understanding

Example 1 (p. 475)

1. **GARDENING** Marigolds x come in containers with 4 flowers and daisies y come individually. Graph the function $4x + y = 15$ to find the number of containers of marigolds and daisies you can get if you want 15 flowers.

Example 2 (p. 476)

Graph each function.

2. $y = x + 5$
3. $y = 3x - 2$
4. $y = -2x + 1$

Example 3 (p. 477)

5. **MULTIPLE CHOICE** Which line graphed best represents the table of values for the ordered pairs (x, y)?

x	−7	−2	2	9
y	−6.5	−4	−2	1.5

A

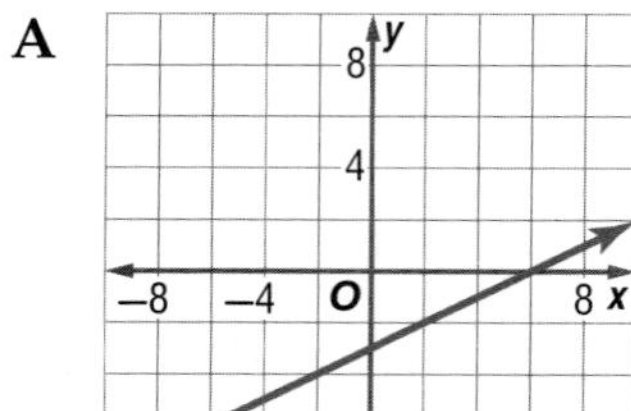

C

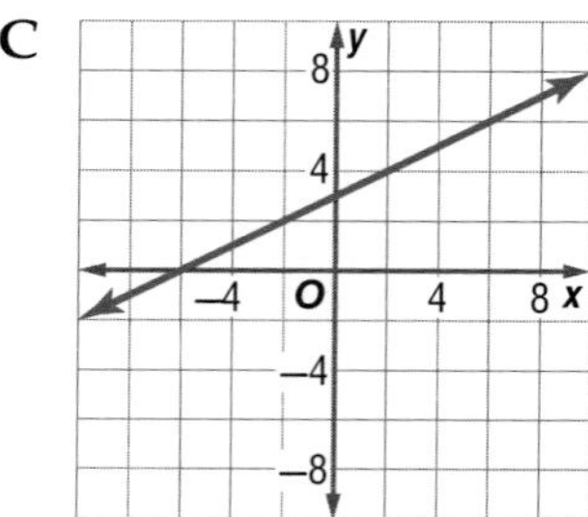

B

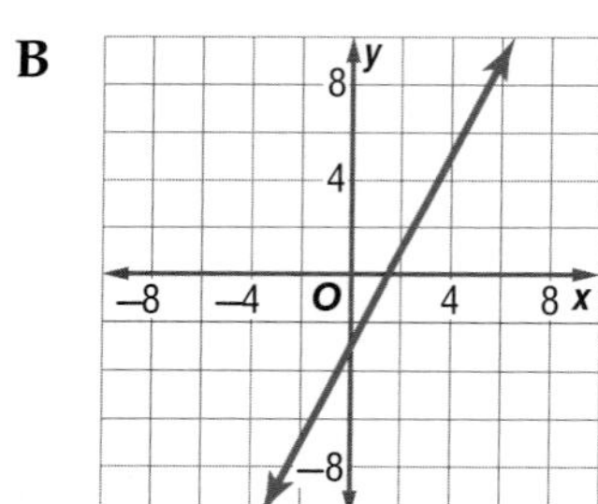

D

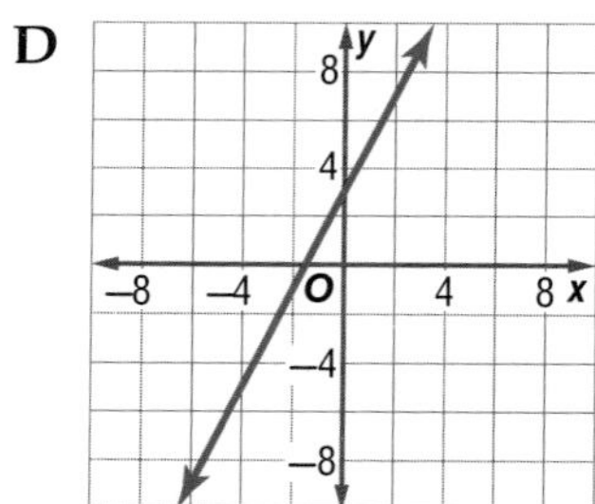

Practice and Problem Solving

HOMEWORK HELP	
For Exercises	**See Examples**
6, 7	1
8–15	2
27, 28	3

6. **PETS** Fancy goldfish x cost \$3 each and common goldfish y cost \$1 each. Graph the function $3x + y = 20$ to determine how many of each type of goldfish Tasha can buy for \$20.

7. **CLOTHES** A store sells T-shirts x in packs of 5 and regular shirts y individually. Graph the function $5x + y = 10$ to determine the number of each type of shirt Bethany can have if she buys 10 shirts.

Graph each function.

8. $y = 4x$
9. $y = -3x$
10. $y = x - 3$
11. $y = x + 1$
12. $y = 3x - 7$
13. $y = 2x + 3$
14. $y = \frac{1}{3}x + 1$
15. $y = \frac{1}{2}x - 3$

16. **TEMPERATURE** The formula $F = 1.8C + 32$ compares temperatures in degrees Celsius C, to temperatures in degrees Fahrenheit F. Find four ordered pairs (C, F) that are solutions of the equation. Then graph the equation.

MEASUREMENT For Exercises 17–19, use the following information.
The equation $y = 1.09x$ describes the approximate number of meters y in x yards.

17. Would negative values of x have any meaning in this situation? Explain.
18. Graph the function.
19. About how many meters is a 40-yard race?

ELEVATION For Exercises 20 and 21, use the following information and the table at the right.
If the temperature is 80°F at sea level, the function $t = 80 - 3.6h$ describes the temperature t at a height of h thousand feet above sea level.

Eastern U.S. Mountains	
Mountain	**Elevation (ft)**
Mount Mitchell, NC	6,684
Mount Rogers, VA	5,729
Black Mountain, KY	4,139
Sassafras Mountain, SC	3,560

Source: *New York Times Almanac*

20. Graph the temperature function.
21. What is the temperature at each peak on a day that is 80°F at sea level?

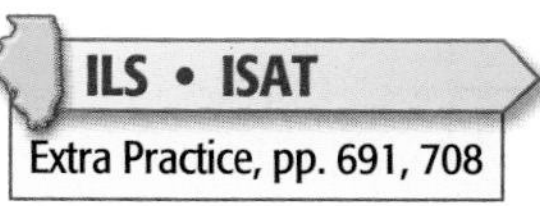

Extra Practice, pp. 691, 708

22. **MONEY** Drake is saving money to buy a new computer for $1,200. He already has $450 and plans to save $30 a week. The function $f(x) = 30x + 450$ represents the amount Drake has saved after x weeks. Graph the function to determine the number of weeks it will take Drake to save enough money to buy the computer.

H.O.T. Problems

23. **OPEN ENDED** Draw a graph of a linear function. Name three solutions of the function.

24. **Which One Doesn't Belong?** Identify the ordered pair that is not a solution of $y = -4x + 3$. Explain your reasoning.

(2, 5)	(0, 3)	(−1, 7)	(1, −1)

25. **CHALLENGE** Name the coordinates of four points that satisfy each function. Then give the function rule.

a. 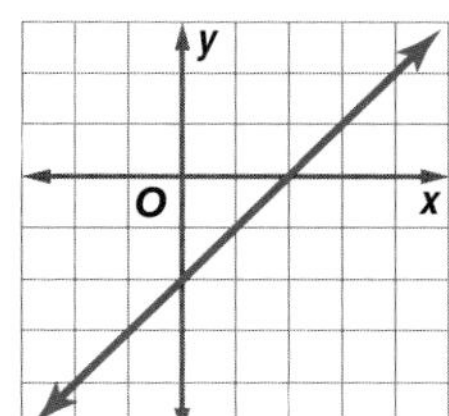

b. 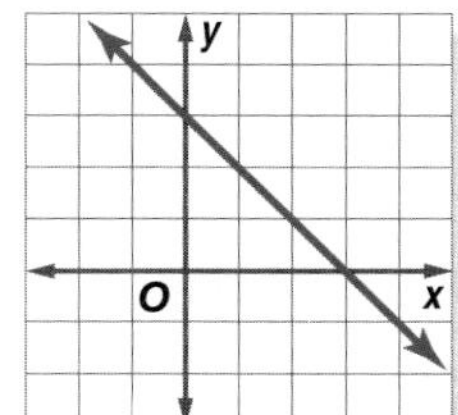

26. **WRITING IN MATH** Explain how a function table can be used to graph a function.

ISAT PRACTICE 8.D.3a, 8.D.3b

27. Which line graphed below best represents the table of values for the ordered pairs (x, y)?

x	−4	0	4	8
y	−2	−1	0	1

A 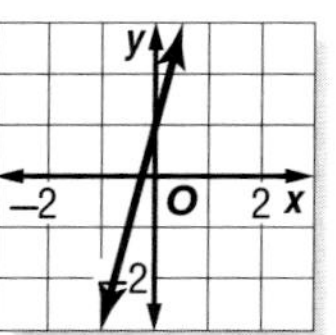

C 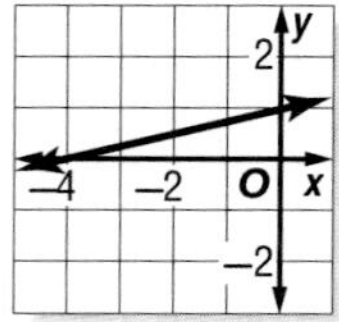

B 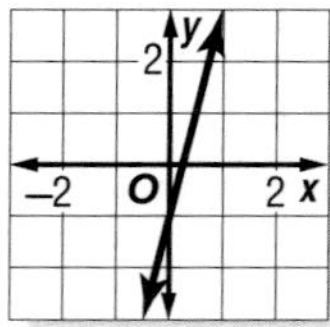

D 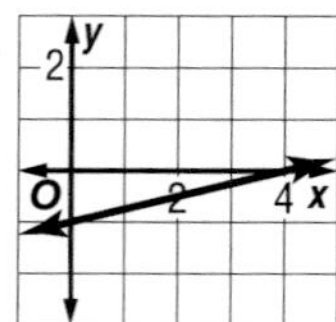

28. The graph shows the line $y = 5x - 1$.

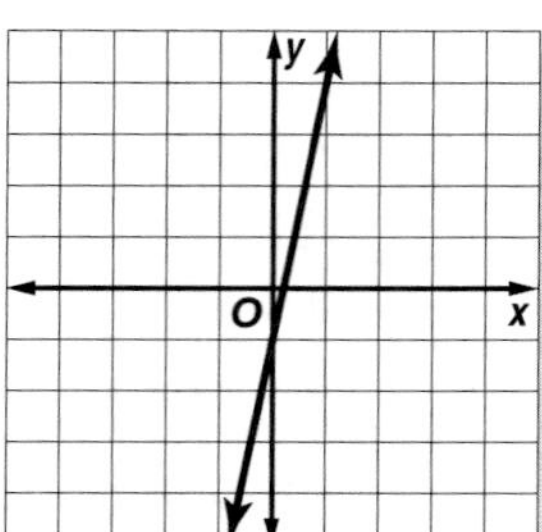

Which table of ordered pairs contains only points on this line?

F

x	−2	−1	0	1
y	−9	−4	1	6

G

x	−3	−2	−1	0
y	−8	−7	−6	−5

H

x	0	1	2	3
y	−1	0	1	2

J

x	−1	0	1	2
y	−6	−1	4	9

Spiral Review

Find each function value. (Lesson 9-2)

29. $f(6)$ if $f(x) = 7x - 3$

30. $f(-5)$ if $f(x) = 3x + 15$

31. $f(3)$ if $f(x) = 2x - 7$

32. Write an expression that can be used to find the nth term of the arithmetic sequence 15, 30, 45, 60, … . Then write the next three terms. (Lesson 9-1)

33. **BAND** The school band makes \$0.50 for every flower they sell. They want to make at least \$500 on the flower sale. Write and solve an inequality to find how many flowers they can sell and meet their goal. (Lesson 8-8)

GET READY for the Next Lesson

PREREQUISITE SKILL Find the constant rate of change for each graph. (Lesson 4-4)

34. 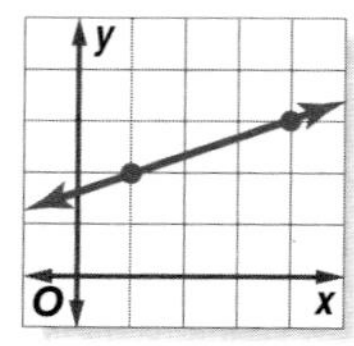

35. 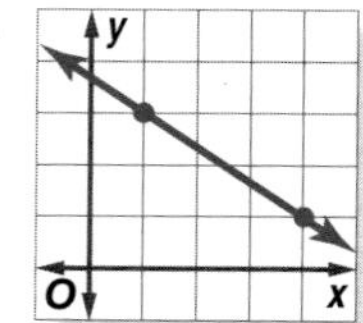

36. 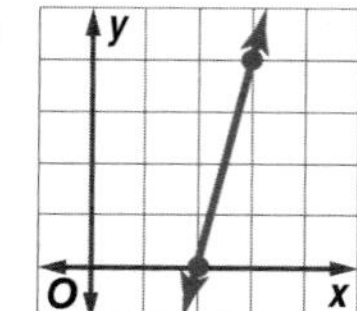

9-4 Slope

MAIN IDEA

Find the slope of a line.

IL Learning Standards

6.D.3 Apply ratios and proportions **to solve practical problems. 8.D.3a Solve problems using numeric, graphic or symbolic representations of variables,** expressions, **equations** and inequalities. *Also addresses 8.A.3b, 8.B.3.*

New Vocabulary

slope
rise
run

IL Math Online

glencoe.com

- Extra Examples
- Personal Tutor
- Self-Check Quiz

GET READY for the Lesson

SAFETY A ladder truck uses a moveable ladder to reach upper levels of houses and buildings.

1. The rate of change of the ladder compares the height it is raised to the distance of its base from the building. Write this rate as a fraction in simplest form.
2. Find the rate of change of a ladder that has been raised 100 feet and has a base of 50 feet from the building.

The term slope is used to describe how steep a straight line is *numerically*. **Slope** is the ratio of the **rise**, or vertical change, to the **run**, or horizontal change. In linear functions, no matter which two points you choose, the slope, or rate of change, of the line is always constant.

$$\text{slope} = \frac{\text{rise}}{\text{run}}$$

rise ← vertical change between any two points
run ← horizontal change between the same two points

Real-World EXAMPLE

1 EXERCISE Find the slope of the treadmill at the right.

slope	$= \frac{\text{rise}}{\text{run}}$	Definition of slope
	$= \frac{10 \text{ in.}}{48 \text{ in.}}$	rise = 10 in., run = 48 in.
	$= \frac{5}{24}$	Simplify.

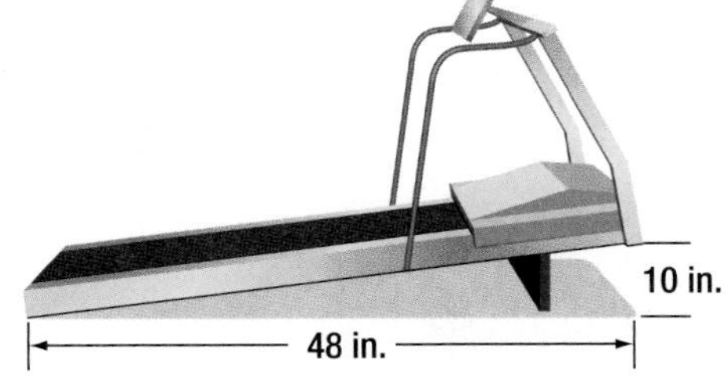

The slope of the treadmill is $\frac{5}{24}$.

CHECK Your Progress

a. **HIKING** A hiking trail rises 6 feet for every horizontal change of 100 feet. What is the slope of the hiking trail?

Since slope is a rate of change, it can be positive (slanting upward) or negative (slanting downward).

 Find Slope Using a Graph

Study Tip

Translating Rise and Run
up → positive
down → negative
right → positive
left → negative

2 **Find the slope of the line.**

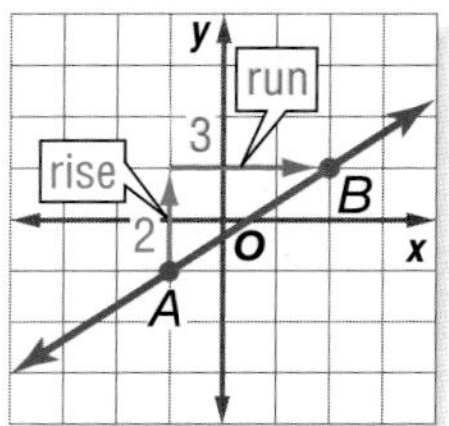

Choose two points on the line. The vertical change is 2 units while the horizontal change is 3 units.

$\text{slope} = \frac{\text{rise}}{\text{run}}$ Definition of slope

$= \frac{2}{3}$ rise = 2, run = 3

The slope of the line is $\frac{2}{3}$.

 **CHECK Your Progress**

b. 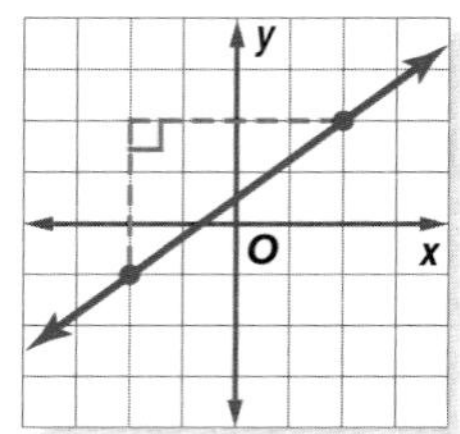

c. 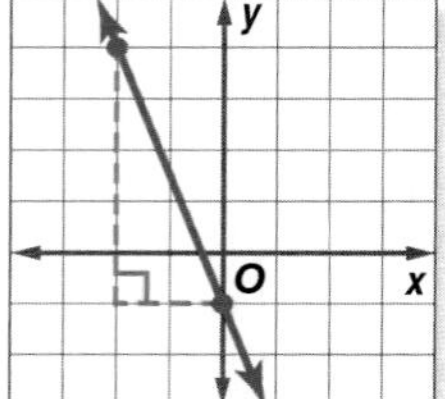

Slope can be found by finding the ratio of the change in y-values (rise) to the change in x-values (run) for any two points on a line.

 EXAMPLE Find Slope Using a Table

3 **The points given in the table lie on a line. Find the slope of the line. Then graph the line.**

x	1	3	5	7
y	12	9	6	3

+2 +2 +2 (changes in x); −3 −3 −3 (changes in y)

Choose two points from the table to find the changes in the x- and y-values.

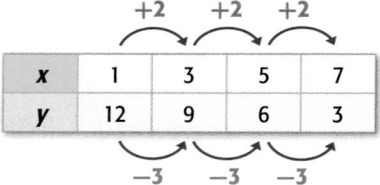

$\text{slope} = \frac{\text{change in } y}{\text{change in } x}$

$= \frac{9 - 12}{3 - 1}$

$= \frac{-3}{2} \text{ or } -\frac{3}{2}$

The slope is $-\frac{3}{2}$.

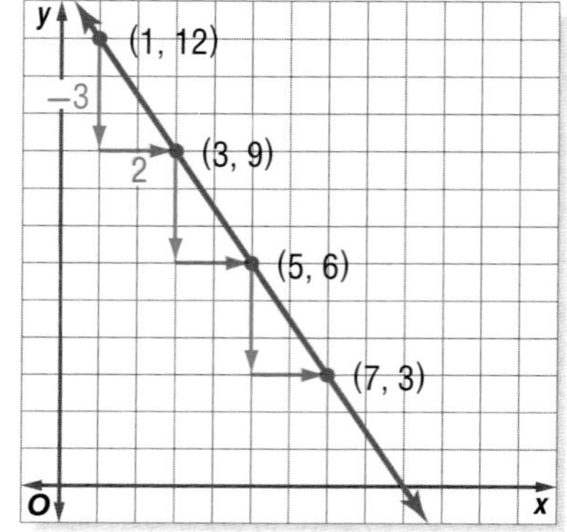

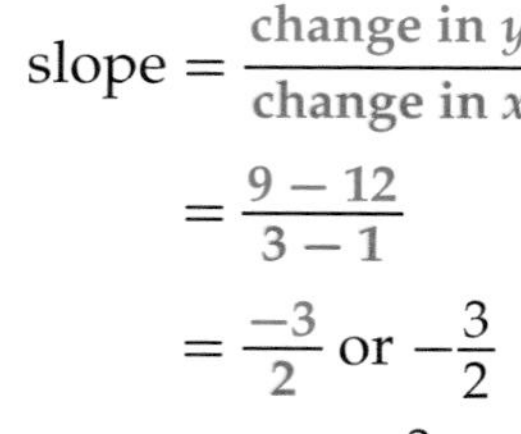

Study Tip

Slope
You can choose any two points to calculate slope. Whichever y-value you use first, be sure to use the corresponding x-value first.

CHECK Your Progress

d.

x	−6	−2	2	6
y	−2	−1	0	1

e.

x	−4	0	4	8
y	−1	−2	−3	−4

Reading Math

Subscripts x_1 is read *x sub one* and x_2 is read *x sub two*. They are used to indicate two different *x*-coordinates.

You have found slope by using $\frac{\text{rise}}{\text{run}}$ and $\frac{\text{change in } y}{\text{change in } x}$. You can also find the slope of a line by using the coordinates of any two points on the line. One point can be represented by (x_1, y_1) and the other by (x_2, y_2). The small numbers slightly below x and y are called *subscripts*.

Slope Formula — Key Concept

Words The slope m of a line passing through points (x_1, y_1) and (x_2, y_2) is the ratio of the difference in the *y*-coordinates to the corresponding difference in the *x*-coordinates.

Model

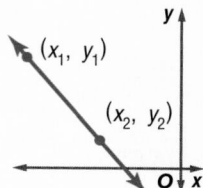

(x_1, y_1), (x_2, y_2), O, x, y

Symbols $m = \frac{y_2 - y_1}{x_2 - x_1}$, where $x_2 \neq x_1$

EXAMPLES Find Slope Using Coordinates

Find the slope of the line that passes through each pair of points.

4 $C(-1, -4), D(2, 2)$

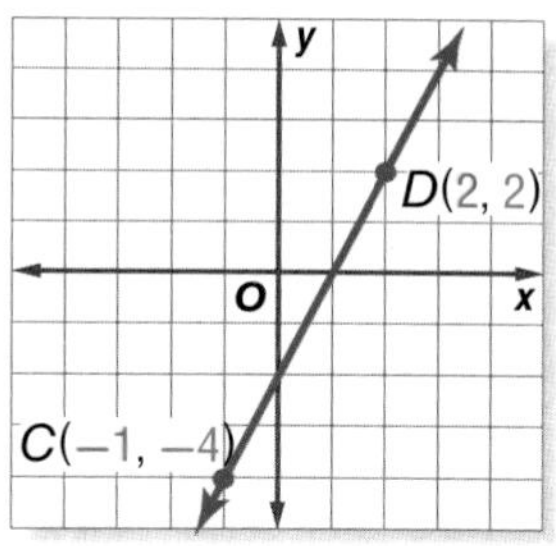

$m = \frac{y_2 - y_1}{x_2 - x_1}$ Slope formula

$m = \frac{2 - (-4)}{2 - (-1)}$ $(x_1, y_1) = (-1, -4)$, $(x_2, y_2) = (2, 2)$

$m = \frac{6}{3}$ or 2 Simplify.

Check When going from left to right, the graph of the line slants upward. This is correct for positive slope.

Study Tip

Using the Slope Formula

- It does not matter which point you define as (x_1, y_1) and (x_2, y_2).
- However, the coordinates of both points must be used in the same order.

To check Example 5, let $(x_1, y_1) = (-4, 3)$ and $(x_2, y_2) = (1, 2)$. Then find the slope.

5 $R(1, 2), S(-4, 3)$

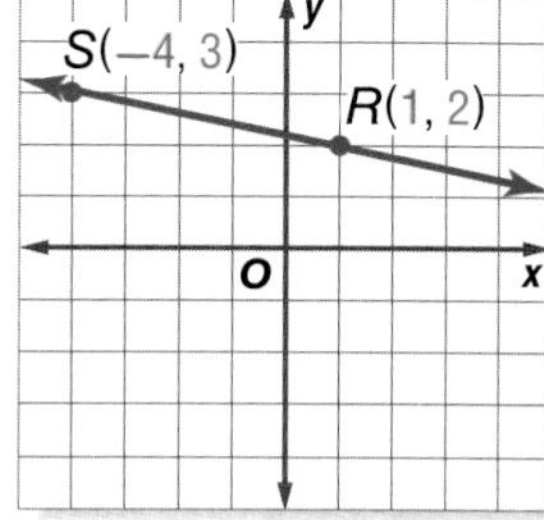

$m = \frac{y_2 - y_1}{x_2 - x_1}$ Slope formula

$m = \frac{3 - 2}{-4 - 1}$ $(x_1, y_1) = (1, 2)$, $(x_2, y_2) = (-4, 3)$

$m = \frac{1}{-5}$ or $-\frac{1}{5}$ Simplify.

Check When going from left to right, the graph of the line slants downward. This is correct for negative slope.

CHECK Your Progress

f. $A(2, 2), B(5, 3)$ **g.** $C(-2, 1), D(0, -3)$ **h.** $J(-7, -4), K(-3, -2)$

Example 1 (p. 481)

1. **BUILDINGS** Find the slope of the roof of the storage shed.

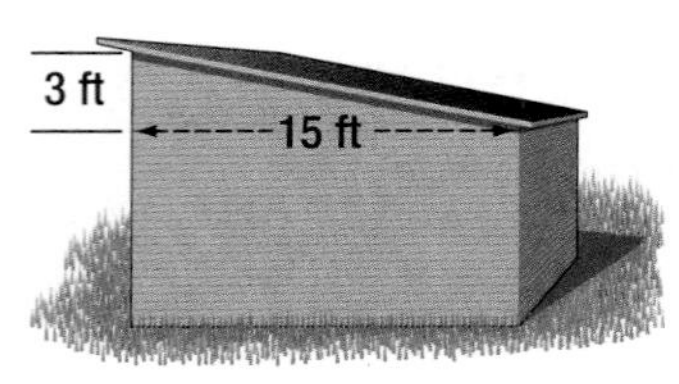

Example 2 (p. 482)

Find the slope of each line.

2. 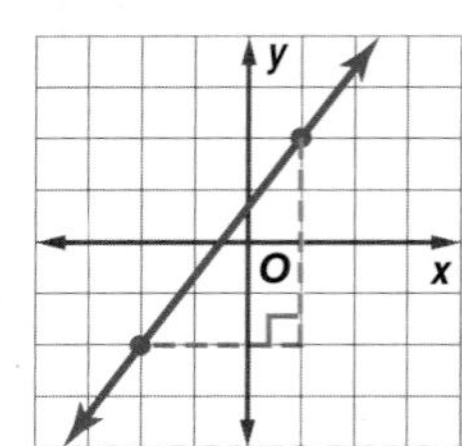

3. 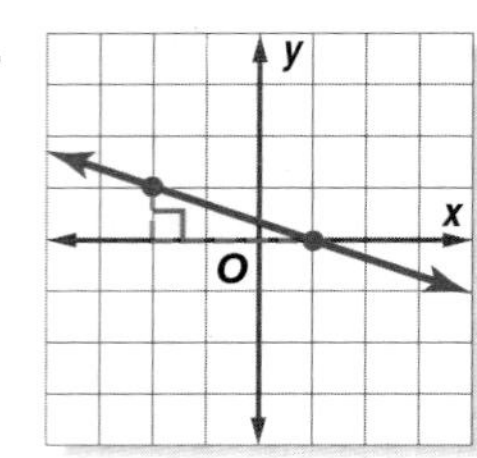

Example 3 (p. 482)

4. The points given in the table lie on a line. Find the slope of the line. Then graph the line.

x	0	1	2	3
y	1	3	5	7

Examples 4, 5 (p. 483)

Find the slope of the line that passes through each pair of points.

5. $A(-3, -2), B(5, 4)$
6. $C(-4, 2), D(1, 5)$
7. $E(-6, 5), F(3, -3)$
8. $G(1, 5), H(4, -3)$

Practice and Problem Solving

HOMEWORK HELP

For Exercises	See Examples
9, 10	1
11–14	2
15, 16	3
17–22	4, 5

9. **SKIING** Find the slope of a ski run that descends 15 feet for every horizontal change of 24 feet.

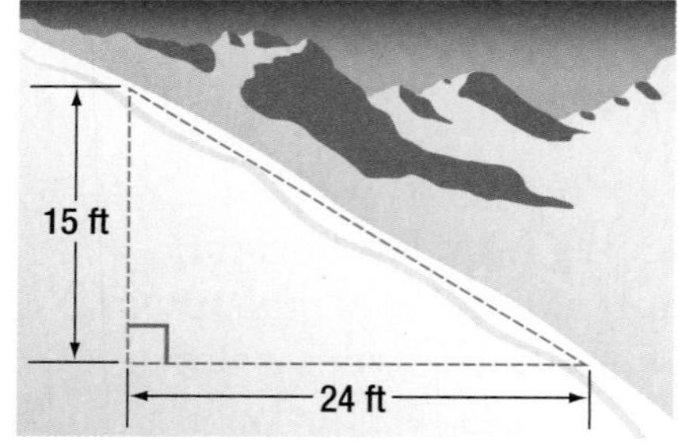

10. **ROADS** Find the slope of a road that rises 12 feet for every horizontal change of 100 feet.

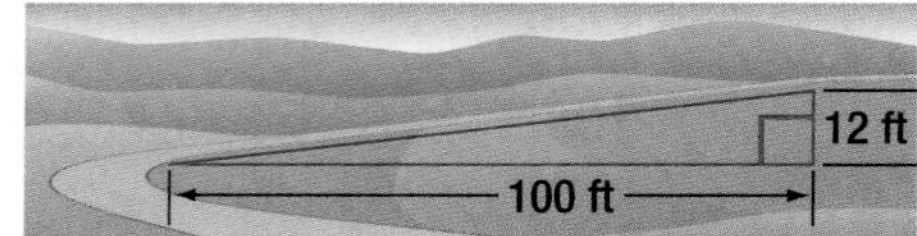

Find the slope of each line.

11.  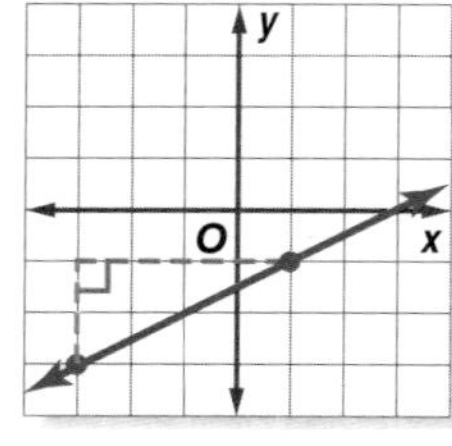

12. 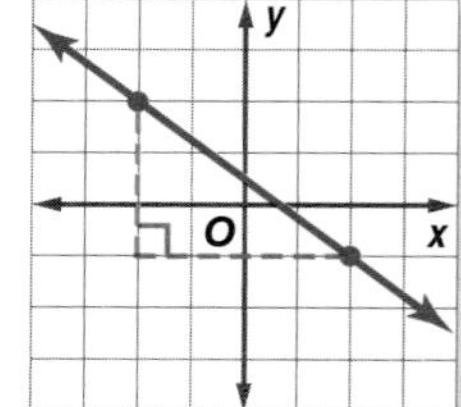

13.  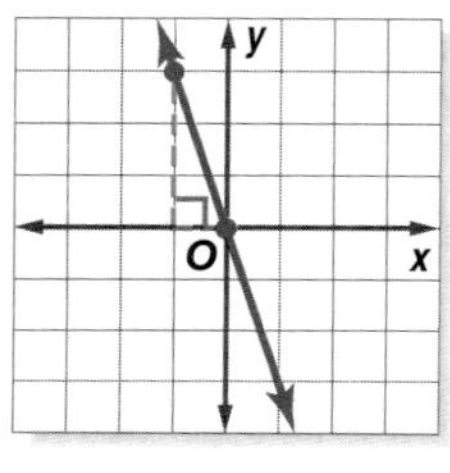

14.  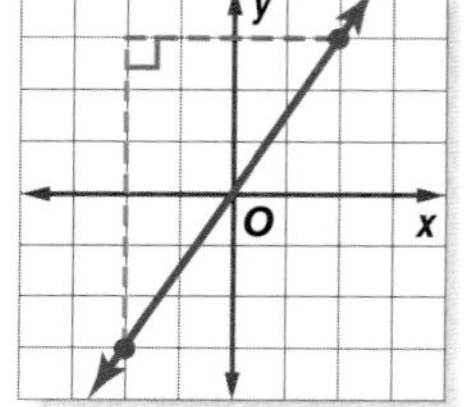

The points given in each table lie on a line. Find the slope of the line. Then graph the line.

15.

x	0	2	4	6
y	9	4	−1	−6

16.

x	−3	3	9	15
y	−3	1	5	9

Find the slope of the line that passes through each pair of points.

17. $A(0, 1), B(2, 7)$
18. $C(2, 5), D(3, 1)$
19. $E(1, 2), F(4, 7)$
20. $G(-6, -1), H(4, 1)$
21. $J(-9, 3), K(2, 1)$
22. $M(-2, 3), N(7, -4)$

23. **AQUARIUMS** The graph shows the depth of water in an aquarium over several days. Find the slope of the line and explain its meaning as a rate of change.

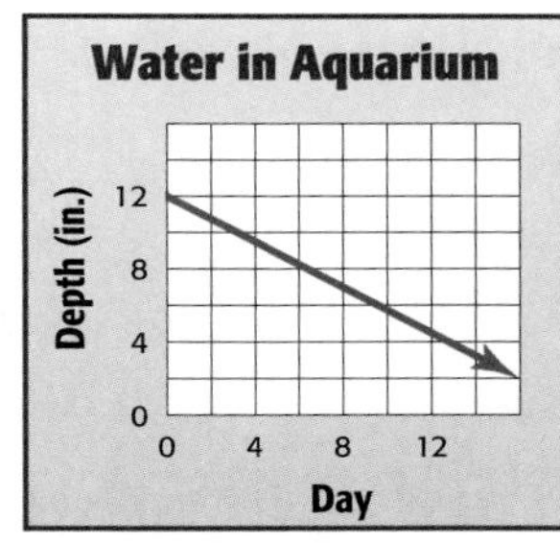

JOBS For Exercises 24–26, use the following information.
For working 3 hours, Sofia earns \$30.60.
For working 5 hours, she earns \$51.
For working 6 hours, she earns \$61.20.

24. Graph the information with the hours on the horizontal axis and money earned on the vertical axis. Draw a line through the points.
25. What is the slope of the graph?
26. What does the slope of the graph represent?

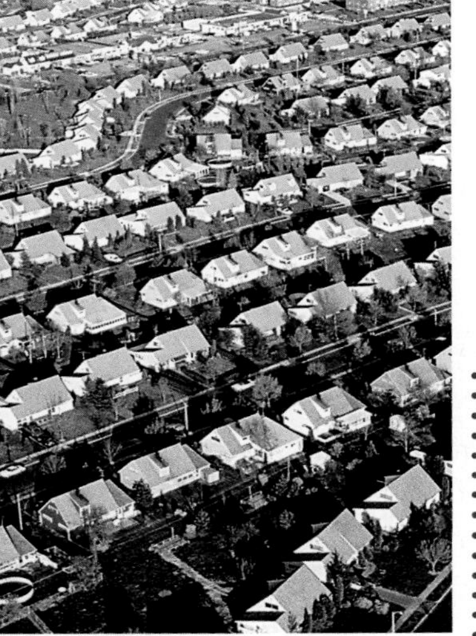

Real-World Link
After World War II, the rate of home ownership in the U.S. rose steadily for three decades, from 44% in the late 1940s to 65.6% in 1980.
Source: U.S. Census Bureau

HOUSING For Exercises 27–29, use the graph at the right.

27. Find the slope of the line representing the change between each three-year period.

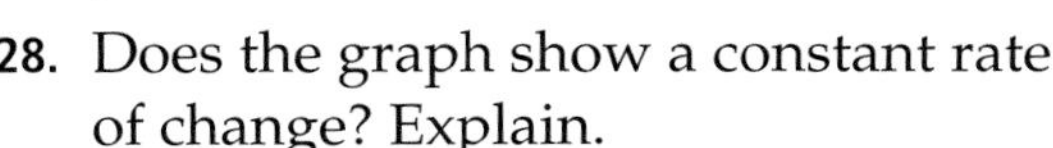

28. Does the graph show a constant rate of change? Explain.
29. If the graph is extended in each direction, could you expect the slope to remain constant throughout the graph? Explain.

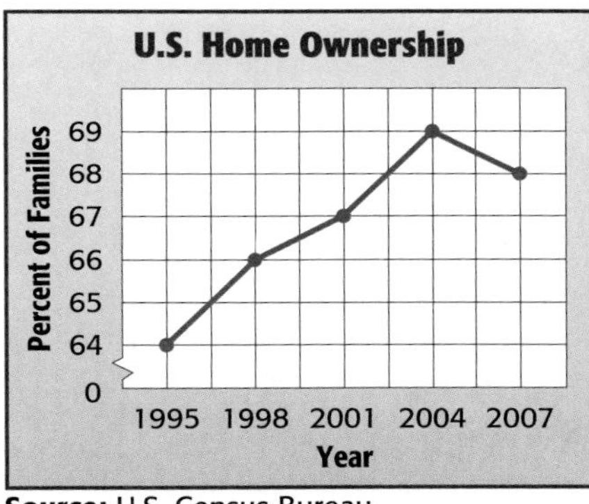

Source: U.S. Census Bureau

30. **GEOMETRY** Two lines that are parallel have the same slope. Determine whether quadrilateral $ABCD$ is a parallelogram. Justify your reasoning.

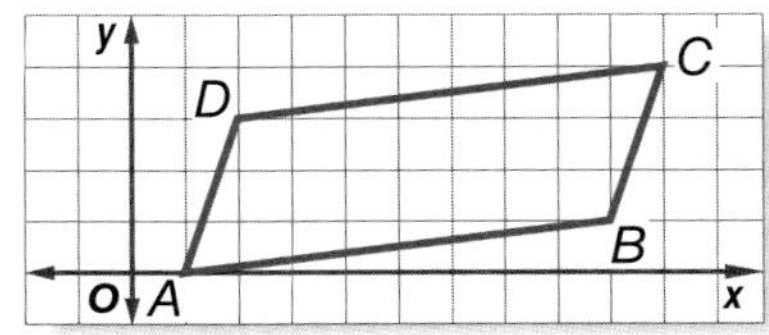

31. **DISABILITIES** Wheelchair ramps for access to public buildings are allowed a maximum of one inch of vertical increase for every one foot of horizontal distance. Would a ramp that is 10 feet long and 8 inches tall meet this guideline? Explain your reasoning.

ILS • ISAT
Extra Practice, pp. 692, 708

H.O.T. Problems

32. **OPEN ENDED** Write the coordinates of two points. Show that you can define either point as (x_1, y_1) and the slope of the line containing the points will be the same.

33. **FIND THE ERROR** Jabali and Joel are finding the slope of the line that passes through $X(0, 2)$ and $Y(2, 3)$. Who is correct? Explain.

Jabali

Joel

34. **CHALLENGE** Find the slope of the straight line that is the graph of the function expressing the circumference of a circle as a function of the radius.

35. **WRITING IN MATH** For the slope of a linear function, explain why the vertical change (rise) and the horizontal change (run) is always the same.

ISAT PRACTICE

6.D.3, 8.D.3a

36. Which line graphed below has a slope of -2?

A 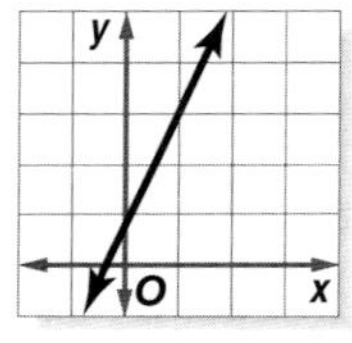

C 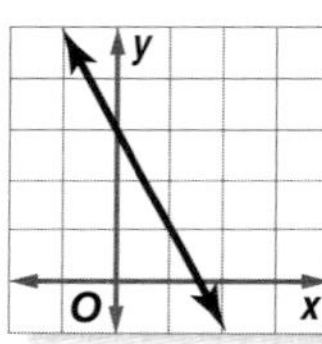

B 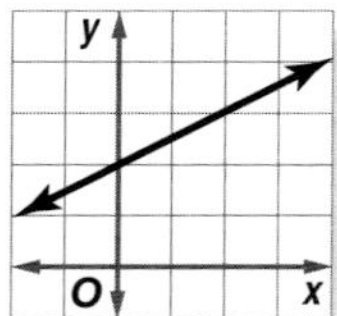

D 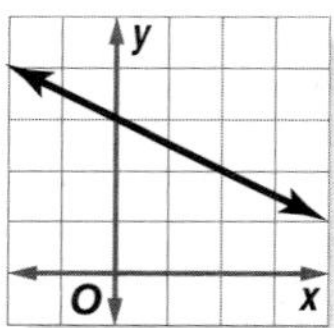

37. What is the slope of the linear function shown in the graph?

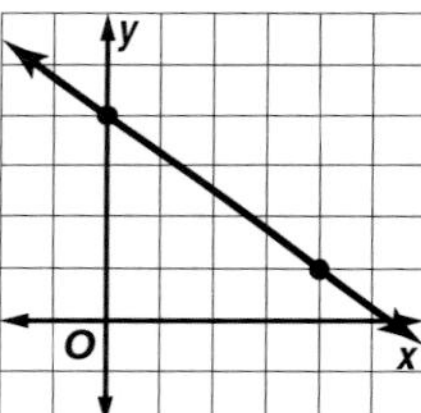

F $-\frac{4}{3}$

G $-\frac{3}{4}$

H $\frac{3}{4}$

J $\frac{4}{3}$

Spiral Review

Graph each function. (Lesson 9-3)

38. $y = 5x$

39. $y = x - 2$

40. $y = 2x - 1$

41. $y = 3x + 2$

42. **TEMPERATURE** The function used to change a Celsius temperature C to a Fahrenheit temperature F is $F = \frac{9}{5}C + 32$. Change 25° Celsius to Fahrenheit. (Lesson 9-2)

GET READY for the Next Lesson

PREREQUISITE SKILL Solve each equation. (Lesson 1-10)

43. $42 = -14x$

44. $144 = 18a$

45. $\frac{n}{3} = 7$

46. $-6 = \frac{t}{9}$

9-5 Direct Variation

MAIN IDEA

Use direct variation to solve problems.

IL Learning Standards

8.D.3a Solve problems using numeric, graphic or symbolic representations of variables, expressions, **equations** and inequalities.
8.D.3b Propose and solve problems using proportions, formulas and linear functions.
Also addresses 6.D.3, 8.A.3b, 8.B.3.

New Vocabulary

direct variation
constant of variation

IL Math Online

glencoe.com

- Extra Examples
- Personal Tutor
- Self-Check Quiz

GET READY for the Lesson

COMPUTERS Use the graph at the right that shows the output of a color printer.

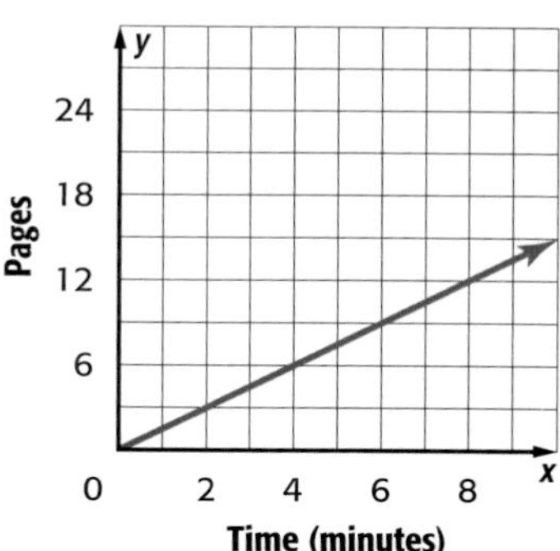

1. What is the constant rate of change, or slope, of the line?
2. Is the total number of pages printed always proportional to the printing time? If so, what is the constant ratio?
3. Compare the constant rate of change to the constant ratio.

In the example above, the number of minutes and the number of pages printed both vary, while the ratio of pages printed to minutes, 1.5 pages per minute, remains constant.

When the ratio of two variable quantities is constant, their relationship is called a **direct variation**. The constant ratio is called the **constant of variation**.

Real-World EXAMPLE Find a Constant Ratio

1 **FUNDRAISER The amount of money Robin has raised for a bike-a-thon is shown in the graph at the right. Determine the amount that Robin raises for each mile she rides.**

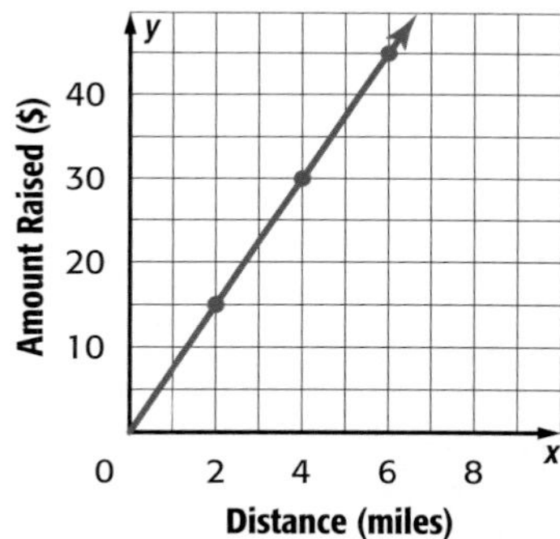

Since the graph of the data forms a line, the rate of change is constant. Use the graph to find the constant ratio.

$\frac{\text{amount raised}}{\text{distance}} \rightarrow \frac{15}{2} \text{ or } \frac{7.5}{1} \quad \frac{30}{4} \text{ or } \frac{7.5}{1} \quad \frac{45}{6} \text{ or } \frac{7.5}{1} \quad \frac{60}{8} \text{ or } \frac{7.5}{1}$

Robin raises $7.50 for each mile she rides.

CHECK Your Progress

a. **SKYDIVING** Two minutes after a skydiver opens his parachute, he has descended 1,900 feet. After 5 minutes, he has descended 4,750 feet. If the distance varies directly as the time, at what rate is the skydiver descending?

In a direct variation equation, the constant rate of change, or slope, is assigned a special variable, k.

Direct Variation

Key Concept

Words A direct variation is a relationship in which the ratio of y to x is a constant, k. We say y varies directly with x.

Symbols $k = \frac{y}{x}$ or $y = kx$, where $k \neq 0$

Example $y = 3x$

Model

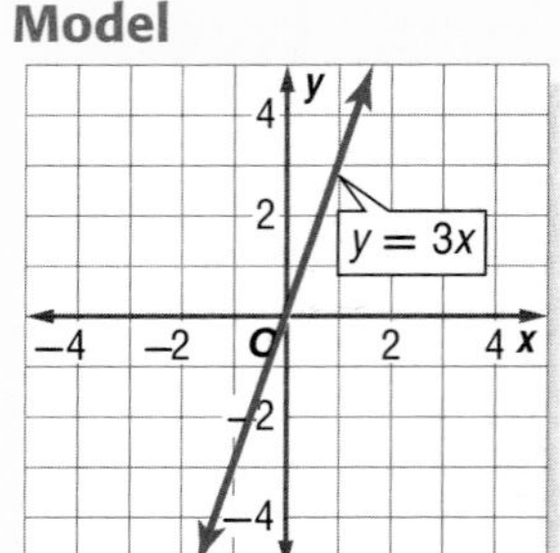

Real-World Link Most pets age at a different rate than their human companions. For example, a 3-year-old dog is often considered to be 21 in human years.

Real-World EXAMPLE Solve a Direct Variation

2 **PETS Refer to the information at the left. Assume that the age of a dog varies directly as its equivalent age in human years. What is the human-year age of a dog that is 6 years old?**

Write an equation of direct variation. Let x represent the dog's actual age and let y represent the human-equivalent age.

$y = kx$	Direct variation
$21 = k(3)$	$y = 21, x = 3$
$7 = k$	Simplify.
$y = 7x$	Substitute for $k = 7$.

Use the equation to find y when $x = 6$.

$y = 7x$	
$y = 7(6)$	$x = 6$
$y = 42$	Multiply.

A dog that is 6 years old is 42 years old in human-equivalent years.

Study Tip

Proportions In Example 2, you can also use a proportion to solve direct variation problems. Write ratios comparing the human equivalent age to the actual age.

$$\frac{21}{3} = \frac{x}{6}$$
$$126 = 3x$$
$$42 = x$$

CHECK Your Progress

b. **SHOPPING** A grocery store sells 6 oranges for $2. How much would it cost to buy 10 oranges? Round to the nearest cent if necessary.

In a direct variation, the constant of variation k is a constant rate of change. When the x-value changes by an amount a, then the y-value will change by the corresponding amount ka. In the previous example, when x changed by a factor of 6, y changed by 7(6) or 42.

Study Tip

Look Back
To review proportional relationships, see Lessons 4-2 and 4-5.

Not all relationships with a constant rate of change are proportional. Likewise, not all linear functions are direct variations.

EXAMPLES Identify Direct Variation

Determine whether each linear function is a direct variation. If so, state the constant of variation.

Miles, x	25	50	75	100
Gallons, y	1	2	3	4

Compare the ratios to check for a common ratio.

$\frac{\text{gallons}}{\text{miles}} \rightarrow \frac{1}{25} \quad \frac{2}{50} \text{ or } \frac{1}{25} \quad \frac{3}{75} \text{ or } \frac{1}{25} \quad \frac{4}{100} \text{ or } \frac{1}{25}$

Since the ratios are the same, the function is a direct variation. The constant of variation is $\frac{1}{25}$.

Hours, x	2	4	6	8
Earnings, y	36	52	68	84

$\frac{\text{earnings}}{\text{hours}} \rightarrow \frac{36}{2} \text{ or } \frac{18}{1} \quad \frac{52}{4} \text{ or } \frac{13}{1} \quad \frac{68}{6} \text{ or } \frac{11.33}{1} \quad \frac{84}{8} \text{ or } \frac{10.50}{1}$

The ratios are not the same, so the function is not a direct variation.

CHECK Your Progress

c.

Days, x	5	10	15	20
Height, y	12.5	25	37.5	50

d.

Time, x	4	6	8	10
Distance, y	12	16	20	24

Study Tip

Direct Variations
Notice that the graph of a direct variation, which is a proportional linear relationship, is a line that passes through the origin.

Proportional Linear Function

Concept Summary

Table

x	−2	−1	1	2
y	−4	−2	2	4
$\frac{y}{x}$	2	2	2	2

Graph

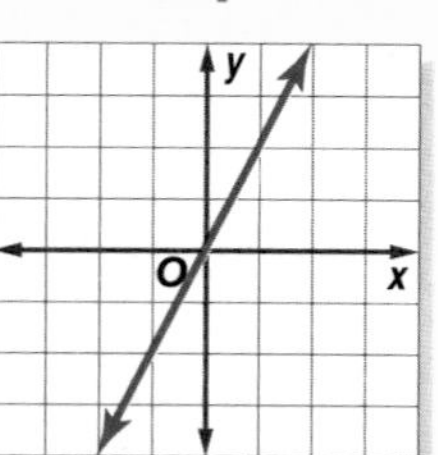

Equation

$y = 2x$

Nonproportional Linear Function

Table

x	−2	−1	1	2
y	−5	−3	1	3
$\frac{y}{x}$	$\frac{5}{2}$	3	1	$\frac{3}{2}$

Graph

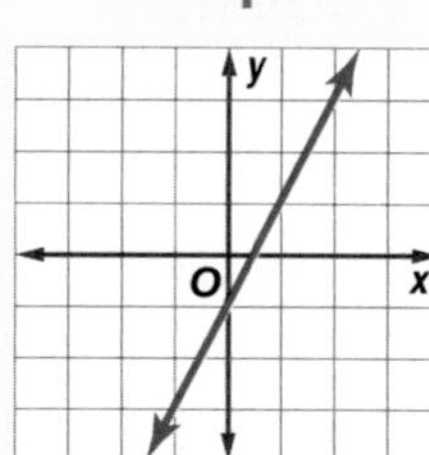

Equation

$y = 2x - 1$

CHECK Your Understanding

Example 1 (p. 487)

1. **MANUFACTURING** The number of computers built varies directly as the number of hours the production line operates. What is the ratio of computers built to hours of production?

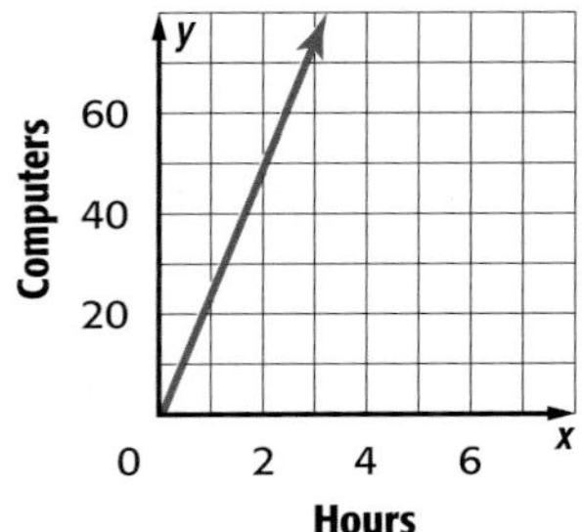

Example 2 (p. 488)

2. **TRANSPORTATION** A charter bus travels 210 miles in $3\frac{1}{2}$ hours. Assuming that the distance traveled is directly proportional to the time traveled, how far will the bus travel in 6 hours?

Examples 3, 4 (p. 489)

3. Determine whether the linear function is a direct variation. If so, state the constant of variation.

Hours, x	2	3	4	5
Miles, y	116	174	232	290

Practice and Problem Solving

HOMEWORK HELP	
For Exercises	See Examples
4–5	1
6–11	2
12–15	3, 4

4. **GARDENING** Janelle planted ornamental grass seeds. After the grass breaks the soil surface, its height varies directly with the number of days. What is the rate of growth?

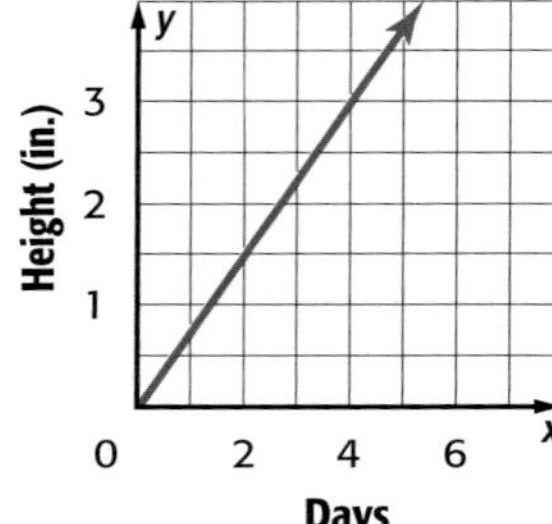

5. **JOBS** The amount Dusty earns is directly proportional to the number of newspapers he delivers. How much does Dusty earn for each newspaper delivery?

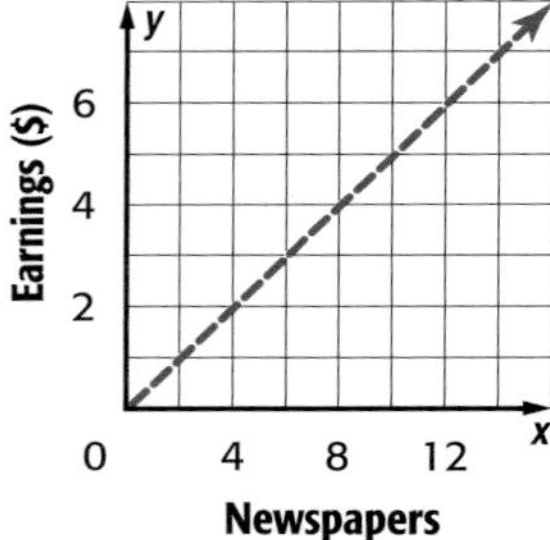

6. **SUBMARINES** Ten minutes after a submarine is launched from a research ship, it is 25 meters below the surface. After 30 minutes, the submarine has descended 75 meters. At what rate is the submarine diving?

7. **MOVIES** The Stratton family rented 3 DVDs for \$10.47. The next weekend, they rented 5 DVDs for \$17.45. What is the rental fee for a DVD?

8. **MEASUREMENT** Morgan used 3 gallons of paint to cover 1,050 square feet and 5 gallons to paint an additional 1,750 square feet. How many gallons of paint would she need to cover 2,800 square feet?

9. **MEASUREMENT** The weight of an object on Mars varies directly with its weight on Earth. An object that weighs 70 pounds on Mars weighs 210 pounds on Earth. If an object weighs 160 pounds on Earth, how much would it weigh on Mars?

Real-World Link The aspect ratio of a television screen describes the ratio of the width of the screen to the height. Standard screens have an aspect ratio of 4:3 while wide-screen televisions have an aspect ratio of 16:9.

10. **ELECTRONICS** The height of a wide-screen television screen is directly proportional to its width. A manufacturer makes a television screen that is 60 centimeters wide and 33.75 centimeters high. Find the height of a television screen that is 90 centimeters wide.

11. **BAKING** A cake recipe requires $2\frac{3}{4}$ cups of flour for 12 servings. How much flour is required to make a cake that serves 30?

Determine whether each linear function is a direct variation. If so, state the constant of variation.

12.

Pictures, x	5	6	7	8
Profit, y	20	24	28	32

13.

Minutes, x	200	400	600	800
Cost, y	65	115	165	215

14.

Age, x	10	11	12	13
Grade, y	5	6	7	8

15.

Price, x	10	15	20	25
Tax, y	0.70	1.05	1.40	1.75

ALGEBRA If y varies directly with x, write an equation for the direct variation. Then find each value.

16. If $y = -12$ when $x = 9$, find y when $x = -4$.
17. Find y when $x = 10$ if $y = 8$ when $x = 20$.
18. If $y = -6$ when $x = -14$, what is the value of x when $y = -4$?
19. Find x when $y = 25$, if $y = 7$ when $x = 8$.
20. Find y when $x = 5$, if $y = 12.6$ when $x = 14$.

21. **MEASUREMENT** The number of centimeters in a measure varies directly as the number of inches. Find the measure of an object in centimeters if it is 50 inches long.

Inches, x	6	9	12	15
Centimeters, y	15.24	22.86	30.48	38.10

Extra Practice, pp. 692, 708

22. **MEASUREMENT** The length of the rectangle shown varies directly as its width. What is the perimeter of a rectangle that is 10 meters long?

$\ell = 4$ m

$w = 6.4$ m

H.O.T. Problems

23. **OPEN ENDED** Identify values for x and y in a direct variation relationship where $y = 9$ when $x = 16$.

24. **CHALLENGE** The amount of stain needed to cover a wood surface is directly proportional to the area of the surface. If 3 pints are required to cover a square deck with a side of 7 feet, how many pints of stain are needed to paint a square deck with a side of 10 feet 6 inches?

25. **WRITING IN MATH** Write a direct variation equation. Then triple the x-value and explain how to find the corresponding change in the y-value.

ISAT PRACTICE 8.D.3a, 8.D.3b

26. Students in a science class recorded lengths of a stretched spring, as shown in the table below.

Length of Stretched Spring	
Distance Stretched, x (centimeters)	Mass, y (grams)
0	0
2	12
5	30
9	54
12	72

Which equation best represents the relationship between the distance stretched x and the mass of an object on the spring y?

A $y = -6x$ **C** $y = -\frac{x}{6}$

B $y = 6x$ **D** $y = \frac{x}{6}$

27. **SHORT RESPONSE** Nicole read 24 pages during a 30-minute independent reading period. How many pages would she read in 45 minutes?

28. To make fruit punch, Kelli must add 8 ounces of pineapple juice for every 12 ounces of orange juice. If she uses 32 ounces of orange juice, which proportion can she use to find x, the number of ounces of pineapple juice she should add to make the punch?

F $\frac{8}{12} = \frac{32}{x}$ **H** $\frac{8}{12} = \frac{x}{32}$

G $\frac{8}{x} = \frac{32}{12}$ **J** $\frac{x}{12} = \frac{8}{32}$

Spiral Review

Find the slope of each line. (Lesson 9-4)

29. 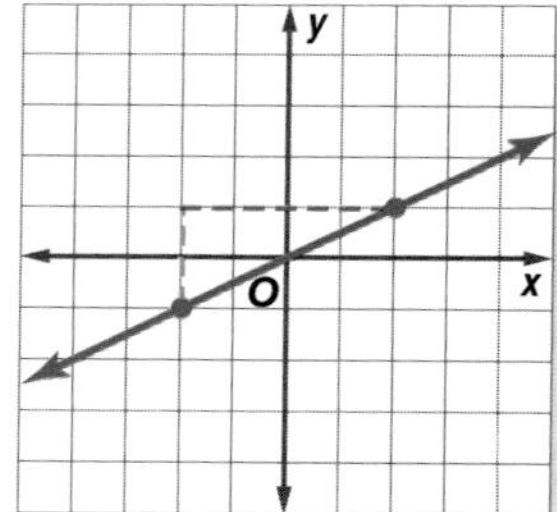

30. 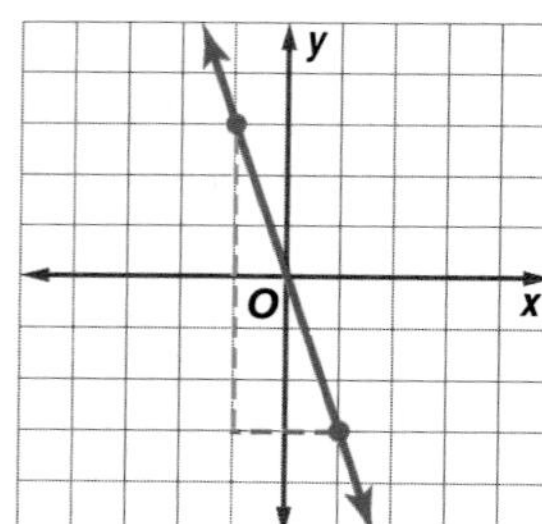

31. 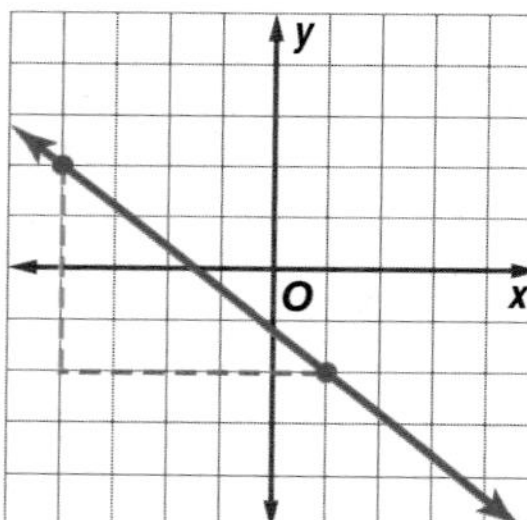

32. **JOBS** The function $p = 7.5h$ describes the relationship between the number of hours h Callie works and the amount she is paid p. Graph the function. Then use your graph to determine how much Callie can expect to earn if she works 20 hours. (Lesson 9-3)

33. **HEALTH** Many health authorities recommend that a healthy diet contains no more than 30% of its Calories from fat. If Jennie consumes 1,500 Calories each day, what is the maximum number of Calories she should consume from fat? (Lesson 5-3)

GET READY for the Next Lesson

PREREQUISITE SKILL Solve each equation. (Lesson 1-9)

34. $7 + a = 15$

35. $23 = d + 44$

36. $28 = n - 14$

37. $t - 22 = -31$

Extend 9-5

Geometry Lab
Slope Triangles

MAIN IDEA

Graph and analyze slope triangles.

IL Learning Standards

6.D.3 Apply ratios and proportions **to solve** practical **problems.** **8.D.3a Solve problems using numeric, graphic or symbolic representations of variables,** expressions, **equations** and inequalities. *Also addresses 7.A.3a, 7.B.3, 8.B.3.*

New Vocabulary

slope triangle

Refer to the graph at the right. Triangle *ABC* is formed by the rise, run, and section of the line between points *A* and *B*. If $A(x_1, y_1)$ and $B(x_2, y_2)$, such that $x_1 < x_2$, are two points on a line, then the right triangle *ABC* is called the **slope triangle** for the line. In this lab, you will investigate the relationship among slope triangles.

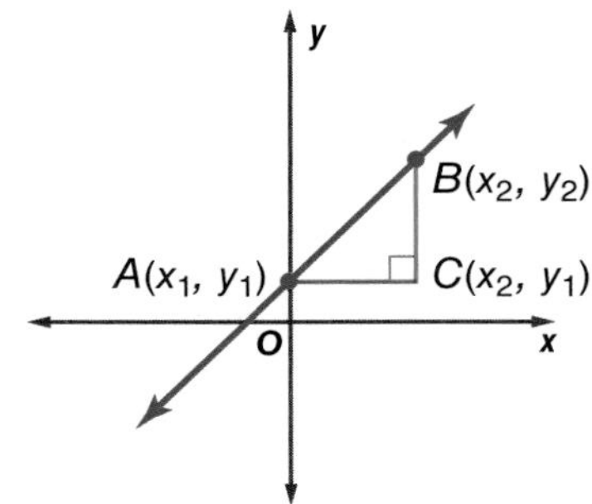

ACTIVITY

STEP 1 Graph $y = x + 1$ on a sheet of grid paper. Make the graph as large as possible. Draw and label two slope triangles anywhere along the line as shown.

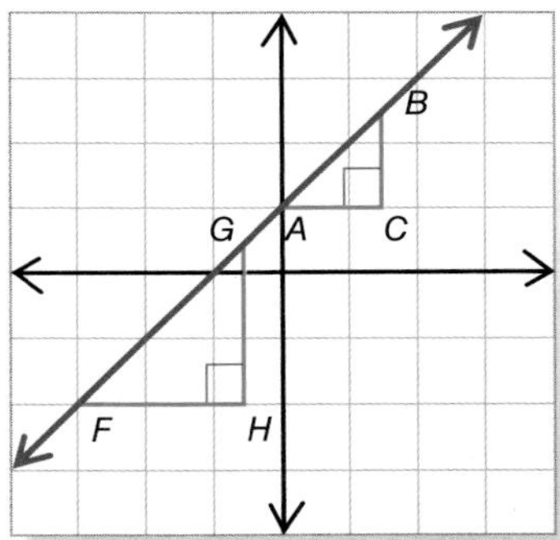

STEP 2 Use a protractor to measure the angles of each triangle.

STEP 3 Use a ruler to measure the side lengths.

Analyze the Results

1. What do you notice about the measures of the corresponding angles?
2. Are the corresponding sides of $\triangle ABC$ and $\triangle FGH$ proportional? Explain.
3. What can you conclude about $\triangle ABC$ and $\triangle FGH$? Explain.
4. Draw another slope triangle on the same line. Compare this triangle with $\triangle ABC$ and $\triangle FGH$. What can you conclude?
5. Repeat the activity above and Exercises 1–4 using several other linear equations.
6. **MAKE A CONJECTURE** Based on this activity, what can you conclude about all slope triangles on a given line?
7. **WRITING IN MATH** Find the slopes of each slope triangle. How are these slopes related to the slope of each line?

Chapter 9 Mid-Chapter Quiz

Lessons 9-1 through 9-5

IL Learning Standards
8.B.3, 8.D.3b

State whether each sequence is arithmetic. Write *yes* or *no*. If it is, state the common difference. Write the next three terms of the sequence. (Lesson 9-1)

1. 13, 17, 21, 25, 29, …
2. 64, −32, 16, −8, 4, …
3. −7, −16, −25, −34, −43, …

Find each function value. (Lesson 9-2)

4. $f(9)$ if $f(x) = 12x$
5. $f(6)$ if $f(x) = x + 7$
6. $f(8)$ if $f(x) = 2x - 8$
7. $f(2)$ if $f(x) = 6x + 1$

8. **MEASUREMENT** The perimeter of a square is 4 times the length of one side. Write a function using two variables to represent the situation. Find the perimeter if a side measures 6 feet. (Lesson 9-2)

9. **MULTIPLE CHOICE** Which equation describes the function represented by the table? (Lesson 9-2)

x	y
−2	−7
0	−3
2	1
4	5

A $y = 2x - 3$ **C** $y = x + 4$
B $y = x - 3$ **D** $y = 2x + 3$

Graph each function. (Lesson 9-3)

10. $y = x + 6$
11. $y = 2x - 5$

12. **WATER** A store sells bottles of water x in packs of 6 and individual bottles of water y. Graph the function $6x + y = 17$ to determine the number of each type of bottled water Sophia can have if she buys 17 bottles of water. (Lesson 9-3)

Find the slope of the line that passes through each pair of points. (Lesson 9-4)

13. $A(2, 5)$, $B(3, 1)$
14. $C(-1, 2)$, $D(-5, 2)$
15. $E(5, 2)$, $F(2, -3)$

16. **MULTIPLE CHOICE** Which graph has a negative slope? (Lesson 9-4)

F
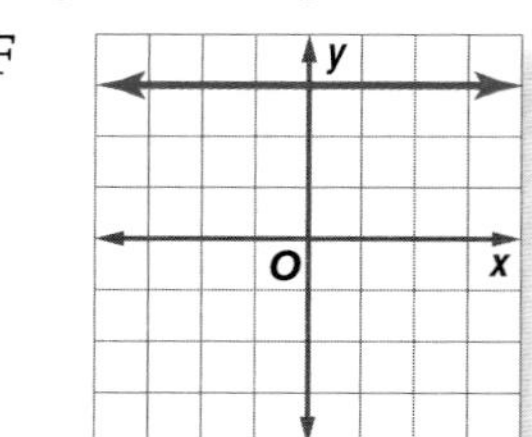

H
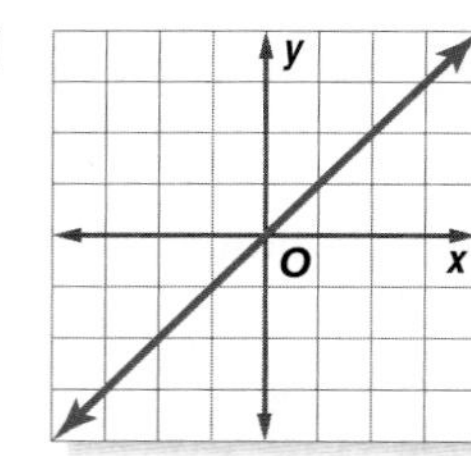

G
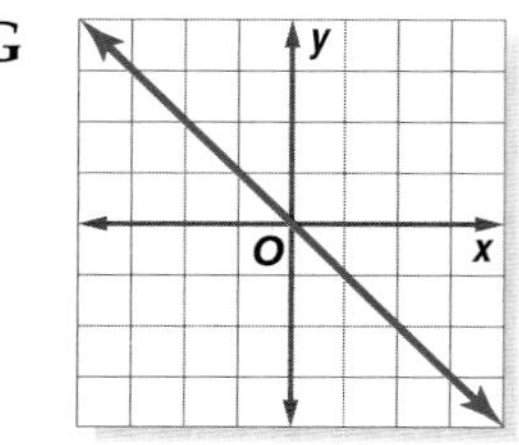

J
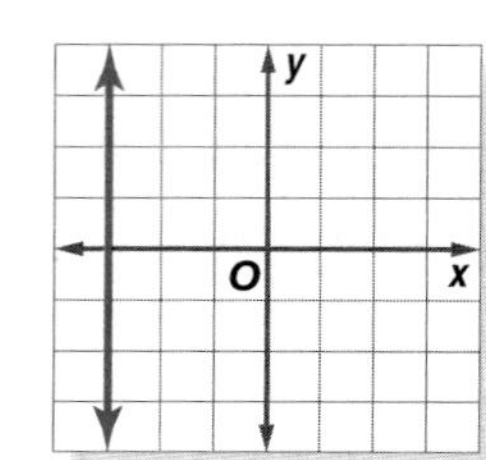

17. **BAKING** Ernesto baked 3 cakes in $2\frac{1}{2}$ hours. Assuming that the number of cakes baked is directly proportional to the number of hours, how many cakes can he bake in $7\frac{1}{2}$ hours? (Lesson 9-5)

18. **JOBS** The number of gallons of water Fina uses is directly proportional to the number of dogs she washes. How many gallons of water does she use for each dog she washes? (Lesson 9-5)

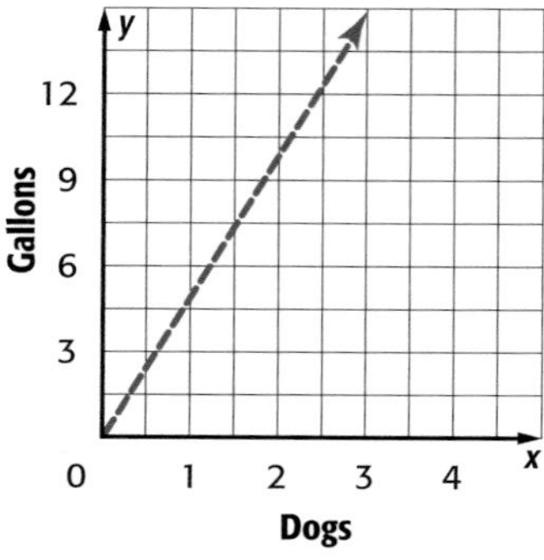

9-6 Slope-Intercept Form

MAIN IDEA

Graph linear equations using the slope and y-intercept.

IL Learning Standards

8.A.3b Solve problems using linear expressions, **equations** and inequalities.
8.D.3b Propose and solve problems using proportions, **formulas and linear functions.**
Also addresses 8.B.3, 8.D.3a.

New Vocabulary

slope-intercept form
y-intercept

IL Math Online

glencoe.com

- Extra Examples
- Personal Tutor
- Self-Check Quiz

GET READY for the Lesson

GASOLINE The graph represents the cost of gasoline at \$3 per gallon.

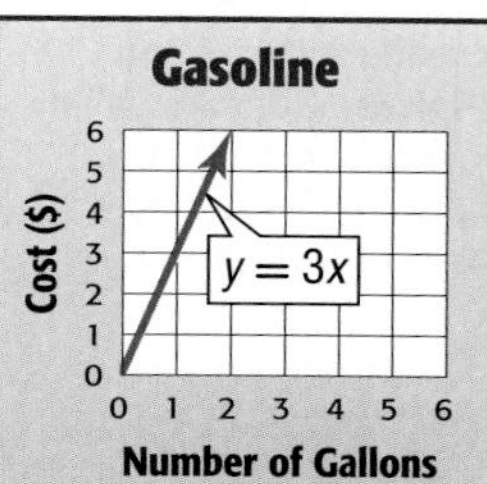

1. Write an equation that represents the cost of gasoline at \$3 per gallon and a drink that costs \$2.
2. Graph the equation from Exercise 1.

Proportional linear functions can be written in the form $y = kx$, where k is the constant of variation, or slope of the line. Nonproportional linear functions can be written in the form $y = mx + b$. This is called the **slope-intercept form**. When an equation is written in this form, m is the slope and b is the y-intercept. The **y-intercept** of a line is the y-coordinate of the point where the line crosses the y-axis.

EXAMPLES Find Slopes and y-intercepts of Graphs

State the slope and the y-intercept of the graph of each equation.

1 $y = \frac{2}{3}x - 4$

$y = \frac{2}{3}x + (-4)$ Write the equation in the form $y = mx + b$.
$y = mx + b$ $m = \frac{2}{3}, b = -4$

The slope of the graph is $\frac{2}{3}$, and the y-intercept is -4.

2 $x + y = 6$

$x + y = 6$ Write the original equation.
$x - x + y = 6 - x$ Subtract x from each side.
$y = 6 - x$ Simplify.
$y = -1x + 6$ Write the equation in the form $y = mx + b$. Recall that $-x$ means $-1x$.
$y = mx + b$ $m = -1, b = 6$

The slope of the graph is -1, and the y-intercept is 6.

CHECK Your Progress

a. $y = -5x + 3$ **b.** $y = \frac{1}{4}x - 6$ **c.** $y - x = 5$

EXAMPLE Graph Using Slope-Intercept Form

3 Graph $y = -\frac{3}{2}x - 1$ using the slope and y-intercept.

Step 1 Find the slope and y-intercept.

$y = -\frac{3}{2}x - 1$ slope $= -\frac{3}{2}$, y-intercept $= -1$

Step 2 Graph the y-intercept -1.

Step 3 Write the slope $-\frac{3}{2}$ as $\frac{-3}{2}$. Use it to locate a second point on the line.

$m = \frac{-3}{2}$ ← change in y: down 3 units ← change in x: right 2 units

Step 4 Draw a line through the two points.

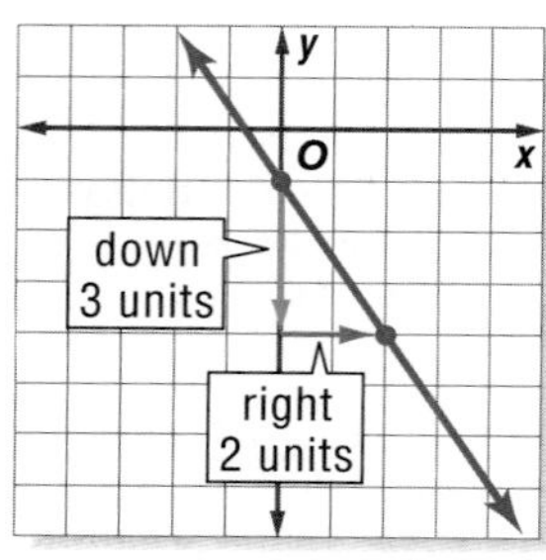

Study Tip

Check for Accuracy To check your graph, substitute the x- and y-values of another point on your graph into the equation. For Example 3, test the point $(2, -4)$.

$y = -\frac{3}{2}x - 1$

$-4 = -\frac{3}{2}(2) - 1$

$-4 = -3 - 1$

$-4 = -4$ ✓

CHECK Your Progress **Graph each equation.**

d. $y = x + 3$ e. $y = \frac{1}{2}x - 1$ f. $y = -\frac{4}{3}x + 2$

EXAMPLES Graph an Equation to Solve Problems

ACTIVITIES The Student Council is selling spirit T-shirts during spirit week. It costs \$20 for the design and \$5 to print each shirt. The cost y to print x shirts is given by $y = 5x + 20$.

4 Graph the equation to find the number of shirts that can be printed for \$50.

$y = 5x + 20$ slope $= 5$, y-intercept $= 20$

Plot the point (0, 20). Locate another point up 5 and right 1. Draw the line. The x-coordinate is 6 when the y-coordinate is 50, so the number of T-shirts is 6.

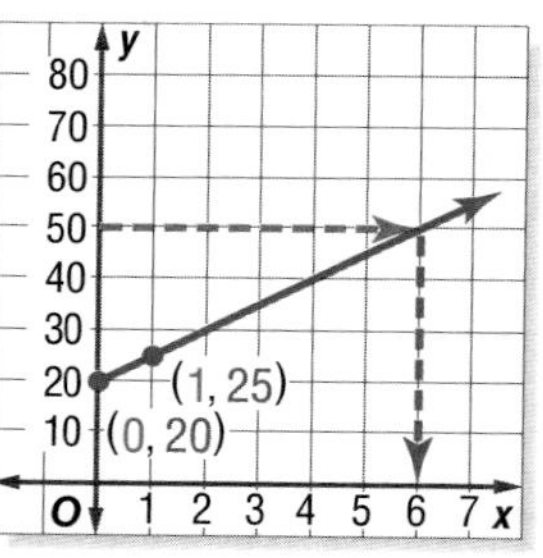

Real-World Link Shirt designs can be created on a computer then sent to a company to screen print the shirts. Each color requires a separate screen for the ink to pass through.

5 Describe what the slope and y-intercept represent.

The slope 5 represents the cost in dollars per T-shirt, and the y-intercept 20 is the one-time charge in dollars for preparing the design.

6 Is the total cost proportional to the number of T-shirts? Explain.

Compare the ratio of total cost to number of T-shirts for two points.

$\frac{25}{1}$ = \$25 per T-shirt $\frac{50}{6} \approx$ \$8.33 per T-shirt The ratios are different.

So, the total cost is not proportional to the number of T-shirts.

CHECK Your Progress

TRANSPORTATION A taxi fare y can be determined by the equation $y = 0.50x + 3.50$, where x is the number of miles traveled.

g. Graph the equation to find the cost of traveling 8 miles.

h. What do the slope and y-intercept represent?

i. Is the total fare proportional to the number of miles? Explain.

CHECK Your Understanding

Examples 1, 2 (p. 495)

State the slope and the y-intercept for the graph of each equation.

1. $y = x + 2$
2. $y = -\frac{1}{6}x - \frac{1}{2}$
3. $2x + y = 3$

Example 3 (p. 496)

Graph each equation using the slope and the y-intercept.

4. $y = \frac{1}{3}x - 2$
5. $y = -\frac{5}{2}x + 1$
6. $y = -2x + 5$

Examples 4–6 (p. 496)

SCHOOL For Exercises 7–9, use the following information.
Liam is reading a 254-page book for school. He can read 40 pages in one hour. The equation for the number of pages he has left to read is $y = 254 - 40x$, where x is the number of hours he reads.

7. Graph the equation to find how many pages Liam has left to read after 3 hours.
8. What do the slope and y-intercept represent?
9. Is the number of pages left to read proportional to the time read? Explain.

Practice and Problem Solving

HOMEWORK HELP	
For Exercises	See Examples
10–15	1, 2
16–21	3
22–27	4–6

State the slope and the y-intercept for the graph of each equation.

10. $y = 3x + 4$
11. $y = -5x + 2$
12. $y = \frac{1}{2}x - 6$
13. $y = -\frac{3}{7}x - \frac{1}{7}$
14. $y - 2x = 8$
15. $3x + y = -4$

Graph each equation using the slope and the y-intercept.

16. $y = \frac{1}{3}x - 5$
17. $y = -x + \frac{3}{2}$
18. $y = -\frac{4}{3}x + 1$
19. $y = \frac{3}{2}x - 4$
20. $y + 2x = -3.5$
21. $1.5 = y - 3x$

BOATING For Exercises 22–24, use the following information.
The Lakeside Marina charges a \$35 rental fee for a boat, in addition to charging \$15 an hour for usage. The total cost y of renting a boat for x hours can be represented by the equation $y = 15x + 35$.

22. Graph the equation to find the total cost for a 3-hour rental.
23. What do the slope and the y-intercept represent?
24. Is the total cost proportional to the number of hours? Explain.

TRAVEL For Exercises 25–27, use the following information.
The Viera family is traveling from Philadelphia, Pennsylvania, to Orlando, Florida, for vacation. The equation $y = 1{,}000 - 65x$ represents the distance remaining in their trip after x hours.

25. Graph the equation to find the distance remaining after 6 hours.
26. What do the slope and y-intercept represent?
27. Is the distance remaining proportional to the hours driven? Explain.

28. **INSECTS** The equation $y = 15x + 37$ can be used to approximate the temperature y in degrees Fahrenheit based on the number of chirps x a cricket makes in 15 seconds. Graph the equation to estimate the number of chirps a cricket will make in 15 seconds if the temperature is 80°F.

GEOMETRY For Exercises 29–31, use the supplementary angles at the right.

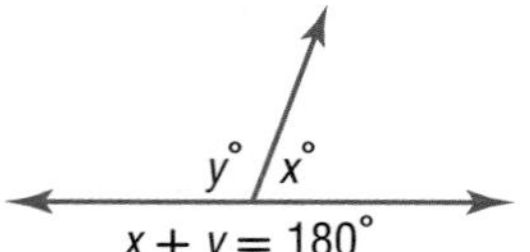

29. Write the equation in slope-intercept form.

30. Graph the equation.

31. Is the relationship between supplementary angles proportional? Explain your reasoning.

For Exercises 32–35, use the graph at the right.

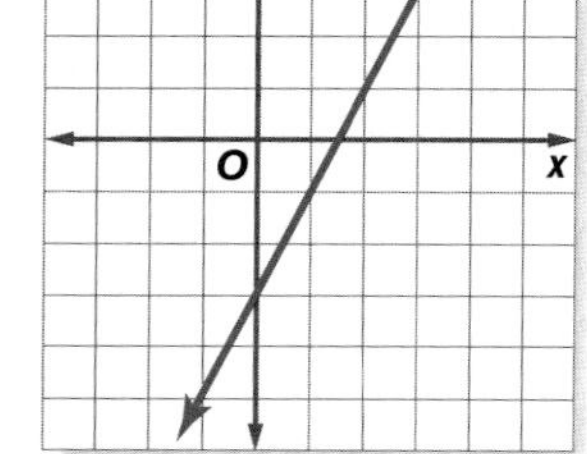

32. What is the slope and y-intercept of the line?

33. Describe how the slope and y-intercept appear on the graph.

34. Use the slope and y-intercept to write the equation of the line in slope-intercept form.

35. The *x-intercept* of a line is the x-coordinate of the point where the line crosses the x-axis. What are the coordinates of the x- and y-intercepts?

WEATHER For Exercises 36–38, use the following information.
The equation $y = 1.5x + 2$ can be used to find the total rainfall in y inches x hours after 12:00 P.M. during a tropical storm.

36. What is the slope and y-intercept of the line?

37. Describe how the slope and y-intercept appear on the graph of the equation. Then explain their meaning.

38. What are the coordinates of the x- and y-intercepts?

For Exercises 39 and 40, complete parts a–d for each table. The points given in the table lie on a line.

a. Find the slope and y-intercept of the line.

b. Describe how the slope and y-intercept appear on the graph of the line.

c. Use the slope and y-intercept to find the equation of the line in slope-intercept form.

d. Find the coordinates of the x- and y-intercepts.

ILS • ISAT
Extra Practice, pp. 692, 708

39.

x	0	1	2	3
y	1	5	9	13

40.

x	2	4	6	8
y	−4	−8	−12	−16

H.O.T. Problems

41. **OPEN ENDED** Draw the graph of a line that has a y-intercept but no x-intercept. What is the slope of the line?

42. **CHALLENGE** A triangle's original vertices are located at (3, 0), (4, −3), and (1, −4). The triangle is translated 1 unit to the right and 3 units up. It is then reflected across the graph of $y = x + 1$. Determine the new vertices of the triangle.

43. **REASONING** What is the slope and y-intercept of a vertical line?

44. **WRITING IN MATH** Write a real-world problem that involves a linear relationship. Describe how the slope and y-intercept would appear in these three different representations of the problem: table, equation, and graph.

ISAT PRACTICE 8.A.3b, 8.D.3b

45. Which *best* represents the graph of $y = 3x + 4$?

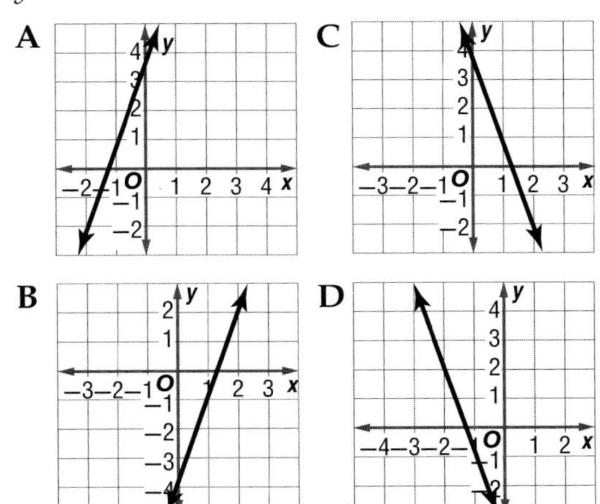

46. Which statement could be true for the graph below?

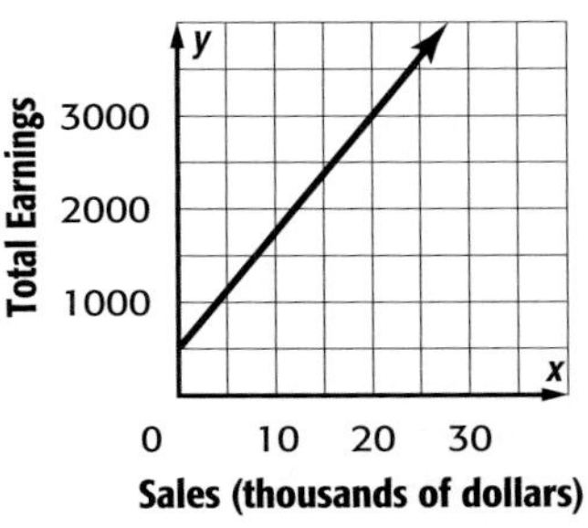

F Mr. Blackwell will earn $1,750 if his sales are $10,000.

G Ms. Chu will not earn any money if she has no sales.

H Mr. Montoya earns $250 for every $1,000 he sells.

J Ms. James earns $2,500 if she sells $2,500 worth of merchandise.

Spiral Review

47. **BICYCLING** Angel rides her bike 25 miles in $2\frac{1}{2}$ hours. How long will it take her to ride 60 miles? (Lesson 9-5)

Find the slope of the line that passes through each pair of points. (Lesson 9-4)

48. $M(4, 3)$, $N(-2, 1)$
49. $S(-5, 4)$, $T(-7, 1)$
50. $X(-9, 5)$, $Y(-2, 5)$

51. **MEASUREMENT** The function $y = 0.39x$ approximates the number of centimeters y in x inches. Make a function table. Then graph the function. (Lesson 9-3)

GET READY for the Next Lesson

PREREQUISITE SKILL Solve each equation. Check your solution. (Lesson 8-2)

52. $3a - 12 = -3$
53. $-2 = -n + 4$
54. $-\frac{1}{3}p - 7 = -3$
55. $4 - \frac{1}{5}x = 20$

Extend 9-6

Graphing Calculator Lab
Modeling Linear Behavior

MAIN IDEA

Use technology to investigate situations to determine if they display linear behavior.

IL Learning Standards

8.B.3 Use graphing technology and algebraic methods to analyze and predict linear relationships and make generalizations from linear patterns.
8.D.3b Propose and solve problems using proportions, formulas and **linear functions.**
Also addresses 8.A.3b, 8.D.3a.

Many situations in the real world exhibit *linear behavior* or behavior in which equal changes in one quantity produce approximately equal changes in another quantity. In this activity, you will examine a situation using a data collection device and a graphing calculator to determine if this situation displays linear behavior.

ACTIVITY

1

STEP 1 Connect a motion detector to your calculator. Start the data collection program by pressing APPS (CBL/CBR) ENTER, and then select RANGER, Applications, Meters, Dist Match.

STEP 2 Place the detector on a desk or table so that it can read the motion of a walker.

STEP 3 Mark the floor at a distance of 1 and 6 meters from the detector. Have a partner stand at the 1-meter mark.

STEP 4 When you press the button to begin collecting data, have your partner begin to walk away from the detector at a slow but steady pace.

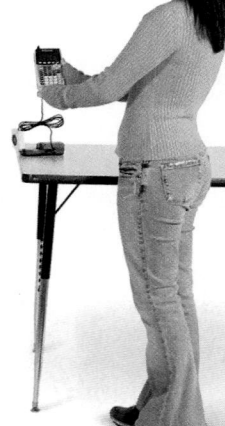

STEP 5 Stop collecting data when your partner passes the 6-meter mark.

STEP 6 Press ENTER to display a graph of the data. The x-values represent equal intervals of time in seconds. The y-values represent the distances from the detector in meters.

Analyze the Results

1. Describe the DISTANCE graph of the collected data. Does the relationship between time and distance appear to be linear? Explain.
2. Use the TRACE feature on your calculator to find the y-intercept on the graph. Interpret its meaning.

3. Press STAT 1 and record the time data from L1 and the distance data from L2 in a table like the one shown. Then use these data to calculate the rate of change $\frac{\text{distance}}{\text{time}}$ for several pairs of points. What do you notice?

List L1	List L2

4. Does your answer to Exercise 3 support your conclusion about the graph in Exercise 1? Explain.

5. **MAKE A PREDICTION** Predict how your graph and answers to Exercise 3 would change if the person in the activity were to
   a. move at a steady but *quick* pace away from the detector.
   b. move at a steady but slow pace *toward* the detector.

6. **COLLECT THE DATA** Repeat the activity and answer Questions 1 through 3 again for each of the situations described in Exercise 5.

7. **MAKE A CONJECTURE** How could you change the situation to be one that does not display linear behavior?

8. **COLLECT THE DATA** Repeat the activity and answer Questions 1 through 3 again for the situation you described in Exercise 7.

Families of graphs are graphs that are related in some manner. In this activity, you will study families of linear graphs.

Study Tip

Window
Pressing ZOOM 6 changes the viewing window for a graph to be [−10, 10] scl: 1 by [−10, 10] scl: 1.

ACTIVITY

2 **STEP 1** Clear any existing equations from the Y= list by pressing Y= CLEAR.

STEP 2 Enter each of the following equations: $y = -2x + 4$, $y = -2x + 1$, and $y = -2x - 3$.

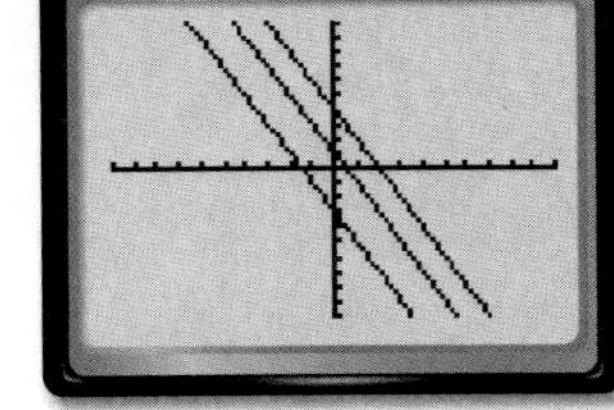

STEP 3 Press ZOOM 6 to graph the equations.

Analyze the Results

9. Compare the three equations and their graphs.

10. **MAKE A CONJECTURE** Consider equations of the form $y = ax + b$, where the value of a is constant but the value of b varies. What do you think is true for the graphs of these equations?

11. Use your calculator to graph $y = 2x + 3$, $y = -x + 3$, and $y = -3x + 3$. Compare the three equations and their graphs.

12. **MAKE A CONJECTURE** Consider equations of the form $y = ax + b$, where the value of a varies but the value of b remains constant. What do you think is true for the graphs of these equations?

9-7 Systems of Equations

MAIN IDEA

Solve systems of equations by graphing.

IL Learning Standards

8.A.3b Solve problems using linear expressions, **equations** and inequalities.
8.D.3a Solve problems using numeric, graphic or symbolic representations of variables, expressions, **equations** and inequalities. *Also addresses 8.B.3.*

New Vocabulary

system of equations

IL Math Online

glencoe.com

- Extra Examples
- Personal Tutor
- Self-Check Quiz

GET READY for the Lesson

Two Internet sites sell the same product for the same price, but their shipping charges differ as shown in the table.

Internet Site	Base Charge	Charge per Pound
A	\$3.00	\$1.00
B	\$1.00	\$2.00

The shipping charges can be represented by the following equations and tables where x represents the number of pounds, and y represents the shipping charge.

Internet Site A

$y = x + 3$

x	$y = x + 3$	y	(x, y)
0	$0 + 3$	3	(0, 3)
1	$1 + 3$	4	(1, 4)
2	$2 + 3$	5	(2, 5)
3	$3 + 3$	6	(3, 6)

Internet Site B

$y = 2x + 1$

x	$y = 2x + 1$	y	(x, y)
0	$2(0) + 1$	1	(0, 1)
1	$2(1) + 1$	3	(1, 3)
2	$2(2) + 1$	5	(2, 5)
3	$2(3) + 1$	7	(3, 7)

For Exercises 1–3, refer to the tables above.

1. For what number of pounds are the shipping charges the same?
2. For what number of pounds are the shipping charges for Internet Site A less than the ones for Internet Site B?
3. For what number of pounds are the shipping charges for Internet Site A greater than Internet Site B?

For Exercises 4 and 5, refer to the graphs of the equations at the right.

4. At what point do the two lines intersect?
5. What does this ordered pair represent?

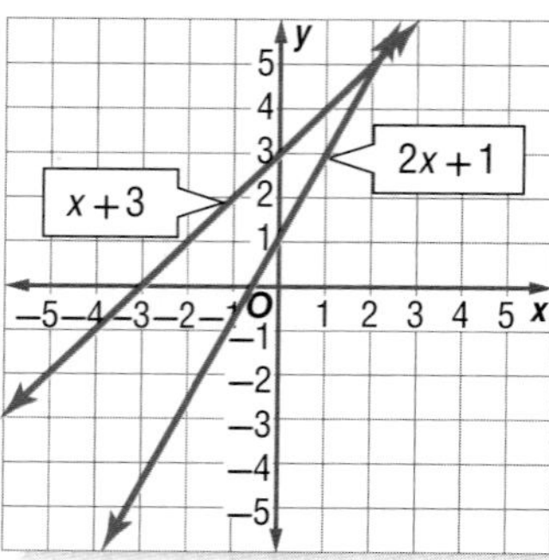

Together, the equations $y = x + 3$ and $y = 2x + 1$ are called a **system of equations**. There are two equations and two different unknowns, x and y.

The solution of a system of equations is an ordered pair that satisfies each equation. The ordered pair for the point of intersection of the graphs is the solution of the system.

Study Tip

Systems of Equations A system of equations can have one solution, infinitely many solutions, or no solutions.

EXAMPLE One Solution

1 **Solve the system $y = -2x - 3$ and $y = 2x + 5$ by graphing.**

Graph each equation on the same coordinate plane.

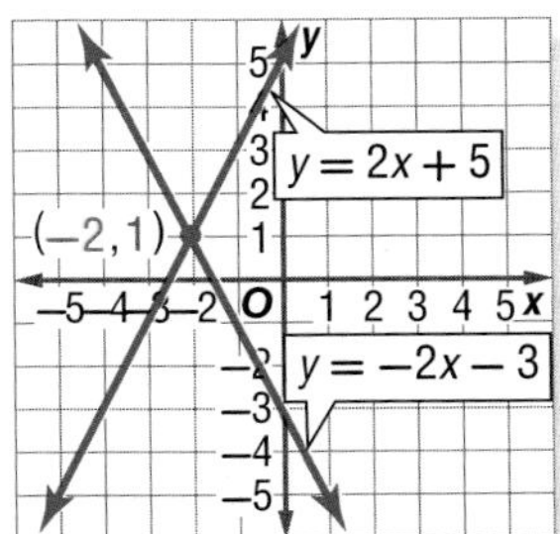

The graphs appear to intersect at (–2, 1).

Check in both equations by replacing x with –2 and y with 1.

Check

$y = -2x - 3$	$y = 2x + 5$
$1 \stackrel{?}{=} -2(-2) - 3$	$1 \stackrel{?}{=} 2(-2) + 5$
$1 = 1$ ✓	$1 = 1$ ✓

The solution of the system is (–2, 1).

CHECK Your Progress

a. Solve the system $y = x - 1$ and $y = 2x - 2$ by graphing.

EXAMPLE No Solution

2 **Solve the system $y = 2x + 1$ and $y = 2x - 3$ by graphing.**

Graph each equation on the same coordinate plane.

The graphs appear to be parallel lines. Since there is no coordinate point that is a solution of both equations, there is no solution for this system of equations.

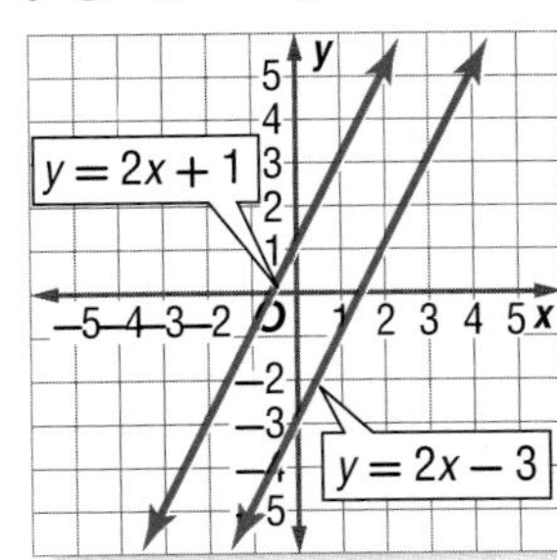

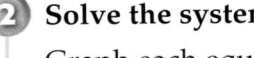

CHECK Your Progress

b. Solve the system $y = -4x - 1$ and $y = -4x + 2$ by graphing.

EXAMPLE Infinitely Many Solutions

3 **Solve the system $y = 2x + 1$ and $y - 3 = 2x - 2$ by graphing.**

Write $y - 3 = 2x - 2$ in slope-intercept form.

$y - 3 = 2x - 2$	Write the equation.
$y - 3 + 3 = 2x - 2 + 3$	Add 3 to both sides.
$y = 2x + 1$	Simplify.

Both equations are the same. Graph the equation.

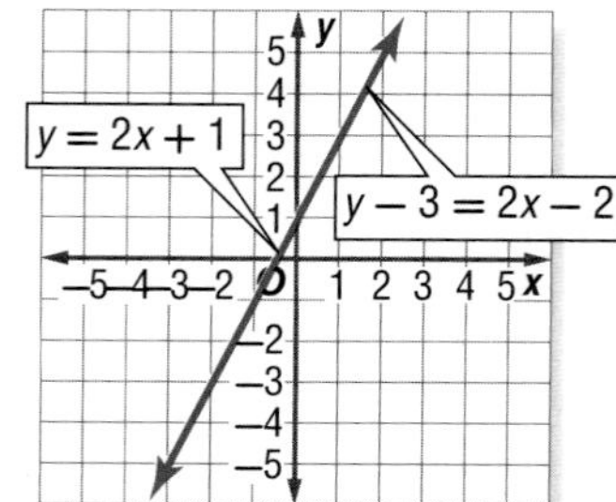

The solution of the system is all the ordered pairs of the points on the line $y = 2x + 1$.

Study Tip

Slopes and Intercepts When a linear system of equations has:

- different slopes and y-intercepts, there is one and only one solution.
- the same slope and different y-intercepts, there is no solution.
- the same slope and the same y-intercept, there is an infinite number of solutions.

CHECK Your Progress

c. Solve the system $y - x = 1$ and $y = x - 2 + 3$ by graphing.

Real-World EXAMPLE Writing and Solving Systems of Equations

4 **MOVIES** **Seven adults and children went to the movies. The number of adults was one more than the number of children. Write a system of equations that represents the number of adults and children. Solve the system by graphing.**

Let x = the number of children, and let y = the number of adults.

number of adults	equals	number of children	plus	one.
y	$=$	x	$+$	1

number of adults	plus	number of children	equals	total number of people.
y	$+$	x	$=$	7

So, the system of equations is $y + x = 7$ and $y = x + 1$.

Write $y + x = 7$ in slope-intercept form.

$y + x = 7$	Write the equation.
$y + x - x = 7 - x$	Subtract x from each side.
$y = -1x + 7$	Write in slope-intercept form.

Study Tip

Systems of Equations When writing the system, it is important to keep like variables lined up in relation to each other.

Study Tip

Check for Reasonableness Check the solution in the words of the problem to be sure the solution makes sense.

Graph $y = -1x + 7$ and $y = x + 1$ on the same coordinate plane.

The graphs appear to intersect at (3, 4).

Check in both equations by replacing x with 3 and y with 4.

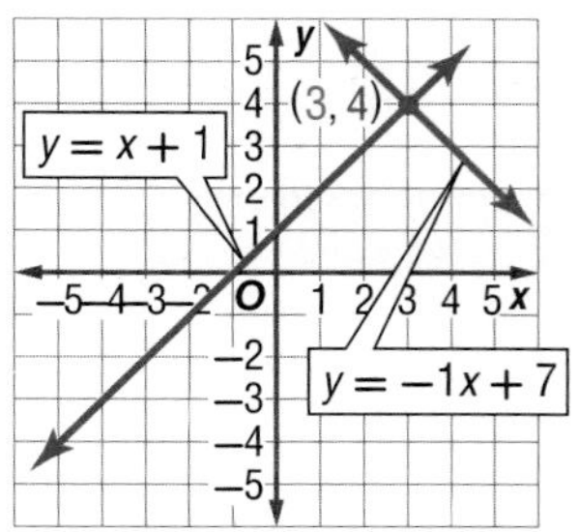

Check

$$y = -1x + 7 \qquad y = x + 1$$
$$4 \stackrel{?}{=} -1(3) + 7 \qquad 4 \stackrel{?}{=} 3 + 1$$
$$4 = 4 \checkmark \qquad 4 = 4 \checkmark$$

The solution of the system is (3, 4). So, 3 children and 4 adults went to the movies.

CHECK Your Progress

d. **MONEY** Jerry has a total of five nickels and dimes in his pocket. He has one more nickel than dime. Write a system of equations that represents the number of coins Jerry has. Solve the system by graphing.

Systems of Equations

Concept Summary

Number of Solutions	one solution	no solutions	infinitely many solutions
Graph	Intersecting Lines	Parallel Lines	Same Line

CHECK Your Understanding

Examples 1–3 (pp. 503–504)

Solve each system of equations by graphing.

1. $y = x + 3$
   $y = -2x - 3$

2. $y = 3x$
   $y - 4 = 3x$

3. $y - 6 = 2x$
   $y = 2(x + 1) + 4$

4. $y = \frac{1}{2}x + 2$
   $2y = 6x + 4$

Example 4 (pp. 504–505)

Write and solve a system of equations that represents each situation.

5. **AGE** The sum of Sally's age plus twice Jason's age is 12. The difference of Sally's age minus Jason's age is 3. Find their ages.

6. **BASKETBALL** In 2006, the New Jersey Nets paid Vince Carter and Jason Kidd combined salaries of $33 million. If Jason Kidd earned $3 million more than Vince Carter, find their salaries.

Practice and Problem Solving

HOMEWORK HELP	
For Exercises	See Examples
7–15	1–3
16–21	4

Solve each system of equations by graphing.

7. $y = x$
   $y = 2x - 4$

8. $y = -\frac{1}{2}x + 5$
   $y = 3x - 2$

9. $y = 4x - 15$
   $y - 4x = 16$

10. $y - 2x = 4$
    $y = 2x$

11. $x + y = 7$
    $3x - y = 5$

12. $x + y = -3$
    $y = x - 2x - 3$

13. $y - 4x = 8$
    $y = 2(2x + 4)$

14. $x + y = 3$
    $x = 4$

15. $-x + y = -2$
    $y = 2$

Write and solve a system of equations that represents each situation.

16. **PETS** A pet store currently has a total of 45 cats and dogs. There are 7 more cats than dogs. Find the number of cats and dogs in the store.

17. **PHONES** A certain wireless company charges $10 a month plus $0.25 per minute. A competitor charges $25 a month plus $0.15 per minute. When would the monthly costs be equal?

18. **TRACK** There are 23 athletes on the middle school track team. There are 7 more girls than boys on the team. Find the number of girls and boys on the team.

19. **JEWELRY** Janelle is ordering materials for beaded bracelets. Bab's Beads charges $0.12 per bead with a shipping cost of $3.25. Jewels by Jo charges $0.25 per bead with no shipping costs. When would the costs be the same?

20. **GEOMETRY** The length of the rectangle is 3 meters more than the width. The perimeter is 26 meters. What are the dimensions of the rectangle?

Perimeter = 26 meters

21. **MONEY** Brad has nickels and dimes in his pocket. He has 3 more dimes than nickels. The coins have a total value of 90¢. Find how many of each coin he has.

ANALYZE GRAPHS For Exercises 22–24, use the information below and the graph at the right.

Ajay and Sophia are biking along the same trail.

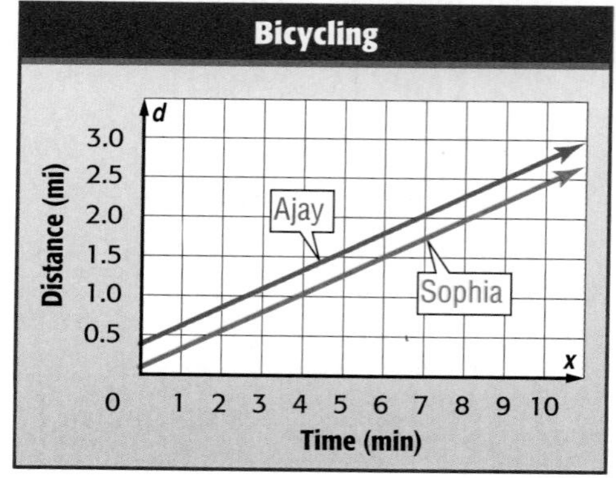

22. Which person rode the farthest after ten minutes?

23. Which person had the greater speed in miles per minute?

24. If the bicycling rates continue, will Sophia catch up to Ajay? Explain your reasoning.

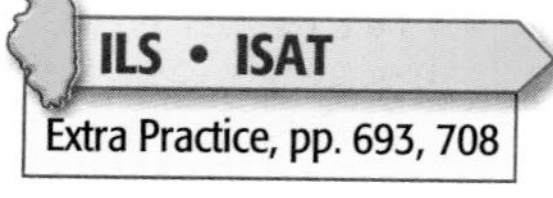

H.O.T. Problems

25. **CHALLENGE** One equation in a system of equations is $y = 2x + 1$.
    a. Write a second equation so that the system has (1, 3) as its only solution.
    b. Write an equation so that the system has no solution.
    c. Write an equation so that the system has many solutions.

26. **WRITING IN MATH** Write a real-world problem that could be represented by a system of equations. What does the point of intersection represent?

ISAT PRACTICE 8.A.3b, 8.D.3a

27. Claire baked 36 cookies. There are 8 more chocolate chip cookies than peanut butter. Which system can be used to find the number of each type of cookie?

    A $c + p = 36$, $p = c + 8$
    C $c + p = 8$, $p = c + 36$
    B $c + p = 36$, $c = p + 8$
    D $c + p = 8$, $c = p + 36$

28. Two equations in a system are shown in the graph. Which of the following statements is true?

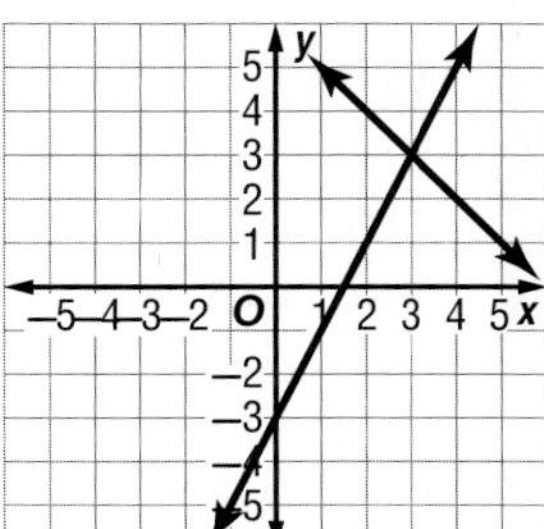

F The solution of the system is (0, −3).
G The solution of the system is (3, 3).
H The system has no solution.
J The system has infinitely many solutions.

Spiral Review

READING For Exercises 29–31, use the following information. (Lesson 9-6)

Eric has read 30 pages of a novel. He plans to read 50 pages every evening until he is finished. The equation $y = 30 + 50x$ can be used to represent the number of pages y Eric has read after x days.

29. Graph the equation.
30. Use the graph to find the number of pages Eric will have read after 6 days.
31. What do the slope and y-intercept represent?
32. **TRAVEL** One and a half hours after leaving its main station, a train has traveled 202.5 miles. At this rate, how far will the train travel after 5 hours? (Lesson 9-5)

For the given value, state whether each inequality is *true* or *false*. (Lesson 8-6)

33. $18 - n > 4, n = 11$
34. $13 + x < 21, x = 8$
35. $34 \leq 5p, p = 7$
36. $\frac{a}{-4} \geq 3, a = -12$

GET READY for the Next Lesson

37. **PREREQUISITE SKILL** A display of video game boxes is stacked in the shape of a pyramid. There are 5 boxes in the top row, 7 boxes in the second row, 9 boxes in the third row, and so on. The display contains 10 rows of boxes. How many boxes are in the display? Use the *look for a pattern* strategy. (Lesson 2-8)

Problem-Solving Investigation

MAIN IDEA: Solve problems by using a graph.

ILS **8.B.3 Use** graphing technology and **algebraic methods to analyze and predict linear relationships and make generalizations from linear patterns.**

P.S.I. TEAM +

e-MAIL: USE A GRAPH

AURELIO: Our science class ranked ten research Web sites from 1 to 10 with a ranking of 1 being the most popular. I created a graph with the average download time in seconds of these Web sites.

YOUR MISSION: Use a graph to find out if the most popular Web site has the fastest download time.

Understand	You want to know whether the most popular Web site ranked by the science class has the fastest download time. **Most Popular Web Sites** Average Download Time (s): 0, 1, 2, 3, 4, 5 Ranking: 1, 2, 3, 4, 5, 6, 7, 8, 9, 10
Plan	Make a graph and study the data.
Solve	The graph shows that, in general, the more popular Web sites are faster than the less popular Web sites. However, the fastest Web site, represented by (3,1), is not the most popular Web site. So, there are some exceptions to this pattern.
Check	Look at the graph. Two Web sites have a higher rating than the fastest Web site.

Analyze The Strategy

1. Explain what the ordered pair (1, 1.4) represents in terms of the question posed.
2. Find a graph in a newspaper, magazine, or on the Internet. Write a sentence describing any patterns in the data.

Mixed Problem Solving

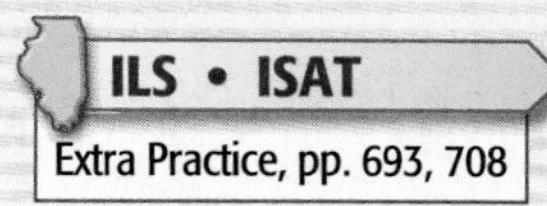

For Exercises 3 and 4, solve by using a graph.

3. **ALGEBRA** The blue line shows the weekly cost of a car rental at Company A. The green line shows the weekly cost of a car rental at Company B. If you wish to rent a car for one week and drive 60 miles, which company charges the lesser amount?

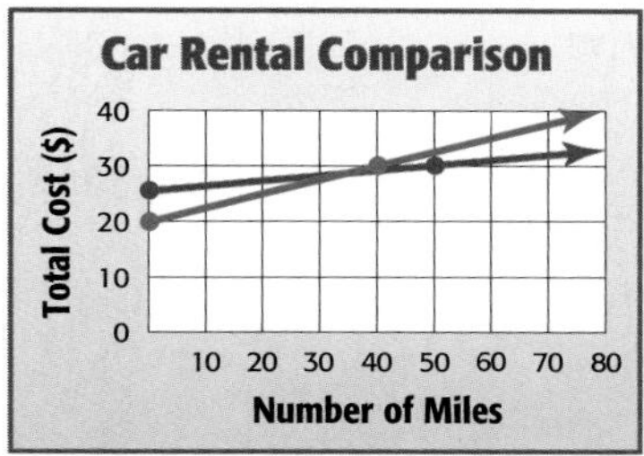

4. **JOBS** A popular Web site listed the results of a survey about the top 10 most glamorous jobs. Make a graph of the data. Does the most glamorous job have the highest median salary?

Job	Votes (%)	Median Salary ($)
Meteorologist	3.8	85,000
Photographer	7.2	50,000
Airline Pilot	7.2	105,000
Event Planner	4.5	52,000
Fashion Designer	24.8	42,000
Investment Banker	5.9	234,000
Surgeon	8.3	270,000
Public Relations Specialist	4.8	78,000
Interior Designer	5.5	48,000
Commercial Real Estate Developer	3.8	184,000

Use any strategy to solve Exercises 5–11. Some strategies are shown below.

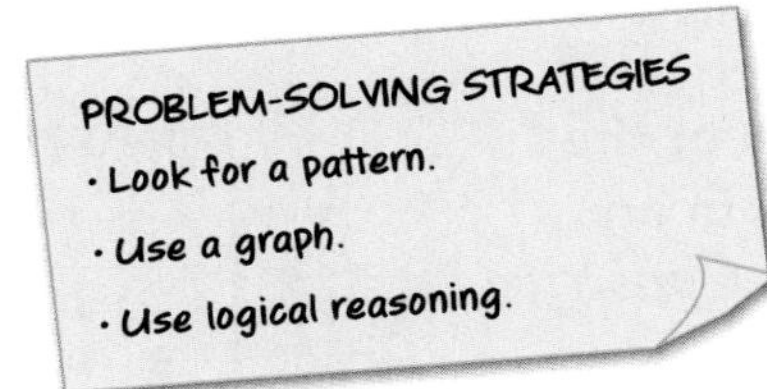

5. **NUMBERS** Find the next two numbers in the sequence 4, 0, −4, −8, … .

CLUBS For Exercises 6–8, use the table that shows the math club membership from 2001 to 2006.

Math Club Membership	
Year	Number of Students
2001	20
2002	21
2003	30
2004	34
2005	38
2006	45

6. Make a graph of the data.

7. Describe how the number of math club memberships changed from 2001 to 2006.

8. What is a reasonable prediction for the membership in 2007 if this membership trend continues?

9. **SCHOOL COLORS** The graph shows the results of a favorite color survey. To the nearest percent, what percent of the students chose purple and orange?

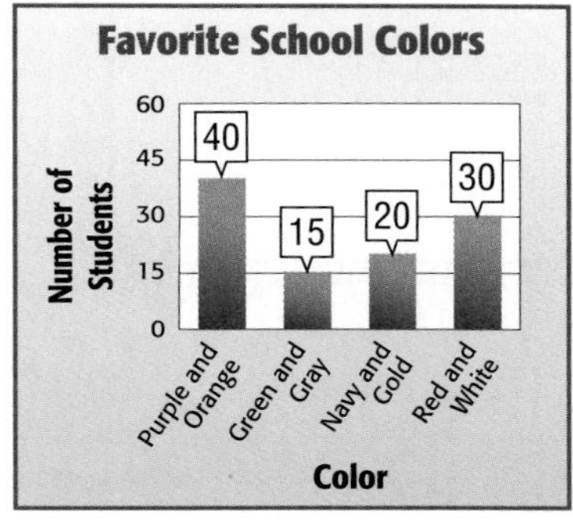

10. **MEASUREMENT** You need 2 cups of water to mix paint. You have an empty 3-cup container and an empty 5-cup container that do not have any markings on them. Explain how you can use these containers to measure the 2 cups of water you need.

11. **STATISTICS** The results of a survey showed that 34% of eighth graders wanted to take an extra language class. The school's policy says that there must be at least 32 students interested in the class. If 105 eighth graders were surveyed, is this enough students for an extra language class?

9-9 Scatter Plots

MAIN IDEA

Construct and interpret scatter plots.

IL Learning Standards

8.B.3 Use graphing technology and **algebraic methods to analyze and predict linear relationships and make generalizations from linear patterns.**

New Vocabulary

scatter plot
line of fit

IL Math Online

glencoe.com

- Extra Examples
- Personal Tutor
- Self-Check Quiz

MINI Lab

Measure a partner's height in inches. Then ask your partner to stand with his or her arms extended parallel to the floor. Measure the distance from the end of the longest finger on one hand to the longest finger on the other hand. Write these measures as the ordered pair (height, arm span) on the board.

1. Graph each of the ordered pairs listed on the board.
2. Examine the graph. Do you think there is a relationship between height and arm span? Explain.

A **scatter plot** is a graph that shows the relationship, if any relationship exists, between two sets of data. In this type of graph, two sets of data are graphed as ordered pairs on a coordinate plane. Scatter plots often show a pattern, trend, or relationship between the variables.

Types of Relationships — Concept Summary

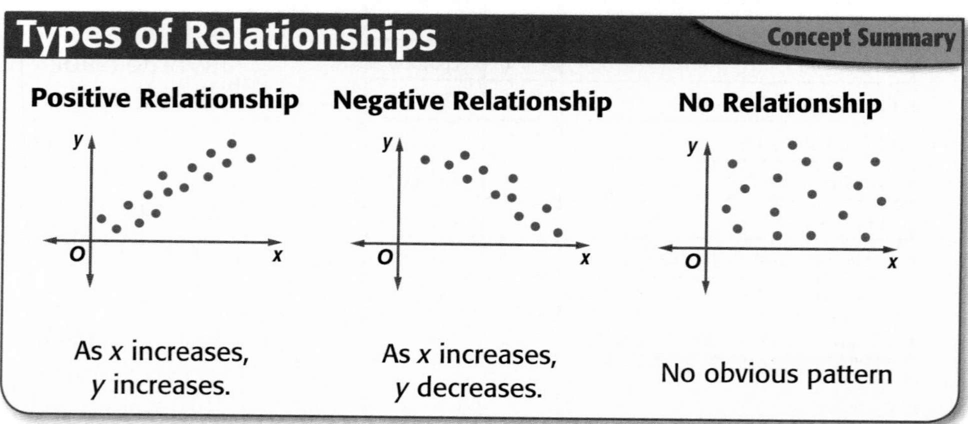

EXAMPLES Identify a Relationship

1 **Explain whether the scatter plot of the data for the amount of memory in an MP3 player and the cost shows a *positive, negative,* or *no* relationship.**

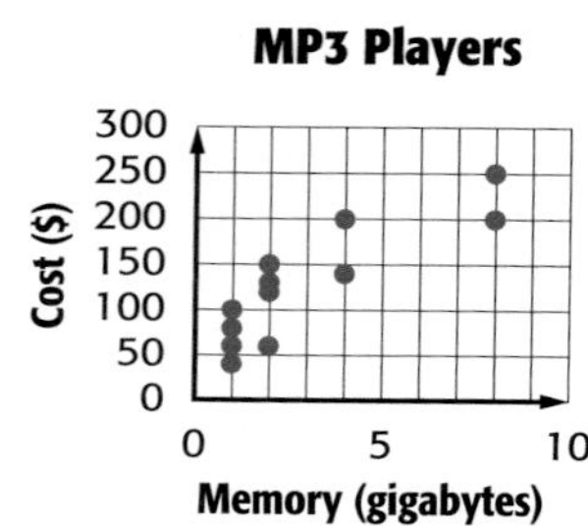

As the amount of memory increases, the cost increases. Therefore, the scatter plot shows a positive relationship.

2 **Explain whether the scatter plot of the date in May and the number of pints of ice cream sold show a *positive, negative,* or *no* relationship.**

Ice cream sales do not depend on the date. Therefore, the scatter plot shows no relationship.

CHECK Your Progress

a. Explain whether the scatter plot of the data for time and temperature shows a *positive, negative,* or *no* relationship.

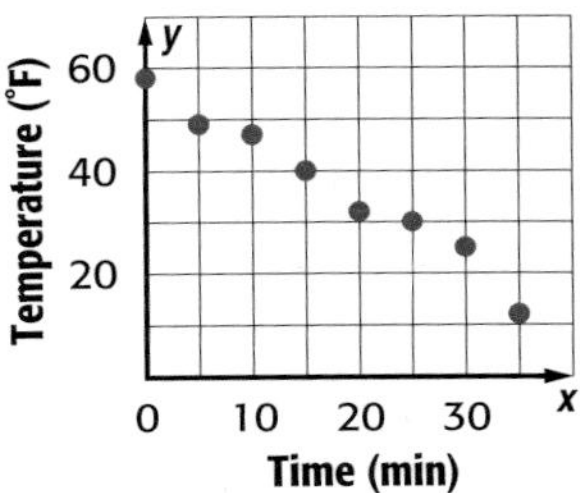

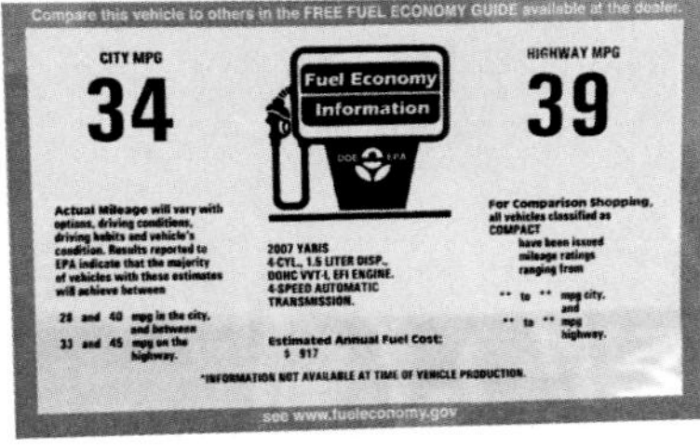

Real-World Link

The Environmental Protection Agency's new guidelines for fuel economy became effective with model year 2008. The new ratings lowered miles per gallon (MPG) estimates for most vehicles. Estimates reflect the use of air conditioning and faster speeds, both of which lower fuel efficiency.

A **line of fit** is a line that is very close to most of the data points.

EXAMPLES Line of Fit

CARS The MPG ratings for a certain car company are given.

Engine Size	1.8	2	2.2	2.4	2.4	2.4	3.4	3.4	3.5	3.6	3.8	3.9	5.3
MPG	29	22	24	20	24	23	19	19	20	20	19	17	18

3 **Make a scatter plot using the data. Then draw a line that best seems to represent the data.**

Graph each of the data points. Draw a line that fits the data.

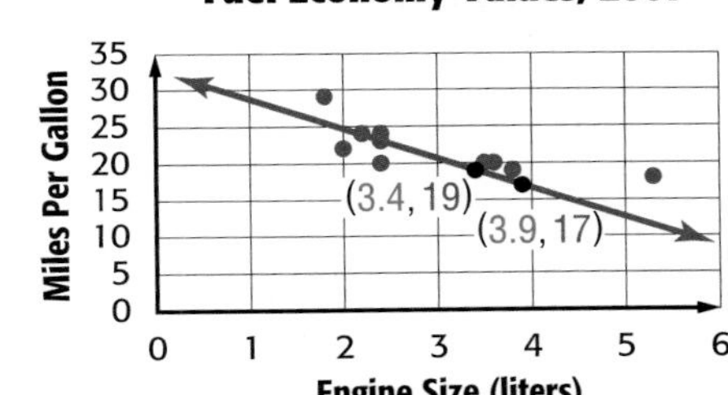

Study Tip

Estimation

Drawing a line of fit using the method in this lesson is an estimation. Therefore, it is possible to draw different lines to approximate the same data.

4 **Write an equation for this line of fit.**

The line passes through points at (3.9, 17) and (3.4, 19). Use these points to find the slope, or rate of change, of the line.

$m = \frac{y_2 - y_1}{x_2 - x_1}$ Definition of slope

$m = \frac{19 - 17}{3.4 - 3.9}$ $(x_1, y_1) = (3.9, 17), (x_2, y_2) = (3.4, 19)$

$m = \frac{2}{-0.5}$ or -4 The slope is -4, and the y-intercept is 35.

The y-intercept is 35 because the line of fit crosses the y-axis at about the point (0, 35).

$y = mx + b$ Slope-intercept form

$y = -4x + 35$ The equation for the line of fit is $y = -4x + 35$.

5 **Use the equation to predict the MPG for a 5.5-liter engine.**

$y = -4x + 35$ Equation for the line of fit

$y = -4(5.5) + 35$ or 13 The MPG will be about 13.

CHECK Your Progress

EDUCATION The approximate numbers of high school graduates in Texas over a 10-year period are shown in the table.

Graduating Class	Number of Graduates	Graduating Class	Number of Graduates
1994	163,000	1999	203,000
1995	169,000	2000	213,000
1996	172,000	2001	215,000
1997	182,000	2002	225,000
1998	197,000	2003	238,000

Source: Texas Education Agency

b. Make a scatter plot of the data. Then draw a line that represents the data.

c. Write an equation for a line of fit.

d. Use the equation to predict the number of graduates for the graduating class of 2015.

CHECK Your Understanding

Examples 1, 2 (pp. 510–511)

Explain whether the scatter plot of the data for each of the following shows a *positive*, *negative*, or *no* relationship.

1.

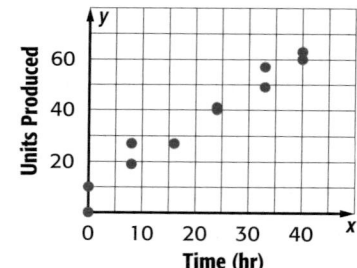

y
Units Produced
60
40
20
0 10 20 30 40 x
Time (hr)

2.

y
Fuel Remaining (gal)
12
8
4
0 100 200 300 x
Distance Traveled (mi)

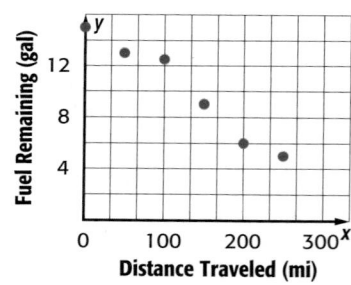

Examples 3–5 (pp. 511–512)

NUTRITION For Exercises 3–5, use the table.

Fast Food Nutritional Information												
Sandwich	A	B	C	D	E	F	G	H	I	J	K	L
Fat (grams)	21	10	14	21	30	34	32	37	27	26	18	7
Calories	490	280	330	430	530	590	540	590	550	470	450	340

3. Draw a scatter plot for the data and draw a line of fit.
4. Write an equation for the line of fit.
5. Estimate the number of grams of fat in a sandwich with 350 calories.

Practice and Problem Solving

HOMEWORK HELP	
For Exercises	See Examples
6–9	1, 2
10–15	3–5

Explain whether the scatter plot of the data for each of the following shows a *positive, negative,* or *no* relationship.

6. 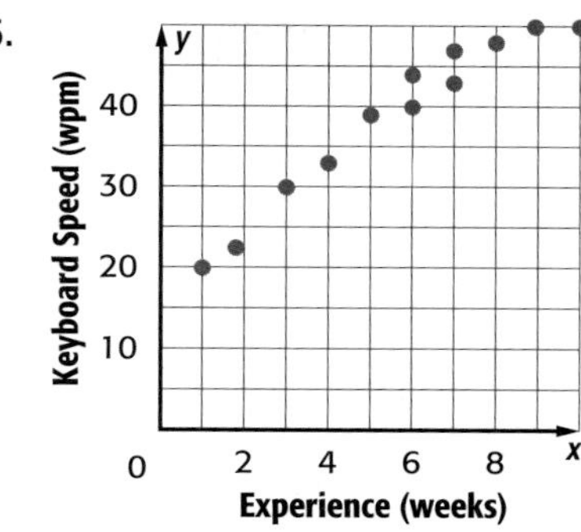

7. 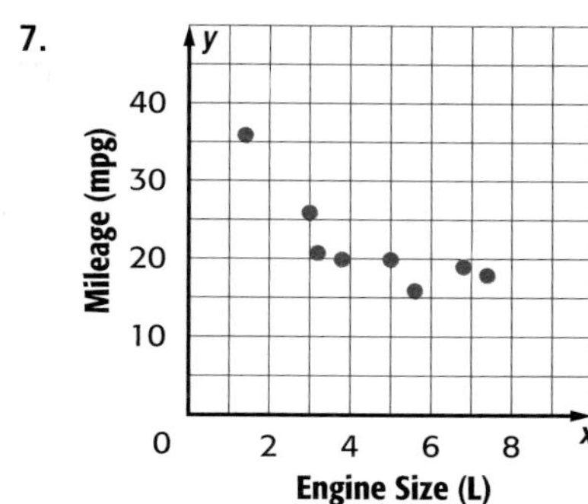

8. 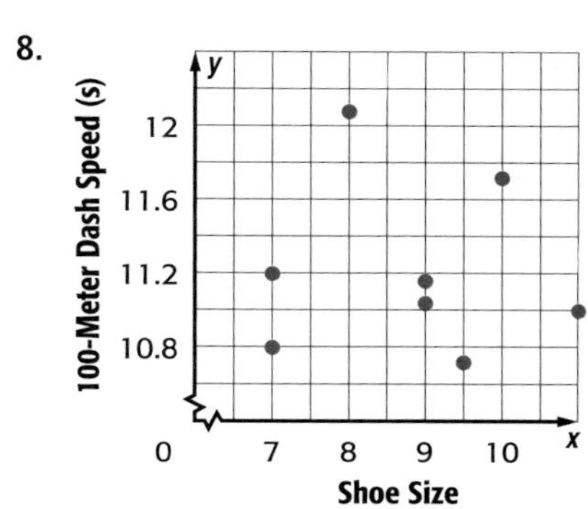

9. 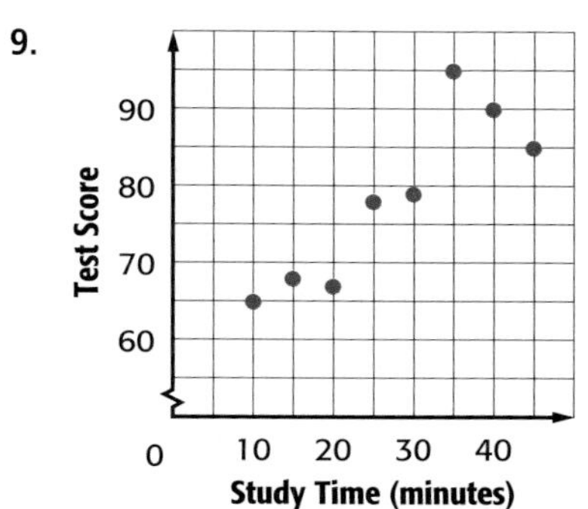

BUSINESS For Exercises 10–12, use the following information. The results of a survey about women's shoe sizes and heights are shown.

Height (inches) and Shoe Size

Shoe Size	8	8	$7\frac{1}{2}$	7	7	10	7	9	9	9
Height	66	65	65	62	61	70	62	65	65	68
Shoe Size	$6\frac{1}{2}$	9	$6\frac{1}{2}$	7	$5\frac{1}{2}$	5	9	6	$7\frac{1}{2}$	$9\frac{1}{2}$
Height	65	68	62	64	62	60	67	59	63	66

10. Draw a scatter plot for the data. Then draw a line of fit.
11. Write an equation for the line of fit.
12. Use your equation to estimate the height of a female who wears a size 5 shoe.

LIFE EXPECTANCY For Exercises 13–15, use the following table.

Year Born	1900	1910	1920	1930	1940	1950	1960	1970	1980	1990	1999	2000
Life Expectancy	47.3	50.0	54.1	59.7	62.9	68.2	69.7	70.8	73.7	75.4	76.7	77.1

Source: U.S. Census Bureau

13. Draw a scatter plot for the data. Then draw a line that seems to best fit the data.
14. Write an equation for your line of fit.
15. Use the equation to predict the life expectancy for a person born in 2020.

Explain whether a scatter plot of the data for each of the following would show a *positive*, *negative*, or *no* relationship.

16. length of a side of a square and perimeter of the square
17. grade in school and number of pets
18. length of time for a shower and amount of water used
19. outside temperature and amount of heating bill

BASEBALL For Exercises 20–22, use the table at the right.

20. Make a scatter plot of the data to show the relationship between home runs and runs batted in.
21. Explain whether you can draw a line of fit to approximate the data.
22. Could you predict the number of runs batted in for a player if you are given the number of home runs hit by that player? Explain.

Player	Home Runs	Runs Batted In
A. Jones	51	128
A. Rodriguez	48	130
D. Ortiz	47	148
D. Lee	46	107
M. Ramirez	45	144
M. Teixeira	43	144
A. Pujols	41	117
A. Dunn	40	101
P. Konerko	40	100
R. Sexton	39	121

Source: Major League Baseball

23. **SCHOOL** Determine the relationship a scatter plot of the data might show. Explain.

Week	1	2	3	4	5	6	7	8	9
Quiz Score	91	91	84	85	90	87	86	97	97

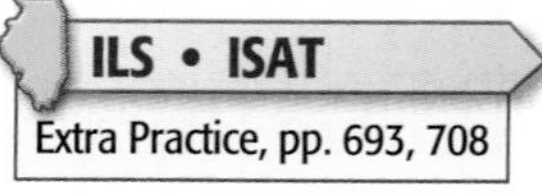

24. **FIND THE DATA** Refer to the Data File on pages 16–19. Choose some data and make a scatter plot with a line of fit. Use your graph to make predictions about unlisted data.

H.O.T. Problems

25. **OPEN ENDED** Give an example of data that could be represented by the scatter plot at the right. Explain the outlying value.

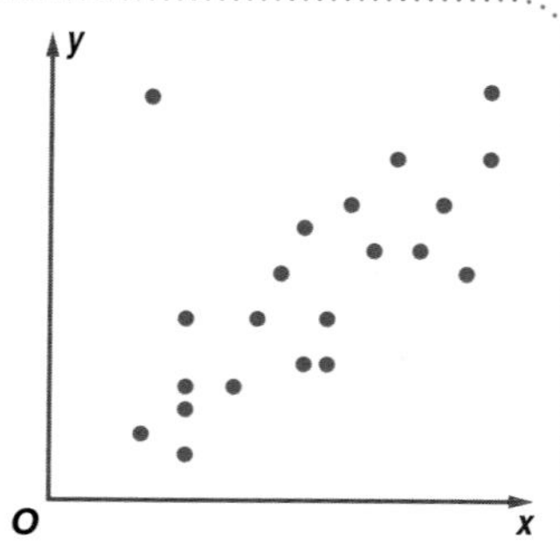

26. **NUMBER SENSE** Suppose a scatter plot shows that as the values of x decrease, the values of y decrease. Does the scatter plot show a *positive*, *negative*, or *no* relationship?

27. **CHALLENGE** Determine whether the following statement is *always*, *sometimes*, or *never* true. Justify your answer.

A scatter plot that shows a positive relationship suggests that the relationship is proportional.

28. **WRITING IN MATH** Explain why a scatter plot of skateboard sales and swimsuit sales for each month of the year might show a positive relationship. Does this mean that one factor caused the other? Explain.

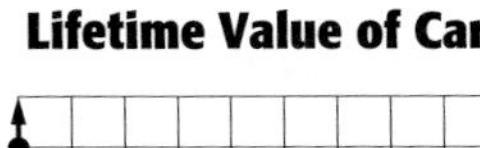

8.B.3

29. A car owner tracked the value of a car using a scatter plot.

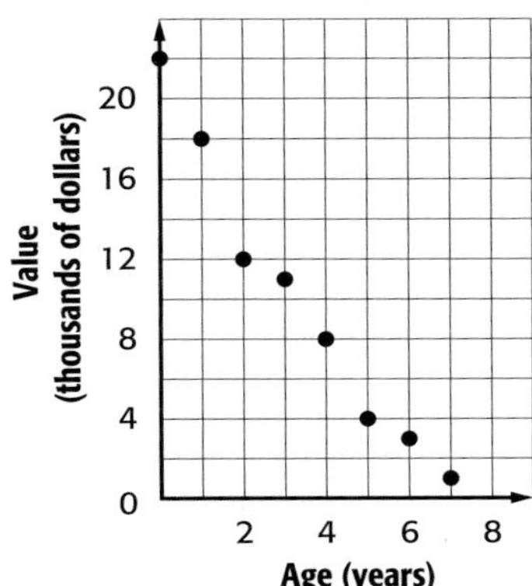

Which description best represents the relationship of the car's value?

A negative trend

B no trend

C positive trend

D cannot be determined

30. The scatter plot shows the cost of fruit Franco bought from a produce stand in relation to the weight of the fruit.

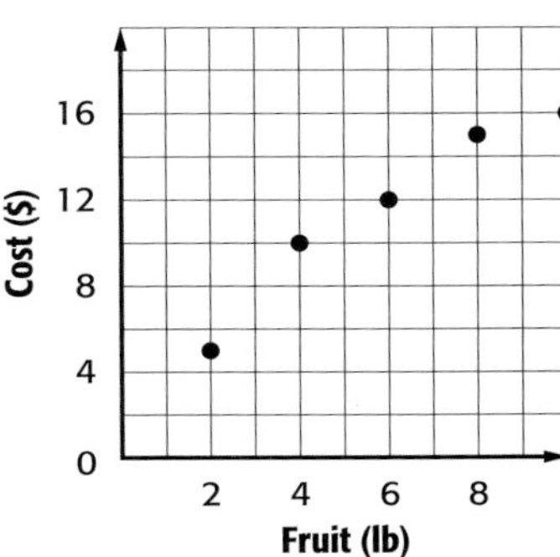

Based on the information in the graph, which statement is a valid conclusion?

F As Franco bought more pieces of fruit, the cost of the fruit increased.

G As Franco bought fewer pieces of fruit, the cost of the fruit decreased.

H As Franco bought fewer pounds of fruit, the number of pieces of fruit decreased.

J As Franco bought more pounds of fruit, the cost of the fruit increased.

Spiral Review

CITIES For Exercises 31–33, use the table. (Lesson 9-8)

31. Make a graph of the data.

32. Describe how the population of Detroit, Michigan, changed from 1950 to 2000.

33. Which city had the greatest percent increase from 1950 to 2000?

Largest U.S. Cities

City	2000	1950
New York, NY	8,010,000	7,890,000
Los Angeles, CA	3,690,000	1,970,000
Chicago, IL	2,900,000	3,620,000
Houston, TX	1,950,000	600,000
Philadelphia, PA	1,520,000	2,070,000
Phoenix, AZ	1,320,000	110,000
San Diego, CA	1,220,000	330,000
Dallas, TX	1,190,000	430,000
San Antonio, TX	1,150,000	410,000
Detroit, MI	950,000	1,850,000

Source: U.S. Census Bureau

34. **SPORTS** There are a total of 36 baseballs and softballs in a bin. There are 5 more softballs than baseballs. Write a system of equations that represents the situation. (Lesson 9-7)

Solve each equation. Check your solution. (Lesson 8-5)

35. $2x + 16 = 6x$

36. $4a - 9 = 7a + 6$

37. $5y - 1 = 3y + 11$

38. $n + 0.8 = -n + 1$

Extend 9-9

Graphing Calculator Lab
Scatter Plots

MAIN IDEA

Create scatter plots and calculate lines of fit using technology.

IL Learning Standards

8.B.3 Use graphing technology and algebraic methods **to analyze and predict linear relationships and make generalizations from linear patterns.**

A graphing calculator is useful for creating and analyzing scatter plots of large sets of data.

ACTIVITY

1 **LEISURE The tables give the weekly number of hours spent watching television and weekly number of hours spent exercising for each person in a survey. Make a scatter plot of the data.**

Weekly Television (h)	17	20	11	10	15	38	5	25
Weekly Exercise (h)	5	4.5	7.5	8	6.5	1	7.5	3

Weekly Television (h)	25	32	5	17	40	28	20	30
Weekly Exercise (h)	2.5	3.5	6	7	0.5	5	4	1.5

STEP 1 Clear the existing data by pressing STAT ENTER ▲ CLEAR ENTER.

STEP 2 Next enter the data. Input the number of weekly hours spent watching television in L1 and press ENTER. Then enter the weekly hours spent exercising in L2.

STEP 3 Turn on the statistical plot by pressing 2nd [STAT PLOT] ENTER ENTER. Select the scatter plot and confirm L1 as the Xlist, L2 as the Ylist, and the square as the mark.

STEP 4 Graph the data by pressing ZOOM 9. Use the Trace feature and the left and right arrow keys to move from one point to another.

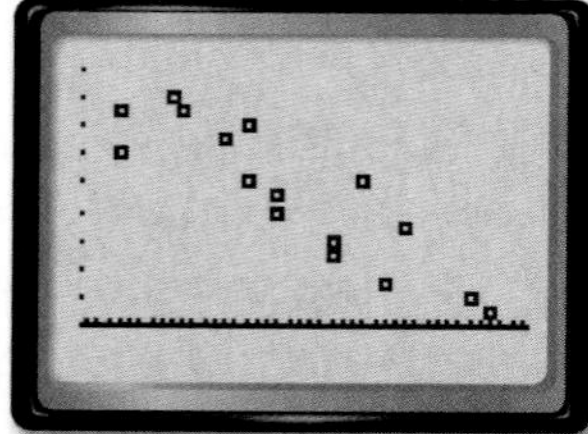

Analyze the Results

1. Describe how the data are related. Explain your reasoning.

2. **WEATHER** Use a graphing calculator to make a scatter plot of the following weather data. Store the data in L3 and L4 and use Plot 2 to create the graph. Then determine whether the data have a *positive, negative,* or *no relationship.* Explain your reasoning.

Average Monthly Temperature (°F)	77	42	45	55	57	63	76	65
Average Monthly Rainfall (in.)	6.0	4.8	7	3.2	6.8	4.8	5.7	7.2

Average Monthly Temperature (°F)	67	73	51	81	84	86	64	43
Average Monthly Rainfall (in.)	2.6	5.5	5.9	6.3	7.9	4.2	6.3	4.5

ACTIVITY

2 LEISURE Find and graph a line of fit for the data in Activity 1.

STEP 1 Access the CALC menu by pressing STAT ▶.

STEP 2 Select 4 to find a line of fit in the form $y = ax + b$. Press 2nd [L1] , 2nd [L2] ENTER to find a line of fit for the data in lists L1 and L2.

STEP 3 Graph the line of fit in Y1 by pressing Y= and then VARS 5 to access the Statistics... menu. Use the ▶ and ENTER keys to select EQ and then press 1 to select RegEQ, the line of fit equation. Finally, press GRAPH.

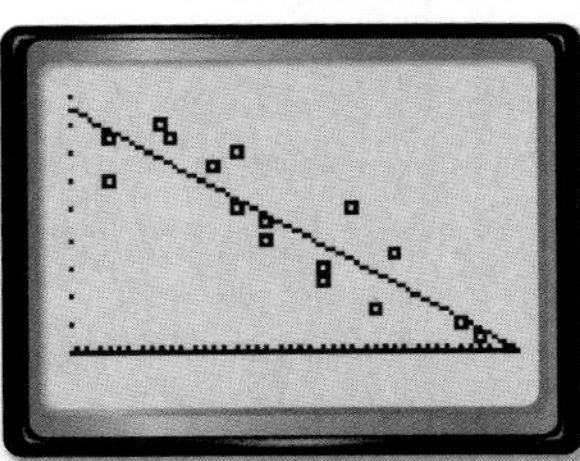

Analyze the Results

3. **MAKE A PREDICTION** Use the TRACE feature to predict the average number of hours of exercise someone who watches 35 hours of television would get.

4. **COLLECT THE DATA** Collect a set of data that can be represented in a scatter plot. Enter the data in a graphing calculator. Determine whether the data have a *positive, negative,* or *no relationship* and whether there appears to be any outlying values. Then use the calculator to find a line of fit and to make a prediction.

CHAPTER 9

Study Guide and Review

IL Math Online glencoe.com
- STUDY TO GO
- Vocabulary Review

GET READY to Study

Be sure the following Big Ideas are noted in your Foldable.

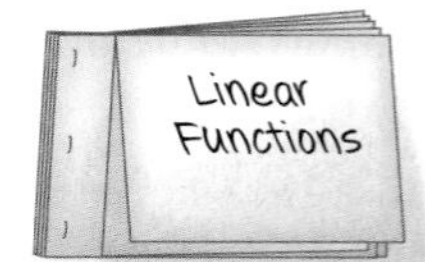

BIG Ideas

Sequences (Lesson 9-1)
- An arithmetic sequence is a sequence in which the difference between any two consecutive terms is the same.

Functions (Lessons 9-2 and 9-3)
- A function is a relationship in which one value is dependent upon another.
- Functions can be represented by words, equations, tables, ordered pairs, and graphs.

Slope (Lesson 9-4)
- The slope m of a line passing through points (x_1, y_1) and (x_2, y_2) is the ratio of the difference in the y-coordinates to the corresponding difference in the x-coordinates.

Direct Variation (Lesson 9-5)
- A direct variation is a relationship in which the ratio of y to x is a constant, k.

Slope-Intercept Form (Lesson 9-6)
- An equation written in slope-intercept form is written as $y = mx + b$, where m is the slope and b is the y-intercept.

Systems of Equations (Lesson 9-7)
- Two equations together are called a system of equations.

Scatter Plots (Lesson 9-9)
- In a positive relationship, x increases and y increases.
- In a negative relationship, x increases and y decreases.
- In a no relationship, no obvious pattern exists between x and y.

Key Vocabulary

arithmetic sequence (p. 464)
common difference (p. 464)
constant of variation (p. 487)
direct variation (p. 487)
domain (p. 470)
function (p. 469)
function table (p. 470)
linear function (p. 476)
line of fit (p. 511)
range (p. 470)
rise (p. 481)
run (p. 481)
scatter plot (p. 510)
sequence (p. 464)
slope (p. 481)
slope-intercept form (p. 495)
system of equations (p. 502)
term (p. 464)
y-intercept (p. 495)

Vocabulary Check

Choose the correct term or number to complete each sentence.

1. The (domain, range) is the set of input values of a function.
2. A (common difference, sequence) is an ordered list of numbers.
3. A relationship where one thing depends on another is called a (function, slope).
4. A (scatter plot, function table) is a graph that shows the relationship between two sets of data.
5. The (x-intercept, y-intercept) has the coordinates $(0, b)$.
6. The slope formula is $\left(\frac{y_2 - y_1}{x_2 - x_1}, \frac{x_2 - x_1}{y_2 - y_1}\right)$.
7. A line that is very close to most of the data points in a scatter plot is called a (line of fit, y-intercept).
8. The (rise, run) is the vertical change between two points on a line.
9. A(n) (dependent, independent) variable is the variable for the output of a function.

Lesson-by-Lesson Review

9-1 Sequences (pp. 464–468)

8.B.3

Write an expression that can be used to find the *n*th term in each sequence. Then write the next three terms.

10. 12, 24, 36, 48, …
11. −8, −16, −24, −32, …
12. 9, 18, 27, 36, …
13. −10, −20, −30, −40, …

Example 1 **Write an expression that can be used to find the *n*th term of the sequence 5, 10, 15, 20, 25, …. Then write the next three terms.**

Term Number (n)	1	2	3	4	5
Term	5	10	15	20	25

+5 +5 +5 +5

The terms have a common difference of 5, so the expression is $5n$. The next three terms are 5(6) or 30, 5(7) or 35, and 5(8) or 40.

9-2 Functions (pp. 469–473)

8.B.3, 8.D.3b

Find each function value.

14. $f(3)$ if $f(x) = 3x + 1$
15. $f(-11)$ if $f(x) = -2x$
16. $f(2)$ if $f(x) = \frac{1}{2}x - 4$
17. Complete the function table for $f(x) = 3x + 2$. Then state the domain and the range of the function.

x	$3x + 2$	y
−2		
0		
1		
5		

Example 2 **Complete the function table for $f(x) = 2x - 1$. Then state the domain and range of the function.**

x	$2x - 1$	$f(x)$
−2	2(−2) − 1	−5
0	2(0) − 1	−1
1	2(1) − 1	1
5	2(5) − 1	9

Domain: {−2, 0, 1, 5}
Range: {−5, −1, 1, 9}

9-3 Representing Linear Functions (pp. 475–480)

8.D.3a, 8.D.3b

Graph each function.

18. $y = -2x + 1$
19. $y = \frac{1}{2}x - 2$
20. **CANDY** A regular fruit smoothie x costs \$1.50, and a large fruit smoothie y costs \$3. Graph the function $1.5x + 3y = 12$ to determine how many of each type of fruit smoothie Lisa can buy with \$12.

Example 3 **Graph $y = 3 - x$.**

x	$3 - x$	y	(x, y)
−1	3 − (−1)	4	(−1, 4)
0	3 − 0	3	(0, 3)
2	3 − 2	1	(2, 1)
3	3 − 3	0	(3, 0)

y
$y = 3 - x$
O
x

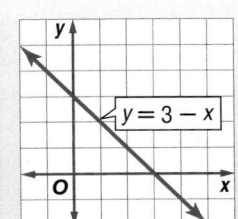

9-4 Slope (pp. 481–486)

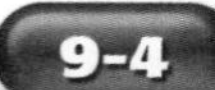

6.D.3, 8.D.3a

Find the slope of each line that passes through each pair of points.

21. $A(-2, 3), B(-1, 5)$
22. $G(6, 2), H(1, 5)$
23. $Q(2, 1), R(3, -5)$
24. **SLIDES** Find the slope of a slide that descends 8 feet for every horizontal change of 14 feet.

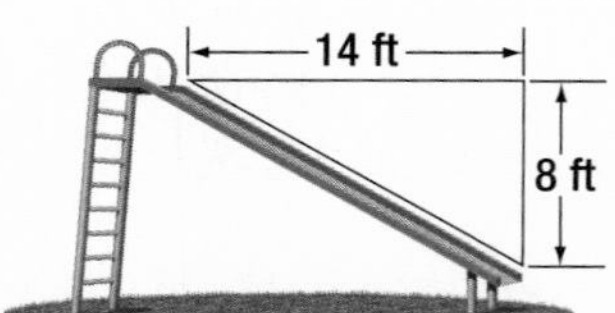

25. **ANIMALS** A lizard is crawling up a hill that rises 5 feet for every horizontal change of 30 feet. Find the slope of the hill.

Example 4 **Find the slope of the line that passes through $A(-3, 2)$ and $B(5, -1)$.**

$m = \frac{y_2 - y_1}{x_2 - x_1}$ Slope formula

$m = \frac{-1 - 2}{5 - (-3)}$ $(x_1, y_1) = (-3, 2)$, $(x_2, y_2) = (5, -1)$

$m = \frac{-3}{8}$ or $-\frac{3}{8}$ Simplify.

9-5 Direct Variation (pp. 487–492)

8.D.3a, 8.D.3b

26. **TIME** It takes Gabriella 4 hours to knit 6 scarves. Assuming that the number of scarves made varies directly as the time spent knitting, how many scarves will she make in 6 hours?
27. **MONEY** Josiah spent $15.60 on 3 comic books. The next time, he spent $10.40 on 2 comic books. What is the cost for each comic book?
28. **FRUIT** The cost of peaches varies directly with the number of pounds bought. If 3 pounds of peaches cost $4.50, find the cost of 5.5 pounds.

Example 5 **Mrs. Dimas paid $6.48 for 8 apples. The next weekend, she paid $9.72 for 12 apples. What is the cost of each apple?**

$\frac{\$6.48}{8 \text{ apples}}$ or $\frac{\$0.81}{1 \text{ apple}}$ $\frac{\$9.72}{12 \text{ apples}}$ or $\frac{\$0.81}{1 \text{ apple}}$

So, each apple costs $0.81.

Mixed Problem Solving
For mixed problem-solving practice, see page 708.

9-6 Slope-Intercept Form (pp. 495–499)

(pp. 495–499)

8.A.3b, 8.D.3b

State the slope and y-intercept for the graph of each equation.

29. $y = 2x + 5$
30. $y = -\frac{1}{5}x + 6$
31. $y - 4x = 7$
32. $3x + y = -2$
33. **MONEY** Malik had \$100 in his savings account. He plans to add \$25 each week. The equation for the amount of money y Malik has in his savings account is $y = 100 + 25x$, where x is the number of weeks. Graph the equation.
34. **BIRDS** The altitude in feet y of an albatross that is slowly landing can be given by $y = 400 - 100x$, where x represents the time in minutes. State the slope and y-intercept of the graph of the equation and describe what they represent.

Example 6 **State the slope and y-intercept of the graph of $y = -\frac{1}{2}x + 3$.**

$y = -\frac{1}{2}x + 3$ Write the equation.

$y = mx + b$

The slope of the graph is $-\frac{1}{2}$, and the y-intercept is 3.

9-7 Systems of Equations (pp. 502–507)

8.A.3b, 8.D.3a

Solve each system of equations by graphing.

35. $y = -2x - 7$
    $y = x + 8$
36. $y - 4 = 2x + 3$
    $y - 2x = 5$
37. **FOOD** Twenty-five teenagers were surveyed. There were five more who preferred pizza than preferred steak. Write and solve a system of equations to find how many preferred steak and how many preferred pizza.
38. **MOVIES** Sheryl is considering two different movie rental plans. The first plan charges \$10 per month plus \$2 per movie to rent. The second plan charges \$4 per movie with no monthly base fee. Write and solve a system of equations to find the cost of these two plans. What does your solution represent?

Example 7 **Solve the system $y + x = 20$ and $y = x + 8$ by graphing.**

Graph each equation on the same coordinate plane.

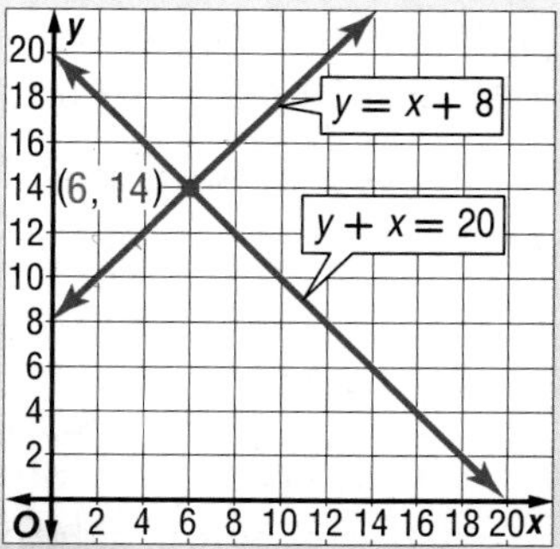

Since the graphs intersect at (6, 14), the solution of the system is (6, 14).

PSI: Use a Graph (pp. 508–509)

8.B.3

39. **BASKETBALL** The graph shows the number of points scored in the first seven basketball games. What is the average number of points scored so far this season?

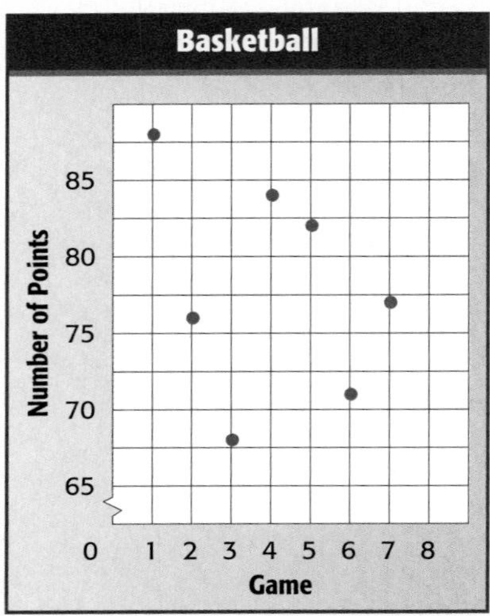

Example 8 **The graph shows the heights of maple trees. Find the average height of the trees. Round to the nearest tenth.**

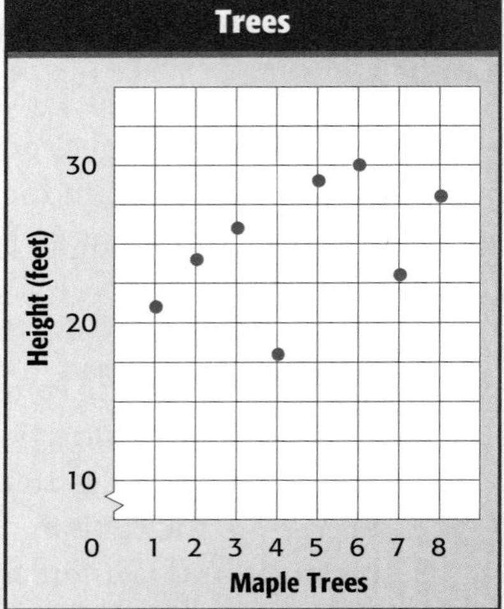

Add the heights: $21 + 24 + 26 + 18 + 29 + 30 + 23 + 28$ or 199

Divide: $\frac{199}{8}$ or 24.9

So, the average height is 24.9 feet.

Scatter Plots (pp. 510–515)

8.B.3

Determine whether a scatter plot of the data for the following might show a *positive*, *negative*, or *no* relationship.

40. day of the week and temperature
41. child's age and grade level in school
42. temperature outside and amount of clothing
43. **ATTENDANCE** Use the table to draw a scatter plot and a line of fit for the data.

Volleyball Game	1	2	3	4	5	6	7
Number of Students	28	30	37	35	36	39	40

Example 9 **Determine whether the graph below shows a *positive*, *negative*, or *no* relationship.**

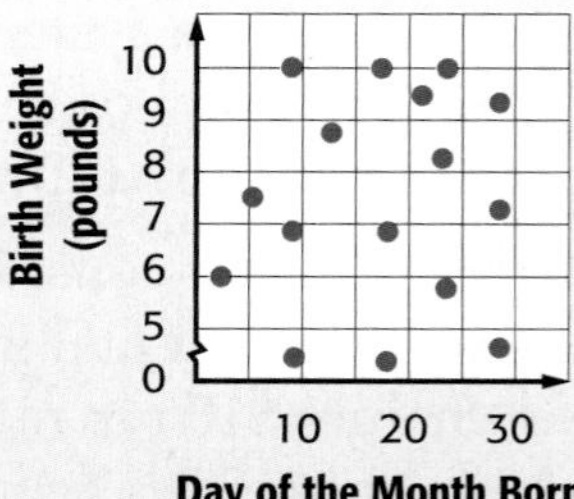

Since there is no obvious pattern, there is no relationship.

CHAPTER 9

Practice Test

IL Math Online glencoe.com
• Chapter Test

Write an expression that can be used to find the *n*th term in each sequence. Then write the next three terms.

1. 4, 8, 12, 16, …
2. −7, −14, −21, −28, …

Find each function value.

3. $f(3)$ if $f(x) = -2x + 6$
4. $f(-2)$ if $f(x) = \frac{x}{2} + 5$

5. **JOBS** The amount Jerri earns working is directly proportional to the time she works. If she earns $187.50 after working 25 hours, how much will she earn working 30 hours?

6. **RAIN** By 6 P.M., 3 inches of rain had fallen. For the next 3 hours, 0.5 inch of rain fell per hour. How many inches fell by 9 P.M.?

Graph each function.

7. $y = -2x + 5$
8. $y = \frac{1}{3}x - 1$

Find the slope of the line that passes through each pair of points.

9. $A(-2, 5), B(-2, 1)$
10. $E(2, -1), F(5, -3)$

11. **MULTIPLE CHOICE** Rico planted 18 flowers in 30 minutes. At the same rate, how many flowers would he plant in 55 minutes?

    A 30 **B** 33 **C** 36 **D** 38

MONEY For Exercises 12–14, use the following information.

The equation that represents the amount of money y Simon owes his grandfather after x months is $y = 120 - 15x$.

12. Graph the equation to find how much Simon will owe after 6 months.
13. What do the slope and y-intercept represent?
14. Is the amount of money owed proportional to the number of months? Explain.

15. **MONEY** Robert has 26 coins that are all nickels and dimes. The value of the coins is $1.85. Write and solve a system of equations that represents this situation.

16. **MULTIPLE CHOICE** Which ordered pair is a solution of $y = -3x$?

    F (3, 1)

    G (−3, 1)

    H (1, 3)

    J (1, −3)

SALES For Exercises 17 and 18, use the table.

New Customers			
Month	Customers	Month	Customers
Jan	542	Jul	631
Feb	601	Aug	620
Mar	589	Sep	723
Apr	610	Oct	754
May	648	Nov	885
June	670	Dec	1,027

17. Make a graph of the data.
18. Describe how the number of new customers changed from January to December.

TRAVEL For Exercises 19–21, use the table.

Distance (mi)	50	100	150	200	250
Gas (gal)	2	6	8	15	18

19. Draw a scatter plot for the data and draw a line of fit.
20. Write an equation for the line of fit.
21. Use your equation to estimate the amount of gas needed to travel 375 miles.

ISAT Practice

Cumulative, Chapters 1–9

PART 1 Multiple Choice

Read each question. Then fill in the correct answer on the answer sheet provided by your teacher or on a sheet of paper.

1. A pattern of equations is shown below. Which statement best describes this pattern of equations?

   80% of 62.5 is 50
   40% of 125 is 50
   20% of 250 is 50
   10% of 500 is 50

   A When the percent is halved and the other number is doubled, the answer is 50.

   B When the percent is halved and the other number is halved, the answer is 50.

   C When the percent is increased by 2 and the other number remains the same, the answer is 50.

   D When the percent remains the same and the other number is increased by 2, the answer is 50.

2. The area of a square is 20 square inches. Which best represents the length of a side of the square?

   F 4.5 inches

   G 5 inches

   H 10 inches

   J 11 inches

3. Beth's monthly charge for Internet access c can be found using the equation $c = 12 + 2.50h$, where h represents the number of hours of usage during a month. What is the total charge for a month in which Beth used the Internet for 9 hours?

   A \$39.95 **C** \$27.00

   B \$34.50 **D** \$22.50

4. Which statement is true about the slope of line $\overleftrightarrow{RT}$?

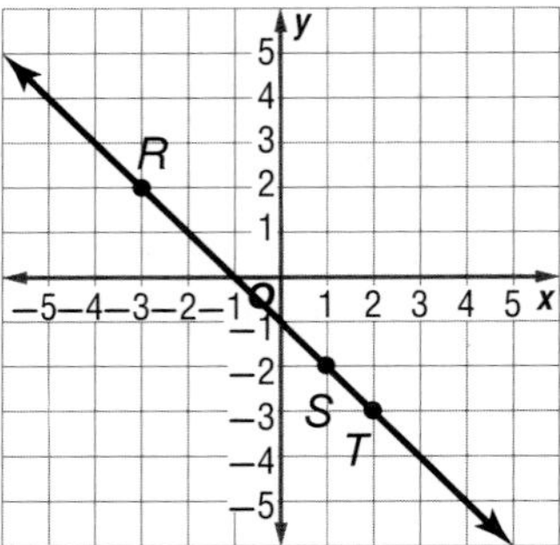

   F The slope is the same between any two points.

   G The slope between point R and point S is greater than the slope between point S and point T.

   H The slope between point R and point T is greater than the slope between point S and point T.

   J The slope is positive.

5. The graph of the line $y = -2x + 1$ is shown below. Which table of ordered pairs contains only points on this line?

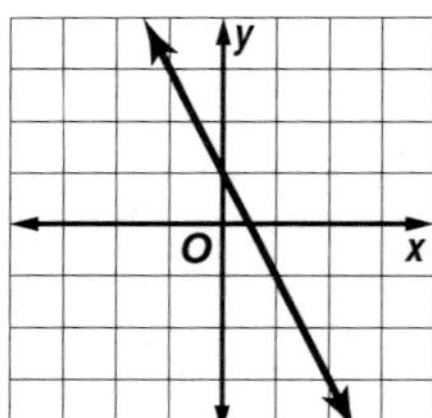

   A

x	−2	−1	0
y	5	3	−1

   B

x	−2	−1	0
y	3	1	−1

   C

x	−1	0	1
y	−3	−1	1

   D

x	−1	0	1
y	3	1	−1

Preparing for ISAT
For test-taking strategies and practice, see pages 712–729.

6. A truck used 6.3 gallons of gasoline to travel 107 miles. How many gallons of gasoline would it need to travel 250 miles more?

F 8.4 gal H 18.9 gal
G 14.7 gal J 21.0 gal

TEST-TAKING TIP

Question 6 When working with units of measurement, remember to write the units to ensure that the numbers are compared correctly.

7. Which of the following conclusions about the number of rebounds per game and the height of a player is best supported by the scatter plot below?

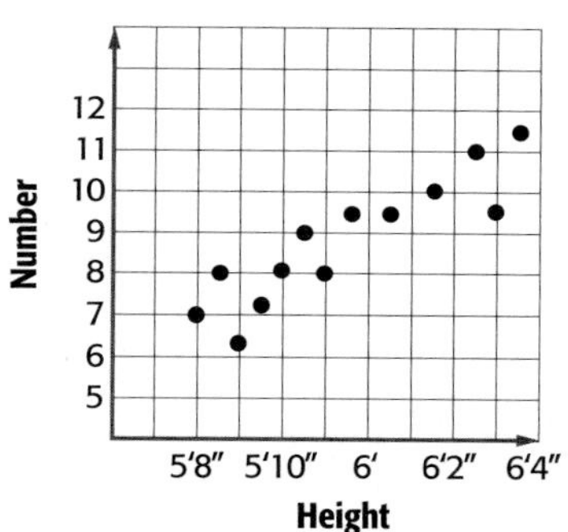

A The number of rebounds increases as the player's height decreases.

B The number of rebounds is unchanged as the player's height increases.

C The number of rebounds increases as the player's height increases.

D There is no relationship between the number of rebounds and the player's height.

PART 2 Short Response/Grid In

Record your answers on the answer sheet provided by your teacher or on a sheet of paper.

8. The slope of the line shown below is $\frac{4}{5}$. What is the value of n?

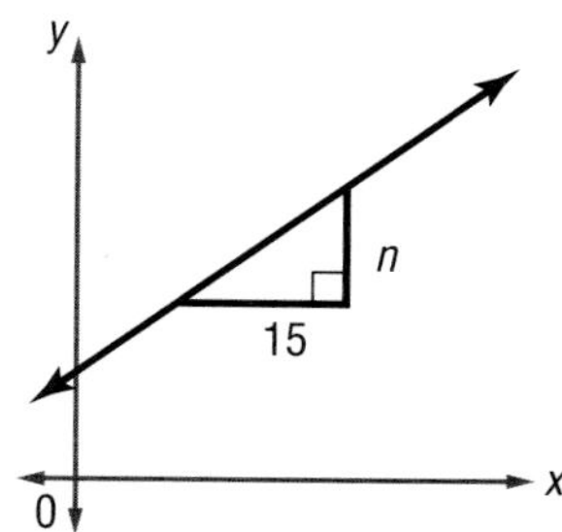

PART 3 Extended Response

Record your answers on the answer sheet provided by your teacher or on a sheet of paper. Show your work.

9. Study the data in the table.

Student	Study Time	Test Score
Patrick	30 min	75
LaDonne	50 min	89
Marlena	1 hr 10 min	93
Jason	25 min	72
Joaquim	1 hour	91
Carla	45 min	83
Heather	1 hr 15 min	90

a. Why is a scatter plot a good representation of the data?

b. Graph the data. Describe the relationship of the data.

NEED EXTRA HELP?									
If You Missed Question...	1	2	3	4	5	6	7	8	9
Go to Lesson...	2-8	3-2	9-2	9-4	9-6	9-5	9-9	9-4	9-9
IL Learning Standards	6.B.3a	8.D.3c	8.B.3	8.D.3a	8.D.3a	6.D.3	8.B.3	8.D.3a	8.B.3

Algebra: Nonlinear Functions and Polynomials

Illinois Learning Standards

8.D.3b Propose and solve problems using proportions, formulas and linear functions.
8.D.3a Solve problems using numeric, graphic or symbolic representations of variables, expressions, equations and inequalities.

Key Vocabulary

cube root (p. 560)
nonlinear function (p. 528)
quadratic function (p. 534)

Real-World Link

Fountains Many real-world situations, such as Buckingham Fountain in Chicago, Illinois, cannot be modeled by linear functions. These can be modeled using nonlinear functions.

Algebra: Nonlinear Functions and Polynomials Make this Foldable to help you organize your notes. Begin with eight sheets of grid paper.

1. **Cut** off one section of the grid paper along both the long and short edges.

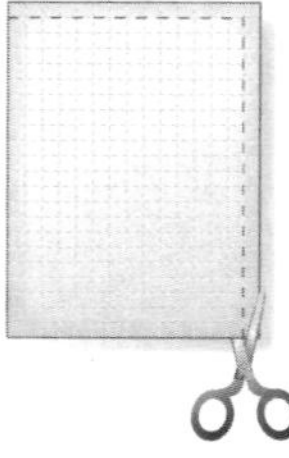

2. **Cut** off two sections from the second sheet, three sections from the third sheet, and so on to the eighth sheet.

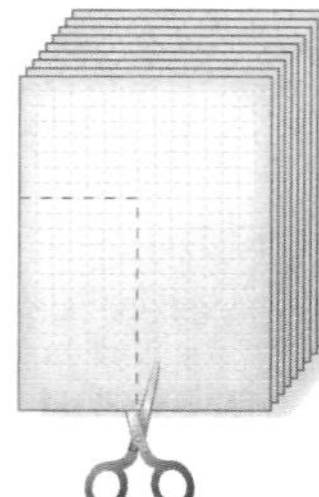

3. **Stack** the sheets from narrowest to widest.

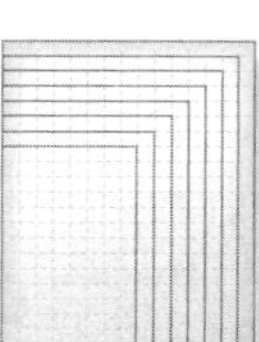

4. **Label** each of the right tabs with a lesson number.

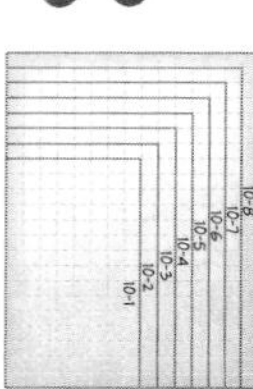

GET READY for Chapter 10

Diagnose Readiness You have two options for checking Prerequisite Skills.

Option 2

IL Math Online Take the Online Readiness Quiz at glencoe.com.

Option 1

Take the Quick Check below. Refer to the Quick Review for help.

QUICK Practice

Graph each equation. (Lesson 9-3)

1. $y = x - 4$
2. $y = 2x$
3. $y = x + 2$
4. **MEASUREMENT** The equation $y = 2.54x$ describes about how many centimeters y are in x inches. Graph the function. (Lessons 9-3)

Write each expression using a positive exponent. (Lesson 2-9)

5. a^{-9}
6. 6^{-4}
7. x^{-5}
8. 5^{-2}

Write each expression using exponents. (Lesson 2-9)

9. $6 \cdot 6 \cdot 6 \cdot 6$
10. $3 \cdot 7 \cdot 7 \cdot 3 \cdot 7$
11. **FUNDRAISER** The students at Hampton Middle School raised $8 \cdot 8 \cdot 2 \cdot 8 \cdot 2$ dollars to help build a new community center. How much money did they raise? (Lesson 2-9)

QUICK Review

Example 1

Graph $y = x + 1$.

First, make a table of values. Then, graph the ordered pairs and connect the points.

x	y	(x, y)
0	1	(0, 1)
1	2	(1, 2)
2	3	(2, 3)
3	4	(3, 4)

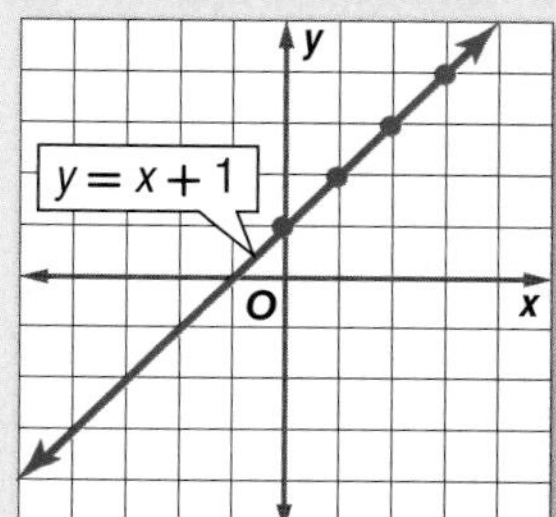

Example 2

Write n^{-3} using a positive exponent.

$n^{-3} = \frac{1}{n^3}$ Definition of negative exponent

Example 3

Write $5 \cdot 4 \cdot 5 \cdot 4 \cdot 5$ using exponents.

5 is multiplied by itself 3 times and 4 is multiplied by itself 2 times.

So, $5 \cdot 4 \cdot 5 \cdot 4 \cdot 5 = 5^3 \cdot 4^2$.

10-1 Linear and Nonlinear Functions

MAIN IDEA

Determine whether a function is linear or nonlinear.

IL Learning Standards

8.A.3b Solve problems using linear expressions, **equations** and inequalities.
8.D.3b Propose and solve problems using proportions, formulas and **linear functions.**
Also addresses 8.B.3, 8.D.3a.

New Vocabulary

nonlinear function

IL Math Online

glencoe.com

- Extra Examples
- Personal Tutor
- Self-Check Quiz

GET READY for the Lesson

FOOTBALL The table shows the approximate height and length traveled by a football thrown at an angle of 30° with an initial velocity of 30 yards per second.

Time (s)	Height (yd)	Length (yd)
0.00	0	0
0.50	6.2	13.0
1.00	9.7	26.0
1.50	10.5	39.0
2.00	8.7	52.0
2.50	4.2	65.0

1. Did the football travel the same height each half-second? Justify your answer.
2. Did the football travel the same length each half-second? Justify your answer.
3. Graph the ordered pairs (time, height) and (time, length) on separate grids. Connect the points with a straight line or smooth curve. Then compare the graphs.

In Lesson 9-3, you learned that linear functions have graphs that are straight lines. These graphs represent constant rates of change. This occurs when the rate of change between any two data points is proportional. **Nonlinear functions** are functions that do not have constant rates of change. Therefore, their graphs are not straight lines.

EXAMPLES Identify Functions Using Tables

Determine whether each table represents a *linear* or *nonlinear* function. Explain.

1

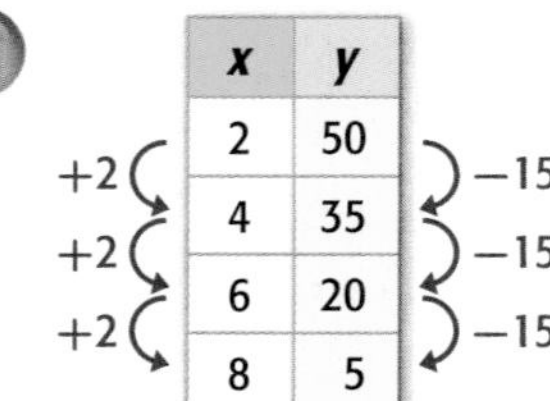

x	y
2	50
4	35
6	20
8	5

As x increases by 2, y decreases by 15 each time. The rate of change is constant, so this function is linear.

2

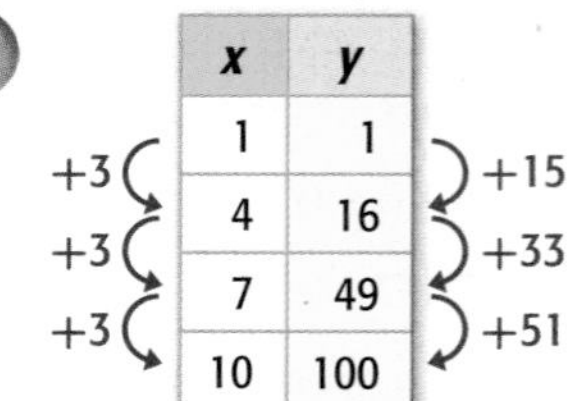

x	y
1	1
4	16
7	49
10	100

As x increases by 3, y increases by a greater amount each time. The rate of change is not constant, so this function is nonlinear.

CHECK Your Progress **Determine whether each table represents a *linear* or *nonlinear* function. Explain.**

a.

x	0	5	10	15
y	20	16	12	8

b.

x	0	2	4	6
y	0	2	8	18

EXAMPLES Identify Functions Using Graphs

Determine whether each graph represents a *linear* or *nonlinear* function. Explain.

3

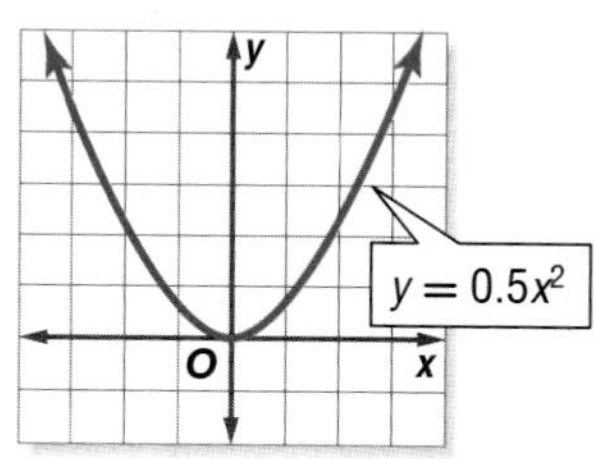

The graph is a curve, not a straight line. So, it represents a nonlinear function.

4

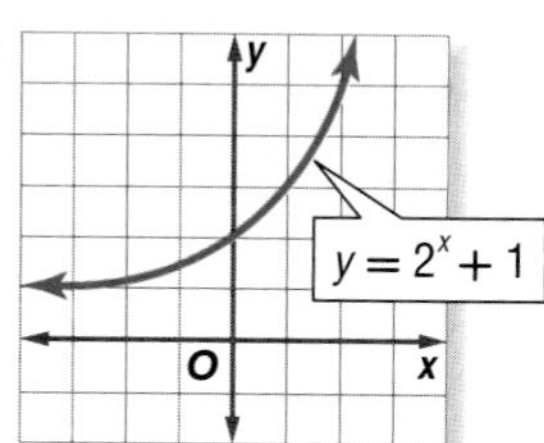

This graph is also a curve. So, it represents a nonlinear function.

CHECK Your Progress

c.

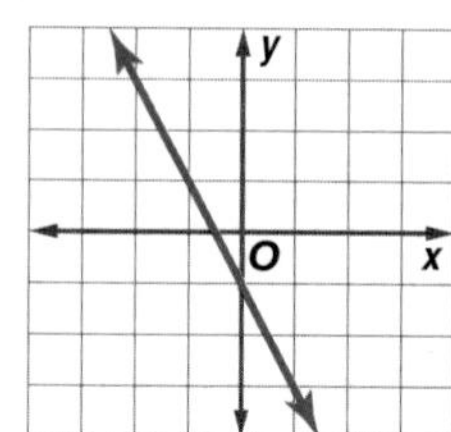

d.

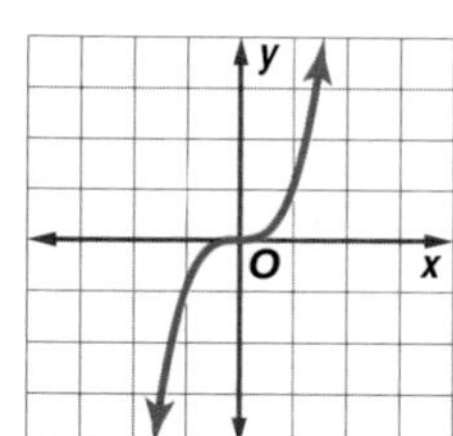

e.

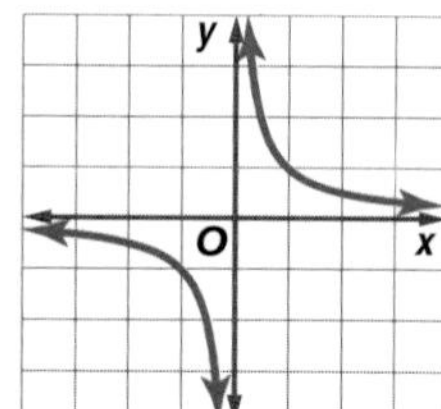

Study Tip

Identifying Linear Equations
Always examine an equation after it has been solved for y to see that the power of x is 1 or 0. Then check to see that x does not appear in the denominator.

Recall that the equation for a linear function can be written in the form $y = mx + b$, where m represents the constant rate of change.

EXAMPLES Identify Functions Using Equations

Determine whether each equation represents a *linear* or *nonlinear* function. Explain.

5 $y = x + 4$

Since the equation can be written as $y = 1x + 4$, this function is linear.

6 $y = \frac{6}{x}$

The equation cannot be written in the form $y = mx + b$. So, this function is nonlinear.

CHECK Your Progress

f. $y = 2x^3 + 1$

g. $y = 3x$

h. $y = \frac{x}{5}$

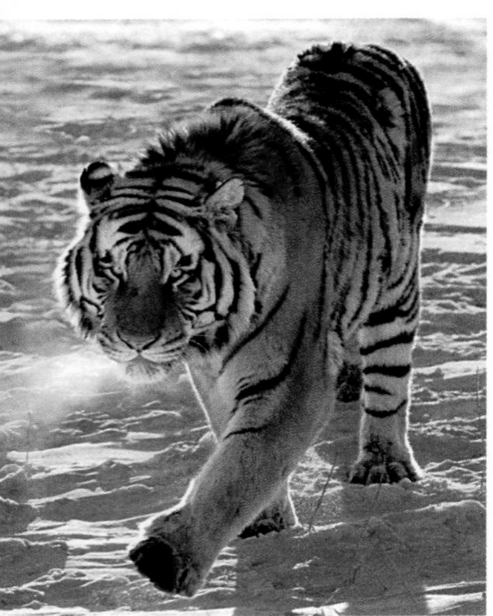

Real-World Link An adult Siberian tiger can weigh as much as 660 pounds and eats about 10,000 Calories per day.
Source: National Geographic

Real-World EXAMPLE

7 TIGERS Use the table to determine whether the minimum number of Calories a tiger cub should eat is a linear function of its age in weeks.

Age (weeks)	Minimum Calorie Intake
1	825
2	1,000
3	1,185
4	1,320
5	1,420

Examine the differences between the number of Calories for each week.

$1{,}000 - 825 = 175$ $\quad 1{,}185 - 1{,}000 = 185$
$1{,}320 - 1{,}185 = 135$ $\quad 1{,}420 - 1{,}320 = 100$

The difference in Calories is not the same. Therefore, this function is nonlinear.

Check Graph the data to verify the ordered pairs do not lie on a straight line.

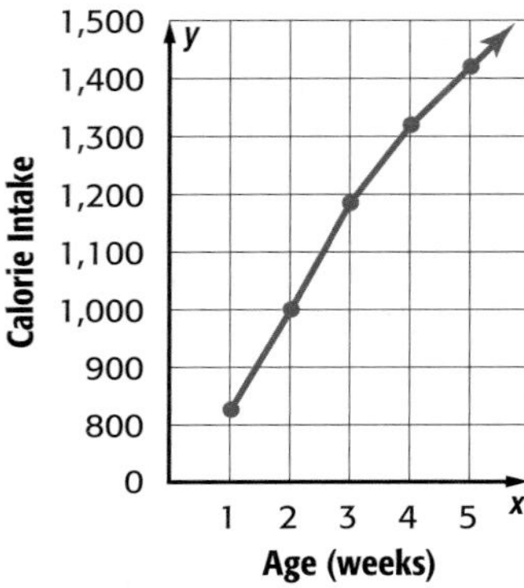

CHECK Your Progress

i. **TICKETS** Tickets to the school dance cost $5 per student. Are the ticket sales a linear function of the number of tickets sold? Explain.

Number of Tickets Sold	1	2	3
Ticket Sales	$5	$10	$15

CHECK Your Understanding

Determine whether each table, graph, or equation represents a *linear* or *nonlinear* function. Explain.

Examples 1–6 (pp. 528–529)

1.

x	0	1	2	3
y	1	3	6	10

2.

x	0	3	6	9
y	−3	9	21	33

3. 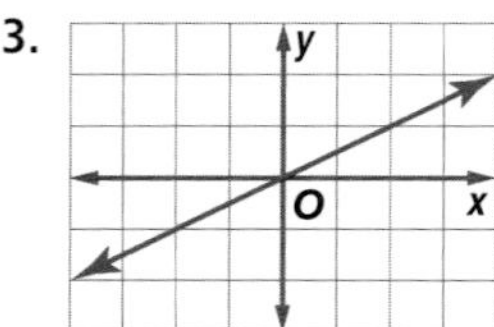

4. 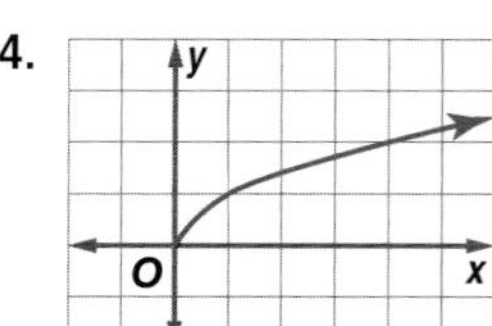

5. $y = \frac{x}{3}$

6. $y = 2x^2$

Example 7 (p. 530)

7. **MEASUREMENT** The table shows the measures of the sides of several rectangles. Are the widths of the rectangles a linear function of the lengths? Explain.

Length (in.)	1	4	8	10
Width (in.)	64	16	8	6.4

Practice and Problem Solving

HOMEWORK HELP	
For Exercises	See Examples
8–13	1, 2
14–19	3, 4
20–25	5, 6
26–29	7

Determine whether each table, graph, or equation or represents a *linear* or *nonlinear* function. Explain.

8.

x	3	6	9	12
y	12	10	8	6

9.

x	1	2	3	4
y	1	4	9	16

10.

x	5	10	15	20
y	13	28	43	58

11.

x	1	3	5	7
y	−2	−18	−50	−98

12.

x	2	4	6	8
y	10	12	16	24

13.

x	4	8	12	16
y	3	0	−3	−6

14. 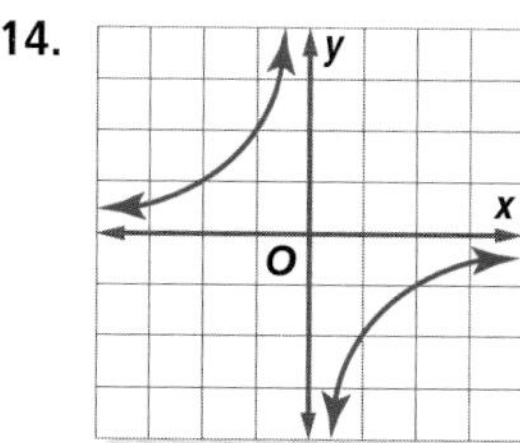

15. 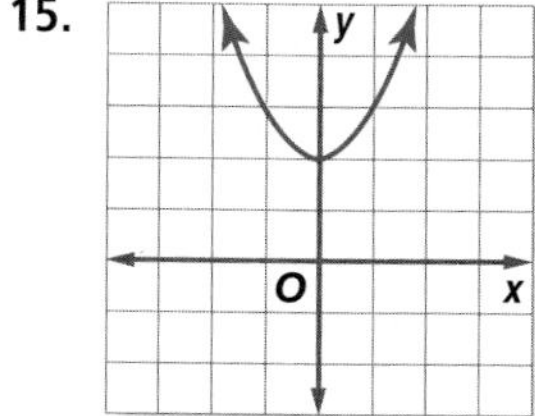

16. 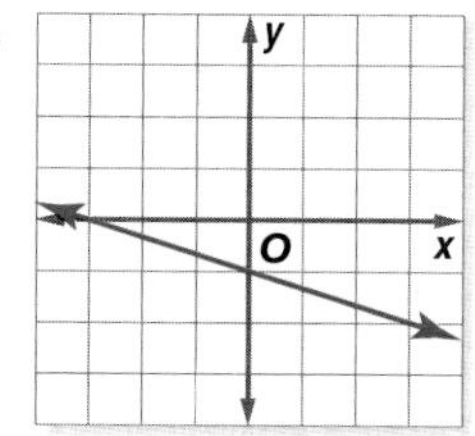

17. 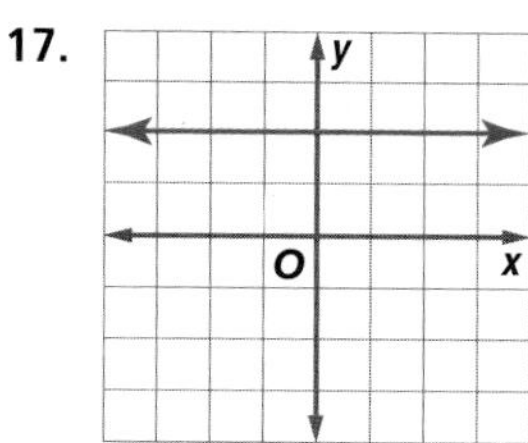

18. 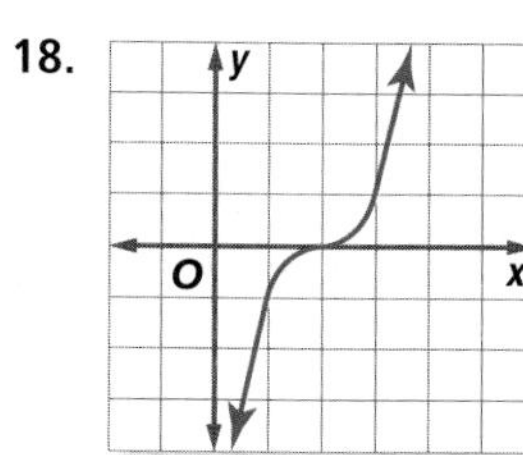

19. 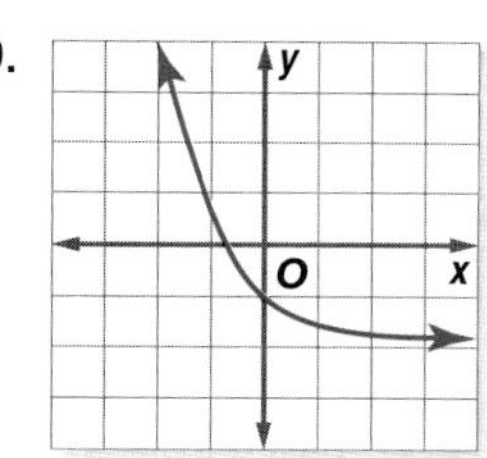

20. $y = x^3 - 1$

21. $y = 4x^2 + 9$

22. $y = 0.6x$

23. $y = \frac{3x}{2}$

24. $y = \frac{4}{x}$

25. $y = \frac{8}{x} + 5$

26. **TRAVEL** The Guzman family drove from Anderson to Myrtle Beach. Use the table to determine whether the distance driven is a linear function of the hours traveled. Explain.

Time (h)	1	2	3	4
Distance (mi)	65	130	195	260

27. **BUILDINGS** The table shows the height of several buildings in Chicago, Illinois. Use the table to determine whether the height of the building is a linear function of the number of stories. Explain.

Building	Stories	Height (ft)
Harris Bank III	35	510
One Financial Place	40	515
Kluczynski Federal Building	45	545
Mid Continental Plaza	50	582
North Harbor Tower	55	556

Source: *The World Almanac*

MEASUREMENT For Exercises 28 and 29, use the following information. Recall that the circumference of a circle is equal to pi times its diameter and that the area of a circle is equal to pi times the square of its radius.

28. Is the circumference of a circle a linear or nonlinear function of its diameter? Explain your reasoning.

29. Is the area of a circle a linear or nonlinear function of its radius? Explain your reasoning.

For Exercises 30–34, determine whether each equation or table represents a *linear* or *nonlinear* function. Explain.

30. $y - x = 1$

31. $xy = -9$

32. $y = 2^x$

33.

x	0.5	1	1.5	2
y	15	8	1	−6

34.

x	−4	0	4	8
y	2	1	−1	−4

35. **FOOTBALL** The graphic shows the average attendance at college bowl games from 2001 to 2006. Would you describe the graph as linear or nonlinear? Explain your reasoning.

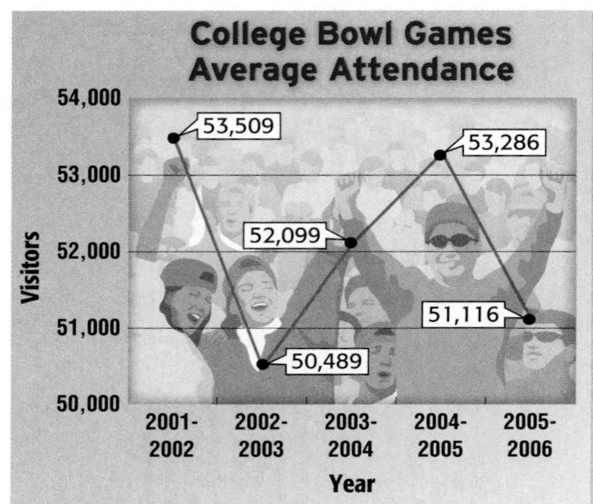

Source: Football Bowl Association

36. **MEASUREMENT** Make a graph showing the area of a square as a function of its perimeter. Explain whether the function is linear.

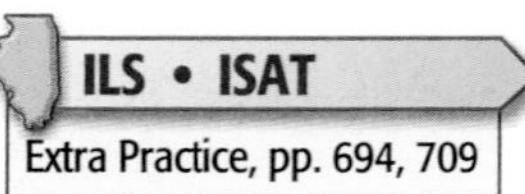

Extra Practice, pp. 694, 709

37. **GRAPHING** Water is poured at a constant rate into the vase at the right. Draw a graph of the water level as a function of time. Is the water level a linear or nonlinear function of time? Explain.

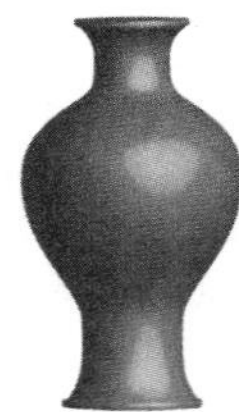

H.O.T. Problems

38. **CHALLENGE** Does the graph of $x = 2$ represent a linear function? Explain your reasoning.

39. **Which One Doesn't Belong?** Identify the function that is not linear. Explain your reasoning.

$y = 3x + 5$	$y = 5x^3$	$y + 3 = 5x$	$3x - y = 5$

40. **OPEN ENDED** Give an example of a nonlinear function using an equation.

41. **WRITING IN MATH** Describe two methods for determining whether a function is linear given its equation.

ISAT PRACTICE 8.A.3b, 8.D.3b

42. Which equation describes the data in the table?

x	−7	−5	−3	0	4
y	50	26	10	1	17

A $5x + 1 = y$ **C** $x^2 + 1 = y$

B $xy = 68$ **D** $-2x^2 + 8 = y$

43. Which equation represents a nonlinear function?

F $y = 3x + 1$

G $y = \frac{x}{3}$

H $2xy = 10$

J $y = 3(x - 5)$

Spiral Review

STATISTICS Determine whether a scatter plot of the data for the following might show a *positive, negative,* or *no* relationship. (Lesson 9-9)

44. grade on a test and amount of time spent studying

45. age and number of siblings

46. number of Calories burned and length of time exercising

47. LANGUAGES The graph shows the top five languages spoken by at least 100 million native speakers worldwide. What conclusions can you make about the number of Mandarin native speakers and the number of English native speakers? (Lesson 9-8)

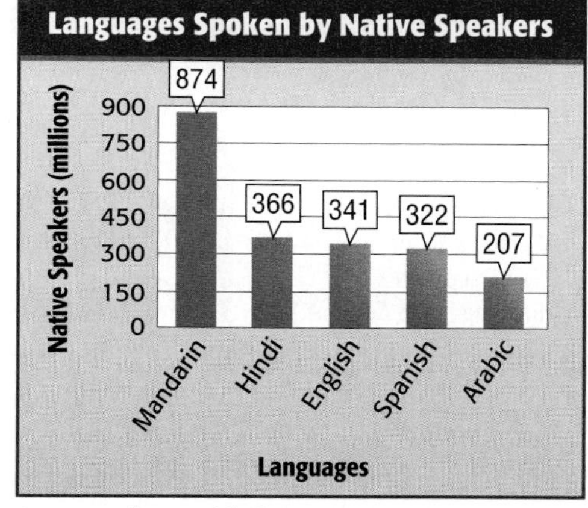

Source: *The World Almanac For Kids*

Solve each equation. Check your solution. (Lesson 8-4)

48. $1 - 3c = 9c + 7$

49. $7k + 12 = 8 - 9k$

50. $13.4w + 17 = 5w - 4$

51. $8.1a + 2.3 = 5.1a - 3.1$

52. $4.1x - 23 = -3.9x - 1$

53. $3.2n + 3 = -4.8n - 29$

54. PARKS A circular fountain in a park has a diameter of 8 feet. The park director wants to build a fountain that has an area four times that of the current fountain. What will be the diameter of the new fountain? (Lesson 7-1)

55. MEASUREMENT The cylindrical air duct of a large furnace has a diameter of 30 inches and a height of 120 feet. If it takes 15 minutes for the contents of the duct to be expelled into the air, what is the volume of the substances being expelled each hour? (Lesson 7-5)

GET READY for the Next Lesson

PREREQUISITE SKILL Graph each equation. (Lesson 9-3)

56. $y = 2x$

57. $y = x + 3$

58. $y = 3x - 2$

59. $y = \frac{1}{3}x + 1$

10-2 Graphing Quadratic Functions

MAIN IDEA

Graph quadratic functions.

IL Learning Standards

8.A.3b Solve problems using linear expressions, **equations** and inequalities.
8.D.3a Solve problems using numeric, graphic or symbolic representations of variables, expressions, **equations** and inequalities.

New Vocabulary

quadratic function

IL Math Online

glencoe.com

- Extra Examples
- Personal Tutor
- Self-Check Quiz
- Reading in the Content Area

MINI Lab

You know that the area A of a square is equal to the length of a side s squared, or $A = s^2$.

STEP 1 Copy and complete the table.

STEP 2 Graph the ordered pairs from the table. Connect them with a smooth curve.

s	s^2	(s, A)
0	0	(0, 0)
1	1	(1, 1)
2		
3		
4		
5		
6		

1. Is the relationship between the side length and the area of a square linear or nonlinear? Explain.
2. Describe the shape of the graph.

A **quadratic function**, like $A = s^2$, is a function in which the greatest power of the variable is 2. Its graph is U-shaped, opening upward or downward. The graph opens upward if the coefficient of the variable that is squared is *positive*, downward if it is *negative*.

EXAMPLES Graph Quadratic Functions

1 **Graph $y = x^2$.**

To graph a quadratic function, make a table of values, plot the ordered pairs, and connect the points with a smooth curve.

x	x^2	y	(x, y)
−2	$(-2)^2 = 4$	4	(−2, 4)
−1	$(-1)^2 = 1$	1	(−1, 1)
0	$(0)^2 = 0$	0	(0, 0)
1	$(1)^2 = 1$	1	(1, 1)
2	$(2)^2 = 4$	4	(2, 4)

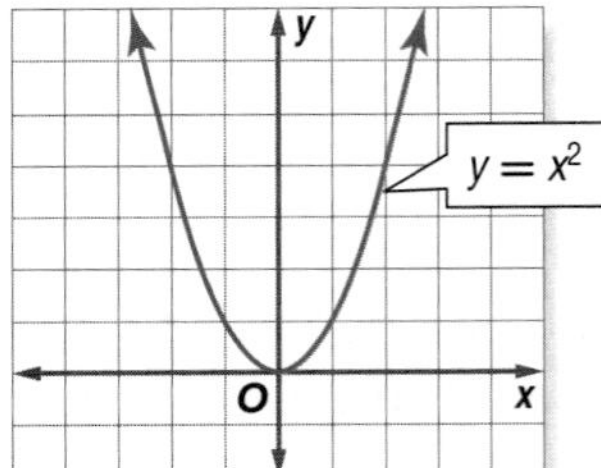

2 **Graph $y = -2x^2$.**

x	$-2x^2$	y	(x, y)
−2	$-2(-2)^2 = -8$	−8	(−2, −8)
−1	$-2(-1)^2 = -2$	−2	(−1, −2)
0	$-2(0)^2 = 0$	0	(0, 0)
1	$-2(1)^2 = -2$	−2	(1, −2)
2	$-2(2)^2 = -8$	−8	(2, −8)

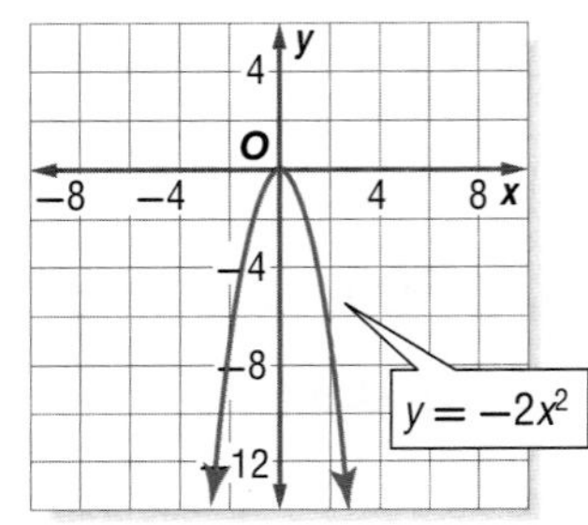

Study Tip

Quadratic Functions The graph of a quadratic function is called a *parabola*.

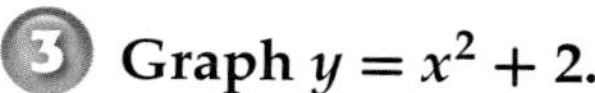

3 Graph $y = x^2 + 2$.

x	$x^2 + 2$	y	(x, y)
−2	$(-2)^2 + 2 = 6$	6	(−2, 6)
−1	$(-1)^2 + 2 = 3$	3	(−1, 3)
0	$(0)^2 + 2 = 2$	2	(0, 2)
1	$(1)^2 + 2 = 3$	3	(1, 3)
2	$(2)^2 + 2 = 6$	6	(2, 6)

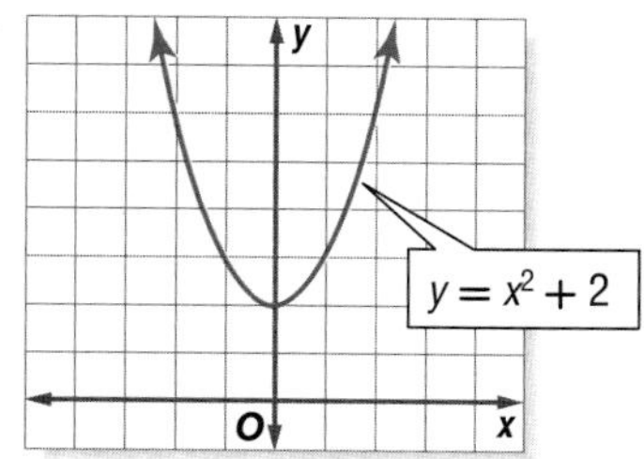

4 Graph $y = -x^2 + 4$.

x	$-x^2 + 4$	y	(x, y)
−2	$-(-2)^2 + 4 = 0$	0	(−2, 0)
−1	$-(-1)^2 + 4 = 3$	3	(−1, 3)
0	$-(0)^2 + 4 = 4$	4	(0, 4)
1	$-(1)^2 + 4 = 3$	3	(1, 3)
2	$-(2)^2 + 4 = 0$	0	(2, 0)

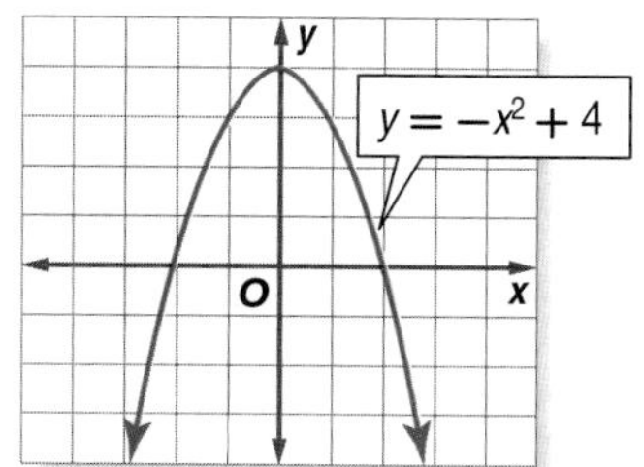

CHECK Your Progress

a. $y = 6x^2$ b. $y = x^2 - 2$ c. $y = -2x^2 - 1$

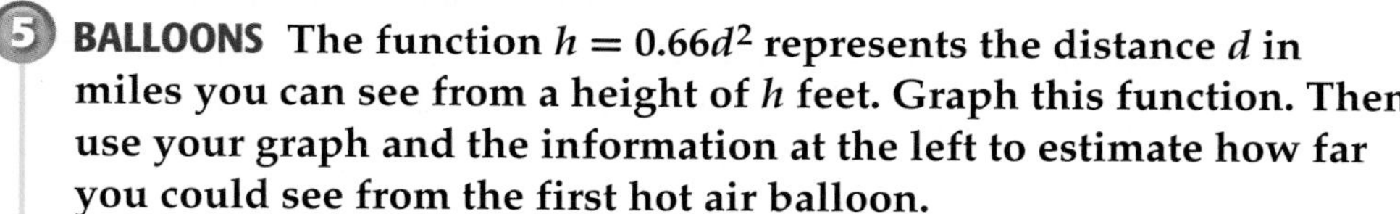

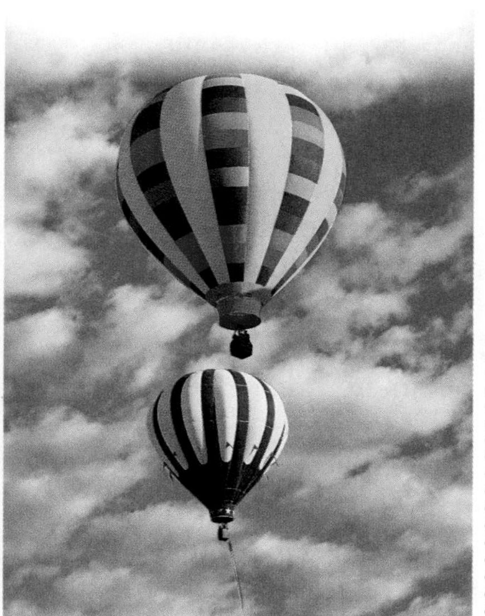

Real-World Link In 1783, one of the first hot air balloons to take flight flew about 1,000 feet in the air.

Source: *Scholastic Book of Firsts*

5 **BALLOONS The function $h = 0.66d^2$ represents the distance d in miles you can see from a height of h feet. Graph this function. Then use your graph and the information at the left to estimate how far you could see from the first hot air balloon.**

Distance cannot be negative, so use only positive values of d.

d	$h = 0.66d^2$	(d, h)
0	$0.66(0)^2 = 0$	(0, 0)
10	$0.66(10)^2 = 66$	(10, 66)
20	$0.66(20)^2 = 264$	(20, 264)
25	$0.66(25)^2 = 412.5$	(25, 412.5)
30	$0.66(30)^2 = 594$	(30, 594)
35	$0.66(35)^2 = 808.5$	(35, 808.5)
40	$0.66(40)^2 = 1,056$	(40, 1,056)

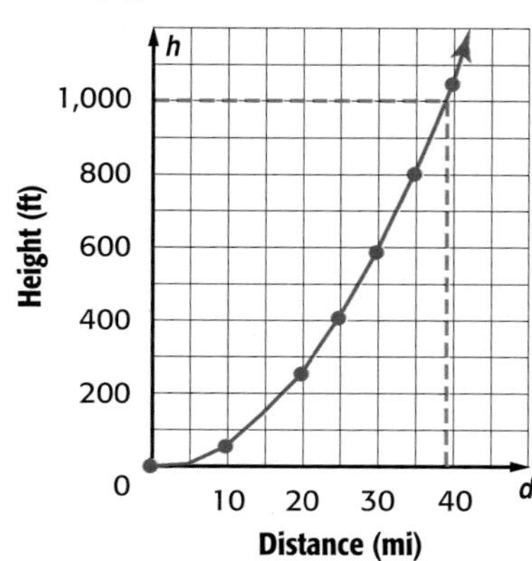

At a height of 1,000 feet, you could see approximately 39 miles.

CHECK Your Progress

d. **TOWERS** The outdoor observation deck of the Space Needle in Seattle, Washington, is 520 feet above ground level. Estimate how far you could see from the observation deck.

CHECK Your Understanding

Examples 1–4 (pp. 534–535)

Graph each function.

1. $y = 3x^2$
2. $y = -5x^2$
3. $y = -4x^2$
4. $y = -x^2 + 1$
5. $y = x^2 - 3$
6. $y = -x^2 + 2$

Example 5 (p. 535)

7. **CARS** The function $d = 0.006s^2$ represents the braking distance d in meters of a car traveling at a speed s in kilometers per second. Graph this function. Then use your graph to estimate the speed of the car if its braking distance is 12 meters.

Practice and Problem Solving

HOMEWORK HELP

For Exercises	See Examples
8–11	1, 2
12–19	3, 4
20, 21	5

Graph each function.

8. $y = 4x^2$
9. $y = 5x^2$
10. $y = -3x^2$
11. $y = -6x^2$
12. $y = x^2 + 6$
13. $y = x^2 - 4$
14. $y = -x^2 + 2$
15. $y = -x^2 - 5$
16. $y = 2x^2 - 1$
17. $y = 2x^2 + 3$
18. $y = -4x^2 - 1$
19. $y = -3x^2 + 2$

20. **CARNIVAL RIDES** The function $a = 0.2v^2$ models the acceleration of the passengers on a certain carnival ride, where a is the acceleration toward the center of the ride in meters per second every second, and v is the velocity in meters per second. Graph this function. Then use your graph to estimate the velocity of the ride at an acceleration of 1 meter per second every second.

21. **BRIDGES** A penny is dropped from a height of 196 feet off the Astoria-Megler Bridge near Astoria, Oregon. The function $d = -16t^2 + 196$ models the distance d in feet the penny is from the surface of the water at time t seconds. Graph this function. Then use your graph to estimate the time it will take for the penny to reach the water.

Graph each function.

22. $y = 0.5x^2 + 1$
23. $y = 1.5x^2$
24. $y = 4.5x^2 - 6$
25. $y = \frac{1}{3}x^2 - 2$
26. $y = \frac{1}{2}x^2$
27. $y = -\frac{1}{4}x^2 + 1$

MEASUREMENT For Exercises 28 and 29, write a function for each of the following. Then graph the function in the first quadrant.

28. The surface area of a cube is a function of the edge length a. Use your graph to estimate the edge length of a cube with a surface area of 54 square centimeters.

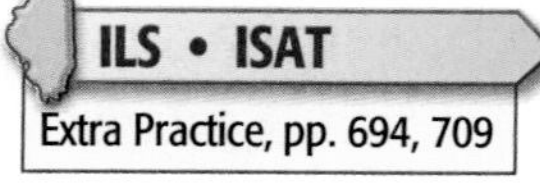

Extra Practice, pp. 694, 709

29. The volume V of a rectangular prism with a square base and a fixed height of 5 inches is a function of the base edge length s. Use your graph to estimate the base edge length of a prism whose volume is 180 cubic inches.

H.O.T. Problems

CHALLENGE The graphs of quadratic functions may have exactly one highest point, called a *maximum*, or exactly one lowest point, called a *minimum*. Graph each quadratic equation. Determine whether each graph has a maximum or a minimum. If so, give the coordinates of each point.

30. $y = 2x^2 + 1$ **31.** $y = -x^2 + 5$ **32.** $y = x^2 - 3$

33. **OPEN ENDED** Write and graph a quadratic function that opens upward and has its minimum at (0, −3.5).

34. **WRITING IN MATH** Write a quadratic function of the form $y = ax^2 + c$ and explain how to graph it.

ISAT PRACTICE 8.A.3b, 8.D.3a

35. Which graph represents the function $y = -0.5x^2 - 2$?

A 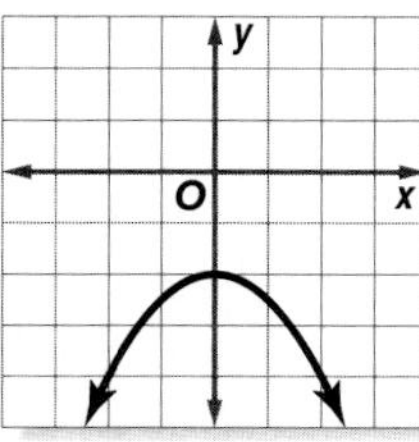

B 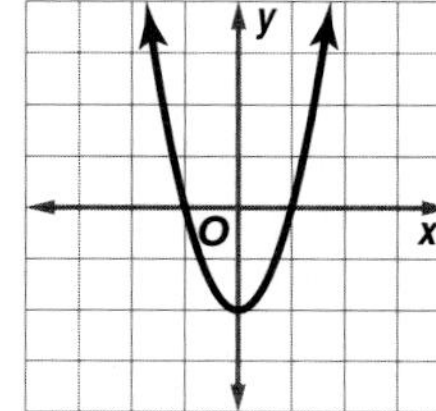

C 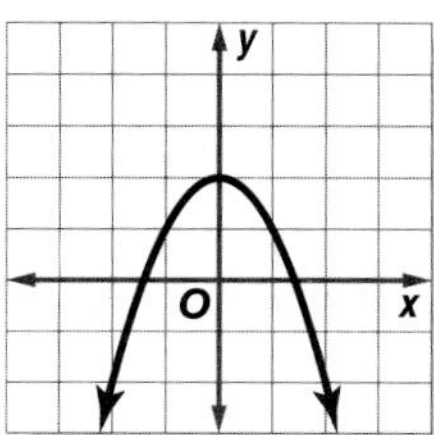

D 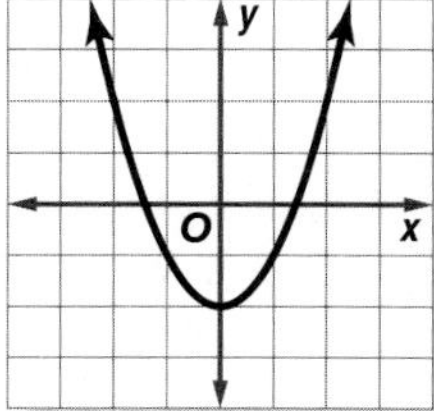

Spiral Review

Determine whether each equation represents a *linear* or *nonlinear* function. (Lesson 10-1)

36. $y = x - 5$ **37.** $y = 3x^3 + 2$ **38.** $x + y = -6$ **39.** $y = -2x^2$

STATISTICS For Exercises 40–42, use the information at the right. (Lesson 9-9)

Whooping Cranes	
Year	**Population**
2002	181
2003	194
2004	197
2005	216
2006	227

40. Draw a scatter plot of the data and draw a line of fit.

41. Does the scatter plot show a *positive, negative,* or *no* relationship?

42. Use your graph to estimate the population of the whooping crane at the refuge in 2007.

43. **SAVINGS** Anna's parents put $750 into a college savings account. After 6 years, the investment had earned $540. Write an equation that you could use to find the simple interest rate. Then find the simple interest rate. (Lesson 5-9)

GET READY for the Next Lesson

44. **PREREQUISITE SKILL** A section of a theater is arranged so that each row has the same number of seats. You are seated in the 5th row from the front and the 3rd row from the back. If your seat is 6th from the left and 2nd from the right, how many seats are in this section of the theater? Use the *draw a diagram* strategy. (Lesson 4-6)

10-3 Problem-Solving Investigation

MAIN IDEA: Solve problems by making a model.

ILS **9.C.3b Develop and solve problems using geometric relationships and models,** with and **without the use of technology.**

P.S.I. TEAM +

e-Mail: MAKE A MODEL

ALICIA: For computer class, we are designing a computer game where players are required to make arrangements of five squares.

YOUR MISSION: Make a model to find how many different ways five squares can be arranged to form a single shape so that touching squares border on a full side.

Understand	You know each of the five squares needs to be arranged so that touching squares border a full side. You need to determine how many arrangements are possible.
Plan	Make models showing the different arrangements.
Solve	There are 12 possible arrangements.
Check	Check the diagram carefully to make sure it includes all possible arrangements. Notice that rotations are not counted as a separate arrangement, but reflections are counted.

Analyze The Strategy

1. Suppose the students had to make arrangements of six squares. How many different arrangements of six squares are possible?
2. **WRITING IN MATH** Describe when you should use the *make a model* problem-solving strategy to solve a problem.

Mixed Problem Solving

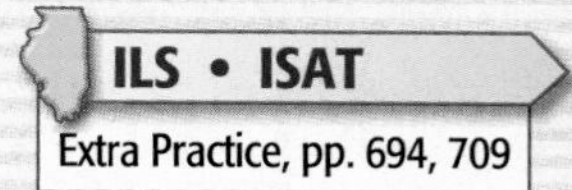

For Exercises 3–5, solve by making a model.

3. **ART** Jeffrey is making a model of his backyard for an art class. His backyard measures 72 feet by 96 feet. If he uses a scale of 8 feet = $1\frac{1}{2}$ inches, what are the dimensions of the backyard on the model?

4. **PATTERNS** Mrs. Hollern is making a quilt using the following pattern. How many squares would be in the 20th figure in this pattern?

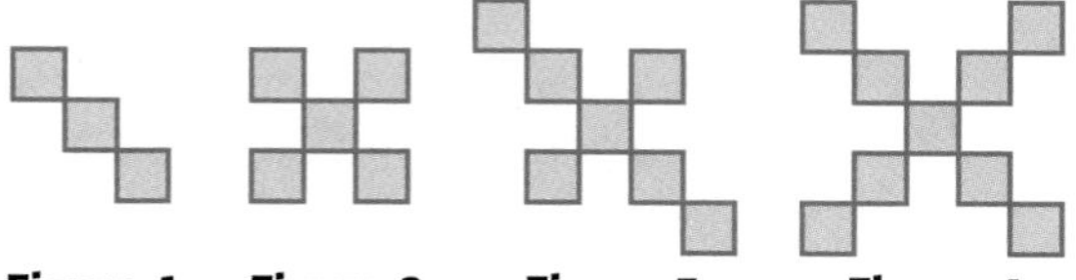

5. **POPCORN** A box of popcorn is made from rectangular sheets of cardboard measuring $8\frac{1}{2}$ inches by 11 inches. To make the box, each corner of the cardboard has a $1\frac{1}{2}$-inch square cut out. Find the volume of the box of popcorn.

Use any strategy to solve Exercises 6–13. Some strategies are shown below.

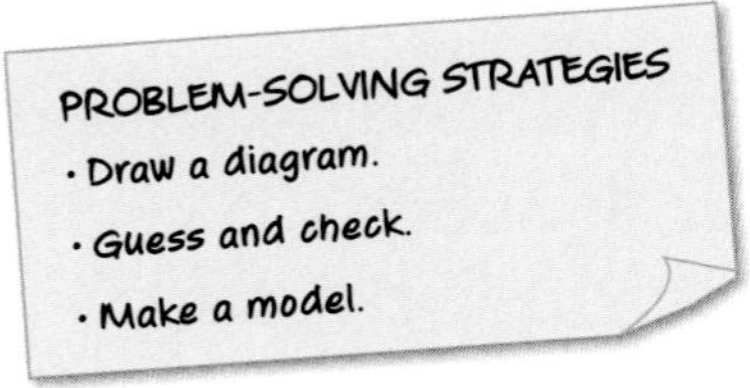

6. **VOLLEYBALL** A total of 8 players came to volleyball practice on Monday. How many different teams of 3 players can be made from the total number of players that came to practice?

7. **PRINTS** A store sells digital 4 x 6 prints without corrections for $0.20 and with corrections for $0.28. Mitchell spent $16.44, not including tax, on prints. How many of each type of print did he buy?

8. **TABLES** Student Council is setting up tables end-to-end for an awards banquet. How many square tables will they need to put together for 32 people? Each table will seat one person on each side.

9. **MONEY** Jeremy borrowed $250 from his parents for a camping trip. He has already repaid them $82. If he plans to pay them $14 each week, how many weeks will it take Jeremy to repay his parents?

10. **POSTERS** Jacinda has 3 posters that she wants to hang on her bedroom wall. Each poster measures 2 feet wide. She wants the gaps between each poster and the ends of the wall to be the same distance. If her wall measures 18 feet, how wide should each gap be?

TILE For Exercises 11 and 12, use the diagram below that shows the design of a tile border around a rectangular swimming pool that measures 7 feet by 4 feet. Each tile is a square measuring 1 foot on a side.

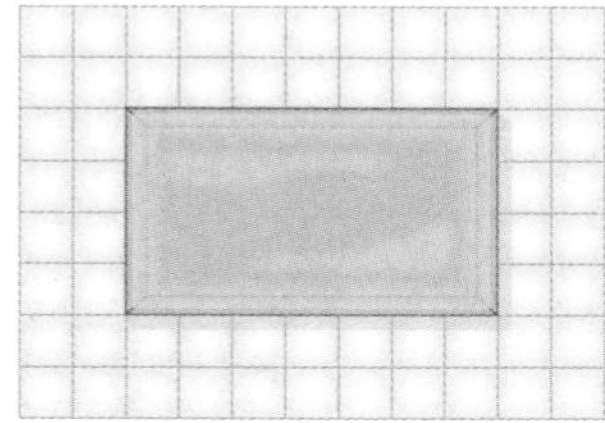

11. Using the model above, how many tiles are needed if the pool is 18 feet long and 12 feet wide?

12. How many tiles are needed for a pool 32 feet long and 20 feet wide?

13. **LAUNDRY** You need two clothespins to hang one towel on a clothesline. One clothespin can be used on a corner of one towel and a corner of the towel next to it. What is the least number of clothespins you need to hang 8 towels?

10-4 Graphing Cubic Functions

MAIN IDEA

Graph cubic functions.

IL Learning Standards

8.A.3b Solve problems using linear expressions, **equations** and inequalities.
8.D.3a Solve problems using numeric, graphic or symbolic representations of variables, expressions, **equations** and inequalities.

IL Math Online

glencoe.com

- Extra Examples
- Personal Tutor
- Self-Check Quiz

GET READY for the Lesson

MEASUREMENT You can find the area A of a square by squaring the length of a side s. This relationship can be represented in different ways.

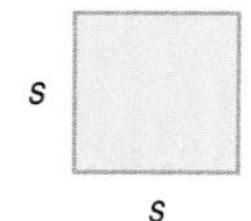

Words and Equation

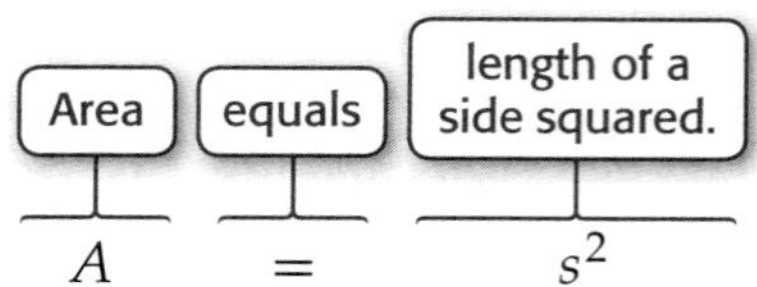

Table

s	s^2	(s, A)
0	$0^2 = 0$	(0, 0)
1	$1^2 = 1$	(1, 1)
2	$2^2 = 4$	(2, 4)

Graph

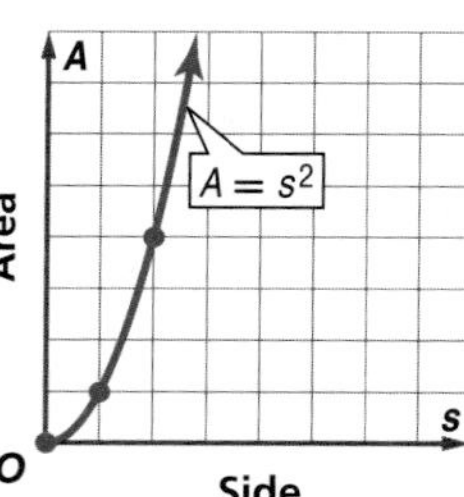

1. The volume V of a cube is found by cubing the length of a side s. Write a formula to represent the volume of a cube as a function of side length.

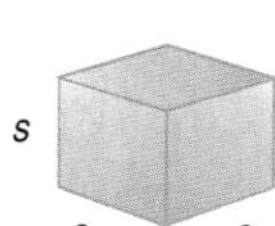

2. Graph the volume as a function of side length. (*Hint*: Use values of s such as 0, 0.5, 1, 1.5, 2, and so on.)
3. Would it be reasonable to use negative numbers for x-values in this situation? Explain.

You can graph cubic functions such as the formula for the volume of a cube by making a table of values.

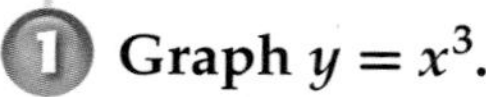

EXAMPLE Graph a Cubic Function

1 **Graph $y = x^3$.**

x	$y = x^3$	(x, y)
−1.5	$(-1.5)^3 \approx -3.4$	(−1.5, −3.4)
−1	$(-1)^3 = -1$	(−1, −1)
0	$(0)^3 = 0$	(0, 0)
1	$(1)^3 = 1$	(1, 1)
1.5	$(1.5)^3 \approx 3.4$	(1.5, 3.4)

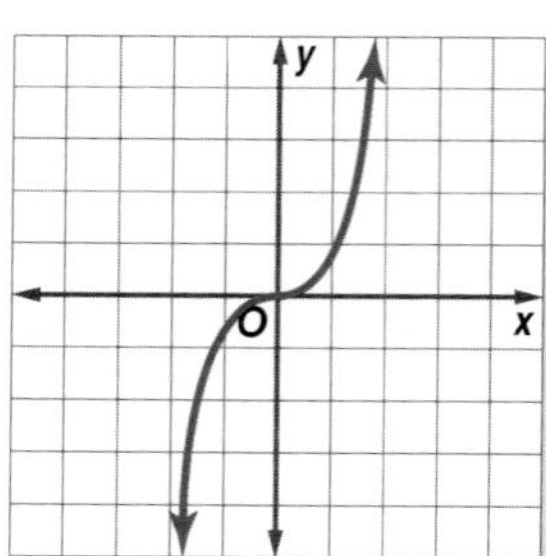

CHECK Your Progress

Graph each function.

a. $y = x^3 - 1$
b. $y = -4x^3$
c. $y = x^3 + 4$

Real-World Link

Packaging is the nation's third largest industry, with over \$130 billion in sales each year.

Source: San Jose State University

Real-World EXAMPLE

2 PACKAGING A packaging company wants to manufacture a cardboard box with a square base of side length x inches and a height of $(x - 3)$ inches as shown.

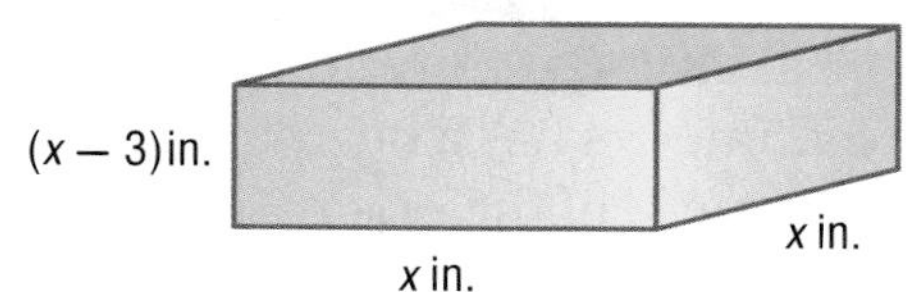

Write the function for the volume V of the box. Graph the function. Then estimate the dimensions of the box that would give a volume of approximately 8 cubic inches.

$V = \ell wh$	Volume of a rectangular prism
$V = x \cdot x \cdot (x - 3)$	Replace ℓ with x, w with x, and h with $(x - 3)$.
$V = x^2(x - 3)$	$x \cdot x = x^2$
$V = x^3 - 3x^2$	Distributive Property and Commutative Property

The function for the volume V of the box is $V = x^3 - 3x^2$. Make a table of values to graph this function. You do not need to include negative values of x since the side length of the box cannot be negative.

x	$V = x^3 - 3x^2$	(x, V)
0	$(0)^3 - 3(0)^2 = 0$	(0, 0)
0.5	$(0.5)^3 - 3(0.5)^2 \approx -0.6$	(0.5, –0.6)
1	$(1)^3 - 3(1)^2 = -2$	(1, –2)
1.5	$(1.5)^3 - 3(1.5)^2 \approx -3.4$	(1.5, –3.4)
2	$(2)^3 - 3(2)^2 = -4$	(2, –4)
2.5	$(2.5)^3 - 3(2.5)^2 \approx -3.1$	(2.5, –3.1)
3	$(3)^3 - 3(3)^2 = 0$	(3, 0)
3.5	$(3.5)^3 - 3(3.5)^2 \approx 6.1$	(3.5, 6.1)
4	$(4)^3 - 3(4)^2 = 16$	(4, 16)

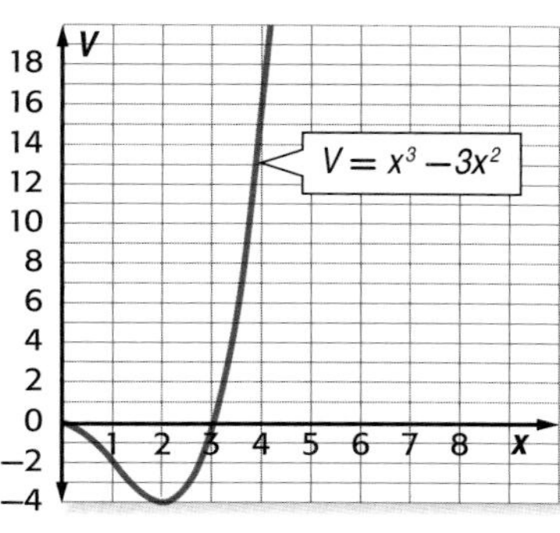

Looking at the graph, we see that the volume of the box is approximately 8 cubic inches when x is about 3.6 inches.

When the volume is about 8 cubic inches, the dimensions of the box are 3.6 inches, 3.6 inches, and 3.6 – 3 or 0.6 inch.

Study Tip

Analyze the Graph

Notice that the graph is *below* the x-axis for values of $x < 3$. This means that the "volume" of the box is negative for $x < 3$. To have a box with a positive height and a positive volume, x must be greater than 3.

CHECK Your Progress

d. **PACKAGING** A packaging company wants to manufacture a cardboard box with a square base of side length x feet and a height of $(x - 2)$ feet. Write the function for the volume V of the box. Graph the function. Then estimate the dimensions of the box that would give a volume of about 1 cubic foot.

CHECK Your Understanding

Example 1 (p. 540)

Graph each function.

1. $y = -x^3$
2. $y = 0.5x^3$
3. $y = x^3 - 2$
4. $y = 2x^3 + 1$

Example 2 (p. 541)

5. **MEASUREMENT** A rectangular prism with a square base of side length x centimeters has a height of $(x + 1)$ centimeters. Write the function for the volume V of the prism. Graph the function. Then estimate the dimensions of the prism that would give a volume of approximately 9 cubic centimeters.

Practice and Problem Solving

HOMEWORK HELP	
For Exercises	See Examples
6–17	1
18, 19	2

Graph each function.

6. $y = -2x^3$
7. $y = -3x^3$
8. $y = 0.2x^3$
9. $y = 0.1x^3$
10. $y = x^3 + 1$
11. $y = 2x^3 + 1$
12. $y = x^3 - 3$
13. $y = 2x^3 - 2$
14. $y = \frac{1}{4}x^3$
15. $y = \frac{1}{3}x^3 + 2$
16. $y = -x^3 - 2$
17. $y = -x^3 + 1$

18. **MEASUREMENT** Jorge built a scale model of the Great Pyramid. The base of the model is a square with side length s and the model's height is $(s - 1)$ feet. Write the function for the volume V of the model. Graph this function. Then estimate the length of one side of the square base of the model if the model's volume is approximately 8 cubic feet.

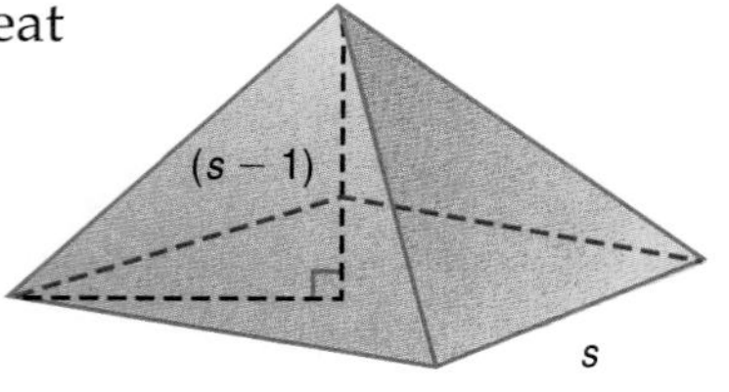

19. **MEASUREMENT** The formula for the volume V of a tennis ball is given by the equation $V = \frac{4}{3}\pi r^3$ where r represents the radius of the ball. Graph this function. Use 3.14 for π. Then estimate the length of the radius if the volume of the tennis ball is approximately 11 cubic inches.

Graph each pair of equations on the same coordinate plane. Describe their similarities and differences.

20. $y = x^3$
    $y = 3x^3$
21. $y = x^3$
    $y = x^3 - 3$
22. $y = 0.5x^3$
    $y = 2x^3$
23. $y = 2x^3$
    $y = -2x^3$

FARMING For Exercises 24 and 25, use the following information.

A grain silo consists of a cylindrical main section and a hemispherical roof. The cylindrical main section has a radius of r units and a height h equivalent to the radius. The volume V of a cylinder is given by the equation $V = \pi r^2 h$.

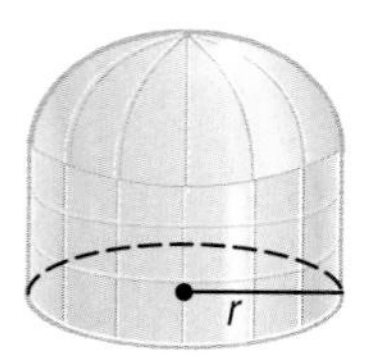

24. Write the function for the volume V of the cylindrical main section of the grain silo in terms of its radius r.

25. Graph this function. Use 3.14 for π. Then estimate the radius and height in meters of the cylindrical main section of the grain silo if the volume is approximately 15.5 cubic meters.

ILS • ISAT

Extra Practice, pp. 695, 709

H.O.T. Problems

26. **OPEN ENDED** Write the equation of a cubic function whose graph in the first quadrant shows faster growth than the function $y = x^3$.

CHALLENGE The *zeros* of a cubic function are the x-coordinates of the points at which the function crosses the x-axis. Find the zeros of each function below.

27. $y = x^3$

28. $y = x^3 + 1$

29. **WRITING IN MATH** The volume V of a cube with side length s is given by the equation $V = s^3$. Explain why negative values are not necessary when creating a table or a graph of this function.

ISAT PRACTICE 8.A.3b, 8.D.3a

30. Which equation could represent the graph shown below?

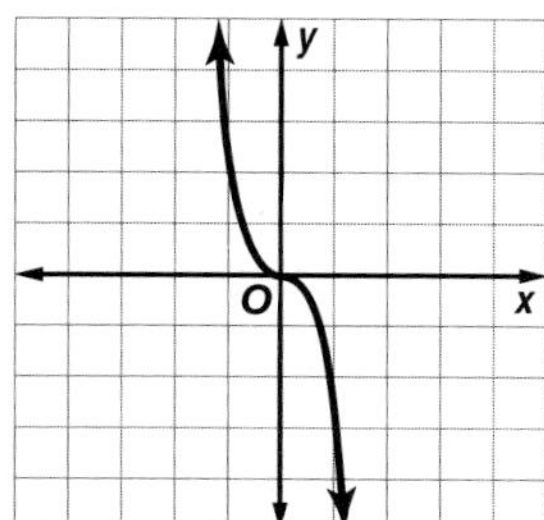

A $y = x^3$

B $y = -x^3$

C $y = 2x^3$

D $y = -2x^3$

31. Which equation could represent the graph shown below?

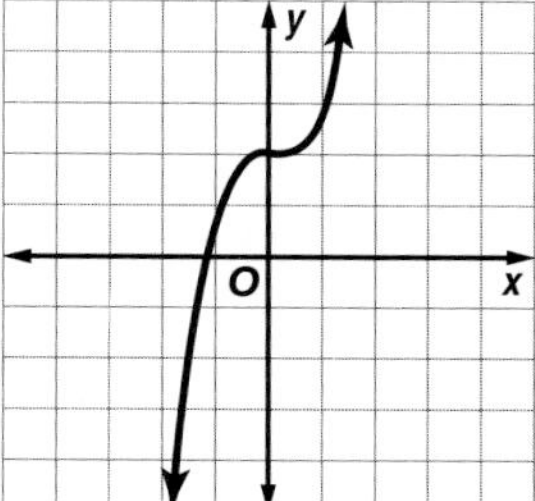

F $y = x^3 - 2$

G $y = x^3 + 2$

H $y = -2x^3$

J $y = 2x^3 + 1$

Spiral Review

32. **MANUFACTURING** A company packages six small books for a children's collection in a decorated 4-inch cube. They are shipped to bookstores in cartons. Twenty cubes fit in a carton with no extra space. What are the dimensions of the carton? Use the *make a model* strategy. (Lesson 10-3)

Graph each function. (Lesson 10-2)

33. $y = -2x^2$

34. $y = x^2 + 3$

35. $y = -3x^2 + 1$

36. $y = 4x^2 + 3$

Estimate each square root to the nearest whole number. (Lesson 3-2)

37. $\sqrt{54}$

38. $\sqrt{126}$

39. $\sqrt{8.67}$

40. $\sqrt{19.85}$

GET READY for the Next Lesson

PREREQUISITE SKILL Write each expression using exponents. (Lesson 2-9)

41. $3 \cdot 3 \cdot 3 \cdot 3 \cdot 3$

42. $5 \cdot 4 \cdot 5 \cdot 5 \cdot 4$

43. $7 \cdot (7 \cdot 7)$

44. $(2 \cdot 2) \cdot (2 \cdot 2 \cdot 2)$

Extend 10-4

Graphing Calculator Lab
Families of Nonlinear Functions

MAIN IDEA

Use a graphing calculator to graph families of nonlinear functions.

IL Learning Standards

8.A.3b Solve problems using linear expressions, **equations** and inequalities.
8.D.3a Solve problems using numeric, graphic or symbolic representations of variables, expressions, **equations** and inequalities.

Families of nonlinear functions share a common characteristic based on a parent function. The parent function of a family of quadratic functions is $y = x^2$. You can use a graphing calculator to investigate families of quadratic functions.

ACTIVITY

Graph $y = x^2$, $y = x^2 + 5$, and $y = x^2 - 3$ on the same screen.

STEP 1 Clear any existing equations from the Y= list by pressing [Y=] [CLEAR].

STEP 2 Enter each equation. Press [X,T,θ,n] [x^2] [ENTER], [X,T,θ,n] [x^2] [+] 5 [ENTER], and [X,T,θ,n] [x^2] [−] 3 [ENTER].

STEP 3 Graph the equations in the standard viewing window. Press [ZOOM] 6.

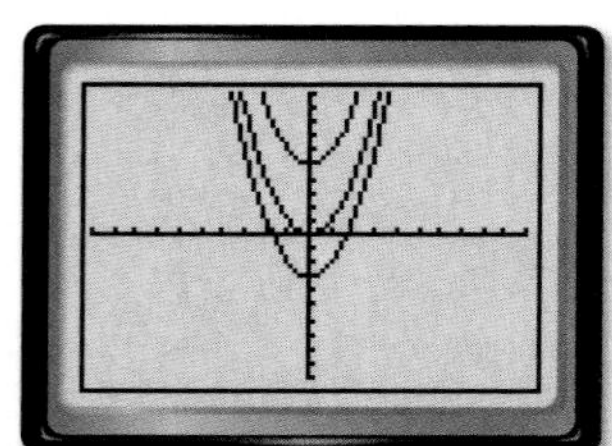

Analyze the Results

1. Compare and contrast the three equations you graphed.
2. Describe how the graphs of the three equations are related.
3. **MAKE A CONJECTURE** How does changing the value of c in the equation $y = x^2 + c$ affect the graph?
4. Use a graphing calculator to graph $y = 0.5x^2$, $y = x^2$, and $y = 2x^2$.
5. Compare and contrast the three equations you graphed in Exercise 4.
6. Describe how the graphs of the three equations are related.
7. **MAKE A CONJECTURE** How does changing the value of a in the equation $y = ax^2$ affect the graph?
8. Use a graphing calculator to graph $y = 0.5x^3$, $y = x^3$, and $y = 2x^3$.
9. Compare and contrast the three equations you graphed in Exercise 8 to the equations you graphed in Exercise 4.

10-5 Multiplying Monomials

MAIN IDEA

Multiply monomials.

IL Learning Standards

8.A.3b Solve problems using linear **expressions,** equations and inequalities.
8.D.3c Apply properties of powers, perfect squares and square roots.

New Vocabulary

monomial

IL Math Online

glencoe.com
- Extra Examples
- Personal Tutor
- Self-Check Quiz

GET READY for the Lesson

MEASUREMENT The edge of a dime is approximately 1 millimeter thick. The table shows how other metric measurements of length are related to the millimeter.

Unit of Length	Times Longer than a Millimeter	Written Using Powers
Millimeter	1	10^0
Centimeter	$1 \times 10 = 10$	10^1
Decimeter	$10 \times 10 = 100$	$10^1 \times 10^1 = 10^2$
Meter	$100 \times 10 = 1{,}000$	$10^1 \times 10^2 = 10^3$
Dekameter	$1{,}000 \times 10 = 10{,}000$	$10^1 \times 10^3 = 10^4$
Hectometer	$10{,}000 \times 10 = 100{,}000$	$10^1 \times 10^4 = 10^5$
Kilometer	$100{,}000 \times 10 = 1{,}000{,}000$	$10^1 \times 10^5 = 10^6$

1. Examine the exponents of the factors and the exponents of the products in the last column. What do you observe?

A **monomial** is a number, a variable, or a product of a number and one or more variables. Exponents are used to show repeated multiplication. You can use this fact to find a rule for multiplying monomials.

$$3^2 \cdot 3^4 = \underbrace{(3 \cdot 3)}_{\text{2 factors}} \cdot \underbrace{(3 \cdot 3 \cdot 3 \cdot 3)}_{\text{4 factors}} \text{ or } 3^6 \quad \text{(6 factors)}$$

Notice that the sum of the original exponents is the exponent in the final product. This relationship is stated in the following rule.

Product of Powers — Key Concept

Words To multiply powers with the same base, add their exponents.

Examples

Numbers	Algebra
$2^4 \cdot 2^3 = 2^{4+3}$ or 2^7	$a^m \cdot a^n = a^{m+n}$

EXAMPLES Multiply Powers

1 **Find $5^2 \cdot 5$. Express using exponents.**

$5^2 \cdot 5 = 5^2 \cdot 5^1$ — $5 = 5^1$

$= 5^{2+1}$ — The common base is 5.

$= 5^3$ — Add the exponents.

Check $5^2 \cdot 5 = (5 \cdot 5) \cdot 5$
$= 5 \cdot 5 \cdot 5$
$= 5^3$ ✓

2 **Find $-3x^2(4x^5)$. Express using exponents.**

$-3x^2(4x^5) = (-3 \cdot 4)(x^2 \cdot x^5)$	Commutative and Associative Properties
$= (-12)(x^{2+5})$	The common base is x.
$= -12x^7$	Add the exponents.

CHECK Your Progress

Multiply. Express using exponents.

a. $9^3 \cdot 9^2$ b. $\left(\frac{3}{5}\right)^2 \left(\frac{3}{5}\right)^9$ c. $-2m(-8m^5)$

Real-World Link . . . . A census is taken every ten years by the U.S. Census Bureau to determine population. The government uses the data from the census to make many decisions.

Source: U.S. Census Bureau

Real-World EXAMPLE

3 **The population of Groveton is 6^5. The population of Putnam is 6^3 times as great. How many people are in Putnam?**

To find out the number of people, multiply 6^5 by 6^3.

$6^5 \cdot 6^3 = 6^{5+3}$ or 6^8 Product of Powers

The population of Putnam is 6^8 or 1,679,616 people.

CHECK Your Progress

d. **RIVERS** The Guadalupe River is 2^8 miles long. The Amazon River is almost 2^4 times as long. Find the length of the Amazon River.

In Lesson 2-9, you learned to evaluate negative exponents. Remember that any nonzero number to the negative n power is the multiplicative inverse of that number to the nth power. The Product of Powers rule can be used to multiply powers with negative exponents.

EXAMPLE Multiply Negative Powers

4 **Find $x^4 \cdot x^{-2}$. Express using exponents.**

METHOD 1

$x^4 \cdot x^{-2} = x^{4+(-2)}$	The common base is x.
$= x^2$	Add the exponents.

METHOD 2

$x^4 \cdot x^{-2}$

$= x \cdot x \cdot x \cdot x \cdot \frac{1}{x} \cdot \frac{1}{x}$	$x^{-2} = \frac{1}{x^2}$
$= x^2$	Simplify.

CHECK Your Progress

Simplify. Express using positive exponents.

e. $3^8 \cdot 3^{-2}$ f. $n^9 \cdot n^{-4}$ g. $5^{-1} \cdot 5^{-2}$

CHECK Your Understanding

Examples 1–4 (pp. 545–546)

Simplify. Express using exponents.

1. $4^5 \cdot 4^3$
2. $n^2 \cdot n^9$
3. $-2a(3a^4)$
4. $5^2x^2y^4 \cdot 5^3xy^3$
5. $r^7 \cdot r^{-3}$
6. $6m \cdot 4m^2$

Example 3 (p. 546)

7. **AGE** Angelina is 2^3 years old. Her grandfather is 2^3 times her age. How old is her grandfather?

Practice and Problem Solving

HOMEWORK HELP

For Exercises	See Examples
8–25	1, 2, 4
26–28	3

Simplify. Express using exponents.

8. $6^8 \cdot 6^5$
9. $2^9 \cdot 2$
10. $n \cdot n^7$
11. $b^{13} \cdot b$
12. $2g \cdot 7g^6$
13. $(3x^8)(5x)$
14. $-4a^5(6a^5)$
15. $(8w^4)(-w^7)$
16. $(-p)(-9p^2)$
17. $-5y^3(-8y^6)$
18. $4m^{-2}n^5(3m^4n^{-2})$
19. $(-7a^4bc^3)(5ab^4c^2)$
20. $x^6 \cdot x^{-3}$
21. $y^{-1} \cdot y^4$
22. $z^{-2} \cdot z^{-3}$
23. $m^2n^{-1} \cdot m^{-3}n^3$
24. $3f^{-4} \cdot 5f^2$
25. $-3ab \cdot 4a^{-3}b^3$

26. **INSECTS** The number of ants in a nest was 5^3. After the eggs hatched, the number of ants increased 5^2 times. How many ants are there after the eggs hatch?

27. **COMPUTERS** The processing speed of a certain computer is 10^{11} instructions per second. Another computer has a processing speed that is 10^3 times as fast. How many instructions per second can the faster computer process?

28. **MOVIES** An online movie rental company has 4^5 comedy movie titles available to its members. The company also carries 4^2 times as many action movie titles. How many action movie titles does the company carry?

Simplify. Express using exponents.

29. $xy^2(x^3y)$
30. $2^6 \cdot 2 \cdot 2^3$
31. $4a^2b^3(7ab^2)$
32. $\left(\frac{2}{3}\right)^4\left(\frac{2}{3}\right)^3$
33. $\left(\frac{7}{8}\right)^{-5}\left(\frac{7}{8}\right)^{13}$
34. $\left(\frac{2}{5}\right)^4\left(\frac{2}{5}\right)^{-7}\left(\frac{2}{5}\right)^6$
35. $\left(\frac{1}{4}\right)^{-4}\left(\frac{1}{4}\right)$
36. $\left(\frac{2}{5}\right)^3\left(\frac{2}{5}\right)^{-2}$
37. $\left(\frac{2}{7}\right)^{-2}\left(\frac{7}{2}\right)^{-3}$

ILS • ISAT

Extra Practice, pp. 695, 709

H.O.T. Problems

38. **CHALLENGE** What is twice 2^{30}? Write using exponents.

39. **OPEN ENDED** Write a multiplication expression whose product is 5^{13}

40. **WRITING IN MATH** Determine whether the following statement is *true* or *false*. Explain your reasoning or give a counterexample.

If you change the order in which you multiply two monomials, the product will be different.

ISAT PRACTICE 8.A.3b, 8.D.3c

41. Which expression is equivalent to $8x^2y \cdot 8yz^2$?
    A $64x^2y^2z^2$
    B $64x^2yz^2$
    C $16x^2y^2z^2$
    D $384x^2y^2z^2$

42. **SHORT RESPONSE** What is the area in square feet of the rectangle below?

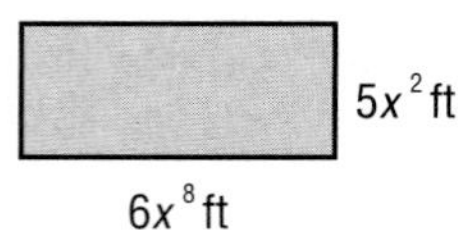

Spiral Review

Graph each function. (Lessons 10-2 and 10-4)

43. $y = -x^3$
44. $y = 0.5x^3$
45. $y = x^3 - 2$
46. $y = 5x^2$
47. $y = x^2 + 5$
48. $y = x^2 - 4$

49. **BIOLOGY** The table shows how long it took for the first 400 bacteria cells to grow in a petri dish. Is the growth of the bacteria a linear function of time? Explain. (Lesson 10-1)

Time (min)	46	53	57	60
Number of cells	100	200	300	400

Express each number in scientific notation. (Lesson 2-10)

50. The flow rate of some Antarctic glaciers is 0.00031 mile per hour.

51. A human blinks about 6.25 million times a year.

ALGEBRA Solve each equation. Check your solution. (Lesson 2-7)

52. $k - 4.1 = -9.38$
53. $1\frac{3}{4} + p = -6\frac{1}{2}$
54. $\frac{c}{10} = 0.845$

Find each sum or difference. Write in simplest form. (Lesson 2-6)

55. $\frac{7}{8} - \frac{3}{10}$
56. $-\frac{1}{5} + \frac{5}{12}$
57. $9\frac{2}{3} + \frac{1}{6}$
58. $-2\frac{3}{4} - 1\frac{1}{8}$

GET READY for the Next Lesson

PREREQUISITE SKILL **Write each expression using exponents.** (Lesson 2-9)

59. $3 \cdot 3 \cdot 3 \cdot 3$
60. $5 \cdot 4 \cdot 4 \cdot 5 \cdot 4$
61. $8 \cdot (8 \cdot 8)$
62. $(5 \cdot 5 \cdot 5) \cdot (5 \cdot 5)$

CHAPTER 10

Mid-Chapter Quiz

Lessons 10-1 through 10-5

IL Learning Standards
8.A.3b, 8.D.3a

Determine whether each equation or table represents a *linear* or *nonlinear* function. Explain. (Lesson 10-1)

1. $3y = x$
2. $y = 5x^3 + 2$
3.

x	1	3	5	7
y	−5	−6	−7	−8

4.

x	−1	0	1	2
y	1	0	1	4

5. **LONG DISTANCE** The graph shows the amount of data transferred as a function of time. Is this a linear or nonlinear function? Explain your reasoning. (Lesson 10-1)

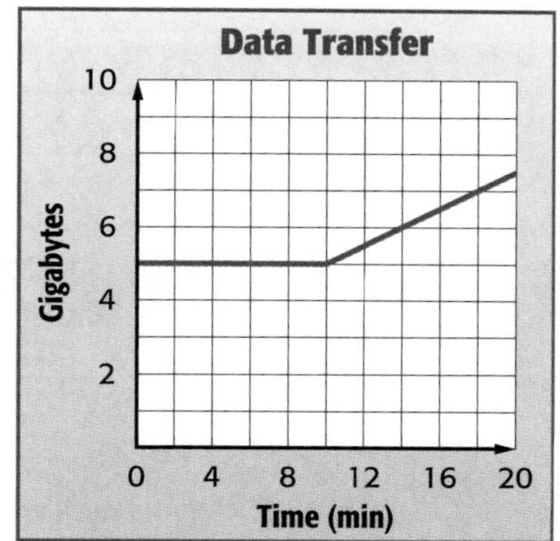

Graph each function. (Lesson 10-2)

6. $y = 2x^2$
7. $y = -x^2 + 3$
8. $y = 4x^2 - 1$
9. $y = -3x^2 + 1$

10. **SKYDIVING** The function $d = 4.9t^2$ models the distance d in meters fallen by a skydiver t seconds after jumping from a plane. Graph this function. After about how many seconds will the skydiver fall 130 feet? (Lesson 10-2)

11. **MULTIPLE CHOICE** Which graph shows $y = x^2 + 1$? (Lesson 10-2)

A
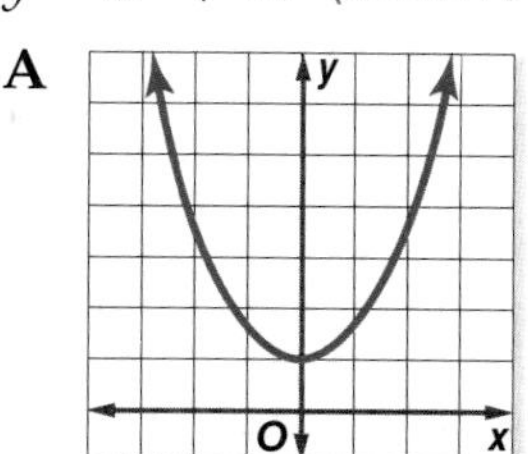

C
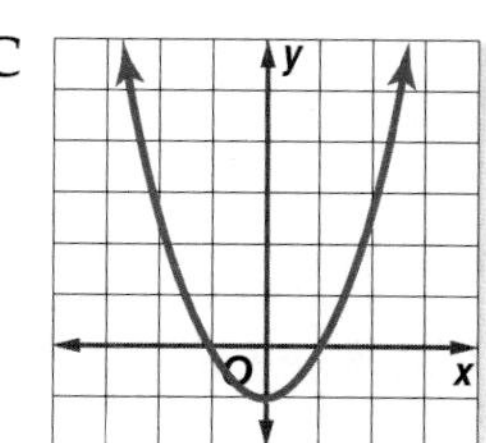

B
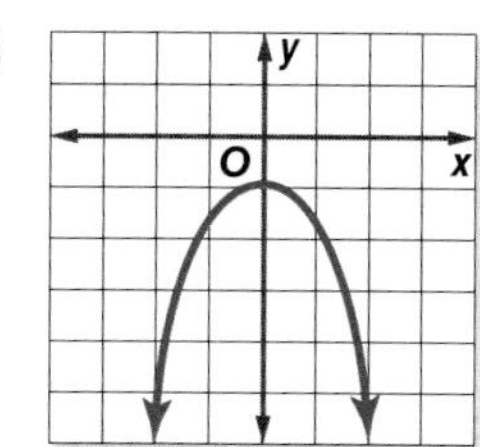

D
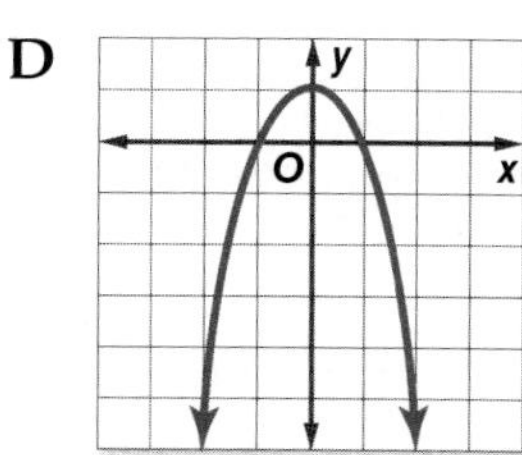

12. **MEASUREMENT** Brenda has a photograph that is 10 inches by 13 inches. She decides to frame it using a frame that is $2\frac{1}{4}$ inches wide on each side. Find the total area of the framed photograph. Use the *make a model* strategy. (Lesson 10-3)

Graph each function. (Lesson 10-4)

13. $y = -2x^3$
14. $y = 3x^3$
15. $y = 2x^3$
16. $y = 0.1x^3$

Simplify. Express using exponents. (Lesson 10-5)

17. $10^4 \cdot 10^7$
18. $3^{-3} \cdot 3^5 \cdot 3^2$
19. $2^3a^7 \cdot 2a^{-3}$
20. $(3^2xy^4z^2)(3^5x^3y^{-2}z^3)$

21. **MULTIPLE CHOICE** Which expression below has the same value as $5m^2$? (Lesson 10-5)

F $5m$

G $5 \cdot m \cdot m$

H $5 \cdot 5 \cdot m \cdot m$

J $5 \cdot m \cdot m \cdot m$

10-6 Dividing Monomials

MAIN IDEA

Divide monomials.

IL Learning Standards

8.A.3b Solve problems using linear **expressions,** equations and inequalities.
8.D.3c Apply properties of powers, perfect squares and square roots.

IL Math Online

glencoe.com

- Extra Examples
- Personal Tutor
- Self-Check Quiz

GET READY for the Lesson

NUMBER SENSE Refer to the table shown that relates division sentences using the numbers 2, 4, 8, and 16, and the same sentences written using powers of 2.

Division Sentence	Written Using Powers of 2
$4 \div 2 = 2$	$2^2 \div 2^1 = 2^1$
$8 \div 2 = 4$	$2^3 \div 2^1 = 2^2$
$8 \div 4 = 2$	$2^3 \div 2^2 = 2^1$
$16 \div 2 = 8$	$2^4 \div 2^1 = 2^3$
$16 \div 4 = 4$	$2^4 \div 2^2 = 2^2$
$16 \div 8 = 2$	$2^4 \div 2^3 = 2^1$

1. Examine the exponents of the divisors and dividends. Compare them to the exponents of the quotients. What do you notice?
2. **MAKE A CONJECTURE** Write the quotient of 2^5 and 2^2 using powers of 2.

As you know, exponents are used to show repeated multiplication. You can use this fact to find a rule for dividing powers with the same base.

Notice that the difference of the original exponents is the exponent in the final quotient. This relationship is stated in the following rule.

$$\frac{5^7}{5^4} = \frac{\overbrace{5 \cdot 5 \cdot 5 \cdot 5 \cdot 5 \cdot 5 \cdot 5}^{7 \text{ factors}}}{\underbrace{5 \cdot 5 \cdot 5 \cdot 5}_{4 \text{ factors}}} \text{ or } 5^3$$

Quotient of Powers — Key Concept

Words To divide powers with the same base, subtract their exponents.

Examples

Numbers	Algebra
$\frac{3^7}{3^3} = 3^{7-3}$ or 3^4	$\frac{a^m}{a^n} = a^{m-n}$, where $a \neq 0$

EXAMPLES Divide Powers

Simplify. Express using exponents.

1 $\frac{4^8}{4^2}$

$\frac{4^8}{4^2} = 4^{8-2}$ The common base is 4.

$= 4^6$ Simplify.

2 $\frac{n^9}{n^4}$

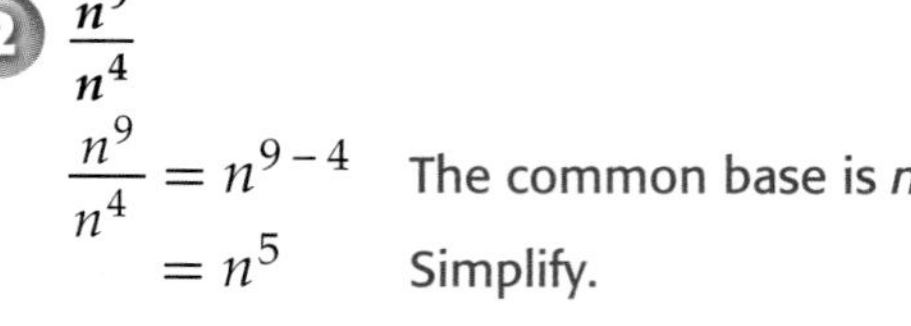

$\frac{n^9}{n^4} = n^{9-4}$ The common base is n.

$= n^5$ Simplify.

CHECK Your Progress

Simplify. Express using exponents.

a. $\frac{5^7}{5^4}$

b. $\frac{x^{10}}{x^3}$

c. $\frac{12w^5}{2w}$

The Quotient of Powers rule can also be used to divide powers with negative exponents. It is customary to write final answers using positive exponents.

EXAMPLES Use Negative Exponents

Simplify. Express using positive exponents.

Study Tip

Look Back
To review adding and subtracting integers, see Lessons 1-4 and 1-5.

3 $\dfrac{6^9}{6^{-3}}$

$\dfrac{6^9}{6^{-3}} = 6^{9-(-3)}$ Quotient of Powers

$= 6^{9+3}$ or 6^{12} Simplify.

4 $\dfrac{w^{-1}}{w^{-4}}$

$\dfrac{w^{-1}}{w^{-4}} = w^{-1-(-4)}$ Quotient of Powers

$= w^{-1+4}$ or w^3 Simplify.

CHECK Your Progress

Simplify. Express using positive exponents.

d. $\dfrac{11^{-8}}{11^2}$ e. $\dfrac{b^{-4}}{b^{-7}}$ f. $\dfrac{6h^5}{3h^{-5}}$

ISAT EXAMPLE 8.A.3b, 8.D.3c

5 $\dfrac{2^2 \cdot 4^5 \cdot 5^2}{2^5 \cdot 4^4 \cdot 5^2} =$

A 2 **B** 1 **C** $\frac{1}{2}$ **D** 0

Test-Taking Tip

Remember that the Quotient of Powers Rule allows you to simplify $\frac{5^2}{5^2}$.

$\frac{5^2}{5^2} = 5^{2-2} = 5^0 = 1$

When dividing powers, do not divide the bases.

$\frac{4^5}{4^4} = 4^1$, not 1^1.

Read the Item

You are asked to divide one monomial by another.

Solve the Item

$\dfrac{2^2 \cdot 4^5 \cdot 5^2}{2^5 \cdot 4^4 \cdot 5^2} = \left(\dfrac{2^2}{2^5}\right)\left(\dfrac{4^5}{4^4}\right)\left(\dfrac{5^2}{5^2}\right)$ Group by common base.

$= 2^{-3} \cdot 4^1 \cdot 5^0$ Subtract the exponents.

$= \dfrac{1}{2^3} \cdot 4 \cdot 1$ $2^{-3} = \dfrac{1}{2^3}$

$= \dfrac{4}{8}$ or $\dfrac{1}{2}$ Simplify.

The answer is C.

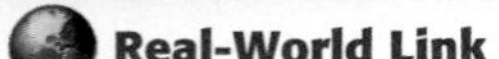

Real-World Link The Hawaiian Islands contain 1,052 miles of shoreline.

Source: *The World Almanac*

CHECK Your Progress

g. Simplify $\dfrac{\left(\frac{1}{6}\right)^4 \times \left(\frac{1}{6}\right)^{-12}}{\left(\frac{1}{6}\right)^{-3}}$.

F $\left(\frac{1}{6}\right)^5$ G $\frac{1}{6}$ H 6^4 J 6^5

Real-World EXAMPLE

6 SHORELINES Outer coasts, offshore islands, sounds, bays, rivers and creeks are used to measure shorelines. Hawaii's total shoreline is about 2^{10} miles long. New Hampshire contains about 2^7 miles of shoreline. About how many times as long is Hawaii's shoreline than New Hampshire's shoreline?

To find how many times as long, divide 2^{10} by 2^7.

$\dfrac{2^{10}}{2^7} = 2^{10-7}$ or 2^3 Quotient of Powers

Hawaii's shoreline is about 2^3 or 8 times as long as New Hampshire's shoreline.

CHECK Your Progress

h. **SOUND** The loudness of a vacuum cleaner is 10^4 times as intense as the loudness of a mosquito buzzing, while the loudness of a jack hammer is 10^9 times as intense. How many times as intense is the loudness of a jack hammer than that of a vacuum cleaner?

CHECK Your Understanding

Examples 1–4 (pp. 550-551)

Simplify. Express using positive exponents.

1. $\dfrac{7^6}{7}$
2. $\dfrac{2^9}{2^{13}}$
3. $\dfrac{y^8}{y^5}$
4. $\dfrac{z}{z^2}$
5. $\dfrac{9c^7}{3c^2}$
6. $\dfrac{24k^9}{6k^6}$
7. $\dfrac{15^{-6}}{15^2}$
8. $\dfrac{35p^1}{5p^{-4}}$

Example 5 (p. 551)

9. Simplify $\dfrac{2^2 \cdot 3^3 \cdot 4^4}{2 \cdot 3^3 \cdot 4^5}$.

A 2^2 B 2 C $\frac{1}{2}$ D $\left(\frac{1}{2}\right)^2$

Example 6 (p. 552)

10. **LANGUAGES** French is spoken by 2^6 million people. Sicilian is spoken by 2^2 million people. How many times as many people speak French than Sicilian?

Practice and Problem Solving

HOMEWORK HELP	
For Exercises	See Examples
11–26	1–4
27–30	5
31–34	6

Simplify. Express using positive exponents.

11. $\frac{8^{15}}{8^4}$ 12. $\frac{2^9}{2}$ 13. $\frac{4^3}{4^7}$ 14. $\frac{13^2}{13^5}$

15. $\frac{h^7}{h^6}$ 16. $\frac{g^{18}}{g^6}$ 17. $\frac{x^8}{x^{11}}$ 18. $\frac{n}{n^8}$

19. $\frac{36d^{10}}{6d^5}$ 20. $\frac{16t^4}{8t}$ 21. $\frac{20m^7}{5m^5}$ 22. $\frac{75r^6}{25r^5}$

23. $\frac{22^{-9}}{22^4}$ 24. $\frac{3^{-1}}{3^{-5}}$ 25. $\frac{42w^{-6}}{7w^{-2}}$ 26. $\frac{12y^{-6}}{2y^{-10}}$

27. $\frac{x^6y^{14}}{x^4y^9}$ 28. $\frac{6^3 \cdot 6^6 \cdot 6^4}{6^2 \cdot 6^3 \cdot 6^4} =$ 29. $\frac{\left(\frac{1}{5}\right)^2 \times \left(\frac{1}{5}\right)^{-6}}{\left(\frac{1}{5}\right)^2}$ 30. $\frac{3x^4}{3^4x^{-2}}$

Real-World Career
How Does a Food Scientist Use Math? Food scientists analyze food to determine how processing and storage affects its flavor, texture, appearance, and nutritional value.

31. **SEATING** A typical movie theater can seat about 3^5 people. Madison Square Garden in New York City has a capacity of about 3^9 people. About how many times as great is the capacity of Madison Square Garden than a typical movie theater?

32. **FOOD** The pH of a solution describes its acidity. Each one-unit decrease in pH means that the solution is 10 times more acidic. An apple is 10^3 times as acidic as milk, while a lemon is 10^4 times as acidic. How many times as acidic is a lemon than an apple?

33. **ANIMALS** A common flea 2^{-4} inch long can jump about 2^3 inches high. About how many times its body size can a flea jump?

34. **MEDICINE** The mass of a molecule of penicillin is 10^{-18} kilograms and the mass of a molecule of insulin is 10^{-23} kilograms. How many times as great is a molecule of penicillin than a molecule of insulin?

IL Math Online

For more information, go to glencoe.com.

Find each missing exponent.

35. $\frac{17^{\bullet}}{17^4} = 17^8$ 36. $\frac{k^6}{k^{\bullet}} = k^2$ 37. $\frac{5^{\bullet}}{5^{-9}} = 5^3$ 38. $\frac{p^{-1}}{p^{\bullet}} = p^{10}$

ANALYZE TABLES For Exercises 39 and 40, use the information in the table.

39. How many times as great is one quadrillion than one million?

40. One quintillion is one trillion times as great as what number?

Power of Ten	U.S. Name
10^3	one thousand
10^6	one million
10^9	one billion
10^{12}	one trillion
10^{15}	one quadrillion
10^{18}	one quintillion

ILS • ISAT

Extra Practice, pp. 695, 709

H.O.T. Problems

41. **NUMBER SENSE** Is $\frac{3^{100}}{3^{99}}$ *greater than*, *less than*, or *equal to* 3? Explain your reasoning.

42. **OPEN ENDED** Write a division expression with a quotient of 10^9.

43. **CHALLENGE** What is half of 2^{30}? Write using exponents.

44. **WRITING IN MATH** Explain why the Quotient of Powers Rule cannot be used to simplify the expression $\frac{x^5}{y^2}$.

ISAT PRACTICE 8.A.3b, 8.D.3c

45. Which expression below is equivalent to $\frac{9m^8}{3m^2}$?

A $6m^4$ C $3m^4$
B $6m^6$ D $3m^6$

46. The area of a rectangle is 2^6 square feet. If the length is 2^3 feet, find the width of the rectangle.

F 2 feet H 2^3 feet
G 2^2 feet J 2^9 feet

47. One meter is 10^3 times longer than one millimeter. One kilometer is 10^6 times longer than one millimeter. How many times longer is one kilometer than one meter?

A 10^9
B 10^6
C 10^3
D 10

Spiral Review

Simplify. Express using positive exponents. (Lesson 10-5)

48. $6^4 \cdot 6^7$ 49. $18^3 \cdot 18^{-5}$ 50. $(-3x^{11})(-6x^3)$ 51. $(-9a^4)(2a^{-7})$

Graph each function. (Lesson 10-4)

52. $y = x^3 + 2$ 53. $y = \frac{1}{3}x^3$ 54. $y = -2x^3$ 55. $y = -0.1x^3$

State the slope and the y-intercept for the graph of each equation. (Lesson 9-6)

56. $y = x - 3$ 57. $y = \frac{2}{3}x + 7$ 58. $3x + 4y = 12$ 59. $x + 2y = 10$

60. **COIN COLLECTING** Jada has 156 coins in her collection. This is 12 more than 8 times the number of nickels in the collection. How many nickels does Jada have in her collection? (Lesson 8-3)

GET READY for the Next Lesson

Simplify. Express using positive exponents. (Lesson 10-5)

61. $5n \cdot 3n^4$ 62. $(-x)(-8x^3)$ 63. $(-5b^7)(-2b^4)$ 64. $(-4w)(6w^{-2})$

10-7 Powers of Monomials

MAIN IDEA

Find powers of monomials.

IL Learning Standards

8.A.3b Solve problems using linear **expressions,** equations and inequalities.
8.D.3c Apply properties of powers, perfect squares and square roots.

IL Math Online

glencoe.com
- Extra Examples
- Personal Tutor
- Self-Check Quiz

GET READY for the Lesson

MEASUREMENT Suppose the side length of a cube is 2^2 centimeters.

1. Write a multiplication expression for the volume of the cube.
2. Simplify the expression. Write as a single power of 2.
3. Using 2^2 as the base, write the multiplication expression $2^2 \cdot 2^2 \cdot 2^2$ using an exponent.
4. Explain why $(2^2)^3 = 2^6$.

You can use the rule for finding the *product* of powers to discover the rule for finding the *power* of a power.

$$(6^4)^5 = \overbrace{(6^4)\,(6^4)\,(6^4)\,(6^4)\,(6^4)}^{5\text{ factors}}$$

$$= 6^{4+4+4+4+4} \leftarrow \text{Apply the rule for the product of powers.}$$

$$= 6^{20}$$

Notice that the product of the original exponents, 4 and 5, is the final power 20. This relationship is stated in the following rule.

Power of a Power — Key Concept

Words	To find the power of a power, multiply the exponents.	
Examples	**Numbers**	**Algebra**
	$(5^2)^3 = 5^{2 \cdot 3}$ or 5^6	$(a^m)^n = a^{m \cdot n}$

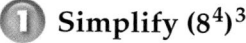

EXAMPLES Find the Power of a Power

1 Simplify $(8^4)^3$.

$(8^4)^3 = 8^{4 \cdot 3}$ Power of a Power

$= 8^{12}$ Simplify.

2 Simplify $(k^7)^5$.

$(k^7)^5 = k^{7 \cdot 5}$ Power of a Power

$= k^{35}$ Simplify.

CHECK Your Progress

Simplify. Express using exponents.

a. $(2^5)^2$ b. $(w^4)^6$ c. $[(3^2)^3]^2$

Study Tip

Common Error
When finding the power of a power, do not add the exponents.
$(8^4)^3 = 8^{12}$, not 8^7.

Extend the power of a *power* rule to find the power of a *product*.

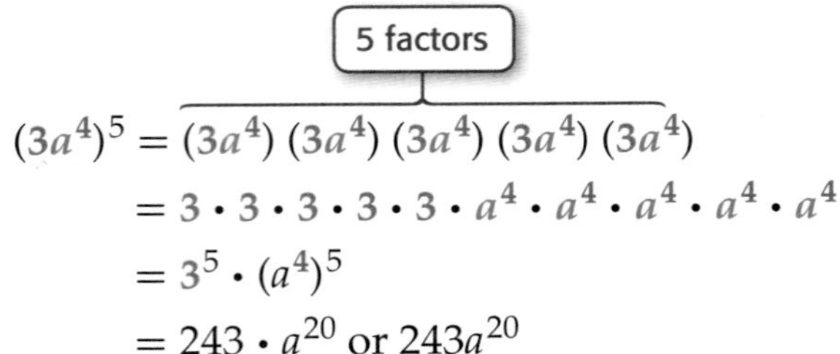

$(3a^4)^5 = (3a^4)(3a^4)(3a^4)(3a^4)(3a^4)$

$= 3 \cdot 3 \cdot 3 \cdot 3 \cdot 3 \cdot a^4 \cdot a^4 \cdot a^4 \cdot a^4 \cdot a^4$ — Associative and Commutative Properties of Multiplication

$= 3^5 \cdot (a^4)^5$ — Write using powers.

$= 243 \cdot a^{20}$ or $243a^{20}$ — Apply the rule for power of a power.

This example suggests the following rule.

Power of a Product

Key Concept

Words To find the power of a product, find the power of each factor and multiply.

Examples

Numbers	Algebra
$(6x^2)^3 = (6)^3 \cdot (x^2)^3$ or $216x^6$	$(ab)^m = a^m b^m$

Study Tip

Alternative Method
$(4p^3)^4$ can also be expressed as
$(4p^3)(4p^3)(4p^3)(4p^3)$
or $(4 \cdot 4 \cdot 4 \cdot 4)$
$(p \cdot p \cdot p)(p \cdot p \cdot p)$
$(p \cdot p \cdot p)(p \cdot p \cdot p)$
which is $256p^{12}$.

EXAMPLES Power of a Product

3 **Simplify $(4p^3)^4$.**

$(4p^3)^4 = 4^4 \cdot p^{3 \cdot 4}$

$= 256p^{12}$ — Simplify.

4 **Simplify $(-2m^7n^6)^5$.**

$(-2m^7n^6)^5 = (-2)^5 m^{7 \cdot 5} n^{6 \cdot 5}$

$= -32m^{35}n^{30}$ — Simplify.

CHECK Your Progress

Simplify.

d. $(8b^9)^2$

e. $(6x^5y^{11})^4$

f. $(-5w^2z^8)^3$

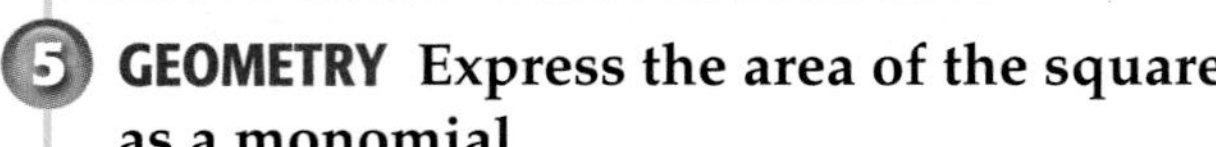

Real-World EXAMPLE

5 **GEOMETRY Express the area of the square as a monomial.**

$A = s^2$ — Area of a square

$A = (7a^4b)^2$ — Replace s with $7a^4b$.

$A = 7^2(a^4)^2(b^1)^2$ — Power of a Product

$A = 49a^8b^2$ — Simplify.

The area of the square is $49a^8b^2$ square units.

$7a^4b$

CHECK Your Progress

g. **GEOMETRY** Find the volume of a cube with sides of length $8x^3y^5$. Express as a monomial.

CHECK Your Understanding

Examples 1–4 (pp. 555-556)

Simplify.

1. $(3^2)^5$
2. $(h^6)^4$
3. $[(2^3)^2]^3$

Example 5 (p. 556)

4. $(7w^7)^3$
5. $(5g^8k^{12})^4$
6. $(-6r^5s^9)^2$
7. **MEASUREMENT** Express the volume of the cube at the right as a monomial.

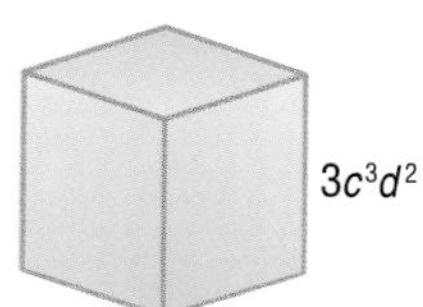

Practice and Problem Solving

HOMEWORK HELP	
For Exercises	See Examples
8–27	1–4
28–31	3

Simplify.

8. $(4^2)^3$
9. $(2^2)^7$
10. $(5^3)^3$
11. $(3^4)^2$
12. $(d^7)^6$
13. $(m^8)^5$
14. $(h^4)^9$
15. $(z^{11})^5$
16. $[(3^2)^2]^2$
17. $[(4^3)^2]^2$
18. $[(5^2)^2]^2$
19. $[(2^3)^3]^2$
20. $(5j^6)^4$
21. $(8v^9)^5$
22. $(11c^4)^3$
23. $(14y)^4$
24. $(6a^2b^6)^3$
25. $(2m^5n^{11})^6$
26. $(-3w^3z^8)^5$
27. $(-5r^4s^{12})^4$

GEOMETRY Express the area of each square below as a monomial.

28. $8g^3h$

29. $12d^6e^7$

GEOMETRY Express the volume of each cube below as a monomial.

30.

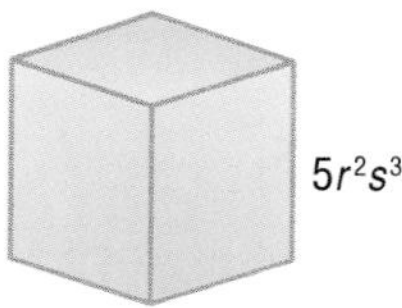

31.

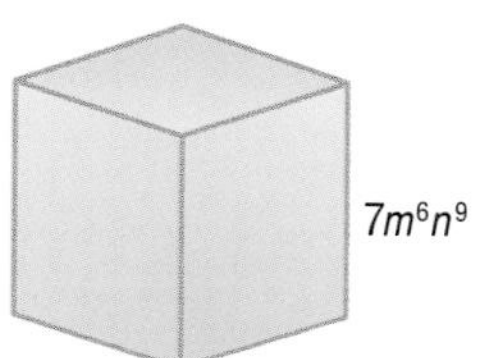

Simplify.

32. $(0.5k^5)^2$
33. $(0.3p^7)^3$
34. $(\frac{1}{4}w^5z^3)^2$
35. $(\frac{3}{5}a^{-6}b^9)^2$
36. $(3x^{-2})^4(5x^6)^2$
37. $(-2v^7)^3(-4v^{-2})^4$
38. **PHYSICS** A ball is dropped from the top of a building. The expression $4.9x^2$ gives the distance in meters the ball has fallen after x seconds. Write and simplify an expression that gives the distance in meters the ball has fallen after x^2 seconds. Then write and simplify an expression that gives the distance the ball has fallen after x^3 seconds.
39. **BACTERIA** A certain culture of bacteria doubles in population every hour. At 1 P.M., there are 5 cells. The expression $5(2^x)$gives the number of bacteria that are present x hours after 1 P.M. Simplify the expressions $[5(2^x)]^2$ and $[5(2^x)]^3$ and describe what they each represent.

ILS • ISAT

Extra Practice, pp. 695, 709

MEASUREMENT For Exercises 40-42, use the table that gives the area and volume of a square and cube, respectively, with side lengths shown.

Side Length (units)	Area of Square (units^2)	Volume of Cube (units^3)
x	x^2	x^3
$2x$		
$3x$		
x^2		
x^3		

40. Copy and complete the table.

41. Describe how the area and volume are each affected if the side length is doubled. Then describe how they are each affected if the side length is tripled.

42. Describe how the area and volume are each affected if the side length is squared. Describe how they are each affected if the side length is cubed.

H.O.T. Problems

43. **OPEN ENDED** A *googol* is 10^{100}. Use the Power of a Power rule to write three different expressions that are equivalent to a googol where each expression uses exponents.

CHALLENGE Solve each equation for x.

44. $(7^x)^3 = 7^{15}$

45. $(-2m^3n^4)^x = -8m^9n^{12}$

46. **WRITING IN MATH** Compare and contrast how you would correctly simplify the expressions $(2a^3)(4a^6)$ and $(2a^3)^6$.

ISAT PRACTICE 8.A.3b, 8.D.3c

47. Which expression is equivalent to $(10^4)^8$?

    A 10^2 C 10^{12}

    B 10^4 D 10^{32}

48. Which expression has the same value as $81h^8k^6$?

    F $(9h^6k^4)^2$ H $(6h^5k^3)^3$

    G $(9h^4k^3)^2$ J $(3h^2k)^6$

49. Which of the following has the same value as $64m^6$?

    A the area in square units of a square whose side length is $8m^2$

    B the expression $(32m^3)^2$

    C the expression $(8m^3)^2$

    D the volume in cubic units of a cube whose side length is $4m^3$

Spiral Review

Simplify. Express using positive exponents. (Lesson 10-6)

50. $\frac{15^7}{15^4}$

51. $\frac{y^{10}}{y^2}$

52. $\frac{18m^9}{6m^4}$

53. $\frac{24g^3}{3g^8}$

54. **MEASUREMENT** Find the area of a rectangle with a length of $9xy^2$ and a width of $4x^2y$. (Lesson 10-5)

GET READY for the Next Lesson

Find each square root. (Lesson 3-1)

55. $\sqrt{49}$

56. $\sqrt{121}$

57. $\sqrt{225}$

58. $\sqrt{400}$

10-8 Roots of Monomials

MAIN IDEA

Find roots of monomials.

IL Learning Standards

8.A.3b Solve problems using linear **expressions,** equations and inequalities.
8.D.3c Apply properties of powers, perfect squares and **square roots.**

New Vocabulary

cube root

IL Math Online

glencoe.com

- Extra Examples
- Personal Tutor
- Self-Check Quiz

GET READY for the Lesson

NUMBER THEORY The square root of a number is a number whose square is that number. Some perfect squares can be factored into the product of two other perfect squares.

1. Find two factors of 100 that are also perfect squares.
2. Find the square roots of 4 and 25. Then find their product.
3. How does the product relate to 100?
4. Repeat Questions 1–3 using 144.

The pattern you discovered about the factors of a perfect square is true for any number.

Product Property of Square Roots — Key Concept

Words For any numbers a and b, where $a \geq 0$ and $b \geq 0$, the square root of the product ab is equal to the product of each square root.

Examples

Numbers	Algebra
$\sqrt{9 \cdot 16} = \sqrt{9} \cdot \sqrt{16}$ $= 3 \cdot 4$ or 12	$\sqrt{ab} = \sqrt{a} \cdot \sqrt{b}$

Review Vocabulary

square root: a number whose square is that number (Lesson 3-1)

The square root of a monomial is a monomial whose square is that monomial. You can use the product property of square roots to find the square roots of monomials.

$$\sqrt{x^2} = \sqrt{x \cdot x} = |x|$$

Since x represents an unknown value, absolute value is used to indicate the positive value of x.

$$\sqrt{x^4} = \sqrt{x^2 \cdot x^2} = x^2$$

Absolute value is not necessary since the value of x^2 will never be negative.

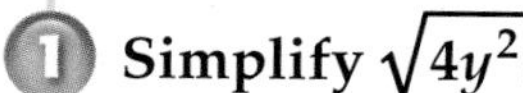

EXAMPLES Simplify Square Roots

1 Simplify $\sqrt{4y^2}$.

$$\sqrt{4y^2} = \sqrt{4} \cdot \sqrt{y^2}$$
$$= \sqrt{2 \cdot 2} \cdot \sqrt{y \cdot y}$$
$$= 2|y|$$

2 Simplify $\sqrt{36q^6}$.

$$\sqrt{36q^6} = \sqrt{36} \cdot \sqrt{q^6}$$
$$= \sqrt{6 \cdot 6} \cdot \sqrt{q^3 \cdot q^3}$$
$$= 6|q^3|$$

CHECK Your Progress

a. $\sqrt{v^2}$ b. $\sqrt{c^6d^8}$ c. $\sqrt{121x^4z^{10}}$

Reading Math

Cube Root Symbol The cube root of a is shown by the symbol $\sqrt[3]{a}$.

The process of simplifying expressions involving square roots can be extended to cube roots. The **cube root** of a monomial is a monomial whose cube is that monomial.

$$\sqrt[3]{8} = \sqrt[3]{2 \cdot 2 \cdot 2} = 2 \qquad \sqrt[3]{a^3} = \sqrt[3]{a \cdot a \cdot a} = a$$

Product Property of Square Roots

Key Concept

Words For any numbers a and b, the cube root of the product ab is equal to the product of each cube root.

Examples

Numbers	Algebra
$\sqrt[3]{216} = \sqrt[3]{8} \cdot \sqrt[3]{27}$ $= 2 \cdot 3$ or 6	$\sqrt[3]{ab} = \sqrt[3]{a} \cdot \sqrt[3]{b}$

EXAMPLES Simplify Cube Roots

3 Simplify $\sqrt[3]{c^3}$.

$\sqrt[3]{c^3} = c$ $\quad (c)^3 = c^3$

4 Simplify $\sqrt[3]{64g^6}$.

$\sqrt[3]{64g^6} = \sqrt[3]{64} \cdot \sqrt[3]{g^6}$ Product Property of Cube Roots

$= \sqrt[3]{4 \cdot 4 \cdot 4} \cdot \sqrt[3]{g^2 \cdot g^2 \cdot g^2}$

$= 4 \cdot g^2$ or $4g^2$ Simplify.

Study Tip

Absolute Value Because a cube root can be negative, absolute value is not necessary when simplifying cube roots.

CHECK Your Progress

d. $\sqrt[3]{s^3}$ e. $\sqrt[3]{27y^3}$ f. $\sqrt[3]{216k^{12}}$

Real-World EXAMPLE

5 GEOMETRY Express the length of one side of the square whose area is $81y^2z^6$ square units in simplified form.

$A = s^2$ Area of a square

$81y^2z^6 = s^2$ Replace A with $81y^2z^6$.

$\sqrt{81y^2z^6} = s$ Definition of square root.

$\sqrt{81} \cdot \sqrt{y^2} \cdot \sqrt{z^6} = s$ Product Property of Square Roots

$9|yz^3| = s$ Simplify. Add absolute value.

The length of one side of the square is $9|yz^3|$ units.

CHECK Your Progress

g. **GEOMETRY** Find the length of one side of a cube whose volume is $125a^{15}$ cubic units.

Examples 1–2 (p. 559)

Simplify.

1. $\sqrt{d^2}$
2. $\sqrt{25a^2}$
3. $\sqrt{49x^6y^2}$
4. $\sqrt{121h^8k^{10}}$

Example 3–4 (p. 560)

5. $\sqrt[3]{m^3}$
6. $\sqrt[3]{8p^3}$
7. $\sqrt[3]{125r^6s^9}$
8. $\sqrt[3]{64\,x^{12}y^3}$

Example 5 (p. 560)

9. **GEOMETRY** Express the length of one side of the square whose area is $256u^2v^6$ square units as a monomial.

10. **GEOMETRY** Express the length of one side of a cube whose volume is $27b^3c^{12}$ cubic units as a monomial.

Practice and Problem Solving

HOMEWORK HELP

For Exercises	See Examples
11–18	1–2
19–26	3–4
27–34	5

Simplify.

11. $\sqrt{n^2}$
12. $\sqrt{y^4}$
13. $\sqrt{g^8k^{14}}$
14. $\sqrt{64a^2}$
15. $\sqrt{36z^{12}}$
16. $\sqrt{144k^4m^6}$
17. $\sqrt{9p^8q^4}$
18. $\sqrt{225x^4y^6}$
19. $\sqrt[3]{h^3}$
20. $\sqrt[3]{v^3}$
21. $\sqrt[3]{27b^3}$
22. $\sqrt[3]{64k^3}$
23. $\sqrt[3]{125d^9e^3}$
24. $\sqrt[3]{8q^9r^{18}}$
25. $\sqrt[3]{343m^3n^{21}}$
26. $\sqrt[3]{216x^{12}w^{15}}$

GEOMETRY Express the length of one side of each square whose area is given as a monomial.

27.

$A = 121a^2b^2$

28.
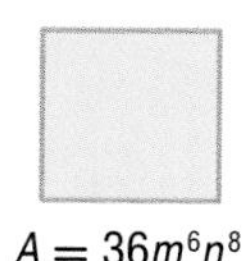
$A = 36m^6n^8$

29.

$A = 400x^2y^{10}$

30.

$A = 49p^4q^6$

GEOMETRY Express the length of one side of each cube whose volume is given as a monomial.

31.

$V = 64w^3z^3$

32.
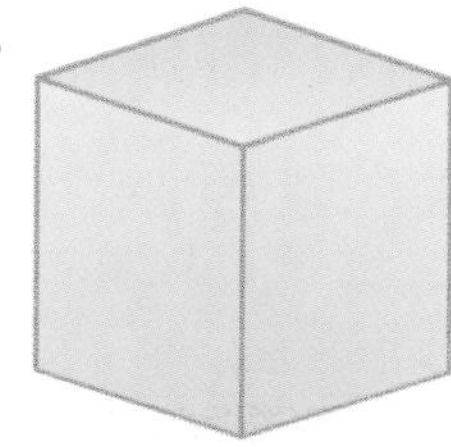
$V = 343c^6d^{12}$

33.

$V = 27g^{24}h^3$

34.
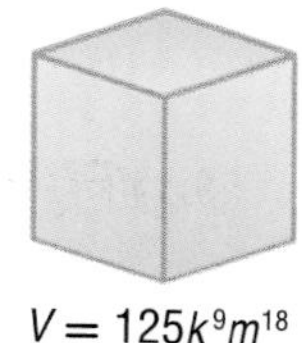
$V = 125k^9m^{18}$

Simplify.

35. $\sqrt{0.25x^2}$
36. $\sqrt[3]{0.008p^9}$
37. $\sqrt[3]{\frac{8}{27}w^3x^6}$

Simplify each expression if $\sqrt{\frac{a}{b}} = \frac{\sqrt{a}}{\sqrt{b}}$.

38. $\sqrt{\frac{x^2}{16}}$
39. $\sqrt{\frac{81}{m^4}}$
40. $\sqrt{\frac{121}{h^8k^6}}$

Extra Practice, pp. 696, 709

H.O.T. Problems

41. **OPEN ENDED** Write a monomial and its square root.

CHALLENGE Solve each equation for x.

42. $\sqrt{25a^x} = 5|a^3|$

43. $\sqrt[3]{64a^3b^x} = 4ab^7$

44. $\sqrt{81a^4b^x} = 9a^2|b^5|$

45. **WRITING IN MATH** Explain why absolute value is necessary when simplifying the expression $\sqrt{y^2}$ and not necessary when simplifying $\sqrt{y^4}$.

ISAT PRACTICE 8.A.3b, 8.D.3c

46. Which expression is equivalent to $\sqrt{144g^2}$?

A $12g$ C $12g^2$

B $12|g|$ D $12|g^2|$

47. Which expression has the same value as $\sqrt{400h^2k^4}$?

F $20hk^2$ H $20h^2k^4$

G $20|h|k^2$ J $200|h|k^2$

48. Which of the following has the same value as $\sqrt[3]{27m^3n^6}$?

A the length of the side of a square whose area is $27m^3n^6$

B the expression $9mn^3$

C the expression $3mn^2$

D the length of the side of a cube whose volume is $3mn^2$

Spiral Review

Simplify. (Lesson 10-7)

49. $(6^3)^5$

50. $(n^7)^2$

51. $(2a^3b^2)^4$

52. $(-4p^{11}q)^3$

Simplify. Express using positive exponents. (Lesson 10-6)

53. $\frac{9^5}{9^3}$

54. $\frac{k^{15}}{k^6}$

55. $\frac{24y^4}{4y^2}$

56. $\frac{45g^3}{3g^7}$

57. **GROCERIES** A grocery cart in the shape of a rectangular prism has a volume of $18\frac{3}{4}$ cubic feet. After shopping, the empty space measures $1\frac{1}{2}$ feet by 1 foot by $1\frac{1}{2}$ feet. How much space was taken up by groceries? (Lesson 7-5)

58. **RETAIL** Find the discount to the nearest cent for a flat-screen television that costs $999 and is on sale at 15% off. (Lesson 5-8)

Problem Solving in Social Studies

Web Design 101 It's time to complete your project. Use the information and data you have gathered about another country to create your Web page. Since your job responsibility also includes making the Web page visually appealing, be sure to include the appropriate tables, graphs, and photos.

IL Math Online **Unit Project at** glencoe.com

CHAPTER 10

Study Guide and Review

IL Math Online glencoe.com
- STUDY TO GO
- Vocabulary Review

GET READY to Study

Be sure the following Big Ideas are noted in your Foldable.

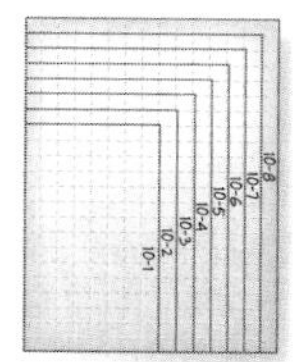

BIG Ideas

Functions (Lessons 10-1, 10-2, and 10-4)

- Linear functions have constant rates of change.
- Nonlinear functions do not have constant rates of change.
- Quadratic functions are functions in which the greatest power of the variable is 2.
- Cubic functions are functions in which the greatest power of the variable is 3.

Monomials (Lessons 10-5 through 10-8)

- To multiply powers with the same base, add their exponents.
- To divide powers with the same base, subtract their exponents.
- To find the power of a power, multiply the exponents.
- To find the power of a product, find the power of each factor and multiply.

Key Vocabulary

cube root (p. 560)
monomial (p. 545)
nonlinear function (p. 528)
quadratic function (p. 534)

Vocabulary Check

State whether each sentence is *true* or *false*. If *false*, replace the underlined word or number to make a true sentence.

1. The equation $y = x^2 - 3x$ is an example of a <u>monomial</u>.
2. A <u>nonlinear</u> function has a constant rate of change.
3. A quadratic function is a function whose greatest power of the variable is <u>2</u>.
4. The product of $3x$ and $x^2 + 3x$ will have <u>3</u> terms.
5. A quadratic function is a <u>nonlinear</u> function.
6. The graph of a linear function is a <u>curve</u>.
7. To divide powers with the same base, <u>subtract</u> the exponents.
8. The Quotient of Powers states when dividing powers with the same base, <u>subtract</u> their exponents.
9. The graph of a cubic function is a <u>straight line</u>.

Lesson-by-Lesson Review

10-1 Linear and Nonlinear Functions (pp. 528–533)

8.A.3b, 8.D.3b

Determine whether each equation or table represents a *linear* or *nonlinear* function. Explain.

10. $y - 4x = 1$

11. $y = x^2 + 3$

12.

Time (h)	2	3	4	5
Number of Pages	98	147	199	248

Example 1 **Determine whether the table represents a *linear* or *nonlinear* function.**

x	y
−2	−3
−1	−1
0	1
1	3

As x increases by 1, y increases by 2. The rate of change is constant, so this function is linear.

10-2 Graphing Quadratic Functions (pp. 534–537)

8.A.3b, 8.D.3a

Graph each function.

13. $-4x^2$

14. $y = x^2 + 4$

15. $y = -2x^2 + 1$

16. $y = 3x^2 - 1$

17. **CLIFFS** The function $d = -4.9t^2 + 43$ models the distance d in meters a rock is from the surface of the water t seconds after being dropped from a 43-meter tall cliff. Graph this function. How long does it take for the rock to reach the water?

Example 2 **Graph $y = -x^2 - 1$.**

Make a table of values. Then plot and connect the ordered pairs with a smooth curve.

x	$y = -x^2 - 1$	(x, y)
−2	$-(-2)^2 - 1$	(−2, −5)
−1	$-(-1)^2 - 1$	(−1, −2)
0	$-(0)^2 - 1$	(0, −1)
1	$-(1)^2 - 1$	(1, −2)
2	$-(2)^2 - 1$	(2, −5)

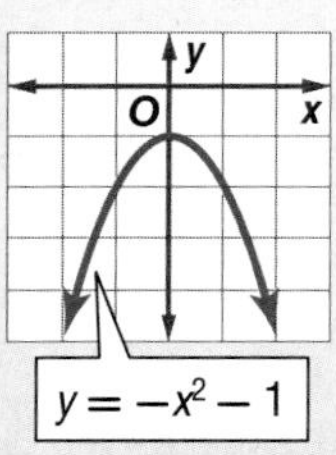

10-3 PSI: Make a Model (pp. 538-539)

9.C.3b

Solve the problem by using the make a model strategy.

18. **MEASUREMENT** Sydney has a postcard that measures 5 inches by 3 inches. She decides to frame it, using a frame that is $1\frac{3}{4}$ inches wide. What is the perimeter of the framed postcard?

19. **MAGAZINES** A book store arranges it best-seller magazines in the front window. In how many different ways can five best-seller magazines be arranged in a row?

Example 3

DISPLAYS **Cans of oil are displayed in the shape of a pyramid. The top layer has 2 cans in it. One more can is added to each layer, and there are 4 layers in the pyramid. How many cans are there in the display?**

So, based on the model there are 14 cans.

Mixed Problem Solving
For mixed problem-solving practice, see page 709.

10-4 Graphing Cubic Functions (pp. 540-543)

8.A.3b, 8.D.3a

Graph each function.

20. $y = 2x^3 - 4$
21. $y = 0.25x^3 - 2$
22. $y = 2x^3 + 4$
23. $y = 0.25x^3 + 2$
24. **MEASUREMENT** A rectangular prism with a square base of side length x inches has a height of $(x - 1)$ inches. Write the function for the volume V of the prism. Graph the function. Then estimate the dimensions of the box that would give a volume of approximately 18 cubic inches.

Example 4 Graph $y = -x^3$.

x	$y = -x^3$	(x, y)
−2	$-(-2)^3$	(−2, 8)
−1	$-(-1)^3$	(−1, 1)
0	$-(0)^3$	(0, 0)
1	$-(1)^3$	(1, −1)
2	$-(2)^3$	(2, −8)

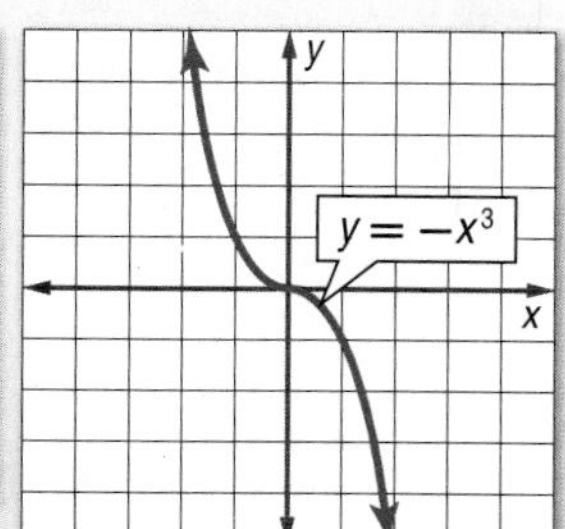

10-5 Multiplying Monomials (pp. 545-548)

8.A.3b, 8.D.3c

Simplify. Express using exponents.

25. $4 \cdot 4^5$
26. $x^6 \cdot x^2$
27. $-9y^2(-4y^9)$
28. $\left(\frac{3}{7}\right)^{-4} \cdot \left(\frac{3}{7}\right)^2$
29. **LIFE SCIENCE** The number of bacteria after t cycles of reproduction is 2^t. Suppose a bacteria reproduces every 30 minutes. If there are 1,000 bacteria in a dish now, how many will there be in 1 hour?

Example 5 Find $4 \cdot 4^3$. Express using exponents.

$4 \cdot 4^3 = 4^1 \cdot 4^3$ $4 = 4^1$
$= 4^{1+3}$ The common base is 4.
$= 4^4$ Add the exponents.

Example 6 Find $3a^3 \cdot 4a^7$.

$3a^3 \cdot 4a^7 = (3 \cdot 4)a^{3+7}$ Commutative and Associative Properties
$= 12a^{10}$

10-6 Dividing Monomials (pp. 550-554)

8.A.3b, 8.D.3c

Simplify. Express using exponents.

30. $\frac{5^9}{5^2}$
31. $\frac{n^5}{n}$
32. $\frac{21c^{11}}{-7c^8}$
33. $\frac{\left(\frac{4}{7}\right)^3 \times \left(\frac{4}{7}\right)^{-1}}{\frac{4}{7}}$
34. **MEASUREMENT** The area of the family room is 3^4 square feet. The area of the kitchen is 4^3 square feet. What is the difference in area between the two rooms?

Example 7

Simplify $\frac{6^8}{6^3}$. Express using exponents.

$\frac{6^8}{6^3} = 6^{8-3}$ The common base is 6.
$= 6^5$ Simplify.

Example 8

Simplify $\frac{s^{-8}}{s^{-4}}$. Express using exponents.

$\frac{s^{-8}}{s^{-4}} = s^{-8-(-4)}$ Quotient of Powers
$= s^{-8+4}$ or $\frac{1}{s^4}$ Simplify.

Study Guide and Review

10-7 Powers of Monomials (pp. 555-558)

8.A.3b, 8.D.3c

Simplify.

35. $(9^2)^3$
36. $(d^6f^3)^4$
37. $(5y^5)^4$
38. $(6z^4x^3)^5$
39. $(\frac{3}{4}n^{-1})^2$
40. $[(p^2)^3]^2$
41. $(5^{-1})^2$
42. $(-3k^2)^2(4k^{-3})^2$
43. **GEOMETRY** Find the volume of a cube with sides of length $5s^2t^4$ as a monomial.
44. **GEOMETRY** Find the area of a square with sides of length $6a^3b^5$ as a monomial.

Example 9

Simplify $(7^3)^5$.

$(7^3)^5 = 7^{3 \cdot 5}$ Power of a Power

$= 7^{15}$ Simplify.

Example 10

Simplify $(2x^2y^3)^3$.

$(2x^2y^3)^3 = 2^3 \cdot x^{2 \cdot 3} y^{3 \cdot 3}$ Power of a Product

$= 8x^6y^9$ Simplify.

10-8 Roots of Monomials (pp. 559-562)

8.A.3b, 8.D.3c

Simplify.

45. $\sqrt{a^2}$
46. $\sqrt{49n^4}$
47. $\sqrt{36x^2y^6}$
48. $\sqrt{81q^{14}}$
49. $\sqrt[3]{p^6}$
50. $\sqrt[3]{8m^{18}}$
51. $\sqrt[3]{64c^6d^{21}}$
52. $\sqrt[3]{125r^9s^{15}}$
53. **GEOMETRY** Express the length of one side of the square whose area is $64b^{16}$ square units as a monomial.
54. **GEOMETRY** Express the length of one side of a cube whose volume is $216a^9c^3$ cubic units as a monomial.

Example 11

Simplify $\sqrt{16f^8g^6}$.

$\sqrt{16f^8g^6}$

$= \sqrt{16} \cdot \sqrt{f^8} \cdot \sqrt{g^6}$ Product Property of Square Roots

$= 4 \cdot f^4 \cdot |g^3|$ or $4f^4|g^3|$ Use absolute value to indicate the positive value of g^3.

Example 12

Simplify $\sqrt[3]{x^9}$.

$\sqrt[3]{x^9} = x^3$ $(x^3)^3 = x^9$

CHAPTER 10 Practice Test

IL Math Online glencoe.com
• Chapter Test

Determine whether each graph, equation, or table represents a *linear* or *nonlinear* function. Explain.

1. 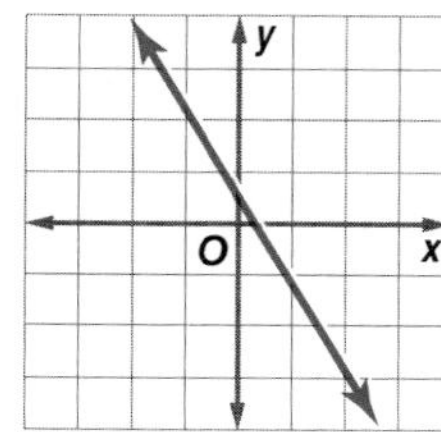

2. $2x = y$

3.

x	−3	−1	1	3
y	2	10	18	26

Graph each function.

4. $y = \frac{1}{2}x^2$

5. $y = -2x^2 + 3$

6. **BUSINESS** The function $p = 60 + 2d^2$ models the profit made by a manufacturer of digital audio players. Graph this function. Then use your graph to estimate the profit earned after making 20 players.

7. **MULTIPLE CHOICE** Simplify the algebraic expression $(3x^3y^2)(7x^3y)$.

   A $21x^9y^2$
   B $21x^6y^2$
   C $21x^6y^3$
   D $21x^6y^6$

Graph each function.

8. $y = x^3 + 4$

9. $y = x^3 - 4$

10. $y = \frac{1}{3}x^3$

11. **MEASUREMENT** A neighborhood group would like Jacob to fertilize their lawns. The average area of each lawn is 6^4 square feet. If there are 6^2 lawns in this neighborhood, how many total square feet of lawn does Jacob need to fertilize?

12. **CRAFTS** Martina is making cube-shaped gift boxes from decorative cardboard. Each side of the cube is to be 6 inches long, and there is a $\frac{1}{2}$-inch overlap on each side. How much cardboard does Martina need to make each box?

Simplify. Express using exponents.

13. $15^3 \cdot 15^5$

14. $-5m^6(-9m^8)$

15. $\frac{3^{15}}{3^7}$

16. $\frac{-40w^8}{8w}$

Simplify.

17. $\sqrt{m^2}$

18. $\sqrt{144a^2b^6}$

19. $\sqrt[3]{64x^3y^{15}}$

20. **MULTIPLE CHOICE** Which expression is equivalent to $\frac{(12x^4)(4x^3)}{8x^5}$?

    F $12x^7$
    G $12x^2$
    H $6x^4$
    J $6x^2$

21. **MEASUREMENT** Find the area of the rectangle at the right.

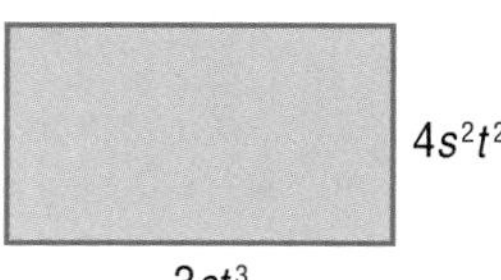

Simplify.

22. $[(x^2)^4]^3$

23. $(-2b^3)^2(4b^2)^2$

24. $(3^{-3})^2$

25. **GEOMETRY** Express the length of one side of a square with an area of $121x^4y^{10}$ square units in simplified form.

CHAPTER 10 ISAT Practice
Cumulative, Chapters 1–10

IL Math Online glencoe.com
• Test Practice

PART 1 Multiple Choice

Read each question. Then fill in the correct answer on the answer sheet provided by your teacher or on a sheet of paper.

1. A car used 4.2 gallons of gasoline to travel 126 miles. How many gallons of gasoline would it need to travel 195 miles?

   A 2.7

   B 5.0

   C 6.5

   D 7.6

2. The scatter plot below shows the cost of computer repairs in relation to the number of hours the repair takes. Based on the information in the scatter plot, which statement is a valid conclusion?

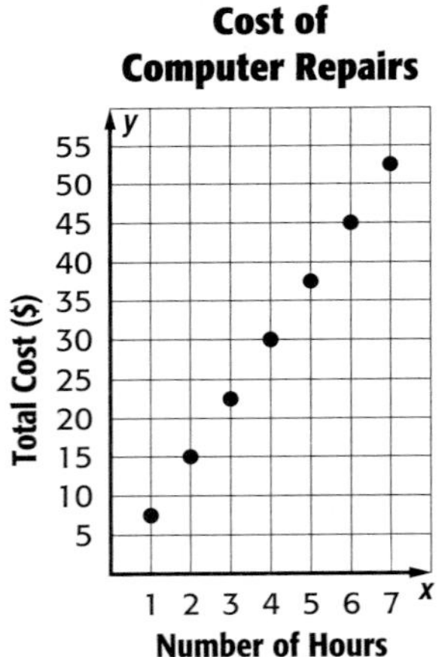

   F As the length of time increases, the cost of the repair increases.

   G As the length of time increases, the cost of the repair stays the same.

   H As the length of time decreases, the cost of the repair increases.

   J As the length of time increases, the cost of the repair decreases.

3. The equation $c = 0.8t$ represents c, the cost of t tickets on a ferry. Which table contains values that satisfy this equation?

A

Cost of Ferry Tickets				
t	1	2	3	4
c	$0.80	$1.00	$1.20	$1.40

B

Cost of Ferry Tickets				
t	1	2	3	4
c	$0.80	$1.60	$2.40	$3.20

C

Cost of Ferry Tickets				
t	1	2	3	4
c	$0.75	$1.50	$2.25	$3.00

D

Cost of Ferry Tickets				
t	1	2	3	4
c	$1.80	$2.60	$3.40	$4.20

4. Shanelle purchased a new computer for $1,099 and a computer desk for $699 including tax. She plans to pay the total amount in 24 equal monthly payments. What is a reasonable amount for each monthly payment?

   F $50

   G $75

   H $150

   J $1,800

TEST-TAKING TIP

Question 4 You can often use estimation to eliminate incorrect answers. In this question, Shanelle's total spent can be estimated by adding $1,100 and $700, then dividing by 24. The sum of $1,100 and $700 is $1,800 before dividing by 24, so choice J can be eliminated.

Preparing for ISAT
For test-taking strategies and practice, see pages 712–729.

5. Which of the following is the graph of $y = \frac{2}{3}x^2$?

A 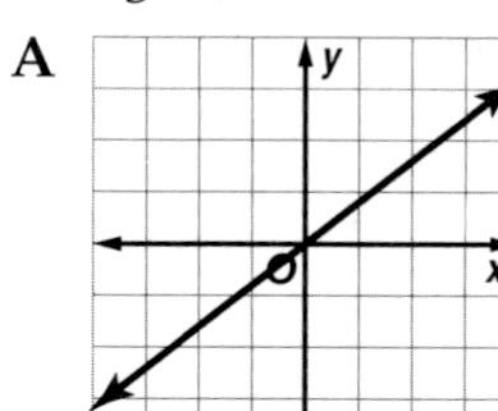

C 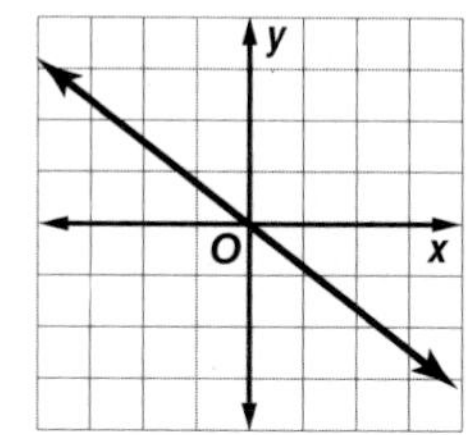

B 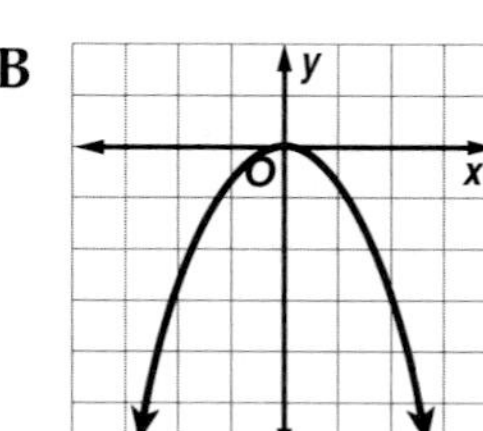

D 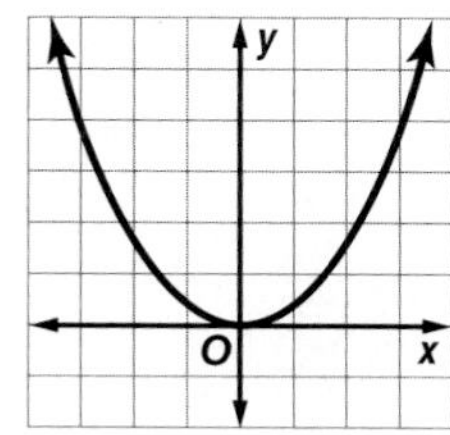

6. Simplify the expression shown below.

$$(3m^3n^2)(6m^4n)$$

F $18m^{12}n^2$
G $18\ m^7n^2$
H $18\ m^7n^3$
J $18\ m^7n^6$

7. What is the height h of the gutter in the figure below?

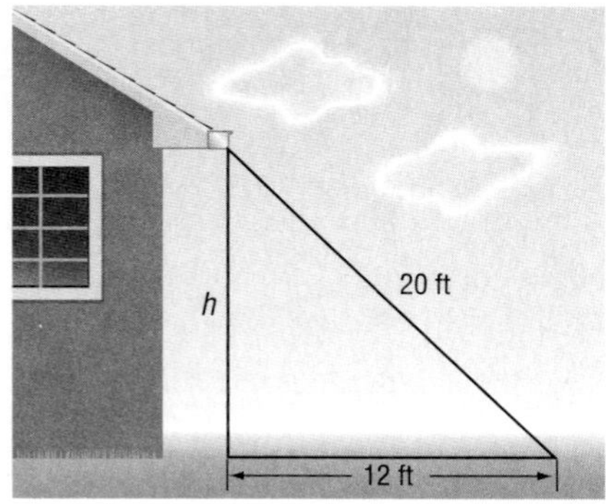

A 10 ft
B 14 ft
C 16 ft
D 18 ft

PART 2 Short Response/Grid In

Record your answers on the answer sheet provided by your teacher or on a sheet of paper.

8. The area of a rectangle is $30m^{11}$ square feet. If the length of the rectangle is $6m^4$ feet, what is the width of the rectangle?

9. Find $5^2 \times 5^4$.

PART 3 Extended Response

Record your answers on the answer sheet provided by your teacher or on a sheet of paper. Show your work.

10. An electronics store is having a sale on certain models of televisions. Mr. Castillo would like to buy a television that is on sale. This television normally costs $679.

a. What price, not including tax, will Mr. Castillo pay if he buys the television on Saturday?

b. What price, not including tax, will Mr. Castillo pay if he buys the television on Wednesday?

c. How much money will Mr. Castillo save if he buys the television on Saturday?

NEED EXTRA HELP?										
If You Missed Question...	1	2	3	4	5	6	7	8	9	10
Go to Lesson...	4-5	9-9	9-2	5-5	10-2	10-5	3-6	10-6	10-5	5-8
IL Learning Standards	6.D.3	8.B.3	8.B.3	6.C.3b	8.A.3b	8.A.3b	8.A.3b	8.A.3b	8.A.3b	6.D.3

Unit 5

Statistics, Data Analysis, and Probability

Focus

Use statistical procedures and probability to analyze data and make predictions.

CHAPTER 11
Statistics

BIG Idea Use statistical measures, including mean, median, and range, to summarize data, compare data sets, and organize and display data.

CHAPTER 12
Probability

BIG Idea Use theoretical probability and proportions to make predictions about events.

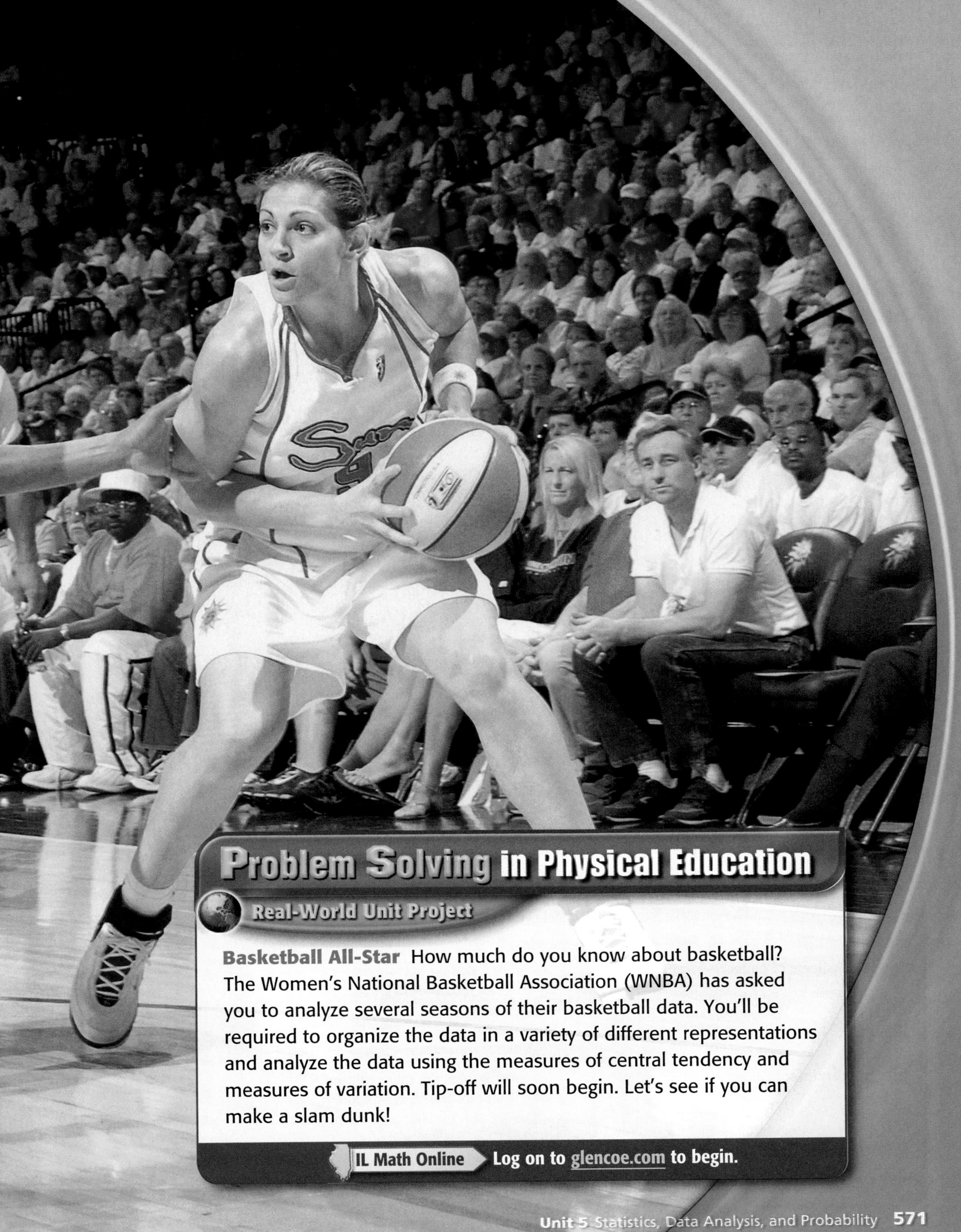

Problem Solving in Physical Education

Real-World Unit Project

Basketball All-Star How much do you know about basketball? The Women's National Basketball Association (WNBA) has asked you to analyze several seasons of their basketball data. You'll be required to organize the data in a variety of different representations and analyze the data using the measures of central tendency and measures of variation. Tip-off will soon begin. Let's see if you can make a slam dunk!

IL Math Online Log on to glencoe.com to begin.

CHAPTER 11

Statistics

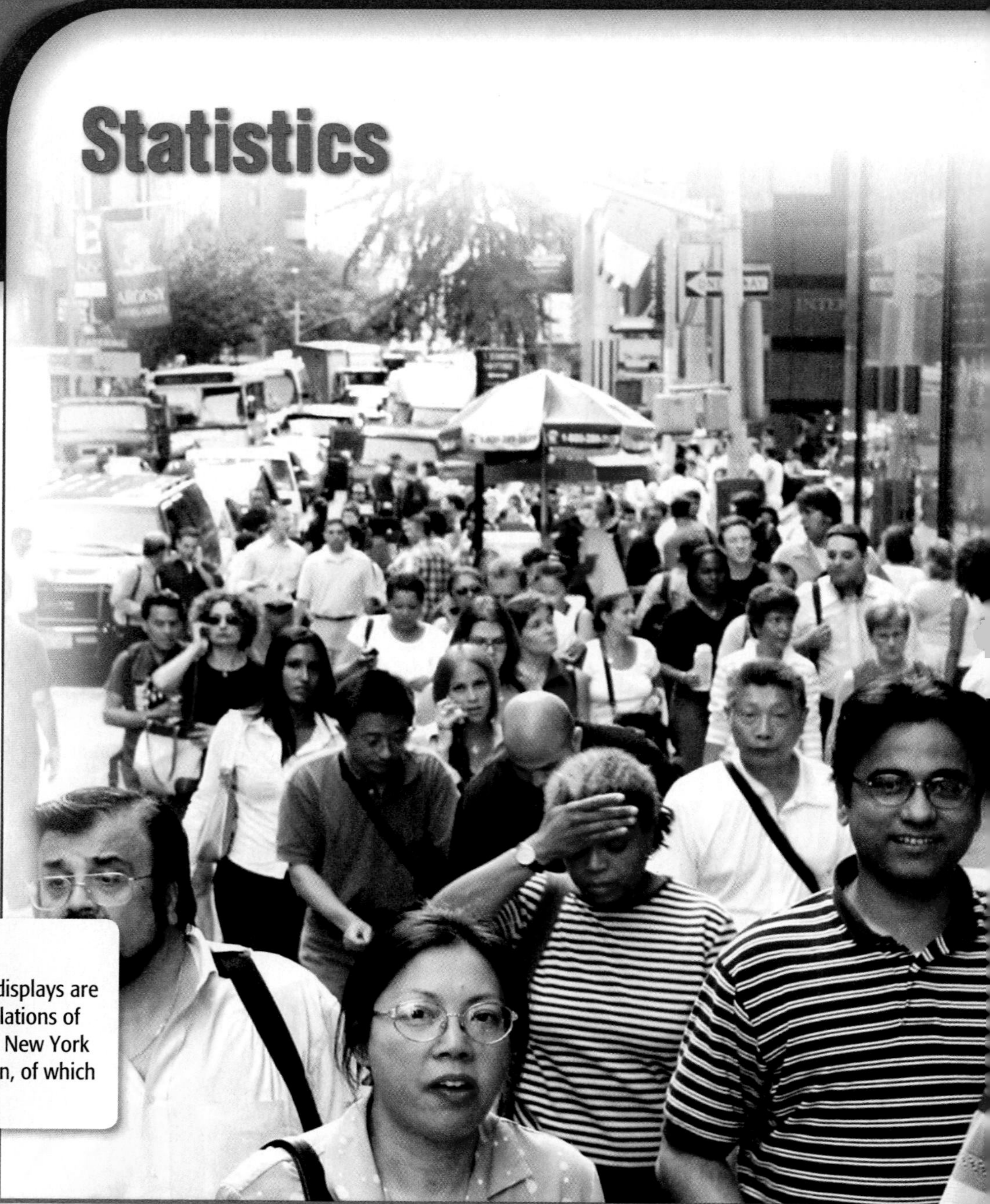

Illinois Learning Standards

10.A.3a Construct, read and interpret tables, graphs (including circle graphs) and charts to organize and represent data.
10.A.3b Compare the mean, median, mode and range, with and without the use of technology.

Key Vocabulary

circle graph (p. 582)
histogram (p. 576)
measures of central tendency (p. 591)
measures of variation (p. 599)

Real-World Link

Population Statistics and statistical displays are frequently used to describe the populations of a country, state, or city. For example, New York has a population of about 19.3 million, of which 51.6% are female.

FOLDABLES® Study Organizer

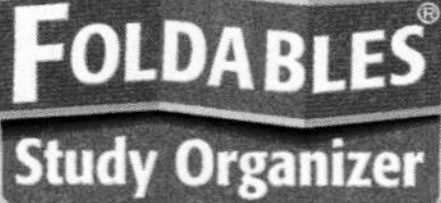

Statistics Make this Foldable to help you organize your notes. Begin with five pieces of $8\frac{1}{2}'' \times 11''$ paper.

1. **Place** 5 sheets of paper $\frac{3}{4}$ inch apart.

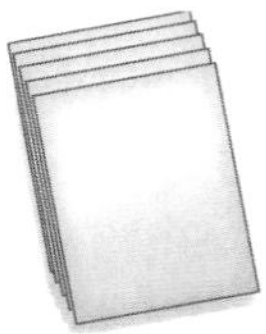

2. **Roll** up bottom edges. All tabs should be the same size.

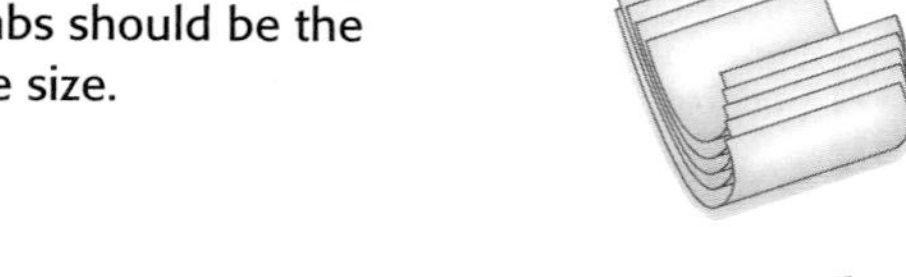

3. **Crease** and staple along the fold.

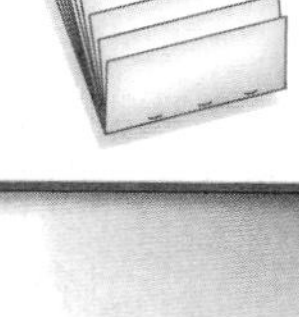

4. **Label** the tabs with the topics from the chapter. Label the last tab Vocabulary.

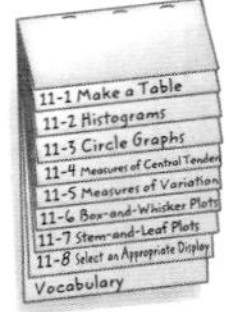

GET READY for Chapter 11

Diagnose Readiness You have two options for checking Prerequisite Skills.

Option 2

IL Math Online Take the Online Readiness Quiz at glencoe.com.

Option 1

Take the Quick Check below. Refer to the Quick Review for help.

QUICK Practice

Graph each set of points on a number line. (Lesson 1-3)

1. {7, 8, 10, 15, 16}
2. {15, 20, 21, 25, 30}

Add or subtract. (Lessons 1-4 and 1-5)

3. $-4 + (-8)$
4. $-5 + 2$
5. $7 + (-3)$
6. $1 - (-5)$
7. **GOLF** Gary's golf scores relative to par on two holes were 3 and −2. Find his total score relative to par for the two holes. (Lesson 1-4)

Order each set of rational numbers from least to greatest. (Lesson 2-2)

8. 0.23, 2.03, 0.32
9. 5.4, 5.64, 5.46, 5.6
10. 0.01, 1.01, 0.10, 1.10
11. **LUNCH** Horace's lunch cost \$3.71, Susan's cost \$3.17, and Paul's cost \$3.07. Write these costs in order from least to greatest. (Lesson 2-2)

Solve each problem. (Lesson 5-7)

12. Find 52% of 360.
13. What is 36% of 360?
14. Find 14% of 360.

QUICK Review

Example 1

Graph the set {2, 4, 5, 9} on a number line.

0 2 4 6 8 10

Example 2

Find $6 + (-4)$.

$6 + (-4) = 2$ — 6 and −4 have opposite signs. Subtract the absolute values, 6 and 4. The difference, 2, has the sign of the number with the larger absolute value, 6.

Example 3

Order 6.08, 0.68, and 8.60 from least to greatest.

Line up the decimal points.

6.08
0.68
8.60

Compare the digits in each place-value position.

The order from least to greatest is 0.68, 6.08, and 8.60.

Example 4

What is 72% of 360?

$72\% \text{ of } 360 = 0.72 \times 360$ — Use the percent equation.

$= 259.2$ — Multiply.

Problem-Solving Investigation

MAIN IDEA: Solve problems by making a table.

ILS **10.A.3a Construct, read and interpret tables,** graphs (including circle graphs) and charts **to organize and represent data.**

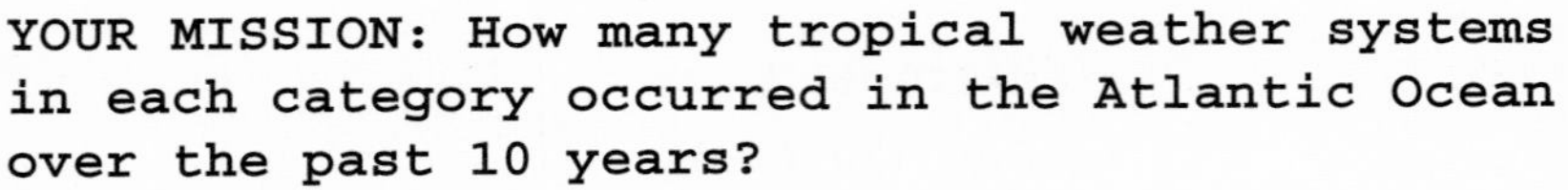

P.S.I. TEAM +

e-Mail: MAKE A TABLE

EMILIO: In science class, we examined the effects of ocean temperature on the weather by researching tropical weather systems in the Atlantic Ocean over the past ten years. They fall into one of four categories: 1–10 or little activity, 11–20 or average activity, 21–30 or high activity, and over 30 or unusually high activity.

YOUR MISSION: How many tropical weather systems in each category occurred in the Atlantic Ocean over the past 10 years?

Understand You have a list of the Atlantic tropical weather systems for the past 10 years. You need to know how many fall into each category.

Plan Make a table to show the *frequency*, or number, of weather systems in each category.

8	14
12	15
15	14
21	16
31	10

Source: NOAA

Category	Tally	Frequency
1–10	‖	2
11–20	𝍸 |	6
21–30	|	1
over 30	|	1

Solve There were 2 years with little activity, 6 years of average activity, 1 year of high activity, and 1 year of unusually high activity.

Check Emilio wanted to list 10 years of activity. Since $2 + 6 + 1 + 1 = 10$, the table seems reasonable.

Analyze The Strategy

1. Tell an advantage and disadvantage of listing the values in a table.
2. Describe two types of information you have seen recorded in a table.
3. WRITING IN MATH Write a problem that can be answered using a table. Then solve the problem by making a table.

Mixed Problem Solving

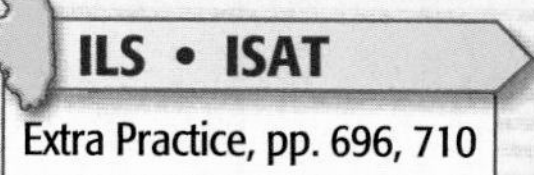

Extra Practice, pp. 696, 710

Solve Exercises 4 and 5. Use the *make a table* strategy.

4. **SCHOOL** The list shows the times several students arrived at school on Monday. Organize the data in a table using intervals 7:00–7:14, 7:15–7:29, 7:30–7:44, and so on. What is the most common time interval for students to arrive at school?

7:35	7:10	7:35	7:30	7:15
7:30	7:00	7:20	7:40	7:30
7:25	7:20	7:00	7:25	7:05
7:25	7:40	7:25	7:10	7:45
7:10	7:15	7:30	7:05	7:40

5. **HOCKEY** The list shows the number of goals made by the Anaheim Ducks in thirty of their regular season games in 2007. Find the number that was made most frequently.

4	3	5	2	1	0
1	0	4	3	2	0
2	3	4	3	3	2
3	1	5	3	2	7
5	3	2	5	5	0

Source: The National Hockey League

Use any strategy to solve Exercises 6–11. Some strategies are shown below.

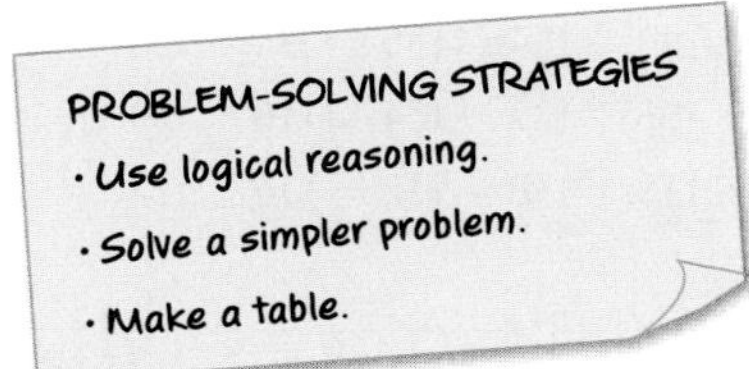

6. **PHOTOGRAPHY** How many ways are there to arrange five French club members for a yearbook photo if the president and vice president must be seated in front with the other three members behind them?

7. **COUSINS** William, Michael, Sophia, and Christina are all cousins that live in different states: Ohio, Idaho, Colorado, and Arizona. Over the summer, William and Michael visited Sophia in Ohio. Christina likes to snowboard in her hometown of Denver. Michael lives the farthest south. Who lives in Idaho?

8. **TELEVISION** The first sitcom in the United States aired in 1949. If it aired 30 new episodes per year, how many new episodes did it air until the sitcom went off the air in 1956?

9. **COUNTIES** About what percent of the counties in Utah are from 3,001 to 7,000 square miles?

Land Area of Utah Counties		
Land Area (sqare miles)	**Tally**	**Frequency**
1–1,000	~~IIII~~ I	6
1,001–2,000	~~IIII~~ III	8
2,001–3,000	III	3
3,001–4,000	~~IIII~~	5
4,001–5,000	II	2
5,001–6,000	II	2
6,001–7,000	II	2
7,001–8,000	I	1

Source: *The World Almanac*

10. **E-MAIL** About 97 billion e-mails are sent daily worldwide. Over 40 billion of them are spam messages. At this rate, how many spam messages are sent yearly in a non-leap year?

11. **ANIMALS** The graph shows the maximum length of several animals. The maximum length of a walrus is twice the maximum length of a lion, which is 0.4 meter longer than the maximum length of a giant panda. Find the maximum length of a walrus.

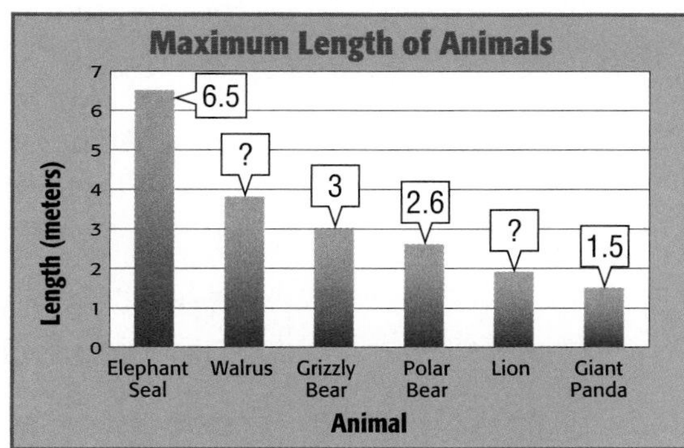

Source: *Top 10 of Everything*

11-2 Histograms

MAIN IDEA

Display and interpret data in a histogram.

IL Learning Standards

10.A.3a Construct, read and interpret tables, graphs (including circle graphs) and charts **to organize and represent data.**

New Vocabulary

histogram

IL Math Online

glencoe.com

- Extra Examples
- Personal Tutor
- Self-Check Quiz
- Reading in the Content Area

GET READY for the Lesson

BASKETBALL Kylie researched the average ticket prices to NBA basketball games for 30 teams. The frequency table shows the results.

Price Interval ($)	Tally	Frequency
20.00–29.99	|	1
30.00–39.99	卌 卌 |	11
40.00–49.99	卌 卌	10
50.00–59.99	卌	5
60.00–69.99	|	1
70.00–79.99	||	2

1. What do you notice about the price intervals in the table?
2. How many tickets were at least $20.00 but less than $50.00?

Data from a frequency table can be displayed as a histogram. A **histogram** is a type of bar graph used to display numerical data that have been organized into equal intervals.

EXAMPLE Construct a Histogram

1 **MOVIES Choose intervals and make a frequency table of the data shown. Then construct a histogram to represent the data.**

Running Time of Movies (minutes)				
135	89	142	219	96
144	104	135	94	155
106	127	134	116	91
118	138	118	110	101

The least value in the data is 89 and the greatest is 219. An interval size of 30 minutes would yield the frequency table at the right.

Running Time of Movies (minutes)		
Time	Tally	Frequency
81–110	卌 |||	8
111–140	卌 |||	8
141–170	|||	3
171–200		0
201–230	|	1

To construct a histogram, follow these steps.

Step 1 Draw and label a horizontal and vertical axis. Include a title.

Step 2 Show the intervals from the frequency table on the horizontal axis.

Step 3 For each time interval, draw a bar whose height is given by its frequency.

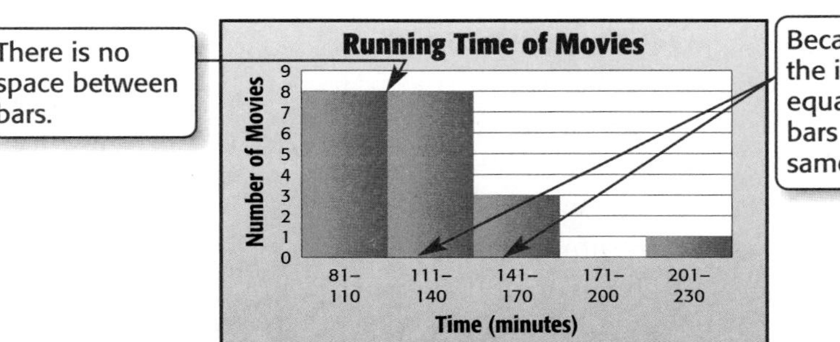

Study Tip

Gaps
Intervals with a frequency of 0 have a bar height of 0. This is referred to as a gap.

CHECK Your Progress

a. **SCHOOL** The list at the right gives a set of test scores. Choose intervals, make a frequency table, and construct a histogram to represent the data.

Test Scores							
94	85	73	93	75	77	89	80
89	83	79	81	87	85	90	83
88	86	83	91	93	93	92	90
91	88	96	97	98	82	90	100

EXAMPLES Analyze and Interpret Data

2 **BASEBALL How many Cincinnati Reds players were at bat at least 400 time in 2006?**

Five players were at bat 400–499 times, and 2 players were at bat 500–599 times. Therefore, 5 + 2 or 7 players were at bat at least 400 times.

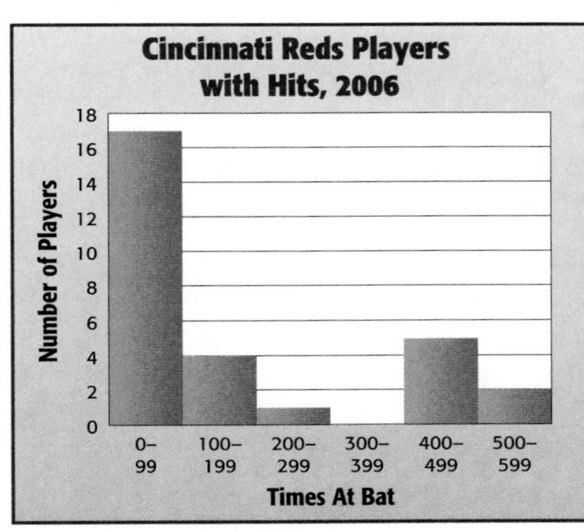

Source: Major League Baseball

3 **BASEBALL What percent of the players were at bat 199 times or fewer?**

There were 17 + 4 + 1 + 5 + 2 or 29 total players with hits, and there were 17 + 4 or 21 total players that were at bat 199 times or fewer. Since $\frac{21}{29}$ is about 0.72 or 72%, about 72% of the players were at bat 199 times or fewer.

CHECK Your Progress

b. What was the greatest number of times at bat of any one player?

c. Based on the data above, how many times is a Cincinnati Reds player most likely to be at bat?

CHECK Your Understanding

Example 1 (pp. 576–577)

1. **POPULATION** The list gives the approximate population density for each state. Choose intervals and make a frequency table. Then construct a histogram to represent the data.

U.S. State Population Density (per square mile)									
88	42	189	33	810	6	15	50	10	179
1	703	16	102	175	22	402	36	138	89
45	401	223	103	62	18	165	274	80	75
51	296	170	41	61	138	9	1,003	27	99
217	141	52	542	81	1,135	277	133	66	5

Source: *The World Almanac*

Examples 2, 3 (p. 577)

VOLCANOES For Exercises 2–4, use the histogram at the right.

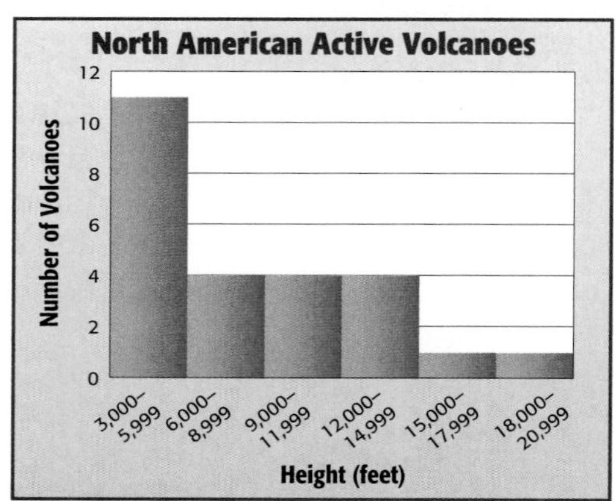

Source: *The World Almanac*

2. What percent of the volcanoes are 8,999 feet or less?
3. How likely is it that any given volcano is at least 15,000 feet tall? Explain your reasoning.
4. What is the height of the tallest volcano?

Practice and Problem Solving

HOMEWORK HELP	
For Exercises	See Examples
5, 6	1
7–14	2, 3

For each problem, choose intervals and make a frequency table. Then construct a histogram to represent the data.

5.

Hours Spent Exercising per Week						
3	0	9	1	4	2	0
3	6	14	4	2	5	3
7	3	0	8	3	10	

6.

Average Speed (mph), Selected Animals						
70	61	50	50	50	45	8
43	42	40	40	40	35	0.17
35	32	32	30	30	30	1.17
30	25	20	9	18	12	200

COUNTRIES For Exercises 7–10, use the histogram below.

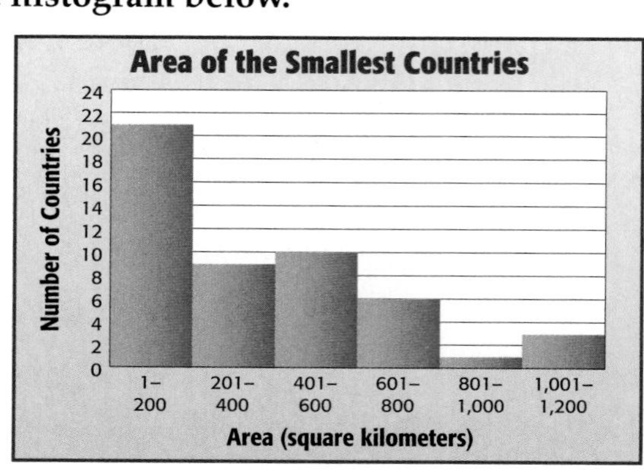

7. How many countries have an area less than 401 square kilometers?
8. What percent of the countries have an area of 201–600 square kilometers?
9. How likely is it that any given country will have an area greater than 800 square kilometers?
10. Which country is the smallest?

Real-World Link Total solar eclipses occur about 3 times every 4 years.
Source: *The World Almanac*

ECLIPSES For Exercises 11–14, use the histogram at the right.

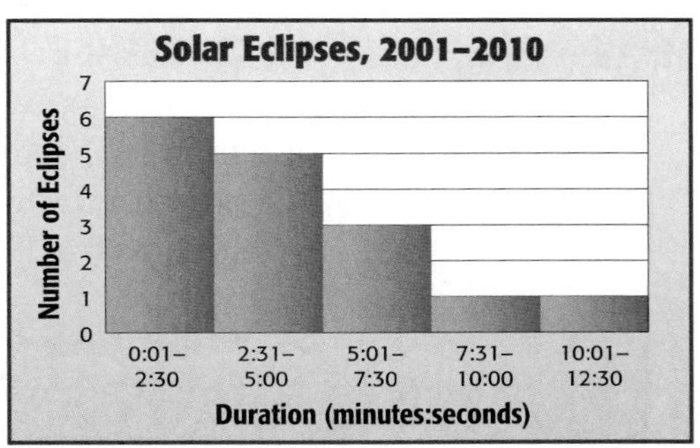

Source: NASA

11. What percent of the solar eclipses lasted at least 7 minutes 31 seconds?
12. How long was the shortest solar eclipse?
13. What is the duration of a typical solar eclipse during the decade? Explain your reasoning.
14. How many solar eclipses lasted between 1 second and 5 minutes?

BUILDINGS For Exercises 15–18, use the histograms shown.

Tall Buildings in Pittsburgh and Seattle

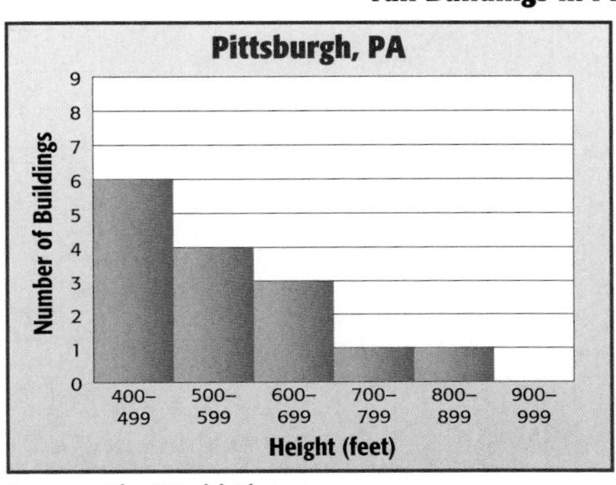

Source: *The World Almanac*

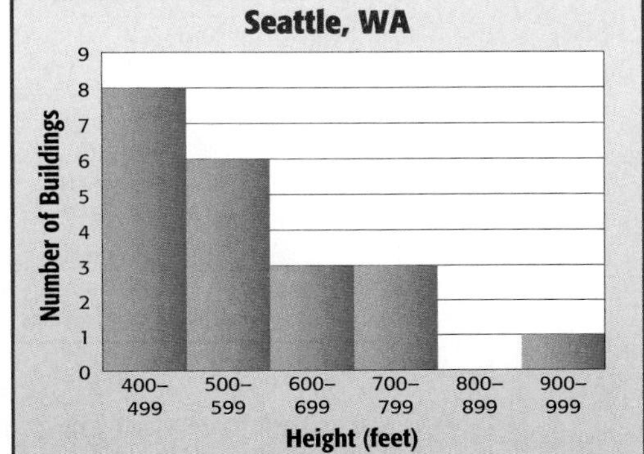

Source: *The World Almanac*

15. Which city has the tallest building?
16. Determine which city has more buildings that are 800–899 feet tall.
17. Determine which city has more buildings that are at least 600 feet tall. What percent of the buildings in that city are at least 600 feet tall?
18. What is the height of the shortest building in each city?

19. **COLLECT THE DATA** Conduct a survey of your classmates to determine the number of hours each person spends on the Internet during a typical week. Then choose intervals, make a frequency table, and construct a histogram to represent the data.

20. **RESEARCH** Use the Internet or other resource to find the populations of each county, census division, or parish in your state. Make a histogram using your data. How does your county, census division, or parish compare with others in your state?

ILS • ISAT
Extra Practice, pp. 696, 710

21. **OPEN ENDED** Construct a histogram that has a vertical line of symmetry and two gaps. Then construct a histogram that has a vertical line of symmetry and one gap.

H.O.T. Problems

22. **CHALLENGE** Describe how the histogram at the right would change if larger intervals, such as 0–9 and 10–19, were used. Describe how it would change if smaller intervals, such as 0–2, 3–5, 6–8, and so on, were used.

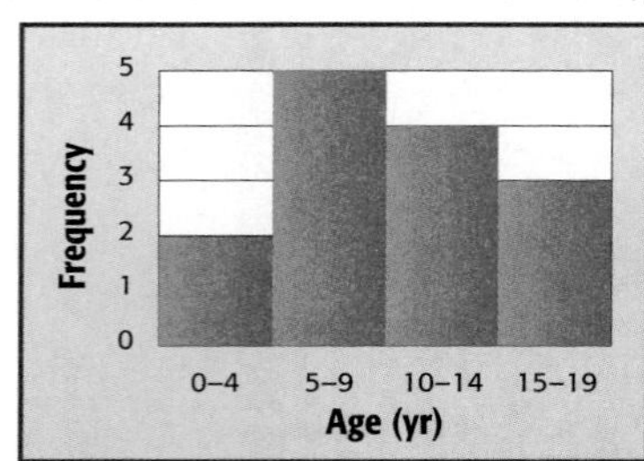

23. **WRITING IN MATH** Describe when a histogram might be more useful than a table with individual data. Then describe when a table of data might be more useful.

ISAT PRACTICE 10.A.3a

24. Which statement can be concluded from the histogram?

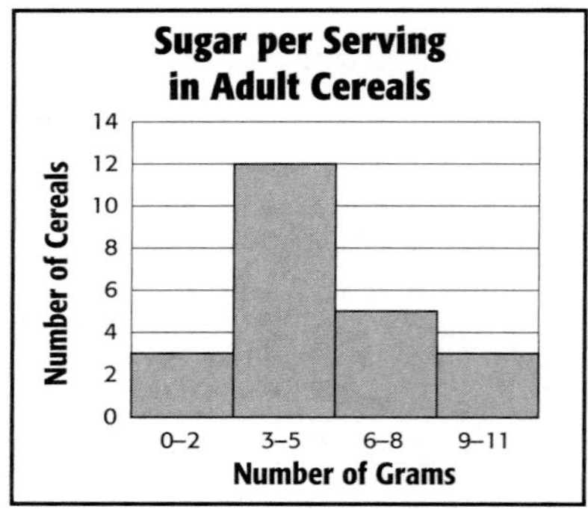

A The least number of grams of sugar per serving is 0.

B The greatest number of grams of sugar per serving is 11.

C Most of the cereals have 6–11 grams of sugar per serving.

D Most of the cereals have 3–5 grams of sugar per serving.

25. **SHORT RESPONSE** A group of mothers reported when their children got their first tooth.

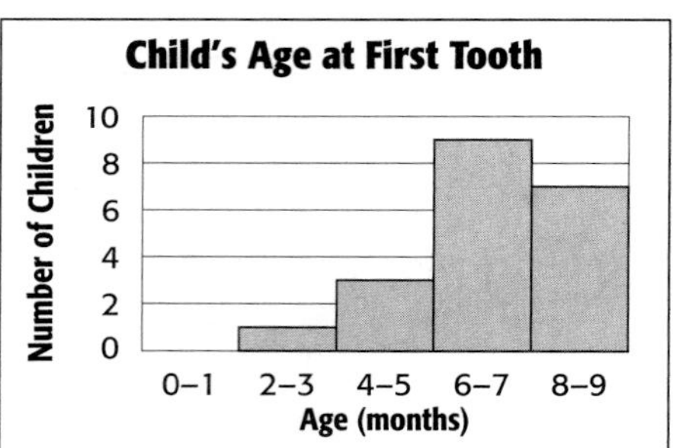

What fraction of the number of children reported got their first tooth when they were six months old or older?

Spiral Review

26. **THEME PARKS** The list gives the annual attendance in millions of persons for various theme parks in the United States. Use the *make a table* strategy to organize the data into intervals. (Lesson 11-1)

14.0	12.7	8.6	7.9	7.3	6.9
6.1	5.3	5.2	4.6	4.3	4.3
4.0	3.5	3.3	3.3	3.2	3.2
3.1	3.0	2.6	2.6	2.6	2.5

Source: *The World Almanac*

27. **GEOMETRY** Express the length of one side of a cube with a volume of $64x^3$ cubic units as a monomial. (Lesson 10-8)

GET READY for the Next Lesson

PREREQUISITE SKILL Solve each problem. (Lessons 5-3 and 5-7)

28. Find 26% of 360.

29. What is 53% of 360?

30. Find 73% of 360.

Extend 11-2

Graphing Calculator Lab
Histograms

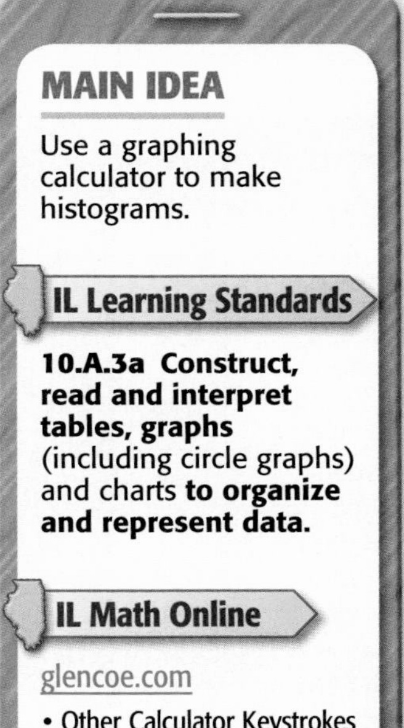

MAIN IDEA

Use a graphing calculator to make histograms.

IL Learning Standards

10.A.3a Construct, read and interpret tables, graphs (including circle graphs) and charts **to organize and represent data.**

IL Math Online

glencoe.com

- Other Calculator Keystrokes

You can make a histogram using a graphing calculator.

ACTIVITY

The Moapa Middle School basketball team listed each player's average points per game. Make a histogram of the data.

Average Points per Game											
15	3	11	7	4	6	18	1	2	21	10	3
9	2	1	12	24	5	13	20	4	12	1	2

STEP 1 Clear any existing data in list L1 by pressing STAT ENTER ▲ CLEAR ENTER.

Then enter the data in L1. Input each number and press ENTER.

STEP 2 Turn on the statistical plot by pressing 2nd [STAT PLOT] ENTER ENTER.

Select the histogram and L1 as the Xlist by pressing ▼ ▶ ▶ ENTER ▼ 2nd L1 ENTER.

STEP 3 Press WINDOW. To set the viewing window to be [0, 25] scl: 5 by [0, 12] scl: 1, press WINDOW 0 ENTER 25 ENTER 5 ENTER 0 ENTER 12 ENTER 1 ENTER GRAPH.

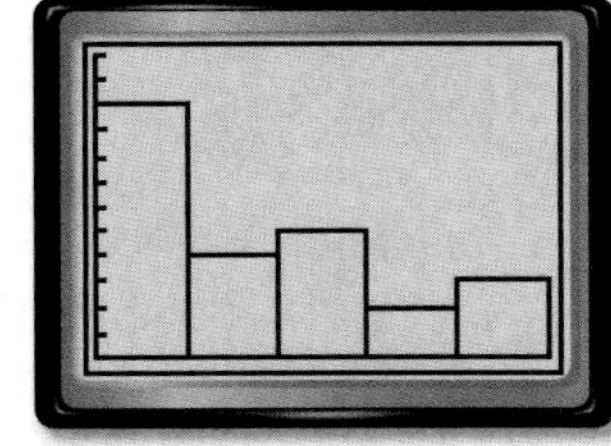

STEP 4 Press GRAPH to create the histogram.

Analyze the Results

1. Press TRACE. Find the frequency of each interval using the right arrow key.
2. Explain why the x-values for this data set were chosen as 0 to 25.
3. **COLLECT THE DATA** Use the graphing calculator to make a histogram of your classmates' heights in inches.

11-3 Circle Graphs

MAIN IDEA

Construct and interpret circle graphs.

IL Learning Standards

10.A.3a Construct, read and interpret tables, graphs (including circle graphs) and charts **to organize and represent data.**
10.A.3c Test the reasonableness of an argument based on data and communicate their findings.

New Vocabulary

circle graph

IL Math Online

glencoe.com
- Extra Examples
- Personal Tutor
- Self-Check Quiz

GET READY for the Lesson

MOVIES The graphic shows the results of a recent survey of 1,100 U.S. movie-goers.

Behaviors Americans Find Most Annoying at a Movie Theater

Behavior	Percent
Someone talking on a cell phone during a movie	73%
A cell phone ringing during a movie	10%
Someone talking to their seatmate during a movie	10%
Someone saving seats in a crowded theater	4%
Someone loudly eating popcorn or some other snack during a movie	3%

Source: Braun Research

1. What percent of U.S. movie-goers found a ringing cell phone the most annoying behavior at a movie theater?
2. What percent of U.S. movie-goers were annoyed with some kind of noise disturbance?
3. Which behavior was reported as the most annoying?
4. Are all the behaviors surveyed accounted for in the graphic? Explain.

A **circle graph** can be used to compare parts of a data set to the whole set of data. The entire circle represents the whole set, so the percents in a circle graph add up to 100.

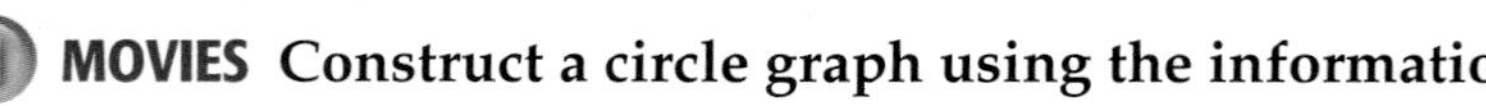

Construct a Circle Graph from Percents

1 MOVIES Construct a circle graph using the information above.

Step 1 There are 360° in a circle. So, multiply each percent written as a decimal by 360° to find the number of degrees for each section of the graph.

Talking on a cell phone:	73% of $360° = 0.73 \cdot 360° \approx 263°$
Ringing cell phone:	10% of $360° = 0.10 \cdot 360°$ or $36°$
Talking to seatmate:	10% of $360° = 0.10 \cdot 360°$ or $36°$
Saving seats:	4% of $360° = 0.04 \cdot 360° \approx 14°$
Eating loudly:	3% of $360° = 0.03 \cdot 360° \approx 11°$

Step 2 Use a compass to draw a circle and a radius. Then use a protractor to draw an 11° angle. This section represents someone eating loudly. From the new radius, draw the next angle. Repeat for each of the remaining angles. Label each section. Then give the graph a title.

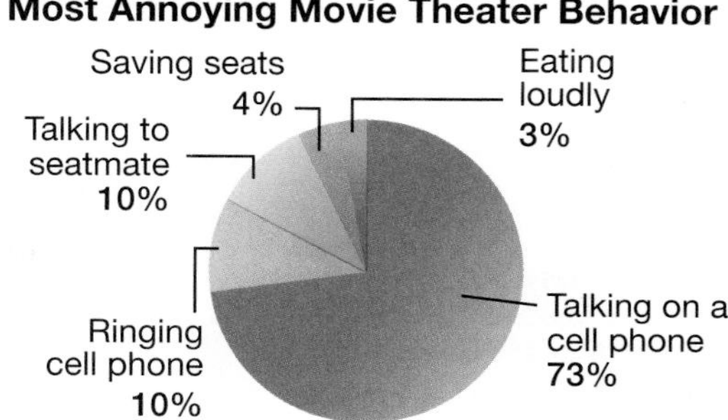

CHECK Your Progress

a. **CELL PHONES** The table gives the percentage share of the top five wireless-subscribing countries in the world. Construct a circle graph to represent the data.

Global Wireless Subscribers

Country	Percentage Share
China	19.3
U.S.A.	9.9
Russia	5.6
Japan	4.6
Brazil	4.1
Other	56.5

Source: *Computer Industry Almanac*

Real-World Link At the 2006 Winter Olympics, Apolo Anton Ohno of the United States won a gold medal in the men's 500-meter short track. His time was 41.935 seconds.
Source: MSNBC

When percents are not known, you must first determine what part of the whole each item represents.

EXAMPLE Construct a Circle Graph from Data

2 **OLYMPICS** **Construct a circle graph of the data in the histogram at the right.**

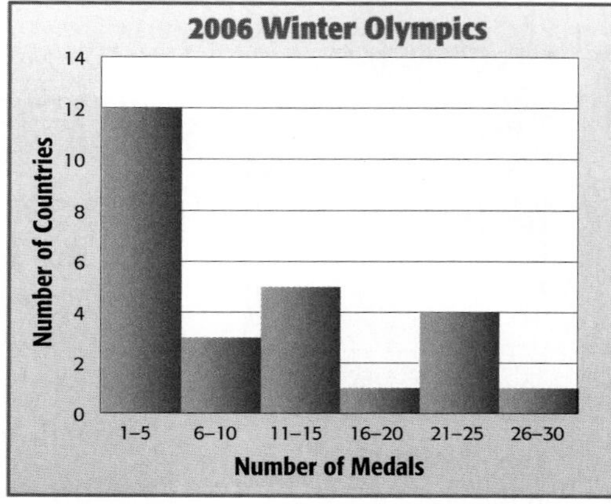

Source: MSNBC

Step 1 Find the total number of countries.

$12 + 3 + 5 + 1 + 4 + 1 = 26$

Step 2 Find the ratio that compares the number in each medal count to the total number of countries. Round to the nearest hundredth.

1 to 5: $12 \div 26 \approx 0.46$	16 to 20: $1 \div 26 \approx 0.04$
6 to 10: $3 \div 26 \approx 0.12$	21 to 25: $4 \div 26 \approx 0.15$
11 to 15: $5 \div 26 \approx 0.19$	26 to 30: $1 \div 26 \approx 0.04$

Step 3 Use these ratios to find the number of degrees of each section. Round to the nearest degree if necessary.

1 to 5: $0.46 \cdot 360 = 165.6$ or about 166
6 to 10: $0.12 \cdot 360 = 43.2$ or about 43
11 to 15: $0.19 \cdot 360 = 68.4$ or about 69
16 to 20: $0.04 \cdot 360 = 14.4$ or about 14
21 to 25: $0.15 \cdot 360 = 54$
26 to 30: $0.04 \cdot 360 = 14.4$ or about 14

Study Tip

Rounding
In Step 3, 68.4 was rounded to 69 so that the total number of degrees would equal 360°.

Step 4 Use a compass and a protractor to draw a circle and the appropriate sections. Label each section and give the graph a title. Write the ratios as percents.

2006 Winter Olympics Medal Count

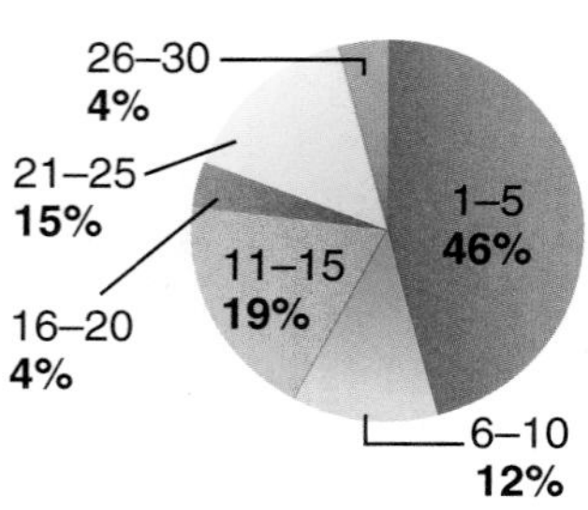

 **CHECK Your Progress**

b. **BIRTHPLACES** The table gives the region of birth and number of people living in the United States who were born in a different country. Construct a circle graph of the data.

Foreign-Born Residents of the United States

Region of Birth	Number of People
Europe	4,915,557
Asia	8,226,254
Africa	881,300
Oceania	168,046
Latin America	16,086,974
North America	829,442

Source: U.S. Census Bureau

Real-World Link
In the academic year 2003–2004, 57% of all degrees awarded by 4-year institutions and 62% of all degrees awarded by 2-year institutions were awarded to women.
Source: National Center for Education Statistics

EXAMPLE Analyze and Interpret Data

3 SCHOOL Use the circle graph at the right to describe the makeup of the school enrollment of persons 3 years or older who are enrolled in school in the United States.

School Enrollment of Persons 3 Years or Older Enrolled in School

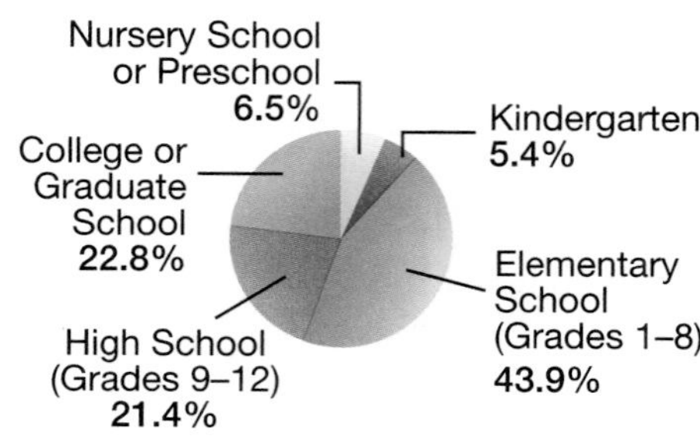

Source: U.S. Census Bureau

More persons were enrolled in elementary school than in any other category. More than $\frac{3}{4}$ of the total enrolled are in a preK-12 program. The number of persons enrolled in high school and the number of persons enrolled in college or graduate school are about the same.

Your Progress

c. **PETS** Use the circle graph at the right to describe the makeup of the dollar amount Americans pay for their pets.

How Much Did You Pay For Your Pet?

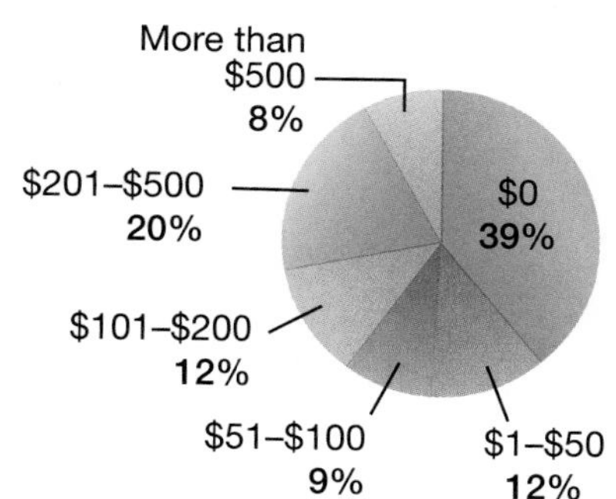

Source: American Animal Hospital Association

CHECK Your Understanding

Examples 1, 2 (pp. 582–584)

Construct a circle graph for each set of data.

1.

Frequency of Exercise	
Several Times a Day or Once a Day	32%
Several Times a Week	33%
Several Times a Month or Once a Month	15%
A Few Times a Year or Never	19%
Not Sure	1%

Source: FOX News

2.

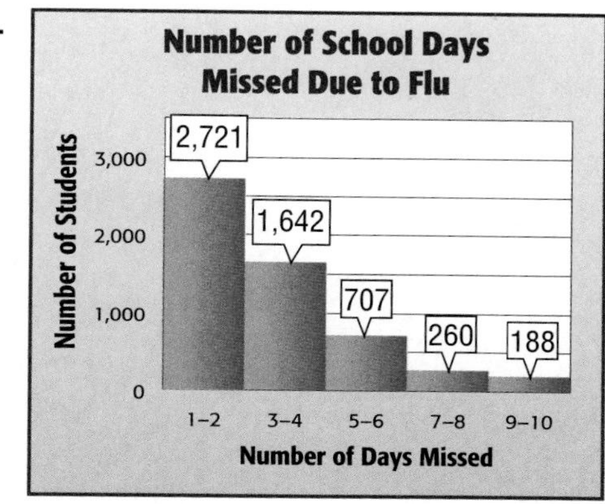

Source: PBS Kids

Example 3 (pp. 584–585)

3. **ACTIVITIES** Use the circle graph to describe the activities teens say they are willing to give up.

Activity Teenagers Are Most Willing to Give Up

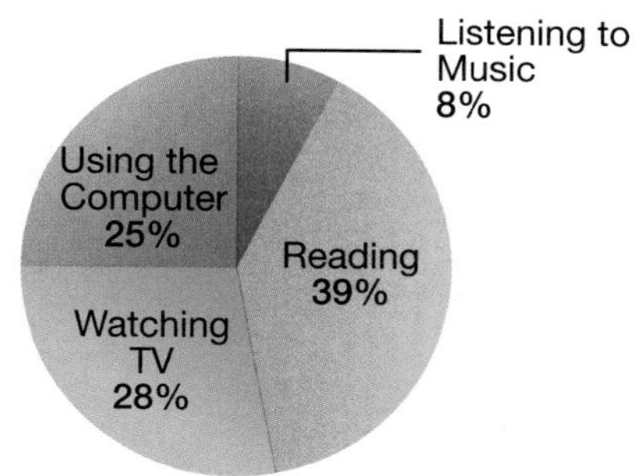

Source: National Education Association

4. **POPULATION** Use the circle graph to describe the population of North Carolina by age.

Percent of North Carolina Population by Age

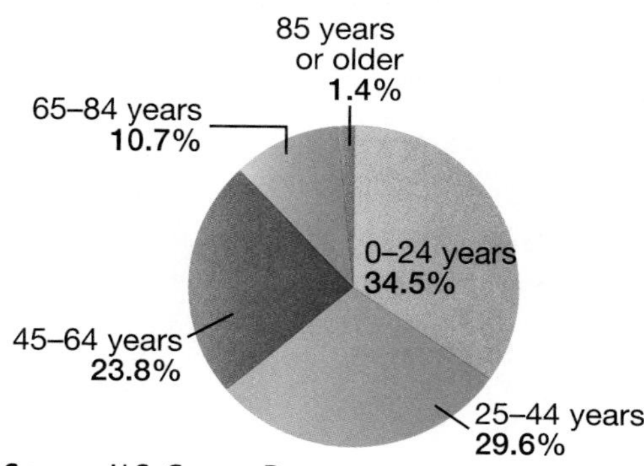

Source: U.S. Census Bureau

Practice and Problem Solving

HOMEWORK HELP	
For Exercises	See Examples
5–8	1
9–12	2
13–15	3

Construct a circle graph for each set of data.

5.

Countries with the Most Internet Users	
United States	45%
Japan	18%
China	15%
Germany	8%
United Kingdom	7%
South Korea	7%

Source: *Time for Kids Almanac*

6.

Where Is the Best Place to Go Clothes Shopping?	
Malls	79%
Other	8%
Online	6%
Flea Markets	4%
Vintage Stores	3%

Source: PBS Kids

7.

How Old Do You Wish You Were?

Number of Persons
Age (years)
21–30: 354
31–40: 167
41–50: 112
51–60: 64
61–70: 53
71–80: 25
81–90: 10
91–100: 2

8.

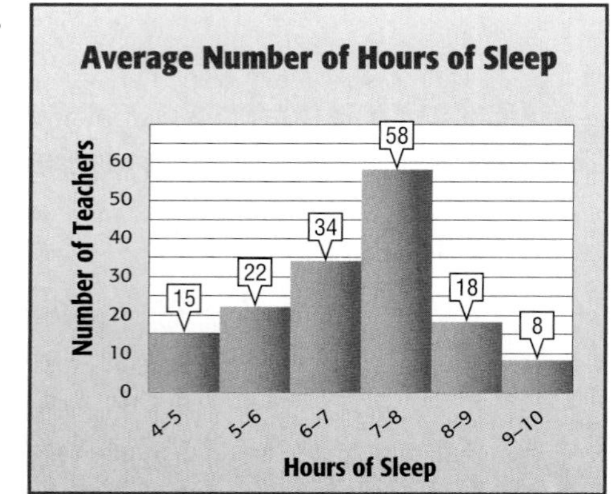

Describe the data in each circle graph.

9.

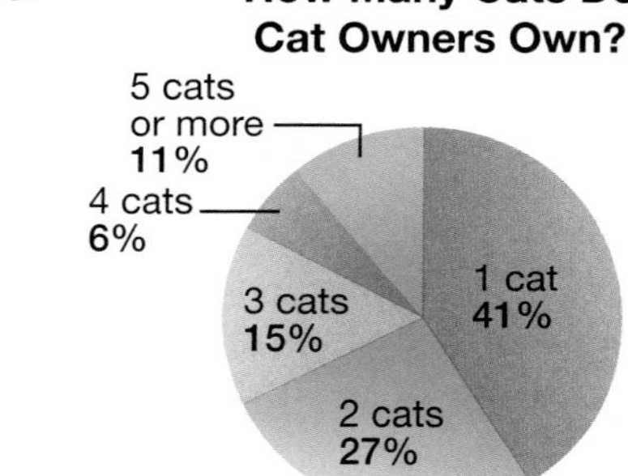

Source: American Animal Hospital Association

10.

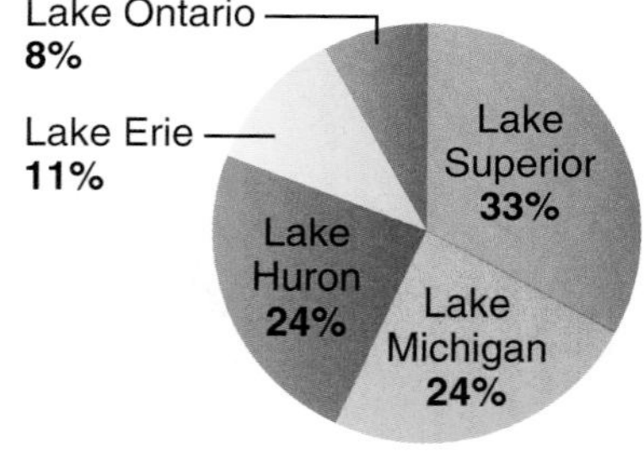

Source: *The World Almanac*

Real-World Link Americans eat about 100 acres of pizza daily, which averages to about 350 slices per second.

11.

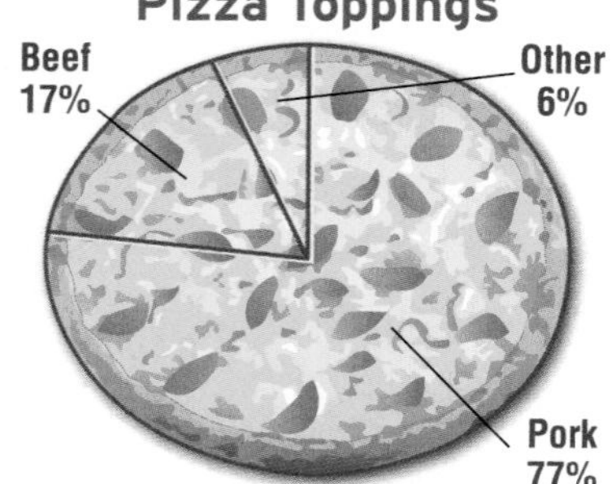

Source: The National Pork Board

12.

Source: Serta

Real-World Link The Eastern Hemisphere includes Asia, Africa, Europe, and Oceania while the Western Hemisphere includes North and South America.

13. **EARTH SCIENCE** Use the circle graph at the right to determine the percent of aluminum in Earth's crust. Then find the measure in degrees of the angle of the aluminum section of the circle graph.

Elements in Earth's Crust

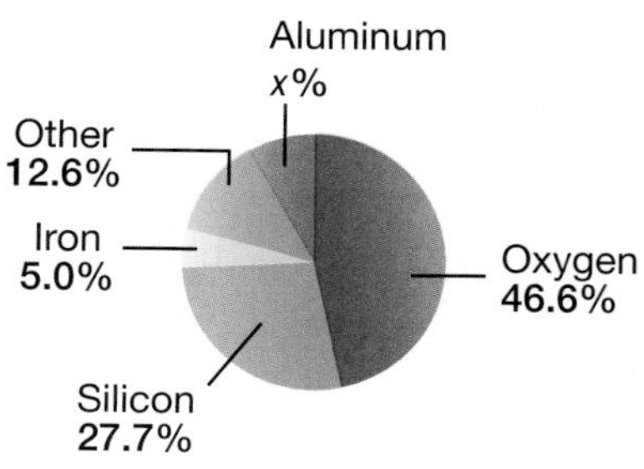

Source: Texas A&M University

14. **COLLECT THE DATA** Conduct a survey of your classmates to determine the number of hours they watch TV in a particular week. Construct a histogram of the data. Then construct a circle graph of the data.

15. **TOURISM** Use the information at the left and the circle graph at the right to determine the percent of foreign visitors to the United States from the Eastern Hemisphere. Then find the number of visitors from the Eastern Hemisphere if there was a total of 50 million foreign visitors to the United States.

Place of Origin for Foreign Visitors to the U.S.

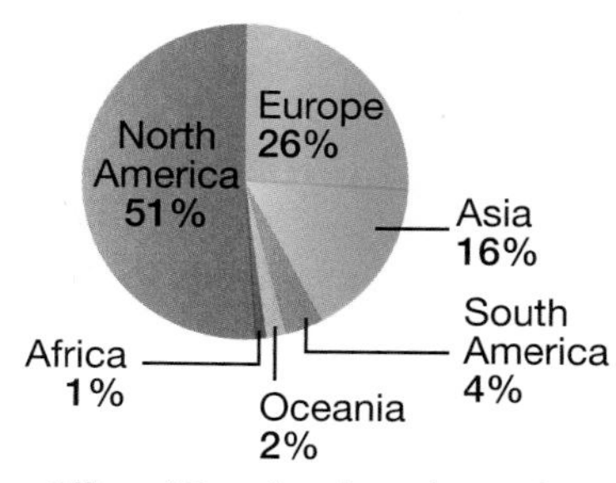

Source: Office of Travel and Tourism Industries

SPRING BREAK For Exercises 16–18, use the table below.

16. Construct a circle graph of the data.
17. Conduct a survey of your classmates to determine their favorite activity during Spring Break. Then construct a circle graph of the data.
18. Describe any similarities and differences between the two circle graphs you made.

Favorite Activity During Spring Break	
Outdoor Activities	27%
Shopping	22.5%
Traveling	14%
Playing Video Games	13.2%
Watching Movies/TV	12%

ILS • ISAT
Extra Practice, pp. 697, 710

H.O.T. Problems

19. **NUMBER SENSE** What percent of the circle graph at the right is represented by Section A? by Section B? by Section C?

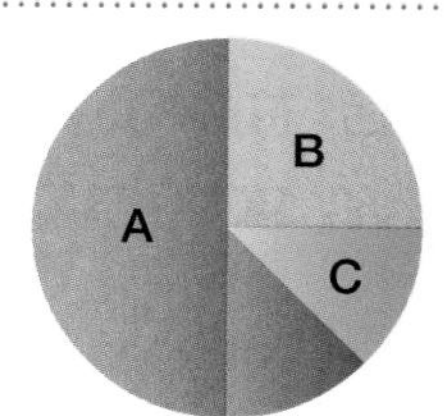

20. **OPEN ENDED** Construct a circle graph with five categories showing how you spend 24 hours in a typical weekday.

21. **REASONING** Explain why a circle graph could *not* be made of the data in the table at the right.

Most Popular Newspaper Section Read by Teens	
Comics	56%
Entertainment	51%
Sports	45%
Advertising	42%
Local News	35%
Classifieds	28%

Source: Newspaper Association of America

22. **WRITING IN MATH** Write a word problem about a real-world situation in which you could construct a circle graph to solve the problem. Explain why the circle graph would be helpful.

ISAT PRACTICE 10.A.3a, 10.A.3c

23. Ms. Horace surveyed the students in the 8th grade about their favorite type of television program. The table shows the results of the survey. Which circle graph best represents the data in the table?

Type of Program	Number of Students
Comedy	120
Drama	180
Reality	240
Action	60

A

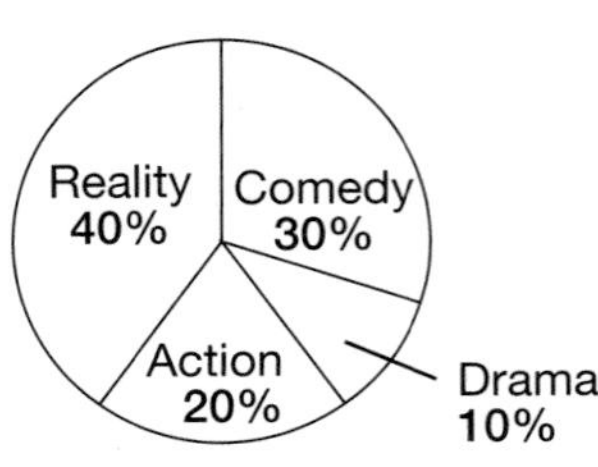

C

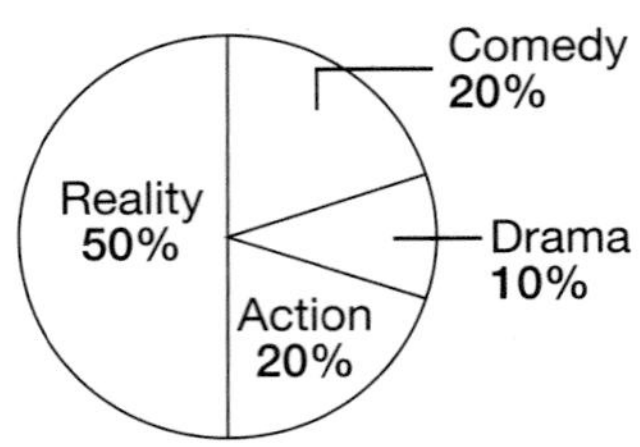

B

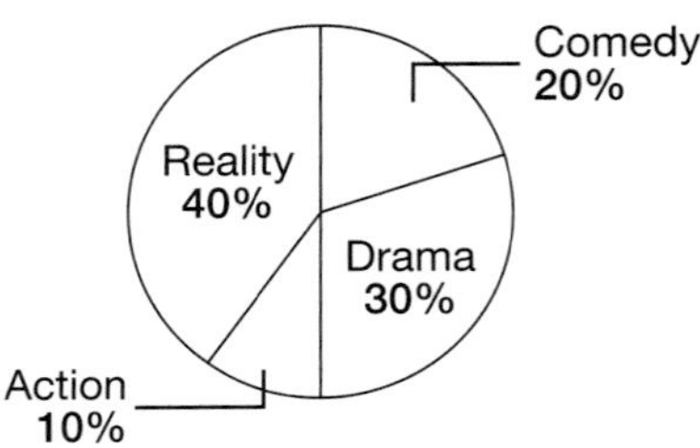

D

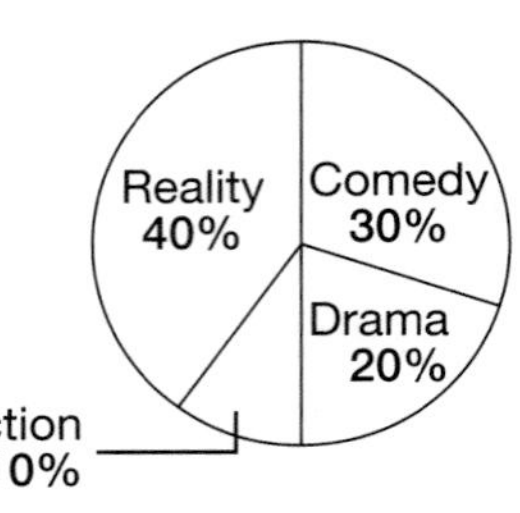

Spiral Review

24. **ANIMALS** The number of years various types of animals are expected to live are listed below. Construct a histogram of the data. (Lesson 11-2)

1, 3, 5, 5, 6, 7, 8, 8, 10, 10, 10, 12, 12, 12,
12, 15, 15, 15, 15, 16, 18, 20, 20, 25, 35

25. Find the length of a side of a square with an area of $36x^2y^6$. (Lesson 10-8)

26. **SKYDIVING** The distance d a skydiver falls in t seconds is given by the function $d = 16t^2$. Graph this function and estimate how far a skydiver will fall in 5.5 seconds. (Lesson 10-2)

Find the volume of each prism or cylinder. Round to the nearest tenth, if necessary. (Lesson 7-5)

27. rectangular prism: length 4 cm, width 8 cm, height 2 cm

28. cylinder: diameter 1.6 in., height 5 in.

GET READY for the Next Lesson

PREREQUISITE SKILL Evaluate each expression.

29. $\frac{57 + 25 + 32 + 46}{4}$

30. $\frac{14(107) + 342 + 10(13)}{3}$

31. $\frac{500 - 125 + 205 - 20}{8}$

Extend 11-3

Spreadsheet Lab
Line, Bar, and Circle Graphs

MAIN IDEA

Use technology to create line, bar, and circle graphs.

IL Learning Standards

10.A.3a Construct, read and interpret tables, graphs (including circle graphs) and charts **to organize and represent data.**

A computer spreadsheet is useful to construct line, bar, and circle graphs.

ACTIVITY

1 The table gives the number of Bachelor's degrees awarded to women by U.S. colleges and universities.

Year	'97–'98	'00–'01	'03–'04	'06–'07
Degrees (in thousands)	664.5	713.3	804.1	870.0

Source: National Center for Education Statistics

To construct a line graph of the data, follow these steps.

STEP 1 Set up a spreadsheet, with the years in column A and the number of degrees in column B.

STEP 2 Highlight the data in column B, from B2 through B5. This tells the spreadsheet to read the data in column B.

STEP 3 Click on the Chart Wizard icon, choose the line graph, and click Next.

STEP 4 To set the *x*-axis, choose the Series tab and press the icon next to the Category (X) axis labels.

STEP 5 On the spreadsheet, select the data in column A, from A2 through A5. Press the icon on the bottom of the Chart Wizard box to automatically paste the data.

STEP 6 Click Next and enter the chart title and labels for the *x*- and *y*-axes. Click Next again and then Finish.

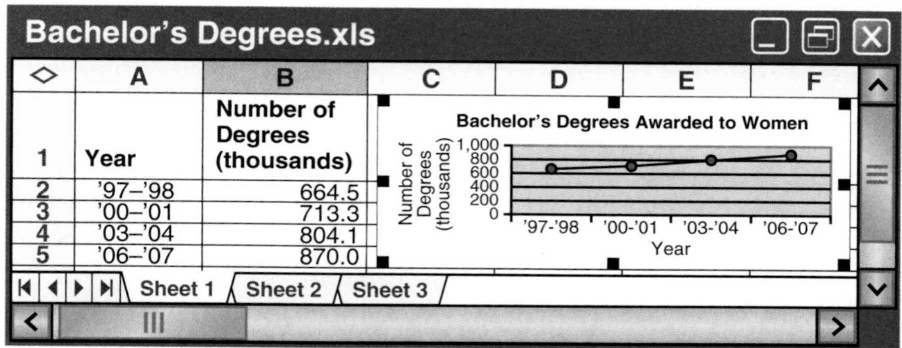

2 **STEP 1** To make a bar graph, highlight the data in B2 through B5.

STEP 2 Click on the Chart Wizard and choose the vertical bar graph.

STEP 3 Complete steps 3–5 from Activity 1.

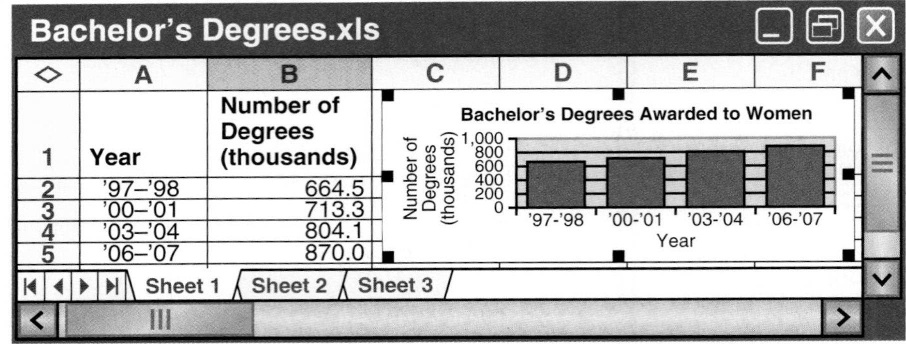

ACTIVITY

3 **STEP 1** To make a circle graph, highlight the data in A2 through B5.

STEP 2 Click on the Chart Wizard and choose Pie.

STEP 3 Click Next to enter the chart title. Then click Next and Finish.

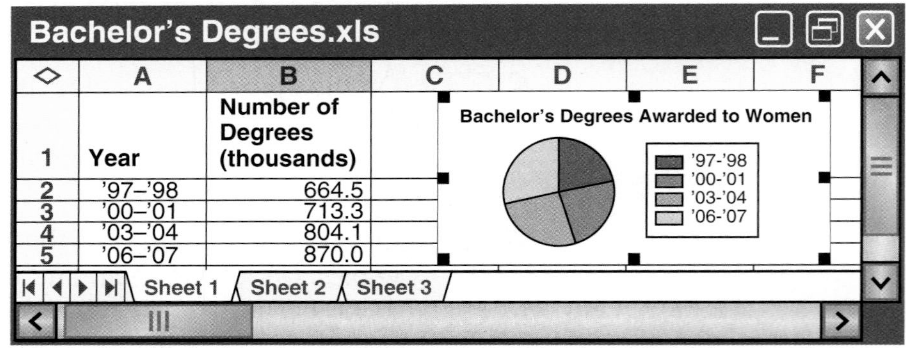

Analyze the Results

1. **MAKE A CONJECTURE** Use one of the graphs to predict the approximate number of bachelor's degrees that would be awarded to women from U.S. colleges and universities in the year 2018–2019. Which graph(s) did you use to make this conjecture? Justify your selection(s).
2. **COLLECT THE DATA** Collect some data that can be displayed in a line, bar, and circle graph. Use a spreadsheet to construct each graph.

Measures of Central Tendency and Range

MAIN IDEA

Find the mean, median, mode, and range of a set of data

IL Learning Standards

10.A.3b Compare the mean, median, mode and range, with and **without the use of technology.**

New Vocabulary

measures of central tendency
mean
median
mode
range

IL Math Online

glencoe.com

- Extra Examples
- Personal Tutor
- Self-Check Quiz

GET READY for the Lesson

OLYMPIC MEDALS Use the table to answer each question.

1. What number(s) appear the most in the bronze category?
2. What is the *average* number of medals won by the United States in the bronze category?
3. Place the numbers in the bronze category in order from least to greatest. What is the middle number?

United States' Summer Olympics Medals 1972–2004

Year	Gold	Silver	Bronze
1972	33	31	30
1976	34	35	25
1980	0	0	0
1984	83	61	30
1988	36	31	27
1992	37	34	37
1996	44	32	25
2000	40	24	33
2004	35	39	29

Source: United States Olympic Committee

Measures of central tendency are numbers that describe the center of a set of data. The most common measures are **mean**, **median**, and **mode**. The **range** is also used to describe a set of data.

Measures of Central Tendency and Range — Concept Summary

Measure	Description
mean	sum of the data divided by the number of items in the set
median	middle number of the data ordered from least to greatest, or the mean of the middle two numbers
mode	number or numbers that occur most often
range	difference between the greatest number (maximum) and least number (minimum) in a set of data

EXAMPLE Find Measures of Central Tendency and Range

1 **The ages, in years, of the people seated at a table are 22, 18, 24, 32, 24, 18. Find the mean, median, mode, and range of the set of data.**

Mean $\frac{22 + 18 + 24 + 32 + 24 + 18}{6} = \frac{138}{6}$ or 23 years old

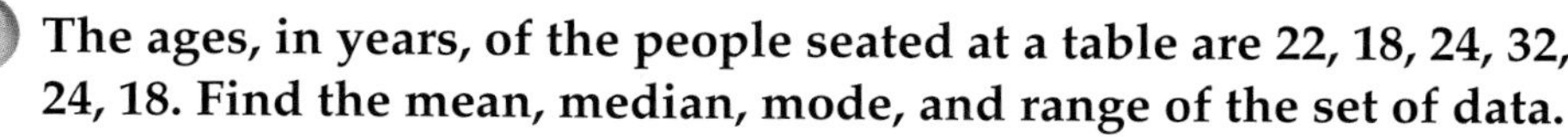

Median 18, 18, 22, 24, 24, 32 — Arrange in order from least to greatest.

$\frac{22 + 24}{2} = 23$ years old

Mode The data set has two modes, 18 and 24 years old.

Range 32 − 18 or 14 years

CHECK Your Progress

a. The prices of parking at several lots are listed below. Find the mean, median, mode, and range. Round to the nearest cent.
$3, $2.50, $6, $5.50, $3, $4.25

Sometimes one or two measures of central tendency or the range are more representative of the data than the other measure(s).

Real-World Link
There are at least one million insects for each of the world's humans.
Source: *Top Ten of Everything*

Real-World EXAMPLE

2 INSECTS Select the appropriate measure of central tendency or range to describe the data in the table. Justify your reasoning.

Most Common Insects	
Species	**Number of Known Species (thousands)**
Beetles	400
Butterflies and Moths	165
Ants, Bees, and Wasps	140
True Flies	120
Bugs	90
Caddisflies	10

Source: *Top Ten of Everything*

Find the mean, median, mode, and range of the data.

Mean

$$\frac{400 + 165 + 140 + 120 + 90 + 10}{6}$$

$$= \frac{924}{6} \approx 154.2$$

The mean is about 154.2 thousand.

Study Tip
Median
Since there are two middle numbers, the median is the mean of the middle two numbers.

Median Arrange the numbers from least to greatest.
10, 90, 120, 140, 165, 400

The median is $\frac{120 + 140}{2}$ or 130 thousand.

Mode Since each number only occurs once, there is no mode.

Range 400 − 10 or 390 thousand

Since beetles, butterflies, and moths are the only insects with a greater number of known species than the mean, the mean is *not* the appropriate measure of central tendency.

Since there is no mode, the median is the appropriate measure of central tendency. The range tells us that the spread of the data is 390 thousand.

CHECK Your Progress

b. **COMPUTERS** Select the appropriate measure of central tendency or range to describe the data in the table. Justify your reasoning.

Computer Model	Hard Drive (gigabytes)
L100	40
L150	80
NX250	40
NX300	120
PC150	40
PC250	40

Different circumstances determine which measure of central tendency or range is most appropriate to describe a set of data.

Study Tip

Range
The range of a data set gives the spread, or how far the values are spread out. Use the range when you want to describe the spread.

Using Mean, Median, and Mode

Concept Summary

Measure	Most Useful When...
mean	the data have no extreme values
median	the data have extreme values there are no big gaps in the middle of the data
mode	the data have many identical numbers

ISAT EXAMPLE 10.A.3b

3 Spencer has the following scores on five quizzes: 90, 85, 80, 75, and 90. If his teacher drops his lowest score, which of the following statements would be true?

A The mean would decrease.

B The mean would increase.

C The median would decrease.

D The median would not change.

Read the Item

You need to find which statement would be true if the lowest score, 75, is dropped.

Solve the Item

The mean of the five quizzes is $\frac{90 + 85 + 80 + 75 + 90}{5}$ or 84. The mean of the four quizzes is $\frac{90 + 85 + 80 + 90}{4}$ or 86.25. Since the mean increased, you can eliminate answer choice A.

Find the median to check the other answer choices. Arrange the numbers from least to greatest, with and without the lowest score.

75, 80, (85), 90, 90   80, 85, 90, 90 → (87.5)

Since the median increased from 85 to 87.5, you can eliminate answer choices C and D. So, the answer is B.

CHECK Your Progress

c. Darci deposited $35, $10, $25, and $50 into her savings account last month. If she deposits $44 this week, which of the following statements about the data set would be true?

F The mean would decrease.

G The mean would not change.

H The median would increase.

J The mode would increase.

CHECK Your Understanding

Find the mean, median, mode, and range of each set of data. Round to the nearest tenth if necessary.

Example 1 (pp. 591–592)

1. the number of minutes spent on cell phone calls in one day
   19, 21, 18, 17, 18, 22, 46

2. the number of miles several employees commute to work
   10, 3, 17, 1, 8, 6, 12, 15

Example 2 (p. 592)

3. **TEACHERS** Select the appropriate measure of central tendency or range to describe the data in the table. Justify your reasoning.

Number of Years Teaching at South Middle School	
Ms. Malan	27
Mr. Sliger	11
Mrs. Lindley	9
Ms. Nolasco	6
Mr. Wyatt	5
Mrs. Clarke	3

Example 3 (p. 593)

4. **MULTIPLE CHOICE** Brianna studied 1 hour, 3 hours, 2 hours, and 2 hours over four days. If she would have studied 2 hours instead of 1 hour one of the days, which of the following would decrease?

   A mean **C** mode

   B median **D** range

Practice and Problem Solving

HOMEWORK HELP	
For Exercises	See Examples
5–8	1
9, 10	2
22, 23	3

Find the mean, median, mode, and range of each set of data. Round to the nearest tenth if necessary.

5. the number of points scored each by five basketball players
   9, 8, 15, 8, 20

6. the ages, in years, of the Henderson family children
   23, 16, 5, 6, 14

7. the prices, in dollars, of several pairs of running shoes
   78, 80, 75, 73, 84, 81, 84, 79

8. the number of channels for various cable television plans
   36, 38, 33, 34, 32, 30, 34, 35

For Exercises 9 and 10, select the appropriate measure of central tendency or range to describe the data in each table. Justify your reasoning.

9.

Fastest Roller Coasters	
Coaster	Speed (mph)
Dodonpa	107
Kingda Ka	128
Millennium Force	93
Phantom's Revenge	82
Steel Dragon 2000	95
Superman: The Escape	100
Top Thrill Dragster	120
Tower of Terror	100

Source: Info Please

10.

Known Moons of Planets	
Planet	Number of Moons
Mercury	0
Venus	0
Earth	1
Mars	2
Jupiter	63
Saturn	34
Uranus	27
Neptune	13

Source: NASA

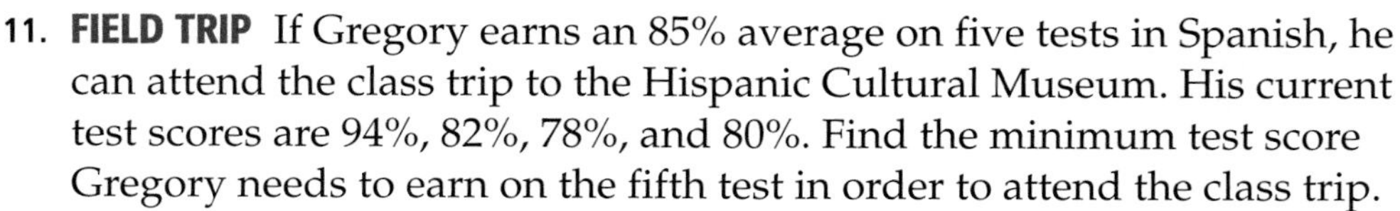

11. **FIELD TRIP** If Gregory earns an 85% average on five tests in Spanish, he can attend the class trip to the Hispanic Cultural Museum. His current test scores are 94%, 82%, 78%, and 80%. Find the minimum test score Gregory needs to earn on the fifth test in order to attend the class trip.

Real-World Link The 2004 Paralympic Summer Games were held in Greece and consisted of 19 sports, including the men's 100-meter race.

BIRDS **For Exercises 12–14, use the table at the right.**

12. Find the mean, median, mode, and range of the incubation periods of all the birds.

13. Select the appropriate measure of central tendency or range to describe the data. Justify your reasoning.

14. Using the measures of central tendency and the range of the parrots and of the cockatoos, determine which species, parrot or cockatoo, seems to have the greater incubation period. Justify your reasoning.

Number of Days of Incubation Periods for Pet Birds	
Australian King Parrot	20
Glossy Cockatoo	30
Major Mitchell's Cockatoo	26
Princess Parrot	21
Red-Tailed Cockatoo	30
Red-Winged Parrot	21
Regent Parrot	21
Superb Parrot	20
White-Tailed Cockatoo	29
Yellow-Tailed Cockatoo	29

15. **BASEBALL** The table gives the seating capacity of several baseball parks. Describe how the mean, median, mode, and range are each affected if the data for Yankee Stadium are not included.

Seating Capacity of Baseball Parks	
Comerica Park	40,120
Tropicana Field	43,772
Jacobs Field	43,405
Yankee Stadium	56,937
Kauffman Stadium	40,793
U.S. Cellular Field	40,615

Source: *Major League Baseball Teams*

16. **RUNNING** Natalie runs 4 miles on Mondays, 3.5 miles on Wednesdays, and 4.5 miles on Fridays. Describe how the mean, median, mode, and range would each be affected if Natalie chooses to add a 3.5-mile jog on Sundays.

Extra Practice, pp. 697, 710

H.O.T. Problems

17. **OPEN ENDED** Construct a set of data that has a mode of 10 and a median of 7.

18. **FIND THE ERROR** Miles and Horacio are finding the median of 62, 64, 63, 60, 65, 65, and 70. Who is correct? Explain.

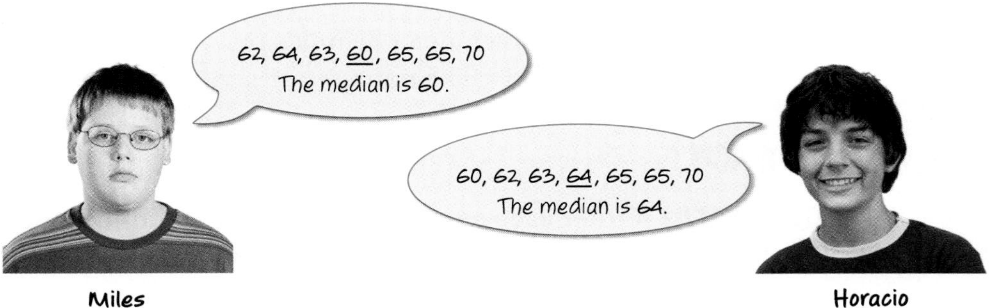

62, 64, 63, 60, 65, 65, 70
The median is 60.
60, 62, 63, 64, 65, 65, 70
The median is 64.
Miles
Horacio

19. **REASONING** Determine whether the following statement is *sometimes*, *always*, or *never* true. Explain your reasoning.

All measures of central tendency must be members of the set of data.

20. **CHALLENGE** Give a counterexample to show that the following statement is false.

The median is always representative of the data.

21. **WRITING IN MATH** Write a problem that asks for the measures of central tendency. Use data from a newspaper or magazine. Tell which measure is most representative of the data.

ISAT PRACTICE 10.A.3b

22. The speeds, in miles per hour, of several cars on a busy street were clocked as 42, 38, 44, 35, 50, and 38. Which measure of data would make the speeds appear the fastest?

A mode

B median

C mean

D range

23. Isaac earned the following by mowing lawns: \$25, \$20, \$30, and \$25. If he earns another \$30, which of the following statements would be true?

F The mode would not be affected.

G The mean would decrease.

H The median would decrease.

J The mean would increase.

Spiral Review

24. **FOOD** Makayla surveyed the students in her class regarding their favorite school lunch. Fifty-two percent voted for pizza, 25% voted for nachos, 15% voted for cheeseburgers, and 8% voted for salad. Make a circle graph of the data. (Lesson 11-3)

HEIGHTS For Exercises 25 and 26, use the histogram at the right. (Lesson 11-2)

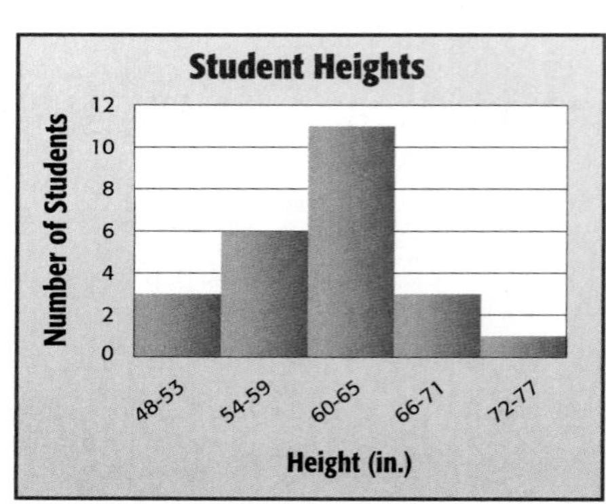

25. How many students are at least 60 inches tall?

26. How many students are between 54 and 71 inches tall?

27. **SPEED** If a car travels an average of 58 miles per hour, how far will it travel in 3.5 hours? (Lesson 4-3)

GET READY for the Next Lesson

PREREQUISITE SKILL Order each set of rational numbers from least to greatest. (Lesson 2-2)

28. 3.1, 3.25, 3.2, 2.9, 2.89

29. 91.3, 93.1, 94.7, 93.11, 93

30. 17.4, 16.8, 16.79, 15.01, 15.1

Spreadsheet Lab
Mean, Median, and Mode

MAIN IDEA

Use a spreadsheet to find mean, median, and mode.

IL Learning Standards

10.A.3b Compare the mean, median, mode and range, with and without **the use of technology.**

You can use a spreadsheet to find the mean, median, and mode of data.

ACTIVITY

BASKETBALL The following is a list of the top ten number of wins by NBA coaches. Make a spreadsheet for the data.

Number of Wins by NBA Coaches				
1,372	1,165	999	953	938
1,265	1,037	991	948	908

Source: *Top Ten of Everything*

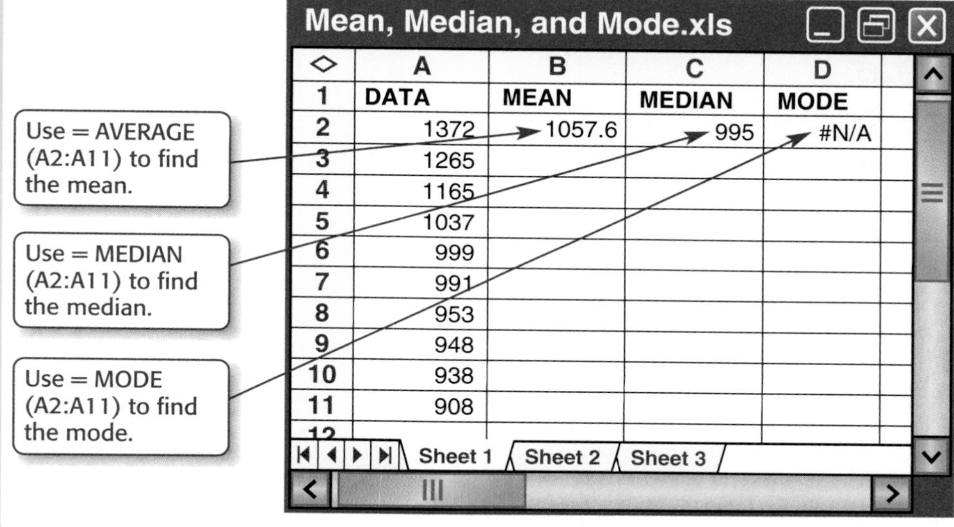

Mean, Median, and Mode.xls
A
B
C
D
1 DATA MEAN MEDIAN MODE
2 1372 1057.6 995 #N/A
3 1265
4 1165
5 1037
6 999
7 991
8 953
9 948
10 938
11 908
Sheet 1
Sheet 2
Sheet 3
Use = AVERAGE (A2:A11) to find the mean.
Use = MEDIAN (A2:A11) to find the median.
Use = MODE (A2:A11) to find the mode.

EXERCISES

For Exercises 1–3, use the following tables.

NBA Western Conference Top Ten Scoring Leaders 2006-2007	
2,430	1,704
1,916	1,671
1,881	1,642
1,747	1,618
1,709	1,608

NBA Eastern Conference Top Ten Scoring Leaders 2006-2007	
2,132	1,561
2,105	1,540
2,070	1,485
1,753	1,443
1,576	1,426

1. Use spreadsheets to find the mean, median, and mode of the top ten points scored for each confrence.
2. Compare the highest points scored for the two conferences.
3. Compare the mean and median of the two conferences.

CHAPTER 11 Mid-Chapter Quiz

Lessons 11-1 through 11-4

IL Learning Standards
10.A.3a, 10.A.3b

1. **TEMPERATURE** Organize the data below in a frequency table using intervals 60–69, 70–79, 80–89, and 90–99. What is the most common interval of monthly high temperatures? (Lesson 11-1)

Average Monthly High Temperatures (°F) for Tucson, Arizona					
66	82	99	70	90	99
97	66	94	85	74	74

2. **MUSIC** Choose intervals and make a frequency table of the data below. Then construct a histogram to represent the data. (Lesson 11-2)

Number of Days Students Practiced Musical Instruments Last Week								
7	5	7	6	5	7	6	3	6
4	2	0	6	4	5	2	5	7
4	0	7	5	3	7	1	3	0

JOBS For Exercises 3–5, use the histogram below which shows the age, in years, at which several people surveyed started their first job. (Lesson 11-2)

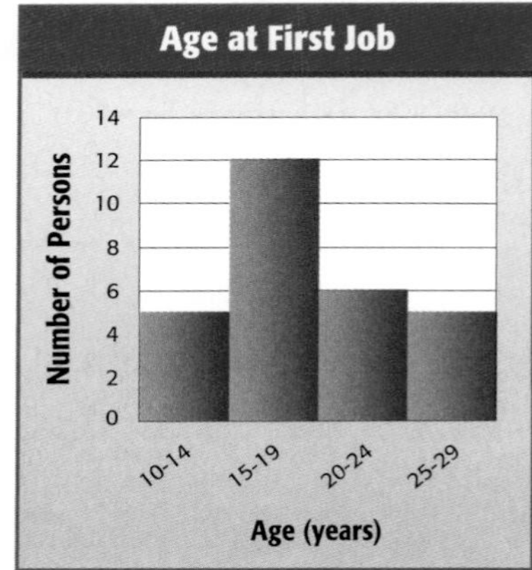

3. How many people surveyed started their first job after their 20th birthday but before their 30th birthday?
4. Based on this histogram, at what age is a person most likely to start their first job?
5. Construct a circle graph for this set of data. (Lesson 11-3)

6. **MULTIPLE CHOICE** Which statement *cannot* be determined by the graph? (Lesson 11-3)

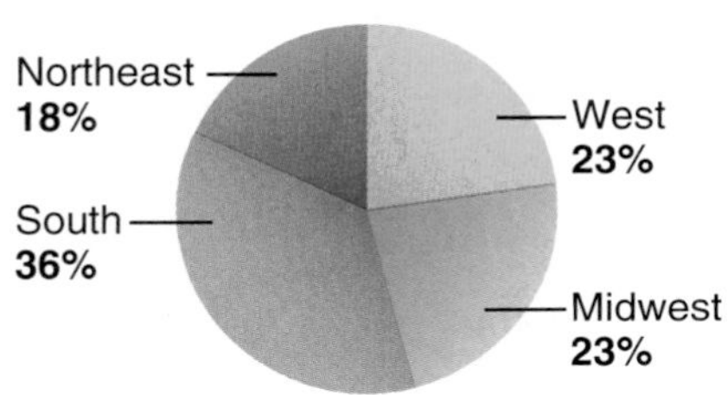

A About one fifth of the labor force works in the Northeast.

B More people work in the Southern region than any other region.

C The same number of people work in the West as in the Midwest.

D Half of the labor force works in the West.

Find the mean, median, mode, and range of each set of data. Round to the nearest tenth if necessary. (Lesson 11-4)

7. sales tax, as a percent, for several states
4.5, 6, 5.75, 5, 6.25, 5.5

8. length, in seconds, of several commercials
35, 41, 17, 22, 25, 33, 17

9. **MULTIPLE CHOICE** The list gives the scores on a recent history test. Which measure of data would make the scores appear highest? (Lesson 11-4)

History Test Scores									
77	82	65	92	77	87	100	83	77	78
45	73	67	87	82	59	75	77	68	85
82	75	87	52	87	79	85	82	87	

F mode

G mean

H median

J range

11-5 Measures of Variation

MAIN IDEA

Find the measures of variation of a set of data.

IL Learning Standards

10.A.3a Construct, read and interpret tables, graphs (including circle graphs) and charts **to organize and represent data.** **10.A.3b Compare the mean, median, mode and range,** with and **without the use of technology.**

New Vocabulary

measures of variation
quartiles
lower quartile
upper quartile
interquartile range
outlier

IL Math Online

glencoe.com

- Extra Examples
- Personal Tutor
- Self-Check Quiz

GET READY for the Lesson

TEEN SPENDING The average amount of money teens spend each week is given in the table.

1. Find the median of the data.
2. Organize the data into two groups: the top half and the bottom half. How many data values are in each group?
3. What is the median of each group?
4. Find the difference between the two numbers from Question 3.
5. Find the range of the data.
6. What does the range tell you about the amount of money spent each week for those ten countries?

Top Ten Countries Average Weekly Teen Spending	
Norway	$49.70
Sweden	$41.70
Brazil	$41.30
Argentina	$40.50
Hong Kong	$38.00
United States	$37.60
Denmark	$37.40
Singapore	$34.10
Greece	$32.90
France	$31.30

Source: Media Wiley

Measures of variation are used to describe the distribution of the data. In Lesson 11-4, you used the range to describe how "spread out" the data are. The range is one measure of variation. **Quartiles** are values that divide a set of data into four equal parts. Recall that the median separates a set of data in two equal parts.

lower half — median — upper half

$31.30 $32.90 $34.10 $37.40 $37.60 ↓ $38.00 $40.50 $41.30 $41.70 $49.70

The median of the lower half of a set of data is the **lower quartile** or LQ.

The median of the upper half of a set of data is the **upper quartile** or UQ.

So, one half of the data lie between the lower quartile and the upper quartile. Another measure of variation is the **interquartile range**.

Interquartile Range — Key Concept

The interquartile range is the range of the middle half of the data. It is the difference between the upper quartile and the lower quartile.

EXAMPLE Find Measures of Variation

1 **MOVIES Find the measures of variation for the data in the table.**

Themes of Sports Films	
Sport	**Films**
Auto Racing	85
Baseball	85
Basketball	41
Boxing	204
Football	123
Golf	24
Horse Racing	139
Wrestling	20

Source: *Top Ten of Everything*

Range 204 − 20 or 184 films

Median, Upper Quartile, and Lower Quartile

Order the numbers from least to greatest.

lower quartile ↓ median ↓ upper quartile ↓

20 24 41 85 85 123 139 204

$\frac{24+41}{2} = 32.5$ $\frac{85+85}{2} = 85$ $\frac{123+139}{2} = 131$

The median is 85, the lower quartile is 32.5, and the upper quartile is 131.

Interquartile Range upper quartile − lower quartile
= 131 − 32.5 or 98.5

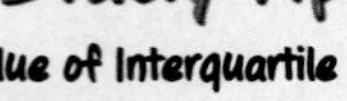

Value of Interquartile Range
A small interquartile range means that the data in the middle of the set are close together. A large interquartile range means that the data in the middle are spread out.

CHECK Your Progress

a. **ENTERTAINMENT** Determine the measures of variation for the data in the table.

DVD Prices in Dollars at Various Stores			
14.95	19.99	24.99	17.99
14.99	14.95	23.49	15.89
15.99	21.95	17.99	15.99

Data that are more than 1.5 times the value of the interquartile range beyond either quartile are called **outliers**. An outlier is a data value that is either much *larger* or much *smaller* than the median.

EXAMPLE Find Outliers

2 **WINDS Find any outliers for the data in the table.**

Find the interquartile range.
12.4 − 9.0 = 3.4

Multiply the interquartile range by 1.5.
3.4 × 1.5 = 5.1

Now subtract 5.1 from the lower quartile and add 5.1 to the upper quartile.
9.0 − **5.1** = 3.9
12.4 + **5.1** = 17.5

Average Speeds of Winds		
	Station	**Speed (mph)**
	Mt. Washington, NH	35.1
upper quartile →	Boston, MA	12.4
	Buffalo, NY	11.8
median →	Detroit, MI	10.2
	Lexington, KY	9.1
lower quartile →	Pittsburgh, PA	9.0
	Phoenix, AZ	6.2

Source: *The World Almanac*

The only outlier is 35.1 because it is greater than 17.5.

CHECK Your Progress

b. **BUILDINGS** Find any outliers for the data in the table.

Tallest Buildings (ft), Houston, Texas					
1,002	972	901	780	748	762
725	714	691	685	741	732

Real-World Link The brain of a dolphin appears to sleep one hemisphere at a time.
Source: Neuroscience for Kids

EXAMPLE Use Measures of Variation to Describe Data

3 **SLEEP Use the measures of variation to describe the data in the table at the right.**

Number of Hours of Sleep for Selected Animals	
Brown Bat	19.9
Giant Armadillo	18.1
Infant Human	16.0
Cat	12.1
Bottle-Nosed Dolphin	10.4
Gray Seal	6.2
Horse	2.9
Giraffe	1.9

Source: Neuroscience for Kids

Find the measures of variation.

The range is 19.9 − 1.9, or 18.

The median is 11.25.

The upper quartile is 17.05.

The lower quartile is 4.55.

The interquartile range is 17.05 − 4.55, or 12.5.

The spread of the data is 18 hours. The median is 11.25 hours. One fourth of the animals got at or below 4.55 hours of sleep and one fourth of the animals got at or above 17.05 hours of sleep. The number of hours of sleep for half of the animals was in the interval 4.55–17.05.

CHECK Your Progress

c. **CYCLING** Use the measures of variation to describe the data in the table at the right.

Number of Tour de France Wins	
France	36
Belgium	18
Italy	9
Spain	8
United States	8

Source: *World Almanac for Kids*

CHECK Your Understanding

LANGUAGE For Exercises 1–5, use the data in the table on the right.

U.S. Non-English Language Spoken at Home	
Language	**Speakers (millions)**
Spanish	28.1
Chinese	2.0
French	1.6
German	1.4
Tagalog	1.2
Vietnamese	1.0
Italian	1.0
Korean	0.9

Source: U.S. Census Bureau

Example 1 (p. 600)

1. Determine the range of the data.
2. Find the median and the upper and lower quartiles.
3. What is the interquartile range of the data?

Example 2 (p. 600)

4. Identify any outliers.

Example 3 (p. 601)

5. Use the measures of variation to describe the data in the table.

Practice and Problem Solving

HOMEWORK HELP	
For Exercises	**See Examples**
6, 7, 10, 11, 14, 15, 18, 19	1
8, 12, 16, 20	2
9, 13, 17, 21	3

SYRUP For Exercises 6–9, use the data in the table at the right.

Annual Production of Maple Syrup (gallons)	
Vermont	430,000
Maine	265,000
New York	210,000
Wisconsin	76,000
Michigan	59,000

Source: *World Almanac for Kids*

6. What is the range of the data?
7. Find the median, the upper and lower quartiles, and the interquartile range of the data.
8. Identify any outliers.
9. Use the measures of variation to describe the data in the table.

EXERCISE For Exercises 10–13, use the data in the table at the right.

Calories Burned per Minute of Exercise	
Jogging (6 mph)	8
Jumping Rope	7
Basketball	7
Soccer	6
Bicycling (9.4 mph)	5
Downhill Skiing	5
Walking (4 mph)	4

Source: *World Almanac for Kids*

10. What is the range of the data?
11. Find the median, upper and lower quartiles, and the interquartile range of the data.
12. Identify any outliers.
13. Use the measures of variation to describe the data in the table.

SPACE For Exercises 14–17, use the data in the table at the right.

Number of U.S. Shuttle Launches 1981–2005	
1981–1985	23
1986–1990	15
1991–1995	28
1996–2000	28
2001–2005	13

Source: NASA

14. What is the range of the data?
15. Find the median, upper and lower quartiles, and the interquartile range for the data.
16. Identify any outliers.
17. Use the measures of variation to describe the data in the table.

Real-World Link Crustaceans, insects, and spiders are all arthropods. There are about 750,000 species of insects alone.
Source: *World Almanac for Kids*

ANIMALS For Exercises 18–21, use the data in the table at the right.

Number of Species in the Animal Kingdom	
Arthropods	1,100,000
Fish	24,500
Birds	9,000
Mammals	9,000
Reptiles	8,000
Amphibians	5,000

Source: *World Almanac for Kids*

18. What is the range of the data?
19. Find the median, upper and lower quartiles, and the interquartile range for the data.
20. Identify any outliers.
21. Use the measures of variation to describe the data in the table.

22. **GOLF** Brandon's golf scores relative to par were −1, −2, 4, −6, 3, −1, and −3. Rashan's scores were −5, 5, 0, 4, −1, −4, and −3. Find the measures of variation of both person's scores. Then describe any similarities or differences in the measures of variation.

Real-World Link The Verrazano Narrows Bridge in New York City is the longest bridge in the United States. Each of its two towers weighs 27,000 tons.

Source: Metropolitan Transit Authority

RIVERS For Exercises 23–27, use the table at the right.

23. Which continent has a greater range of length of rivers?
24. Find the measures of variation for each continent.
25. Compare the modes and the interquartile ranges of the length of rivers.
26. Select the appropriate measure of central tendency or range to describe the length of rivers for each continent. Justify your response.
27. Describe the length of rivers of Africa and South America, using both the measures of central tendency and variation.

Length (miles) of Principal Rivers			
Africa		South America	
4,160	700	4,000	1,300
2,900	660	2,485	1,100
2,590	500	2,100	1,000
1,700		2,013	1,000
1,300		1,988	1,000
1,100		1,750	956
1,100		1,677	910
1,020		1,600	808
1,000		1,584	400
1,000		1,400	150

Source: *The World Almanac*

EARTHQUAKES For Exercises 28–30, use the line plot.

28. Find the range, mean, median, mode, upper and lower quartiles, and the interquartile range for the data.
29. Identify any outliers.
30. Use the measures of variation to describe the data in the table.

Magnitude of Earthquakes in the Central U.S. for September 2005

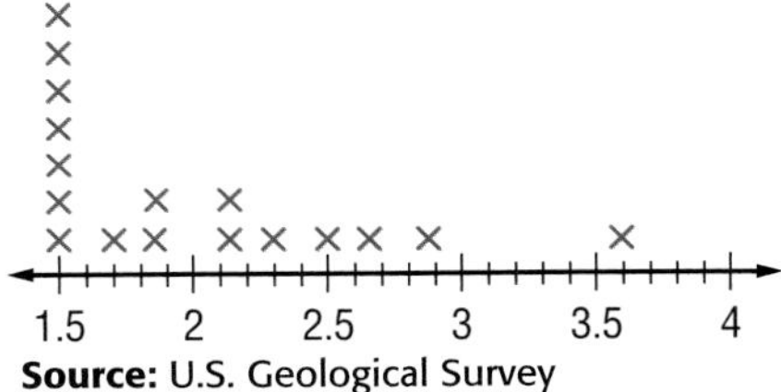

Source: U.S. Geological Survey

BRIDGES For Exercises 31–33, use the table at the right.

31. Find the length of the Golden Gate Bridge if the median is 4,000 feet.
32. Find the length of the Akashi Kaikyo Bridge if the range is 2,566 feet.
33. The 11th longest suspension bridge in the world is the Tagus River Bridge in Portugal, with a length of 3,323 feet. Describe how the measures of variation are affected if this data value is included.

10 Longest Suspension Bridges in the World		
Bridge	Country	Length (ft)
Akashi Kaikyo	Japan	y
Great Belt Link	Denmark	5,328
Humber River	England	4,626
Verrazano Narrows	United States	4,260
Golden Gate	United States	x
Mackinac Straits	United States	3,800
Minami Bian-Seto	Japan	3,668
Second Bosphorous	Turkey	3,576
First Bosphorous	Turkey	3,524
George Washington	United States	3,500

Source: *Structural Steel Designer's Handbook*

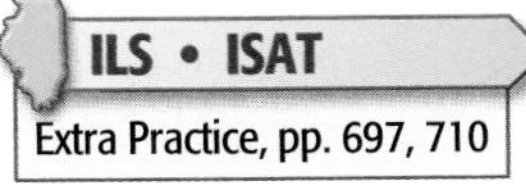

Extra Practice, pp. 697, 710

34. **FIND THE DATA** Refer to the Data File on pages 16–19. Choose some data and write a real-world problem in which you would determine measures of central tendency and measures of variation.

H.O.T. Problems

35. **OPEN ENDED** Create a list of data with at least eight numbers that has an interquartile range of 20 and one outlier.

36. **CHALLENGE** Create two different sets of data that have the same range but different interquartile ranges. Then create two different sets of data that have the same median and same quartiles, but different ranges.

37. **WRITING IN MATH** Explain why the interquartile range is not affected by very high or low values in the data.

ISAT PRACTICE 10.A.3a, 10.A.3b

38. Which of the following statements is never true concerning the measures of variation of a set of data?

    A Half the data lie within the interquartile range.

    B Three fourths of the data lie above the lower quartile.

    C The median, the lower quartile, and the upper quartile separate the data into three equal parts.

    D 50% of the data lie below the median.

39. The number of Grand Slam singles titles won by twelve tennis players are 14, 8, 7, 6, 5, 5, 10, 11, 8, 8, 6, and 7. Which of the following statements is *not* supported by these data?

    F Half of the titles won are below 7.5 and half are above 7.5.

    G The spread of the data is 9 titles.

    H An outlier of the data is 11 titles.

    J About one fourth of the titles won are at or above 9 titles.

Spiral Review

40. **HEIGHTS** The heights, in inches, of the Allen family are 72, 68, 48, 71, and 67. Find the mean, median, mode, and range. Round to the nearest tenth if necessary. (Lesson 11-4)

41. **NATIONAL PARKS** Wyoming has 3,159 square miles of Yellowstone National Park while Montana has 264 square miles and Idaho has 49 square miles. Construct a circle graph to show what part of Yellowstone National Park is in each state. (Lesson 11-3)

MEASUREMENT Find the area of each figure. Round to the nearest tenth. (Lesson 7-2)

42.

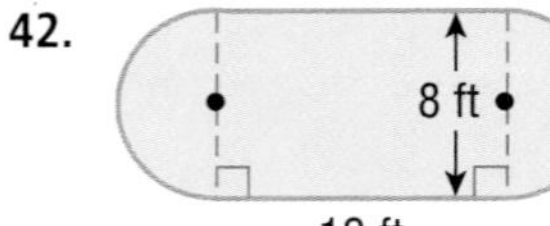

43.

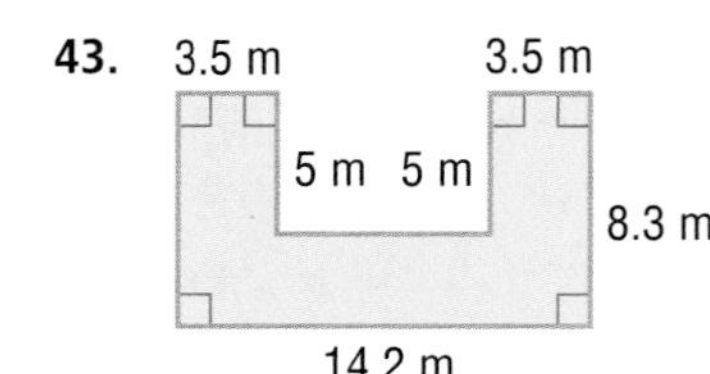

GET READY for the Next Lesson

PREREQUISITE SKILL Graph each set of points on a number line. (Lesson 1-3)

44. {3, 5, 8, 9, 10}
45. {13, 15, 20, 27, 31}
46. {9, 13, 16, 17, 21}
47. {3, 9, 10, 15, 19}

Box-and-Whisker Plots

MAIN IDEA

Display and interpret data in a box-and-whisker plot.

IL Learning Standards

10.A.3a Construct, read and interpret tables, graphs (including circle graphs) and charts **to organize and represent data.**
10.A.3c Test the reasonableness of an argument based on data and communicate their findings.

New Vocabulary

box-and-whisker plot

IL Math Online

glencoe.com

- Extra Examples
- Personal Tutor
- Self-Check Quiz

GET READY for the Lesson

ELEVATION The table gives the elevation of several cities.

1. What is the least value in the data?
2. What is the lower quartile of the data?
3. What is the median of the data?
4. What is the upper quartile of the data?
5. What is the greatest value in the data?
6. Name any outliers.

Elevation of Selected United States Cities

City	Elevation (feet)
Mobile, AL	209
Baltimore, MD	193
Richmond, VA	164
Hartford, CT	162
New York, NY	158
Anchorage, AK	130
Atlantic City, NJ	114
Wilmington, DE	92

Source: *The World Almanac*

A **box-and-whisker plot** uses a number line to show the distribution of a set of data. The *box* is drawn around the quartile values, and the *whiskers* extend from each quartile to the extreme data points that are not outliers.

EXAMPLE Construct a Box-and-Whisker Plot

1 **ELEVATION Use the data in the table above to construct a box-and-whisker plot.**

Step 1 Draw a number line that includes the least and greatest number in the data.

Step 2 Mark the extremes, the median, and the upper and lower quartile above the number line.

Step 3 Draw the box and the whiskers.

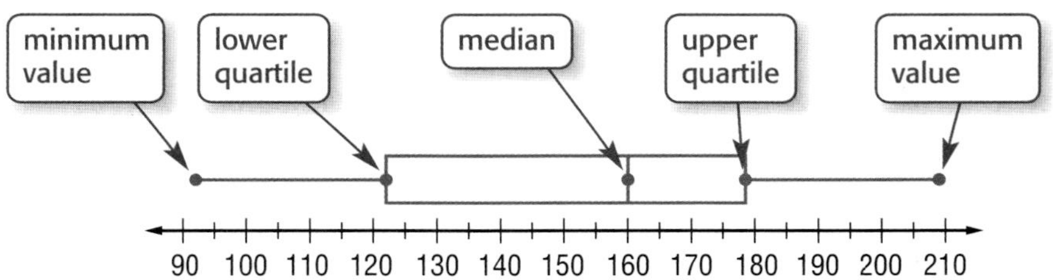

CHECK Your Progress

Construct a box-and-whisker plot for each set of data.

a. Prices, in dollars, of admission to a hockey game:
42, 38, 42, 45, 43, 65, 55, 50, 34, 36, 40, 35

b. Low temperatures for various cities:
52, 58, 67, 63, 47, 44, 52, 28, 49, 65, 52, 59

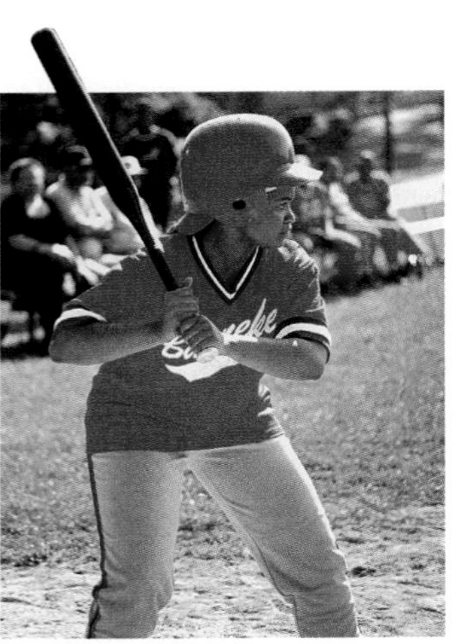

Box-and-whisker plots separate data into four parts. Although the parts usually differ in length, each part contains one fourth of the data.

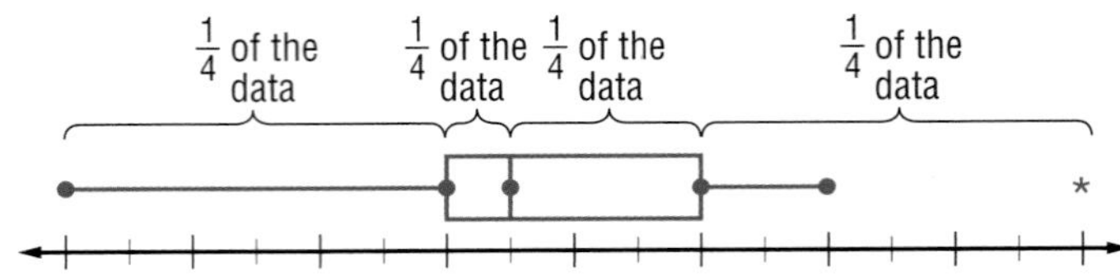

A long whisker or box indicates that the data have a greater range. A short whisker or box indicates the data have a lesser range. An asterisk (*) indicates an outlier and is not connected to be part of a whisker.

Real-World Link According to a recent survey, about 5 million girls, ages 6–17, listed softball as their favorite sport.
Source: *World Almanac for Kids*

EXAMPLE Interpret Data

2 **SOFTBALL** **What does the length of the box-and-whisker plot tell you about the data?**

Home Runs Hit in a Softball Season

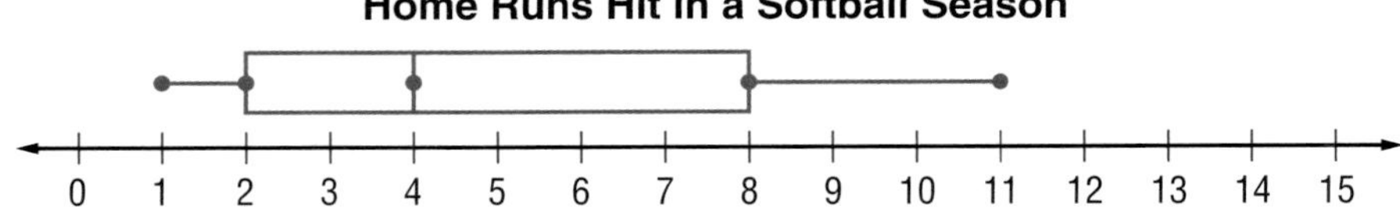

The data between the median and the upper quartile are more spread out than the data between the median and the lower quartile. The whisker at the right is longer than the whisker at the left, so the data above the upper quartile are more spread out than the data below the lower quartile.

CHECK Your Progress

c. **WORK** Compare data between the median and the upper quartile and the data between the median and the lower quartile.

Average Daily Commute Time (minutes) to Work for Selected U.S. States

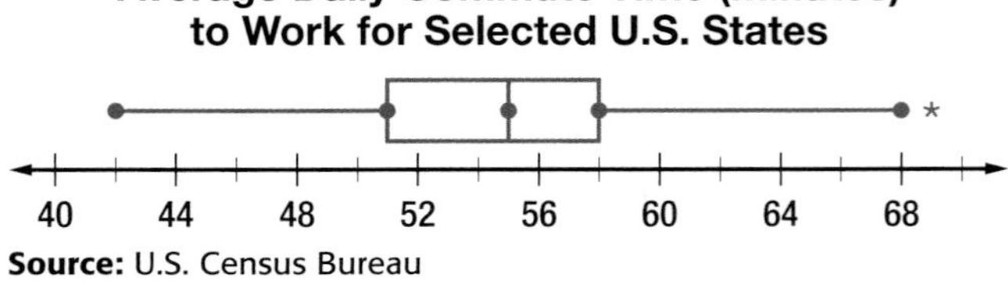

Source: U.S. Census Bureau

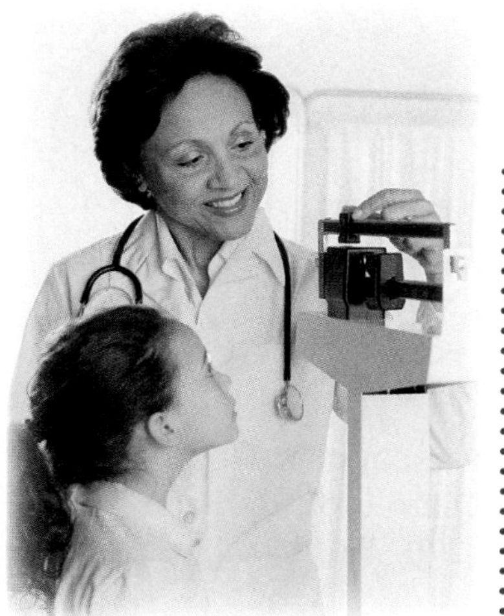

Real-World Career
How Does a Pediatrician Use Math?
Pediatricians chart the growth of infants, children, and adolescents. They use this information to monitor proper growth and development.

IL Math Online

For more information, go to glencoe.com.

EXAMPLE Compare Data

3 **HEIGHT Refer to the double box-and-whisker plot below that shows the height of girls and boys in a class. Compare the heights of the girls versus the boys.**

In general, the girls are shorter than the boys. The upper quartile for the girl's height is 67 inches, meaning 75% of the girls were 67 inches or shorter. The lower quartile for the boys is 66 inches, meaning 75% of the boys were at least 66 inches tall.

CHECK Your Progress

d. **HEIGHT** In the double box-and-whisker plot above, what percent of the girls and what percent of the boys are 67 inches or shorter?

CHECK Your Understanding

Example 1 (p. 605)

Draw a box-and-whisker plot for each set of data.

1. Hours per month volunteering at the community center: 38, 43, 36, 37, 32, 37, 29, 51
2. Points earned on a test: 100, 70, 70, 90, 50, 90, 50, 90, 100, 50, 90, 100, 90, 50, 25, 80

Example 2 (p. 606)

FISH For Exercises 3 and 4, use the following box-and-whisker plot.

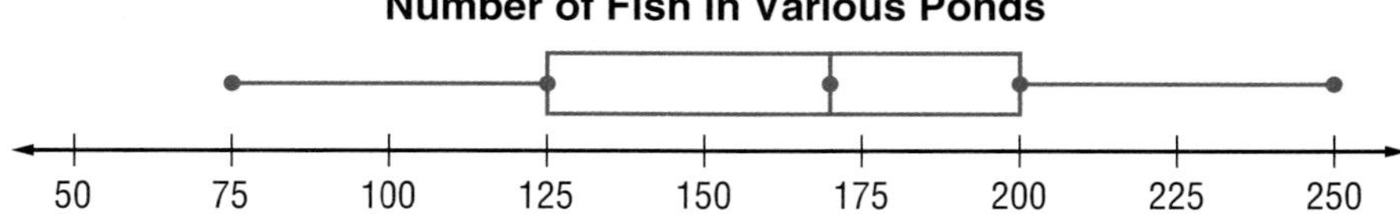

3. What is the interquartile range of the data?
4. Three fourths of the ponds have at least how many fish?

Example 3 (p. 607)

5. **BASEBALL** Refer to the box-and-whisker plot. In which league did more than half of the teams win more games than the other league? Justify your reasoning.

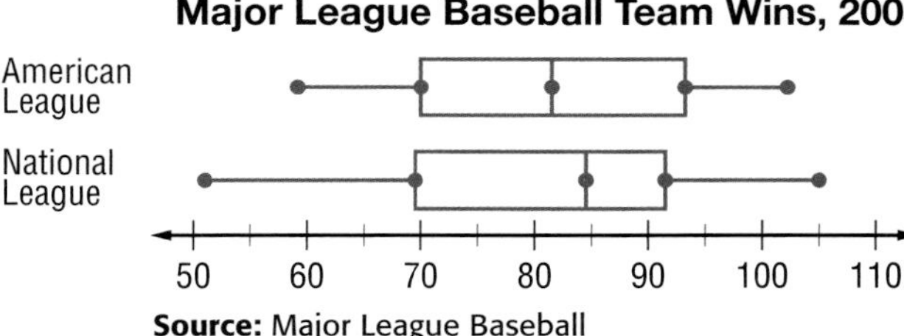

Practice and Problem Solving

For Exercises	See Examples
6–9	1
10–13, 15	2
14, 16–18	3

Construct a box-and-whisker plot for each set of data.

6. Ages of persons in line for a jazz concert:
49, 45, 55, 32, 28, 53, 26, 38, 35, 35, 51

7. Number of miles between rest stops on a highway:
77, 85, 72, 76, 95, 90, 73, 82, 82, 80, 73

8. Speed, in miles per hour, of commercial airliners:
540, 460, 520, 350, 500, 480, 475, 525, 450, 515

9. Prices, in dollars, of plane tickets from Detroit to Atlanta:
225, 245, 220, 270, 350, 280, 230, 240, 225, 270

HISTORY For Exercises 10 and 11, use the box-and-whisker plot at the right.

Population of Thirteen Original States, 1790 (thousands)

100 200 300 400 500 600 700

Source: U.S. Census Bureau

10. Approximately what percent of the states had populations greater than 100,000?

11. How does the length of the whisker after the upper quartile represent the data?

ZOOS For Exercises 12 and 13, use the following box-and-whisker plot.

Areas (acres) of the Ten Largest Zoos in the United States

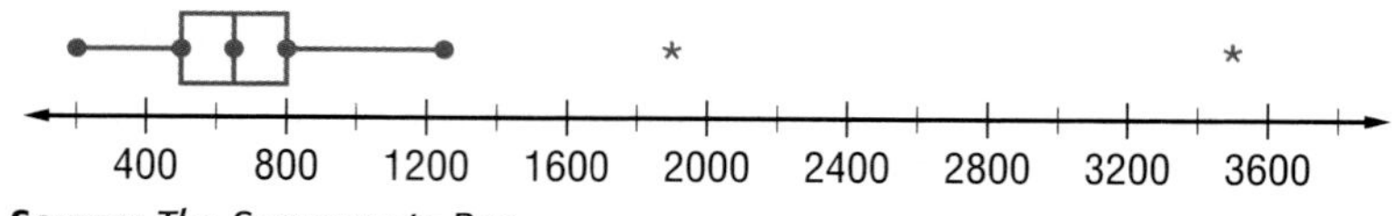

Source: *The Sacramento Bee*

12. How many outliers are in the data?

13. Describe the distribution of the data. What can you say about the areas of the major zoos in the U.S.?

ROLLER COASTERS For Exercises 14–18, use the box-and-whisker plot below.

Speed (miles per hour) of Roller Coasters

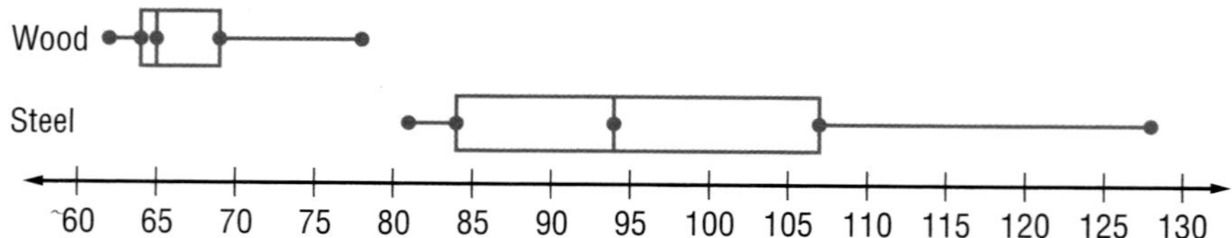

14. Which set of data has a greater range?

15. How many outliers are in the data?

16. What percent of wood roller coasters travel at least 69 miles per hour?

17. What percent of steel roller coasters travel at least 84 miles per hour?

18. In general, do metal roller coasters travel faster or slower than wood roller coasters? Justify your reasoning.

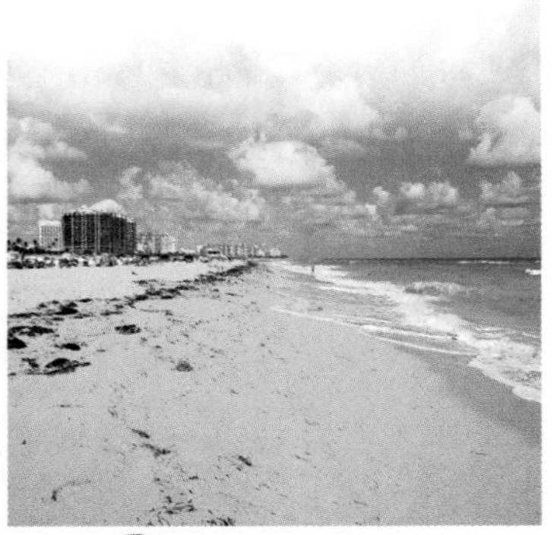

Real-World Link Florida, the "Sunshine State," actually ranks sixth in the average number of sunny days per year. In fact, Florida has more partly cloudy days than anywhere else in the United States.

Source: *Washington Times*

PARKS For Exercises 19 and 20, use the table at the right.

19. Construct a box-and-whisker plot for the set of data. Then determine in which interval the data are the most spread out.

20. Describe how the box-and-whisker plot would change if the data for California and Florida were not included.

State and National Parkland of Selected States

State	Total Acres per 10 Square Miles of Land
California	616.6
Florida	611.2
Arizona	412.8
Michigan	176.6
North Carolina	172.8
Minnesota	79.5
Texas	72.7
Ohio	58.3
Georgia	25.1

Source: Indiana Chamber

WEATHER For Exercises 21–23, use the box-and-whisker plot below.

Average Number of Sunny Days Per Year for Selected U.S. Cities

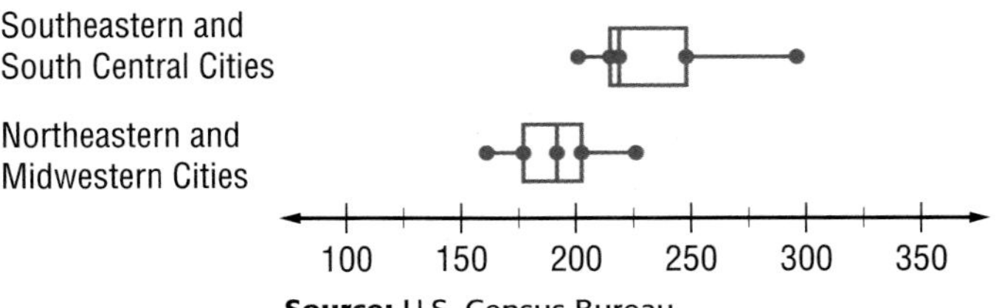

Source: U.S. Census Bureau

21. What percent of the data for the Southeastern and South Central cities is above the lower quartile for the Northeastern and Midwestern cities?

22. Boston, Massachusetts, has an average number of 98 sunny days a year. If this city is added to the data for the Northeastern and Midwestern cities, describe how the box-and-whisker plots would change.

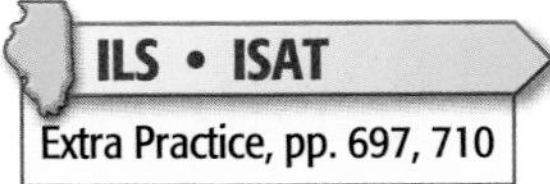

23. Write one or two sentences comparing the average number of sunny days of Southeastern and South Central U.S. cities versus Northeastern and Midwestern U.S. cities.

H.O.T. Problems

24. **OPEN ENDED** Write a set of data that could be represented by the box-and-whisker plot at the right.

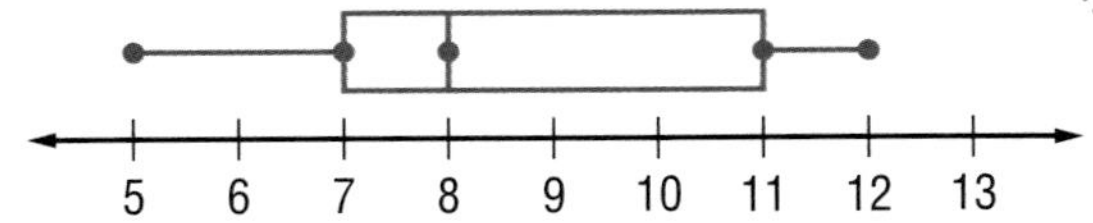

25. **FIND THE ERROR** Ebony and Chance are making a box-and-whisker plot for the following set of data. Who is correct? Explain.

72, 85, 89, 90, 90, 95, 97, 97, 98, 99, 99

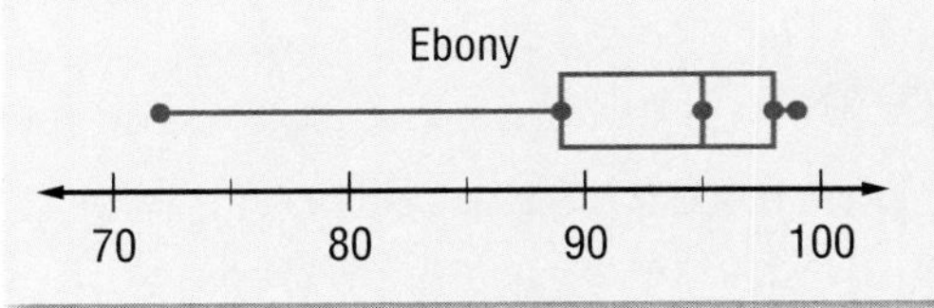

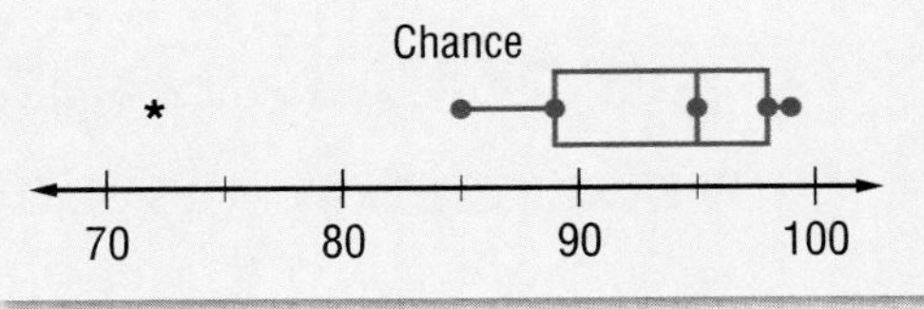

26. **REASONING** The lower quartile, median, and upper quartile of a data set are x, y, and 70, respectively. If a box-and-whisker plot were to be made from this data, give possible values for x and y according to each of the following conditions.

a. The median separates the box into two equal parts.

b. The box between the median and the upper quartile is twice as long as the box between the median and the lower quartile.

27. **WRITING IN MATH** Explain the advantage of using a box-and-whisker plot to display data.

ISAT PRACTICE 10.A.3a, 10.A.3c

28. Which box-and-whisker plot represents the data set 18, 22, 31, 25, 30, 19, 26, 24, and 35?

A
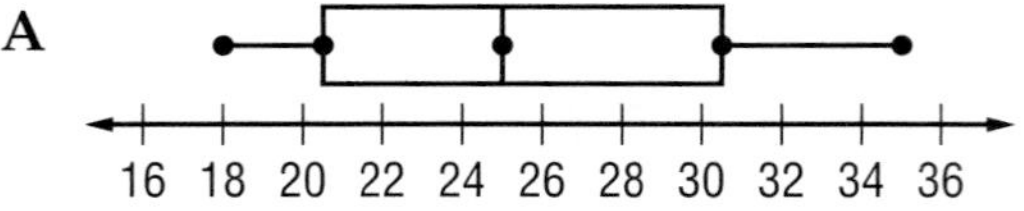

B
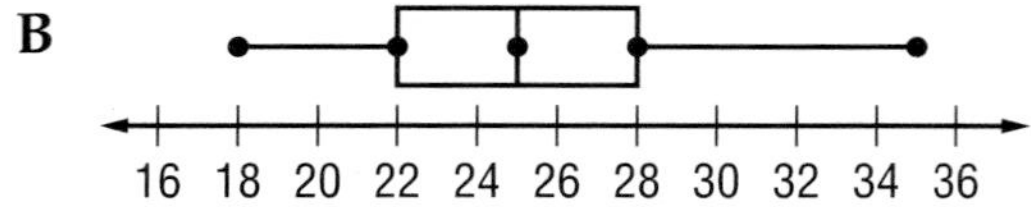

C
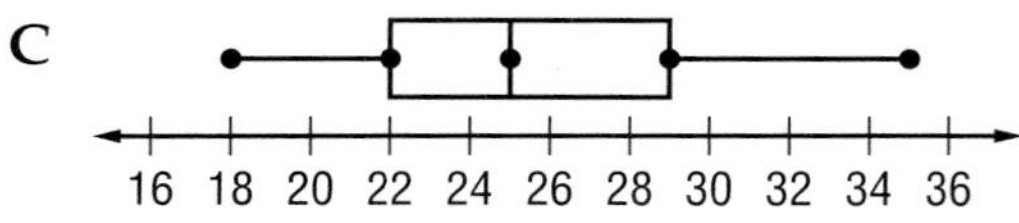

D
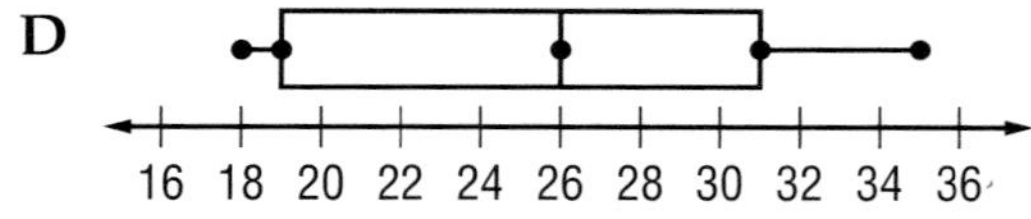

29. Which of the following statements is *not* true concerning the box-and-whisker plot below?

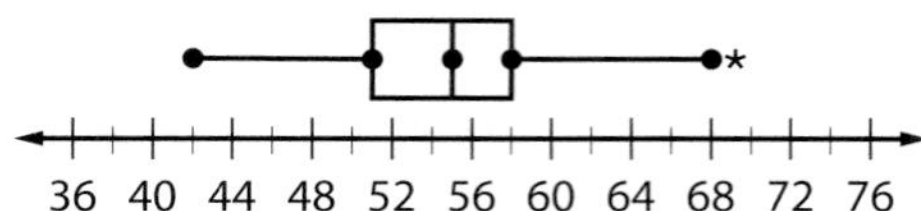

F The value 69 is an outlier.

G Half of the data is above 55.

H $\frac{1}{4}$ of the data is in the interval 58–69.

J There are more data values in the interval 42–51 than there are in the interval 55–58.

Spiral Review

Find the range, median, upper and lower quartiles, interquartile range, and any outliers for each set of data. (Lesson 11-5)

30. 73, 52, 31, 54, 46, 28, 47, 49, 58

31. 87, 63, 84, 94, 89, 74, 50, 85, 91, 78, 99, 81, 77, 86, 65, 81, 74

32. **TEMPERATURES** Find the mean, median, mode, and range of the temperatures 76, 65, 91, 34, 23, 45, 74, 65, 82, 31, 65 and 24 degrees. Round to the nearest tenth if necessary. (Lesson 11-4)

GET READY for the Next Lesson

PREREQUISITE SKILL Make a line plot for each set of data. (Page 749)

33. 2, 5, 9, 8, 2, 6, 2, 5, 8, 10

34. 14, 12, 9, 7, 12, 10, 14, 7, 8, 12

Graphing Calculator Lab
Box-and-Whisker Plots

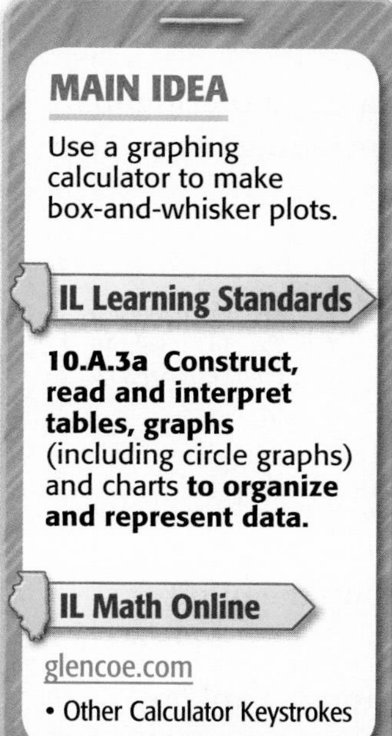

MAIN IDEA

Use a graphing calculator to make box-and-whisker plots.

IL Learning Standards

10.A.3a Construct, read and interpret tables, graphs (including circle graphs) and charts **to organize and represent data.**

IL Math Online

glencoe.com

• Other Calculator Keystrokes

You can create a box-and-whisker plot using a graphing calculator.

ACTIVITY

Make a box-and-whisker plot of the data at the right. It shows the grades on Miss Romero's last math test.

Miss Romero's Math Test Scores							
78	94	85	92	72	56	89	92
90	84	98	82	75	100	94	87
92	85	94	70	78	95	70	80

STEP 1 Clear list L1 by pressing STAT ENTER ▲ CLEAR ENTER. Then enter the data into L1. Input each number and press ENTER.

STEP 2 Press 2nd [STAT PLOT] ENTER to choose the first plot. Highlight On, the modified box-and-whisker plot for the type, L1 for the Xlist, and 1 as the frequency.

STEP 3 Press WINDOW and choose an appropriate range for the x values. The window 50 to 110 with a scale of 4 includes all of these data.

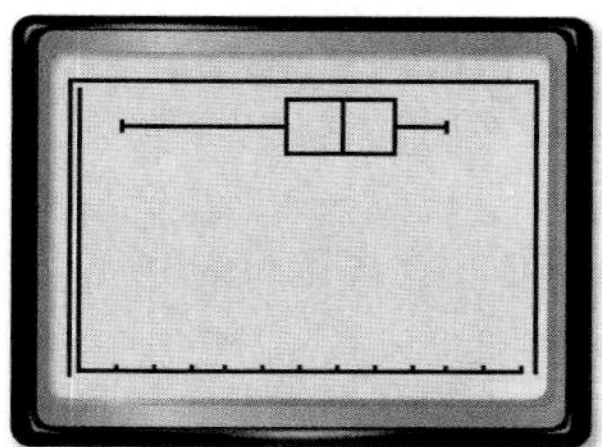

STEP 4 Press GRAPH. Press TRACE and the arrow keys to determine the five key data points of your graph.

ANALYZE THE RESULTS

1. What are the values of the five key data points of the graph? What do they represent?
2. What percent of the test scores are below 78?
3. What percent of the test scores are above the median? What percent of the test scores are below the median?
4. What percent of the scores are between 56 and 86?
5. Suppose you earned a grade of 80. Describe what percent of students scored higher and what percent scored lower than you.

11-7 Stem-and-Leaf Plots

MAIN IDEA

Display data in stem-and-leaf plots. Interpret data in stem-and-leaf plots.

IL Learning Standards

10.A.3a Construct, read and interpret tables, graphs (including circle graphs) and charts **to organize and represent data.**
10.A.3c Test the reasonableness of an argument based on data and communicate their findings.

New Vocabulary

stem-and-leaf plot
stems
leaves
back-to-back stem-and-leaf plot

IL Math Online

glencoe.com

- Extra Examples
- Personal Tutor
- Self-Check Quiz

GET READY for the Lesson

An elector is a voter that represents his or her state in a presidential election. The number of electors for each state, including the District of Columbia, is shown in the table below.

Number of Electors								
AL: 9	CT: 7	ID: 4	LA: 9	MS: 6	NJ: 15	OK: 7	TN: 11	WV: 5
AK: 3	DE: 3	IL: 21	ME: 4	MO: 11	NM: 5	OR: 7	TX: 34	WI: 10
AZ: 10	DC: 3	IN: 11	MD: 10	MT: 3	NY: 31	PA: 21	UT: 5	WY: 3
AR: 6	FL: 27	IA: 7	MA: 12	NE: 5	NC: 15	RI: 4	VT: 3	
CA: 55	GA: 15	KS: 6	MI: 17	NV: 5	ND: 3	SC: 8	VA: 13	
CO: 9	HI: 4	KY: 8	MN: 10	NH: 4	OH: 20	SD: 3	WA: 11	

Source: *The World Almanac*

Write each number on a self-stick note. Then group the numbers: 0–9, 10–19, 20–29, 30–39, 40–49, 50–59.

1. Is there an equal number of electors in each group? Explain.
2. Name an advantage of displaying the data in groups.

In a **stem-and-leaf plot**, numerical data are listed in ascending or descending order. The digits in the greatest place value of the data are used for the **stems**. The digits in the next greatest place value form the **leaves**.

Real-World EXAMPLE Draw a Stem-and-Leaf Plot

1 **OLYMPICS The table shows the total points scored in the first beach volleyball match played by each team in the 2004 Olympics. Display the data for the men's teams in a stem-and-leaf plot.**

Beach Volleyball Scores		
Country	**Men**	**Women**
Greece	52	47
United States	61	42
Brazil	42	42
Canada	44	42
South Africa	60	17
Cuba	50	54
Germany	55	52
Australia	42	42
Switzerland	49	29
Norway	46	37

Source: Athens 2004

Step 1 Find the least and the greatest number. Then identify the greatest place value digit in each number.

- The least number, 42, has 4 in the tens place.
- The greatest number, 61, has 6 in the tens place.

Step 2 Draw a vertical line and write the stems from 4 to 6 to the left of the line.

Stem	Leaf
4	
5	
6	

Step 3 Write the leaves to the right of the the corresponding stem on the *other* side of the line. For example, for 42, write 2 to the right of 4.

Stem	Leaf
4	2 4 2 9 6
5	2 0 5
6	1 0

Step 4 Rearrange the leaves so they are ordered from least to greatest. Repeat a leaf as often as it occurs. Then include a key to explain how to interpret the data.

Beach Volleyball Scores

Stem	Leaf
4	2 2 4 6 9
5	0 2 5
6	0 1

5|2 = 52 points

CHECK Your Progress

a. Display the data for the women's teams in a stem-and-leaf plot.

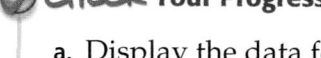

Real-World Link The first president was George Washington. He was 57 years old at the time of his inauguration. He served as president from 1789 to 1797 and earned $25,000 per year.
Source: *Info Please*

Real-World EXAMPLE Interpret Data

2 **PRESIDENTS The stem-and-leaf plot lists the ages of the U.S. Presidents at the time of their first inauguration.**

Age at Inauguration

Stem	Leaf
4	2 3 6 6 7 8 9 9
5	0 0 1 1 1 1 2 2 4 4 4 4 4 5 5 5 5 6 6 6 7 7 7 7 8
6	0 1 1 1 2 4 4 6 8 9

5|0 = 50 years

Source: *The World Almanac*

Based on the data, what inferences can be made about the ages of the U.S. Presidents at their first inauguration?

- Most of the data occur in the 50–59 interval.
- The youngest age is 42. The oldest age is 69. The range is 27.
- The median age is 55.

CHECK Your Progress

Refer to the stem-and-leaf plot in Example 1.

b. In which interval(s) do most of the scores occur?

c. What is the range of the data?

d. What is the median score?

Two sets of data can be compared using a **back-to-back stem-and-leaf plot**. The back-to-back stem-and-leaf plot below shows the scores of two basketball teams for the games in one season.

The leaves for one set of data are on one side of the stem.

Points Scored

Falcons	Stem	Cardinals
7 6 5 5 4 2 2 2	6	4 2
8 8 8 5 4	7	0 2 2 5 7 9
1 0 0	8	1 3 4 6 8 9 9

1|8 = 81 points *8|6 = 86 points*

The leaves for the other set of data are on the other side of the stem.

Real-World EXAMPLE Compare Data

3 **WEATHER The average monthly temperatures for Helena, Montana, and Seattle, Washington, are shown. Which city has more varied temperatures? Explain.**

The data for Helena are spread out, while the data for Seattle are clustered. So, Helena has the more varied temperatures.

Average Monthly Temperatures

Seattle, WA	Stem	Helena, MT
	2	0 1 6
	3	2 4
7 6 4 2 1	4	3 5
6 4 0	5	3 5
6 5 1 1	6	2 7 9

1|6 = 61° *4|5 = 45°*

CHECK Your Progress **Use the test score data below.**

e. Which class had higher test scores? Explain.

f. Which class had more varied test scores? Explain.

3rd Period	Stem	7th Period
8 8 3 2 2	7	3
7 6 3 1 0 0	8	1 2 5 6 6 8 9 9
3 2 1 1 0	9	0 2 2 3 3 3 3 5 6

8|7 = 78% *7|3 = 73%*

CHECK Your Understanding

Example 1 (pp. 612–613)

Display each set of data in a stem-and-leaf plot.

1.

Average Life Span					
Animal	**Years**	**Animal**	**Years**	**Animal**	**Years**
Asian Elephant	40	African Elephant	35	Lion	15
Horse	20	Red Fox	7	Chipmunk	6
Moose	12	Cow	15	Hippopotamus	41

Source: *The World Almanac*

2.

Summer Paralympic Games Participating Countries												
Year	'60	'64	'68	'72	'76	'80	'84	'88	'92	'96	'00	'04
Countries	23	22	29	44	42	42	42	61	82	103	128	136

Source: International Paralympic Committee

Example 2 (p. 613)

SCHOOL For Exercises 3–5, use the test score data shown at the right.

3. Find the lowest and highest scores.
4. What is the median score?
5. Write a statement that describes the data.

Test Scores

Stem	Leaf
5	0 9
6	4 5 7 8
7	0 4 4 5 5 6 7 8 8
8	2 3 3 5 7 8
9	0 1 5 5 9

5|9 = 59%

Example 3 (p. 614)

FOOD For Exercises 6 and 7, use the food data shown in the back-to-back stem-and-leaf plot.

6. What is the greatest number of fat grams in each sandwich?
7. In general, which type of sandwich has a lower amount of fat? Explain.

Fat (g) of Various Burgers and Chicken Sandwiches

Chicken		Burgers
8	0	
9 8 5 5 3 3	1	0 5 9
0	2	0 6
	3	0 3 6

8|0 = 8 g *2|6 = 26 g*

Practice and Problem Solving

HOMEWORK HELP	
For Exercises	See Examples
8–9	1
10–15	2
16–19	3

Display each set of data in a stem-and-leaf plot.

8.

State Representatives Largest States	
State	Number
California	53
Florida	25
Illinois	19
Michigan	15
New York	29
Ohio	18
Pennsylvania	19
Texas	32

Source: *The World Almanac*

9.

2005–2006 Big 12 Women's Softball	
University	Wins
Baylor	38
Iowa State	23
Kansas	36
Missouri	26
Nebraska	44
Oklahoma	40
Oklahoma State	21
Texas	55
Texas A&M	34
Texas Tech	19

Source: Big 12 Sports

ANALYZE TABLES For Exercises 10–15, use the table shown.

10. What is the mean number of home runs hit by a single season home run leader?
11. Display the number of home runs in a stem-and-leaf plot.
12. What is the most home runs hit between 1994 and 2005?
13. How many of the season leaders hit fewer than 50 home runs?
14. What is the median number of home runs hit by a single season home run leader?
15. Write a sentence that describes the data.

National League Single Season Home Run Leaders, 1994–2005		
Year	Player	Home Runs
1994	Matt Williams	43
1995	Dante Bichette	40
1996	Andres Galarraga	47
1997	Larry Walker	49
1998	Mark McGwire	70
1999	Mark McGwire	65
2000	Sammy Sosa	50
2001	Barry Bonds	73
2002	Sammy Sosa	49
2003	Jim Thome	47
2004	Adrian Beltre	48
2005	Andruw Jones	51
2006	Ryan Howard	58

Source: Major League Baseball

Real-World Link The Louisiana Tech women's basketball team has the best-winning percentage in Division I. Over a 31-year period, the team has 873 wins and 149 losses.
Source: NCAA

ANALYZE TABLES For Exercises 16–19, use the information shown in the back-to-back stem-and-leaf plot.

NCAA Women's Basketball Statistics Overall Games Won, 2006–2007

Big Ten Conference	Stem	Big East Conference
8 7 7 7 6 6 3 2	0	2 3 3 3 4 6 8 9 9
5 4 3	1	0 0 0 1 2 2 6
$3 \vert 1 = 13$		$1 \vert 0 = 10$

16. What is the greatest number of games won by a Big Ten Conference team?
17. What is the least number of games won by a Big East Conference team?
18. How many teams are in the Big East Conference?
19. Compare the median number of games won by each conference.

ILS • ISAT
Extra Practice, pp. 698, 710

H.O.T. Problems

20. **COLLECT THE DATA** Display the foot lengths, in inches, of the students in your class in a stem-and-leaf plot. Then write a few sentences that analyze the data.

21. **CHALLENGE** Create a stem-and-leaf plot of at least 10 pieces of data in which the maximum value is 70, the range is 50, and the median is 25.

22. **WRITING IN MATH** Data about the ages of U.S. Presidents on their inauguration can be displayed in both a histogram and in a stem-and-leaf plot. Discuss the advantages and disadvantages of using each display.

ISAT PRACTICE 10.A.3a, 10.A.3c

23. The back-to-back stem-and-leaf plot shows the amount of protein in certain foods.

Amount of Protein (g)

Dairy Products	Stem	Legumes, Nuts, Seeds
9 8 8 7 7 6 2 2	0	5 6 9
0	1	4 5 8
6	2	
	3	9

6 | 2 = 26 grams *3 | 9 = 39 grams*

Which of the following is a true statement?

A The median amount of protein in dairy products is 9 grams.

B The difference between the greatest and least amount of protein in dairy products is 28 grams.

C The average amount of protein in legumes, nuts, and seeds is more than the average amount in dairy products.

D The greatest amount of protein in legumes, nuts, and seeds is 93 grams.

Spiral Review

Draw a box-and-whisker plot for each set of data. (Lesson 11-6)

24. 22, 25, 36, 42, 33, 76, 45, 53, 44, 36, 37, 29

25. 61, 67, 76, 72, 56, 53, 61, 24, 58, 74, 61, 68

RIVERS For Exercises 26–28, use the table at the right. (Lesson 11-5)

26. Determine the measures of variation for the data.

27. Find any outliers of the data.

28. Use the measures of variation to describe the data.

Major U.S. Rivers

River	Length (mi)
Arkansas	1,459
Colorado	1,450
Columbia	1,243
Mississippi	2,348
Ohio	981
Rio Grande	1,900

Source: *The World Almanac*

GET READY for the Next Lesson

PREREQUISITE SKILL Find the mean and median for each set of data. (Lesson 11-4)

29. 75, 66, 67, 85, 86, 74, 74, 62, 72

30. 20, 28, 21, 16, 16, 15, 20, 21, 56, 17, 16, 18

11-8 Select an Appropriate Display

MAIN IDEA

Select an appropriate display for a set of data.

IL Learning Standards

10.A.3a Construct, read and interpret tables, graphs (including circle graphs) and charts **to organize and represent data.**
10.A.3c Test the reasonableness of an argument based on data and communicate their findings.

IL Math Online

glencoe.com

- Concepts In Motion
- Extra Examples

GET READY for the Lesson

WEATHER Mr. Watkin's class charted the high temperatures in various cities. The following graphs are four ways they displayed the daily high temperatures.

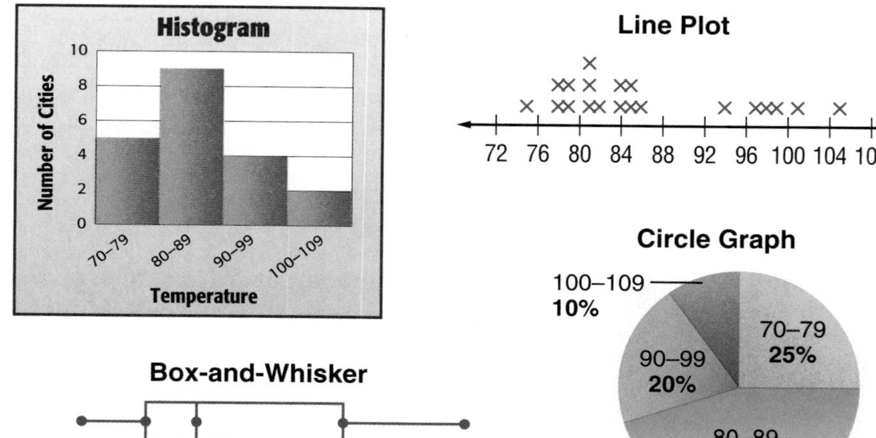

1. Which display(s) show how many cities had a temperature of exactly 79° F?
2. Which display(s) show the interval of temperatures for half of the cities?

As you decide what type of display to use, ask the following questions.

- What type of information is this?
- What do I want my graph or display to show?

EXAMPLE Select an Appropriate Display

1 **SCHEDULES Select an appropriate display to show the parts of a day taken up by many activities. Justify your reasoning.**

Since the display will show the parts of a whole, a circle graph would be an appropriate display to represent this data.

CHECK Your Progress

Select an appropriate display.

a. the population of the United States arranged by age intervals

b. the spread of the average top speeds of 100 selected cars

Study Tip

Look Back
You can review bar graphs on p. 749, line graphs on p. 749, and Venn diagrams in Lesson 3-3.

Statistical Displays

Concept Summary

Type of Display	Best Used to...
Bar Graph	show the number of items in specific categories
Box-and-Whisker Plot	show measures of variation for a set of data
Circle Graph	compare parts of the data to the whole
Histogram	show frequency of data divided into equal intervals
Line Graph	show change over a period of time
Line Plot	show how many times each number occurs in the data
Stem-and-Leaf Plot	list all individual numerical data in condensed form
Venn Diagram	show how elements among sets of data are related

Real-World Link . . .
In 2006, the motion picture industry made $9.49 billion in movie ticket sales.
Source: *The Hollywood Reporter*

EXAMPLE Construct an Appropriate Display

2 **MOVIES Select an appropriate type of display for the data below to predict the average movie admission charge in 2010. Justify your reasoning. Then construct the display.**

Movie Admission							
Year	1940	1950	1960	1970	1980	1990	2000
Cost of Admission ($)	0.24	0.53	0.69	1.55	2.69	4.23	5.39

Source: *New York Times Almanac*

These data deal with changes over a period of time. A broken line graph would be an appropriate display to show the change over time.

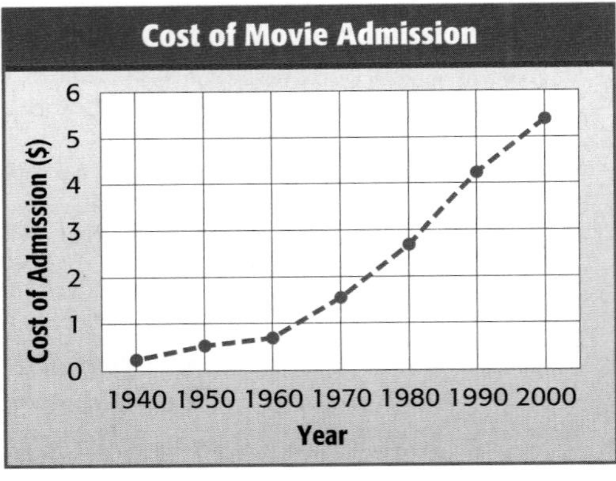

CHECK Your Progress

c. **OCEANS** The table lists the areas in square miles of five oceans. Select an appropriate type of display to compare the areas of the oceans. Then construct the display.

Ocean Areas	
Ocean	**Area (sq. mi)**
Arctic	5,427,000
Atlantic	29,637,900
Indian	26,469,900
Pacific	60,060,700
Southern	7,848,300

Source: Info Please

CHECK Your Understanding

Example 1 (p. 617)

Select an appropriate display for each situation. Justify your reasoning.

1. the number of students ordering yearbooks by grade
2. the sales of a particular brand of shoes compared to the total

Example 2 (p. 618)

3. **SCHOOL** Select an appropriate type of display for showing how the data varies. Justify your reasoning. Then construct the display.

Test Scores Period 4														
98	77	89	63	71	79	81	96	81	85	81	92	77	68	72
74	85	72	85	92	91	73	85	77	78	67	91	88	74	88

Practice and Problem Solving

HOMEWORK HELP	
For Exercises	See Examples
4–9	1
10–13	2

Select an appropriate display for each situation. Justify your reasoning.

4. the number of cell phone subscribers for the past 5 years
5. point totals for the top 10 NASCAR drivers
6. the portion of a family's budget assigned to each category
7. the median of the exam scores for one class
8. gas mileage for 2008 cars
9. number of Americans who speak Spanish, French, and/or German

Select an appropriate display for each situation. Justify your reasoning. Then construct the display.

10.

Favorite Sports for Girls (ages 6–17, in millions)	
Bicycling	10.1
Walking/Hiking	9.0
Bowling	8.9
Volleyball	7.6
Basketball	6.2
Soccer	6.2
In-Line Skating	5.5

Source: *World Almanac for Kids*

11.

Average Height of Females	
Age (years)	Height (inches)
10	56.4
11	59.6
12	61.4
13	62.6
14	63.7
15	63.8

Source: *National Health and Nutrition Examination Survey*

12. **ANIMALS** Refer to the table at the right. Construct an appropriate display of the data.

13. **MUSIC** A survey asked teens what they liked most about a song. Of those who responded, 59 said the music only, 41 said the lyrics only, 18 said they liked both equally, and 5 said they did not like either. Construct an appropriate display of this data.

Federally Endangered Animals, U.S.	
Type	Number of Species
Mammals	68
Fish	74
Reptiles and Amphibians	26
Birds	77
Invertebrates	153

Source: U.S. Fish and Wildlife Service

MUSIC **For Exercises 14 and 15, refer to the displays below. Select which display is most appropriate to answer each question. Justify your reasoning. Then answer the question.**

8th Grade Music Preference

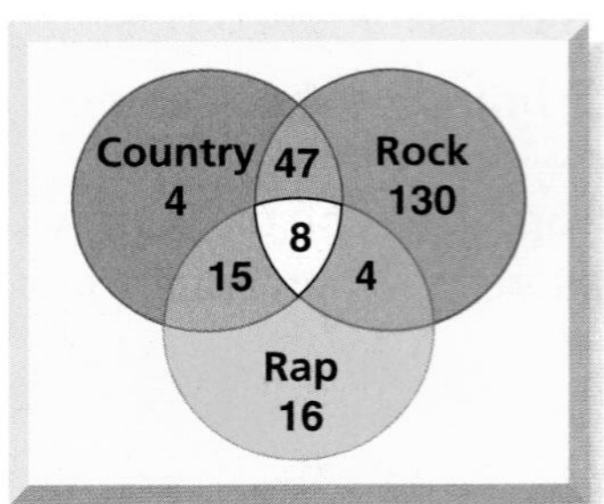

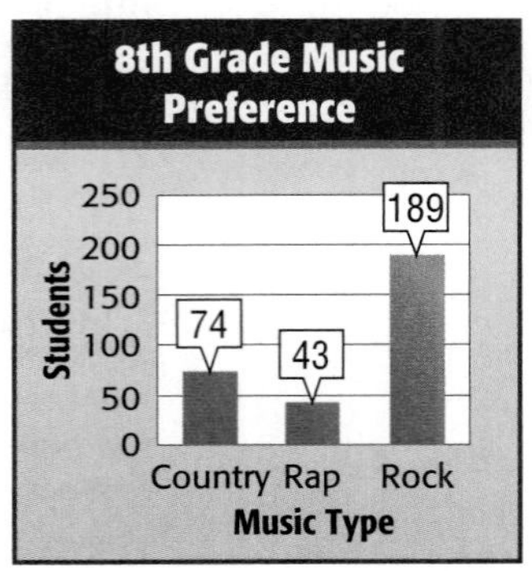

14. How many students like only country music?

15. How many students like rock music?

16. **COLLECT THE DATA** Conduct a survey of your classmates about sports using data that can be presented in a Venn diagram. Then draw the Venn diagram.

COMPUTERS **For Exercises 17 and 18, use the plot at the right. Construct another type of display appropriate to represent this data to answer each of the following questions. Then answer the question.**

Number of Text Messages Received on Saturday

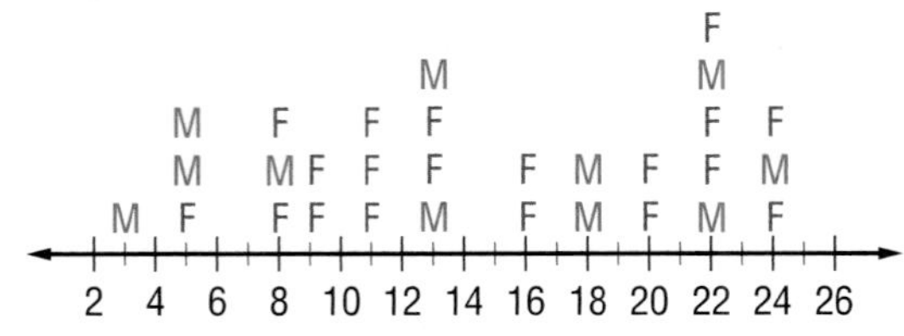

M = male F = female

17. Compare the median for the number of text messages received by males and females.

18. What fraction of people are female and received more than 10 text messages that day?

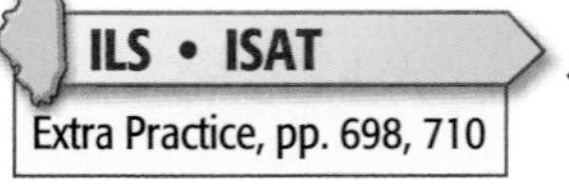

19. **FIND THE DATA** Refer to the Data File on pages 16–19. Choose some data, select an appropriate display for the data, and construct the display.

H.O.T. Problems

20. **OPEN ENDED** Give an example of data that could be represented using a circle graph.

CHALLENGE **For Exercises 21–23, state whether the following statements are *always, sometimes,* or *never* true. Justify your response.**

21. A circle graph can be used to display data from a histogram.

22. A line graph can be used to display data from a Venn diagram.

23. A box-and-whisker plot can be used to display data from a line plot.

24. **WRITING IN MATH** Compare and contrast bar graphs and histograms. Explain when it is appropriate to use a histogram rather than a bar graph.

ISAT PRACTICE 10.A.3a, 10.A.3c

25. Roger polled 24 classmates to find out the average number of hours each spends online each week. Which of the following displays would be most appropriate to show the individual student responses?

A **Number of Hours Spent Online Each Week**

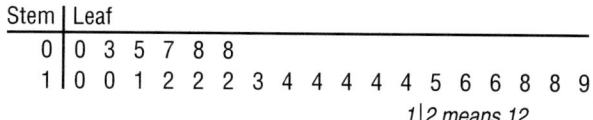

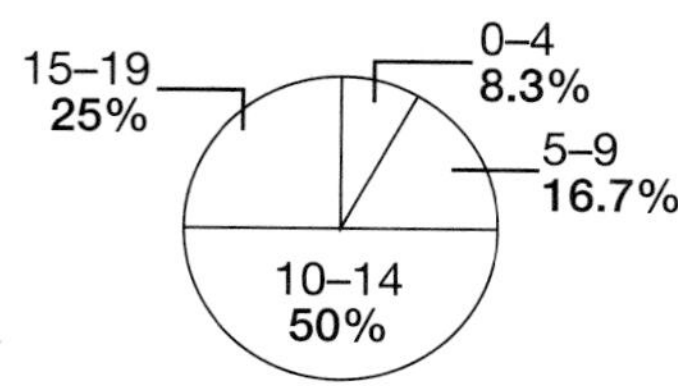

C **Number of Hours Spent Online Each Week**

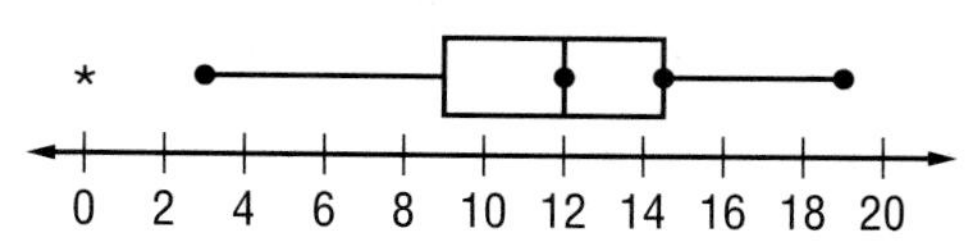

B **Number of Hours Spent Online Each Week**

Stem	Leaf
0	0 3 5 7 8 8
1	0 0 1 2 2 2 3 4 4 4 4 4 5 6 6 8 8 9

1|2 means 12

D **Number of Hours Spent Online Each Week**

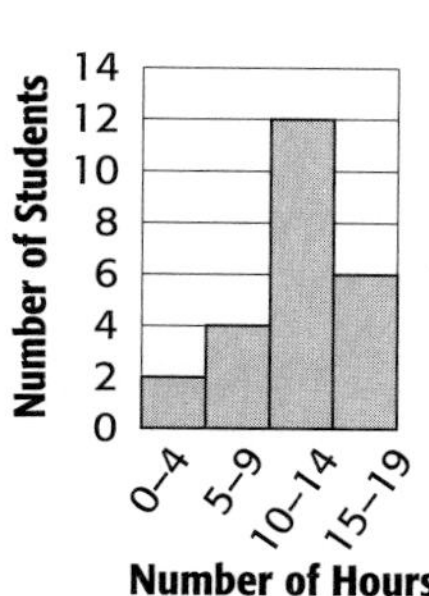

Spiral Review

26. Display the data set {\$12, \$15, \$18, \$21, \$14, \$37, \$27, \$9} in a stem-and-leaf plot. (Lesson 11-7)

Draw a box-and-whisker plot for each set of data. (Lesson 11-6)

27. 42, 38, 42, 45, 43, 80, 55, 50, 34, 36, 40, 35

28. 52, 58, 67, 63, 47, 44, 52, 15, 49, 65, 52, 59

POPULATION For Exercises 29–31, use the table at the right. (Lesson 11-5)

29. Determine the measures of variation for the data.

30. Find any outliers of the data.

31. Use the measures of variation to describe the data.

Ancestral Origins of America (millions)	
German	42.8
Irish	30.5
African American	24.9
English	24.5
American	20.2
Mexican	18.4
Other	120.7

Source: U.S. Census Bureau

32. **CRAFTS** It takes Carolyn two hours to complete a cross-stitch pattern. Carolyn can spend no more than fourteen hours cross-stitching. Write an inequality that represents this situation and use it to determine whether Carolyn can complete 8 cross-stitch patterns. (Lesson 8-6)

ALGEBRA Use the Distributive Property to rewrite each expression. (Lesson 8-1)

33. $8(y + 6)$

34. $-5(a - 10)$

35. $(9 + k)(-2)$

36. $(n - 3)5$

CHAPTER 11 Study Guide and Review

IL Math Online glencoe.com
- STUDY TO GO
- Vocabulary Review

FOLDABLES® Study Organizer GET READY to Study

Be sure the following Big Ideas are noted in your Foldable.

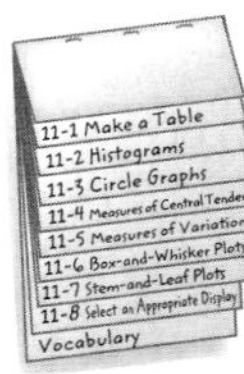

BIG Ideas

Displays (Lessons 11-2, 11-3, and 11-6 to 11-8)
- Bar graphs show the number of items in specific categories.
- Box-and-whisker plots use a number line to show the distribution of a set of data.
- Circle graphs compare parts of the data to the whole.
- Histograms show the frequency of data that has been organized into equal intervals.
- Line graphs show change over a period of time.
- Line plots show how many times each number occurs in the data.
- Stem-and-leaf plots list all individual numerical data in a condensed form.

Measures of Central Tendency (Lesson 11-4)
- The mean of a set of data is the sum of the data divided by the number of items in a data set.
- The median of a set of data is the middle number of the ordered data, or the mean of the middle two numbers.
- The mode or modes of a set of data is the number or numbers that occur most often.

Measures of Variation (Lesson 11-5)
- The range of a set of data is the difference between the greatest and the least numbers in the set.
- The interquartile range is the range of the middle half of the data. It is the difference between the upper quartile and the lower quartile.

Key Vocabulary

box-and-whisker plot (p. 605)
circle graph (p. 582)
histogram (p. 576)
interquartile range (p. 599)
lower quartile (p. 599)
mean (p. 591)
measures of central tendency (p. 591)
measures of variation (p. 599)
median (p. 591)
mode (p. 591)
outlier (p. 600)
quartiles (p. 599)
range (p. 591)
stem-and-leaf plot (p. 612)
upper quartile (p. 599)

Vocabulary Check

State whether each sentence is *true* or *false*. If *false*, replace the underlined word or number to make a true sentence.

1. A <u>histogram</u> is a bar graph that shows the frequency of data in intervals.
2. A <u>variation</u> is a piece of data that is more than 1.5 times the value of the interquartile range beyond the quartiles.
3. The range is one of the <u>measures of central tendency</u>.
4. The <u>mean</u> is the sum of the data divided by the number of pieces of data.
5. If you want to show how the parts compare to the whole, use a <u>circle graph</u>.
6. The <u>mode</u> is the middle number of a set of data.
7. The <u>range</u> is the difference between the greatest and the least values in a set of data.
8. The <u>median</u> is a data value that is quite separated from the rest of the data.

Lesson-by-Lesson Review

11-1 PSI: Make a Table (pp. 574–575)

10.A.3a

Solve. Use the *make a table* strategy.

9. **SPEEDS** About what percent of the speeds in the table below were from 20–24 miles per hour?

Car Speeds (mph)	Tally	Frequency
20–24	卌	5
25–29	卌 卌 ||	12
30–34	卌 ||||	9

10. **MAIL** The list shows the cost to mail letters of various weights. Organize the data in a table using the intervals \$0.00–\$0.49, \$0.50–\$0.99, \$1.00–\$1.49, and \$1.50–\$1.99. What is the most common interval of costs?

\$0.75	\$0.41	\$1.31	\$0.58	\$0.41	\$1.31
\$1.48	\$1.31	\$0.41	\$0.41	\$0.41	\$1.31
\$0.41	\$1.65	\$0.41	\$1.31	\$1.99	\$0.75
\$0.41	\$0.41	\$0.75	\$0.41	\$0.75	\$0.41

Example 1 **About what percent of the temperatures below are from 80°F–84°F? Round to the nearest percent. Use the *make a table* strategy.**

Temperature (°F)	Tally	Frequency
70–74	卌 卌	10
75–79	卌 ||	7
80–84	卌	5
85–89	||||	4
90–95	||	2

Find the total number of temperatures listed in the table.

$10 + 7 + 5 + 4 + 2$ or 28 — Add frequencies.

Find the percent of 80°F–84°F.

$5 \div 28$ or 0.179 — Divide.

0.179×100 or 17.9 — Multiply.

So, 18% of the temperatures were in the 80°F–84°F range.

11-2 Histograms (pp. 576–580)

10.A.3a

For Exercises 11–14, use the histogram at the right.

11. How large is each interval?
12. What percent of the runners ran slower than 74 seconds?
13. What was the most likely time?
14. What was the greatest time?
15. **PLANTS** The heights in inches of various types of plants are listed below. Choose intervals and construct a histogram to represent the data.

    1, 1, 2, 4, 4, 5, 6, 7, 7, 8, 9, 10, 11, 12, 12, 12, 13, 14, 17, 18, 18, 19, 21, 23, 24

Example 2 **Choose intervals and construct a histogram to represent the following 400-meter dash times.**

61	71	68	68	69	72	73	61	76	70
64	64	63	82	68	78	74	80	62	75

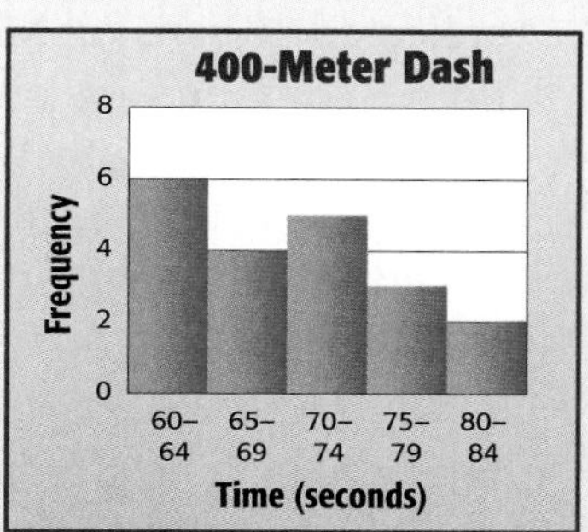

 Circle Graphs (pp. 582–588)

10.A.3a, 10.A.3c

16. **SCHOOL** At Washington Middle School 60 students play football, 20 are on the soccer team, 70 students are in the marching band, 50 are in the school choir, and 120 participate in other activities. Each student is in only one activity. Make a circle graph showing what percent of the total students in extracurricular activities is represented by each activity.

17. **SCIENCE** Use the graph to describe the makeup of Earth's atmosphere.

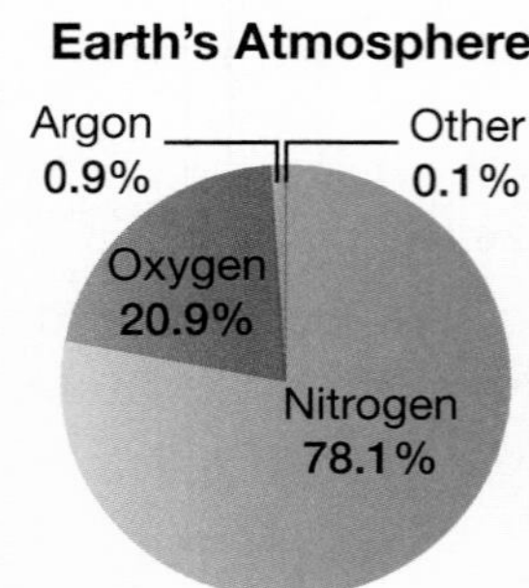

Example 3 Use the circle graph to describe Americans' spending on cats and dogs.

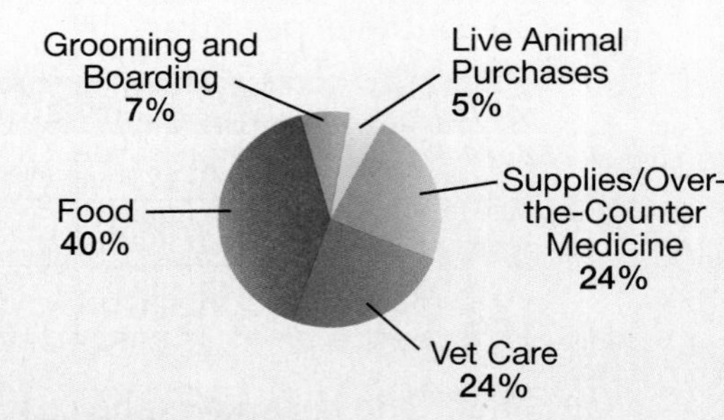

Source: *BusinessWeek*

The majority of spending on cats and dogs is on food, which accounts for two fifths of the total spending. Spending on veterinarian care and supplies and over-the-counter medicine is the same.

11-4 Measures of Central Tendency and Range (pp. 591–596)

10.A.3b

Find the mean, median, mode, and range for each set of data. Round to the nearest tenth if necessary.

18. the height in feet of various slides
    20, 19, 15, 15, 18, 15, 3
19. the number of pounds of recycled newspaper
    6.5, 5.6, 6.8, 10.1, 9.6
20. **FOOD DRIVE** Miss Hollern's homeroom collected 18 cans on Monday, 22 cans on Tuesday, 34 cans on Wednesday, 17 cans on Thursday, and 5 cans on Friday. Select the appropriate measure of central tendency or range to describe the data. Justify your answer.

Example 4 The numbers of grams of fat in various candy bars are listed below. Find the mean, median, mode, and range. Round to the nearest tenth if necessary. Then select the appropriate measure of central tendency or range to describe the data. Justify your answer.

9, 8, 9, 8, 9, 13, 24

mean: $\frac{8 + 8 + 9 + 9 + 9 + 13 + 24}{7}$ or 11.4 g

median: 8, 8, 9, (9), 9, 13, 24

mode: 9 g occurs most frequently

range: 24 − 8 or 16 g

The appropriate measure of central tendency or range to describe the data is the median or the mode. The mean is affected by the highest value, 24 grams.

Mixed Problem Solving
For mixed problem-solving practice, see page 710.

11-5 Measures of Variation (pp. 599–604)

10.A.3a, 10.A.3b

Find the range, median, upper and lower quartiles, interquartile range, and any outliers for each set of data.

21. the number of miles from school to home: 12, 2, 3, 2, 3, 3, 4, 5, 4, 6, 1
22. the number of hours spent listening to music: 7, 5, 7, 3, 7, 8, 9, 8
23. **MOVIES** The number of times Jean's friends have been to the movie theater over the last six months is 8, 9, 5, 10, 7, 6, 2, and 4. Use the measures of variation to describe this data.

Example 5 **The numbers of hours spent studying for the French exam are listed below. Find the range, median, upper and lower quartiles, interquartile range, and any outliers for the set of data.**

10, 9, 2, 9, 3, 9, 4, 5, 6, 9, 9

range: 10 – 2 or 8

median: 2, 3, 4, 5, 6, (9), 9, 9, 9, 9, 10

lower quartile: 2, 3, (4), 5, 6

upper quartile: 9, 9, (9), 9, 10

interquartile range: 9 – 4 or 5

outliers: 5 × 1.5 = 7.5. Since none of the data are less than 4 – 7.5 or –3.5, or greater than 9 + 7.5 or 16.5, there are no outliers.

11-6 Box-and-Whisker Plots (pp. 605–610)

10.A.3a, 10.A.3c

Construct a box-and-whisker plot for each set of data.

24. the number of miles an athlete ran: 0, 5, 7, 11, 13, 13, 13, 14, 15
25. the number of hours spent grading papers: 7, 2, 7, 8, 8, 9, 7, 5
26. **PETS** The numbers of pets various students have are 3, 6, 2, 3, 1, 3, 6, 4, 5, 4, and 2. Construct a box-and-whisker plot for the data. What do the lengths of the parts of the plot tell you?

Example 6 **The hours of various plane flights are listed below. Draw a box-and-whisker plot for the set of data.**

9, 2, 3, 9, 5, 6, 7, 9, 4, 10, 9

Lengths of Plane Flights (hours)

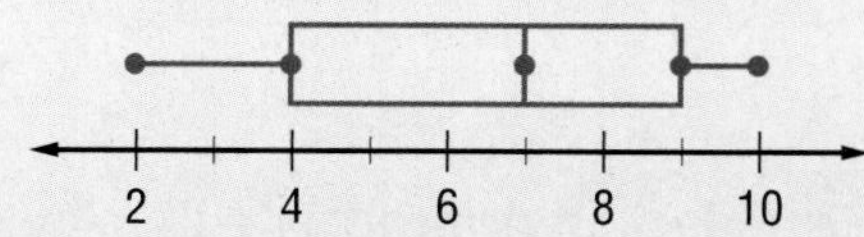

11-7 Stem-and-Leaf Plots (pp. 612–616)

10.A.3a, 10.A.3c

Display each set of data in a stem-and-leaf plot.

27.

Grade	9th	10th	11th	12th
Students	77	65	72	84

28.

Favorite Color	Green	Yellow	Red	Blue
Number	12	17	33	25

WEATHER For Exercises 29–32, use the temperature data shown below.

Average Montly High Temperatures (°F) for Lake Tahoe, CA

Stem	Leaf
4	1 2 2 6 9
5	3
6	1 2
7	0 2 9 9

7|9 = 79°

Source: The Weather Channel

29. In which interval(s) do most of the temperatures occur?
30. What is the lowest average monthly temperature? the highest?
31. What is the range of the data?
32. What is the median temperature?

Example 7 The costs of various cell phone plans are listed below. Draw a stem-and-leaf plot for the set of data.

\$35, \$43, \$57, \$39, \$46

Stem	Leaf
3	
4	
5	

Write the stems from 3 to 5 to the left of the vertical line.

Stem	Leaf
3	5 9
4	3 6
5	7

5|7 = \$57

Write the leaves to the right of the line, with the corresponding stem. Include a key.

11-8 Select an Appropriate Display (pp. 617–621)

10.A.3a, 10.A.3c

33. **TEST SCORES** Select an appropriate display to show individual student scores on an English test in numerical order.
34. **CHORES** Is a circle graph an appropriate display to represent how many hours in a day are spent on certain chores? Justify your answer.

Example 8 Select an appropriate display for the number of hockey players compared to the total number of athletes.

An appropriate display would be a circle graph because you are comparing a part to the whole.

Chapter 11 Practice Test

IL Math Online glencoe.com
• Chapter Test

1. **NUTRITION** Make a table to determine the number of grams of carbohydrates listed most often.

Carbohydrates (g) in Various Cereals							
15	34	44	38	24	32	22	44
32	15	32	15	24	33	22	32
34	24	32	24	33	44	33	32

EXERCISE For Exercises 2–5, use the list below.

Points Scored During a Football Game									
7	3	14	17	10	21	35	6	24	7
3	42	2	6	7	20	9	13	5	38

2. Choose intervals and construct a frequency table of this data.
3. Construct a histogram.
4. How many teams are represented?
5. What percent of the teams scored more than 20 points?

PICNICS For Exercises 6–11, use the list below of the ages of the people at a picnic.

75, 36, 25, 26, 19, 32, 35, 38, 16, 23, 22, 40, 17

6. Find the mean, median, mode, and range.
7. Select the appropriate measure of central tendency or range to describe the data. Justify your reasoning.
8. Find the upper and lower quartiles and the interquartile range.
9. Identify any outliers.
10. Construct a box-and-whisker plot.
11. When one more person joined the picnic, the mean age was 30. How old was the person who joined the picnic?

12. **MULTIPLE CHOICE** Marsha has the following scores on four quizzes: 70, 85, 85, and 90. If her teacher drops her lowest score, which of the following would increase?

    A mode
    B mean
    C median
    D range

13. **MULTIPLE CHOICE** A grocery store had daily sales of \$15,696, \$23,400, \$19,080, \$18,000, \$23,400, \$17,604, and \$15,228 last week. Which data measure would make the sales last week appear the most profitable?

    F mean
    G median
    H mode
    J range

14. **SCORES** About what percent of the scores in the display below are greater than or equal to 78?

Scores on a Recent Biology Test

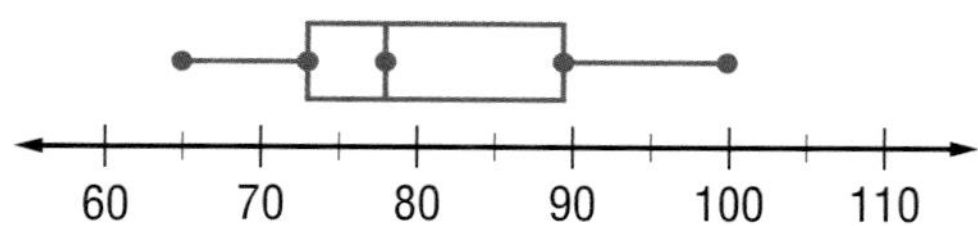

15. **DVDs** Select an appropriate type of display to represent the average prices of DVDs over the last 10 years. Justify your answer.

16. **SCHOOL** Display the data for the number of students with a "B" average at Jefferson Elementary School by grade in a stem-and-leaf plot.

Grade	Jackson	Jefferson
1st	27	13
2nd	22	28
3rd	17	36
4th	12	9
5th	33	27
6th	26	30

ISAT Practice

Cumulative, Chapters 1–11

IL Math Online glencoe.com
• Test Practice

PART 1 Multiple Choice

Read each question. Then fill in the correct answer on the answer sheet provided by your teacher or on a sheet of paper.

1. Clarence surveyed the students in his class about their favorite cafeteria food. The table shows the results of the survey.

Favorite Cafeteria Food				
Food	Chili	Pizza	Chicken	Soup
Votes	3	12	6	3

Which circle graph best represents the data?

A Favorite Cafeteria Food

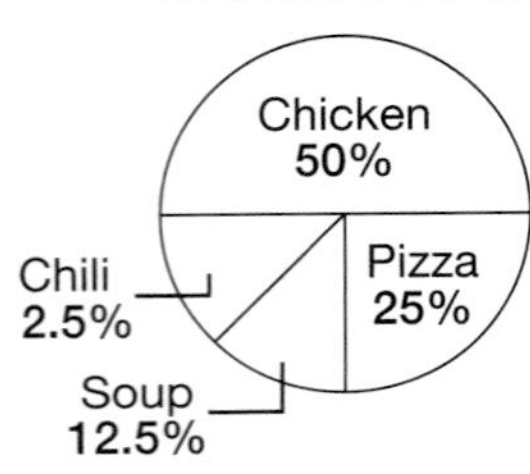

C Favorite Cafeteria Food

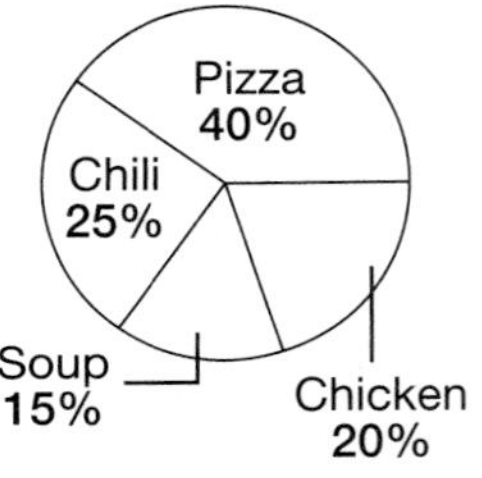

B Favorite Cafeteria Food

D Favorite Cafeteria Food

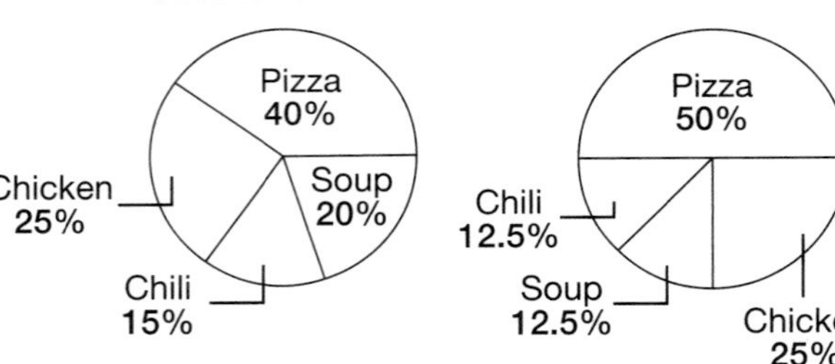

2. Cindy's bowling average is 192 for 12 games. If she drops her lowest score of 174, which equation can be used to find n, Cindy's new bowling average?

F $n = \frac{(192 \times 12) - 174}{11}$

G $n = \frac{(192 \times 12) - 174}{12}$

H $n = \frac{(174 \times 12) - 192}{12}$

J $n = \frac{(192 - 174) \times 12}{11}$

3. Janelle wants to buy a new television. She will finance the total cost of $600 by making 12 equal monthly payments to pay back this amount plus interest. What other information is needed to determine the amount of Janelle's monthly payment?

A the interest rate being charged

B the amount of money Janelle has in her savings account

C the brand of the computer

D the amount of Janelle's weekly income

4. The table shows the number of hours students have volunteered at a community center over several months. If the students volunteer 290 hours during the month of September, which measure of data will change the most?

Student Volunteer Hours						
Month	Jan	Feb	Mar	Apr	May	Jun
Hours	145	150	125	165	160	155

F the mean

G the median

H the mode

J They will all change the same amount.

5. Marcia's average math test score was 82. Which of the following students has the same average math test score as Marcia?

A Jenny earned 492 points on 6 tests.

B Frankie earned 352 points on 4 tests.

C Jeremiah earned 468 points on 6 tests.

D Julieanne earned 344 points on 4 tests.

6. Which is an irrational number?

F -2

G $-\frac{7}{8}$

H $\sqrt{3}$

J $\sqrt{4}$

Preparing for ISAT
For test-taking strategies and practice, see pages 712–729.

7. Before the last soccer game of the season, Tony scored a total of 45 goals. He scored 3 goals in the final game, making his season average 2 goals per game. To find the total number of games that Tony played, first find the sum of 45 and 3, and then —

   A add the sum to 2.
   B subtract 3 from 145.
   C multiply the sum by 2.
   D divide the sum by 2.

8. Rakim's French test scores were 86, 84, 80, 75, 90, 75, and 88. Which measure of data would give Rakim the highest test score?

   F mode
   G median
   H mean
   J range

TEST-TAKING TIP

Question 8 Review any terms that you have learned before you take a test. For example, for a test on data and statistics, be sure that you understand such terms as *mean*, *median*, and *mode*.

9. The cost of a pair of rollerblades is \$33. If the rollerblades are on sale for 35% off, what is the sale price of the rollerblades?

   A \$11.55
   B \$15.45
   C \$21.45
   D \$23.55

PART 2 Short Response/Grid In

Record your answers on the answer sheet provided by your teacher or on a sheet of paper.

10. The histogram shows the results of a survey on the distance students travel to school. To the nearest percent, what percent of the students ride the bus 16 miles or more?

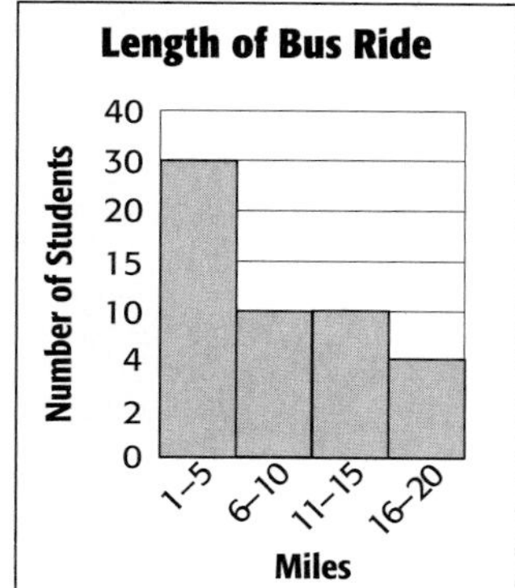

PART 3 Extended Response

Record your answers on the answer sheet provided by your teacher or on a sheet of paper. Show your work.

11. A bicycle shop has 15 men's bicycles, 22 women's bicycles, 19 girls' bicycles, and 24 boys' bicycles.
    a. Make a graph that shows the number of each type of bicycle the bike shop has.
    b. Make a graph that shows what part of the total number of bicycles is represented by each type of bicycle.
    c. Describe an advantage of each type of graph you drew.

NEED EXTRA HELP?											
If You Missed Question...	1	2	3	4	5	6	7	8	9	10	11
Go to Lesson...	11-3	11-4	1-1	11-4	11-4	3-4	11-4	11-4	5-7	11-2	11-8
IL Learning Standards	10.A.3a	10.A.3b	6.B.3a	10.A.3b	10.A.3b	6.B.3c	10.A.3b	10.A.3b	8.A.3b	10.A.3a	10.A.3a

CHAPTER 12

Probability

Illinois Learning Standards

10.C.3a Determine the probability and odds of events using fundamental counting principles.
10.C.3b Analyze problem situations (e.g., board games, grading scales) and make predictions about results.

Key Vocabulary

dependent events (p. 638)
independent events (p. 637)
outcome (p. 632)

Real-World Link

Baseball A baseball player from Clemson University in Clemson, South Carolina, had 59 hits out of 161 times at bat in a recent season. You can use past performance to predict the number of hits the player should make next season.

Probability Make this Foldable to help you organize your notes. Begin with a plain sheet of 11″ × 17″ paper.

1. **Fold** the sheet in half lengthwise. Cut along the fold.

2. **Fold** each half in quarters along the width.

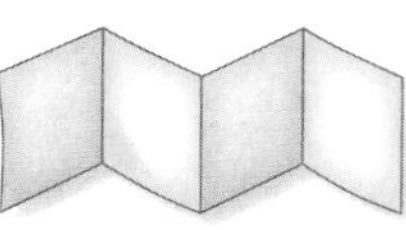

3. **Unfold** each piece and tape to form one long piece.

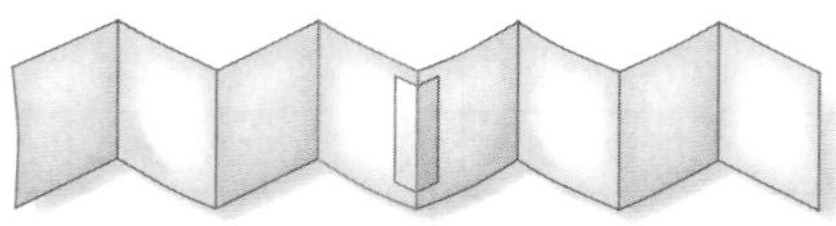

4. **Label** each page with a key topic as shown. Refold to form a booklet.

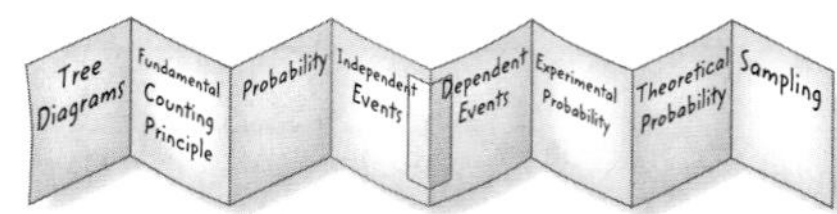

GET READY for Chapter 12

Diagnose Readiness You have two options for checking Prerequisite Skills.

Option 2

IL Math Online Take the Online Readiness Quiz at glencoe.com.

Option 1

Take the Quick Check below. Refer to the Quick Review for help.

QUICK Practice

Write each fraction in simplest form. (Prior Grade)

1. $\frac{48}{72}$
2. $\frac{35}{60}$
3. $\frac{21}{99}$
4. **TRAVEL** On a family trip to San José, California, Dustin drove 4 hours out of 18 hours. Write this portion of time spent driving as a fraction in simplest form. (Prior Grade)

Multiply. Write in simplest form. (Lesson 2-3)

5. $\frac{3}{4} \cdot \frac{8}{9}$
6. $\frac{5}{6} \cdot \frac{1}{2}$
7. $\frac{2}{4} \cdot \frac{2}{7}$
8. $\frac{7}{8} \cdot \frac{4}{6}$

Solve each problem. (Lesson 5-7)

9. Find 35% of 90.
10. Find 42% of 340.
11. What is 60% of 220?
12. What is 5% of 72?
13. **SURVEY** Anna surveyed 144 students in her school. She found that 82% of the students said pizza is their favorite lunch. How many students surveyed said their favorite lunch is pizza? (Lesson 5-7)

QUICK Review

Example 1

Write $\frac{45}{51}$ in simplest form.

$\frac{45}{51} = \frac{15}{17}$ ($\div 3$) Divide the numerator and denominator by their GCF, 3.

Example 2

Find $\frac{3}{7} \cdot \frac{1}{6}$. Write in simplest form.

$\frac{3}{7} \cdot \frac{1}{6} = \frac{\overset{1}{\cancel{3}}}{7} \cdot \frac{1}{\underset{2}{\cancel{6}}}$ Divide 3 and 6 by their GCF, 3.

$= \frac{1 \cdot 1}{7 \cdot 2}$ or $\frac{1}{14}$

Example 3

Find 20% of 170.

$\frac{a}{b} = \frac{p}{100}$ Use the percent proportion.

$\frac{a}{170} = \frac{20}{100}$ Replace b with 170 and p with 20.

$a \cdot 100 = 170 \cdot 20$ Find the cross products.

$100a = 3{,}400$ Multiply.

$\frac{100a}{100} = \frac{3{,}400}{100}$ Divide each side by 100.

$a = 34$

34 is 20% of 170.

12-1 Counting Outcomes

MAIN IDEA

Count outcomes by using a tree diagram or the Fundamental Counting Principle.

IL Learning Standards

Preparation for 10.C.3a Determine the probability and odds of events using fundamental counting principles.

New Vocabulary

outcome
event
sample space
tree diagram
Fundamental Counting Principle
random
probability

IL Math Online

glencoe.com

- Extra Examples
- Personal Tutor
- Self-Check Quiz

GET READY for the Lesson

BANQUET At an awards banquet for the school track team, each person can select a meal from the options shown.

1. How many different appetizers are available? main dishes? desserts?
2. Make a list showing all of the different meals you could have at the banquet.

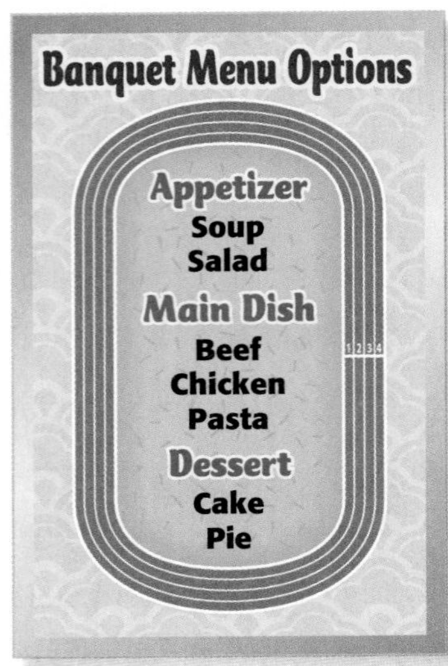

Banquet Menu Options
Appetizer
Soup
Salad
Main Dish
Beef
Chicken
Pasta
Dessert
Cake
Pie

An **outcome** is any one of the possible results of an action. For selecting a specific appetizer, main dish, and dessert, there are 12 total outcomes. An **event** is an outcome or a collection of outcomes.

An organized list of outcomes, called a **sample space**, can help you determine the total number of possible outcomes for an event. One type of organized list is a **tree diagram**.

EXAMPLE Use a Tree Diagram

1 **BANQUET Draw a tree diagram to determine the number of different meals described in the real-world example above.**

Appetizer	Main Dish	Dessert	Outcome
soup	beef	cake	soup, beef, cake
		pie	soup, beef, pie
	chicken	cake	soup, chicken, cake
		pie	soup, chicken, pie
	pasta	cake	soup, pasta, cake
		pie	soup, pasta, pie
salad	beef	cake	salad, beef, cake
		pie	salad, beef, pie
	chicken	cake	salad, chicken, cake
		pie	salad, chicken, pie
	pasta	cake	salad, pasta, cake
		pie	salad, pasta, pie

There are 12 different meal choices for the banquet.

CHECK Your Progress

a. A dime and a penny are tossed. Draw a tree diagram to determine the number of outcomes.

You can also find the total number of outcomes by multiplying. This principle is known as the **Fundamental Counting Principle**.

Fundamental Counting Principle

Key Concept

If event M has m possible outcomes and event N has n possible outcomes, then event M followed by event N has $m \cdot n$ possible outcomes.

Real-World Link For the 2007 MLB All-Star game, 14 players were nominated for each position in the infield (1st base, 2nd base, short stop, 3rd base, and catcher) for the American League.
Source: Major League Baseball

Real-World EXAMPLE

2 **BASEBALL Use the information at the left to determine how many different infield teams are possible when one player is selected for each position.**

There are 14 choices for each position. Use the Fundamental Counting Principle.

$$14 \times 14 \times 14 \times 14 \times 14 = 537{,}824$$

There are 537,824 possible infield teams.

CHECK Your Progress

b. **DINING** A restaurant offers a choice of 3 types of pasta with 5 types of sauce. Each pasta entrée comes with or without a meatball. How many different entrées are available?

Outcomes occur at **random** if each outcome is equally likely to occur. In this situation, the **probability** of an event is the ratio of the number of outcomes in that event to the total number of outcomes.

Real-World EXAMPLE Find Probability

3 **CLASSES Students at East Valley Middle School take six classes each day: math, science, social studies, English, Spanish, and music. What is the probability Julio's first three classes are science, music, and math, in that order?**

First, find the number of possible outcomes.

$$6 \times 5 \times 4 = 120$$

There are 120 possible outcomes. There is one way Julio's classes can be science, music, and math, in that order.

$P(\text{science, music, math}) = \frac{1}{120}$ There is 1 order out of 120.

This can also be written as a decimal, 0.008, or a percent, 0.8%.

CHECK Your Progress

c. Two number cubes are rolled. What is the probability that the sum of the numbers on the cubes is 12?

CHECK Your Understanding

Example 1 (p. 632) 1. The number cube shown is tossed twice. Draw a tree diagram to determine the number of possible outcomes.

Example 2 (p. 633) 2. **CODES** At Wyler Middle School, a student's identification code is the first two letters of the student's last name followed by the last four numbers of his or her Social Security number. How many different student identification codes are possible?

Example 3 (p. 633) 3. **GAMES** In a lottery game, you pick a 4-digit number. One of these numbers is the winning number. What is the probability of winning?

Practice and Problem Solving

HOMEWORK HELP

For Exercises	See Examples
4–7	1
8–13	2
14–15	3

Draw a tree diagram to determine the number of possible outcomes.

4. A penny, a nickel, and a dime are tossed.
5. A number cube is rolled and a penny is tossed.
6. A white or red ball cap comes in small, medium, large, or extra large.
7. The Sweet Treats Shoppe offers single-scoop ice cream in chocolate, vanilla, or strawberry, and two types of cones, regular or sugar.

Use the Fundamental Counting Principle to find the number of possible outcomes.

8. The day of the week is picked at random and a number cube is rolled.
9. A number cube is rolled 3 times.
10. There are 5 true-false questions on a history quiz.
11. There are 4 choices for each of 5 multiple-choice questions on a science quiz.

12. **BAGELS** At Bonnie's Bagels, you can choose from five different types of bagels, four different spreads, and four different toppings. How many different bagel combinations are possible?

13. **VEHICLES** A state's license plates are issued with 2 letters, followed by 2 numbers and a letter. How many different license plates could the state issue?

14. **FLOWERS** Tatiana and her brother are each looking for flowers to give their aunt for her birthday. Tatiana likes either red roses or yellow tulips. Her brother likes blue irises, yellow daisies, red tulips, or white gardenias. If they each choose a flower at random, what is the probability that they select the same color flower?

15. **PHONE NUMBERS** The first three digits of a phone number are based on the area of the state you live in. The next four digits are random numbers. What is the probability of the last four digits being the current year?

ELECTRONICS For Exercises 16 and 17, use the table that shows various options for a digital music player.

16. How many different players are available, based on storage capacity and color?

17. If an FM radio tuner is also available as an option, how many players are available?

Storage Capacity	Colors	
256 megabytes	blue	purple
512 megabytes	red	pink
1 gigabyte	green	silver
2.5 gigabytes	white	black

For Exercises 18 and 19, one marble is drawn from each bag. Use a tree diagram to answer each question.

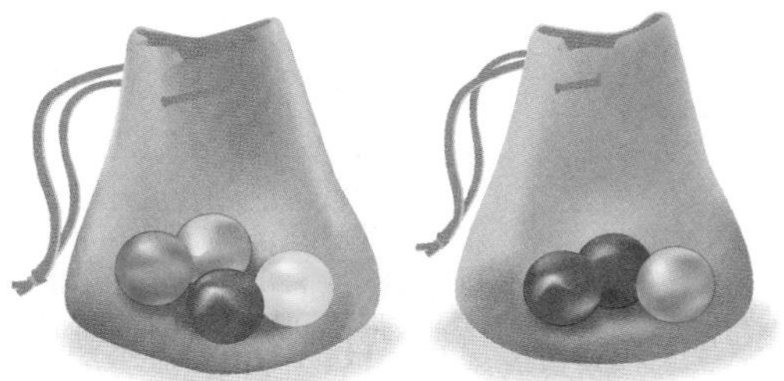

18. What is the probability that at least one marble will be blue?

19. What is the probability that at least one marble will be yellow?

LUNCHES For Exercises 20–24, use the following information.
Parent volunteers made lunches for an 8th-grade field trip. Each lunch had a peanut butter and jelly or a deli-meat sandwich; a bag of potato chips or pretzels; an apple, an orange, or a banana; and juice, water, or soda. One of each possible lunch combinations was made.

20. How many different lunch combinations were made?

21. How many of these combinations contained an apple?

22. If the lunches are handed out randomly, what is the probability that a student receives a lunch containing a banana?

23. What is the probability of a student receiving a lunch with potato chips and soda?

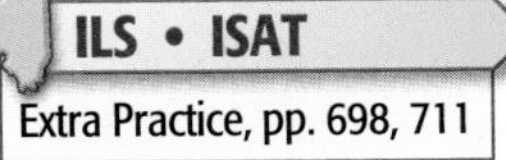

24. Suppose 4 types of meat were used for the deli-meat sandwiches. What is the probability that a student receives one specific type of sandwich?

H.O.T. Problems

25. **OPEN ENDED** Give an example of a situation that has 15 possible outcomes.

26. **NUMBER SENSE** A pizza shop has regular, hand-tossed, and thin crusts; two different cheeses; and four toppings. Without calculating the number of possible outcomes, how many more pizzas can they make if they add a deep-dish crust to their menu?

27. **CHALLENGE** Write an algebraic expression to find the number of outcomes if a number cube is rolled x times.

28. **WRITING IN MATH** Describe a possible advantage for using a tree diagram rather than the Fundamental Counting Principle.

ISAT PRACTICE Preparation for 10.C.3a

29. A school cafeteria offers sandwiches with three types of meat and two types of bread. Which table shows all possible sandwich combinations available?

A

Bread	Meat
White	Ham
Wheat	Turkey
White	Ham
Wheat	Turkey

B

Bread	Meat
White	Ham
White	Turkey
White	Beef
Wheat	Ham
Wheat	Turkey
Wheat	Beef
Rye	Ham
Rye	Turkey
Rye	Beef

C

Bread	Meat
White	Ham
White	Turkey
White	Beef
Wheat	Ham
Wheat	Turkey
Wheat	Beef

D

Bread	Meat
White	Ham
White	Turkey
White	Beef
White	Bologna
Wheat	Ham
Wheat	Turkey
Wheat	Beef
Wheat	Bologna

Spiral Review

Choose an appropriate type of display for each situation. (Lesson 11-8)

30. the amount of each flavor of ice cream sold relative to the total sales

31. the number of people attending a fair for specific intervals of ages

32. **STATISTICS** Display the data set {\$12, \$15, \$18, \$21, \$14, \$37, \$27, \$9} in a stem-and-leaf plot. (Lesson 11-7)

33. **GRADES** Mr. Francis has told his students that he will remove the lowest exam score for each student at the end of the grading period. Seki received grades of 43, 78, 84, 85, 88, and 90 on her exams. What will be the difference between the mean of her original grades and the mean of her five grades after Mr. Francis removes one grade? (Lesson 11-4)

34. What is 35% of 130? (Lesson 5-3)

GET READY for the Next Lesson

PREREQUISITE SKILL Multiply. Write in simplest form. (Lesson 2-3)

35. $\frac{4}{5} \cdot \frac{3}{8}$

36. $\frac{3}{10} \cdot \frac{5}{6}$

37. $\frac{7}{12} \cdot \frac{3}{14}$

38. $\frac{2}{3} \cdot \frac{9}{10}$

12-2 Probability of Compound Events

MAIN IDEA

Find the probability of independent and dependent events.

IL Learning Standards

6.D.3 Apply ratios and proportions **to solve practical problems.** **10.C.3a Determine the probability** and odds **of events** using fundamental counting principles. *Also addresses 10.C.3b.*

New Vocabulary

compound event
independent events
dependent events

IL Math Online

glencoe.com

- Concepts in Motion
- Extra Examples
- Personal Tutor
- Self-Check Quiz

GET READY for the Lesson

SALES A sale advertises that if you buy an item from the column on the left, you get a tote bag free. Suppose you choose items at random.

Type of Item	Tote Bag Colors
T-shirt	green
jacket	red
hat	white
beach towel	
visor	
polo shirt	

1. What is the probability of buying a beach towel? receiving a red tote bag?
2. What is the product of the probabilities in Exercise 1?
3. Draw a tree diagram to determine the probability that someone buys a beach towel and receives a red tote bag.

The combined action of buying an item and receiving a free tote bag is a compound event. A **compound event** consists of two or more simple events.

The color of the tote bag does not depend on the item purchased. These events are independent. For **independent events**, the outcome of one event does not affect the other event.

Probability of Independent Events — Key Concept

Words The probability of two independent events can be found by multiplying the probability of the first event by the probability of the second event.

Symbols $P(A \text{ and } B) = P(A) \cdot P(B)$

EXAMPLE Independent Events

1 **One letter tile is selected and the spinner is spun. What is the probability that both will be a vowel?**

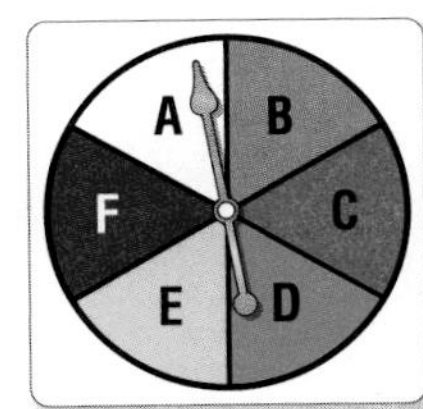

$P(\text{selecting a vowel}) = \frac{2}{7}$

$P(\text{spinning a vowel}) = \frac{1}{3}$

$P(\text{both letters are vowels}) = \frac{2}{7} \cdot \frac{1}{3} = \frac{2}{21}$

CHECK Your Progress

Use the letters and spinner above to find each probability.

a. $P(\text{both letters are As})$

b. $P(\text{both are consonants})$

Test-Taking Tip

Mental Math You may wish to simplify individual probabilities before multiplying them.

ISAT EXAMPLE 6.D.3, 10.C.3a

2 A spinner and a number cube are used in a game. The spinner has an equal chance of landing on one of five colors: red, yellow, blue, green, and purple. The faces of the cube are labeled 1 through 6. What is the probability of a player spinning blue and then rolling a 3 or 4?

A $\frac{3}{11}$ **B** $\frac{1}{4}$ **C** $\frac{1}{15}$ **D** $\frac{1}{30}$

Read the Item

You are asked to find the probability of the spinner landing on blue and rolling a 3 or 4 on a number cube. The events are independent because spinning the spinner does not affect the outcome of rolling a number cube.

Solve the Item

First, find the probability of each event.

$P(\text{blue}) = \frac{1}{5}$ $\quad \frac{\text{number of ways to spin blue}}{\text{number of possible outcomes}}$

$P(3 \text{ or } 4) = \frac{2}{6} \text{ or } \frac{1}{3}$ $\quad \frac{\text{number of ways to roll 3 or 4}}{\text{number of possible outcomes}}$

Then, find the probability of both events occurring.

$P(\text{blue and 3 or 4}) = \frac{1}{5} \cdot \frac{1}{3}$ $\quad P(A \text{ and } B) = P(A) \cdot P(B)$

$= \frac{1}{15}$ $\quad$ Multiply.

The probability is $\frac{1}{15}$, which is answer C.

CHECK Your Progress

c. A game requires players to roll two fair number cubes to move the game pieces. The faces of the cubes are labeled 1 through 6. What is the probability of rolling a 2 or 4 on the first number cube and then rolling a 5 on the second?

F $\frac{1}{3}$ **G** $\frac{1}{2}$ **H** $\frac{1}{12}$ **J** $\frac{1}{18}$

If the outcome of one event affects the outcome of another event, the events are called **dependent events**.

Vocabulary Link
Dependent
Everyday Use under the control of others
Math Use relying on another quantity or action

Probability of Dependent Events — Key Concept

Words	If two events, A and B, are dependent, then the probability of both events occurring is the product of the probability of A and the probability of B after A occurs.
Symbols	$P(A \text{ and } B) = P(A) \cdot P(B \text{ following } A)$

Real-World EXAMPLE Dependent Events

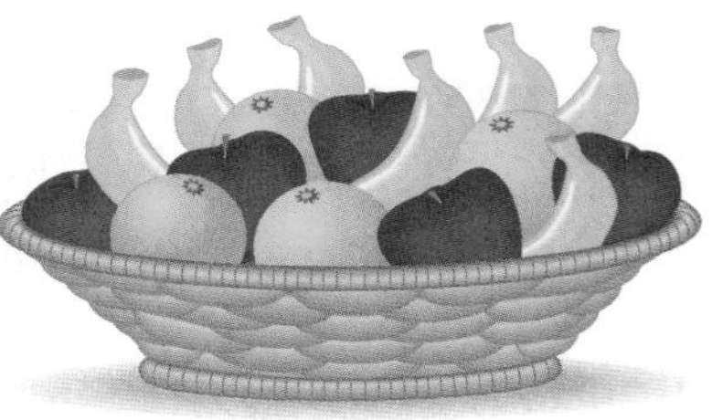

3 **FRUIT There are 4 oranges, 7 bananas, and 5 apples in a fruit basket. Megan selects a piece of fruit at random and then Terrance selects a piece of fruit at random. Find the probability that two apples are chosen.**

Since the first piece of fruit is not replaced, the first event affects the second event. These are dependent events.

$P(\text{first piece is an apple}) = \frac{5}{16}$ ← number of apples ← total pieces of fruit

$P(\text{second piece is an apple}) = \frac{4}{15}$

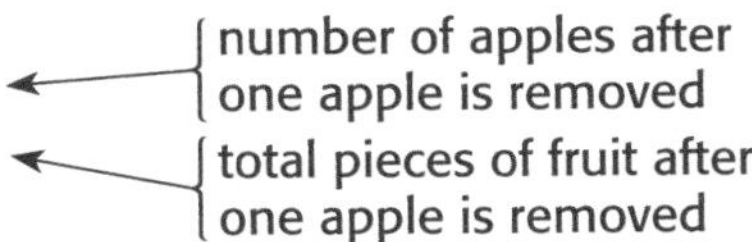

$P(\text{two apples}) = \frac{\overset{1}{\cancel{5}}}{\underset{4}{\cancel{16}}} \cdot \frac{\overset{1}{\cancel{4}}}{\underset{3}{\cancel{15}}} \text{ or } \frac{1}{12}$

CHECK Your Progress

Refer to the situation above. Find each probability.

d. P(two bananas)

e. P(orange then apple)

f. P(apple then banana)

g. P(two oranges)

CHECK Your Understanding

Example 1 (p. 637)

A penny is tossed and a number cube is rolled. Find each probability.

1. P(tails and 3)
2. P(heads and odd)

Example 2 (p. 638)

3. **MULTIPLE CHOICE** A spinner and a number cube are used in a game. The spinner has an equal chance of landing on 1 of 3 colors: red, yellow, and blue. The faces of the cube are labeled 1 through 6. What is the probability of a player spinning red and then rolling an even number?

   A $\frac{2}{5}$ B $\frac{1}{3}$ C $\frac{1}{6}$ D $\frac{1}{12}$

Example 3 (p. 639)

A card is drawn from the cards shown and not replaced. Then, a second card is drawn. Find each probability.

1 2 3 4
5 6 7 8 9

4. P(two even numbers)
5. P(a number less than 4 and then a number greater than 4)

Practice and Problem Solving

HOMEWORK HELP	
For Exercises	See Examples
6–11	1
12, 13	2
14–19	3

A number cube is rolled, and a marble is selected from the bag at the right. Find each probability.

6. P(1 and red)
7. P(3 and purple)
8. P(even and yellow)
9. P(odd and *not* green)
10. P(less than 4 and blue)
11. P(greater than 1 and red)

12. **LAUNDRY** A laundry basket contains 18 blue socks and 24 black socks. What is the probability of randomly picking 2 black socks from the basket?

13. **GAMES** Beth is playing a board game that requires rolling two number cubes to move a game piece. She needs to roll a sum of 6 on her next turn and then a sum of 10 to land on the next two bonus spaces. What is the probability that Beth will roll a sum of 6 and then a sum of 10 on her next two turns?

Mrs. Ameldo's class has 5 students with blue eyes, 7 with brown eyes, 4 with hazel eyes, and 4 with green eyes. Two students are selected. Find each probability.

14. P(two blue)
15. P(green then brown)
16. P(hazel then blue)
17. P(brown then blue)
18. P(two green)
19. P(*not* hazel)

20. **MARKETING** A discount supermarket has found that 60% of their customers spend more than $75 each visit. What is the probability that the next two customers will each spend more than $75?

SCHOOL For Exercises 21 and 22, use the information below and in the table.

At Clearview Middle School, 56% of the students are girls and 44% are boys.

Clearview Middle School Favorite Subject	
Art	16%
Language Arts	13%
Math	28%
Music	7%
Science	21%
Social Studies	15%

21. If two students are chosen at random, what is the probability that the first student is a girl and that the second student's favorite subject is science?

22. What is the probability that of two randomly selected students, one is a boy and the other is a student whose favorite subject is *not* art or math?

23. **MOVIES** You and a friend plan to see 2 movies over the weekend. You can choose from 6 comedy, 2 drama, 4 romance, 1 science fiction, or 3 action movies. You write the movie titles on pieces of paper and place them in a bag, and you each randomly select a movie. What is the probability that neither of you selects a comedy? Is this a dependent or independent event? Explain.

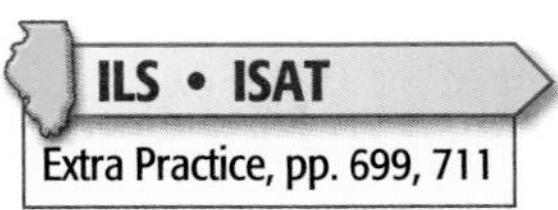

24. **MONEY** Donoma had 8 dimes and 6 pennies in her pocket. If she took out 1 coin and then a second coin without replacing the first, what is the probability that both coins were dimes? Is this a dependent or independent event? Explain.

POPULATION For Exercises 25 and 26, use the information in the table.

Assume that age is *not* dependent on the region.

Lewburg County Population	
Demographic Group	**Fraction of the Population**
Under age 18	$\frac{3}{10}$
18 to 64 years old	$\frac{3}{5}$
65 years or older	$\frac{1}{10}$
Rural Area	$\frac{4}{5}$
Urban Area	$\frac{1}{5}$

25. A resident of Lewburg County is picked at random. What is the probability that the person is under 18 years old or 18 to 64 years old and from an urban area?

26. What is the probability that the person is less than 18 years old or 65 years or older and from a rural area?

Real-World Link The game of dominoes is believed to have originated in 12th century China.

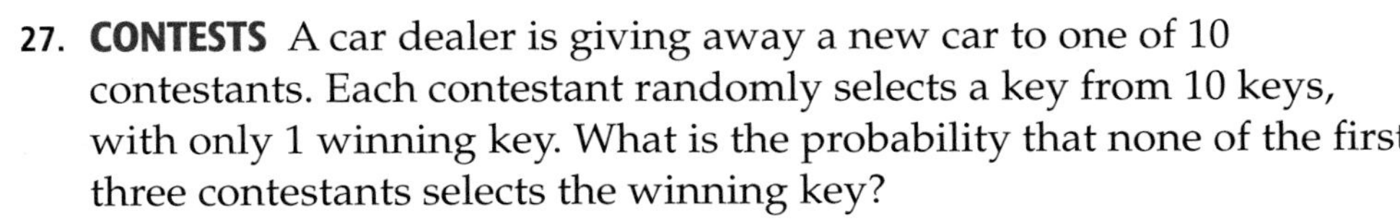

27. **CONTESTS** A car dealer is giving away a new car to one of 10 contestants. Each contestant randomly selects a key from 10 keys, with only 1 winning key. What is the probability that none of the first three contestants selects the winning key?

28. **DOMINOES** A standard set of dominoes contains 28 tiles, with each tile having two sides of dots from 0 to 6. Of these tiles, 7 have the same number of dots on each side. If four players each randomly choose a tile, what is the probability that each chooses a tile with the same number of dots on each side?

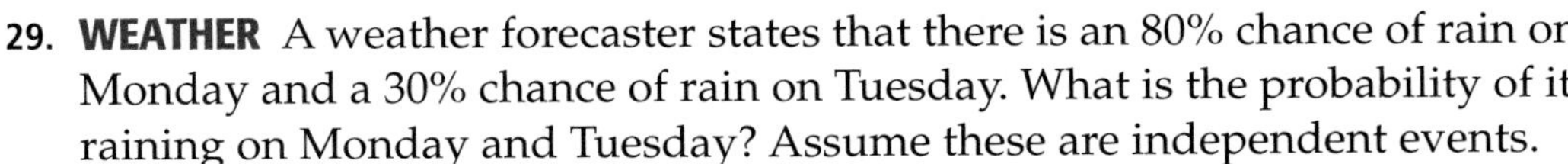

29. **WEATHER** A weather forecaster states that there is an 80% chance of rain on Monday and a 30% chance of rain on Tuesday. What is the probability of it raining on Monday and Tuesday? Assume these are independent events.

30. **FIND THE DATA** Refer to the Data File on pages 16–19. Choose some data and write a real-world problem in which you would find a compound probability.

H.O.T. Problems

31. **OPEN ENDED** There are 9 marbles representing 3 different colors. Write a problem where 2 marbles are selected at random without replacement and the probability is $\frac{1}{6}$.

32. **FIND THE ERROR** The spinner at the right is spun twice. Felisa and Tamera are finding the probability that both spins will result in an even number. Who is correct? Explain.

$\frac{2}{5} \cdot \frac{2}{5} = \frac{4}{25}$

Felisa

$\frac{2}{5} \cdot \frac{1}{4} = \frac{2}{20}$

Tamera

33. **CHALLENGE** Determine whether the following statement is *true* or *false*. If the statement is false, provide a counterexample.
If two events are independent, then the probability of both events is less than 1.

34. **WRITING IN MATH** What is the difference between independent events and dependent events?

ISAT PRACTICE 6.D.3, 10.C.3a

35. Mr. Fernandez is holding four straws of different lengths. He has asked four students to each randomly pick a straw to see who goes first in a game. John picks first, gets the second longest straw, and keeps it. What is the probability that Jeremy will get the longest straw if he picks second?

A $\frac{1}{4}$ C $\frac{1}{3}$

B $\frac{1}{2}$ D $\frac{1}{5}$

36. The spinners below are each spun once.

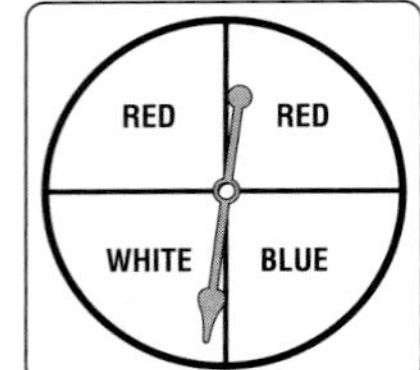

What is the probability of spinning 2 and white?

F $\frac{1}{16}$ H $\frac{2}{5}$

G $\frac{1}{4}$ J $\frac{3}{5}$

Spiral Review

37. **SCHOOL** Doli can take 4 different classes first period, 3 different classes second period, and 5 different classes third period. How many different schedules can she have? (Lesson 12-1)

38. **RADIO LISTENING** Choose an appropriate display for the data at the right. Then make a display. Justify your reasoning. (Lesson 11-8)

Adult Audience of Oldies Radio

Age	18 to 24	25 to 34	35 to 44	45 to 54	55 or older
Percent of Audience	10%	14%	29%	33%	14%

Source: Interep Research Division

MEASUREMENT Find the volume of each solid described. Round to the nearest tenth if necessary. (Lessons 7-5 and 7-6)

39. rectangular pyramid: length, 14 m; width, 12 m; height 7 m

40. cone: diameter, 22 cm; height, 24 cm

GET READY for the Next Lesson

PREREQUISITE SKILL Write each fraction in simplest form.

41. $\frac{52}{120}$ 42. $\frac{33}{90}$ 43. $\frac{49}{70}$ 44. $\frac{24}{88}$

12-3 Experimental and Theoretical Probability

MAIN IDEA

Find experimental and theoretical probabilities and use them to make predictions.

IL Learning Standards

6.D.3 Apply ratios and proportions **to solve practical problems. 10.C.3a Determine the probability** and odds **of events** using fundamental counting principles. *Also addresses 10.C.3b.*

New Vocabulary

experimental probability
theoretical probability

IL Math Online

glencoe.com

- Concepts In Motion
- Extra Examples
- Personal Tutor
- Self-Check Quiz

MINI Lab

Draw one marble from a bag containing 10 different-colored marbles. Record its color, and replace it in the bag. Repeat 50 times.

1. Find the ratio $\frac{\text{number of times color was drawn}}{\text{total number of draws}}$ for each color.
2. Is it possible to have a certain color marble in the bag and never draw that color?
3. Open the bag and count the marbles. Find the ratio $\frac{\text{number of each color marble}}{\text{total number of marbles}}$ for each color of marble.
4. Are the ratios in Exercises 1 and 3 the same? Explain.

In the Mini Lab above, you determined a probability by conducting an experiment. Probabilities that are based on the outcomes obtained by conducting an experiment are called **experimental probabilities**.

Probabilities based on known characteristics or facts are called **theoretical probabilities**. For example, you can compute the theoretical probability of picking a certain color marble from a bag. Theoretical probability tells you what *should* happen in an experiment.

EXAMPLES Theoretical and Experimental Probability

1 **What is the theoretical probability of rolling a double 1 using two number cubes?**

The theoretical probability is $\frac{1}{6} \cdot \frac{1}{6}$ or $\frac{1}{36}$.

2 **The graph shows the results of an experiment in which two number cubes were rolled. According to the experimental probability, is a sum of 12 likely to occur?**

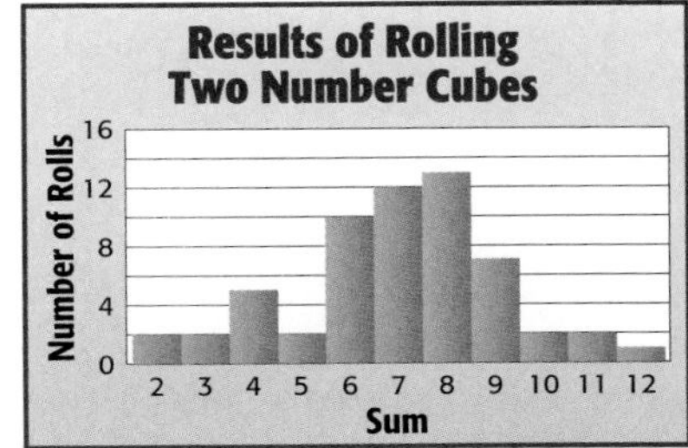

Only 1 of the 58 sums is 12. So, the experimental probability of rolling a sum of 12 is $\frac{1}{58}$. It is not likely that a sum of 12 will occur.

CHECK Your Progress

a. Refer to the graph above. According to the experimental probability, which sum is most likely to occur?

Real-World Career . . .
How Does a Cell Phone Designer Use Math?
Industrial Designers use information from surveys to help them decide the features and styles customers prefer.

IL Math Online

For more information, go to glencoe.com.

Real-World EXAMPLE

3 **TIME Three hundred people were surveyed as to how they keep track of time. What is the experimental probability that a person uses his or her cell phone?**

Method	Number Who Use This Method
cell phone	185
clock	58
watch	57

There were 300 people surveyed and 185 use their cell phone to keep track of time. The experimental probability is $\frac{185}{300}$ or about 62%.

CHECK Your Progress

b. What is the experimental probability that a person uses his or her watch to keep track of time?

You can use past performance to predict future events.

EXAMPLE Use Probability to Predict

4 **MANUFACTURING At a plant that manufactures light bulbs, an inspector finds that the probability that a light bulb is *not* defective is $\frac{8}{11}$. Is this probability experimental or theoretical? Explain.**

This is an experimental probability since it is based on what has already happened.

If the company wants to have 10,000 non-defective light bulbs, how many light bulbs will they need to make?

This problem can be solved using a proportion.

8 out of 11 light bulbs are *not* defective. → $\frac{8}{11} = \frac{10{,}000}{x}$ ← 10,000 out of x light bulbs should *not* be defective.

Solve the proportion.

$\frac{8}{11} = \frac{10{,}000}{x}$	Write the proportion.
$8 \cdot x = 11 \cdot 10{,}000$	Find the cross products.
$8x = 110{,}000$	Multiply.
$\frac{8x}{8} = \frac{110{,}000}{8}$	Divide each side by 8.
$x = 13{,}750$	The company should make 13,750 light bulbs.

CHECK Your Progress

c. **SURVEYS** In a recent survey of 150 people, 18 responded that they were left-handed. If an additional 2,500 people are surveyed, how many would be expected to be left-handed?

CHECK Your Understanding

Example 1 (p. 643)

For Exercises 1–3, use the table that shows the results of tossing three coins, one at a time, 50 times.

Result	Frequency	Result	Frequency
HHH	6	TTT	3
HHT	5	TTH	6
HTH	10	THT	5
HTT	5	THH	10

1. What is the theoretical probability of tossing exactly two heads?

Example 2 (p. 643)

2. Find the experimental probability of tossing exactly two heads.
3. How likely is it that a toss of three coins will have two heads? Explain.

For Exercises 4 and 5, use the table at the right showing the results of a survey of shoes that students are wearing.

Shoe	Number of Students
athletic	48
sandals	33
dress	28
boots	11

Example 3 (p. 644)

4. What is the probability that the next student to walk by will be wearing athletic shoes?

Example 4 (p. 644)

5. Out of the next 75 students, how many would you expect to be wearing dress shoes?

Practice and Problem Solving

HOMEWORK HELP

For Exercises	See Examples
6, 9	1, 2
8, 11	3
7, 10	4

TENNIS For Exercises 6 and 7, use the following information.

During the first four weeks of tennis season, Jeanette won 24 out of 30 matches.

6. What is the probability that she will win her next match?
7. If she competes in 50 matches this season, how many should she be expected to win?

8. **SURVEYS** In a survey, 120 out of 200 students said their favorite food was pizza. What is the experimental probability that a student chose pizza as his or her favorite food?

AWARDS For Exercises 9 and 10, use the table that shows how many films from each category won the Best Picture award.

Category	Number of Films
Drama	32
Historical/Epic	13
Comedy	10
Musical	9
War	6
Action	4
Western	3
Suspense	2

9. What is the probability that the next movie to win will be a comedy?
10. Out of 100 winners, how many would you expect to be action films?
11. **CARS** Of the last 80 cars sold at a dealership, 35 of them were SUVs. What is the experimental probability that the next car they sell will be an SUV?
12. **SPORTS** In a survey of 90 students at Genoa Middle School, 42 liked to watch basketball and 24 liked to watch soccer. If there are 300 students in the middle school, how many would you expect to like to watch soccer?

For Exercises 13–15, use the table that shows the results of spinning an equally divided 8-section spinner.

Number on Spinner	Frequency
1	8
2	5
3	9
4	4
5	10
6	6
7	5
8	3

13. Compare the theoretical and experimental probabilities of the spinner landing on 5.
14. Based on the experimental probability, how many times would you expect the spinner to land on 3 if the spinner is spun 200 times?
15. Jarred predicts that the spinner will land on 4 or 8 on the next spin. Is this a reasonable prediction? Explain.

BASEBALL For Exercises 16 and 17, use the table which shows the batting results of a baseball player for a season.

Result	Frequency
Single	32
Double	18
Triple	14
Home Run	5
Walk	11
Out	120

16. Based on the results, how likely is it that the player would be out after his next turn batting?
17. The next time the player is at bat, how likely is it for him to hit a single or a double?

18. **FOOD** The manager of a school cafeteria asked selected students to pick their favorite menu item. The results of the survey are shown in the table. If the cafeteria serves 350 lunches, and students can choose only one lunch, how many hamburgers could the manager expect to sell?

Menu Item	Students
Hot Dog	22
Hamburger	19
Pizza	30
Taco	16
Chicken Strips	13

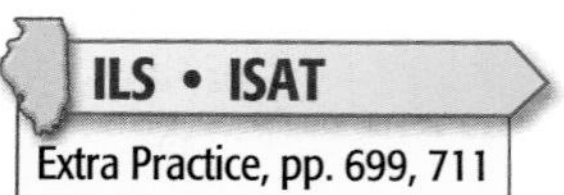

Extra Practice, pp. 699, 711

19. **ODDS** The *odds* of an event occurring is a ratio that compares the number of favorable outcomes to the number of unfavorable outcomes. Suppose a number cube is rolled. What are the odds of rolling a 2? an even number? a number greater than 4?

H.O.T. Problems

20. **OPEN ENDED** Two hundred fifty people are surveyed about their favorite color. Make a table of possible results if the experimental probability that the favorite color is blue is 40%.
21. **CHALLENGE** A survey found that 75 students out of 200 own a skateboard and that 280 students out of 400 own a bicycle. What is the probability that a student has both a skateboard and a bicycle?
22. **WRITING IN MATH** Explain why you would *not* expect the theoretical probability of an event and the experimental probability of the same event to always be the same.

ISAT PRACTICE 6.D.3, 10.C.3a

23. The results of a survey about what students say is the hardest part of going to school are shown in the table.

Issue	Number of Students
Tests	72
Paying Attention	38
Homework	36
Organization	32
Presentations	22

Based on the results, what is the probability that the next student surveyed will choose "organization"?

A $\frac{8}{25}$ C $\frac{4}{25}$

B $\frac{9}{50}$ D $\frac{4}{50}$

24. **SHORT RESPONSE** Shannon spun the spinner shown and recorded her results.

Number on Spinner	Frequency
1	20
2	10
3	2
4	40
5	8

What is the experimental probability of landing on the number five?

Spiral Review

Eight cards numbered 1–8 are shuffled together. Once a card is drawn, it is not replaced. Find each probability. (Lesson 12-2)

25. 8 then 4

26. even then odd

27. **SCHOOL** At the school cafeteria, students can choose from 4 entrées and 3 beverages. How many different lunches of one entrée and one beverage can be purchased at the cafeteria? (Lesson 12-1)

28. **STATISTICS** Find the range, median, upper and lower quartiles, interquartile range, and any outliers of the set of data. (Lesson 11-5)

115, 117, 111, 121, 110, 127, 116, 126, 105,
115, 100, 103, 122, 130, 101, 100, 108, 130

ALGEBRA Write an inequality for each sentence. (Lesson 8-6)

29. **HEALTH** Your heart beats over 100,000 times a day.

30. **BIRDS** A peregrine falcon can spot a pigeon up to 8 kilometers away.

GET READY for the Next Lesson

31. **PREREQUISITE SKILL** Lawanda was assigned some math exercises for homework. She answered half of them in study period. After school, she answered 7 more exercises. If she still has 11 exercises to complete, how many exercises were assigned? Use the *work backward* strategy. (Lesson 1-8)

Extend 12-3

Probability Lab
Fair Games

MAIN IDEA

Use experimental and theoretical probabilities to decide whether a game is fair.

IL Learning Standards

10.C.3b Analyze problem situations (e.g., board **games,** grading scales) **and make predictions about results.**

Mathematically speaking, a two-player game is fair if each player has an equally likely chance of winning. In this lab, you will analyze two simple games and determine whether each game is fair.

ACTIVITY

1 **In a counter-toss game, players toss three two-color counters. The winner of each game is determined by how many counters land with either the red or yellow side facing up. Play this game with a partner.**

STEP 1 Player 1 tosses the counters. If 2 or 3 chips land red-side up, Player 1 wins. If 2 or 3 chips land yellow-side up, Player 2 wins. Record the results in a table like the one shown below. Place a check in the winner's column for each game.

Game	Player 1	Player 2
1		
2		

STEP 2 Player 2 then tosses the counters and the results are recorded.

STEP 3 Continue alternating the tosses until each player has tossed the counters 10 times.

Analyze the Results

1. Make an organized list of all the possible outcomes resulting from one toss of the 3 counters. Explain your method.
2. Calculate the theoretical probability of each player winning. Write each probability as a fraction and as a percent.
3. **MAKE A CONJECTURE** Based on the theoretical probabilities of each player winning, is this a fair game? Explain your reasoning.
4. Calculate the experimental probability of each player winning. Write each probability as a fraction and as a percent.
5. Compare the probabilities in Exercises 2 and 4.
6. **GRAPH THE DATA** Make a graph of the experimental probabilities of Player 1 winning for 5, 10, 15, and 20 games. Graph the ordered pairs (games played, Player 1 wins) using a blue pencil, pen, or marker. Describe how the points appear on your graph.

7. Add to the graph you created in Exercise 6 the theoretical probabilities of Player 1 winning for 5, 10, 15, and 20 games. Graph the ordered pairs (games played, Player 1 wins) using a red pencil, pen, or marker. Connect these red points and describe how they appear on your graph.

8. As the number of games played increases, how does the experimental probability compare to the theoretical probability?

9. **MAKE A PREDICTION** Predict the number of times Player 1 would win if the game were played 100 times.

ACTIVITY

2 **In a number-cube game, players roll two number cubes. Play this game with a partner.**

STEP 1 Player 1 rolls the number cubes. Player 1 wins if the total of the numbers rolled is 5 or if a 5 is shown on one or both number cubes. Otherwise, Player 2 wins. Record the results in a table like the one shown below.

Game	Player 1	Player 2
1		
2		

STEP 2 Player 2 then rolls the number cubes and the results are recorded.

STEP 3 Continue alternating the rolls until each player has rolled the number cubes 10 times.

Analyze the Results

10. Make an organized list of all the possible outcomes resulting from one roll. Explain your method.

11. Calculate the theoretical probability of each player winning and the experimental probability of each player winning. Write each probability as a fraction and as a percent. Then compare these probabilities.

12. **MAKE A CONJECTURE** Based on the theoretical and experimental probabilities of each player winning, is this a fair game? Explain your reasoning.

13. **WRITING IN MATH** If the game is fair, explain how you could change the game so that it is not fair. If the game is not fair, explain how you could change the game to make it fair. Explain.

Problem-Solving Investigation

MAIN IDEA: Solve problems by acting it out.

ILS **10.C.3b Analyze problem situations** (e.g., board games, grading scales) **and make predictions about results.**

P.S.I. TEAM +

e-Mail: ACT IT OUT

SETH: I have a quiz in Spanish class this Friday. I wonder if tossing a coin would be a good way to answer a 5-question true-false quiz.

YOUR MISSION: Act it out to determine if tossing a coin is a good way to answer a true-false quiz.

Understand	You know there are five true-false questions on the quiz. You can carry out an experiment to test if tossing a coin would be a good way to answer the questions and get a good grade.
Plan	Toss a coin 5 times. If the coin shows tails, the answer is T. If the coin shows heads, the answer is F. Do three trials.
Solve	Suppose the correct answers are T, F, F, T, F. Let's circle them in each trial. (See table below.) Since the experiment produced 2–3 correct answers on a 5-question quiz, it shows that tossing a coin to answer a true-false quiz is *not* the way to get a good grade.
Check	Check by doing several more trials.

Answers	T	F	F	T	F	Number Correct
Trial 1	(T)	T	(F)	F	T	2
Trial 2	F	(F)	T	(T)	(F)	3
Trial 3	(T)	(F)	T	F	T	2

Analyze The Strategy

1. Explain an advantage of using the *act it out* strategy to solve a problem.
2. **WRITING IN MATH** Write a problem that could be solved by acting it out. Then use the strategy to solve the problem. Explain your reasoning.

Mixed Problem Solving

ILS • ISAT
Extra Practice, pp. 699, 711

For Exercises 3–5, solve using the *act it out* strategy.

3. **MONEY** Miguel bought an apple juice and a bag of pretzels for \$4.55. If he paid the cashier with a \$5 bill, in how many different ways can he receive his change if the cashier only gives him quarters, dimes, and nickels?

4. **FITNESS** The length of a basketball court is 84 feet long. Hector runs 20 feet forward and then 8 feet back. How many more times will he have to do this until he reaches the end of the basketball court?

5. **PHOTOGRAPHS** Omar is taking a picture of the French club's five officers. The club secretary will always stand on the left and the treasurer will always stand on the right. How many different ways can he arrange the officers in a single row for the picture?

Use any strategy to solve Exercises 6–12. Some strategies are shown below.

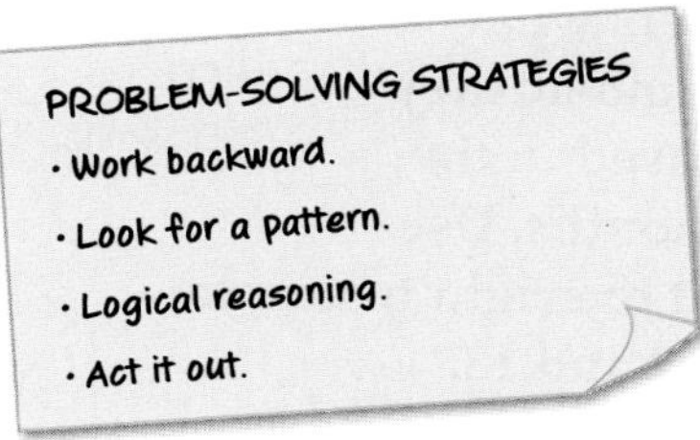

6. **MEASUREMENT** Mrs. Lopez is designing her garden in the shape of a rectangle. The perimeter of her garden is $2\frac{1}{4}$ times greater than the perimeter of the rectangle shown. Find the perimeter of Mrs. Lopez's garden.

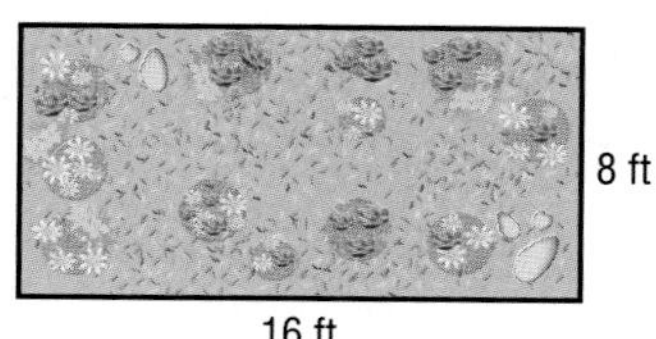

7. **ALGEBRA** Complete the pattern.

   100, 98, 94, ■, 80, ■.

8. **MONEY** Carmen received money for a birthday gift. She loaned \$5 to her sister Emily and spent half of the remaining money. The next day she received \$10 from her uncle. After spending \$9 at the movies, she still had \$11 left. How much money did she receive for her birthday?

9. **UNIFORMS** Nick has to wear a uniform to school. He can wear either navy blue, black, or khaki pants with a green, white, or yellow shirt. How many uniform combinations can Nick wear?

10. **TICKETS** Abbey, Constance, Miranda, and Jasmine are standing in a line to buy tickets for a concert. In how many different ways can they stand in the line?

11. **THEME PARKS** Refer to the graphic below. How does the attendance of the Magic Kingdom compare with the attendance of Disney's Animal Kingdom?

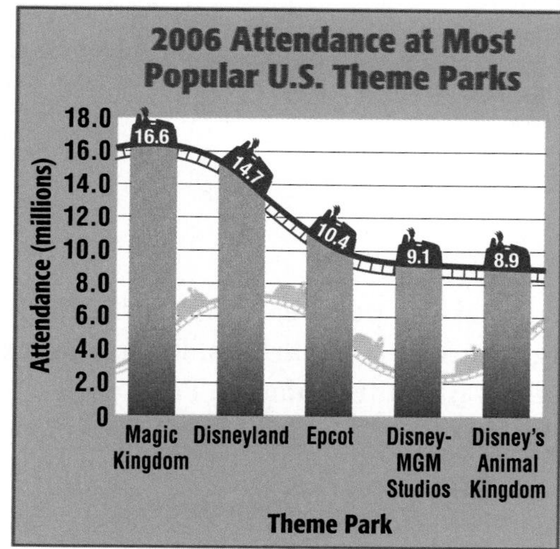

12. **NUMBER SENSE** The probability of selecting a blue marble from a bag is $\frac{2}{5}$. The probability of selecting a red marble is $\frac{3}{10}$. The number of green marbles in the bag is double the number of yellow marbles. What is one possibility for the number of each marble in the bag?

CHAPTER 12 Mid-Chapter Quiz

Lessons 12-1 through 12-4

IL Learning Standards
10.C.3a, 10.C.3b

1. **BREAKFAST** Draw a tree diagram to determine the number of one-bread and one-beverage outcomes using the breakfast choices listed below. (Lesson 12-1)

2. **FASHION** Reina has three necklaces, three pairs of earrings, and two bracelets. How many combinations of the three types of jewelry are possible? (Lesson 12-1)

3. **MULTIPLE CHOICE** Roman has ten cards numbered 1 to 10. What is the probability of picking two even-numbered cards one after the other, if the first card picked is replaced? (Lesson 12-2)

   A $\frac{1}{5}$ C $\frac{1}{4}$

   B $\frac{2}{9}$ D $\frac{3}{8}$

A box contains 3 purple, 2 yellow, 4 pink, 3 orange, and 2 blue markers. Once a marker is selected, it is *not* replaced. Find each probability. (Lesson 12-2)

4. P(two purple markers)
5. P(two orange markers)
6. P(a pink marker then an orange marker)
7. P(two markers that are *not* blue)
8. P(two markers that are neither yellow nor pink)
9. P(two markers that are neither purple nor pink)

10. **MULTIPLE CHOICE** A bag contains 4 red, 20 blue, and 6 green marbles. Kevin picks one at random and keeps it. Then Amy picks a marble. What is the probability that they each select a red marble? (Lesson 12-2)

    F $\frac{1}{150}$ H $\frac{2}{145}$

    G $\frac{1}{15}$ J $\frac{1}{870}$

11. **FOOD** Two hundred twenty-five high school freshman were asked to name their favorite hot lunch. One hundred thirty-five students named tacos as their favorite. If an additional 80 freshman are asked, how many would be expected to choose tacos? (Lesson 12-3)

MUSIC A survey asked 500 teenagers what formats of music they had purchased in the past two months. Use the table at the right to answer Exercises 12 and 13. (Lesson 12-3)

Format	Number Purchased
CD	380
Download	415

12. What is the experimental probability that a teenager purchased a CD in the past two months?

13. What is the experimental probability that a teenager purchased a music download in the past two months?

14. A coin is tossed three times, and it landed heads up all three times. What is the theoretical probability that the next toss will land tails up? (Lesson 12-3)

15. **BOOKS** Jackie has two math books and two English books that she wants to place on a shelf. Use the *act it out* strategy to determine how many different ways she can organize the books. (Lesson 12-4)

12-5 Using Sampling to Predict

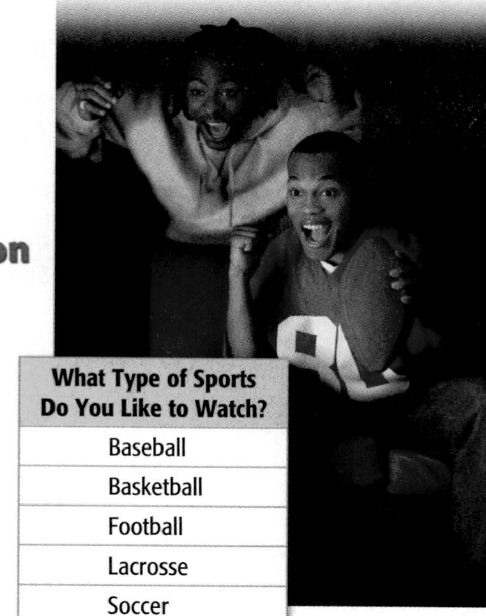

What Type of Sports Do You Like to Watch?
Baseball
Basketball
Football
Lacrosse
Soccer

MAIN IDEA

Predict the actions of a larger group by using a sample.

IL Learning Standards

10.B.3 Formulate questions (e.g., relationships between car age and mileage, average incomes and years of schooling), **devise and conduct experiments or simulations, gather data, draw conclusions and communicate** results to an audience using traditional methods and contemporary technologies.

New Vocabulary

sample
population
unbiased sample
simple random sample
stratified random sample
systematic random sample
biased sample
convenience sample
voluntary response samplent ratios

IL Math Online

glencoe.com

- Extra Examples
- Personal Tutor
- Self-Check Quiz
- Reading in the Content Area

GET READY for the Lesson

ENTERTAINMENT The manager of a television station wants to conduct a survey to determine what type of sports people like to watch.

1. Suppose she decides to survey a group of people at a basketball game. Do you think the results would represent all of the people in the viewing area? Explain.
2. Suppose she decides to survey students at your middle school. Do you think the results would represent all of the people in the viewing area? Explain.
3. Suppose she decides to call every 100th household in the telephone book. Do you think the results would represent all of the people in the viewing area? Explain.

The manager of the radio station cannot survey everyone in the listening area. A smaller group called a **sample** must be chosen. A sample is used to represent a larger group called a **population**.

To get valid results, a sample must be chosen very carefully. An **unbiased sample** is selected so that it accurately represents the entire population. Three ways to pick an unbiased sample are listed below.

Unbiased Samples — Concept Summary

Type	Description	Example
Simple Random Sample	Each item or person in the population is as likely to be chosen as any other.	Each student's name is written on a piece of paper. The names are placed in a bowl, and names are picked without looking.
Stratified Random Sample	The population is divided into similar, non-overlapping groups. A simple random sample is then selected from each group.	Students are picked at random from each grade level at a school.
Systematic Random Sample	The items or people are selected according to a specific time or item interval.	Every 20th person is chosen from an alphabetical list of all students attending a school.

Vocabulary Link
Bias
Everyday Use a tendency or prejudice.
Math Use error introduced by selecting or encouraging a specific outcome.

In a **biased sample**, one or more parts of the population are favored over others. Two ways to pick a biased sample are listed below.

Biased Samples

Concept Summary

Type	Description	Example
Convenience Sample	A convenience sample consists of members of a population that are easily accessed.	To represent all the students attending a school, the principal surveys the students in one math class.
Voluntary Response Sample	A voluntary response sample involves only those who want to participate in the sampling.	Students at a school who wish to express their opinions complete an online survey.

EXAMPLES Determine Validity of Conclusions

Determine whether each conclusion is valid. Justify your answer.

1 **To determine what music their customers like, every tenth person to walk into the music store is surveyed. Out of 150 customers, 70 stated that they prefer rock music. The manager concludes that about half of all customers prefer rock music.**

The conclusion is valid. Since the population is the customers of the music store, the sample is a systematic random sample. It is an unbiased sample.

2 **To determine what people like to do in their leisure time, the customers of a music store are surveyed. Of these, 85% said that they like to listen to music, so the store manager concludes that most people like to listen to music in their leisure time.**

The conclusion is not valid. The customers of a music store probably like to listen to music in their leisure time. This is a biased sample. The sample is a convenience sample since all of the people surveyed are in one specific location.

CHECK Your Progress

Determine whether each conclusion is valid. Justify your answer.

a. A radio station asks its listeners to call one of two numbers to indicate their preference for two candidates for mayor in an upcoming election. Seventy-two percent of the listeners who responded preferred candidate A, so the radio station announced that candidate A would win the election.

b. To award prizes at a sold-out hockey game, four seat numbers are picked from a barrel containing individual papers representing each seat number. Tyler concludes that he has as good a chance as everyone else to win a prize.

A valid sampling method uses unbiased samples. If a sampling method is valid, you can use the results to make predictions.

Study Tip

Misleading Probabilities Probabilities based on biased samples can be misleading. If the people surveyed were all women, the probabilities generated by the survey would not be valid, since both women and men purchase pants at the store.

Real-World EXAMPLE Using Sampling to Predict

3 STORES A store sells 4 main styles of pants: jeans, capris, cargos, and khakis. The people who work in the store survey 50 customers at random. The types of pants they prefer are indicated at the right. If 450 pairs of pants are to be ordered, how many should be jeans?

Type	Number
jeans	25
capris	10
cargos	8
khakis	7

First, determine whether the sample method is valid. The sample is a simple random sample since customers were randomly selected. Thus, the sample method is valid.

$\frac{25}{50}$ or 50% of the customers prefer jeans. So, find 50% of 450.

$0.5 \times 450 = 225$ About 225 pairs of jeans should be ordered.

CHECK Your Progress

c. **RECREATION** A swimming instructor at a community pool asked her students if they would be interested in an advanced swimming course, and 60% stated that they would. If there are 870 pool members, how many people can the instructor expect to take the course?

CHECK Your Understanding

Examples 1, 2 (p. 654)

Determine whether each conclusion is valid. Justify your answer.

1. To determine how much money the average family in the United States spends to cool their home, a survey of 100 households from Alaska are picked at random. Of the households, 85 said that they spend less than $75 a month on cooling. The researcher concluded that the average household in the United States spends less than $75 on cooling per month.

2. To determine the benefits that employees consider most important, one person from each department of the company is chosen at random. Medical insurance was listed as the most important benefit by 67% of the employees. The company managers conclude that medical insurance should be provided to all employees.

Example 3 (p. 655)

3. **GOLF** Zach is trying to decide which of three different golf courses is the best. He randomly surveyed some people at a golf store and recorded the results in the table. If he surveyed 150 people, how many would be expected to vote for Rolling Meadows?

Course	Number
Whispering Trail	10
Tall Pines	8
Rolling Meadows	7

Practice and Problem Solving

HOMEWORK HELP	
For Exercises	See Examples
4–9	1, 2
10, 11	3

Determine whether each conclusion is valid. Justify your answer.

4. To evaluate the quality of their product, a manufacturer of cell phones pulls every 50th phone off the assembly line to check for defects. Out of 200 phones tested, 4 are defective. The manager concludes that about 2% of the cell phones produced will be defective.

5. To determine whether the students will attend an arts festival at the school, Manuel surveys his friends in the art club. All of his friends plan to attend, so Manuel assumes that all the students at his school will also attend.

6. To determine the most popular television stars, a magazine asks its readers to complete a questionnaire and send it back to the magazine. The majority of those who replied liked one actor the most, so the magazine decides to write more articles about that actor.

7. To determine what people in California think about a proposed law, 2 people from each county in the state are surveyed at random. Of those surveyed, 42% said that they do not support the proposal. The legislature concludes that the law should not be passed.

Do You Support Proposed Law?	
Yes	30%
No	42%
Not sure	28%

8. Megan needs to buy two different packages of bread from a store to conduct an experiment. She closes her eyes and picks one package and then takes two steps to the left and chooses another package.

9. Mr. Roberts asks the five students sitting in the front row of his classroom if they plan on attending the pep rally. Because all five students say yes, Mr. Roberts concludes that all of the students will be attending the pep rally.

Real-World Link
63% of teens prefer to use a telephone to talk to their friends.
Source: *Pew Internet & American Life Project*

10. **COMMUNICATION** The Student Council advisor asked every tenth student in the lunch line how they preferred to be contacted with school news. The results are shown in the table. If there are 680 students at the school, how many can be expected to prefer e-mail?

Method	Number
E-mail	16
Newsletter	12
Announcement	5
Telephone	3

11. **TRAVEL** A random survey of people at a mall shows that 22 prefer to take a family trip by car, 18 prefer to travel by plane, and 4 prefer to travel by bus. If 500 people are surveyed, how many should say they prefer to travel by plane?

12. **AIRPORTS** An airport is considering building an Internet café in the terminal. They surveyed 500 random passengers in the airport, and 425 agree the Internet café is a good idea. Should the airport add this area? Explain your reasoning.

13. **ACTIVITIES** Patrick wants to conduct a survey about who stays for after-school activities. Describe a valid sampling method he could use.

MUSIC **For Exercises 14 and 15, use the following information.**

The manager of a music store sent out 1,000 survey forms to households near her store. The results of the survey are shown in the graph at the right.

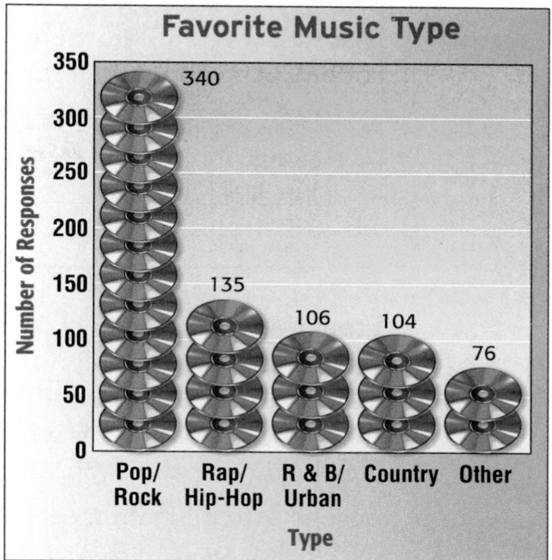

14. Based on this survey, if the manager orders 2,500 CDs, how many pop/rock CDs should be ordered?

15. Based on the survey results, the manager concludes that 25% of customers will buy either rap/hip-hop or R&B/urban CDs. Is this a valid conclusion? Explain.

SURVEYS **A survey is also biased if it contains questions that are worded to influence people's responses. Explain whether each survey question may result in bias.**

16. "Due to overcrowding, should another school be built?"

17. "Which snack do you most frequently purchase at the movies?"

18. "This semester, we read the popular *Journey* series. Did you enjoy the books?"

19. "Name your favorite baseball team."

COLLECT THE DATA **For Exercises 20–23, conduct a survey of the students in your math class to determine whether they prefer the Winter Olympics or the Summer Olympics.**

20. What percent prefer the Winter Olympics?

21. Use your survey to predict how many students in your school prefer the Winter Olympics.

22. Is your survey a good way to determine the preferences of the students in your school? Explain.

23. How could you improve your survey?

ILS • ISAT

Extra Practice, pp. 699, 711

24. **FIND THE DATA** Refer to the Data File on pages 16–19. Choose some data and write a real-world problem in which you would make a prediction based on samples.

H.O.T. Problems

25. **CHALLENGE** How could the wording of a question or the tone of voice of the interviewer affect a survey? Give at least two examples.

26. **WRITING IN MATH** Compare taking a survey and finding an experimental probability.

ISAT PRACTICE 10.B.3

27. Maci surveyed all the members of her softball team about their favorite sport.

Sport	Number of Members
Softball	12
Basketball	5
Soccer	3
Volleyball	8

From these results, Maci concluded that softball was the favorite sport among all her classmates. Which is the best explanation for why her conclusion might *not* be valid?

A The softball team meets only on weekdays.

B She should have asked only people who do not play sports.

C The survey should have been done daily for a week.

D The sample was not representative of all of her classmates.

28. Ms. Hernandez determined that 60% of the students in her classes brought an umbrella to school when the weather forecast predicted rain. If she has a total of 150 students, which statement does *not* represent Ms. Hernandez's data?

F On days when rain is forecast, less than $\frac{2}{5}$ of her students bring an umbrella to school.

G On days when rain is forecast, 90 of her students bring an umbrella to school.

H On days when rain is forecast, more than $\frac{1}{2}$ of her students bring an umbrella to school.

J On days when rain is forecast, 60 of her students do not bring an umbrella to school.

Spiral Review

29. PIZZA A pizza parlor has thin crust and thick crust, 2 different cheeses, and 4 toppings. Use the *act it out* strategy to determine how many different one-cheese and one-topping pizzas can be ordered. (Lesson 12-4)

30. BASKETBALL In practice, Gina made 80 out of 100 free throws. What is the experimental probability that she will make a free throw? (Lesson 12-3)

31. CAR RENTAL You can rent a car for either \$35 a day plus \$0.40 per mile or for \$20 a day plus \$0.55 per mile. Write and solve an equation to find the number of miles that result in the same cost for one day. (Lesson 8-4)

Problem Solving in Physical Education

Real-World Unit Project

Basketball All-Star It's time to complete your project. Use the data you have gathered about your basketball teams to prepare a poster that contains several graphs. Be sure to include a spreadsheet with your project.

IL Math Online **Unit Project at** glencoe.com

CHAPTER 12 Study Guide and Review

IL Math Online glencoe.com
- STUDY TO GO
- Vocabulary Review

FOLDABLES® Study Organizer — GET READY to Study

Be sure the following Big Ideas are noted in your Foldable.

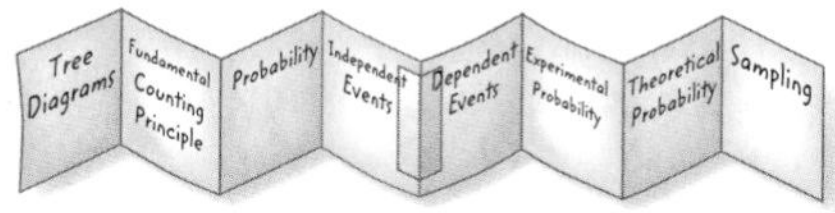

BIG Ideas

Counting Outcomes (Lesson 12-1)

- If event *M* can occur in *m* ways and is followed by event *N* that can occur in *n* ways, then the event *M* followed by the event *N* can occur in $m \cdot n$ ways.

Probability (Lessons 12-2 and 12-3)

- The probability of two independent events can be found by multiplying the probability of the first event by the probability of the second event.
- If two events, *A* and *B*, are dependent, then the probability of both events occurring is the product of the probability of *A* and the probability of *B* after *A* occurs.

Statistics (Lesson 12-5)

- An unbiased sample is representative of an entire population.
- A biased sample favors one or more parts of a population over others.

Key Vocabulary

biased sample (p. 654)
compound events (p. 637)
convenience sample (p. 654)
dependent events (p. 638)
event (p. 632)
experimental probability (p. 643)
Fundamental Counting Principle (p. 633)
independent events (p. 637)
outcome (p. 632)
population (p. 653)
probability (p. 633)
random (p. 633)
sample (p. 653)
sample space (p. 632)
simple random sample (p. 653)
stratified random sample (p. 653)
systematic random sample (p. 653)
theoretical probability (p. 643)
tree diagram (p. 632)
unbiased sample (p. 653)
voluntary response sample (p. 654)

Vocabulary Check

Choose the correct term to complete each sentence.

1. A list of all possible outcomes is called the (sample space, event).
2. The (population, probability) of an event is the ratio of a specific outcome to the total number of outcomes.
3. A (combination, compound event) consists of two or more simple events.
4. For (independent, dependent) events, the outcome of one does not affect the other.
5. (Theoretical, Experimental) probability is based on known characteristics or facts.
6. A (simple random sample, convenience sample) is a biased sample.

Lesson-by-Lesson Review

12-1 Counting Outcomes (pp. 632–636)

10.C.3a

For Exercises 7–9, use the following informaton.

A spinner with three equal sections labeled A, B, and C is spun and a number cube is rolled.

7. Draw a tree diagram to show the possible outcomes.
8. Find the probability of spinning a B and rolling a 3.
9. Find the probability of spinning a vowel and rolling an even number.

10. **BIKES** A bicycle shop has two styles of boys' bikes. They each come in one of three colors and one of two sizes. How many different bicycles are available?

Example 1 **A bakery sells 5 different flavors of cake in 3 different sizes with 1, 2, or 3 layers. How many choices does a customer have?**

number of flavors	×	number of sizes	×	number of layers	=	total number of cakes
5	×	3	×	3	=	45

The customer has 45 choices.

12-2 Probability of Compound Events (pp. 637–642)

6.D.3, 10.C.3a

A bag of marbles contains 3 red, 4 blue, 2 yellow, and 1 green marble. Once selected, the marble is not replaced. Find each probability.

11. P(2 yellow)
12. P(red then blue)
13. P(green then red)
14. P(yellow then blue)

15. **TIES** Mr. Dominguez has 4 black ties, 3 gray ties, 2 maroon ties, and 1 brown tie. If he selects two ties without looking, what is the probability that he will pick two black ties?

Example 2 **A spinner that is equally divided into eight sections labeled 1–8 is spun and a coin is tossed. What is the probability of spinning an even number and tossing heads?**

$P(\text{spinning an even number}) = \frac{1}{2}$

$P(\text{tossing heads}) = \frac{1}{2}$

$P(\text{even and heads}) = \frac{1}{2} \cdot \frac{1}{2}$

$= \frac{1}{4}$

Mixed Problem Solving
For mixed problem-solving practice, see page 711.

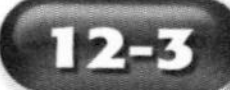

12-3 Experimental and Theoretical Probability (pp. 643–647)

6.D.3, 10.C.3a

A number cube is rolled. The table shows the results of the last 50 rolls. Find each experimental probability.

Number	Times Rolled
1	7
2	9
3	10
4	12
5	6
6	6

16. *P*(five)
17. *P*(one or two)
18. *P*(less than 6)
19. Compare the theoretical and experimental probabilities of rolling a four.

SPELLING For Exercises 20 and 21, use the following information.
On a spelling test, Angie misspells 2 out of the first 10 words.

20. What is the probability that she will misspell the next spelling word?
21. If the spelling test has 25 words on it, how many words would you expect Angie to misspell?

For Exercises 22 and 23, use the following information.
A group of three coins are each tossed 20 times. The results are shown in the table.

Outcome	Frequency
0 heads, 3 tails	2
1 head, 2 tails	8
2 heads, 1 tail	6
3 heads, 0 tails	4

22. What is the experimental probability that there will be one head and two tails?
23. What is the experimental probability that there will be three heads and zero tails?

Example 3 **A nickel and a dime are tossed. What is theoretical probability of tossing two tails?**

The theoretical probability is $\frac{1}{2} \cdot \frac{1}{2}$ or $\frac{1}{4}$.

Example 4 **In an experiment, the same two coins are tossed 50 times. Ten of those times, tails were both showing. Find the experimental probability of tossing two tails.**

Since tails were showing 10 out of the 50 tries, the experimental probability is $\frac{10}{50}$ or $\frac{1}{5}$.

Example 5 **Compare the theoretical and experimental probabilities of tossing two tails.**

The theoretical probability $\frac{1}{4}$ is greater than the experimental probability $\frac{1}{5}$.

12-4 PSI: Act It Out (pp. 650–651)

10.C.3b

Solve. Use the *act it out* strategy.

24. **READING** In English class, each student must select 4 short stories from a list of 5 short stories to read. How many different combinations of short stories could a student read?
25. **CARPENTRY** Jaime has $14\frac{1}{4}$ feet of lumber. She uses $2\frac{7}{8}$ feet for a bookshelf. Does Jaime have enough lumber for four more identical shelves? Explain.

Example 6 **The Spirit Club is making a banner using three sheets of paper. How many different banners can they make using their school colors of black, orange, and white?**

Use three index cards labeled black, orange, and white to model the different banners.

There are six different combinations they can make.

12-5 Using Sampling to Predict (pp. 653–658)

10.B.3

DANCES For Exercises 26 and 27, use the following information.

Mrs. Jenkins is taking a survey to find how many students would attend a school dance.

26. Describe the sample if Mrs. Jenkins asks every tenth student in the eighth grade.
27. Suppose 7 out of 12 students surveyed said they would attend a school dance. How many out of 350 students would be expected to attend a dance?

Example 7 **In a survey of store customers, the owners of a grocery determined that 25 out of 40 customers prefer the store brand oatmeal over the name brand oatmeal. If there is space for 500 boxes of oatmeal, how many store brand containers of oatmeal should the store order?**

25 out of 40 or 62.5% of the customers prefer the store brand oatmeal.

Find 62.5% of 500.

$0.625 \times 500 = 312.5$

The store should order about 313 boxes of store brand oatmeal.

Chapter 12 Practice Test

IL Math Online glencoe.com
• Chapter Test

1. **PICTURES** Students who are posing for their school pictures have the following options. How many different pictures can be taken?

Choices for School Pictures
5 different backgrounds
3 different poses
2 different treatments

2. **MULTIPLE CHOICE** Ms. Hawthorne randomly selects 2 students from 6 volunteers to be on the school activities committee. If Roberto and Joel volunteer, what is the probability that they will both be selected?

   A $\frac{1}{3}$ C $\frac{1}{30}$

   B $\frac{1}{15}$ D $\frac{1}{60}$

A jar contains 4 blue, 7 red, 6 yellow, 8 green, and 3 white tiles. Once a tile is selected, it is not replaced. Find each probability.

3. P(2 blue)
4. P(red then white)
5. P(white then green)
6. P(two tiles that are neither yellow nor red)

Two coins are tossed 20 times. No heads were tossed 4 times, one head was tossed 9 times, and 2 heads were tossed 7 times.

7. What is the experimental probability of two heads?
8. What is the experimental probability of one head?
9. Draw a tree diagram to show the outcomes of tossing two coins.
10. Compare the experimental probability with the theoretical probability of getting two heads when two coins are tossed.

11. **SHOES** A tennis shoe comes in men's and women's sizes; cross training, walking, and running styles; and blue, black, or white. What is the number of possible outcomes?

12. **SOFTBALL** Miranda had the opportunity to bat 15 times during the tournament. Of those at bats, she made an out 6 times, hit a single 5 times, a double three times, and a home run once. What is the experimental probability that Miranda hit a double?

13. **VOLUNTEERING** Student Council surveyed four homerooms to find out how many hours students volunteer each year. The results are shown in the table. If there are 864 students at the school, how many can be expected to volunteer 21–40 hours?

Number of Hours	Number of Students
0–10	38
11–20	26
21–40	10
40 or more	6

14. **MULTIPLE CHOICE** Mr. Delgadillo wants to know if the eighth-grade students want to take a field trip to the art museum. How should he conduct a valid survey?

   F Ask students in the art club.
   G Ask the parents of the students.
   H Ask every tenth eighth grader who enters the school.
   J Make an announcement and ask students to come and tell him.

15. **BASEBALL** To determine the favorite sport, a random survey is administered at a baseball game. Of those surveyed, 72% responded that baseball is their favorite sport. It is concluded that baseball is the favorite sport of most people. Is this conclusion valid?

ISAT Practice
Cumulative, Chapters 1–12

IL Math Online glencoe.com
• Test Practice

PART 1 Multiple Choice

Read each question. Then fill in the correct answer on the answer sheet provided by your teacher or on a sheet of paper.

1. The table below shows all of the possible outcomes of a 3-panel light switch being turned on or off.

1st switch	2nd switch	3rd switch
ON	ON	ON
ON	ON	OFF
ON	OFF	ON
ON	OFF	OFF
OFF	ON	ON
OFF	ON	OFF
OFF	OFF	ON
OFF	OFF	OFF

Which of the following statements must be true if an outcome is chosen at random?

A The probability that all of the switches will be on is the same as the probability that all of the switches will be off.

B The probability that one light switch is on is higher than the probability that two light switches are on.

C The probability that exactly two switches have the same outcome is $\frac{1}{2}$.

D The probability of having at least one light switch on is higher than the probability of having at least one light switch off.

2. The probability that Maryanne gets a hit in softball is $\frac{3}{5}$. How many hits would you expect her to get in her next 60 at bats?

F 50

G 36

H 30

J 24

3. Of the 32 students surveyed in J.T.'s homeroom, 14 recycle at home. How many students would you expect to recycle at home if a total of 880 students were surveyed?

A 495 C 281

B 385 D 123

4. A car tire travels about 100 inches in 1 full rotation. What is the radius of the tire, to the nearest inch?

F 32 inches H 24 inches

G 28 inches J 16 inches

5. What is the volume of a rectangular prism with a length of 7 centimeters, a width of 14 centimeters, and a height of 10 centimeters?

A 31 cm^3 C 980 cm^3

B 108 cm^3 D 1,000 cm^3

6. An ice cream store surveyed 100 of its customers about their favorite flavor. The results are shown in the table. If the store uses only these data to order ice cream, what conclusion can be drawn from the data?

Favorite Flavor	
Flavor	Frequency
Chocolate Chip	40
Vanilla	15
Cookie Dough	20
Chocolate	15
Other	10

F More than half of each order should be chocolate chip and cookie dough ice cream.

G Half of the order should be vanilla and chocolate ice cream.

H Only chocolate, cookie dough, and vanilla ice cream should be ordered.

J About one third of the order should be vanilla and chocolate chip ice cream.

Preparing for ISAT

For test-taking strategies and practice, see pages 712–729.

7. A drawer contained two blue, three black, and four white socks. Michael removed one blue sock from the drawer and did *not* put the sock back in the drawer. He then randomly removed another sock from the drawer. What is the probability that the second sock Michael removed was blue?

   A $\frac{1}{18}$ **C** $\frac{1}{8}$

   B $\frac{1}{9}$ **D** $\frac{1}{4}$

8. The net below forms a cylinder when folded. What is the surface area of the cylinder?

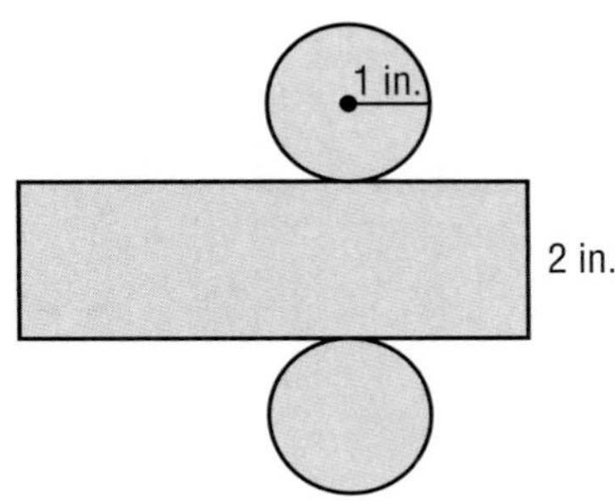

   F 6.3 in^2 **H** 21.3 in^2

   G 18.8 in^2 **J** 42.6 in^2

9. If three coins are tossed, what is the probability that they all show tails?

   A 6.25% **C** 25%

   B 12.5% **D** 50%

10. What is the solution of the inequality $4n - 8 \leq 40$?

   F $n \leq 8$ **H** $n \geq 8$

   G $n \leq 12$ **J** $n \geq 12$

PART 2 Short Response/Grid In

Record your answers on the answer sheet provided by your teacher or on a sheet of paper.

11. A sporting goods company ships basketballs in cube-shaped boxes. What is the surface area of the box to the nearest tenth?

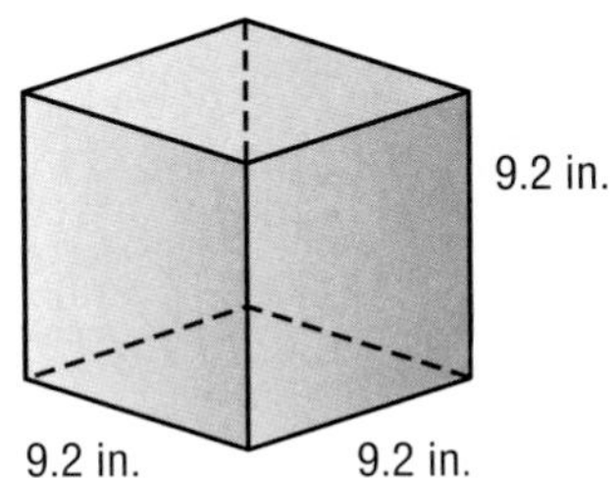

PART 3 Extended Response

Record your answers on the answer sheet provided by your teacher or on a sheet of paper. Show your work.

12. In a cookie jar, there are 5 chocolate chip, 5 peanut butter, and 5 oatmeal cookies. Two cookies are pulled out of the jar.

    a. What is the probability of choosing 2 chocolate chip cookies?

    b. From the cookies left, what is the probability of choosing an oatmeal cookie next?

TEST-TAKING TIP

Question 12 Extended-response questions often involve several parts. When one part of the question involves the answer to a previous part of the question, make sure to check your answer to the first part before moving on.

NEED EXTRA HELP?												
If You Missed Question...	1	2	3	4	5	6	7	8	9	10	11	12
Go to Lesson...	12-2	12-3	12-5	7-1	7-5	12-5	12-2	7-7	12-2	8-8	7-7	12-2
IL Learning Standards	6.D.3	6.D.3	10.B.3	7.A.3b	7.A.3b	10.B.3	6.D.3	7.C.3b	6.D.3	8.A.3b	7.C.3b	6.D.3

Looking
Ahead

Let's Look Ahead

Polynomials

MAIN IDEA

Use physical models to simplify polynomials.

IL Learning Standards

8.A.3b Solve problems using linear **expressions,** equations and inequalities.
8.D.3a Solve problems using numeric, graphic or symbolic representations of variables, expressions, equations and inequalities.

New Vocabulary

polynomial

IL Math Online

glencoe.com

- Personal Tutor
- Self-Check Quiz
- Extra Examples

GET READY for the Lesson

COINS The value of x dimes is $10x$ cents.

1. Write an expression to represent the value in cents of y quarters.
2. Write an expression to represent the total value of x dimes, y quarters, and z pennies.

You can use algebra tiles to model monomials. A tile that is 1 unit by 1 unit represents the integer 1. A tile that is 1 unit by x units represents the variable x. A tile that is x units by x units represents the expression x^2.

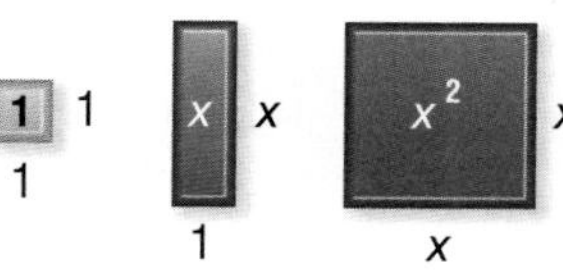

Red tiles with the same shapes are used to represent -1, $-x$, and $-x^2$.

You can also use these tiles to model **polynomials**, which are algebraic expressions that contain more than one monomial.

EXAMPLE Model Polynomials

1 **Use algebra tiles to model $x^2 - 3x + 4$.**

$x^2 - 3x + 4 = x^2 + (-3x) + 4$ Use the definition of subtraction to write the polynomial as the sum of terms.

$x^2 + (-3x) + 4$

CHECK Your Progress

Use algebra tiles to model each polynomial.

a. $5x - 6$

b. $2x^2 + 4x + 3$

When simplifying polynomials, it is customary to write the result in *standard form*. That is, write the powers of the variable decreasing from left to right.

Standard form	**Not standard form**
$-3x^2 + 4x + 1$	$4x - 3x^2 + 1$

Study Tip

Like Terms
Tiles or groups of tiles with the same shape represent *like terms*. In other words, like terms are expressions that contain the same variable to the same power.

EXAMPLE Simplify Polynomials

2 **Simplify $-3 + 4x + x^2 + x$.**

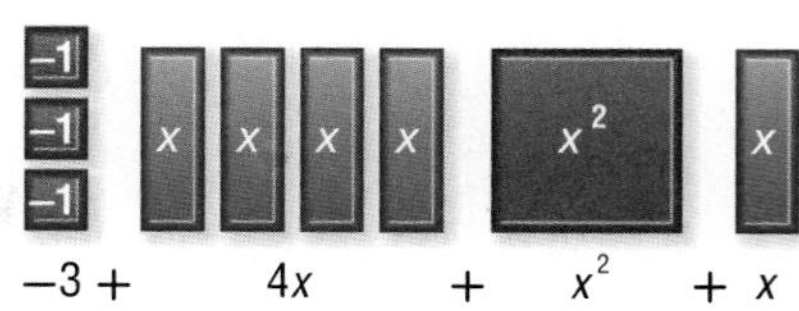

Group tiles with the same shape. Write a polynomial for the tiles.

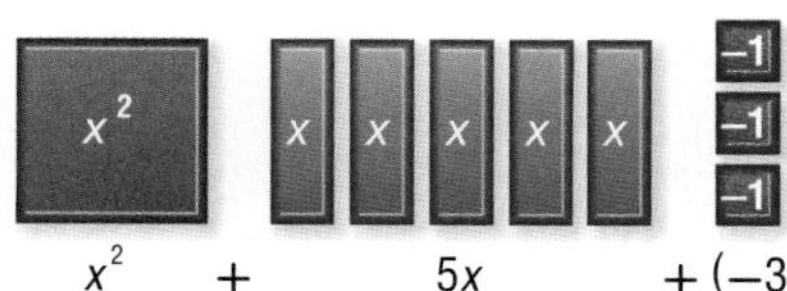

So, $-3 + 4x + x^2 + x = x^2 + 5x + (-3)$ or $x^2 + 5x - 3$.

CHECK Your Progress

Simplify each polynomial. Use models if needed.

c. $-x + 1 - 2x + 5$

d. $x^2 + 4 + 3x + x^2$

When a positive tile and a negative tile of the same shape are paired, the result is called a *zero pair*. Remove any zero pairs when simplifying polynomials.

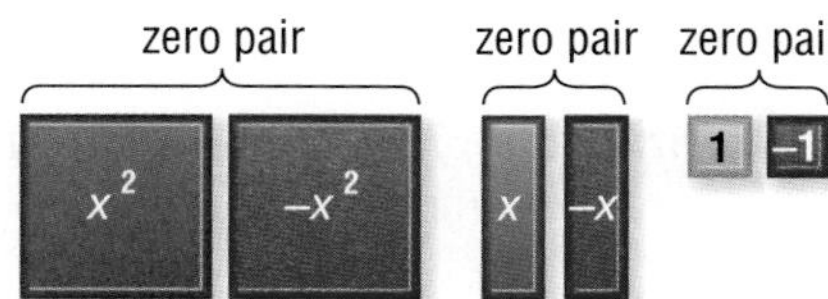

EXAMPLE Remove Zero Pairs to Simplify Polynomials

3 **Simplify $2x^2 - 3x - x^2$.**

$2x^2 - 3x - x^2 = 2x^2 + (-3x) + (-x^2)$ Write the polynomial as the sum of terms.

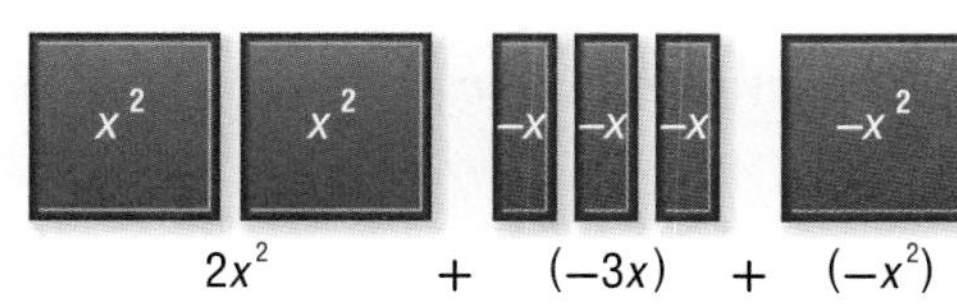

Group tiles with the same shape. Remove the zero pair.

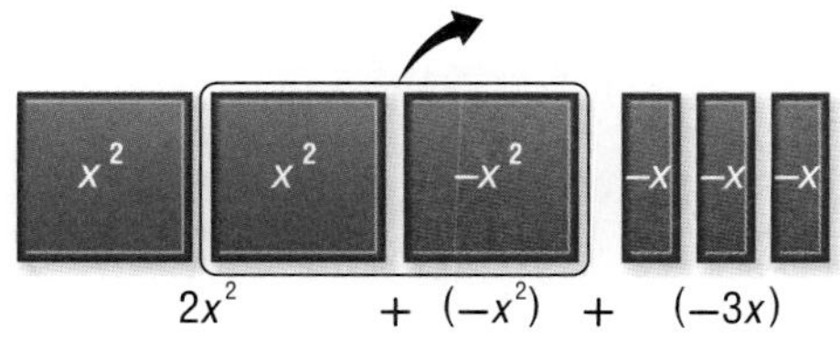

So, $2x^2 - 3x - x^2 = x^2 - 3x$.

CHECK Your Progress

Simplify each polynomial. Use models if needed.

e. $6 - 2x + 3x$

f. $-2x^2 + 5 - 1 + x^2$

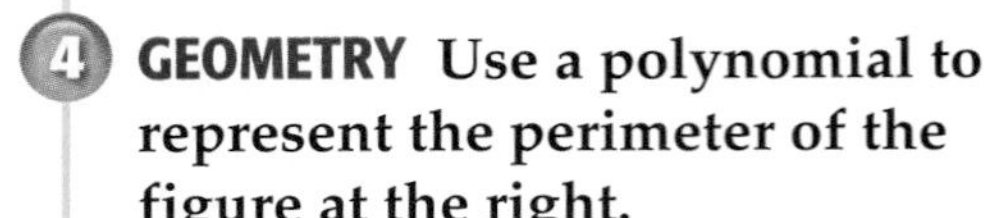

Use a Polynomial to Represent Problems

4 **GEOMETRY** **Use a polynomial to represent the perimeter of the figure at the right.**

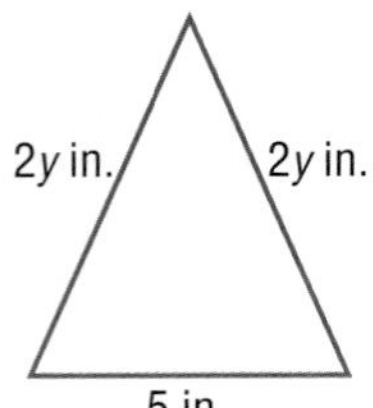

perimeter $= 2y + 2y + 5$ Definition of perimeter

$= (4y + 5)$ in. Combine like terms.

g. **SHOPPING** Jenna bought a bottled water for \$2, four notebooks for \$$x$ each, and a pack of gum for \$1. Write and simplify a polynomial expression to represent the total amount of money she spent.

CHECK Your Understanding

Example 1 (p. LA2)

Use algebra tiles to model each polynomial.

1. $3x^2 + 4x$
2. $-x^2 + 2x + 5$

Examples 2, 3 (p. LA3)

Simplify each polynomial.

3. $2x + 3 + 3x$
4. $x^2 - 3x + x$

Example 4 (p. LA4)

5. **GEOMETRY** Use a polynomial to represent the perimeter of the figure at right.

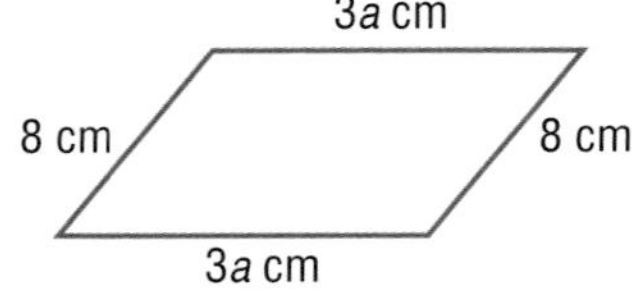

Examples 2, 3 (p. LA3)

Simplify each polynomial. Use models if needed.

6. $1 + 2x + 4 + x$
7. $x^2 - 6x + 4x$
8. $3x^2 + 5x - x^2 + 2x$
9. $-2x^2 + 7 + 3x - x^2 - 5x$

Practice and Problem Solving

HOMEWORK HELP

For Exercises	See Examples
10–13	1
14–17, 20–27	2, 3
18, 19	4

Use algebra tiles to model each polynomial.

10. $5x - 1$
11. $x^2 + 6$
12. $2x^2 - x + 3$
13. $-x^2 + 6x - 4$

Simplify each polynomial.

14. $5 + x + 2$
15. $-x^2 + 4x - x^2$

Simplify each polynomial.

16. $x^2 - x + 4 + 2x - 3$

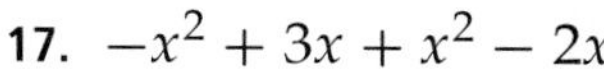

17. $-x^2 + 3x + x^2 - 2x$

18. **GEOMETRY** Use a polynomial to represent the perimeter of the figure at right.

2k mm

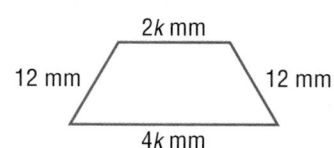

12 mm 12 mm

4k mm

19. **EXERCISE** Taylor jogged x miles after school. Seth jogged twice the distance that Taylor jogged. Rashida jogged 4 miles. Write and simplify a polynomial expression to represent the total number of miles that the three people jogged.

Simplify each polynomial. Use models if needed.

20. $x^2 + 7 + 3x^2$

21. $9 - 5x - 2x + 2$

22. $-2x^2 + x - 3x^2 - 6$

23. $7x - 8 + 2x + 4x^2 + x^2$

24. $-6x + 4 + 2x + 7$

25. $5 - x^2 + 7x + 4x^2$

26. $4x^2 + 5x + 1 - 4x^2 - 6x$

27. $6 + 2x^2 - 3x - 4x - x^2$

28. **PIZZA** For a party, one classroom orders 4 large pizzas, 2 medium pizzas, and 6 submarine sandwiches. Another classroom orders 6 large pizzas and 8 submarine sandwiches. If ℓ represents the cost of a large pizza, m represents the cost of a medium pizza, and s represents the cost of a submarine sandwich, write an expression in simplest form for the total amount of money that the two classrooms spent on food.

29. **JOBS** Michael and Olivia each earn x dollars per lawn that they mow and y dollars per swimming pool that they clean. The table shows how many lawns they mowed and how many pools they cleaned. Write an expression in simplest form for the total amount of money they earned.

Person	Number of Lawns	Number of Pools
Michael	8	6
Olivia	9	4

Simplify each polynomial.

30. $1.5t^2 - 7.6 + 4t - 2t^2 + t - 5.1$

31. $10 + 6c^3 - c^2 - 2c^3 + 2c^2 - 4c^2$

32. $\frac{1}{2}n^2 - 6n - \frac{3}{4}n + 7n$

33. $4a^2 + 2b - b^2 - 6b + 3a^2 - 5a$

H.O.T. Problems

34. **CHALLENGE** Determine whether $x^2 + 6x = 7x^2$ is *sometimes, always,* or *never* true. Explain your reasoning.

35. **REASONING** Explain how you can tell from a model whether a polynomial will have one term, two terms, or three terms when it is simplified.

36. **OPEN ENDED** Write a polynomial with four terms that simplifies to $x^2 + 3x$.

37. **WRITING IN MATH** Describe how to use models to simplify polynomials.

Adding Polynomials

MAIN IDEA

Add polynomials.

IL Learning Standards

8.A.3b Solve problems using linear **expressions,** equations and inequalities.
8.D.3a Solve problems using numeric, graphic or symbolic representations of variables, expressions, equations and inequalities.

IL Math Online

glencoe.com

- Personal Tutor
- Self-Check Quiz
- Extra Examples

GET READY for the Lesson

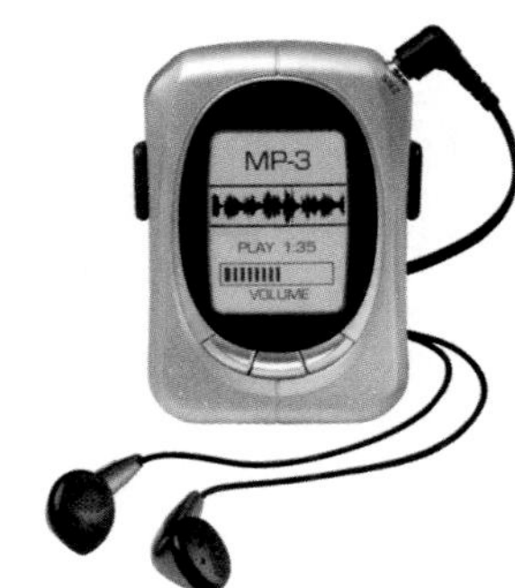

MUSIC Lauren has 82 songs and 6 music videos on her MP3 player. Javier has 125 songs and 2 music videos on his MP3 player.

1. The expression 82 songs + 6 videos represents the items on Lauren's MP3 player. Write an expression for the items on Javier's MP3 player.
2. Add the two expressions to find the total number of songs and videos.

You can use models to add polynomials.

EXAMPLES Add Polynomials

1 **Find $(3x + 4) + (2x + 1)$.**

Step 1 Model each polynomial.

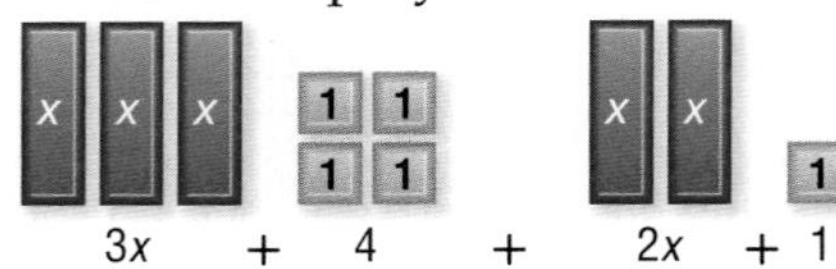

Step 2 Combine the tiles that have the same shape.

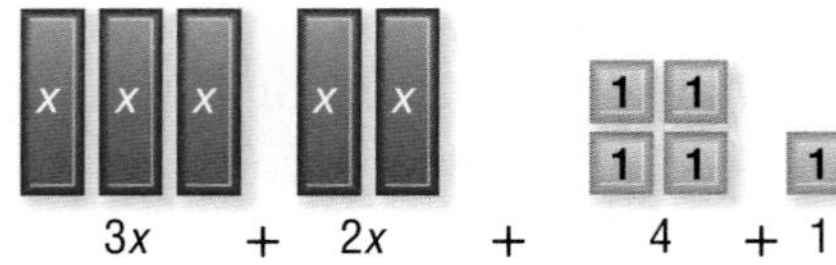

Step 3 Write the polynomial for the combined tiles.

$(3x + 4) + (2x + 1) = 5x + 5$

2 **Find $(2x^2 - 4x + 2) + (-2x + 2)$.**

$$\begin{array}{rl} 2x^2 - 4x + 2 & \\ + \quad\quad -2x + 2 & \text{Arrange like terms in columns.} \\ \hline 2x^2 - 6x + 4 & \text{Add.} \end{array}$$

So, $(2x^2 - 4x + 2) + (-2x + 2) = 2x^2 - 6x + 4$.

CHECK Your Progress **Add. Use models if needed.**

a. $(x^2 + x - 3) + (3x^2 - 4)$ b. $(-2x^2 - x + 1) + (-x^2 - 3x)$

When adding polynomials, remove any zero pairs.

EXAMPLES Use Zero Pairs to Add Polynomials

3 **Find $(x^2 - 3) + (x^2 - 2x + 1)$.**

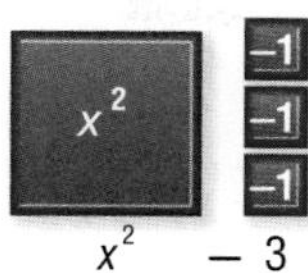

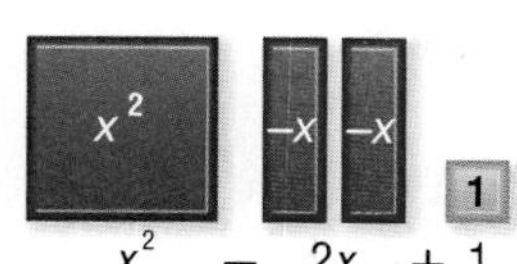

Group tiles with the same shape. Then remove any zero pairs.

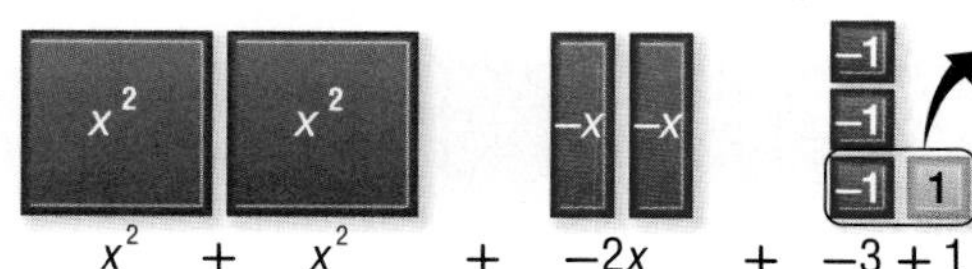

Write the polynomial for the tiles that remain.

So, $(x^2 - 3) + (x^2 - 2x + 1) = 2x^2 - 2x - 2$.

4 **Find $(-2x^2 + 3x + 2) + (x^2 - x + 4)$.**

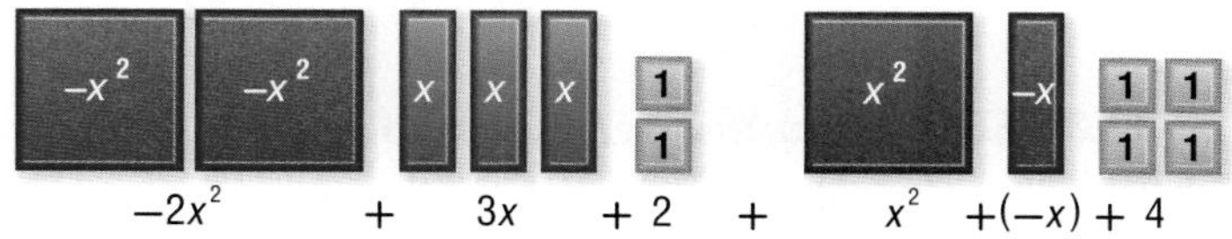

Group tiles with the same shape. Then remove any zero pairs.

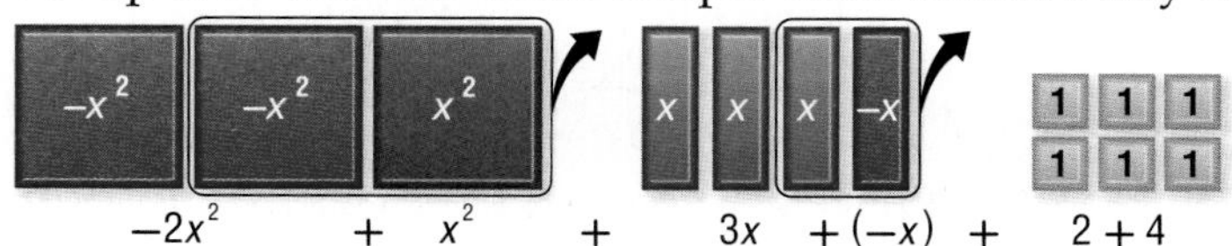

So, $(-2x^2 + 3x + 2) + (x^2 - x + 4) = -x^2 + 2x + 6$.

CHECK Your Progress **Add. Use models if needed.**

c. $(-3x^2 + 2x) + (3x^2 + 4x)$

d. $(x^2 - 4x - 1) + (-2x^2 + 5x - 3)$

Real-World EXAMPLE Use Polynomials to Find Perimeter

5 **GEOMETRY Find the perimeter of the figure at the right.**

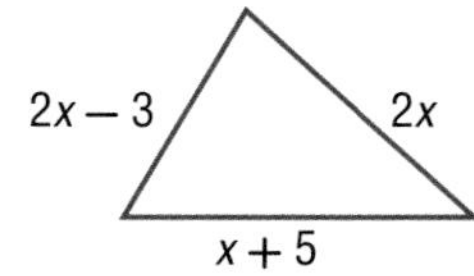

perimeter $= (2x - 3) + 2x + (x + 5)$

$= (2x + 2x + x) + (-3 + 5)$ Combine like terms.

$= 5x + 2$ Simplify.

> **Study Tip**
> **Like Terms**
> Recall that like terms are terms that have the same variable.

CHECK Your Progress

e. **GEOMETRY** A rectangle has side lengths of $(x^2 - 5x)$ units and $(2x^2 + x)$ units. What is the perimeter of the rectangle?

CHECK Your Understanding

Examples 1–4 (pp. LA6, LA7)

Add. Use models if needed.

1. $(x + 5) + (2x + 3)$
2. $(x^2 - 4x) + (x^2 - 5x)$
3. $(2x^2 - 6) + (-x^2 + 3x - 1)$
4. $(x^2 - 7x + 2) + (-3x^2 + x + 4)$

Example 5 (p. LA7)

5. **GEOMETRY** Find the perimeter of the figure at the right.

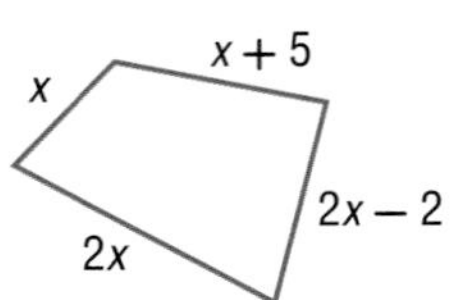

Practice and Problem Solving

HOMEWORK HELP	
For Exercises	See Examples
6–13	1–4
14, 15	5

Add. Use models if needed.

6. $(7x + 5) + (x + 2)$
7. $(-x + 3) + (-5x + 6)$
8. $(3x^2 - 7x + 1) + (x^2 - x)$
9. $(x - 1) + (3x + 7)$
10. $(6x^2 + 5x) + (-9x + 4)$
11. $(-4x^2 - 2x) + (-x^2 + 2x + 10)$
12. $(-3x^2 + x - 1) + (x^2 + x - 4)$
13. $(2x^2 - 5x + 3) + (x^2 - 6x - 8)$

GEOMETRY Find the perimeter of each figure.

14.

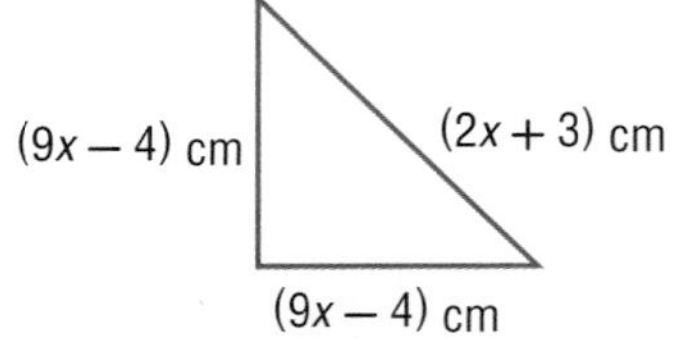

15.

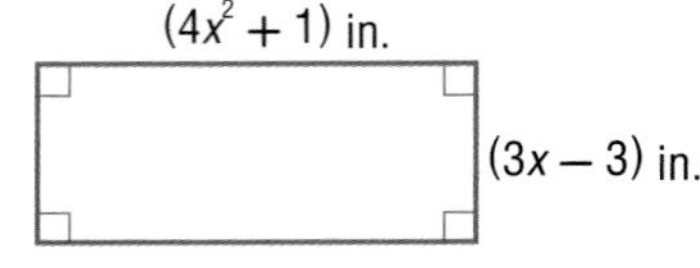

16. **NEWSPAPERS** Anna and Cole each earn x cents per newspaper that they deliver, plus tips. Anna delivered 55 newspapers and earned $12 in tips. Cole delivered 68 newspapers and earned $15 in tips.
   a. Write a polynomial expression to represent Anna's total earnings.
   b. Write a polynomial expression to represent Cole's total earnings.
   c. Write a polynomial expression to represent their total earnings.

17. **GEOMETRY** The angle measures of a triangle are $(x + 15)°$, $(2x - 20)°$, and $2x°$. What are the actual angle measures of the triangle?

Add.

18. $(-2x^3 + 3x^2 + 6x + 1) + (x^3 - 10x^2 - 6x + 9)$
19. $(b^2 + a + 7 - 2b) + (4a^2 + 6b + 4b^2 - 8)$
20. $(-n^2 + 6) + (4n^2 - 5n - 2) + (2n^2 - 3n)$

H.O.T. Problems

21. **CHALLENGE** Find the product of 3 times $(x^2 + 2x + 5)$.
22. **REASONING** Explain how algebra tiles represent like terms and zero pairs.
23. **OPEN ENDED** Write two polynomials that have a sum of $3x^2 - 8x$.
24. **WRITING IN MATH** Compare and contrast finding the sum of polynomials with finding the sum of integers.

Subtracting Polynomials

MAIN IDEA

Subtract polynomials.

IL Learning Standards

8.A.3b Solve problems using linear **expressions,** equations and inequalities.
8.D.3a Solve problems using numeric, graphic or symbolic representations of variables, expressions, equations and inequalities.

IL Math Online

glencoe.com

- Personal Tutor
- Self-Check Quiz
- Extra Examples

GET READY for the Lesson

PETS A pet store had 6 puppies and then received x more puppies.

1. Write an expression for the total number of puppies.
2. The pet store sold 2 of the puppies. Write and simplify an expression to represent the number of puppies the pet store has left.

As with adding polynomials, to subtract polynomials, you subtract the like terms. You can also use models to subtract polynomials.

EXAMPLES Subtract Polynomials

1 Find $(5x + 4) - (3x + 2)$.

Step 1 Model the polynomial $5x + 4$.

Step 2 To subtract $3x + 2$, remove 3 x-tiles and 2 1-tiles.

Step 3 Write the polynomial for the remaining tiles.

$(5x + 4) - (3x + 2) = 2x + 2$

2 Find $(x^2 - 4x - 6) - (-x - 3)$.

Step 1 Model the polynomial $x^2 - 4x - 6$.

$x^2 - 4x - 6 =$
$x^2 + (-4x) + (-6)$

Step 2 To subtract $-x - 3$, remove 1 negative x-tile and 3 negative 1-tiles.

Step 3 Write the polynomial for the remaining tiles.

$(x^2 - 4x - 6) - (-x - 3) = x^2 - 3x - 3$

CHECK Your Progress **Subtract. Use models if needed.**

a. $(7x - 5) - (2x - 1)$

b. $(2x^2 + 6x - 4) - (x^2 + 2x - 4)$

EXAMPLE Use Zero Pairs to Subtract Polynomials

3 **Find $(2x^2 + 3x + 2) - (x^2 - 2x)$.**

Step 1 Model the polynomial $2x^2 + 3x + 2$.

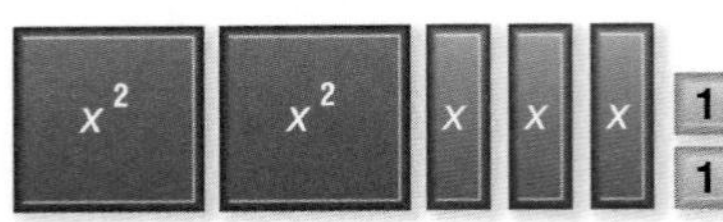

Step 2 Since there are no negative x-tiles to remove, add 2 zero pairs of x-tiles.

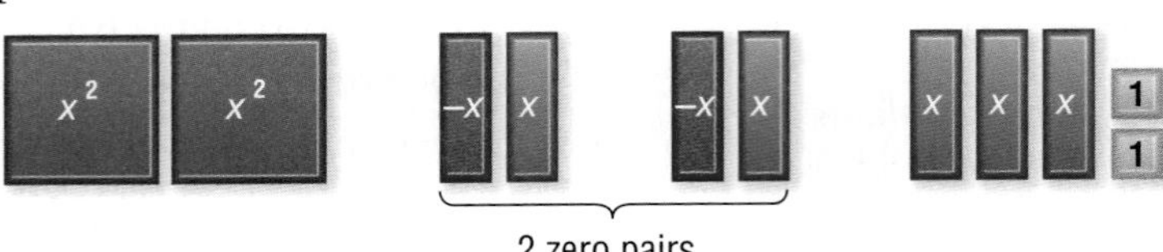

Step 3 Remove 1 x^2-tile and 2 negative x-tiles.

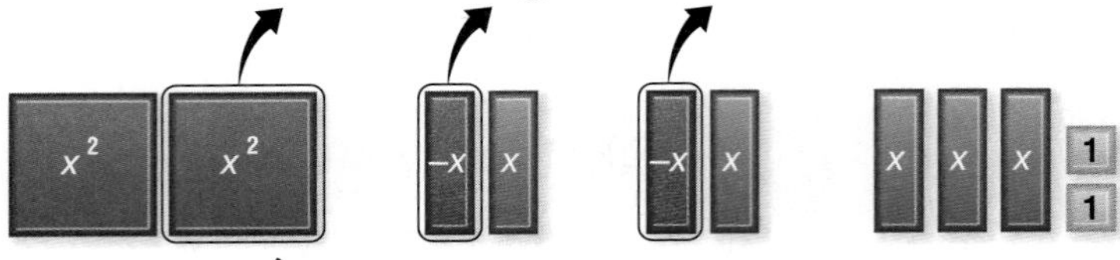

So, $(2x^2 + 3x + 2) - (x^2 - 2x) = x^2 + 5x + 2$.

Study Tip

Zero Pairs
In Step 2, to subtract $x^2 - 2x$, you need to remove 1 x^2-tile and 2 negative x-tiles. You can add zero pairs of x^2-tiles, x-tiles, or 1-tiles.

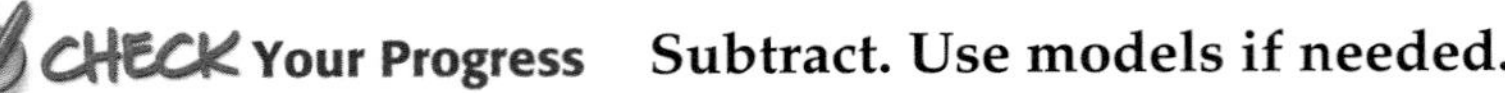

CHECK Your Progress **Subtract. Use models if needed.**

c. $(x - 5) - (2x - 1)$

d. $(3x^2 + 7x + 4) - (2x^2 + 5)$

Real-World EXAMPLE

4 **EXERCISE After x seconds, Cyclist A travels $(16x + 2)$ feet and Cyclist B travels $(19x - 1)$ feet. After 120 seconds, how many more feet does Cyclist B travel?**

Step 1 Write an expression to represent the difference in distances.

Distance B − Distance A	$= (19x - 1) - (16x + 2)$	Subtract the distances.
	$= 19x - 1 - 16x - 2$	Distributive Property
	$= 3x - 3$	Simplify.

Step 2 Evaluate the expression for a time of 120 seconds.

$3x - 3$	$= 3(120) - 3$	Replace x with 120.
	$= 360 - 3$ or 357	Simplify.

So, Cyclist B travels 357 feet farther.

CHECK Your Progress

e. **MONEY** After x hours at their jobs, Kayla earns $9x$ dollars and Abigail earns $(7x + 3)$ dollars. After 5 hours, how much more money does Kayla earn?

CHECK Your Understanding

Examples 1–3 (pp. LA9, LA10)

Subtract. Use models if needed.

1. $(6x + 5) - (3x + 1)$
2. $(3x^2 - 4x + 2) - (x^2 - 2x)$
3. $(x^2 + 9x - 4) - (x^2 - 2x + 1)$
4. $(5x^2 + 7) - (x^2 + 2x + 4)$

Example 4 (p. LA10)

5. **FUNDRAISING** The expression $8x + 50$ represents the total amount of money the soccer team earned from selling x T-shirts.
   a. If the team had to pay $(2x + 24)$ dollars in expenses, write an expression to represent their profit.
   b. If the soccer team sold 54 T-shirts, what was their profit?

Practice and Problem Solving

HOMEWORK HELP	
For Exercises	See Examples
6–13	1–3
14, 15	4

Subtract. Use models if needed.

6. $(3x + 7) - (x + 5)$
7. $(2x^2 - 4x) - (x^2 - x)$
8. $(x^2 + 8x - 9) - (3x - 1)$
9. $(-4x^2 + x + 7) - (-2x^2 + x + 2)$
10. $(6x^2 + 4x) - (3x^2 - x)$
11. $(4x^2 - 3) - (x^2 + x + 1)$
12. $(5x + 6) - (x^2 + 2x)$
13. $(-4x^2 + x + 5) - (x^2 + 2x + 3)$

14. **EXERCISE** In x days, the expression $5x + 2$ represents the number of miles that Celeste rode her bike and $10x$ represents the number of miles that Kimiko rode her bike. After 7 days, how many more miles did Kimiko ride her bike than Celeste?
15. **CARS** A car accelerates for t seconds. The expression $2t + t^2$ represents the distance the car travels in meters. Another car has twice the acceleration and travels $(2t + 2t^2)$ meters in t seconds. After 10 seconds, how much farther does the second car travel?

Subtract. Then evaluate the difference if $a = 2$ and $b = -3$.

16. $(5a + 12b) - (4a - 2b)$
17. $(3a - 8) - (-a + 6b)$

18. **MONEY** Eric had \$25 and bought 3 packs of baseball cards for b dollars each. Kyle had \$22 and bought 4 packs of baseball cards for b dollars each.
    a. Write an expression to represent how much money each person had left after he bought the pack of cards.
    b. If each pack cost \$2, how much more money did Eric have than Kyle?

H.O.T. Problems

19. **CHALLENGE** The sum of $(x^2 - 8)$ and another polynomial equals $(3x^2 - 4)$. What is the other polynomial? Explain how you found the answer.
20. **REASONING** Explain how to subtract $x^2 + 5x + 7$ from $2x^2$.
21. **OPEN ENDED** Write two polynomials that have a difference of $4x + 1$.
22. **WRITING IN MATH** Explain how subtracting polynomials is similar to subtracting measurements such as 5 feet 8 inches − 4 feet 2 inches.

Cube Roots

MAIN IDEA

Estimate and use cube roots.

New Vocabulary

cube root

IL Math Online

glencoe.com

- Personal Tutor
- Self-Check Quiz
- Extra Examples

GET READY for the Lesson

GEOMETRY The volume of the cube at the right is represented by $x \cdot x \cdot x$.

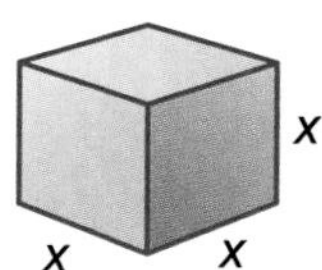

1. Write the volume of the cube as a power.
2. If the volume of the cube is 8 cubic inches, what is the side length x?

Numbers like 8, 27, and 64 are perfect cubes because they are the cubes of integers.

$8 = 2 \cdot 2 \cdot 2$ or 2^3 $\quad 27 = 3 \cdot 3 \cdot 3$ or 3^3 $\quad 64 = 4 \cdot 4 \cdot 4$ or 4^3

Cube Roots — Key Concept

Words A **cube root** of a number is one of its three equal factors.

Symbols If $x^3 = y$, then x is the cube root of y.

Examples Since $4 \cdot 4 \cdot 4$ or $4^3 = 64$, 4 is a cube root of 64.
Since $-5 \cdot (-5) \cdot (-5) = -125$, -5 is a cube root of -125.

The symbol $\sqrt[3]{}$ is used to indicate a cube root of a number.

EXAMPLE Use a Calculator to Estimate Cube Roots

1 Use a calculator to find $\sqrt[3]{200}$ to the nearest tenth.

[MATH] 4 200 [ENTER] 5.848035476 — Use a calculator.

$\sqrt[3]{200} \approx 5.8$ — Round to the nearest tenth.

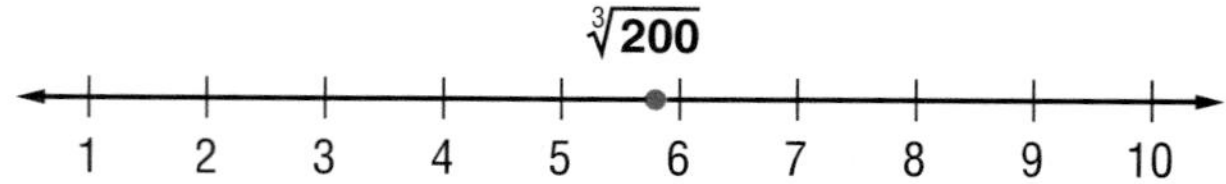

Check Since $6^3 = 216$, the answer is reasonable.

CHECK Your Progress

a. $\sqrt[3]{75}$

b. $\sqrt[3]{-310}$

You can also estimate cube roots mentally by using perfect cubes. The first ten perfect cubes are shown at the right.

$1 = 1^3$	$216 = 6^3$
$8 = 2^3$	$343 = 7^3$
$27 = 3^3$	$512 = 8^3$
$64 = 4^3$	$729 = 9^3$
$125 = 5^3$	$1{,}000 = 10^3$

EXAMPLES Estimate Cube Roots Mentally

Study Tip

Appropriate Forms of Numbers
Express a number as a cube root if an exact answer is needed. Express a number as a decimal if an approximation is sufficient.

Estimate each cube root to the nearest integer.

2 $\sqrt[3]{180}$

The first perfect cube less than 180 is 125. $\sqrt[3]{125} = 5$

The first perfect cube greater than 180 is 216. $\sqrt[3]{216} = 6$

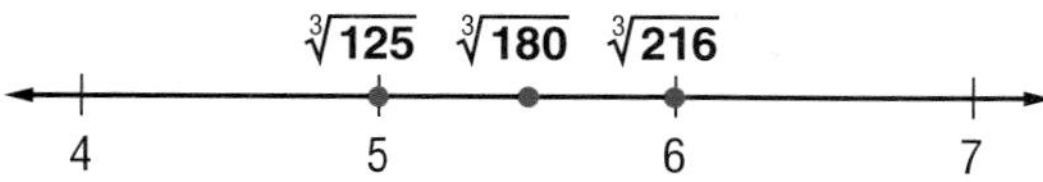

The cube root of 180 is between the whole numbers 5 and 6. Since 180 is closer to 216 than to 125, $\sqrt[3]{180}$ is closer to 6 than to 5.

3 $\sqrt[3]{-320}$

The first perfect cube less than 320 is 216. $\sqrt[3]{216} = 6$

The first perfect cube greater than 320 is 343. $\sqrt[3]{343} = 7$

$\sqrt[3]{-343}$ $\sqrt[3]{-320}$ $\sqrt[3]{-216}$

−8 −7 −6 −5

The negative cube root of 320 is between the integers −6 and −7. Since 320 is closer to 343 than to 216, $\sqrt[3]{-320}$ is closer to −7 than to −6.

CHECK Your Progress

c. $\sqrt[3]{62}$

d. $\sqrt[3]{-25}$

Real-World EXAMPLE Estimate Side Lengths of Cubes

4 **GEOMETRY The volume of the cube at the right is given. Estimate the side length of the cube to the nearest integer.**

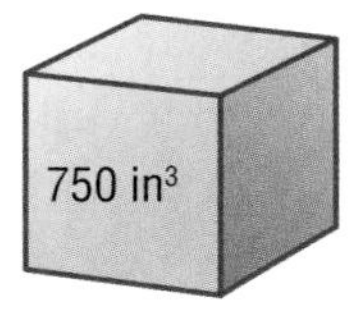

The side length of the cube equals the cube root of the volume, or $\sqrt[3]{750}$.

750 is between the perfect cubes 729 and 1,000. So, the cube root of 750 is between 9 and 10. Since 750 is closer to 729 than to 1,000, $\sqrt[3]{750}$, or the side length of the cube, is closer to 9 inches.

CHECK Your Progress

e. **GEOMETRY** A cube has a volume of 500 cubic centimeters. Estimate the side length of the cube to the nearest integer.

CHECK Your Understanding

Example 1 (p. LA12)

Use a calculator to find each cube root to the nearest tenth.

1. $\sqrt[3]{95}$
2. $\sqrt[3]{7}$
3. $\sqrt[3]{-360}$

Example 4 (p. LA13)

4. **GEOMETRY** The volume of the cube at the right is given. Estimate the side length of the cube to the nearest integer.

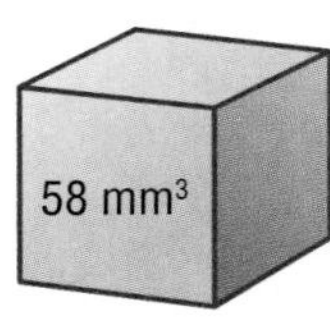

Examples 2, 3 (p. LA13)

Estimate each cube root to the nearest integer. Do not use a calculator.

5. $\sqrt[3]{51}$
6. $\sqrt[3]{-145}$
7. $\sqrt[3]{400}$

Practice and Problem Solving

HOMEWORK HELP	
For Exercises	See Examples
8–13	1
14, 15	4
16–21	2, 3

Use a calculator to find each cube root to the nearest tenth.

8. $\sqrt[3]{18}$
9. $\sqrt[3]{526}$
10. $\sqrt[3]{294}$
11. $\sqrt[3]{105}$
12. $\sqrt[3]{-86}$
13. $\sqrt[3]{-600}$

GEOMETRY The volume of each cube is given. Estimate the side length of the cube to the nearest integer.

14. 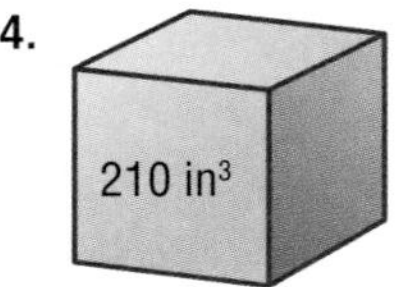

15. 

Estimate each cube root to the nearest integer. Do not use a calculator.

16. $\sqrt[3]{199}$
17. $\sqrt[3]{22}$
18. $\sqrt[3]{475}$
19. $\sqrt[3]{-34}$
20. $\sqrt[3]{-802}$
21. $\sqrt[3]{989}$

Complete mentally.

22. The number $\sqrt[3]{488}$ lies between which two consecutive integers?
23. Find a cube root that lies between 4 and 5.
24. Order $\sqrt[3]{-45}$, 3.8, $\sqrt[3]{60}$, −4, and $\sqrt[3]{51}$ from least to greatest.

H.O.T. Problems

25. **CHALLENGE** Every positive number has both a positive square root and a negative square root. Is it also true that every positive number has both a positive cube root and a negative cube root? Explain.

26. **REASONING** Without using a calculator, determine which is greater, $\sqrt[3]{900}$ or 10? Explain your reasoning.

27. **OPEN ENDED** Give two numbers that have cube roots between 3 and 4.

28. **WRITING IN MATH** Explain how to estimate the cube root of 10.

Matrices

MAIN IDEA

Use matrices to organize data.

New Vocabulary

matrix
element
dimensions

IL Math Online

glencoe.com

- Personal Tutor
- Self-Check Quiz
- Extra Examples

GET READY for the Lesson

AMUSEMENT PARK The table shows the costs of different passes to an amusement park.

1. How many different types of passes are there for juniors/seniors?
2. What does the number 110 represent?

Cost of Amusement Park Passes

Pass	Regular ($)	Junior/ Senior ($)
1-Day	42	12
1-Day Plus Water Park	71	31
Season	110	50

The table above has rows and columns of data. A rectangular arrangement of numerical data in rows and columns is called a **matrix**. Each number in a matrix is called an **element**.

$$\underbrace{\begin{bmatrix} 42 & 12 \\ 71 & 31 \\ 110 & 50 \end{bmatrix}}_{\text{2 columns}} \Big\} \text{3 rows}$$

- This matrix has 3 rows and 2 columns.
- The number 110 is an element in the third row and the first column.

A matrix is described by its **dimensions**, or the number of rows and columns, with the number of rows stated first. The dimensions of the matrix above are 3 by 2.

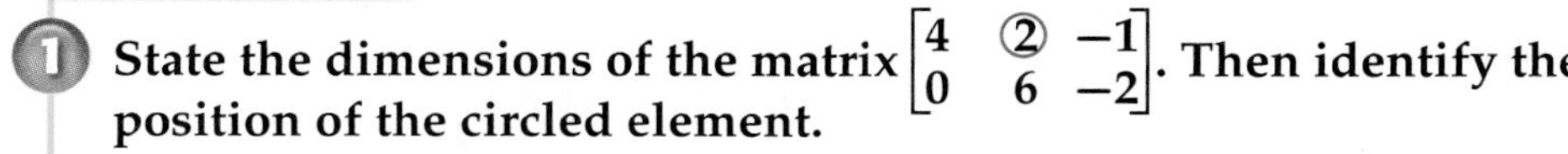

EXAMPLE Identify Dimensions and Elements

1 **State the dimensions of the matrix $\begin{bmatrix} 4 & \textcircled{2} & -1 \\ 0 & 6 & -2 \end{bmatrix}$. Then identify the position of the circled element.**

$$\underbrace{\begin{bmatrix} 4 & \textcircled{2} & -1 \\ 0 & 6 & -2 \end{bmatrix}}_{\text{3 columns}} \Big\} \text{2 rows}$$

The matrix has 2 rows and 3 columns. So, the dimensions of the matrix are 2 by 3. The circled element is in the first row, second column.

CHECK Your Progress

State the dimensions of each matrix. Then identify the position of the circled element.

a. $\begin{bmatrix} 9 & 0 & 7 \\ \textcircled{-2} & 1 & 8 \\ 16 & 1 & 5 \end{bmatrix}$

b. $\begin{bmatrix} 11 & -3 & \textcircled{16} & 1 \\ 20 & 10 & -4 & 2 \end{bmatrix}$

Use a Matrix to Organize Data

GYMNASTICS The table shows the scores of two gymnasts at a gymnastics meet.

Gymnast	Event			
	Bars	Beam	Floor	Vault
Katelyn	9.50	9.40	9.45	9.75
Britt	9.25	9.55	9.65	9.35

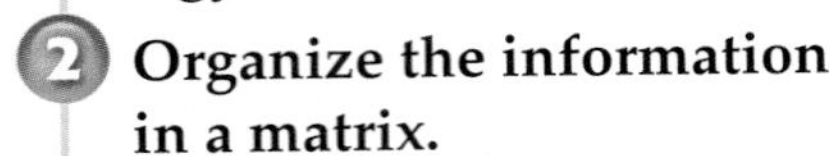

2 Organize the information in a matrix.

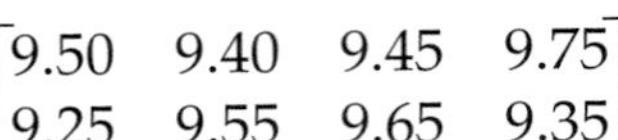

$$\begin{bmatrix} 9.50 & 9.40 & 9.45 & 9.75 \\ 9.25 & 9.55 & 9.65 & 9.35 \end{bmatrix}$$

The matrix has 2 rows and 4 columns, like the information in the table.

3 Name the element in the first row, third column. What does it represent?

The element in the first row, third column is 9.45. It is Katelyn's score for the floor event.

Real-World Link
The earliest known chili recipe dates back to 1737.

CHECK Your Progress

FOOD The table shows the cost of soup and chili at a restaurant.

Item	Cup ($)	Bowl ($)
Soup	1.75	2.50
Chili	2.00	3.00

c. Make a matrix of the information. What are the dimensions?
d. What is the element in the second row, first column? What does it represent?

You can add or subtract matrices if they have the same dimensions. To do this, add or subtract corresponding elements of the matrices.

Study Tip

Matrices
The plural of matrix is *matrices*. Matrices with different dimensions cannot be added or subtracted because not all the elements would be paired.

Add or Subtract Matrices

Key Concept

Words Two matrices with the same dimensions can be added or subtracted by adding or subtracting their corresponding elements.

Symbols

$$\begin{bmatrix} a & b \\ c & d \end{bmatrix} + \begin{bmatrix} e & f \\ g & h \end{bmatrix} = \begin{bmatrix} a+e & b+f \\ c+g & d+h \end{bmatrix}$$

$$\begin{bmatrix} a & b \\ c & d \end{bmatrix} - \begin{bmatrix} e & f \\ g & h \end{bmatrix} = \begin{bmatrix} a-e & b-f \\ c-g & d-h \end{bmatrix}$$

Example

$$\begin{bmatrix} 1 & 4 \\ 0 & 2 \end{bmatrix} + \begin{bmatrix} 5 & 5 \\ 1 & 3 \end{bmatrix} = \begin{bmatrix} 1+5 & 4+5 \\ 0+1 & 2+3 \end{bmatrix} \text{ or } \begin{bmatrix} 6 & 9 \\ 1 & 5 \end{bmatrix}$$

EXAMPLES Add and Subtract Matrices

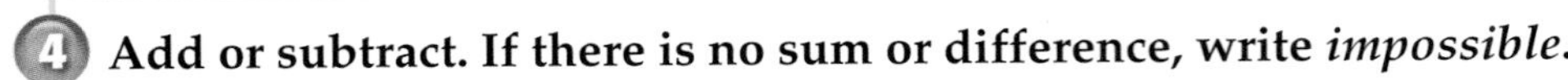

4 Add or subtract. If there is no sum or difference, write *impossible*.

$$\begin{bmatrix} 8 & -2 & 5 \\ 9 & 0 & 1 \end{bmatrix} + \begin{bmatrix} 10 & 4 \\ -1 & 7 \end{bmatrix}$$

The first matrix is 2 by 3. The second matrix is 2 by 2. The matrices do not have the same dimensions, so, it is impossible to add them.

5 $\begin{bmatrix} 0 & 2 \\ -3 & 4 \\ 1 & 4 \end{bmatrix} + \begin{bmatrix} 7 & 5 \\ 2 & 1 \\ -3 & 5 \end{bmatrix}$

$$\begin{bmatrix} 0 & 2 \\ -3 & 4 \\ 1 & 4 \end{bmatrix} + \begin{bmatrix} 7 & 5 \\ 2 & 1 \\ -3 & 5 \end{bmatrix} = \begin{bmatrix} 0+7 & 2+5 \\ -3+2 & 4+1 \\ 1+(-3) & 4+5 \end{bmatrix}$$

$$= \begin{bmatrix} 7 & 7 \\ -1 & 5 \\ -2 & 9 \end{bmatrix}$$

6 $\begin{bmatrix} 12 & 5 & 2 \\ 0 & 1 & -1 \end{bmatrix} - \begin{bmatrix} 3 & 5 & 1 \\ 9 & -6 & 0 \end{bmatrix}$

$$\begin{bmatrix} 12 & 5 & 2 \\ 0 & 1 & -1 \end{bmatrix} - \begin{bmatrix} 3 & 5 & 1 \\ 9 & -6 & 0 \end{bmatrix} = \begin{bmatrix} 12-3 & 5-5 & 2-1 \\ 0-9 & 1-(-6) & -1-0 \end{bmatrix}$$

$$= \begin{bmatrix} 9 & 0 & 1 \\ -9 & 7 & -1 \end{bmatrix}$$

CHECK Your Progress

e. $\begin{bmatrix} 1 & 0 & -1 \end{bmatrix} + \begin{bmatrix} 6 & 8 & 10 \end{bmatrix}$

f. $\begin{bmatrix} 1 & 8 \\ 7 & 1 \end{bmatrix} - \begin{bmatrix} 2 & 2 & 3 \\ -6 & 7 & 1 \end{bmatrix}$

CHECK Your Understanding

Example 1 (p. LA15)

State the dimensions of each matrix. Then identify the position of the circled element.

1. $\begin{bmatrix} 8 & -2 & \textcircled{1} \end{bmatrix}$

2. $\begin{bmatrix} 6 & 0 \\ \textcircled{4} & 5 \end{bmatrix}$

3. $\begin{bmatrix} 22 & 18 & 20 & -5 & 1 \\ -9 & 11 & -1 & 6 & \textcircled{2} \end{bmatrix}$

Examples 2, 3 (p. LA16)

4. **WEATHER** The table shows the high and low temperatures in a city for five days.

Temperature (F°)	Mon.	Tues.	Wed.	Thurs.	Fri.
High	81	83	66	69	77
Low	55	47	40	45	52

a. Organize the data in a matrix.
b. What are the dimensions of the matrix?
c. What is the element in the first row, fourth column? What does it represent?

Examples 4–6 (pp. LA16, LA17)

Add or subtract. If there is no sum or difference, write *impossible*.

5. $\begin{bmatrix} 2 & 1 \\ -3 & 7 \end{bmatrix} + \begin{bmatrix} 4 & -1 \\ 4 & 0 \end{bmatrix}$

6. $\begin{bmatrix} 10 \\ 15 \\ 3 \end{bmatrix} - \begin{bmatrix} 8 \\ 20 \\ 3 \end{bmatrix}$

7. $\begin{bmatrix} 5 & 8 & 2 \end{bmatrix} - \begin{bmatrix} 1 & 10 & 6 \\ 2 & -2 & 1 \end{bmatrix}$

8. $\begin{bmatrix} -7 & 8 & -1 \\ 6 & 8 & 11 \end{bmatrix} + \begin{bmatrix} 0 & 2 & 5 \\ -3 & 1 & 6 \end{bmatrix}$

Practice and Problem Solving

HOMEWORK HELP	
For Exercises	See Examples
9–14	1
15, 16	2, 3
17–22	4–6

State the dimensions of each matrix. Then identify the position of the circled element.

9. $\begin{bmatrix} \textcircled{6} \\ -1 \\ 8 \end{bmatrix}$

10. $\begin{bmatrix} 11 & \textcircled{12} & 15 \end{bmatrix}$

11. $\begin{bmatrix} -5 & 8 & \textcircled{1} & 0 \end{bmatrix}$

12. $\begin{bmatrix} -2 & 14 & 12 \\ 6 & 8 & 9 \\ 0 & \textcircled{1} & 0 \end{bmatrix}$

13. $\begin{bmatrix} -3 & 7 & 2 & 6 \\ \textcircled{5} & -4 & 0 & 9 \end{bmatrix}$

14. $\begin{bmatrix} 1 & -3 & 8 & 9 \\ 9 & 10 & 2 & \textcircled{0} \\ 7 & 5 & 6 & -2 \end{bmatrix}$

Organize each set of data in a matrix. Then state the dimensions of the matrix.

15.

Nutritional Information		
Snack	Fat	Protein
Pretzels	1 g	3 g
Sunflower Seeds	15 g	7 g

16.

Concert Tickets		
Seats	Concert A	Concert B
Upper Level	$65	$118
Lower Level	$110	$177
Premier Seating	$280	$320

Add or subtract. If there is no sum or difference, write *impossible*.

17. $\begin{bmatrix} -2 & 0 & 9 & 1 \end{bmatrix} + \begin{bmatrix} 0 & 1 & 6 & 5 \end{bmatrix}$

18. $\begin{bmatrix} 2 & 0 & 2 \\ 3 & 8 & 1 \end{bmatrix} + \begin{bmatrix} 6 & -2 \\ 10 & 7 \end{bmatrix}$

19. $\begin{bmatrix} 15 & 9 \\ -1 & 1 \end{bmatrix} - \begin{bmatrix} 5 & 10 \\ 1 & 8 \end{bmatrix}$

20. $\begin{bmatrix} 0 & -4 \\ 16 & 13 \\ 12 & -2 \end{bmatrix} + \begin{bmatrix} -3 & -4 \\ 0 & -8 \\ -9 & 2 \end{bmatrix}$

21. $\begin{bmatrix} 4 & 11 \\ 18 & 7 \\ -1 & 9 \end{bmatrix} - \begin{bmatrix} 0 & -5 & 2 \\ 1 & 6 & 4 \end{bmatrix}$

22. $\begin{bmatrix} -5 & 20 & 10 \\ 10 & 6 & 1 \\ 0 & -3 & 1 \end{bmatrix} - \begin{bmatrix} 4 & 10 & -3 \\ 7 & 0 & 2 \\ 2 & 12 & 1 \end{bmatrix}$

23. **ACTIVITIES** Juliana practices piano 1 hour on Monday, 0 hours on Tuesday, and 1.5 hours on Wednesday. She practices lacrosse 1 hour on Monday, 2 hours on Tuesday, and 1 hour on Wednesday.
   a. Organize this information in a matrix.
   b. Name the element in the second row, third column and describe what it represents.

24. Find $\begin{bmatrix} -6 \\ 13 \end{bmatrix} + \begin{bmatrix} 7 \\ 4 \end{bmatrix} - \begin{bmatrix} 11 \\ 9 \end{bmatrix}$.

25. Find $\begin{bmatrix} 3.6 & 0.7 \\ -9.0 & 2.5 \end{bmatrix} - \begin{bmatrix} -1.4 & 6.8 \\ -7.3 & 0.9 \end{bmatrix}$.

H.O.T. Problems

26. **CHALLENGE** Find the values of w, x, y, and z in the following sentence.
$$\begin{bmatrix} 8 & 2 \\ 0 & -3 \end{bmatrix} + \begin{bmatrix} w & x \\ y & z \end{bmatrix} = \begin{bmatrix} 11 & -1 \\ 7 & -2 \end{bmatrix}$$

27. **REASONING** Describe the difference between a 1-by-4 matrix and a 4-by-1 matrix.

28. **OPEN ENDED** Write two matrices with a sum of $\begin{bmatrix} 7 & -3 \\ 1 & 0 \end{bmatrix}$.

29. **WRITING IN MATH** Describe the similarities and differences between using a table and using a matrix to organize information.

Different Forms of Linear Equations

MAIN IDEA

Write the equation of a line in point-slope form and in standard form.

IL Learning Standards

8.A.3b Solve problems using linear expressions, **equations** and inequalities.
8.D.3a Solve problems using numeric, graphic or symbolic representations of variables, expressions, **equations** and inequalities.
Also addresses 8.B.3, 8.D.3b.

New Vocabulary

point-slope form
standard form

IL Math Online

glencoe.com

- Personal Tutor
- Self-Check Quiz
- Extra Examples

GET READY for the Lesson

SOCCER On a penalty kick in soccer, the ball comes in at about 80 feet per second, as shown in the graph at the right. In the graph, $(x_1, y_1) = (2, 160)$, $(x_2, y_2) = (x, y)$, and the slope is 80.

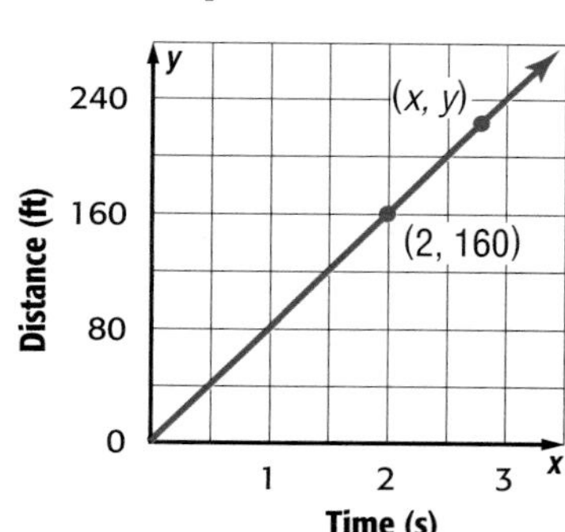

1. Substitute the given values into the formula $\frac{y_2 - y_1}{x_2 - x_1} = m$.
2. Multiply each side of the equation that you wrote in Exercise 1 by $x - 2$. Write the resulting equation.

An equation like $y - 160 = 80(x - 2)$ is written in **point-slope form**. You can write an equation in point-slope form if you know the coordinates of a point (x_1, y_1), and the slope m of a line.

$$y - \underset{y_1}{\underset{\uparrow}{160}} = \underset{m}{\underset{\uparrow}{80}}(x - \underset{x_1}{\underset{\uparrow}{2}})$$

Point-Slope Form — Key Concept

Words The linear equation $y - y_1 = m(x - x_1)$ is written in point-slope form, where (x_1, y_1) is a given point on a nonvertical line and m is the slope of the line.

Symbols $y - y_1 = m(x - x_1)$

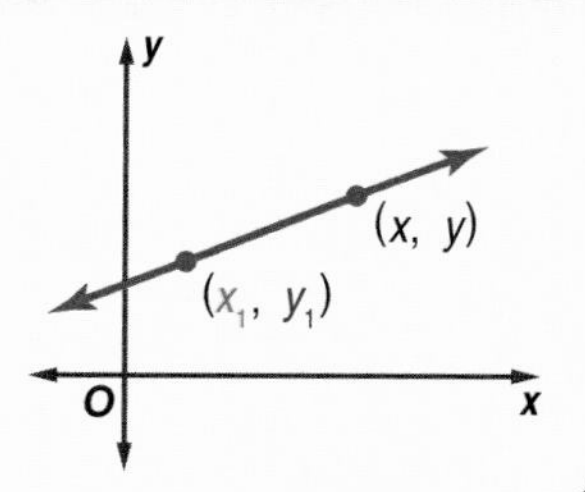

EXAMPLE Write an Equation Given Slope and a Point

1 **Write the point-slope form of an equation for the line that passes through (–2, 3) with slope $-\frac{3}{4}$.**

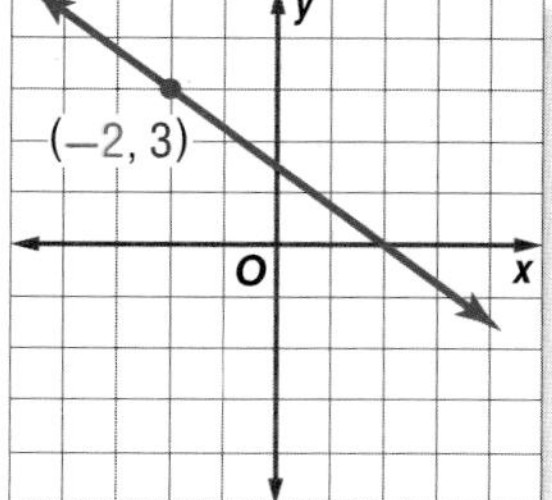

$y - y_1 = m(x - x_1)$	Point-slope form
$y - 3 = -\frac{3}{4}[x - (-2)]$	$(x_1, y_1) = (-2, 3)$, $m = -\frac{3}{4}$
$y - 3 = -\frac{3}{4}(x + 2)$	Simplify

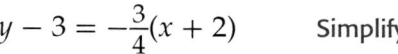

CHECK Your Progress

a. Write the point-slope form of an equation for the line that passes through (1, 5) with slope 4.

EXAMPLE Write an Equation of a Horizontal Line

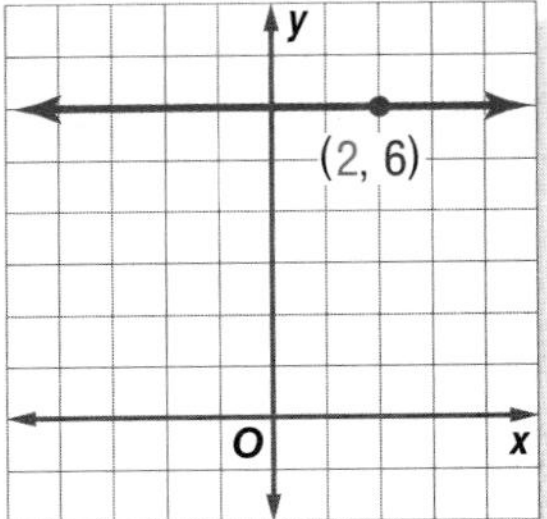

2 **Write the point-slope form for the horizontal line that passes through (2, 6).**

$y - y_1 = m(x - x_1)$	Point-slope form
$y - 6 = 0(x - 2)$	$(x_1, y_1) = (2, 6), m = 0$
$y - 6 = 0$	Simplify.

CHECK Your Progress

b. Write the point-slope form of an equation for the horizontal line that passes through (6, –1).

In Lesson 9-6, you studied equations in slope-intercept form, $y = mx + b$. In addition to slope-intercept form and point-slope form, equations can also be written in the form $Ax + By = C$, called **standard form**.

Real-World EXAMPLE Write an Equation in Standard Form

> **Study Tip**
> **Standard Form**
> Regardless of which point is used to find the point-slope form, the standard form results in the same equation.

3 **SOCCER Refer to the application at the beginning of the lesson. Write the equation $y - 160 = 80(x - 2)$ in standard form.**

$y - 160 = 80(x - 2)$	Original equation
$y - 160 = 80x - 160$	Distributive Property
$y = 80x$	Add 160 to each side.
$-80x + y = 0$	Subtract $80x$ from each side.
$80x - y = 0$	Multiply each side by -1.

CHECK Your Progress

c. Write $y + 3 = \frac{1}{2}(x + 4)$ in standard form.

CHECK Your Understanding

Example 1 (p. LA19)

Write the point-slope form of an equation for the line that passes through each point with the given slope.

1. $(2, 5), m = 4$
2. $(-3, 1), m = -2$
3. $(6, -4), m = \frac{1}{2}$

Example 2 (p. LA20)

4. Write the point-slope form of an equation for the horizontal line that passes through (–4, 3).

Example 3 (p. LA20)

5. **BUTTONS** The equation $y - 70 = 5(x - 10)$ represents the cost y of manufacturing school spirit buttons. In the equation, x is the number of buttons made. Write the equation in standard form.

Write each equation in standard form.

6. $y - 10 = -2(x - 1)$
7. $y + 4 = -3(x - 5)$
8. $y - 3 = \frac{3}{2}(x + 2)$

Practice and Problem Solving

HOMEWORK HELP	
For Exercises	See Examples
9–14	1
15, 16	2
17–24	3

Write the point-slope form of an equation for the line that passes through each point with the given slope.

9. $(1, 9), m = 2$
10. $(-2, 3), m = 5$
11. $(4, -1), m = -3$
12. $(6, 2), m = \frac{2}{3}$
13. $(-4, -5), m = \frac{3}{4}$
14. $(-7, 10), m = -4$
15. Write the point-slope form of an equation for the horizontal line that passes through (8, 1).
16. A horizontal line passes through (0, −5). Write the point-slope form of its equation.
17. **PARTIES** The equation $y - 146 = 12(x - 8)$ represents the cost y of having a party for x people. Write the equation in standard form.
18. **PLANTS** The equation $y - 11 = \frac{1}{5}(x + 5)$ represents the height of a plant y after x weeks. Write the equation in standard form.

Write each equation in standard form.

19. $y - 4 = -3(x - 3)$
20. $y - 12 = -6(x + 1)$
21. $y + 9 = 2(x + 5)$
22. $y + 1 = \frac{4}{5}(x - 3)$
23. $y - 8 = \frac{1}{2}(x + 2)$
24. $y + 2 = -\frac{1}{4}(x - 7)$

Write each equation in slope-intercept form, point-slope form, and standard form.

25. The line passes through (0, 20) and (−2, 8).
26. The line has a slope of 0.5 and a y-intercept of −1.
27. The line has a slope of −0.25 and passes through (7, 0.75)

Write the point-slope form of an equation for each line graphed.

28.
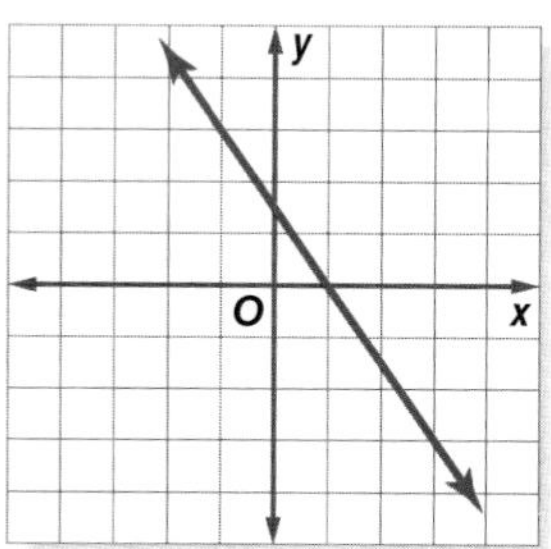

29.
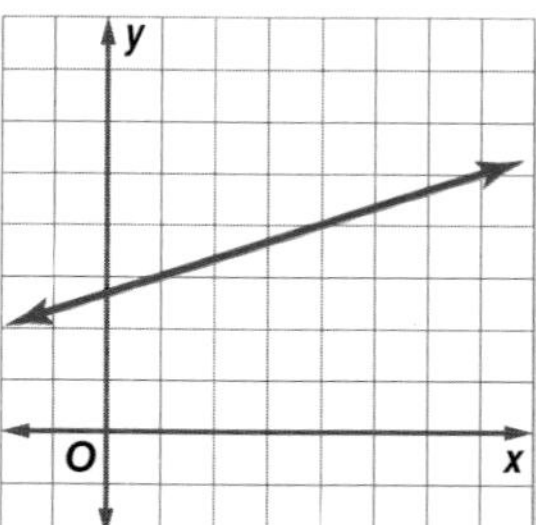

30.
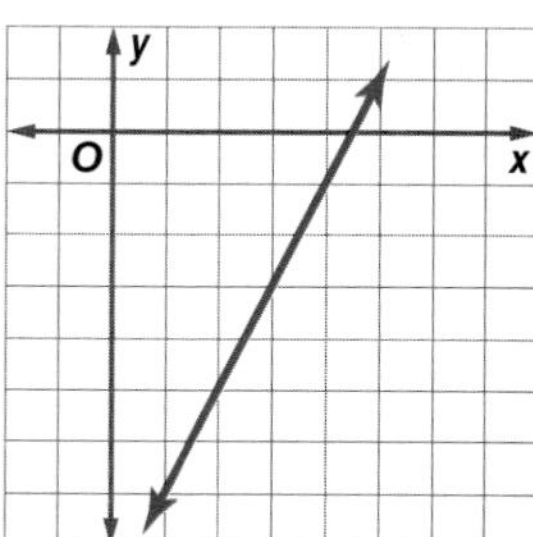

H.O.T. Problems

31. **CHALLENGE** A line has the equation $y = -\frac{1}{2}x + 6$. Write an equation in point-slope form for the same line. Explain the steps that you used.
32. **REASONING** Find an equation in point-slope form for the line that passes through (2, 9) and (5, −1). What is the slope?
33. **OPEN ENDED** Write a linear equation that is in point-slope form. Describe the slope and name a point on the line.
34. **WRITING IN MATH** Name three different forms of a linear equation and give an example of each. From which equation or equations is it easiest to determine the slope? Explain.

Student Handbook

Built-In Workbooks

Reference

How to Use the Student Handbook

A Student Handbook is the additional skill and reference material found at the end of books. The Student Handbook can help answer these questions.

What If I Need More Practice?

The **Extra Practice** section provides additional problems for each lesson so you have ample opportunity to practice new skills.

What If I Have Trouble with Word Problems?

The **Mixed Problem Solving** pages provide additional word problems that use the skills in each chapter.

What If I Need to Prepare for a Standardized Test?

The **Preparing for Standardized Tests** section provides worked-out examples and practice problems for multiple-choice, gridded-response, short-response, and extended-response questions.

What If I Forget What I Learned Last Year?

Use the **Concepts and Skills** section to refresh your memory about topics you have learned in other math classes.

What If I Forget a Vocabulary Word?

The **English-Spanish Glossary** provides a list of important, or difficult, words used throughout the textbook. It provides a definition in English and Spanish as well as the page number(s) where the word can be found.

What If I Need to Check a Homework Answer?

The answers to the odd-numbered problems are included in **Selected Answers**. Check your answers to make sure you understand how to solve all of the assigned problems.

What If I Need to Find Something Quickly?

The **Index** alphabetically lists the subjects covered throughout the entire textbook and the pages on which each subject can be found.

What If I Forget a Formula?

Inside the back cover of your math book is a list of **Formulas and Symbols** that are used in the book.

Extra Practice

Lesson 1-1

Pages 24–28

Use the four-step plan to solve each problem.

1. Joseph is planting bushes around the perimeter of his lawn. If the bushes must be planted 4 feet apart and Joseph's lawn is 64 feet wide and 124 feet long, how many bushes will Joseph need to purchase?
2. At the bookstore, pencils cost \$0.15 each and erasers cost \$0.25 each. What combination of pencils and erasers can be purchased for a total of \$0.65?
3. Cheap Wheels Car Rental rents cars for \$50 per day plus \$0.15 per mile. How much will it cost to rent a car for 2 days and to drive 200 miles?
4. At Smart's Car Rental, it costs \$57 per day plus \$0.10 per mile to rent a certain car. How much will it cost to rent the car for 1 day and drive 180 miles?

Lesson 1-2

Pages 29–34

Evaluate each expression if $x = 5$, $y = 3$, and $z = 4$.

1. $2y + 3x$
2. $4z - 2y$
3. $12 + 8y - x$
4. $4y - z + x$
5. $7y + 5z - 2x$
6. $(xy)^2$
7. xy^2
8. $\frac{2x^2}{3y + 1}$

Evaluate each expression if $a = 3$, $b = 6$, and $c = 5$.

9. $2a + bc$
10. ba^2
11. $\frac{bc}{a}$
12. $3a + c - 2b$
13. $(2c + b) \cdot a$
14. $\frac{2(ac)^2}{b}$
15. abc
16. $(3b + a)c$

Name the property shown by each statement.

17. $2(a + b) = 2a + 2b$
18. $3 \times 5 = 5 \times 3$
19. $(2 + 6) + 5 = 2 + (6 + 5)$
20. $3(4 + 1) = (4 + 1)3$
21. $(7 \times 5)2 = 7(5 \times 2)$
22. $8(2x + 1) = 8(2x) + 8(1)$
23. $5(x + 2) = (x + 2)5$
24. $(3x + 2) + 0 = 3x + 2$
25. $5 \cdot 1 = 5$

Lesson 1-3

Pages 35–39

Replace each ● with >, <, or = to make a true sentence.

1. -3 ● 0
2. -1 ● -2
3. -5 ● -4
4. 6 ● -7
5. -13 ● -12
6. -6 ● 6
7. $|13|$ ● $|-19|$
8. $|-6|$ ● $|2|$
9. $|14|$ ● $|-14|$
10. $|0|$ ● $|-4|$
11. $|23|$ ● $|-20|$
12. $|-12|$ ● -12

Evaluate each expression.

13. $|-1|$
14. $|3|$
15. $|160 + 32|$
16. $|0|$
17. $|7 - 3|$
18. $|3| + |-7|$
19. $|8 - 6| - |7 - 9|$
20. $|102| - |-2|$
21. $|80 + 100|$

Lesson 1-4

Pages 41–45

Add.

1. $-7 + (-7)$
2. $-36 + 40$
3. $18 + (-32)$
4. $47 + 12$
5. $-69 + (-32)$
6. $-120 + (-2)$
7. $-56 + (-4)$
8. $14 + 16$
9. $-18 + 11$
10. $-42 + 29$
11. $-13 + (-11)$
12. $95 + (-5)$
13. $-120 + 2$
14. $25 + (-25)$
15. $-4 + 8$
16. $-9 + (-6)$
17. $42 + (-18)$
18. $-33 + (-12)$
19. $7 + (-13) + 6 + (-7)$
20. $-6 + 12 + (-20)$
21. $4 + 9 + (-14)$
22. $-20 + 0 + (-9) + 25$
23. $5 + 9 + 3 + (-17)$
24. $-36 + 40 + (-10)$
25. $(-2) + 2 + (-2) + 2$
26. $6 + (-4) + 9 + (-2)$
27. $9 + (-7) + 2$

Lesson 1-5

Pages 46–49

Subtract.

1. $3 - 7$
2. $-5 - 4$
3. $-6 - 2$
4. $12 - 9$
5. $0 - (-14)$
6. $58 - (-10)$
7. $-41 - 15$
8. $-81 - 21$
9. $26 - (-14)$
10. $6 - (-4)$
11. $63 - 78$
12. $-5 - (-9)$
13. $72 - (-19)$
14. $-51 - 47$
15. $-99 - 1$
16. $8 - 13$
17. $-2 - 23$
18. $-20 - 0$
19. $55 - 33$
20. $84 - (-61)$
21. $-4 - (-4)$
22. $-2 - (-3)$
23. $65 - (-2)$
24. $0 - (-3)$
25. $0 - 5$
26. $-2 - 6$
27. $-4 - 7$

Lesson 1-6

Pages 51–56

Multiply.

1. $5(-2)$
2. $-11(-5)$
3. $-5(-5)$
4. $-12(6)$
5. $2(-2)$
6. $-3(2)(-4)$
7. $(-4)(-4)$
8. $4(21)$
9. $-50(0)$
10. $3(-13)$
11. $2(2)$
12. $-2(-2)$
13. $5(-12)$
14. $2(2)(-2)$
15. $6(-4)$

Divide.

16. $4 \div (-2)$
17. $16 \div (-8)$
18. $-14 \div (-2)$
19. $-18 \div 3$
20. $-25 \div 5$
21. $-56 \div (-8)$
22. $81 \div 9$
23. $-55 \div 11$
24. $-42 \div (-7)$
25. $18 \div (-3)$
26. $0 \div (-1)$
27. $-32 \div 8$
28. $81 \div (-9)$
29. $18 \div (-2)$
30. $-21 \div 3$

Lesson 1-7

Pages 57–61

Define a variable. Then write an equation to model each situation.

1. When the marbles were divided among the 3 players, each player received 48 marbles.
2. The low temperature of –2°F was 20 degrees less than the high temperature.
3. A team of 84 football players separated into equal-size groups results in 12 players per group.
4. Jack's time of 43 seconds was 8 seconds more than Clarissa's time.

Define a variable. Then write an equation that could be used to solve each problem.

5. **TICKETS** The total cost of concert tickets is equally divided among 4 friends. If the cost of 1 ticket is \$56, what was the total cost of the 4 concert tickets?
6. **READING** Natalie has read 163 pages in her book. If the book has a total of 395 pages, how many more pages does Natalie have to read?
7. **SCORES** Simon's score of –12 was one-fifth of Tabitha's score. What is Tabitha's score?
8. **BASEBALL CARDS** Adam's baseball card collection has 76 more cards than Kerry's baseball card collection. If Kerry has 349 baseball cards, how many baseball cards does Adam have?

Lesson 1-8

Pages 62–63

Solve using the *work backward* strategy.

1. **SCHEDULE** The closing day activities at camp must be over by 2:45 P.M. Trent needs $1\frac{1}{2}$ hours to hold the field competitions, 45 minutes for the awards ceremony, and an hour and 15 minutes for the cookout. Then everyone will need an hour to pack and check out. What time will Trent need to start the camp activities?
2. **BOWLING** Alexia's bowling scores are 166, 176, 172, 171, and 159. What is the minimum score she can bowl in her next game to maintain an average of at least 170?
3. **STOCK** A share of stock increased in value by 25%. Then it decreased in value by \$4 and then it doubled. If the stock is now worth \$32, how much was the stock worth originally?

Lesson 1-9

Pages 65–69

Solve each equation. Check your solution.

1. $g - 3 = 10$
2. $b + 7 = 12$
3. $a + 3 = 15$
4. $r - 3 = 4$
5. $t + 3 = 21$
6. $s + 10 = 23$
7. $9 + n = 13$
8. $13 + v = 31$
9. $-4 + b = 12$
10. $z - 10 = -8$
11. $-7 = x + 12$
12. $a + 6 = -9$
13. $c - 18 = 13$
14. $r - (-8) = 14$
15. $m + (-2) = 6$

Lesson 1-10

Pages 70–73

Solve each equation. Check your solution.

1. $4x = 36$
2. $39 = 3y$
3. $4z = 16$
4. $\frac{t}{5} = 6$
5. $100 = 20b$
6. $8 = \frac{w}{8}$
7. $10a = 40$
8. $\frac{s}{9} = 8$
9. $420 = 5s$
10. $8k = 72$
11. $2m = 18$
12. $\frac{m}{8} = 5$
13. $\frac{r}{7} = -8$
14. $\frac{w}{7} = 8$
15. $18q = 36$
16. $9w = 54$
17. $4 = p \div 4$
18. $14 = 2p$
19. $12 = 3t$
20. $\frac{m}{4} = 12$
21. $6h = 12$
22. $-2a = -8$
23. $0 = 6r$
24. $\frac{y}{12} = -6$
25. $3m = -15$
26. $\frac{c}{-4} = 10$
27. $-6f = -36$

Lesson 2-1

Pages 84–89

Write each fraction or mixed number as a decimal.

1. $\frac{2}{5}$
2. $2\frac{3}{11}$
3. $-\frac{3}{4}$
4. $\frac{5}{7}$
5. $\frac{3}{4}$
6. $-\frac{2}{3}$
7. $\frac{7}{11}$
8. $\frac{1}{2}$
9. $\frac{5}{6}$
10. $1\frac{3}{5}$
11. $-2\frac{1}{4}$
12. $\frac{8}{9}$

Write each decimal as a fraction or mixed number in simplest form.

13. 0.5
14. $0.\overline{8}$
15. 0.32
16. −0.75
17. $2.\overline{2}$
18. $0.\overline{38}$
19. −0.486
20. 20.08
21. −9.36
22. $10.1\overline{8}$
23. 1.24
24. $-5.\overline{7}$

Lesson 2-2

Pages 91–95

Replace each ● with <, >, or = to make a true sentence.

1. −5.6 ● 4.2
2. 4.256 ● 4.25
3. 0.233 ● $0.\overline{23}$
4. $\frac{5}{7}$ ● $\frac{2}{5}$
5. $\frac{6}{7}$ ● $\frac{7}{9}$
6. $\frac{2}{3}$ ● $\frac{2}{5}$
7. $\frac{3}{8}$ ● 0.375
8. $-\frac{1}{2}$ ● 0.5
9. 12.56 ● $12\frac{3}{8}$
10. −0.25 ● −0.26
11. 1.31 ● $1.\overline{31}$
12. $\frac{3}{5}$ ● $\frac{2}{3}$

Order each set of rational numbers from least to greatest.

13. 0.24, 0.2, 0.245, 2.24, 0.25
14. $0.\overline{3}$, 0.3, $0.3\overline{4}$, $0.\overline{34}$, 0.33
15. $\frac{2}{5}, \frac{2}{3}, \frac{2}{7}, \frac{2}{9}, \frac{2}{1}$
16. $\frac{1}{2}, \frac{5}{7}, \frac{2}{9}, \frac{8}{9}, \frac{6}{6}$
17. 0.25, 0.2, 0.02, 0.251, $\frac{253}{1{,}000}$
18. $\frac{3}{10}, \frac{3}{2}, \frac{3}{5}, \frac{3}{1}, \frac{3}{8}, \frac{3}{7}, \frac{3}{4}$
19. $\frac{3}{5}, \frac{2}{3}$, 0.61, 0.65, $\frac{33}{50}$
20. $-\frac{3}{5}, -\frac{2}{3}, -\frac{1}{2}, -\frac{3}{4}, -\frac{5}{6}$
21. $\frac{4}{9}$, 0.4, 0.44, $\frac{3}{5}$
22. 7.5, $7\frac{2}{3}$, $6\frac{5}{6}$, 6.8
23. Graph the following set of numbers on a number line.
    −4.14, −4.3, $-4\frac{1}{3}$, −4.1, $-2\frac{7}{8}$

Extra Practice

Lesson 2-3

Pages 96–101

Multiply. Write in simplest form.

1. $\frac{2}{11} \cdot \frac{3}{4}$
2. $4\left(-\frac{7}{8}\right)$
3. $-\frac{4}{7} \cdot \frac{3}{5}$
4. $\frac{6}{7}\left(-\frac{7}{12}\right)$
5. $\frac{7}{8} \cdot \frac{1}{3}$
6. $\frac{3}{4} \cdot \frac{4}{5}$
7. $-1\frac{1}{2} \cdot \frac{2}{3}$
8. $\frac{5}{6} \cdot \frac{6}{7}$
9. $8\left(-2\frac{1}{4}\right)$
10. $-3\frac{3}{4} \cdot \frac{8}{9}$
11. $\frac{10}{21}\left(-\frac{7}{8}\right)$
12. $-1\frac{4}{5}\left(-\frac{5}{6}\right)$
13. $5\frac{1}{4} \cdot 6\frac{2}{3}$
14. $-8\frac{3}{4} \cdot 4\frac{2}{5}$
15. $6 \cdot 8\frac{2}{3}$
16. $\left(\frac{3}{5}\right)\left(\frac{3}{5}\right)$
17. $-4\frac{1}{5}\left(-3\frac{1}{3}\right)$
18. $-8\left(\frac{3}{4}\right)$
19. $3\frac{2}{3}\left(-3\frac{1}{2}\right)$
20. $\left(-\frac{2}{5}\right)\left(-\frac{2}{5}\right)$
21. $4\frac{1}{2}\left(-1\frac{1}{3}\right)$
22. $-5\left(-3\frac{1}{5}\right)$
23. $4\frac{1}{3} \cdot 1\frac{1}{2}$
24. $-5\left(3\frac{1}{3}\right)$

Lesson 2-4

Pages 102–107

Write the multiplicative inverse of each number.

1. 3
2. -5
3. $\frac{2}{3}$
4. $2\frac{1}{8}$
5. $\frac{1}{15}$
6. -8
7. $1\frac{1}{3}$
8. $-\frac{4}{5}$

Divide. Write in simplest form.

9. $\frac{2}{3} \div \frac{3}{4}$
10. $-\frac{4}{9} \div \frac{5}{6}$
11. $\frac{7}{12} \div \frac{3}{8}$
12. $\frac{5}{18} \div \frac{2}{9}$
13. $\frac{1}{3} \div 4$
14. $5\frac{1}{4} \div \left(-2\frac{1}{2}\right)$
15. $-6 \div \left(-\frac{4}{7}\right)$
16. $-6\frac{3}{8} \div \frac{1}{4}$
17. $\frac{6}{7} \div \frac{3}{5}$
18. $3\frac{1}{3} \div (-4)$
19. $2\frac{5}{12} \div 7\frac{1}{3}$
20. $\frac{5}{6} \div 1\frac{1}{9}$
21. $8 \div \left(-1\frac{4}{5}\right)$
22. $-5 \div \frac{2}{7}$
23. $\frac{3}{5} \div \frac{6}{7}$
24. $4\frac{8}{9} \div \left(-2\frac{2}{3}\right)$
25. **BUILDING** Mr. Thompson and his two children are building a tree house in their backyard. It took them 15 days to complete the project. How long would it take Mr. Franklin and 4 children to build a similar tree house?

Lesson 2-5

Pages 108–112

Add or subtract. Write in simplest form.

1. $\frac{17}{21} + \left(-\frac{13}{21}\right)$
2. $\frac{5}{11} + \frac{6}{11}$
3. $-\frac{8}{13} + \left(-\frac{11}{13}\right)$
4. $-\frac{7}{12} + \frac{5}{12}$
5. $\frac{13}{28} - \frac{9}{28}$
6. $-1\frac{2}{9} - \frac{7}{9}$
7. $\frac{15}{16} + \frac{13}{16}$
8. $2\frac{1}{3} - \frac{2}{3}$
9. $-\frac{4}{35} - \left(-\frac{17}{35}\right)$
10. $\frac{3}{8} + \left(-\frac{5}{8}\right)$
11. $\frac{8}{15} - \frac{2}{15}$
12. $-2\frac{4}{7} - \frac{3}{7}$
13. $-\frac{29}{9} - \left(-\frac{26}{9}\right)$
14. $2\frac{3}{5} + 7\frac{3}{5}$
15. $\frac{5}{18} - \frac{13}{18}$
16. $-2\frac{2}{7} + \left(-1\frac{6}{7}\right)$
17. $-\frac{3}{10} + \frac{7}{10}$
18. $\frac{4}{11} + \frac{9}{11}$
19. $\frac{1}{8} + 1\frac{7}{8}$
20. $\frac{5}{6} - \frac{7}{6}$
21. $5 - 3\frac{5}{7}$
22. $-3 - 4\frac{5}{8}$
23. $5\frac{3}{7} + 2\frac{6}{7}$
24. $-9\frac{3}{4} - \left(-2\frac{3}{4}\right)$
25. $4\frac{5}{9} - 1\frac{2}{9}$
26. $2\frac{5}{12} - 8\frac{7}{12}$
27. $-5\frac{1}{4} + 1\frac{3}{4}$
28. $6\frac{1}{5} - 2\frac{4}{5}$

Lesson 2-6

Pages 114–118

Add or subtract. Write in simplest form.

1. $\frac{7}{12} + \frac{7}{24}$
2. $-\frac{3}{4} + \frac{7}{8}$
3. $\frac{2}{5} + \left(-\frac{2}{7}\right)$
4. $-\frac{3}{5} - \left(-\frac{5}{6}\right)$
5. $\frac{5}{24} - \frac{3}{8}$
6. $-\frac{7}{12} - \frac{3}{4}$
7. $-\frac{3}{8} + \left(-\frac{4}{5}\right)$
8. $\frac{2}{15} + \left(-\frac{3}{10}\right)$
9. $-\frac{2}{9} - \left(-\frac{2}{3}\right)$
10. $-\frac{7}{15} - \frac{5}{12}$
11. $\frac{3}{8} + \frac{7}{12}$
12. $-2\frac{1}{4} + \left(-1\frac{1}{3}\right)$
13. $3\frac{2}{5} - 3\frac{1}{4}$
14. $\frac{3}{4} + \left(-\frac{4}{15}\right)$
15. $-1\frac{2}{3} + 4\frac{3}{4}$
16. $-\frac{1}{8} - 2\frac{1}{2}$
17. $3\frac{2}{5} - 1\frac{1}{3}$
18. $5\frac{1}{3} + \left(-8\frac{3}{7}\right)$
19. $\frac{3}{5} - \frac{2}{3}$
20. $1\frac{1}{3} - 2\frac{5}{6}$

Lesson 2-7

Pages 119–123

Solve each equation. Check your solution.

1. $434 = -31y$
2. $6x = -4.2$
3. $\frac{3}{4}a = -12$
4. $-10 = \frac{b}{-7}$
5. $7.2 = \frac{3}{4}c$
6. $r + 0.4 = 1.4$
7. $-2.4n = 7.2$
8. $7 = \frac{1}{2}d$
9. $n - 0.64 = -5.44$
10. $\frac{t}{3} = 2$
11. $\frac{3}{8} = \frac{1}{2}x$
12. $\frac{1}{2}h = -14$
13. $k - 1.18 = 1.58$
14. $4\frac{1}{2}s = -30$
15. $\frac{2}{3}f = \frac{8}{15}$
16. $\frac{2}{3}m = 22$
17. $\frac{2}{3}g = 4\frac{5}{6}$
18. $7 = \frac{1}{3}v$
19. $\frac{g}{1.2} = -6$
20. $z - 4\frac{5}{8} = 15\frac{3}{8}$
21. $-12 = \frac{1}{5}j$

Lesson 2-8

Pages 124–125

Look for a pattern. Then use the pattern to solve the problem.

1. **NUMBERS** Find the next two integers in the pattern 48, 36, 25, 15, 6, ■, ■.

2. **MONEY** A car rental company charges a flat rate of $24.95 and $0.12 per mile. If the total cost of renting a car was $60.95, how many miles were driven?

Number of Miles	Charges	Cost ($)
0	24.95 + 0(0.12)	24.95
50	24.95 + 50(0.12)	30.95
100	24.95 + 100(0.12)	36.95
150	24.95 + 150(0.12)	42.95

3. **DISPLAYS** A display of laundry detergent boxes are stacked in the shape of a pyramid. There are 3 boxes in the first row, 5 boxes in the second row, 7 boxes in the next row, and so on. The display contains 8 rows of boxes. How many boxes are in the display?

Lesson 2-9

Pages 126–129

Write each expression using exponents.

1. $4 \cdot 4 \cdot 4 \cdot 4$
2. $\frac{3}{4} \cdot \frac{3}{4}$
3. $7 \cdot 7 \cdot 7 \cdot 7 \cdot 7 \cdot 7$
4. $4 \cdot 4 \cdot 4 \cdot 4 \cdot 4 \cdot 5 \cdot 5 \cdot 5 \cdot 5 \cdot 5 \cdot 5 \cdot 5 \cdot 5$
5. $3 \cdot 2 \cdot \frac{5}{6} \cdot \frac{5}{6} \cdot \frac{5}{6} \cdot 2 \cdot 2 \cdot 2 \cdot 3 \cdot \frac{5}{6}$
6. $b \cdot b \cdot b \cdot b \cdot c \cdot c \cdot c \cdot c \cdot c \cdot c$
7. $3 \cdot 2 \cdot 5 \cdot 5 \cdot 5 \cdot 2 \cdot 2 \cdot 2 \cdot 3 \cdot 5$
8. $a \cdot a \cdot a \cdot b \cdot b \cdot b \cdot a \cdot a \cdot a \cdot b$
9. $6 \cdot 6 \cdot 6 \cdot 6 \cdot 6 \cdot 6 \cdot 6 \cdot 6$

Evaluate each expression.

10. 4^3
11. 6^2
12. $\left(\frac{2}{5}\right)^3$
13. $5^2 \cdot 6^2$
14. $3 \cdot 2^4$
15. $10^4 \cdot 3^2$
16. $5^3 \cdot 1^9$
17. $2^2 \cdot 2^4$
18. $2 \cdot 3^2 \cdot 4^2$
19. 7^3
20. $\left(\frac{1}{2}\right)^3 \cdot 4^5$
21. $3^5 \cdot 4^2$
22. $7^2 \cdot 3^4$
23. 3^{-3}
24. 2^{-4}
25. 5^{-2}

Lesson 2-10

Pages 130–133

Write each number in standard form.

1. 4.5×10^3
2. 2×10^4
3. 1.725896×10^6
4. 9.61×10^2
5. 1×10^7
6. 8.256×10^8
7. 5.26×10^4
8. 3.25×10^2
9. 6.79×10^5
10. 3.1×10^{-4}
11. 2.51×10^{-2}
12. 6×10^{-1}
13. 2.15×10^{-3}
14. 3.14×10^{-6}
15. 1×10^{-2}

Write each number in scientific notation.

16. 720
17. 7,560
18. 892
19. 1,400
20. 91,256
21. 51,000
22. 0.012
23. 0.0002
24. 0.054
25. 0.231
26. 0.0000056
27. 0.000123

Lesson 3-1

Pages 144–147

Find each square root.

1. $\sqrt{9}$
2. $\sqrt{81}$
3. $-\sqrt{625}$
4. $\sqrt{36}$
5. $-\sqrt{169}$
6. $\sqrt{144}$
7. $\sqrt{961}$
8. $\sqrt{324}$
9. $-\sqrt{225}$
10. $-\sqrt{4}$
11. $\sqrt{529}$
12. $-\sqrt{484}$
13. $\sqrt{196}$
14. $\sqrt{729}$
15. $\sqrt{289}$
16. $\sqrt{0.04}$
17. $\sqrt{2.25}$
18. $\sqrt{0.01}$
19. $-\sqrt{0.09}$
20. $\sqrt{0.49}$
21. $\sqrt{1.69}$
22. $-\sqrt{\frac{4}{9}}$
23. $-\sqrt{\frac{81}{64}}$
24. $\sqrt{\frac{25}{81}}$

Lesson 3-2

Pages 148–151

Estimate to the nearest whole number.

1. $\sqrt{229}$
2. $\sqrt{63}$
3. $\sqrt{290}$
4. $\sqrt{27}$
5. $\sqrt{333}$
6. $\sqrt{23}$
7. $\sqrt{96}$
8. $\sqrt{200}$
9. $\sqrt{117}$
10. $\sqrt{47}$
11. $\sqrt{1.30}$
12. $\sqrt{8.4}$
13. $\sqrt{18.35}$
14. $\sqrt{25.70}$
15. $\sqrt{14.1}$
16. $\sqrt{15.3}$

Lesson 3-3

Pages 152–153

Use a Venn diagram to solve.

1. **CLASSES** The guidance counselor surveyed 42 seventh graders to find out their interest in photography or ceramics. The results showed that 32 students liked photography, 24 favored ceramics, and 18 were interested in both photography and ceramics. How many students liked neither photography nor ceramics?
2. **CLUBS** At Harding Middle School, 28 students are in the Spanish club, 32 students are in the art club, and 21 students are in the math club. Of those students who are in exactly two clubs, 7 are in Spanish and art, 5 are in math and art, and 3 are in Spanish and math. If there are 2 students who are in all three clubs, how many students are only in the art club?
3. **PETS** Miss Coughlin surveyed her students about their pets. The results showed that 18 students owned a dog, 12 students had a cat, and 7 students owned both a cat and a dog. If there are 29 students in Miss Coughlin's class, how many students do not own a cat or a dog?

Lesson 3-4

Pages 155–159

Name all sets of numbers to which each real number belongs.

1. 6.5
2. $\sqrt{25}$
3. $\sqrt{3}$
4. -7.2
5. $-0.\overline{61}$
6. $\frac{1}{2}$
7. $\frac{16}{4}$
8. -102.1
9. $\sqrt{29}$

Estimate each square root to the nearest tenth. Then graph the square root on a number line.

10. $-\sqrt{12}$
11. $\sqrt{23}$
12. $\sqrt{2}$
13. $\sqrt{10}$
14. $-\sqrt{30}$
15. $\sqrt{5}$
16. $\sqrt{21}$
17. $-\sqrt{202}$
18. $-\sqrt{10}$

Replace each ● with <, >, or = to make a true sentence.

19. $\sqrt{7}$ ● 2.8
20. $2\frac{1}{3}$ ● $2.\overline{3}$
21. $\sqrt{121}$ ● 11
22. 5.6 ● $\sqrt{30}$
23. 9.45 ● $9.\overline{4}$
24. $\sqrt{5}$ ● 2.23
25. $\sqrt{6.25}$ ● $2\frac{1}{2}$
26. $5\frac{1}{3}$ ● $\sqrt{30}$
27. $4\frac{2}{3}$ ● $\sqrt{22}$

Lesson 3-5

Pages 162–166

Write an equation you could use to find the length of the missing side of each right triangle. Then find the missing length. Round to the nearest tenth if necessary.

1. 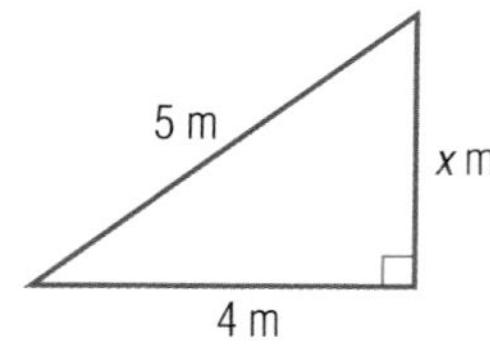

2. 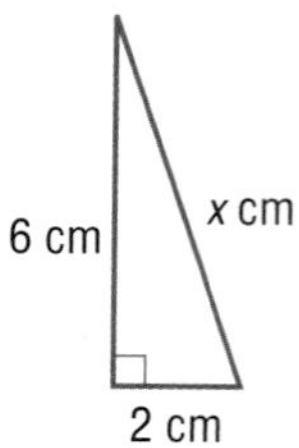

3. 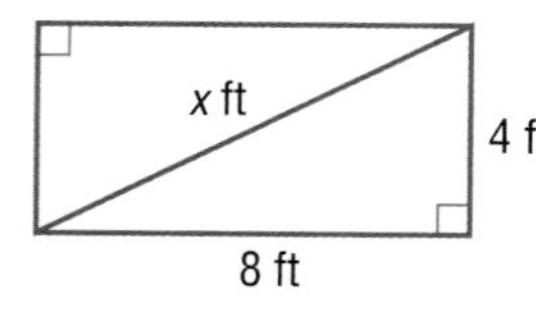

4. a, 6 cm; b, 5 cm
5. a, 12 ft; b, 12 ft
6. a, 8 in.; b, 6 in.
7. a, 20 m; c, 25 m
8. a, 9 mm; c, 14 mm
9. b, 15 m; c, 20 m

Determine whether each triangle with sides of given lengths is a right triangle.

10. 15 m, 8 m, 17 m
11. 7 yd, 5 yd, 9 yd
12. 5 in., 12 in., 13 in.
13. 9 in., 12 in., 16 in.
14. 10 ft, 24 ft, 26 ft
15. 2 ft, 2 ft, 3 ft

Lesson 3-6

Pages 167–171

Write an equation that can be used to answer each question. Then solve. Round to the nearest tenth if necessary.

1. How far apart are the boats?

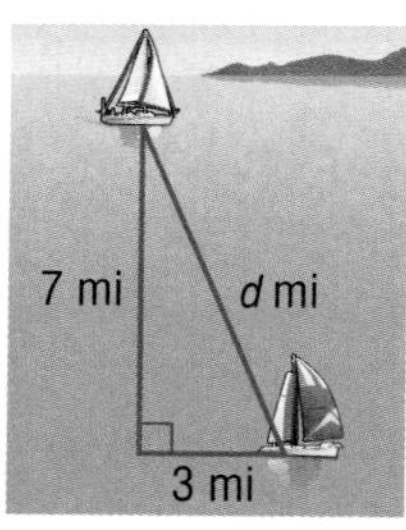

2. How high does the ladder reach?

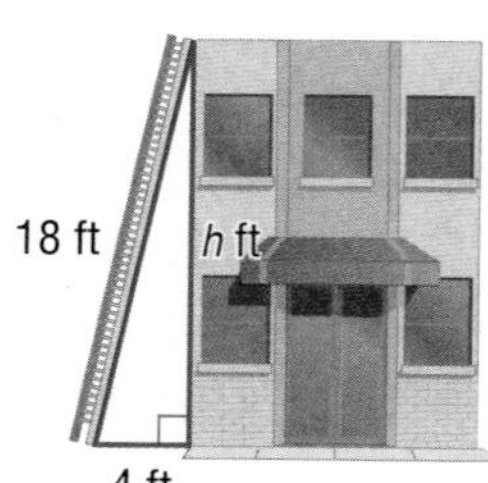

3. How long is each rafter?

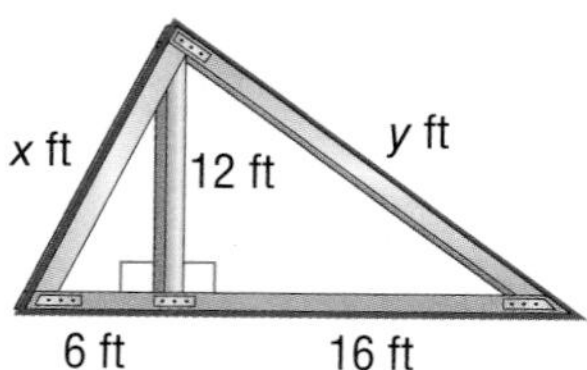

Lesson 3-7

Pages 173–178

Graph and label each point.

1. $A\left(4\frac{1}{2}, 2\frac{2}{3}\right)$
2. $B(-2.75, 3.5)$
3. $C(-1.5, 0.25)$
4. $D\left(3\frac{1}{4}, \frac{3}{4}\right)$
5. $E(2.4, -1.75)$
6. $F\left(-2\frac{1}{3}, -3\frac{2}{5}\right)$

Graph each pair of ordered pairs. Then find the distance between the points. Round to the nearest tenth if necessary.

7. $(-4, 2), (4, 17)$
8. $(5, -1), (11, 7)$
9. $(-3, 5), (2, 7)$
10. $(7, -9), (4, 3)$
11. $(5, 4), (-3, 8)$
12. $(-8, -4), (-3, 8)$
13. $(2, 7), (10, -4)$
14. $(9, -2), (3, 6)$
15. $(2, 3), (-1, 6)$
16. $(-5, 1), (2, -3)$
17. $(0, 1), (5, 2)$
18. $(-1, 2), (-2, 3)$

Lesson 4-1

Pages 190–193

Express each ratio in simplest form.

1. 10 losses out of 50 games
2. 27 empty chairs to 9 open
3. 4 out of 12 people agree
4. 8 quarts for 1 gallon of oil
5. 2 cups water in 4 pints soda
6. 11 dimes to 5 quarters
7. 660 feet wide: 1 mile long
8. 12 players to 1 coach

Express each rate as a unit rate.

9. 6 pounds gained in 12 weeks
10. $800 for 40 tickets
11. $6.50 for 5 pounds
12. 6 inches of rain in 3 weeks
13. 20 preschoolers to 2 teachers
14. 10 inches of snow in 2 days
15. $500 for 50 tickets
16. $360 for 100 dinners

Lesson 4-2

Pages 194–197

1. **POPCORN** Fun Center rents popcorn machines for $20 per hour. In addition to the hourly charge, there is a rental fee of $32. Is the number of hours you rent the popcorn machine proportional to the total cost?
2. **BAKING** Mrs. Govin is making cakes for the school bake sale. She needs 2 cups of sugar for every cake she makes. Is the number of cakes Mrs. Govin makes proportional to the number of cups of sugar?
3. **MUSIC** At a local music store, CDs cost $11.99 including tax. Is the number of CDs purchased proportional to the cost of the CDs?
4. **SAVINGS** Jean has $280 in her savings account. Starting next week, she will deposit $30 in her account every week. Is the amount of money in her account proportional to the number of weeks?

Lesson 4-3

Pages 198–203

For Exercises 1 and 2, use the following information.

Time (P.M.)	1:00	2:00	2:30	3:00	3:15
Temperature	88°F	89°F	80°F	76°F	76°F

1. Find the rate of change between 2:00 and 2:30.
2. Find the rate of change between 3:00 and 3:15. Explain the meaning of this rate of change.

For Exercises 3–5, use the following information.

Time (P.M.)	6:00	6:30	6:45	7:00	7:10	7:30	8:00	8:15	8:30
Number of Tickets Sold	2	32	77	137	139	140	142	142	142

3. Find the rate of change between 6:45 and 7:00.
4. Find the rate of change between 6:00 and 8:30.
5. During which time period was the greatest rate of change?

Lesson 4-4

Pages 204–209

Determine whether the relationship between the two quantities described in each table is linear. If so, find the constant rate of change. If not, explain your reasoning.

1.

Calories Burned				
Time (min)	1	2	3	4
Calories	4.3	8.6	12.9	16.3

2.

Punch Recipe				
Soda (c)	2	4	6	8
Juice (c)	$1\frac{1}{4}$	$2\frac{1}{2}$	$3\frac{3}{4}$	5

Find the constant rate of change for each graph and interpret its meaning.

3.

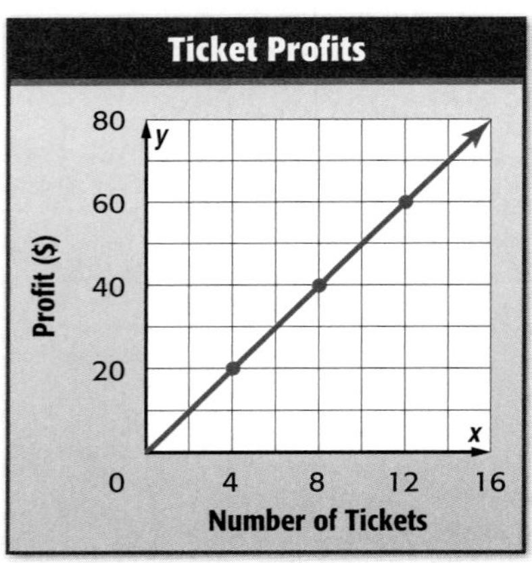

4.

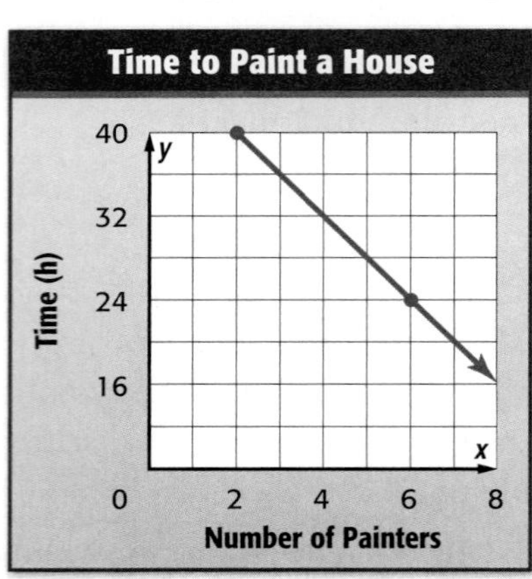

Lesson 4-5

Pages 210–214

Solve each proportion.

1. $\frac{x}{15} = \frac{4}{5}$
2. $\frac{a}{11} = \frac{24}{8}$
3. $\frac{19}{p} = \frac{16}{32}$
4. $\frac{5}{t} = \frac{0.5}{0.3}$
5. $\frac{5}{19} = \frac{c}{57}$
6. $\frac{3.6}{3} = \frac{b}{2.5}$
7. $\frac{18}{4.5} = \frac{8}{f}$
8. $\frac{36}{7} = \frac{a}{21}$
9. $\frac{9}{8} = \frac{36}{a}$
10. $\frac{b}{126} = \frac{3}{14}$
11. $\frac{n}{6} = \frac{1}{4}$
12. $\frac{7}{9} = \frac{c}{54}$
13. $\frac{2}{3} = \frac{a}{12}$
14. $\frac{7}{8} = \frac{c}{16}$
15. $\frac{3}{7} = \frac{21}{d}$
16. $\frac{2}{5} = \frac{18}{x}$
17. $\frac{3}{5} = \frac{n}{21}$
18. $\frac{5}{12} = \frac{b}{5}$
19. $\frac{4}{36} = \frac{2}{y}$
20. $\frac{16}{8} = \frac{y}{12}$

Lesson 4-6

Pages 216–217

Use the *draw a diagram* strategy to solve the problem.

1. **PICTURE FRAMES** Mr. Francisco has 4 picture frames that he wants to hang on the wall. In how many different ways can he hang the picture frames on the wall?
2. **PONDS** Carter is filling the pond in his backyard. After 2 minutes and 20 seconds, the pond is only $\frac{1}{7}$ full. If the pond can hold 280 gallons, how much longer will it take to fill the pond?
3. **MARCHING BAND** The marching band is in formation on the field. In the first row, there are 10 band members. Each additional row has 6 more members in it. If there are a total of 6 rows, how many band members are there?

Lesson 4-7

Pages 218–223

Determine whether each pair of polygons is similar. Explain your reasoning.

1. 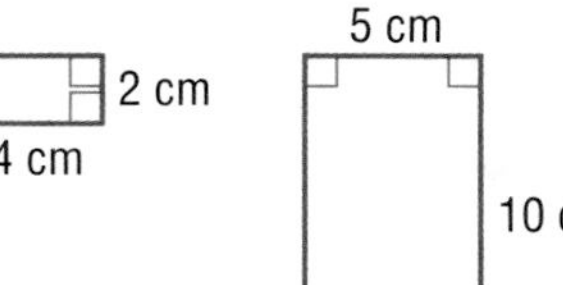

2. 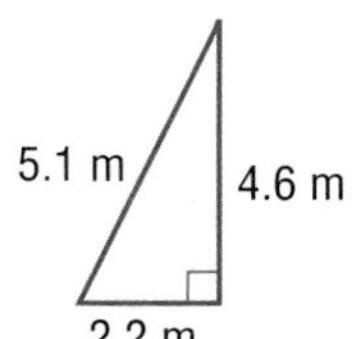

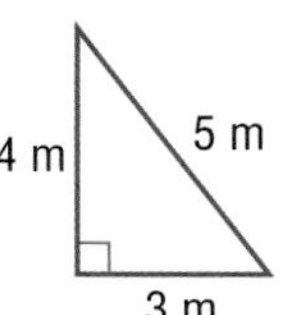

Each pair of polygons is similar. Write and solve a proportion to find each missing measure.

3. 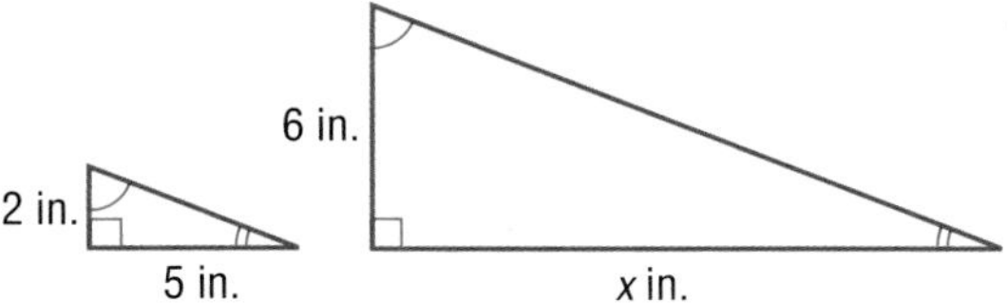

4. 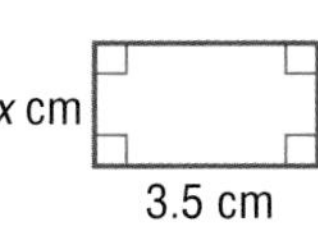

Lesson 4-8

Pages 225–230

Find the coordinates of the vertices of triangle $A'B'C'$ after triangle ABC is dilated using the given scale factor. Then graph triangle ABC and its dilation.

1. $A(-1, 0)$, $B(2, 1)$, $C(2, -1)$; scale factor 2
2. $A(4, 6)$, $B(0, -2)$, $C(6, 2)$; scale factor $\frac{1}{2}$
3. $A(1, -1)$, $B(1, 2)$, $C(-1, 1)$; scale factor 3
4. $A(2, 0)$, $B(0, -4)$, $C(-2, 4)$; scale factor $\frac{3}{2}$

In each figure, the green figure is a dilation of the blue figure. Find the scale factor of each dilation and classify each dilation as an *enlargement* or as a *reduction*.

5. 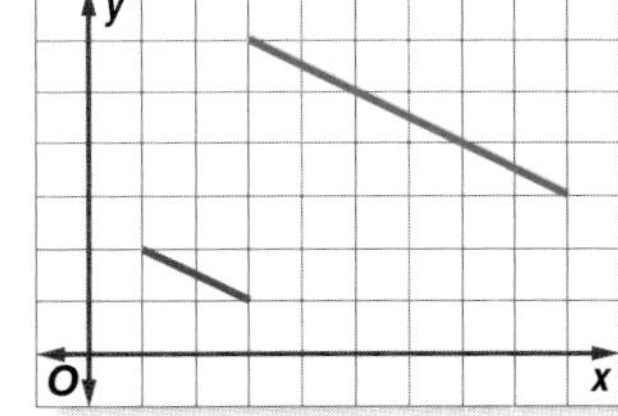

6. 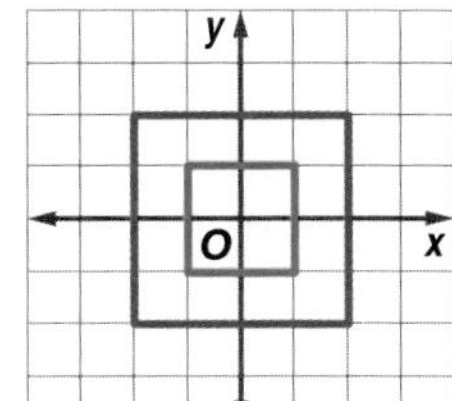

7. 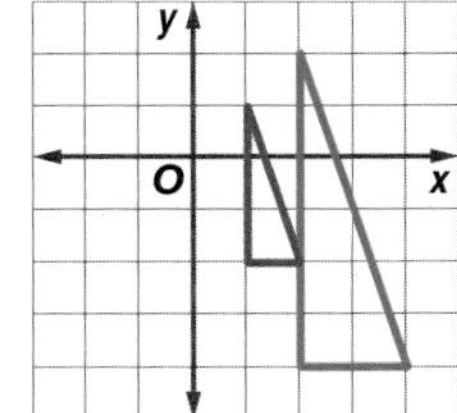

Lesson 4-9

Pages 232–235

Write and solve a proportion to find the missing measure.

1. A road sign casts a shadow 14 meters long, while a tree nearby casts a shadow 27.8 meters long. If the road sign is 3.5 meters high, how tall is the tree.
2. Use the map to find the distance across Catfish Lake. Assume the triangles are similar.
3. A 7-foot tall golf flag casts a shadow 21 feet long. A golfer standing nearby casts a shadow 16.5 feet long. How tall is the golfer?

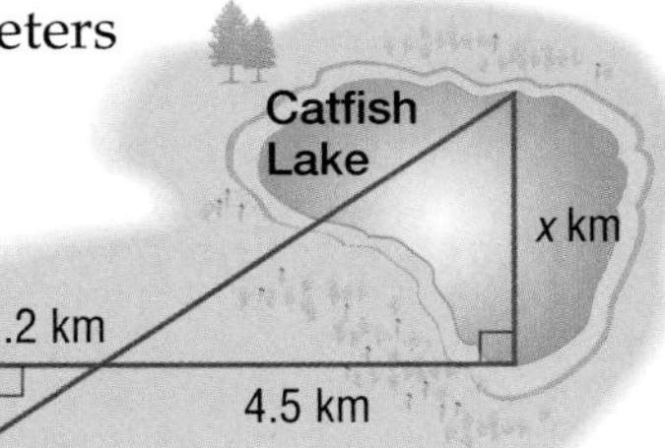

Lesson 4-10

Pages 236–241

Solve.

1. The distance between two cities on a map is 3.2 centimeters. If the scale on the map is 1 centimeter = 50 kilometers, find the actual distance between the two cities.
2. A scale model of the Empire State Building is 10 inches tall. If the Empire State Building is 1,250 feet tall, find the scale of this model.
3. On a scale drawing of a house, the dimensions of the living room are 4 inches by 3 inches. If the scale of the drawing is 1 inch = 6 feet, find the actual dimensions of the living room.
4. Columbus, Ohio, is approximately 70 miles from Dayton, Ohio. If a scale on an Ohio map is 1 inch = 11 miles, about how far apart are the cities on the map?

Lesson 5-1

Pages 252–255

Write each ratio or fraction as a percent.

1. 3 out of 5	2. $\frac{1}{4}$	3. $\frac{7}{10}$	4. 39:100
5. 11 out of 25	6. 72.5:100	7. 3 out of 4	8. $\frac{1}{2}$
9. 8:10	10. 45 per 100	11. 15 out of 100	12. 1:5

Write each percent as a fraction in simplest form.

13. 30%	14. 4%	15. 20%	16. 85%
17. 3%	18. 80%	19. 17%	20. 55%
21. 10%	22. 6%	23. 8%	24. 7%

Lesson 5-2

Pages 256–261

Write each percent as a decimal.

1. 2%	2. 25%	3. 29%	4. 6.2%
5. 16.8%	6. 14%	7. 23.7%	8. 42%
9. 3%	10. 0.7%	11. 375%	12. 90%

Write each decimal as a percent.

13. 0.35	14. 14.23	15. 0.9	16. 0.13
17. 6.21	18. 0.08	19. 0.036	20. 2.34
21. 0.4	22. 0.75	23. 0.125	24. 0.01

Write each fraction as a percent.

25. $\frac{2}{5}$	26. $\frac{1}{3}$	27. $\frac{2}{25}$	28. $\frac{9}{75}$
29. $\frac{7}{3}$	30. $\frac{14}{25}$	31. $\frac{11}{40}$	32. $\frac{9}{20}$

Lesson 5-3

Pages 263–267

Write a percent proportion and solve each problem. Round answers to the nearest tenth if necessary.

1. 39 is 5% of what number?
2. What is 19% of 200?
3. 6 is what percent of 30?
4. 24 is what percent of 72?
5. 9 is $33\frac{1}{3}$% of what number?
6. Find 55% of 134.
7. 8 is what percent of 32?
8. What is 35% of 215?
9. 62 is 50% of what number?
10. 93 is what percent of 186?
11. 90 is 36% of what number?
12. 15 is 60% of what number?
13. What is 15% of 60?
14. 15 is 20% of what number?
15. 66 is 75% of what number?
16. 31 is what percent of 155?
17. 22 is 25% of what number?
18. What is 65% of 150?
19. 6 is 75% of what number?
20. 27 is what percent of 100?

Lesson 5-4

Pages 268–271

Compute mentally.

1. 10% of 206
2. 1% of 19.3
3. 20% of 15
4. 87.5% of 80
5. 50% of 46
6. 12.5% of 56
7. $33\frac{1}{3}$% of 93
8. 90% of 2,000
9. 30% of 70
10. 40% of 95
11. $66\frac{2}{3}$% of 48
12. 80% of 25
13. 25% of 400
14. 75% of 72
15. 37.5% of 96
16. 40% of 35
17. 60% of 85
18. 62.5% of 160
19. 90% of 205
20. 1% of 2,364
21. 20% of 85
22. 75% of 12
23. 12.5% of 800
24. 30% of 90
25. 1% of 70
26. 40% of 45
27. 62.5% of 88

Lesson 5-5

Pages 272–273

Determine reasonable solutions for the following problems.

1. **TIME** Mario estimates that he spends 30% of his work day answering e-mails. If he worked 8.7 hours in one day, did he answer e-mails for 2, 3, or 4 hours?
2. **SEWING** Norma is making scarves for the craft show. Each scarf needs 48 inches of material. If she has 676 inches of material, about how many scarves can she make: 14, 16, or 18?
3. **POPCORN** The cost of renting a popcorn machine is $134.99. If the student council sells bags of popcorn for $0.85, should they sell 125, 140, or 150 bags of popcorn to pay for the popcorn machine?
4. **TRAVEL** The Hernandez family has traveled 310 miles. If this is 77% of the trip, would the number of miles left to travel be about 70, 90, or 240?

Lesson 5-6

Pages 275–278

Estimate.

1. 33% of 12
2. 24% of 84
3. 39% of 50
4. 19% of 135
5. 21% of 50
6. 49% of 121

Estimate each percent.

7. 11 out of 99
8. 28 out of 89
9. 9 out of 20
10. 25 out of 270
11. 5 out of 49
12. 7 out of 57

Estimate the percent of the area shaded.

13. 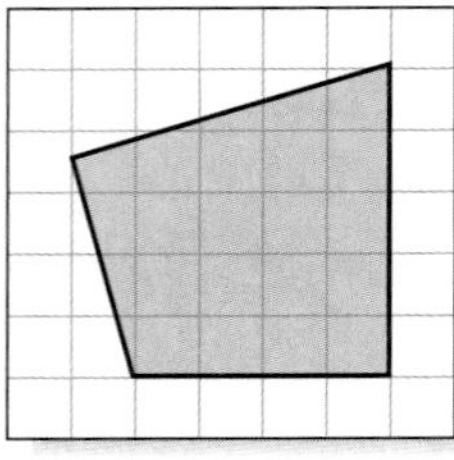

14. 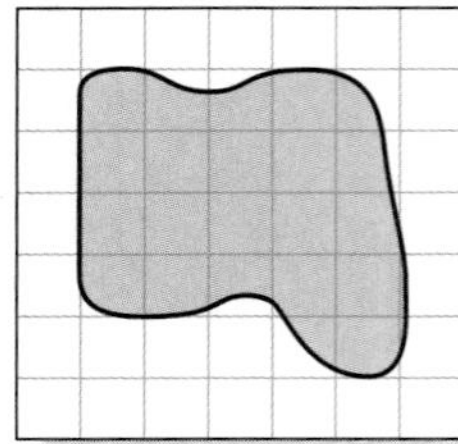

15. 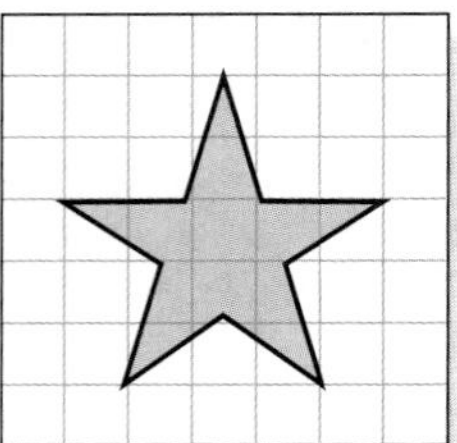

Lesson 5-7

Pages 279–283

Solve each problem using a percent equation.

1. Find 5% of 73.
2. What is 15% of 15?
3. Find 80% of 12.
4. What is 7.3% of 500?
5. Find 0.3% of 155.
6. What is 75% of 450?
7. Find 7.2% of 10.
8. What is 10.1% of 60?
9. 20 is what percent of 64?
10. Sixty-nine is what percent of 200?
11. Seventy is what percent of 150?
12. 26 is 30% of what number?
13. 7 is 14% of what number?
14. 35.5 is what percent of 150?
15. 17 is what percent of 25?
16. 152 is 2% of what number?

Lesson 5-8

Pages 284–289

Find each percent of change. Round to the nearest tenth if necessary. State whether the percent of change is an *increase* or a *decrease*.

1. original: 35
   new: 29
2. original: 550
   new: 425
3. original: 72
   new: 88

Find the selling price for each item given the cost to the store and the markup.

4. golf clubs: $250, 30% markup
5. compact disc: $17, 15% markup
6. shoes: $57, 45% markup
7. book: $26, 20% markup

Find the sale price of each item to the nearest cent if necessary.

8. piano: $4,220, 35% off
9. scissors: $14, 10% off
10. book: $29, 40% off
11. sweater: $38, 25% off

Lesson 5-9

Pages 290–293

Find the simple interest to the nearest cent if necessary.

1. \$500 at 7% for 2 years
2. \$2,500 at 6.5% for 36 months
3. \$8,000 at 6% for 1 year
4. \$1,890 at 9% for 42 months
5. \$760 at 4.5% for $2\frac{1}{2}$ years
6. \$12,340 at 5% for 6 months

Find the total amount in each account to the nearest cent if necessary.

7. \$300 at 10% for 3 years
8. \$3,200 at 8% for 6 months
9. \$20,000 at 14% for 20 years
10. \$4,000 at 12.5% for 4 years
11. \$450 at 11% for 5 years
12. \$17,000 at 15% for $9\frac{1}{2}$ years

Lesson 6-1

Pages 306–311

Find the value of x in each figure.

1. 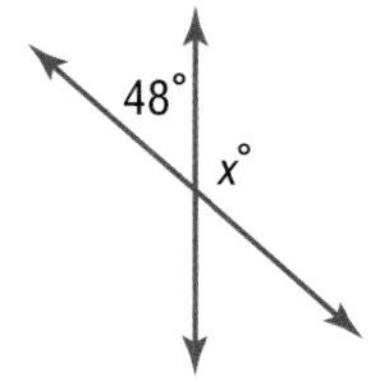

2. 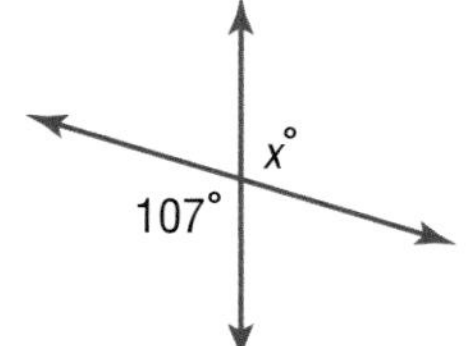

3. 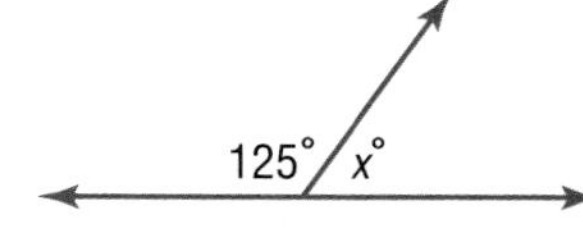

4. 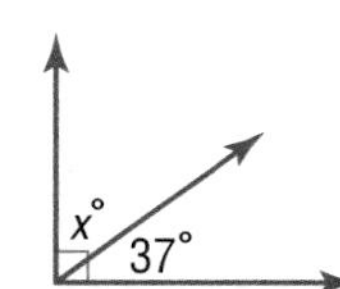

5. 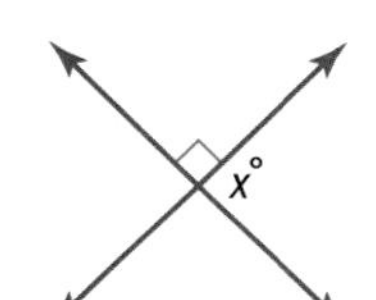

6. 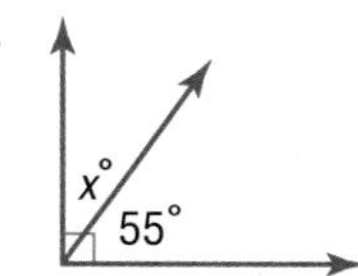

Classify each pair of angles as *alternate interior, alternate exterior,* or *corresponding.*

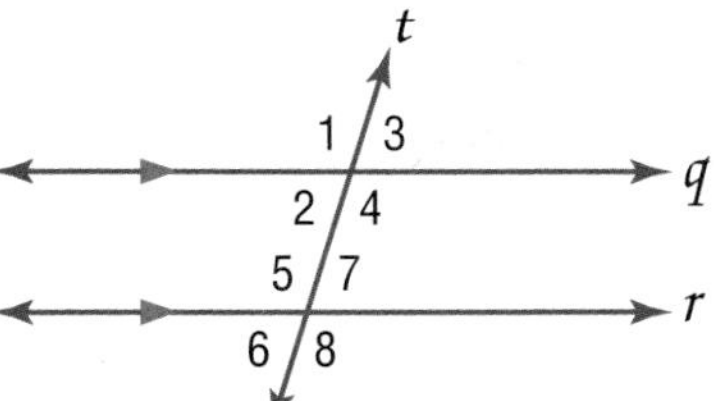

7. $\angle 3$ and $\angle 6$
8. $\angle 7$ and $\angle 3$
9. $\angle 5$ and $\angle 4$
10. $\angle 8$ and $\angle 1$

Lesson 6-2

Pages 314–315

Solve each problem using logical reasoning.

1. **GEOMETRY** Can a polygon containing two right angles be a triangle? Explain your reasoning. Can it be a quadrilateral? Explain.
2. **HEIGHT** Kristina is $\frac{2}{3}$ the height of Pedro, who is $\frac{3}{4}$ as tall as Destini. If Destini is 4 feet tall, how tall are the others?
3. **SPELLING** The top 4 finishers in the spelling bee were Kina, Niko, Gia, and Martez. Niko and the first place winner studied with Kina for the spelling bee. Gia is not the first place winner. Who is the first place winner?

Lesson 6-3

Pages 316–319

Find the sum of the measures of the interior angles for each polygon.

1. dodecagon (12-gon)
2. 17-gon
3. 21-gon

Find the measure of each interior angle for the regular polygons listed below.

4. 18-gon
5. 22-gon
6. octagon

Find the missing angle measurement for each shape described below.

7. quadrilateral: $\angle G = 110°$, $\angle H = 75°$, $\angle I = 110°$, and $\angle J =$ ■
8. pentagon: $\angle K = 112°$, $\angle L = 90°$, $\angle M = 123°$, $\angle N = 77°$, and $\angle O =$ ■

Lesson 6-4

Pages 320–323

Determine whether the polygons shown are congruent. If so, name the corresponding parts and write a congruence statement.

1. 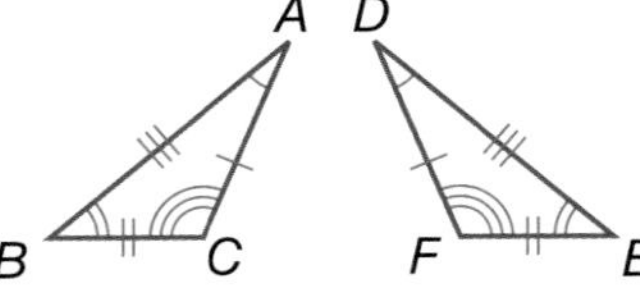

2. 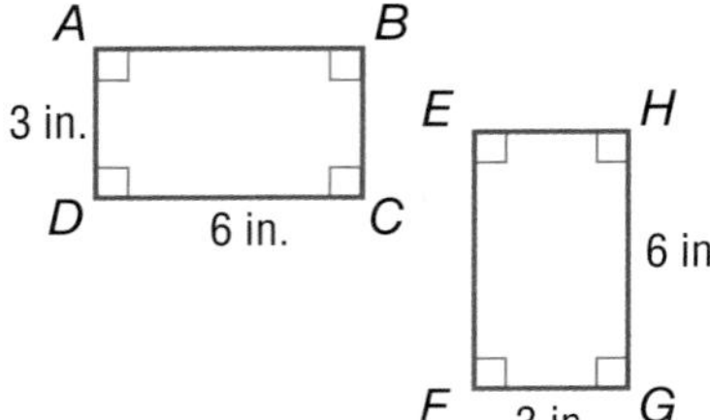

3. 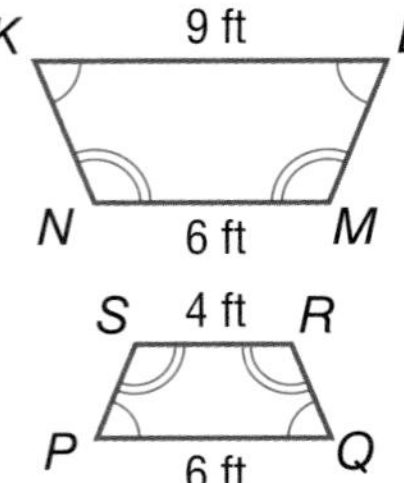

In the figure, quadrilateral *ABCD* is congruent to quadrilateral *EFGH*. Find each measure.

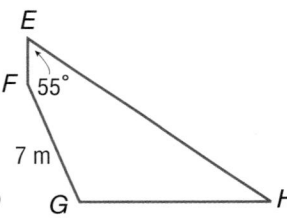

4. $m\angle A$
5. BC

Lesson 6-5

Pages 327–331

Complete parts a and b for each figure.

a. **Determine whether the figure has line symmetry. If it does, trace the figure and draw all lines of symmetry. If not, write *none*.**

b. **Determine whether the figure has rotational symmetry. Write *yes* or *no*. If *yes*, name its angle(s) of rotation.**

1. 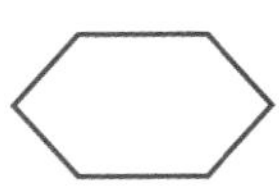
2. 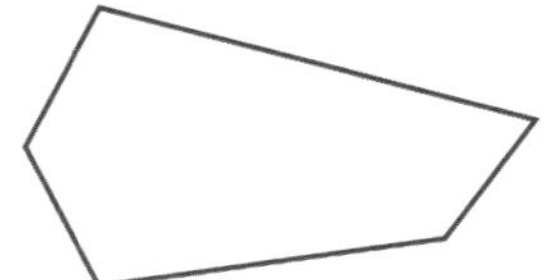
3. 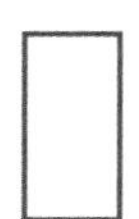
4. 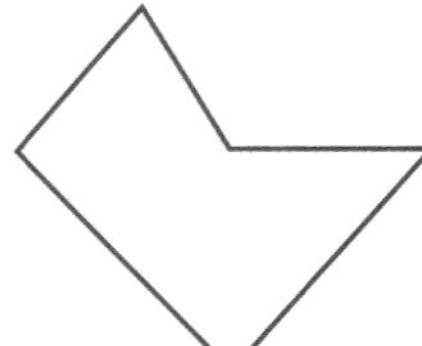
5. 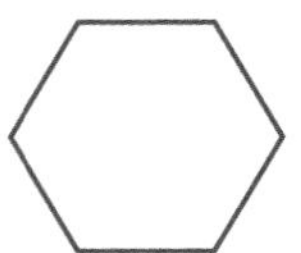
6. 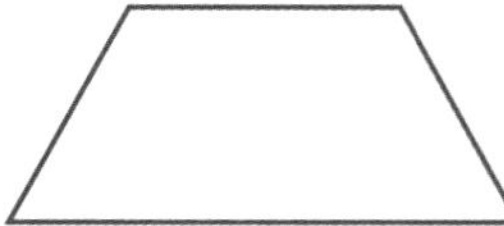

Lesson 6-6

Pages 332–336

Copy the figure onto graph paper. Then draw the reflection of the image over the given line.

1. 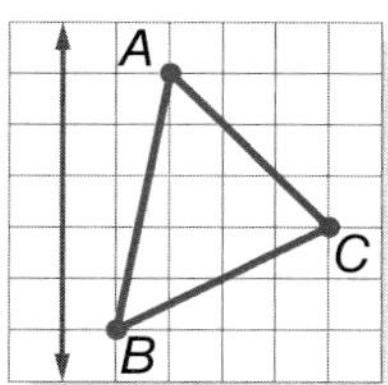

2. 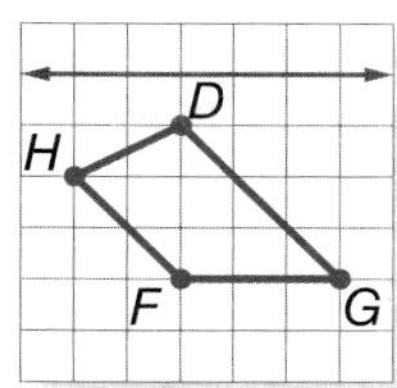

Graph the figure with the given vertices. Then graph the image of the figure after a reflection over the given axis, and write the coordinates of its vertices.

3. triangle CAT with vertices $C(2, 3)$, $A(8, 2)$, and $T(4, -3)$; x-axis
4. trapezoid $TRAP$ with vertices $T(-2, 5)$, $R(1, 5)$, $A(4, 2)$, and $P(-5, 2)$; y-axis

Lesson 6-7

pages 337–341

Graph the figure with the given vertices. Then graph the image of the figure after the indicated translation, and write the coordinates of its vertices.

1. rectangle $PQRS$ with vertices $P(-7, 6)$, $Q(-5, 6)$, $R(-5, 2)$, and $S(-7, 2)$ translated 9 units right and 1 unit down
2. pentagon $DGLMR$ with vertices $D(1, 3)$, $G(2, 4)$, $L(4, 4)$, $M(5, 3)$ and $R(3, 1)$ translated 5 units left and 7 units down
3. triangle TRI with vertices $T(2, 1)$, $R(0, 3)$, and $I(-1, 1)$ translated 2 units left and 3 units down
4. quadrilateral $QUAD$ with vertices $Q(3, 2)$, $U(3, 0)$, $A(6, 0)$ and $D(6, 2)$, translated 3 units left and 1 unit down

Lesson 7-1

Pages 352–357

Find the circumference and area of each circle. Round to the nearest tenth.

1. 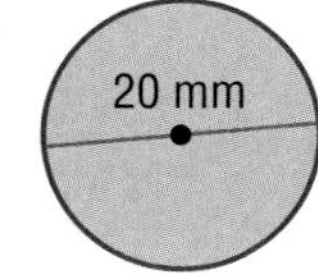

2. 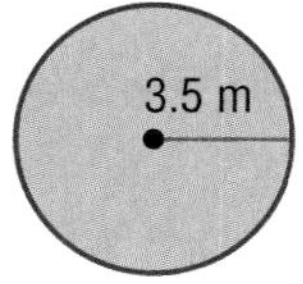

3. 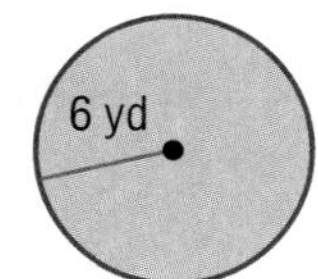

4. 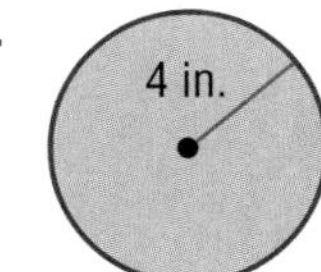

5. 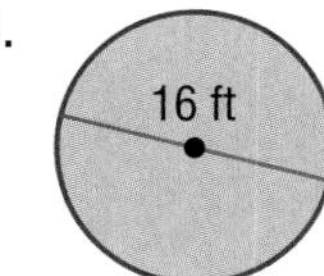

6. 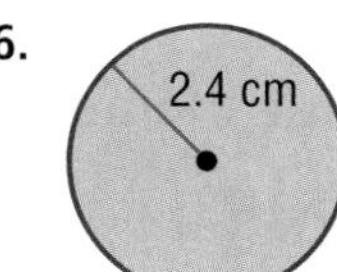

7. 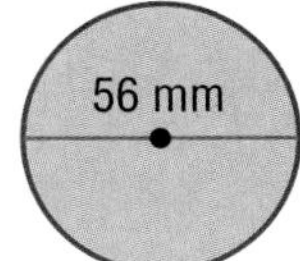

8. 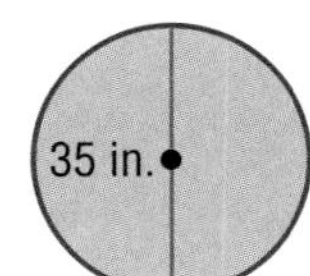

9. 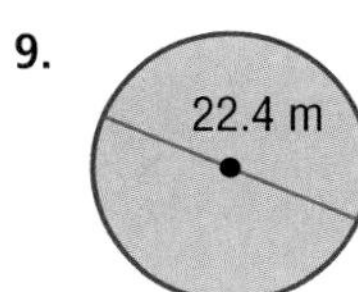

Extra Practice

Lesson 7-2

Pages 360–361

Use the *solve a simpler problem* strategy to solve the following problems.

1. **MEASUREMENT** Describe a method that could be used to determine the thickness of one sheet of paper in a textbook.
2. **HEALTH** A human heart beats an average of 72 times in one minute. Estimate the number of times a human heart beats in one year.
3. **GIFT WRAPPING** During the holidays, Tyler and Abigail earn extra money by wrapping gifts at a department store. Tyler wraps 8 packages an hour and Abigail wraps 10 packages an hour. Working together, about how long will it take them to wrap 40 packages?

Lesson 7-3

Pages 363–367

Find the area of the shaded region. Round to the nearest tenth if necessary.

1. 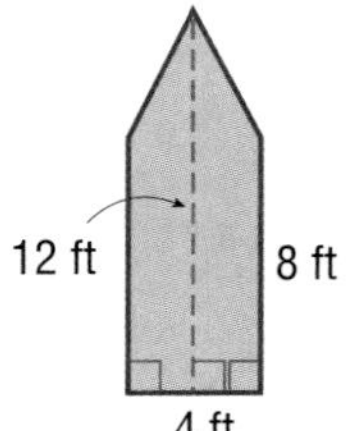

2. 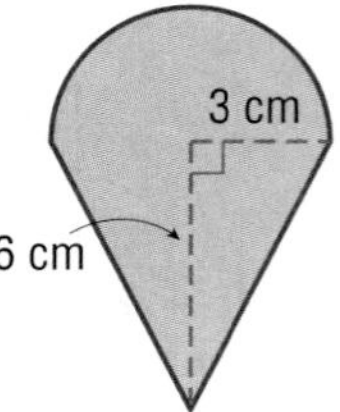

3. 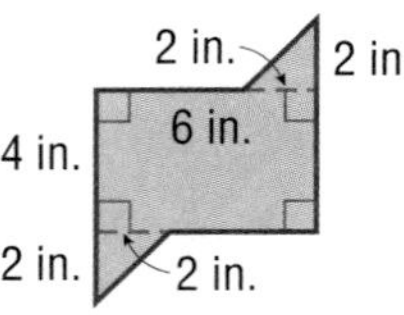

4. 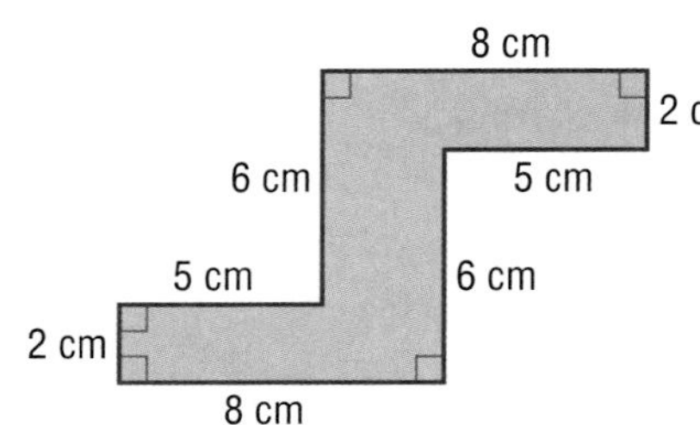

5. 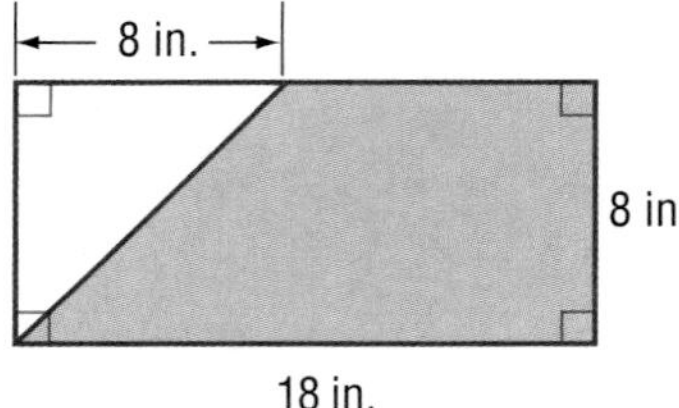

6. 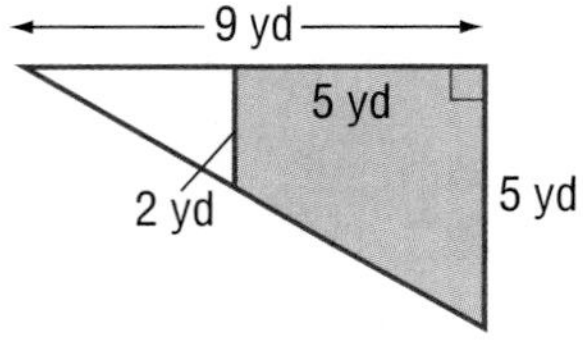

Lesson 7-4

Pages 368–372

For Exercises 1–4, use the figure at the right.

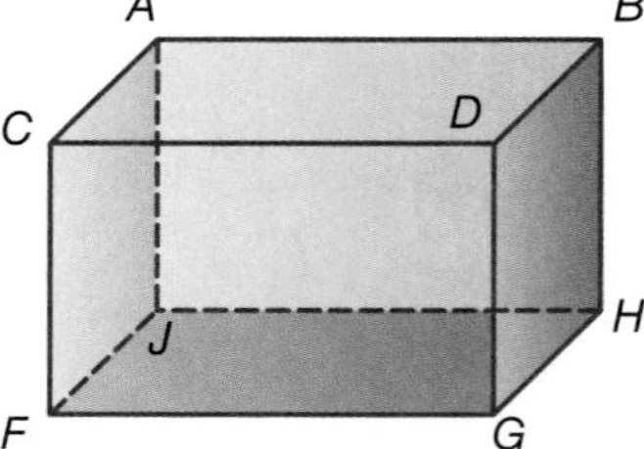

1. Name all planes that are parallel to plane *FGH*.
2. Identify a segment that is skew to *BH*.
3. Identify two sets of points between which a diagonal can be drawn.
4. Identify the intersection of planes *FCD* and *ABD*.

Identify each solid. Name the number and shapes of the faces. Then name the number of edges and vertices.

5. 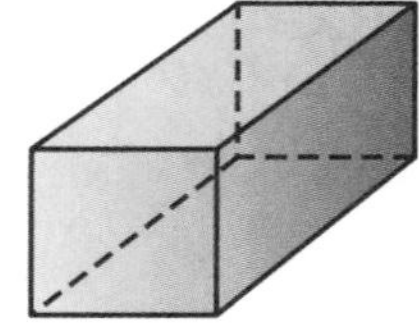

6. 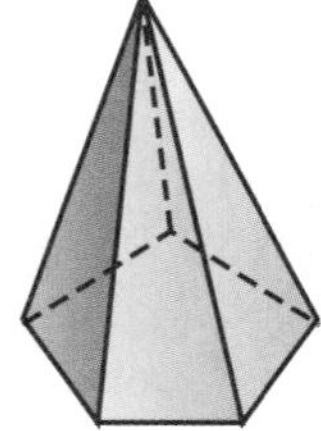

7. 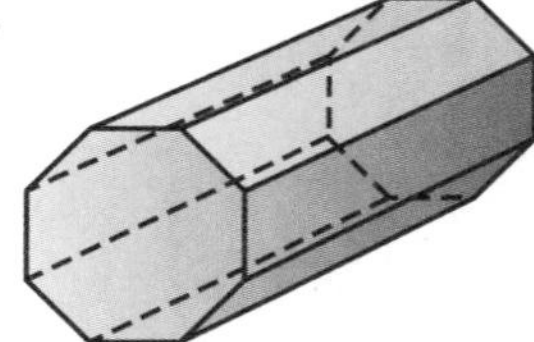

Lesson 7-5

Pages 373–378

Find the volume of each solid. Round to the nearest tenth if necessary.

1. 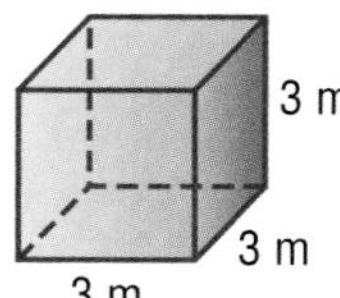

2. 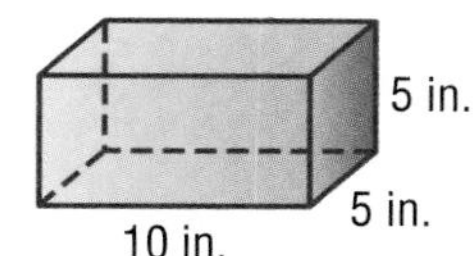

3. 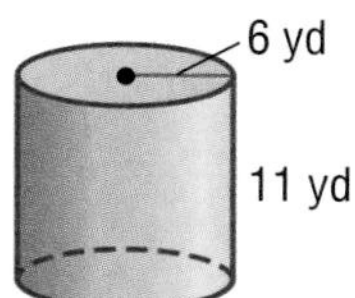

4. 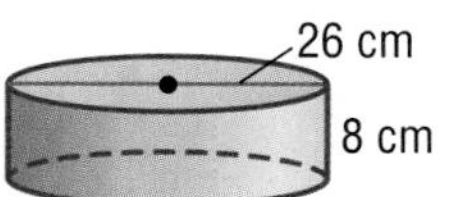

5. 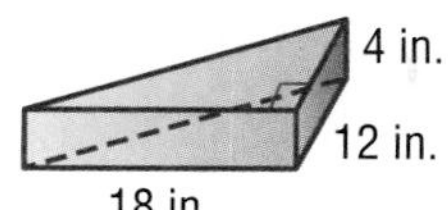

6. 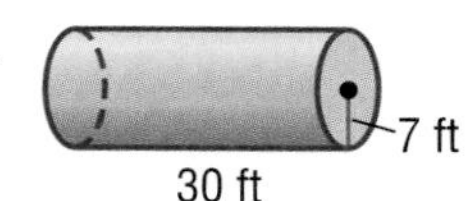

7. triangular prism: base of triangle, 7 yd; altitude, 18 yd; height of prism, $5\frac{1}{3}$ yd.

Lesson 7-6

Pages 380–384

Find the volume of each solid. Round to the nearest tenth if necessary.

1. 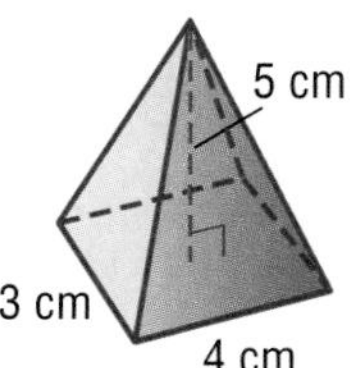

2. 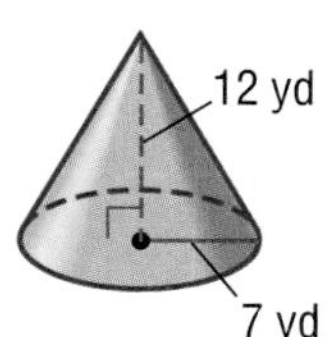

3. 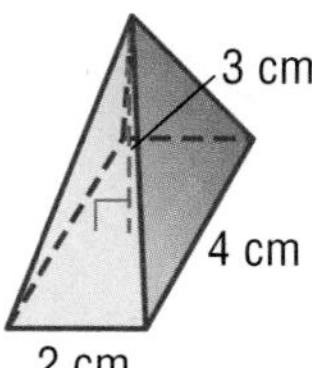

4. 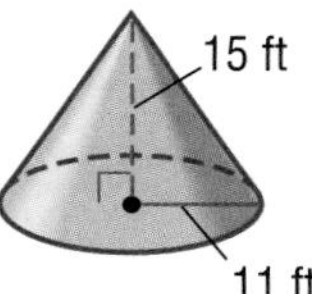

5. 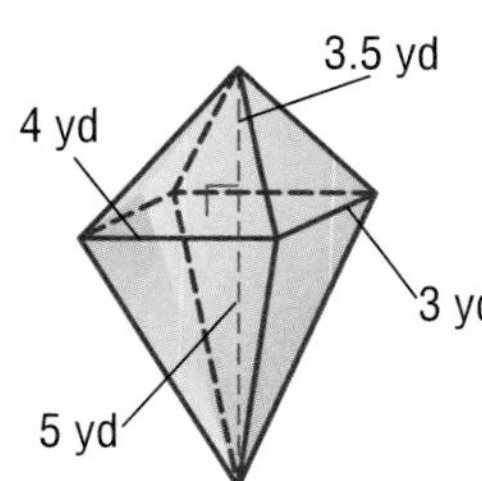

6. 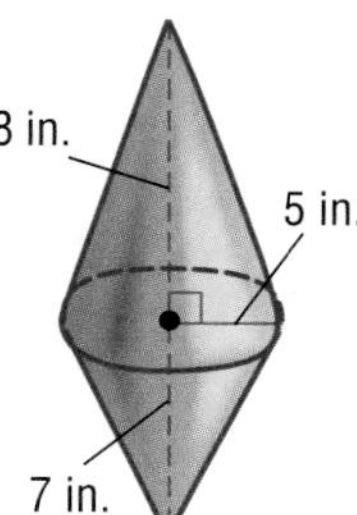

Lesson 7-7

Pages 386–391

Find the lateral and total surface areas of each solid. Round to the nearest tenth if necessary.

1. 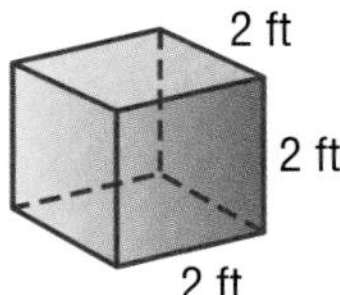

2. 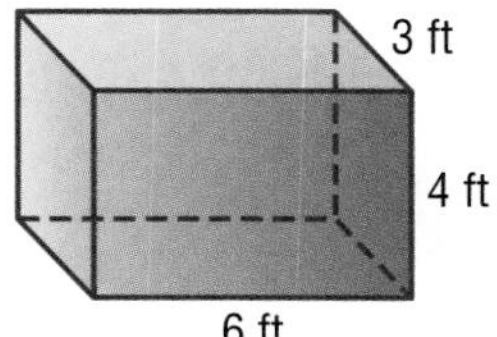

3. 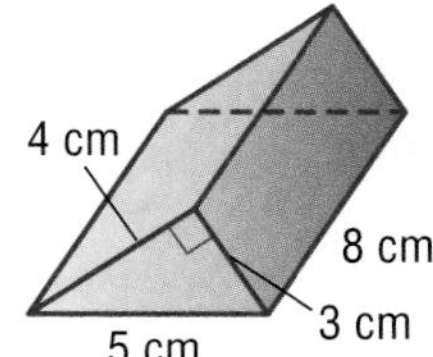

4. 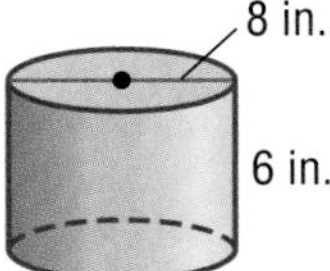

5. 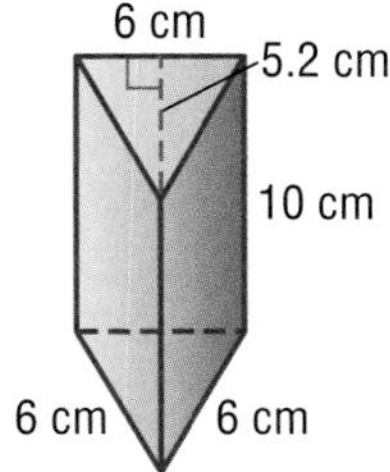

6. 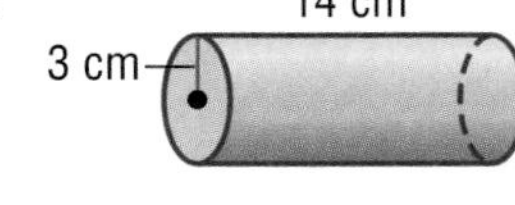

7. cylinder: diameter, 25 m; height, 30 m

Lesson 7-8

Pages 393–396

Find the lateral and total surface area of each regular pyramid. Round to the nearest tenth if necessary.

1. 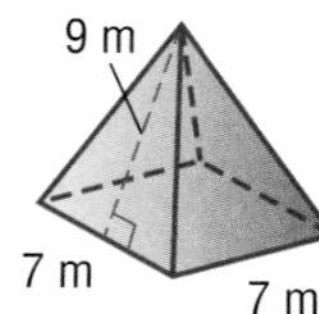

2. 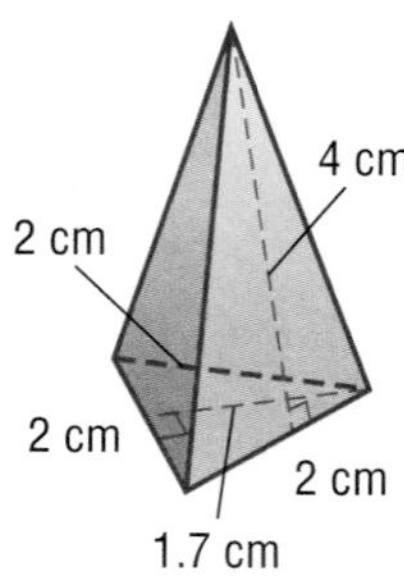

3. 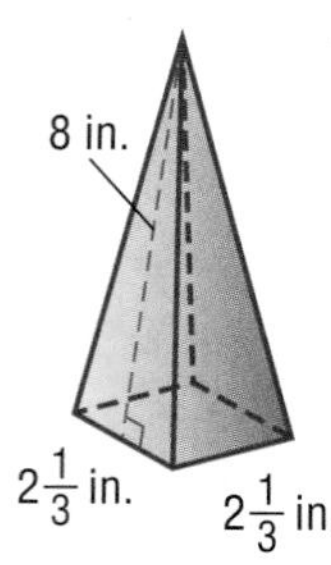

Lesson 7-9

Pages 399–404

Find the missing measure for each pair of similar solids. Round to the nearest tenth if necessary.

1. 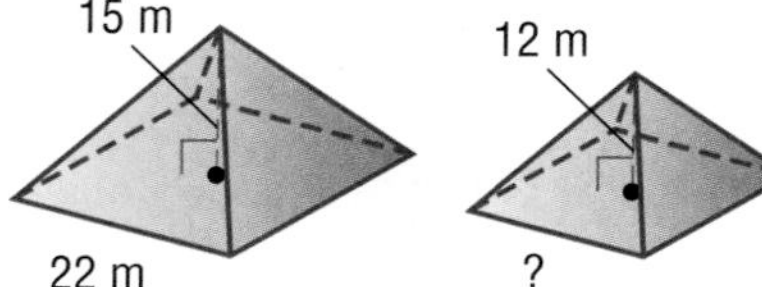

2. 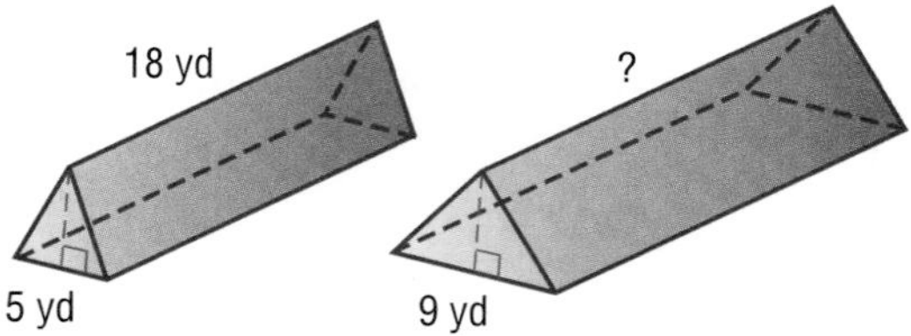

3. 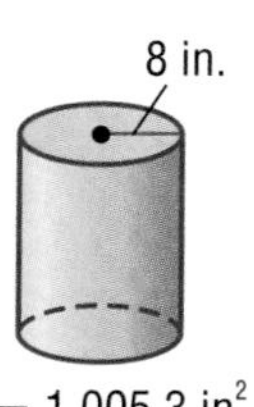

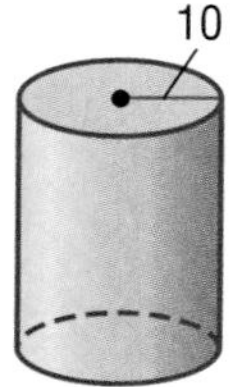

= 1,005.3 in^2 $S = ?$

4. 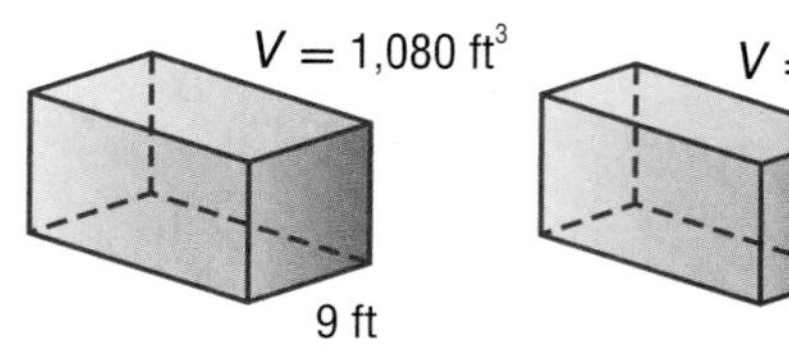

Lesson 8-1

Pages 416–421

Use the Distributive Property to rewrite each expression.

1. $2(x + 3)$
2. $3(a + 7)$
3. $3(g - 6)$
4. $-2(a + 3)$
5. $-1(x - 6)$
6. $4(a - 5)$

Identify the terms, like terms, coefficients, and constants in each expression.

7. $8b + 7b - 4 - 6b$
8. $9 + 8z - 3 + 5z$
9. $11q - 5 + 2q - 7$
10. $a + 1 + 2a + 8a$
11. $1 - 2c - 3c + 100$
12. $14j - 6 + 8j - 5$

Simplify each expression.

13. $3x + 2x$
14. $6x - 3x$
15. $2a - 5a$
16. $5x - 6x$
17. $8a - 3a$
18. $a - 4a$
19. $3a + 2a - 6$
20. $6x + 2x - 3$
21. $5a - 3 + 2a$
22. $3x + 7 - 5x$
23. $x - 3 + 5x$
24. $6x - 3x - 2$
25. $a - 2a + 5$
26. $6x - 2 + 7x$
27. $5a - 7a + 2$
28. $4a + 2 - 7a - 5$
29. $3a - 2 + 5a - 7$
30. $5x - 3x + 2 - 5$

Lesson 8-2

Pages 422–426

Solve each equation. Check your solution.

1. $2x + 4 = 14$
2. $5p - 10 = 0$
3. $5 + 6a = 41$
4. $\frac{x}{3} - 7 = 2$
5. $18 = 6q - 24$
6. $18 = 4m - 6$
7. $3r - 3 = 9$
8. $2x + 3 = 5$
9. $0 = 4x - 28$
10. $3x - 1 = 5$
11. $3z + 5 = 14$
12. $3x - 15 = 12$
13. $9a - 8 = 73$
14. $2x - 3 = 7$
15. $3t + 6 = 9$
16. $2y + 10 = 22$
17. $15 = 2y - 5$
18. $3c - 4 = 2$
19. $6 + 2p = 16$
20. $8 = 2 + 3x$
21. $4b + 24 = 24$
22. $2x + 3x - 6 = 19$
23. $-2x - 6 = 14$
24. $3x - 9 = -18$
25. $2a - 3a + 1 = 15$
26. $5x - 3x + 6 = -10$
27. $3a - 5a + a = 11$
28. $5a - 3a - 5 + 1 = -10$
29. $3 = 7a - 6a + 2$
30. $3y + 5y - 1 = 15$

Lesson 8-3

Pages 427–431

Translate each sentence into an equation. Then find each number.

1. The sum of a number and 7 is 11.
2. Seven more than the quotient of a number and -2 is 6.
3. The sum of a number and 6 is 21.
4. The difference of a number and 2 is 4.
5. Twice a number plus 5 is -3.
6. The product of a number and 3 is 18.
7. The product of a number and 4 plus 2 is 14.
8. Eight less than the quotient of a number and 3 is 5.
9. The difference of twice a number and 3 is 11.
10. The sum of 3 times a number and 7 is 25.

Lesson 8-4

Pages 434–437

Solve each equation. Check your solution.

1. $6x + 10 = 1x$
2. $2a - 5 = -3a$
3. $7a - 5 = 2a$
4. $3a + 7 = 10$
5. $8x + 3 = 2x$
6. $5x - 3 = -18$
7. $3a - 1 = 2a$
8. $7a - 2 = 12$
9. $3x + 6 = x$
10. $2x + 7 = 11 - 2x$
11. $8x + 10 = 3x$
12. $7a + 4 = 3a$
13. $7x + 8 = 11x$
14. $21x + 11 = 10x$
15. $5x + 5 = 14 + 2x$
16. $7b - 4 = 2b + 16$
17. $2y - 3 = 5 - 2y$
18. $3m = 2m + 7$
19. $9t + 1 = 4t - 9$
20. $-2a + 3 = a - 12$
21. $3x = 9x - 12$
22. $2c + 3 = 3c - 4$
23. $s - 3 = 5 - s$
24. $3w - 5 = 5w - 7$
25. $4x - 7 = 11 + x$
26. $5x + 2 = 10 + x$
27. $3x + 2 = 2x + 5$

Lesson 8-5

Pages 439–440

Solve Exercises 1–4. Use the *guess and check* strategy.

1. **NUMBER THEORY** A number squared is 529. Find the number.
2. **VOLUME** The volume of a right triangular prism is 216 cubic centimeters. The legs of the triangular base are half the height of the prism. Find the dimensions of the prism.
3. **MONEY** Edwin has $2.35 in quarters, dimes, nickels, and pennies. He has 31 coins. The number of pennies is twice as great as the number of quarters, and $\frac{5}{6}$ as great as the number of nickels. He has fewer dimes than any other coin. How many of each coin does he have?
4. **LEGS** On a farm, there are 100 total legs on people and animals. Each cow and horse has 4 legs, and each person has 2 legs. There are 4 more than ten times as many cows and horses than people. How many cows and horses, and how many people are there?

Lesson 8-6

Pages 441–444

Write an inequality for each sentence.

1. A number is less than 10.
2. A number is greater than or equal to −7.
3. A number is less than −2.
4. A number is more than 5.
5. A number is less than or equal to 11.
6. A number is no more than 8.

Graph each inequality on a number line.

7. $x > 5$
8. $y > 0$
9. $z < -2$
10. $a \geq 6$
11. $b \leq 2$
12. $x \geq 1$
13. $a \leq 3$
14. $b \geq 1$
15. $x < -2$
16. $n \geq -3$
17. $t > -1$
18. $y \leq -5$

Lesson 8-7

Pages 445–448

Solve each inequality. Check your solution.

1. $y + 3 > 7$
2. $c - 9 < 5$
3. $x + 4 \geq 9$
4. $y - 3 < 15$
5. $t - 13 \geq 5$
6. $x + 3 < 10$
7. $y - 6 \geq 2$
8. $x - 3 \geq -6$
9. $a + 3 \leq 5$
10. $c - 2 \leq 11$
11. $a + 15 \geq 6$
12. $y + 3 \geq 18$
13. $y + 16 \geq -22$
14. $x - 3 \geq 17$
15. $y - 6 > -17$
16. $y - 11 < 7$
17. $a + 5 \geq 21$
18. $c + 3 > -16$
19. $x - 12 \geq 12$
20. $x + 5 \geq 5$
21. $y - 6 > 31$
22. $a - 6 > 17$
23. $y + 7 > 3$
24. $a + 13 \geq -16$
25. $y - 6 > 5$
26. $y + 6 < -5$
27. $x - 17 \geq 34$
28. $y + 1 \leq 16$
29. $a - 14 \geq 16$
30. $x + 14 \leq 20$

Lesson 8-8

Pages 449–453

Solve each inequality and check your solution. Then graph the solution on a number line.

1. $5p \geq 25$
2. $4x < 12$
3. $15 \leq 3m$
4. $\frac{d}{3} > 15$
5. $8 < \frac{r}{7}$
6. $9g < 27$
7. $4p \geq 24$
8. $5p > 25$
9. $-4 > \frac{-k}{3}$
10. $\frac{-z}{5} > 2$
11. $-3x \leq 9$
12. $-5x > -35$
13. $\frac{a}{-6} < 1$
14. $\frac{x}{-5} \leq -2$
15. $-2x < 16$

Lesson 9-1

Pages 464–468

State whether each sequence is arithmetic. Write *yes* or *no*. If it is, state the common difference. Write the next three terms of the sequence.

1. $1, 5, 9, 13, \ldots$
2. $2, 6, 18, 54, \ldots$
3. $1, 4, 9, 16, 25, \ldots$
4. $729, 243, 81, \ldots$
5. $2, -3, -8, -13, \ldots$
6. $5, -5, 5, -5, \ldots$
7. $810, -270, 90, -30, \ldots$
8. $11, 14, 17, 20, 23, \ldots$
9. $33, 27, 21, \ldots$
10. $21, 15, 9, 3, \ldots$
11. $\frac{1}{8}, -\frac{1}{4}, \frac{1}{2}, -1, \ldots$
12. $\frac{1}{81}, \frac{1}{27}, \frac{1}{9}, \frac{1}{3}, \ldots$
13. $\frac{3}{4}, 1\frac{1}{2}, 3, \ldots$
14. $2, 5, 9, 14, \ldots$
15. $-1\frac{1}{4}, -1\frac{3}{4}, -2\frac{1}{4}, -2\frac{3}{4}, \ldots$

Lesson 9-2

Pages 469–473

Find each function value.

1. $f\left(\frac{1}{2}\right)$ if $f(x) = 2x - 6$
2. $f(-4)$ if $f(x) = -\frac{1}{2}x + 4$
3. $f(1)$ if $f(x) = -5x + 1$
4. $f(6)$ if $f(x) = \frac{2}{3}x - 5$
5. $f(0)$ if $f(x) = 1.6x + 4$
6. $f(2)$ if $f(x) = 2x - 8$

Copy and complete each function table. Then give the domain and range.

7. $f(x) = -4x$

x	−4x	f(x)
−2		
−1		
0		
1		

8. $f(x) = x + 6$

x	x + 6	f(x)
−6		
−4		
−2		
0		

9. $f(x) = 3x + 2$

x	3x + 2	f(x)
−3		
−2		
−1		
0		

Lesson 9-3

Pages 475–480

Graph each function.

1. $y = 6x + 2$
2. $y = -2x + 3$
3. $y = -5x$
4. $y = 10x - 2$
5. $y = -2.5x - 1.5$
6. $y = 7x + 3$
7. $y = \frac{x}{4} - 8$
8. $y = 3x + 1$
9. $y = 25 - 2x$
10. $y = \frac{x}{6}$
11. $y = -2x + 11$
12. $y = 7x - 3$

Lesson 9-4

Pages 481–486

Find the slope of the line that passes through each pair of points.

1. $A(2, 3), B(1, 5)$
2. $C(-6, 1), D(2, 1)$
3. $E(3, 0), F(5, 0)$
4. $G(-1, -3), H(-2, -5)$
5. $I(6, 7), J(11, 1)$
6. $K(5, 3), L(5, -2)$
7. $M(10, 2), N(-3, 5)$
8. $O(6, 2), P(1, 7)$
9. $Q(5, 8), R(-3, -2)$
10. $S(-1, 7), T(3, 8)$
11. $U(4, -1), V(-5, -2)$
12. $W(3, -2), X(7, -1)$
13. $Y(0, 5), Z(2, 1)$
14. $A(6, 5), B(-3, -5)$
15. $C(2, 1), D(7, -1)$
16. $E(-5, 2), F(0, 2)$
17. $G(-3, 5), H(-2, 5)$
18. $I(2, 0), J(3, 5)$

Lesson 9-5

Pages 487–492

TRAVEL **Use the graph to answer Exercises 1 and 2.**

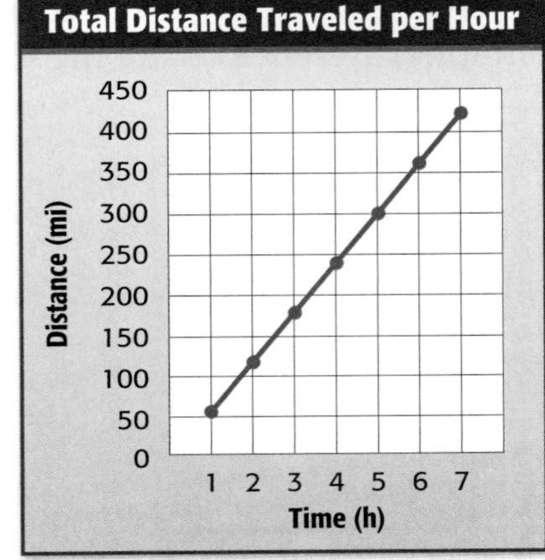

1. The number of miles traveled varies directly with the number of hours traveled. What is the rate of speed in miles per hour?
2. Going at the rate shown, what distance would one travel in 39 hours?
3. **GAS MILEAGE** Pilar's car can travel about 100 miles on 3 gallons of gas. Assuming that the distance traveled remains constant to the amount of gas used, how many gallons of gas would be needed to travel 650 miles?
4. **MONEY** Determine whether the linear function shown is a direct variation. If so, state the constant of variation.

Savings, x	\$2,154	\$3,231	\$4,308	\$5,385
Years, y	2	3	4	5

Lesson 9-6

Pages 495–499

State the slope and y-intercept for the graph of each equation.

1. $y = 3x - 5$
2. $y = 2x - 6$
3. $y = -6x + \frac{1}{2}$
4. $y = -7x + \frac{5}{2}$
5. $y = \frac{1}{2}x + 7$
6. $y = \frac{3}{4}x + 8$
7. $y = -\frac{2}{3}x - \frac{1}{3}$
8. $y = -\frac{1}{8}x - \frac{3}{8}$
9. $y = \frac{2}{3}x + 5$
10. $y = -\frac{2}{7}x - 1$
11. $3x + y = 6$
12. $y - 4x = 7$

Graph each equation using the slope and y-intercept.

13. $y = -2x + 5$
14. $y = -3x + 1$
15. $y = -x + 1$
16. $y = -x + 3$
17. $y = x - 3$
18. $y = x - 5$
19. $y = 3x - 6$
20. $y = \frac{5}{2}x - 1$
21. $y = \frac{1}{2}x + 3$
22. $y = -2x - 2$
23. $y - 4x = -1$
24. $2x + y = 3$

Lesson 9-7

Pages 502–507

Write and solve a system of equations that represents each situation.

1. **BAND** The school band has a total of 125 students. There are 25 more girls than boys.

2. **PIZZA** Pearson Middle School ordered a total of 75 cheese and pepperoni pizzas. The total cost of the pizzas was $445. Each cheese pizza cost $5, and each pepperoni pizza cost $7.

Solve each system of equations by graphing.

3. $y = x - 1$
 $y = -x + 11$

4. $y = -x$
 $y = 2x$

5. $y = -x + 3$
 $y = x + 3$

6. $y = x - 3$
 $y = 2x$

7. $y = -x + 6$
 $y = x + 2$

8. $y = -x + 2$
 $y = x - 4$

9. $y = -3x + 6$
 $y = x - 2$

10. $y = 3x - 4$
 $y = -3x - 4$

11. $y = 2x + 1$
 $y = 3x$

12. $y = -x + 4$
 $y = x - 10$

13. $y = -x + 6$
 $y = 2x$

14. $y = x - 4$
 $y = -2x + 5$

Lesson 9-8

Pages 508–509

CLUBS For Exercises 1–3, use the table that shows the math club membership from 2001 to 2006.

1. Make a graph of the data.

2. Describe how the number of math club memberships changed from 2001 to 2006.

3. What is a reasonable prediction for the membership in 2007 if this membership trend continues?

Math Club Membership

Year	Number of Students
2001	20
2002	21
2003	30
2004	34
2005	38
2006	45

Lesson 9-9

Pages 510–515

Explain whether a scatter plot of the data for each of the following might show a *positive*, *negative*, or *no* relationship.

1. height and hair color

2. hours spent studying and test scores

3. income and month of birth

4. child's age and height

5. age and eye color

6. number of hours worked and earnings

7. 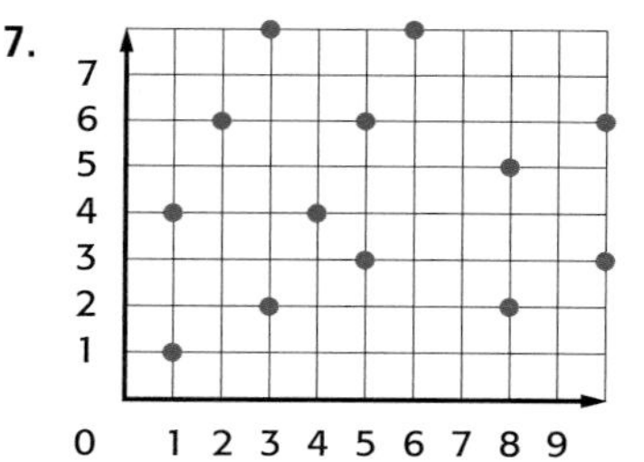

8. 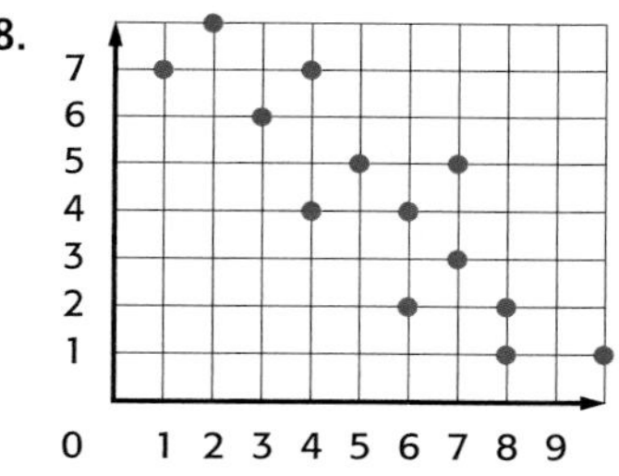

9. 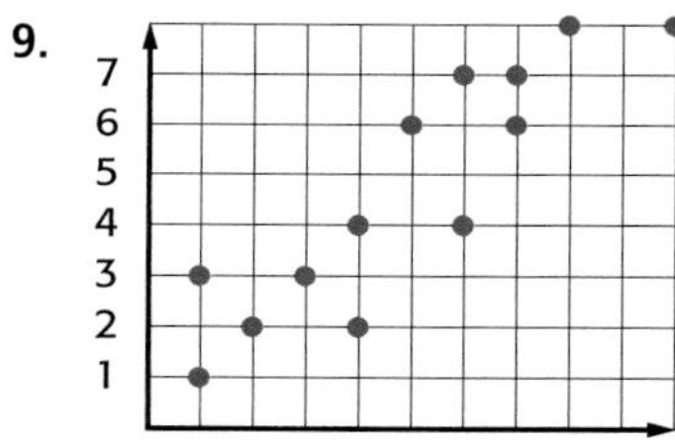

Extra Practice

Lesson 10-1

Pages 528–533

Determine whether each graph, equation, or table represents a *linear* or *nonlinear* function. Explain.

1.

x	−1	0	1	2
y	2	0	2	8

2.

x	−1	0	1	2
y	−1	0	1	8

3.

x	−1	0	1	2
y	−3	0	3	6

4. 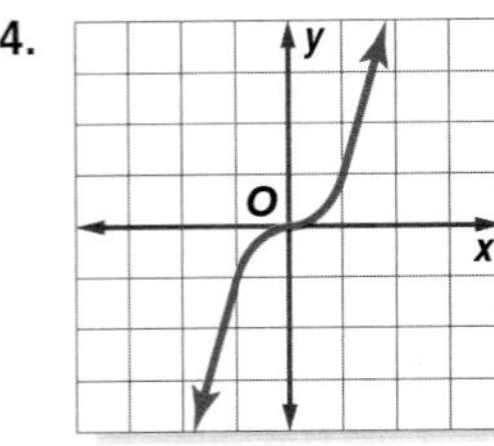

5. 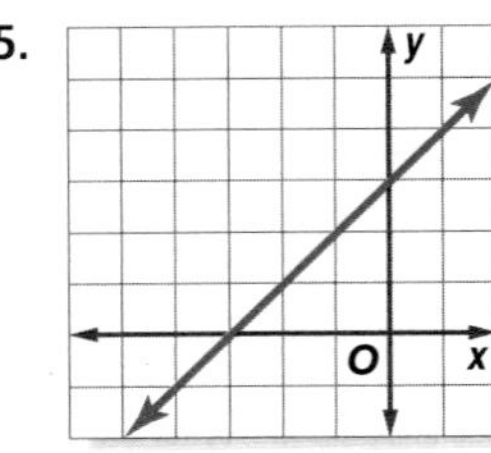

6. 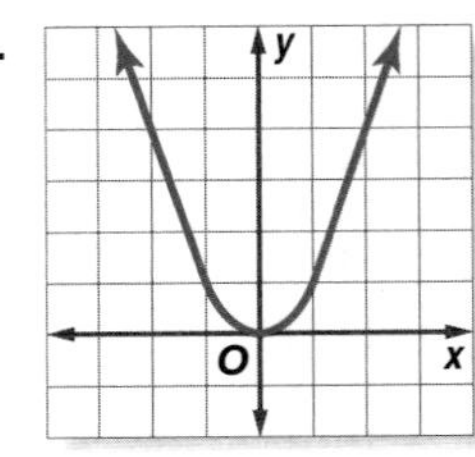

7. $y = 3x$
8. $y = \frac{2}{3}x$
9. $y = x^2 + 5$
10. $y = 4^x$
11. $y = -\frac{3}{x}$
12. $xy = -3$
13. $y = x^3 + 2$
14. $y = 2$
15. $y = 3x + 5$

Lesson 10-2

Pages 534–537

Graph each function.

1. $y = x^2 - 1$
2. $y = 1.5x^2 + 3$
3. $y = x^2 - x$
4. $y = 2x^2$
5. $y = x^2 + 3$
6. $y = -3x^2 + 4$
7. $y = -x^2 + 7$
8. $y = 3x^2$
9. $y = 3x^2 + 9x$
10. $y = -x^2$
11. $y = \frac{1}{2}x^2 + 1$
12. $y = 5x^2 - 4$
13. $y = -x^2 + 3x$
14. $y = 2.5x^2$
15. $y = -2x^2$
16. $y = 8x^2 + 3$
17. $y = -x^2 + \frac{1}{2}x$
18. $y = -4x^2 + 4$
19. $y = 4x^2 + 3$
20. $y = -4x^2 + 1$
21. $y = 2x^2 + 1$
22. $y = x^2 - 4x$
23. $y = 3x^2 + 5$
24. $y = 0.5x^2$
25. $y = 2x^2 - 5x$
26. $y = \frac{3}{2}x^2 - 2$
27. $y = 6x^2 + 2$
28. $y = 5x^2 + 6x$

Lesson 10-3

Pages 538–539

For Exercises 1–2, solve by making a model.

1. **GEARS** The set of gears shown has diameters of 10 inches, 12 inches, 12 inches, and 20 inches. After how many complete revolutions of the smaller gear will the larger gear make one complete revolution?

2. **PACKAGING** Cecil needs packing tape to ship a number of identically-shaped packages. The packages are cubes. He needs to tape all the way around the box, in both directions, and have 2 inches of overlap in each direction. Write an expression that can be used to find the amount of tape needed to wrap p such packages.

Lesson 10-4

Pages 540–543

Graph each function.

1. $y = 2x^3 - 3$
2. $y = -x^3 + 2$
3. $y = \frac{1}{2}x^3$
4. $y = -4x^3 + 3$
5. $y = -\frac{1}{4}x^3 - 1$
6. $y = x^3 - 2$
7. $y = \frac{1}{3}x^3 - 2$
8. $y = -3x^3 + 1$
9. $y = x^3 + 2$

Lesson 10-5

Pages 545–548

Simplify. Express using exponents.

1. $2^3 \cdot 2^4$
2. $5^6 \cdot 5$
3. $t^{-4} \cdot t^2$
4. $y^5 \cdot y^3$
5. $(-3x^3)(-2x^2)$
6. $b^{12} \cdot b$
7. $3^5 \cdot 3^8$
8. $(-2y^3)\,(5y^{-7})$
9. $(6a^5)(-3a^6)$
10. $(-x)(-6x^3)$
11. $(3x^2)(2x^5)$
12. $(-6y^2)(-2y^5)$
13. $(-3a)(-2a^6)$
14. $8a^{-3}\,(5a^5)$
15. $(6x^2)(2x^{11})$

Lesson 10-6

Pages 550–554

Simplify. Express using positive exponents.

1. $\frac{x^{11}}{x^2}$
2. $\frac{a^6}{a^3}$
3. $\frac{b^4}{b^{-5}}$
4. $\frac{7^9}{7^6}$
5. $\frac{2^5}{2^2}$
6. $\frac{11^{10}}{11}$
7. $\frac{16x^3}{4x^2}$
8. $\frac{25y^5}{5y^2}$
9. $\frac{-48y^3}{-8y}$
10. $\frac{12y^{-5}}{3y^2}$
11. $\frac{39x^7y^5}{3x^3y}$
12. $\frac{21a^7b^2}{7ab^2}$
13. $\frac{22a^{-4}b^3}{2a^2b^{-2}}$
14. $\frac{15x^2y}{3xy}$
15. $\frac{20a^3b^2}{2a^2b}$

Lesson 10-7

Pages 555–558

Simplify.

1. $(2^3)^2$
2. $(4^3)^3$
3. $(6^2)^4$
4. $(a^4)^3$
5. $(m^7)^8$
6. $(k^5)^7$
7. $[(3^2)^2]^3$
8. $[(4^2)^2]^2$
9. $[(2^3)^2]^3$
10. $(6z^4)^5$
11. $(8c^8)^3$
12. $(-3a^5b^{12})^5$

Lesson 10-8

Pages 559–562

Simplify.

1. $\sqrt{b^2}$
2. $\sqrt{c^4d^8}$
3. $\sqrt{m^2p^6}$
4. $\sqrt{k^4}$
5. $\sqrt{49x^2}$
6. $\sqrt{81w^4}$
7. $\sqrt{64y^4z^8}$
8. $\sqrt{36b^6c^{10}}$
9. $\sqrt[3]{j^3}$
10. $\sqrt[3]{27k^6}$
11. $\sqrt[3]{64d^9}$
12. $\sqrt[3]{8m^{15}}$
13. $\sqrt[3]{125c^6}$
14. $\sqrt[3]{512h^{21}}$
15. $\sqrt[3]{343j^{12}}$
16. $\sqrt[3]{216p^3}$

Lesson 11-1

Pages 574–575

Solve Exercises 1 and 2. Use the *make a table* strategy.

1. **BEDTIME** The list shows the times eighth graders in Mr. Garcia's homeroom went to sleep the previous night. Organize the data in a table using intervals 9:00–9:29, 9:30–9:59, and so on. What is the most common interval for students to go to sleep?

9:35	10:45	10:20	10:50
9:10	11:00	10:23	10:00
10:05	10:15	9:55	9:40
10:39	10:33	9:59	9:43
10:04	11:05	9:00	9:24
10:37	9:30	9:50	11:15
10:01	10:58		

2. **PETS** Ms. Smith's class listed the number of pets they have in their homes as shown below. Organize the list to determine what the most common number of pets per household is for the class.

0	1	2	5	4
3	2	2	3	0
1	10	3	4	2
1	0	9	2	6
3	2	2	0	1
5	12	0	2	3

Lesson 11-2

Pages 576–580

ARCHITECTURE For Exercises 1–4, use the histogram.

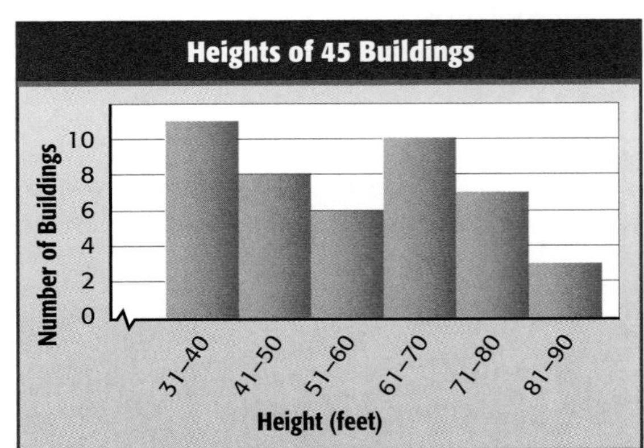

1. How many buildings are represented in the histogram?
2. Which interval represents the most number of buildings?
3. What percent of the buildings are taller than 70 feet?
4. What is the height of the tallest building?

Lesson 11-3

Pages 582–588

Construct a circle graph for each set of data.

1.

Students in North High School	
freshmen	30%
sophomores	28%
juniors	24%
seniors	18%

2.

Number of Siblings	
0	25%
1	45%
2	20%
3	5%
4	2%
5+	3%

3.

Household Expenses	
food	45%
housing	30%
utilities	15%
other	10%

Lesson 11-4

Pages 591–596

Find the mean, median, mode, and range for each set of data. Round to the nearest tenth if necessary.

1. 2, 7, 9, 12, 5, 14, 4, 8, 3, 10
2. 58, 52, 49, 60, 61, 56, 50, 61
3. 122, 134, 129, 140, 125, 134, 137
4. 36, 41, 43, 45, 48, 52, 54, 56, 56, 57, 60, 64, 65
5. 11, 15, 21, 11, 6, 10, 11
6. 21, 20, 19, 20, 18, 21, 23, 25
7. 1, 3, 2, 1, 1, 2, 2, 2, 3
8. 23, 35, 42, 26, 27, 29, 31, 29, 27

Lesson 11-5

Pages 599–604

Find the range, median, upper and lower quartiles, interquartile range, and any outliers for each set of data.

1. 15, 12, 21, 18, 25, 11, 17, 19, 20
2. 2, 24, 6, 13, 8, 6, 11, 4
3. 189, 149, 155, 290, 141, 152
4. 451, 501, 388, 428, 510, 480, 390
5. 22, 18, 9, 26, 14, 15, 6, 19, 28
6. 245, 218, 251, 255, 248, 241, 250
7. 46, 45, 50, 40, 49, 42, 64
8. 128, 148, 130, 142, 164, 120, 152, 202

Lesson 11-6

Pages 605–610

Draw a box-and-whisker plot for each set of data.

1. 2, 3, 5, 4, 3, 3, 2, 5, 6
2. 6, 7, 9, 10, 11, 11, 13, 14, 12, 11, 12
3. 15, 12, 21, 18, 25, 11, 17, 19, 20
4. 2, 24, 6, 13, 8, 6, 11, 4

ZOOS **For Exercises 5 and 6, use the following box-and-whisker plot.**

Area (acres) of Major Zoos in the United States

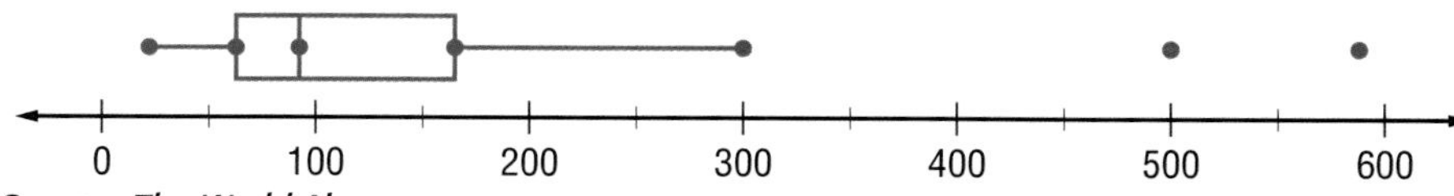

Source: *The World Almanac*

5. How many outliers are in the data?
6. Describe the distribution of the data. What can you say about the areas of the major zoos in the United States?

Lesson 11-7

Pages 612–616

Display each set of data in a stem-and-leaf plot.

1. 37, 44, 32, 53, 61, 59, 49, 69
2. 3, 26, 35, 8, 21, 24, 30, 39, 35, 5, 38
3. 15.7, 7.4, 0.6, 0.5, 15.3, 7.9, 7.3
4. 172, 198, 181, 182, 193, 171, 179, 186, 181
5. 55, 62, 81, 75, 71, 69, 74, 80, 67
6. 121, 142, 98, 106, 111, 125, 132, 109, 117, 126
7. 17, 54, 37, 86, 24, 69, 77, 92, 21
8. 7.3, 6.1, 8.9, 6.7, 8.2, 5.4, 9.3, 10.2, 5.9, 7.5, 8.3

For Exercises 9–11, use the stem-and-leaf plot shown at the right.

Stem	Leaf
7	2 2 3 5 9
8	0 1 1 4 6 6 8 9
9	3 4 8

9|4 = 94

9. What is the greatest value?
10. In which interval do most of the values occur?
11. What is the median value?

Lesson 11-8

Pages 617–621

FITNESS For Exercises 1 and 2, use the graphs.

1. Do both graphs contain the same information? Explain.
2. Which graph would you use to indicate that many more eighth graders finished the obstacle course than sixth or seventh graders? Explain.

Graph A

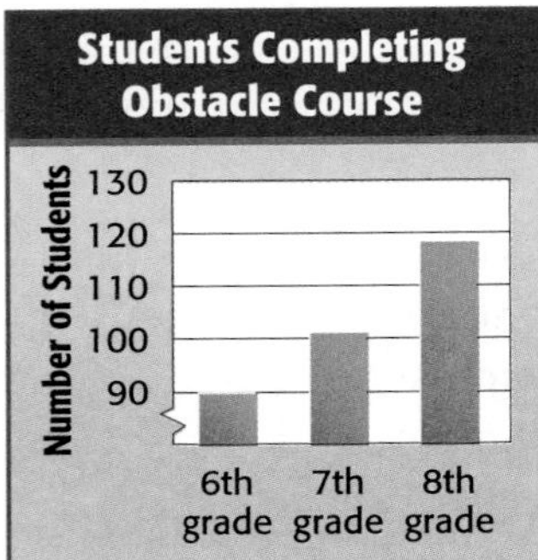

Graph B

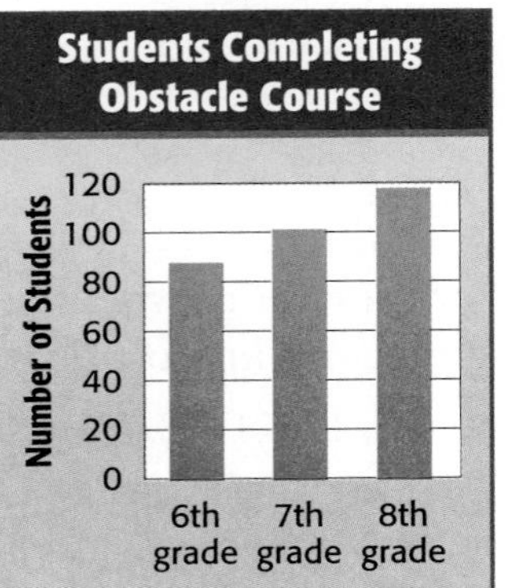

Lesson 12-1

Pages 632–636

Draw a tree diagram to determine the number of possible outcomes.

1. A car comes in white, black, or red with standard or automatic transmission and with a 4-cylinder or 6-cylinder engine.
2. A customer can buy roses or carnations in red, yellow, pink, or white.
3. A pizza can be ordered with a regular or deep dish crust and with a choice of one topping, two toppings, or three toppings.

Use the Fundamental Counting Principle to find the number of possible outcomes.

4. A woman's shoe comes in red, white, blue, or black with a choice of high, medium, or low heels.
5. Sugar cookies, chocolate chip, or oatmeal raisin cookies can be ordered either with or without icing.

Lesson 12-2

Pages 637–642

Two socks are drawn from a drawer which contains one red sock, three blue socks, two black socks, and two green socks. Once a sock is selected, it is not replaced. Find each probability.

1. P(a black sock and then a green sock)
2. P(two blue socks)

There are three quarters, five dimes, and twelve pennies in a bag. Once a coin is drawn from the bag, it is not replaced. If two coins are drawn at random, find each probability.

3. P(a quarter and then a penny)
4. P(a nickel and then a dime)

Lesson 12-3

Pages 643–647

FOOD For Exercises 1–3, use the survey results at the right.

1. What is the probability that a person's favorite pizza topping is pepperoni?
2. Out of 280 people, how many would you expect to have pepperoni as their favorite pizza topping?
3. What is the probability that a person's favorite pizza topping is pepperoni or sausage?

Favorite Pizza Topping

Topping	Number
pepperoni	45
sausage	25
green pepper	15
mushrooms	5
other	10

Lesson 12-4

Pages 650–651

Use the *act it out* strategy to solve the following problems.

1. **BRIDGES** One third of a bridge support is underground, another one sixth of it is covered by water, and 325 feet are out of the water. What is the total height of the bridge support?
2. **GAMES** Cesar is playing a game with his little sister that requires him to arrange cards face down into an array of columns and rows. When he puts 4 cards in each row, he has 3 left over. When he puts 5 cards in each row, he has 1 left over. Give two possible numbers of cards Cesar might have.

Lesson 12-5

Pages 653–658

Determine whether the conclusions are valid. Justify your answer.

1. To award prizes at a hockey game, four tickets with individual seat numbers printed on them are picked from a barrel. Since Jose's section was not selected for any of the four prizes, he assumes that they forgot to include the entire section in the drawing.
2. To evaluate the quality of the televisions coming off the assembly line, the manufacturer takes one every half hour and tests it. About 1 out of every 10,000 is found to have a minor mechanical problem. The company assumes from this data that about 1 out of every 10,000 televisions they produce will be returned for mechanical problems after being purchased.

Mixed Problem Solving

Chapter 1 Algebra: Integers

Pages 22–81

1. **PATTERNS** Draw the next two figures in the pattern below. (Lesson 1-1)

TEMPERATURE For Exercises 2 and 3, use the following information.

The formula $F = \frac{9}{5}C + 32$ is used to convert degrees Celsius to degrees Fahrenheit. (Lesson 1-2)

2. Find the degrees Fahrenheit if it is 30°C outside.
3. A local newscaster announces that today is his birthday. Rather than disclose his true age on air, he states that his age in degrees Celsius is 10. How old is he?

4. **SPORTS** In football, a penalty results in a loss of yards. Write an integer to describe a loss of 10 yards. (Lesson 1-3)

BILLS For Exercises 5 and 6, use the table below. (Lesson 1-4)

Description	Amount ($)
Beginning Balance	435
Gas Company	−75
Electric Company	−75
Phone Company	−100
Deposit	75
Rent	−200

5. How much is in the account?
6. Kirsten owes the cable company $65. Does she have enough to pay this bill?

7. **WEATHER** For the month of August, the highest temperature was 98°F. The lowest temperature was 54°F. What was the range of temperatures for the month? (Lesson 1-5)

8. **WEATHER** During a thunderstorm, the temperature dropped by 5 degrees per half hour. What was the temperature change after 3 hours? (Lesson 1-6)

HISTORY For Exercises 9 and 10, use the following information.

To be president of the United States, a person must be at least 35 years old. (Lesson 1-7)

9. If y is the year a person was born, write an expression for the earliest year that he or she could be president.
10. If a person became president in 2004, write an equation to find the latest year he or she could have been born.

11. **TIME** Lo arrived home at 5:45 P.M. from the store. At the store, she spent half an hour trying on clothes, 15 minutes looking at shoes, and 10 minutes waiting in line. If it took her 35 minutes to drive home, what time did she arrive at the store? Use the *work backward* strategy. (Lesson 1-8)

12. **BANKING** After you withdraw $75 from your checking account, the balance is $205. Write and solve a subtraction equation to find your balance before the withdrawal. (Lesson 1-9)

13. **MONEY** Janelle babysits and charges $5 per hour. Write and solve a multiplication equation to find how many hours she needs to babysit in order to make $55. (Lesson 1-10)

14. **PHYSICAL SCIENCE** Work is done when a force acts on an object and the object moves. The amount of work, measured in foot-pounds, is equal to the amount of force applied, measured in pounds, times the distance, in feet, the object moved. Write and solve a multiplication equation that could be used to find how far you have to lift a 45-pound object to produce 180 foot-pounds of work. (Lesson 1-10)

1. **HEALTH** A newborn baby weighs $6\frac{3}{4}$ pounds. Write this weight as a decimal. (Lesson 2-1)

MEASUREMENT For Exercises 2 and 3, use the figure below. (Lesson 2-1)

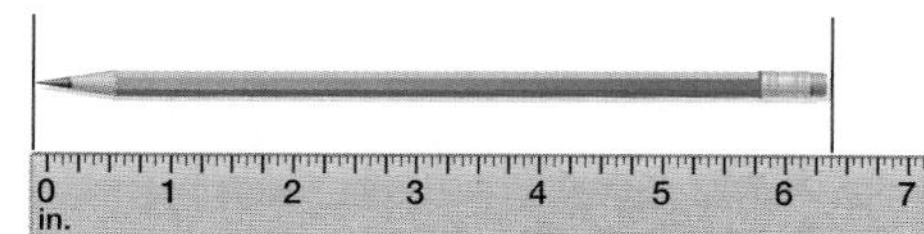

2. Write the length of the pencil as a fraction.
3. Write the length of the pencil as a decimal.
4. **SEWING** Which is the smallest seam: $\frac{1}{4}$ inch, $\frac{1}{2}$ inch, or $\frac{1}{8}$ inch? (Lesson 2-2)

Find the area of each rectangle. (Lesson 2-3)

5. 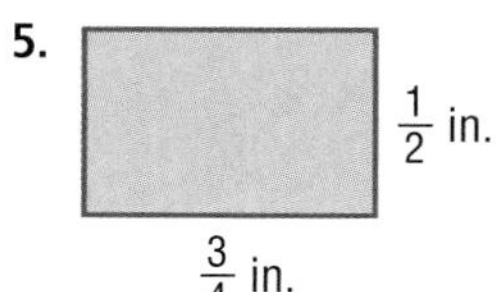

6. 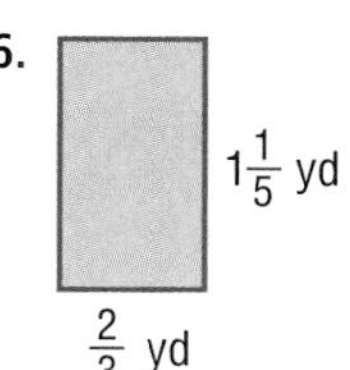

7. **COOKING** Giovanni is increasing his double chocolate chip cookie recipe to $1\frac{1}{2}$ batches. If the original recipe calls for $3\frac{1}{2}$ cups of flour, how much flour does he need for $1\frac{1}{2}$ batches? (Lesson 2-3)

8. **MEDICINE** A baby gets 1 dropper of medicine for each $2\frac{1}{4}$ pounds of body weight. If a baby weighs $11\frac{1}{4}$ pounds, how many droppers of medicine should she get? (Lesson 2-4)

9. **LIBRARIES** Lucas is storing a set of art books on a shelf that has $11\frac{1}{4}$ inches of space. If each book is $\frac{3}{4}$ inch wide, how many books can be stored on the shelf? (Lesson 2-4)

10. **HEIGHT** Molly is $64\frac{1}{4}$ inches tall. Minya is $62\frac{3}{4}$ inches tall. How much taller is Molly than Minya? (Lesson 2-5)

GEOMETRY Find the perimeter of each figure. (Lesson 2-5)

11. 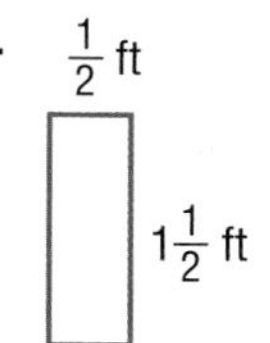

12. 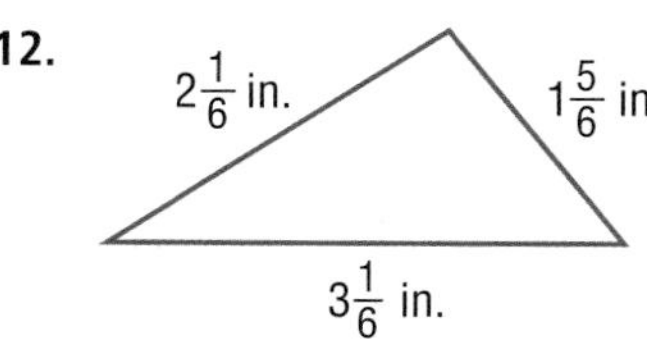

13. **ELECTIONS** In the Student Council elections, Janie won $\frac{1}{5}$ of the votes, and Jamal won $\frac{2}{3}$ of the votes. What fraction of the votes did the only other candidate receive? (Lesson 2-6)

14. **CONSTRUCTION** Three pieces of wood are $4\frac{3}{4}$, $5\frac{1}{8}$, and $7\frac{3}{16}$ inches long. If these pieces of wood are laid end to end, what is their total length? (Lesson 2-6)

FINANCES For Exercises 15 and 16, use the following information.
Jenna makes $3.25 per hour delivering newspapers. (Lesson 2-7)

15. Write a multiplication equation you can use to determine how many hours she must work to earn $35.75.
16. How many hours does Jenna need to work to earn $35.75?

17. **SCHEDULES** Buses arrive at the station at 11:10 A.M., 11:32 A.M., 11:54 A.M., and 12:16 P.M. If this pattern continues, what time will the next bus arrive at the station? Use the *look for a pattern* strategy. (Lesson 2-8)

18. **BIOLOGY** If one cell splits in two every $\frac{1}{2}$ hour, how many cells will there be after $4\frac{1}{2}$ hours? (Lesson 2-9)

19. **HAIR** There are an estimated 100,000 hairs on a person's head. Write this number in scientific notation. (Lesson 2-10)

20. **LIFE SCIENCE** A petri dish contains 2.53×10^{11} bacteria. Write the number of bacteria in standard form. (Lesson 2-10)

1. **GARDENING** A square garden has an area of 576 square feet. What is the length of each side of the garden? (Lesson 3-1)

GEOMETRY The formula for the perimeter of a square is $P = 4s$, where s is the length of the side. Find the perimeter of each square. (Lesson 3-1)

2. 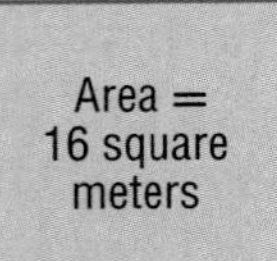

3. Area = 144 square inches

SCIENCE The formula $t = \frac{\sqrt{h}}{4}$ represents the time t in seconds that it takes an object to fall from a height of h feet. (Lesson 3-2)

4. If a ball is dropped from a height of 100 feet, estimate how long it will take to reach the ground.

5. If a ball is dropped from a height of 500 feet, estimate how long it will take to reach the ground.

6. **SUMMER** Mrs. Thorne surveyed her students about their summer plans. The results showed that 42 students wanted to go on vacation, 53 students hoped to get a summer job. Of those students, 17 planned to do both. If 93 students were surveyed, how many students are not planning to go on vacation or get a summer job? Use a Venn diagram. (Lesson 3-3)

7. **WAVES** The speed s in knots of a wave can be estimated using the formula $s = 1.34\sqrt{\ell}$, where ℓ is the length of the wave in feet. Find the estimated speed of a wave of length 5 feet. (Lesson 3-4)

8. **GEOMETRY** To approximate the radius of a circle, you can use the formula $r = \sqrt{\frac{A}{3.14}}$, where A is the area of the circle. To the nearest tenth, find the radius of a circle that has an area of 60 square feet. (Lesson 3-4)

9. **GEOGRAPHY** In Ohio, a triangle is formed by the cities Cleveland, Columbus, and Toledo. From the distances given below, is this triangle a right triangle? Explain your reasoning. (Lesson 3-5)

10. **INTERIOR DESIGN** A room is 20 feet by 15 feet. Find the length of the diagonal of the room. (Lesson 3-5)

11. **KITES** A kite string is 25 yards long. The horizontal distance between the kite and the person flying it is 12 yards. How high is the kite? (Lesson 3-6)

12. **REPAIRS** Shane is painting his house. He has a ladder that is 10 feet long. He places the base of the ladder 6 feet from the house. How far up the side of the house will the top of the ladder reach? (Lesson 3-6)

13. **ARCHAEOLOGY** A dig uncovers an urn at (1, 1) and a bracelet at (5, 3). How far apart were the two items if one unit on the grid equals 1 mile? (Lesson 3-7)

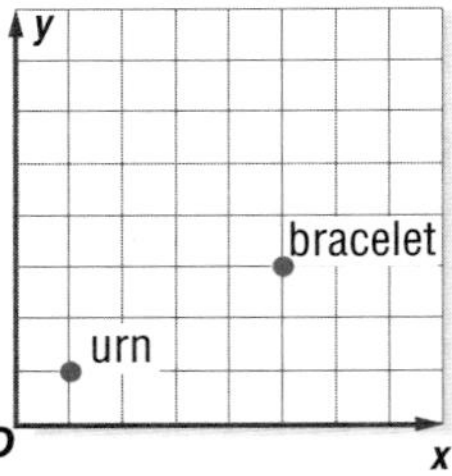

14. **TRAVEL** A unit on the grid below is 0.25 mile. Find the distance from point A to point B. (Lesson 3-7)

Chapter 4 Proportions and Similarity

1. **SHOPPING** You can buy 3 used CDs at The Music Shoppe for $12.99, or you can buy 5 of the same for $19.99 at Quality Sounds. Which is the better buy? Explain your reasoning. (Lesson 4-1)

2. **TRAVEL** On a trip, you drive 1,565 miles on 100 gallons of gas. Find your car's gas mileage. (Lesson 4-1)

3. **MUSIC** A music store is having a sale on CDs. If you buy 4 CDs, you get 1 CD free. If all CDs are priced at $9.99, is the amount of money spent proportional to the number of CDs you take home? (Lesson 4-3)

4. **WEATHER** The temperature is 88°F at 2 P.M. and 72°F at 3:30 P.M. What was the rate of change in temperature between these two time periods? (Lesson 4-3)

5. **LOANS** Find the slope of the line below and interpret its meaning as a rate of change. (Lesson 4-4)

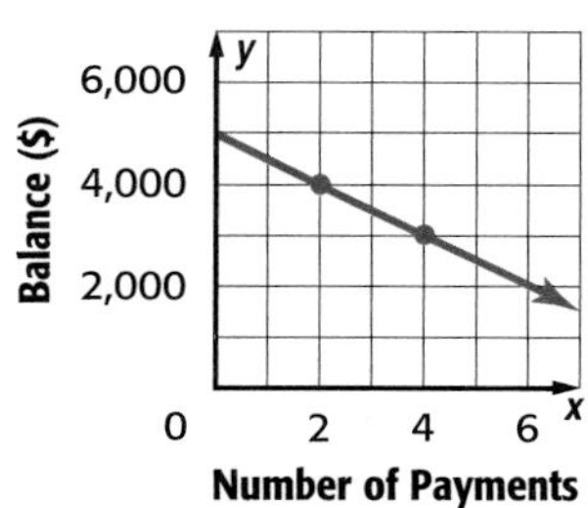

6. **ELECTIONS** About $\frac{2}{3}$ of the eighth-grade class voted for Dominic to be Student Council president. If there are 350 students in the eighth-grade class, how many voted for Dominic? (Lesson 4-5)

7. **GIFTS** Tammy wants to buy a card and a balloon for her mother's birthday. She is deciding among 5 different cards and 4 different balloons. If she buys only one card and one balloon, how many different combinations can be purchased? Use the *draw a diagram* strategy. (Lesson 4-6)

8. **PHOTOGRAPHY** Eva wants to enlarge the picture below and frame it. The scale factor from the original picture to the enlarged picture is to be 5:2. Find the dimensions of the enlarged picture. (Lesson 4-7)

9. **MURAL** A design 10 inches long and 7 inches wide is to be enlarged to appear as a wall mural that is 36 inches long. How wide will the mural be and what is the scale factor for this enlargement? (Lesson 4-8)

10. **FLAGPOLE** A 10-foot-tall flagpole casts a 4-foot shadow. At the same time, a nearby tree casts a 25-foot shadow. Draw a diagram of this situation. Then write and solve a proportion to find the height of the tree. (Lesson 4-9)

11. **SURVEYING** Write and solve a proportion to find the distance across the river shown in the diagram below. (Lesson 4-9)

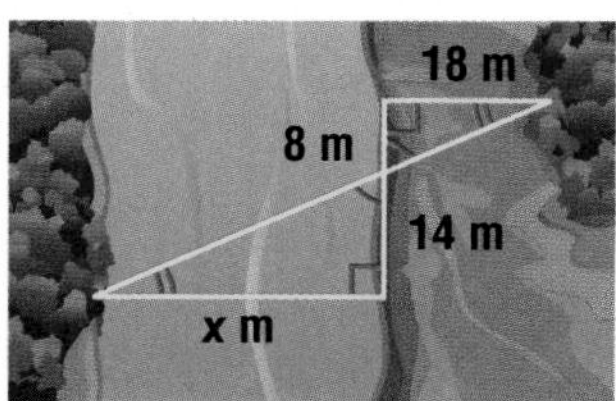

12. **ARCHITECTURE** The Eiffel Tower is 986 feet tall. If Caroline built a scale model that is 6 inches tall, what is the scale of the model? (Lesson 4-10)

13. **CARS** A model is being built of a car. The car is 12 feet long and 6 feet wide. If the length of the model is 4 inches, how wide should the model be? (Lesson 4-10)

1. **SCHOOL** Two out of five children entering kindergarten can read. Write this ratio as a percent. (Lesson 5-1)

2. **ELECTIONS** About 25% of the school voted for yellow and red to be the school colors. Write this percent as a fraction. (Lesson 5-1)

3. **FOOD** About $\frac{17}{25}$ of Americans eat fast food at least two times a week. Write $\frac{17}{25}$ as a percent. (Lesson 5-2)

4. **MEASUREMENT** What percent of the area of the rectangle is shaded? (Lesson 5-2)

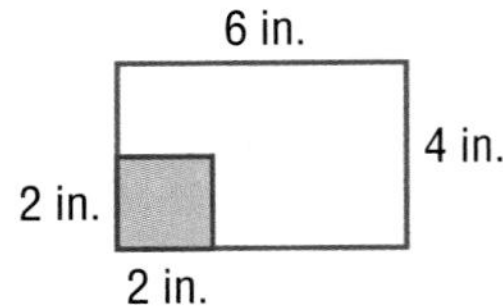

5. **EXAMS** Lexie answered 75% of the exam questions correctly. If she answered 30 questions correctly, how many questions were on the exam? (Lesson 5-3)

COLORS For Exercises 6 and 7, use the table listing the number of each color of candies in a jar. (Lesson 5-3)

Color	Number
yellow	4
brown	12
red	2
green	5
orange	1
blue	1

6. What percent of the candies are brown?

7. What percent of the candies are green?

8. **MOVIES** The results of a survey asking children ages 3 to 6 if they liked a recent animated movie are shown below.

If 120 children were surveyed, how many said they liked the movie? (Lesson 5-4)

9. **FARMING** A farmer receives 25% of the cost of a bag of flour. Determine the amount of money a farmer receives from a bag of flour that sells for $1.60. (Lesson 5-4)

10. **MONEY** Julianne earned $272, $298, and $304 on her last 3 paychecks. If she saved 28% of her earnings, would the amount of money she saved be closer to $260, $460, or $600? (Lesson 5-5)

11. **LIFE SCIENCE** The table below lists the elements found in the human body. If Jacinta weighs 120 pounds, estimate how many pounds of each element are in her body. (Lesson 5-6)

Element	Percent of Body
Oxygen	63
Carbon	19
Hydrogen	9
Nitrogen	5
Calcium	1.5
Phosphorus and Sulfur	1.2

Source: *The New York Public Library Science Desk Reference*

12. **RETAIL** A pair of shoes costs $50. If a 5.75% sales tax is added, what is the total cost of the shoes? (Lesson 5-7)

13. **DISCOUNT** A watch that regularly sells for $35 is on sale for $26.95. Find the percent of discount. (Lesson 5-8)

14. **WEATHER** The average wind speed on Mount Washington is 35.3 miles per hour. The highest wind speed ever recorded there is 231 miles per hour. Find the percent of change from the average wind speed to the highest wind speed. (Lesson 5-8)

15. **LOANS** Cleo paid off a $2,000 loan from her parents in 3 years. If she paid a total of $2,030 back to her parents, what was the interest rate of her loan? (Lesson 5-9)

Chapter 6 Geometry and Spatial Reasoning

FURNITURE For Exercises 1–3, use the following information.

A single piece of wood is used for both the backrest of a chair and its rear legs. The inside angle that the wood makes with the floor is 100°, and the seat is parallel to the floor. (Lesson 6-1)

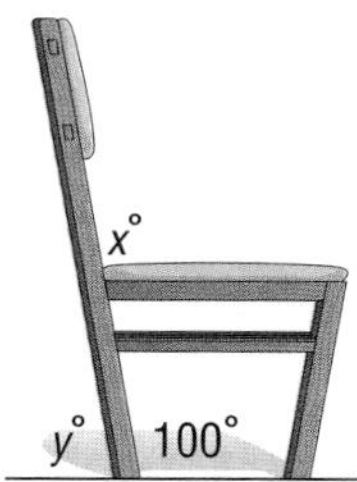

1. Find the values of x and y.
2. Classify the angle measuring $x°$.
3. Classify the angle pair measuring 100° and $x°$.

4. **TRANSPORTATION** The angle at the corner where two streets intersect is 125°. If a bus cannot make a turn at an angle of less than 70°, can bus service be provided on a route that includes turning that corner in both directions? Explain. (Lesson 6-1)

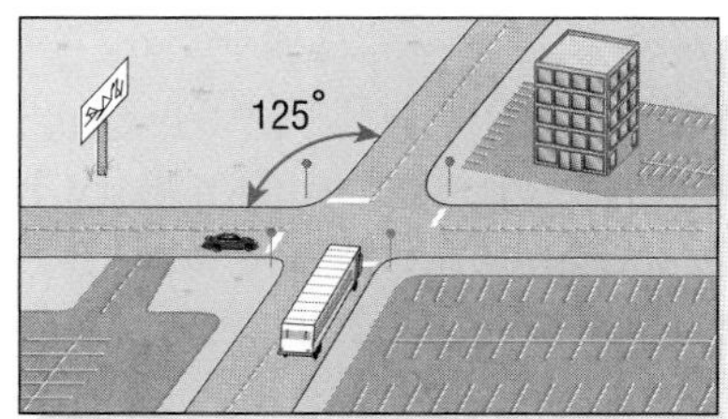

5. **MEASUREMENT** If 45 milligrams equals 0.045 gram and 0.045 gram equals 0.000045 kilogram, then how many milligrams are in 9.87 kilograms? Use logical reasoning. (Lesson 6-2)

6. **SALES** A card store is selling cards for $1.55 each. If you buy 3, you get 1 free. How many cards did Tamara get if she spent $18.60? Use logical reasoning. (Lesson 6-2)

7. **GEOMETRY** Use the table to find the sum of the measures of the interior angles of a 17-gon. (Lesson 6-3)

Polygon	Sum of the Interior Angles
Triangle	180°
Quadrilateral	360°
Pentagon	540°
Hexagon	720°

8. **GEOMETRY** The floor of a playhouse is in the shape of a regular hexagon. What is the measure of an interior angle of the floor? (Lesson 6-3)

9. **GARDENING** Two triangular gardens have congruent shapes. If 36 bricks are needed to border the first garden, how many bricks are needed to border the second garden? Explain your reasoning. (Lesson 6-4)

QUILT PATTERNS For Exercises 10 and 11, use the diagrams below. (Lesson 6-5)

a. 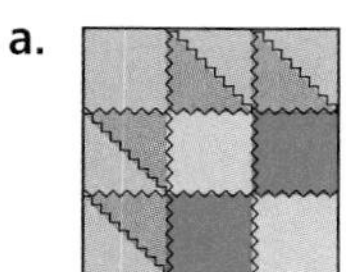

b. 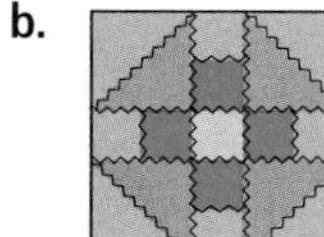

10. Determine whether each pattern has line symmetry. If it does, trace the pattern and draw all lines of symmetry. If not, write *none*.
11. Which pattern has rotational symmetry? Name its angles of rotation.

ART For Exercises 12 and 13, copy and complete the design shown at the right so that each finished four-paneled piece of art fits the given description.

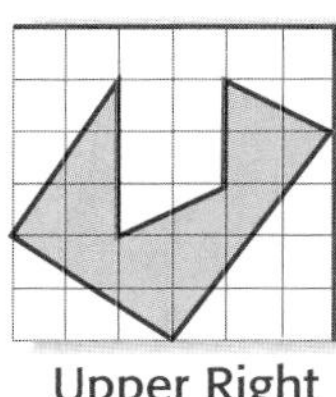

Upper Right Corner

12. The finished art has only a vertical line of symmetry. (Lesson 6-6)
13. The finished art shows translations of the first design to each of the other 3 panels. (Lesson 6-7)

1. **FOOD** An apple pie has a diameter of 8 inches. If 1 slice is $\frac{1}{6}$ of the pie, what is the area of each slice? (Lesson 7-1)

2. **MONEY** The diameter of a dime is about 17.9 millimeters. If the dime is rolled on its edge, how far will it roll after one complete rotation? (Lesson 7-1)

3. **AREA** The school courtyard is 48 feet long and 32 feet wide. The Student Council planted a garden that covered 18.9% of the courtyard. About how much of the courtyard is covered by the garden? Use the *solve a simpler problem* strategy. (Lesson 7-2)

4. **FURNITURE** The top of a desk is shown below. How much workspace does the desktop provide? (Lesson 7-3)

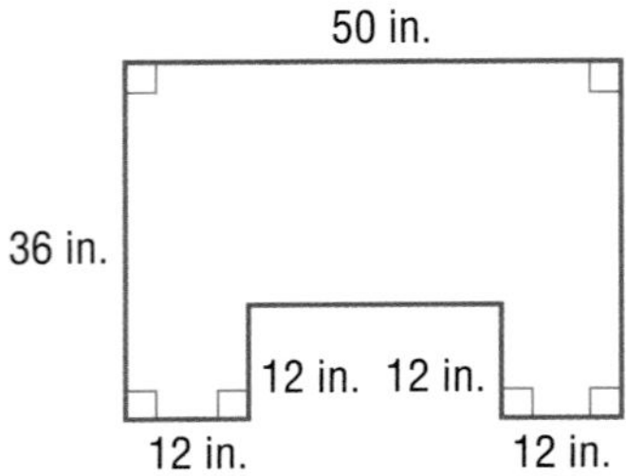

5. **STORAGE** Denise has a hatbox in the shape of a hexagonal prism. How many faces, edges, and vertices are on the hatbox? (Lesson 7-4)

ANT FARM For Exercises 6 and 7, use the following information.

A 3-foot by 2-foot by 1.5-foot terrarium is to be filled with dirt for an ant farm. (Lesson 7-5)

6. How much dirt will the terrarium hold?

7. If each bag from the store holds 3 cubic feet of dirt, how many bags will be needed to fill the terrarium?

8. **BATTERY** A size D battery is cylinder-shaped, with a diameter of 33.3 millimeters and a height of 61.1 millimeters. Find the battery's volume in cubic centimeters. (*Hint*: 1 cm^3 = 1,000 mm^3) (Lesson 7-5)

9. **FROZEN CUSTARD** You are filling cone-shaped glasses with frozen custard. Each glass has the dimensions shown. One gallon of custard is equivalent to 4,000 cubic centimeters. About how many glasses can you completely fill using one gallon of custard? (Lesson 7-6)

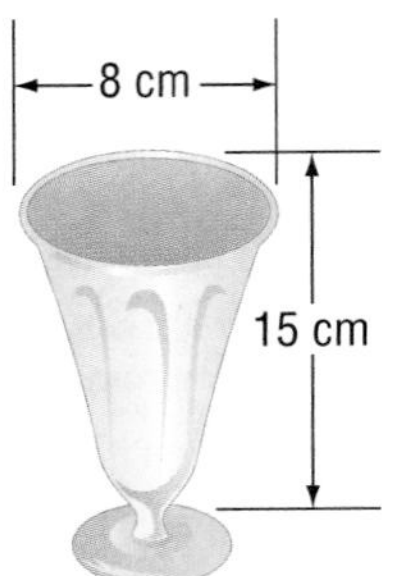

10. **PRESENTS** Viviana wants to wrap a gift in a box that is 5 inches by 3 inches by 3 inches. How much wrapping paper will she need? Assume that the paper does not overlap. (Lesson 7-7)

11. **PAINTING** The front of a government building has four columns that are each 15 feet tall and 6 feet in diameter. If the columns are to be painted, find the total surface area to be painted. (*Hint:* The tops and bottoms of the columns will not be painted.) (Lesson 7-7)

12. **HISTORY** The Pyramid of Cestius in Rome is a square pyramid with a slant height of 39.9 meters and a base length of 30 meters. What is its lateral surface area? Round to the nearest tenth if necessary. (Lesson 7-8)

13. **FAMOUS BUILDINGS** The front of the Rock and Roll Hall of Fame in Ohio is a square pyramid made out of glass. The pyramid has a slant height of 120 feet and a base length of 230 feet. Find the lateral area of the pyramid. (Lesson 7-8)

14. **PYRAMIDS** A square pyramid has a slant height of 150 feet. Alejandro built a model of the pyramid. On the model, 3 inches represents 54 feet. What is the slant height of the model? (Lesson 7-9)

1. **SCHOOL SUPPLIES** You buy two gel pens for x dollars each, a spiral-bound notebook for \$1.50, and a large eraser for \$1. Write an expression in simplest form for the total amount of money you spent on school supplies. (Lesson 8-1)

2. **ENTERTAINMENT** You buy x CDs for \$15.99 each, a tape for \$9.99, and a video for \$20.99. Write an expression in simplest form for the total amount of money you spent. (Lesson 8-1)

3. **ZOO** Four adults took a trip to the zoo. If they spent \$37 for admission and \$3 for parking, solve the equation $4a + 3 = 37$ to find the cost of admission per person. (Lesson 8-2)

4. **POOLS** There were 820 gallons of water in a 1,600-gallon pool. Water is being pumped into the pool at a rate of 300 gallons per hour. Solve the equation $300t + 820 = 1{,}600$ to find how many hours it will take to fill the pool. (Lesson 8-2)

5. **FOOTBALL** In football, a touchdown with an extra point is worth 7 points and a field goal is worth 3 points. The winning team scored 27 points. The score consisted of two field goals, and the rest were touchdowns with extra points. Write and solve an equation to determine how many touchdowns the winning team scored. (Lesson 8-3)

6. **DIVING** In diving competitions where there are three judges, the sum of the judges' scores is multiplied by the dive's degree of difficulty. A diver's final score is the sum of all the scores for each dive. The degree of difficulty for Angel's final dive is 2.0. Her current score is 358.5, and the current leader's final score is 405.5. Write and solve an equation to determine what the sum of the judges' scores for Angel's last dive must be in order for her to tie the current leader for first place. (Lesson 8-3)

7. **MEASUREMENT** Write an equation to find the value of x so that each pair of polygons has the same perimeter. Then solve. (Lesson 8-4)

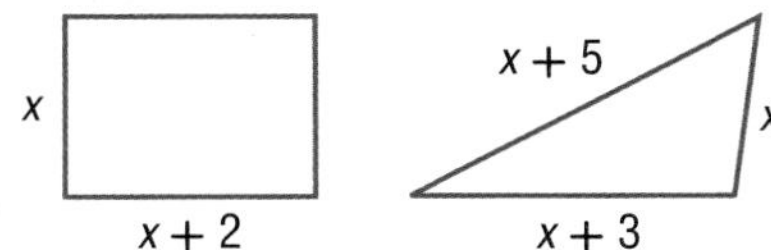

8. **MUSIC** One music club charges \$35 a month plus \$5 per CD. Another club charges \$7 a month plus \$9 per CD. Write and solve an equation to find the number of CD purchases that results in the same monthly cost. (Lesson 8-4)

9. **MEASUREMENT** A cube has a volume of 125 cubic centimeters. The cube is inside another cube with dimensions that are twice that of the smaller cube. Find the dimensions of both the smaller and larger cubes. Use the *guess and check* strategy. (Lesson 8-5)

For Exercises 10 and 11, write an inequality for each sentence. (Lesson 8-6)

10. **AMUSEMENT PARKS** Your height must be over 48 inches tall to ride the roller coaster.

11. **SHOPPING** You can spend no more than \$500 on your vacation.

12. **SCHOOL** Julie has math and English homework tonight. She has no more than 90 minutes to spend on her homework. Suppose Julie spends 35 minutes completing her math homework. Write and solve an inequality to find how much time she can spend on her English homework. (Lesson 8-7)

13. **STATISTICS** The Boston Marathon had more than 2,600,000 spectators along its 26-mile route. Write and solve an inequality to find the average number of spectators per mile. (Lesson 8-8)

1. Annie earns \$6.50 per hour at her job. Make a list of the total amount of money earned for 1, 2, 3, 4, and 5 hours. How much money would she earn for working 7 hours? (Lesson 9-1)

MEASUREMENT For Exercises 2 and 3, use the following information.

A regular pentagon is a polygon with five sides of equal length. (Lessons 9-2 and 9-3)

2. Write and graph a function for the perimeter P of a regular pentagon with side length s.
3. Determine the perimeter of a regular pentagon with sides 3 units long.

WATER FLOW For Exercises 4–6, use the following information.

An empty swimming pool is being filled with water. After 2, 3, and 5 hours, the amount of water in the pool is 144, 216, and 360 cubic meters, respectively. (Lesson 9-4)

4. Graph the information with the hours on the horizontal axis and cubic meters of water on the vertical axis. Draw a line through the points.
5. What is the slope of the graph?
6. What does the slope represent?

For Exercises 7 and 8, use the graph below.

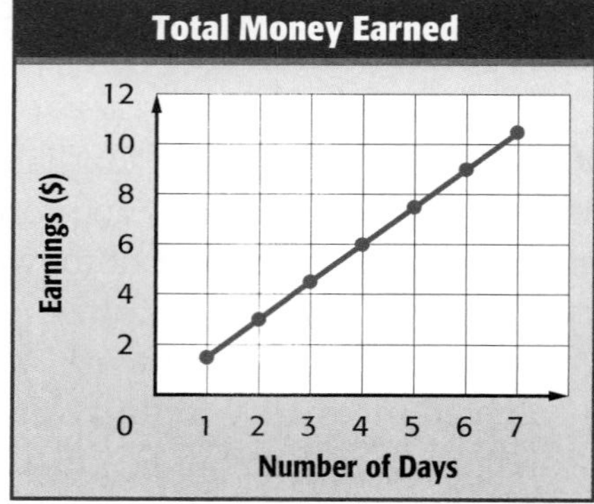

7. The amount of money earned varies directly with the number of days worked. What is the ratio of money earned to days worked? (Lesson 9-5)
8. Find the total amount earned after 16 days. (Lesson 9-5)

9. **SAVINGS** Chen is saving for an \$850 computer. He plans to save \$50 each month. The equation $y = 850 - 50x$ represents the amount Chen still needs to save. Graph the equation. What does the slope of the graph represent? (Lesson 9-6)

10. **SCHOOL CONCERT** Ticket prices for the fall concert are listed on the sign.

Ticket	Cost
Student	\$3
Non-Student	\$5

A total of 140 tickets were sold and \$590 was collected. Write and solve a system of equations that represents this situation. (Lesson 9-7)

11. **TESTS** The graph shows the scores on a recent math test. What was the grade of student number 24? (Lesson 9-8)

Student Grades on Math Test

STATISTICS For Exercises 12 and 13, use the table. (Lesson 9-9)

12. Draw the scatter plot for the data.
13. Does the scatter plot show a *positive, negative,* or *no relationship*?

Year Born	Life Expectancy
1900	47.3
1910	50.0
1920	54.1
1930	59.7
1940	62.9
1950	68.2
1960	69.7
1970	70.8
1980	73.7
1990	75.4
2000	77.1

Source: U.S. Census Bureau

1. **MEASUREMENT** Recall that the volume V of a sphere is equal to four-thirds pi times the cube of its radius. Is the volume of a sphere a *linear* or *nonlinear* function of its radius? Explain. (Lesson 10-1)

2. **PRODUCTION** The table lists the cost of producing a specific number of items at the ABC Production Company. Does this table represent a *linear* or *nonlinear* function? Explain. (Lesson 10-1)

Number of Items	Cost ($)
2	2,507
4	2,514
6	2,521
8	2,528

SCIENCE For Exercises 3–5, use the following information.

The quadratic equation $h = -16t^2 + 200$ models the height of a ball t seconds after it is dropped from a 200-foot cliff. (Lesson 10-2)

3. Graph the function.
4. How high is the ball after 2 seconds?
5. After about how many seconds will the ball reach the ground?

6. **ART** Leah is creating a model of her kitchen. The kitchen measures 18 feet by 12 feet. If she uses a scale of 2 feet = $1\frac{1}{2}$ inch, what are the dimensions of her kitchen on the model? Use the *make a model* strategy. (Lesson 10-3)

7. **POPULATION** The population growth of a particular species of insect is given by the function $y = 2x^3$, where x represents time elapsed in days and y represents the population size. Graph this function. (Lesson 10-4)

8. **AGE** Felipe's age was 2^3 times Joey's age. If Joey is 2^3 years old, how old is Felipe? (Lesson 10-5)

9. **LIFE SCIENCE** The number of cells in a petri dish starts at 2^5. By the end of the day, the number will be 2^7 times greater. How many cells will be in the dish at the end of the day? (Lesson 10-5)

10. **EARTHQUAKES** The table below describes different earthquake intensities.

Earthquake	Richter Scale	Intensity
A	8	10^7
B	4	10^3

Determine how many times more intense Earthquake A was than Earthquake B. (Lesson 10-6)

SCIENCE For Exercises 11 and 12, use the following information.

Kitchen Items	pH
Lemon Juice	2
Vinegar	3
Tomatoes	4
Water	7
Baking Soda	9

11. The pH of a solution describes its acidity. Each one-unit *decrease* in the pH means that the solution is 10 times more acidic. How much more acidic is vinegar than baking soda? (Lesson 10-6)

12. Cola is 10^4 times more acidic than water. What is the pH value of cola? (Lesson 10-6)

13. **MEASUREMENT** Express the volume of the cube at the right as a monomial. (Lesson 10-7)

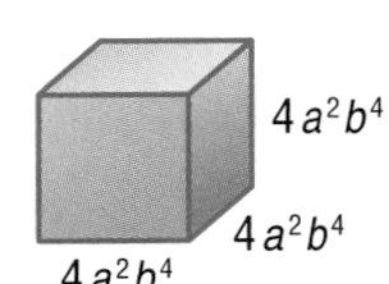

14. **MEASUREMENT** Express the length of one side of a cube whose volume is $8x^6y^9$ cubic units as a monomial. (Lesson 10-8)

Mixed Problem Solving

1. **AGES** The list shows ages of people at a movie. Organize the data in a table using intervals 0–10, 11–17, 18–35, 36–44 and 45 and older. What is the most common age group? (Lesson 11-1)

5	3	32	35	14	25	28	63	4	7
18	50	45	10	9	70	30	45	8	7
6	36	38	3	7	10	11	29	33	5
6	80	75	10	8	28	30	6	4	39
40	12	8	35	10	5	3	42	11	38
14	13	12	9	11	17	45	11	18	9

ADVERTISING For Exercises 2 and 3, use the histogram below. (Lesson 11-2)

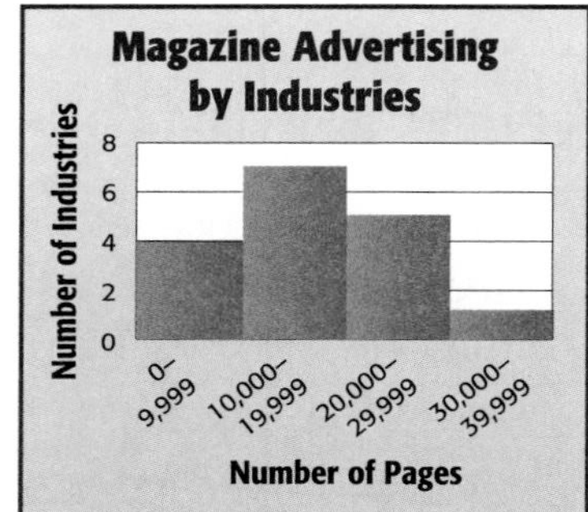

Source: Publisher Information Bureau, Inc.

2. How many industries used 20,000 pages or more of magazine advertising?

3. What percent of industries used less than 30,000 pages of magazine advertising?

4. **AIR** Use the circle graph below to describe the makeup of the air we breathe. (Lesson 11-3)

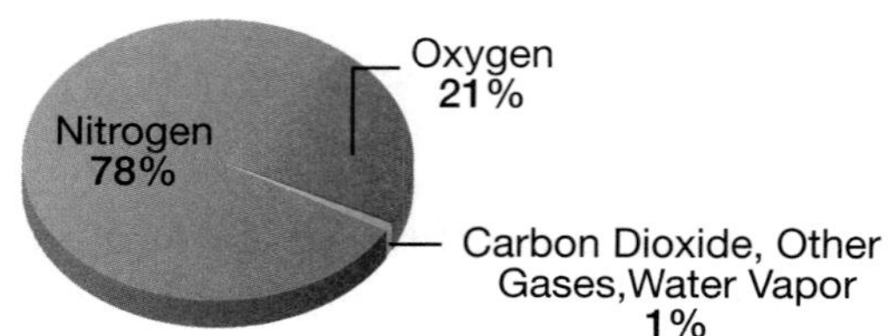

Source: *The World Almanac for Kids*

5. **BOWLING** Find the mean, median, and mode of the bowling scores for the bowling club members listed. Then select the appropriate measure of central tendency to describe the data. Justify your answer. (Lesson 11-4)

Club Member	Score
A	118
B	125
C	115
D	198
E	125
F	131
G	127
H	135

POPULATION The populations of the smallest countries in 2000 were 860, 10,838, 11,845, 18,766, 26,937, 31,693, and 32,204. (Lessons 11-5 and 11-6)

6. Find the range and median of the data.

7. Find the upper quartile, lower quartile, and interquartile range of the data.

8. Make a box-and-whisker plot of the data.

9. **ARCHITECTURE** The number of floors in each of the fifteen tallest buildings in a U.S. city is listed below.

51	53	45	39	36
47	42	33	32	31
33	28	28	25	23

Make a stem-and-leaf plot of the data. (Lesson 11-7)

For Exercises 10 and 11, select an appropriate type of display for each situation. Then make a display. (Lesson 11-8)

10. **MUSIC** A survey asked teens what they liked most about a song. 59% said the sound, and 41% said the lyrics.

11.

Tax Returns Filed Electronically				
Year	1990	1991	1992	1993
Percent	3.7%	6.6%	9.6%	11.0%
Year	1994	1995	1996	1997
Percent	12.2%	10.5%	12.6%	15.8%
Year	1998	1999	2000	2001
Percent	19.9%	23.3%	27.6%	30.7%

Source: Internal Revenue Service

Pages 630–665

1. **MONEY** A dime, a penny, a nickel, and a quarter are tossed. How many different outcomes are there? (Lesson 12-1)

2. **PHONE NUMBERS** How many seven-digit phone numbers can be made using the numbers 0 through 9 if the first number cannot be 0? (Lesson 12-1)

3. **YOGURT** The Yogurt Spot advertises that there are 1,512 ways to enjoy a one-topping sundae. They offer six flavors of frozen yogurt, six different serving sizes, and several different toppings. How many toppings do they offer? (Lesson 12-1)

4. **MUSIC** Kurt is listening to a CD that contains 12 songs. If he presses the random button on his CD player, what is the probability that the first two songs will be the same? (Lesson 12-2)

5. **BUSINESS** An auto dealer finds that 70% of the cars coming in for service need a tune up, and 50% need a new air filter. What is the probability that a car brought in for service needs both a tune up and a new air filter? (Lesson 12-2)

ELECTRONICS For Exercises 6 and 7, use the following information.

The table shows the percent of students at a school who have various electronic devices in their bedrooms. (Lesson 12-2)

Electronic Device	Percent
TV	60
DVD Player	15
Computer	20
Game Station	75

6. What is the probability that a student has both a TV and a computer?

7. What is the probability that a student has a TV, a DVD player, and a computer?

8. **ECONOMICS** Thirty-one percent of minimum-wage workers are between 16 and 19 years old. Twenty-two percent of the minimum-wage workers are between 20 and 24 years old. If a person who makes minimum wage is selected at random, what is the probability that he or she will be between 16 and 24 years old? (Lesson 12-2)

TELEVISION For Exercises 9 and 10, use the table below. (Lesson 12-3)

Television Show	Number Who Selected as Favorite Show
Show A	35
Show B	25
Show C	20
Show D	10
Show E	10

9. What is the probability a person's favorite prime-time TV show is Show A?

10. Out of 320 people, how many would you expect to say that Show A is their favorite prime-time TV show?

11. **FOOD** How many different two-scoop ice cream cones can be created from the list of flavors shown? Use the *act it out* strategy. (Lesson 12-4)

Ice Cream Flavors		
Vanilla	Chocolate	Strawberry
Chocolate Chip	Cookie Dough	Neopolitan
Peanut Butter	Rocky Road	Banana Split
Raspberry	Butter Pecan	Mint

CONCERTS For Exercises 12 and 13, use the following information.

As they leave a concert, 50 people are surveyed at random. Six people say they would buy a concert T-shirt. (Lesson 12-5)

12. What percent say they would buy a T-shirt?

13. If 6,330 people attend the next concert, how many would you expect to buy T-shirts?

Preparing for Standardized Tests

Throughout the year, you may be required to take several standardized tests, and you may have some questions about them. Here are some answers to help you get ready.

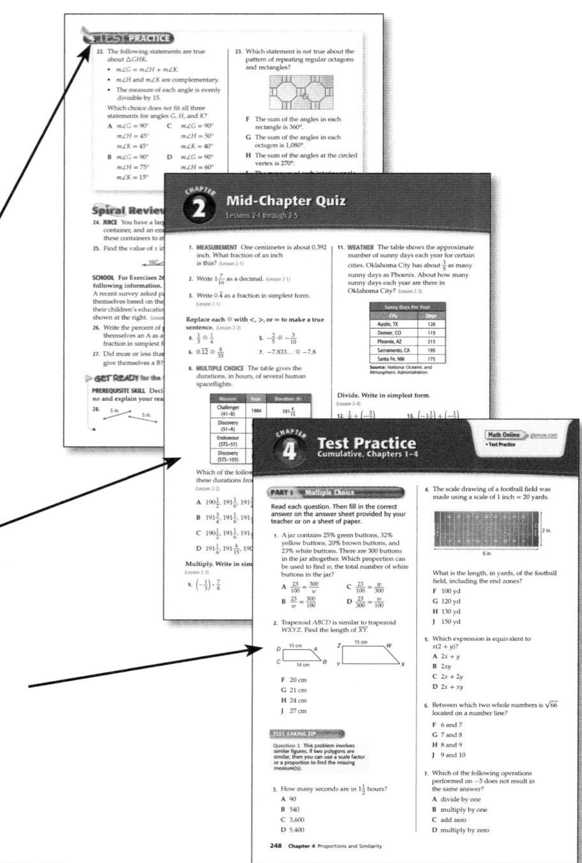

How Should I Study?

The good news is that you've been studying all along—a little bit every day. Here are some of the ways your textbook has been preparing you.

- **Every Day** Each lesson had multiple-choice practice questions.
- **Every Week** The Mid-Chapter Quiz and Practice Test also had several multiple-choice practice questions.
- **Every Month** The Test Practice pages at the end of each chapter had even more questions, including short-response/grid-in and extended-response questions.

Are There Other Ways to Review?

Absolutely! The following pages contain even more practice for standardized tests.

Tips for SUCCESS

Prepare

- Go to bed early the night before the test. You will think more clearly after a good night's rest.
- Become familiar with common formulas and when they should be used.
- Think positively.

During the Test

- Read each problem carefully. Underline key words and think about different ways to solve the problem.
- Watch for key words like NOT. Also look for order words like *least, greatest, first,* and *last.*
- Watch for units of measurement. The units in the possible answers may be different from the units in the problem.
- Answer questions you are sure about first. If you do not know the answer to a question, skip it and go back to that question later.
- Check your answer to make sure it is reasonable.
- Make sure that the number of the question on the answer sheet matches the number of the question on which you are working in your test booklet.

Whatever you do...

- Don't try to do it all in your head. If no figure is provided, draw one.
- Don't rush. Try to work at a steady pace.
- Don't give up. Some problems may seem hard to you, but you may be able to figure out what to do if you read each question carefully or try another strategy.

Multiple-Choice Questions

Multiple-choice questions are the most common type of question on standardized tests. These questions are sometimes called *selected-response questions*. You are asked to choose the best answer from four or five possible answers.

Incomplete shading
(A) (B) (C) (D)

Too light shading
(A) (B) (C) (D)

Correct shading
(A) (B) (C) (D)

To record a multiple-choice answer, you may be asked to shade in a bubble that is a circle or an oval or just to write the letter of your choice. Always make sure that your shading is dark enough and completely covers the bubble.

The answer to a multiple-choice question may not stand out from the choices. However, you may be able to eliminate some of the choices. Another answer choice might be that the correct answer is not given.

ISAT EXAMPLE

1 Kent places a ladder at a 60° angle against the wall as shown in the diagram. What is the measure of ∠1?

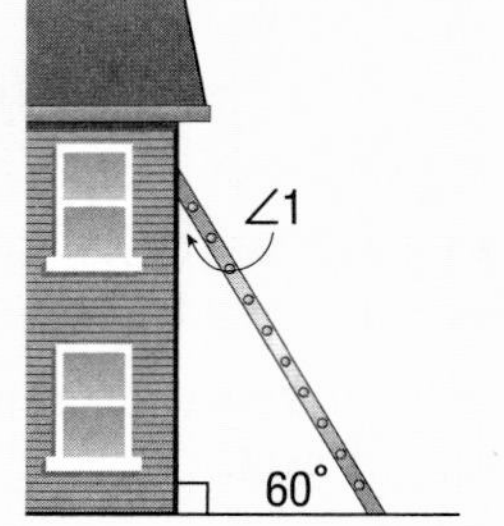

A 15°
B 30°
C 60°
D 90°

STRATEGY

Elimination
Can you eliminate any of the choices?

You know that the ground and wall meet at a 90° angle. You can eliminate choice D because you know that a triangle cannot have two angles measuring 90°. Find the measure of the third angle by subtracting the measures of the two known angles from 180°, the sum of the angles of a triangle.

$180° - 90° - 60° = 30°$ The measure of ∠1 is 30°, and the answer is B.

ISAT EXAMPLE

2 Sam's Store sells 8 cans of soup for $2.25 while Midtown's Mart sells the same soup at 10 cans for $3.00. Which statement is true?

F Midtown's Mart has the lower price per can.
G Sam's Store has the lower price per can.
H Both stores have the same cost per can.
J None of these can be determined.

Find the price per can at Sam's Store and Midtown's Mart.

Sam's Store:

$$\frac{\$2.25}{8 \text{ cans}} = \$0.28125 \text{ per can}$$

Midtown's Mart:

$$\frac{\$3.00}{10 \text{ cans}} = \$0.30 \text{ per can}$$

Since $0.28 < 0.30$, Sam's Store has the lower cost per can. The answer is G.

Preparing for Standardized Tests

ISAT EXAMPLE

3 **The charges for adult ski passes at Logan Ski Slopes are shown in the table. What is the minimum number of days that an adult must ski in order for the yearly pass to be less expensive than buying daily passes?**

A 4 days

B 6 days

C 7 days

D 8 days

Type of Ski Pass	Cost ($)
Daily	38
Yearly	247

You need to find the minimum number of daily passes that will cost more than $247.

STRATEGY

Backsolving
Use the answer choices to work backward to find the answer.

METHOD 1 Multiply.

Multiply each answer choice by $38 to determine which answer choices result in a cost greater than $247.

A $4 \times \$38 = \$152$

B $6 \times \$38 = \$228$

C $7 \times \$38 = \$266$

D $8 \times \$38 = \$304$

Answer choices C and D are both greater than $247. However, the problem asks for the minimum number of days. So answer choice C, 7 days, is correct.

METHOD 2 Use an inequality.

Write an inequality comparing the costs of a daily ski pass and a yearly ski pass.

Each daily pass costs $38, so after d days of skiing a person will have spent $38d$.

You want to find when $38d$ is greater than $247, the cost of a yearly pass. Write and solve the inequality.

$38d > 247$ Original inequality

$\frac{38d}{38} > \frac{247}{38}$ Divide each side by 38.

$d > 6.5$ Simplify.

Read the problem a second time just to be sure whether you want the cost to be greater or less than $247.

Since the ski passes are only sold by the day and not by a partial day, the number of days must be a whole number. The next whole number greater than 6.5 is 7. So, 7 days is the minimum number of days in which the yearly pass will be less expensive. The answer is choice C.

Multiple-Choice Practice

Choose the best answer.

Number and Operations

1. Dillon can run at a rate of 9 miles per hour. How many feet per minute is this?

   A 13.2 C 4,752
   B 792 D 47,520

2. Danielle mows lawns for a part-time job in the summer. She charges $8 an hour. If Mrs. Taylor paid Danielle $44, how long did it take Danielle to mow Mrs. Taylor's lawn?

   F 4.5 h H 5.5 h
   G 5 h J 6 h

3. Mario had 18 CDs. On Saturday he bought 4 more CDs. What is the percent of change in the number of CDs he owns? Round to the nearest percent.

   A 18% B 22% C 29% D 82%

Algebra

4. To raise money for new uniforms, the soccer team is selling shirts that have the team's logo on them. The company making the shirts charges $20 for the design and $5 for each shirt made. The total cost y to the soccer team can be represented by the equation $y = 5x + 20$, where x represents the number of shirts made. Which graph represents this equation?

F
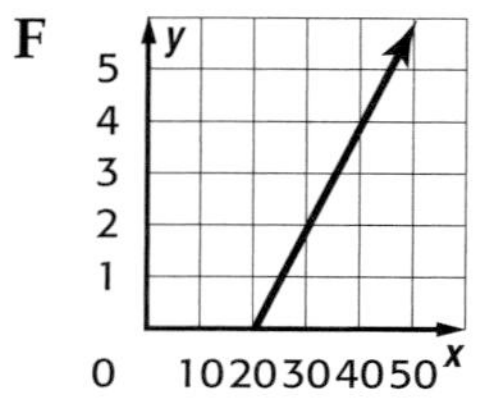

H
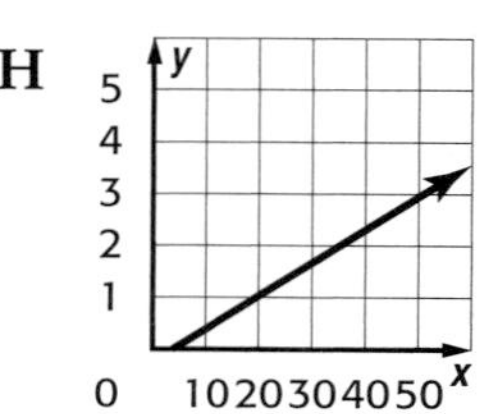

G
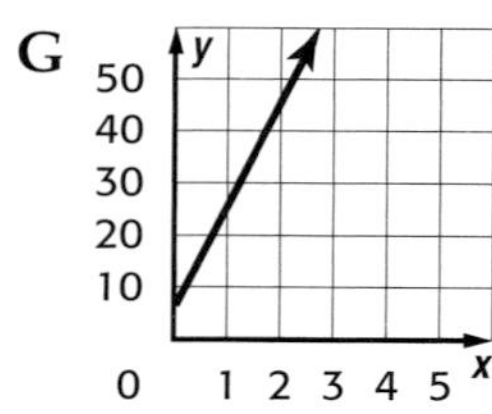

J
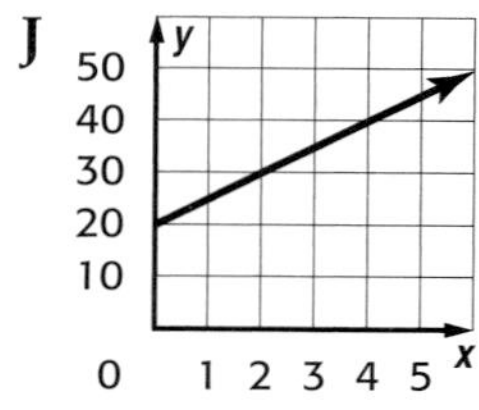

5. Emilia received her allowance on Saturday and took it to the mall. After she spent $5.49 for lunch, she still had $26.51. Which equation could be used to find how much she received for her allowance?

   A $x - 5.49 = 26.51$ C $26.51 - x = 5.49$
   B $x + 5.49 = 26.51$ D $x + 26.51 = 5.49$

6. At the water park you buy your friends a pizza for $15, an order of breadsticks for $3.50, and 4 drinks that cost x dollars each. Which expression represents this situation?

   F $15 + 7.50x$ H $4x + 18.50$
   G $22.50x$ J 22.50

Geometry

7. Sarah is building a kite out of crepe paper and balsa wood. What is the measure of ∠1?

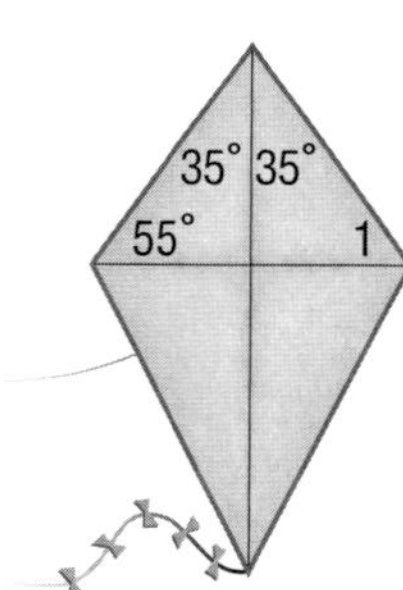

   A 25° B 35° C 45° D 55°

8. Alysha wants to hang decorative lights diagonally across her ceiling for a party. What should be the minimum length of the light strand? Round to the nearest tenth of a foot if necessary.

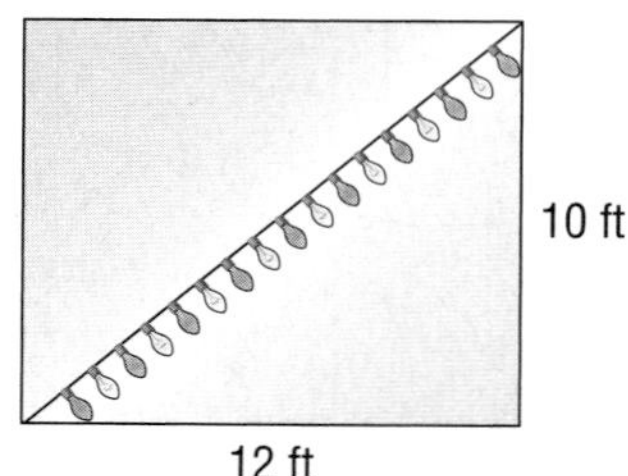

   F 6.6 ft G 12.0 ft H 15.6 ft J 22.0 ft

Preparing for Standardized Tests

9. Alonso has a template to make paver bricks for a patio. He needs to enlarge the template by a scale factor of 5. He placed the template on a coordinate grid and labeled the vertices A, B, C, and D. What will be the new x-coordinate of vertex A after the enlargement?

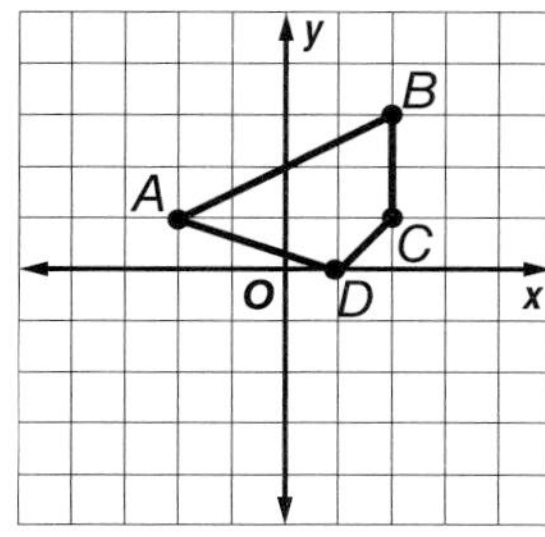

A 210 B 25 C 5 D 10

Measurement

10. Keegan rode his bike 49 miles in 3 hours. What was his average speed in miles per hour? Round to the nearest whole number if necessary.

F 16 mph H 55 mph
G 25 mph J 147 mph

11. How much grain will the bin below hold? Round to the nearest tenth of a cubic foot.

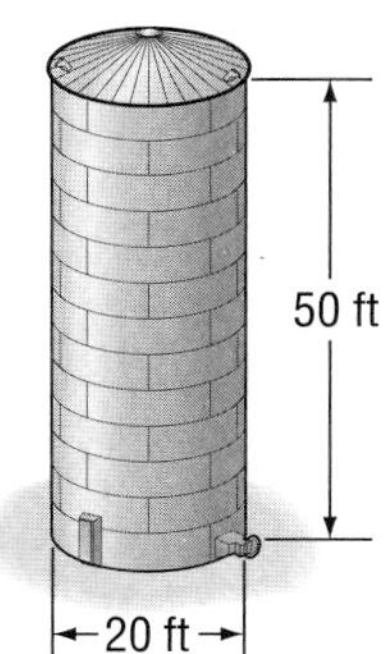

A 314.2ft^3 C 3141.6 ft^3
B $1{,}570.8\text{ ft}^3$ D $15{,}708.0\text{ ft}^3$

12. One kilogram is approximately 2.2 pounds. If Sara weighs 105 pounds, how many kilograms does she weigh? Round to the nearest tenth of a kilogram.

F 40.8 kg H 209.5 kg
G 47.7 kg J 231.0 kg

Data Analysis and Probability

13. Which situation *best* describes the scatter plot?

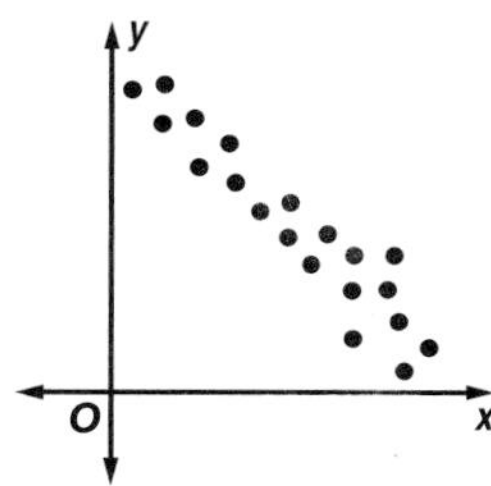

A number of hours worked at a job and amount of money earned
B number of gallons of water taken out of a swimming pool and height of water in swimming pool
C length of hair and age
D year of birth and age

TEST-TAKING TIP

Question 13 When a question asks for the best answer, read all the answer choices first and eliminate any unreasonable answer choices.

14. Mileah was comparing the amount of caffeine in six different popular soft drinks. She found that a 12-ounce serving contained the following milligrams of caffeine: 55, 47, 45, 41, 40, and 37. What is the mean of this data set? Round to the nearest milligram.

F 37 mg
G 43 mg
H 44 mg
J 55 mg

15. Braden has 32 movies. Eight of these movies are action movies. If he randomly chooses a movie to watch, what is the probability that it is *not* an action movie?

A $\frac{1}{4}$ C $\frac{1}{2}$
B $\frac{1}{3}$ D $\frac{3}{4}$

Gridded-Response Questions

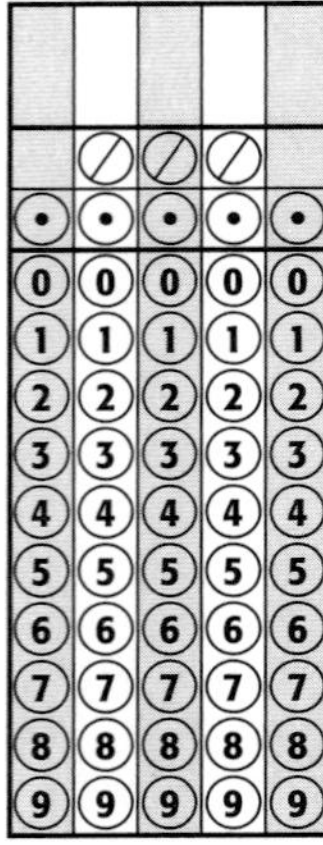

Gridded-response questions are another type of question on standardized tests. These questions are sometimes called *student-produced response* or *grid in*.

For gridded response, you must mark your answer on a grid printed on an answer sheet. The grid contains a row of four or five boxes at the top, two rows of ovals or circles with decimal and fraction symbols, and four or five columns of ovals, numbered 0–9. An example of a grid from an answer sheet is shown.

ISAT EXAMPLE

1 **Zach is in charge of ordering hot dogs for the concession stand for the home football games. If he needs 70 hot dogs for 2 games, how many will he need for all 8 home games?**

What value do you need to find?

You need to find the total number of hot dogs needed for 8 games given the number needed for 2 games.

Write and solve a proportion. Let d represent the number of hot dogs needed for 8 games.

$$\begin{matrix} \text{hot dogs} \rightarrow \\ \text{games} \rightarrow \end{matrix} \quad \frac{70}{2} = \frac{d}{8} \quad \begin{matrix} \leftarrow \text{hot dogs} \\ \leftarrow \text{games} \end{matrix}$$

$70 \cdot 8 = 2d$ Find the cross products.

$560 = 2d$ Multiply.

$280 = d$

Zach will need 280 hot dogs for 8 games.

How do you fill in the grid for the answer?

- Print your answer in the answer boxes.
- Print only one digit or symbol in each answer box.
- Do not write any digits or symbols outside the answer boxes.
- You may print your answer with the first digit in the left answer box, or with the last digit in the right answer box. You may leave blank any boxes you do not need on the right or the left side of your answer.
- Fill in only one bubble for every answer box that you have written in. Be sure not to fill in a bubble under a blank answer box.

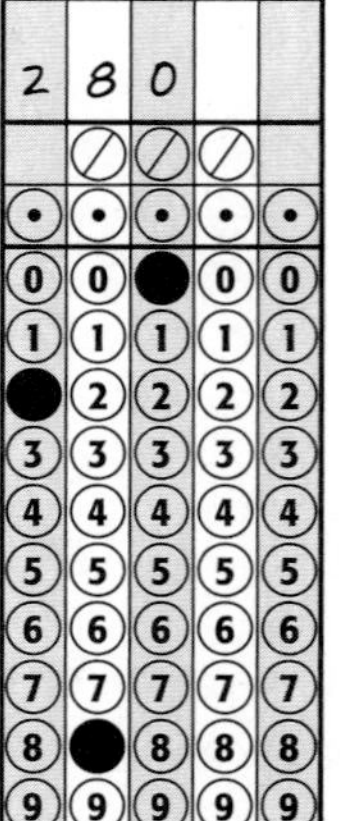

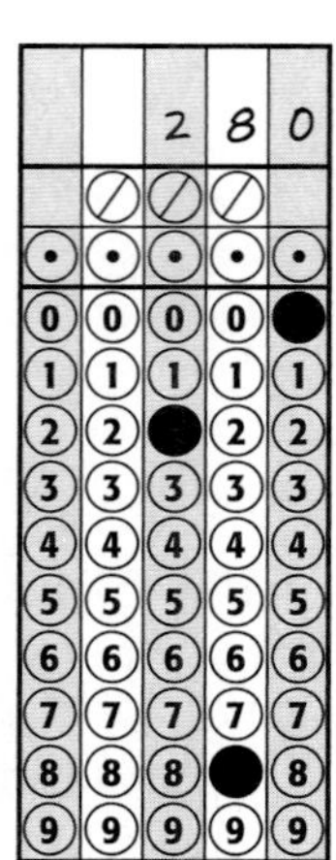

Many gridded-response questions result in an answer that is a fraction or a decimal. These values can also be filled in on the grid.

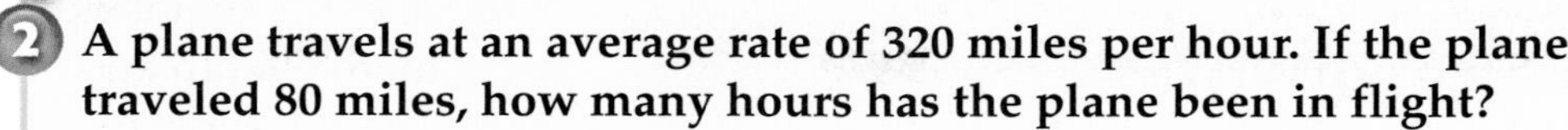

2 **A plane travels at an average rate of 320 miles per hour. If the plane traveled 80 miles, how many hours has the plane been in flight?**

$r \times t = d$ Use the distance formula.

$320t = 80$ Replace r with 320 and d with 80.

$\frac{320t}{320} = \frac{80}{320}$ Divide each side by 320.

$t = \frac{1}{4}$ Simplify.

The plane has been traveling for $\frac{1}{4}$ of an hour.

How do you fill in the answer grid?

You can either grid the fraction $\frac{1}{4}$, or the decimal, 0.25.

The following are acceptable answer responses.

Notice that the question asks for the time in hours, not minutes. So an answer of 15 would be incorrect.

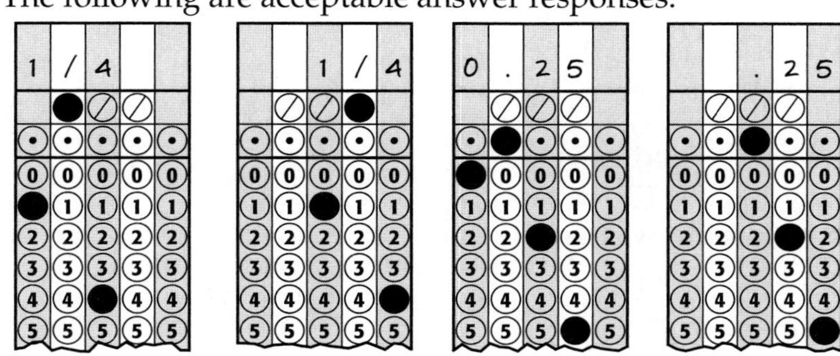

Before filling in the grid, change any mixed numbers to equivalent improper fractions or decimals.

ISAT EXAMPLE

3 **Triangle *ABC* is similar to $\triangle QRS$. What is the value of x?**

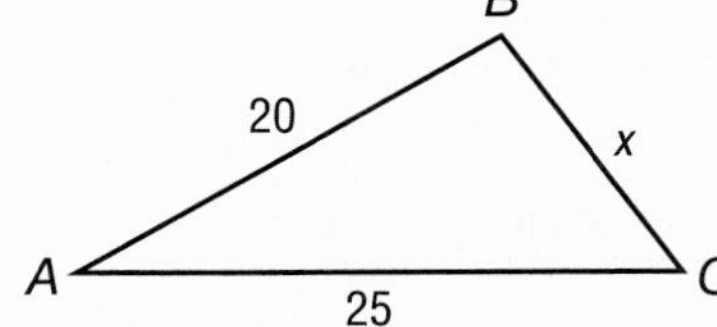

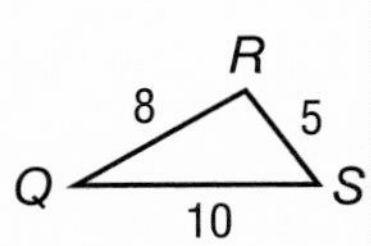

$\frac{BC}{RS} = \frac{AC}{QS}$ Write a proportion.

$\frac{x}{5} = \frac{25}{10}$ $BC = x$, $RS = 5$, $AC = 25$, $QS = 10$

$x \cdot 10 = 5 \cdot 25$ Find the cross products.

$\frac{10x}{10} = \frac{125}{10}$ Multiply. Then divide each side by 10.

$x = \frac{25}{2}$ or $12\frac{1}{2}$

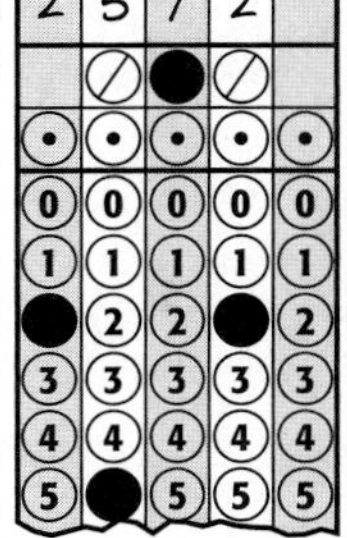

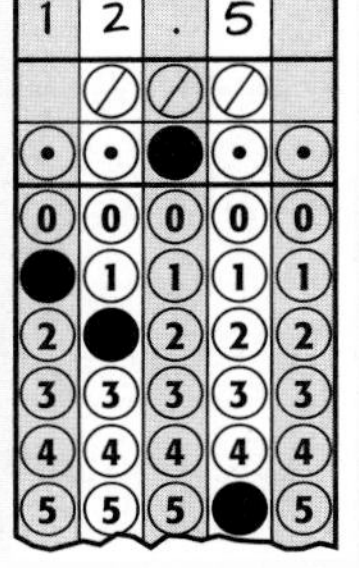

Do not enter 121/2, as this will be interpreted as $\frac{121}{2}$.

You can either grid the improper fraction $\frac{25}{2}$ or the decimal 12.5.

Gridded-Response Practice

Solve each problem. Then copy and complete a grid like the one shown on page 718.

Number and Operations

1. John ran $3\frac{1}{2}$ miles on Monday. On Tuesday, he ran $2\frac{1}{4}$ miles. How many more miles did he run on Monday?

2. Maria's Fashions is having a sale on shoes. She is discounting every pair of shoes by 35%. If a pair of sandals regularly sell for \$32, what will be the sale price of the sandals in dollars?

3. There are approximately 2.54 centimeters in one inch. If the width of a piece of paper is 8 inches, what is the approximate width of the paper in centimeters?

4. The atomic weight of iodine is approximately 1.269×10^2. What is iodine's atomic weight written in standard notation?

5. Austin's Sandwich Shop offers a lunchtime sandwich special. A customer has a choice of bread, meat, and cheese as shown in the table. How many different sandwich choices are there?

Bread	Meat	Cheese
Sourdough	Turkey	Swiss
Wheat	Ham	American
Rye	Roast Beef	Provolone

Algebra

6. Evaluate $\frac{y^2 - 1}{x + 2}$ if $x = -1$ and $y = 6$.

7. Find $f(-1)$ if $f(x) = 3x + 7$.

8. After a half hour, Kara had walked 1.5 miles. After 1 hour, she had walked 3 miles. If you graph this information with hours on the x-axis and miles on the y-axis, what is the slope of the graph?

9. A video rental store charges \$20 for a membership and \$3 to rent each video. The total cost y can be represented by the equation $y = 3x + 20$, where x represents the number of videos rented. What is the y-intercept of the graph of the equation?

10. The graph shows the enrollment of students grades Pre-K through 8 from 1980 to 2010. What is the rate of change between 2000 and 2010?

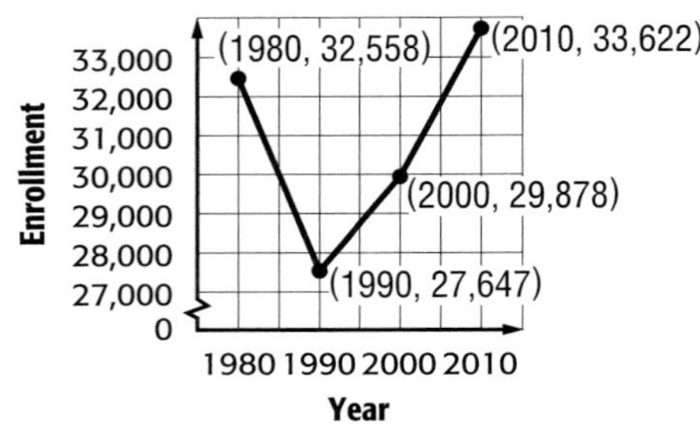

11. If $\frac{5a^5b^3}{ab}$ is simplified, what is the exponent of a?

Geometry

12. What is the distance between point A and point B? Round to the nearest tenth of a unit.

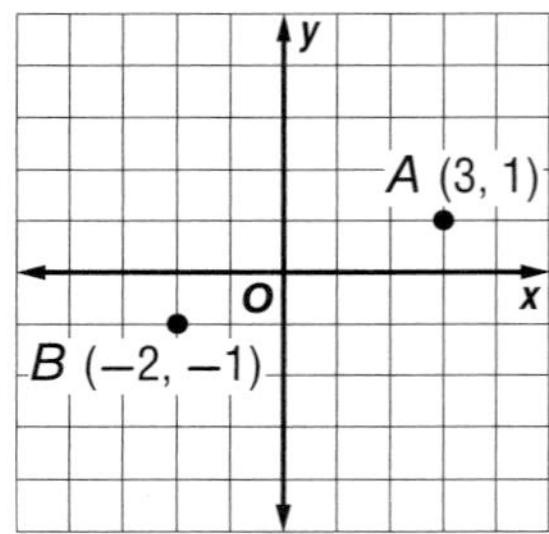

13. What is the measure of $\angle 3$ in degrees?

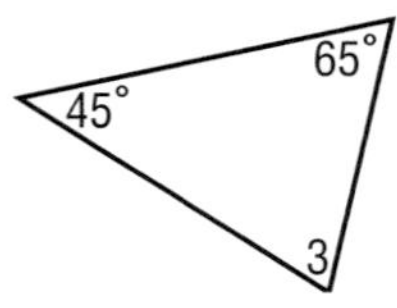

Preparing for Standardized Tests

14. Triangle MNO is dilated with a scale factor of 2. What is the x-coordinate of M on the dilated image?

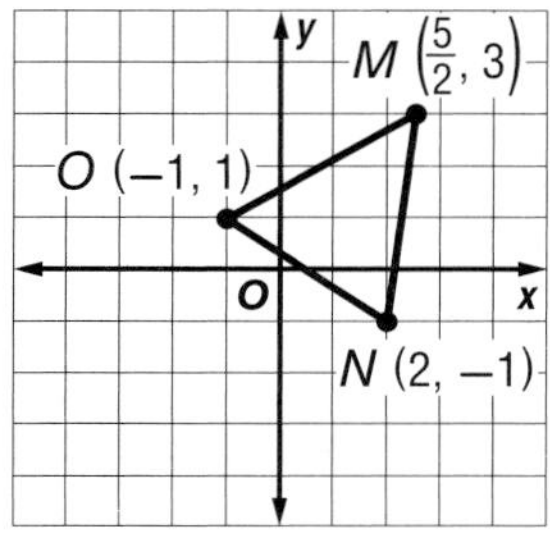

15. If polygon $ABCD$ is similar to polygon $RSTU$, what is the measure of $\overline{AB}$?

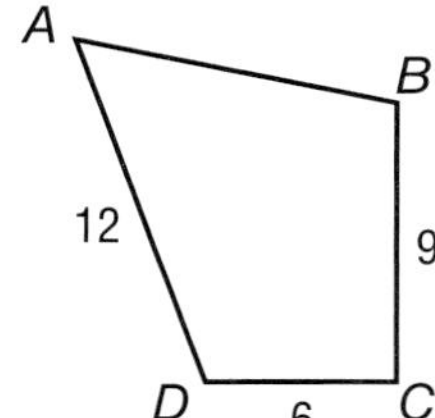

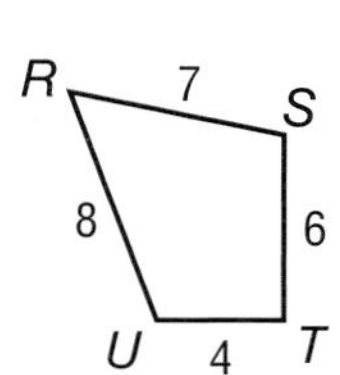

16. Triangle QRS is congruent to $\triangle XYZ$. Find the value of a.

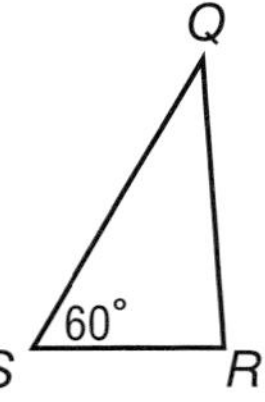

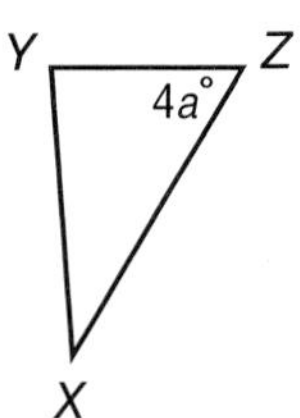

Measurement

17. The distance from Little Rock, Arkansas, to Albuquerque, New Mexico, is 882 miles. What is this distance to the nearest kilometer? (1 kilometer $\approx$ 0.62 miles)

18. Giant Value sells 8 bottles of fruit juice for \$6.00. Express this as a unit rate in dollars per bottle.

19. The Bakers need a cover for their swimming pool. If the swimming pool is round and has a diameter of 15 feet, what will be the area of the cover? Round to the nearest tenth of a square foot.

20. What is the volume of the cone? Round to the nearest cubic inch.

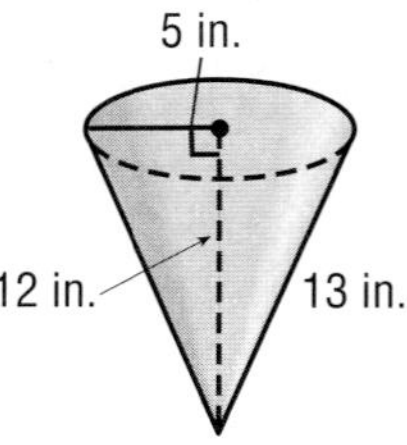

TEST-TAKING TIP

Question 20 A figure may give you more information than you need to solve the problem. Before solving, circle any information in the figure that is needed to find the answer.

Data Analysis and Probability

21. Last week Toya worked the following hours per day: 5, 6, 9, 4, 3, and 9. What is the mean number of hours that she worked per day?

22. The spinner is divided into 8 equal sections. If Megan spins the spinner, what is the probability that the spinner will land on yellow or red?

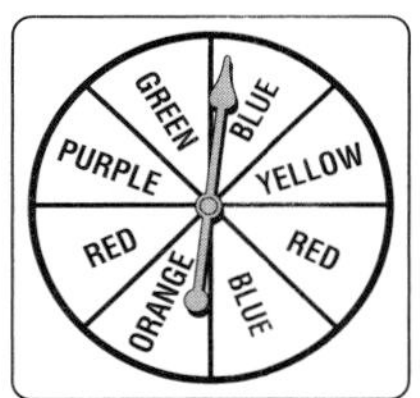

23. The table shows the height in inches of 15 students in Mrs. Garcia's class. What is the interquartile range of the data?

63	62	65	64	69
65	68	68	67	60
64	67	65	70	68

24. A bag contains 2 green marbles, 6 yellow marbles, 5 red marbles, and 9 blue marbles. How many yellow marbles must be added to the bag so that the probability of randomly picking a yellow marble is $\frac{1}{3}$?

25. In Mr. Firewalk's class, 24 of the 30 students said they owned a pet. If the entire school has 890 students, how many of the total students in the school would you expect own pets?

Short-Response Questions

Short-response questions require you to provide a solution to the problem as well as any method, explanation, and/or justification you used to arrive at the solution. These are sometimes called *constructed-response, open-response, open-ended, free-response*, or *student-produced questions*.

The following is a sample rubric, or scoring guide.

Credit	Score	Criteria
Full	2	Full credit: The answer is correct and a full explanation is provided that shows each step in arriving at the final answer.
Partial	1	Partial credit: There are two different ways to receive partial credit. • The answer is correct, but the explanation provided is incomplete or incorrect. • The answer is incorrect, but the explanation and method of solving the problem is correct.
None	0	No credit: Either an answer is not provided or the answer does not make sense.

On some standardized tests, no credit is given for a correct answer if your work is not shown.

ISAT EXAMPLE

1 **Sophia wants to retile her kitchen floor. If the tiling costs \$3.50 per square foot, what will be the cost to tile the entire floor?**

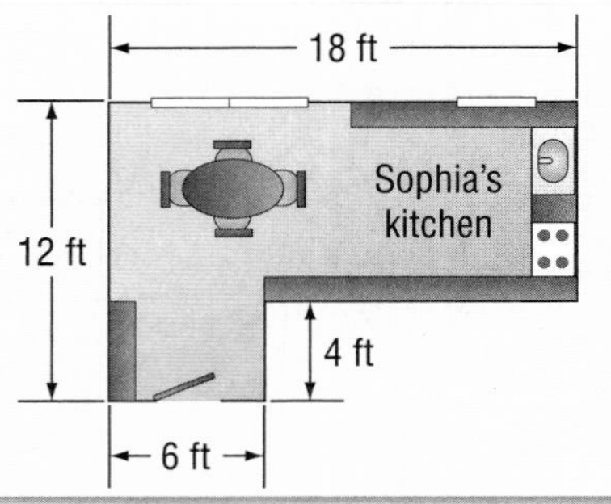

Full Credit Solution

I will break the kitchen into two rectangular regions and find the area of each region.

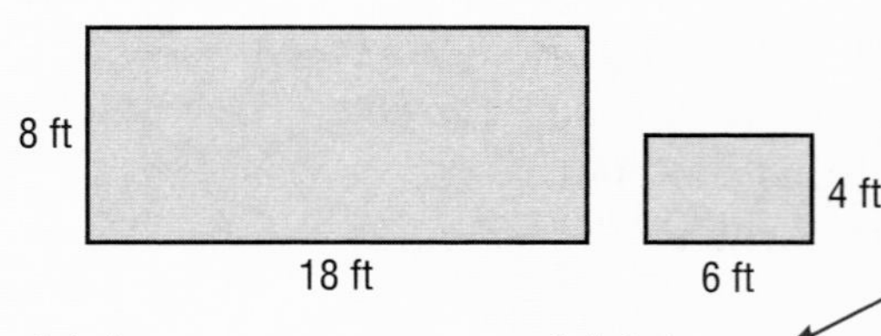

$A = lw = (18)(8)$ $\quad$ $A = lw = (4)(6)$

$= 144$ square feet $\quad$ $= 24$ square feet

Total area $= 144 + 24 = 168$ square feet

Since it costs \$3.50 for each square foot, I will multiply the total square feet (168) by \$3.50.

$168 \times \$3.5 = \$588$

It will cost Sophia \$588 to tile her kitchen.

The steps, calculations, and reasoning are clearly stated.

Be sure to complete this final step to answer the question asked.

Partial Credit Solution

In this sample solution, there are no explanations for finding the lengths or for the calculations.

There is no explanation of how the lengths were found.

$$A = lw$$
$$= (18)(12) - (4)(12)$$
$$= 216 - 48$$
$$= 168$$

There are 168 square feet in her kitchen.

$168 + 3.5 = 588$

It will cost $588 to tile the kitchen.

Partial Credit Solution

In this sample solution, the answer is incorrect because the area was calculated incorrectly. However, the process for finding the area and then the cost was correct.

The area calculated was incorrect, but an explanation was given for each step.

Since the tiling is charged in square feet, I will first find the area of the kitchen in square feet.

$$A = lw$$
$$= (18)(12)$$
$$= 216$$

The area of the kitchen is 216 square feet.

Since it costs $3.50 for each square foot, I will multiply the total square feet (216) by $3.50.

$216 + 3.5 = 756$

It will cost $756 to tile the kitchen.

No Credit Solution

In this sample solution, there are no explanations, the area is calculated incorrectly, and the cost for the tile was not found.

$$A = lw$$
$$= (18)(12)$$
$$= 216$$

It will cost $216 to tile the kitchen.

Short-Response Practice

Solve each problem. Show all your work.

Number and Operations

1. Mr. Collins is the supervisor of the eighth grade basketball league. He has 72 students signed up to play. Each team needs to have the same number of students, but cannot have more than 15 students. What is the greatest number of students that can be on each team? How many teams will Mr. Collins have?

2. Mika buys a jacket for \$45 plus 6% sales tax. She decided that she didn't want it anymore so she sold it to her friend for \$50. How much did she gain or lose from her sale?

3. Karla is baking cookies to take to a bake sale. Her recipe calls for $3\frac{1}{2}$ cups of flour. If she plans on taking $4\frac{1}{2}$ batches to the sale, how much flour will she need?

4. The Student Council has saved \$200 for a field trip to the Discovery Science Museum. If the admission is \$8 per student and lunch for each student will cost \$5.25, how many students will be able to go?

5. Kory is five feet tall. When she stands next to a tree, she casts a 6-foot shadow. How tall is the tree if it casts a 36-foot shadow?

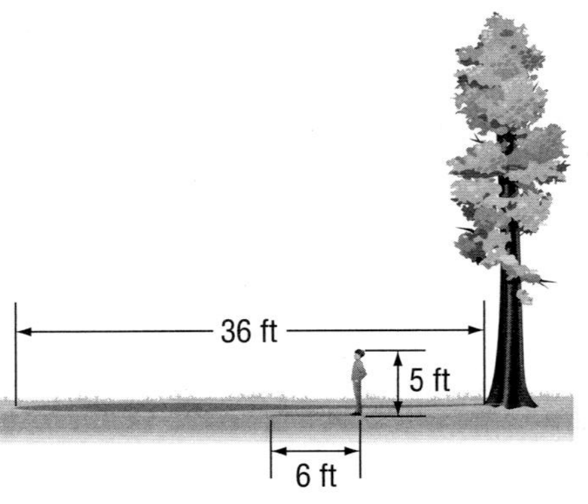

Algebra

6. Miguel has \$400. He plans to spend \$5 per day on lunch. The equation for the amount of money y Miguel has at any time is $y = 400 - 5x$, where x is the number of days from today. If this equation is graphed, what is the slope? What does the slope mean?

7. Tyree wants to hire a landscaper. JR's Landscaping Service charges \$200 for a design layout and \$50 an hour for working on a yard. Great Landscapers charges \$400 for a design layout and \$25 an hour for working on the yard. If it will take 6 hours to landscape Tyree's yard, which company should he hire? Explain.

8. The points in the table all lie on one line. Find the slope of the line. Then graph the line.

x	y
−1	4
0	6
1	8
2	10

9. Lucy is helping her father run his campaign for city mayor. If she can make and mail 45 flyers in half an hour, how long will it take her to make and mail 150 flyers?

10. Kyle bought x shirts for \$24.99 each, a pair of shoes for \$49.99, and a pair of jeans for \$51.99. If Kyle spent a total of \$201.94, how many shirts did he buy?

Geometry

11. Find the value of x so that the polygons have the same perimeter.

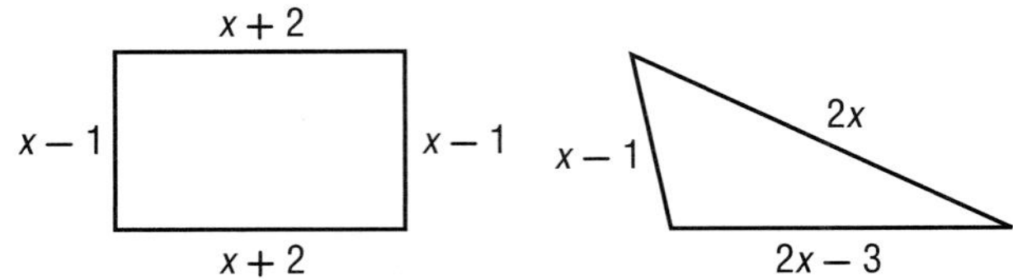

12. Find the measures of a and b.

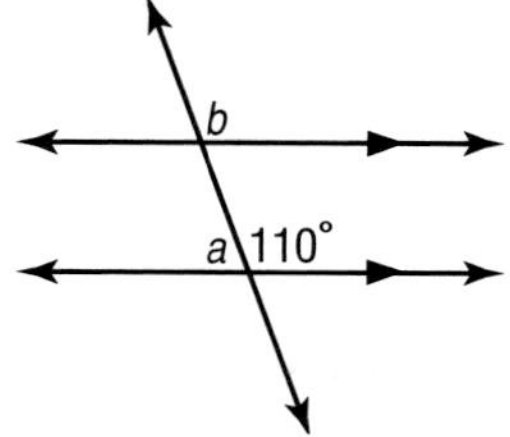

13. From the distances given, do the three cities in Iowa form a right triangle? Explain.

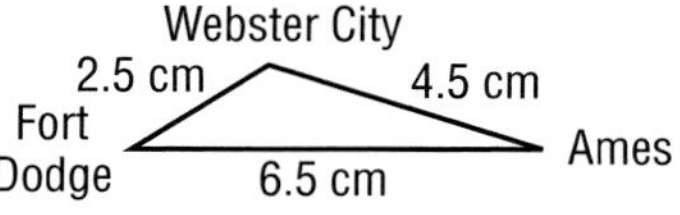

Measurement

14. Find the value of x in the figure.

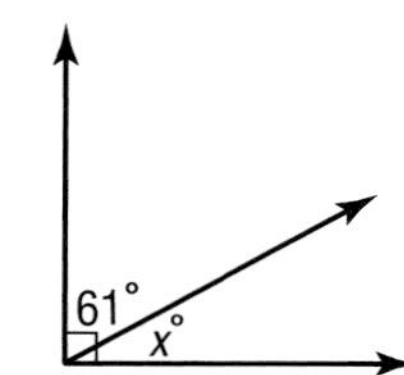

15. What is the ratio of the surface area of the smaller box to the surface area of the larger box?

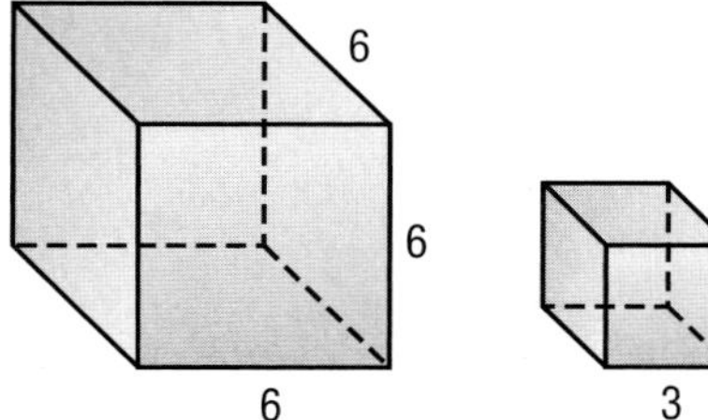

16. Find the area of the figure below. Round to the nearest tenth.

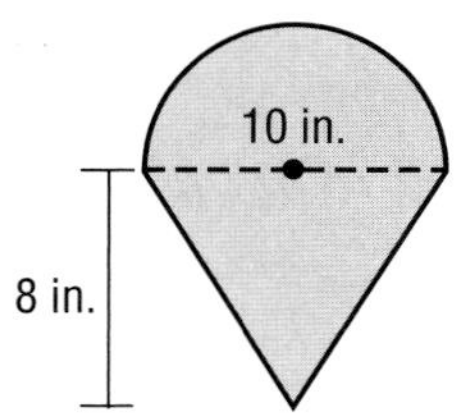

TEST-TAKING TIP

Questions 13 and 16 Be sure to read the instruction of each problem carefully. Some questions require an explanation or specify how to round answers.

17. The basketball team receives cups of water at every timeout. The cups are shaped as cones as shown below. What is the volume of one cup? Use 3.14 for π.

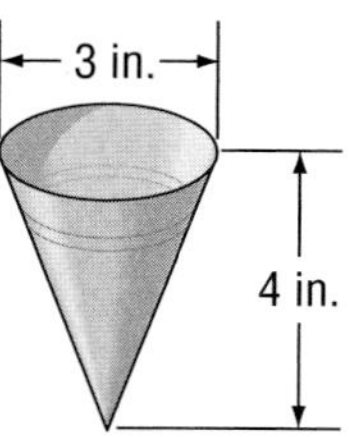

Data Analysis and Probability

18. Lee has 8 pairs of shoes. He is flying to see his brother and can only fit 2 pairs in his suitcase. How many different combinations of 2 pairs of shoes can he take?

19. The table shows a list of favorite sports of the students in Mr. Murray's class.

Sport	Number of Students
swimming	5
basketball	3
golf	2
volleyball	7
football	8
soccer	5
other	5

What is the probability that a randomly selected student has a favorite sport that is swimming or soccer?

20. Shari's Boutique has 15 employees. They would like to hire more people since they are expanding their store. The current salaries of the employees are listed in the table.

Position	Yearly Salary	Number of Employees
Manager	\$75,000	1
Supervisor	\$30,000	4
Clerk	\$12,000	10

Which measure of central tendency should Shari use to encourage people to apply? Explain.

Extended-Response Questions

Extended-response questions are often called *open-ended* or *constructed-response questions*. Most extended-response questions have multiple parts. You must answer all parts to receive full credit.

In extended-response questions you must show all of your work in solving the problem. A rubric is used to determine if you receive full, partial, or no credit. The following is a sample rubric.

Credit	Score	Criteria
Full	4	Full credit: A correct solution is given that is supported by well-developed, accurate explanations.
Partial	3, 2, 1	Partial credit: A generally correct solution is given that may contain minor flaws in reasoning or computation, or an incomplete solution is given. The more correct the solution, the greater the score.
None	0	No credit: An incorrect solution is given indicating no mathematical understanding of the concept, or no solution is given.

On some standardized tests, no credit is given for a correct answer if your work is not shown.

Make sure that you show every part of your solution. This includes figures, graphs, and any explanations for your calculations.

ISAT EXAMPLE

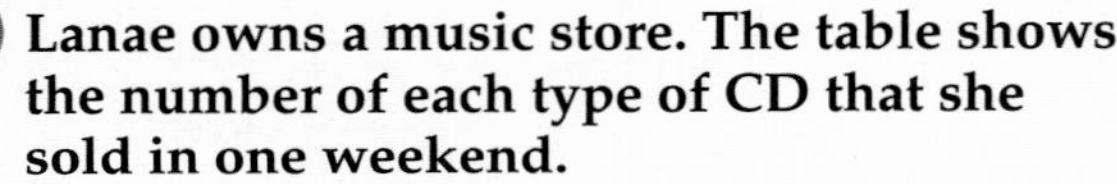

1 **Lanae owns a music store. The table shows the number of each type of CD that she sold in one weekend.**

a. Find the percent of CDs sold for each music type. Round to the nearest percent.

b. Make a circle graph of the data.

c. If Lanae sells 250 CDs the following weekend, how many would you expect to be Jazz?

Music Type	Number of CDs Sold
Classical	12
Country	9
Hip-Hop	15
Jazz	24
R&B	35

Full Credit Solution

Part a

I will first find the total number of CDs sold.

$$15 + 9 + 12 + 35 + 24 = 95$$

To find each percent, I will divide the number of CDs in the category by the total number of CDs sold:

Classical: $\frac{12}{95} \approx 13\%$

Country: $\frac{9}{95} \approx 9\%$

Hip-Hop: $\frac{15}{95} \approx 16\%$

Jazz: $\frac{24}{95} \approx 25\%$

R&B: $\frac{35}{95} \approx 37\%$

Part b

I will multiply each percent by 360 to find the number of degrees for each section of the circle.

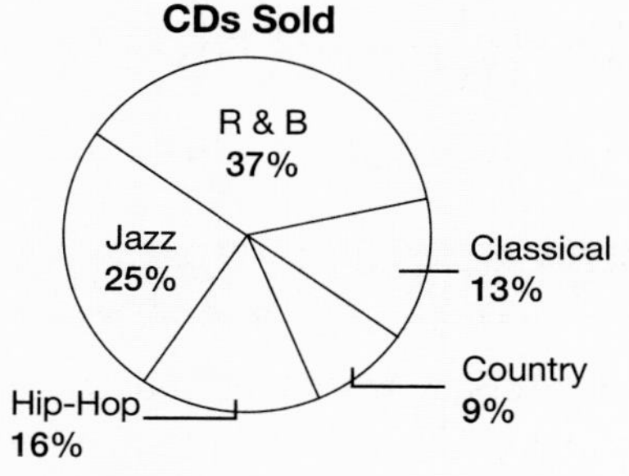

Classical: 13% of 360 = $0.13 \times 360 = 46.8$

Country: 9% of 360 = $0.09 \times 360 = 32.4$

Hip-Hop: 16% of 360 = $0.16 \times 360 = 57.6$

Jazz: 25% of 360 = $0.25 \times 360 = 90$

R&B: 37% of 360 = $0.37 \times 360 = 133.2$

Part c

Since 25% of the CDs sold the weekend before were Jazz, you would expect about 25% of the 250 CDs to be Jazz.
25% of 250 = $0.25 \times 250 = 62.5$.
You should expect about 63 of the CDs sold to be Jazz.

Partial Credit Solution

Part a This answer includes no explanation of how the percents were found.

Classical: ≈ 13% Country: ≈ 9% R&B: ≈ 37%
Hip-Hop: ≈ 16% Jazz: ≈ 25%

Part b

This sample answer only includes part of the answer. The circle graph is missing.

To make a circle graph of the data, I first need to find the number of degrees that represent each section.
Classical: 13% of 360 = 0.13×360 or 46.8
Country: 9% of 360 = 0.09×360 or 32.4
Hip-Hop: 16% of 360 = 0.16×360 or 57.6
Jazz: 25% of 360 = 0.25×360 or 90
R&B: 37% of 360 = 0.037×360 or 133.2

Part c Partial credit is given since no work is shown, but the answer is correct.

About 63 CDs should be Jazz.

No Credit Solution

A student who demonstrates no understanding of how to find the percents, does not make a circle graph, or draws an incorrect graph, and does not understand how to use the information to make predictions receives no credit.

Extended-Response Practice

Solve each problem. Show all your work.

Number and Operations

1. Ellen has a postcard that she wants to enlarge. The dimensions of the postcard are 5 inches by 7 inches.
   - **a.** Suppose she enlarges the postcard by a scale factor of 6. What will be the new dimensions?
   - **b.** Ellen found that after enlarging the picture with a scale factor of 6, it still was not the right size. She decided to try to enlarge it so the scale factor from the original picture to the enlarged picture is 3:5. What will be the new dimensions?
   - **c.** Using the dimensions found in Part a, what is the ratio of the area of the smaller picture to the area of the enlarged picture?

2. The table shows the number of computer users in seven different countries in a recent year.

Country	Computer Users (millions)
United States	168.84
Japan	48.00
Germany	31.59
United Kingdom	25.91
France	21.81
China	21.31
Canada	17.20

Source: U.S. Census Bureau

   - **a.** Which country had approximately $\frac{1}{8}$ the number of computer users that the United States had?
   - **b.** How many more computer users did China have than Canada?
   - **c.** If the total number of computer users in the top 15 countries is 420.20 million, what percent of these users are from Germany? Round to the nearest tenth of a percent.

Algebra

3. The table shows the annual average temperatures and snowfalls for several cities.

City	Annual Averages	
	Temperature (F°)	Snowfall (in.)
Albuquerque, NM	56.2	10.6
Atlanta, GA	61.3	1.9
Chicago, IL	49.0	40.3
Des Moines, IA	49.9	34.7
Houston, TX	67.9	0.4
Louisville, KY	56.1	17.5
Memphis, TN	62.3	5.5
Miami, FL	75.9	0.0
New York, NY	54.7	26.1

   - **a.** Draw a scatter plot of the data. Let the x-axis be the average temperature and the y-axis be the average snowfall.
   - **b.** Does the scatter plot show a *positive, negative,* or *no* relationship? Explain.
   - **c.** Use your scatter plot to estimate the amount of annual snowfall you would expect in Cincinnati which has an annual average temperature of 51.7°F.

4. Kyung works at a golf course for his summer job. The table shows the amount of money that he earns after various numbers of hours worked.

Time (h)	Amount ($)
2	15.00
5	37.50
8	60.00

   - **a.** Graph the information with hours on the x-axis and dollars on the y-axis. Draw a line through the points.
   - **b.** What is the slope of the graph? Explain what the slope means.
   - **c.** If Kyung works 34 hours in one week, how much money will he make?

Geometry

5. Chelsea leans a 10-foot ladder on the side of her house. The base of the ladder is 4 feet from the house.

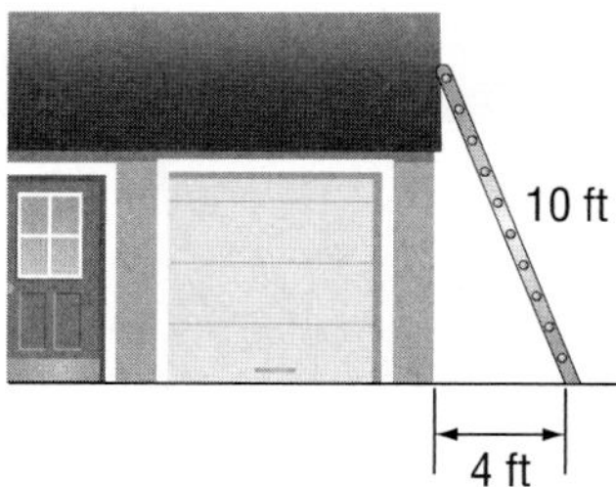

a. How high up the wall does the ladder reach? Round to the nearest tenth of a foot.

b. If Chelsea needs the ladder to reach 11 feet up the wall, is this possible? If so, how far from the base of the house should the ladder be?

c. Use the diagram to find the measures of the angles in the triangle formed by the ladder, the ground, and the wall. Round to the nearest degree.

TEST-TAKING TIP

Question 5 After finding the solutions, always go back and read the problem again to make sure your solution answers what the problem is asking.

6. Use $\triangle ABC$ and $\triangle JKL$ below.

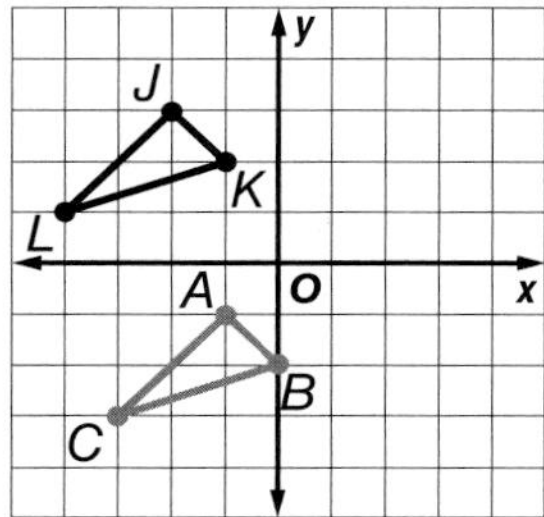

a. Graph the image of $\triangle ABC$ after it is reflected over the y-axis. Write the coordinates of its vertices.

b. Graph the image of $\triangle JKL$ after it is translated 2 units up. Write the coordinates of its vertices.

c. What translation(s) would transform $\triangle ABC$ to $\triangle JKL$?

Measurement

7. The table shows the winning men's marathon times, rounded to the nearest minute, at five Olympic games.

Year	Runner	Time (min)
1988	Gelindo Bordin	131
1992	Hwang Young-Cho	133
1996	Josia Thugwane	133
2000	Gezahgne Abera	130
2004	Stefano Baldino	131

Source: *The World Almanac*

a. A marathon is 26.2 miles. What rate did the 2000 winner run the marathon in miles per hour? Round to the nearest tenth.

b. If the 2004 winner could keep up his average rate, how long would it take him to run 50 miles? Round to the nearest minute.

Data Analysis and Probability

8. The data represent the magnitudes of recent earthquakes.

6.8	6.4	6.4	7.6
5.9	6.5	5.9	5.0
6.1	7.4	6.5	8.1

Source: *The World Almanac*

a. Make a box-and-whisker plot of the data.

b. What is the interquartile range of the data?

c. What is the median and mean of the data?

9. Forty customers were surveyed as they left Super Slides Water Park. The results are in the table below.

Item	Number Purchased
T-shirt	16
Beverage	36
Food	21

a. What percent of the customers purchased a beverage?

b. If 215 people attend the park on Monday, about how many of the customers would you expect will purchase food?

Concepts and Skills Bank

9.B.3 **Identify, describe, classify and compare two- and three-dimensional geometric figures and models according to their properties.**

Geometric Figures

The table below shows basic geometric figures.

Geometric Figures — Key Concept

Definition	Model
A **point** is an exact location in space, represented by a dot.	A **Words:** point *A*
A **line** is a set of points that form a straight path that goes in opposite directions without ending.	C D **Words:** line *CD* or line *DC* **Symbols:** $\overleftrightarrow{CD}$ or $\overleftrightarrow{DC}$, line ℓ
A **ray** is a line that has an endpoint and goes in one direction without ending.	S T **Words:** ray *ST* **Symbols:** $\overrightarrow{ST}$
A **line segment** is part of a line between two endpoints.	G H **Words:** line segment *GH* or line segment *HG* **Symbols:** $\overline{GH}$ or $\overline{HG}$
A **plane** is a flat surface that goes on forever in all directions.	M O N **Words:** plane *MNO*, plane *OMN*, plane *NMO*, plane *MON*, plane *ONM*, plane *NOM*
An **angle** is formed by two rays with a common endpoint. The two rays that make up the angle are called the sides of the angle. The common endpoint is called the **vertex**.	A side B vertex side C **Words:** angle *ABC* or angle *CBA*, angle *B* **Symbols:** $\angle ABC$ or $\angle CBA$, $\angle B$

EXAMPLES Name Geometric Figures

Use the figure to name each of the following.

1 a line containing point *A*.

There are four points on the line. Any two of the points can be used to name the line.

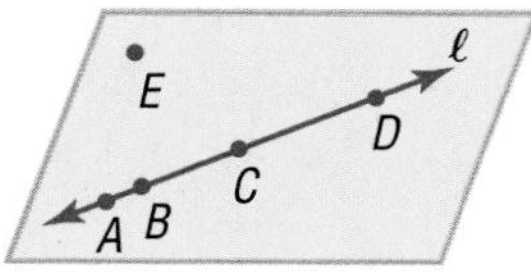

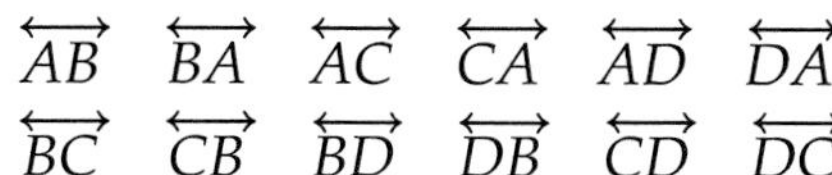

$\overleftrightarrow{AB}$ $\overleftrightarrow{BA}$ $\overleftrightarrow{AC}$ $\overleftrightarrow{CA}$ $\overleftrightarrow{AD}$ $\overleftrightarrow{DA}$

$\overleftrightarrow{BC}$ $\overleftrightarrow{CB}$ $\overleftrightarrow{BD}$ $\overleftrightarrow{DB}$ $\overleftrightarrow{CD}$ $\overleftrightarrow{DC}$

2 a line segment.

There are 6 line segments: $\overline{AB}$, $\overline{AC}$, $\overline{AD}$, $\overline{BC}$, $\overline{BD}$, $\overline{CD}$.

Exercises

For Exercises 1–5, refer to the figure at the right.

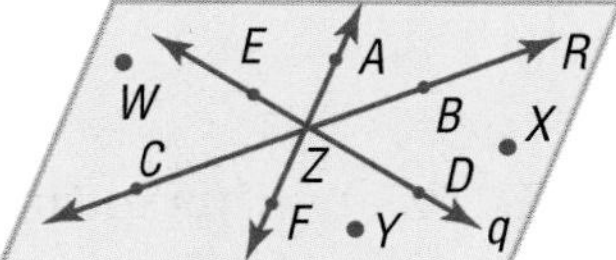

1. Name a line containing point *E*.
2. Identify two rays.
3. What is another name for $\angle BZD$?
4. Name the plane shown.
5. List three line segments.

For Exercises 6–10, refer to the figure at the right.

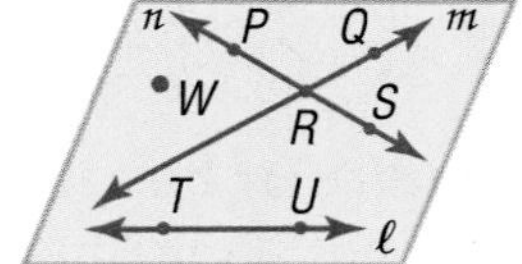

6. Name a line that contains point *S*.
7. Identify two angles.
8. List three line segments.
9. Name a point *not* contained in lines ℓ, *m*, or *n*.
10. What is another name for line *m*?

Draw and label a figure for each of the following.

11. point *J*
12. line *AB*
13. $\overline{AB}$ and $\overline{BC}$
14. plane *XYZ*

Name the geometric term(s) modeled by each object.

15. 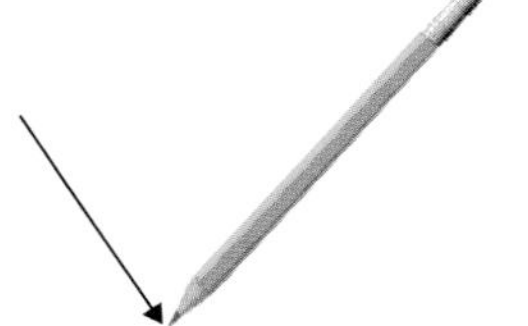

16. 

17. 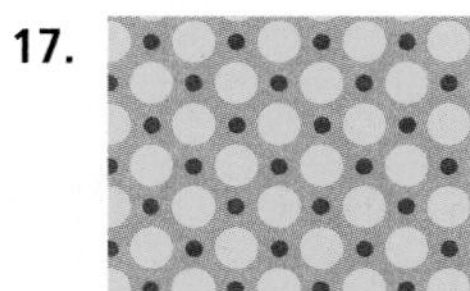

18. a blanket
19. the end of a pushpin
20. woven threads in a placemat
21. Describe a real-life example of a plane containing points, lines, and angles.

2 Geometric Constructions

A compass is a drawing instrument used for drawing circles and arcs. A straightedge, such as a ruler, is used to draw segments. You can use a compass and a straightedge to construct basic elements of geometric figures. You know a line segment is part of a line with two endpoints. Line segments that have the same length are called **congruent segments**.

ILS **7.A.3a Measure length,** capacity, weight/mass **and angles using sophisticated instruments** (e.g., **compass,** protractor, trundle wheel). *Also addresses 7.B.3, 9.A.3c.*

ACTIVITY Construct Congruent Segments

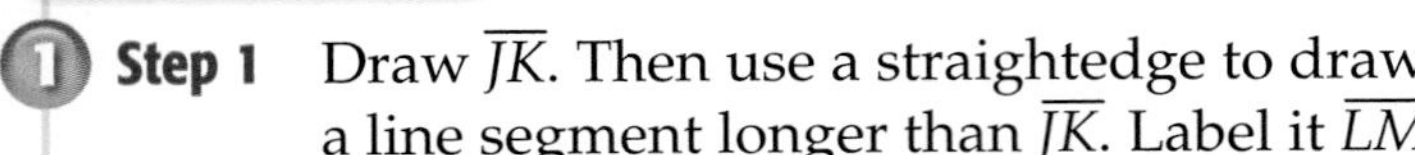

1 **Step 1** Draw $\overline{JK}$. Then use a straightedge to draw a line segment longer than $\overline{JK}$. Label it $\overline{LM}$.

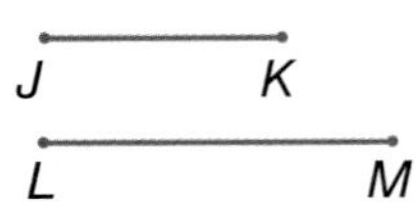

Step 2 Place the compass at J and adjust the compass setting so you can place the pencil tip on K. The compass setting equals the length of $\overline{JK}$.

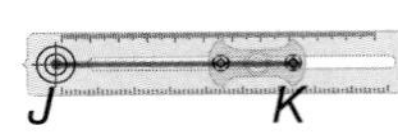

Step 3 Using this setting, place the compass tip at L. Draw an arc to intersect $\overline{LM}$. Label the intersection P.

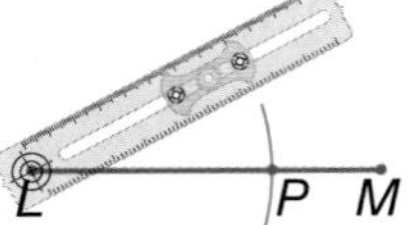

$\overline{LP}$ is congruent to $\overline{JK}$.

A **perpendicular bisector** is a perpendicular line that divides a line segment into two congruent segments.

ACTIVITY Construct Perpendicular Bisectors

2 **Step 1** Draw $\overline{AB}$. Then place the compass at point A. Using a setting greater than one half the length of $\overline{AB}$, draw an arc above and below $\overline{AB}$.

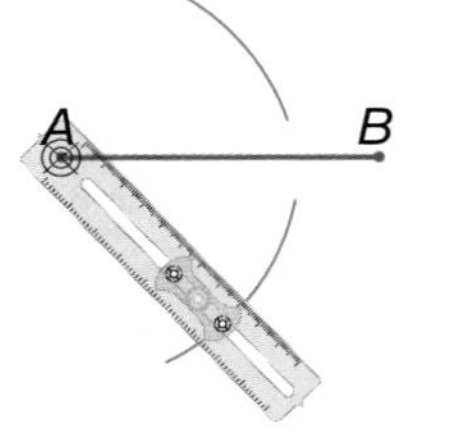

Step 2 Using this setting, place the compass at point B. Draw another set of arcs above and below $\overline{AB}$ as shown.

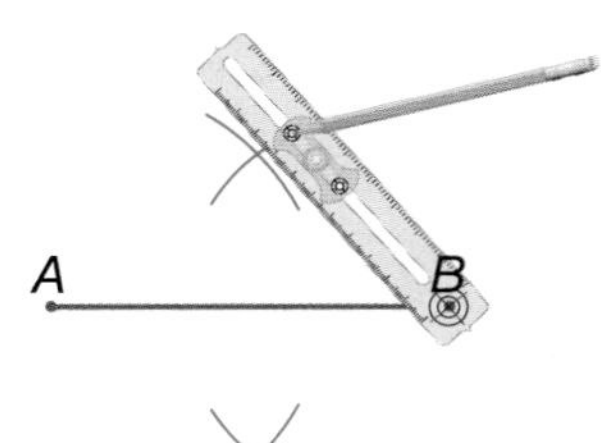

Step 3 Label the intersection of these arcs X and Y as shown.

Step 4 Draw $\overline{XY}$. Label the intersection of $\overline{AB}$ and this new line M.

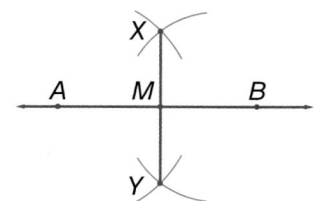

$\overline{XY}$ is the perpendicular bisector of $\overline{AB}$.

Two angles that have the same measure are called **congruent angles**.

Construct Congruent Angles

3 **Step 1** Draw $\angle ABC$.

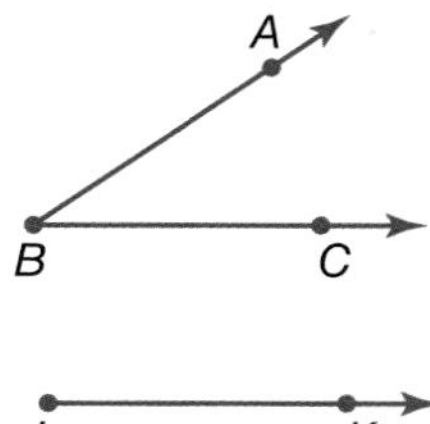

Step 2 Use a straightedge to draw $\overrightarrow{LK}$.

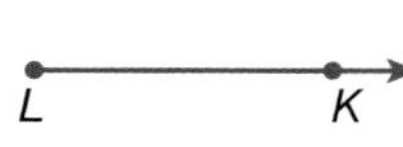

Step 3 With the compass at point B, draw an arc that intersects both sides of $\angle ABC$. Label the two points of intersection as X and Y.

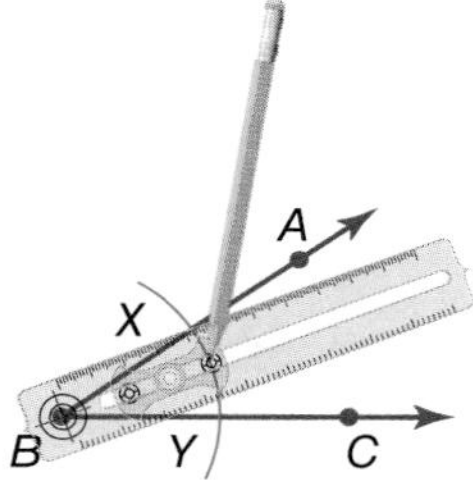

Step 4 With the same setting on your compass, place your compass at point L. Draw another arc. Label the intersection R.

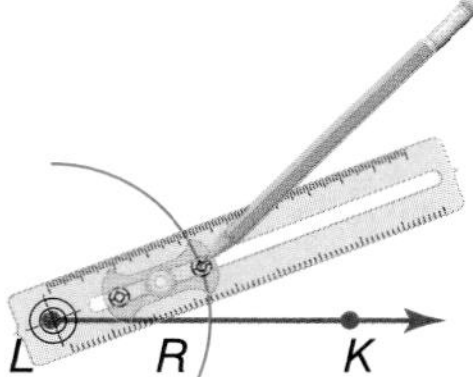

Step 5 Open your compass to the same width as the distance between points X and Y. Then place the compass at point R. Draw an arc that intersects the arc you drew in Step 4. Label this point of intersection S.

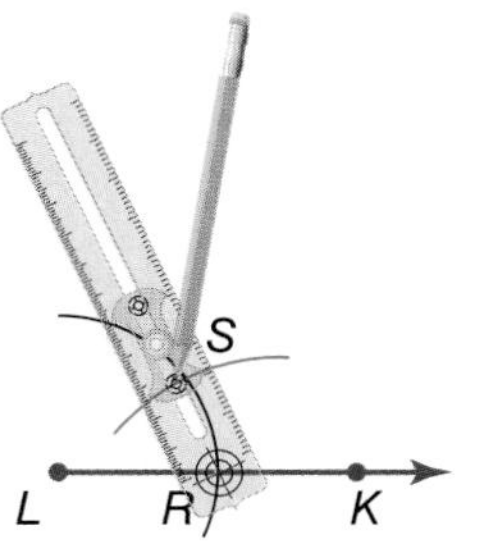

Step 6 Draw $\overrightarrow{LM}$ through point S. Angle MLK is congruent to $\angle ABC$.

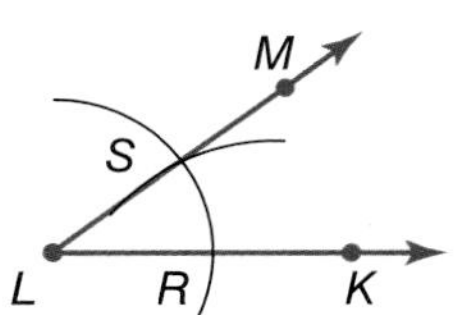

Concepts and Skills Bank

An **angle bisector** is a ray that divides an angle into two congruent angles.

ACTIVITY Construct an Angle Bisector

4 **Step 1** Draw $\angle JKL$.

Step 2 Place the compass at point K and draw an arc that intersects both sides of the angle. Label the intersections X and Y.

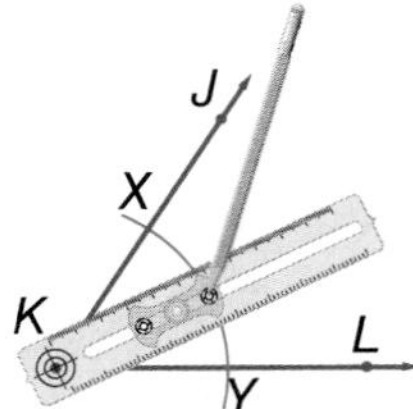

Step 3 With the compass at point X, draw an arc in the interior of $\angle JKL$.

Step 4 Using this setting, place the compass at point Y. Draw another arc.

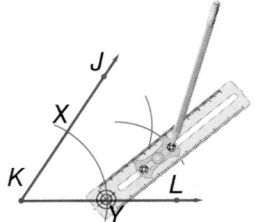

Step 5 Label the intersection of these arcs H. Then draw $\overrightarrow{KH}$.

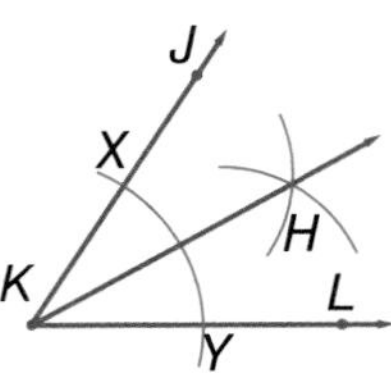

$\overrightarrow{KH}$ is the **bisector** of $\angle JKL$.

Exercises

Trace each segment. Then construct a segment congruent to it.

1.

2.

3.

Trace each segment. Then construct the segment's perpendicular bisector.

4.

5.

6.

Trace each angle. Then construct an angle congruent to it.

7. 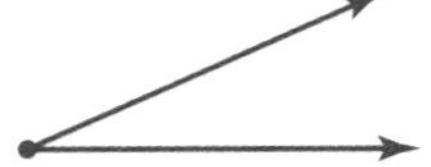

8. 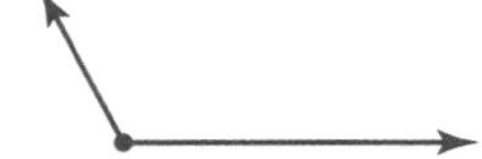

9. 

10. Construct the angle bisector for Exercise 7.

11. Construct the angle bisector for Exercise 8.

12. Construct the angle bisector for Exercise 9.

ILS **7.A.3a Measure** length, capacity, weight/mass and **angles using sophisticated instruments (e.g.,** compass, **protractor,** trundle wheel). *Also addresses 7.A.3b, 7.B.3, 9.A.3c.*

3 Measuring and Drawing Angles

Two rays that have a common endpoint form an **angle**. The common endpoint is called the **vertex**, and the two rays that make up the angle are called the **sides** of the angle.

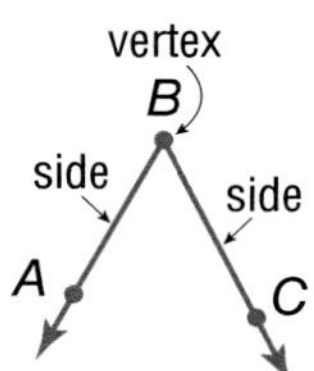

A circle can be divided into 360 equal sections. Each section is one **degree**. You can use a **protractor** to measure an angle in degrees and draw an angle with a given degree measure.

EXAMPLE Measure an Angle

1 Use a protractor to measure ∠*FGH*.

Step 1 Place the center point of the protractor's base on vertex *G*. Align the straight side with side $\overrightarrow{GH}$ so that the marker for 0° is on the ray.

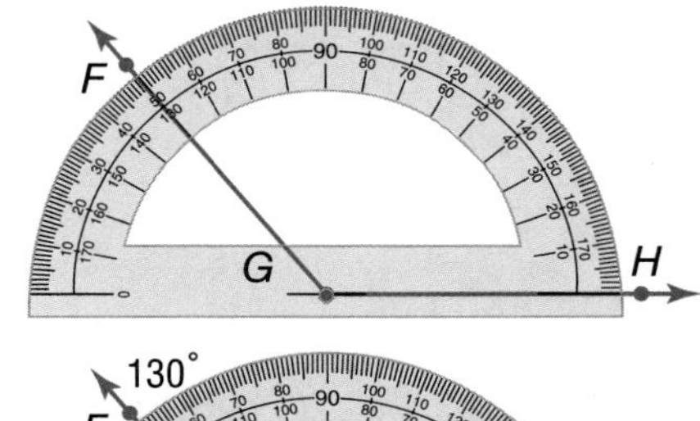

Step 2 Use the scale that begins with 0° at $\overrightarrow{GH}$. Read where the other side of the angle, $\overrightarrow{GF}$, crosses this scale.

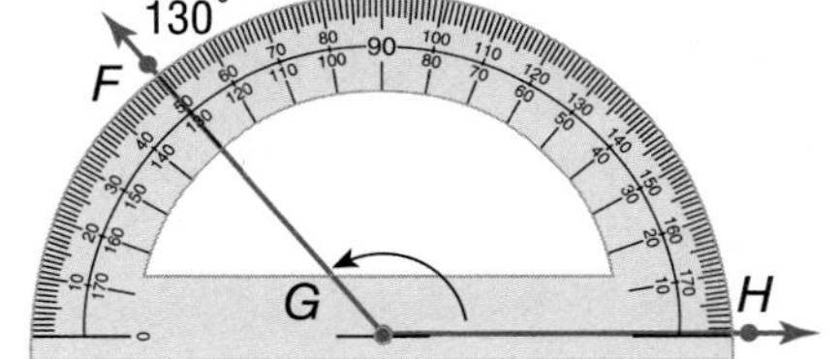

The measure of angle *FGH* is 130°.
Using symbols, $m\angle FGH = 130°$.

EXAMPLE Draw an Angle

2 Draw ∠*X* having a measure of 75°.

Step 1 Draw a ray. Label the endpoint *X*.

Step 2 Place the center point of the protractor's base on point *X*. Align the mark labeled 0 with the ray.

Step 3 Use the scale that begins with 0. Locate the mark labeled 75. Then draw the other side of the angle.

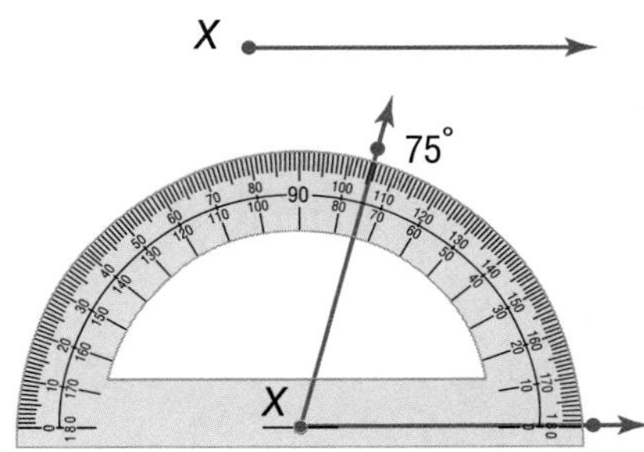

Exercises

Estimate the measure of each angle. Then use a protractor to find the actual measure.

1. ∠*XZY*
2. ∠*SZT*
3. ∠*SZY*
4. ∠*UZX*
5. ∠*TZW*
6. ∠*UZV*

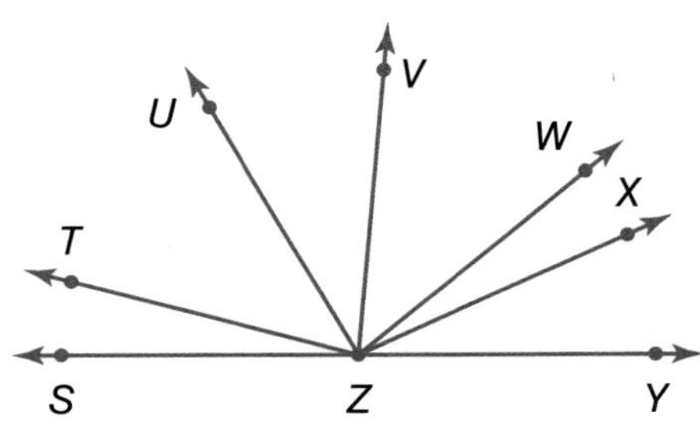

Use a protractor to draw an angle having each measurement.

7. 110°
8. 85°
9. 90°
10. 155°
11. 140°
12. 117°

Concepts and Skills Bank

Accuracy and Precision

7.B.3 Select and apply instruments including rulers and protractors **and units of measure to the degree of accuracy required.** *Also addresses 7.A.3a, 7.A.3b.*

All measurements taken in the real world are approximations. The greater the care in which a measurement is taken, the more accurate it will be. **Accuracy** is how close the measurement is to the actual value. **Precision** is the ability of a measurement to be consistently reproduced. A measurement is precise only to one-half of the smallest unit used in a measurement.

EXAMPLE Determine Precision

1 **Which is a more precise measurement of the line segment—3 centimeters or 2.9 centimeters? Explain.**

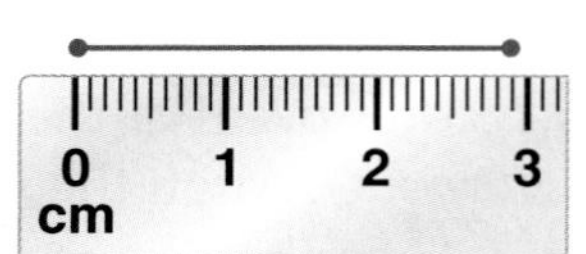

Estimate 3 cm
measurement: 3 cm
precision: nearest 0.5 cm

Estimate 3 cm
measurement: 2.9 cm
precision: nearest 0.05 cm or 0.5 mm

Since 3 is measured to the nearest 0.5 centimeter and 2.9 is measured to the nearest 0.05 centimeter, 2.9 is a more precise measurement.

Exercises

Choose the correct term(s) to determine the degree of accuracy needed in each measurement situation.

1. In a travel brochure, the length of a cruise ship would be described in (millimeters, meters).
2. A person making a jacket measures the fabric to the nearest (inch, eighth of an inch).
3. In a science experiment, the mass of one drop of solution is found to the nearest 0.01 (gram, kilogram).
4. The weight of a bag of apples in a grocery store would be given to the nearest (tenth of a pound, tenth of an ounce).
5. **HEIGHT** Which is the more precise measure for the height of a child: $49\frac{1}{2}$ inches or 4 feet? Explain.
6. **CAPACITY** Which unit is more precise for the capacity of a container: gallons or ounces? Explain.
7. **GEOMETRY** Draw a line segment. Estimate the length of the line segment. Then measure using two different units. Which measuring unit gave the more precise measurement?
8. **CONSTRUCTION** A construction company is ordering cement to complete all the sidewalks in a new neighborhood. Would you say that precision or accuracy is more important in the completion of their order? Explain.

5 Triangles

ILS **9.B.3 Identify, describe, classify** and compare **two-** and three-**dimensional geometric figures** and models **according to their properties.** *Also addresses 9.A.3c.*

A **triangle** is a figure formed by three line segments that intersect only at their end points. The sum of the measures of angles of a triangle is 180°.

EXAMPLE Find a Missing Angle Measurement

1 Find the value of x in $\triangle RST$.

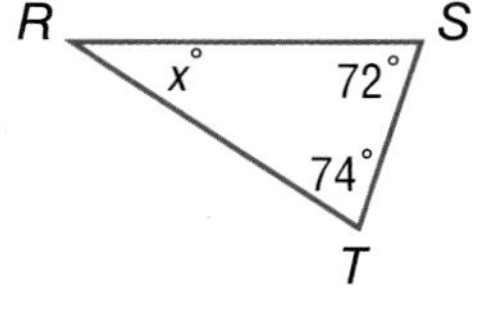

$m\angle R + m\angle S + m\angle T = 180$	The sum of the measures is 180.
$x + 72 + 74 = 180$	Replace $m\angle R$ with x, $m\angle S$ with 72, and $m\angle T$ with 74.
$x + 146 = 180$	Simplify.
$-146 = -146$	Subtract 146 from each side.
$x = 34$	

The value of x is 34.

All triangles have at least two acute angles and can be classified by the measure of the third angle.

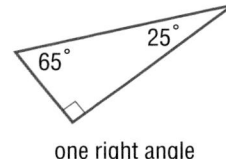

Acute Triangle	Obtuse Triangle	Right Triangle
70°, 50°, 60°	40°, 110°, 30°	65°, 25°
three acute angles	one obtuse angle	one right angle

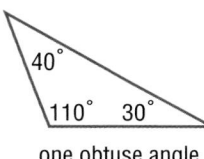

Triangles can also be classified by the number of congruent sides.

- **Scalene triangles** have no congruent sides
- **Isosceles triangles** have at least two sides congruent
- **Equilateral triangles** have 3 congruent sides

EXAMPLE Classify Triangles

2 Classify each triangle by its angles and by its sides.

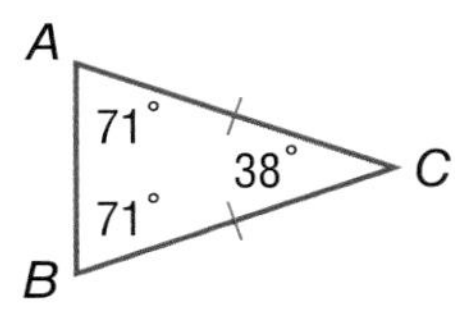

Angles $\triangle ABC$ has all acute angles.

Sides $\triangle ABC$ has two congruent sides.

So, $\triangle ABC$ is an acute isosceles triangle.

Exercises

Find the value of x in each triangle. Then, classify each triangle by its angles and by its sides.

1. 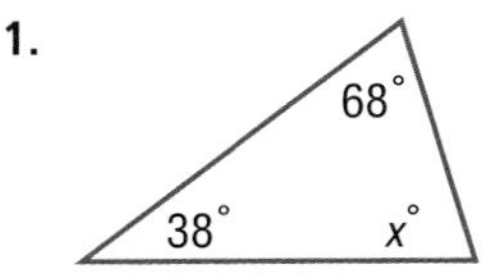

2. 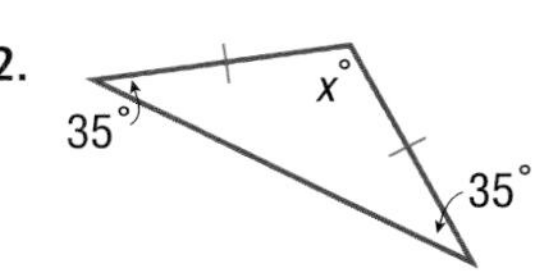

3. 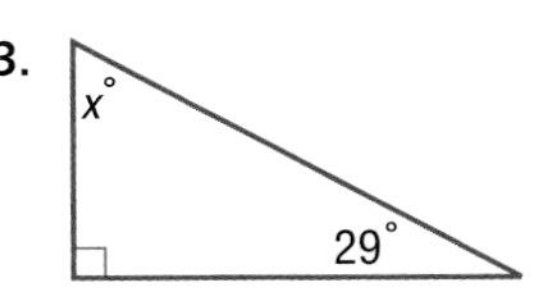

4. 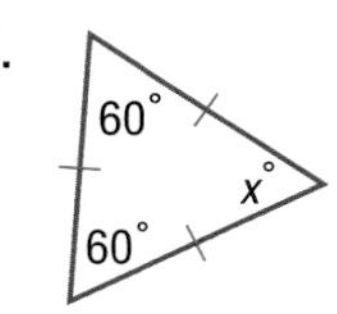

Concepts and Skills Bank

6 Classifying Quadrilaterals

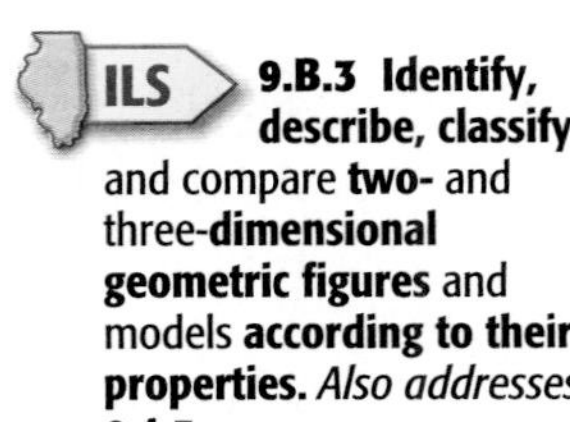

9.B.3 Identify, describe, classify and compare **two-** and three-**dimensional geometric figures** and models **according to their properties.** *Also addresses 9.A.3c.*

A **quadrilateral** is a polygon that has four sides and four angles. The concept map below shows how quadrilaterals are classified. Notice that the diagram goes from the most general type of quadrilateral to most specific.

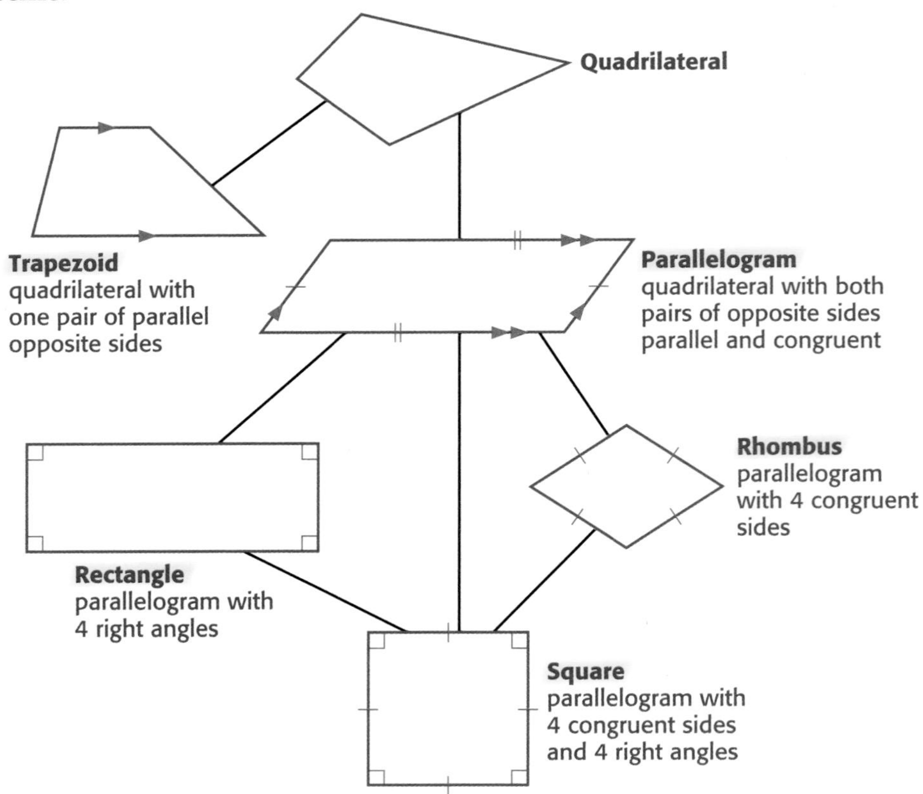

EXAMPLES Classifying Quadrilaterals

Classify each quadrilateral using the name that *best* describes it.

1

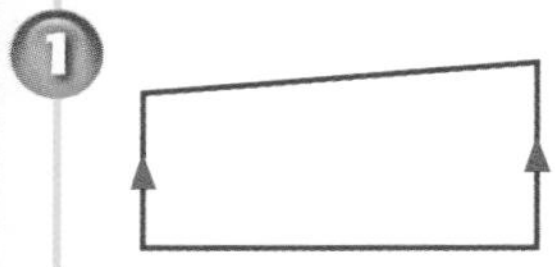

The quadrilateral has one pair of parallel sides. It is a trapezoid.

2

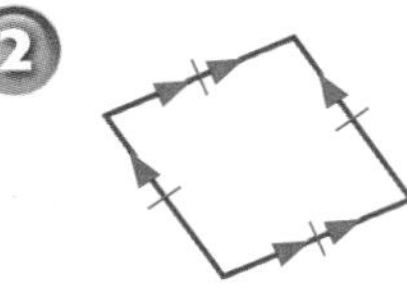

The quadrilateral is a parallelogram with four congruent sides. It is a rhombus.

Exercises

Classify each quadrilateral using the best name that describes it.

1. 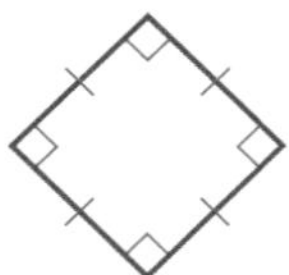
2. 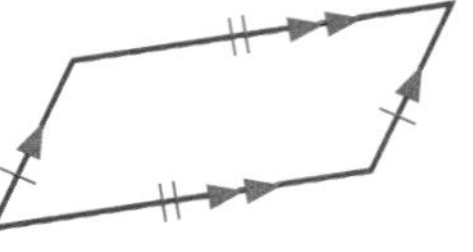
3. 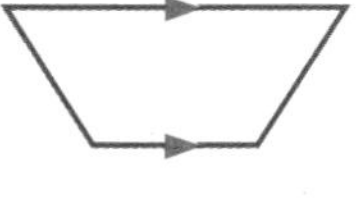
4. 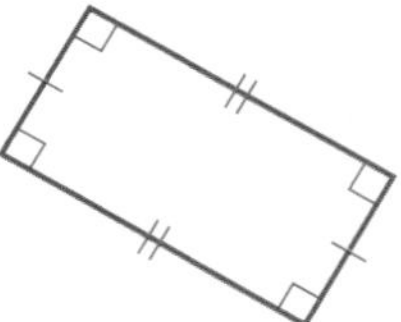
5. 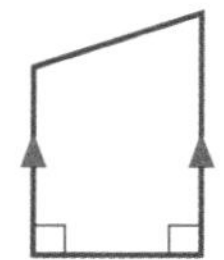
6. 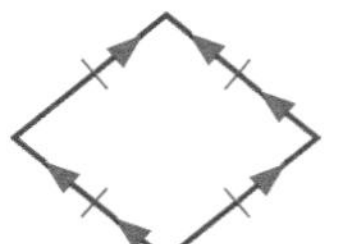
7. 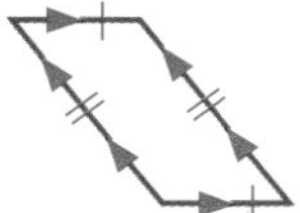
8. 

Perimeter and Area of Parallelograms, Triangles, and Trapezoids

7.A.3b Apply the concepts and attributes of length, capacity, weight/mass, **perimeter, area,** volume, time, temperature and angle measures in practical situations.
7.C.3b Use concrete and graphic **models and appropriate formulas to find perimeters, areas,** surface areas and volumes **of two-** and three-**dimensional regions.**

Several formulas for perimeter are shown in the table.

Shape	Formula	Model
Parallelogram	$P = 2(b) + 2(c)$	b, c, h
Triangle	$P = b + c + d$	c, h, d, b
Trapezoid	$P = b_1 + b_2 + c + d$	b_1, d, c, b_2

EXAMPLE Find Perimeter of a Triangle

1 Find the perimeter of the triangle.

The length of the base is 30 meters. The length of the two sides are 24 and 16 meters.

24 m, 16 m, 30 m

Estimate $P = 20 + 20 + 30$ or 70 m

$P = b + c + d$ Perimeter of a triangle

$P = 30 + 24 + 16$ Replace b with 30, c with 24, and d with 16.

$P = 30 + 24 + 16$ or 70 Simplify.

The perimeter of the triangle is 70 meters. Compare to the estimate.

Exercises

Measure the sides of each figure to the nearest $\frac{1}{16}$ inch. Then find the perimeter.

1. 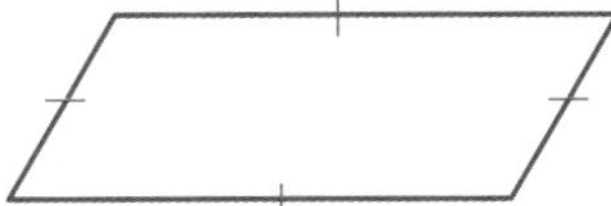

2. 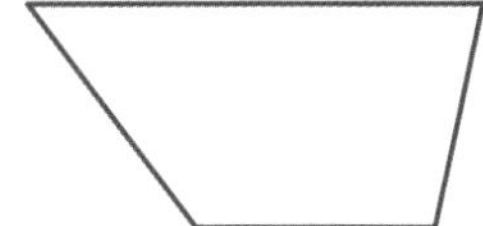

3. 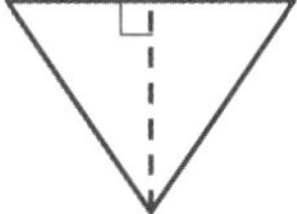

Measure the sides of each figure to the nearest millimeter. Then find the perimeter.

4. 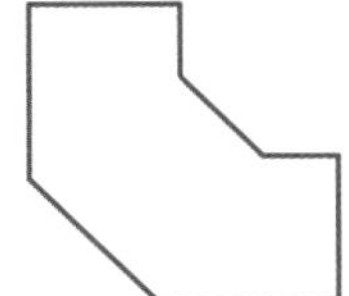

5. 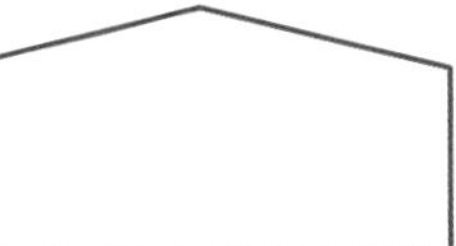

6. 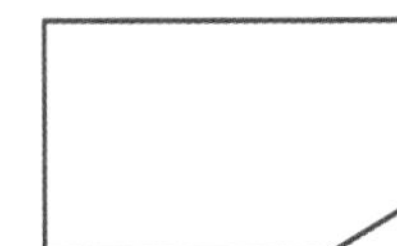

Area formulas are shown in the table below.

Shape	Formula	Model
Parallelogram	$A = bh$	
Triangle	$A = \frac{1}{2}bh$	
Trapezoid	$A = \frac{1}{2}h(b_1 + b_2)$	

EXAMPLE Find the Area of a Trapezoid

2 Find the area of the trapezoid.

The height is 4 yards. The lengths of the bases are 7 yards and 3 yards.

$A = \frac{1}{2}h(b_1 + b_2)$ Area of a trapezoid

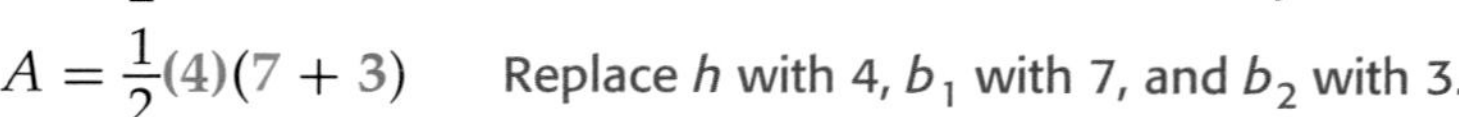

$A = \frac{1}{2}(4)(7 + 3)$ Replace h with 4, b_1 with 7, and b_2 with 3.

$A = \frac{1}{2}(4)(10)$ or 20 Simplify.

The area is 20 square yards.

Exercises

Find the area of each figure.

7.

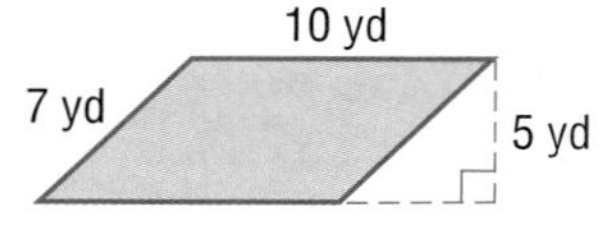

8.

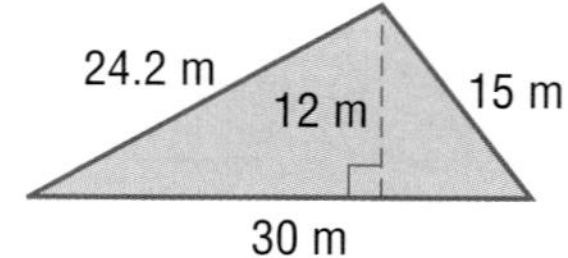

9.

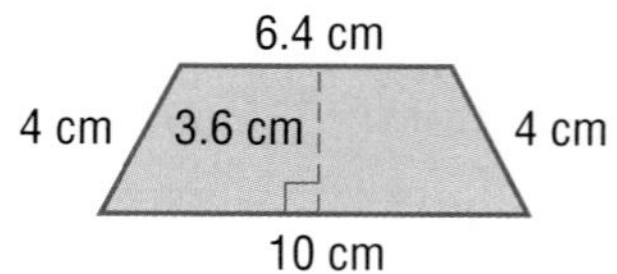

10.

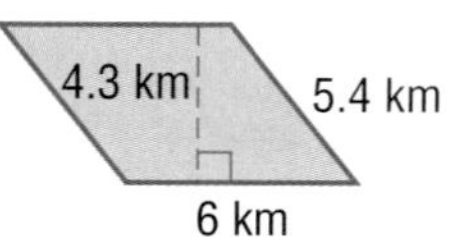

11.

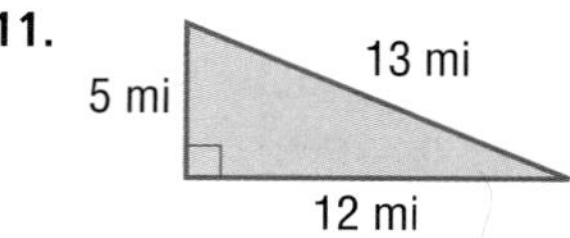

12.

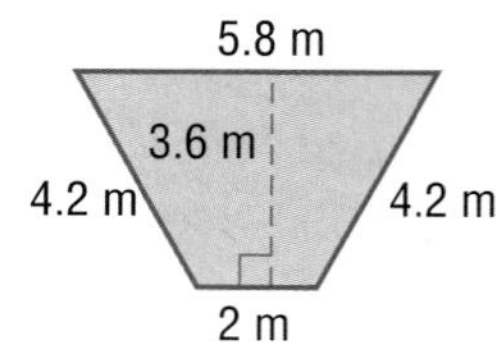

13. Compare the formulas for the perimeter and area of parallelograms, triangles, and trapezoids.

ILS **7.C.3b Use** concrete and graphic models and **appropriate formulas to find** perimeters, areas, surface areas and **volumes of** two- and **three-dimensional regions.** *Also addresses 7.A.3b, 9.B.3.*

8 Properties and Volumes of Spheres

A **sphere** is the set of all points in space that are a given distance from a given point, called the center. A sphere does not contain any bases. To find the volume of a sphere, use the following formula.

Volume of a Sphere

Key Concept

Words The volume V of a sphere is four thirds the product of π and the cube of the radius r.

Model

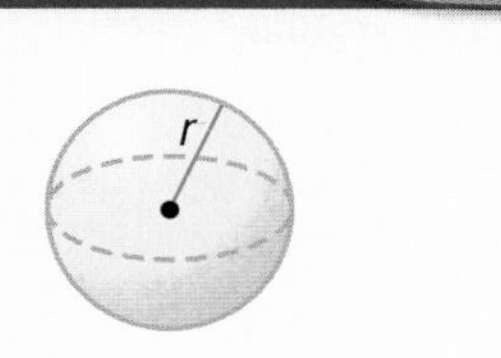

Symbols $V = \frac{4}{3}\pi r^3$

EXAMPLE Find the Volume of a Sphere

1 TOYS Find the volume of the soccer ball.

$V = \frac{4}{3}\pi r^3$ Volume of a sphere

$V = \frac{4}{3} \cdot \pi \cdot 11^3$ Replace r with 11.

$V = 5{,}575.3$ Simplify.

The volume of the soccer ball is about 5,575.3 cubic centimeters.

Exercises

Find the volume of each sphere. Round to the nearest tenth.

1. 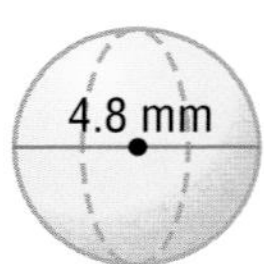

2. 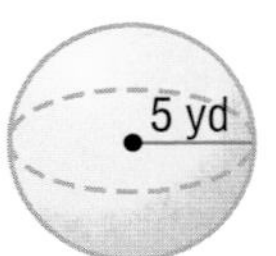

3. 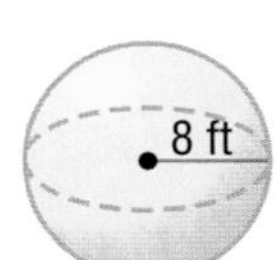

4. 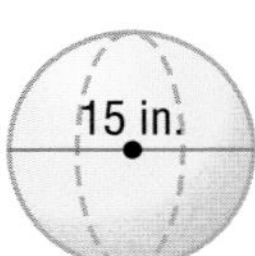

5. 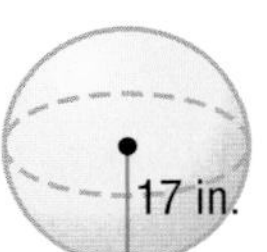

6. 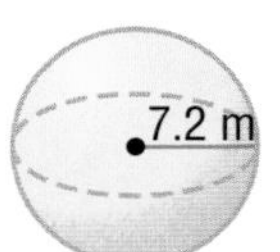

7. **NATURE** The eggs of a hummingbird are nearly spherical in shape. If the hummingbird's eggs are 1 centimeter in diameter, find the volume of one egg. Round to the nearest tenth.

8. **CIRCUS** A clown is juggling 4 balls. If the diameter of each ball is 2 inches, what is the volume of one ball? Round to the nearest tenth.

9. Write about a real-world situation that can be solved by finding the volume of a sphere.

Converting Within Measurement Systems

ILS **7.A.3b Apply the concepts and attributes of length, capacity, weight/mass,** perimeter, area, volume, time, temperature and angle measures **in practical situations.**

The relationships among the most commonly used customary and metric units of measurement are shown in the table.

Measurement Conversions	
Customary Units	**Metric Units**
Length	
1 foot (ft) = 12 inches (in.) 1 yard (yd) = 3 feet 1 mile (mi) = 5,280 feet	1 meter (m) = 1,000 millimeters (mm) 1 meter (m) = 100 centimeters (cm) 1 kilometer (km) = 1,000 meters
Weight	**Mass**
1 pound (lb) = 16 ounces (oz) 1 ton (T) = 2,000 pounds	1 gram (g) = 1,000 milligrams (mg) 1 kilogram (kg) = 1,000 grams
Capacity	
1 cup (c) = 8 fluid ounces (fl oz) 1 pint (pt) = 2 cups 1 quart (qt) = 2 pints 1 gallon (gal) = 4 quarts	1 liter (L) = 1,000 milliliters (mL) 1 kiloliter (kL) = 1,000 liters
Time	
1 minute (min) = 60 seconds (s) 1 hour (h) = 60 minutes 1 day (d) = 24 hours	1 week (wk) = 7 days 1 year (yr) = 365 days
Temperature	
Fahrenheit to Celsius	$C = \frac{5}{9}(F - 32)$
Celsius to Fahrenheit	$F = \frac{9}{5}C + 32$

Each relationship in the table can be written as a ratio. To convert measurements, you can use a proportion or a ratio.

EXAMPLES Convert Measurements

1 Convert 12 yards to feet.

Let x represent the number of feet in 12 yards.

$\frac{12 \text{ yards}}{x \text{ feet}} = \frac{1 \text{ yard}}{3 \text{ feet}}$ Write a proportion.

$12 \cdot 3 = x \cdot 1$ Find the cross products.

$36 = x$ Simplify.

So, 12 yards = 36 feet.

2 Convert 750 milliliters to liters.

Since 1 liter = 1,000 milliliters, multiply 750 milliliters by the ratio $\frac{1 \text{ L}}{1{,}000 \text{ mL}}$.

$750 \text{ mL} = 750 \text{ mL} \cdot \frac{1 \text{ L}}{1{,}000 \text{ mL}}$ Multiply by $\frac{1 \text{ L}}{1{,}000 \text{ mL}}$.

$= 750 \text{ \cancel{mL}} \cdot \frac{1 \text{ L}}{1{,}000 \text{ \cancel{mL}}}$ Divide out common units, leaving the desired unit, liters.

$= \frac{750}{1{,}000} \text{ L or } 0.75 \text{ L}$ Divide.

So, 750 milliliters = 0.75 liter.

You can also use unit analysis to convert measurements.

EXAMPLE Multi-Step Conversions

3 Convert 2 hours to seconds.

$$2\text{ h} = 2\text{ h} \cdot \frac{60\text{ min}}{1\text{ h}} \cdot \frac{60\text{ s}}{1\text{ min}}$$

$$= 2\cancel{\text{h}} \cdot \frac{60\cancel{\text{min}}}{1\cancel{\text{h}}} \cdot \frac{60\text{ s}}{1\cancel{\text{min}}}$$ Divide out common units, leaving the desired unit, seconds.

$$= 2 \cdot 60 \cdot 60\text{ s or } 7{,}200\text{ s}$$ Multiply.

So, 2 hours = 7,200 seconds.

Exercises

Complete.

1. 2 mi = ■ ft
2. 2500 g = ■ kg
3. 120 min = ■ h
4. 5 gal = ■ qt
5. 8.25 kg = ■ g
6. 8000 mg = ■ g
7. 150 ft = ■ yd
8. 80°F = ■ °C
9. 9.25 L = ■ mL
10. 655 mL = ■ L
11. 49 d = ■ wk
12. 72 in. = ■ ft
13. 20 wk = ■ d
14. 14 lb = ■ oz
15. 15°C = ■ °F
16. 4,570 mm = ■ m
17. 8.5 T = ■ lb
18. 72.6 cm = ■ mm
19. 79 m = ■ km
20. 63,360 ft = ■ mi
21. 0.625 km = ■ m

Use unit analysis to make each conversion.

22. 24 c = ■ gal
23. 25 km = ■ mm
24. 60,000 mg = ■ kg
25. 5 T = ■ oz
26. 5 d = ■ min
27. 190,080 in. = ■ mi
28. 5 km = ■ cm
29. 12 gal = ■ c
30. 425,000 mg = ■ kg
31. 10 pt = ■ gal
32. 14,080 yd = ■ mi
33. 82,500 cm = ■ km
34. 4,500 min = ■ d
35. 12 kg = ■ mg
36. 1 d = ■ s
37. 15.5 km = ■ cm
38. 1 mi = ■ yd
39. 24,000 oz = ■ T

40. **FISH** The average weight of bass in a certain pond is 40 ounces. About how many pounds does a bass weigh?

WORLD RECORDS For Exercises 41–43, use the table at the right.

41. How many centimeters long is the longest distance jumped on a pogo stick?
42. How many meters long are the longest ears on a dog?
43. How many meters long is the longest distance ridden on a lawn mower?

Record	Length
Longest Distance Jumped on a Pogo Stick	37.18 km
Greatest Distance Walked with a Milk Bottle Balanced on the Head	130.3 km
Longest Lawn Mover Ride	23,487.5 km
Longest Ears on a Dog	34.9 cm

Source: Guinness World Records

Concepts and Skills Bank

10 Converting Between Measurement Systems

ILS **7.A.3b Apply the concepts and attributes of length, capacity, weight/mass,** perimeter, area, volume, time, temperature and angle measures **in practical situations.**

Dimensional analysis is the process of including units of measurement as factors when you compute. You can use dimensional analysis to convert measurements between the two common measurement systems. The table shows conversion factors for units of length, capacity, and mass or weight.

Conversion Factors for Length	
1 in. ≈ 2.54 cm	1 yard ≈ 0.914 m
1 ft ≈ 0.305 m	1 mi ≈ 1.609 km
Conversion Factors for Capacity and Mass or Weight	
1 fl oz ≈ 29.574 mL	1 qt ≈ 0.946 L
1 pt ≈ 0.473 L	1 gal ≈ 3.785 L
1 oz ≈ 28.35 g	1 lb ≈ 0.454 kg

EXAMPLE Convert Between Systems

1 Convert 9 centimeters to inches.

Use 1 in. ≈ 2.54 cm.

$9 \text{ cm} \approx 9 \text{ cm} \cdot \frac{1 \text{ in.}}{2.54 \text{ cm}}$ Since 1 in. ≈ 2.54 cm, multiply by $\frac{1 \text{ in.}}{2.54 \text{ cm}}$.

$\approx 9 \cancel{\text{cm}} \cdot \frac{1 \text{ in.}}{2.54 \cancel{\text{cm}}}$ Divide out common units, leaving the desired unit, inch.

$\approx \frac{9 \text{ in.}}{2.54}$ or 3.54 in. Multiply.

So, 9 centimeters is approximately 3.54 inches.

EXAMPLE Convert Units Using Multi-Steps

2 SLOTHS A sloth's top speed is 1.9 kilometer per hour. How fast is this in feet per second?

To convert kilometers to feet, use conversion factors relating kilometers to miles and miles to feet.

To convert hours to seconds, use conversion factors relating hours to minutes and minutes to seconds.

$\frac{1.9 \text{ km}}{1 \text{ h}} \cdot \frac{1 \text{ mi}}{1.6093 \text{ km}} \cdot \frac{5{,}280 \text{ ft}}{1 \text{ mi}} \cdot \frac{1 \text{ h}}{60 \text{ min}} \cdot \frac{1 \text{ min}}{60 \text{ s}}$

$= \frac{1.9 \cancel{\text{km}}}{1 \cancel{\text{h}}} \cdot \frac{1 \cancel{\text{mi}}}{1.6093 \cancel{\text{km}}} \cdot \frac{5{,}280 \text{ ft}}{1 \cancel{\text{mi}}} \cdot \frac{1 \cancel{\text{h}}}{60 \cancel{\text{min}}} \cdot \frac{1 \cancel{\text{min}}}{60 \text{ s}}$ Divide out common units.

$= \frac{10{,}032 \text{ ft}}{5{,}793.48 \text{ s}}$ Multiply.

$= \frac{1.73 \text{ ft}}{1 \text{ s}}$ Divide.

The sloth's top speed is 1.73 feet per second.

Exercises

Complete each conversion. Round to the nearest hundredth.

1. 5 in. ≈ ■ cm	**2.** 12 in. ≈ ■ cm
3. 15 cm ≈ ■ in.	**4.** 8.2 cm ≈ ■ in.
5. 20 oz/min ≈ ■ qt/day	**6.** 70 mph ≈ ■ ft/sec
7. 2 L ≈ ■ qt	**8.** 10 mL ≈ ■ fl oz
9. 2,000 lb ≈ ■ kg	**10.** 63.5 kg ≈ ■ lb
11. 16 fl oz/h ≈ ■ mL/min	**12.** 150 fl oz/day ≈ ■ L/h
13. 52 mi/h ≈ ■ km/min	**14.** 15 gal/h ≈ ■ L/min
15. 6 in. ≈ ■ cm	**16.** 1.6 cm ≈ ■ in.
17. 4 qt ≈ ■ L	**18.** 50 mL ≈ ■ fl oz
19. 50 mph ≈ ■ ft/sec	**20.** 50 gal/h ≈ ■ L/min
21. 350 cm/sec ≈ ■ in/min	**22.** 15 km/min ≈ ■ mph

23. How many inches are in 54 centimeters?

24. Convert 17 miles to kilometers

25. How many pounds are there in 19 kilograms?

26. Convert 1.4 quarts to milliliters.

27. In meters per second, how fast is 1,550 feet per minute?

28. A storage bin is being filled at a rate of 2,350 lb/h. What is the rate in kg/min?

Determine which is greater.

29. 3 gal, 10 L **30.** 14 oz, 0.4 kg **31.** 4 mi, 6.2 km

32. COMPUTERS A notebook computer has a mass of 2.25 kilograms. About how many pounds does the notebook weigh?

33. MILEAGE A certain SUV can travel an average of 18 miles per gallon of gasoline. How many kilometers can the SUV travel with one liter of gasoline?

34. COOKING When preparing to cook, Joanna can chop 2 pounds of carrots in 3 minutes. How many ounces can she chop per second?

35. CARS A vehicle can travel 11 kilometers per liter of gasoline. How many miles per gallon is this?

36. WATER Which is greater, a bottle containing 64 fluid ounces of water or a bottle containing 2 liters of water?

37. FOOD Which is greater, a 1.5-pound box of raisins or a 650-gram box of raisins?

11 Probability of Simple Events

ILS **10.C.3a Determine the probability** and odds **of events** using fundamental counting principles.

A **simple event** is a specific outcome or type of outcome. **Probability** is the chance that something will happen. The probability of an event is a ratio that compares the number of favorable outcomes to the number of possible outcomes. The probability that an event will happen is between 1 and 0. A probability can be expressed as a fraction, a decimal, or a percent.

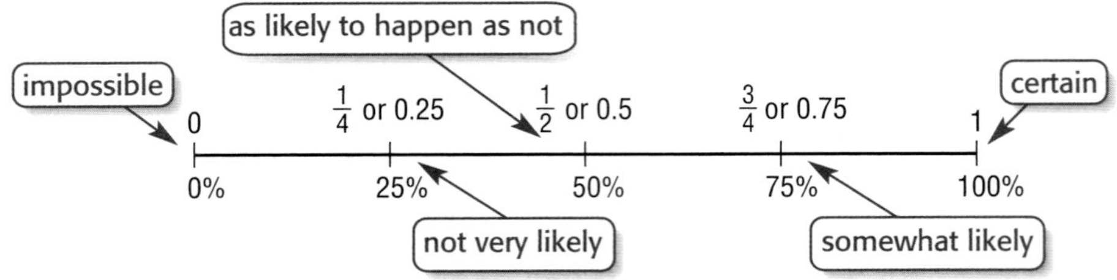

EXAMPLE Find Probabilities

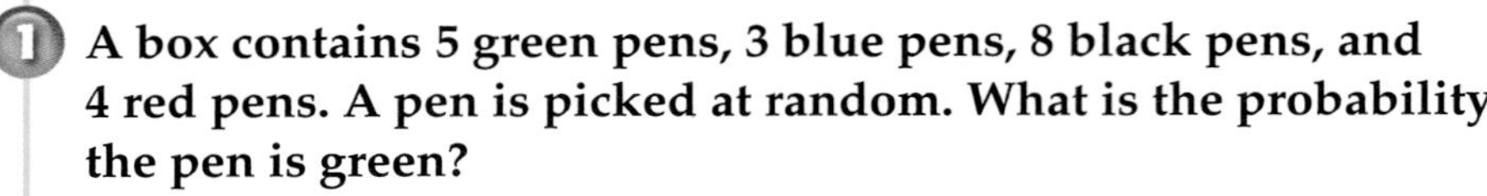

1 A box contains 5 green pens, 3 blue pens, 8 black pens, and 4 red pens. A pen is picked at random. What is the probability the pen is green?

There are 5 + 3 + 8 + 4 or 20 pens in the box.

$$P(\text{green}) = \frac{\text{green pens}}{\text{total number of pens}} \quad \text{Definition of probability}$$

$$= \frac{5}{20} \text{ or } \frac{1}{4} \quad \text{There are 5 green pens out of 20 pens.}$$

The probability the pen is green is $\frac{1}{4}$. The probability can also be written as 0.25 or 25%.

Exercises

The spinner is used for a game. Write each probability as a fraction, a decimal, and a percent.

1. $P(5)$
2. $P(\text{even})$
3. $P(\text{greater than } 5)$
4. $P(\textit{not } 2)$
5. $P(\text{an integer})$
6. $P(\text{less than } 7)$
7. **COINS** A jar has 11 nickels, 28 dimes, 39 pennies, 22 quarters, and 8 silver dollars. What is the probability that the first coin picked is a silver dollar?

A beanbag is tossed on the square at the right. It lands at random in a small square. Write each probability as a fraction, a decimal, and a percent.

8. $P(\text{red})$
9. $P(\text{blue})$
10. $P(\text{white or yellow})$
11. $P(\text{blue or red})$
12. $P(\textit{not } \text{green})$
13. $P(\text{brown})$
14. **MONTHS** What is the probability that a month picked at random starts with the letter J?

12 Geometric Probability

ILS 10.C.3b Analyze problem situations (e.g., board games, grading scales) and make predictions about results.

Recall that the probability of an event is defined as the ratio of the number of ways an event can happen to the number of possible outcomes. Probability can also be related to the area of a figure.

Probability and Area — Key Concept

Words The probability of landing in a specific region of a target is the ratio of the area of the specific region to the area of the target.

Symbols $P(\text{specific region}) = \dfrac{\text{area of specific region}}{\text{area of the target}}$

EXAMPLES Find Probability Using Area Models

1 **Find the probability that a randomly thrown dart will land in the shaded region of the dartboard. Assume all darts land on the dartboard.**

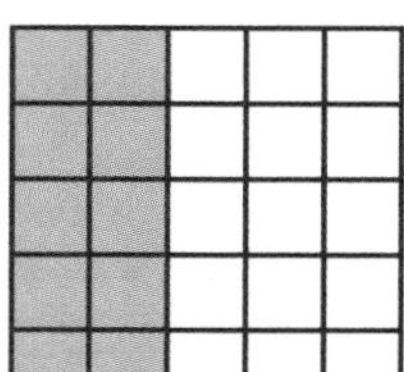
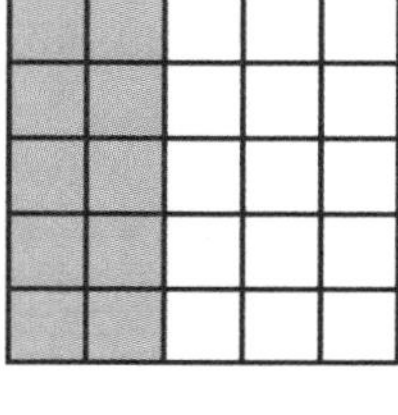

$$P(\text{shaded region}) = \frac{\text{area of shaded region}}{\text{area of the target}}$$
$$= \frac{10}{25} \text{ or } \frac{2}{5}$$

So, the probability is $\frac{2}{5}$, 0.4, or 40%.

2 **To win a penny toss game at the school carnival, you must toss a penny in the red section of the square board. What is the probability that a penny that lands on the board will land in the red section?**

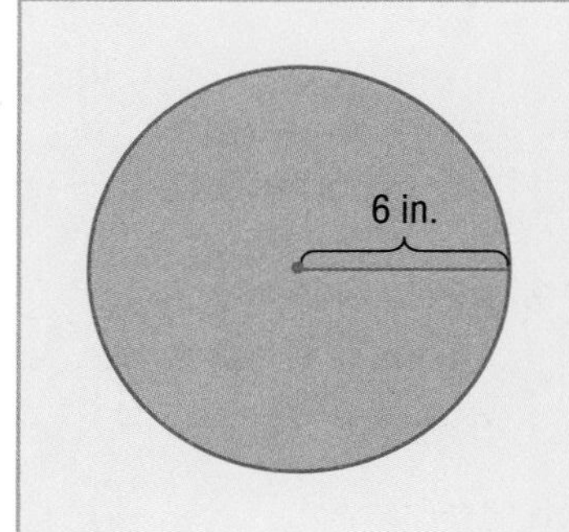

To find the probability of landing in the red section, find the area of the red section and the area of the entire board.

Area of red section $= \pi \cdot r^2$	Area of a circle
$= \pi \cdot 6^2$	Replace r with 6.
$= 36\pi$	Multiply 6 by 6.
≈ 113	Simplify.

The area of the red circle is about 113 square inches.

Area of the square $= s^2$
$= 16^2$ or 256

$$P(\text{landing in the red section}) = \frac{\text{area of red section}}{\text{total area}}$$
$$\approx \frac{113}{256}$$

So, the probability is about $\frac{113}{256}$ or 44%.

Concepts and Skills Bank

Exercises

Find the probability that a randomly thrown dart will land in the shaded region of each dartboard. Write the probability as a fraction, decimal, and percent.

1. 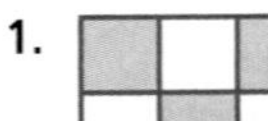
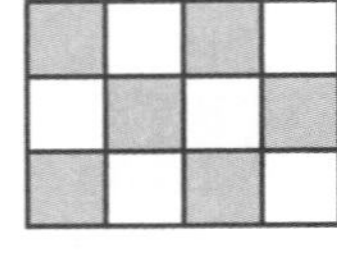

2. 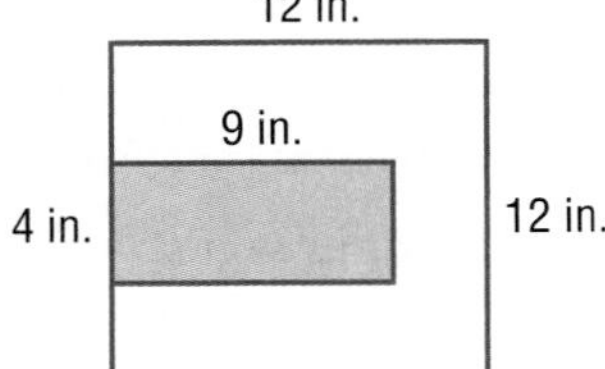

3. 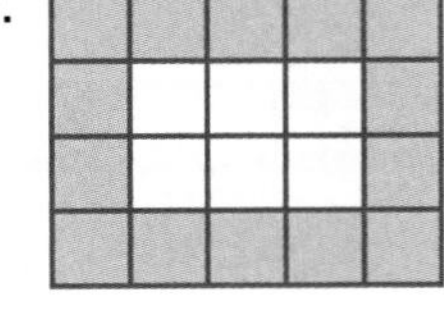

4. 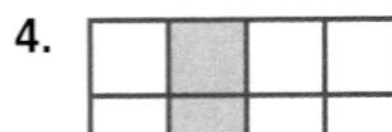

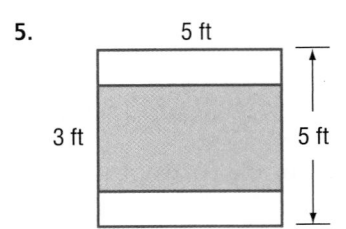

5.
5 ft
3 ft
5 ft

6. 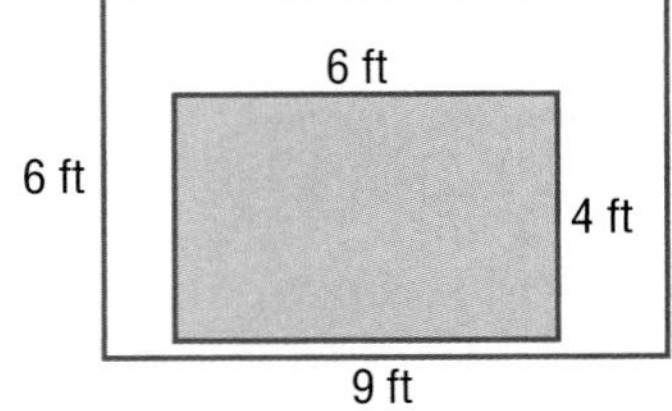

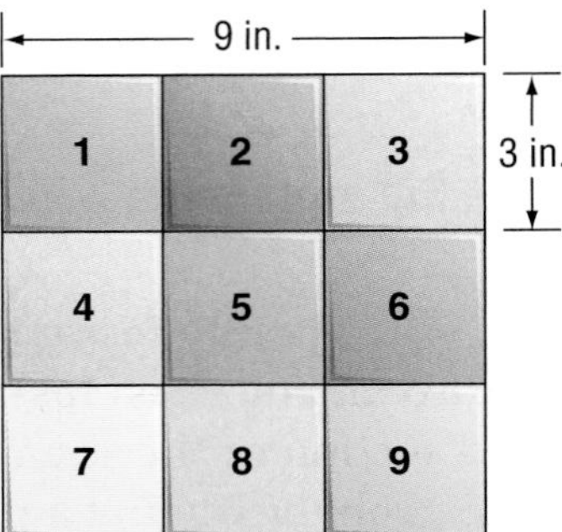

7. **GAMES** To win a prize, a beanbag must land on an even number. It is equally likely that the beanbag will land anywhere on the board shown. What is the probability of winning a prize?

8. **PATIOS** A rectangular patio is 8 feet by 10 feet. At the center of the patio is a rectangular rug that is 4 feet wide and 6 feet long. If a coin is dropped at random on the patio, what is the probability that the coin lands on the rug?

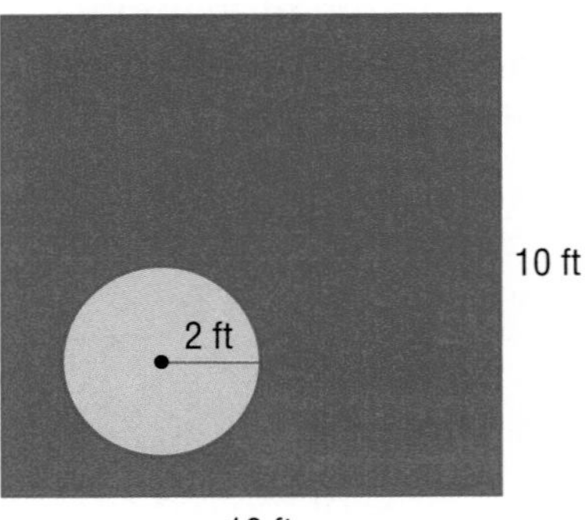

9. **KEYS** A key was lost in the backyard shown. What is the probability that the key is in the circle of freshly planted grass?

10. **FOUNTAINS** A circular flower garden has a diameter of 16 feet. At the center of the garden is a fountain 5 feet in diameter. If a coin is tossed at random into the garden and lands in the garden, what is the probability that the coin will land in the fountain?

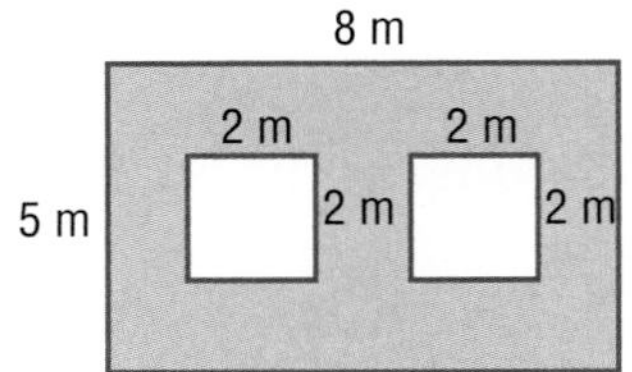

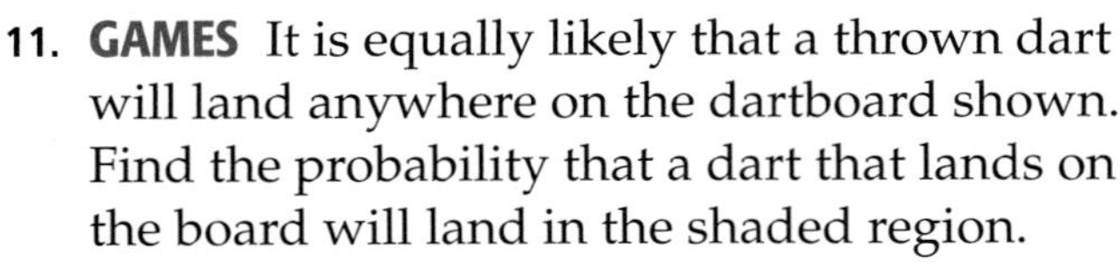

11. **GAMES** It is equally likely that a thrown dart will land anywhere on the dartboard shown. Find the probability that a dart that lands on the board will land in the shaded region.

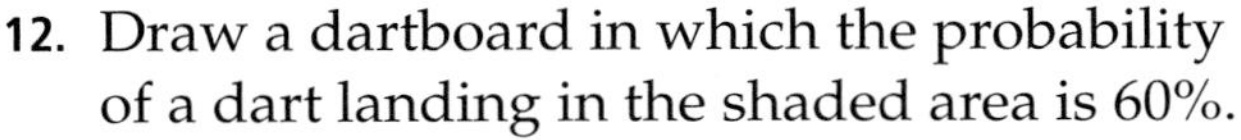

12. Draw a dartboard in which the probability of a dart landing in the shaded area is 60%.

13 Displaying Data in Graphs

10.A.3a Construct, read and interpret tables, graphs (including circle graphs) **and charts to organize and represent data.**

Statistics involves collecting, analyzing, and presenting information, called **data**. Graphs display data to help readers make sense of the information.

- **Bar graphs** are used to compare the frequency of data. The bar graph below compares the average number of vacation days given by countries to their workers.

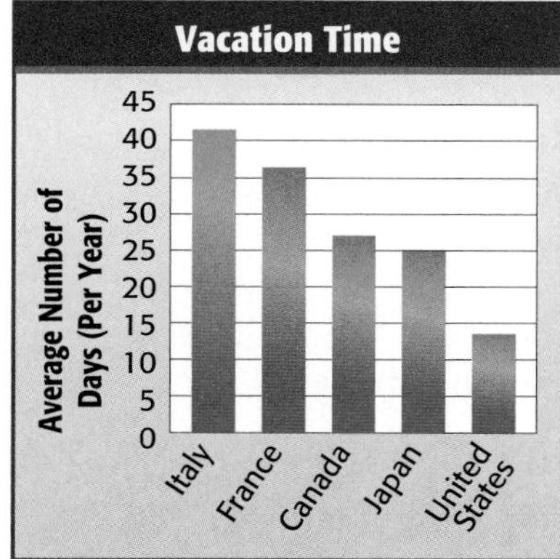

Source: *The World Almanac*

- **Double bar graphs** compare two sets of data. The double bar graph below shows the percent of men and women 65 and older who held jobs in various years.

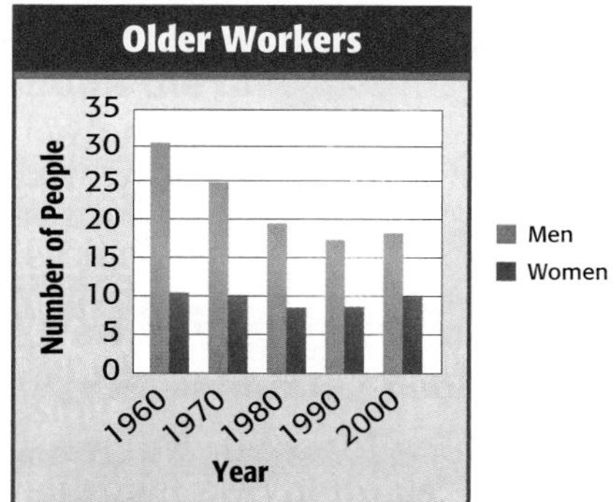

Source: *The World Almanac*

- **Line plots** are diagrams that show the frequency of data on a number line. The line plot below shows the prices of DVDs.

- **Double line graphs**, like double bar graphs, show two sets of data. The double line graph below compares the amount of money spent by both domestic and foreign U.S. travelers.

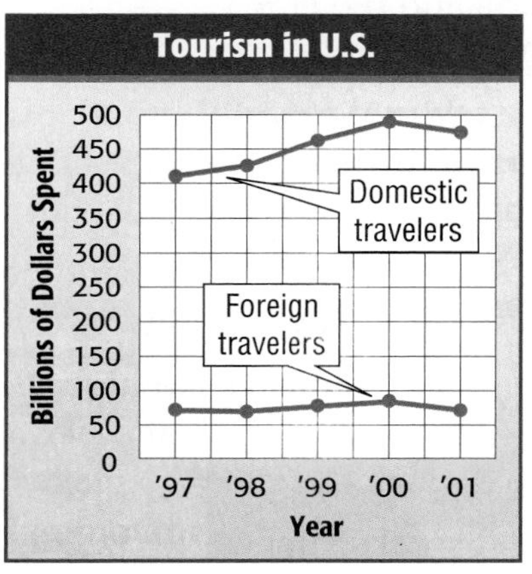

Source: *The World Almanac*

- **Stem-and-leaf plots** are used to condense a set of data where the greatest place value of the data is used for the **stems** and the next greatest place value forms the **leaves**. Each data value can be seen in this type of graph.

The stem-and-leaf plot below contains this list of mathematics test scores:

95 76 64 88 93 68 99 96 74 75 92 80 76 85 91 70 62 81

The least number has 6 in the tens place.

The greatest number has 9 in the tens place.

The stems are 6, 7, 8, and 9.

The leaves are ordered from least to greatest.

Stem	Leaf	
6	2 4 8	
7	0 4 5 6 6	
8	0 1 5 8	
9	1 2 3 5 6 9	*6 | 2 = 62*

EXAMPLE Choose a Display

1 **Shonny is writing a research paper about the Olympics for her social studies class. She wants to include a graph that shows the number of participants from each country in the 2006 Winter Olympics. Should she use a line plot, bar graph, or stem-and-leaf plot?**

Since the data would compare the number of participants from each country, she should choose a bar graph.

Exercises

For Exercises 1–4, determine whether a bar graph, double bar graph, line plot, double line graph, or stem-and-leaf plot is the best way to display each of the following sets of data. Explain your reasoning.

1. the number of cell phones per household in a neighborhood
2. the income of an average household in six different countries
3. the prices for a loaf of bread in twenty different supermarkets
4. the number of boys and the number of girls participating in six different school sports

For Exercises 5–9, refer to the bar graph, double bar graph, line plot, double line graph, and stem-and-leaf plot on page 749.

5. Write several sentences to describe the data shown in the graph titled "Vacation Time." Include a comparison of the days worked for Canada and the U.S.
6. Write several sentences to describe the data shown in the graph titled "Older Workers." What other type or types of graphs could you use to display this data? Explain your reasoning.
7. Write several sentences to describe the data shown in the graph titled "Tourism in U.S." What other type or types of graphs could you use to display this data? Explain your reasoning.
8. Write several sentences to describe the data shown in the graph titled "DVD Prices." What other type or types of graphs could you use to display this data? Explain your reasoning.
9. Write several sentences to describe the data shown in the stem-and-leaf plot of mathematics test scores. What is an advantage of showing the scores in this type of graph?

For Exercises 10–12, use the stem-and-leaf plot that shows the number of stories in the tallest buildings in Dallas, Texas.

10. How many buildings does the stem-and-leaf plot represent?
11. How many stories are there for the shortest building in the stem-and-leaf plot? the tallest building?
12. What is the median number of stories for these buildings? the mean number?

Stem	Leaf
2	7 9 9
3	0 1 1 1 3 3 4 4 6 6 7
4	0 2 2 5 9
5	0 0 0 0 2 5 6 8
6	0
7	2 2 | 7 = 27

Concepts and Skills Bank

14 Outliers

10.A.3c Test the reasonableness of an argument based on data and communicate their findings.

Data that is more than 1.5 times the value of the interquartile range beyond the quartiles are called **outliers**. Outliers affect measures of central tendency.

EXAMPLE

1 WAGES The hourly wages of employees at a coffee shop are: \$6, \$5, \$5.75, \$6.50, \$20, \$5.75, and \$7. How does the outlier affect the mean, median, mode, and range?

Calculate each measure with and without the outlier, \$20. Then compare.

	including the outlier	**without the outlier**
mean:	$\frac{\$6 + \$5 + \ldots + \$7}{7} = \$8$	$\frac{\$6 + \$5 + \ldots + \$7}{6} = \$6$
median:	\$6	\$5.88
mode:	\$5.75	\$5.75
range:	\$20 − \$5 = \$15	\$7 − \$5 = \$2

Including the outlier increases the mean by \$8 − \$6 or \$2. The median was affected by \$6 − \$5.88 or \$0.12. The mode was not affected. The range was increased by \$15 − \$2 or \$13.

Exercises

Determine how the inclusion of the outlier affects the mean, median, mode, and range.

1. length in yards of spools of ribbon: 60, 48, 36, 144, and 72
2. cost in dollars of concert tickets: 37, 50, 40, 15, 50, and 48
3. number of words in a magazine article: 100, 118, 115, 97, 40, and 100
4. cost in dollars of a scarf and hat set: 25, 22, 18, 16, 60, 30, and 25

5. **E-MAIL** The table shows the number of junk e-mails Petra received over the last 10 days. Which measure of central tendency is most affected by the exclusion of the outlier for the number of e-mails received?

Junk E-Mails				
10	12	15	10	11
8	30	10	10	9

6. **CAPACITY** The table shows the maximum capacity of classrooms at Monroe Middle School. Which is most affected by the inclusion of the outlier: mean, median, mode, or range?

Room Capacity				
40	42	35	41	39
36	38	41	36	35
38	16	40	37	48
39	35	42	10	40

7. Find real-world data that includes an outlier. Display the data in a graph. Then make the same graph without the inclusion of the outlier. Compare the two graphs.

Concepts and Skills Bank

Misleading Statistics

10.A.3a Construct, read and interpret tables, graphs (including circle graphs) **and charts to organize and represent data.**
10.A.3c Test the reasonableness of an argument based on data and communicate their findings.

Two graphs that represent the same data may look quite different. If different vertical scales are used, each graph will give a different visual impression.

EXAMPLES Misleading Graphs

TRAVEL The graphs show the growth of the cruise industry.

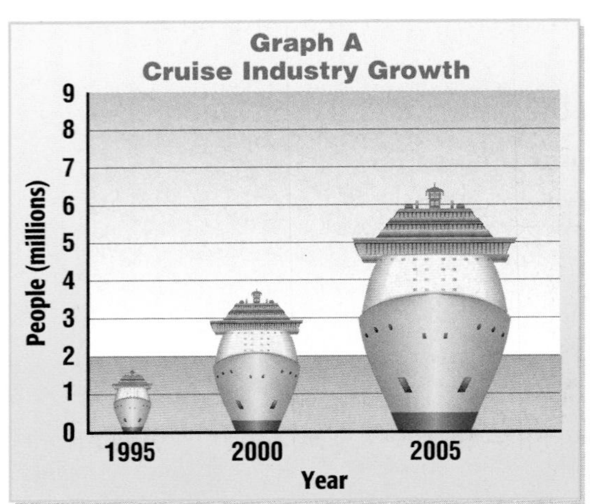

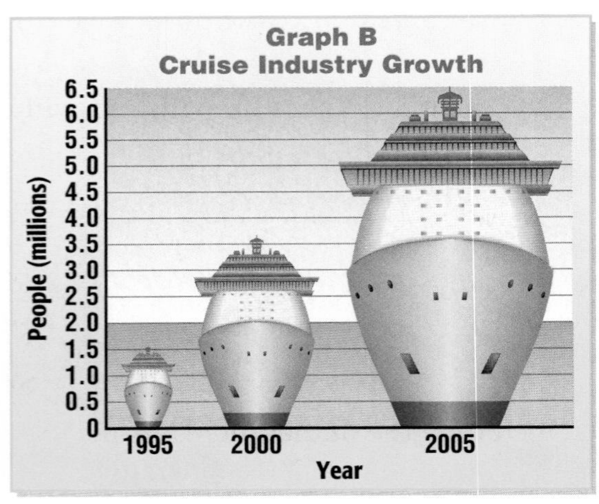

1. **Why do the graphs look different?**

   The vertical scales differ.

2. **Which graph appears to show a greater increase in the growth of the cruise industry? Explain.**

   Graph B; the size of the ship makes the increase appear more dramatic because both the height and width of the ship are increasing.

When reading a statistical graph, you must interpret the information carefully and determine whether the inference made from the data is valid.

EXAMPLE Accuracy of Predictions and Conclusions

3. **FAIRS According to the graph, the number of people did not increase as fast from 2005–2009 as it did from 1990–2005. Determine whether this statement is accurate. Justify your reasoning.**

   No, the statement is not accurate. The horizontal scale is inconsistent; from 1990 to 2005, the interval is 5 years, but the interval is 1 year from 2005 to 2009.

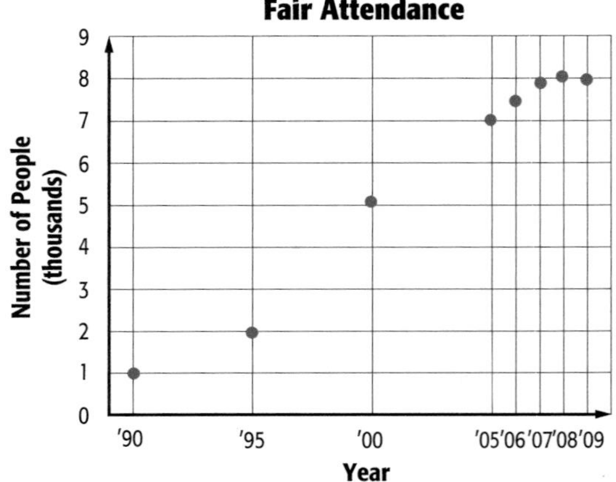

Concepts and Skills Bank

Area formulas are shown in the table below.

Shape	Formula	Model
Parallelogram	$A = bh$	b, h
Triangle	$A = \frac{1}{2}bh$	h, b
Trapezoid	$A = \frac{1}{2}h(b_1 + b_2)$	b_1, h, b_2

EXAMPLE Find the Area of a Trapezoid

2 Find the area of the trapezoid.

The height is 4 yards. The lengths of the bases are 7 yards and 3 yards.

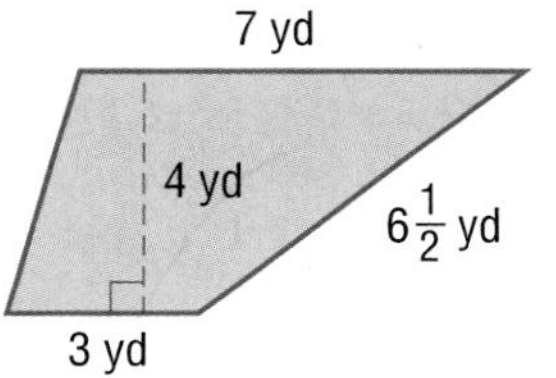

$A = \frac{1}{2}h(b_1 + b_2)$ Area of a trapezoid

$A = \frac{1}{2}(4)(7 + 3)$ Replace h with 4, b_1 with 7, and b_2 with 3.

$A = \frac{1}{2}(4)(10)$ or 20 Simplify.

The area is 20 square yards.

Exercises

Find the area of each figure.

7.
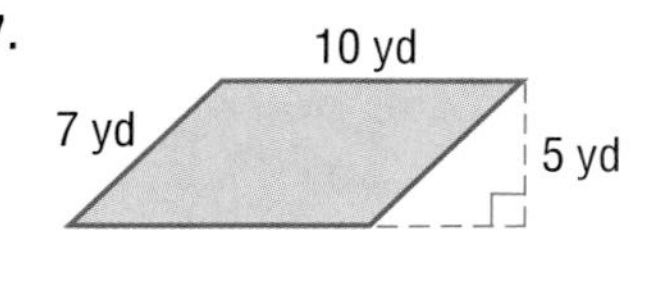

8.
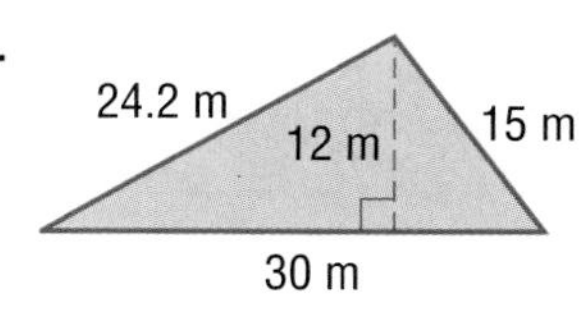

9.
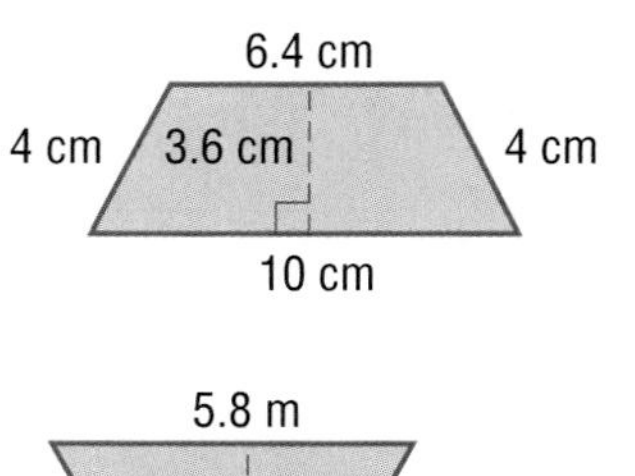

10. 4.3 km 5.4 km 6 km

11.
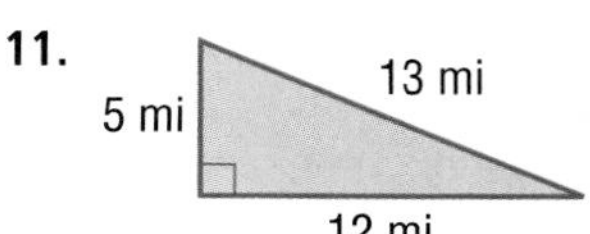

12.
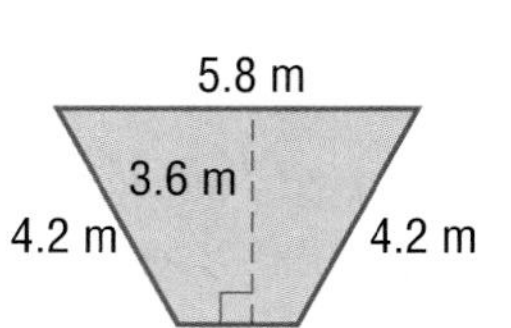

13. Compare the formulas for the perimeter and area of parallelograms, triangles, and trapezoids.

7 Perimeter and Area of Parallelograms, Triangles, and Trapezoids

ILS 7.A.3b Apply the concepts and attributes of length, capacity, weight/ mass, **perimeter, area,** volume, time, temperature and angle measures in practical situations.
7.C.3b Use concrete and graphic **models and appropriate formulas to find perimeters, areas,** surface areas and volumes **of two-** and three-**dimensional regions.**

Several formulas for perimeter are shown in the table.

Shape	Formula	Model
Parallelogram	$P = 2(b) + 2(c)$	
Triangle	$P = b + c + d$	
Trapezoid	$P = b_1 + b_2 + c + d$	

EXAMPLE Find Perimeter of a Triangle

1 Find the perimeter of the triangle.

The length of the base is 30 meters. The length of the two sides are 24 and 16 meters.

24 m, 16 m, 30 m

Estimate $P = 20 + 20 + 30$ or 70 m

$P = b + c + d$ Perimeter of a triangle

$P = 30 + 24 + 16$ Replace b with 30, c with 24, and d with 16.

$P = 30 + 24 + 16$ or 70 Simplify.

The perimeter of the triangle is 70 meters. Compare to the estimate.

Exercises

Measure the sides of each figure to the nearest $\frac{1}{16}$ inch. Then find the perimeter.

1. 2. 3.

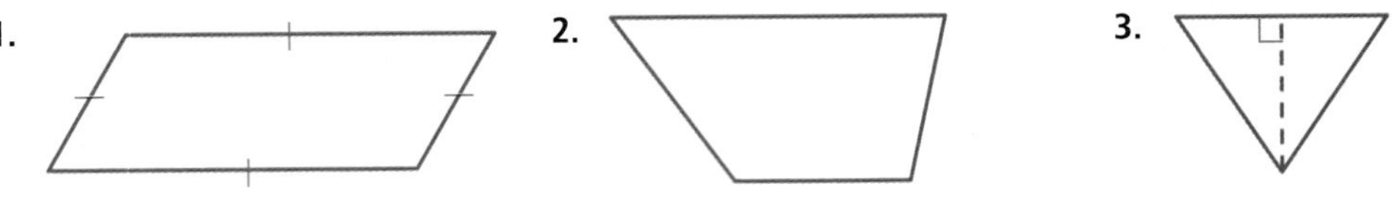

Measure the sides of each figure to the nearest millimeter. Then find the perimeter.

4. 5. 6.

Exercises

MOVIES For Exercises 1 and 2, refer to the graphs below.

Top Five All Time Movies Graph A

Top Five All Time Movies Graph B

1. Which graph gives the impression that the top all-time movie made far more money than any other top all-time movie?
2. Which graph shows that movie C made nearly as much money as the other top movies?

JOBS For Exercises 3 and 4, refer to the graphs below.

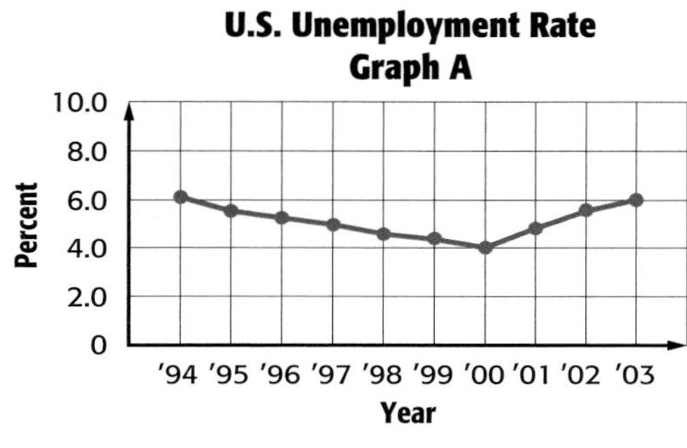

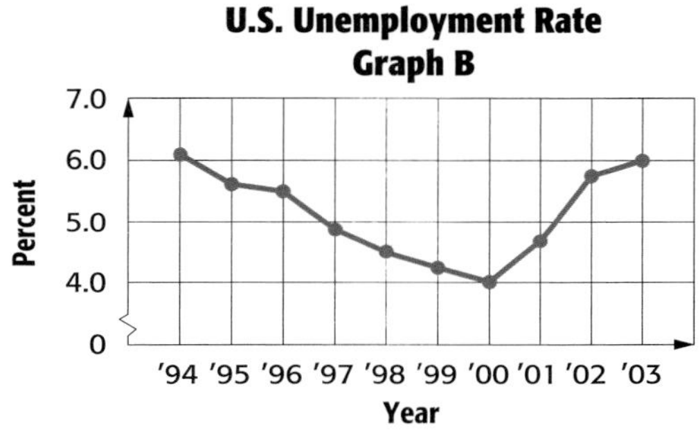

3. What causes the graphs to differ in their appearance?
4. Which graph appears to show that unemployment rates have increased rapidly since 2000? Explain your reasoning.
5. **COMMUNICATION** The graph shows the number of area codes in the U.S. in two years. According to the graph, it appears that the number of area codes increased by about four times between 1995 and 2005. Determine whether this statement is accurate. Justify your reasoning.

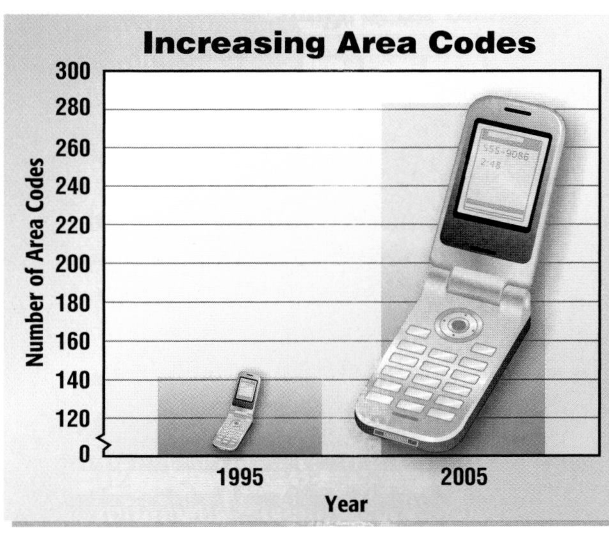

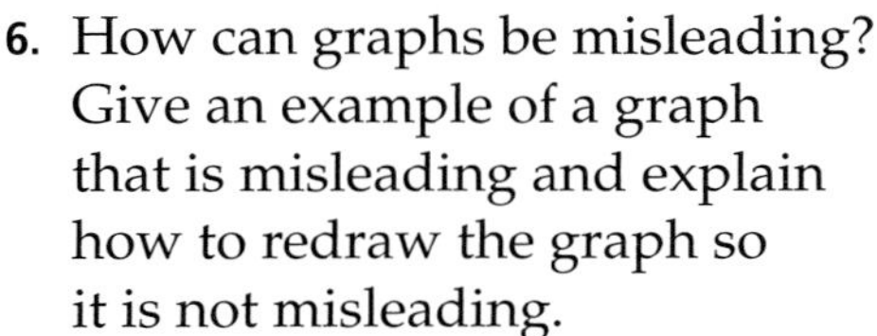

6. How can graphs be misleading? Give an example of a graph that is misleading and explain how to redraw the graph so it is not misleading.

Photo Credits

Cover: Moodboard/CORBIS; **v** Digital Vision/Getty Images; **vi** (tl tc tr bl bc br)Aaron Haupt; **vii** (bl)File Photo, (others)Aaron Haupt; **viii-ix** Panoramic Images/Getty Images; **xv** Panoramic Images/Getty Images; **xvi** EPH/isifa Image Service s.r.o./Alamy; **xviii–xix** Art Wolfe/Stone/Getty Images; **xx–xxi** Pixtal/age fotostock; **xxii–xxiii** Darron Cummings/AP Images; **xxiv–xxv** Beverly Joubert/Getty Images; **xxvi–xxvii** Douglas Peebles Photography/Alamy; **xxviii–xxix** Joe Sohm/Getty Images; **xxx** Gabe Palmer/CORBIS; **IL7** Flip Chalfant/Getty Images; **1** John Evans; **3** Walter Bibikow/CORBIS; **4** John Tomlinson/GreatRiverRoad.com; **5** Chuck Eckert/Alamy; **6** Alan Look/Icon SMI/CORBIS; **7** Dennis Banks; **8** Phil Degginger/Alamy; **9** Reinhard Dirscherl/Getty Images; **10** Peter Beers; **11** Peter Beers; **12** Izzy Schwartz/Photodisc/Getty Images; **13** Ben Bloom/Getty Images; **14** Jerry Lai/AP Images; **15** Brian Kersey/Landov; **16** (l) Jonathan Daniel/Getty Images; (r) Hisham Ibrahim/Getty Images; **17** (tl) Jeff Haynes/AFP/Getty Images; (br) Creatas/PunchStock; **18** (t) Peter Pearson/Getty Images; (bl) Jason Lindsey/Alamy; (br) Chuck Eckert/Alamy; **19** (tl) Kim Karpeles/Alamy, (br) Scott Boehm/Getty Images; **20–21** JupiterImages/Brand X/Alamy; **22** Solstice Photography/Brand X/CORBIS; **24** IT Stock/age fotostock; **25** Gerry Ellis/Digital Vision/Getty Images; **33** Gabe Palmer/CORBIS; **34** (l)Cleve Bryant/PhotoEdit, (r)David Young-Wolff/PhotoEdit; **37** Peter Arnold, Inc./Alamy; **38** David Taylor/Photo Researchers, Inc.; **43** Ross M. Horowitz/The Image Bank/Getty Images; **49** (l)age fotostock/SuperStock, (r)David Young-Wolff/PhotoEdit; **51** Mike Fizer/Transtock Inc./Alamy; **58** AP Images; **60** Joseph Sohm/Visions of America/CORBIS; **61** (l)Andrew Olney/Masterfile, (r)Michael Newman/PhotoEdit; **62** Amos Morgan/Photodisc/Getty Images; **63** Chris Bacon/AP/Wide World Photos; **70** EPH/isifa Image Service s.r.o./Alamy; **71** Aaron Haupt; **72** Paul A. Souders/CORBIS; **82** STScI/NASA/CORBIS; **84** Alexis Rosenfeld/Photo Researchers, Inc.; **86** Michael Zagaris/Stringer/Getty Images; **92** BananaStock/SuperStock; **94** Kevin C. Cox/Getty Images; **98** Joe Marquette/AP Images; **100** (l)Thinkstock/CORBIS, (r)Richard Hutchings/Photo Researchers; **102** Art Wolfe/Stone/Getty Images; **104** Brand X Pictures/PunchStock; **105** (l)Rick and Nora Bowers/Visuals Unlimited, (r)Handout/NABU/M. Delpho/Reuters/CORBIS; **106** Phanie/Photo Researchers; **109** Ian Walton/Staff/Getty Images Sport/Getty Images; **111** (l)Jack Hollingsworth/CORBIS, (r)Skjold Photographs/The Image Works; **114** Kim Karpeles/Alamy; **119** Chris Graythen/Stringer/Getty Images Sport/Getty Images; **120** Kay Nietfeld/epa/CORBIS; **122** Stephen Dunn/Getty Images Sport/Getty images; **124** CMCD/Getty Images; **142** Damir Frkovic/Masterfile; **145** Roger Ressmeyer/CORBIS; **147** Foxtrot ©2002 Bill Amend. Reprinted with permission of Univeral Press Syndicate. All rights reserved.; **149** (l)Yellow Dog Productions/Photodisc/Getty images, (r)Photodisc/Getty Images; **151** (l)JupiterImages/BananaStock/Alamy, (r)Michelle D. Bridwell/PhotoEdit; **152** Kevin Peterson/Photodisc/Getty Images; **157** Chris Ryan/Taxi/Getty Images; **166** (l)First Light/ImageState, (r)Sean Justice/Riser/Getty Images; **167** Profimedia. CZ s.r.o./Alamy Images; **170** Justin Kase/Alamy; **175** Stan Honda/AFP/Getty Images; **186–187** Richard Klune/CORBIS; **188** Jim Zuckerman/CORBIS; **191** Brendan Smialowski/Stringer/Getty; **192** JupiterImages/Comstock; **196** age fotostock/SuperStock; **198** Gary Atkinson/Photonica/Getty Images; **200** Will Kincaid/AP Images; **202** Jim Reed/Photo Researchers; **205** Susie M. Eising/StockFood Creative/Getty Images; **210** Stockbyte/Getty Images; **211** Jeff Greenberg/PhotoEdit; **216** Ryan McVay/Photodisc/Getty Images; **223** Annabella Bluesky/Photo Researchers, Inc.; **224** Mimmo Jodice/CORBIS; **227** Adam Hart-Davis/Photo Researchers; **229** BARNpix.com/Alamy Images; **236** BananaStock/PunchStock; **237** DK Limited/CORBIS; **240** (tl)NASA, (tr)Handout/Reuters/CORBIS, (bl)RubberBall/SuperStock, (br)PNC/Digital Vision/Getty Images; **250** CORBIS; **253** Bettmann/CORBIS; **256** Brooklyn Productions/The Image Bank/Getty Images; **258** David Forbert/SuperStock; **260** (t)Ben Blankenburg/CORBIS, (bl)Bill Aron/PhotoEdit, (br)C Squared Studios/Getty Images; **262** Josh Devins Photography; **265** John Cancalosi/Peter Arnold, Inc.; **269** Underwood & Underwood/CORBIS; **271** (l)Darren Modricker/CORBIS, (r)SW Productions/Photodisc/Getty Images; **272** Barbara Penoyar/Getty Images; **277** Purestock/SuperStock; **279** David Muench/CORBIS; **281** Juan Silva/The Image Bank/Getty Images; **284** Frank Cezus/Photographer's Choice/Getty Images; **285** Hal Pierce, Laboratory for Atmospheres, NASA Goddard Space Flight Center/NOAA; **287** Zave Smith/CORBIS; **289** (l)photodisc/First Light, (r)photodisc/First Light; **290** (t)Car Culture/CORBIS, (b)James Woodson/Digital Vision/Getty Images; **291** PHOTOEDIT/PhotoEdit; **302–303** Chris Windsor/Taxi/Getty Images; **304** Mike Dobel/Alamy; **308** Benelux Press/Taxi/Getty Images; **310** (l)age fotostock/SuperStock, (c)Mike MacCarter, (r)image100/CORBIS; **314** Brand X Pictures/PunchStock; **317** (l)Roger Wood/CORBIS, (r)Bill Aron/PhotoEdit; **318** (tl)George W. Hart, (tr)E.S. Ross/Visuals Unlimited, (b)Allan Friedlander/SuperStock; **322** (l)Peter Bowater/Photo Researchers, Inc., (r)Gjon Mili/Time Life Pictures/Getty Images; **323** Pete Turner/The Image Bank/Getty Images; **327** spaceimaging.com/Getty Images; **328** (l)Michael Newman/PhotoEdit, (b)Photick/SuperStock; **329** Courtesy Ramona Maston/FolkArt.com; **330** (l)Vanni Archive/CORBIS, (r)Samuel R. Maglione/Photo Researchers, Inc.; **334** Don Emmert/AFP/Getty Images; **335** (l)Liu Liqun/CORBIS, (r)Daryl Benson/Masterfile; **340** Silvia Otte/Photonica/Getty Images; **341** David Davis Photoproductions/Alamy; **345** Plate decorated with flame pattern. 16th century, Islamic School, Turkey. Ceramic.;/Louvre, Paris, France, Giraudon/Bridgeman Art Library; **350** Todd Gipstein/CORBIS; **354** Andre Jenny/Alamy; **356** Jonathan Nourok/PhotoEdit; **360** Amos Morgan/Photodisc/Getty Images; **363** AP Photo/Darron Cummings; **364** Bill Bachmann/Photo Researchers, Inc.; **368** Brand X Pictures/Alamy; **370** (tl)Rachel Epstein/PhotoEdit, (tr)Terrance Klassen/Alamy, (c)Steve Hamblin/Alamy, (b)Ken Cavanagh; **371** (l)Atlantide Phototravel/CORBIS, (r)Carsten Reisinger/Alamy; **377** (l)DreamPictures/Taxi/Getty Images, (r)Stewart Cohen/Getty Images; **379** Todd Yarrington; **381** Paul Hardy/CORBIS; **387** Roy Toft/National Geographic/Getty Images; **393** Interfoto Pressebildagentur/Alamy; **394** Charles & Josette Lenars/CORBIS; **395** Ablestock/Alamy; **399** Tim O'Hara/CORBIS; **412–413** JupiterImages/Brand X/Alamy; **414** David Muench/CORBIS; **418** AFP/Getty Images; **426** (l)RubberBall/Alamy Images, (r)CORBIS; **428** Jeff Greenberg/The Image Works Image; **430** Tim Fitzharris/Masterfile; **434** Purestock/Punchstock; **435** MPI/Getty Images; **438** CORBIS; **444** (l)Robin Lynne Gibson/Getty Images, (r)Richard Hutchings/Photo Researchers; **446** Antoine Gyori/AGP/CORBIS; **449** (t bl br)United States coin images from the United States Mint; **451** Otto Greule Jr/Stringer; **462** Eric Gieszl/Ultimate Rollercoaster; **465** Bob Daemmrich/The Image Works; **469** Michael Newman/PhotoEdit; **470** CORBIS; **496** Stew Milne/AP Images; **508** RubberBall Productions/Getty Images; **511** Robin Nelson/PhotoEdit; **526** age fotostock/SuperStock; **528** Greg Trott/Getty Images; **530** Steve Bloom Images/Alamy; **535** ImageState/Alamy; **538** Amos Morgan/Getty Images; **545** Michael Newman/PhotoEdit; **552** Douglas Peebles Photography/Alamy; **553** Maximilian Stock Ltd/Photo Researchers, Inc.; **570–571** David Dow/NBAE via Getty Images; **574** Digital Vision/PunchStock; **579** Digital Vision/PunchStock; **583** Eric Gay/AP Images; **592** Mark Moffett; **595** (t)Alexandros Vlachos/epa/CORBIS, (bl)Ryan McVay/Getty Images, (br)Jenny Acheson/Getty Images; **599** SW Productions/Getty Images; **606** Cleve Bryant/PhotoEdit; **607** CORBIS; **618** Chuck Savage/CORBIS; **630** Mark Crammer/The Anderson Independent-Mail/AP Images; **633** Kimberly White/Reuters/Landov; **644** Stockbyte/SuperStock; **650** RubberBall Productions/Alamy Images; **666** Eclipse Studios; **713** Tim Fuller; **LA0–LA1** Digital Vision/PunchStock; **LA2** United States coin images from the United States Mint; **LA6** Don Farrall/Getty Images; **LA9** images-of-france/Alamy; **LA16** Brian Leatart/Getty Images

Glossary/Glosario

Glossary/Glosario

IL Math Online A mathematics multilingual glossary is available at glencoe.com. The glossary includes the following languages.

Arabic	Cantonese	Korean	Tagalog
Bengali	English	Portuguese	Urdu
Brazilian Portuguese	Haitian Creole	Russian	Vietnamese
	Hmong	Spanish	

Cómo usar el glosario en español:

1. Busca el término en inglés que desees encontrar.
2. El término en español, junto con la definición, se encuentran en la columna de la derecha.

English — Español

A

abscissa (p. 173) The first number of an ordered pair; the x-coordinate.

abscisa El primer número de un par ordenado. La coordenada x.

absolute value (p. 36) The distance a number is from zero on the number line.

valor absoluto Número de unidades en la recta numérica que un número dista de cero.

Addition Property of Equality (p. 66) If you add the same number to each side of an equation, the two sides remain equal.

propiedad de adición de la igualdad Si sumas el mismo número a ambos lados de una ecuación, los dos lados permanecen iguales.

additive inverse (p. 43) Two integers that are opposite of each other are called additive inverses. The sum of any number and its additive inverse is zero.

inverso aditivo Dos enteros que son opuestos mutuos reciben el nombre de inversos aditivos. La suma de cualquier número y su inverso aditivo es cero.

Additive Inverse Property (p. 43) The sum of a number and its additive inverse is zero.

propiedad del inverso de la adición La suma de un número y su inverso aditivo es cero.

algebra (p. 29) The branch of mathematics that involves expressions with variables.

álgebra Rama de las matemáticas que trabaja con expresiones con variables.

algebraic expression (p. 29) A combination of variables, numbers, and at least one operation.

expresión algebraica Una combinación de variables, números y por lo menos una operación.

alternate exterior angles (p. 308) In the figure, transversal t intersects lines ℓ and m. $\angle 1$ and $\angle 7$, and $\angle 2$ and $\angle 8$ are alternate exterior angles. If line ℓ and m are parallel, then these pairs of angles are congruent.

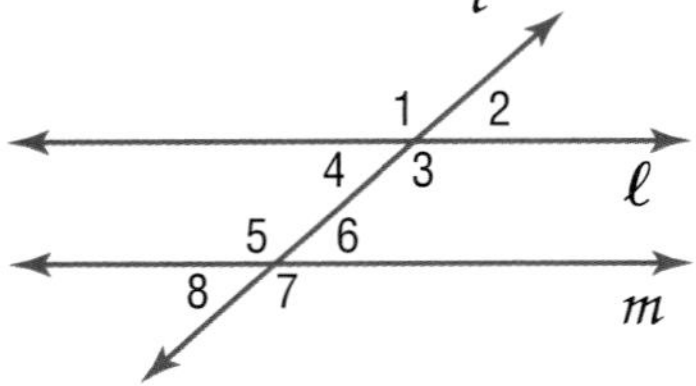

ángulos alternos externos En la figura, la transversal t interseca las rectas ℓ y m. $\angle 1$ y $\angle 7$, y $\angle 2$ y $\angle 8$ son ángulos alternos externos. Si las rectas ℓ y m son paralelas, entonces estos ángulos son pares de ángulos congruentes.

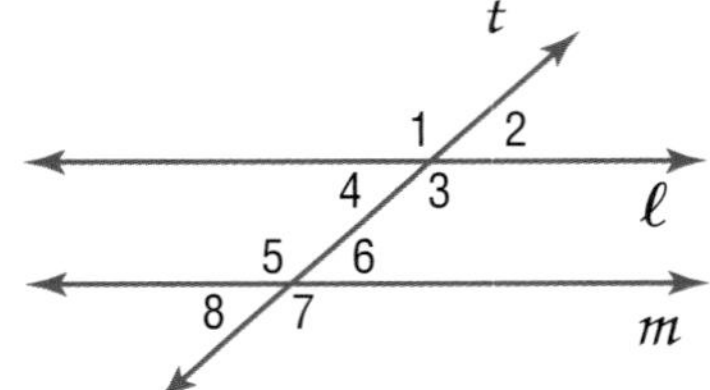

alternate interior angles (p. 308) In the figure below, transversal t intersects lines ℓ and m. $\angle 3$ and $\angle 5$, and $\angle 4$ and $\angle 6$ are alternate interior angles. If lines ℓ and m are parallel, then these pairs of angles are congruent.

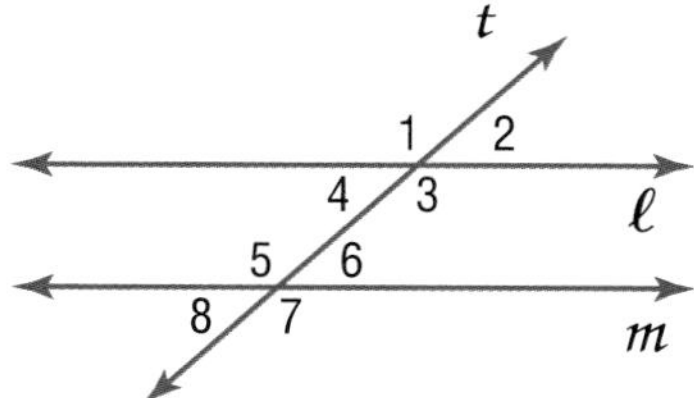

ángulos alternos internos En la figura, la transversal t interseca las rectas ℓ y m. $\angle 3$ y $\angle 5$, y $\angle 4$ y $\angle 6$ son ángulos alternos internos. Si las rectas ℓ y m son paralelas, entonces estos ángulos son pares de ángulos congruentes.

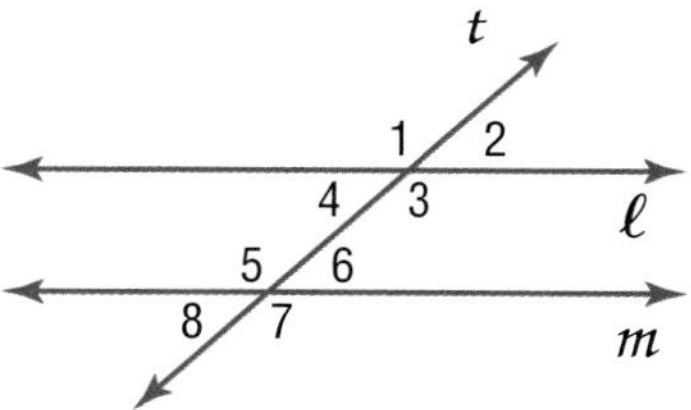

angle of rotation (p. 328) The angle through which a preimage is rotated to form the image.

ángulo de rotación El ángulo a través del cual se rota una preimagen para formar la imagen.

arithmetic sequence (p. 464) A sequence in which the difference between any two consecutive terms is the same.

sucesión aritmética Sucesión en la cual la diferencia entre dos términos consecutivos es constante.

Associative Property (p. 31) The way in which three numbers are grouped when they are added or multiplied does not change their sum or product.

propiedad asociativa La forma en que se agrupan tres números al sumarlos o multiplicarlos no altera su suma o producto.

B

bar notation (p. 85) In repeating decimals, the line or bar placed over the digits that repeat. Another way to write 2.6363636… is $2.\overline{63}$.

notación de barra En decimales periódicos, la línea o barra que se coloca sobre los dígitos que se repiten. Otra manera de escribir 2.6363636... es $2.\overline{63}$.

base (p. 126) In a power, the number used as a factor. In 10^3, the base is 10. That is, $10^3 = 10 \times 10 \times 10$.

base Número que se usa como factor en un potencia. En 10^3, la base es 10. Es decir, $10^3 = 10 \times 10 \times 10$.

base (p. 365) The bases of a prism are the two parallel congruent faces.

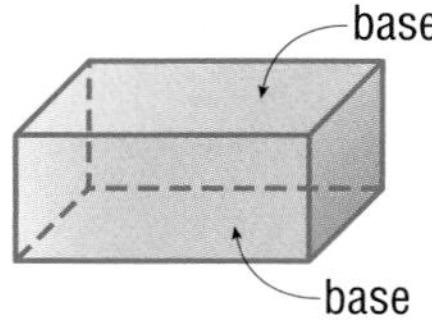

base Las bases de un prisma son las dos caras congruentes paralelas.

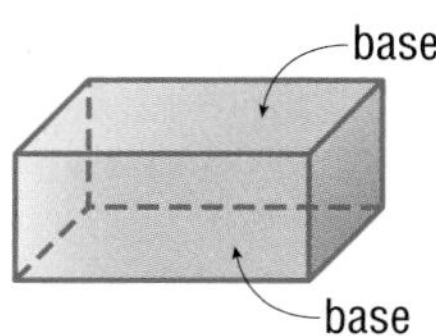

biased sample (p. 654) A sample drawn in such a way that one or more parts of the population are favored over others.

muestra sesgada Muestra en que se favorece una o más partes de una población.

box-and-whisker plot (p. 605) A diagram that summarizes data using the median, the upper and lower quartiles, and the extreme values. A box is drawn around the quartile values and whiskers extend from each quartile to the extreme data points.

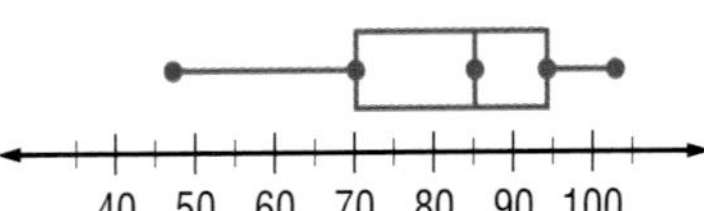

diagrama de caja y patillas Diagrama que resume información usando la mediana, los cuartiles superior e inferior y los valores extremos. Se dibuja una caja alrededor de los cuartiles y se trazan patillas que los unan a los valores extremos respectivos.

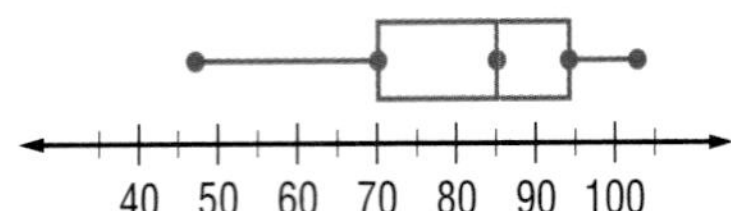

C

center (p. 225) The given point from which all points on a circle are the same distance.

centro Un punto dado del cual equidistan todos los puntos de un círculo.

circle (p. 352) The set of all points in a plane that are the same distance from a given point called the center.

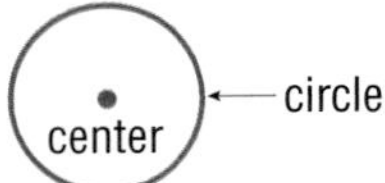

círculo Conjunto de todos los puntos en un plano que equidistan de un punto dado llamado centro.

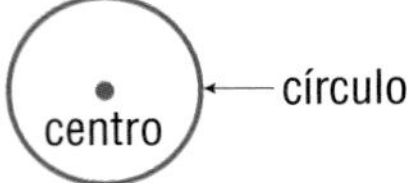

circle graph (p. 582) A type of statistical graph used to compare parts of a whole. The entire circle represents the whole.

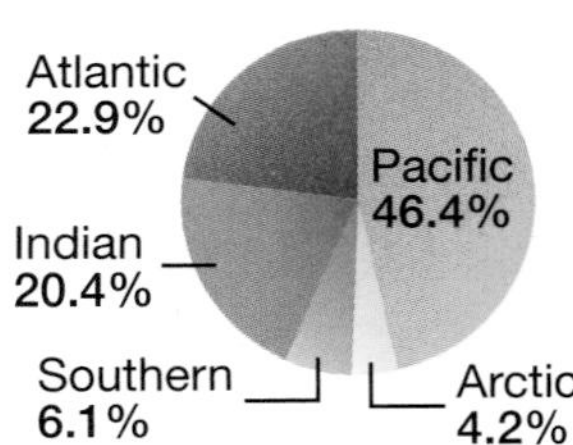

gráfica circular Tipo de gráfica estadística que se usa para comparar las partes de un todo. El círculo completo representa el todo.

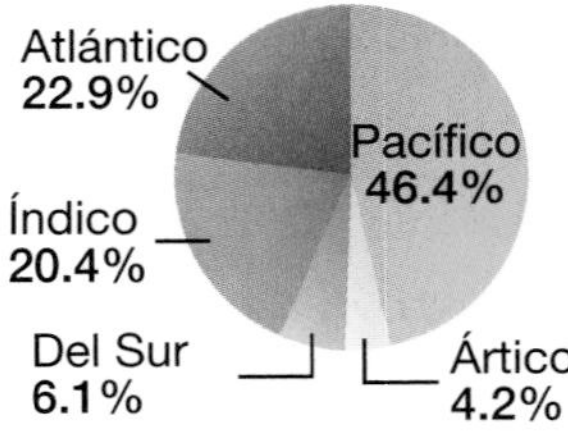

circumference (p. 352) The distance around a circle.

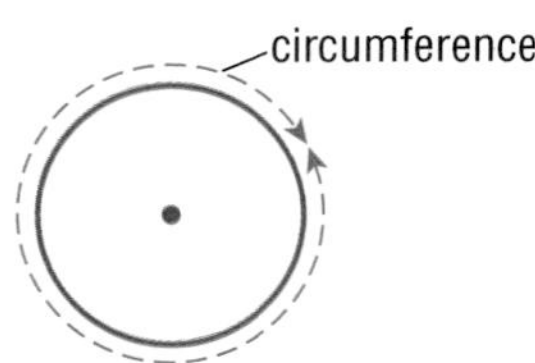

circunferencia La distancia alrededor de un círculo.

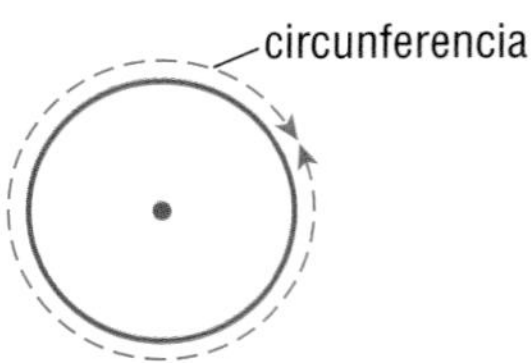

chord (p. 352) A segment with endpoints that are on a circle.

cuerda Segmento cuyos extremos están sobre un círculo.

coefficient (p. 417) The numerical factor of a term that contains a variable.

coeficiente Factor numérico de un término que contiene una variable.

common difference (p. 464) The difference between any two consecutive terms is an arithmetic sequence.

diferencia común La diferencia entre cualquier par de términos consecutivos en una sucesión aritmética.

Commutative Property (p. 31) The order in which two numbers are added or multiplied does not change their sum or product.

propiedad conmutativa La forma en que se suman o multiplican dos números no altera su suma o producto.

compatible numbers (p. 275) Two numbers that are easy to add, subtract, multiply, or divide mentally.

números compatibles Dos números que son fáciles de sumar, restar, multiplicar o dividir mentalmente.

complementary angles (p. 306) Two angles are complementary if the sum of their measures is 90°.

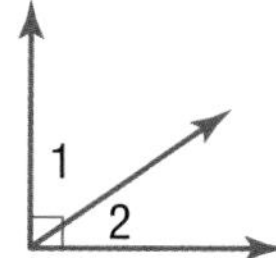

∠1 and ∠2 are complementary angles.

ángulos complementarios Dos ángulos son complementarios si la suma de sus medidas es 90°.

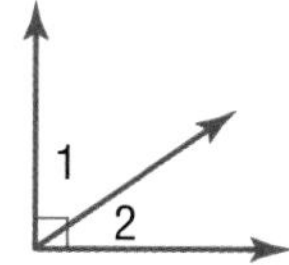

∠1 y ∠2 son complementarios.

composite figure (p. 363) A figure that is made up of two or more shapes.

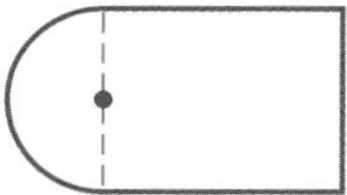

figura compleja Figura compuesta de dos o más formas.

composite solid (p. 375) An object made up of more than one type of solid.

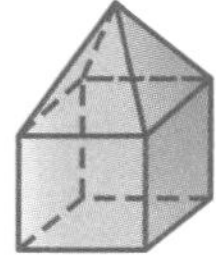

sólido complejo Cuerpo compuesto de más de un tipo de sólido.

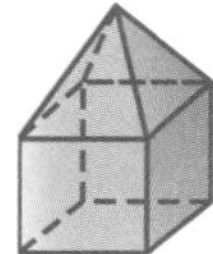

compound event (p. 637) An event that consists of two or more simple events.

evento compuesto Evento que consta de dos o más eventos simples.

compound interest (p. 294) Interest paid on the initial principal and on interest earned in the past.

interés compuesto Interés que se paga por el capital inicial y sobre el interés ganado en el pasado.

cone (p. 380) A three-dimensional figure with one circular base. A curved surface connects the base and the vertex.

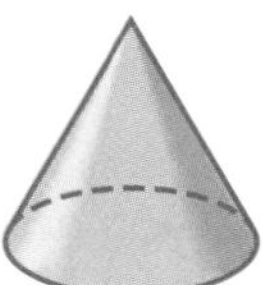

cono Figura tridimensional con una base circular. Una superficie curva conecta la base con el vértice.

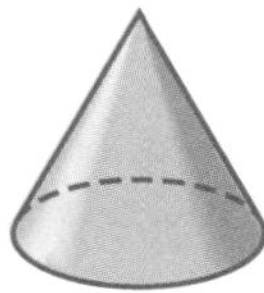

congruent (p. 219) Having the same measure.

congruente Que tienen la misma medida.

congruent polygons (p. 320) Polygons that have the same size and shape.

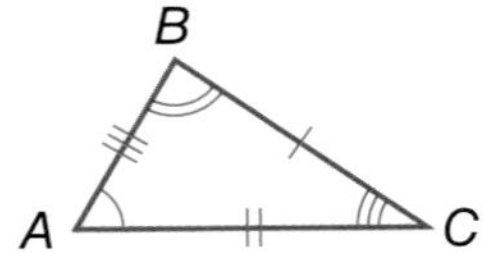

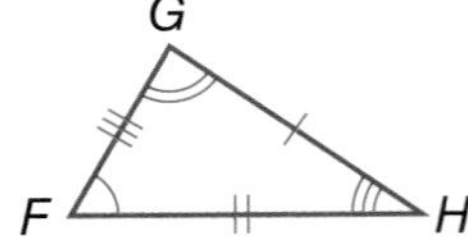

polígonos congruentes Polígonos que tienen la misma medida y la misma forma.

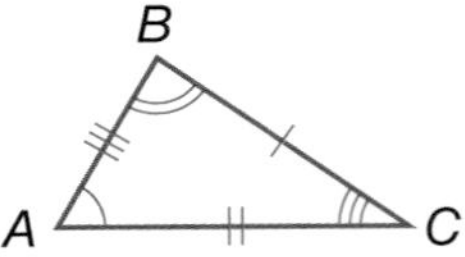

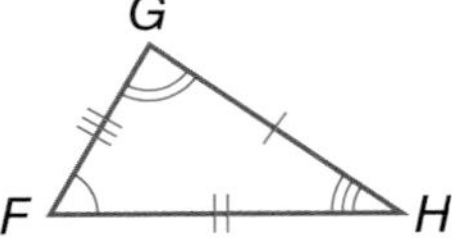

conjecture (p. 24) An educated guess.

conjetura Suposición informada.

constant (p. 417) A term without a variable.

constante Término sin variables.

constant of proportionality (p. 212) A constant ratio or unit rate in a proportion.

constante de proporción Razón constante o tasa unitaria en una proporción.

constant rate of change (p. 204) The rate of change in a linear relationship.

tasa constante de cambio Tasa de cambio en una relación lineal.

constant of variation (p. 487) A constant ratio in a direct variation.

constante de variación Razón constante en una relación de variación directa.

convenience sample (p. 654) A sample which includes members of the population that are easily accessed.

muestra de conveniencia Muestra que incluye miembros de una población fácilmente accesibles.

converse (p. 164) The converse of a theorem is formed when the parts of the theorem are reversed. The converse of the Pythagorean Theorem can be used to test whether a triangle is a right triangle. If the sides of the triangle have lengths a, b, and c, such that $c^2 = a^2 + b^2$, then the triangle is a right triangle.

recíproco El recíproco de un teorema se forma cuando se invierten las partes del teorema. El recíproco del teorema de Pitágoras puede usarse para averiguar si un triángulo es un triángulo rectángulo. Si las longitudes de los lados de un triángulo son a, b y c, tales que $c^2 = a^2 + b^2$, entonces el triángulo es un triángulo rectángulo.

coordinate (p. 35) A number associated with a point on the number line.

coordenada Número asociado con un punto en la recta numérica.

coordinate plane (p. 173) A plane in which a horizontal number line and a vertical number line intersect at their zero points.

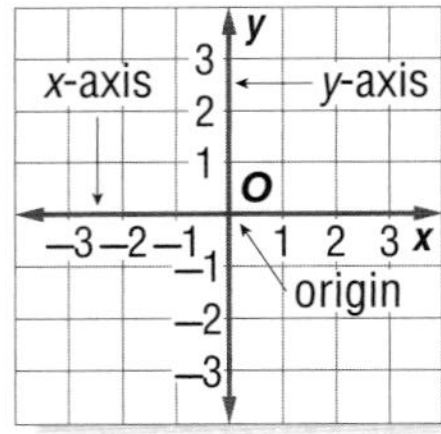

plano de coordenadas Plano en que una recta numérica horizontal y una recta numérica vertical se intersecan en sus puntos cero.

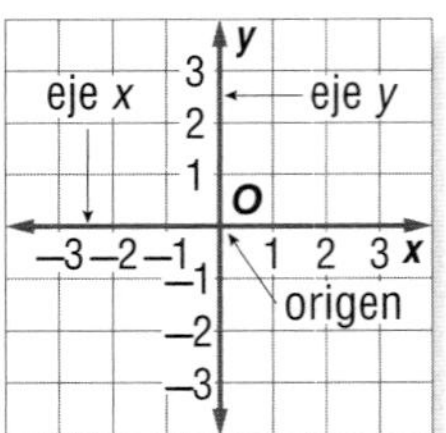

corresponding angles (p. 308) Angles that have the same position on two different parallel lines cut by a tranversal.

ángulos correspondientes Ángulos que ocupan la misma posición en dos rectas paralelas distintas cortadas por una transversal.

corresponding parts (p. 218) Parts of congruent or similar figures that match.

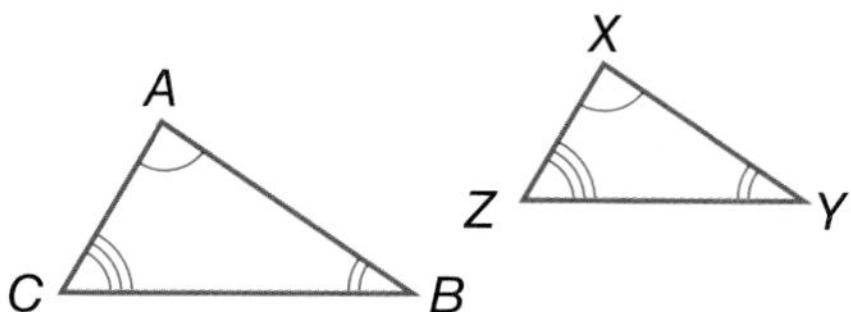

$\overline{AB}$ and $\overline{XY}$ are corresponding sides.
$\angle C$ and $\angle Z$ are corresponding angles.

partes correspondientes Partes de figuras congruentes o semejantes que coinciden.

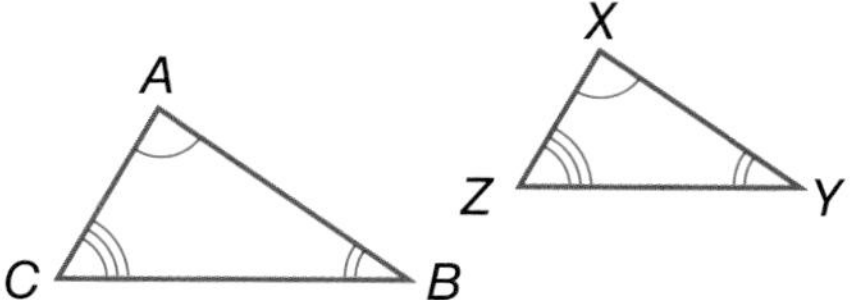

$\overline{AB}$ y $\overline{XY}$ son lados correspondientes.
$\angle C$ y $\angle Z$ son ángulos correspondientes.

counterexample (p. 31) A statement or example that shows a conjecture is false.

contraejemplo Ejemplo o enunciado que demuestra que una conjetura es falsa.

cross products (p. 210) The products of the terms on the diagonals when two ratios are compared. If the cross products are equal, then the ratios form a proportion. In the proportion $\frac{2}{3} = \frac{8}{12}$, the cross products are 2×12 and 3×8.

productos cruzados Productos que resultan de la comparación de los términos de las diagonales de dos razones. Si los productos son iguales, las razones forman una proporción. En la proporción $\frac{2}{3} = \frac{8}{12}$, los productos cruzados son 2×12 y 3×8.

cube root (p. 560) A number that can be raised to the third power to create another number.

raíz cúbica Número que se puede elevar a la tercera potencia para crear otro número.

cylinder (p. 372) A solid whose bases are congruent, parallel circles, connected with a curved side.

cilindro Sólido cuyas bases son círculos congruentes y paralelos, conectados por un lado curvo.

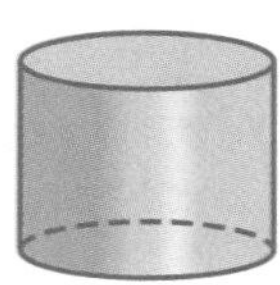

D

defining a variable (p. 58) Choosing a variable and a quantity for the variable to represent in an expression or equation.

definir una variable El elegir una variable y una cantidad que esté representada por la variable en una expresión o en una ecuación.

dependent events (p. 638) Two or more events in which the outcome of one event does affect the outcome of the other event or events.

eventos dependientes Dos o más eventos en que el resultado de uno de ellos afecta el resultado de los otros eventos.

diameter (p. 352) The distance across a circle through its center.

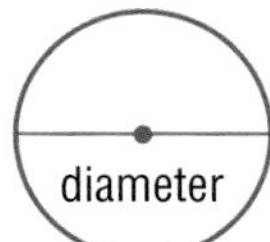

diámetro La distancia a través de un círculo pasando por el centro.

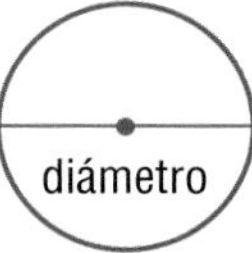

dilation (p. 225) A transformation that results from the reduction or enlargement of an image.

dilatación Transformación que resulta de la reducción o ampliación de una imagen.

dimensional analysis (p. 98) The process of including units of measurement when you compute.

análisis dimensional Proceso que incorpora las unidades de medida al hacer cálculos.

direct variation (p. 487) A relationship between two variable quantities with a constant ratio.

variación directa Relación entre dos cantidades variables con una razón constante.

discount (p. 286) The amount by which a regular price is reduced.

descuento La cantidad de reducción del precio normal.

Distributive Property (p. 31) To multiply a sum by a number, multiply each addend by the number outside the parentheses.

propiedad distributiva Para multiplicar una suma por un número, multiplica cada sumando por el número fuera de los paréntesis.

Division Property of Equality (p. 70) If you divide each side of an equation by the same nonzero number, the two sides remain equal.

propiedad de división de la igualdad Si cada lado de una ecuación se divide entre el mismo número no nulo, los dos lados permanecen iguales.

domain (p. 470) The set of input values in a function.

dominio Conjunto de valores de entrada de una función.

E

edge (p. 365) The intersection of two faces of a three-dimensional figure.

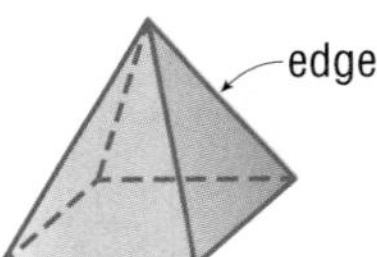

arista La intersección de dos caras de una figura tridimensional.

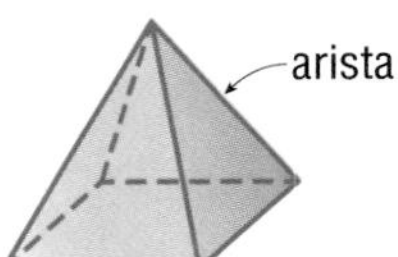

enlargement (p. 226) A dilation with a scale factor greater than 1.

ampliación Dilatación con un factor de escala mayor que 1.

equation (p. 57) A mathematical sentence that contains an equals sign, =.

ecuación Un enunciado matemático que contiene un signo de igualdad (=).

equiangular (p. 317) A polygon in which all angles are congruent.

equiangular Polígono en el cual todos los ángulos son congruentes.

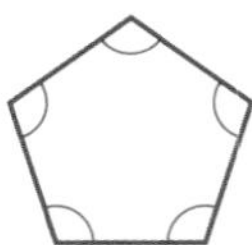

equilateral (p. 317) A polygon in which all sides are congruent.

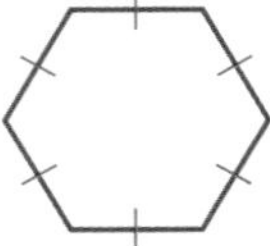

equilátero Polígono en el cual todos los lados son congruentes.

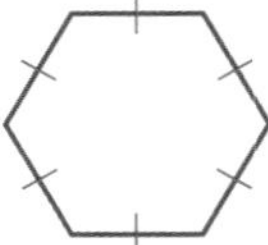

Glossary/Glosario

equivalent expressions (p. 416) Expressions that have the same value regardless of the value(s) of the variable(s).

expresiones equivalentes Expresiones que poseen el mismo valor, sin importar los valores de la(s) variable(s).

equivalent ratios (p. 210) Two ratios that have the same value.

razones equivalentes Dos razones que tienen el mismo valor.

evaluate (p. 29) To find the value of an expression by replacing the variables with numerals.

evaluar Calcular el valor de una expresión sustituyendo las variables por números.

event (p. 632) An outcome is a possible result.

evento Un resultado posible.

experimental probability (p. 643) An estimated probability based on the relative frequency of positive outcomes occurring during an experiment.

probabilidad experimental Probabilidad de un evento que se estima basándose en la frecuencia relativa de los resultados favorables al evento en cuestión, que ocurren durante un experimento.

exponent (p. 126) In a power, the number of times the base is used as a factor. In 10^3, the exponent is 3.

exponente En una potencia, el número de veces que la base se usa como factor. En 10^3, el exponente es 3.

exterior angles (p. 307) The four outer angles formed by two lines cut by a transversal.

ángulo externo Los cuatro ángulos exteriores que se forman cuando una transversal corta dos rectas.

F

face (p. 365) Any surface that forms a side or a base of a prism.

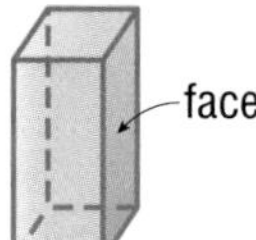

cara Cualquier superficie que forma un lado o una base de un prisma.

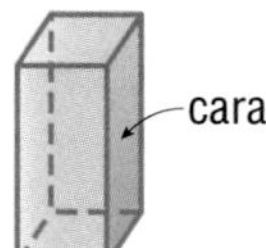

function (p. 469) A relation in which each element of the input is paired with exactly one element of the output according to a specified rule.

función Relación en que cada elemento de entrada se relaciona con un único elemento de salida, según una regla específica.

function table (p. 470) A table organizing the input, rule, and output of a function.

tabla de funciones Tabla que organiza las entradas, la regla y las salidas de una función.

Fundamental Counting Principle (p. 633) Uses multiplication of the number of ways each event in an experiment can occur to find the number of possible outcomes in a sample space.

principio fundamental de contar Método que usa la multiplicación del número de maneras en que cada evento puede ocurrir en un experimento, para calcular el número de resultados posibles en un espacio muestral.

H

histogram (p. 576) A special kind of bar graph that displays the frequency of data that has been organized into equal intervals. The intervals cover all possible values of data, therefore, there are no spaces between the bars of the graph.

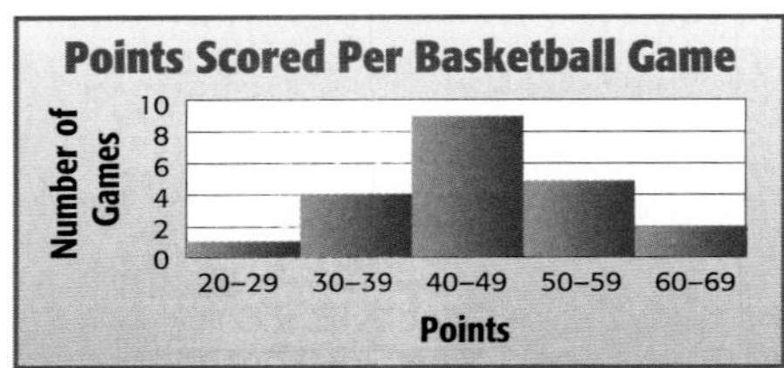

histograma Tipo especial de gráfica de barras que exhibe la frecuencia de los datos que han sido organizados en intervalos iguales. Los intervalos cubren todos los valores posibles de datos, sin dejar espacios entre las barras de la gráfica.

hypotenuse (p. 162) The side opposite the right angle in a right triangle.

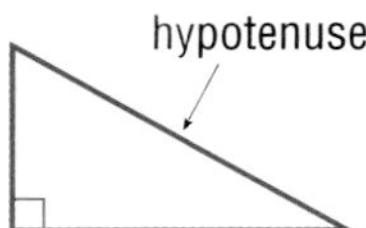

hipotenusa El lado opuesto al ángulo recto de un triángulo rectángulo.

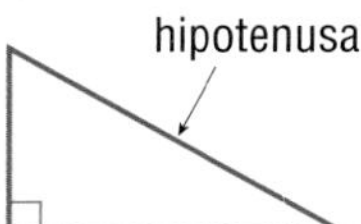

I

image (p. 332) The position of a figure after a transformation.

imagen La posición de una figura después de una transformación.

independent events (p. 637) Two or more events in which the outcome of one event does not affect the outcome of the other event(s).

eventos independientes Dos o más eventos en los cuales el resultado de un evento no afecta el resultado de otro evento o eventos.

indirect measurement (p. 232) A technique using proportions to find a measurement.

medición indirecta Técnica que usa proporciones para calcular una medida.

inductive reasoning (p. 312) Reasoning based on a pattern of examples or past events.

razonamiento inductivo Razonamiento que se basa en un patrón de ejemplos o eventos pasados.

inequality (p. 35) A mathematical sentence that contains $<$, $>$, $\neq$, $\leq$, or $\geq$.

desigualdad Enunciado matemático que contiene $<$, $>$, $\neq$, $\leq$, o $\geq$.

integers (p. 35) The set of whole numbers and their opposites.

$$\ldots, -3, -2, -1, 0, 1, 2, 3, \ldots$$

enteros El conjunto de los números enteros y sus opuestos.

$$\ldots, -3, -2, -1, 0, 1, 2, 3, \ldots$$

interest (p. 290) The amount of money paid or earned for the use of money.

interés Cantidad que se cobra o se paga por el uso del dinero.

interior angle (p. 316) An angle inside a polygon.

ángulo interno Ángulo ubicado dentro de un polígono.

interquartile range (p. 599) The range of the middle half of a set of data. It is the difference between the upper quartile and the lower quartile.

rango intercuartílico El rango de la mitad central de un conjunto de datos. Es la diferencia entre el cuartil superior y el cuartil inferior.

inverse operations (p. 66) Pairs of operations that undo each other. Addition and subtraction are inverse operations. Multiplication and division are inverse operations.

peraciones inversas Pares de operaciones que se anulan mutuamente. La adición y la sustracción son operaciones inversas. La multiplicación y la división son operaciones inversas.

irrational number (p. 155) A number that cannot be expressed as $\frac{a}{b}$, where a and b are integers and $b \neq 0$.

números irracionales Un número que no se puede expresar como el cociente $\frac{a}{b}$, donde a y b son enteros y $b \neq 0$.

L

lateral surface area (p. 386) The sum of the areas of the lateral faces of a pyramid.

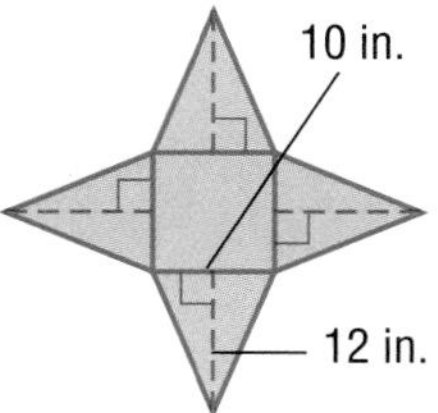

lateral area $= 4\left(\frac{1}{2} \times 10 \times 12\right) = 240$ square inches

área lateral La suma de las áreas de las caras laterales de una pirámide.

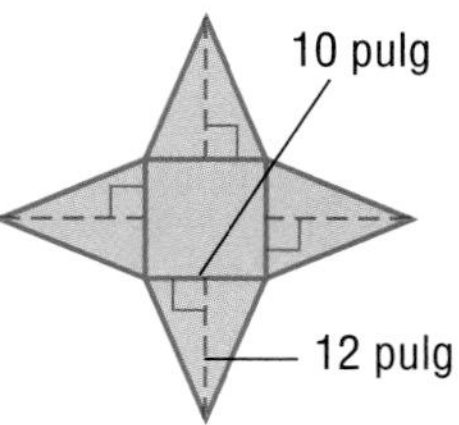

área lateral $= 4\left(\frac{1}{2} \times 10 \times 12\right) = 240$ pulgadas cuadradas

lateral face (p. 386) A triangular side of a pyramid.

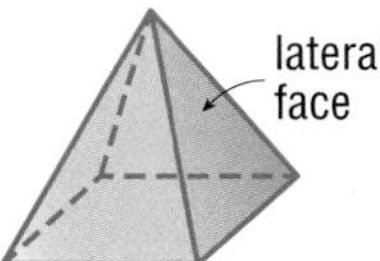

cara lateral Un lado triangular de una pirámide.

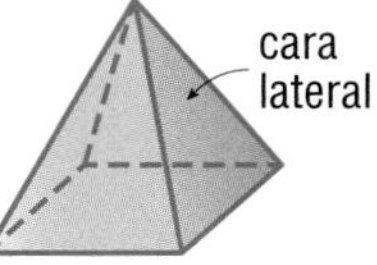

legs (p. 162) The two sides of a right triangle that form the right angle.

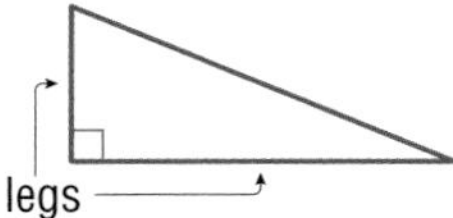

catetos Los dos lados de un triángulo rectángulo que forman el ángulo recto.

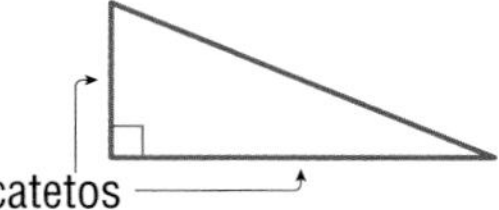

like fractions (p. 108) Fractions that have the same denominator.

fracciones semejantes Fracciones que tienen el mismo denominador.

like terms (p. 417) Terms that contain the same variable(s).

términos semejantes Términos que contienen la(s) misma(s) variable(s).

line of fit (p. 511) A line that is very close to most of the data points in a scatter plot.

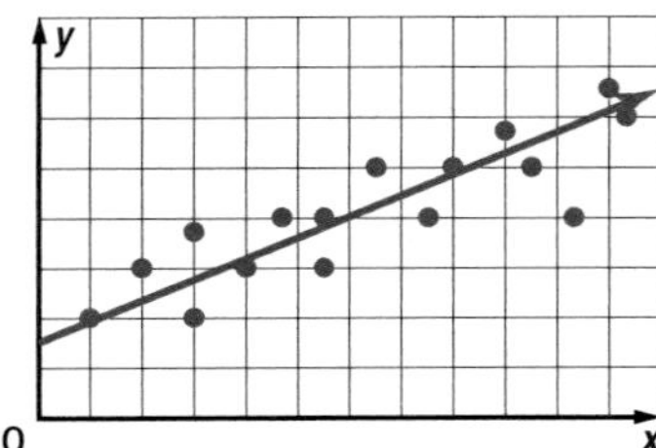

recta de ajuste Recta que mejor aproxima a los puntos de los datos de una gráfica de dispersión.

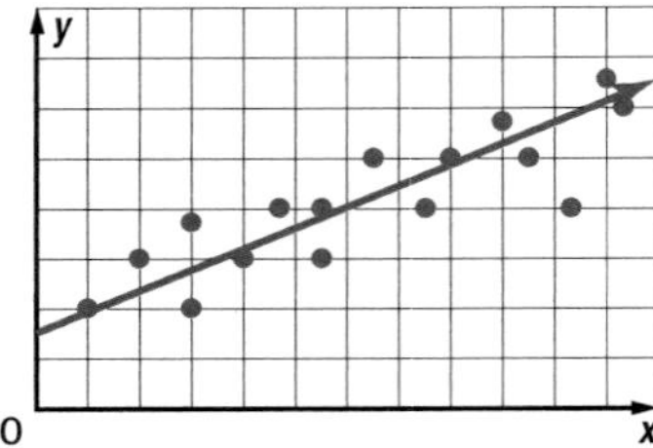

linear function (p. 472) A function in which the graph of the solutions forms a line.

función lineal Función en la cual la gráfica de las soluciones forma un recta.

linear relationship (p. 204) A relationship that has a straight-line graph.

relación lineal Relación cuya gráfica es una recta.

line of reflection (p. 332) The line a figure is flipped over in a reflection.

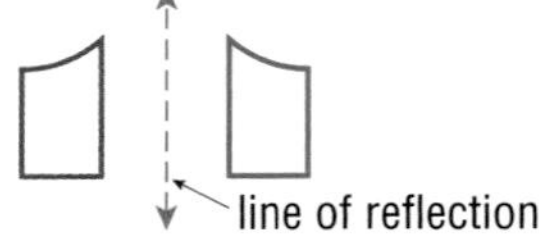

línea de reflexión Línea a través de la cual se le da vuelta a una figura en una reflexión.

line of symmetry (p. 327) A line that divides a figure into two halves that are reflections of each other.

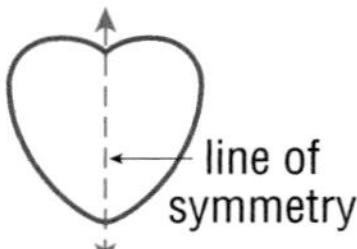

eje de simetría Recta que divide una figura en dos mitades que son reflexiones una de la otra.

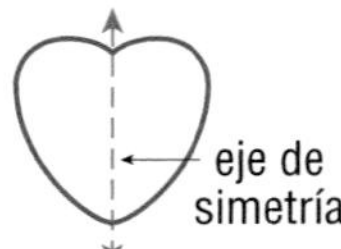

line symmetry (p. 327) Figures that match exactly when folded in half have line symmetry.

simetría lineal Exhiben simetría lineal las figuras que coinciden exactamente al doblarse una sobre otra.

lower quartile (p. 599) The median of the lower half of a set of data, represented by LQ.

cuartil inferior La mediana de la mitad inferior de un conjunto de datos, la cual se denota por CI.

M

markup (p. 286) The amount the price of an item is increased above the price the store paid for the item.

margen de utilidad Cantidad de aumento en el precio de un artículo por encima del precio que paga la tienda por dicho artículo.

mean (p. 591) The sum of the numbers in a set of data divided by the number of items in the data set.

media La suma de los números de un conjunto de datos dividida entre el número total de artículos.

measures of central tendency (p. 591) Numbers or pieces of data that can represent the whole set of data.

medidas de tendencia central Números o fragmentos de datos que pueden representar el conjunto total de datos.

measures of variation (p. 599) Numbers used to describe the distribution or spread of a set of data.

medidas de variación Números que se usan para describir la distribución o separación de un conjunto de datos.

median (p. 591) The middle number in a set of data when the data are arranged in numerical order. If the data set has an even number, the median is the mean of the two middle numbers.

mediana El número central de un conjunto de datos, una vez que los datos han sido ordenados numéricamente. Si hay un número par de datos, la mediana es el promedio de los dos datos centrales.

mode (p. 591) The number(s) or item(s) that appear most often in a set of data.

moda El número(s) o artículo(s) que aparece con más frecuencia en un conjunto de datos.

monomial (p. 545) A number, a variable, or a product of a number and one or more variables.

monomio Un número, una variable o el producto de un número por una o más variables.

Multiplication Property of Equality (p. 71) If you multiply each side of an equation by the same number, the two sides remain equal.

propiedad de multiplicación de la igualdad Si cada lado de una ecuación se multiplica por el mismo número, los lados permanecen iguales.

multiplicative inverse (p. 102) A number times its multiplicative inverse is equal to 1. The multiplicative inverse of $\frac{2}{3}$ is $\frac{3}{2}$.

inverso multiplicativo Un número multiplicado por su inverso multiplicativo es igual a 1. El inverso multiplicativo de $\frac{2}{3}$ es $\frac{3}{2}$.

Multiplicative Inverse Property (p. 102) The product of a number and its multiplicative inverse is 1.

propiedad del inverso multiplicativo El producto de un número por su inverso multiplicativo es 1.

negative number (p. 35) A number that is less than zero.

número negativo Número menor que cero.

net (p. 385) A two-dimensional pattern of a three-dimensional figure.

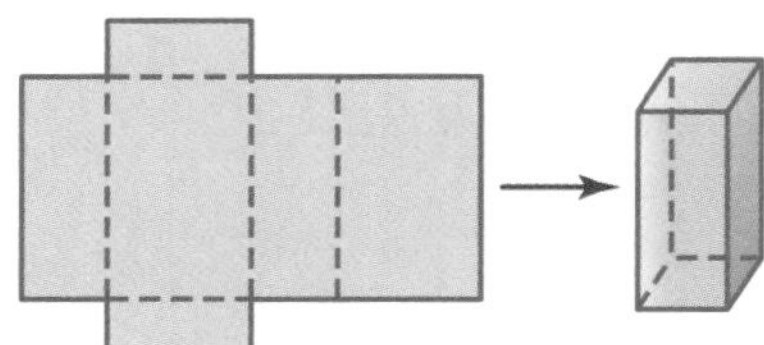

red Patrón bidimensional de una figura tridimensional.

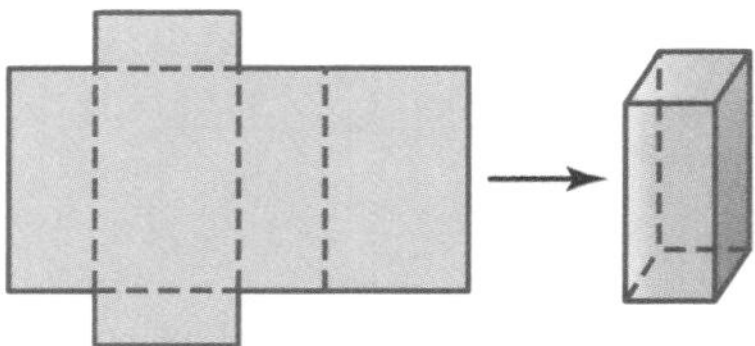

nonlinear function (p. 528) A function that does not have a constant rate of change. The graph of a nonlinear function is not a straight line.

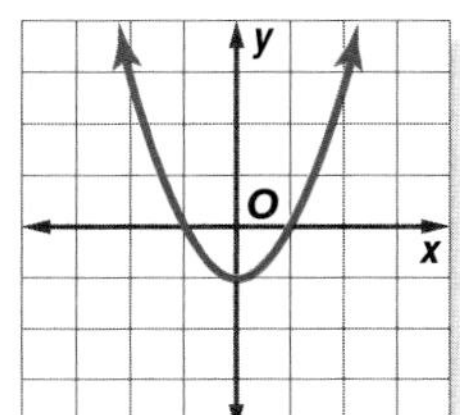

función no lineal Función que no tiene una tasa constante de cambio. La gráfica de una función no lineal no es una recta.

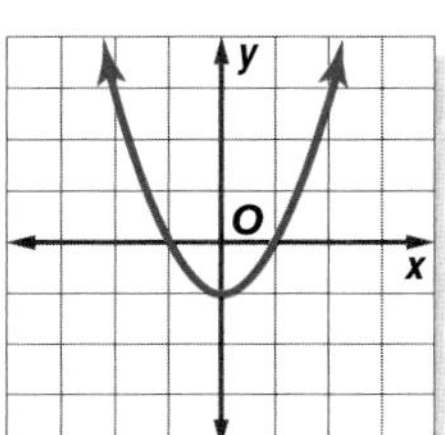

nonproportional (p. 194) A relationship in which two quantities do not have a constant ratio.

noproporcional Una relación en la que dos cantidades no tienen una razón constante.

numerical expression (p. 29) A mathematical expression that has a combination of numbers and at least one operation. 4 + 2 is a numerical expression.

expresión numérica Expresión matemática que tiene una combinación de números y por lo menos una operación. 4 + 2 es una expresión numérica.

O

opposites (p. 43) Two numbers with the same absolute value but different signs. The sum of opposites is zero.

opuestos Dos números con el mismo valor absoluto, pero distintos signos. La suma de opuestos es cero.

order of operations (p. 29) The rules to follow when more than one operation is used in an expression.

1. Do all operations within grouping symbols first; start with the innermost grouping symbols.
2. Evaluate all powers before other operations.
3. Multiply and divide in order from left to right.
4. Add and subtract in order from left to right.

orden de las operaciones Reglas a seguir cuando se usa más de una operación en una expresión.

1. Primero ejecuta todas las operaciones dentro de los símbolos de agrupamiento.
2. Evalúa todas las potencias antes que las otras operaciones.
3. Multiplica y divide en orden de izquierda a derecha.
4. Suma y resta en orden de izquierda a derecha.

ordered pair (p. 173) A pair of numbers used to locate a point in the coordinate plane. The ordered pair is written in this form: (x-coordinate, y-coordinate).

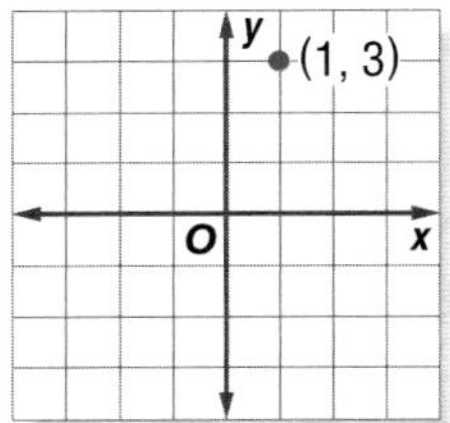

par ordenado Par de números que se utiliza para ubicar un punto en un plano de coordenadas. Se escribe de la siguiente forma: (coordenada x, coordenada y).

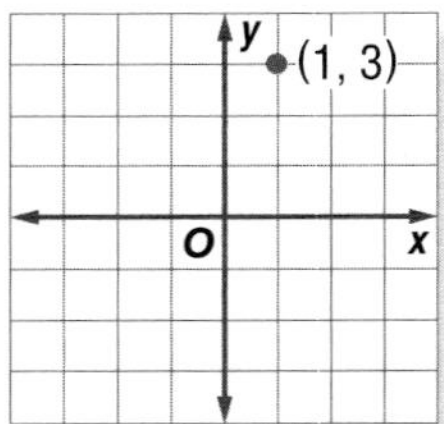

ordinate (p. 173) The second number of an ordered pair; the y-coordinate.

ordenada El segundo número de un par ordenado; la coordenada y.

origin (p. 173) The point of intersection of the x-axis and y-axis in a coordinate plane.

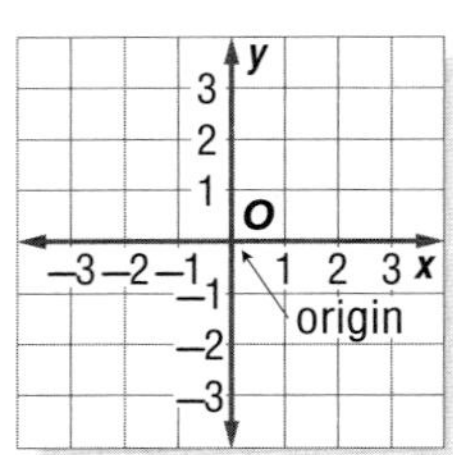

origen Punto en que el eje x y el eje y se intersecan en un plano de coordenadas.

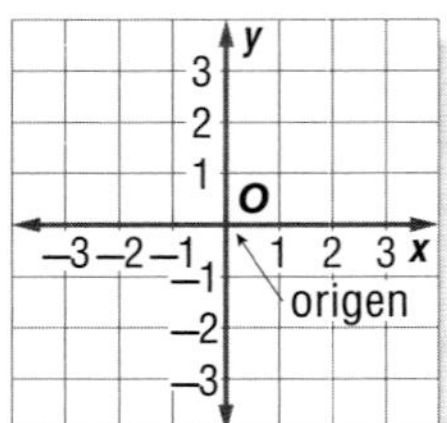

outcome (p. 632) One possible result of a probability event. For example, 4 is an outcome when a number cube is rolled.

resultado Uno de los resultados posibles de un evento probabilístico. Por ejemplo, 4 es un resultado posible cuando se lanza un dado.

outlier (p. 599) Data that are more than 1.5 times the interquartile range from the upper or lower quartiles.

valor atípico Datos que distan de los cuartiles respectivos más de 1.5 veces la amplitud intercuartílica.

P

parallel lines (p. 307) Lines in the same plane that never intersect or cross. The symbol || means parallel.

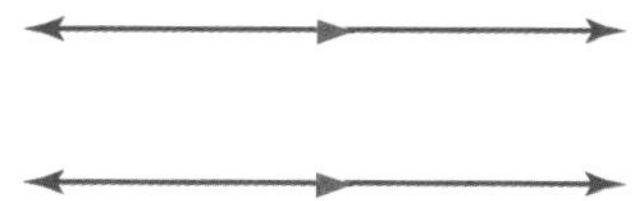

rectas paralelas Rectas que yacen en un mismo plano y que no se intersecan. El símbolo || significa paralela a.

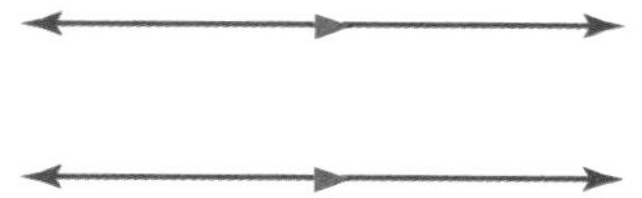

percent (p. 252) A ratio that compares a number to 100.

por ciento Razón que compara un número con 100.

percent equation (p. 279) An equivalent form of the percent proportion in which the percent is written as a decimal. Part = Percent • Whole

ecuación porcentual Forma equivalente de proporción porcentual en la cual el por ciento se escribe como un decimal. Parte = Por ciento • Entero

percent of change (p. 284) A ratio that compares the change in quantity to the original amount.

porcentaje de cambio Razón que compara el cambio en una cantidad a la cantidad original.

percent of decrease (p. 285) The percent of change when the new amount is less than the original.

porcentaje de disminución El porcentaje de cambio cuando la nueva cantidad es menos que la cantidad original.

percent of increase (p. 285) The percent of change when the new amount is greater than the original.

porcentaje de aumento El porcentaje de cambio cuando aumenta la nueva cantidad es mayor que la cantidad original.

percent proportion (p. 263) Compares part of a quantity to the whole quantity using a percent. $\frac{\text{part}}{\text{whole}} = \frac{\text{percent}}{100}$

proporción porcentual Compara parte de una cantidad con la cantidad total mediante un por ciento. $\frac{\text{parte}}{\text{entero}} = \frac{\text{por ciento}}{100}$

perfect square (p. 144) A rational number whose square root is a whole number. 25 is a perfect square because its square root is 5.

cuadrados perfectos Número racional cuya raíz cuadrada es un número entero. 25 es un cuadrado perfecto porque su raíz cuadrada es 5.

perpendicular lines (p. 307) Two lines that intersect to form right angles.

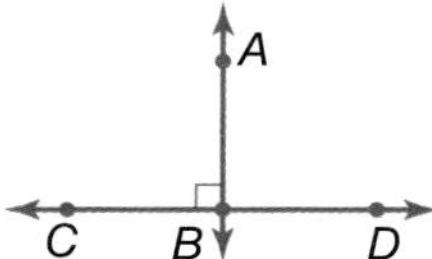

rectas perpendiculares Dos rectas que se intersecan formando ángulos rectos.

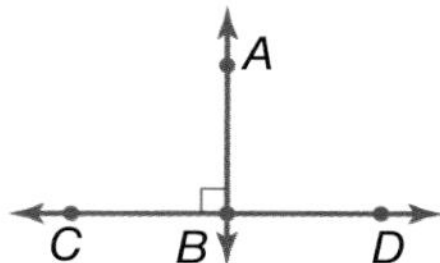

perspective (p. 364) A point of view.

perspectiva Un punto de vista.

pi (p. 352) The ratio of the circumference of a circle to its diameter. The Greek letter π represents this number. The value of pi is always 3.1415926… .

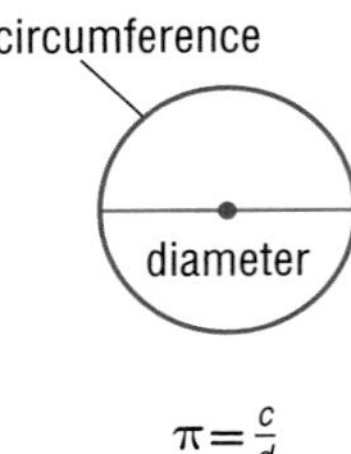

$\pi = \frac{c}{d}$

pi Razón de la circunferencia de un círculo al diámetro del mismo. La letra griega π representa este número. El valor de pi es siempre 3.1415926… .

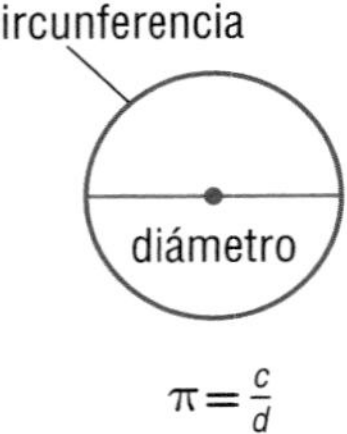

$\pi = \frac{c}{d}$

polygon (p. 218) A simple closed figure in a plane formed by three or more line segments.

polígono Figura simple y cerrada en el plano formada por tres o más segmentos de recta.

polyhedron (p. 365) A solid with flat surfaces that are polygons.

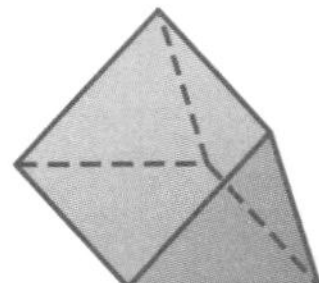

poliedro Sólido cuyas superficies planas son polígonos.

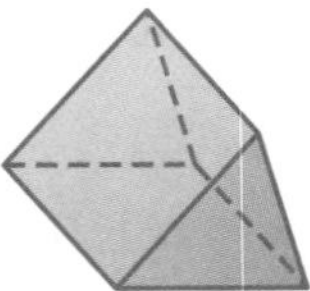

population (p. 653) The entire group of items or individuals from which the samples under consideration are taken.

población El grupo total de individuos o de artículos del cual se toman las muestras bajo estudio.

positive number (p. 35) Any number that is greater than zero.

número positivo Todo número mayor que cero.

powers (pp. 30, 126) Numbers written using exponents. Powers represent repeated multiplication. The power 7^3 is read *seven to the third power,* or *seven cubed.*

potencias Números que se expresan usando exponentes. Las potencias representan multiplicación repetida. La potencia 7^3 se lee *siete a la tercera potencia,* o *siete al cubo.*

principal (p. 290) The amount of money invested or borrowed.

capital Cantidad de dinero que se invierte o que se toma prestada.

prism (p. 365) A polyhedron with two parallel, congruent faces called bases.

prisma Poliedro con dos caras congruentes y paralelas llamadas bases.

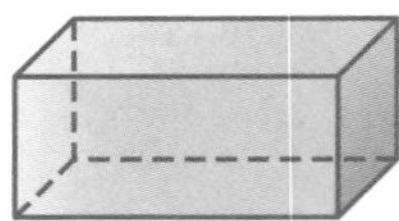

probability (p. 633) The chance that some event will happen. It is the ratio of the number of ways a certain event can occur to the number of possible outcomes.

probabilidad La posibilidad de que suceda un evento. Es la razón del número de maneras en que puede ocurrir un evento al número total de resultados posibles.

property (p. 31) An open sentence that is true for any numbers.

propiedad Enunciado abierto que se cumple para cualquier número.

proportion (p. 210) An equation that shows that two ratios are equivalent.

proporción Ecuación que muestra que dos razones son equivalentes.

proportional (p. 194) A statement of equality of two ratios with a constant ratio.

proporcional Enunciado que establece la igualdad de dos razones con una razón constante.

pyramid (p. 365) A polyhedron with one base that is a polygon and faces that are triangles.

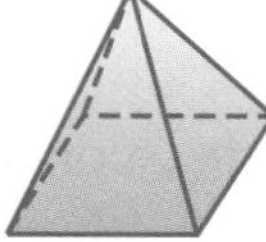

pirámide Poliedro cuya base tiene forma de polígono y caras en forma de triángulos.

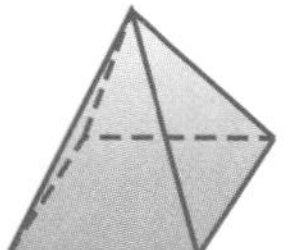

Pythagorean Theorem (p. 162) In a right triangle, the square of the length of the hypotenuse c is equal to the sum of the squares of the lengths of the legs a and b. $c^2 = a^2 + b^2$

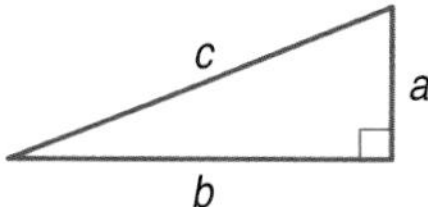

Teorema de Pitágoras En un triángulo rectángulo, el cuadrado de la longitud de la hipotenusa es igual a la suma de los cuadrados de las longitudes de los catetos. $c^2 = a^2 + b^2$

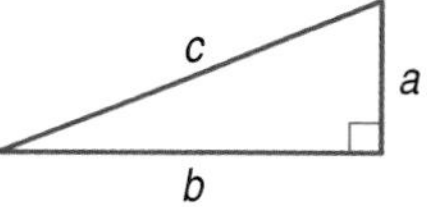

Q

quadrants (p. 173) The four regions into which the two perpendicular number lines of the coordinate plane separate the plane.

y-axis
Quadrant II
Quadrant I
O
x-axis
Quadrant III
Quadrant IV

cuadrantes Las cuatro regiones en que las dos rectas numéricas perpendiculares dividen el plano de coordenadas.

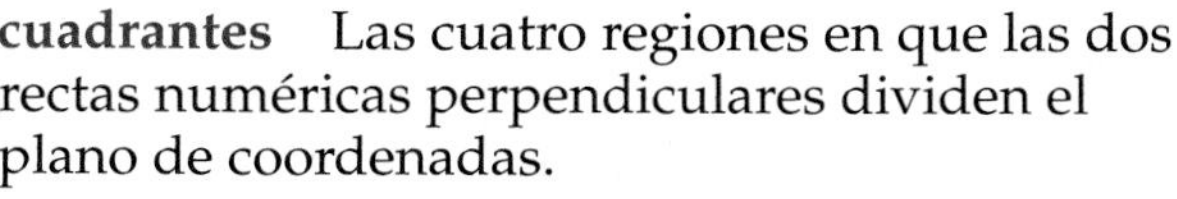

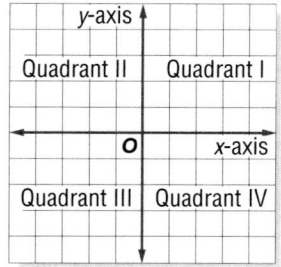

quadratic function (p. 534) A function in which the greatest power of the variable is 2.

función cuadrática Función en la cual la potencia mayor de la variable es 2.

quartiles (p. 599) Values that divide a set of data into four equal parts.

cuartiles Valores que dividen un conjunto de datos en cuatro partes iguales.

R

radical sign (p. 144) The symbol used to indicate a nonnegative square root, $\sqrt{\ }$.

signo radical Símbolo que se usa para indicar una raíz cuadrada no negativa, $\sqrt{\ }$.

radius (p. 352) The distance from the center of a circle to any point on the circle.

radio Distancia desde el centro de un círculo hasta cualquier punto del mismo.

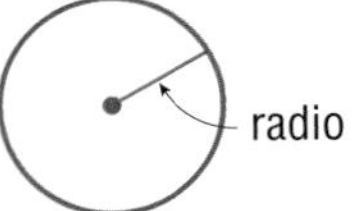

random (p. 633) Outcomes occur at random if each outcome is equally likely to occur.

azar Los resultados ocurren al azar si todos los resultados son equiprobables.

range (p. 591) The difference between the greatest number and the least number in a set of data.

rango La diferencia entre el número mayor y el número menor en un conjunto de datos.

range (p. 470) The set of output values in a function.

rango El conjunto de valores de salida en una función.

rate (p. 191) A ratio of two measurements having different units.

tasa Razón que compara dos cantidades que tienen distintas unidades de medida.

rate of change (p. 198) A rate that describes how one quantity changes in relation to another.

tasa de cambio Tasa que describe cómo cambia una cantidad con respecto a otras.

ratio (p. 190) A comparison of two numbers by division. The ratio of 2 to 3 can be stated as 2 out of 3, 2 to 3, 2:3, or $\frac{2}{3}$.

razón Comparación de dos números mediante división. La razón de 2 a 3 puede escribirse como 2 de cada 3, 2 a 3, 2:3, o $\frac{2}{3}$.

rational number (p. 84) Numbers of the form $\frac{a}{b}$, where a and b are integers and $b \neq 0$.

número racional Números de la forma $\frac{a}{b}$, donde a y b son enteros y $b \neq 0$.

real numbers (p. 155) The set of rational numbers together with the set of irrational numbers.

número real El conjunto de números racionales junto con el conjunto de números irracionales.

reciprocals (p. 102) The multiplicative inverse of a number. The product of reciprocals is 1.

recíproco El inverso multiplicativo de un número. El producto de recíprocos es 1.

reduction (p. 226) A dilation with a scale factor between 0 and 1.

reducción Dilatación con un factor de escala entre 0 y 1.

reflection (p. 332) A type of transformation in which a mirror image is produced by flipping a figure over a line.

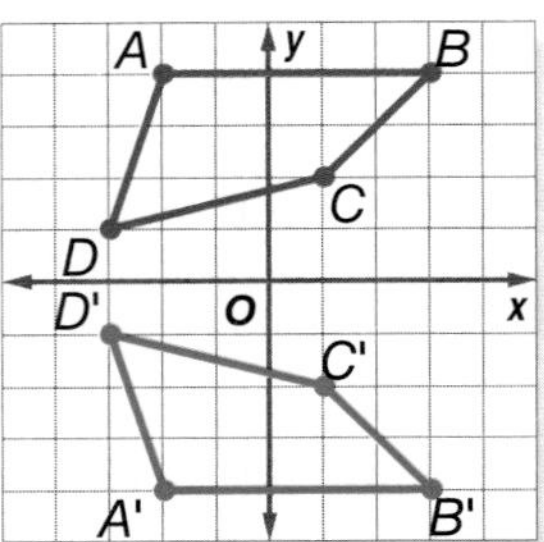

reflexión Tipo de transformación en que se produce una imagen especular al darle vuelta de campana a una figura por encima de una línea.

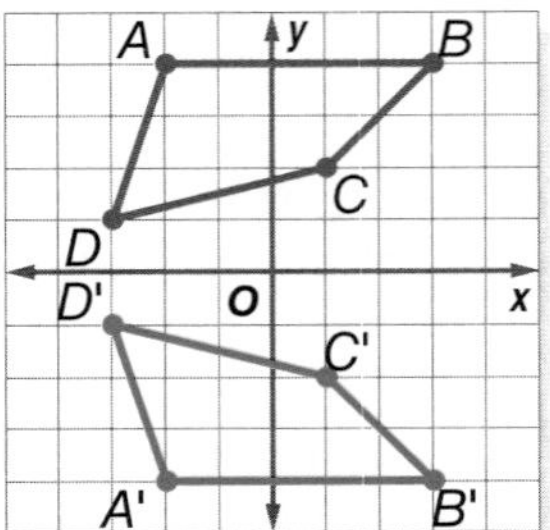

regular polygon (p. 317) A polygon that is equilateral and equiangular.

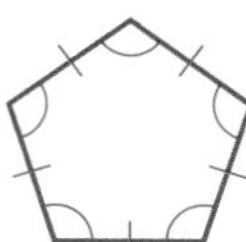

polígono regular Polígono equilátero y equiangular.

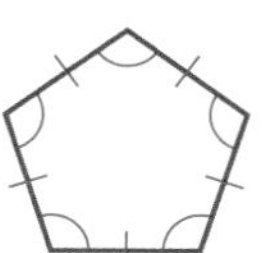

regular pyramid (p. 393) A pyramid whose base is a regular polygon.

pirámide regular Pirámide cuya base es un polígono regular.

repeating decimal (p. 85) A decimal whose digits repeat in groups of one or more. Examples are 0.181818… and 0.8333… .

decimal periódico Decimal cuyos dígitos se repiten en grupos de uno o más. Por ejemplo: 0.181818… y 0.8333… .

rise (p. 481) The vertical change between any two points on a line.

elevación El cambio vertical entre cualquier par de puntos en una recta.

rotational symmetry (p. 328) A figure has rotational symmetry if it can be turned less than 360° about its center and still look like the original.

simetría rotacional Una figura posee simetría rotacional si se puede girar menos de 360° en torno a su centro sin que esto cambie su apariencia con respecto a la figura original.

run (p. 481) The horizontal change between any two points on a line.

carrera El cambio horizontal entre cualquier par de puntos en una recta.

S

sample (p. 653) A randomly-selected group chosen for the purpose of collecting data.

muestra Grupo escogido al azar o aleatoriamente que se usa con el propósito de recoger datos.

sample space (p. 632) The set of all possible outcomes of a probability experiment.

espacio muestral Conjunto de todos los resultados posibles de un experimento probabilístico.

scale (p. 236) The ratio of a given length on a drawing or model to its corresponding actual length.

escala Razón de una longitud dada en un dibujo o modelo a su longitud real correspondiente.

scale drawing (p. 236) A drawing that is similar, but either larger or smaller than the actual object.

dibujo a escala Dibujo que es semejante, pero más grande o más pequeño que el objeto real.

scale factor (p. 219) The ratio of the lengths of two corresponding sides of two similar polygons.

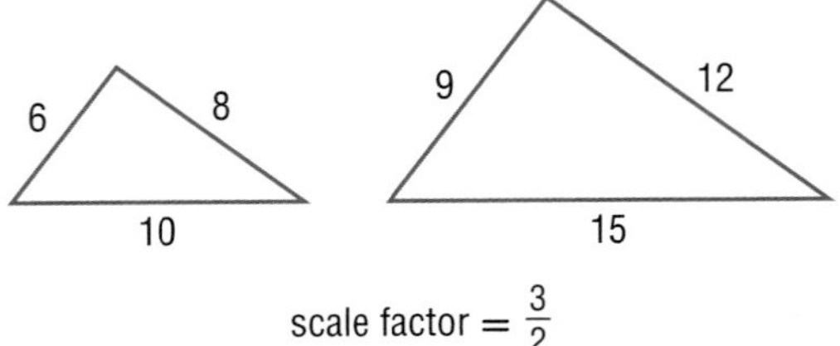

factor de escala La razón de las longitudes de dos lados correspondientes de dos polígonos semejantes.

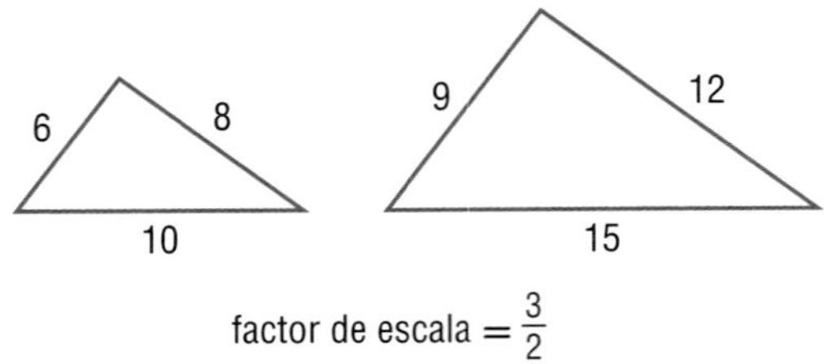

scale model (p. 236) A replica of an original object that is too large or too small to be built at actual size.

modelo a escala Una replica del objeto original, el cual es demasiado grande o demasiado pequeño como para construirlo de tamaño natural.

scatter plot (p. 510) A graph that shows the general relationship between two sets of data.

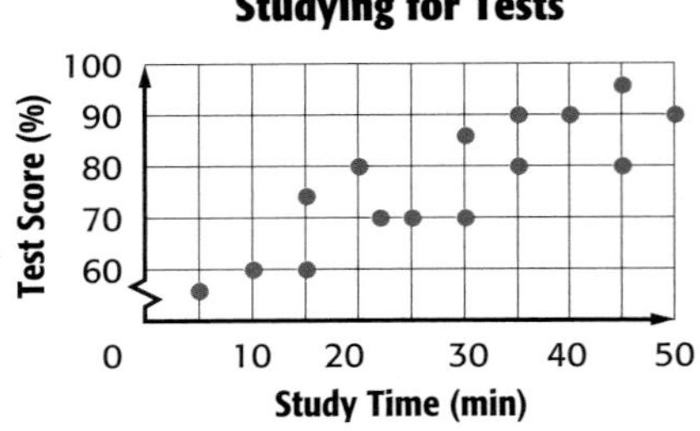

diagrama de dispersión Gráfica que muestra la relación general entre dos conjuntos de datos.

scientific notation (p. 130) A way of expressing numbers as the product of a number that is at least 1 but less than 10 and a power of 10. In scientific notation, 5,500 is 5.5×10^3.

notación científica Manera de expresar números como el producto de un número que es al menos igual a 1, pero menor que 10, por una potencia de 10. En notación científica, 5,500 es 5.5×10^3.

selling price (p. 286) The amount the customer pays for an item.

precio de venta Cantidad de dinero que paga un consumidor por un artículo.

sequence (p. 464) An ordered list of numbers, such as 0, 1, 2, 3 or 2, 4, 6, 8.

sucesión Lista ordenada de números, tales como 0, 1, 2, 3 o 2, 4, 6, 8.

similar (p. 218) Polygons that have the same shape are called similar polygons.

semejante Los polígonos que tienen la misma forma se llaman polígonos semejantes.

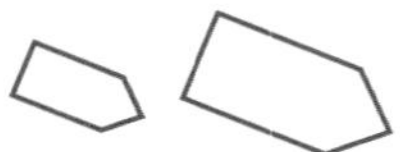

similar solids (p. 399) Solids that have the same shape and their corresponding linear measures are proportional.

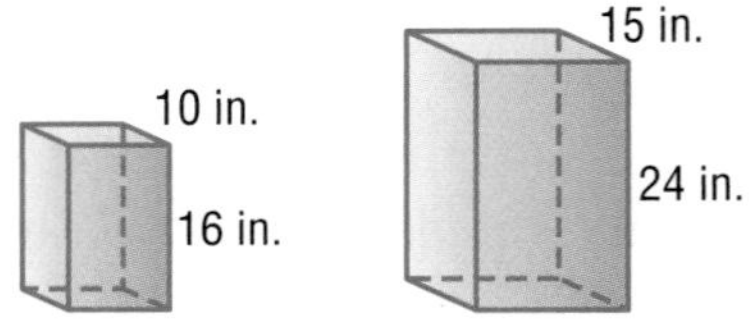

sólidos semejantes Sólidos que tienen la misma forma y cuyas medidas lineales correspondientes son proporcionales.

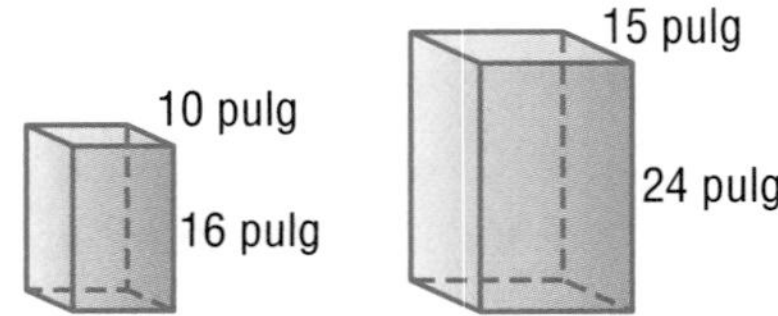

simple random sample (p. 653) A sample where each item or person in the population is as likely to be chosen as any other.

muestra aleatoria simple Muestra de una población que tiene la misma probabilidad de escogerse que cualquier otra.

simplest form (p. 418) An algebraic expression that has no like terms and no parentheses.

forma reducida Expresión algebraica que carece de términos semejantes y de paréntesis.

simplifying the expression (p. 418) Using properties to combine like terms.

simplificar una expresión El uso de propiedades para combinar términos semejantes.

slant height (p. 393) The altitude or height of each lateral face of a pyramid.

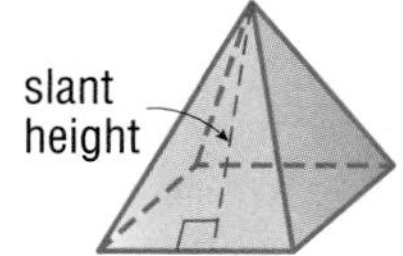

altura oblicua La longitud de la altura de cada cara lateral de una pirámide.

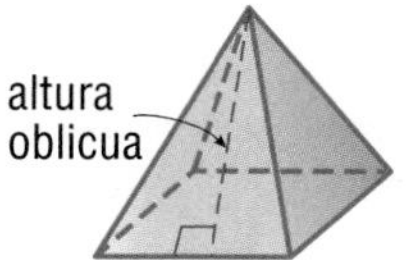

slope (p. 481) The rate of change between any two points on a line. The ratio of vertical change to horizontal change.

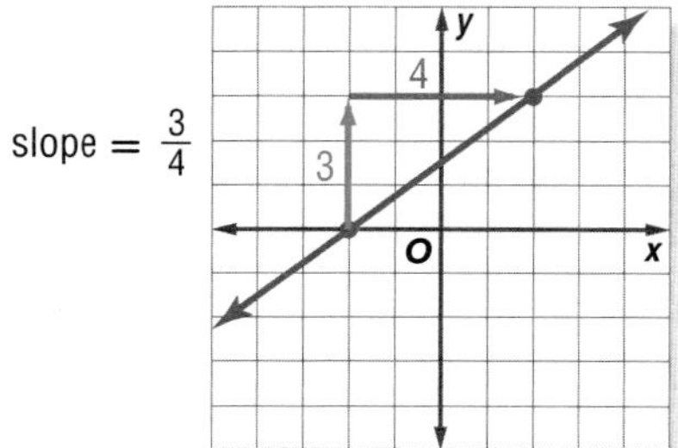

pendiente Razón de cambio entre cualquier par de puntos en una recta. La razón del cambio vertical al cambio horizontal.

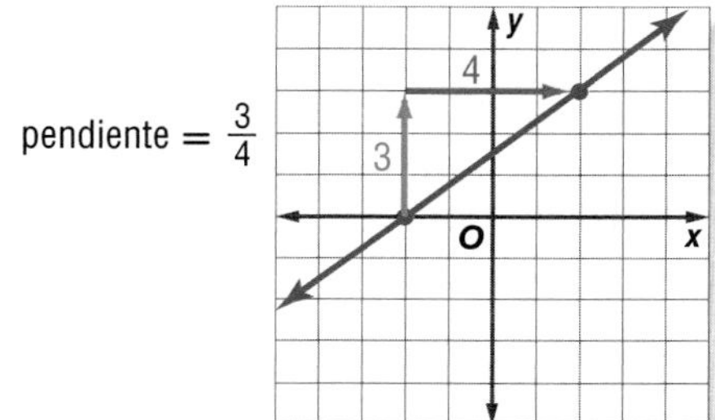

slope-intercept form (p. 495) An equation written in the form $y = mx + b$, where m is the slope and b is the y-intercept.

forma pendiente intersección Ecuación de la forma $y = mx + b$, donde m es la pendiente y b es la intersección y.

slope triangle (p. 493) In the figure, if $A(x_1, y_1)$ and $B(x_2, y_2)$, such that $x_1 < x_2$, are two points on a line, then the right triangle ABC is the slope triangle for the line.

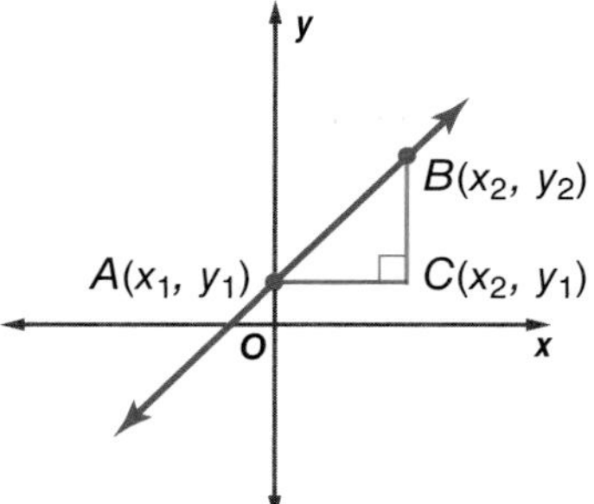

triángulo de la pendiente En la figura, si $A(x_1, y_1)$ y $B(x_2, y_2)$, tal que $x_1 < x_2$, son dos puntos sobre la recta, entonces el triángulo rectángulo ABC es el triángulo de la pendiente para la recta.

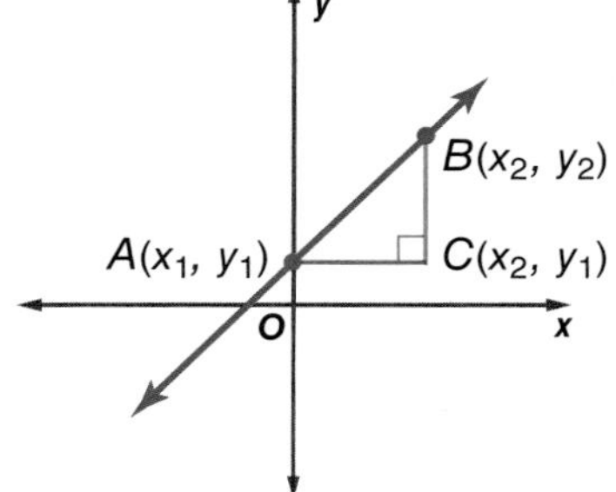

solid (p. 365) A three-dimensional figure formed by intersecting planes.

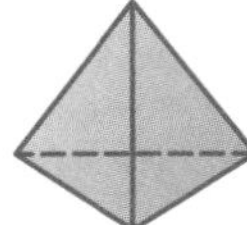

sólido Figura tridimensional formada por planos que se intersecan.

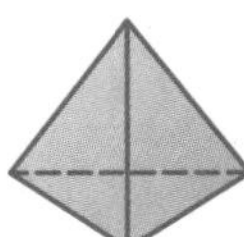

solution (p. 65) The value for the variable that makes an equation true. The solution of $10 + y = 25$ is 15.

solve (p. 65) Find the value of the variable that makes the equation true.

square root (p. 144) One of the two equal factors of a number. If $a^2 = b$, then a is the square root of b. A square root of 144 is 12 since $12^2 = 144$.

stem-and-leaf plot (p. 612) A system used to condense a set of data where the greatest place value of the data forms the stem and the next greatest place value forms the leaves.

stratified random sample (p. 653) A sampling method in which the population is divided into similar, non-overlapping groups. A simple random sample is then selected from each group.

Subtraction Property of Equality (p. 65) If you subtract the same number from each side of an equation, the two sides remain equal.

supplementary angles (p. 306) Two angles are supplementary if the sum of their measures is 180°.

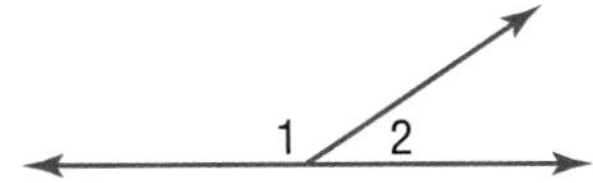

∠1 and ∠2 are supplementary angles.

systematic random sample (p. 653) A sampling method in which the items or people are selected according to a specific time or item interval.

system of equations (p. 502) A set of two or more equations with the same variables.

term (p. 464) A number, a variable, or a product of numbers and variables.

terminating decimal (p. 85) A decimal whose digits end. Every terminating decimal can be written as a fraction with a denominator of 10, 100, 1,000, and so on.

theoretical probability (p. 643) Probability based on known characteristics or facts.

solución El valor de la variable de una ecuación que hace que se cumpla la ecuación. La solución de $10 + y = 25$ es 15.

resolver Proceso de encontrar la variable que satisface una ecuación.

raíz cuadrada Uno de dos factores iguales de un número. Si $a^2 = b$, la a es la raíz cuadrada de b. Una raíz cuadrada de 144 es 12 porque $12^2 = 144$.

diagrama de tallo y hojas Sistema que se usa para condensar un conjunto de datos, en donde el mayor valor de posición de los datos forma el tallo y el siguiente valor de posición mayor forma las hojas.

muestra aleatoria estratificada Método de muestreo en que la población se divide en grupos semejantes que no se sobreponen. Luego se selecciona una muestra aleatoria simple de cada grupo.

propiedad de sustracción de la igualdad Si sustraes el mismo número de ambos lados de una ecuación, los dos lados permanecen iguales.

ángulos suplementarios Dos ángulos son suplementarios si la suma de sus medidas es 180°.

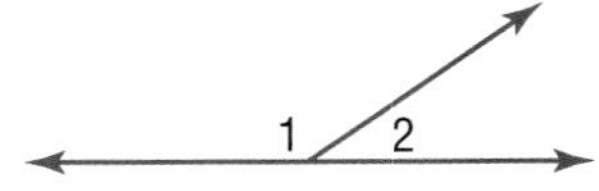

∠1 y ∠2 son ángulos suplementarios

muestra aleatoria sistemática Muestra en que los elementos de la muestra se escogen según un intervalo de tiempo o elemento específico.

sistema de ecuaciones Sistema de ecuaciones con las mismas variables.

término Un número, una variable o un producto de números y variables.

decimal terminal Decimal cuyos dígitos terminan. Todo decimal terminal puede escribirse como una fracción con un denominador 10, 100, 1,000, etc.

probabilidad teórica Probabilidad que se basa en características o hechos conocidos.

total surface area (p. 386) The sum of the areas of the surfaces of a solid.

área de superficie total La suma del área de las superficies de un sólido.

transformation (p. 332) A mapping of a geometric figure.

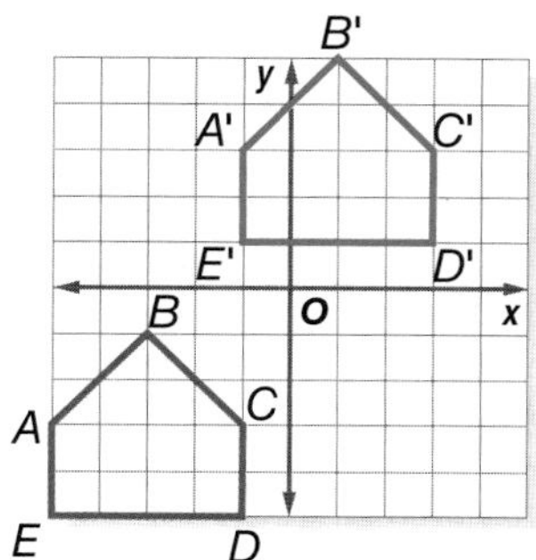

transformación Movimiento de una figura geométrica.

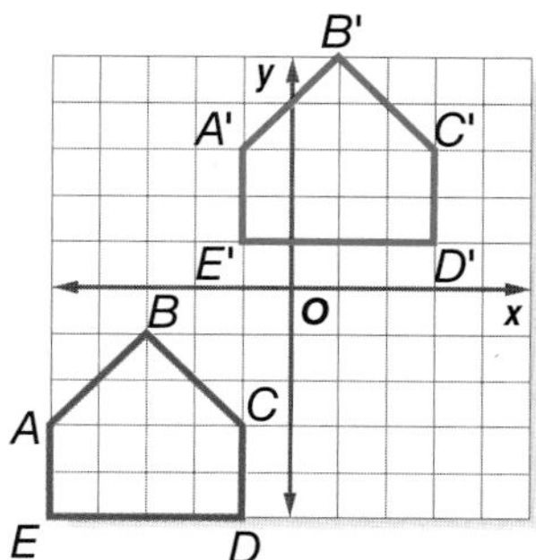

translation (p. 337) A transformation in which a figure is slid horizontally, vertically, or both.

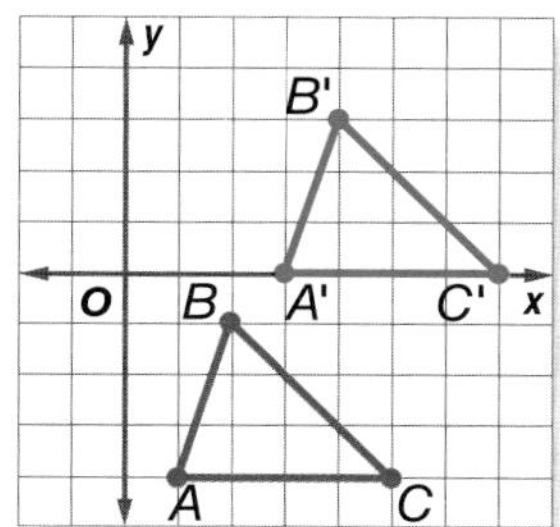

traslación Transformación en que una figura se desliza horizontal o verticalmente o de ambas maneras.

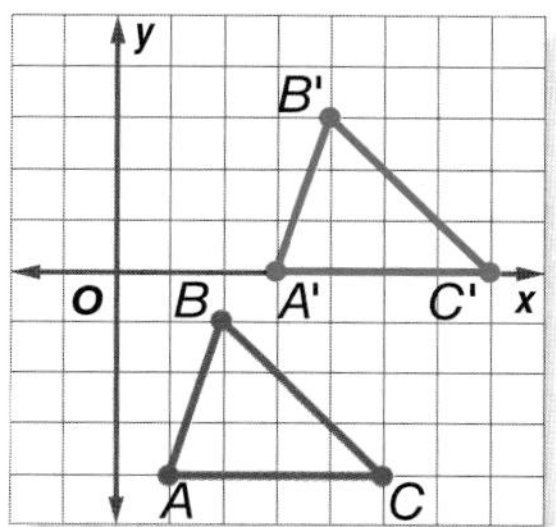

transversal (p. 307) A line that intersects two or more other lines to form eight angles.

transversal Recta que interseca dos o más rectas formando ocho ángulos.

tree diagram (p. 632) A diagram used to show the total number of possible outcomes in a probability experiment.

diagrama de árbol Diagrama que se usa para mostrar el número total de resultados posibles en experimento probabilístico.

two-step equation (p. 422) An equation that contains two operations.

ecuación de dos pasos Ecuación que contiene dos operaciones.

U

unbiased sample (p. 653) A sample that is selected so that it is representative of the entire population.

muestra no sesgada Muestra que se selecciona de modo que sea representativa de la población entera.

unit rate/ratio (pp. 191, 214) A rate with a denominator of 1.

razón unitaria Una tasa con un denominador de 1.

unlike fractions (p. 114) Fractions whose denominators are different.

fracciones con distinto denominador Fracciones cuyos denominadores son diferentes.

upper quartile (p. 599) The median of the upper half of a set of data, represented by UQ.

cuartil superior La mediana de la mitad superior de un conjunto de números, denotada por CS.

V

variable (p. 29) A symbol, usually a letter, used to represent a number in mathematical expressions or sentences.

variable Un símbolo, por lo general, una letra, que se usa para representar números en expresiones o enunciados matemáticos.

Venn diagram (p. 152) A diagram that uses circles to show how elements among sets of numbers or objects are related.

diagrama de Venn Diagrama que utiliza círculos para mostrar la relación entre elementos dentro de un conjunto de números.

vertex (p. 365) The vertex of a prism is the point where three or more planes intersect.

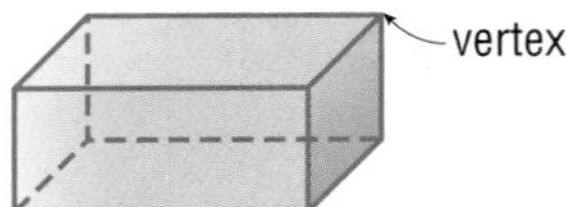

vértice El vértice de un prisma es el punto en que se intersecan dos o más planos del prisma.

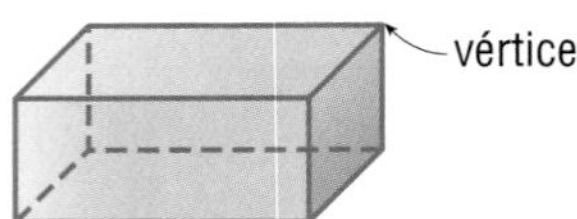

vertical angles (p. 306) Opposite angles formed by the intersection of two lines. Vertical angles are congruent. In the figure, the vertical angles are $\angle 1$ and $\angle 3$, and $\angle 2$ and $\angle 4$.

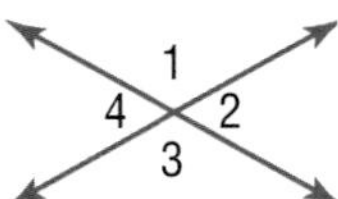

ángulos opuestos por el vértice Ángulos congruentes que se forman de la intersección de dos rectas. En la figura, los ángulos opuestos por el vértice son $\angle 1$ y $\angle 3$, y $\angle 2$ y $\angle 4$.

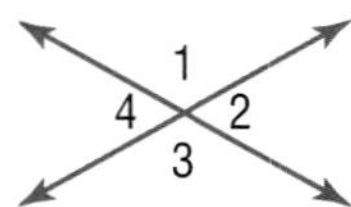

volume (p. 371) The number of cubic units needed to fill the space occupied by a solid.

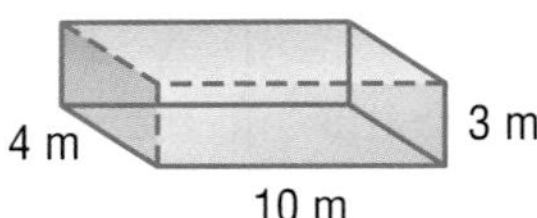

$V = 10 \times 4 \times 3 = 120$ cubic meters

volumen El número de unidades cúbicas que se requieren para llenar el espacio que ocupa un sólido.

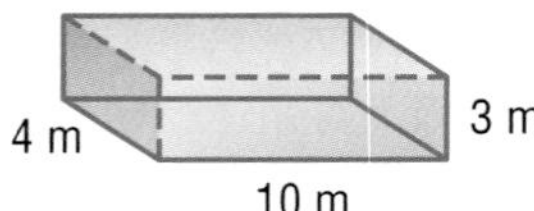

$V = 10 \times 4 \times 3 = 120$ metros cúbicos

voluntary response sample (p. 654) A sample which involves only those who want to participate in the sampling.

muestra de respuesta voluntaria Muestra que involucra sólo aquellos que quieren participar en el muestreo.

X

***x*-axis** (p. 173) The horizontal number line that helps to form the coordinate plane.

eje *x* La recta numérica horizontal que ayuda a formar el plano de coordenadas.

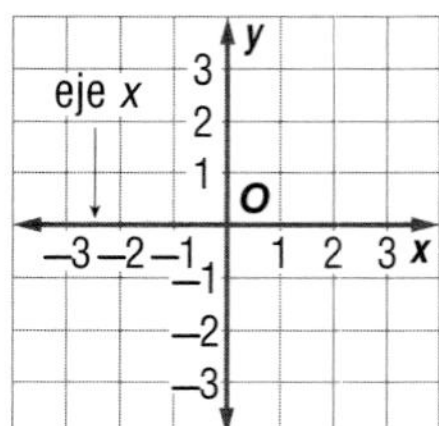

***x*-coordinate** (p. 173) The first number of an ordered pair.

coordenada *x* El primer número de un par ordenado.

Y

y-axis (p. 173) The vertical number line that helps to form the coordinate plane.

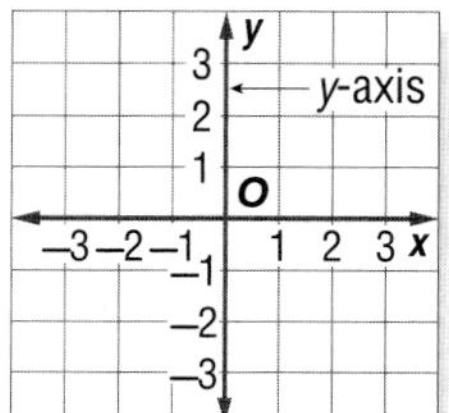

y-coordinate (p. 173) The second number of an ordered pair.

y-intercept (p. 495) The value of *y* where the graph crosses the *y*-axis.

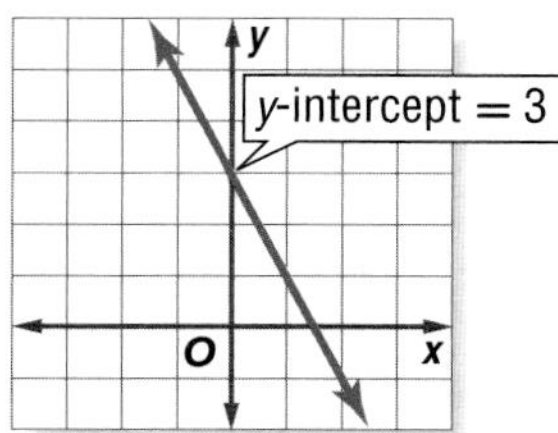

eje *y* La recta numérica vertical que ayuda a formar el plano de coordenadas.

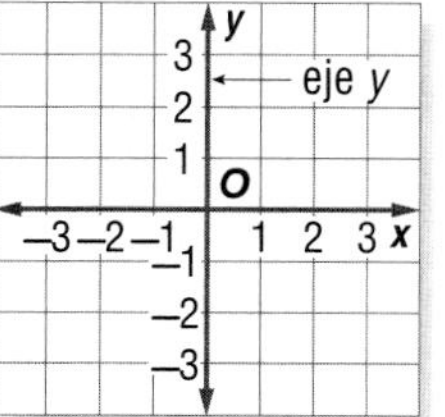

coordenada *y* El segundo número de un par ordenado.

intersección *y* El valor de y donde la gráfica cruza el eje *y*.

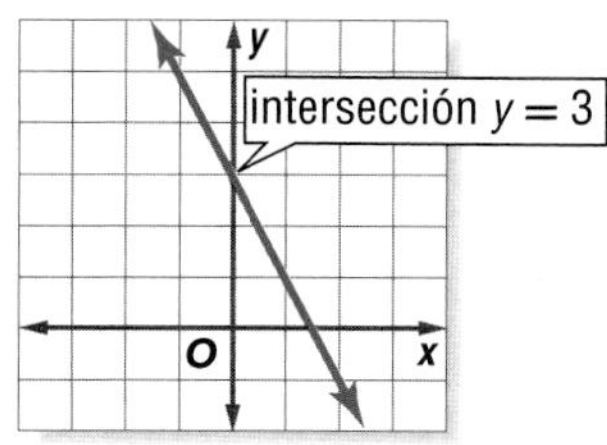

Selected Answers

For Homework Help, go to Hotmath.com
Complete, step-by-step solutions of most odd-numbered exercises are provided free of charge.

Chapter 1 Algebra: Integers

Page 23 ***Chapter 1*** ***Getting Ready***

1. 77 **3.** 79.5 **5.** \$281.50 **7.** 33 **9.** 72.63 **11.** 14 **13.** 108 **15.** 1,220 **17.** 32 **19.** 0.4 **21.** \$0.79

Pages 27–28 ***Lesson 1-1***

1. 12 units **3.** about 500 points **5.** 21 **7.** Delaware; 236 people per square mile **9.** 18

11. 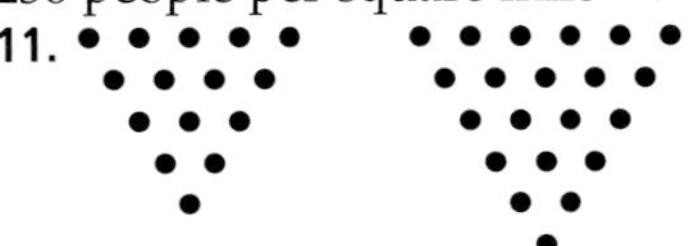

13. 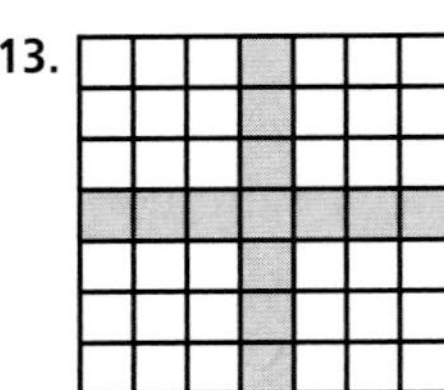

100; Sample answer: Each figure contains 4 squares made up of white tiles with side lengths 1 less than the figure number. The sixth figure contains 21 green tiles. So, it has four squares with side lengths 5 white tiles by 5 white tiles. $5 \times 5 = 25$ tiles in each square and $4 \times 25 = 100$ white tiles total. **15.** Explore — Identify what information is given and what you need to find. Plan — Estimate the answer and then select a strategy for solving. Solve — Carry out the plan and solve. Check — Compare the answer to the estimate and determine if it is reasonable. If not, make a new plan. **17.** G **19.** 309 **21.** 700

Pages 32–34 ***Lesson 1-2***

1. 81 **3.** 13 **5.** 14 **7.** 72°F **9.** Assoc. (×) **11.** 16 **13.** 47 **15.** 72 **17.** 3 **19.** 23 **21.** 26 **23.** 10° C **25.** Iden. (×) **27.** Comm. (+) **29.** Distributive Property **31.** Assoc. (×) **33.** true **35.** false; $(24 \div 4) \div 2 \neq 24 \div (4 \div 2)$ **37.** 6,966 households **39.** $2 \cdot n - 1$; 19

41.

Fun World			
Number of People	**Total Cost (\$)**	**Number of People**	**Total Cost (\$)**
10	370	18	666
11	407	19	703
12	444	20	740
13	481	21	777
14	518	22	814
15	555	23	851
16	592	24	888
17	629	25	925

43. Sample answer: If the group size is 10–14 people, then Fun World would cost less. If the group size is 15–25, then Coaster City costs less. **45.** true **47.** false; $6 + 7 \cdot (2 + 5) = 55$ **49.** The everyday meaning of variable is something that is likely to change or vary, and the mathematical meaning of a variable is a placeholder for a value that can change or vary. **51.** H **53.** \$1.33 **55.** < **57.** >

Pages 37–39 ***Lesson 1-3***

1. > **3.** < **5.** 5 **7.** 1 **9.** 13 **11.** 4 **13.** > **15.** < **17.** < **19.** > **21.** < **23.** = **25.** 14 **27.** 18 **29.** 6 **31.** 15 **33.** 17

35. {5, 25} 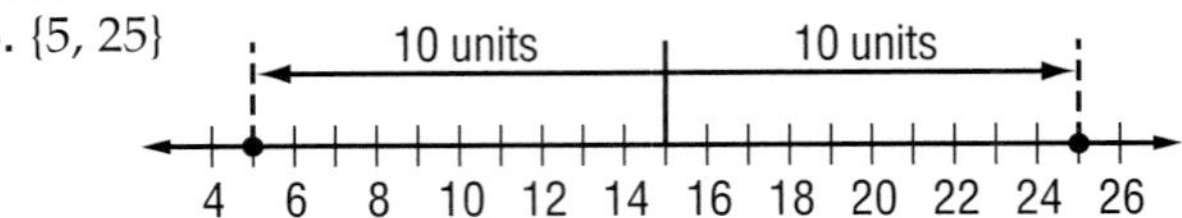

37. {19, 33} 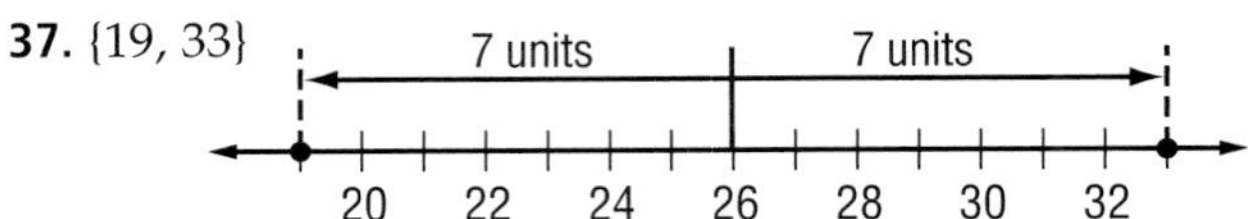

39. helium

41. −169°F

100 100

−469° −369° −269° −169°

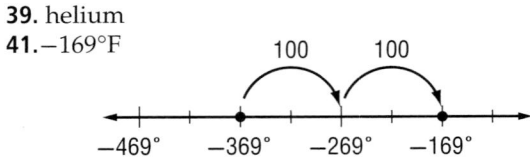

43. Never; the absolute value of a positive number is always positive. **45.** Always; if $b \geq 0$, then $a - |b| = a - b$ which is less than or equal to $a + b$. If $b < 0$, then $a - |b| = a - (-b) = a + b$. **47.** The absolute value of a number is its distance from 0 on a number line. Since distance can never be negative, the absolute value of a number can never be negative. **49.** H **51.** 7 **53.** 3 **55.** 23 **57.** 28

Pages 44–45 ***Lesson 1-4***

1. −9 **3.** −15 **5.** −11 **7.** 17 **9.** −11 **11.** 22 **13.** −20 **15.** −36 **17.** 15 **19.** −7 **21.** 24 **23.** 1 **25.** −11 **27.** −18 **29.** Mon, −2 feet; Tues, −3 feet; Wed, -2 feet **31.** $-350 + 400 = 50$; The elevation of the plane was 50 feet higher **33.** \$48 **35.** −133 **37.** −2 **39.** −20 **41.** Sometimes; If x and y have different signs, then $|x + y| \neq |x| + |y|$. If x and y have the same sign, then $|x + y| = |x| + |y|$. $|-2 + 5| = |3|$ or 3, $|-2| + |5| = 2 + 5$ or 7, and $3 \neq 7$ **43.** B **45.** > **47.** < **49.** Sample answer: about 134.37 million **51.** 17 **53.** 4

Pages 46–49 ***Lesson 1-5***

1. −5 **3.** −14 **5.** 10 **7.** 4 **9.** +49°F **11.** 8 **13.** 6 **15.** −4 **17.** −20 **19.** −17 **21.** 14 **23.** 16 **25.** −1 **27.** 3 **29.** Asia; 30,367 ft **31.** −6 **33.** 5 **35.** 17 **37.** 281 **39.** Christie Kerr; 8 **41.** 52 **43.** 36 **45.** David; only the second integer should be replaced with its opposite. **47.** false; $3 - 2 \neq 2 - 3$ **49.** B **51.** \$705.04 **53.** 15 **55.** 37 **57.** 15

Pages 54–56 ***Lesson 1-6***

1. −20 **3.** −21 **5.** 9 **7.** −4 **9.** 9 **11.** 5 **13.** −11 **15.** −1 **17.** −56 **19.** −40 **21.** −36 **23.** 24 **25.** 16 **27.** −84 **29.** 207°F **31.** −10 **33.** 5 **35.** −21 **37.** 12 **39.** −4 cm **41.** −21 **43.** 1 **45.** −3 **47.** −4 **49.** 288 min or 4 h 48 min **51.** −64 **53.** 0 **55.** −89
57. 1,230 million admissions; The average change in admissions from 2002 to 2004 was −50 million admissions per year. If this average change per year remains the same, then 2010 − 2004 or 6 years later in 2010 the number of admissions will be $6 \cdot (-50) + 1{,}530$ or 1,230 million. **59.** Positive; the product of two negative numbers is always a positive number.
61. Positive; the product of four negative numbers is always a positive number. **63.** false; $3 - 5 = -2$
65. When multiplying $-2(-3)(-4)$, you can work from left to right since the signs are the same. First multiply -2×-3. The signs are the same, so you get a positive 6. Next multiply 6×-4, which gives you −24 because the signs are different. **67.** G **69.** 9 **71.** 22 **73.** −11 **75.** −4 **77.** Sample answer: difference **79.** Sample answer: separated

Pages 59–61 ***Lesson 1-7***

1. s = Corey's score; $20 = 4s$ **3.** d = original depth; $d - 75 = -600$ **5.** C **7.** a = class average; $a - 5 = 82$ **9.** d = number of days; $\frac{-75}{d} = 15$ **11.** m = amount of money; $\frac{m}{4} = 235$ **13.** h = height; $15 = \frac{h}{4}$ **15.** s = score; $s + 5 = -3$ **17.** $d = 24g$ **19.** $t = m + \frac{1}{2}$ **21.** $f = 3y$

23.

Map Distance, *m* (inches)	Actual Distance, *a* (miles)
1	20
2	40
3	60
4	80
m	20*m*

$a = 20m$

25. Sample answer: Let n represent the number in the sequence and p the position of the number in the sequence; $n = 2p$. **27.** Zoe; Toshi's expression is the translation of *14 is 6 less n*, instead of 14 is 6 less than n. **29.** C **31.** −90 **33.** −2 **35.** −1,080°F

Pages 62–63 ***Lesson 1-8***

1. Sample answer: The students had an ending number and the operations that led to that number. They need to work their way back to the beginning number.
3. Sample answer: Jacob spent a third of his money as a deposit on a campsite. Then he bought sports equipment that cost $21. Finally, he spent $16 at the grocery store. How much money did Jacob have initially if he now has $2 left?
Start with 2 and add 16. $\longrightarrow 2 + 16 = 18$
Add 21. $\longrightarrow 18 + 21 = 39$
Divide by $\frac{1}{3} \longrightarrow 39 \div \frac{1}{3} = 117$
5. 6:15 A.M. **7.** week 12 **9.** $600 **11.** Subtraction followed by subtraction; 69 years old

Pages 68–69 ***Lesson 1-9***

1. 6 **3.** −12 **5.** 7 **7.** 3 **9.** 17 **11.** −6 **13.** −14 **15.** 1 **17.** −10 **19.** 7 **21.** $b - 50 = 124$; $74 **23.** $(-18) + h = 54$; $h = 72$ in. or 6 ft **25.** $a = 21.9 - 6.4$; 15.5 **27.** Sample answer: $n + 5 = 2$, $n - 6 = -9$ **29.** Subtract 5 from each side to get $|x| = 2$. If $|x| = -2$, $|-2| = 2$ and if $x = 2$, $|2| = 2$. **31.** C **33.** James will need to drive 615 miles the third day. **35.** $x \div 2 = 3$ **37.** −36 **39.** −60

Pages 72–73 ***Lesson 1-10***

1. 8 **3.** 6 **5.** −36 **7.** $\frac{3}{4}x = 1{,}350$; $1,800 **9.** 8 **11.** −2 **13.** −7 **15.** 54 **17.** −100 **19.** −72 **21.** $1{,}200t = 6{,}000$; $5 **23.** $16c = 64$; 4 **25.** $8g = 120$; 15 **27.** −8 **29.** 6 **31.** $180 = 45d$; 4 ft **33.** Sample answer: it is greater than 300. **35.** Sample answer: Divide each side by −4. Apply the Division Prop. of Equality because the inverse operation of multiplication is division. **37.** H **39.** $8 + j = 15$ **41.** $3p = 9$ **43.** −175 **45.** −448 **47.** −7 **49.** 13 **51.** +45 **53.** −5

Pages 74–78 ***Chapter 1*** ***Study Guide and Review***

1. false; inverse operations **3.** false; equation **5.** false; counterexample **7.** true **9.** true **11.** $70 **13.** 36 **15.** 23 **17.** 3 mi **19.** > **21.** 5 **23.** −33 **25.** −34 **27.** 5 **29.** 3 **31.** 79 ft **33.** −21 **35.** −12 **37.** −11 **39.** p = length of her best jump; $670 = p - 5$ **41.** 4:45 P.M. **43.** 50 **45.** 12 **47.** −15 **49.** $x + 32 = 150$; 118 people **51.** −5 **53.** 294 **55.** $28x = 168$, 6 mo

Chapter 2 Algebra: Rational Numbers

Page 83 ***Chapter 2*** ***Getting Ready***

1. −9 **3.** −14 **5.** 17°F **7.** −9 **9.** 27 **11.** 28 **13.** 125 **15.** 72 **17.** 63

Pages 87–89 ***Lesson 2-1***

1. 0.8 **3.** −1.725 **5.** $4.8\overline{3}$ **7.** 0.429 **9.** $\frac{8}{25}$ **11.** $-\frac{5}{9}$ **13.** $2\frac{5}{33}$ **15.** 0.4 **17.** 0.825 **19.** −0.15625 **21.** 5.3125 **23.** $-0.\overline{54}$ **25.** $-7.1\overline{7}$ **27.** $0.1\overline{6}$ **29.** 0.417 **31.** $\frac{1}{2}$ **33.** $-7\frac{8}{25}$ **35.** $-\frac{5}{11}$ **37.** $2\frac{7}{9}$ **39.** See students' work. **41.** $2\frac{2}{5}$ **43.** $\frac{7}{8}$ in.; 0.875 in. **45.** $8\frac{9}{10}$ cm; 8.9 cm **47.** $1.06 = 1\frac{3}{50}$; $0.24 = \frac{6}{25}$; $-2.72 = -2\frac{18}{25}$; $-3.40 = -3\frac{2}{5}$ **49.** Sample answer: $0.\overline{12}$; Since $0.\overline{12} = \frac{4}{33}$, it is a rational number. **51.** When dividing, there are two possibilities for the remainder. If the remainder is 0, the decimal terminates. If the remainder is not 0, then at the point where the remainder repeats or equals the original dividend, the decimal begins to repeat. **53.** D **55.** G **57.** −22 **59.** −4 **61.** 3h **63.** 15 **65.** 24

Pages 93–95 ***Lesson 2-2***

1. > **3.** > **5.** > **7.** > **9.** Gulfport, Galveston, Mobile, Baltimore, Key West, Washington **11.** <
13. > **15.** = **17.** 0.004, $\frac{1}{125}$, $\frac{1}{60}$, $0.0\overline{6}$, 0.125, $\frac{1}{4}$
19. < **21.** > **23.** > **25.** > **27.** < **29.** >
31.

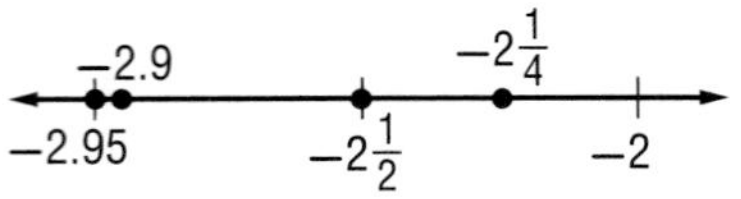

33.

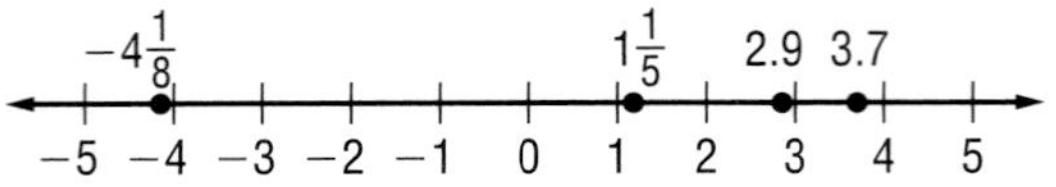

35. University of North Carolina **37.** Greatest to least; since the numerators are the same, the values of the fractions decrease as the denominators increase.
39. No; $0.\overline{2} = \frac{2}{9}$. **41.** C **43.** 0.875 in. **45.** −15
47. −27 **49.** 24 **51.** 28 **53.** −51

Pages 99–101 ***Lesson 2-3***

1. $\frac{3}{7}$ **3.** 1 **5.** $-\frac{1}{12}$ **7.** $7\frac{1}{3}$ **9.** −12
11. $\frac{2 \text{ dollars}}{1 \text{ pound}} \cdot 2\frac{5}{8}$ pounds = \$5.25 **13.** $\frac{1}{48}$ **15.** $\frac{3}{5}$
17. $-\frac{9}{40}$ **19.** $\frac{1}{35}$ **21.** $14\frac{1}{6}$ **23.** $1\frac{1}{2}$ **25.** $2\frac{1}{3}$ in. by $3\frac{1}{3}$ in.
27. $\frac{150{,}000 \text{ people}}{1 \text{ square mile}} \cdot 2.25$ square miles = 337,500 people
29. $-\frac{2}{9}$ **31.** $\frac{4}{27}$ **33.** $\frac{3}{20}$ **35.** $8\frac{8}{15}$ **37.** $7\frac{14}{25}$
39. $-\frac{2}{27}$ **41.** about 4 million square miles **43.** $\frac{33}{2{,}000}$
45. $39\frac{1}{16}$ **47.** $101\frac{1}{4}$ **49.** Jorge; to multiply mixed numbers, you must first rename them as fractions.
51. $\frac{6}{7}$ **53.** B **55.** < **57.** = **59.** $\frac{11}{100}$ oz. **61.** $C = 150s$
63. −3 **65.** −23

Pages 105–107 ***Lesson 2-4***

1. $\frac{7}{5}$ **3.** $-\frac{4}{11}$ **5.** $1\frac{1}{4}$ **7.** $\frac{1}{2}$ **9.** $\frac{3}{10}$ **11.** $-\frac{43}{82}$ **13.** $-\frac{9}{7}$
15. $\frac{1}{15}$ **17.** $\frac{5}{17}$ **19.** $\frac{8}{15}$ **21.** $\frac{4}{5}$ **23.** $-1\frac{1}{15}$ **25.** $\frac{5}{6}$
27. $\frac{1}{10}$ **29.** $\frac{2}{15}$ **31.** $1\frac{1}{2}$ **33.** $-2\frac{5}{8}$ **35.** $3\frac{2}{3}$
37. $1\frac{1}{2}$ hours **39.** 4 hummingbirds **41.** 8.5 m
43. Sample answer: $\frac{2}{3}$; The additive inverse of $\frac{2}{3}$ is $-\frac{2}{3}$ since $\frac{2}{3} + -\frac{2}{3} = 0$, and the multiplicative inverse is $\frac{3}{2}$ since $\frac{2}{3} \cdot \frac{3}{2} = 1$. **45.** $30 \div \frac{3}{4}$; 30 times a number less than 1 will be less than 30. However, 30 divided by a number less than 1 will be greater than 30. **47.** $\frac{53}{72}$
49. B **51.** $\frac{3}{8}$ **53.** 7 **55.** play sports **57.** −10
59. 8 **61.** −18

Pages 110–112 ***Lesson 2-5***

1. $-\frac{2}{5}$ **3.** $-1\frac{2}{9}$ **5.** $-\frac{1}{2}$ **7.** $3\frac{2}{9}$ **9.** $6\frac{11}{16}$ **11.** $\frac{1}{3}$
13. $\frac{1}{6}$ **15.** $-1\frac{2}{5}$ **17.** $-\frac{1}{2}$ **19.** $11\frac{1}{4}$ **21.** $5\frac{1}{5}$ **23.** $-5\frac{2}{3}$
25. $1\frac{3}{5}$ **27.** $18\frac{2}{3}$ ft **29.** $-7\frac{1}{5}$ **31.** 76 in. **33.** $7\frac{2}{3}$
35. $-8\frac{1}{3}$ **37.** $56\frac{3}{5}$ seconds **39.** $60\frac{3}{8}$ in. **41.** Heather; to add like fractions, add the numerators and write the sum over the denominator. **43.** Sample answer: You are 2 miles away from your destination. You travel $1\frac{3}{10}$ miles. How far are you from your destination?; $\frac{7}{10}$ mi
45. G **47.** $\frac{5}{16}$ **49.** $\frac{3}{4}$ **51.** 3 **53.** 14 **55.** 21,600
57. 18 **59.** 20

Pages 116–118 ***Lesson 2-6***

1. $\frac{7}{12}$ **3.** $-1\frac{1}{9}$ **5.** $\frac{37}{117}$ **7.** $-1\frac{17}{30}$ **9.** $-1\frac{35}{72}$ **11.** $-\frac{1}{3}$
13. $-1\frac{5}{14}$ **15.** $-\frac{13}{24}$ **17.** $-\frac{5}{99}$ **19.** $-5\frac{3}{10}$ **21.** $14\frac{13}{14}$
23. $-10\frac{3}{8}$ **25.** $-3\frac{23}{24}$ **27.** $2\frac{3}{5}$ mi **29.** $-3\frac{11}{24}$
31. $45\frac{1}{2}$ in^2 **33.** $x = 6\frac{1}{8}$ **35.** Sample answer: $\frac{3}{4} - \frac{1}{3} = \frac{5}{12}$ **37.** $\frac{8}{15}$ **39.** $\frac{2}{3} + \frac{3}{4} = 1\frac{5}{12}$
41. $\frac{2}{3} \div \frac{3}{4} = \frac{8}{9}$ **43.** H **45.** $-\frac{11}{15}$ **47.** −4
49. $24d = 2{,}967$; about 124 days **51.** −31 **53.** −56

Pages 121–123 ***Lesson 2-7***

1. −4.37 **3.** $\frac{3}{8}$ **5.** −54 **7.** 5 **9.** $0.24n = 27.3$; 113.75 revolutions **11.** 7.53 **13.** $-\frac{8}{9}$ **15.** −7.42
17. 36 **19.** −7 **21.** 12.65 **23.** $9.4t = 13.9$; 1.5 visitors **25.** $\frac{4}{9}$ **27.** −29.4 **29.** 2 min 12 sec
31. 31.832 m^2 **33.** $s = 108 \div 9\frac{5}{8}$; 11 shelves
35. 13.72 cm **37.** $-\frac{1}{4}\left(\frac{1}{4}x\right)$ does not belong because $-\frac{1}{4}$ and $\frac{1}{4}$ are not reciprocals. **39.** Sample answer: Use the Multiplication Property of Equality to multiply each side of the equation by $-\frac{3}{2}$ which is the multiplicative inverse of $-\frac{2}{3}$. **41.** G **43.** $\frac{13}{42}$ **45.** $-12\frac{3}{10}$
47. $198\frac{3}{4}$ ft **49.** $x + (-6) = 24$; 30 **51.** 27 **53.** −29

Pages 124–125 ***Lesson 2-8***

1. You are adding 4, 6, and 8, to columns 1, 2, and 3, respectively, to get the answer in the next column. Add 10 to column 4 to get the answer in column 5. He will complete 78 curl-ups in week 8. **3.** Each height is $\frac{2}{3}$ times the previous height; 5th bounce **5.** 44 people
7. \$4,500 **9.** 1 hour 36 minutes **11.** eighth note; sixteenth note; thirty-second note **13.** 8,388,608

Pages 128–129 ***Lesson 2-9***

1. $2^3 \cdot 3^3$ **3.** $\left(\frac{1}{2}\right)^2 p^3 k^2$ **5.** $\frac{1}{343}$ **7.** $\frac{1}{243}$ **9.** 40,000
11. $3^2 \cdot 5 \cdot q^3$ **13.** $2^2 \cdot d^3 \cdot k^2$ **15.** $5^2 \cdot \left(\frac{1}{6}\right)^3 \cdot x^2 \cdot y^5$
17. $\frac{1}{81}$ **19.** $\frac{9}{25}$ **21.** $\frac{1}{729}$ **23.** $\frac{1}{64}$ **25.** 81 **27.** 67.5
29. 887,000,000 miles **31.** 1.913×10^9 or 1,913,000,000 mi
33. 280,000 **35.** $\frac{1}{3{,}200}$ **37.** $\frac{5}{3{,}087}$ **39.** 1

41. $6^{-3}, 6^0, 6^2$; Sample answer: the exponents in order from least to greatest are −3, 0, 2. **43.** Sample answer: 3^{-2}; $3^{-2} = \frac{1}{3^2}$ or $\frac{1}{9}$ **45.** Sample answer: The expression $(-4)^2$ means negative 4 to the second power. $(-4)^2 = (-4)(-4) = 16$. The expression 4^{-2} means 4 to the negative second power. $4^{-2} = \frac{1}{4^2}$ or $\frac{1}{16}$
47. G **49.** 12 mi **51.** 2,000,000 **53.** 2,600

Pages 132–133 ***Lesson 2-10***

1. 73,200 **3.** 0.455 **5.** 2.77×10^5 **7.** 4.955×10^{-5} **9.** 2006, 2003, 2005, 2004 **11.** 3,160 **13.** 4,265,000 **15.** 0.00011 **17.** 0.0000252 **19.** 4.3×10^4 **21.** 1.47×10^8 **23.** 7.2×10^{-3} **25.** 9.01×10^{-5} **27.** Arctic, Southern, Indian, Atlantic, Pacific **29.** $-4.56 \times 10^2, -4.56 \times 10^{-2}, -4.56 \times 10^{-3}, 4.56 \times 10^2$ **31.** 5.0444986×10^{13} **33.** about 1,454.5 times heavier

35a. $\frac{(1.3 \times 10^5)(5.7 \times 10^{-3})}{4 \times 10^{-4}} = 1.8525 \times 10^6$

35b. $\frac{(9 \times 10^4)(1.6 \times 10^{-3})}{(2 \times 10^5)(3 \times 10^4)(1.2 \times 10^{-4})} = 2 \times 10^{-4}$

37. D **39.** 288 **41.** −21 **43.** $2\frac{5}{12}$

Pages 134–138 ***Chapter 2*** ***Study Guide and Review***

1. true **3.** true **5.** false; rational numbers **7.** true **9.** true **11.** $1.\overline{3}$ **13.** −2.3 **15.** $\frac{3}{10}$ **17.** $4\frac{1}{3}$ **19.** 0.26 **21.** < **23.** = **25.** $-\frac{3}{4}, -\frac{1}{2}$, 0, 0.75 **27.** 1 **29.** $\frac{1}{2}$ **31.** $5\frac{1}{4}$ c **33.** $-\frac{7}{8}$ **35.** $-3\frac{7}{10}$ **37.** 1 **39.** $-\frac{3}{4}$ **41.** $2\frac{1}{2}$ h **43.** $\frac{53}{60}$ **45.** $3\frac{3}{5}$ **47.** $-6\frac{9}{10}$ **49.** 3.2 **51.** $1\frac{1}{6}$ **53.** $15 = \frac{3}{8}m$; 40 **55.** 15.2 minutes or 15 minutes 12 seconds **57.** 3^5 **59.** x^4y **61.** 625 **63.** $\frac{1}{125}$ **65.** 216 **67.** 67,100 **69.** 0.015 **71.** 6.4×10^{-5} **73.** 8.75×10^7 **75.** 93,000,000 mi; 9.3×10^7 mi

Chapter 3 Real Numbers and the Pythagorean Theorem

Page 143 ***Chapter 3*** ***Getting Ready***

1–4.

y
A(−1, 3)
D(−4, 0)
O
x
C(−2, −3)
B(2, −4)

5. 20 **7.** 164 **9.** 394 **11.** 15 **13.** 17

Pages 146–147 ***Lesson 3-1***

1. 5 **3.** −1.3 **5.** ±10 **7.** 6 or −6 **9.** 2.5 *or* −2.5 **11.** 4 **13.** −22 **15.** $\frac{11}{18}$ **17.** $\pm\frac{3}{7}$ **19.** −1.6 **21.** 0.5 **23.** 9 or −9 **25.** 12 or −12 **27.** $\frac{3}{5}$ or $-\frac{3}{5}$ **29.** 0.13 or −0.13 **31.** 13 students **33.** 25 **35.** 110.25 **37.** 20 ft

39. Sample answer: $x^2 = 100$ **41.** When $x > 25$. **43.** D **45.** 696,000,000 **47.** $2^4 \cdot 3^2$ **49.** 18 **51.** 64, 81 **53.** 36, 49

Pages 150–151 ***Lesson 3-2***

1. 5 **3.** 12 **5.** 6 **7.** about 59.3 swings **9.** 5 **11.** 14 **13.** 5 **15.** 6 **17.** about 2.75 seconds **19.** 5 **21.** 7, $\sqrt{50}$, 9, $\sqrt{85}$ **23.** $\sqrt{34}$, 6, $\sqrt{62}$, 8 **25.** 10 or −10 **29.** 10; since 94 is less than 100, $\sqrt{94}$ is less than 10. **31.** Jordan; $14^2 = 196$ or about 200, but $100^2 = 10{,}000$. **33.** Since $8^2 < 78 < 9^2$, the square root of 78 is between 8 and 9. Since 78 is closer to 81 than 64, graph $\sqrt{78}$ closer to 9 than to 8. **35.** J **37.** 8.36×10^8 **39.** −70 **41.** 5

Pages 152–153 ***Lesson 3-3***

1. Add the number of students in math and the number of students in Spanish, then subtract the number of students who are in both. **3.** 26 people **5.** 6 owners **7.** 12 cars, 7 SUVs **9.** 6, 10 **11.** 27 runs

Pages 158–159 ***Lesson 3-4***

1. rational **3.** irrational **5.** 1.4

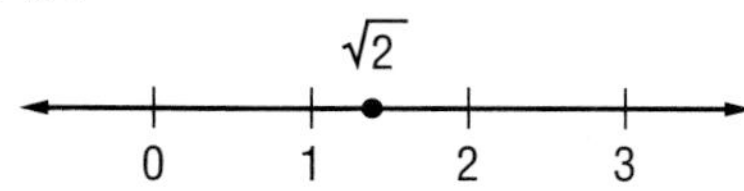

7. > **9.** < **11.** whole, integer, rational **13.** integer, rational **15.** rational **17.** irrational **19.** 2.4

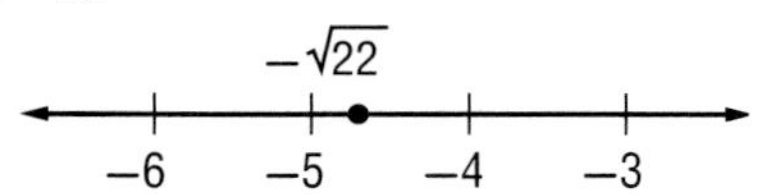

21. −4.7

−√22
−6 −5 −4 −3

23. < **25.** > **27.** = **29.** Yes; $\sqrt{30 \cdot 0.8 \cdot 90} \approx 46$; so the car was speeding. **31.** 36 **33.** $\sqrt{9}$, 3.01, $3.\overline{01}$, $3.\overline{1}$ **35.** −2.5, $-\sqrt{5}$, $\sqrt{6}$, 2.5 **37.** always **39.** sometimes; Sample answer: the product of the rational number 0 and any irrational number is the rational number 0. **41.** D **43.** 62 students **45.** 5 or −5 **47.** 0.8 or −0.8 **49.** 52 **51.** 65

Pages 164–166 ***Lesson 3-5***

1. $c^2 = 12^2 + 16^2$; 20 m **3.** $25^2 = 7^2 + b^2$; 24 ft **5.** about 9.7 in. **7.** yes; $9^2 + 40^2 = 41^2$ **9.** $c^2\ 5^2 + 12^2$; 13 in. **11.** $60^2 = a^2 + 51^2$; 31.5 yd **13.** $18^2 = 8^2 + b^2$; 16.1 m **15.** no **17.** no **19.** no **21.** about 457.0 mi **23.** $c^2 = 48^2 + 55^2$; 73 yd **25.** $c^2 = 23^2 + 18^2$; 29.2 in. **27.** $12.3^2 = a^2 + 5.1^2$; 11.2 m **29.** Sample answer: 3, 4, 5; $3^2 + 4^2 = 5^2$, $9 + 16 = 25$, $25 = 25$ **31.** Sample answer: 6, 8, 10; 5, 12, 13; 10, 24, 26 **33.** C **35.** < **37.** = **39.** 9 or −9 **41.** 28 **43.** 37

Pages 169–171 ***Lesson 3-6***

1. $5^2 = 3^2 + h^2$; 4 ft **3.** about 5.7 in. **5.** $12^2 = 5^2 + h^2$; 10.9 ft **7.** $x^2 = 70^2 + 20^2$; 72.8 ft

9. 25 yd **11.** 2 blocks **13.** about 28.5 in. **15.** 42.7 units **17.** Sample answer: Sam leaves his house. He walks 2 miles north, and then turns and walks 3 miles west. How far is Sam from his house? Using the Pythagorean Theorem, $c^2 = 2^2 + 3^2$. Solving for c, Sam is about 3.6 miles from his house. **19.** about 0.6 ft; By solving $20^2 = x^2 + 5^2$, you find that the ladder reaches approximately 19.4 ft up the wall. Therefore, the top of the ladder would move down 20 ft − 19.4 ft or 0.6 ft. by pulling out the bottom of the ladder 5 feet. **21.** C **23.** yes; $20^2 + 48^2 = 52^2$ **25.** $-9\frac{5}{12}$ **27.** $-3\frac{9}{10}$ **29.** $2{,}500{,}000 = a + 700{,}000$ 1.8 million years

31.

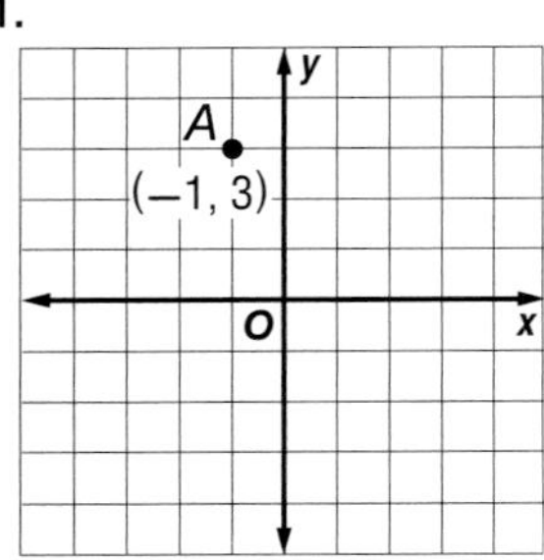

33.

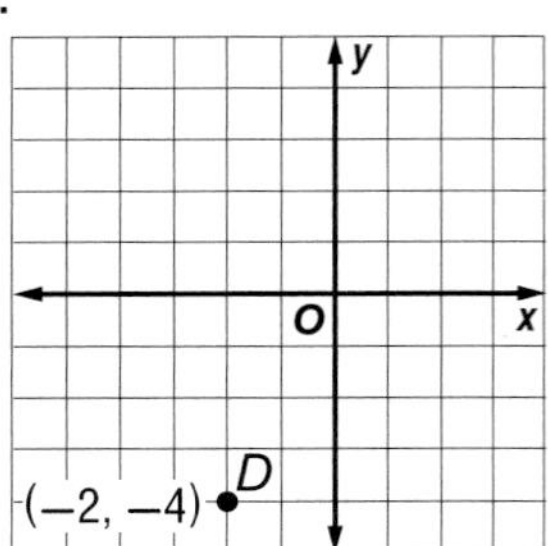

Pages 176–178 ***Lesson 3-7***

1. $\left(-1\frac{1}{3}, 1\frac{1}{3}\right)$ **3.** $\left(1, -\frac{2}{3}\right)$ **5–8.**

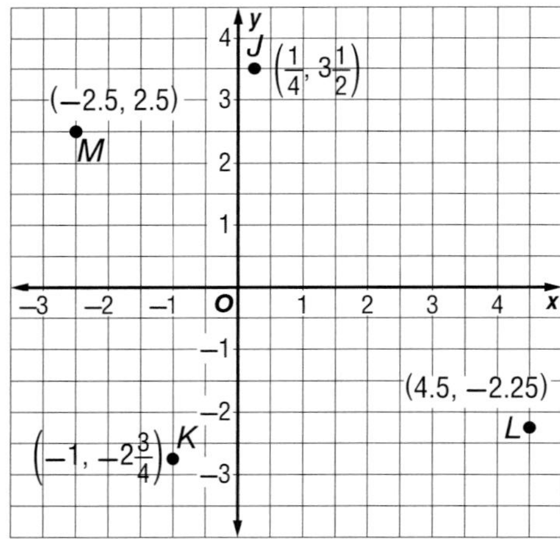

9.

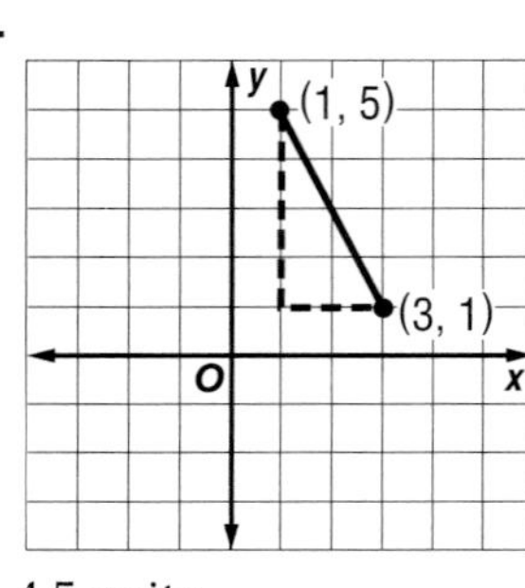

4.5 units

11.

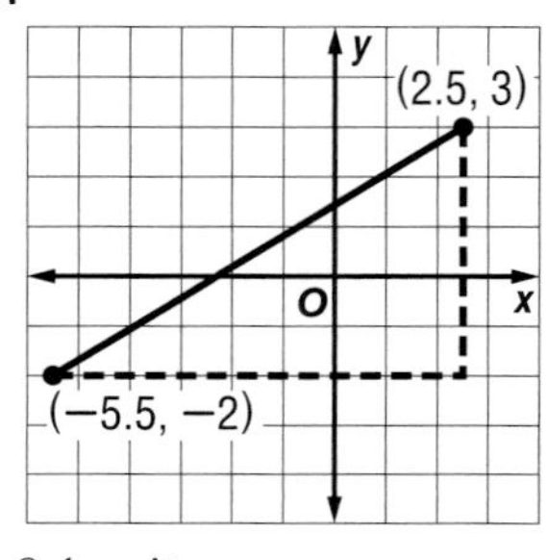

9.4 units

13.

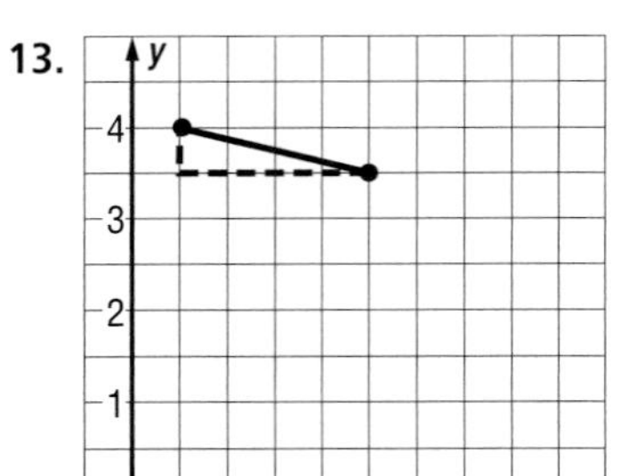

about 1.0 mi

15. $\left(\frac{3}{4}, \frac{1}{2}\right)$

17. $\left(1, -\frac{3}{4}\right)$

19. $\left(-\frac{1}{2}, -\frac{1}{2}\right)$

21. $\left(-1, \frac{1}{4}\right)$

22–27.

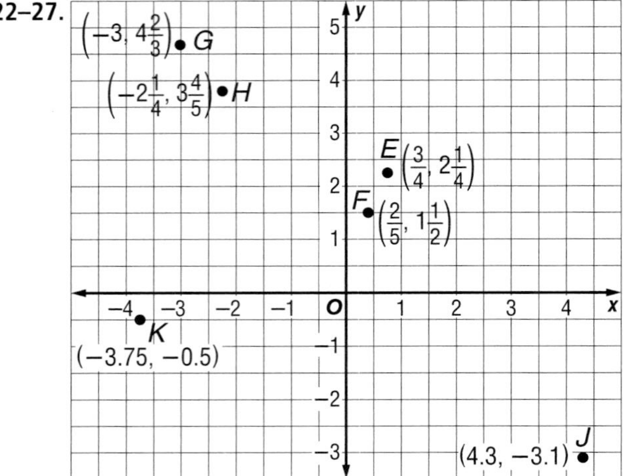

29.

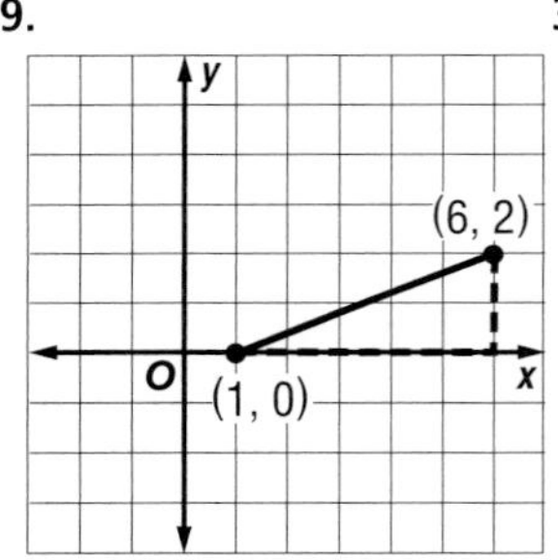

5.4 units

31.

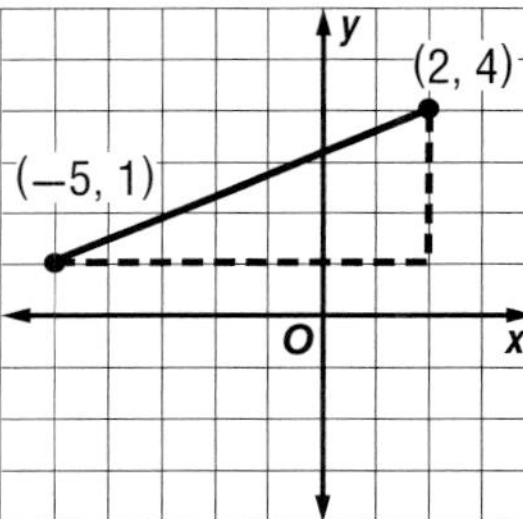

7.6 units

33.

6.4 units

35. about 217.8 mi **37.** 13 units^2 **39.** about 6.7 units **41.** Calculator; it will be most helpful when squaring and finding the square root involving decimals; about 8.6 units **43.** C **45.** 4.5 spaces **47.** 9.6 in. **49.** $\frac{1}{2}$ **51.** $\frac{n}{7} = -14; -98$

Pages 179–182 ***Chapter 3*** ***Study Guide and Review***

1. false; 9 **3.** false; irrational **5.** false; square root **7.** false; longest **9.** 9 **11.** −8 **13.** 16 small squares in each row **15.** 6 **17.** 10 **19.** 3 **21.** 4 **23.** 9 **25.** irrational **27.** rational **29.** irrational **31.** 75.89 m **33.** $20^2 = a^2 + 16^2$; 12 m **35.** $9.5^2 = 4^2 + b^2$; 8.6 m **37.** $c^2 = 6^2 + 7^2$; 9.2 cm **39.** $15^2 = 3^2 + h^2$; 14.7 ft **41.** $55^2 = w^2 + 27^2$; 48 in. **43.** about 13.9 m

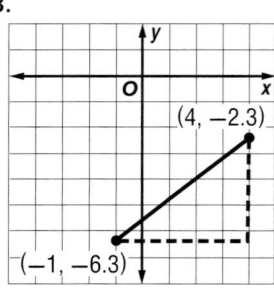

45.

(–1, 2), (4, 8)

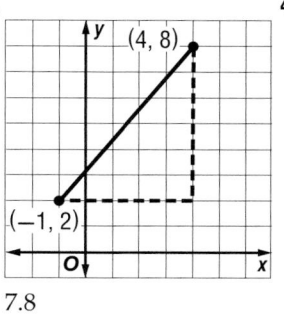

7.8

47.

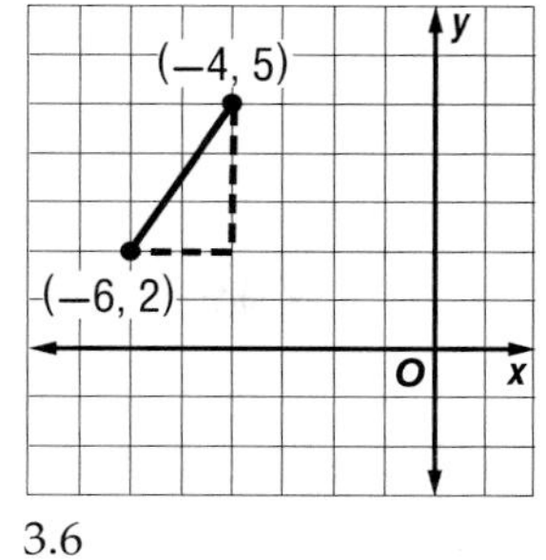

3.6

49.

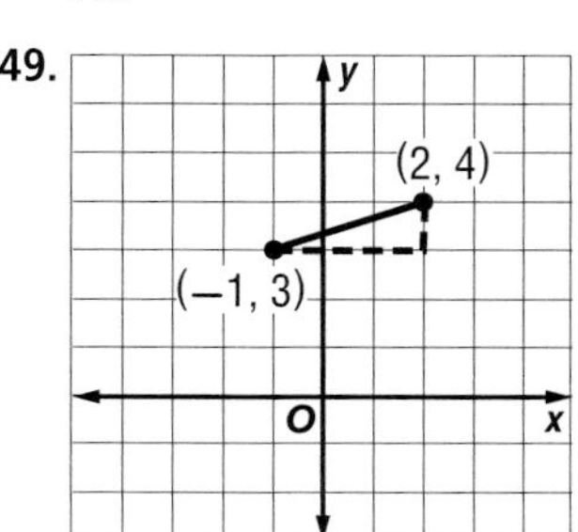

3.2

Chapter 4 Proportions and Similarity

Page 189 ***Chapter 4*** ***Getting Ready***

1. $\frac{5}{12}$ **3.** $\frac{4}{9}$ **5.** $\frac{2}{5}$ **7.** $\frac{3}{4}$ **9.** 6 **11.** 14 **13.** 1.75 **15.** 10.5

Pages 192–193 ***Lesson 4-1***

1. $\frac{1}{15}$ or 1:15 **3.** $\frac{1}{14}$ or 1:14 **5.** \$12.50/day **7.** 34-ounce bottle; The cost per ounce of the 34-ounce bottle is \$1.07 while the cost per ounce of the 9-ounce bottle is \$1.09. **9.** $\frac{7}{25}$ **11.** 7:8 **13.** $\frac{3}{5}$ or 3:5 **15.** $\frac{5}{4}$ or 5:4 **17.** 18 mi/gal **19.** 23.3 miles per gallon **21.** 491 people per hour **23.** Logan; he ran at a rate of 0.126 meter per second and Scott ran at a rate of 0.132 meter per second. **25.** Leon; Sample answer: pick a sample distance such as 30 miles. Then find the overall time for each runner. The person with the lowest overall time finished first. **27.** 20 dimes; Sample answer: use the guess-and-check strategy to check several combinations of coins to find one to fit the situation.

29. D

31.

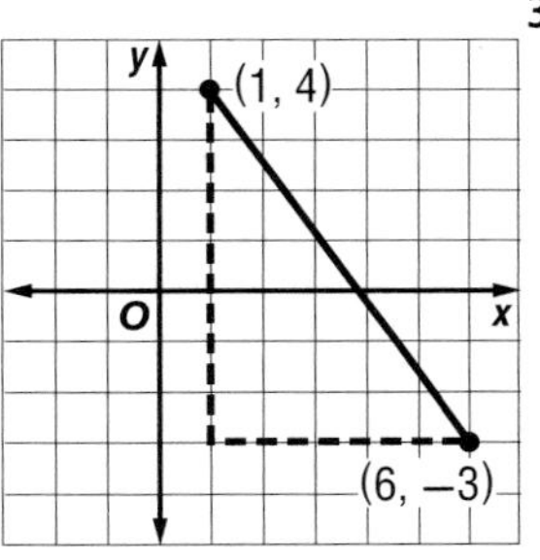

8.6 units

33.

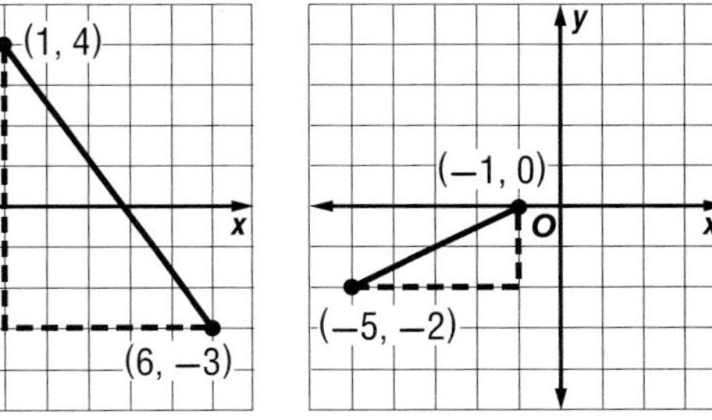

4.5 units

35. 56.6 ft **37.** 0.375 **39.** 0.5

Pages 195–197 ***Lesson 4-2***

1. Yes; Sample answer:

Time (days)	1	2	3	4
Water (L)	225	450	675	900

The earnings to time ratio for 1, 2, 3, and 4 hours is $\frac{1}{225}$, $\frac{2}{450}$ or $\frac{1}{225}$, $\frac{3}{675}$ or $\frac{1}{225}$, and $\frac{4}{900}$ or $\frac{1}{225}$. Since these ratios are all equal to $\frac{1}{225}$, the number of days the supply lasts is proportional to the amount of water the elephant drinks. **3.** No; Sample answer:

Number of Teachers	4	5	6	7
Number of Students	28	56	84	112

The ratio of students to teachers for 4, 5, 6, and 7 teachers is $\frac{28}{4}$ or 7, $\frac{56}{5}$ or 11.2, $\frac{84}{6}$ or 14, and $\frac{112}{7}$ or 16. Since these ratios are not all equal, the number of students at the school is not proportional to the number of teachers.

5. No; Sample answer:

Rental Time (h)	1	2	3	4
Cost (\$)	37	62	87	112

The cost to time ratio for 1, 2, 3, and 4 hours is $\frac{37}{1}$ or 37, $\frac{62}{2}$ or 31, $\frac{87}{3}$ or 29, and $\frac{112}{4}$ or 28. Since these ratios are not all equal, the cost of a rental is not proportional to the number of hours you rent the boat.

7. Yes; Sample answer:

Time (days)	5	10	15	20
Length (in.)	7.5	15	22.5	30

The length to time ratio for 5, 10, 15, and 20 days is $\frac{7.5}{5}$ or 1.5, $\frac{15}{10}$ or 1.5, $\frac{22.5}{15}$ or 1.5, and $\frac{30}{20}$ or 1.5. Since these ratios are all equal to 1.5 ft per day, the length of vine is proportional to the number of days of growth.

9. Yes; Sample answer:

Number of Hours Worked on Sunday	1	2	3	4
Number of Coupons Given Away on Sunday	52	104	156	208

The coupons to hours ratios for 1, 2, 3, and 4 hours of work on Sunday are $\frac{52}{1}$ or 52, $\frac{104}{2}$ or 52, $\frac{156}{3}$ or 52, and $\frac{208}{4}$ or 52. Since these ratios are all equal to 52 coupons per hour, the number of coupons given away is proportional to the number of hours worked on Sunday. **11.** Yes; Sample answer:

Retail Price (\$)	16	32	48	64
Tax Collected (\$)	1	2	3	4

The cost to tax ratios for 16, 32, 48, and 64 dollars are $\frac{16}{1}$ or 16, $\frac{32}{2}$ or 16, $\frac{48}{3}$ or 16, and $\frac{64}{4}$ or 16. Since these ratios are all equal, the amount of tax is proportional to the cost of the item.

13. Yes; Sample answer:

Side length (units)	1	2	3	4
Perimeter (units)	4	8	12	16

Selected Answers

The side length to perimeter ratio for side lengths of 1, 2, 3, and 4 units is $\frac{1}{4}$, $\frac{2}{8}$ or $\frac{1}{4}$, $\frac{3}{12}$ or $\frac{1}{4}$, and $\frac{4}{16}$ or $\frac{1}{4}$. Since these ratios are all equal to $\frac{1}{4}$, the measure of the side length of a square is proportional to the square's perimeter. **15.** No; the cost to weight ratio for 1, 2, 3, 4, and 5 oz is $\frac{0.39}{1}$ or 0.39, $\frac{0.63}{2}$ or about 0.32, $\frac{0.87}{3}$ or 0.29, $\frac{1.11}{4}$ or about 0.28, and $\frac{1.35}{5}$ or 0.27. Since these ratios are not all equal, the cost to mail a letter is not proportional to its weight. **17.** Sample answer: Proportional: the total cost of buying CDs at $11.99 each; The cost to number of CDs ratio for 1, 2, 3, and 4 CDs are all $11.99. Non-proportional: the monthly cost of a cellular phone at $29.95 per month plus $0.25 per minute; The cost to number of minutes ratio for 1, 2, 3, and 4 minutes, $\frac{30.17}{1}$ or 30.17, $\frac{30.42}{2}$ or 15.21, $\frac{30.67}{3}$ or about 10.22, and $\frac{30.92}{4}$ or 7.73, respectively, are not all equal. **19.** Luke is incorrect; Sample answer:

DVDs purchased	1	2	3	4
Amount of Money Remaining	180	160	140	120

The ratio of DVDs purchased to money remaining for 1, 2, 3, and 4 DVDs, $\frac{180}{1}$ or 180, $\frac{160}{2}$ or 80, $\frac{140}{3}$ or about 46.67, $\frac{120}{4}$ or 30. Since these ratios are not all equal, the two quantities are not proportional. The number of DVDs purchased, however, is proportional to the total cost of the DVDs. **21.** $\frac{5}{21}$ or 5:21 **23.** about 27.5 units **25.** $\frac{n}{4} = -16$; -64 **27.** 3 **29.** 0.2

Pages 201–203 ***Lesson 4-3***

1. 4 points/test

3.

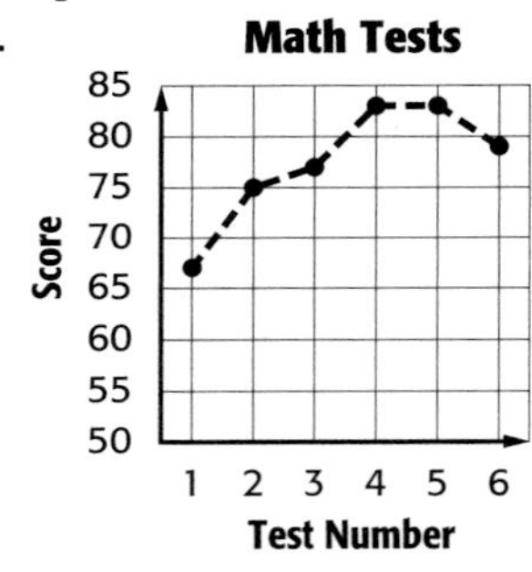

The rate of increase is greatest between Test 1 and Test 2 because the segment between those two points is the steepest. **5.** −1.8 tickets per half hour **7.** −$3.62

9.

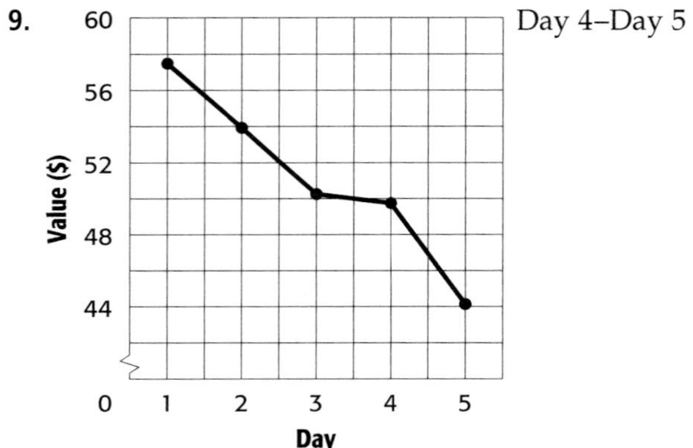

Day 4–Day 5

11. −1.05 million viewers per year **13.** 40.5 radio stations/year **15.** 2001–2002 **17.** $26.2 billion per year **19.** 491.96 million; multiply the yearly rate by 8 years, then add that amount to the number for 2004.

21.

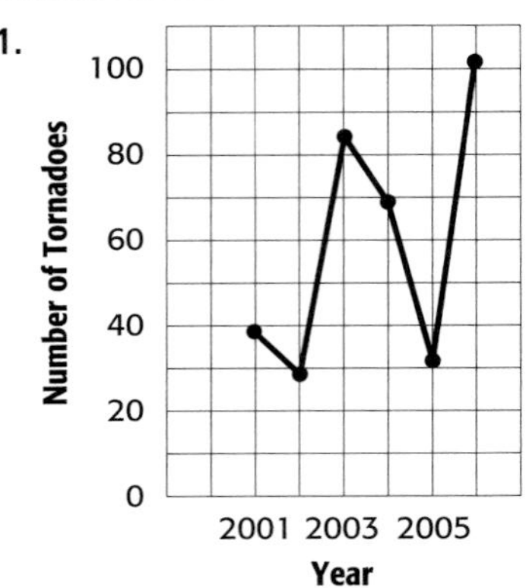

between 2005 and 2006; between 2001 and 2002

23. Sample answer: $2.60 on Day 1, $2.92 on Day 5

25.

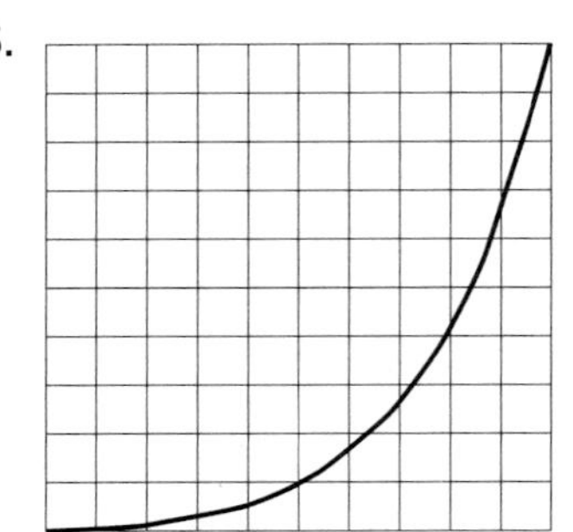

27. C **29.** C **31.** 1 lb 4 oz for $4.99; 1 lb 4 oz for $4.99 costs about $0.25 per ounce and 2 lb 6 oz for $9.75 costs about $0.26 per ounce.

Pages 207–209 ***Lesson 4-4***

1. No; the rate of change from 2 to 3 cm, $\frac{8-27}{3-2}$ or 19 cm^3 per cm, is not the same as the rate of change from 3 to 4 cm, $\frac{64-27}{4-3}$ or 37 cm^3 per cm, so the rate of change is not constant. **3.** 7.5 in./cm; 7.5 miles for each inch on the map **5.** Yes; the graph is a line, so the relationship is linear. The ratio of map distance to actual distance is a constant 7.5 mi/cm, so the relationship is proportional. **7.** Yes; the rate of change between cost and time for each hour is a constant 3¢ per hour. **9.** No; the rate of change from 1 to 2 meters, $\frac{19.6-4.9}{2-1}$ or 14.7 m/s, is not the same as the rate of change from 2 to 3 meters, $\frac{44.1-19.6}{3-2}$ or 24.5 m/s, so the rate of change is not constant. **11.** 2 in./1 m; The level of the aquarium goes up 2 inches every minute. **13.** −250 ft/min; a decrease of 250 feet each minute **15.** 0.25; $\frac{1}{4}$ of retail price **17.** Yes; the graph is a line, so the relationship is linear. The ratio of cost to number of pizza is a constant $10 per pizza, so the relationship is proportional. **19.** No; the graph is a line, so the relationship is linear.

However, the ratios of altitude to time for 2 and 6 minutes are $\frac{3000}{2}$ or 1,500 and $\frac{1500}{4}$ or 375, respectively. Since these ratios are not the same, the relationship is not proportional. **21.** No; the graph is a line, so the relationship is linear. However, the ratios of retail price to sale price for \$20 and \$40 retail prices are $\frac{10}{20}$ or 0.5 and $\frac{15}{40}$ or 0.375, respectively. Since these ratios are not the same, the relationship is not proportional.
23. Luis; he is spending \$0.50 per minute while Miriam is only paying about \$0.17 per minute.
25.

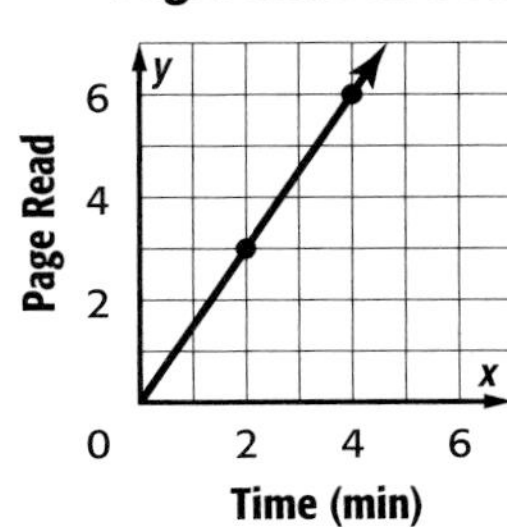

Sample answer: The rate of change between any two pieces of data is $\frac{3}{2}$ or 1.5 pages per min, so the relationship is linear. Since the ratio of pages to minutes is a constant 1.5 pages per min, the relationship is proportional.
27. Sample answer: Melodie decided to keep track of the number of miles she walked each day. The table shows her progress.

Total Number of Days	1	2	3	4
Total Number of Miles Walked	2	4	6	8

What was the constant rate of change in the number of miles she walked per day? Solution: She walked a constant 2 miles per day. This is a proportional relationship, since the ratio of miles to days walked is a constant 2 miles per day. **29.** H **31.** Yes; Sample answer:

Time (weeks)	1	2	3	4
Allowance (\$)	20	40	60	80

The allowance to time ratio for 1, 2, 3, and 4 weeks is $\frac{20}{1}$ or 20, $\frac{40}{2}$ or 20, $\frac{60}{3}$ or 20, and $\frac{80}{4}$ or 20. Since these ratios are all equal to 20, the amount of allowance is proportional to the number of weeks. **33.** 33.3 cups

Pages 212–214 ***Lesson 4-5***

1. 40 **3.** 16.4 **5.** $m = 9.5h$; \$19; \$42.75 **7.** 6 **9.** 3.5 **11.** 3.75 **13.** 13.5 **15.** $\frac{14}{483} = \frac{x}{600}$; about 17.4 gal **17.** $\frac{4}{5} = \frac{x}{30}$; 24 people **19.** $\frac{62}{100} = \frac{20}{s}$; 32 kph **21.** 73 inches **23.** e = weight on Earth; $\frac{120}{45.6} = \frac{e}{55}$; $e \approx 144.7$ **25.** m = weight on Mercury; $\frac{109.2}{45.6} = \frac{115}{m}$; $m \approx 48$ **27.** Yes; Solve the proportion $\frac{5}{2000} = \frac{3}{x}$, where x is the area covered by the 3 remaining pounds of seed. The 3 remaining pounds will cover an area of 1,200 ft^2. The area to be seeded is $(8 \cdot 3) \cdot (14 \cdot 3)$ or 1,008 ft^2. Since $1{,}008 < 1{,}200$, there is enough left to seed the area. **29.** 22 **31.** 5 **33.** C **35.** $\frac{n}{515} = \frac{12}{35}$ **37.** \$30.94

Pages 216–217 ***Lesson 4-6***

1. She is sitting in the 3rd row from the back so there are 2 rows behind her. Since she is in the 5th row, there are 5 + 2 or 7 rows. She is sitting in the 2nd seat from the right so there is one seat next to her on the right. Since she is in the 6th seat, there are 6 + 1 or 7 seats in each row. $7 \times 7 = 49$ seats **3.** 63 seats **5.** 55 **7.** 0.6 mile **9.** 15 people **11.** 7.5 gal. **13.** 10 min

Pages 222–223 ***Lesson 4-7***

1. No; the corresponding angles are congruent, but $\frac{5}{3} \neq \frac{13}{5}$. **3.** $\frac{x}{6} = \frac{6}{3}$, 12; $\frac{9}{y} = \frac{6}{3}$, 4.5 **5.** No; the corresponding angles are congruent, but $\frac{3}{7} \neq \frac{4}{8}$.
7. Yes; the corresponding angles are congruent and $\frac{20}{15} = \frac{16}{12} = \frac{24}{18}$. **9.** Sample proportion: $\frac{8}{x} = \frac{12}{3}$, 2 **11.** Sample proportion: $\frac{x}{10} = \frac{21}{10.5}$, 20 **13.** 0.3 cm
15. They are proportional; Sample answer: If $\triangle ABC \sim \triangle XYW$ then corresponding sides are proportional, so $\frac{a}{x} = \frac{c}{z}$.

$\frac{a}{x} = \frac{c}{z}$	Write the proportion.
$az = xc$	Find the cross products.
$\frac{az}{cz} = \frac{xc}{cz}$	Divide each side by cz.
$\frac{a}{c} = \frac{x}{z}$	Divide out common factors.

17. Always; all corresponding angles between squares are congruent since all four angles in a square are right angles. In addition, all sides in a square are congruent. Therefore, all four ratios of corresponding sides are equal. **19.** J **21.** 15 **23.** 12.5
25.

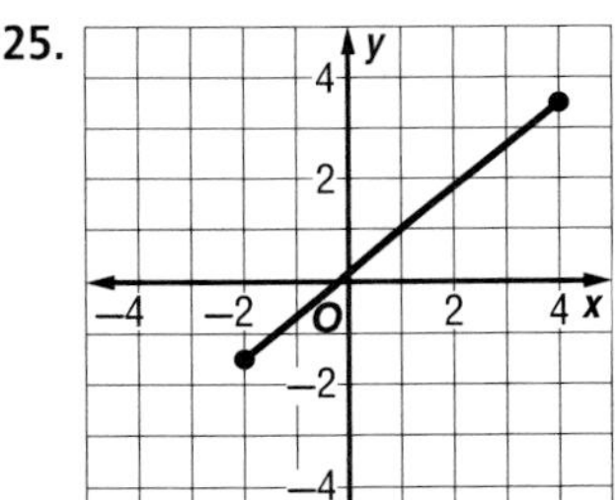

Pages 228–230 ***Lesson 4-8***

1.

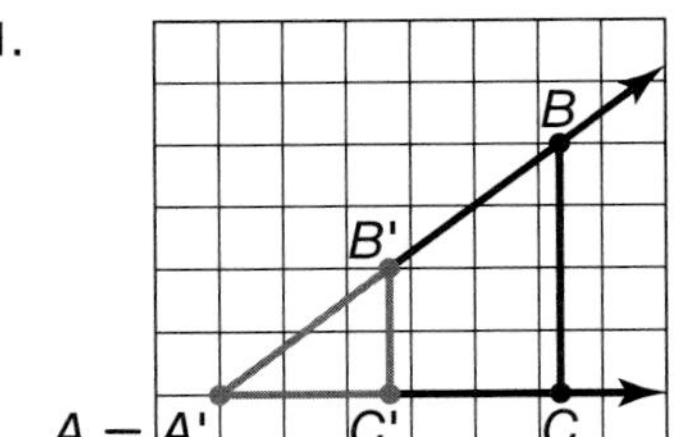

3. $A'(-12, 6)$, $B'(-6, -12)$, $C'(9, 18)$;

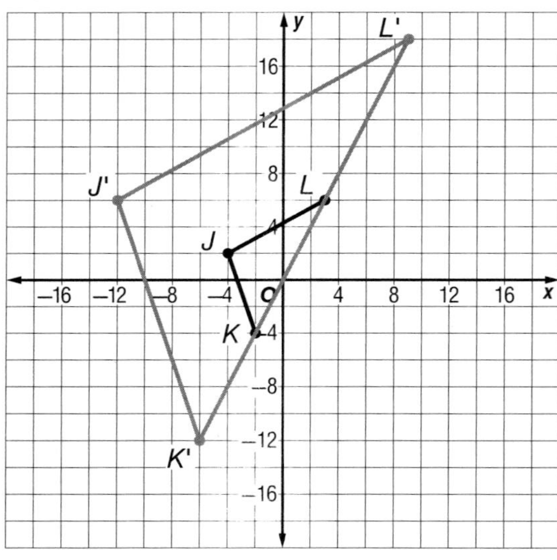

5. 3; enlargement

7.

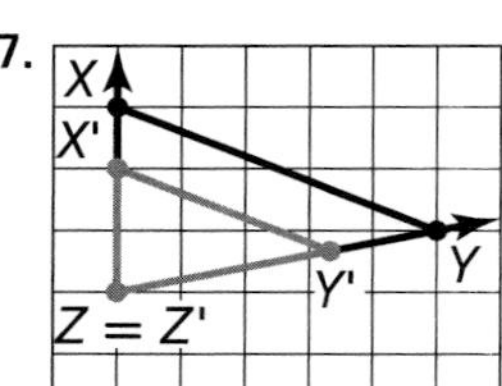

9.

11. $H'(-2, 6)$, $J'(6, 4)$, $K'(4, -6)$ $L'(-4, -4)$

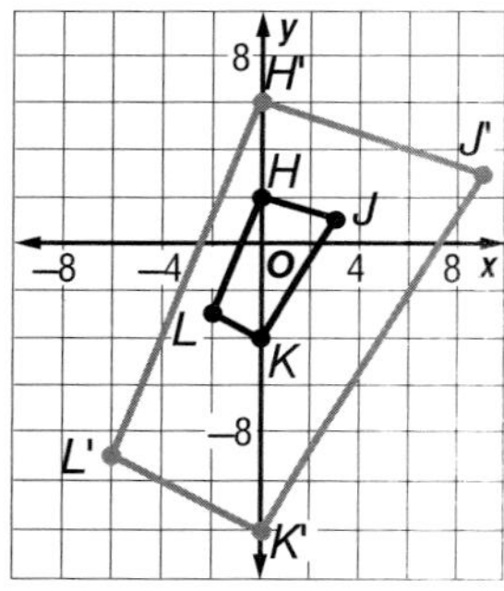

13. $H'(-3, 1)$, $J'(2, 2)$, $K'\left(3\frac{1}{2}, -1\right)$ $L'(-1, -2)$

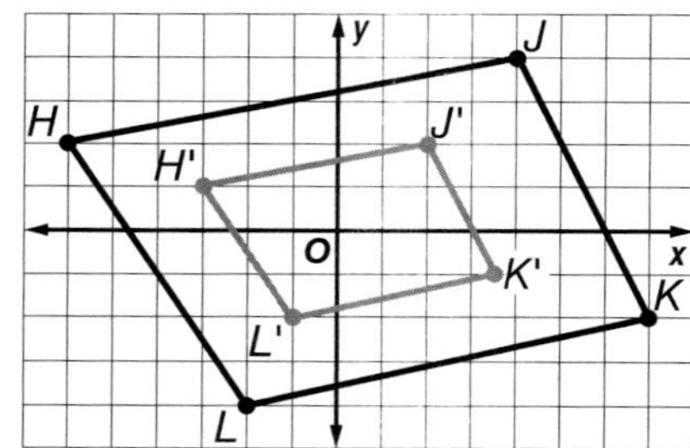

15. $\frac{3}{5}$, reduction **17.** 2, enlargement **19.** 4.5 cm by 3 cm
21. 48; $\frac{20 \text{ ft}}{5 \text{ in.}} = \frac{240 \text{ in.}}{5 \text{ in.}}$ or 48

23.

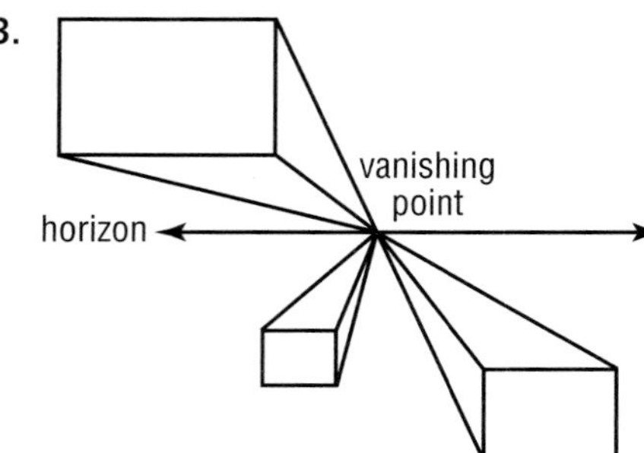

25. The figure is enlarged and turned 180°. **27.** B
29. $\frac{4.5}{m} = \frac{3}{8}$; 12 **31.** about 7.2 mi **33.** $\frac{4}{5} = \frac{5}{x}$; 6.25

Pages 233–235 Lesson 4-9

1. 3.3 m **3.** $\frac{h}{50} = \frac{50}{12.5}$; 200 ft **5.** $\frac{8}{25} = \frac{12}{x}$; 37.5 m
7. $\frac{9}{h} = \frac{15}{7}$; 4.2 feet
9. 6 feet tall

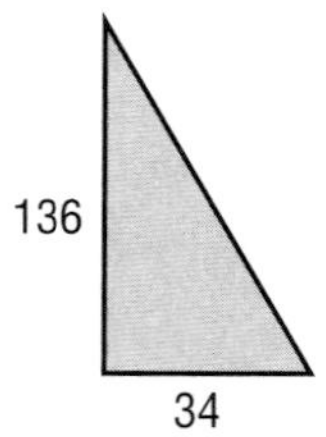

11. Sample answer: At the same time a baby giraffe casts a 3.2-foot shadow, a 15-foot adult giraffe casts an 8-foot shadow. How tall is the baby giraffe? Solving the proportion $\frac{x}{3.2} = \frac{15}{8}$ gives a height of 6 ft for the baby giraffe. **13.** Sample answer: the length of the tall object's shadow, the length of the shadow of a nearby object whose height is directly measurable, and the height of the nearby object **15.** H **17.** $13\frac{1}{3}$ in.
19. 7 **21.** 4.2 **23.** 20.7

Pages 239–241 Lesson 4-10

1. about 113 mi **3.** 1 in. = 50 ft **5.** Sample answer: 1 in. = 1.25 ft; 8 in. by 9.6 in. **7.** 9 ft; 12 ft **9.** 12 ft; 12 ft **11.** 12 ft; 12 ft **13.** 1 cm = 1.6 mm **15.** 1:16
17. Sample answer: 1 in. = 8 ft; length: $22\frac{3}{4}$ in., width: $19\frac{3}{8}$ in. **19.** A tennis ball; sample answer: If the diameter of the model is d then $\frac{d}{11{,}000} = \frac{3}{4{,}000}$, so $d = 8.25$. **23.** Measure the distance between two places on the map for which you already know the actual distance. Set up a ratio of the map distance to the known distance. Then simplify.
25. C **27.** 18 feet **29.** (0,0), $(2, -\frac{4}{3})$, $(-4, -2)$
31. 7 **33.** 3 cups **35.** $\frac{1}{12}$ or $-\frac{1}{12}$

Pages 242–246 Chapter 4 Study Guide and Review

1. false; shape **3.** false; different **5.** true **7.** 1 for 28
9. 1 out of 7 **11.** No; sample answer:

Months	1	2	3	4
Cost ($)	60	90	120	150

The cost to months ratio for 1, 2, 3, and 4 months is

$\frac{60}{1} = 60, \frac{90}{2} = 45, \frac{120}{3} = 40, \frac{150}{4} = 37.5$. Since these ratios are not all equal, the total cost is not proportional to the number of months of high-speed Internet. **13.** \$0.67/yr **15.** No; the rate of change from 1 to 2 hr, $\frac{4-2}{2-1}$ or 2 in. per hr, is not the same as the rate of change from 2 to 3 hr, $\frac{7-4}{3-2}$ or 3 in. per hr, so the rate of change is not constant **17.** 4 **19.** 3.5 **21.** 3.2 miles **23.** $\frac{3}{4}$ ft **25.** $\frac{13}{x} = \frac{5}{1}$; 2.6 **27.** $\frac{7}{8}$ **29.** 4; enlargement **31.** 60 ft **33.** 21 km **35.** 1 in. = 24 in. or 1 in. = 2 ft

Chapter 5 Percent

Page 251 ***Chapter 5*** ***Getting Ready***

1. 101 **3.** 55 **5.** 0.4 **7.** 0.75 **9.** 0.9 **11.** 0.25 **13.** 450 **15.** 31.5

Pages 254–255 ***Lesson 5-1***

1. 17% **3.** 6.25% **5.** 45% **7.** $\frac{19}{100}$ **9.** $\frac{9}{50}$ **11.** 110% **13.** 35% **15.** 18% **17.** 90% **19.** 2% **21.** $\frac{43}{100}$ **23.** $\frac{7}{10}$ **25.** $\frac{7}{25}$ **27.** $\frac{13}{20}$ **29.** $75\% = \frac{3}{4}$; $46\% = \frac{23}{50}$; $45\% = \frac{9}{20}$; $42\% = \frac{21}{50}$; $37\% = \frac{37}{100}$ **31.** 160% **33.** Sample answer: 60%. Since $\frac{1}{2} = 50\%$ and $\frac{3}{4} = 75\%$, $50\% < 60\% < 75\%$. **35.** Birds: 2.8%, mammals: 3.6%, fish: 0.3%, reptiles: 1%, amphibians: 0.4%; by writing the ratios as percents, it is easier to determine which group has the greatest ratio because all of the percents are numbers that are compared to 100. **37.** H **39.** 52 ft **41.** 1.07, $1\frac{1}{2}$, 1.8, $1\frac{8}{9}$ **43.** 0.75 **45.** $0.\overline{3}$

Pages 258–261 ***Lesson 5-2***

1. 0.4 **3.** 0.003 **5.** 123% **7.** 44% **9.** $83.\overline{3}\%$ **11.** 0.062, 60%, $\frac{13}{20}$, $\frac{17}{25}$ **13.** 0.9 **15.** 1.72 **17.** 0.004 **19.** 0.07 **21.** 0.11 **23.** 62% **25.** 47.5% **27.** 0.7% **29.** 275% **31.** 21% **33.** 85% **35.** 160% **37.** 2.5% **39.** $44.\overline{4}\%$ **41.** 20% **43.** $33\frac{1}{3}\%$ **45.** no summer camp **47.** 8%, $\frac{7}{10}$, $\frac{3}{4}$, 0.8 **49.** $\frac{1}{20}$, 7%, $\frac{2}{25}$, 0.09 **51.** $\frac{3}{13}$, $\frac{3}{10}$, 0.305, 31% **53.** Mora 0.340; Abreu 0.301; 0.301, 0.308, 0.340 **55.** < **57.** The daily value of carbohydrates is 12% or $\frac{3}{25}$ which is less than $\frac{1}{5}$ or $\frac{5}{25}$. **59.** Fraction; $\frac{1}{8}$ is already in fraction form and $0.25 = \frac{1}{4}$ or $\frac{2}{8}$. Since $\frac{1}{8} < \frac{2}{8}$, Lisa did not eat more cookies than she gave to Kaitylin. **61.** Toni; 0.9 is 9 tenths, not 9 hundredths. **63.** Sample answer: 65% **65.** D **67.** 31.25% **69.** 0.6% **71.** 66% **73.** $\frac{1}{8}$ **75.** {−56, −13, 13, 42, 101} **77.** 20 **79.** 17.5

Pages 266–267 ***Lesson 5-3***

1. $\frac{70}{280} = \frac{n}{100}$; 25% **3.** $\frac{n}{90} = \frac{60}{100}$; 54 **5.** $\frac{151.5}{n} = \frac{75}{100}$; 202 **7.** $\frac{48}{30} = \frac{n}{100}$; 160% **9.** about 500 pounds **11.** $\frac{120}{360} = \frac{n}{100}$; 33.3% **13.** $\frac{n}{350} = \frac{17}{100}$; 59.5 **15.** $\frac{95}{n} = \frac{95}{100}$; 100 **17.** $\frac{n}{57} = \frac{250}{100}$; 142.5 **19.** about 20% **21.** $\frac{4}{550} = \frac{n}{100}$; 0.7% **23.** $\frac{n}{42} = \frac{5.8}{100}$; 2.4 **25.** $\frac{57}{n} = \frac{13.5}{100}$; 422.2 **27.** 25% **29.** Sample answer: Let x be 2 and y be 5. 2% of 5 is 0.1 and 5% of 2 is 0.1. The result will always be the same for any two numbers x and y. x% of $y = x(0.01) \cdot y$ and y% of $x = y(0.01) \cdot x$. By the Commutative Property of Multiplication, $x(0.01) \cdot y = y(0.01) \cdot x$. **31.** D **33.** 0.016, 16%, $\frac{1}{6}$ **35.** 3.63 **37.** 60 in. **39.** 213 **41.** 340

Pages 270–271 ***Lesson 5-4***

1. 60 **3.** 27 **5.** 35 **7.** \$12,000 **9.** 31 **11.** 9 **13.** 9 **15.** 100 **17.** 12.5 **19.** 0.283 **21.** 14.7 **23.** 1.02 **25.** about 92 million **27.** = **29.** 900 teens **33.** Sample answer: 6 and 24: Since $66\frac{2}{3}\% = \frac{2}{3}$, any multiple of 3 would make computation easier. **35.** Since 75% equals $\frac{3}{4}$, find $\frac{3}{4}$ of 40. $\frac{1}{4}$ of 40 is 10. So, $\frac{3}{4}$ of 40 is $3 \cdot 10$ or 30. **37.** J **39.** 45% **41.** 0.6% **43.** 0.8 mile

Pages 272–273 ***Lesson 5-5***

1. An exact cost was not needed. **3.** \$90; \$30 is less than 50% of 129 and \$60 is about 50%. The sale price must be \$90 because it is greater than 50%. **5.** 40; Sample answer: $300 \div 8 = 37.5$, which is about 40. **7.** 1,234,567,654,321 **9.** \$40 **11.** about 36,000,000 **13.** 1,875 boxes

Pages 277–278 ***Lesson 5-6***

1. Sample answer: $\frac{1}{2}$ of 160 or 80 **3.** Sample answer: $\frac{3}{4}$ of 64 or 48 **5.** Sample answer: $\frac{6}{35} \approx \frac{7}{35}$ or 20% **7.** Sample answer: $\frac{14}{19} \approx \frac{15}{20}$ or 75% **9.** Sample answer: $\frac{2}{3}$ of 93 or 62 **11.** Sample answer: $\frac{1}{4}$ of 64 or 16 **13.** Sample answer: $\frac{9}{10}$ of 40 or 36 **15.** Sample answer: $\frac{3}{4}$ of 80 or 60 **17.** Sample answer: $\frac{6}{59} \approx \frac{6}{60}$ or 10% **19.** Sample answer: $\frac{5}{36} \approx \frac{6}{36}$ or $16\frac{2}{3}\%$ **21.** Sample answer: $\frac{7}{11} \approx \frac{8}{12}$ or $66\frac{2}{3}\%$ **23.** Sample answer: $\frac{9}{55} \approx \frac{9}{54}$ or $16\frac{2}{3}\%$ **25.** Sample answer: $\frac{3}{4}$ of 48 or 36 field goals **27.** Sample answer for New York: $\frac{8{,}143{,}197}{19{,}254{,}630} \approx \frac{8{,}000{,}000}{20{,}000{,}000}$ or 40%

Sample answer for California: $\frac{3{,}844{,}829}{36{,}132{,}147} \approx \frac{4{,}000{,}000}{36{,}000{,}000}$ or 11.1%

Sample answer for Illinois: $\frac{2{,}842{,}518}{12{,}763{,}371} \approx \frac{3{,}000{,}000}{12{,}000{,}000}$ or 25%

New York has the greatest percent of its population living in New York City. **29.** Sample answer: $1\frac{1}{4}$ of 40 or 50 **31.** 51% of 240; 24% of 480 is less than $\frac{1}{4}$ of 480 or 120. 51% of 240 is greater than $\frac{1}{2}$ of 240 or 120. **33.** sometimes; Sample answer: it will depend on the amount that each value is rounded. **35.** D **37.** 48 **39.** 5 **41.** 0.4 **43.** 0.1

Pages 282–283 **Lesson 5-7**

1. 782 **3.** 4% **5.** 2,000 **7.** \$7,420 **9.** 36 **11.** 30% **13.** 200 **15.** 20.16 **17.** 0.12% **19.** 500 **21.** 27.2 mi/gal **23.** 28 games **25.** 9.375 **27.** Always; $a\%$ of b is $\frac{a}{100} \cdot b$ or $\frac{ab}{100}$ and $b\%$ of a is $\frac{b}{100} \cdot a$ or $\frac{ab}{100}$. **29.** Sample answer: Suppose an item costs \$100. A 5% discount would be a discount of \$5, so the discounted price would be \$95. Adding 5% sales tax to \$95 adds \$4.75. \$95 + \$4.75 is not \$100. **31.** H **33.** \$40 **35.** 63 **37.** 3.6 **39.** 7.1 **41.** −270 **43.** 720 **45.** 87 **47.** 229

Pages 287–289 **Lesson 5-8**

1. 20%; decrease **3.** 23.1%; increase **5.** \$115.71 **7.** 50%; increase **9.** 20%; decrease **11.** 25%; decrease **13.** 6.7% **15.** \$910.00 **17.** \$36.25 **19.** \$56.25 **21.** \$83.97 **23.** 5.2 seconds **27.** \$8.50 **29.** Chris; the change must be compared to the original price \$5.75, not the new price \$6.25. **31.** D **33.** 39 pets **35.** Sample answer: $\frac{1}{4}$ of 84 or 21 **37.** Sample answer: $\frac{1}{3}$ of 96 or 32 **39.** 0.3 in./month **41.** 3

Pages 292–293 **Lesson 5-9**

1. \$112.50 **3.** \$729.30 **5.** C **7.** \$45 **9.** \$10.08 **11.** \$2,587.50 **13.** \$587.22 **15.** 45% **17.** \$23,250 **19.** \$1,029.60 **21.** 25-year mortgage loan **23.** Sample answer: \$1,000 principal with a 22% interest rate **25.** B **27.** \$180 **29.** 60 **31.** 8.4×10^{-5}

Pages 295–298 **Chapter 5** **Study Guide and Review**

1. percent **3.** markup **5.** principal **7.** discount **9.** 1.5% **11.** 80% **13.** 20% **15.** $1\frac{1}{5}$ **17.** 1.47 **19.** 70% **21.** 255% **23.** 96% **25.** Andrea: $\frac{7}{8} = 87.5\%$, $87.5\% < 88\%$ **27.** $\frac{n}{18} = \frac{45}{100}$; 8.1 **29.** 16 **31.** 1.83 **33.** 12 **35.** 84 shoppers; Sample answer: 10% of 1,413 is about 140, and 6% is a little more than half of 140 or 70. Since 84 is slightly greater than 70, it is a reasonable answer. **37.** Sample answer: $\frac{2}{3}$ of 60 or 40 **39.** Sample answer: $\frac{33}{98} \approx \frac{33}{99}$ or $33\frac{1}{3}\%$ **41.** about 68°F **43.** 12.3 **45.** 633 movies **47.** 25%; increase **49.** 33.3%; decrease **51.** \$17.00 **53.** \$68.25

Chapter 6 Geometry and Spatial Reasoning

Page 305 **Chapter 6** **Getting Ready**

1. 86 **3.** 98 **5.** 180 **7.** 1,260 **9.** 540 **11.** 64 **13.** 52

Pages 309–311 **Lesson 6-1**

1. 27 **3.** 104 **5.** alternate exterior **7.** alternate interior **9.** corresponding angles; since ∠2 and ∠3 are supplementary, $m\angle 2 = 140°$; since ∠1 and ∠2 are corresponding angles they are congruent so $m\angle 1 = 140°$ **11.** 103 **13.** 131 **15.** 112 **17.** 79 **19.** alternate interior **21.** alternate interior **23.** alternate exterior **25.** corresponding angles **27.** ∠1 and ∠3 are corresponding angles. Since ∠2 and ∠3 are supplementary, $m\angle 2 = 180° - 84.5°$ or 95.5°. **29.** 40 **31.** 135°; The lines are parallel, so alternate interior angles are congruent. **33.** 38°; The lines are parallel, so alternate exterior angles are congruent. **35.** 150°; The lines are parallel, so corresponding angles are congruent. **37.** Always; if a 90° angle is formed by the transversal and one line, then the corresponding angle formed by the transversal and a parallel line must be 90°. **41.** F **43.** 35%; increase **45.** 95%; decrease **47.** 360

Pages 314–315 **Lesson 6-2**

1. Yes, Chris used inductive reasoning. Chris observed that the acute angles of several different examples of right triangle were complementary to decide that the acute angles of all right triangles are complementary. **3.** The diagonals in a rectangle are congruent.

5.

Fraction	$\frac{1}{11}$	$\frac{4}{11}$	$\frac{8}{11}$	$\frac{3}{11}$	$\frac{6}{11}$	$\frac{9}{11}$
Decimal	$0.\overline{09}$	$0.\overline{36}$	$0.\overline{72}$	$0.\overline{27}$	$0.\overline{54}$	$0.\overline{81}$

7. Sample answer: Ajay: 2 hours; his sister: 4 hours **9.** one 1-lb package and three $2\frac{1}{2}$-lb packages **11.** Multiplication; $21{,}750 \times 20 = 435{,}000$ miles

Pages 317–319 **Lesson 6-3**

1. 360° **3.** 1,800° **5.** 540° **7.** 1,620° **9.** 3,060° **11.** 108° **13.** 140° **15.** 152.3° **17.** 90°, 120°, 150°; 360° **19.** The measure of each angle in each outlined triangle is 60°. If a triangle is equilateral, the measure of each angle will be 60° regardless of the size of the triangle. **21.** Sample answer: There are $n - 2$ triangles inside a regular polygon. Every triangle has an angle measure sum of 180°. So, every polygon has an angle measure sum of $(n - 2)180°$. If a polygon has n sides, it has n angles also. Therefore, divide the angle measure sum by the number of angles to find an individual angle measure. **23.** H **25.** 20 **27.** more **29.** Yes; the angles have the same measure.

Pages 322–323 **Lesson 6-4**

1. yes; $\angle A \cong \angle G$, $\angle C \cong \angle H$, $\angle E \cong \angle F$, $\overline{AC} \cong \overline{GH}$, $\overline{CE} \cong \overline{HF}$, $\overline{AE} \cong \overline{GF}$; $\triangle ACE \cong \triangle GHF$ **3.** 73° **5.** 7 yd **7.** yes; $\angle H \cong \angle P$, $\angle K \cong \angle Q$, $\angle J \cong \angle M$, $\overline{HK} \cong \overline{PQ}$, $\overline{KJ} \cong \overline{QM}$, $\overline{HJ} \cong \overline{PM}$; $\triangle HJK \cong \triangle PMQ$ **9.** 13 in. **11.** 113° **13.** Sample answer; $\overline{MK} \cong \overline{SN}$, Since you know both quadrilaterals are squares, you know that all angles are 90° and therefore congruent to each other. You also know that the sides of each quadrilateral are congruent. You need to know whether a side of quadrilateral $JMKL$ is congruent to a side of quadrilateral $PSNO$. **15.** quadrilateral $ABCD \cong$ quadrilateral $WXYZ$, $m\angle A = 80°$. **17.** Sample answer: If the scale factor between two similar polygons is 1 then the lengths of the corresponding sides would be the same. Therefore, the polygons would be congruent. **19.** 300 ft **21.** 108° **23.** 140° **25.** A

Pages 329–331 ***Lesson 6-5***

1a.

1b. no **3.**

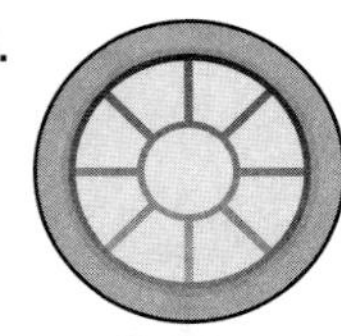

5a.

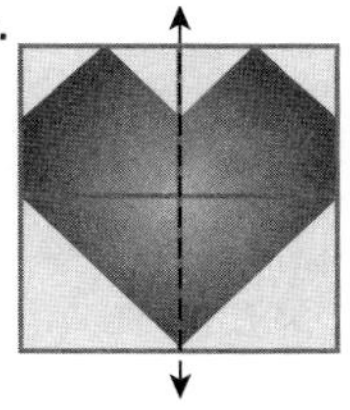

7a.

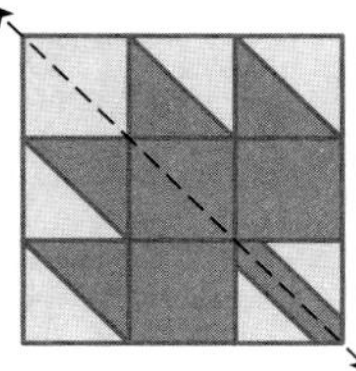

5b. yes; 180° **7b.** no

9. none

11. 6 pieces

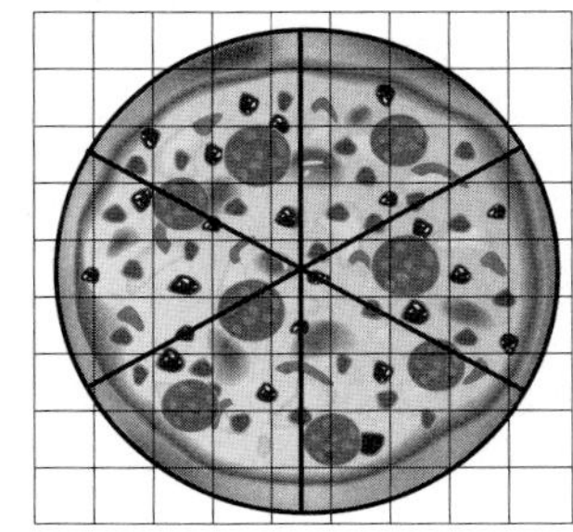

13. The window has 16 lines of symmetry. The window has rotational symmetry. The angles of rotation are 22.5°, 45°, 67.5°, 90°, 112.5°, 135°, 157.5°, 180°, 202.5°, 225°, 247.5°, 270°, 292.5°, 315°, 337.5°, and 360°. **15.** rectangle, rhombus, square; parallelogram, rectangle, rhombus, square

17. false

19. D **21.** 720° **23.** 2,160° **25.** $19.50

Pages 334–336 ***Lesson 6-6***

1.

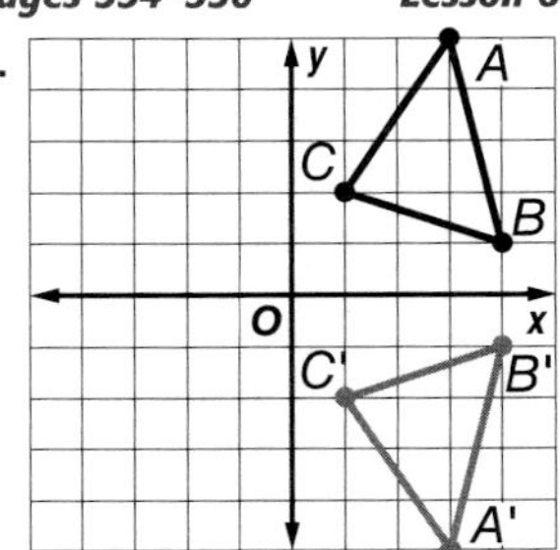

$A'(3, -5)$, $B'(4, -1)$, $C'(1, -2)$

2.

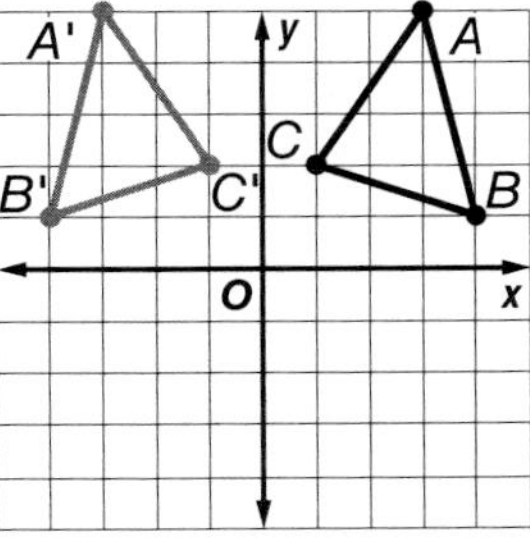

$A'(-3, 5)$, $B'(-4, 1)$, $C'(-1, 2)$

3.

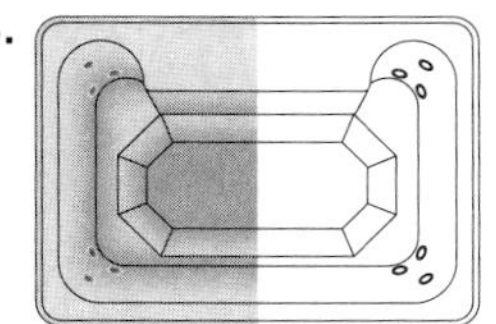

5.

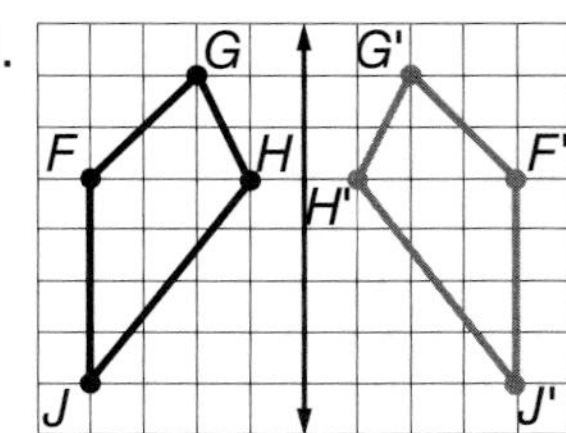

7.

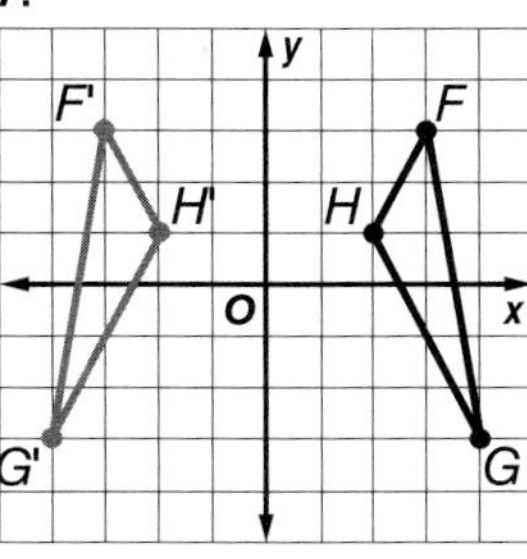

$F'(-3, 3)$, $G'(-4, -3)$, $H'(-2, 1)$

9.

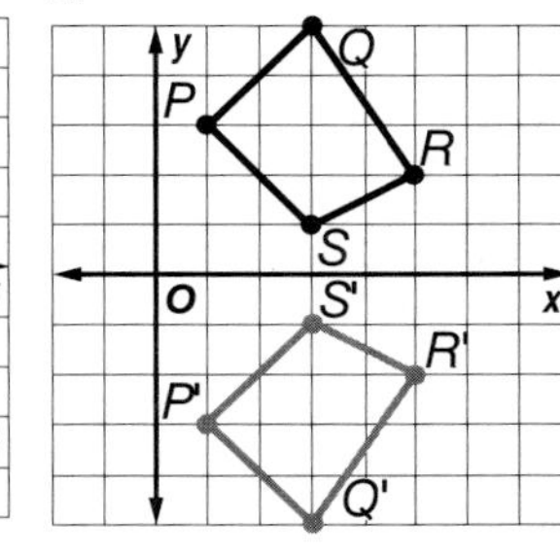

$P'(1, -3)$, $Q'(3, -5)$, $R'(5, -2)$, $S'(3, -1)$

11.

13. $X'(1, -3)$, $Y'(-2, -5)$, $Z'(-3, 2)$

15.

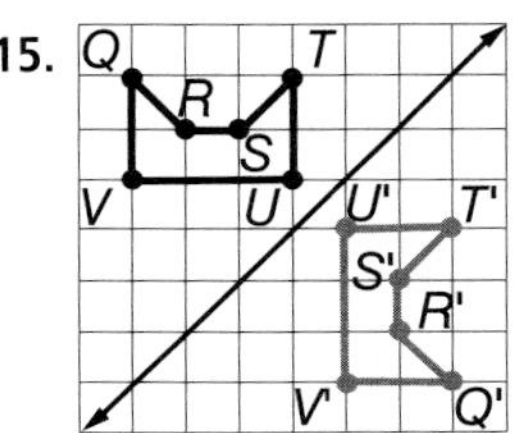

19. (x, y) becomes $(x, -y)$ after being reflected over the x-axis. The x-coordinate is the same and the y-coordinate changes sign. (x, y) becomes $(-x, y)$ after being reflected over the y-axis. The y-coordinate is the same and the x-coordinate changes sign.
21. yes; 90°, 180°, 270° **23.** yes; 60°, 120°, 180°, 240°, 300° **25.** −5 **27.** 3

Pages 339–341 ***Lesson 6-7***

1.

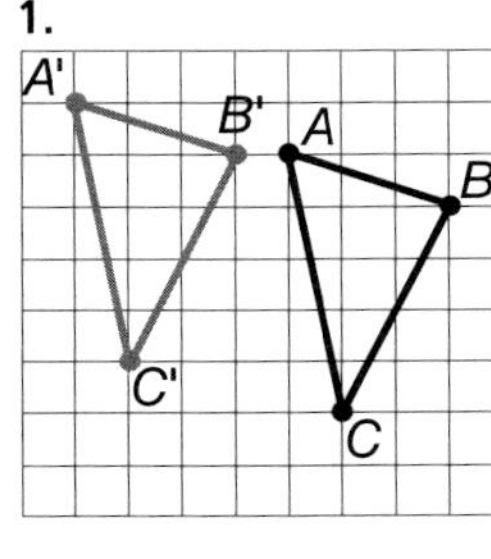

3.

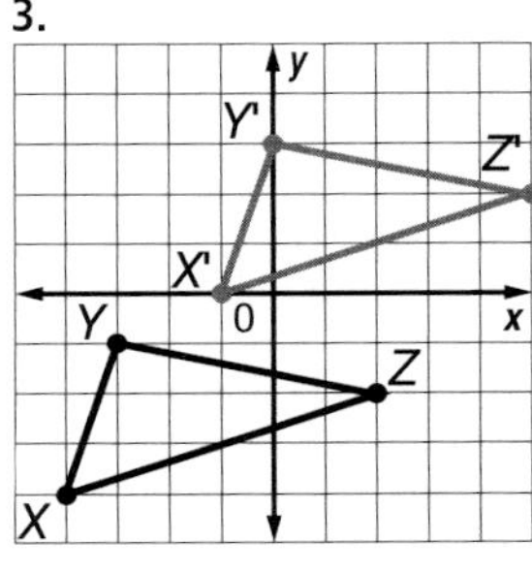

$X'(-1, 0)$, $Y'(0, 3)$, $Z'(5, 2)$

5. C

7.

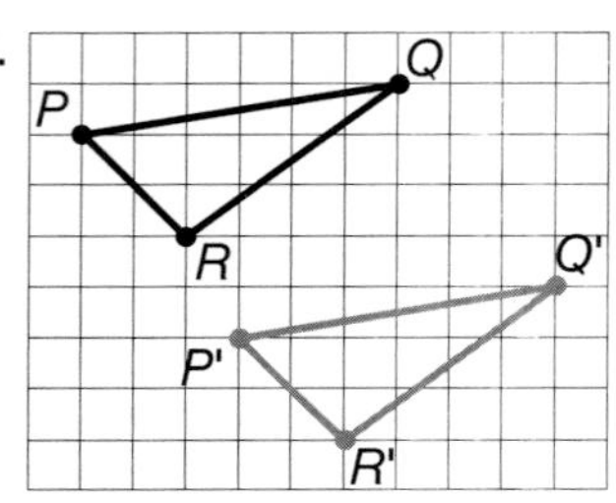

9.

11.

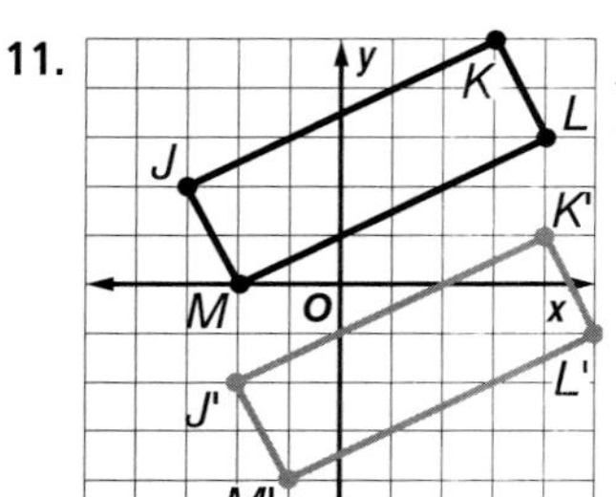

$J'(-2, -2)$, $K'(4, 1)$, $L'(5, -1)$, $M'(-1, -4)$

13.

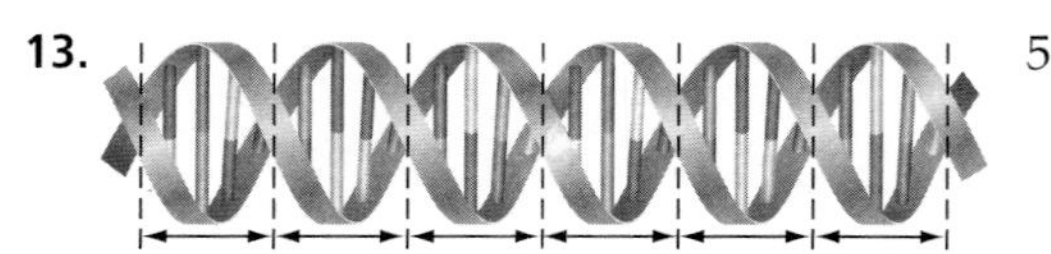

5

15. $B'(-12, 0)$, $C'(1, 5)$; The translation is to the left 5 units. **17.** $(x - m, y + n)$ **19.** B

21.

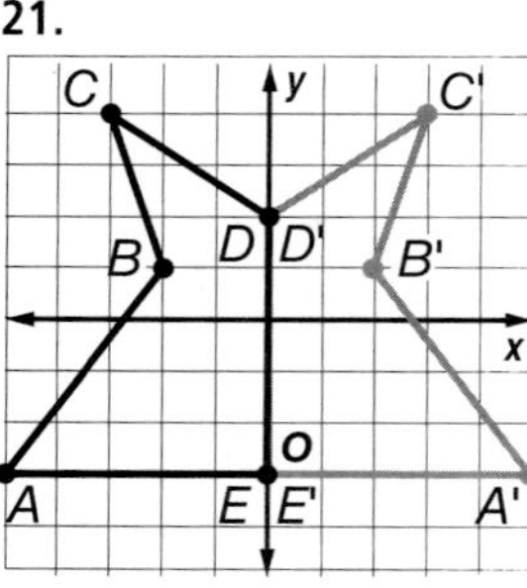

$A'(5, -3)$, $B'(2, 1)$, $C'(3, 4)$, $D'(0, 2)$, $E'(0, -3)$

23. no

25. $\frac{3}{8}$, 38%, $\frac{5}{8}$, 0.65

Pages 342–346 ***Chapter 6*** ***Study Guide and Review***

1. True **3.** False, $\angle B$ **5.** False, equiangular **7.** True **9.** 125 **11.** 58 **13.** corresponding **15.** corresponding **17.** $\angle 2$ and $\angle 3$ are supplementary angles, $m\angle 2 = 94°$.

19. 1,440° **21.** 128.6° **23.** 135° **25.** Yes; $\angle A \cong \angle P$, $\angle B \cong \angle Q$, $\angle C \cong \angle R$, and $\angle D \cong \angle S$; $\overline{AB} \cong \overline{PQ}$, $\overline{BC} \cong \overline{QR}$, $\overline{CD} \cong \overline{RS}$, $\overline{DA} \cong \overline{SP}$; $ABCD \cong PQRS$

27.

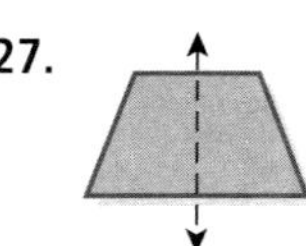

29. None **31.** Yes; 90°, 180°, 270°

33.

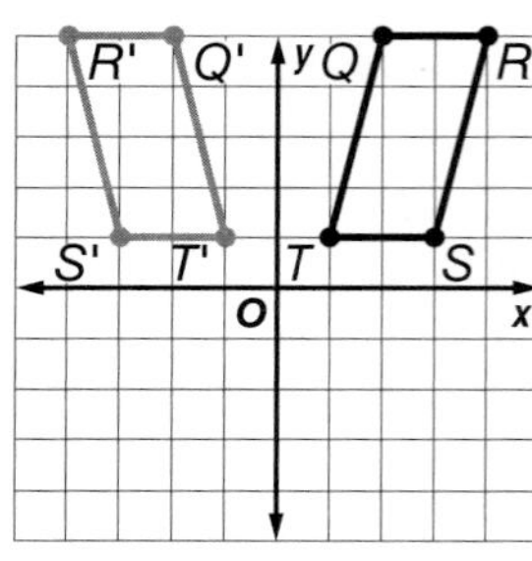

35.

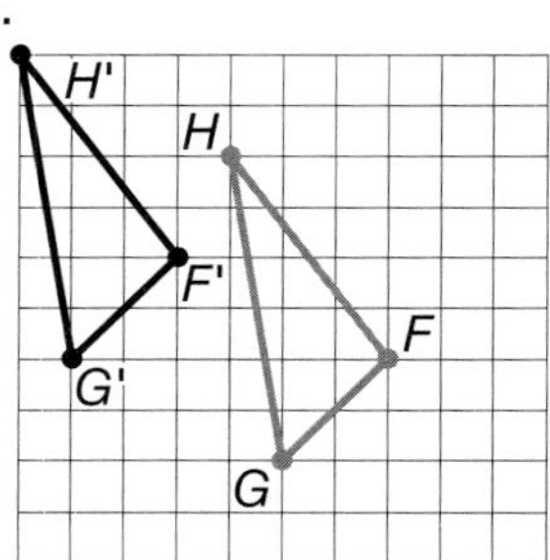

37.

$A'(3, -2)$, $B'(4, 1)$, $C'(6, -1)$

39. $P'(-2, 6)$

Chapter 7 Measurement: Area and Volume

Page 351 ***Chapter 7*** ***Getting Ready***

1. 32 **3.** 8 **5.** 102 **7.** 227.68 **9.** 20.1 **11.** 283.4

Pages 355–357 ***Lesson 7-1***

1. 56.5 cm **3.** 7.9 mi **5.** 346.4 ft^2 **7.** 2.5 inches **9.** 119.4 mi **11.** 106.8 km **13.** 22.1 mi^2 **15.** 70.9 in^2 **17.** about 14.1 feet **19.** 8,168 in. or $680\frac{2}{3}$ ft **21.** 8.6π km; 18.49π km^2 **23.** 1.2π mi; 0.36π mi^2 **25.** 21 bags **27.** $14\frac{2}{3}$ in.; $17\frac{1}{9}$ in^2 **29.** circumference; height = $3d$, $C = 3.14d$ **31.** about 15.7 ft^2

33. Sample answer:

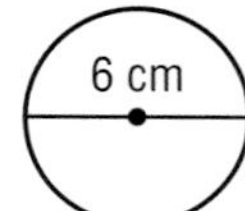

The circumference of the circle is $C = p \cdot 6$ or 18.8 cm.

35. 88.0 cm^2 **37.** 18.2 m^2 **39.** B

41.

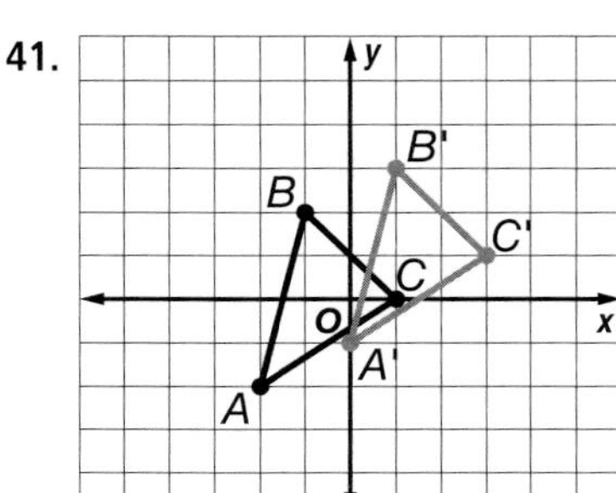

43. about $471,000/in^2

Pages 360–361 ***Lesson 7-2***

1. There would be too many squares to count in the 5×5 square. **3.** 210 **5.** 3 packages of 30 and 2 packages of 80 **7.** 165 hours **9.** 52 students **11.** $17.53 **13.** No, the total is $12.49.

Pages 365–367 ***Lesson 7-3***

1. 216 in^2 **3.** 3.9 ft^2 **5.** 64 cm^2 **7.** 220.5 cm^2 **9.** 38.6 ft^2 **11.** 119.5 ft^2 **13.** 610 m^2 **15.** 120 cm^2 **17.** 218 ft^2 **19.** Divide the composite figure horizontally into two trapezoids, find the area of each, and then find the sum of their areas. Divide the complex figure up vertically into two triangles and a square, find the area of each figure, then find the sum of their areas.

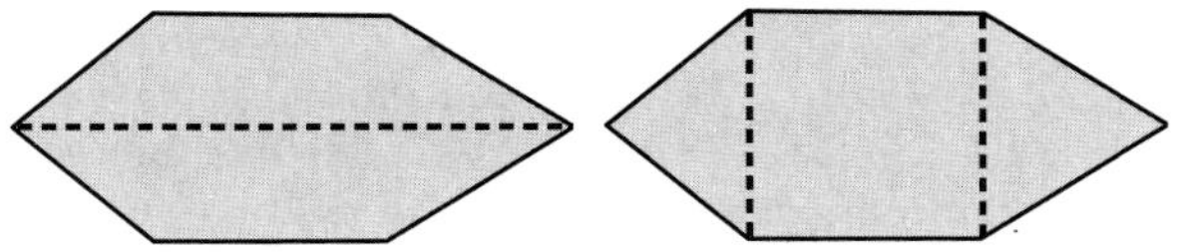

21. H **23.** 314.2 ft^2 **25.** triangle **27.** pentagon

Pages 370–372 ***Lesson 7-4***

1. Planes *ABCD* and *EFGH* **3.** points *D* and *F* **5.** rectangular prism; 6 faces, all rectangles; 12 edges; 8 vertices **7.** rectangular pyramid; 5 faces, 1 rectangle and 4 triangles; 8 edges; 5 vertices **9.** Sample answer: planes *RSTU* and *VYXW* **11.** Sample answer: points *S* and *W* **13.** triangular pyramid; 4 faces, all triangles; 6 edges; 4 vertices **15.** triangular prism; 5 faces, 2 triangles and 3 rectangles; 9 edges; 6 vertices

17.

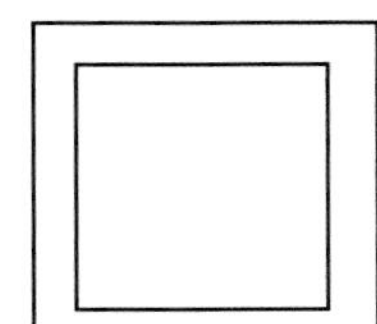

top view

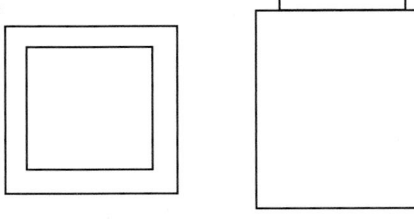

front and side views

19a. triangular based pyramid

19b. top view side view

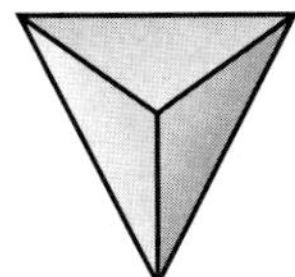

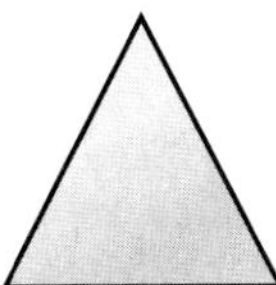

21a. 2 square pyramids

21b. top view side view

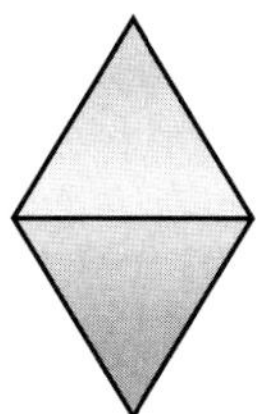

25. Never; a pyramid has all sides, except the base, intersecting at one vertex. **27.** A **29.** 161.1 in^2 **31.** 15 in^2 **33.** 27.5 cm^2

Pages 376–378 ***Lesson 7-5***

1. 36 ft^3 **3.** 1,272.3 yd^3 **5.** 14,790 cm^3 **7.** 216 mm^3 **9.** 768 m^3 **11.** 55.4 m^3 **13.** 297.5 ft^3 **15.** 236.1 cm^3 **17.** 3,864.9 cm^3 **19.** 6 in. **21.** Sample answer: 5.6 inches; the height remains the same, so πr^2 must equal 24. Solve the equation for *r*, then double it to get the diameter. **23.** 1,728 **25.** 1,000,000 **27.** The base of the prism is a hexagon, which can be separated into two congruent trapezoids. So, the area of the base is $2 \times \frac{1}{2}(4)(11 + 5)$ or 64 m^2. The height of the prism is 7 m, so the volume of the prism is 64×7 or 448 m^3. **29.** Volume quadruples **31.** Volume quadruples **33.** Ana; the base of the prism is a triangle and the area of a triangle is one-half the product of the base times altitude of the triangle. The height of the prism is 9 in. **35.** $V = Bh$ and $V = \ell wh$; Sample answer: $V = \ell wh$ because you can see exactly which values you need to substitute into the formula. **37.** 10 **39.** 284.52 ft^2 **41.** 22 million pounds **43.** $2\frac{1}{4}$ **45.** $\frac{3}{800}$ **47.** 35 **49.** 240

Pages 383–384 ***Lesson 7-6***

1. 410.7 cm^3 **3.** 376,041.7 cm^3 **5.** 71 ft **7.** 2,948.9 in^3 **9.** 2,261.9 cm^3 **11.** 195 yd^3 **13.** 175 cm^3 **15.** 2.6 mi^3 **17.** 188.5 m^3 **19.** 840 yd^3 **21.** 103.7 mm^3 **23.** 165 min **25.** Sample answer:

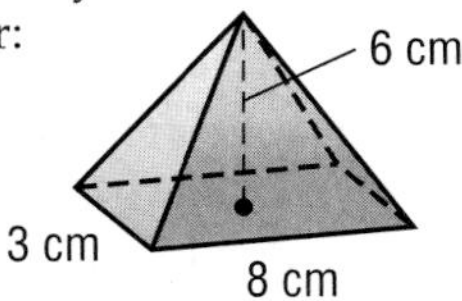

27. Sample answer: finding the amount of ice cream inside a cone **29.** J **31.** trapezoidal prism; 6 faces, 2 trapezoids, 4 rectangles; 12 edges; 8 vertices **33.** $240 **35.** 17.3 ft **37.** 23.9 cm

Pages 389–391 ***Lesson 7-7***

1. 64 yd^2; 94 yd^2 **3.** 236.2 m^2; 336.8 m^2 **5.** 81.7 in^2 **7.** 30 in^2; 58 in^2 **9.** 265.05 m^2; 332.25 m^2 **11.** 202.3 mm^2; 335.3 mm^2 **13.** 635.4 in^2 **15.** 1,358.4 in^2 **17.** 363.2 in^2 **19.** Double the radius; consider the expression for the surface area of a cylinder, $2\pi r^2 + 2\pi rh$. If you double the height, you will double the second addend. If you double the radius, you will quadruple the first addend and double the second addend. **21.** Surface area is the area of all the surfaces of a solid.

Lateral area is the surface area minus the area of the bases. **23.** H **25.** 3,041.1 cm^3 **27.** 1.4 **29.** 20

Pages 395–396 ***Lesson 7-8***

1. 48 ft^2; 64 ft^2 **3.** 572,400 ft^2 **5.** 35 ft^2; 47.3 ft^2 **7.** 105.3 mm^2; 140.4 mm^2 **9.** 1,536 ft^2; 2,112 ft^2 **11.** 1,280 ft^2 **13.** 829,503 ft^2 **15.** 17 in. **17.** Sample answer: 2 in. by 3 in. by 2.1 in. **19.** D **21.** 61.3 in^2 **23.** $53\frac{1}{3}$ **25.** $2\frac{1}{3}$

Pages 402–404 ***Lesson 7-9***

1. 21.4 in. **3.** B **5.** 2.7 ft **7.** 1,040 in^2 **9.** 52.1 cm^3 **11.** 133.6 in^3 **13.** 90 ft^2 **15.** $\frac{1}{2}$ **17.** 58,679.1 cm^3, 139,091.2 cm^3, 469,432.8 cm^3 **19.** Sample answer: The cones are similar because the ratios comparing their radii and heights are equal: $\frac{3}{1.5} = \frac{8}{4}$.

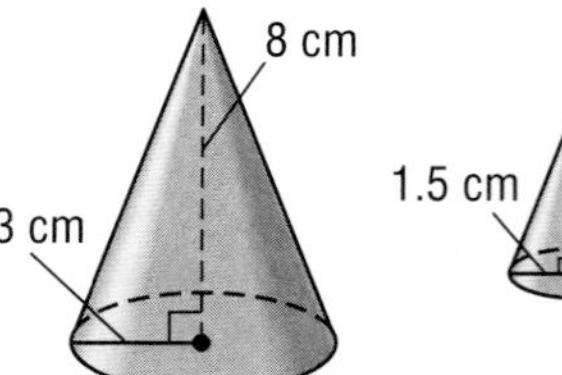

21. true; Sample answer: all spheres are the same shape, and since the radii or diameters are the only linear measures, they are always proportional. **23.** A **25.** 925,041.6 ft^2 **27.** $Q'(-3, -3)$, $R'(2, -4)$, $S'(3, -2)$, $T'(-2, -1)$ **29.** 12%

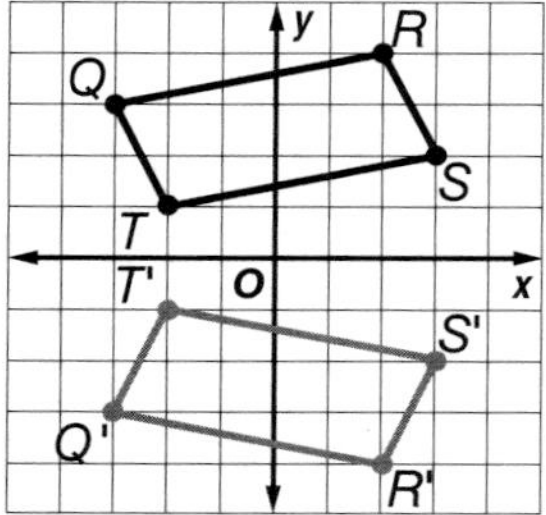

Pages 405–408 ***Chapter 7*** ***Study Guide and Review***

1. true **3.** false, volume **5.** false, three **7.** false, diameter **9.** 18.8 cm; 28.3 cm^2 **11.** 66,123 mi^2 **13.** 57.5 mm^2 **15.** triangular prism; 5 faces, 2 triangles, 3 rectangles; 9 edges; 6 vertices **17.** 6 faces, 10 edges, 6 vertices **19.** 660 yd^3 **21.** 163.3 ft^3 **23.** 445.3 yd^3 **25.** 636.2 in^2 **27.** 33,947.5 m^2

Chapter 8 Algebra: More Equations and Inequalities

Page 415 ***Chapter 8*** ***Getting Ready***

1. true **3.** true **5.** Des Moines; $-5 > -7$ **7.** $-5 - 3x = 32$ **9.** \$29 **11.** -15 **13.** -4 **15.** 7 **17.** -84

Pages 419–421 ***Lesson 8-1***

1. $5x + 20$ **3.** $3y + 18$ **5.** $2p - 6$ **7.** $-6g + 12$ **9.** terms: $5n, -2n, -3, n$; like terms: $5n, -2n$, and n; coefficients: 5, -2, 1; constant: -3 **11.** terms: 7, $-3d$, -8, d; like terms: $-3d$ and d, 7 and -8; coefficients: -3, 1; constants: 7, -8 **13.** 5 **15.** $3x + 4.50$ **17.** $-8a - 8$ **19.** $-2p - 14$ **21.** $30 - 6q$ **23.** $-15 + 3b$ **25.** $-4n + 12$ **27.** $18 + 3z$ **29.** terms: 7, $-5x$, 1; like terms: 7, 1; coefficients: -5; constants: 7, 1 **31.** terms: $n, 4n, -7n, -1$; like terms: $n, 4n, -7n$; coefficients: 1, 4, -7; constant: -1 **33.** terms: 9, $-z$, 3, $-2z$; like terms: 9 and 3, $-z$ and $-2z$; coefficients: -1, -2; constants: 9, 3 **35.** $11c$ **37.** $2 + 4d$ **39.** $-8j + 5$ **41.** $2x + 30$ **43.** $2y - 5$ **47.** $-12x - 20$ **49.** $4x - 4y$ **51.** $14 + 7n$ **53.** $-12ab - 30ac$ **55.** Sample answer: you are 14 years younger than 6 times your brother's age, a. **57.** $n(4.75 + 2.50) + 30$; $7.25n + 30$ **59.** $12(x - 7)$; $12x - 84$ **61.** $7m - 20$ **63.** $4(x - 2)$; $4(x - 2)$ is equivalent to $4x - 8$, while the other three expressions are equivalent to $4x - 2$. **65.** true; $2(x - 1) + 3(x - 1) = 2x - 2 + 3x - 3$ or $5x - 5$ which is equivalent to $5(x - 1)$. **67.** G **69.** 137.7 cm^2; 172.8 cm^2 **71.** 51 in^2; 69.1 in^2 **73.** no **75.** 57.3 mph **77.** -4 **79.** -45

Pages 424–426 ***Lesson 8-2***

1. 4 **3.** 28 **5.** 8 **7.** 16 payments **9.** -7 **11.** 7 people **13.** -3 **15.** -2 **17.** 5 **19.** -64 **21.** 7 **23.** -52 **25.** 5 **27.** 4 **29.** -1 **31.** -1 **33.** 15 rounds **35.** 11 **37.** 64 **39.** -26 **41.** $x = 39.75$; No, it satisfies the equation, but it is not a solution of the problem, because you cannot have 0.75 animals. **43.** Juan; Jeanie did not undo the operations in reverse order. **45.** You identify the order in which operations would be performed on the variable, then you undo each operation using its inverse operation in reverse order. **47.** F **49.** $-3x - 15$ **51.** $-8p + 56$ **53.** 12 ft **55.** $n + 5 = 17$

Pages 429–431 ***Lesson 8-3***

1. $3n + 1 = 7$ **3.** $\frac{n}{5} - 10 = 3$ **5.** $121 = s + (s + 45)$; \$38 **7.** $2n + 15 = 9$ **9.** $7n - 6 = -20$ **11.** $3x + 1.99 = 55.99$; \$18 **13.** $13 + 1.50r = 35.50$; 15 rides **15.** $2x + 2(134) = 360$; 46 **17.** 34 miles per hour **19.** 4 **21.** 10, 12, 14 **23.** $7.50h + 150 = 600$; 60 h; $12h = 600$; 50 h **25.** Sample answer: You and your friend spent \$25 at the mall. You spent \$6 less than your friend. How much did your friend spend? **27.** $n + 2n + (n + 3) = 27$; 6, 9, 12 **29.** Sample answer: To rent a locker at the gym it costs \$7 a week. You will save an extra \$4 once you return the key. If your total cost is \$24, how many weeks did you rent the locker? $7x - 4 = 24$; 4 weeks. **31.** J **33.** -2 **35.** 6 **37.** 8 **39.** $3 + 5y$ **41.** 146.9%; increase **43.** 7 **45.** $-15a$

Pages 436–437 ***Lesson 8-4***

1. -3 **3.** -4 **5.** 5 **7.** 75 mi **9.** 8 **11.** -9 **13.** 10 **15.** 1 **17.** 5 **19.** 3.6 **21.** Let n = the number; $4n + 11 = n - 7$; -6 **23.** $483 + 18p = 462 + 21p$; 7 games **25.** $60x = 8x + 26$; 0.5 **27.** $10 + 0.07(15x) + 9x = 15x$;

3 sweatshirts **29.** 147 units^2 **31.** C **33.** \$7.95 **35.** −5 **37.** 4 **39.** Enrique can invite two friends.

Pages 439–440 ***Lesson 8-5***

1. There are 30 people going to the museum, not 23 + 5 or 28 people. **3.** 24 or −24 **5.** 3 rings, 5 toys **7.** Sample answer: 3, 8, 12 **9.** Sample answer: 8 in. by 5 in. by 10 in.; 10 in. by 10 in. by 4 in. **11.** 32, 36, 40 **13.** 45

Pages 443–444 ***Lesson 8-6***

1. $s \le 55$ **3.** false **5.** true

7. 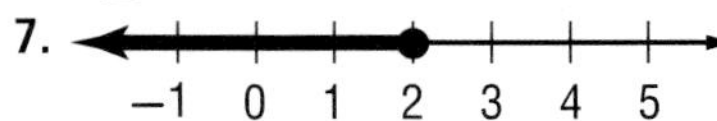

9. 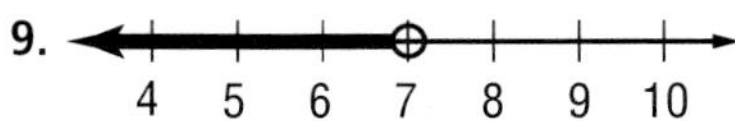

11. $t \ge 10$ **13.** $c \le 25$ **15.** $w > 200$ **17.** true **19.** true **21.** false

23. −3 −2 −1 0 1 2 3

25. −1 0 1 2 3 4 5

27. 4 5 6 7 8 9 10

29. 1 2 3 4 5 6 7

31. all except skateboarding **33.** 85,000 < 185,000 **35.** True; 12 = 12 meets one of the conditions of greater than or equal to. **37.** D **39.** two 5-card packages and two 3-card packages **41.** 16 **43.** 33

Pages 447–448 ***Lesson 8-7***

1. $b > 4$ **3.** $x < 14$ **5.** C **7.** $n \ge -12$ **9.** $y > -5$ **11.** $g \ge 17$ **13.** $s \le 7$ **15.** $x \le -16$ **17.** $g < -7$ **19.** $q \le -1.3$ **21.** $p > -1.2$ **23.** $f < 3\frac{3}{4}$ **25.** $n - 11 < 8$; $n < 19$ **27.** $n + 17 \le 6$; $n \le -11$ **29.** $2{,}200 + w \le 5{,}300$; $w \le 3{,}100$ lb **31.** $12 > x + 4$; $x < 8$; x must be any number less than 8 ft. **33.** more than one **35.** more than one **37.** Sample answer: $x + 4 < 13$, $x - 6 < 3$ **39.** $m \le 55$ **41.** true **43.** true **45.** −5 **47.** 48

Pages 452–453 ***Lesson 8-8***

1. $x > 4$ **3.** $x \le -9$ **5.** $y < -8$ **7.** $g > 14$ **9.** $45 + 0.19m \le 100$; $m \le 289.5$; He can drive 289.5 miles. **11.** $n \le 5$ **13.** $g < -4$ **15.** $y < -11$ **17.** $r < -3$ **19.** $c \le 1$ **21.** $a \le -15$ **23.** $n < -98$ **25.** $t \ge 10$ **27.** $k < 20$ **29.** $6.25h \ge 89$; $h \ge 14.24$; Max must work at least 15 hours.

31. $k \le -1$ −4 −3 −2 −1 0 1 2 3 4

33. $n < -9$ −12 −11 −10 −9 −8 −7 −6 −5 −4

35. $x \le -3$ −6 −5 −4 −3 −2 −1 0 1 2

37. $\frac{x}{-5} + 1 \le 7$; $x \ge -30$ **39.** $-2x - 6 > -18$; $x < 6$ **41.** Kendra; when dividing by a positive number, do not reverse the inequality symbol. **43.** Reverse the inequality symbol when multiplying or dividing by a negative number. **45.** F **47.** $a \le 7$ **49.** $n < -22$ **51.** $b \le 200$

Pages 454–458 ***Chapter 8*** ***Study Guide and Review***

1. false; the same **3.** false; constant **5.** true **7.** false; equivalent expressions **9.** $4a + 12$ **11.** $7p$ **13.** $2n - 5$ **15.** −2 **17.** 4 **19.** $2n + 6 = -4$ **21.** $8 + 4d = 28$; 5 more days **23.** −7 **25.** 1.5 **27.** Sample answer: 125 candy bars and 105 pretzels **29.** fingers: 14; wrist: 8; palm: 5 **31.** $p \le 15$ **33.** false

35. 88 89 90 91 92 93 94 95 96

37. $b \ge 17$ **39.** $x \le -2.8$ **41.** $t < 3\frac{1}{2}$ **43.** $920 + n \le 1{,}800$; the elevator can carry at most an additional 880 pounds. **45.** $k \le 5.1$ **47.** $y \le -7$ **49.** $a \ge -2.4$ **51. a.** $8h \ge 1{,}200$ **b.** $h \ge 150$ **c.** at least 150 h

Chapter 9 Algebra: Linear Functions

Page 463 ***Chapter 9*** ***Getting Ready***

1–4. 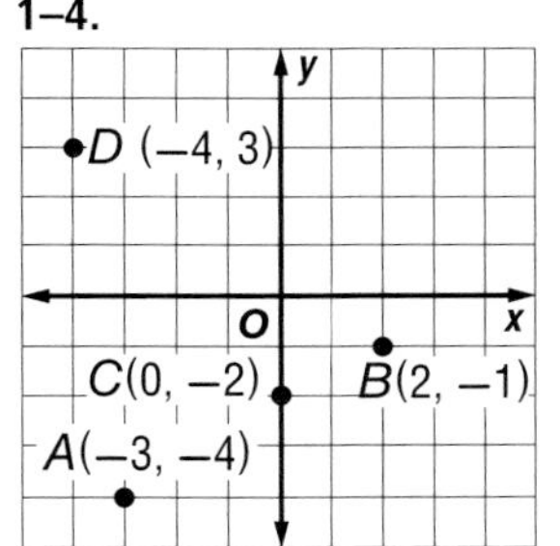

5. 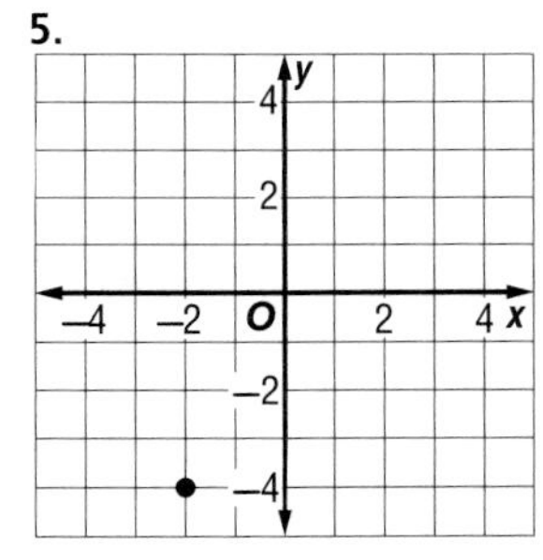

7. 15 **9.** 11 **11.** 5 **13.** 4

Pages 464–468 ***Lesson 9-1***

1. yes; 2; 12, 14, 16 **3.** yes; −6, −22, −28, −34 **5.** $-5m$; −25, −30, −35 **7.** 11 **9.** B **11.** no **13.** yes; 2; 4, 6, 8 **15.** yes; $2\frac{1}{2}$; $16\frac{1}{2}$, 19, $21\frac{1}{2}$ **17.** $12n$; 60, 72, 84 **19.** $\frac{2}{5}n$; 2, $2\frac{2}{5}$, $2\frac{4}{5}$ **21.** $3n - 2$; 13, 16, 19 **23.** 45 **25.** −101 **27.** 1,264 **29.** Yes; sample answer: the ratio of time to weeks is $\frac{1}{8}$ for every week. **31.** No; sample answer: the ratio of squares to figure number is not constant. **33.** Yes; the common difference is 0. **35.** Sample answer: −1, $-1\frac{1}{3}$, $-1\frac{2}{3}$, −2, ... **37.** $3n + 5$ **39.** C **41.** $5.25h \ge 42$; $h \ge 8$ **43.** $k > -11$ **45.** $y > -3$

Pages 469–474 ***Lesson 9-2***

1. −2

Selected Answers

3.

x	8 − x	f(x)
−3	8 − (−3)	11
−1	8 − (−1)	9
2	8 − 2	6
4	8 − 4	4

Domain: {−3, −1, 2, 4}
Range: {11, 9, 6, 4}

5.

x	3x − 2	f(x)
−5	3(−5) − 2	−17
−2	3(−2) − 2	−8
2	3(2) − 2	4
5	3(5) − 2	13

Domain: {−5, −2, 2, 5}
Range: {−17, −8, 4, 13}

7. 35 **9.** 11 **11.** –21

13.

x	6x − 4	f(x)
−5	6(−5) − 4	−34
−1	6(−1) −4	−10
2	6(2) − 4	8
7	6(7) − 4	38

Domain: {−5, −1, 2, 7}
Range: {−34, −10, 8, 38}

15.

x	7 + 3x	f(x)
−3	7 + 3(−3)	−2
−2	7 + 3(−2)	1
1	7 + 3(1)	10
6	7 + 3(6)	25

Domain: {−3, −2, 1, 6}
Range: {−2, 1, 10, 25}

17.

x	7x	f(x)
−5	7(−5)	−35
−3	7(−3)	−21
2	7(2)	14
6	7(6)	41

Domain: {−5, −3, 2, 6}
Range: {−35, −21, 14, 41}

19. $s = b + 30$; 215 **21.** 2 **23.** 7 h **25.** $f(x) = 2x - 2$; $f(0) = -2, f(-4) = -10, f(3) = 4$ **27.** Sample answer: If the rate remains constant, increasing the time by a factor of *f* increases the distance by a factor of *f*.
29. H **31.** $x \leq 6$ **33.** $g < -3$ **35.** 574.7 in^2 **37.** 5

38–41.

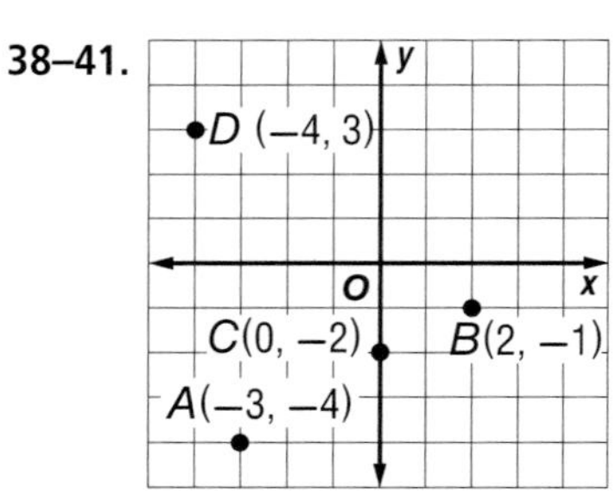

Pages 475–480 **Lesson 9-3**

1.

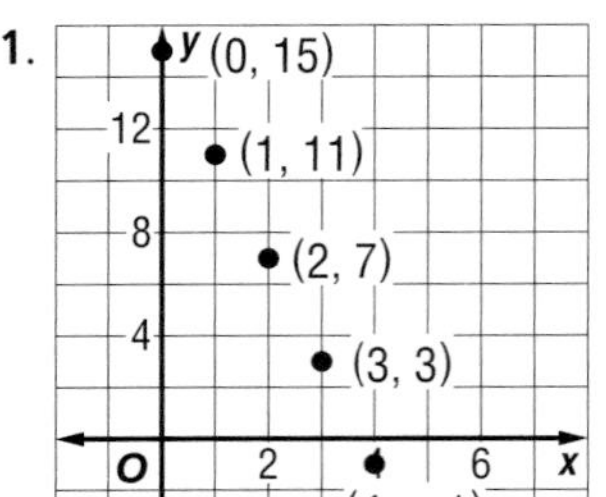

3.

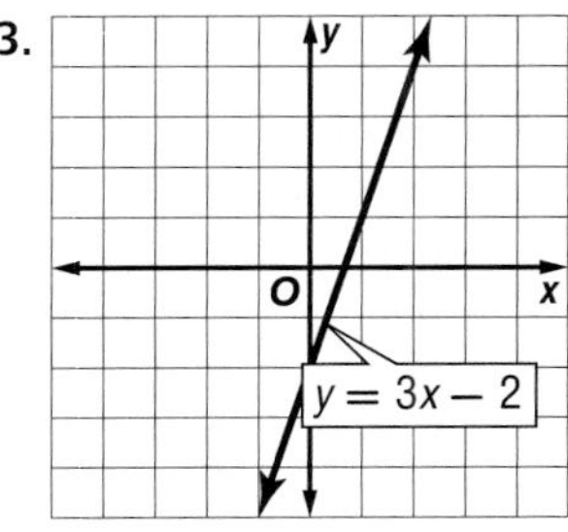

5. A

7.

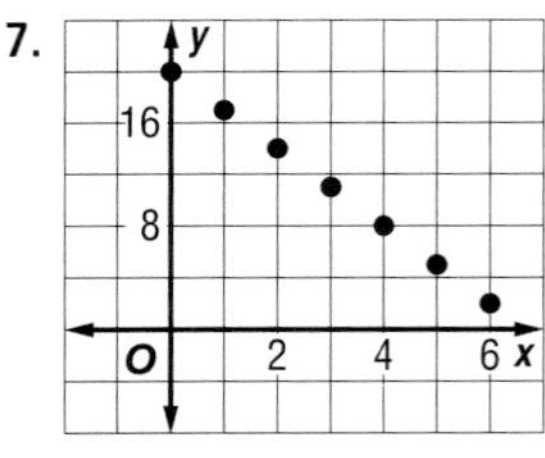

9.

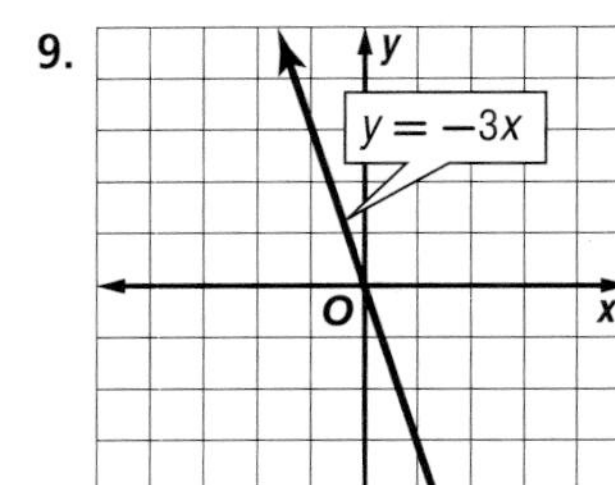

11.

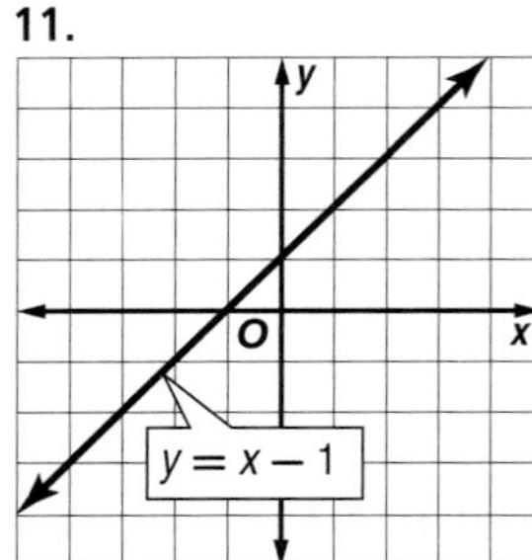

13.

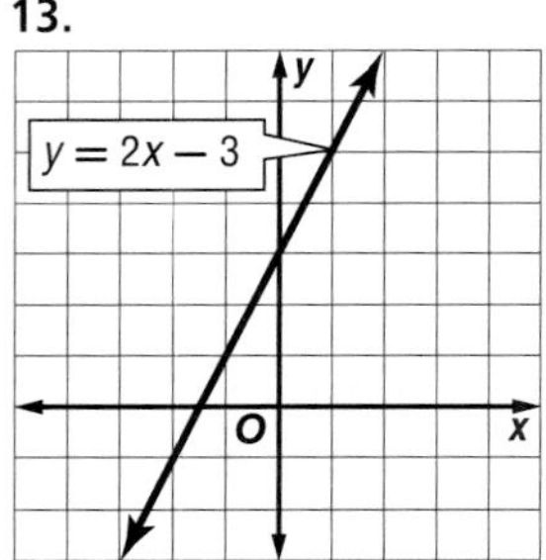

15.

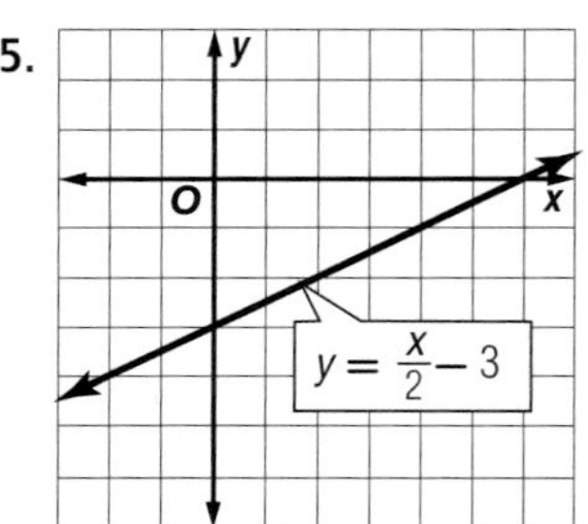

17. No; you could not have a negative distance.
19. 43.6 m **21.** Mitchell: 55.9°F; Rogers: 59.4°F; Black: 65.1°F; Sassafras: 67.2°F

23.

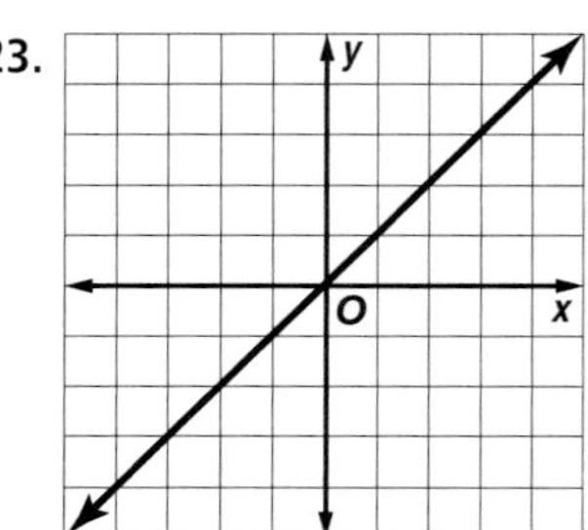

25a. Sample answer: (−2, −4), (0, −2), (2, 0), (4, 2); $y = x - 2$ **25b.** Sample answer: (−1, 4), (0, 3), (1, 2),

(3, 0); $y = 3 - x$ **27.** D **29.** 39 **31.** −1
33. $0.50x \geq 500$; at least 1,000 flowers **35.** $-\frac{2}{3}$

Pages 481–486 ***Lesson 9-4***

1. $\frac{1}{5}$ or $-\frac{1}{5}$ **3.** $-\frac{1}{3}$ **5.** $\frac{3}{4}$ **7.** $-\frac{8}{9}$ **9.** $-\frac{5}{8}$ **11.** $\frac{1}{2}$
13. −3 **15.** $-\frac{5}{2}$;

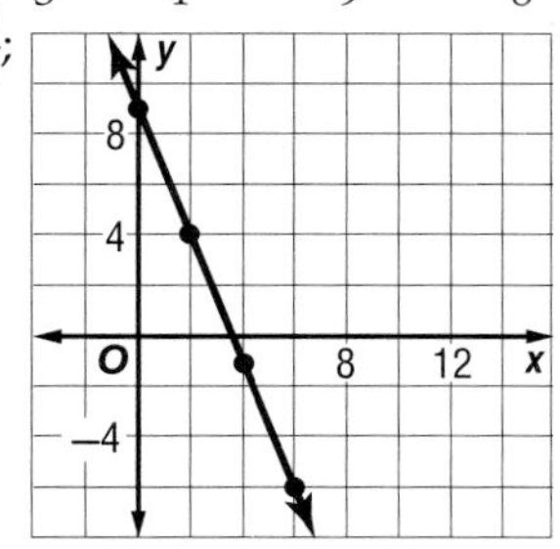

17. 3 **19.** $\frac{5}{3}$ **21.** $-\frac{2}{11}$ **23.** $-\frac{5}{8}$; the depth of the water is decreasing $\frac{5}{8}$ inch per day. **25.** 10.2 **27.** '95–'98: $\frac{2}{3}$; '98–'01: $\frac{1}{3}$; '01–'04: $\frac{2}{3}$; 04–07: $\frac{-0.8}{3}$ **29.** No; the percent of families owning homes cannot exceed 100%. The closer the percent reaches 100, the slower the growth will be. **31.** Yes; $\frac{1}{15} < \frac{1}{12}$ **33.** Joel; Jabali did not use the x-coordinates in the same order as the y-coordinates. **35.** The rise and the run must always be the same or the line will not be straight. **37.** G

39.

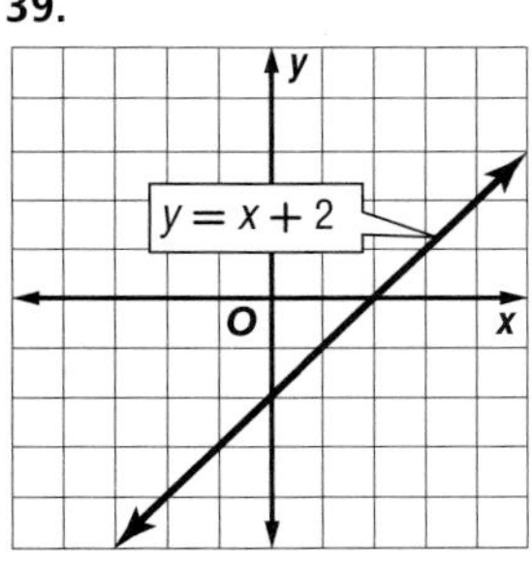

41.

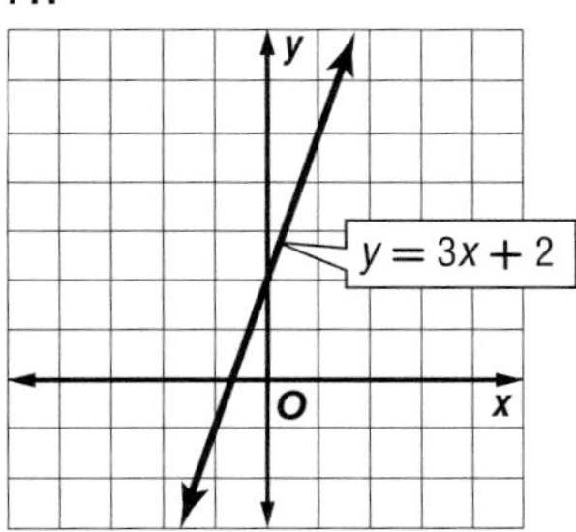

43. −3 **45.** 21

Pages 487–493 ***Lesson 9-5***

1. 25 computers per hour **3.** yes; 58
5. $0.50/newspaper **7.** $3.49/DVD **9.** $53\frac{1}{3}$ lb
11. $6\frac{7}{8}$ c **13.** no **15.** yes; 0.07 **17.** $y = \frac{2}{5}x$; 4
19. $y = 78x$; $28\frac{4}{7}$ **21.** 127 cm **23.** Sample answer: $x = 3$, $y = 1\frac{11}{16}$ **25.** Sample answer: $y = 6x$; If you multiply x by 3, the value of y is 6 • 3 or 18. **27.** 36
29. $\frac{1}{2}$ **31.** $-\frac{4}{5}$ **33.** 450 calories **35.** −21 **37.** −9

Pages 495–501 ***Lesson 9-6***

1. 1; 2 **3.** −2; 3 **5.**

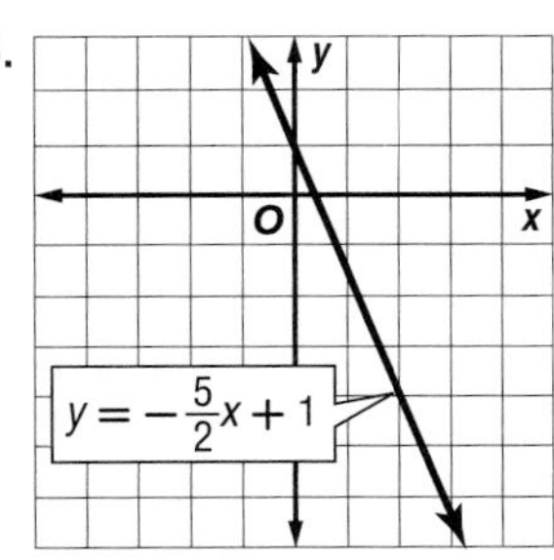

7. 134 pages

9. No; the ratios of the pages left to read to the time read are not equal. **11.** −5; 2 **13.** $-\frac{3}{7}$; $-\frac{1}{7}$
15. −3; −4

17.

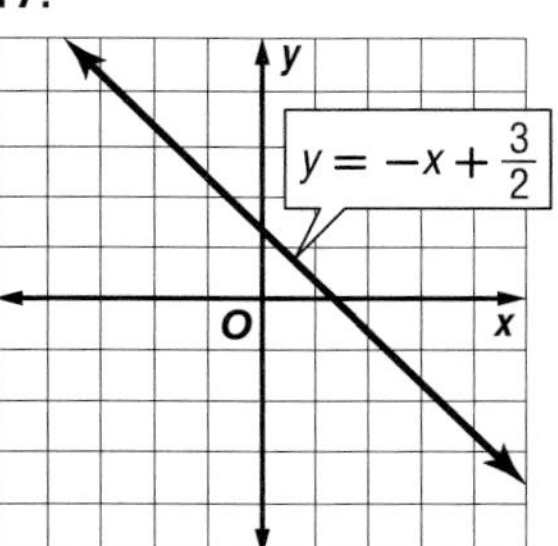

19.

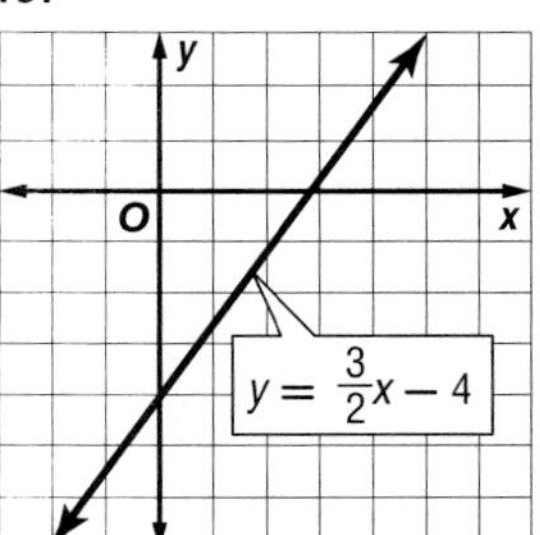

21.

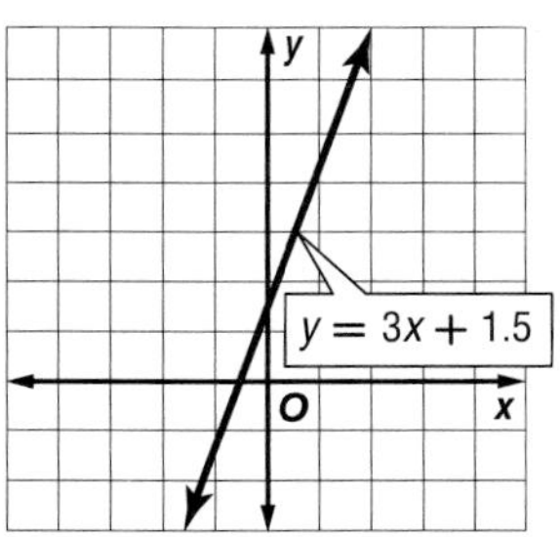

23. the hourly rental charge, $15, and the base rental fee, $35

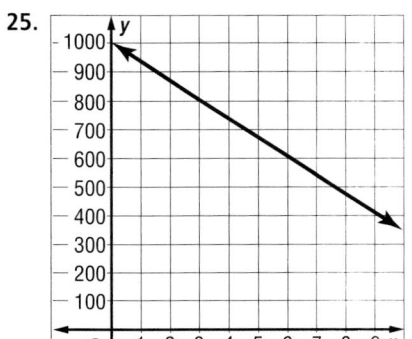

25. 610 miles

27. No; the ratio of the distance remaining to the hours driven are not equal. **29.** $y = -x + 180$ **31.** No; the ratios of the angle measures are not equal.
33. Sample answer: The y-intercept of −3 means the graph will cross the y-axis at −3, and the slope of 2 means the graph will rise as x increases.
35. (1.5, 0), (0, −3) **37.** Sample answer: The y-intercept of 2 means the graph will cross the y-axis at 2 and the slope of 1.5 means the graph will rise as x increases. The y-intercept represents the rainfall at noon, and the slope represents the hourly rate of rainfall. **39a.** 4; 1
39b. Sample answer: The y-intercept of 1 means the

graph will cross the y-axis at 1. The slope of 4 means the graph will rise as x increases. **39c.** $y = 4x + 1$ **39d.** $\left(\frac{-1}{4}, 0\right)$, (0, 1) **43.** The slope is undefined. There is no y-intercept unless the graph of the line is the y-axis. **45.** A **47.** 6 h **49.** $\frac{3}{2}$

51.

x	$0.39x$	y	(x, y)
0	0.39(0)	0	(0, 0)
1	0.39(1)	0.39	(1, 0.39)
2	0.39(2)	0.78	(2, 0.78)
3	0.39(3)	1.17	(3, 1.17)
4	0.39(4)	1.56	(4, 1.56)

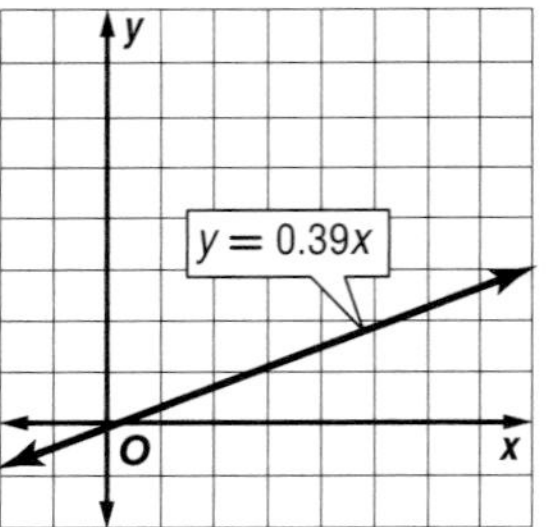

53. 6 **55.** −80

Pages 502–507 ***Lesson 9-7***

1.

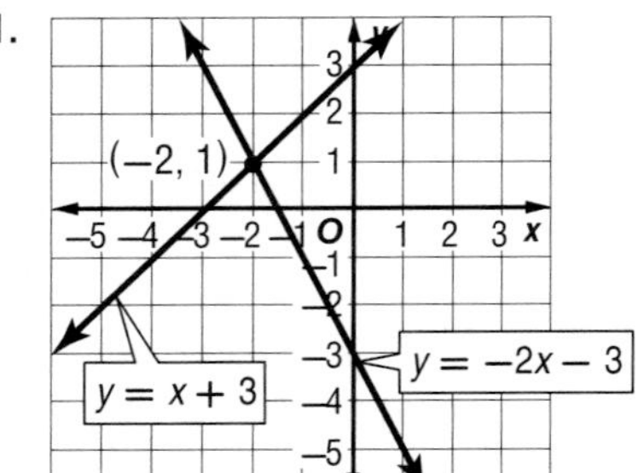

(−2, 1)

3.

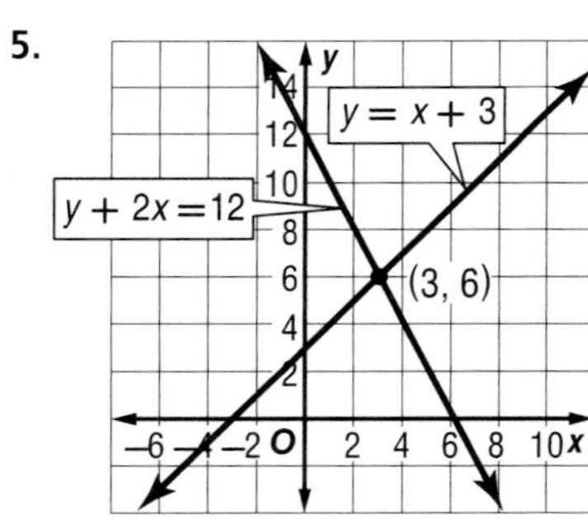

All points on the line $y = 2x + 6$.

5.

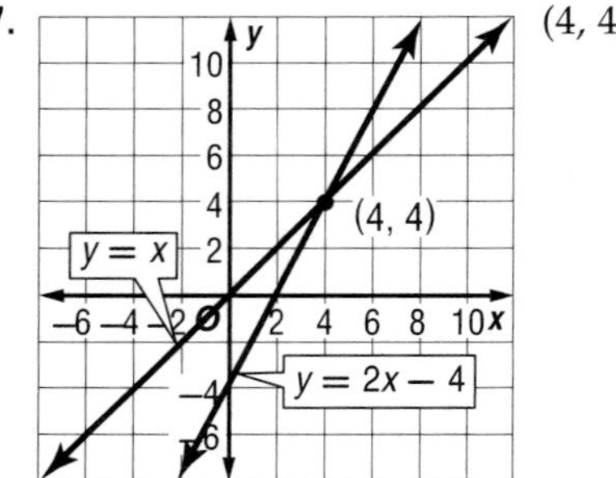

Let x = Jason's age and y = Sally's age; $y + 2x = 12$; $y = x + 3$; Sally is 6 years old, and Jason is 3 years old.

7.

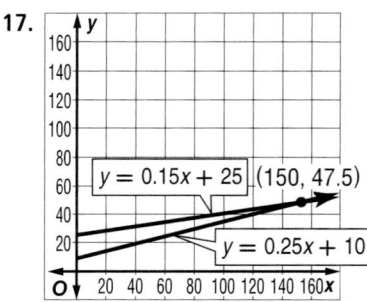

(4, 4)

9.

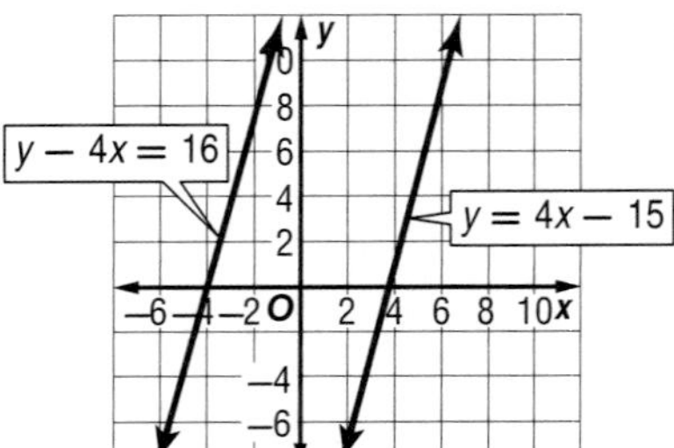

no solution

11.

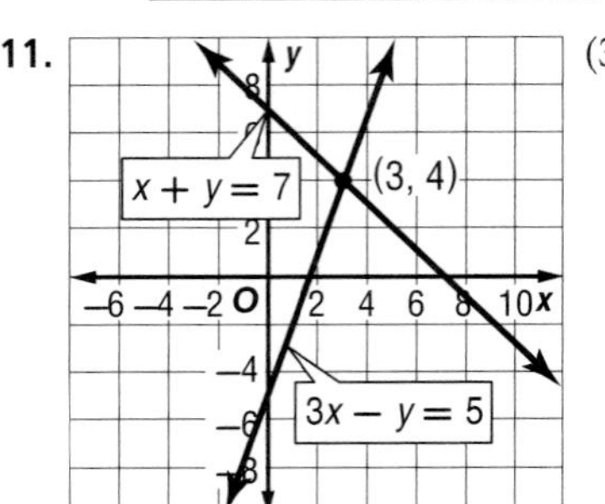

(3, 4)

13.

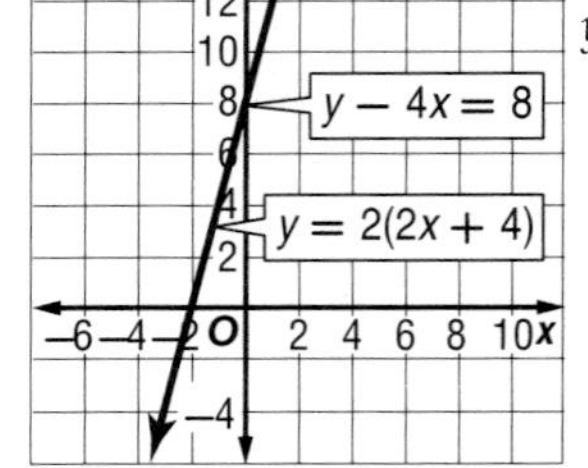

All points on the line $y = 4x + 8$.

15.

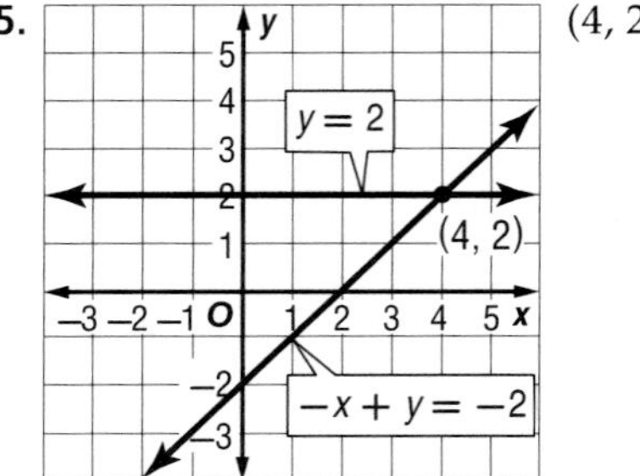

(4, 2)

17.

Let x = the number of minutes used and y = the total monthly cost; $y = 0.25x + 10$; $y = 0.15x + 25$; At 150 minutes, the monthly costs are equal.

19.

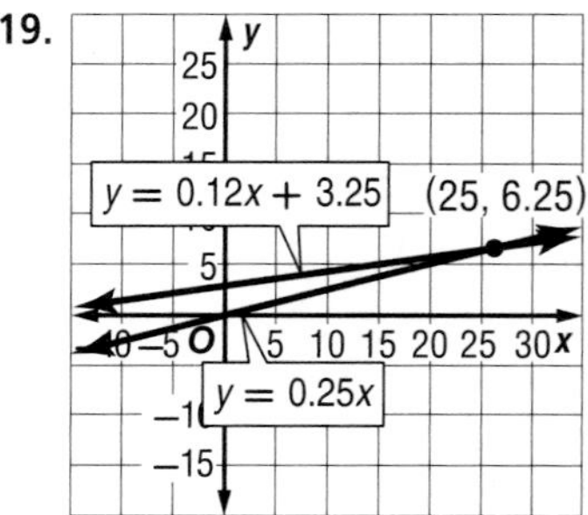

Let x = the number of beads purchased and y = the total cost; $y = 0.12x + 3.25$; $y = 0.25x$; At 25 beads, the costs would be the same.

21. Let x = the number of nickels and y = the number of dimes; $y = x + 3$; $5x + 10y = 90$; Brad has 4 nickels and 7 dimes.

23. neither **25a.** Sample answer: $y = -x + 4$ **25b.** Sample answer: $y = 2x - 1$ **25c.** Sample answer: $y = 2x - 1$ **27.** B

29.

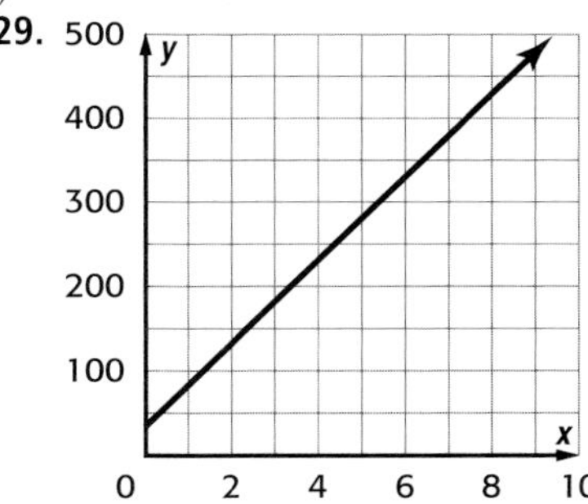

31. the number of pages read each day; the number of pages read initially **33.** true **35.** true **37.** 140 boxes

Pages 508–509 ***Lesson 9-8***

1. Sample answer: The most popular Web site has an average download time of 1.4 seconds, which is not the fastest download time. This ordered pair is an exception to the general statement that the most popular Web sites are faster than the less popular Web sites. **3.** company B **5.** −12, −16 **7.** The membership increased steadily from 2001 to 2006. **9.** 38% **11.** yes

Pages 510–517 ***Lesson 9-9***

1. As the number of hours increases, the number of units produced increases. Therefore, the scatter plot shows a positive relationship.

3. **Fast Food Nutritional Information**

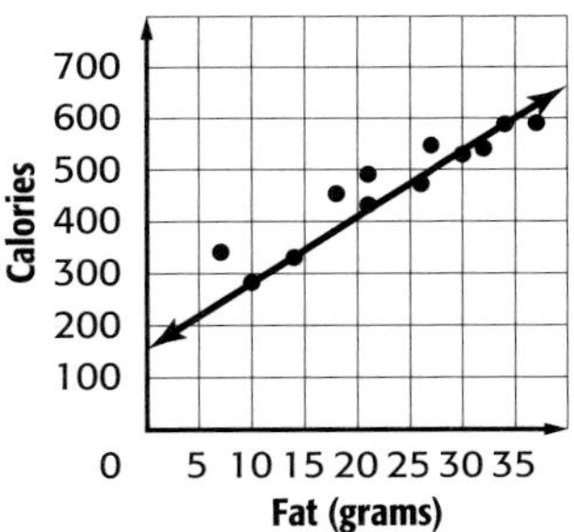

5. Sample answer: 18 g

7. As the engine size increases, the mileage decreases. Therefore, the scatter plot shows a negative relationship. **9.** As the study time increases, the test scores increase. Therefore, the scatter plot shows a positive relationship.

11. $y = 2.5x + 45$ **13.** Sample answer: positive

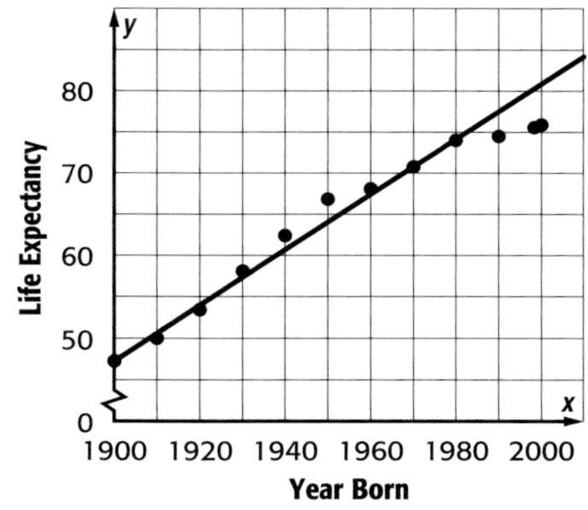

15. Sample answer: about 88.1 yr

17. The number of pets does not depend on a student's grade level. Therefore, a scatter plot of the data would show no relationship. **19.** As the outside temperature increases, the amount of a heating bill decreases. Therefore, a scatter plot of the data would show a negative relationship. **21.** Sample answer: there is no relationship between home runs hit and runs batted in. Therefore, you cannot draw a line of fit to represent the data. **23.** no relationship; sample answer: the data appears random on a scatter plot **25.** Sample answer: the number of trees in an orchard and the number of apples harvested. The outlying value could represent an orchard with a large number of apples.
27. Sometimes; sample answer: the price per gallon of gasoline would increase proportionally as the number of gallons bought increases. But, as the level of education increases, salary may or may not increase proportionally. **29.** A

31.

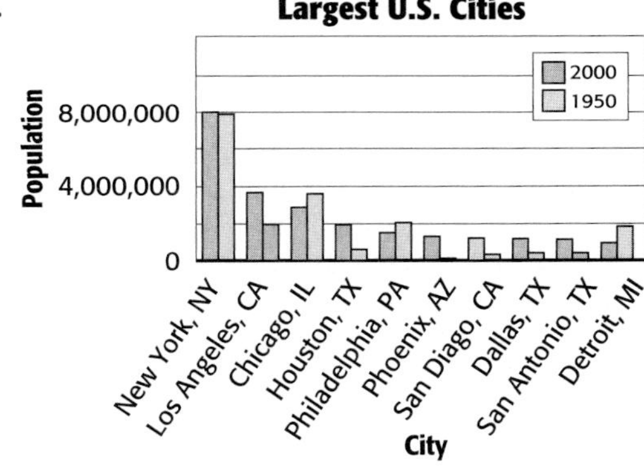

33. Phoenix **35.** 4 **37.** 6

Pages 518–522 ***Chapter 9*** ***Study Guide and Review***

1. domain **3.** function **5.** y-intercept **7.** line of fit **9.** dependent **11.** $-8n$; −40, −48, −56 **13.** $-10n$; −50, −60, −70 **15.** 22
17. Domain: {−2, 0, 1, 5}; Range: {−4, 2, 5, 17}

x	$3x + 2$	y
−2	3(−2) + 2	−4
0	3(0) + 2	2
1	3(1) + 2	5
5	3(5) + 2	17

19.

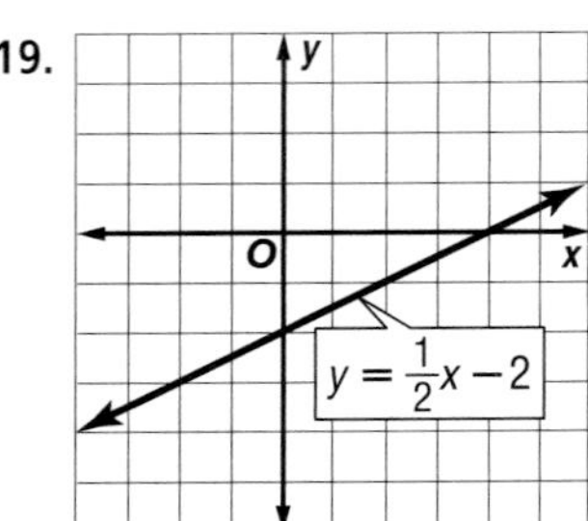

21. 2 **23.** −6 **25.** $\frac{1}{6}$ **27.** \$5.20 **29.** 2; 5 **31.** 4; 7

33.

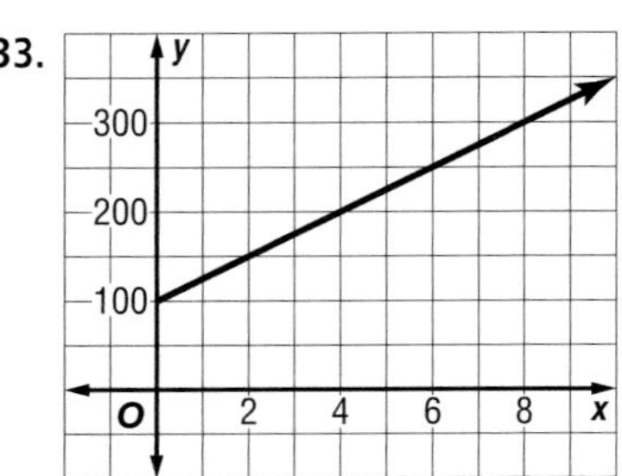

35. (−5, 3)

(−5, 3)
$y = x + 8$
$y = -2x - 7$

37.

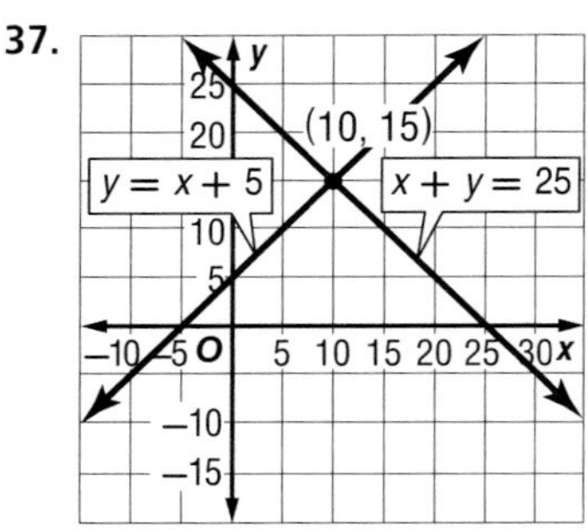

Let x = the number that preferred steak and y = the number that preferred pizza; $x + y = 25$; $y = x + 5$; (10, 15); ten students preferred steak and 15 students preferred pizza.

39. 78 **41.** positive

43.

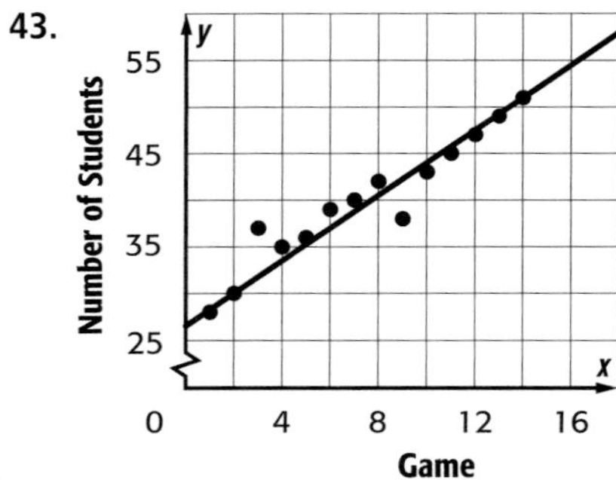

Chapter 10 Algebra: Nonlinear Functions and Polynomials

Page 527 ***Chapter 10*** ***Getting Ready***

1.

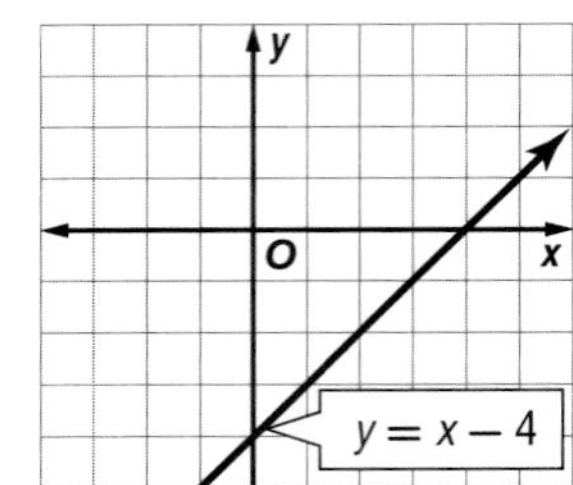

Line $y = x - 4$ goes through points (0, −4), (1, −3), (2, −2), (3, −1).

3.

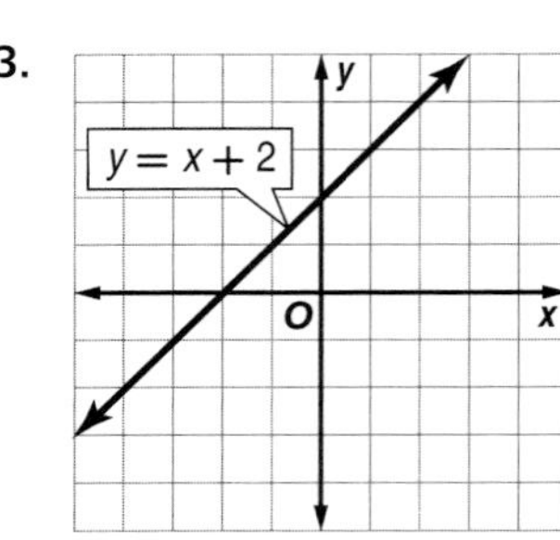

Line $y = x + 2$ goes through points (0, 2), (1, 3), (2, 4), (3, 5), and (4, 6).

5. $\frac{1}{a^9}$ **7.** $\frac{1}{x^5}$ **9.** 6^4 **11.** \$2,048

Pages 530–533 ***Lesson 10-1***

1. Nonlinear; as x increases by 1, y increases by a greater amount each time. **3.** Linear; graph is a straight line **5.** Linear; can be written as $y = \frac{1}{3}x + 0$ **7.** No; the rate of change is not constant. **9.** Nonlinear; rate of change is not constant. **11.** Nonlinear; rate of change is not constant. **13.** Linear; rate of change is constant; as x increases by 4, y decreases by 3 **15.** Nonlinear; graph is a curve **17.** Linear; graph is a straight line **19.** Nonlinear; graph is a curve **21.** Nonlinear; power of x is greater than 1 **23.** Linear; can be written in the form $y = \frac{3}{2}x + 0$. **25.** Nonlinear; x is in the denominator, so the equation cannot be written in the form $y = mx + b$. **27.** No; the rate of change is not constant. **29.** Nonlinear; the power of r in the function $A = \pi r^2$ is greater than 1. **31.** Nonlinear; when solved for y, x appears in the denominator so the equation cannot be written in the form $y = mx + b$. **33.** Linear; rate of change is constant, as x increases by 0.5, y decreases by 7. **35.** Nonlinear; the points (year, attendance) would lie on a curved line, not on a straight line and the rate of change is not constant.

37.

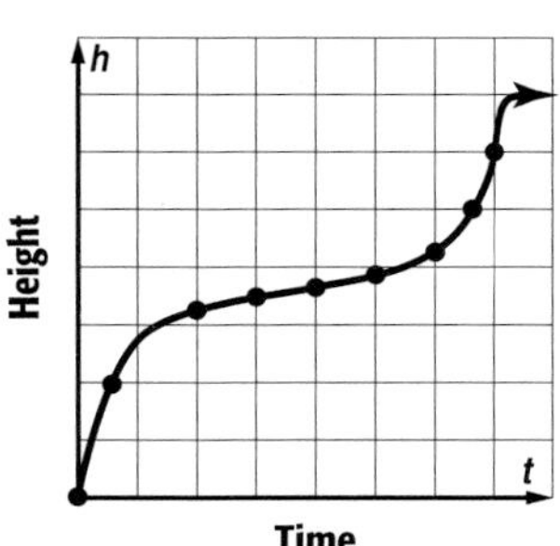

Nonlinear; the water level is not changing at a constant rate.
39. $y = 5x^3$; $y = 5x^3$ cannot be written in the form $y = mx + b$. **41.** Sample answer: the function is linear if its equation can be written in the form $y = mx + b$; the function is linear if a table of values constructed using its equation indicates a constant rate of change.
43. H **45.** no relationship **47.** Sample answer: The number of Mandarin native speakers is about $2\frac{1}{2}$ times the number of English native speakers. **49.** -0.25
51. -1.8 **53.** -4 **55.** 2,356.2 ft^3

57.

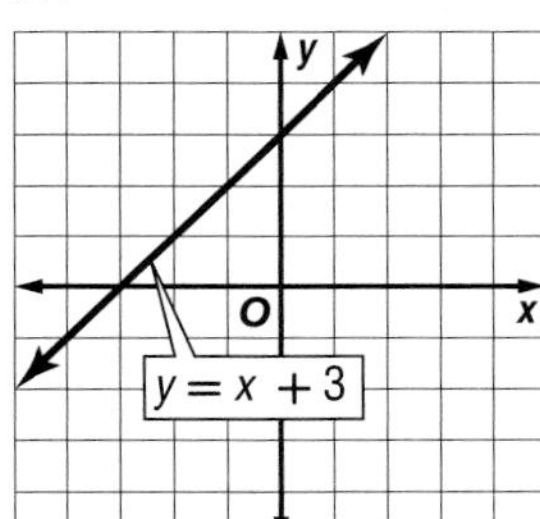

59.

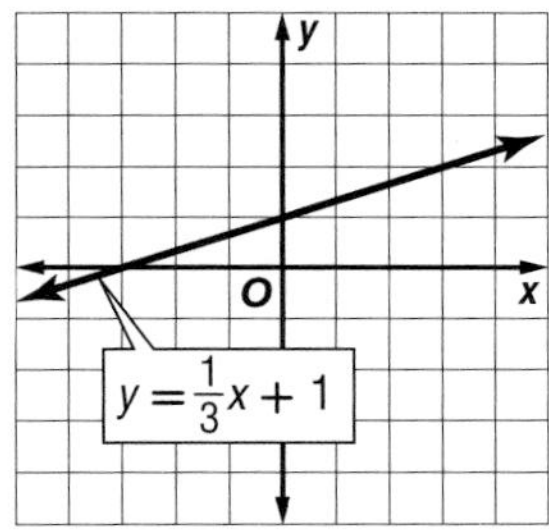

Pages 536–537 ***Lesson 10-2***

1.

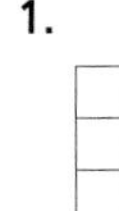

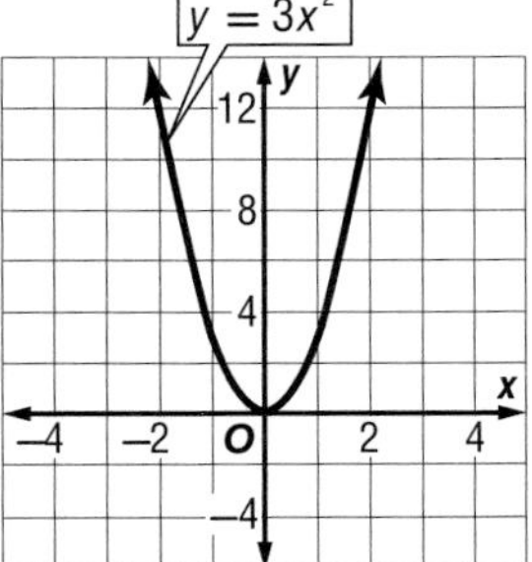

3.

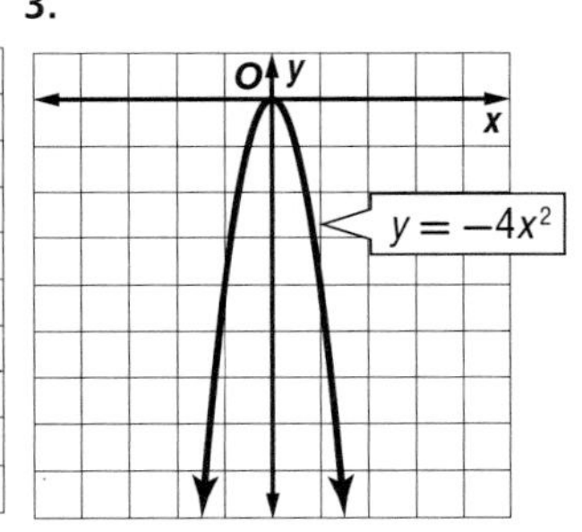

5.

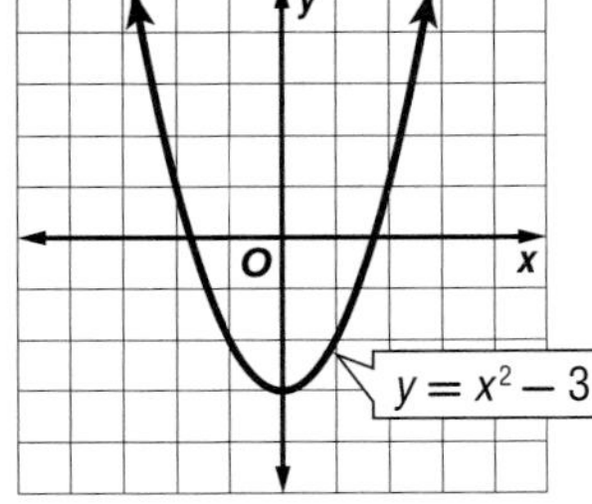

7.

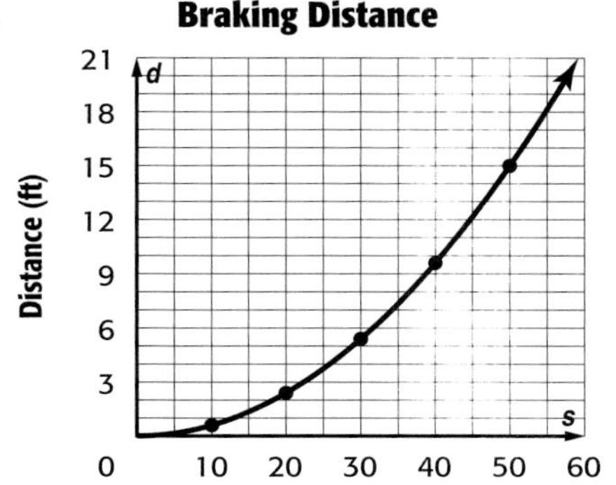

about 45 km/s

9.

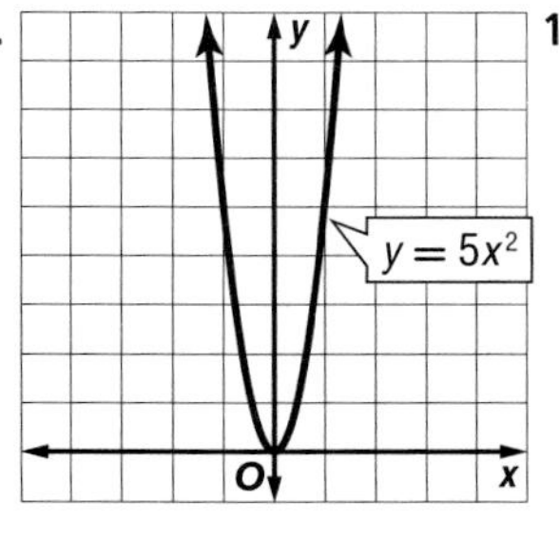

11.

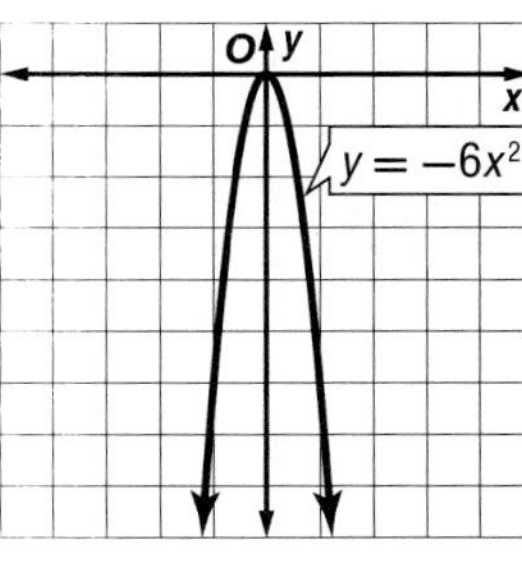

13.

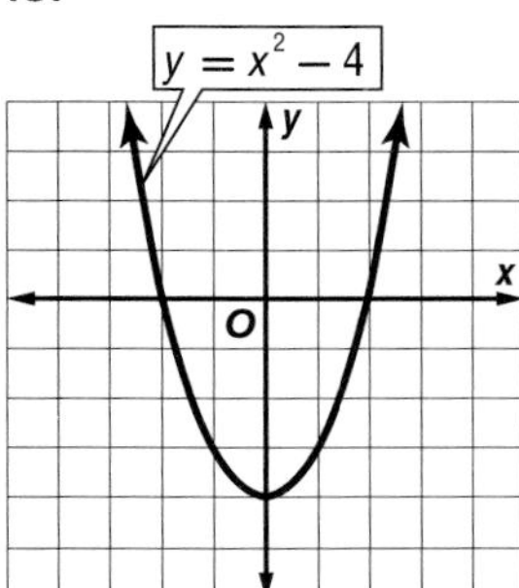

15.

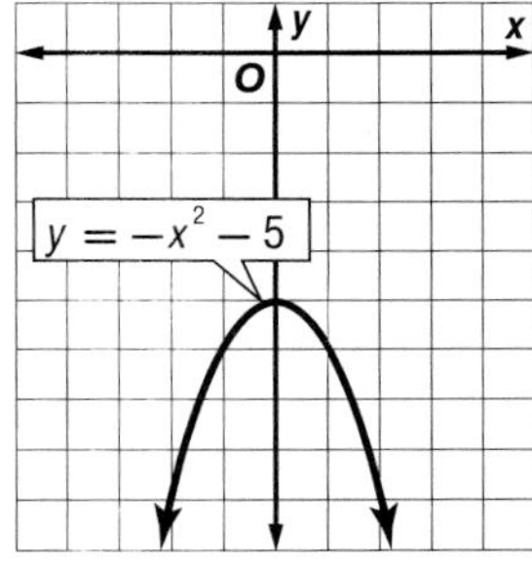

17.

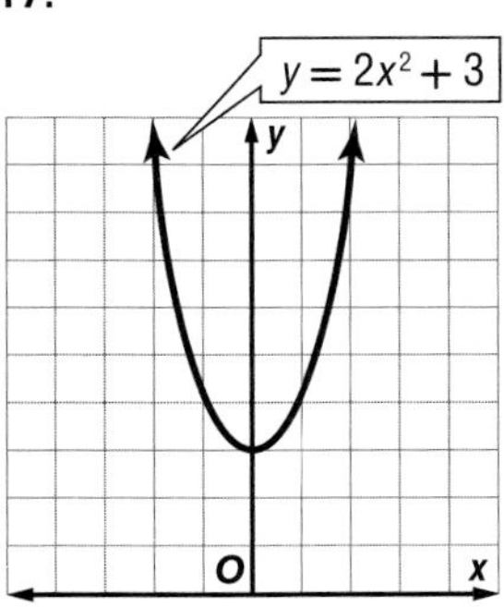

19.

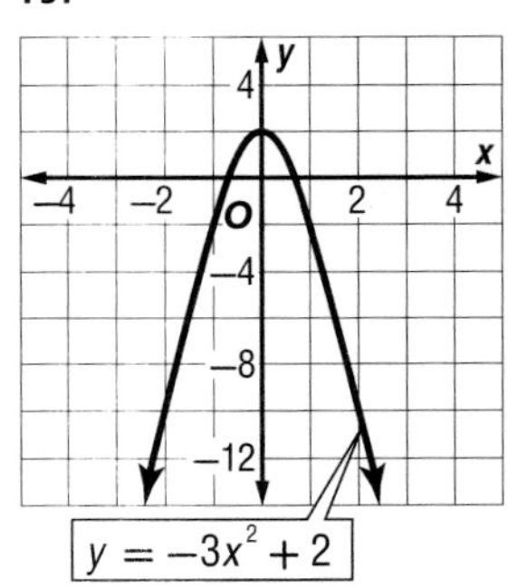

21.

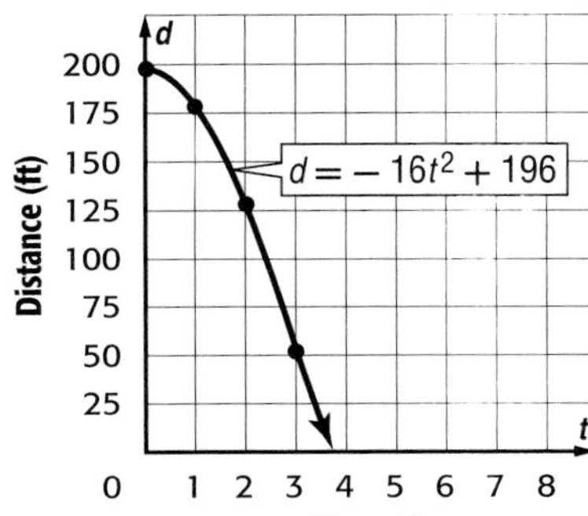

about 3.5 s

Selected Answers

23.

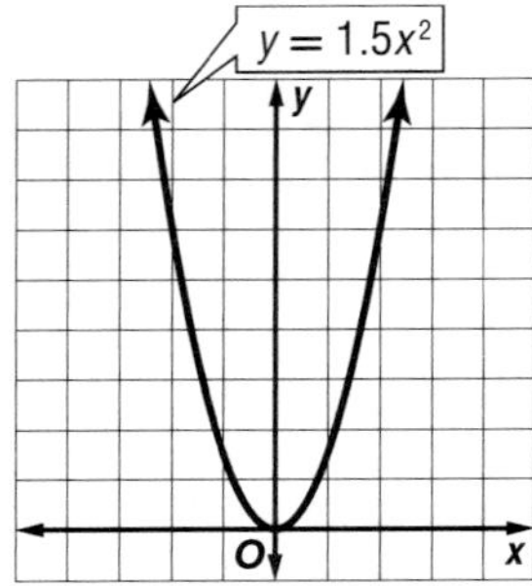

25.

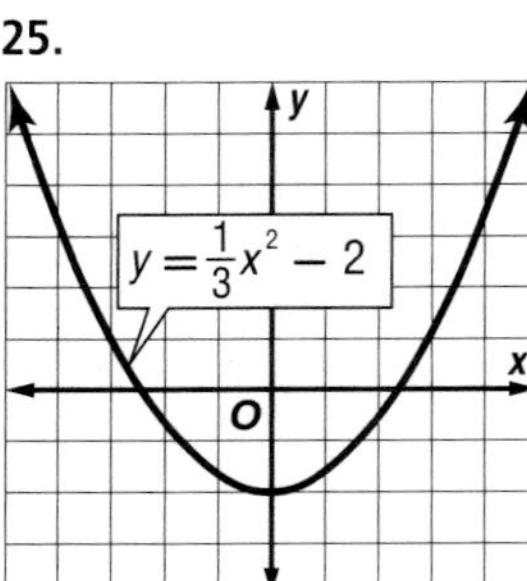

27.

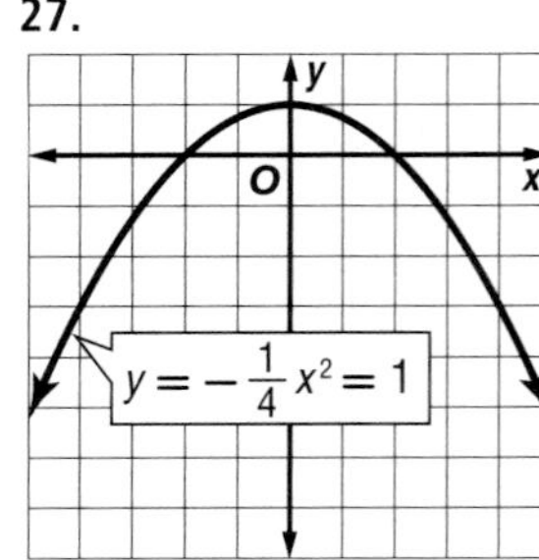

29. $V = 5s^2$ 6 in.

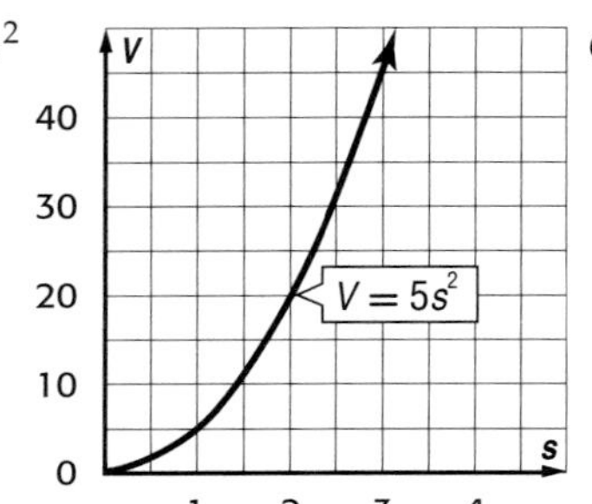

31.

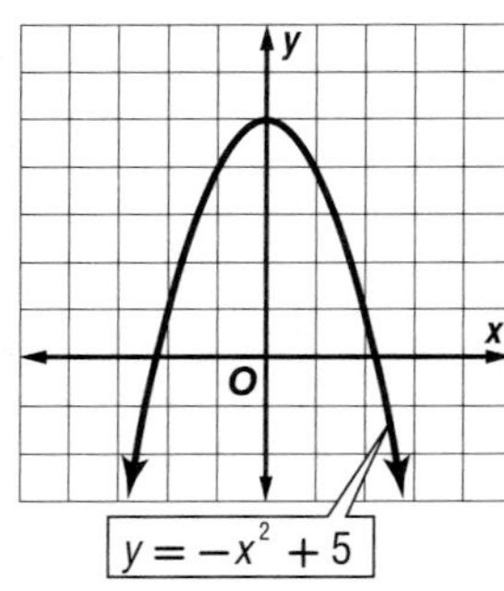

maximum; (0, 5)

33. Sample answer: $y = x^2 - 3.5$

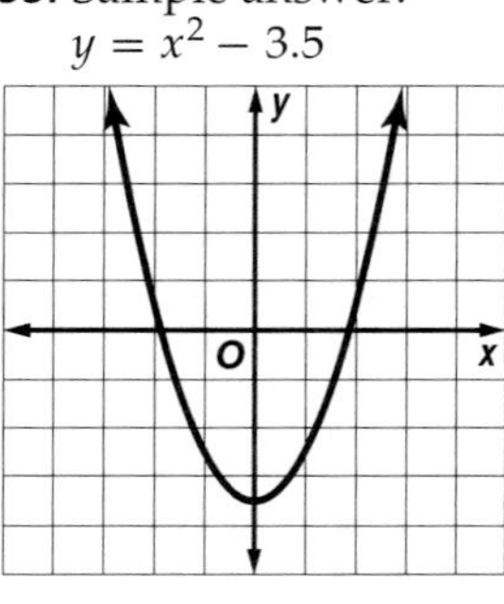

35. A **37.** nonlinear **39.** nonlinear **41.** positive **43.** $540 = 750 \cdot r \cdot 6$; 12% **45.** 64

Pages 538–539 ***Lesson 10-3***

1. 20 **3.** 13.5 in. by 18 in. **5.** 66 in^3 **7.** Sample answer: 38 with corrections and 29 without **9.** 12 **11.** 136 **13.** 9 clothespins

Pages 542–543 ***Lesson 10-4***

1.

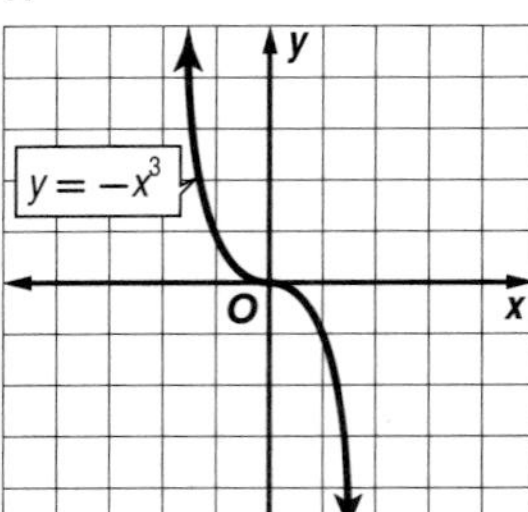

3.

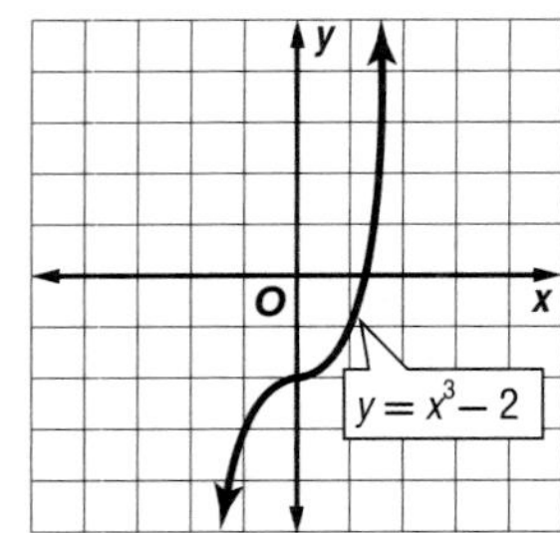

5.

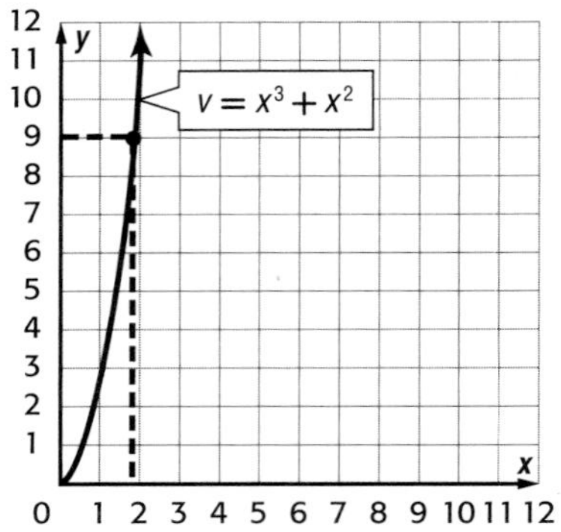

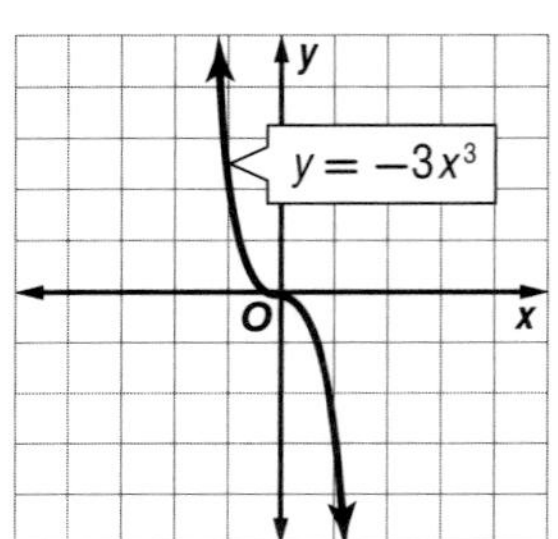

$V = x^3 + x^2$; 1.8 cm × 1.8 cm × 2.8 cm

7.

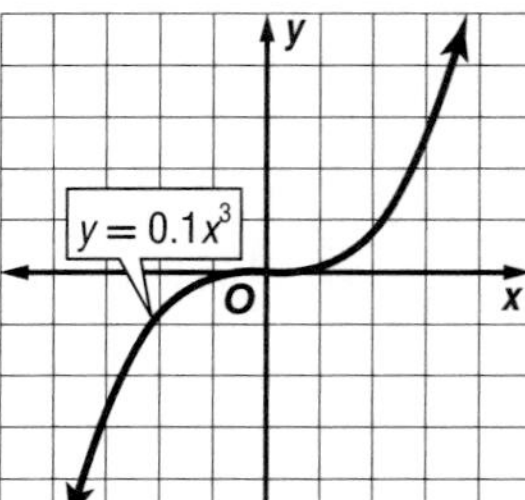

9.

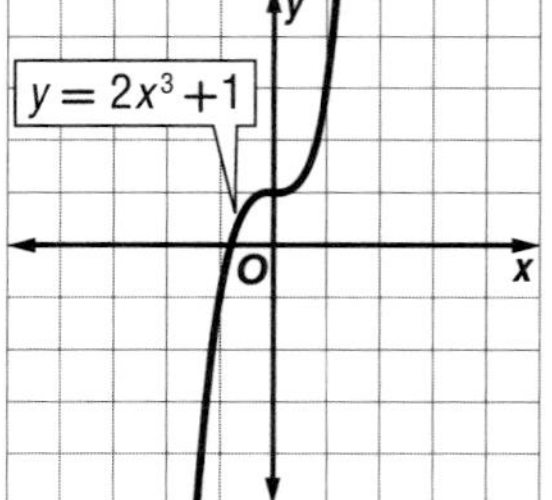

11.

13.

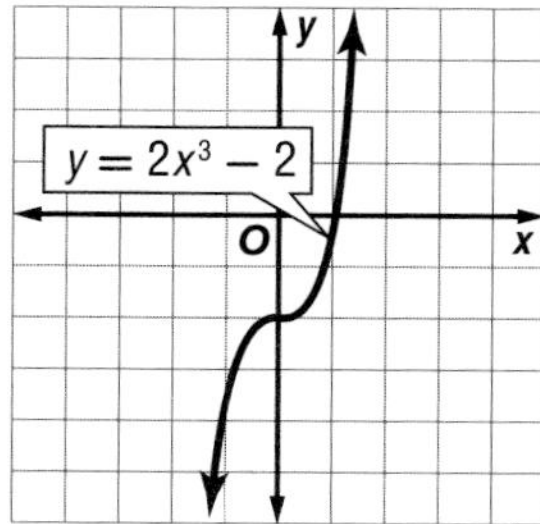

15.

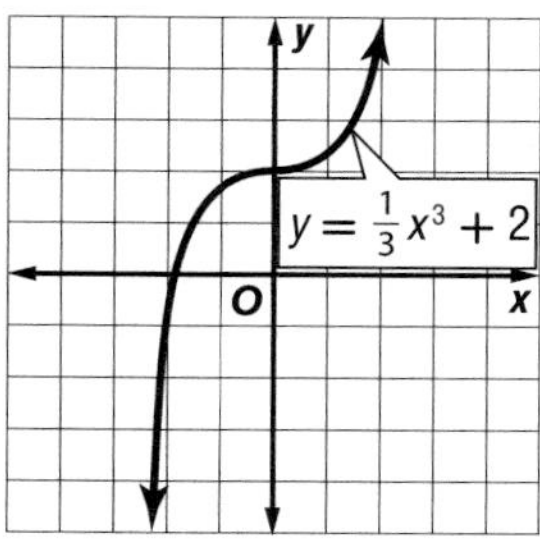

17.

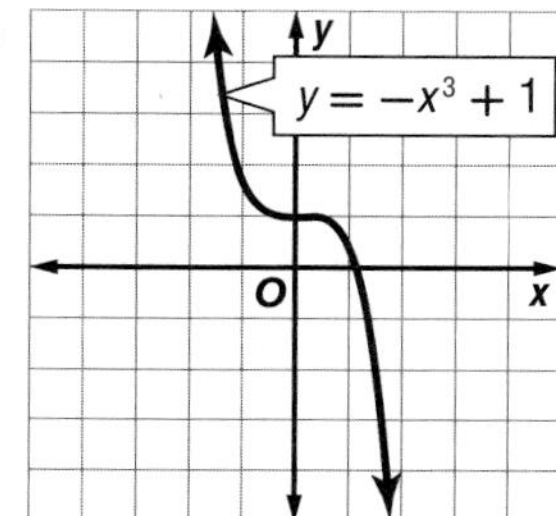

19. about 1.4 in.

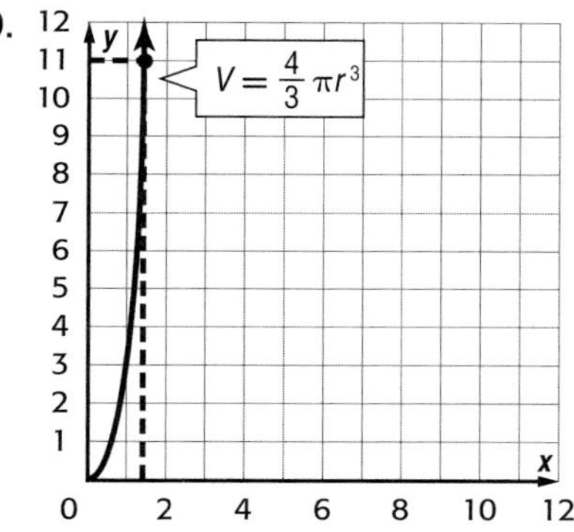

21. different shapes

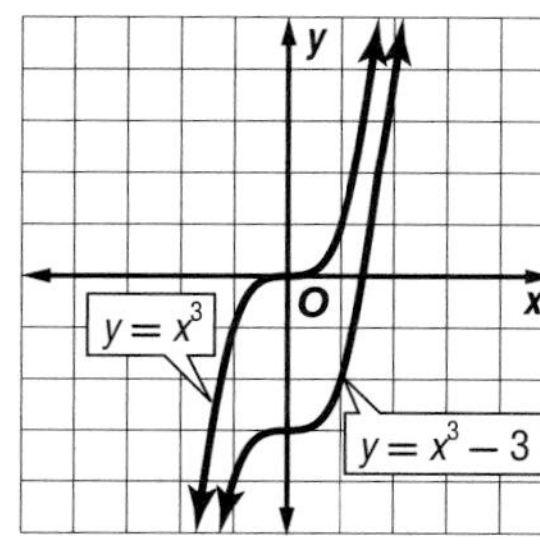

23.

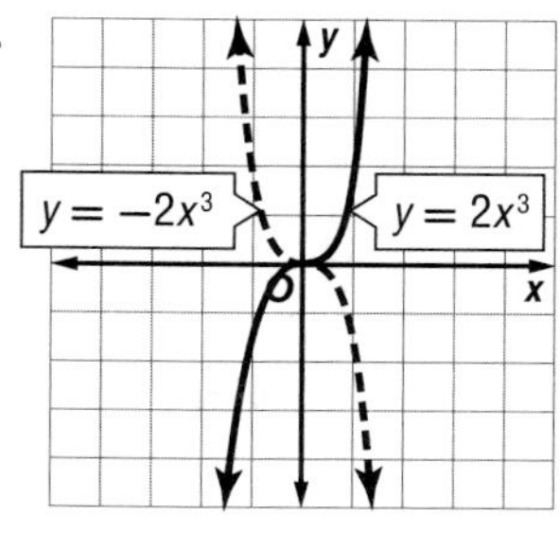

25. about 1.7 m

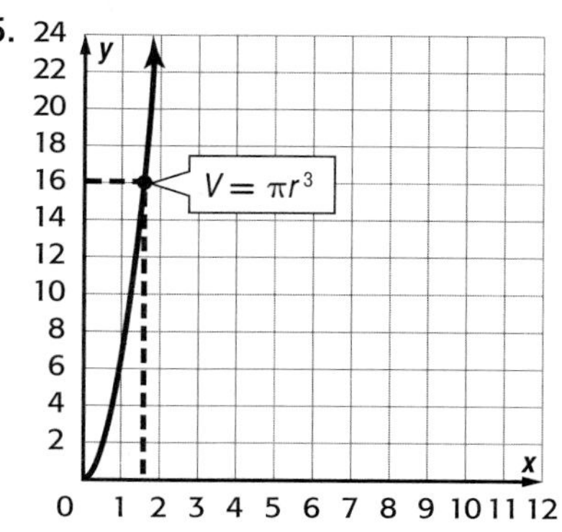

27. 0

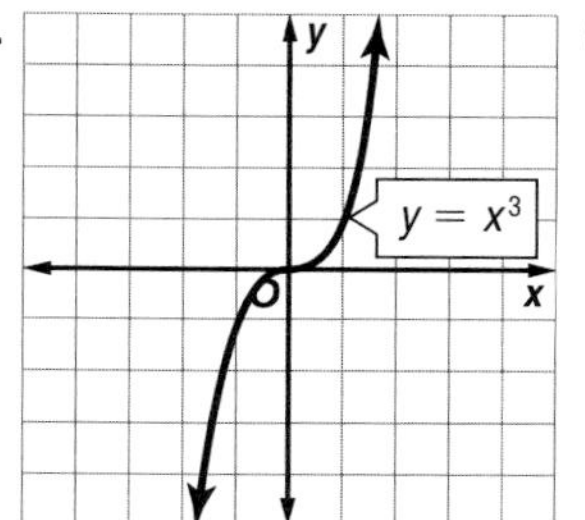

29. Both the side length and the volume of a cube cannot be negative. **31.** G

33.

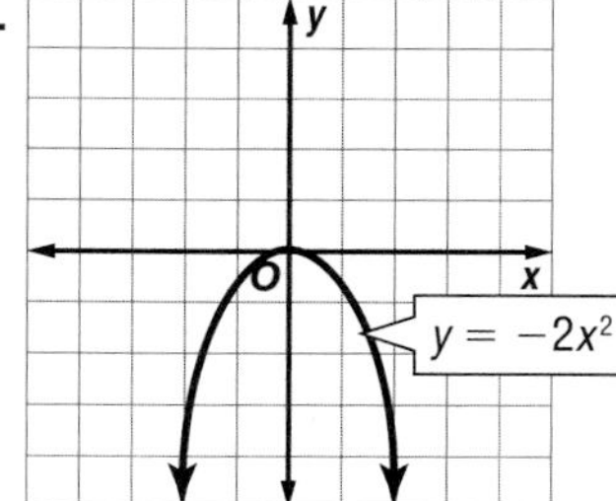

35.

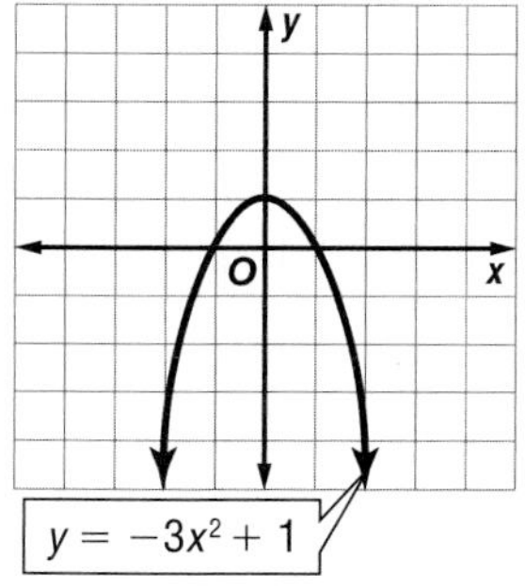

37. 7 **39.** 3 **41.** 3^5 **43.** 7^3

Pages 547–548 **Lesson 10-5**

1. 4^8 **3.** $-6a^5$ **5.** r^4 **7.** 2^6 or 64 years old **9.** 2^{10} **11.** b^{14} **13.** $15x^9$ **15.** $-8w^{11}$ **17.** $40y^9$ **19.** $-35a^5b^5c^5$ **21.** y^3 **23.** $m^{-1}n^2$ **25.** $-12a^{-2}b^4$ **27.** 10^{14} instructions

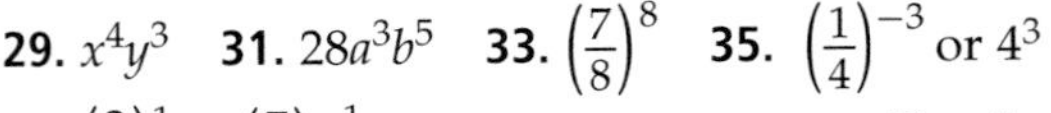

29. x^4y^3 **31.** $28a^3b^5$ **33.** $\left(\frac{7}{8}\right)^8$ **35.** $\left(\frac{1}{4}\right)^{-3}$ or 4^3

37. $\left(\frac{2}{7}\right)^1$ or $\left(\frac{7}{2}\right)^{-1}$ **39.** Sample answer: $5^{10} \cdot 5^3$ **41.** A

43.

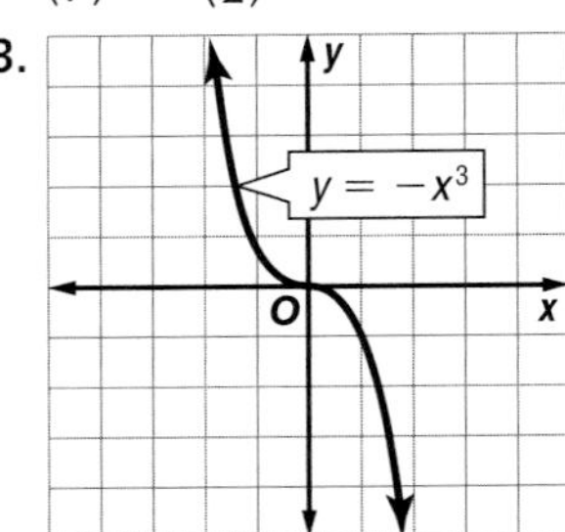

45.

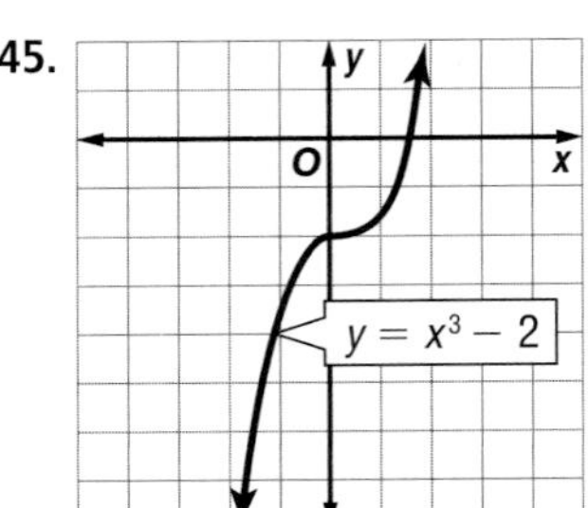

47.

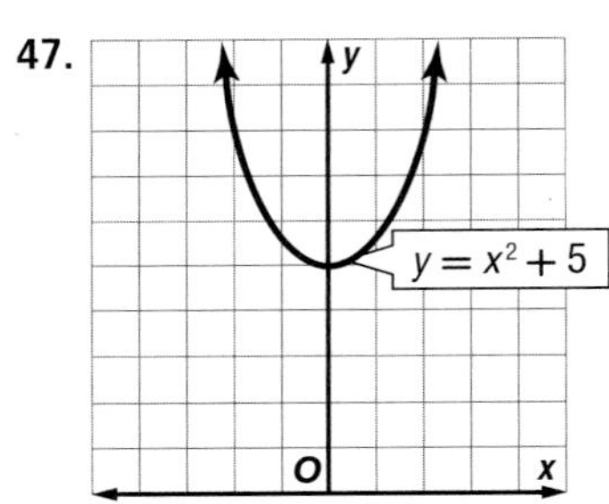

49. No; the difference between the times varies, so the growth is not constant. **51.** 6.25×10^6 **53.** $-8\frac{1}{4}$ **55.** $\frac{23}{40}$ **57.** $9\frac{5}{6}$ **59.** 3^4 **61.** 8^3

Pages 552–554 **Lesson 10-6**

1. 7^5 **3.** y^3 **5.** $3c^5$ **7.** $\frac{1}{15^8}$ **9.** C **11.** 8^{11} **13.** $\frac{1}{4^4}$ **15.** h **17.** $\frac{1}{x^3}$ **19.** $6d^5$ **21.** $4m^2$ **23.** $\frac{1}{22^{13}}$ **25.** $\frac{6}{w^4}$ **27.** x^2y^5 **29.** $\frac{1}{3^{3x^6}}$ **31.** 3^4 or 81 times **33.** 2^7 or 128 times **35.** 12 **37.** -6 **39.** 10^9 times greater **41.** Equal; Sample answer: Using the quotient of powers, $\frac{3^{100}}{3^{99}} = 3^{100-99}$ or 3^1, which is 3. **43.** 2^{29} **45.** D **47.** C **49.** $\frac{1}{18^2}$ **51.** $\frac{18}{a^3}$

53.

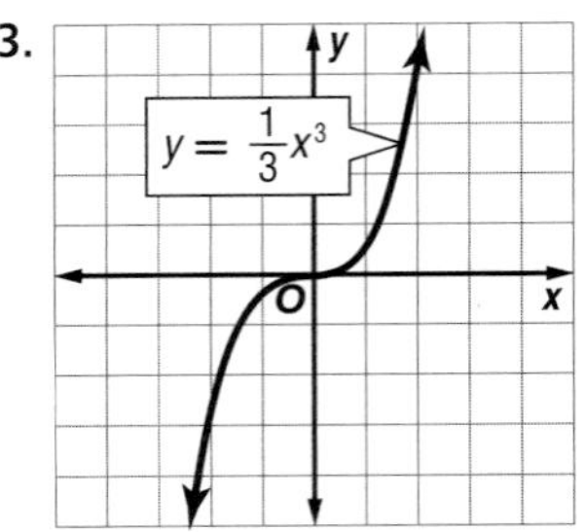

55.

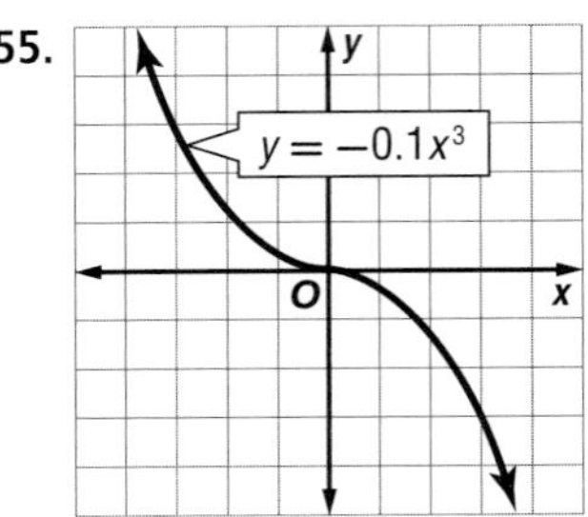

57. $\frac{2}{3}$; 7 **59.** $-\frac{1}{2}$; 5 **61.** $15n^5$ **63.** $10b^{11}$

Pages 557–558 **Lesson 10-7**

1. 3^{10} or 59,049 **3.** 2^{18} or 262,144 **5.** $625g^{32}k^{48}$ **7.** $27c^9d^6$ sq units **9.** 2^{14} or 16,384 **11.** 3^8 or 6,561 **13.** m^{40} **15.** z^{55} **17.** 4^{12} or 16,777,216 **19.** 2^{18} or 262,144 **21.** $32{,}768v^{45}$ **23.** $38{,}416y^4$ **25.** $64m^{30}n^{66}$ **27.** $625r^{16}s^{48}$ **29.** $144d^{12}e^{14}$ **31.** $343m^{18}n^{27}$ **33.** $0.027p^{21}$ **35.** $\frac{9b^{18}}{25a^{12}}$ **37.** $-2{,}048v^{13}$ **39.** $25(2^{2x})$; the number of bacteria present when the population of the culture has been squared; $125(2^{3x})$; the number of bacteria present when the population of the culture has been tripled. **41.** If the side length is doubled, the area is quadrupled and the volume is multiplied by 8. **43.** Sample answer: $(10^2)^{50}$, $(10^4)^{25}$, and $(10^{10})^{10}$ **45.** 3 **47.** D **49.** C **51.** y^8 **53.** $\frac{8}{g^5}$ **55.** 7 **57.** 15

Pages 561–562 **Lesson 10-8**

1. $|d|$ **3.** $7|x^3y|$ **5.** m **7.** $5r^2s^3$ **9.** $16\,|uv^3|$ units **11.** $|n|$ **13.** $g^4|k^7|$ **15.** $6z^6$ **17.** $3p^4q^2$ **19.** h **21.** $3b$ **23.** $5d^3e$ **25.** $7mn^7$ **27.** $11|ab|$ **29.** $20|xy^5|$ **31.** $4wz$ **33.** $3|g^8|h$ **35.** $0.5|x|$ **37.** $\frac{2}{3}wx^2$ **39.** $\frac{9}{m^2}$ **41.** Sample answer: $\sqrt{49m^4n^2} = 7m^2|n|$ **43.** $x = 21$ **45.** Sample answer: The expression $\sqrt{y^2}$ indicates the positive square root. The variable y can either be positive, negative, or zero. If y is negative, then writing the simplified form of $\sqrt{y^2}$ as y would indicate the negative square root. The simplified form must be written as $|y|$ to indicate that the square root is positive, regardless of the value of y. The absolute value is not necessary when simplifying $\sqrt{y^4}$ because it square root is y^2, which is always positive. **47.** G **49.** 6^{15} **51.** $16a^{12}b^8$ **53.** 9^2 **55.** $6y^2$ **57.** $16\frac{1}{2}$ ft^2

Pages 563–566 **Chapter 10** **Study Guide and Review**

1. false; quadratic function **3.** true **5.** true **7.** true **9.** false; curve **10.** true **11.** nonlinear; power of x is greater than 1

13.

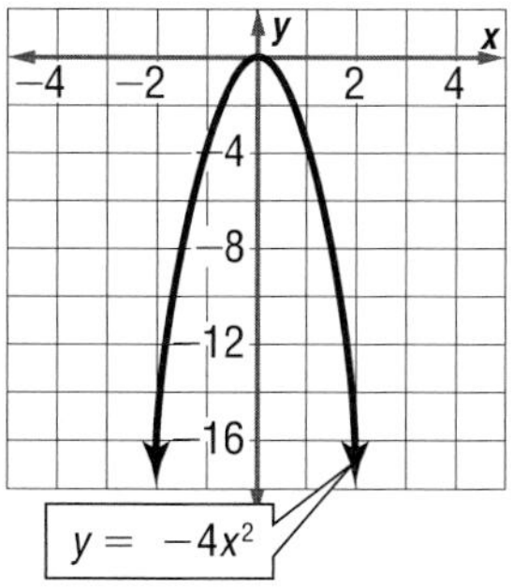

15.

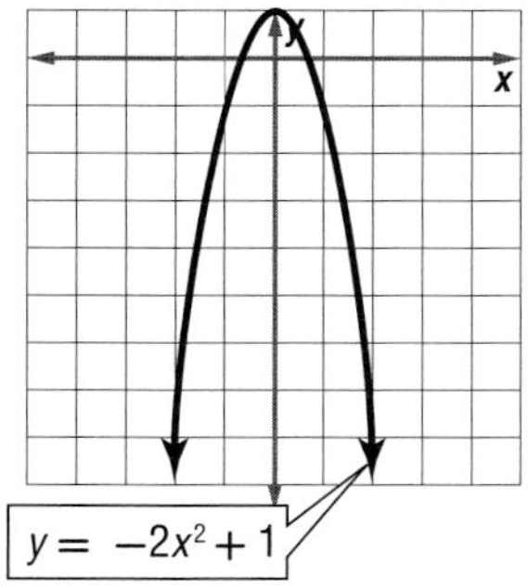

17.

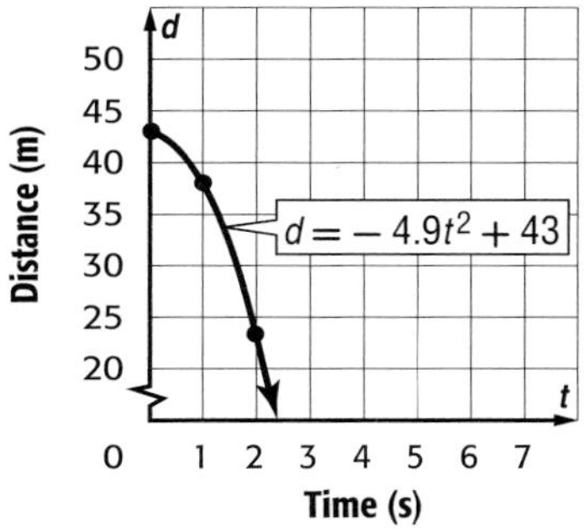

about 3 s

19. 120

21.

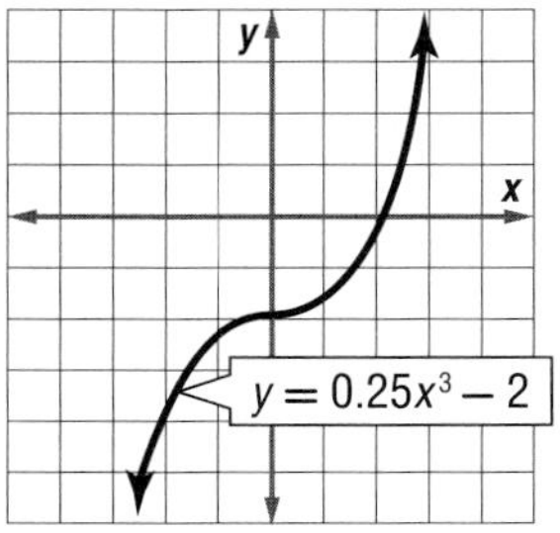

23.

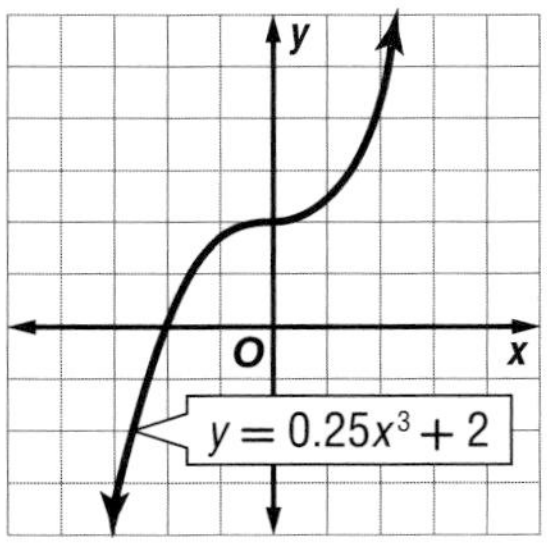

25. 4^6 **27.** $36y^{11}$ **29.** 4,000 **31.** n^4 **33.** $\frac{4}{7}$ **35.** 9^6 or 531,441 **37.** $625y^{20}$ **39.** $\frac{9}{16n^2}$ **41.** 0.04 **43.** $125s^6t^{12}$ **45.** $|a|$ **47.** $6|xy^3|$ **49.** p^2 **51.** $4c^2d^7$ **53.** $8b^8$

Chapter 11 Statistics

Page 573 **Chapter 11** **Getting Ready**

1.

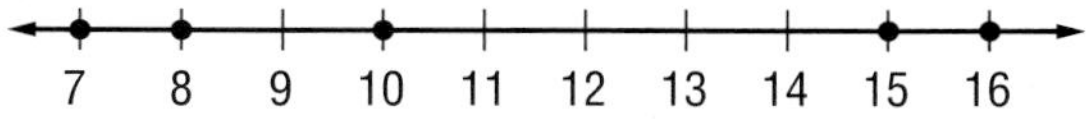

3. −12 **5.** 4 **7.** 1 **9.** 5.4, 5.46, 5.6, 5.64 **11.** \$3.07, \$3.17, \$3.71 **13.** 129.6

Pages 574–575 **Lesson 11-1**

1. Sample answer: An advantage is that it organizes the data into classes; a disadvantage is that individual values of data are lost. **3.** Sample answer: Pat recorded the color of cars as they pass his house as shown. How many of each color car passed his house? Red, Green, Black, Red, Red, Green, White, Red, White, Black, Green, Red, White, Black, Red, Blue, Green, White, Red, Red, Green, Black, Black, Red, Green

Color	Frequency
Red	9
Green	6
Black	5
White	4
Blue	1

There were 9 red cars, 6 green cars, 5 black cars, 4 white cars, and 1 blue car. **5.** 3 **7.** William **9.** about 37.9% **11.** 3.8 meters

Pages 578–580 **Lesson 11-2**

1. Sample answer:

State Population Density (per square mile)		
Density	**Tally**	**Frequency**
0–199	卌 卌 卌 卌 卌 卌 卌 III	38
200–399	卌	5
400–599	III	3
600–799	I	1
800–899	I	1
900–1,099	I	1
1,100–1,299	I	1

Source: National Climatic Data Center

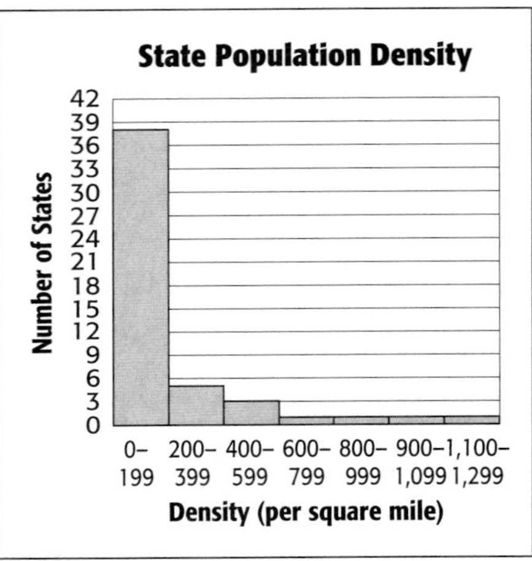

3. Not very likely. Only two volcanoes out of 25 are 15,000 feet or taller.

5. Sample answer:

Hours Spent Exercising per Week		
Hours	**Tally**	**Frequency**
0–2	𝍸 I	6
3–5	𝍸 III	8
6–8	III	3
9–11	II	2
12–14	I	1

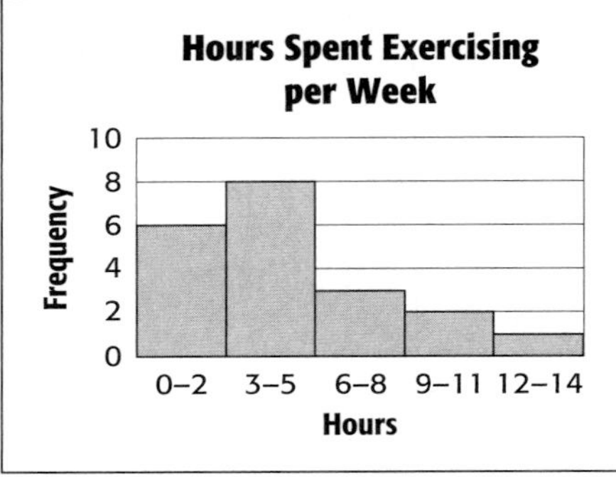

7. 30 countries **9.** Not very likely. Only 4 out of the 50 countries in the histogram have an area greater than 800 square kilometers. **11.** 12.5% **13.** Sample answer: A typical solar eclipse lasted from 1 second to 5 minutes. Eleven solar eclipses lasted from 1 second to 5 minutes while five solar eclipses lasted from 5 minutes 1 second to 12 minutes 30 seconds.
15. Seattle **17.** Seattle; about 33%
21. Sample answer:

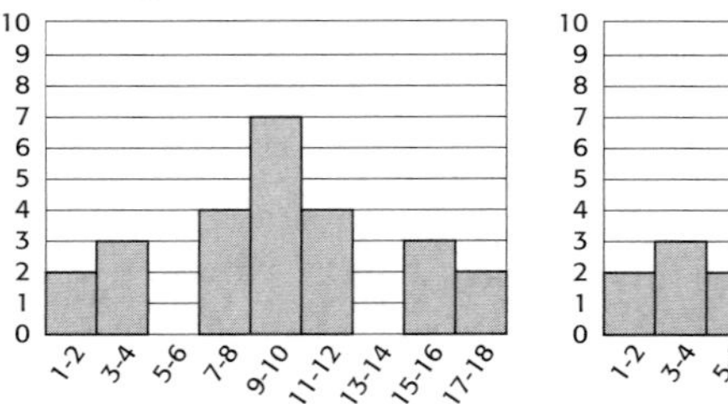

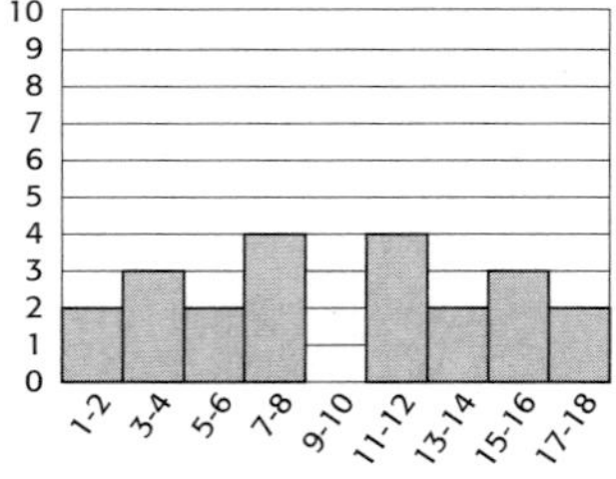

23. Because it is more visual, a histogram is more useful than a table when you are trying to show a general trend. Because the individual data are shown, a table is more useful when you need to know exact numbers.

25. $\frac{4}{5}$ **27.** $4x$ units **29.** 190.8

Pages 585–588 ***Lesson 11-3***

1.

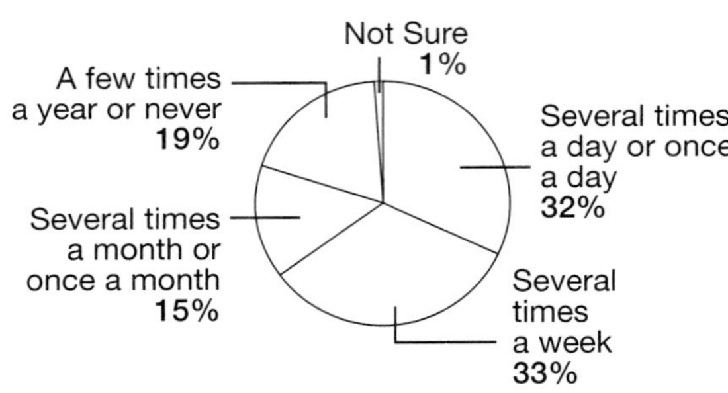

3. Sample answer: The vast majority of teens (92%) would rather give up activities such as reading, watching TV, and using the computer than listening to music. The activity that teens would most readily give up is reading.

5.

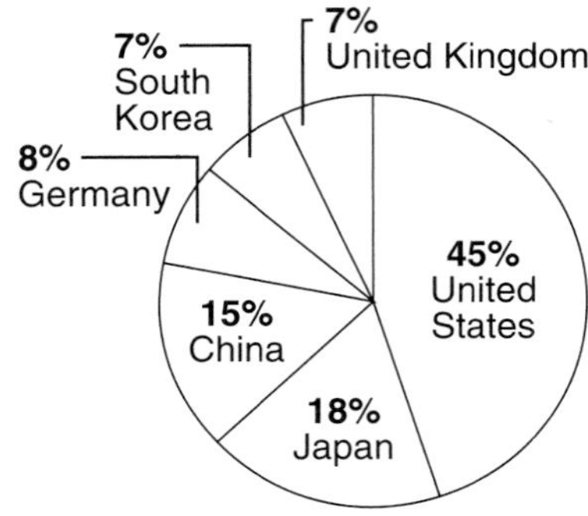

7.

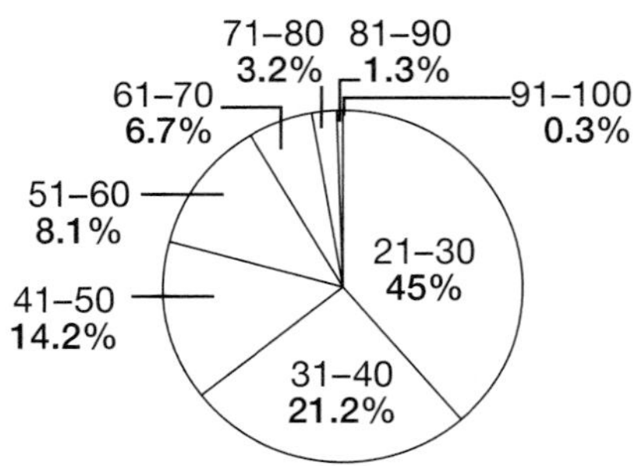

9. Sample answer: More American cat owners own 1 cat than any other category. A little over $\frac{1}{4}$ of American cat owners own 2 cats. **11.** Sample answer: Over $\frac{3}{4}$ of Americans prefer pork as a meat topping on their pizza. A little less than $\frac{1}{5}$ of Americans prefer beef as a meat topping on their pizza. **13.** $x = 8.1\%$; 29.16°
15. 45%; 22.5 million **19.** 50%; 25%; 12.5%

21. Sample answer: The percentages do not add up to 100%. **23.** B **25.** $6|xy^3|$ **27.** 64 cm^3 **29.** 40 **31.** 70

Pages 594–596 ***Lesson 11-4***

1. 23; 19; 18; 29 **3.** The median; the mean is affected by the value of 27, and there is no mode. **5.** 12; 9; 8; 12 **7.** 79.3; 79.5; 84; 11 **9.** the mean, 103.1, median, 97.5 and mode, 100 equally represent the data as most of the data is near 100. **11.** 91% **13.** Mean or median; the mode is the greatest number in the set of data, but the mean and median seem to be central numbers. **15.** If the data for the Yankee Stadium is not included, the mean decreases from about 44,273.7 to 41,741. The median decreases from 42,099 to 40,793. There still is no mode. The range decreases from 16,817 to 3,652. **17.** Sample answer: 4, 6, 7, 10, 10 **19.** Never; the mode must always be a member of the set of data, but the mean and median may or may not be a member of the set of data. **23.** J **25.** 15 students **27.** 203 miles **29.** 91.3, 93, 93.1, 93.11, 94.7

Pages 601–604 ***Lesson 11-5***

1. 27.2 million **3.** 0.8 million **5.** Sample answer: The spread of the data is 27.2 million speakers. The middle number is 1.3 million speakers. About one fourth of the languages had at or below 1.0 million speakers and about one fourth of the languages had at or above 1.8 million speakers. The number of speakers for half of the languages was in the interval 1.0–1.8 million. **7.** Median: 210,000; Upper Quartile: 347,500; Lower Quartile: 67,500; Interquartile Range: 280,000 **9.** Sample answer: The spread of the data is 371,000 gallons. The middle number is 210,000 gallons. About one-fourth of the states had a maple syrup production at or above 347,500 gallons and about one fourth of the states had a maple syrup production at or below 67,500 gallons. The number of gallons of maple syrup produced by half of the states was in the interval 67,500–347,500. **11.** Median: 6; Upper Quartile: 7; Lower Quartile: 5; Interquartile Range: 2 **13.** Sample answer: The spread of the data is 4 calories. The middle number is 6 calories. About one fourth of the activities burn at or above 7 calories per minute and about one-fourth of the activities burn at or below 5 calories per minute. The number of calories burned per minute by half of the activities is in the interval 5–7. **15.** Median: 23; Upper Quartile: 28; Lower Quartile: 14; Interquartile Range: 14 **17.** Sample answer: The spread of the data is 15 launches. The middle number is 23 launches. About one-fourth of the year intervals had at or above 28 launches and about one fourth of the year intervals had at or below 14 launches. The number of launches for half of the year intervals was in the interval 14–28. **19.** Median: 9,000; Upper Quartile: 24,500; Lower Quartile: 8,000; Interquartile Range: 16,500 **21.** Sample answer: The spread of the data is 1,095,000 species. The middle number is 9,000 species. About one fourth of the animal groups had at or above 24,500 species and about one fourth of the animal groups had at or below 8,000 species. The number of species for half of the animal groups was in the interval 8,000–24,500. **23.** South America **25.** Sample answer: One of the modes for Africa, 1,000 miles, is the same as the mode for South America. The interquartile range for Africa is 1,295 miles, while the interquartile range for South America is 891, so the middle 50% of rivers in South America are more spread out than the middle 50% of rivers in Africa. **27.** Sample answer: South America has a greater range, or spread, of river lengths. South America's median river length is greater than Africa's. Since the upper quartile and the lower quartile of Africa's river lengths are higher and lower, respectively, than South America's, it follows that South America has more rivers about the same length. Half of Africa's river lengths are within 1,295 miles of each other while half of South America's river lengths are within 891 miles of each other. **29.** There are no outliers. **31.** 4,200 ft **33.** The range increases from 2,542 ft to 2,566 ft. The median decreases from 4,000 ft to 3,800 ft. The upper quartile decreases from 4,626 ft to 4,443 ft. The lower quartile decreases from 3,576 ft to 3,550 ft. The interquartile range decreases from 1,050 to 893 ft. **35.** Sample answer: {1, 50, 50, 60, 60, 70, 70, 80} **37.** It only involves the middle half of the data. **39.** H

41. **Yellowstone National Park**

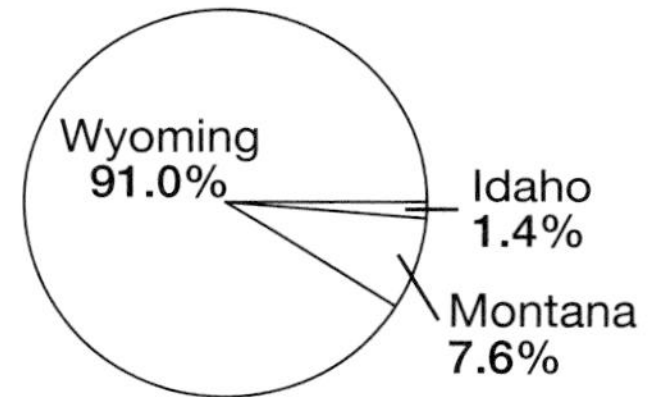

43. 81.9m^2

45.

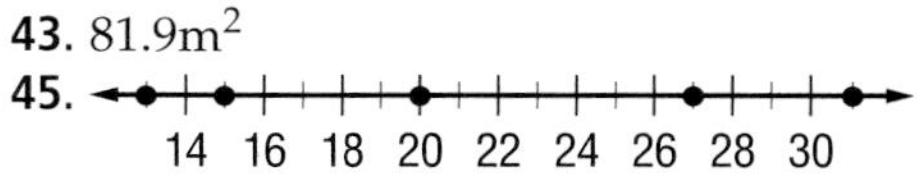

47.

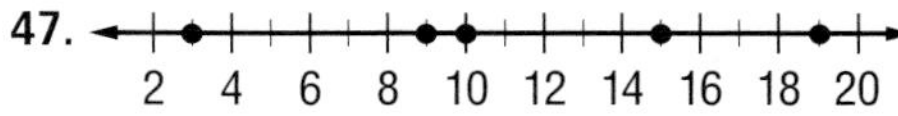

Pages 607–610 ***Lesson 11-6***

1.

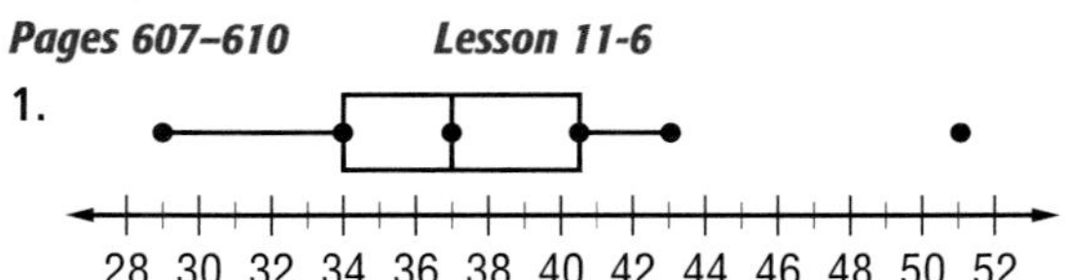

3. 75 **5.** American League; The median of the National League teams is 81 and the median for the American League teams is 81.3.

7.

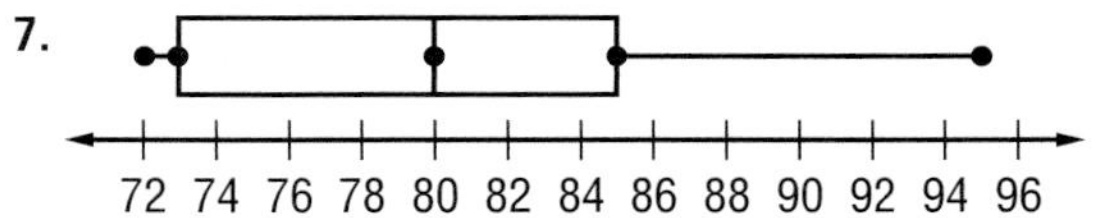

Selected Answers

9.

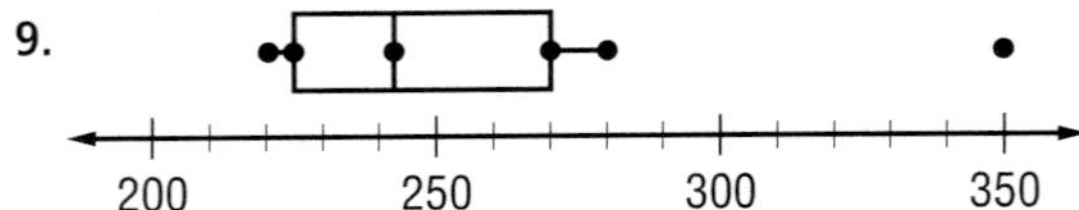

11. Sample answer: the data is very spread out meaning that there is quite a difference in the populations. **13.** The top half of the data is much more spread out than the bottom half of the data. Most major zoos are considerably smaller in area than the few zoos that have very large areas. **15.** none
17. 75%

19.

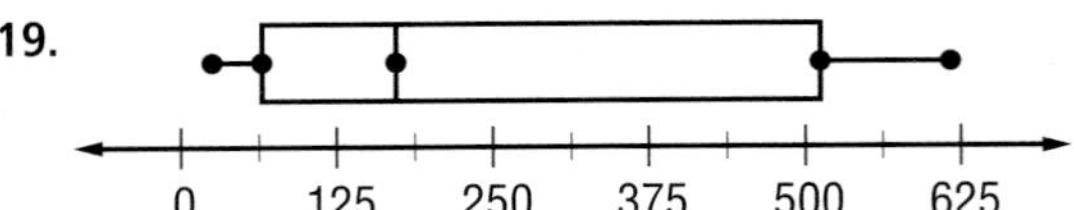

The data in the interval between the median and the upper quartile is the most spread out. **21.** 100%
23. Sample answer: Overall, there seem to be more sunny days in the Southeastern and South Central U.S. cities than there are in the Northeastern and Midwestern U.S. cities. The median number of sunny days in the Southeastern and South Central cities was higher than the median for the Northeastern and Midwestern cities. The data for the Southeastern and South Central cities had a greater spread than the data for the Northeastern and Midwestern cities.
25. Chance; 72 is an outlier. **27.** Sample answer: a box-and-whisker plot gives a visual representation of the spread of a set of data. It can be used to make general conclusions about the data without the need to perform calculations. **29.** J **31.** 49; 81; 88, 74; 14; 50

33.

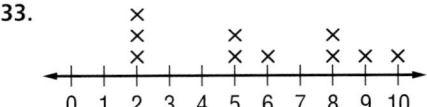

0 1 2 3 4 5 6 7 8 9 10

Pages 614–616 ***Lesson 11-7***

1.

Stem	Leaf
0	6 7
1	2 5 5
2	0
3	5
4	0 1

2 | 0 = 20

3. 50%, 99% **5.** Sample answer: The lowest score was 50%. The highest score was 99%. Most of the scores were in the 70–79% interval. **7.** Chicken; whereas chicken sandwiches have 8–20 grams of fat, burgers have 10–36 grams of fat. 99%

9.

Stem	Leaf
1	9
2	1 3 6
3	4 6 8
4	0 4
5	5

2|3 = 23 wins

11.

Stem	Leaf
4	0 7 7 8 9 9
5	0 1 8
6	5
7	0 3

4 | 7 = 47

13. 7
15. Sample answer: The majority of single-season home run leaders between 1995 and 2006 hit fewer than 50 home runs.
17. 2
19. Sample answer: The median (9) number of games won by the teams in the Big East Conference is greater than the median (7) number of games won by the teams in the Big Ten Conference.
21. Sample answer:

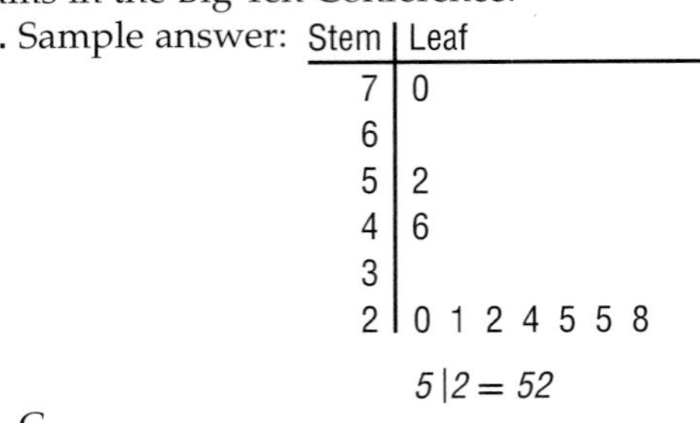

Stem	Leaf
7	0
6	
5	2
4	6
3	
2	0 1 2 4 5 5 8

5 | 2 = 52

23. C

25.

20 24 28 32 36 40 44 48 52 56 60 64 68 72 76

27. no outliers **29.** 73.4; 74

Pages 619–621 ***Lesson 11-8***

1. Bar graph; it shows the number of items in specific categories. **3.** Box-and-whisker plot; it shows how the data are separated into 4 equal sets.

Test Scores Period 4

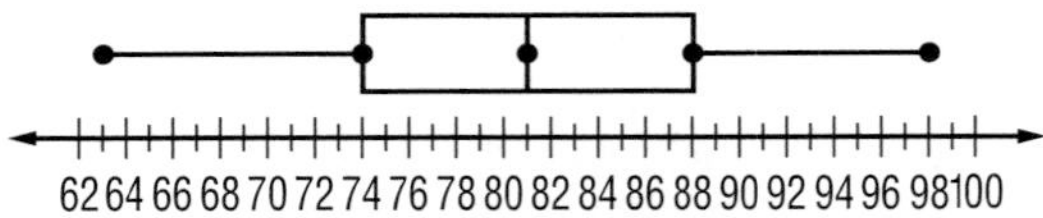

5. Bar graph; it shows the number of items in specific categories. **7.** Box-and-whisker plot; it shows the measures of variation for a set of data. **9.** Venn diagram; it shows how the data is related
11. Sample answer: Line graph:

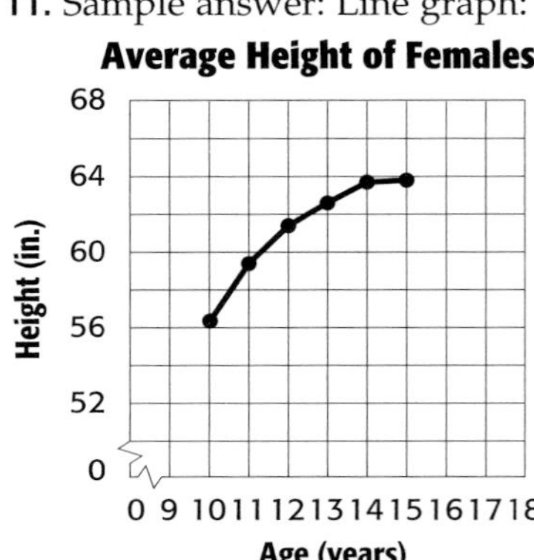

13. 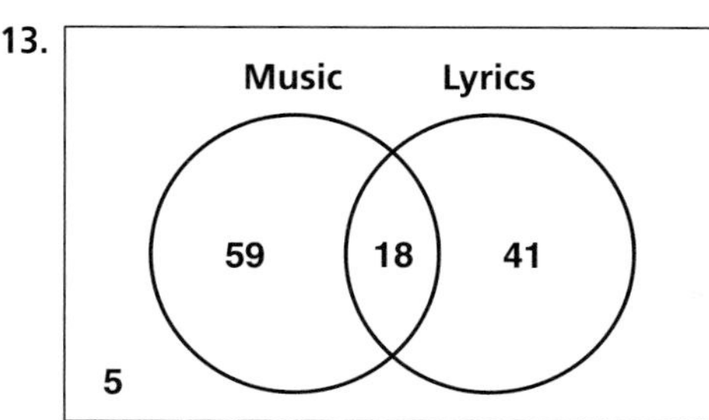

15. Bar graph; sample answer: the bar graph shows the total number of students for each type of music. 189 students like rock music.

17. Number of Text Messages Received on Saturday

Female	Stem	Male
9 9 8 8 5	0	3 5 5 8
6 6 3 3 1 1 1	1	3 3 8 8
4 4 2 2 2 0 0	2	2 2 4
0 | 2 = 20		*2 | 4 = 24*

Sample answer: The median is 13 messages for both males and females. **21.** Always; Sample answer: The sections of the circle graph can be taken from the intervals on the histogram and percents can be found by dividing each interval's frequency by the total number of data values. **23.** Always; Sample answer: The line plot shows individual data values so the measures of variation can be determined and a box-and-whisker plot can be made. **25.** B

27. 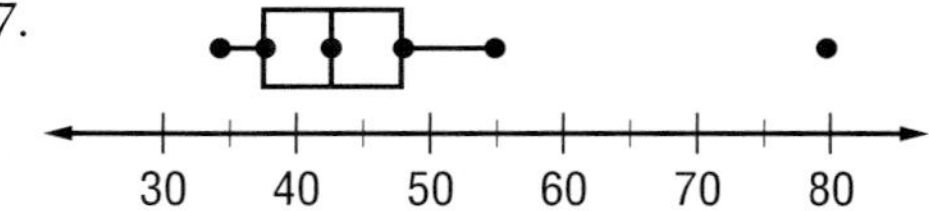

29. range: 102.3 million; median: 24.9 million; UQ: 42.8 million; LQ: 20.2 million; interquartile range: 22.6 million **31.** Sample answer: There are no extreme values. The range of the middle half of the data is about one fourth of the range of all of the data. The median is closer to the lower values than the higher values. **33.** $8y + 48$ **35.** $-18 - 2k$ **37.** $675

Pages 622–626 ***Chapter 11*** ***Study Guide and Review***

1. true **3.** false; measures of variation **5.** true **7.** true **9.** about 19% **11.** 5 seconds **13.** Most runners were in the 60–64 interval.

15. 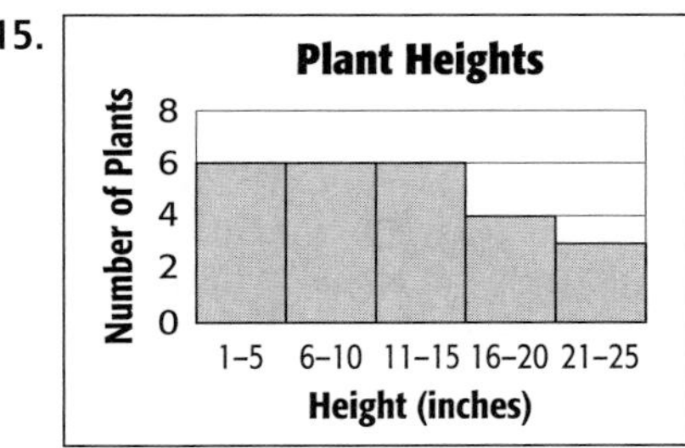

17. The air is mostly nitrogen. A little over a fifth of the air is oxygen. All other gases and water vapor account for only 1% of the air. **19.** 7.7, 6.8, no mode, 4.5 **21.** 11; 3; 5, 2; 3; 12 **23.** The spread of the data is 8. The middle number is 6.5. About one fourth of Jean's friends have been to the movies at or above 8.5 times (9 times) and about one fourth of Jean's friends have been to the movies at or below 4.5 times (4 times). Half of Jean's friends have been to the movies in the interval 4.5 (4) – 8.5 (9) times.

25. 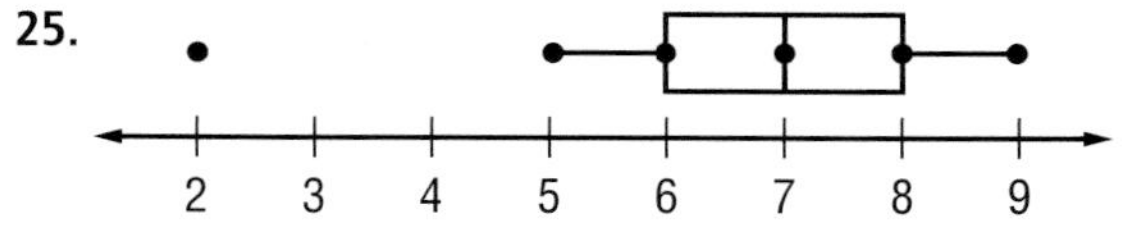

27. 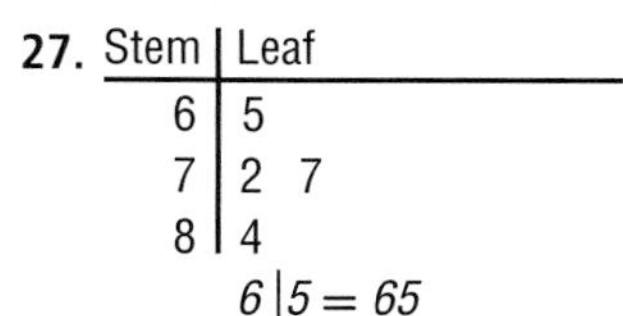

Stem	Leaf
6	5
7	2 7
8	4

6 | 5 = 65

29. 40–49° interval **31.** 38° **33.** stem-and-leaf plot

Chapter 12 Probability

Page 631 ***Chapter 12*** ***Getting Ready***

1. $\frac{2}{3}$ **3.** $\frac{7}{33}$ **5.** $\frac{2}{3}$ **7.** $\frac{1}{7}$ **9.** 31.5 **11.** 3.6 **13.** 118

Pages 634–636 ***Lesson 12-1***

1. Roll 1 Roll 2 Outcome

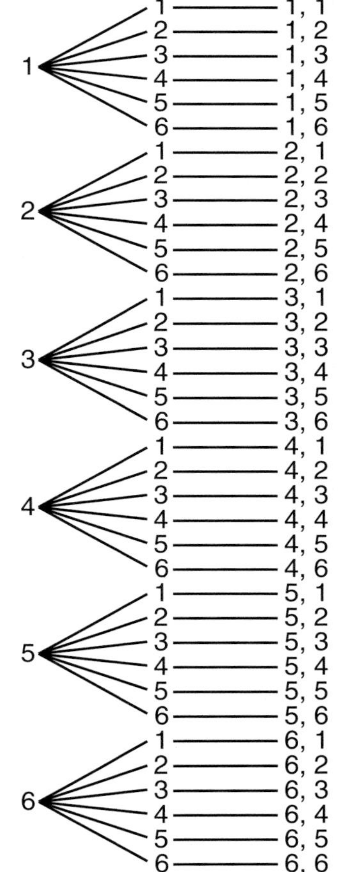

36 outcomes

Selected Answers

3. $\frac{1}{10,000}$

5.

Number Cube	Penny	Outcome
1	Heads	1, Heads
	Tails	1, Tails
2	Heads	2, Heads
	Tails	2, Tails
3	Heads	3, Heads
	Tails	3, Tails
4	Heads	4, Heads
	Tails	4, Tails
5	Heads	5, Heads
	Tails	5, Tails
6	Heads	6, Heads
	Tails	6, Tails

12 outcomes

7.

Flavor	Cone	Outcome
Chocolate	Regular	Chocolate, Regular
	Sugar	Chocolate, Sugar
Vanilla	Regular	Vanilla, Regular
	Sugar	Vanilla, Sugar
Strawberry	Regular	Strawberry, Regular
	Sugar	Strawberry, Sugar

6 outcomes

9. 216 outcomes **11.** 1,024 outcomes **13.** 1,757,600 **15.** $\frac{1}{10,000}$ **17.** 64 players **19.** $\frac{1}{4}$ **21.** 12 **23.** $\frac{1}{6}$ **25.** Sample answer: Maria can choose from 5 flavors of ice cream and 3 different toppings. How many desserts can Maria make with one flavor of ice cream and one topping? **27.** 6^x **29.** C **31.** histogram **33.** 7 points **35.** $\frac{3}{10}$ **37.** $\frac{1}{8}$

Pages 639–642 ***Lesson 12-2***

1. $\frac{1}{12}$ **3.** C **5.** $\frac{5}{24}$ **7.** $\frac{1}{48}$ **9.** $\frac{3}{8}$ **11.** $\frac{5}{24}$ **13.** $\frac{5}{432}$ **15.** $\frac{7}{95}$ **17.** $\frac{7}{76}$ **19.** $\frac{12}{19}$ **21.** 11.76% **23.** $\frac{3}{8}$; dependent event; after the first piece of paper is chosen, there is one less from which to choose. **25.** $\frac{9}{50}$ **27.** $\frac{7}{10}$ **29.** 24% **31.** Sample answer: There are 4 red marbles, 3 green marbles, and 2 blue marbles in a bag. Two marbles are picked at random without replacement. The probability of 2 red marbles is $\frac{4}{9} \cdot \frac{3}{8}$ or $\frac{1}{6}$. **33.** False; Sample answer: the probability of tossing heads or tails on a coin and rolling a 6 or less on a number cube. **35.** C **37.** 60 schedules **39.** 392 m^3 **41.** $\frac{13}{30}$ **43.** $\frac{7}{10}$

Pages 645–647 ***Lesson 12-3***

1. $\frac{3}{8}$ **3.** Likely; half the tosses have two heads. **5.** about 18 **7.** 40 matches **9.** $\frac{10}{79}$ **11.** $\frac{7}{16}$ **13.** Sample answer: the experimental probability $\frac{1}{5}$ is greater than the theoretical probability $\frac{1}{8}$. **15.** The prediction is not reasonable; sample answer: the experimental probability of landing on 4 or 8 is $\frac{7}{50}$. It is much more likely to land on one of the other numbers. **17.** Sample answer: the experimental probability of the player hitting a single or a double is $\frac{1}{4}$, so it is somewhat likely. **19.** 1:6; 1:1; 1:2 **21.** $\frac{21}{80}$ **23.** C **25.** $\frac{1}{56}$ **27.** 12 lunches **29.** $b > 100,000$ **31.** 36 exercises

Pages 650–651 ***Lesson 12-4***

1. Sample answer: You can make a prediction about what will actually happen in the problem. **3.** 8 ways **5.** 6 **7.** 88,70 **9.** 9 **11.** Almost twice as many people visited the Magic Kingdom as Disney's Animal Kingdom.

Pages 655–658 ***Lesson 12-5***

1. The conclusion is invalid. This is a biased sample, since people in other states would spend much more than those in Alaska. The sample is a convenience sample since all the people are from the same state. **3.** This is a simple random survey, so the sample is valid; 42 people. **5.** The conclusion is not valid. This is a biased sample, since only music students were surveyed. This is a convenience sample. **7.** The conclusion is valid. This is an unbiased, stratified random sample. **9.** The conclusion is not valid. This is a biased sample, since only the oranges on the top of the first crate are represented. This is a convenience sample. **11.** This is a simple random survey, so the sample is valid; about 205 people. **13.** Sample answer: Brett could use a systematic random survey, asking every 10th student entering the school. **15.** This is not a valid conclusion. Because the survey is voluntary, not all the survey forms were returned and the results are biased. **17.** This question may not result in bias. **19.** This question may not result in bias. **23.** Sample answer: Ask every 10th student leaving the school which he or she prefers. **25.** Sample answer: If the questions are not asked in a neutral manner, the people may not give their true opinion. For example, the question "You really don't like Brand X, do you?" might not get the same answer as the question "Do you prefer Brand X or Brand Y?" Also, the question "Why would anyone like rock music?" might not get the same answer as the question "What do you think about rock music?" **27.** D **29.** 16 pizzas **31.** $35 + 0.40x = 20 + 0.55x$; 100 mi.

1. Sample space **3.** compound event
5. Theoretical probability
7.

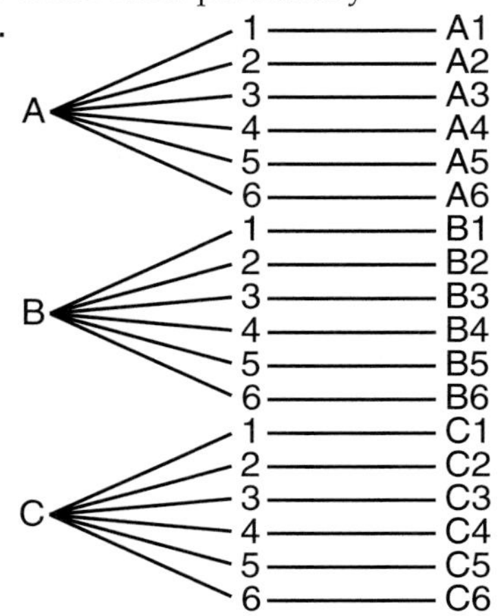

9. $\frac{1}{6}$ **11.** $\frac{1}{45}$ **13.** $\frac{1}{30}$ **15.** $\frac{2}{15}$ **17.** $\frac{8}{25}$ **19.** Sample answer: the theoretical probability of $\frac{1}{6}$ is less than the experimental probability of $\frac{6}{25}$. **21.** 5 words **23.** $\frac{1}{5}$ **25.** No; she needs $14\frac{3}{8}$ ft for 5 shelves and she only has $14\frac{1}{4}$ ft. **27.** about 204 students

Selected Answers

Index

Index

Index

Index

Index

Index

Index

Index

T

Symbols

Number and Operations

$+$	plus or positive
$-$	minus or negative
$a \cdot b$, $a \times b$, ab or $a(b)$	a times b
$\div$	divided by
$\pm$	plus or minus
$=$	is equal to
$\neq$	is not equal to
$>$	is greater than
$<$	is less than
$\geq$	is greater than or equal to
$\leq$	is less than or equal to
$\approx$	is approximately equal to
%	percent
$a:b$	the ratio of a to b, or $\frac{a}{b}$
$0.7\overline{5}$	repeating decimal 0.75555…

Algebra and Functions

$-a$	opposite or additive inverse of a
a^n	a to the nth power
a^{-n}	$\frac{1}{a^n}$
$\lvert x \rvert$	absolute value of x
$\sqrt{x}$	principal (positive) square root of x
$f(n)$	function, f of n

Geometry and Measurement

$\cong$	is congruent to
$\sim$	is similar to
$^\circ$	degree(s)
$\overleftrightarrow{AB}$	line AB
$\overrightarrow{AB}$	ray AB
$\overline{AB}$	line segment AB
AB	length of $\overline{AB}$
⦜	right angle
$\perp$	is perpendicular to
$\parallel$	is parallel to
$\angle A$	angle A
$m\angle A$	measure of angle A
$\triangle ABC$	triangle ABC
(a, b)	ordered pair with x-coordinate a and y-coordinate b
O	origin
π	pi $\left(\text{approximately } 3.14 \text{ or } \frac{22}{7}\right)$

Probability and Statistics

$P(A)$	probability of event A

Formulas

Perimeter	square	$P = 4s$
	rectangle	$P = 2\ell + 2w$ or $P = 2(\ell + w)$
Circumference	circle	$C = 2\pi r$ or $C = \pi d$
Area	square	$A = s^2$
	rectangle	$A = \ell w$
	parallelogram	$A = bh$
	triangle	$A = \frac{1}{2}bh$
	trapezoid	$A = \frac{1}{2}h(b_1 + b_2)$
	circle	$A = \pi r^2$
Surface Area	cube	$S = 6s^2$
	rectangular prism	$S = 2\ell w + 2\ell h + 2wh$
	cylinder	$S = 2\pi rh + 2\pi r^2$
Volume	cube	$V = s^3$
	prism	$V = \ell wh$ or Bh
	cylinder	$V = \pi r^2 h$ or Bh
	pyramid	$V = \frac{1}{3}Bh$
	cone	$V = \frac{1}{3}\pi r^2 h$ or $\frac{1}{3}Bh$
Pythagorean Theorem	right triangle	$a^2 + b^2 = c^2$
Temperature	Fahrenheit to Celsius	$C = \frac{5}{9}(F - 32)$
	Celsius to Fahrenheit	$F = \frac{9}{5}C + 32$

Measurement Conversions

Length	1 kilometer (km) = 1,000 meters (m) 1 meter = 100 centimeters (cm) 1 centimeter = 10 millimeters (mm)	1 foot (ft) = 12 inches (in.) 1 yard (yd) = 3 feet or 36 inches 1 mile (mi) = 1,760 yards or 5,280 feet
Volume and Capacity	1 liter (L) = 1,000 milliliters (mL) 1 kiloliter (kL) = 1,000 liters	1 cup (c) = 8 fluid ounces (fl oz) 1 pint (pt) = 2 cups 1 quart (qt) = 2 pints 1 gallon (gal) = 4 quarts
Weight and Mass	1 kilogram (kg) = 1,000 grams (g) 1 gram = 1,000 milligrams (mg) 1 metric ton = 1,000 kilograms	1 pound (lb) = 16 ounces (oz) 1 ton (T) = 2,000 pounds
Time	1 minute (min) = 60 seconds (s) 1 hour (h) = 60 minutes 1 day (d) = 24 hours	1 week (wk) = 7 days 1 year (yr) = 12 months (mo) or 52 weeks or 365 days 1 leap year = 366 days
Metric to Customary	1 meter ≈ 39.37 inches 1 kilometer ≈ 0.62 mile 1 centimeter ≈ 0.39 inch	1 kilogram ≈ 2.2 pounds 1 gram ≈ 0.035 ounce 1 liter ≈ 1.057 quarts